THE
CHALLENGE
OF
DEMOCRACY

Kenneth Janda
Northwestern University

Jeffrey M. Berry
Tufts University

Jerry Goldman
Northwestern University

THE

CHALLENGE

OF

DEMOCRACY

Government in America

Houghton Mifflin Company   Boston   Dallas   Geneva, Illinois   Lawrenceville, New Jersey   Palo Alto

Printed in the U.S.A.

Library of Congress Catalog Card Number: 86-81451

ISBN: 0-395-34353-4

BCDEFGHIJ-RM-8987

Illustration Credits

Illustrations by Boston Graphics, Inc.
Cover: Gorchev & Gorchev, Inc.
Frontispiece: Douglas Kirkland/Sygma.

Chapter 1: **Page 2 (Opener):** Robert Llewellyn; **6:** J Berndt/Stock, Boston; **9:** By permission of the Houghton Library, Harvard University; **10;** Sygma; **12;** ©Georg Gerster/ Photo Researchers, Inc. **17:** AP/Wide World Photos; **18**(left): Mark Antman/Stock, Boston; **18**(right): Ira Wyman/Sygma; **20:** Copyright 4/29/86. Chicago Tribune Company. All rights reserved. Used with permission; **23:** J.P. Laffont/Sygma; **25:** Bob Daemmrich/TexaStock; **29:** Copyright, 1986, G.B. Trudeau. Reprinted with permission of Universal Press Syndicate. All rights reserved.

Chapter 2: **Page 32 (Opener):** Joan Liftin/Archive; **34:** AP/Wide World Photos; **39:** Jim Wilson/*The Boston Globe;* **40:** Bryce Flynn/Stock, Boston; **41:** Michael Coers. Copyright ©1975 *The Louisville Times.* Reprinted with permission; **48:** Carolyn Hine; **49:** Terry Ashe/*Time Magazine;* **51:** Paul Conklin; **52**(left): Peter Menzel/Stock, Boston; **52**(right): Mark Godfrey/Archive.

Chapter 3: **Page 62 (Opener):** Paul Conklin; **64:** UPI/ Bettman Newsphotos; **65:** J.P. Laffont/Sygma; **67:** National Archives; **69:** Library of Congress; **72:** The Historical Society of Pennsylvania; **77 and 80:** Library of Congress; **87:** UPI/ Bettman Newsphotos; **88:** Lyndon Baines Johnson Library; **96:** National Archives; **102:** AP/Wide World Photos.

Chapter 4: **Page 106 (Opener):** AP/Wide World Photos; **109:** Michael Hayman/Stock, Boston; **111**(left): John Lei/Stock, Boston; **111**(right): Owen Franken/Stock, Boston; **117:** David Hurn/Magnum; **118:** Bruce Davidson/Magnum; **123:** National Archives; **127:** George Tames/NYT Pictures; **132:** Paul Conklin; **135:** Michel Philippot/Sygma.

Chapter 5: **142 (Opener):** Billy E. Barnes/Click/Chicago: **145**(left): Martin Levick/Black Star; **145**(right): Paul Conklin; **147:** *St. Louis Globe-Democrat* Photo; **153:** Michael D. Sullivan/TexaStock; **156:** Max Winter/Picture Group; **163:** Alon Reininger/Woodfin Camp & Associates; **166:** Elizabeth Hamlin/Stock, Boston; **167:** AP/Wide World Photos; **171:** Ashe/Sygma.

Copyright page continues on page A-76

For our children
Susan and Katy
Rachel and Jessica
Jon, Matt, and Josh

Brief Contents

Color Essays and Features

COMPARED WITH WHAT? FEATURES

Contents

19

Foreign and Defense Policy   675

Preface

From the beginning, we wanted to write an American government textbook that students not only would like but also would credit for shaping their thinking about politics. Now finished, we are satisfied. We believe that students will like *The Challenge of Democracy* and that they will use its framework to analyze politics long after the course is over.

We have tried to discuss a complex subject, politics, in a captivating and understandable way. American politics isn't dull, and its textbooks needn't be either. Although writing this book was more work than any of us originally imagined, we also have had more fun along the way than we ever thought possible.

We think that an introductory American government text can go beyond simply offering students basic information about the political process. A text can also teach students how political scientists think about politics. In our profession we try to organize, analyze, and interpret political events, trends, and problems. We want to encourage students to organize, analyze, and interpret American politics and government, too.

THEMATIC FRAMEWORK

It is easy for students to become frustrated with the sheer amount of information assigned each week in an introductory American government course. Our framework provides a way for them to put this information into a broader perspective. Most important, our framework enables students to recognize and to think critically about the difficult choices we face as citizens and voters.

Two themes run through our book. In Chapter 1, we suggest that American politics often reflects conflicts between the values of *freedom* and *order* and between the values of *freedom* and *equality*. These value conflicts are prominent in contemporary American society and they help to explain political controversy and consensus in earlier eras.

In Chapter 3, for example, we argue that the Constitution was designed to promote order and virtually ignored issues of political and social equality. However, equality was later served by several amendments to the Constitution. In Chapter 17, "Order and Civil Liberties," we demonstrate how many of this nation's most controversial issues are conflicts among individuals holding differing values concerning freedom, order, and equality. Views on issues such as school prayer are not just political opinions, but rather choices about a philosophy that we want government to follow. Yet these choices are difficult, sometimes excruciatingly so.

The second theme, introduced in Chapter 2, asks students to consider two competing models of government. One way that government can make decisions is by means of *majoritarian* principles, that is, by taking the actions desired by a majority of citizens. Majoritarianism is a focus of discussion, for example, in Chapter 7, "Political Parties, Campaigns, and Voting," where we treat the real and the ideal roles of political parties. A contrasting model of government, *pluralism,* is built around the interaction of government decisionmakers with groups concerned about issues that directly affect them.

These models are not mere abstractions; we use them to illustrate the dynamics of the American political system. In Chapter 10, "The Congress," and Chapter 15, "The Economics of Public Policy," we discuss the fight for reform of the federal tax code, a monument to pluralism in American politics. Within this context we describe the successful 1986 tax reform effort as reflecting majoritarian instincts counteracting the effects of pluralism. The tension between majoritarianism and pluralism is common in our political system, and we have tried to help students understand the advantages and disadvantages of each model.

As appropriate in other parts of each chapter, we use the themes to discuss relevant issues. All Americans profess a commitment to equality, but "equality" means different things to different people. In Chapter 18, "Equality and Civil Rights," we follow a detailed presentation of the development of affirmative action policy with a discussion of different conceptions of equality, invoking the related concepts introduced in Chapter 1.

Throughout the book we stress that it is the *students* who must choose among the competing values and models of government. Although the three of us have strong opinions about which choices are best, we do not believe it is our role to tell college students our answers to the broad questions we have posed. We hope that students will recognize that maintaining a democracy requires difficult choices; this is why we have titled our book *The Challenge of Democracy.*

FEATURES OF THE BOOK

In many ways, the most important features of the book are the two themes just described, for they provide a consistent thread that underlies the presentation of factual material. We have also used some other strategies to help students understand what they read.

Each chapter begins with a vignette that draws the student into the chapter and suggests the major themes of the book. It is followed by a few focus questions that alert the student to the central ideas that will be addressed in the chapter.

We believe that students can better evaluate how our political system works when they compare it with politics in other countries. Each chapter has at least one boxed feature—called "Compared With What?"—that treats its topic in a comparative perspective. What other countries of the world are commonly considered to be democratic? How much do Americans participate in politics compared with citizens elsewhere? How much does the United States spend on social insurance and defense compared with other countries? These and other questions are addressed by the "Compared With What?" boxes.

Additional boxed features discuss topics in more detail or explain them through illustration. For example, in Chapter 7, on political parties, we discuss *The Wizard of Oz* as a political fable written about the Progressive Party around the turn of the century. In Chapter 15, on the economics of public policy, we illustrate the lack of consensus among economists on key principles of economic theory.

Another feature of *The Challenge of Democracy* is the set of four Color Essays divided among the major parts of the book. The first essay discusses and illustrates political expression in art. The other three contain a series of maps and charts that use color to describe patterns in voting, population composition, presidential greatness and success in Congress, government expenditures, military bases, and so on. Each color essay illustrates and describes important subjects discussed in the accompanying chapters.

The chapters conclude with lists of key terms and suggested readings. Finally, the appendix adds *Federalist Papers* Nos. 10 and 51 to the basic documents of American government and to the glossary of terms.

THE TEACHING PACKAGE

When we began writing *The Challenge of Democracy,* we viewed the book itself as part of a tightly integrated set of instructional materials. We have worked closely with some very talented political scientists and with educational specialists at Houghton Mifflin to produce what we think is a superior set of ancillary materials to help both students and instructors throughout the course.

The primary purpose of the *Instructor's Manual,* written by the authors, is to provide teachers with classroom material that relates directly to the thematic framework and organization of the book. It includes learning objectives, chapter synopses, lecture outlines, and suggested classroom and individual activities. An accompanying *Test Item Bank,* prepared by Edward Sidlow of Northwestern University and Beth Henschen of Loyola University, provides about 1,100 test items — identification, multiple-choice, and essay. A *Study Guide,* written by Melissa Butler of Wabash College, is keyed closely to the book. It contains an overview of each chapter, exercises on reading tables and graphs, suggested topics for student research, and multiple-choice questions for practice.

Ancillaries for the microcomputer include *LectureBank,* an inventory of detailed ideas for lecture topics; *Microtest,* the test items on tape or disk; and *Microstudy Plus,* a computerized study guide. For instructors who want to introduce students to data analysis there is also a disk and workbook called *Crosstabs,* which allows students to do creative research using survey data on the 1984 presidential election and data on voting in Congress. The *Crosstabs* materials were prepared in collaboration with Philip Schrodt of Northwestern University.

The authors (left to right)—
Jeff Berry, Jerry Goldman,
and Ken Janda

ACKNOWLEDGMENTS

Our first thanks must go to Professor Melissa Butler, of Wabash College, who wrote Chapter 4, "Federalism," and Chapter 19, "Foreign and Defense Policy." We could not have worked with a more capable colleague in integrating these chapters with the book's themes. We are also grateful to our friends at Northwestern and Tufts — particularly Timothy Breen, Jay Casper, Richard Eichenberg, Reid Hastie, Herbert Jacob, Don Klein, Kent Portney, Karl de Schweinitz, Wesley Skogan, and Donald Strickland — for their advice and assistance at many points in preparing the manuscript. Special recognition is due Professor Philip Schrodt of Northwestern for writing the data analysis computer program used in *Crosstabs*. We also wish to thank Robert Baumgartner of the Northwestern University Library, Leslie Bailey and Richard Johnson of Northwestern's Language Laboratory, and Lucille Mayer and Jonelle Melton on the staff of the Northwestern political science department for their assistance in completing this project.

We have also been fortunate to obtain the help of many outstanding political scientists across the country who reviewed drafts of our chapters and who made many suggestions for improvement. We found their comments enormously helpful, and we thank them for taking valuable time away from their own teaching and research to write up their detailed reports. More specifically, our thanks go to

David Ahern, University of Dayton

Theodore Arrington, University of North Carolina, Charlotte

Thad Beyle, University of North Carolina, Chapel Hill

Gregory A. Caldeira, University of Iowa

John Chubb, Stanford University

Gary Copeland, University of Oklahoma

Cornelius P. Cotter, University of Wisconsin — Milwaukee

Patricia S. Florestano, University of Maryland

Kenneth Hayes, University of Maine

Ronald Hedlund, University of Wisconsin — Milwaukee

Peter Howse, American River College

Clyde Kuhn, California State University — Sacramento

Michael Maggiotto, University of South Carolina

Bruce Oppenheimer, University of Houston

Richard Pacelle, Indiana University

Robert Pecorella, St. John's University

John Winkle, University of Mississippi

Clifford Wirth, University of New Hampshire

Ann Wynia, North Hennepin Community College

Finally, we want to acknowledge our debt to the superb staff at Houghton Mifflin who worked hard at making this book a reality while having to put up with our shenanigans. They deserve combat pay and Purple Hearts for their efforts.

K.J., J.B., J.G.

PART I

DILEMMAS
OF
DEMOCRACY

Freedom, Order, or Equality?

Which is better: to live under a government that enforces strict law and order or under one that allows individuals complete freedom to do whatever they please? Which is better: to pass laws that impose equality among races and sexes or to allow businesses and private clubs freedom to choose their customers and members?

These questions reflect the fundamental dilemmas—difficult choices between unsatisfactory alternatives—that confront modern government. This book explains American government and politics in light of these dilemmas. Thus it does more than explain the workings of our government. It also encourages thinking about what government should—and should *not*—do. In the course of explaining American government, we also judge our government against democratic ideals. Thus this book also encourages thinking about *how* government should make its decisions. As its title implies, *The Challenge of Democracy* argues that good government often involves tough choices.

UNDERSTANDING AMERICAN GOVERNMENT

A national survey was taken after the 1984 presidential election. It found 72 percent of the respondents agreeing with the statement, "Politics and government seem so complicated that a person like me can't understand what's going on."[1] Young respondents were even more confused: more than 75 percent of those under twenty-one years of age confessed that they did not understand "what's going on" in politics.

What is so difficult about understanding American government? The problem hardly lies in lack of information. Americans have plenty of opportunity to learn about their government. Newspaper, television, and radio commentators report daily on politics in Washington, in state capitals, and in cities and towns across the country. An unending flow of facts about officials, issues, events, and laws bombards us all.

For many people, the problem is in paying attention. Early in life, we learn to tune out these political intrusions on our familiar world of family and playmates. As we grow up, the things that matter most to us are making friends, developing our talents, getting jobs, and finding mates. Eventually, we begin to realize that political events are also important in our lives. We dutifully struggle to pay attention and to learn. For a few, political learning seems to come easily. By high school age, they devour a daily newspaper from front-page news to editorials—while most people start and stop at the comics, entertainment pages, or sports. By voting age, we often become uncomfortable because we know so little about our government. For many citizens, this discomfort eventually passes. Even as mature adults, they continue to skip "hard" political news in favor of sensational stories about crime and corruption or juicy gossip about beautiful people.

Most students regret their lack of knowledge and want to become politically aware. Some are discouraged at the start by the amount and complexity of political news. Lacking a framework for judgment, they see the torrent of facts as a meaningless blur. This book brings these facts into focus by analyzing and evaluating the *norms* or *values* that people use to judge what is good or bad about political events. Its purpose is not to preach what people "ought" to favor. It is to teach what values people *have* favored when pursuing "liberal" or "conservative" brands of politics.

Teaching without preaching is not easy, for no one can exclude personal values completely from political analysis. Our approach minimizes this problem by concentrating on the dilemmas confronting governments that must choose between policies that threaten equally cherished values. For example, people value both freedom and human life. Studies clearly show that seat belts save lives in automobile accidents. Government has the authority—known as its **police power**—to maintain order and otherwise safeguard citizens' health, morals, safety, and welfare. Should a government use its police power and force citizens to wear seat belts to save lives? Or should it allow citizens the freedom *not* to wear seat belts and thus sacrifice lives?

Citizens frequently argue over government policies without dissecting those policies to look for conflicting values. Closer observers of politics engage in **normative analysis** of government policies. They determine which values (norms) are harmed and which are helped by the policy choices. We hope to stimulate readers to analyze specific policy disputes (for example, should seat belts be required?) as conflicts between fundamental values (individual freedom versus safety and order) with broader political overtones (conservative or liberal politics).

By looking beyond specifics to underlying normative principles, students should be able to make more sense out of politics. Our framework for analyzing governmental policies and procedures distinguishes between the human *values* that Americans pursue through government and the institutional *models* that guide our efforts to govern in a "democratic" manner. It does not encompass all the complexities of American government, but it should help your knowledge grow by improving your digestion of political information.

Conceptualizing Politics

Sometimes the closest seat offers the poorest view. Just as people sit back from a wide-screen motion picture to gain perspective, students seeking to understand American government need a broader view. They must raise their thinking to a higher level by *conceptualizing* about politics. A *concept* is a generalized idea. It groups various events, objects, or qualities under a common classification or label. Consider the concept of ideology.

Citizens hold different opinions about the merits of government policies. Sometimes their views are based on pure self-interest. For example, senior citizens who receive retirement payments favor the social security system more than citizens who do not. Policies are also judged according to an individual's values and beliefs. Some people hold a hodgepodge of values and beliefs, producing shallow and even contradictory opinions on government policies. However, others organize their opinions into a **political ideology**—a consistent set of values and beliefs about the proper purpose and scope of government.

Rosa Parks: She Sat for Equality
Rosa Parks had just finished a day's work as a seamstress and was sitting in the front of the bus in Montgomery, Alabama, going home. A white man claimed her seat, which he could do according to the law in December of 1955. When she refused to move and was arrested, angry blacks, led by Dr. Martin Luther King, Jr., began a boycott of the Montgomery bus company, and the civil rights movement for racial equality was born.

Political commentators often describe the ideologies of politicians and voters as "liberal" or "conservative." In popular usage, liberals favor an active role for government in society and conservatives favor a narrow role. For example, liberals favored the Social Security Act of 1935 because they wanted the government to assist the elderly. Conservatives opposed the act because it committed the federal government to a new and costly program of retirement payments. Although relatively few citizens today would advocate scrapping social security, citizens often divide sharply on ideological grounds over the desirability of other government programs. By analyzing their ideological positions more carefully, we can explain their support of and opposition to seemingly diverse government policies.

Our Conceptual Framework

The conceptual framework that guides this book consists of five concepts that figure prominently in political analysis. We regard these five concepts as especially important to a broad understanding of American politics, and we use them repeatedly throughout the book. Learning these concepts and their interrelationships will help you evaluate political happenings long after you have read this text.

The five concepts that we emphasize deal with fundamental issues of *what* government tries to do and *how* it decides to do so. What government tries to do will be evaluated according to the concepts of *order, freedom,* and *equality.* All governments pursue order as a value, because maintaining order is part of the meaning of government. Most governments at least profess to preserve individual freedom while maintaining order, but governments vary widely in the extent to which they succeed. Very few governments even profess to guarantee equality, and governments differ greatly in policies that pit equality against freedom. Our conceptual framework will help us evaluate the extent to which the United States pursues — and achieves — all three values through its government.

How government chooses the proper mix of order, freedom, and equality in its policymaking deals with the *process* of choice rather than the outcome. We shall evaluate the American governmental process according to two alternative models of democratic government: the *pluralist* and the *majoritarian.* Most governments profess to be democracies. Whether they are democracies or not depends on their (and our) meaning of the term. Even countries that Americans agree are democracies — for example, the United States and Britain — differ substantially in the type of democracy they practice. Our conceptual models of democratic government will be used both to classify the type of democracy the United States is and to evaluate its success in fulfilling that model.

These five concepts can be organized under two headings in this outline of the book's conceptual framework:

Concepts identifying the VALUES pursued by government

> ORDER
> FREEDOM
> EQUALITY

Concepts describing MODELS of democratic government

> MAJORITARIAN DEMOCRACY
> PLURALIST DEMOCRACY

The rest of this chapter explains *order, freedom,* and *equality* as conflicting *values* pursued by government. Chapter 2 will discuss *majoritarian democracy* and *pluralist democracy* as alternative *institutional models* for implementing democratic government.

Theories of Politics

For our purposes, **politics** can be defined as competition among people trying to influence government decisions toward different outcomes. Scholars try to make sense out of politics by linking concepts together in general statements called *theories.* Concepts are the ideas; theories interrelate these ideas and help us both to explain and to evaluate politics. Theories about politics are of two main types: *empirical* and *normative.* **Empirical theories** make factual generalizations that can be tested by observation. Consider this empirical generalization: "Democratic voters tend to be liberals and Republican voters tend to be conservatives." We can easily test the validity of this empirical theory by studying voting behavior (which we shall do in Chapter 7).

Normative theories, on the other hand, contain statements that *evaluate* or *prescribe* conditions. Here is an example of a normative evaluation: "Democracy is the best form of government." A normative prescription is: "Election procedures should be devised to maximize voter turnout." Both of these generalizations assert some value or norm. People can argue over the truth of either statement, but that truth cannot be proved through observation, as can generalizations in empirical theories.

Good theory is fundamental to understanding politics. Empirical theories are used to describe and also to predict political behavior. Normative theories are used to judge the desirability of political actions and outcomes. Most of the analyses in this book will involve empirical theories about the way American government actually operates. Evaluating the operation of United States politics requires the use of normative theories about democratic government and about the pursuit of freedom, order, and equality. The existence of government itself is based on different normative theories about the purpose of government.

THE PURPOSES OF GOVERNMENT

Most people do not like being told what to do. Fewer still like being *coerced* into certain actions. Yet every day, millions of American motorists dutifully drive on the right-hand side of the street and obediently stop at red lights. Every year, millions of U.S. citizens struggle to complete income tax forms before midnight, April 15. The coercive power of government underlies both examples. If people do not like coercion, why do they submit to it? In other words, why government?

Government can be defined as the legitimate use of force—including imprisonment and execution—to control human behavior. *All* governments require citizens to surrender some freedom in the process of being governed. Although some governments minimize their infringement on personal freedom, *no* government exists to maximize personal freedom. Governments exist to control; "to govern" *means* "to control." People surrender their freedom to government to obtain its benefits. Throughout history, government seems to have served three major purposes: (1) to maintain order (preserving life and protecting property); (2) to provide public goods; and (3) to promote equality.

To Maintain Order

Maintaining order is the oldest purpose of government. **Order** is rich with meanings as an object of government. Think first of *order* in the phrase, "law and order." To maintain order in this sense means establishing the rule of law to *preserve life* and to *protect property*. The seventeenth-century philosopher Thomas Hobbes (1588–1679) was most concerned about preserving life. In his classic philosophical treatise, *Leviathan* (1651), Hobbes described living without government as life in a "state of nature." Without rules, people would live like animals, stealing and killing for personal benefit. In Hobbes's classic phrase, life in a state of nature would be "solitary, poor, nasty, brutish,

Leviathan, Hobbes's All-Powerful Sovereign
This engraving is from the frontispiece to the 1651 edition of Leviathan, *by Thomas Hobbes. It shows Hobbes's all-powerful sovereign brandishing a sword in one hand and the scepter of justice in the other. The sovereign watches over an orderly town, made peaceful by his absolute authority. But note that his body is composed of tiny images of his subjects. The sovereign exists only through them. Hobbes explains that such awesome governmental power can be created only if men ''confer all their power and strength upon one man, or upon one assembly of men, that may reduce all their wills, by plurality of voices, unto one will.''*

and short.'' He believed that a single ruler, or *sovereign*, must possess unquestioned governmental authority to guarantee the safety of the weak against attacks from the strong. Hobbes characterized his all-powerful government as Leviathan, a biblical sea monster. Any infringement of freedom in obeying Leviathan's laws was a small price to pay for the security of living in a civil society rather than in a state of nature.

For most Americans today, a state of nature can only be imagined. We might think of the storied lawlessness in frontier towns before the Lone Ranger (or John Wayne) established law and order. But, in some parts of the world today, people actually live in a state of lawlessness. For example, the Lebanese have lived for more than ten years without a central government strong enough to control warring religious factions. Films of street fighting in the strife-torn city of Beirut, often shown on television news programs, illustrate what a state of nature might be like.

By focusing on life in the cruel state of nature, Hobbes valued government primarily as a means for survival. Other theorists took survival for

Life in a "State of Nature" in the 1980s

Seventeenth-century philosopher Thomas Hobbes characterized life without government as life in a state of nature — it would be "solitary, poor, nasty, brutish, and short." Some three hundred years later, we get a picture of life in a state of nature in Beirut, Lebanon, where the central government has collapsed and citizens try to survive amidst the gunfire and bombings of warring religious factions.

granted and valued government for preserving private property (goods and land owned by individuals) in their conception of order. Foremost among these was John Locke (1632–1704), whose *Two Treatises of Government* (1690) strongly influenced the Declaration of Independence. In fact, the declaration's famous phrase that identifies "Life, Liberty, and the pursuit of Happiness" as "unalienable Rights" of citizens under government reflects Locke's view of life, liberty, and property as the basic purposes of government. Thomas Jefferson, who wrote the Declaration of Independence, substituted "pursuit of Happiness" for "property."

Not everyone recognizes the protection of all private property as a dominant purpose of government. The theories of the nineteenth-century German philosopher Karl Marx (1818–1883) rejected private ownership of property that is used in production of goods or services. Marx's ideas form the basis of **communism,** a complex theory that gives ownership of all land and productive facilities to the people—that is, the government. The Soviet Union, which is a communist state, operates under a constitution that reflects the following principles of government ownership:

> State property, i.e., the common property of the Soviet people, is the principal form of socialist property.
>
> The land, its minerals, waters, and forests are the exclusive property of the state. The state owns the basic means of production in industry, construction, and agriculture; means of transport and communication; the banks; the property of state-run trade organisations and public utilities, and other state-run undertakings; most urban housing; and other property necessary for state purposes.[2]

In noncommunist societies, the extent to which government must protect property or can take it away is a major political issue that forms the basis of much ideological thinking across the world. As you will see, Americans hold very strong views on the sanctity of private property.

Another meaning of order — *social order* — figures in the purposes of government. Social order refers to established patterns of authority in society and to traditional modes of behavior. It is the accepted way of "doing things." The prevailing social order prescribes proper behavior in many different areas: how students should dress in school (neatly, no purple hair) and behave toward their teachers (respectfully); under what conditions people should have sexual relations (married and of different sexes); what the press should not publish (sexually explicit photos); and what the proper attitude toward religion and country should be (reverential). Note that the social order can change. Today, perfectly respectable men and women appear in public places in bathing suits that would have caused a scandal around the turn of the century. Governments usually act to protect the established order, resisting attempts to change social patterns.

The tendency of governments to resist social change suggests that all governments are inherently conservative. However, some governments aim at restructuring the social order. In fact, social change is most dramatic when one government is overthrown through force and replaced by a revolutionary government. In a less dramatic way, governments may work at changing social patterns more gradually through the legal process. Our use of the term *order* in this book includes all three aspects of the term: preserving life, protecting property, and maintaining traditional patterns of social relationships.

To Provide Public Goods

After governments have established order, they can pursue other purposes. Using their coercive powers, they can tax citizens to raise funds to spend on **public goods.** These are projects that benefit all citizens but that are not likely to be produced by the voluntary acts of individuals. The government of ancient Rome, for example, built aqueducts to carry fresh water from the mountains to Rome's inhabitants. Road building — also a Roman achievement — illustrates another public good provided by government. Government action to provide public goods is often controversial. During President James Monroe's administration in the 1820s, many people thought that building a "national road" was not a proper function of the national government, the Romans notwithstanding.

Over time, the scope of legitimate functions of the national government has expanded. During President Dwight Eisenhower's administration in the 1950s, the national government outdid the Romans' noble road building. Despite his basic conservatism, Eisenhower launched the massive Interstate Highway System at a projected cost of $27 billion. Nevertheless, some government enterprises that are common in other countries are politically controversial or even unacceptable in the United States. Running railroads, operating coal mines, and generating electric power are three good examples. Thus, government action in providing for the public good often generates disagreement. People differ on how far the government ought to go in using

A Concrete Example of a Public Good
Governments use tax money to undertake projects that benefit virtually all citizens but that are not likely to be undertaken by any group of individuals. Expressways are one example of a public good (except when you are stuck in one at rush hour).

its power to tax in providing for public goods and on how much should be done by private business for profit.

To Promote Equality

The promotion of equality is the newest major purpose of government, and this purpose has gained prominence only in this century in the aftermath of industrialization and urbanization. Moved by the contrast of poverty amidst plenty, some political leaders in European nations pioneered extensive government programs to improve life for the lower classes. Under the emerging concept of the welfare state, government's role expanded to provide for individuals' welfare—medical care, education, guaranteed income—"from the cradle to the grave." Some nations, such as Sweden and Britain, adopted welfare programs that aimed at reducing social inequalities. This new purpose of government, to promote equality, has been by far the most controversial government objective. Taxation for public goods (to build roads and schools, for example) is often opposed because of its cost alone. However, taxation for government programs to promote economic and social equality is opposed more strongly *on principle*.

The key issue is government's role in redistributing income—taking from the wealthy to give to the poor. Charity (voluntary giving to the poor) has a strong basis in Western religious traditions. Using the power of the state to support the poor does not. (In Charles Dickens' nineteenth-century British novels, the power of the state was used to *imprison* the poor, not to support them.) Using the state to redistribute income was originally a radical thought. It was expressed at the end of the nineteenth century as the ultimate principle of developed communism: "from each according to his ability, to each according to his needs."[3] This is the extreme expression of the government's role in redistributing wealth. Not even communist governments go this far, but the idea remains: taking from the rich to help the needy.

Especially since the Great Depression of the 1930s, the government's role in redistributing income to promote equality has become a major source of policy debates in the United States. Food stamps and AFDC (Aid to Families with Dependent Children) payments are typical examples of government programs that redistribute income—and generate controversy. Government can also promote social equality through controversial policies that do not redistribute income. For example, government can regulate social behavior to enforce equality—as when the U.S. courts required the local Junior Chamber of Commerce ("Jaycees") in Minneapolis to admit women as members in 1984. Whether it acts to redistribute income or to regulate social behavior, the government's role in promoting social equality inevitably clashes with the value of personal freedom.

IDEOLOGY AND THE SCOPE OF GOVERNMENT

How far should government go to maintain order, provide public goods, or promote equality? In the United States (as in every other nation), citizens, scholars, and politicians have different opinions on this issue. Their opinions can be analyzed according to normative theories about the proper scope of government—the range of its permissible activities. Imagine a continuum ranging from the desire for government to do everything to the fear of government's doing anything. The extreme ideological possibilities on this continuum—*totalitarianism* and *anarchism*—are staked out in Figure 1.1. The

Figure 1.1

Ideology and the Scope of Government
Political ideologies can be classified according to the scope of action that people are willing to give to government in dealing with social and economic matters. The continuum below spans a range of philosophies. Note that capitalism is compatible with a rather broad range of government activity. Note also that conventional politics in the United States spans only a portion of the theoretical possibilities for government action.

In popular usage, liberals favor a greater scope of government, and conservatives favor a narrower scope. However, this traditional distinction has eroded over time and now oversimplifies the difference between liberals and conservatives. See Figure 1.2 for a more discriminating classification of liberals and conservatives.

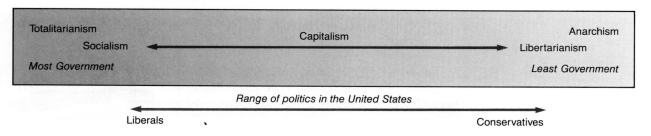

intermediate philosophies—*socialism*, *capitalism*, and *libertarianism*—combine different mixes of concern about the government's role in economic and political matters. The two broad ideological orientations at the bottom—*liberalism* and *conservatism*—are only roughly related to this continuum. They will be explained at greater length later.

Totalitarianism

Totalitarianism represents the most extreme conception of unlimited governmental scope. A totalitarian government controls all sectors of society: business, labor, education, religion, sports, the arts, and so on. A true totalitarian favors a network of laws, rules, and regulations guiding every aspect of individual behavior. The object is to produce a perfect society serving some master plan for "the common good." Totalitarianism has reached its terrifying potential only in literature and films (for example, George Orwell's *1984*), but several real societies have come perilously close to "perfection." One thinks of Hitler's Nazi Germany, Stalin's Soviet Union, and (more recently) the Ayatollah Khomeini's Iran. Not many people openly profess totalitarianism today, but it is a useful concept that anchors one side of the continuum.

Socialism

In its unmodified form, socialism is similar to communism, for both are economic systems based on Marxist theory. Under **socialism** (as under communism), the scope of government extends to ownership or control of the basic industries that produce goods and services. These include communications, mining, heavy industry, transportation, and power. Socialists also favor a strong government role in regulating existing private industry and directing the economy, but socialism draws sharper limits to the scope of government, allowing greater room for private ownership of productive capacity. Nevertheless, socialists—like communists—believe that the state should have a broad scope of authority in the economic life of a nation.

Many Americans simply equate socialism with communism as practiced in the closed societies of the Soviet Union and Eastern Europe, but there is a difference. All communist governments tend toward totalitarianism by controlling both political and social life through a dominant party organization. Some socialist governments, however, practice **democratic socialism**—guaranteeing civil liberties, such as freedom of speech and religion, and allowing citizens to determine the extent of government activity through free elections and competitive political parties. Outside the United States, socialism is not an inherently bad term. In fact, the governments of Britain, Sweden, Germany, and France—among other democracies—have at times been avowedly "socialist" since World War II.

Capitalism

In contrast to both socialism and communism, **capitalism** favors *free enterprise*—private businesses operating without government regulations. Some theorists, most notably the contemporary economist Milton Friedman, argue that free enterprise is necessary for free politics.[4] According to this

Compared With What? 1.1

Government Ownership of Basic Industries

Despite accusations of "big government," the U.S. government owns and operates relatively few enterprises, compared with other major Western countries. The chart below shows that the proportion of eleven basic industries under government ownership in the United States is far smaller than in other democratic nations.

	Posts	Telecommunications	Railways	Electricity	Airlines	Gas	Oil production	Coal	Motor industry	Steel	Shipbuilding
Austria	●	●	●	●	●	●	●	●	●	●	†
Britain	●	●	●	●	●	◕	◔	●	◑	◔	●
Italy	●	●	●	◕	●	†	†	◔	◕	◕	
France	●	●	●	◕	●	†	●	◑	◕	○	
Sweden	●	●	●	◑	◑	●	†	†	○	◕	◕
West Germany	●	●	●	◕	●	◑	◔	◑	◔	○	◔
Australia	●	●	●	●	◔	●	○	○	○	○	†
Canada	●	◔	◔	●	●	◔	○	○	○	○	○
Japan	●	●	●	○	◔	○	†	○	○	○	○
United States	●	○	◔	◔	○	○	○	○	○	○	○

○ Private ownership

◔ Mixed ownership, with private predominating

◑ Basically equal balance between public and private

◕ Mixed ownership, with government predominating

● All or nearly all government ownership

† Not applicable
* Including Conrail

Source: *The Economist*, December 21, 1986–January 3, 1986, p. 72. © 1985 *The Economist*, reprinted by permission of Special Features.

argument, the economic system of capitalism is necessary for democracy—which contradicts those who believe in democratic socialism. Who is right depends partly on one's understanding of democracy, which we shall study in Chapter 2.

The United States is decidedly a capitalist country, far more so than Britain or most other Western countries. Despite the U.S. government's enormous budget, compared with other countries it does not own or operate many public enterprises (see Compared With What? 1.1). Government ownership and operation of basic industries is not popular in the United States. However, our government *does* extend its scope into the economic sphere by regulating private businesses and directing the overall economy. American liberals and conservatives both embrace capitalism, but they differ on the nature and amount of government intervention in the economy they support.

Libertarianism

Libertarianism is opposed to all government action except that which is necessary to protect life and property. Libertarians grudgingly recognize the necessity of government but believe that government should be as limited as possible. For example, libertarians grant the need for traffic laws for safe and efficient automobile travel. But they oppose laws stating a minimum drinking age as a restriction on individual actions. Libertarians believe that government social programs for providing food, clothing, or shelter are outside the permissible scope of government. Instead, they depend on individual action to provide charity for the needy. Libertarians certainly oppose government ownership of basic industries, but they go much further. They oppose *any* government intervention in the economy. Libertarians advocate an economic policy of **laissez faire.** This French phrase means "let (people) do (as they please)." In English and in economics, it translates best as "hands off" the economy. Libertarians are vocal in arguing their laissez-faire policies for economics and for social life in general. Whereas those who favor a broad scope of government action shun description as "socialist," libertarians make no secret of their identity. Libertarians ran their own party candidates for president in 1976, 1980, and 1984 on straight libertarian principles (see Feature 1.1). (Their candidate did best in 1980, winning almost a million votes, which was still less than 1 percent of the total vote cast.)

Don't confuse liber*tarians* with liber*als* because of the terms' linguistic similarity. They are similar, but their meanings are very different. Liber*tarianism* draws on *liberty* as its root and means "absence of governmental constraint." In American political usage, liber*alism* evolved from the root word *liberal.* Over time, it has come to mean something closer to "generous," in the sense that liberals are willing to support government spending on welfare programs.

Anarchism

Anarchism stands opposite totalitarianism on a continuum of governmental scope. Anarchists oppose all government, in any form. As a political philosophy, anarchism values freedom above all else. Because all government involves some restriction on personal freedom (for example, forcing people

Feature 1.1

Philosophy of the 1984 Libertarian Presidential Candidate

The libertarian philosophy of government was espoused in 1984 by David Bergland, the presidential candidate of the Libertarian party, who appeared on the ballot in several states but received less than 1 percent of the vote. According to Bergland, the government has no business doing most of what it now does.

Mr. Bergland would, among other things, bring back American troops and weapons from wherever they may be, turn the public schools into private schools, eliminate Social Security and stop trying to enforce laws on such matters as drugs, pornography, abortion and gun ownership. . . .

The Libertarian candidate differs decisively from his Republican and Democratic rivals on both foreign and domestic policy. This country's foreign policy, as he sees it, should be aimed at safeguarding the security, personal liberties and personal property of Americans. . . .

The theme of people caring for themselves runs strongly through the Libertarian Party's domestic program. As Mr. Bergland sees it, "Government is a conglomerate of service businesses." He asks, "Is it necessary that those performing the services be Government employees and that they be paid through taxes?" His answer in most cases is in the negative.

He would do away with most regulatory agencies as well as with such impositions on the free market as the minimum wage, the Federal Reserve system, zoning regulations and antipollution laws. He would rely instead on individuals and businesses to protect and pursue their own interests. . . .

He is against bailouts for corporations or banks. The way to assist the poor, he maintains, is not by welfare but by breaking down the barriers to their participation in an untrammelled economy.

Prominent among the institutions that Mr. Bergland would eliminate is the public school. As a step toward "the separation of education and the state," he proposes an annual tax credit of $1,500 for any taxpayer who supports any student in any school. He predicts that this would encourage corporations and individuals to subsidize children whose families cannot afford private school and would increase personal choice.

He wants to break up what he calls the "protective monopoly business" of education and remove "coercive measures" such as compulsory attendance, taxation, and all rules as to "who can teach and what is to be taught."

Mr. Bergland sums up the Libertarian creed: "I want to remove coercion as a premise in human relationships."

to drive on one side of the road), a pure anarchist would even object to traffic laws. Like totalitarianism, anarchism is not a popular philosophy, but it does have adherents on the political fringes.

On May 4, 1986, an estimated three hundred to five hundred anarchists gathered in Chicago to commemorate the hundredth anniversary of the riot in Haymarket Square, in which an anarchist's bomb killed several policemen. The modern anarchists, who came from all across the nation, ran amok through Chicago's financial district and along the fashionable Michigan Avenue shopping area, defacing property, shouting anticapitalist slogans, and waving black flags—the symbol of anarchism. One of the thirty-six anarchists arrested gave his name as Tentatively A. Convulsion. Most of the rest declined to give names and refused to be fingerprinted. This unusual gathering was described by one of its planners as "the most significant anarchist event held in America in years"[5]—which indicates that anarchism is more bizarre than it is popular. Anarchism serves to anchor the right side of the government continuum and to indicate that libertarians are not as extreme in opposing government as is theoretically possible.

Protests Reflecting the Two Dilemmas of Government
These two groups of citizens are protesting government's interference with personal freedom, but they have very different objectives. The group on the left objects to outlawing abortions, an area that involves government in promoting order by preserving the life of the unborn — an example of the original dilemma of government (the choice between freedom and order). The group on the right objects to forced busing, which involves government in promoting racial equality — an example of the modern dilemma of government (the choice between freedom and equality).

Liberals and Conservatives—
The Middle Ground

As shown in Figure 1.1, practical politics in the United States ranges over only the central portion of the continuum representing the scope of government action. The totalitarian and anarchist positions at the extreme ends are rarely argued in public debate. Similarly, in this era of distrust of "big government," few American politicians would openly advocate socialism. On the other hand, more than one hundred individuals ran for Congress in 1984 as candidates of the Libertarian party. Although none won, American libertarians are sufficiently vocal to be heard in the debate about how much government should do.

Nevertheless, most debate over public policies in the United States ranges over only a small portion of the possible scope of government action. The opposing sides in this debate are commonly styled as "liberal" and "conservative." In popular usage, liberals favor a broader scope of government, whereas conservatives would narrow the scope. This distinction applies clearly to government action in providing for public goods. Liberals favor generous government support for education, wildlife protection, public transportation, and so forth. Conservatives favor fewer government programs and smaller government budgets. In particular, conservatives favor free enterprise and oppose government activism in economic matters, such as undertaking major job programs, regulating business operations, and legislating working conditions and wage rates.

Despite their usefulness for analyzing positions on government programs that provide for public goods, the liberal and conservative labels no longer fit some of the major divisions in political attitudes. In theory, conservatives oppose government activism, yet conservatives *favor* government control over the publication of sexually explicit magazines. In theory, liberals favor government activism, yet liberals *oppose* government regulation of abortions. What's going on? Are American political attitudes hopelessly contradictory, or is something missing in our analysis of ideologies in the 1980s? Actually, something *is* missing. Liberals can be more accurately distinguished from conservatives if we consider not only the scope of government action, but also its *purpose*. We can resolve many apparent contradictions by considering the purposes of government action and the two major value dilemmas in modern government.

TWO DILEMMAS OF GOVERNMENT

The two major dilemmas of American government in the 1980s arise from the oldest and the newest purposes of government. The oldest purpose is to maintain order. The newest purpose is to promote equality. Both order and equality are important social values, but government cannot pursue either order or equality without sacrificing a third important value: individual freedom. The older clash between freedom and order constitutes the *original* dilemma of government. The newer clash between freedom and equality forms the *modern* dilemma of government. Each dilemma presumes a different purpose of government, but each involves trading off some amount of freedom for another value. Once we understand these dilemmas, we shall be able to resolve some apparent contradictions in the attitudes of liberals and conservatives toward the scope of government in the United States.

The Original Dilemma: Freedom Versus Order

The conflict between freedom and order originates in the very meaning of government as the legitimate use of force to control human behavior. How much freedom must a citizen surrender to government? This dilemma has occupied philosophers for hundreds of years. The eighteenth-century French philosopher Jean Jacques Rousseau (1712–1778) posed the problem of devising the proper government:

> The problem is to find a form of association which will defend and protect with the whole common force the person and goods of each associate, and in which each, while uniting himself with all, may still obey himself alone, and remain free as before.[6]

The original purpose of government was to protect life and property, making citizens safe from violent attacks. How well is government doing today in guaranteeing safety to American citizens? Nearly half the respondents in a 1982 national survey said that they were afraid to walk alone at night within a mile of their homes.[7] In our larger urban areas, their fears seem justified. Nearly three out of ten people interviewed in New York City in 1985 reported that they, or a member of their family, had been a victim of crime within the past year.[8] Visitors to New York are well advised to keep

Make My Day — Draw!
Graffiti-defaced buses and subway cars have become a symbol of the breakdown in law and order in urban areas. Few cities have had much success in dealing with the problem. New York put barbed wire around the yards where the vehicles were kept and unleashed dogs to patrol the area, with mixed results. Chicago launched its ''get-tough'' policy in 1986 with a public relations campaign vowing that ''Sheriff Pride'' would keep the buses clean.

out of Central Park after dark. Simply put, Americans do not trust their urban governments to protect them from crime when they go out alone at night.

Compare this climate of fear in urban America with American tourists' feelings of personal safety when they walk after dark in communist cities, such as Moscow, Warsaw, or Prague. They report that it is common to see senior citizens and young couples strolling along late at night on the streets or in the parks. Of course, communist countries give police greater powers to control guns, to monitor citizens' movements, and to arrest and imprison suspicious people. It is not surprising that they do a better job in maintaining order. Communist governments have deliberately chosen order over freedom.

The value conflict between freedom and order represents the original dilemma of government. In the abstract, people value both order and freedom, but the two values inherently conflict in real life. In democratic countries, citizens differ over the balance between order and freedom. Conflict may come over major matters—whether to employ capital punishment for murder—or over minor matters—how to deal with urban teen-agers who spray-paint subway cars. In either case, the choice hinges on how much citizens value order and how much they value freedom.

The Modern Dilemma: Freedom Versus Equality

Popular opinion has it that freedom and equality go hand in hand. In reality, these two values usually clash when governments enact policies to promote social equality. Because social equality is a relatively recent governmental objective, deciding between policies that promote equality but impair freedom, and vice versa, is the modern dilemma of politics. Consider three examples of this dilemma in recent politics.

■ During the 1960s, Congress (through the Equal Pay Act) required employers to pay women and men the same rate for equal work. Thus government forced some employers to pay women more than the employers would have paid if hiring had been based on a free market.

■ During the 1970s, the courts ordered busing of school children to achieve equal proportions of blacks and whites in public schools. This action was motivated by concern for educational equality, but it also impaired freedom of choice.

■ During the 1980s, some states passed legislation that went beyond the idea of "equal pay for equal worth" to the more radical notion of *pay equity*. Women had to be paid at a rate equal to men's—even if they had *different* jobs—providing the women's jobs were of "comparable worth." For example, if the skills and responsibilities of a female nurse were found comparable to those of a male sanitation engineer in the same hospital, the woman's salary and the man's salary would have to be the same (see Feature 1.2). Equal pay for equal worth was denounced as "the looniest idea since 'Looney Tunes' came on the screen" by the chairman of President Ronald Reagan's Civil Rights Commission, but it was the law in some states. In 1986 Congress itself considered enacting the "looney" idea into law.

Feature 1.2

Promoting Equality by Assessing Comparable Worth

Women's advocates contend that men tend to be paid more than women partly because sex discrimination exists in job classifications and pay rates. They back the idea of pay equity for jobs of comparable worth. If the idea becomes national law, it will involve the government more deeply in promoting social equality. The article below indicates how employers (and government) might determine the comparable worth of two different jobs traditionally held by different sexes.

	Nurse	Sanitary Engineer
Know-how	150	60
Problem solving	75	40
Accountability	175	165
Working conditions	50	185
Total	450	450

Should a nurse, usually a woman, be paid as much as a sanitation engineer, often a man? Questions about providing equal pay for jobs of equal value are being raised as interest grows in the relatively new doctrine called "comparable worth." And attempting to answer them is spawning a new career path, mainly in management consulting firms.

Anton Armbruster, an associate of William M. Mercer-Meidinger, an employee benefit and compensation consulting firm, has come up with the following example of how management consultants are providing answers. He uses a point system based on four factors — know-how, prob-

lem-solving requirements, accountability and working conditions.

The nurse probably needs more know-how and more problem-solving ability, but total accountability is about the same because both are important to community health. Working conditions for the engineer, often outdoors in bad weather, are obviously more difficult than those for the typical nurse, so the engineer is credited with a higher number of points in that category.

Source: Elizabeth M. Fowler, "Comparing the Value of Jobs," *New York Times*, January 23, 1985. Copyright © 1984/85 by The New York Times Company. Reprinted by permission.

These examples illustrate the dilemma in using government power to promote equality. The value clash between freedom and order is obvious, but the conflict between freedom and equality is more subtle. Often the conflict is not even recognized by the American public, which regards freedom and equality as complementary rather than conflicting values. The tension between these concepts explains a great deal of political behavior in the United States. Both the original and the modern dilemmas of government are important in understanding American politics, and we shall refer to both throughout the book. Because the tradeoff between freedom and equality is less obvious, we shall pay more attention to explaining it. We begin by clarifying these two concepts.

THE CONCEPTS OF FREEDOM AND EQUALITY

Both freedom and equality have great symbolic value in American politics. The terms have been used more effectively in arousing public support than in explaining political issues. As is usually the case with positive symbols,

Are Poor People Really Free?
Some critics argue that people are not politically free unless they are socially equal. Those who hold this view believe that government should redistribute income to produce equality of outcome, *not just equality of* opportunity. *The conception of equality that you choose affects your position on the modern dilemma of government.*

politicians have snatched these terms to use for their own advantage. Consequently, freedom and equality mean different things to different people at different times — depending on the political context in which they are used.

Freedom

Freedom has been used in two major senses — *freedom to* and *freedom from*. Both senses appear in the "Four Freedoms" (freedom of religion, of speech, from fear, and from want) that Franklin Delano Roosevelt held out to the American people entering World War II. The noted illustrator Norman Rockwell gave Americans a vision of these freedoms in a classic set of paintings published in the *Saturday Evening Post* (see Color Essay A, plate 6). They were later used in a bond drive to raise funds for the war and exhibited throughout the country.

Freedom to suggests the dictionary definition of *freedom* as the absence of constraints on behavior. In this sense, freedom is synonymous with *liberty*. *Liberty*, however, is an "older" term, which has been superseded in symbolic value by *freedom*. Two of Rockwell's paintings ("Freedom of Speech" and "Freedom of Worship") exemplify this type of freedom.

Freedom from identifies a second usage, as reflected in Rockwell's two other paintings, "Freedom from Fear" and "Freedom from Want." These freedoms suggest *immunity* from fear and want—not freedom *to* fear and want. In the modern political context, "freedom from" often signifies the fight against exploitation or oppression. The cry "Freedom Now!" of the civil rights movement in the 1960s conveyed this meaning. If you recognize that freedom in this sense means immunity from discrimination, you can see that it comes close to the concept of equality.[9] We shall avoid using *freedom* to mean "freedom from"; we shall simply use *equality* instead.

Equality

Like freedom, *equality* has been used in different senses and to support different causes. In fact, we need to make three distinctions in explaining the concept of equality.

Political equality.   In the simple matter of voting, **political equality** is easily defined: each voter has one and only one ballot. This basic concept of political equality is central to democratic theory—a subject we shall explore at length in Chapter 2. But when some people advocate political equality they mean more than equality in casting votes. These critics contend that an urban ghetto dweller and the chairman of the board of General Motors are not politically equal simply because each has one vote. Through occupation or wealth, some citizens are more able than others to influence political decisions. For example, wealthy citizens may exert influence by advertising in the mass media or by contacting friends in high places. Lacking great wealth or political connections, most citizens are denied such influence. Thus, some analysts argue that equality in wealth, education, and status—that is, **social equality**—is necessary for true political equality. There are two routes to achieving social equality: providing equal opportunities and ensuring equal outcomes.

Equality of opportunity.   **Equality of opportunity** means that each person has the same chance to succeed in life. This idea is deeply ingrained in American culture. A prohibition on titles of nobility, the absence of property requirements for public offices, free public schools, free public libraries—all these and other features of our society are designed to advance equality of opportunity. To many people, the concept of social equality is satisfied just by offering *opportunities* for people to advance themselves. Under this conception of social equality, it is not essential that people end up being equal after using their opportunities.

Equality of outcome.   For others, however, true social equality means nothing less than **equality of outcome.**[10] Under this conception, society must see to it that people *are* equal. It is not enough for governments to provide people with equal opportunities for social advancement. Governments should also design policies to redistribute wealth and status so that economic and social equality are actually achieved. Such policies applied to business have led to affirmative action programs to increase minority hiring

Who Says College Sports Are for Men?
The tremendous growth in women's sports on college campuses today is largely a result of a federal law that promoted sexual equality in education. Under Title IX, *part of a law passed in 1972 dealing with educational policy, Congress prohibited sex discrimination in schools and colleges that receive federal funds. Enforced by the Department of Education's Office for Civil Rights, Title IX required schools and colleges to provide "reasonably comparable" activities to students of both sexes. Colleges responded by expanding their competitive sports programs for women, including awarding a comparable number of athletic scholarships.*

by requiring firms to seek out women, blacks, and Hispanics for employment. Taken a step further, equality of outcome has prompted racial quotas for hiring minorities so that the proportion of jobs they occupy is equal to their proportions in the local population. In education, equality of outcome has been translated into comparable funding for men's and women's college sports. In employment, equality of outcome has been translated into equal pay for comparable work.

Some observers link the concept of equality of outcome with the concept of governmental **rights** — the idea that every citizen is *entitled* to certain benefits of government. Under this conception, the government should *guarantee* citizens adequate (if not equal) housing, employment, medical care, and income as a matter of right. Obviously, this broad interpretation of governmental rights serves to legitimize efforts to promote equality of outcome, but it is very different from the narrower concept of civil rights discussed in Chapter 18.

Quite clearly, the concept of equality of outcome is very different from the other two senses of equality (political equality and equality of opportunity), and it requires a much greater degree of government activity. It is also the conception of equality that clashes most directly with the concept of freedom. By "taking from one to give to another" — which is required for redistribution of income and status — the government clearly identifies winners and losers. The winners may believe that justice has been served by the redistribution. The losers often feel strongly that their freedom to enjoy their income and status has suffered.

POLITICAL IDEOLOGIES AND THE PURPOSE OF GOVERNMENT

Much of American politics revolves around two dimensions of value conflicts: freedom versus order and freedom versus equality. These two dimensions do not account for all political conflict, but they figure in a surprising number of issues. By keeping them in mind, you can gain insight into the workings of politics. They can also help organize the seemingly chaotic world of political events, actors, and issues.

Liberals Versus Conservatives: The New Differences

Liberals no longer differ from conservatives mainly on government activism in providing for public goods. Liberals still favor a broader government role and conservatives a smaller one, but that is no longer the distinguishing difference. The new source of difference between American liberals and conservatives stems from different attitudes toward the purposes of government. Conservatives emphasize government's original purpose in maintaining social *order*. They are willing to use the coercive power of the state to *force* citizens to be orderly. They favor aggressive police action, swift and severe punishment for criminals, and more laws regulating behavior. For example, conservatives are more likely than liberals to outlaw explicit sexual materials as pornographic. Conservatism does not stop with defining, preventing, and punishing crime, however. Conservatism also seeks to preserve traditional patterns of social relations, such as the domestic role of women and the importance of religion in school and family life.

Liberals are less likely than conservatives to use government power to maintain order. In general, liberals are more tolerant of deviant lifestyles — for example, homosexual behavior. Liberals do not shy away from using government coercion, but they use it for a different purpose — to promote equality. In fact, liberals are apt to back laws ensuring that homosexuals receive equal treatment in employment, housing, education, and so on. Liberals are more likely to support state coercion in other ways:

- Busing school children to achieve racial equality
- Requiring private businesses to hire and promote women and members of minority groups
- Requiring public carriers to provide equal access to the handicapped
- Ordering cities and states to reapportion election districts so that minority voters will elect minority candidates to public office

Conservatives do not oppose equality per se, but they do not value equality to the extent that liberals do. They certainly oppose government coercion to enforce equality.

A Two-Dimensional Classification of Ideologies

To classify liberal and conservative ideologies more accurately, we need to incorporate all three values—freedom, order, and equality—in the classification. To do so, we shall use the model in Figure 1.2.* It depicts the value clashes along two separate dimensions, each anchored in maximum freedom at the lower left. One dimension extends horizontally from maximum freedom on the left to maximum order on the right. The other extends vertically from maximum freedom at the bottom to maximum equality at the top. The labeled boxes correspond to four different ideological types. The labels exemplify the values emphasized by each type.

The ideological type labeled as **libertarians** in Figure 1.2 values freedom more than order or equality. This term is used for people who have libertarian tendencies but who may not accept the whole philosophy. In practical terms, libertarians want minimal governmental intervention in both the economic and the social spheres—for example, no food stamp programs and no laws against abortion.

Liberals value freedom more than order, but not more than equality. Liberals also oppose laws against abortion but want food stamp programs. **Conservatives** value freedom more than equality but would restrict freedom to preserve social order. Conservatives oppose food stamps but favor laws against abortion.

Finally, we have the logically possible ideology at the upper right in Figure 1.2. This group values *both* equality and order more than freedom. Its members support both food stamps *and* laws against abortion. We shall call this new group **populists.** The term derives from a rural reform movement that was active in the late 1800s. Populists viewed government as an instrument to promote the advancement of common people against moneyed or vested interests. They used their voting power both to regulate businesses and to enforce their moral judgments on minorities.[11] Their name aptly describes those who favor government action both to reduce inequalities and to ensure social order.

---

* The ideological groupings conform to the classification in William S. Maddox and Stuart A. Lilie, *Beyond Liberal and Conservative* (Washington, D.C.: Cato Institute, 1984), p. 5. However, this formulation in terms of the values of equality, order, and freedom is quite different.

By analyzing political ideologies on two dimensions rather than one, we can explain why people seem to be "liberal" on one issue (favoring a broader scope of government action) and "conservative" on another (favoring less government action). The answer hinges on the action's *purpose:* which value does it promote—order or equality? According to the typology, only libertarians and populists are consistent in their attitudes toward the scope of government—regardless of its purpose. Libertarians value freedom so highly that they oppose most government efforts to enforce either order or equality. Populists are inclined to trade off freedom for both order and equality. Liberals and conservatives, on the other hand, switch between favoring and opposing government action—depending on its purpose. As you will learn later (in Chapter 5), large groups of Americans fall into each of the four ideological categories. Because Americans choose four different resolutions

Figure 1.2

Two-Dimensional Framework of Ideological Orientations
The four ideological types below are defined by the values they favor in resolving the two major dilemmas of government: how much freedom should be sacrificed in pursuit of (1) order and (2) equality? You may want to test yourself by reflecting on which values are most important to you. Which box in the figure below best represents your combination of values?

DOONESBURY

Garry Trudeau

Doonesbury "Blow for Individual Freedom"

to the original and modern dilemmas of government, the simple labels of
"liberal" and "conservative" do not fit contemporary politics as well as they
did in the 1930s, 1940s, and 1950s.

SUMMARY

The challenge of democracy involves making difficult choices between important values when they conflict in government. *The Challenge of Democracy*
outlines a normative framework for analyzing policy choices that arise in
pursuing the purposes of government.

The three major purposes of government are to maintain order, to provide public goods, and to promote equality. Every government infringes on
individual freedom in pursuing these purposes. While minor controversies
arise over government's provision of public goods, the major dilemmas of
government involve the other two purposes of government. The original
dilemma centers on the conflict between freedom and order. The modern
dilemma focuses on the conflict between freedom and equality.

Some people have political ideologies that help them resolve dilemmas
that arise in specific policy decisions. At the broadest level, ideologies can be
classified according to the scope of government activism. At opposite extremes are totalitarianism, which supports government intervention in every
aspect of society, and anarchism, which rejects government entirely. An important step back from totalitarianism is socialism. Democratic socialism favors government ownership of basic industries but preservation of civil liberties.

A significant step short of anarchism is libertarianism, which allows government to protect life and property, but little else.

We can classify ideologies more accurately by considering both the scope and the purpose of government action. Based on scope alone, liberals support a broader role for government than do conservatives. Using both scope and purpose, we derive a sharper classification. Conservatives would sacrifice freedom for order. Liberals would surrender freedom for equality. Libertarians would choose freedom over both order and equality. Populists would give up freedom for both order and equality.

These concepts dealing with government purposes, values, and political ideologies will appear repeatedly as we determine who favors what government action and why. So far, we have said little about *how* government should make its decisions. In Chapter 2, we complete our normative framework for evaluating American politics by examining the nature of democratic theory. There we shall introduce two key concepts for analyzing how democratic governments make decisions.

Key Terms

police power	libertarianism
normative analysis	laissez faire
political ideology	anarchism
politics	freedom to
empirical theory	freedom from
normative theory	political equality
government	social equality
order	equality of opportunity
communism	equality of outcome
public goods	rights
totalitarianism	libertarian
socialism	liberal
democratic socialism	conservative
capitalism	populist

Selected Readings

Corbett, Michael. *Political Tolerance in America: Freedom and Equality in Public Attitudes.* New York: Longman, 1982. Corbett summarizes research on support for civil liberties and civil rights in America. Drawing heavily on public opinion surveys, he shows the generally upward trend in political tolerance and analyzes tolerant attitudes by social groups.

Ebenstein, William, and Edwin Fogelman. *Today's Isms: Communism, Fascism, Capitalism, Socialism.* 9th ed. Englewood Cliffs, N.J.: Prentice-Hall, 1985. This standard brief source describes the history of each of the four major "isms" and relates each to developments in contemporary politics. It is concise, informative, and readable.

Herson, Lawrence. *The Politics of Ideas: Political Theory and American Public Policy.* Homewood, Ill.: Dorsey Press, 1984. Herson guides a lively journey through American political history, culture, and thought. It has especially good sections on populism, democracy, and the contemporary nature of liberals and conservatives.

Maddox, William S., and Stuart A. Lilie. *Beyond Liberal and Conservative: Reassessing the Political Spectrum*. Washington, D.C.: Cato Institute, 1984. Unsatisfied with the conventional labels of liberal and conservative, Maddox and Lilie devise a typology of ideologies based on two dimensions: expansion of personal freedom, and government intervention in economic affairs. It is similar to our framework, but less theoretical.

McClosky, Herbert, and John Zaller. *The American Ethos: Public Attitudes Toward Capitalism and Democracy*. Cambridge, Mass.: Harvard University Press, 1985. This book analyzes survey data on citizens and opinion leaders. It argues that conflicts between capitalism and democracy have been a feature of American politics. When these conflicts have occurred, they have tended to be resolved in favor of democracy, producing a form of "welfare capitalism."

Medcalf, Linda J., and Kenneth M. Dolbeare. *Neopolitics: American Political Ideas in the 1980s*. Philadelphia: Temple University Press, 1985. This slim volume reviews the history of ideological labels in American politics. It explains the changing meanings of various labels and updates their usage in contemporary politics. It also describes more recent ideological types, for example, the "new right."

2

Majoritarian or Pluralist Democracy?

The Theory of Democratic Government

Meaning and Symbolism / The Procedural View of Democracy / A Complication: Indirect Versus Direct Democracy / The Substantive View of Democracy / Procedural Democracy Versus Substantive Democracy

Institutional Models of Democracy

The Majoritarian Model of Democracy / An Alternative Model: Pluralist Democracy / Comparing the Majoritarian and Pluralist Models / An Undemocratic Model: Elite Theory / Comparing Elite and Pluralist Theory

Democracies Around the World

Testing for Democratic Government / American Democracy: More Pluralist Than Majoritarian

A sniper used a rifle to shoot Martin Luther King, Jr., in Memphis on April 4, 1968. An assassin used a handgun to kill Robert Kennedy two months later in Los Angeles. Despite having a police record, King's killer purchased his weapon over the counter. Kennedy's killer bought a cheap "Saturday night special," no questions asked. Both murders vividly recalled President John F. Kennedy's assassination with a mail-order rifle in Dallas in 1963. Now a stunned nation insisted on stricter gun controls. Congress quickly responded by passing the Gun Control Act of 1968, which outlawed the interstate sale of handguns, required gun dealers to maintain records of sales, and otherwise aided in tracing weapons sales. By responding promptly and positively to public opinion, Congress acted as one would expect an elected legislature in a democracy to act.

Americans continued to favor strict laws controlling handguns throughout the 1970s and 1980s. For example, polls consistently showed majorities of nearly three to one in favor of laws requiring a police permit to purchase a gun.[1] But in 1986, Congress turned against public opinion and relaxed the 1968 act. The votes in the Senate and House weren't even close. The key Senate vote to weaken the legislation was 79 to 15, and the House vote was 292 to 130. Under the new law, gun collectors would not have to obtain a license before selling firearms; records of ammunition sales would no longer have to be kept; and federal authorities would be limited to only one unannounced inspection of gun dealers per year.

NRA Aims at State Legislators
Members of the National Rifle Association (NRA) attend a hearing on state legislation for handgun control in Massachusetts. The NRA opposes all aspects of gun control on any level of government, and it carefully keeps track of which legislators are its friends and which are its foes, in anticipation of the next election.

According to the executive director of the International Association of Chiefs of Police, the new legislation would have "a very detrimental effect on law enforcement and public safety."[2] His judgment was echoed by most of the law and order establishment. The National Sheriffs Association, the Police Foundation, the Fraternal Order of Police, the National Troopers Coalition, and the American Bar Association (ABA) also fought the weaker bill. Scores of police officers came to Congress to argue against relaxing the gun control law. Who could possibly defeat this awesome combination of law enforcement officers backed by public opinion?

The winner was the "gun lobby"—a collection of groups devoted to gun usage and united in the belief that gun controls deprive citizens of their constitutional right to bear arms yet fail to reduce crime. The gun lobby includes the National Rifle Association (NRA), Gun Owners of America, the Citizens' Committee for the Right to Keep and Bear Arms, and similar groups.

Without question, the most important group in the gun lobby is the NRA, whose three million members are quick to contact their representatives on the gun control issue. In addition to its own advertising against the old law, the NRA contributed $1.5 million dollars in 1985 to sympathetic political committees. The NRA effort capped its long campaign to relax the gun control act passed after the King and Kennedy assassinations. On this issue, the gun lobby eventually outweighed public opinion and the law enforcement organizations.

The evidence is clear that Congress voted against what a majority of the people wanted on gun control and voted for a position favored by a minority of gun owners but backed by organized interest groups. Was Congress's decision "democratic"? If not, can we really say that the United States is a democracy?

Chapter 1 discussed three basic values that underlie *what* government should do. In this chapter we discuss *how* government should decide what to do. In particular, we set forth criteria for judging whether or not a government's decisionmaking process is democratic.

THE THEORY OF DEMOCRATIC GOVERNMENT

How a government makes decisions depends first on how many citizens are involved in the process. Imagine a continuum running from rule by one person, through rule by a few, to rule by many. Ancient Greek philosophers gave us two different sets of terms for these situations—one set is based on the Greek root *kratein* meaning "to rule" and the other is based on *archy* meaning "supreme power."

At one extreme is an **autocracy** (or **monarchy**), in which one individual has the power to make all important decisions. The concentration of power in the hands of one person (usually a king) was more common in

One	Few	Many
Autocracy	Aristocracy	Democracy
Monarchy	Oligarchy	Polyarchy

earlier historical periods, although some argue that Hitler ruled Germany autocratically.

Aristocracy means literally "rule by the best" citizens; **oligarchy** puts government power in the hands of "the few." Earlier in history, the nobility or the major landowners often ruled as an aristocracy. Today, aristocracy does not properly describe, say, a group of military leaders ruling an under-developed country; oligarchy is more suitable for that situation. Some critics contend that industrialized nations are also really oligarchies. They argue that the few individuals who head a nation's key financial, industrial, and com-munications institutions amount to a **ruling elite** that can govern a modern society as surely as an aristocracy governed a traditional society.

At the other extreme of the continuum is **democracy,** which means "rule by the people," and—a less familiar term—**polyarchy,** which means literally that "the many" hold the power. Most scholars believe that the United States, Britain, France, and other countries in Western Europe are genuine democracies. Dissenters contend that these countries may *appear* to be democracies, because they hold free elections, but that they are actually run by elites for the elites' benefit. Nevertheless, most people today agree that governments *should* be democratic — whatever that means.

Meaning and Symbolism

Americans have a simple answer to the question "who should govern?" It is "the people." Unfortunately, this is too simple an answer. It fails to define who constitutes "the people." Should we include young children? Recent immigrants? Illegal aliens? This answer also fails to tell us how "the people" should *do* the governing. Should they be assembled in a stadium? Vote by mail? Choose others to govern for them? We need to analyze that standard answer carefully to find out what "government by the people" really means.

The term *democracy* originated in Greek writings around the fifth century B.C. *Demos* referred to the common people, the masses. Then, as now, the definition of *democracy* was "authority in (or rule by) the people."[3] However, the ancient Greeks regarded democracy as an inferior form of government compared with aristocracy. This original fear of democracy still shows in the negative term *demagogue,* which describes a politician who appeals to the masses and often deceives them by manipulating their emotions and prejudices.

Many centuries after the golden age of Greek civilization, democracy was still viewed negatively and even feared, as the equivalent to mob rule. During President George Washington's administration, opponents of a new political party sought to stain it by calling it a "democratic" party. No one would do that in politics today. In fact, the term has become so popular that the names of more than 20 percent of the world's political parties—more than one out of every five—contain some variation of *democracy*.[4]

In the United States, democracy has become the apple pie and mother-hood of political discourse. Like *justice* and *decency, democracy* is now a term of reverence adopted by politicians of all persuasions. Even totalita-rian regimes use it. The Soviet Union routinely refers to the communist govern-ments of Eastern Europe as "peoples' democracies." Like other complex social concepts, democracy means different things to different people. There are, however, two major schools of thought about what constitutes democracy.

The first school of thought regards democracy as a form of government. It emphasizes *procedures* for enabling the people to govern, such as meeting to discuss issues, voting in elections, and running for public office. The second school sees democracy in the *substance* of government policies, such as freedom of religion and provision for human needs. The *substantive* approach is concerned with *what* a government does; the *procedural* approach focuses on *how* decisions are made.[5] Each school of thought provides a set of *normative* principles that state how a government *ought* to function if it is to be called a democracy. Normative principles stress pure ideals and create perfect standards of judgment, which in practice are never fully achieved.

The Procedural View of Democracy

Procedural democratic theory prescribes a set of normative principles that state how a government ought to make decisions. These principles come from responses to three distinct questions that need to be answered before any group can agree on how to make decisions:

1. *Who* should participate in decisionmaking?
2. *How much* should each participant's preferences count in voting?
3. *How many* votes are needed to reach a decision?

The procedural conception of democracy states that *everyone* should participate in government decisionmaking. Again, there may be debate over what "everyone" means, but the ideals of democratic theory permit no exclusions. Everyone within the boundaries of the political community should be allowed to participate in its decisions. And everyone really means *everyone* — including the mentally handicapped, convicted felons, new immigrants, and children. If some people are prohibited from participating, they are excluded for practical or political reasons. The theory of democracy itself does not exclude anyone from participation. We refer to this principle as **universal participation.**

Procedural theory also answers the second question by requiring that each person's preference must carry as much weight as any other person's preference. Cast in terms of voting, all votes should be counted *equally*. This is the principle of **political equality.**

Note that universal participation and political equality are logically distinct principles. Even if everyone were allowed to participate in a decision, some votes might be counted more than others. President Abraham Lincoln reportedly once took a vote among his cabinet members and found his position opposed by every one of them. As he summarized the vote and the decision, "The vote is one aye and the rest nay; the aye carries!" Everyone participated, but Lincoln's vote outweighed all the others combined. (No one ever said that presidents had to run their cabinets democratically.)

In answer to the third and last question raised above, procedural theory prescribes that a group should decide to do what the *majority* of its participants (50 percent plus 1 person more) wants to do. This principle is called majority rule. (If participants divide over more than two alternatives, so that a majority does not occur, the principle usually defaults to *plurality rule,* in which the group should do what *most* participants want.)

Note that majority rule does not necessarily go hand in hand with universal participation and political equality. Group decisions can require an *extraordinary majority*—some stated percentage greater than 50. For example, the U.S. Senate grants each of its one hundred senators only one vote on every issue, but some issues—such as approval of treaties with other nations—require a two-thirds majority for passage. However, all three principles are required before we have truly democratic procedures for decision-making.

A Complication: Indirect Versus Direct Democracy

These three principles—universal participation, political equality, and majority rule—are widely recognized as necessary for democratic decision-making in any group. In small, simple societies, these principles can be met in a **direct democracy**—in which all members of the group meet to make decisions, while observing political equality and majority rule. Something close to direct democracy is practiced in some New England villages, where citizens gather in "town meetings" to make community decisions. For example, citizens in Derry, New Hampshire, governed themselves in annual town meetings for 158 years. Usually held the second Tuesday in March, the Derry town meeting was an all-day affair that began with the election of officers and then proceeded to decide such matters as road repairs and building maintenance.

In large, complex societies, however, the people cannot assemble in one place to participate directly in government. Even in Derry, the town meeting failed as the population increased. When Derry grew to 25,000, turnout at town meetings declined to less than 10 percent of the voting population, which still required a hall seating more than a thousand citizens. In 1985, Derry bowed to growth and switched to a different form of government, an elected town council headed by a mayor.[6] The town still followed democratic principles in voting for members of the town council, but the council decided village policies in place of the people.

Thus Derry changed from direct to **indirect democracy:** its citizens participate in government by electing public officials to make government decisions for them. Because their elected officials are expected to represent the voters' views and interests—that is, to serve as the agents of the citizenry—indirect democracy is also known as **representative government.**

The eighteenth-century French philosopher Jean Jacques Rousseau contended that true democracy was impossible unless all citizens gathered together to make their own decisions and to supervise their government.[7] Some theorists today argue the same point.[8] These writers are concerned with democracy in its purest form—direct democracy. Other theorists, such as the nineteenth-century English philosopher John Stuart Mill (1806–1873), accepted the necessity of indirect democracy and saw representative government as the best *possible* form of government.[9]

Direct Democracy in a New England Town Meeting
Adults and children alike attend the town meeting in Pittsfield, Vermont. Citizens use the town meeting to govern the activities of their village, which amounts to direct democracy. Town meetings typically run all day. In Pittsfield, baked goods are available at lunch time to give the citizens food for thought during the rest of the meeting.

If the voting for representatives follows the principles of universal participation, political equality, and majority rule, then at least the election is democratic. After the election, however, the elected representatives might not make the same decisions the people would have made if they had gathered for the same purpose. To cope with this possibility in representative government, procedural theory requires an additional decisionmaking principle: **responsiveness.** Elected representatives should *respond* to public opinion; they should do what the people want. That is, representatives should do what the people would do if they could assemble to act directly.

According to the strict demands of democratic theory, the principle of responsiveness is absolute. The government should do what a majority wants, immediately, and *regardless of what it is*. Suppose that 55 percent of the citizens would permit children to pray in public schools. According to democratic theory, the government should respond promptly by allowing prayers in public schools. To do otherwise would violate the principle of responsiveness.

Adding this principle to deal with the case of indirect democracy, we now have four principles of procedural democracy:

1. Universal participation
2. Political equality
3. Majority rule
4. Government responsiveness to public opinion

. . . Please Help Me Pass This Test!
In reality, prayer in school is a serious matter. Surveys regularly show that most Americans believe that schools should be allowed to start each day with a prayer, but the Supreme Court has held that school-organized prayers would violate the Constitution. By making such decisions, the Court is protecting minority rights, but it is denying majority rule.

If people wish to limit the government's immediate and complete responsiveness to public opinion, they must find reasons outside the *procedural* theory of democracy. Checks on responsiveness usually come from *substantive* democratic theory.

The Substantive View of Democracy

Substantive democratic theory focuses on the *substance* of government policies rather than on the procedures followed in making those policies. For example, Christians account for more than 90 percent of the U.S. population. Suppose that the Christian majority backed a constitutional amendment to require Bible reading in public schools, that the amendment was passed by Congress, and that it was ratified by the states. In a strict procedural view, the action would be accepted as democratic. But most substantive theorists would reject it as violating the substantive principle of freedom of religion. Substantive principles must be embodied in a government's policies if that government is to be considered democratic. *Which* principles (and, thus, which policies) are central to the substantive conception of democracy? Most substantive theorists will accept the following criterion as a least common denominator for classifying a government as democratic: the

Social Equality in the Classroom
Would our government be democratic if it did not provide for equal educational opportunity through integrated schools? Substantive theorists might argue that democratic government in a multiracial society requires integrated schools. Procedural theorists would leave the issue to be decided by public opinion.

government's policies guarantee civil liberties (for example, freedom of religion and freedom of expression) and civil rights (for example, protection against discrimination in employment and housing). According to this standard, the claim that the United States is a democracy rests on its record in ensuring its citizens these rights and liberties. How good this record is will be discussed in Chapters 17 and 18.

Agreement among substantive theorists breaks down when discussion moves from civil rights to *social* rights (adequate health care, quality education, decent housing) and *economic* rights (private property, steady employment). They would disagree most sharply on whether a government must promote social equality to qualify as a democracy. For example, must a state guarantee unemployment benefits and adequate public housing to be called democratic? Some substantive theorists insist that policies leading to social equality are required in a democracy.[10] Others limit their requirements to policies safeguarding civil rights and liberties.

The political ideology of the theorist tends to explain his or her position on what democracy really requires in substantive policies. Conservative theorists have a narrow view of the scope of government and also have a narrow view of the social and economic rights guaranteed to individuals by government. Liberal theorists believe that a democratic government should guarantee its citizens a much broader spectrum of social and economic rights. In Chapters 15 and 16, we will review important economic and social policies that our government has actually followed over time; keep in mind, however, that what the government *has* done is not necessarily a good guide to what a democratic government *should* do.

Procedural Democracy Versus Substantive Democracy

There is a problem with the substantive view of democracy. It does not provide clear and precise criteria that permit us to determine whether a government is or is not democratic. It is, in fact, open to unending arguments over which government policies are truly democratic in the substantive sense.

There is also a problem with the procedural viewpoint. Although it presents specific criteria for democratic government, those criteria may produce undesirable social policies that prey on minorities. This clashes with **minority rights** — the idea that citizens are entitled to certain things that cannot be denied by majority decisions. Opinions differ about which "certain things" constitute minority rights, but freedom of religion is a good example. One way to protect minority rights is by limiting the principle of majority rule — requiring extraordinary majorities when decisions must be made on certain subjects or by putting the subjects in the Constitution, beyond the reach of majority rule.

In effect, the issue of prayers in school illustrates the limits of majority rule. No matter how large, majorities in Congress cannot pass a law to allow organized prayers in public schools, for the Supreme Court has determined that the Constitution forbids such laws. The Constitution could be changed so that it no longer protects religious minorities, but amendment is a cumbersome process that involves extraordinary majorities. Thus, when limits are put on the principle of majority rule, the *minority* often rules instead. Those who are committed to majority rule in the procedural conception of democracy have no alternative: they must insist on *unlimited* majority rule and then trust in government by the people.

Clearly, the substantive and procedural conceptions of democracy are not completely compatible. In choosing one over the other, the theorist chooses to emphasize either policies or procedures. We favor the procedural conception of democracy because it more clearly approaches the classical definition of democracy as government by the people. Moreover, procedural democracy is founded in clear, well-established rules for decisionmaking in social groups. By choosing the procedural conception, we are stuck with its major problem: it permits a democratic government — one based on unlimited majority rule — to enact undesirable, distasteful, or "substantively undemocratic" policies.

But if we are stuck with this problem, it is only because the word *democracy* has come to mean more than one expects from an analytical term. Because we equate democracy with desirable government, we have trouble accepting undesirable policies in a democratic government. Early political theorists did not attach such overtones to the idea of democracy; they saw it simply and realistically as a mechanism for making government decisions.

If we do the same, if we realize that democratic government and desirable policies are not necessarily synonymous, then we can live with a conception that allows decisions made through democratic procedures to be substantively undesirable.

INSTITUTIONAL MODELS OF DEMOCRACY

A small group of people can agree to make democratic decisions directly by using the principles of universal participation, political equality, and majority rule. But even the smallest nations have too many citizens to practice direct democracy. If nations want democracy, they must achieve it through some form of representative government, electing officials to make government decisions. Even then, democratic government is not guaranteed. Governments must have means for determining what the people want, as well as some means for translating those wants into agreeable decisions. In other words, democratic government requires **institutional mechanisms** — established procedures and organizations — to translate public opinion into government policy, thereby fulfilling the fourth principle, responsiveness. Elections, political parties, legislatures, and interest groups (which we shall discuss in separate chapters) are all examples of such institutional mechanisms in politics.

Some democratic theorists favor institutions that tie government decisions very closely to the desires of the majority of citizens. If most citizens want laws against the sale of pornography, then the government should outlaw pornography. If citizens want more money spent on defense and less on social welfare (or vice versa), the government should act accordingly. For these theorists, the essence of democratic government is mass participation in politics and majority rule.

Other theorists place less importance on the principles of majority rule and responsiveness. They doubt the wisdom of relying so heavily on mass opinion, and they favor institutions that allow groups of citizens to defend their interests in government decisions. Both schools hold a procedural view of democracy but differ in how they interpret "government by the people." These theoretical positions can be summarized by alternative models of democratic institutions. As a model, each is an idealized plan for achieving democratic government through institutional mechanisms. The *majoritarian model* values the people in general. The *pluralist model* values the people in groups.

The Majoritarian Model of Democracy

The **majoritarian model of democracy** relies on the classical, textbook theory of democracy. It interprets government by the people as government by the *majority* of the people. The majoritarian model tries to approximate the people's role in a direct democracy within the limitations of representative government. It assumes that mass citizen participation in politics is needed to force government responsiveness to public opinion by threatening officials with election defeat. The majoritarian model depends on institutions that enable the mass of citizens to express their preferences directly in the political system and that count how many people prefer each alternative.

Popular election of government officials is the main mechanism for democratic government in the majoritarian model. Citizens are expected to control their representatives' behavior by choosing wisely in the first place and by re-electing or defeating public officials according to their performance. Elections fulfill the first three principles of democratic theory: universal participation, political equality, and majority rule. The thrill of re-election and the agony of defeat at the polls are expected to motivate public officials to be responsive as well.

Usually we think of elections only as mechanisms for choosing between candidates for public office, but majoritarian theorists also favor elections as mechanisms for deciding on government policies. An election on a policy issue is called a **referendum.** No provision for referenda exists at the national level, but they are common at the state level and appeared on the ballot in most states in the 1984 general elections. Citizens in Missouri, for example, had the opportunity to vote on closing the nuclear power plant in Calloway, Missouri. (They voted against closing it, 67 percent to 33 percent.[11])

In the majoritarian model, citizens are expected to do more than vote. They are expected to inform themselves about issues, to discuss politics in community meetings, and even to propose legislation through a process called the **initiative.** This process allows citizens to gather petitions to place an issue before the legislature or before the people in a referendum. (In fact, the Missouri nuclear plant issue arose from citizen initiative.)

The most fervent advocates of majoritarian democracy have proposed using modern inventions to maximize governmental responsiveness to majority wishes. Some proposed incorporating public opinion polls, first used regularly in the 1930s, as a mechanism for making government decisions. More recently, some theorists have suggested that electronic technology might offer more and better referenda. For instance, citizens could decide many legislative issues simply by using plastic voter identification cards on computer terminals installed in all homes.[12] People disagree about the merits of maximizing responsiveness through "video voting," but it certainly is technically possible (see Feature 2.1).

The majoritarian model contends that citizens can control their government if they have adequate mechanisms for popular participation. It also assumes that citizens show a high degree of (1) knowledge about government and politics; (2) participation in politics; and (3) rationality in voting on the candidates.

If these factors are truly necessary to the smooth functioning of majoritarian democracy, then the majoritarian model is in trouble in the United States. Only 26 percent of a national sample of voters interviewed just after the 1984 election said that they "followed what's going on" in government "most of the time." More respondents (37 percent) said that they followed politics "only now and then" or "hardly at all." Further, as you will see in Chapter 6, voter turnout in presidential elections has fallen to little more than half of the eligible electorate. And those who do vote often choose party candidates more from habit than from rationally examining the candidates'

A Fishin' Petition
*Citizens of New Bedford, Massachusetts, sign a dory (fishing boat, to landlubbers) that
served as a petition protesting the auctioning of oil drilling rights in Georges Bank, a prime
fishing ground off Cape Cod. The dory was towed to the White House for presentation to
then-president Jimmy Carter. Signing petitions to request government action is one way
that people can involve themselves in politics.*

positions on issues. Obviously, the strong assumptions of citizens' political
knowledge and activity that underlie the majoritarian model simply do not
hold.

An Alternative Model: Pluralist Democracy

For years, political scientists struggled valiantly to match the majoritarian
model of democracy with polling data that showed a simple ignorance of
politics in public opinion. One example will illustrate the shallowness of
public opinion. Throughout President Ronald Reagan's administration, the
U.S. government supported the Nicaraguan rebels (the ''contras'') against the
Soviet-backed Sandinista regime. Reagan picturesquely and frequently described the rebels as ''freedom fighters.'' Nevertheless, at the height of
congressional debate on a key vote to grant $100 million in aid to the rebels,
only 38 percent of those polled in a national survey realized that the United
States and the contras were on the same side.[13]

Feature 2.1

Electronic Democracy

Thanks to computers and telecommunications, we could now involve the masses of citizens directly in government decisions by allowing them to vote on issues by using computer terminals in their own homes. Would this be a good idea? A philosopher writing in *PC World*, a computer magazine, sees problems but urges us to trust the people (and the computers).

> Imagine a nationwide interactive communications network that connects with every home's personal computer, telephone, and TV set. On this network local, state, and national issues are debated and decided periodically. Each viewpoint is clearly and fairly framed, and unpopular views are defended vigorously by a "public dissenter." Voters, using individual passwords to prevent fraud, cast their ballots at the keyboard. The true voice of the people is regularly and authoritatively expressed. The electronic referendum becomes a part of our lives—as popular as "Monday Night Football," though with much more at stake. . . .
>
> Electronic democracy would profoundly change the way we view "government by the people." Today we popularly elect representatives, who then make policy affecting our lives. Electronic democracy promises speed, accuracy, and convenience without representation. Every issue of local, state, or national importance can be put directly to the voter. Problems of fairness, of course, would have to be solved in the design of such a system. Problems like ensuring universal access and guarding against fraud—which have been with us since the beginning of our republic—would have to be solved. But the

Source: Carl Cohen, *PC World* (July 1984): 21–22. Copyright © 1984 PC World Communications. Reprinted by permission.

Polling did not become an established research tool for studying public opinion until the 1950s. When repeated polls revealed how little the public actually knew about political affairs, the assumptions of majoritarian democracy came into question. Obviously, the wisdom of government by the people—the very idea of democracy itself—was also questioned. If most voters did not know enough to make rational political judgments, why pretend that they should govern at all? In short, why argue for democracy?

In the 1950s, an alternative interpretation of democracy evolved, one tailored to the limited knowledge and participation of the *real* electorate rather than the perfect qualities of the ideal one. It was based on the concept of **pluralism.** According to pluralism, modern society consists of innumerable groupings of people who share economic, religious, ethnic, or cultural interests. People with similar interests often organize formal groups—such as the Future Farmers of America, the Junior Chamber of Commerce, and the Knights of Columbus. Many of these formal, purely social groups have little contact with government but occasionally find themselves backing or opposing government policy. When an organized group seeks to influence government policy, it is called an **interest group.** Many interest groups key question about electronic democracy is not so much its feasibility as its desirability. . . .

Would "one terminal, one vote" democracy improve the quality of decisions made? Would the First Amendment be defeated if put to a vote of the American people? Would the taking of American hostages by a foreign power cause a government instantly responsive to the will of its citizens to retaliate by reflex? The masses have commonly been judged as being intemperate in war, shortsighted in peace, and unable to deal with the refinements of economic policy. Recent national polls on political issues tend to support this view.

But if we cannot trust ourselves, who can we trust? If genuine self-government is dangerous, are we not saying that democracy is dangerous — unless restrained by the aristocrat? Is government by the terminal what we really want? Or should we honestly admit that we feel competent to choose our leaders but not to guide them? . . .

If we reject computerized, direct democracy because we fear the outcome, then the whole concept of democracy is in question. Perhaps it is not computers that present the real problem, but placing the ultimate authority in the hands of the governed. And so the answer is at hand: too much democracy — in any form — is dangerous.

I reject this answer because I am a democrat. I realize that people can and sometimes do make terrible mistakes, but I trust them in the long run — certainly more than any elite body. A computerized system of direct participation in public affairs might bring about a better, more robust democracy. . . .

Computers cannot produce a spirit of universal participation, but they can support it. If politics becomes more tangible, more countable, and more keenly sensed and effective because of computers, we may yet revive our flagging democracy. The personal computer, tied to a world of computers, can reinforce the spirit of democracy and endear it to us.

regularly spend a great deal of time trying to influence government policy (see Chapter 8). Examples include the AFL-CIO, the Associated Milk Producers, the National Education Association (NEA), the Moral Majority, Operation PUSH, the National Organization for Women (NOW), and — of course — the National Rifle Association.

The **pluralist model of democracy** interprets *government by the people* to mean government by people operating through competing interest groups. According to this model, democracy exists when many (plural) organizations operate separately from the government, press their interests on the government, and even challenge the government.[14] Compared with majoritarian thinking, pluralist theory shifts the focus of democratic government from the mass electorate to the organized group. It changes the criterion for democratic government from responsiveness to mass public opinion to responsiveness to the claims of citizens organized into interest groups.

The two major mechanisms in pluralist democracy are interest groups and a decentralized government structure that provides ready access to public officials and is open to hearing the groups' arguments for and against government policies. In a centralized structure, decisions are made at one point,

Tenants versus Landlords
*Representatives of opposing
interest groups—renters and
realtors—jammed the city hall
in Cambridge, Massachusetts,
when the city council considered
a rent control law. When an
issue is very important to
opposing groups and their
members turn out in large
numbers to confront government
officials, pluralist politics can
become quite heated.*

the top of the hierarchy. The few decisionmakers at the top are too busy to hear the claims of competing interest groups and to consider those claims in making their decisions. A centralized, hierarchical government structure cannot provide the access and openness necessary for pluralist democracy, which is better served by a decentralized and organizationally complex government structure. The ideal is a system that divides government authority among numerous institutions with overlapping authority. Under such a system, competing interest groups have alternative points of access to present and argue their claims.

Our Constitution approaches the pluralist ideal in the way it divides authority among the branches of government. When the NAACP could not get Congress to outlaw segregated schools in the South, it turned to the federal court system, which did what Congress would not. When Reagan submitted a budget that cut funding for Amtrak trains, train travelers organized and protested to Congress, which restored the funding. According to pluralist democracy, if all opposing interests are allowed to organize, and if the system can be kept open so that all substantial claims have an opportunity to be heard, then the diverse needs of a pluralist society will be served when the issue is decided.

Although many scholars have contributed to this alternative model, pluralist democracy has become most closely identified with political scientist Robert Dahl.* According to Dahl, the fundamental axiom of pluralist de-

*Robert A. Dahl, *Pluralist Democracy in the United States* (Chicago: Rand McNally, 1967). In his *A Preface to Democratic Theory* (Chicago: University of Chicago Press, 1956), Dahl had previously used *polyarchy* to refer to his conception of pluralist democracy. We shall use the more common term instead.

mocracy is that "instead of a single center of sovereign power there must be multiple centers of power, none of which is or can be wholly sovereign."[15] Some watchwords of pluralist democracy, therefore, are *divided authority, decentralization,* and *open access.*

Comparing the Majoritarian and Pluralist Models

In majoritarian democracy, individual citizens — not interest groups — control government actions, mainly through electoral mechanisms. Thus majoritarianism requires that voters be knowledgeable about government affairs. Majoritarian democracy relies on institutional mechanisms that harness the majority's capacity to make decisions. Definitive elections and a centralized government structure are mechanisms that aid majority rule.

Pluralism does not demand much knowledge from citizens in general. It requires specialized knowledge only from interest group members, especially from their leaders. In contrast with majoritarian democracy, pluralist democracy seeks to *limit* majority action so that interest groups can have a thorough say. Pluralist democracy relies on strong interest groups and a decentralized government structure. These mechanisms interfere with majority rule and thereby defend minority interests. One could even say that pluralism allows "minorities" to rule.

Why They Are Called Lobbyists
At the national level, interest groups are usually represented by highly paid lobbyists. These people are called lobbyists because they often gather in the lobby outside congressional meeting rooms, positioned to contact senators and representatives coming and going. Here, lobbyists are waiting to help members of the House Ways and Means Committee understand the importance of their pet tax loopholes.

An Undemocratic Model: Elite Theory

If pluralist democracy interferes with majority rule and even allows *minorities* to rule, how does it differ from **elite theory**—the view that a small group of people (a minority) makes most important government decisions? According to elite theory, the important government decisions are made by an identifiable and stable minority with such shared characteristics as vast wealth and business connections.* Elitism contends that these relatively few individuals wield power in America because they control its key financial, communications, industrial, and governmental institutions.

According to elite theory, the United States is not a democracy but an oligarchy. Although the voters may appear to control government through elections, elite theorists argue that the powerful few in society manage to define the issues and to constrain the possible outcomes of government decisions to suit their own interests. Quite clearly, elite theory describes a government that operates in an undemocratic fashion.

Elite theory appeals to many people, especially to those who believe that wealth dominates politics. The theory also provides plausible explanations for specific political decisions. For example, government spending for new military weapons systems—including enormous overruns in estimated costs—often seems controlled by agreements between the military and giant defense contractors, such as General Dynamics and McDonnell-Douglas.[16] Even President Dwight Eisenhower, himself a former five-star general, warned of the influence of the ''military-industrial complex'' on government policy (in Chapter 19, we shall examine that influence in more detail).

Elite theory breaks down, however, when one tries using it to explain a broader range of political decisions. Dahl, the leading pluralist theorist, has suggested that convincing research on the ruling elite model must meet three tests:

1. The hypothetical ruling elite must be a well-defined group.

2. A fair sample of cases involving key political decisions must exist. In those decisions, the preferences of the hypothetical ruling elite must be shown to run counter to the preferences of any other likely group that might be suggested.

3. In such cases, the preferences of the elite must regularly prevail.[17]

Some researchers have indeed attempted the first test, defining the ruling group. One study identified 7,314 ''elite positions'' at the top of twelve categories of institutions in the corporate, public interest, and governmental sectors of society.[18] Although this number represents only a tiny fraction of the nation's population, 7,314 rulers somehow seems many more than ''the few.''

---

*The classic book on elite theory in American politics is C. Wright Mills, *The Power Elite* (New York: Oxford University Press, 1956). Actually, elite theory argues that elite rule is inevitable in *every* government, indeed in every large organization. See Thomas R. Dye, *Who's Running America? The Conservative Years* (Englewood Cliffs, N.J.: Prentice-Hall, 1986), especially pp. 2–6, for a summary of elite theory.

The Power Elite?
This picture symbolizes the underlying notion of elite theory — that government is driven by wealth. In truth, wealthy people usually have more influence in government than do people of ordinary means. Critics of elite theory point out that it is difficult to demonstrate that an identifiable ruling elite usually sticks together and gets its way in government policy.

The second test, identifying numerous government decisions that pit the special interests of this ruling elite against others' interests, has not been seriously performed in research at the national level. Therefore the third test, determining whether or not elite interests regularly prevail in such decisions, also cannot be met. Careful studies of decisionmaking in American cities, which should be even more susceptible to elite rule than the whole nation, have shown that different groups win on different issues.[19] This tendency also seems to be true in some cases at the national level. For instance, the giant oil, chemical, and steel industries do not always triumph over environmental groups on issues of air pollution. What was once the nation's largest corporation, AT&T, was even forced to break up its telephone monopoly by suits brought by much smaller communications companies.

The available evidence of government decisions on many different topics does not generally support elite theory — at least in the sense that an identifiable ruling elite usually gets its way in government policy. Nevertheless, elite theory is not dead, and it is still forcefully argued by radical critics of American politics.[20] We believe, however, that pluralist theory offers a more satisfactory interpretation of American politics.

Comparing Elite and Pluralist Theory

The key difference between elite and pluralist theory lies in the durability of the ruling minority. Unlike elite theory, pluralist theory defines government conflict not in terms of *a* minority versus *the* majority, but in terms of many minorities conflicting with one another in different policy areas. In the management of national forests, for example, many interest groups join the political competition — logging companies, recreational campers, environmentalists, and so on. Their various interests are pressed on government by group representatives who are well informed about the issues as they affect their members (see Feature 2.2). According to elite theory, the financial

How Do You Like Your Wood?
These photos dramatize the conflict between environmentalists and loggers. The environmentalists envision the big trees soaring majestically toward the sky; loggers see them cut into timber. Because people can neither build homes from nor print textbooks on majesty, government must somehow strike a balance between the legitimate interests of these two competing groups.

Feature 2.2

Interest Group Conflict Over Uses of Forests

According to pluralism, modern society is composed of diverse groups struggling to advance their competing interests. The interplay of interest groups trying to influence government policy is clearly seen in the debate over the use of the national forests. Should their prime use be for commerce, recreation, or simply preservation? This news item explains the issues involved.

KALISPELL, Mont., April 12 — The future of the country's 120 national forests is being laid out in a process that has attracted criticism both from people who want more economic development of the forests and from those who want less.

In the big Flathead National Forest here in northern Montana, those issues are drawn as clearly as anywhere. People who believe the forests should produce timber and minerals for local jobs are opposing those who want the forest to be managed more like a national park, as a place for recreation and wildlife. . . .

The plans being drawn up are the first long-range, forest-by-forest management blueprints that were required under the National Forest Management Act of 1976. The act requires forest supervisors to look 50 years ahead and draw up detailed plans for each of the 10- to 15-year intervals between now and that "planning horizon." The plans must spell out how much timber cutting will be allowed, where oil and gas drilling may take place, what roads should be built, if any, and what lands should be set aside to remain wild.

Conservationists argue that the act was drawn up to curb policies that resulted in excessive clear-cutting of lumber, land erosion, infringement on wildlife habitat and the like. . . .

They say their fears that the timber industry would try to circumvent the act in the new forest plans were confirmed when early draft plans envisaged a massive increase in timber harvesting. Only a public outcry forced the service to retreat, say people like Peter Coppleman, senior counsel at the **Wilderness Society,** a conservation group based in Washington. . . .

Edgar B. Brannon, supervisor of the Flathead National Forest, divides the contending forces in this planning process between "the utilitarians" and the "naturists." To varying degrees, he said, their opposing views are reflected in continuing disagreements about the proper use of the more than 400 million acres of public land in the West and in the rest of the country. . . .

The debate over how national forests should be used is not a new one. Early in the century Gifford Pinchot, the country's first forester and founder of the national forest system, stressed the careful management of woodlands to increase their economic benefit to man. Although he is remembered as a conservationist, he was nonetheless opposed by John Muir, who argued for protecting the bulk of American wild lands from any economic use and went on to found the **Sierra Club,** a conservation lobby. . . .

The timber industry, the dominant but declining source of jobs in the interior Northwest, says the trend toward reduced timber harvests reflects the rise in power of the environmental movement, or the "preservationists," as they are beginning to be called by opponents like John Benneth, director of the **American Forest Institute,** an industry group. . . .

Richard Kuhl, head of the Flathead chapter of the **Montana Wilderness Association,** counters that economics, and not forest policy, is what is hurting the lumber industry. . . .

Of the 32 national forests that have completed their 10- to 15-year plans, 22 have attracted 139 separate appeals, and all but a handful of the appeals are from conservation groups. The 10 remaining forest plans have so far drawn no appeals. . . .

Mr. Brannon's plan for the Flathead National Forest has drawn 39 appeals, 37 of them from environmentalists asking for more wilderness, more wildlife sanctuaries and protection of scenic vistas and the like, and two from industry asking for more timber cutting. . . .

"Because this is the first time around and it is precedent-setting," he said, "we're getting a lot of appeals from groups that want to establish a position, a posture, that they hope will influence later decisions."

resources of big logging companies ought to win out over the arguments of campers and environmentalists, but that does not always happen.

The pluralist model holds that similar competition among minority interests occurs in other fields, including transportation, agriculture, public utilities, and urban housing. Although those groups with "better connections" in government may win more often, no identifiable elite wins consistently on issues dealing with forest management, transportation, agriculture, and so on. Thus the pluralist model specifically rejects the main implication of elite theory, that a single group dominates government decisions.

Instead, pluralist democracy makes a virtue of the struggle among minority interests. It argues for a government that will accommodate this struggle and channel the result into government action. According to pluralist democracy, the public is best served if the governmental structure provides access for different groups to press their claims in competition with one another. Clearly, this conception of democracy differs from the classic conception based on universal participation, political equality, and majority rule. These principles fit the majoritarian model much better. However, the pluralist reliance on access is compatible with contemporary thinking that democratic government should be open to groups that seek redress of grievances. The pluralist concept also fits the facts about the limited knowledge of the mass of U.S. citizens. Clearly, pluralist democracy is worthy of being embraced as a rival model to majoritarianism, the traditional model of procedural democracy.

DEMOCRACIES AROUND THE WORLD

We have proposed two models of democratic government. The majoritarian model conforms to classical democratic theory for a representative government. According to this model, democracy is a hypothetical form of government that features prompt and complete responsiveness to majority opinion. According to the pluralist model, a government is democratic if it allows these interests to organize freely and to press their claims freely on government.

No government actually achieves the high degree of responsiveness demanded by the majoritarian model. It is also true that no government offers complete and equal access to the claims of all competing groups, as required by the pluralist model. Nevertheless, some nations approach these ideals closely enough to qualify as practicing democracies in an imperfect world.

Testing for Democratic Government

How can we decide which countries qualify as practicing democracies? A government's degree of responsiveness or access cannot be measured directly, so we must turn to indirect tests of democracy. One such test is to look for traits normally associated with democratic government — whether defined from a procedural or from a substantive viewpoint. One scholar, for example, established five criteria for a democracy:

1. *The government bases its legitimacy on representing the desires of its citizens.* [Compare this with responsiveness.]

2. *Leaders are chosen in free elections, contested by at least two viable political parties.* [Compare this with majority rule.]
3. *Most adults can participate in the electoral process.* [Compare this with universal participation.]
4. *Citizens' votes are secret and are not coerced.* [Compare this with political equality.]
5. *Citizens, leaders, and party officials enjoy basic freedoms of speech, press, assembly, religion, and organization.*[21] [Regard these as substantive government policies that create conditions for the practice of the other criteria.]

Because the United States fits all these criteria to a fairly high degree, it qualifies as a democracy. How about the other nations of the world? Compared With What? 2.1 reports several scholars' listings of thirty-one democratic nations with populations of over three million. Each scholar used standards similar to the above criteria, but the standards varied enough to produce somewhat different lists. Although no two lists were identical, nineteen nations among the thirty-one were rated as democracies by all four scholars. The nineteen democracies on which a consensus was reached rely on widespread participation, political equality, and free elections to choose representatives who pay close attention to public opinion in making their decisions.

Nineteen democracies throughout the world does not seem like very many, especially when ninety-three nations have populations greater than three million.[22] Thus, only about 20 percent of the world's nations qualify as democracies according to all four scholars. Even counting all thirty-one nations classified as democratic by at least one scholar, we find that nearly two-thirds of all major nations are undemocratic. By any reckoning, democratic government is relatively rare across the world.

Four of the five criteria above apply to governmental procedures rather than to the substance of government policy. But all of these criteria apply equally to the majoritarian and to the pluralist models of democracy. Although the United States clearly qualifies as a democracy according to these criteria, we cannot use them to judge whether it is closer to a majoritarian or to a pluralist democracy.

American Democracy: More Pluralist Than Majoritarian

It is not idle speculation to ask what kind of democracy is practiced in the United States. The answer to this question can help us understand why our government can be called democratic despite a low level of citizen participation in politics and despite government actions that run contrary to public opinion.

Through the rest of this book, we will probe more deeply to determine how well the United States fits the two alternative models of democracy: majoritarian and pluralist. If our answer is not already apparent, it will soon become obvious. We will argue that the U.S. political system rates relatively low according to the majoritarian model of democracy, but that it fulfills the pluralist model very well.

Compared With What? 2.1

Rating Democracies Around the World

Out of nearly one hundred larger nations in the world, how many qualify as democracies? Four studies that sought to answer this question classified a total of thirty-one nations as democracies. However, only nineteen nations were consistently rated as democracies in each study, as indicated by the shading in the table. The United States was one of these relatively rare consensus democracies.

	Dahl	Butler et al.	Powell	Lijphart
1. Australia	X	X	X	X
2. Austria	X	X	X	X
3. Belgium	X	X	X	X
4. Canada	X	X	X	X
Chile			X	
Colombia	X	X		
5. Denmark	X	X	X	X
Dominican Rep.		X		
6. Finland	X	X	X	X
7. France	X	X	X	X
8. Germany (West)	X	X	X	X
Greece	X	X	X	
India	X	X	X	
9. Ireland	X	X	X	X
10. Israel	X	X	X	X
11. Italy	X	X	X	X
12. Japan	X	X	X	X
13. Netherlands	X	X	X	X
14. New Zealand	X	X	X	X
15. Norway	X	X	X	X
Philippines			X	
Portugal		X		
Spain		X		
Sri Lanka	X	X	X	
16. Sweden	X	X	X	X
17. Switzerland	X	X	X	X
Turkey		X	X	
18. United Kingdom	X	X	X	X
19. United States	X	X	X	X
Uruguay			X	
Venezuela	X		X	
Totals	24	27	27	19

Sources: Robert A. Dahl, *Democracy in the United States* (Chicago: Rand McNally, 1976), p. 47; David Butler, Howard R. Penniman, and Austin Ranney, eds., *Democracy at the Polls* (Washington, D.C.: American Enterprise Institute, 1981), p. 4; G. Bingham Powell, *Contemporary Democracies* (Cambridge, Mass.: Harvard University Press, 1982), p. 5; and Arend Lijphart, *Democracies* (New Haven, Conn.: Yale University Press, 1984), p. 8.

This evaluation may not mean much to you now. But you will learn that the pluralist model makes the United States look far more democratic than it does in light of the majoritarian model. Eventually, it will be up to *you* to decide the answers to these three questions: is the pluralist model really an adequate expression of democracy, or is it a perversion of classical ideals designed to portray America as democratic when it really is not? Does the majoritarian model result in a more desirable type of democracy? If so, is it possible to devise new mechanisms of government to produce the mix of majority rule and minority rights that you desire? These questions should play in the back of your mind as you read further about the workings of American government in meeting the challenge of democracy.

SUMMARY AND PROLOGUE TO THE BOOK

There are not many democracies in the world. Scholars agree in classifying only about nineteen of the larger countries as democratic. Is the United States a democracy? Most scholars agree that it is. A more interesting question is what *kind* of democracy it is. The answer depends on your conception of democracy. Some theorists hold to the substantive conception, calling a government democratic if it implements certain policies — such as guaranteeing freedom of religion, providing for human needs, and ensuring social equality. Others, who see democracy as procedural in nature, define democracy as a form of government in which the people govern through suitable institutional mechanisms.

In this book, we opt for the *procedural* conception of democracy, distinguishing between direct and indirect democracy. In a direct democracy, all citizens gather to govern themselves according to the principles of (1) universal participation, (2) political equality, and (3) majority rule. In indirect democracy, the citizens elect representatives to govern for them. If a representative government is elected mostly in accordance with the three principles listed above and is also usually responsive to public opinion, then it qualifies as a democracy.

The procedural conception of democracy has produced rival institutional models of democratic government. The classical majoritarian model assumes that government response to popular demands comes through mass citizen participation in politics. This model underlies most casual discussions of democracy. Sample surveys of public opinion and behavior have seriously undercut the majoritarian model by showing that many citizens participate little in politics and know little about political affairs. The pluralist model of democracy was devised to accommodate these findings. It argues that democracy in a complex society requires only that government allow private interests to organize and to press their competing claims openly in the political system. It differs from elite theory by arguing that different minorities win on different issues. Pluralist democracy works better in a decentralized and organizationally complex government structure than in a centralized, hierarchical one.

The two models of democracy — *majoritarian* and *pluralist* — join the three political values — *freedom, order,* and *equality* — to complete our set of five key concepts for understanding American government.

As you will see in the chapters that follow, the American political system is better suited to the pluralist reformulation of democracy than to the traditional majoritarian model, which still serves as the democratic ideal in many people's minds. The first chapter in Part II, "Foundations of American Government," explains how (and why) the framers of the Constitution separated government powers among three branches of government in a "horizontal" division of national powers. Chapter 4 shows how federalism—the sharing of powers between the nation and the states—resulted in a "vertical" division of powers. Clearly, this double separation of government powers results in a structure that is conducive to pluralist democracy.

Part III, "Mechanisms for Linking People with Government," examines the institutional mechanisms that permit participation in American government. Chapter 5 assesses citizens' political attitudes and their ideological thinking. The extent to which people participate in politics, in both conventional and unconventional ways, is explored in Chapter 6. Chapter 7 traces the history and function of political parties and their relationship to elections. These three chapters suggest that the American electorate is not oriented toward majoritarian democracy and that the party system is not prepared to promote mass participation in politics. Then Chapter 8 shows that citizens often pursue their political goals most intensely through interest groups, again in accordance with the pluralist model. Part III concludes with a chapter explaining how the mass media have affected the political lives of citizens and politicians alike, both shaping public opinion and informing government of public opinion.

Part IV deals with "Institutions of Government" in five chapters. Congress is assessed for its contribution to majoritarian democracy—and it comes out short. The presidency emerges as potentially more responsive than Congress to mass opinion. Individual presidents, however, have emphasized their own values of equality and freedom more than the public's priorities. Next, the bureaucracy is shown to be highly resistant to mass opinion but very responsive to organized interests, in accord with pluralist democracy. The courts, which were intended to be insulated from public opinion, clearly do not fit the majoritarian model of democracy. Throughout much of American history, however, the courts have played a major role in promoting democracy in the *substantive* sense by defending personal freedom against government efforts to impose order. More recently, the courts have also defended government efforts to promote social equality. The last chapter in Part IV explores the most atypical city in American politics, Washington, D.C. To look inside the Washington community is to peer into a whirlpool of pluralism.

Part V, "Making Public Policy," contains five chapters that relate public opinion and private interests to the purposes of government and to the models of democracy. Chapter 15, on the economics of public policy, charts limits to the scope of government activity in a capitalist country. Chapter 16, on domestic policy, examines the scope of government activity in providing for social security, in promoting social welfare, and in coping with the farm problem. Chapters 17 and 18, on civil rights and liberties, discuss how freedom has been balanced against both order and equality in government policies. Chapter 19 re-examines the government's role in maintaining order, this time by defending citizens against violent assault from foreign enemies.

At the end of the book, you are on your own, to consider once again the two dilemmas with which the text began:

■ Which is better: to live under a government that enforces strict law and order or under one that allows individuals complete freedom to do whatever they please?

■ Which is better: to pass laws that impose equality among races and sexes or to allow businesses and private clubs freedom to choose their customers and members?

To these questions we will add another from this chapter:

■ Which is better: a government that immediately responds to public opinion on all matters or one that responds deliberately to organized groups that argue their cases effectively?

If, by the end of this book, you understand the issues involved in answering these questions, then you will have learned a great deal about American government.

Key Terms

autocracy (monarchy)
aristocracy (oligarchy)
ruling elite
democracy (polyarchy)
procedural democratic theory
universal participation
political equality
majority rule
direct democracy
indirect democracy
representative government
responsiveness

substantive democratic theory
minority rights
institutional mechanism
majoritarian model of democracy
referendum
initiative
pluralism
interest group
pluralist model of democracy
elite theory

Selected Readings

Barber, Benjamin R. *Strong Democracy: Participatory Politics for a New Age.* Berkeley, Calif.: University of California Press, 1984. Barber favors a "strong democracy," a government that features a high degree of participation by individuals, much as a direct democracy does. He suggests specific institutional reforms to stimulate civic discussion and popular participation in government.

Dahl, Robert A. *Dilemmas of Pluralist Democracy: Autonomy vs. Control.* New Haven, Conn.: Yale University Press, 1982. Dahl is the leading theorist of pluralist democracy. This book clearly explains the pluralist model with reference to governments in other countries, as well as that in the United States.

Green, Philip. *Retrieving Democracy: In Search of Civic Equality.* Totowa, N.J.: Rowman and Allanheld, 1985. Green contends that representative government is "pseudodemocracy" because government is not under the direct control of the people. He argues for "egalitarian democracy," a society of truly equal citizens. The book urges fundamental economic reforms to produce a redistribution of wealth, which would facilitate direct democracy.

Mansbridge, Jane. *Beyond Adversary Democracy*. New York: Basic Books, 1982. Mansbridge contrasts "adversary democracy," the kind of open contest that occurs between groups in a large nation, with "unitary democracy," a cooperative form of decisionmaking based on common rather than opposing interests. She illustrates unitary democracy with two case studies of decisionmaking, one in a New England village, the other in an urban crisis center.

Pateman, Carole. *Participation and Democratic Theory*. Cambridge, Eng.: Cambridge University Press, 1970. This work is a highly respected analysis of the importance of individual participation in government to democratic theory. Many later studies draw heavily on this influential study.

Spitz, Elaine. *Majority Rule*. Chatham, N.J.: Chatham House, 1984. Spitz reviews the various meanings of "majority" and "rule" and the place of majority rule in democratic theory, but she goes beyond the narrow definition of majority rule as a method of deciding between policies. She argues that majoritarianism should be viewed as a "social practice" among people who want to hold their society together when making decisions.

PART II

FOUNDATIONS OF AMERICAN GOVERNMENT

3

The Constitution

The midnight burglars made a mistake. It led to their quick capture in the early hours of June 17, 1972, and triggered a constitutional struggle that eventually involved the president of the United States, the Congress, and the Supreme Court. The burglars' mistake seems minuscule: they left a piece of tape over the lock they had tripped to enter the Watergate office and apartment complex in Washington, D.C. But a security guard at the building discovered their tampering and called the police, who surprised the burglars in the offices of the Democratic National Committee at 2:30 A.M. They arrested five men — four Cuban exiles and a former CIA agent. The well-dressed burglars wore business suits and surgical gloves. They also carried the equipment they needed to photograph the files and bug the conversations of the Democratic National Committee.

The arrests occurred a month before the 1972 Democratic National Convention. Investigative reporting by the *Washington Post*'s Carl Bernstein and Bob Woodward uncovered a link between the Watergate burglary and the forthcoming election.[1] The burglars had carried the telephone number of another former CIA agent, now working in the White House. At a news conference on June 22, President Richard Nixon said, ''The White House has had no involvement whatsoever in this particular incident.''[2] The chairman of his campaign organization, John Mitchell (formerly Nixon's attorney general), ordered an in-house investigation of the incident the same day. Nine days after initiating the investigation, Mitchell himself resigned as chairman of the Nixon campaign, citing family problems. Mitchell's investigation exonerated the Nixon re-election committee.

At its convention in July, the Democratic party nominated Senator George McGovern of South Dakota to oppose Nixon in the presidential election. McGovern tried to use the burglary of the Democratic headquarters against the Republicans in his election campaign, but the voters either didn't understand or didn't care about the point he was making. In November 1972,

The Unwelcome Wagon Calls
Calls for Richard Nixon's impeachment intensified following the release of taped coversations linking the president to a coverup of the Watergate break-in. On August 8, 1974, a crowd jeering ''Jail to the Chief!'' stopped traffic along Pennsylvania Avenue in front of the White House. A moving van drove up, as if to hasten the president's departure. The following day, Nixon resigned.

Senators Investigate a President
The Select Committee on Presidential Campaign Activities was created by the Senate in 1973 to investigate events surrounding Watergate. Its chairman was Democratic Senator Sam J. Ervin (seated at the center); its ranking minority member was Republican Senator Howard Baker (to Ervin's right). Here, the senators, surrounded by the committee staff, examine a White House document.

Richard Nixon was re-elected president of the United States, winning forty-nine of fifty states in one of the largest electoral landslides in American history.

The events that followed are outlined in Feature 3.1. Here we need only note that the Watergate affair posed one of the most serious modern challenges to the constitutional order of American government. The incident ultimately developed into a struggle over the rule of law between the presidency on the one hand and the Congress and the courts on the other. President Nixon had attempted to use the powers of his office to hide an insidious interference with the electoral process. In the end, his coverup was thwarted by the Constitution and by leaders who believed in the Constitution. The constitutional principle of separation of powers among the executive, legislative, and judicial branches prevented the president from controlling the Watergate investigation. The principle of checks and balances allowed Congress to threaten Nixon with impeachment and removal from office. The belief that Nixon had violated the Constitution finally prompted members of his own party to support the move for impeachment.

Nixon resigned from the presidency after little more than a year and a half into his second term. In some countries, such an irregular change in government leadership provides an opportunity for palace coups, armed revolution, or military dictatorships. But here the most serious display of public antagonism occurred the night before Nixon was to resign: one wag drove up in a moving van as though to hasten the president's departure as a crowd chanting "Jail to the Chief!" stopped traffic on Pennsylvania Avenue in front of the White House. And, significantly, no political violence took place following Nixon's resignation; in fact, none was expected. The constitutional order of the United States had been put to a test. It passed with high honors, overcoming a genuine threat to the legitimacy of our government.

Feature 3.1

Watergate

The frightening details of the Watergate story did not unfold until after President Nixon's re-election in November 1972. Two months later, in January 1973, seven men went to trial for the break-in itself. They included all five burglars and two men closely connected with the president: E. Howard Hunt (a former CIA agent and White House consultant) and G. Gordon Liddy (counsel to the Committee to Re-elect the President, or CREEP). The burglars entered pleas of guilty. Hunt and Liddy were convicted by a jury. In a letter to the sentencing judge, one of the burglars charged that they had been pressured to plead guilty, that others were involved, and that perjury had been committed at the trial of Hunt and Liddy. The Senate launched its own investigation of the matter. It set up a Select Committee on Presidential Campaign Activities, chaired by a self-styled constitutional authority, Democratic Senator Sam Ervin from North Carolina.

The Ervin committee's hearings televised shocking testimony. A White House assistant (Jeb Magruder) confessed to perjury and implicated John Mitchell in planning the burglary. Special Counsel to the President John Dean said that the president had been a party to a cover-up of the crime for eight months. There were additional disclosures of other political burglaries and forged State Department cables that were intended to embarrass a possible Democratic candidate, Senator Edward M. Kennedy of Massachusetts.

A stunned nation also learned that President Nixon had secretly tape-recorded all his conversations in the White House. The Ervin committee asked for the tapes. Nixon refused to produce them, asserting the separa-

tion of powers between the legislative and executive branches and claiming "executive privilege" to withhold information from Congress.

In the midst of all this, Nixon's vice president, Spiro T. Agnew, resigned while under investigation for income tax evasion. The Twenty-Fifth Amendment to the Constitution (1967) provided that the president could choose a new vice president with the consent of Congress. Nixon chose Gerald Ford, then the Republican leader in the House of Representatives. On December 6, Ford became the first vice president not chosen through popular election.

Meanwhile, Nixon was fighting subpoenas requesting the White House tapes. Ordered by a federal court to deliver specific tapes, Nixon proposed a "compromise." He would release written summaries of the taped conversations. The special prosecutor of the attorney general's office refused the compromise. Nixon retaliated with the "Saturday Night Massacre," in which Attorney General Elliot L. Richardson resigned, Richardson's deputy attorney general resigned, and Archibald Cox, the special prosecutor, was dismissed.

The ensuing furor forced Nixon to appoint another special prosecutor, Leon Jaworski, who eventually brought indictments against Nixon's closest aides. Nixon himself was named as an unindicted co-conspirator. Both the special prosecutor and the defendants sought the White House tapes, but Nixon continued to resist. Finally, on July 24, 1974, the Supreme Court ruled that Nixon had to hand over the tapes. At almost the same time, the House Judiciary Committee voted to recommend to the full House that Nixon be impeached for

In this chapter, we shall ask some questions about the Constitution—what is it? Why is the United States governed by it? What values are enshrined in the Constitution, and which model of democracy suits it best?

THE REVOLUTIONARY ROOTS OF THE CONSTITUTION

The Constitution specifies the basic structure of our national government. It divides the government into three branches, and it describes the powers of those branches, their relationships, and the interactions between the government and the governed. Most Americans revere the Constitution as political scripture; to charge that a political action is unconstitutional is like claiming

THE WHITE HOUSE
WASHINGTON

August 9, 1974

Dear Mr. Secretary:

I hereby resign the Office of President of the
United States.

Sincerely,

[signature: Richard Nixon]

11.35 AM

HK

The Honorable Henry A. Kissinger
The Secretary of State
Washington, D.C. 20520

or charged with, three offenses, in accordance with a procedure specified in the Constitution.

The Judiciary Committee vote was decisive, but far from unanimous. On August 5, however, the committee and the country learned the contents of the taped conversations released under the Supreme Court order. The tapes revealed that Nixon had been aware of a coverup on June 23, 1972, soon after the original break-in on June 17. He had also issued an order to the FBI, saying, "Don't go any further in this case, period!"* Now even the eleven House Judiciary Committee Republican members who had opposed the first count of the impeachment were ready to vote against Nixon.

Faced with the complete collapse of his support and likely impeachment by the full House, Nixon resigned the presidency on August 8, 1974. Vice President Gerald Ford became the first unelected president of the United States. A month later, acting within his constitutional powers, Ford pardoned private citizen Richard Nixon for all federal crimes that he had committed or may have committed. When questioned by Congress about the circumstances surrounding the pardon, President Ford said, "There was no deal, period."†

---

* *The Encyclopedia of American Facts and Dates* (New York: Thomas Y. Crowell, 1979), p. 946.

† Others were not so fortunate. Three members of the Nixon cabinet (two attorneys general and a secretary of commerce) were convicted and sentenced for their crimes in the Watergate affair. Nixon's White House chief of staff (H. R. Haldeman) and his domestic affairs adviser (John Ehrlichman) were convicted of conspiracy, obstruction of justice, and perjury. Other officials were tried on related charges. Most were convicted. Richard B. Morris, ed., *Encyclopedia of American History* (New York: Harper & Row, 1976), p. 544.

that it is unholy. Thus the Constitution has taken on a political symbolism that has strengthened its authority as the basis for American government. Deep belief in the Constitution has caused many politicians to abandon party for principle when constitutional issues are raised. The power and symbolic value of the Constitution were proved once again in the Watergate affair.

The Constitution of the United States is two hundred years old. In today's culture, few things that old either work very well or have any relevance for contemporary life. Yet this document, written in 1787 for an agricultural society huddled along the coast of a wild new land, now guides the political life of a massive urban society in the nuclear age. The stability of the Constitution—and of the political system it created—is all the more remarkable because the Constitution itself was rooted in *revolution*. In fact, the U.S. Constitution was the first of several national constitutions that resulted from revolutions. Like the U.S. Constitution, three others — the French constitution of 1791, the Mexican constitution of 1917, and the Russian constitution of 1918 — were products of revolutionary movements.

The noted historian Samuel Eliot Morison observed that "the American Revolution was not fought to *obtain* freedom, but to *preserve* the liberties that Americans already had as colonials."[3] The U.S. Constitution was designed to prevent the potential for anarchy in a revolution by forging a union of states. To understand the values enshrined in the Constitution, one must understand its historical roots. They lie in colonial America, in the revolution against British rule, and in the unsuccessful Articles of Confederation that governed the new nation after the Revolution.

Freedom in Colonial America

The American Revolution was, as Morison noted, fought to preserve existing liberty. Although they were British subjects, the American colonists enjoyed a degree of freedom denied to most people in the world. Europeans — but not Americans — lived with many reminders of their feudal past, a time when great landowners ruled over unlanded tenants. Property inheritance in Europe was fraught with conditions; America imposed few, if any, restrictions. In Europe, established churches required the *tithe* (a compulsory contribution) from parishioners; America had no single established church, and tithing was not an important practice. (Even the Church of England enjoyed little influence in America, although it was established in every southern colony.) In England, subjects could be pressed into service in the Royal Navy; Americans were exempt from such service. European guilds and exclusive professional associations restricted access to the trades and professions; American guilds and associations imposed no such restrictions.

Despite these differences, however, the colonists were proud of their relations with the British Empire. They maintained that the rights of Englishmen in England also belonged to Englishmen in America. The English government intervened as necessary to protect minorities and to sort out differences that divided large and small colonies. Moreover, the British military protected Americans on land and sea.

By 1763 Britain and the colonies had settled on a compromise between imperial British control and colonial self-government. America's foreign affairs and overseas trade were controlled by the king and Parliament, the British legislature; the rest was left to home rule. But the cost of administering the colonies — including the conquest of Spanish Florida and French Canada — was substantial. Since Americans benefited the most, contended their English countrymen, Americans should bear the cost. And the means was to be taxation.

The Road to Revolution

Although their English countrymen may have seen taxation of the colonies as the obvious way to meet administrative costs, the colonists did not share that opinion. Like most people, they did not want to be taxed. They especially did not want to be taxed by a distant government in which they

Americans Protest the Stamp Act
The Stamp Act was vehemently denounced in the colonies. The punishment depicted in this cartoon involved smearing a person's body with tar and then covering it with feathers. This punishment was sometimes inflicted by American mobs on an unpopular or scandalous character — in this case, the stamp distributor.

had no representation. The Stamp Act of 1765 was the first direct tax on the colonies. The tax's purposes were to raise revenue for colonial administration and to impose on Americans a portion of the cost of defense. It was a stern measure. Every legal document (such as a complaint or an appeal) was taxed, along with school diplomas, licenses, deeds, newspapers, playing cards, and more. The tax was a nuisance because it required the use of specially stamped or embossed papers, which could be obtained only from official distributors appointed by the Crown.

Opposition to the Stamp Act was widespread and immediate. A group of citizens, calling themselves Sons of Liberty, engaged in acts of resistance including burning stamped paper and forcing official distributors to resign. Massachusetts invited delegates from other colonies to a Stamp Act Congress in New York City. Nine colonies sent delegates to this first spontaneous act of political union.

The strength of opposition to the Stamp Act was such that Parliament repealed it in 1766. This was a stunning political victory, a demonstration that, united, the colonists could turn back the world's most powerful nation. But Britain was determined that the colonies share the cost of their defense. In June 1767, Parliament passed the Townshend Act, which levied import taxes on certain goods entering the colonies. In response, radical leaders organized colonial merchants to boycott taxed British products and untaxed luxuries to put as much economic pressure on the British as possible.

In 1770 there was hope of reconciliation when Parliament repealed the Townshend Act except for the duty on tea. Tea consumption, most of it British-imported tea, fell to a trickle, leaving the East India Company (a British trading house) awash in 18 million pounds of unsold tea. In May 1773, Parliament acted to bolster the floundering company. It passed the Tea Act, which reduced the price of tea by letting the East India Company sell tea directly to its colonial agents. These direct tea sales eliminated the colonial merchants who purchased their tea from other sources and also eliminated the colonial tea smugglers, who bought their tea in Holland. The act retained the hated tax as a test of the king's authority.

Though the act reduced tea prices, it only roused the colonists' ire, for two reasons. First, the act was viewed as a subterfuge, a devious way to win colonial support for Parliament's right to tax the colonists without representation by making the hated tax a condition of the lower tea prices. Second, the act also threatened to undercut the merchants and smugglers who depended for their livelihood on the tea trade. The colonists responded by giving the Boston Tea Party. Disguised as Indians and blacks, a mob emptied 342 chests of valuable tea into Boston Harbor on the night of December 16, 1773. This act of defiance and destruction could not be ignored. "The die is now cast," wrote George III. "The Colonies must either submit or triumph."

Parliament responded by passing the Coercive (or Intolerable) Acts. One component of the acts imposed a blockade on Boston until the tea was paid for; another gave royal governors the power to quarter British soldiers in private homes. Now the taxation issue became secondary as the British demand for order clashed with the American demand for liberty. The colonists drew together. Surprised Bostonians were sent food and money from other colonies. The Virginia and Massachusetts assemblies summoned a **Continental Congress,** an assembly that would speak and act collectively for the people of all the colonies. All the colonies except Georgia sent representatives.

The First Continental Congress met at Philadelphia in September of 1774. Its purpose was to restore harmony between Great Britain and the American colonies. In an effort at unity, all colonies were given the same voting power — one vote each. A leader, called the "president," was elected. (The terms *president* and *Congress* in American government trace their origins to this Continental Congress.) In October 1774, the delegates adopted a statement of rights and principles, many of which later found their way into the Declaration of Independence and the Constitution. For example, the Congress claimed a right "to life, liberty, and property" and a right "peaceably to assemble, consider of their grievances, and petition the king." The Continental Congress then adjourned, to reconvene in May 1775.

Revolutionary Action

By early 1775, however, a movement that the colonists themselves called a revolution had already begun. In March 1775, Patrick Henry predicted the outbreak of fighting in New England, in his famous "give me liberty or give me death" speech. In April, Massachusetts colonists fought the British at Concord and Lexington. Thus, when the Second Continental Congress met in the spring of 1775, it prepared for war as a nation that did not yet exist while it considered reconciliation with Britain. A military force was organized, and George Washington was appointed commander in chief of the army. Sentiment for independence grew, as the colony-states gradually cut tie after tie with Britain. Still, New York, New Jersey, Pennsylvania, and Maryland resisted self-government. The paramount fear was not of revolution, but of the nature of the government that would replace the British monarchy. Tyranny and anarchy were the most likely replacements, and neither one was acceptable. Meanwhile, the Second Continental Congress remained in session, to serve as the government of the colony-states.

In 1776, news reached Virginia that the British had employed twelve thousand German mercenaries (known as "Hessians") to end the rebellion. The Virginia delegation called on the Continental Congress to resolve "That these United Colonies are, and of right ought to be, free and Independent States, that they are absolved from all allegiance to the British Crown, and that all political connection between them and the State of Great Britain is, and ought to be, totally dissolved." The Congress then chose a Committee of Five to prepare a **Declaration of Independence** to proclaim to the world the colonies' reasons for declaring independence.

The Declaration of Independence

Thomas Jefferson, a young Virginia planter and lawyer, was enlisted by the Committee of Five to prepare a draft of the declaration, because of his "peculiar felicity of expression." The document Jefferson drafted was substantially unchanged by the committee and the Continental Congress. It remains a cherished covenant of our heritage because it expresses simply, clearly, and in an orderly fashion an argument in support of separation from Great Britain.

The declaration was a clear statement of principles that were rooted in the writings of the English philosopher John Locke and expressed many times by speakers in Congress and in the colonial assemblies. Locke argued that people have rights that are God-given or natural and thus inalienable, that is, they cannot be taken away. Since these natural rights existed before there was any government, no government can legitimately deny them.

For Locke, the most basic of people's natural rights was property, a concept that encompassed life and liberty as well as external possessions. In addition, Locke believed that all legitimate political authority exists for the preservation of these natural rights and that such authority is based on the consent of those who are governed. The idea of consent is derived from **social contract theory.** This theory states that the people agree to set up rulers for certain purposes and that they have the right to resist or remove rulers who persist in actions that defeat those purposes.[4] In short, government exists not for the benefit of those who govern but for the good of its subjects; and, Locke argued, rebellion is the ultimate sanction against the abuse of government power. (In his writings, Locke was not concerned with justifying any particular form of government; nor was he a believer in social or political equality.)

Jefferson argued similarly in the Declaration of Independence. Although he was not an orator, Jefferson was a brilliant wordsmith. His "impassioned simplicity of statement" reverberates to this day with the democratic faith:

> We hold these truths to be self-evident, that all men are created equal, that they are endowed by their Creator with certain unalienable Rights, that among these are Life, Liberty and the pursuit of Happiness.

The First Continental Congress had declared in 1774 that colonists were entitled to "life, liberty, and property." Jefferson reformulated the ends of

America Votes for Independence on the Second of July
The Second Continental Congress voted independence from Britain on July 2, 1776. John Adams, a leading revolutionary who later became the second president, viewed the day "as the most memorable epocha [significant event] in the history of America." Independence Day falls on July Fourth, the day the Declaration of Independence was approved.

government as the equivalent "Life, Liberty, and the pursuit of Happiness."
He then continued:

> That to secure these rights, Governments are instituted among Men, deriving
> their just powers from the consent of the governed. That whenever any Form of
> Government becomes destructive of these ends, it is the Right of the People to
> alter or to abolish it, and to institute new Government, laying its foundation on
> such principles and organizing its powers in such form, as to them shall seem
> most likely to effect their Safety and Happiness.

The remainder of the declaration offered a long list of deliberate acts of the
king that were destructive of the legitimate ends of government. Finally, it
declared that the colonies were "Free and Independent States," with no
political connection to Great Britain.

The declaration's major premise is that the people have a right to revolt
when they determine that their government is destructive of legitimate rights
("Life, Liberty, and the pursuit of Happiness"). The long list of the king's
acts serves as the minor premise. These deliberate acts destroy government's
legitimate ends. Therefore, the people have a right to revolt.

On July 2, 1776, the Second Continental Congress finally voted for independence. The vote was by state, and the motion carried eleven states to
none. (Rhode Island was not present, and the New York delegation, lacking
instructions, did not cast its "yea" vote until July 15.) Two days later, the
Declaration of Independence was approved with very few changes. Jefferson's original draft had indicted the king for permitting the continuation of
the slave trade. But representatives from Georgia and South Carolina insisted
that this be deleted before they would vote for approval. Other representatives
removed language they thought would arouse excessive ire on the part of
the colonists. But, in the end, Jefferson's compelling composition was retained almost exactly as written.

The vote for independence came on July 2; the Declaration of Independence was adopted, but not signed, on July 4, 1776. By August of that
year, fifty-five revolutionaries had signed it, pledging "our Lives, our Fortunes, and our sacred Honor" in support of rebellion from the world's most
powerful nation. This was no rhetorical pledge, for an act of rebellion was
treason. If they had lost the Revolutionary War, the signers' fate would have
been gruesome. The punishment for treason was hanging, drawing, and
quartering, in which the victim is first hanged until half-dead from stran-
gulation, then disemboweled, and finally cut into four quarters while still
alive. We celebrate the Fourth of July with fireworks and flagwaving, parades
and picnics. We sometimes forget that our Revolution was a matter of life
and death.

The War for Independence lasted far longer than anyone had expected.
It began in a moment of confusion, when a colonist fired a shot at some
passing British soldiers on the road to Concord, Massachusetts, on April 19,
1775. It ended with Lord Cornwallis's surrender of his six-thousand-man
army at Yorktown, Virginia, on October 19, 1781. It was a costly war: there
were more dead and wounded in relation to the population than in any other
conflict except the Civil War.[5] With hindsight, of course, we can see that the
British were engaged in a hopeless conflict. America was simply too vast to

subdue without instituting complete military rule in the colonies. Britain also had to transport men and supplies over the enormous distance of the Atlantic Ocean. Finally, although the Americans had neither paid troops nor professional soldiers, they were fighting for a cause — in defense of their liberty. The British never understood the power of this fighting faith.

FROM REVOLUTION TO GOVERNMENT: THE FIRST TRY

By declaring their independence from England, the colonies would be leaving themselves without any real central government. Thus, in place of the British monarchy, the revolutionaries proclaimed the creation of a *republic*. Strictly speaking, a **republic** is a government without a monarch, but the term had come to mean a government rooted in the consent of the governed, in which power is exercised by representatives who are responsible to the governed. A republic need not be a democracy, and that was fine with the founders; "democracy" was at that time associated with mob rule and instability. The revolutionaries were less concerned with *who* would control their new government than with *limiting* that government. They had revolted in the name of liberty and now wanted a government with sharply defined powers. To make sure they got one, they meant to put the government in writing.

Experience with Written Constitutions

Those who first left England for the New World had had no experience with written constitutions. To this day, Great Britain lacks any single document that specifies the structure and limits of its government. Instead, its "unwritten" constitution consists of some written documents; various parliamentary acts that established a political system and rules of government, such as the English Bill of Rights of 1688–1689; the English common law, which is composed of the collective decisions of its court judges; and various unwritten customs and conventions, for example, that the monarch must agree to all acts passed by Parliament.

The principle of government by written agreement was, however, an early feature of the New World. The best-known agreement among the early settlers is the Mayflower Compact, signed on the *Mayflower* before the ship landed at Plymouth Rock in 1620. Later, in 1639, colonists in Windsor, Wethersfield, and Hartford, Connecticut, produced a more elaborate constitution. Known as the Fundamental Orders of Connecticut, it is generally considered to be the first modern written constitution. The other colonies had routinely adopted written agreements, or "charters," that typically restricted the powers of the royal governor. But now the revolutionaries needed a document that would structure a government for all thirteen colonies.

The Articles of Confederation

When the Second Continental Congress decided to declare independence from Britain, it also began planning a government for the colonies. Barely a week after the signing of the Declaration of Independence, the Congress

Political Expression in Art

Throughout our nation's history, political expressions—both positive and negative—have appeared in art. To convey a message, the artist frequently used an icon or symbol. One of the first and most popular of such icons was Liberty. She was by no means uniquely American however—her origins lie in ancient Rome and she has enjoyed great popularity in France. The fierceness of this Liberty, done just before the Civil War, suggests that both she and the country were still poised to defend their freedom.

"Miss Liberty." Artist unknown, 1850–1860. Courtesy of the Barenholz Collection. Photo by Schecter Lee, courtesy of the Museum of American Folk Art, New York City.

George Washington was not our country's first icon, but he was the first human being to become a symbol. He represented military valor, presidential dignity, and paternal wisdom—the personal attributes of a hero.

Washington was often paired with Liberty, understandably since he was the instrument through which her ideals were achieved. To the right, she places a laurel wreath—a symbol of honor and glory—on a bust of the deceased president. Gazing reverently toward the sky, she seems to contemplate her hero's place in heaven.

In *Centennial Progress,* painted in 1875, Washington is one of many heroes surrounding Columbia, the female personification of the United States. Along with Thomas Jefferson, Washington occupies a prominent position beside the flag and well above the crowd. Former presidents including Abraham Lincoln and Ulysses

"Centennial Progress," by Montgomery Tiers, 1875. Courtesy William Judson.

"Liberty and Washington." Artist unknown, c.1800–1810. New York State Historical Association, Cooperstown.

FIRST in WAR,
FIRST in PEACE,
&
FIRST in the HEARTS
OF HIS
COUNTRYMEN.

"Parson Weem's Fable," by Grant Wood, 1939. Courtesy Amon Carter Museum, Fort Worth.

Grant, as well as various statesmen such as Benjamin Franklin and Frederick Douglass, gather around the pedestal on which Columbia holds a telegraph wire—arguably one of the most important inventions of the century.

By the twentieth century, reverence for Washington still flourished, but at least part of the public had grown sophisticated enough to recognize the humor in Grant Wood's painting (shown above). Here the artist pokes fun at Americans' taste for patriotic myths such as Washington's childhood confession of chopping down a cherry tree. Parson Weems, the creator of this fable, draws aside a curtain to reveal the climactic scene. But this particular scene is not the one that flourishes in popular imagination. A child-sized Washington with the mature head made famous by Gilbert Stuart's portrait suggests the public's inability to conceive of Washington as an ordinary youth. In the minds of adoring patriots, it is as if Washington sprang to life fully grown, much like a mythical god.

"John Brown Going to his Hanging," by Horace Pippin, 1942. Courtesy of The Pennsylvania Academy of the Fine Arts, Lambert Fund Purchase.

Not all public figures who appear in American art have been revered as unanimously as George Washington. In fact, some are not heroes as much as they are martyrs. Their presence alludes to both a darker side of history and a long tradition of public dissent.

For many black Americans, the abolitionist John Brown was a hero. But Southern white people generally regarded him as an assassin and possibly a madman as well. Northern feeling was ambiguous: even those who shared Brown's desire to free slaves questioned the violence of his action and were forced to speculate about his sanity.

Although John Brown is most famous for his armed raid on Harper's Valley, West Virginia, in 1859, for the black artist Horace Pippin, Brown's subsequent hanging was at least as significant. The artist's grandmother allegedly witnessed the execution and frequently described the event to her young grandson. In the painting, white people gather to watch Brown's arrival and chat together nonchalantly. But the lone black slave—presumably Pippin's grandmother—confronts the viewer with an accusing glare.

Sixty-eight years after John Brown's hanging, another execution shook the country. A court convicted two immigrant anarchists named Nicola Sacco and Bartolomeo Vanzetti of murdering a guard and paymaster during a Massachusetts robbery. Since there was insufficient evidence to prove their involvement in the crime, Sacco and Vanzetti's main offense would seem to have been their political convictions and their Italian heritage. The judge openly sided with the prosecution and the defendants clearly failed to receive as fair a trial as were they constitutionally guaranteed. To those who looked to the United States as a land where freedom of belief was honored, Sacco and Vanzetti's execution in 1927 was an outrage. Ben Shahn, only one of several distressed artists and writers, expressed his anger in a series of paintings called *The Passion of Sacco and Vanzetti.*

"Bartolomeo Vanzetti and Nicola Sacco," by Ben Shahn, 1931–32. Collection, The Museum of Modern Art, New York. Gift of Abby Aldrich Rockefeller.

SAVE FREEDOM OF SPEECH

BUY WAR BONDS

SAVE FREEDOM OF WORSHIP
EACH ACCORDING TO THE DICTATES OF HIS OWN CONSCIENCE

BUY WAR BONDS

OURS...to fight for

FREEDOM FROM WANT

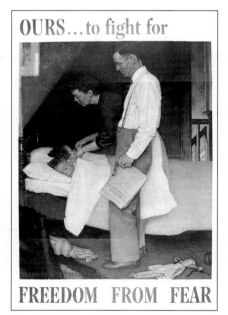

OURS...to fight for

FREEDOM FROM FEAR

"The Four Freedoms," by Norman Rockwell, 1943. Posters by the Office of War Information. Courtesy National Archives.

What starts out as art is sometimes transformed into patriotic propaganda, particularly during times of war. Such was the case with *The Four Freedoms* series Norman Rockwell painted in 1943. Inspired by an address to Congress in which President Franklin Delano Roosevelt outlined his goals for world civilization, these four paintings illustrate the concepts of freedom of speech, freedom of worship, freedom from want, and freedom from fear. Roosevelt's ideals had embraced all of humanity, but Rockwell applied them specifically to the United States. The images of the town meeting and Thanksgiving dinner are especially American in content.

The *Saturday Evening Post* first published *The Four Freedoms* as an inside supplement. The immense popularity of the series led the government to print posters of these illustrations for the Treasury Department's War Bond Drive. The Office of War Information also reproduced *The Four Freedoms* and circulated the posters in schools, club houses, railroad stations, post offices, and other public buildings. Officials even had copies dropped into the European war front to remind soldiers of the liberties for which they were fighting. It is said that no other paintings in the world have ever been reproduced or circulated in such vast numbers as *The Four Freedoms*.

Art tended to protest rather than support the war in Vietnam. Steven Horn's poster for the Committee to End the War reinterprets the familiar World War II poster in which Uncle Sam pointed directly at the viewer and announced "I Want You." Here, Uncle Sam is battered and bandaged—ironically in a way that recalls Revolutionary War patriots. This weary and disillusioned Uncle Sam has simply had enough.

Another American icon—the flag—also appears frequently in images opposing the nation's role in Vietnam. Jaspar John's *Moratorium* is one of the more subtle examples. Strewn across a garish blood orange field are black stars—stars that seem more like dark ashes than points of light. Appearing between black stripes is a mottled green that calls to mind camouflage gear. Note what seems to be a bullet hole placed dead-center in the flag.

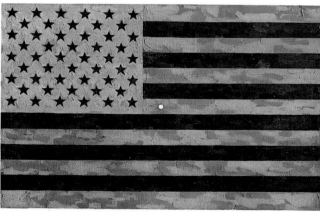

MORATORIUM

"Moratorium," by Jasper Johns, 1969. © Jasper Johns/V.A.G.A., New York, 1986. Photo © 1986 Dorothy Zeidman.

"I Want Out." Steve Horn, photographer; Larry Dunst, art director. Poster for the Committee to End the War.

"Barbara Calling III," by Mike Glier, 1983. Courtesy Barbara Gladstone Gallery. Photo by eeva-inkeri.

One of the dominant political themes of the 1980s has been the threat of nuclear war. Contemporary literature, film, video, and drama have all reflected this concern, but nowhere has it been more apparent than in the visual arts. Many artists have used frightening images of mushroom clouds or sentimental reminders of the beauty of life to depict this issue. But Mike Glier's painting, *Barbara Calling III,* is more mysterious and ultimately more disturbing. Behind the back of a jubilantly shouting protester, a menacing figure with blackened face and hands tosses money into the air. His presence might suggest death, the military establishment, or an unspecified evil force, but in any case, it reminds viewers that, like a shadow, the threat is always with us, just behind our backs.

received a committee report on "Articles of Confederation and Perpetual Union." A **confederation** is a loose association of independent states that agree to cooperate on specified matters. In a confederation, the states retain their **sovereignty,** which means that each has supreme power within its borders. A confederation is thus limited to coordinating the actions of its sovereign states. As a result, the central government is weak in a confederation, and the individual states are strong. The Articles of Confederation created a republic in two senses. First, the absence of a monarch qualified the government as a republic in the strict sense. And, second, power would be exercised by delegates chosen annually by the states, whose consent established the confederation.

Congress debated the **Articles of Confederation,** the compact among the thirteen original states establishing a United States government, for more than a year while the Revolutionary War was going on. Arguments raged between representatives of small states and representatives of large states, between this interest and that interest. The Articles were finally adopted on November 15, 1777, but they were greeted by the states with a mixture of apathy and hostility. Most Americans were more interested in local affairs than in national issues, and even the slightest threat to state sovereignty irritated avid republicans. The Articles did not take effect until they had been ratified by all thirteen states, on March 1, 1781. On March 2, the Continental Congress assumed a new title: "the United States of America in Congress assembled."

The Articles of Confederation jealously guarded state sovereignty; its provisions clearly reflected the delegates' fears that a strong central government might be substituted for British rule. Article II stated:

> Each State retains its sovereignty, freedom, and independence, and every Power, Jurisdiction and right, which is not by this confederation expressly delegated to the United States, in Congress assembled.

Under the Articles of Confederation, each state, regardless of its size, had one vote in the Congress. Votes on important issues, such as financing the war against Britain, required the consent of at least nine of the thirteen states. The common danger—the war—forced the young republic to function under the Articles, but this first try at a government was inadequate to the task. The delegates had succeeded in crafting a national government that was largely powerless.

The Articles failed in at least four ways. First, they did not give the national government the power to tax. As a result, the Congress had to plead for funds with which to conduct the continuing war with Great Britain and carry on the affairs of the new nation. Second, except for the appointment of a presiding officer of the Congress (the president), the Articles made no provision for an independent leadership position to direct the government. This omission was due to the colonists' fear of re-establishing a monarchy, but it left the nation without a leader. Third, the Articles did not permit the national government to regulate interstate and foreign commerce. (When John Adams proposed that the Confederation enter into a commercial treaty with Britain after the war, he was asked, "Would you like one treaty or thirteen, Mr. Adams?"[6]) Finally, the Articles themselves could not be amended without the unanimous agreement of the Congress and the assent of all the state legislatures; thus, each state had the power to veto any changes in the Confederation.

The goal of the delegates who drew up the Articles of Confederation was to retain power in the states. This was consistent with republicanism, which viewed the remote power of a national government as dangerous to liberty. In this sense alone, the Articles were a grand success, because they completely hobbled the infant government.

Once the Revolutionary War ended and independence was a reality, Americans rushed to renew trade with Great Britain. Wartime austerity was replaced by an eagerness to purchase goods from abroad. Debt mounted and, for many, bankruptcy followed. The national government's efforts to restrict foreign imports were blocked by exporting states, which feared retaliation from their foreign customers.

Both the national government and the states issued currency that was virtually worthless because it was not backed by anything of value. Rhode Island went so far as to punish merchants who rejected its own worthless currency. In an ironic twist, harassed creditors were pursued by implacable debtors. Rather than sell their goods for worthless paper, merchants hid their stock or packed up and moved to other states. Those who had lent money to the national government insisted on repayment, and revolutionary soldiers were distressed that the national government would not fund promised pensions.

The national government was withering from lack of power, primarily economic power. By 1785 some states had failed to send delegates to the Congress, and legislative action ground to a halt for lack of a quorum. Obviously, something had to be done to reduce the mounting hostility of the states toward one another. A more satisfactory national government was necessary.

Disorder Under the Confederation

A series of incidents dramatized the weakness of the national government. High interest rates and high state taxes were forcing farmers into bankruptcy in Massachusetts. In 1786, Daniel Shays, a Revolutionary War veteran, marched on a western Massachusetts courthouse with fifteen hundred neighbors armed with barrel staves and pitchforks, to close the courthouse and thus prevent the foreclosure of farms by creditors. Other similar attacks followed, in a series of insurrections that became known as **Shays's Rebellion** and continued into 1787.

Massachusetts appealed to the Confederation for help, but it proved impotent. Horrified by the threat of domestic upheaval that was posed by the rebellion, Congress approved a $530,000 requisition for the establishment of a national army. But that plan was a failure: every state except Virginia rejected the Confederation's request for money. The Massachusetts governor then called out the militia to prevent Shays and his followers from gaining control of a government arsenal in Springfield. The arsenal housed seven thousand muskets with bayonets, thirteen hundred barrels of gunpowder, and large quantities of shot and shell. The farmers' goal was armed rebellion

**Farmers' Protest
Stirs Rebellion**
*Shays's Rebellion (1786–1787)
became a symbol for the urgent
need to maintain order. Daniel
Shays, a destitute farmer who
held the rank of captain during
the Revolution, led the assault.
The uprising demonstrated the
military weakness of the
Confederation: the government
could not muster the funds to
fight the insurgents.*

against established order. Additional Massachusetts militiamen restored order, although Shays escaped to Vermont.[7]

The rebellion left its mark on public opinion by demonstrating the military impotence of the Confederation and the urgent need to suppress insurrection and maintain domestic order. It was proof to skeptics that Americans could not govern themselves. The rebellion alarmed every leader but one. From his diplomatic mission in Paris, Thomas Jefferson wrote, "A little rebellion now and then is a good thing; the tree of liberty must be refreshed from time to time with the blood of patriots and tyrants."

THE CONSTITUTIONAL CONVENTION:
A SECOND TRY

Order, the original purpose of government, was breaking down under the Articles of Confederation. The "league of friendship" envisioned in the Articles seemed inadequate in peacetime to hold a nation together.

Some states had taken halting steps toward a change in government. In 1785 Massachusetts had asked the Congress to revise the Articles of Confederation, but the Congress took no action. In 1786 Virginia had invited the states to attend a convention at Annapolis, to explore revisions aimed at improved commercial regulation. The meeting was both a failure and a success. Although only five states sent delegates to the Annapolis convention, those delegates seized the opportunity to call for another meeting, with a far broader mission, in Philadelphia the next year. The Annapolis delegates called for a new convention that would be charged with "devis[ing] such further provisions as shall appear . . . necessary to render the constitution of the Federal Government adequate to the exigencies of the Union." The Congress then passed a resolution to hold such a convention but limited it to "the sole and express purpose of revising the Articles of Confederation."

Shays's Rebellion lent a sense of urgency to the task before the Philadelphia convention. Congress's inability to confront the rebellion was evidence that a stronger national government was necessary to preserve order and property—to protect the states from internal as well as external dangers. "While the Declaration [of Independence] was directed against an excess of authority," remarked Supreme Court Justice Robert H. Jackson some 150 years later, "the Constitution [that followed the Articles of Confederation] was directed against anarchy."[8]

Twelve of the thirteen states named a total of seventy-four delegates to convene in Philadelphia in May 1787. (Rhode Island, derisively renamed "Rogue Island" by a Boston newspaper, was the one exception.) Fifty-five delegates eventually showed up at the State House in Philadelphia, but no more than thirty were present at any one time during that sweltering summer (see Feature 3.2). Though well versed in ideas, they subscribed to the view that "experience must be our guide. Reason may mislead us."

The Constitutional Convention officially opened on May 25, when representatives of seven states were present to make a quorum. (At the time, it was called the Federal Convention.) Recall that, a year earlier at Annapolis, five states had called for the convention to draft a new and stronger charter for the national government. The spirit of the Annapolis meeting seems to have pervaded the Philadelphia convention, even though the delegates were authorized only to "revise" the Articles of Confederation. Within the first week of debate, Edmund Randolph of Virginia had proposed a long list of changes, which would replace the weak confederation of states with a powerful national government. The delegates unanimously agreed to debate the **Virginia Plan,** as Randolph's proposal became known. Thus they almost immediately rejected the idea of amending the Articles of Confederation and, instead, turned toward writing a new document.

The Virginia Plan

The Virginia Plan served as the basis for the convention's deliberations for the remainder of the summer. Its main elements were as follows:

- The powers of the government would be divided among three separate branches: a **legislative branch,** for making laws; an **executive branch,** for enforcing laws; and a **judicial branch,** for interpreting laws.

- The legislature would consist of two houses. The first would be chosen by the people; the second would be chosen by the members of the first house, from among persons nominated by the state legislatures.

- Representation in the legislature would be in proportion to taxes paid to the national government, or in proportion to the free population of each state.

- A one-person executive would be selected by the legislature and would serve for a single term.

- The executive and a number of federal judges would serve as a council of revision, to approve or veto legislative acts. Their veto (disapproval) could, however, be overridden by a vote of both houses of the legislature.

Feature 3.2

Philadelphia, 1787, Home to the Constitutional Convention

Philadelphia in 1787 was the nation's largest city, with 43,000 inhabitants. The city offered bookstalls, museums, and shops displaying all manner of products. Though regarded by some as silly and possibly worthless, toothbrushes were just coming into fashion. In one sense, the Constitutional Convention was no different from today's political conventions: great amounts of alcoholic beverages were consumed by the delegates. Romantic visions of the period should be tempered, however, by the knowledge that disease was rampant in summer, filth was strewn in the streets, wells were contaminated by backyard privies, and doctors regularly prescribed bleeding, vomiting, and cathartics for common ailments.*

Like other revolutionary assemblies, this one was held in secret. Sentries were posted at the doors, and the windows were shut both for privacy and for protection from the flies that swarmed in when the windows were opened. The summer heat was especially uncomfortable for the New England delegates, who usually dressed in woolens. By noon, the closed-in hall was insufferably hot.

The average age of the delegates was forty-three. Benjamin Franklin was the oldest, at eighty-one; Jonathan Dayton of New Jersey was the youngest, at twenty-three. Franklin suffered from gout and gallstones. He was brought to the convention each day in a sedan chair, which he had acquired in Paris, to reduce the pain of jostling. Four prisoners from the Walnut Street Jail bore the aged cargo.

The delegates were neither short on political experience nor lacking a sense of cause. Half had fought in the Revolutionary War, and three-quarters had sat in the Continental Congress. James Madison of Virginia was there, a political scholar who always dressed in black. He was a small man of thirty-six, with a soft voice. His notes on the convention, which came to light only after his death in 1836, were to provide the most complete available record of the secret sessions. How-

ever, his reliability and veracity as a reporter are today open to doubt.† George Washington of Virginia was unanimously elected as the presiding officer. Alexander Hamilton of New York—at thirty, one of the youngest delegates—came prepared to argue for a strong national government.

Though he took no part in the discussions that followed, Washington's commanding presence and respect left little doubt as to his position.

> It happened one morning in the convention hall, before a quorum had arrived, that some of those present advocated half measures as more likely to meet the approval of the people than any thoroughgoing reform. Washington interrupted the discussion with an expression of opinion that established his position beyond all question: "It is too probable that no plan we propose will be adopted. Perhaps another dreadful conflict is to be sustained. If to please the people, we offer what we ourselves disapprove, how can we afterwards defend our work? Let us raise a standard to which the wise and the honest can repair. The event is in the hand of God."‡

Two of the primary architects of independence, John Adams and Thomas Jefferson, were absent from the convention. Adams was in London on a diplomatic mission for the Congress. Jefferson was in Paris trying to arrange trade agreements and foreign loans in spite of doubts concerning the new nation's ability to meet its obligations. Their influence was, however, felt through their correspondence. Patrick Henry, the firebrand orator from Virginia, was also absent; he "smelt a rat" and refused to attend. By the following year, he was bitterly opposed to the new Constitution.

---

* Catherine Drinker Bowen, *Miracle at Philadelphia* (Boston: Little, Brown, 1966), p. 163.

† W. W. Crosskey and William Jeffrey, Jr. *Politics and the Constitution in the History of the United States*, Vol. III (Chicago: University of Chicago Press, 1980), pp. 404–405.

‡ Max Farrand, *The Framing of the Constitution of the United States* (New Haven, Conn.: Yale University Press, 1913), pp. 64–66.

Virginia Plan

■ The judiciary would include a supreme court and other lower courts whose judges would be lifetime appointees of the legislature.

■ The range of powers of all three branches would be far greater than under the Articles of Confederation and would include the power of the legislature to negate state laws.

By proposing a powerful national legislature that could nullify state laws, the Virginia Plan clearly advocated a new form of government. It was a compound structure, operating on the states and operating on the people.

James Madison of Virginia was a monumental force in the ensuing debates on this and other proposals; he, more than any other person, can be called the "father of the Constitution." He argued well, although he was on the losing side of some issues, including a nine-year term for senators. His reasoning with regard to that issue reveals his concern about equality.

Madison foresaw an increase "of those who will labor under all the hardships of life, and secretly sigh for a more equal distribution of its blessings. These may in time outnumber those who are placed above the feelings of indigence." Power, then, could flow into the hands of the numerous poor. The stability of the Senate, however, with its long elective term of nine years and election by the state legislatures, would provide a barrier against the "sighs of the poor" for more equality. Though Madison lost on the nine-year term, the delegates shared Madison's apprehension of equality.

Many features of the Virginia Plan were ultimately adopted in the Constitution, but not without challenge. The basis of representation in the legislature, the method of choosing legislators, and the structure of the executive branch provoked extensive discussion.

James Madison, a Young But Powerful Force Behind the Constitution
Madison was thirty-six when he participated in the drafting of the Constitution. He earned the title "Father of the Constitution" because he was the most effective advocate of a strong national government.

The New Jersey Plan

When it appeared that much of the Virginia Plan would be carried by the large states, the smaller states united in opposition. William Paterson of New Jersey introduced an alternative set of nine resolutions, written to preserve the spirit of the Articles of Confederation by amending rather than replacing them. This **New Jersey Plan** included the following elements:

■ The single-chamber legislature would have the power to raise revenue and regulate commerce.

■ The states would have equal representation in the legislature, and the members of that body would be chosen by the states.

■ A multiperson executive would be elected by the legislature. Its powers would be similar to those expressed in the Virginia Plan, but without the right to veto legislation.

■ A supreme judiciary would be created with a very limited jurisdiction. (There was no provision for a system of national courts.)

■ The acts of the legislature would be binding on the states; that is, they would be regarded as the "supreme law of the respective states," and force could be used to compel obedience.

The New Jersey Plan was defeated in the first major convention vote, seven states to three. However, the small states had enough support to force a compromise on the issue of representation in the legislature. Table 3.1 compares the two plans.

The Great Compromise

The Virginia Plan provided for a two-chamber legislature, with representation in both chambers based on population. The idea of having two chambers was never seriously challenged, but the idea of representation according to population brought the most heated and prolonged debates. The smaller states demanded equal representation for all states, but another vote rejected that concept for the House of Representatives. The debate continued. Finally, the Connecticut delegation moved that each state have an equal vote in the Senate. Still another poll showed that the delegations were equally divided on this proposal.

A committee was created to resolve the new deadlock; it consisted of one delegate from each state, chosen by secret ballot. The committee worked through the Independence Day recess and then reported a **Great Compromise** (originally proposed by a member of the Connecticut delegation, it is sometimes called the *Connecticut Compromise*): the House of Representatives would initially consist of fifty-six members, apportioned *according to the population of each state*. Money bills, or revenue-raising acts, would originate in the House. Most important, *the states would be represented equally in the Senate*, with two senators each.

In apportioning representatives within the House, the population of each state was to be determined "by adding to the whole Number of free Persons, . . . three fifths of all other Persons." The phrase "all other Persons" is, of course, a euphemism for "slaves." Nowhere does the Constitution mention slaves or slavery by name, despite the fact that slavery was a major issue in the nation and among the delegates. Yet, without mentioning it, the framers allowed slavery—the most undemocratic of all institutions.

It is doubtful that there would have been a Great Compromise—or even a Constitution—if the delegates had had to debate that issue, since southern states would not have ratified a Constitution forbidding slavery. The delegates

Table 3.1

Major Differences Between the Virginia Plan and the New Jersey Plan

Characteristic	Virginia Plan	New Jersey Plan
Legislature	two chambers	one chamber
Legislative power	derived from people	derived from states
Executive	one person	more than one person
Decision rule	majority	extraordinary majority
State laws	legislature can negate	compel obedience
Executive removal	by Congress	by majority of states
Courts	national judiciary	no provision
Ratification	by the people	by the states

themselves appear to have been ambivalent on the slavery issue. They expressed tolerance for slavery by requiring that escaped slaves be returned to their masters; but they also expressed opposition to slavery by permitting the Congress to abolish the slave trade after 1807. Perhaps they believed that a Union with slavery was still a Union; a reckoning on the slavery issue could await another day.

The committee's recommendations, too, were debated without result, but a spirit of compromise was in the air. Yet another committee was appointed to hammer out revisions. It increased the number of representatives in the House to sixty-five and specified the distribution of those representatives among the states. The convention then agreed unanimously that representation would be updated periodically, according to a census of the population to be conducted every ten years. Finally, the delegates accepted the Great Compromise: the smaller states got their equal representation, and the larger states, their proportional representation. The small states might dominate the Senate, and the large states might control the House; but, since all legislation had to be approved by both chambers, neither group of states would be able to dominate the other.

Compromise on the Presidency

Contention replaced compromise when the delegates turned to the executive branch. They did agree to a one-person executive — a president — but disagreed on how the executive would be selected and what the term of office would be. Because the delegates distrusted the judgment of the people, they rejected the idea of popular election. At the same time, representatives of the smaller states feared that election by the legislature would allow the larger states to control the executive.

Once again, a committee of twelve — one member from each participating state — was chosen to effect a compromise. That committee fashioned the cumbersome presidential election system that we know today as the **electoral college.** The "college" consists of a group of electors who are chosen for the sole purpose of selecting the president and vice president. Each state would choose a number of electors equal to the number of representatives it had in Congress. Each elector would then vote for two people. The person with the most votes would become president, provided that that person had a majority of the votes; the person with the next greatest number of votes would become vice president. (This procedure was changed in 1804 by the Twelfth Amendment.) If no candidate won a majority, then the House of Representatives would choose a president, *with each state having one vote.*

The electoral college compromise removed the fear of a popular vote for president. At the same time, it satisfied the small states. If the electoral college failed to produce a president — which the delegates expected would happen — then an election by the House would give every state the same voice in the selection process.

Finally, the delegates agreed that the president should be eligible for re-election and that the term of office should be four years.

The delegates also realized that removing a president from office would be a very serious political matter. For that reason, they involved all other major components of the government in the process. The House alone was empowered to charge a president with "treason, bribery, or other high crimes and misdemeanors," by a majority vote. The Senate was given the sole power to try the president on the House's charges. It could convict, and thus remove, a president only by a two-thirds vote. And the chief justice of the United States was required to preside over the Senate trial.

THE FINAL PRODUCT

Once the delegates resolved their major disagreements, they dispatched the remaining issues relatively quickly. A committee was then appointed to organize and write up the results of the proceedings. Twenty-three resolutions had been debated and approved by the convention; these were reorganized under seven articles in the draft Constitution. The Preamble, which was the last section to be drafted, begins with a phrase that would have been impossible to write when the convention opened. The one-sentence Preamble contains four elements that would form the foundation of the American political tradition.[9] The Preamble

■ *Creates a people*: "We the People of the United States" was a dramatic departure from the loose confederation of states that was to be replaced.

■ *Explains the reason for the Constitution*: "in Order to form a more perfect Union" was an indirect way of saying that the first effort, under the Articles of Confederation, had been inadequate.

■ *Articulates goals*: "establish Justice, insure domestic Tranquility, provide for the common defence, promote the general Welfare, and secure the Blessings of Liberty to ourselves and our Posterity"; in other words, the government exists to promote order and freedom.

■ *And fashions a government*: "do ordain and establish this Constitution for the United States of America."

The Basic Principles

In fashioning the Constitution, the founders advanced four political principles that, taken together, established a novel political order that reflected their revolutionary values. These principles were republicanism, federalism, separation of powers, and checks and balances.

Republicanism. **Republicanism** is a form of government in which power resides in the people and is exercised by their elected representatives. The framers were determined to avoid aristocracy (rule by a hereditary class), monarchy (rule by one), and direct democracy (rule by "mob"). A republic was both novel and daring.

There was no generally accepted model of republican government to follow when the framers advanced their plans. Moreover, at that time, republican government was viewed as suitable only for small territories where the interest of the public would be obvious and where government would be within reach of every citizen. The framers were far from sure that their government could be sustained. After the convention had ended, Benjamin Franklin was asked what sort of government the new nation would have. "A republic," he replied, "if you can keep it."

Federalism. **Federalism** is the division of sovereignty — and hence, power — among two or more governments. It stands in contrast to **unitary government,** in which all power is vested in a central government. The Articles of Confederation embodied a form of federalism in which power was divided between the states and the national government and in which the states possessed the greater share of political power. The federalism of the Constitution conferred more substantial powers on the national government, at the expense of state powers.

The constitutional powers vested in the national and state governments are derived from the people, who remain the ultimate sovereign. These governments could exercise their powers over persons and property within their own spheres of authority. But, at the same time, the people would restrain both national and state governments to preserve their liberty.

The Constitution listed the powers of the national government and the powers that were denied to the states. All other powers remained with the states. Generally, the states were required to give up only the powers necessary to create an effective national government; the national government was limited to the powers specified in the Constitution. In spite of such specific lists, however, the Constitution does not clearly define the spheres of authority within which these powers may be exercised. As you will see in Chapter 4, limits on the exercise of power by the national government and the states have evolved as a result of political and military conflict; moreover, these limits have changed continually.

Separation of powers. **Separation of powers** is the assignment of the lawmaking, law-enforcing, and law-interpreting functions to separate and independent legislative, executive, and judicial branches of government. Nationally, the lawmaking power resides in Congress; the law-enforcing power resides in the presidency; and the law-interpreting power resides in the courts. Separation of powers safeguards liberty by ensuring that all government power does not fall into the hands of a single person or group of people. The Constitution goes so far as to designate different procedures for the selection of the people in each branch (see Figure 3.1), and it stipulates that service in one branch excludes simultaneous service in any other branch.

In theory, separation of powers means that one branch may not exercise the powers of the other branches. In practice, however, the separation is far from complete. One scholar has suggested that what we have instead is "separate institutions *sharing* powers."[10]

Checks and balances. The constitutional system of **checks and balances** is a means of giving each branch of government some scrutiny of and control over the other branches. The framers reasoned that these checks and balances would prevent each branch from ignoring or overpowering the others.

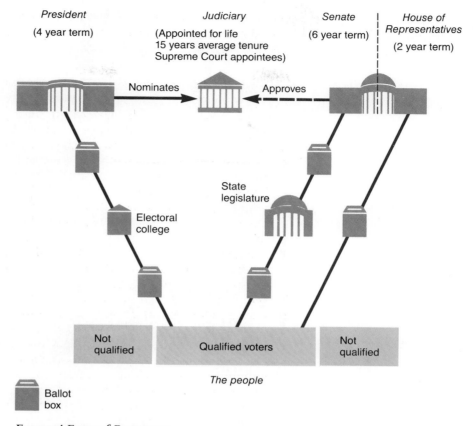

President	Judiciary	Senate	House of Representatives
(4 year term)	(Appointed for life 15 years average tenure Supreme Court appointees)	(6 year term)	(2 year term)

Nominates → ← Approves

State legislature

Electoral college

Not qualified / Qualified voters / Not qualified

The people

Ballot box

Framers' Fears of Democracy

The framers placed limits on majority rule. The people, speaking through the voters, express their choices directly to the House of Representatives. Other elected offices required filtering of the voters' choices through state legislatures and the electoral college. The judiciary is far removed from representative links to the people. Until 1913, when the Seventeenth Amendment was ratified, senators were elected by state legislatures.

Figure 3.1

Checks and balances and separation of powers are distinct principles, but both are needed to ensure that one branch will not dominate the government. Separation of powers divides government responsibilities among the three branches; checks and balances prevent the exclusive exercise of those powers by any one branch. Thus, for example, only the Congress can enact laws, but the president can veto those laws, nullifying them. However, in a "check on a check," the Congress can override the president's veto by an extraordinary (two-thirds) majority in each chamber. In another check on Congress, the courts can declare a law invalid if it violates the Constitution. Furthermore, the president has the power to appoint judges to the courts, even though such appointments must be made with the "advice and consent" of the Senate. Figure 3.2 illustrates the relationship between separation of powers and checks and balances.

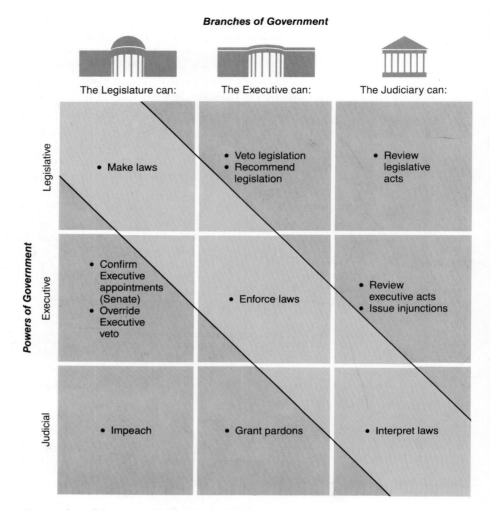

Separation of Powers and Checks and Balances
Separation of powers *is the assignment of lawmaking, law-enforcing, and law-interpreting functions to separate legislative, executive, and judicial branches. This is illustrated by the colored portion of the figure.* Checks and balances *give each branch some power over the other branches. For example, the executive branch possesses some legislative power, and the legislative branch possesses some executive power. These checks and balances are illustrated within the columns and outside the colored section of the figure.*

Figure 3.2

The Articles of the Constitution

Following the Preamble, the Constitution unfolds into seven articles. The first three establish the internal operation and powers of the separate branches. The remaining four articles structure relationships among the states, explain the process of amendment, declare the supremacy of national law, and explain the procedure for ratifying the Constitution.

Article I: The legislative article.   In structuring their new government, the framers began with the legislative branch because they regarded law-making as the paramount function of a republican government. Article I is the most detailed and therefore the longest of all the articles. The first article defines the **bicameral** (two-chambered) character of the Congress and de-scribes the internal operating procedures of the House of Representatives and the Senate. Section 8 of Article I expresses the principle of **enumerated powers,** which means that Congress can exercise only the powers that are granted to it. Eighteen powers are enumerated, of which the first seventeen are specific powers. For example, the third clause of Section 8 gives Congress the power to regulate interstate commerce. (One of the chief deficiencies of the Articles of Confederation was its lack of a means for coping with trade wars waged between states. The solution was to vest control of interstate commerce in the national government.)

The last clause in Section 8, known as the **necessary and proper clause** (also called the **elastic clause**), gives Congress the means to execute the enumerated powers (see the Appendix). This clause is the basis for Congress's **implied powers**—those powers that Congress requires in order to execute its enumerated powers. Thus, the power to levy and collect taxes (Clause 1), when joined with the necessary and proper clause (Clause 18), *implies* that Congress has the power to charter a bank. Otherwise, the national govern-ment would have no means for managing the funds it collected through its

Senators Gramm and Rudman Hold Court
In 1985, Congress passed an automatic budget-cutting proposal to reduce the federal deficit to zero by 1991. The law was drafted by Republican Senators Phil Gramm of Texas and Warren Rudman of New Hampshire, who are seen here in front of the Supreme Court building after the justices heard arguments challenging the law's validity. In 1986, the Court held that the automatic budget-cutting arrangement was a violation of the constitutional separation of powers.

power to tax. Such implied powers clearly expand the enumerated powers conferred on Congress by the Constitution.

The lawmaking power of Congress can be checked and balanced in numerous ways. For example, the president can veto legislation. The president can also recommend legislation and call extraordinary sessions of Congress. The courts can review congressional acts and declare them void because they violate the Constitution. These are just some of the powers shared by other branches.

Article II: The executive article.   Article II describes the qualifications for becoming president, the procedure for electing presidents through the electoral college, and the president's duties and powers. The last include acting as commander in chief of the military; making treaties (which must be ratified by a two-thirds vote of the Senate); and appointing government officers, diplomats, and judges (again, with the advice and consent of the Senate).

The president also possesses legislative powers (as part of the constitutional system of checks and balances). For example, the Constitution requires

May I Have Your Autograph?
A president gives his approval to legislation by signing a bill into law. President Lyndon B. Johnson cultivated the bill-signing ceremony into a high art form that was sure to garner ample attention from the media.

that the president periodically inform the Congress of the "State of the Union" and of the policies and programs that the executive branch intends to advocate in the forthcoming year. This is now done annually, in a State of the Union address. Under special circumstances, the president may also convene or adjourn Congress.

The duty to "take Care that the Laws be faithfully executed" in Section 3 has provided presidents with a reservoir of power extending beyond the powers listed in Article II. Recall that President Nixon refused to turn over the Watergate tapes in response to a judicial subpoena in a criminal trial. Nixon claimed executive privilege to refuse, based on the inherently undefined character of executive power. However, such executive actions can be declared invalid by the courts when they violate the Constitution. Thus, Nixon's attempt to invoke executive privilege was struck down by the Supreme Court; his claim violated the separation of powers because the decision to release or withhold information *in a criminal trial* is a judicial, not an executive, function.

Article III: The judicial article. The third article was cast in vagueness. The Constitution does establish the Supreme Court as the highest court in the land. But beyond that, the framers were unable to agree on the need for, or the composition of, a national judiciary, or on the size, composition, and procedures of the Supreme Court. They left these issues to the Congress; they were resolved when the first Congress established a federal court system.

Short of impeachment, federal judges on Article III courts serve for life. They are appointed to indefinite terms on "good behavior," and their salaries cannot be diminished while they hold office. These stipulations reinforce the separation of powers; they ensure that judges are independent of the other branches and that they need not fear retribution in their exercise of judicial power.

The judicial branch can be checked by Congress through its power to create (and eliminate) lower federal courts. Congress can also restrict the power of the lower courts to decide cases. And, as we have noted, the president appoints — with the advice and consent of the Senate — the justices of the Supreme Court and the judges of the lower federal courts.

Article III does not explicitly empower the courts to invalidate congressional or presidential actions. That power has been inferred from the logic, structure, and theory of the Constitution.

The remaining articles. The remaining four articles of the Constitution cover a lot of ground. Briefly, Article IV requires that the citizens, judicial acts, and criminal warrants of each state be honored in all other states. For example, an Illinois court awards Goldman damages against Janda for $10,000. Janda moves to Alaska to avoid payment. Rather than force Goldman to bring a new suit against Janda in the Alaska courts, the Alaska court (Judge Berry presiding) will, under Article IV's full faith and credit clause, honor the Illinois judgment and enforce it as its own. In other words, you can run but you cannot hide. The origin of this clause can be traced to the Articles of Confederation.

Article IV also permits the addition of new states and stipulates that the national government will protect the states against invasion and domestic violence.

Article V specifies the methods for amending the Constitution. We shall have more to say about this shortly.

An important component of Article VI is the **supremacy clause,** which asserts that the Constitution and national laws take precedence over state and local laws when they conflict. Such a stipulation is vital to the operation of federalism. In keeping with the supremacy clause, Article VI also requires all national and state officials, elected or appointed, to take an oath to support the Constitution. The article also mandates that there be no religious test for holding government office.

Finally, Article VII provided that ratification by conventions held in nine states would be sufficient for the establishment of the Constitution.

The Framers' Motives

Some argue that the Constitution is essentially a conservative document written by wealthy men to advance their own interests. One distinguished historian, Charles A. Beard, maintained that the delegates, who were for the most part wealthy men, had much to gain from a strong national government.[11] Many delegates held government securities that were practically worthless under the Articles of Confederation. A strong national government would protect their property and pay off the nation's debts. Beard argued that the Constitution was crafted to protect the economic interests of such creditor groups.

Beard's argument provoked a generation of historians to examine the financial records of the convention delegates. Their modern scholarship has largely discredited Beard's once-popular view.[12] For example, it turns out that seven of the delegates who quit the convention or refused to sign the Constitution held public securities worth more than twice the holdings of the thirty-nine delegates who did sign. Moreover, the most influential delegates owned no securities. And only a minority of the delegates appeared to benefit economically from the new government.[13]

What did motivate the framers? Surely economic issues were vital, but they were not the major issues. Instead, the single most important factor leading to the Constitutional Convention was the inability of the national or state governments to maintain order under the loose structure of the Articles of Confederation. Certainly order involved the protection of property; but the framers had a broader view of property than their portfolios of government securities. They wished to protect their homes, families, and means of livelihood from impending anarchy under the Articles.

Though there were bitter disagreements on structure, mechanics, and detail, the framers agreed on the most vital issues. For example, three of the most crucial parts of the Constitution—the power to tax, the necessary and proper clause, and the supremacy clause—were unanimously approved without debate. The convention was successful because experience had taught the delegates that a strong national government was essential if the United States was to survive and flourish.

SELLING THE CONSTITUTION

On September 17, 1787, nearly four months from the opening session of the Constitutional Convention, the delegates convened for the last time, to sign the final, carefully written version of their handiwork. Because several delegates were unwilling to sign the document, its final paragraph was craftily worded to give the impression of unanimity: "Done in Convention by the Unanimous Consent *of the States* present."

To take effect, the Constitution still had to be ratified by conventions to be held in each of the states. A minimum of nine states had to ratify it, and the support of such key states as New York and Virginia was crucial. Everywhere, there were differences of opinion regarding the acceptability of the Constitution.

> In Halifax, Virginia, it is reported that a preacher on a Sunday morning had pronounced from the desk a fervent prayer for the adoption of the federal constitution; but he had no sooner ended his prayer than a clever layman ascended the pulpit, invited the people to join a second time in the supplication, and put forth an animated petition that the new scheme be rejected.[14]

The proponents of the new charter, who desired a strong national government, called themselves Federalists. The opponents of the Constitution were quickly dubbed Antifederalists. They claimed, however, that *they* were true Federalists, because they sought to preserve the states from the tyranny of a strong national government. Elbridge Gerry, an Antifederalist, preferred to tar his opponents as "rats" because they favored ratification. He maintained he was an "antirat."[15] Such is the Alice-in-Wonderland character of political discourse. (Nonetheless, the viewpoints of the Federalists and the Antifederalists formed the bases for the first American political parties.)

The Federalist Papers

Beginning in October 1788, a series of eighty-five newspaper articles appeared under the title *The Federalist: A Commentary on the Constitution of the United States*. The articles were reprinted extensively during the ratification period. They bore the pen name "Publius" (Latin for "the people") and were authored primarily by James Madison and Alexander Hamilton, with some assistance from John Jay. In a reasoned, quiet, and intellectual fashion, "Publius" argued in favor of ratification. He was avowedly engaged in an exercise of special pleading, but the articles lacked the thunder that was needed to stir citizens to action. The personal influence of Washington and Franklin probably weighed more heavily than these essays in the ensuing debates. But *The Federalist* (also called the Federalist papers) remains the best single commentary we have on the meaning of the Constitution and the political theory it embodies.

The Antifederalists, not to be outdone, offered their own intellectual basis for rejecting the Constitution. In several essays authored by "Brutus," the Antifederalists attacked the centralization of power in a strong national government, which would obliterate the states and destroy liberty in the process. They were defenders of the status quo, maintaining that the Articles of Confederation established true federal principles.[16]

Of all the Federalist papers, the most magnificent and most frequently cited essay is *The Federalist*, No. 10, by James Madison (see the Appendix). Madison argued that the proposed Constitution was designed "to break and control the violence of faction."

> By a faction, I understand a number of citizens, whether amounting to a majority or minority of the whole, who are united and actuated by some common impulse of passion, or of interest, adverse to the rights of other citizens, or to the permanent and aggregate interests of the community.

Of course, Madison was discussing what we described in Chapter 2 as *pluralism*. What Madison called "factions" we might recognize today as interest groups or even political parties. According to Madison, "The most common and durable source of factions has been the various and unequal distribution of property." Madison was concerned not with reducing inequalities of wealth (which he took for granted), but with controlling the seemingly inevitable conflict among factions. Madison argued that the proposed Constitution was "well-constructed" for this purpose.

The most serious threat was conflict between the wealthy (the minority) and those who lacked wealth (the majority), leading to a tyranny of the majority. On the contrary, wrote Madison, the proposed Constitution would prevent majority tyranny through the mechanism of *representation*. Government would be controlled, not directly by the people, but by their elected representatives. And those representatives would possess the intelligence and discretion to serve the larger interests of the nation. Moreover, the federal system would require that majorities first form within each state and then organize for effective action at the national level. This and the vastness of the country would make it unlikely that a majority would form "to invade the rights of other citizens."

The purpose of *The Federalist*, No. 10, was to demonstrate that the proposed Constitution would establish a republic, not a democracy. People of property need not fear that they would suffer under the tyranny of a majority if they supported ratification.

Madison pressed his argument from a different angle in *The Federalist*, No. 51. Asserting that "Ambition must be made to counteract ambition," he argued that the separation of powers and checks and balances would control tyranny from any source. If power is distributed equally across the three branches, then each branch has the capacity to counteract the other. In Madison's words, "usurpations are guarded against by a division of the government into distinct and separate departments." Because legislative power tends to predominate in republican governments, legislative authority is divided between the Senate and the House of Representatives, with different methods of selection and terms of office. Additional protection comes through federalism, which divides power "between two distinct governments, and the portion allotted to each [is] subdivided among distinct and separate departments."

The Antifederalists argued for additional separation of powers and additional checks and balances, which, they maintained, would eliminate the threat of tyranny entirely. The Federalists maintained that the Antifederalists' proposal would instead make decisive national action virtually impossible.

The purpose of *The Federalist*, No. 51, was to demonstrate that the proposed government was not likely to be ruled by *any* faction. Contrary to conventional wisdom, Madison argued, the key to controlling the evils of faction is to have a large republic—the larger, the better. The more diverse the society, the less likely it is that an unjust majority will form. Madison certainly had no vision of creating a majoritarian democracy. His view of popular government was much more consistent with the model of pluralist democracy discussed in Chapter 2.

A Concession: The Bill of Rights

Despite the eloquence of the Federalist papers, many prominent citizens, including Thomas Jefferson, were distressed that the Constitution lacked a list of basic civil liberties—the individual freedoms that would be guaranteed to citizens. The omission of this list, or bill of rights, was the chief obstacle to the Constitution's adoption by the states. (In fact, seven of the eleven state constitutions that were written in the first five years of the Revolution already contained such a list.) The colonists had just rebelled against the British government to preserve their basic freedoms; why didn't the proposed Constitution spell out those freedoms?

The answer was rooted in logic, not politics. Since the national government was limited to those powers that were granted to it and since no power was granted to abridge the people's liberties, then a list of guaranteed freedoms was logically unnecessary. Hamilton, in *The Federalist*, No. 84, goes even further, arguing that the addition of a bill of rights would be dangerous. To deny the exercise of a nonexistent power might lead to the exercise of a power that is not denied.

Suppose the national government is prohibited, by express declaration, from interfering with the freedom of the press. If the Constitution is silent on other freedoms, the express prohibition on the press fuels inferences in other areas. Since it is not possible to list all prohibited powers, any attempt to provide a partial list makes the remaining areas vulnerable to government abuse.

But logical analysis was no match for political fear. Many states agreed to ratify the Constitution only after Washington proposed that the desired guarantees could be added quickly through amendments. At least 124 such amendments were proposed by the states. These were eventually narrowed down to 12 amendments, which were approved by Congress and sent to the states. Ten of those became part of the Constitution in 1791, when Virginia became the eleventh state to approve them.* (Connecticut, Georgia, and Massachusetts finally approved them in 1939, 150 years after their introduction.) Collectively, these first ten amendments are known as our **Bill of Rights.** They restrain the national government from tampering with fundamental rights and civil liberties and emphasize the limited character of national power (see Table 3.2).

---

* Vermont joined the Union in March 1791, bringing the number of states to fourteen. Three-fourths of the states were necessary for ratification.

Table 3.2
The Bill of Rights (Grouped Conceptually)
The first ten amendments to the Constitution are known as the Bill of Rights. The following is a list of those amendments grouped conceptually. For the actual order and wording of the Bill of Rights, see the Appendix.

Guarantees	Amendment

Guarantees for Participation in the Political Process
No government abridgment of speech or press;
  no government abridgment of peaceable assembly;
  no government abridgment of petitioning government for redress.
	I

Guarantees Respecting Personal Beliefs No government establishment of religion; no government prohibition of free religious exercise.	I
Guarantees of Personal Privacy Owners' consent necessary for peacetime troop quartering in private homes; quartering during war must be lawful.	III
Government cannot engage in unreasonable searches and seizures; warrants to search and seize require probable cause.	IV
No compulsion to testify against oneself in criminal cases.	V

Guarantees Against Government Overreaching
Serious crimes require a grand jury indictment;
  no repeated prosecution for the same offense;
  no loss of life, liberty, or property without due process;
  no government taking of property for public use without just compensation.
	V

Criminal defendants will have a speedy public trial by impartial local jury; defendants informed of accusation; defendants confront witnesses against them; defendants use judicial process to obtain favorable witnesses; defendants have legal assistance for their defense.	VI
Civil lawsuits can be tried by juries if controversy exceeds $20; in jury trials, factfinding is a jury function.	VII
No excessive bail; no excessive fines; no cruel and unusual punishment.	VIII
Other Guarantees No government trespass on unspecified fundamental rights.	IX
The states or the people reserve powers not delegated to the national government or denied to the states.	X
The people have the right to bear arms.	II

Ratification

Delaware was first to ratify the Constitution. (Today, Delaware license plates bear the motto "The First State.") Massachusetts gave its assent after a close contest (187 yeas to 168 nays), but its convention called for the promised bill of rights. New Hampshire, the ninth state to ratify, did so on June 21, 1788. According to Article VII, the Constitution took effect on that date. But this was true only in a technical sense, for two of the remaining states were absolutely critical to the success of the newly formed United States: Virginia and New York together comprised almost 40 percent of its population.

The convention debates in these states were filled with invective. Virginia ratified by a vote of 89 to 79, but it recommended a Declaration of Rights and twenty additional amendments to cure other supposed defects in the

Constitution. The New York convention voted to ratify by the close margin of 30 to 27, a week after Virginia did so. The New Yorkers, too, recommended the addition of a bill of rights, along with thirty-two other amendments. By August 1788, eleven states, including the most influential two, had ratified the Constitution.

But once again, "Rogue Island" was obstinate. The only state that did not send a delegate to the convention became the last state to ratify the Constitution. When Rhode Island did finally vote approval on May 29, 1790, it did so only by a vote of 34 to 32.[17]

CONSTITUTIONAL CHANGE

The founders realized that their Constitution would need to be changed from time to time. To this end, they specified a formal amendment process in Article V — a process that was used almost immediately to add the Bill of Rights. With the passage of time, the Constitution has also been altered through judicial interpretation and through changes in political practice.

The Formal Amendment Process

There are two stages in the amendment process, **proposal** and **ratification;** both must be completed for an amendment to become part of the Constitution. The Constitution provides two alternative methods for completing each stage (see Figure 3.3). Amendments may be proposed (1) by a two-thirds vote of the House of Representatives and of the Senate, or (2) by a national convention, summoned by Congress at the request of two-thirds of the state legislatures. All constitutional amendments have been proposed by the first method; the national convention method of proposal has never been used.

Figure 3.3

Amending the Constitution

There are two stages in amending the Constitution: proposal and ratification. Congress has no control over the proposal stage, but it prescribes the ratification method. Once it has ratified an amendment, a state cannot retract its action. A state's rejection of an amendment does not bar future reconsideration, however.

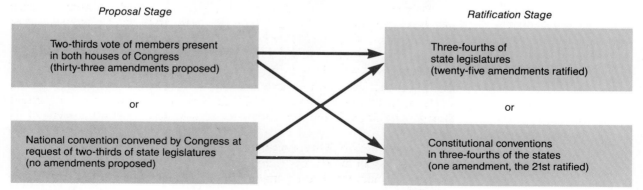

Proposal Stage

Two-thirds vote of members present in both houses of Congress (thirty-three amendments proposed)

or

National convention convened by Congress at request of two-thirds of state legislatures (no amendments proposed)

Ratification Stage

Three-fourths of state legislatures (twenty-five amendments ratified)

or

Constitutional conventions in three-fourths of the states (one amendment, the 21st ratified)

A proposed amendment may be ratified (1) by vote of the legislatures of three-fourths of the states, or (2) by vote of state conventions held in three-fourths of the states. The method of ratification is chosen by Congress; it has employed the state convention method of ratification only once, for the Twenty-First Amendment, which repealed the Eighteenth (Prohibition) Amendment.

Note that the amendment process requires the exercise of **extraordinary majorities** (votes of approval greater than a simple majority). The framers purposely made it difficult to propose and ratify amendments, to ensure that only the most significant issues led to constitutional changes. Note, too, that the president has no formal role in the amendment process. His approval is not required to amend the Constitution, although his political influence affects the success or failure of any amendment effort.

The untried method of calling a national convention to propose an amendment could give rise to several thorny issues. For example, how many delegates should attend, and how should they be chosen? What would be the rules for debating and voting on a proposed amendment? (The Constitution says nothing about this.) But the thorniest issue centers on the limits, if any, on the business of the convention. Recall that the Philadelphia convention of 1787 was charged with revising the Articles of Confederation, yet it drafted an entirely new charter. Would a national convention, called to consider a particular amendment, be within its bounds to rewrite the entire Constitution? No one really knows; constitutional scholars are divided as to the restrictions that would apply. The question may soon be answered by a movement now under way to summon a constitutional convention to write an amendment that would require a balanced budget.

Roll Out the Barrels
The Eighteenth Amendment, which was ratified by the states in 1919, banned the manufacture, sale, or transportation of alcoholic beverages. The amendment was spurred by moral and social reform groups, like the Women's Christian Temperance Union, which was founded by Evanston, Illinois, resident Frances Willard in 1874. The amendment proved to be an utter failure. People continued to drink, but their alcohol came from illegal sources.

Table 3.3
Constitutional Amendments: 11 Through 26

No.	Proposed	Ratified	Intent	Subject
11	1794	1795	D	Prohibits an individual from suing a state in a federal court without the state's consent.
12	1803	1804	D	Requires the electoral college to vote separately for president and vice president.
13	1865	1865	E	Prohibits slavery.
14	1866	1868	E	Gives citizenship to all persons born or naturalized in the U.S. (former slaves); prevents states from depriving any "person of life, liberty, or property, without due process of law."
15	1869	1870	E	Citizens' right to vote shall not be denied "on account of race, color, or previous condition of servitude."
16	1909	1913	E	Gives Congress power to collect an income tax.
17	1912	1913	E	Provides for popular election of senators, who were formerly elected by state legislatures.
18	1917	1919	P	Prohibits making and selling intoxicating liquors.
19	1919	1920	E	Gives women the right to vote.
20	1932	1933	D	Changes the presidential inauguration from March 4 to January 20 and sets January 3 for the opening date of Congress.
21	1933	1933	P	Repeals the 18th Amendment, prohibiting intoxicating beverages.
22	1947	1951	D	Limits a president to two terms.
23	1960	1961	E	Gives citizens of Washington, D.C., the right to vote for president.
24	1962	1964	E	Prohibits charging citizens a poll tax to vote.
25	1965	1967	D	Provides for succession in event of death, removal from office, incapacity, or resignation of the president or vice president.
26	1971	1971	E	Extends voting rights to age 18.

P   Amendments legislating public policy.
D   Amendments correcting perceived deficiencies in government structure.
E   Amendments advancing equality.

Most of the Constitution's twenty-six amendments were adopted to help keep it abreast of changes in political thinking. The first ten amendments (the Bill of Rights) were adopted as the price for ratification, but they have been important to our current system of government. The last sixteen amendments fall into three main categories, as shown in Table 3.3. Amendments have been used to correct deficiencies in government structure, to make public policy, and to advance equality. One attempt to make public policy through a constitutional amendment was disastrous. The Eighteenth Amendment (1919) prohibited the sale or manufacture of intoxicating beverages. Prohibition, as it was called, lasted for about 12 years and was an utter failure. Gangsters began "bootlegging" liquor; people died after drinking home-made booze; and millions of people regularly broke the law by drinking anyway. Congress had to propose another amendment in early 1933 to repeal the Eighteenth. The states ratified the Twenty-First Amendment repealing Prohibition in less than ten months, less time than it took to ratify the Thirteenth Amendment outlawing slavery.

Since 1787, about ten thousand constitutional amendments have been introduced; only a fraction have passed through the proposal stage. Once an amendment has been voted by the Congress, however, the chances of ratification are very high — though not certain. Seven amendments submitted to the states have failed to be ratified. The latest failed amendment, which called for full congressional representation for Washington, D.C., mustered approval in only sixteen states, twenty-two states short of the required three-fourths for ratification.

Interpretation by the Courts

In 1803, in its decision in the case of *Marbury* v. *Madison*, the Supreme Court declared that the courts have the power to nullify government acts when they conflict with the Constitution. (We shall elaborate on this power, which is called **judicial review,** in Chapter 13.) The exercise of this power requires that the courts interpret the Constitution, which is the supreme law of the land and thus is fair game for judicial interpretation. And, in interpreting the Constitution, judges cannot help but give new meaning to its provisions. Hence, judicial interpretation is a form of constitutional change.

What guidelines should judges employ when they interpret constitutional provisions? For one thing, they must realize that our language — particularly the usage and meaning of many words — has changed over the last two hundred years. Judges must be careful to consider the concepts and language of the Constitution as it was written. Should they also consider the intentions of the framers — the so-called original intent? On the one hand, to do so they would need to consult records of the Constitutional Convention and the debates surrounding ratification. But there are many questions about the completeness and accuracy of those records, including even Madison's very detailed notes. On the other hand, the framers were purposely general (and occasionally vague) in writing their document. This vagueness may have resulted from a lack of agreement — or, in some cases, a universal understanding — regarding certain provisions of the Constitution. In any event, politicians and scholars continue to debate a "jurisprudence of original intent," and judges interpret the Constitution as best they can.

Political Practice

The Constitution remains silent on many issues. For example, it says nothing about political parties or the president's cabinet, yet parties and cabinets have exercised considerable influence in American politics. And constitutional provisions may fall out of use. The electors in the electoral college, for example, were supposed to exercise their own independent judgment in voting for president and vice president. Now, however, the electors function simply as a rubber stamp, reflecting the outcome of election contests in their states.

The framers could scarcely imagine an urbanized nation of 240 million people stretching across a land mass some three thousand miles wide. They could never in their wildest nightmares have contemplated the destructiveness of nuclear war or envisioned the influence this would have on the power to declare war. The Constitution gives that power to Congress, which would consider and debate such a momentous step. But with nuclear annihilation perhaps only minutes away, the legislative power to declare war must give way to the president's power to wage war as the nation's commander in chief. Strict adherence to the Constitution could destroy the nation's ability to protect itself from its enemies.

AN EVALUATION OF THE CONSTITUTION

The U.S. Constitution is one of the world's most praised political documents. It is the oldest written national constitution and one of the most widely copied constitutions, sometimes word for word. It is also one of the shortest, containing about 4,300 words, not counting amendments (see Compared With What? 3.1). In fact, the twenty-six amendments (containing about 3,500 words) are nearly as long as the Constitution itself. The brevity of the U.S. Constitution may be one of its greatest strengths. As we noted earlier, the framers simply laid out a structural framework for government, without describing relationships and powers in detail. For example, the Constitution gives Congress the power to regulate "Commerce . . . among the several States," but does not define interstate commerce. Such general phraseology permits interpretations that are in keeping with contemporary political, social, and technological developments. Air travel, for instance, was unknown in 1787, but it now easily falls within Congress's power to regulate interstate commerce.

The generality of the U.S. Constitution stands in stark contrast to the specificity of most state constitutions. The constitution of California, for example, provides that

> Fruit and nut-bearing trees under the age of four years from the time of planting in orchard form and grapevines under the age of three years from the time of planting in vineyard form . . . shall be exempt from taxation. (Article XIII, Section 12)

Because they are so specific, most state constitutions are much longer than the U.S. Constitution.

Freedom, Order, and Equality in the Constitution

The American Revolution was fought to preserve the freedoms that the colonists enjoyed in their new land. The revolutionaries' first try at government was embodied in the Articles of Confederation. The result was a weak government that erred too much toward freedom at the cost of disorder. Deciding that the confederation was beyond correcting, the revolutionaries chose a new form of government—a *federal* government. Their new constitution was aimed at structuring a national government strong enough to maintain order, but not so strong that it could dominate the states or infringe

Compared With What? 3.1

Other Constitutions

In a comparative study of 142 written constitutions from around the world, researchers found that over three-quarters contained more than 6,000 words and nearly half contained more than 12,000 words.* (Compare this with the U.S. Constitution, which contained 4,300 words as written in 1787.) The difference becomes even greater when the constitutions are separated into those of federal nations and those of unitary nations. A federal structure tends to require a longer constitution, for it must specify the relationships between the national and state governments. In the study, the average federal constitution had 26,700 words, compared with 14,300 words for unitary constitutions.

Be thankful you are not studying the Yugoslavian or Indian constitution, the two longest in the world. These two federal constitutions have 60,000 and 54,700 words, respectively. In the Malagasy Republic, on the other hand, students need master only 700 words, less than three pages of double-spaced typewritten text.

What are these constitutions about? The researchers analyzed the constitutions for mentions of political values and found that the number that mentioned freedom or liberty (64 percent) was more than twice the number that mentioned equality (30 percent). In this regard, the U.S. Constitution is quite typical in its emphasis on liberty and its neglect of equality.

The quality of the U.S. Constitution shines brilliantly in comparison with the constitutions of the fifty states.† Only one of the original thirteen states, Massachusetts, still operates under its original constitution. However, Massachusetts's 1780 constitution needed 116 amendments and contains 36,600 words. Georgia, also one of the original thirteen states, has had *ten* constitutions since 1777, including new ones in 1945, 1976, and 1982. Louisiana holds the record: eleven constitutions since 1812, with the latest in 1974.

The U.S. Constitution has also survived with minimum verbiage. Including all twenty-six amendments, the U.S. Constitution contains only about 7,800 words. Only one American state, Vermont, has a shorter constitution. Its 1793 constitution

---

*Hene van Maarseveen and Ger van der Tang. *Written Constitutions: A Computerized Comparative Study* (Dobbs Ferry, N.Y.: Oceana Publications, 1978).

†*Book of the States* (Lexington, Ky.: Council of State Governments, 1985), p. 221.

---

on individual freedoms. In short, the Constitution provided a judicious balance between *order* and *freedom*. It paid virtually no attention to social equality.

The Constitution's silence on social equality is evident in what it failed to specify. First, it failed to mention slavery—a controversial issue even then. In fact, as you saw earlier, the Constitution silently accepted slavery in the wording that specified the results of the Great Compromise. Not until the Thirteenth Amendment's ratification in 1865 was slavery prohibited.

The Constitution also avoided taking a stand on political equality for whites. It left voting qualifications to the states, specifying only that people who could vote for "the most numerous Branch of the State Legislature" could also vote for representatives to Congress (Article I, Section 2). Most states at that time had tax-paying or property-owning requirements for voting by white males; blacks and women were universally excluded from voting.

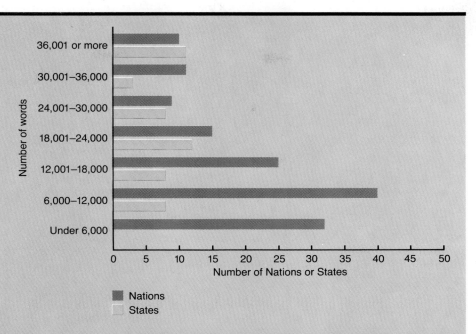

has only 6,660 words. All the other states have longer constitutions, as shown in the accompanying figure. The average state constitution is about *three times* longer than the federal Constitution. In fact, four states (Alabama, New York, Oklahoma, and Texas) have constitutions longer than the 60,000 words in the longest national constitution!

Why are state constitutions so long? Primarily because their framers wrote very specific provisions into those constitutions to protect their special interests. Using the constitution instead of the legislature to make public policy also invites frequent amendments: California's 1879 constitution has 442 amendments, Alabama's has 443, and South Carolina's has 444.

In terms of longevity, brevity, and generality, the U.S. Constitution stands in a class by itself.

These inequalities have been rectified by the equality-advancing amendments (see Table 3.3).

The Constitution did not guarantee blacks citizenship until the Fourteenth Amendment was ratified (1868) and did not give them the right to vote until the Fifteenth Amendment (1870). Women were not guaranteed the right to vote until the Nineteenth Amendment (1920). Finally, the *poll tax* (a tax that people had to pay in order to vote and that tended to disenfranchise blacks) was not eliminated until the Twenty-Fourth Amendment (1964). Two other amendments expanded the Constitution's grant of political equality. The Twenty-Third Amendment (1961) enabled citizens of Washington, D.C., who are not considered to be residents of any state, to vote for president. The Twenty-Sixth Amendment (1971) extended voting rights to all citizens who are at least eighteen years old.

Women Against the ERA
ERA — a constitutional amendment guaranteeing equal rights for men and women — was approved by Congress in 1972, forty-nine years after it was first introduced. The amendment died ten years later, three states short of ratification. An Illinois housewife named Phyllis Schlafly, pictured here with the microphone, was the principal architect for the amendment's defeat. Despite official endorsements of the amendment from a wide spectrum of leaders and groups, opponents argued that it would subject women to the military draft, abolish legislation protecting women from harmful employment, and wipe out privacy rights in public facilities.

What about the Constitution and social equality? The Constitution was designed long before social equality was even a conceivable objective of government. In fact, Madison's famous *The Federalist,* No. 10, held that protection of the "diversities in the faculties of men from which the rights of property originate" is "the first object of government." Over a century later, however, the Constitution was changed to incorporate a key device for the promotion of social equality — the income tax. The Sixteenth Amendment (1913) gave Congress the power to collect an income tax; it was proposed and ratified to replace a law that had been declared unconstitutional in an 1895 court case. The idea of **progressive taxation** (in which the tax rate increases with income) had long been closely linked to the income tax,[18] and the Sixteenth Amendment gave it a constitutional basis. Progressive taxation later helped in the pursuit of social equality through the redistribution of income. That is, higher incomes are taxed at higher rates to help fund social programs that benefit low-income people. Nevertheless, social equality itself had never been, and is not now, a prime *constitutional* value.

Consider the fate of the proposed Equal Rights Amendment (ERA). Proposed by Congress in 1972, the ERA stated simply that "Equality of rights under law shall not be denied or abridged by the United States or any State on account of sex." The ERA was ratified by thirty-five states, but it required approval by thirty-eight states and thus failed to become the Twenty-Seventh Amendment to the Constitution. The remaining state legislatures were content to pursue equal rights for women through legislative policies, rather than through a national constitutional guarantee.

The Constitution and Models of Democracy

It is hard to imagine a governmental framework better suited to the pluralist model of democracy than the Constitution of the United States. It is also hard to imagine a document more frustrating to the majoritarian model of democracy. Consider Madison's view, in *The Federalist,* No. 10, of government involving the inevitable "conflicting factions." This concept fits perfectly with the idea of competing groups in pluralist theory (discussed in Chapter 2). Consider his description in *The Federalist,* No. 51, of the Constitution's ability to guard against "majority tyranny" through its separation of powers and checks and balances. This again fits perfectly with pluralist democracy, which avoids any single center of government power that might fall under majority control.

The delegates to the Constitutional Convention intended to create a republic, a government resting on majority consent; it was not their intent to create a democracy, which rests on majority rule. They succeeded admirably in creating that republic. Along the way, they also produced a government that grew into a democracy, but a particular type of democracy. The framers neither wanted nor got a democracy that fit the majoritarian model. They perhaps wanted, and certainly did get, a government that conforms to the pluralist model of democracy.

SUMMARY

The U.S. Constitution is more than a historic document, an antique curiosity. Although two hundred years old, it still governs the politics of a mighty modern nation. The Constitution has been called "the venerable patriarch of the world's written charters of government."[19] Even a president who won re-election by a landslide was forced from office when he violated its principles.

The Constitution was the final product of a revolutionary movement aimed at preserving existing liberties. The Declaration of Independence argued that everyone is entitled to certain rights (among them, life, liberty, and the pursuit of happiness) that no government can deny. Furthermore, government exists for the good of its subjects, not the other way around.

The Articles of Confederation was the first attempt at government to replace the British monarchy. The states coveted their independence, however; and the loose association of states under the Articles proved impotent when disorder and insurrection threatened. Under the guise of revising the Articles, state delegates met to frame a new charter called the Constitution. Their handiwork specifies the basic structure of the national government.

The Constitution advanced four political principles. Republicanism is a form of government in which power resides in the people and is exercised by their elected representatives. Federalism is a division of power between the states and the national government. Separation of powers is a further division of power into three branches within the government: the legislative (lawmaking) branch; the executive (law-enforcing) branch; and the judiciary (law-interpreting) branch. Finally, the Constitution established a system of checks and balances giving each branch some scrutiny of and control over the other branches.

The paramount, lawmaking power would be exercised by a bicameral (two-chambered) Congress with powers that would be enumerated, which means that Congress can exercise only the powers granted to it. But the Constitution gave Congress the means to execute enumerated powers through the so-called elastic clause.

The stumbling block to ratification (approval) of the Constitution proved to be the absence of a bill of rights, which became the first ten amendments. They restrained the national government from interfering with participation in the political process, personal beliefs, and personal privacy. They embodied guarantees against government overreaching in criminal prosecutions.

The Constitution was designed to strike a balance between order and freedom. It was not designed to advance equality; in fact, it had to be amended to redress inequality. The framers sought order by devising a strong national government, but one whose power could be checked. The framers sought to control the power of the national government through the twin principles of separation of powers and checks and balances. The result was a government that shunned attempts to centralize power, as Richard Nixon learned.

The framers did not set out to create a democracy, for there was little faith in government by the people two centuries ago. Nevertheless, they managed to produce a democratic form of government. Their governmental structure, with its separation of powers and checks and balances, is, however, better suited to the pluralist model of democracy than to the majoritarian model. Simple majority rule, which lies at the basis of the majoritarian model, was precisely what the framers wanted to avoid.

The framers also wanted a government that would balance the powers of the national government and the powers of the state governments. The precise balance was a touchy issue that was skirted by delegates at the convention. For example, they did not settle the issue of secession—whether or not a state had the right to secede from (leave) the "perfect Union" that the people ordained through their Constitution. A civil war was required to demonstrate that states could not secede. Countless political battles over two centuries have demonstrated another point: the national government dominates the state governments in our federal system. In the next chapter, you will see how that has come about.

Key Terms

Continental Congress
Declaration of Independence
social contract theory
republic
confederation
sovereignty
Articles of Confederation
Shays's Rebellion
Virginia Plan
legislative branch
executive branch
judicial branch
New Jersey Plan
Great Compromise
electoral college
republicanism

federalism
unitary government
separation of powers
checks and balances
bicameral
enumerated powers
necessary and proper clause (elastic clause)
implied powers
supremacy clause
Bill of Rights
proposal
ratification
extraordinary majorities
judicial review
progressive taxation

Selected Readings

Beard, Charles A. *Economic Interpretation of the Constitution of the United States*. New York: Macmillan, 1913. The classic argument that economic self-interest animated the framers' actions for or against the Constitution.

Becker, Carl. *The Declaration of Independence: A Study in the History of Political Ideas*. New York: Knopf, 1942. A classic study of the theory and politics of the Declaration of Independence.

Bowen, Catherine Drinker. *Miracle at Philadelphia*. Boston: Atlantic–Little, Brown, 1966. An absorbing and well-written account of the events surrounding the Constitutional Convention.

Kurland, Philip B. *Watergate and the Constitution*. Chicago: University of Chicago Press, 1978. A systematic review of a wide range of consequential issues raised by Watergate.

Rakove, Jack N. *The Beginnings of National Politics: An Interpretive History of the Continental Congress*. New York: Knopf, 1979. This is a history of the Continental Congress and the difficulties of governing under the Articles of Confederation.

Storing, Herbert J. *What the Anti-Federalists Were For*. Chicago: University of Chicago Press, 1981. An analysis of the arguments of the Constitution's opponents.

Wills, Garry. *Explaining America: The Federalist*. Garden City, N.Y.: Doubleday, 1981. This arresting work analyzes the intellectual background of the framers.

Wood, Gordon S. *The Creation of the American Republic, 1776–1787*. Chapel Hill, N.C., University of North Carolina Press, 1969. A penetrating study of political thought in the early period of the new republic.

4

Federalism

Most Friday nights in the spring of 1984, Alberto's was typically crowded with students from the University of Bridgeport. Usually about half the clientele of the popular bar were under twenty-one. The students met friends there, drank a few beers, listened to music, and then walked back to their dorms. In 1984 in the state of Connecticut, this was all perfectly legal. The minimum age for drinking beer and wine there was nineteen.

The scene at Alberto's was no doubt repeated on or near numerous college campuses throughout the United States. In twenty-nine states and the District of Columbia, eighteen-, nineteen-, and twenty-year-olds were completely free to buy and consume alcoholic beverages. That summer, though, the national government threatened to limit their freedom. Congress debated a measure designed to pressure states into raising their minimum drinking ages to twenty-one. Under the proposal, which was part of a highway bill, states would lose 5 percent of their federal highway funds in 1986 and 10 percent in 1987 if they permitted consumption of alcohol by people under twenty-one.

Groups like Mothers Against Drunk Driving (MADD) had fought hard to increase public awareness of the dangers posed by drunken drivers, and this provision of the bill was partly a result of their efforts. Supporters of the bill argued that a uniform drinking age would reduce highway fatalities. Teenagers accounted for 21 percent of alcohol-related traffic deaths, even though they made up only 10 percent of all licensed drivers. The National Transportation Safety Board had estimated that 1,250 lives could be saved by raising the drinking age to twenty-one. Moreover, if there were a uniform national drinking age, there would no longer be an incentive for teenagers from "21-minimum" states to drive to states with lower minimum ages in order to drink or purchase alcohol.

Those who opposed the bill complained that it constituted age discrimination and was an infringement of states' rights. After all, by tradition, states had been responsible for setting their own minimum drinking ages.

After the debate ended, the bill passed handily and was soon presented to President Ronald Reagan for signing. Reagan had pledged to reduce the size and scope of the national government, and he strongly opposed replacing state standards with national ones. Nevertheless, he decided to sign the bill. At the signing ceremony, he remarked, "This problem is bigger than the individual states. It's a grave national problem and it touches all our lives. With the problem so clear cut and the proven solution at hand we have no misgiving about this judicious use of federal power. I'm convinced that it will help persuade state legislators to act in the national interest."[1]

Today the national government plays a critical role in providing funds for highway projects. In 1980, for example, the national government gave $8.8 billion for projects ranging from research, planning, and construction to state and community safety and outdoor advertising control. Few Americans would imagine that, in the early part of the last century, American presidents routinely vetoed bills authorizing roads, canals, and other internal improvements. The reason? They believed these projects exceeded the constitutional authority of the national government.

The 46,000-mile federal interstate highway system is an obvious indication that the nineteenth-century view has not prevailed; the national government has used its authority over interstate commerce and post roads to justify a federal role in highway projects. In the case of the 1984 highway act, however, Congress recognized the formal role of the states as regulators of the minimum drinking age but used its own taxing and spending powers to implement a national standard. Washington lawmakers believed that few states would pass up money offered by the national government, so they used the lever of highway funds to move states to adopt twenty-one as a uniform minimum drinking age. The highway act thus illustrates an important element of federalism, or the dual sovereignty of national and state governments. States will give up a little power and responsibility in exchange for needed revenues. As long as this remains true, it seems, there are few areas where national power cannot reach. In this chapter, we shall examine the concept of federalism as it has been viewed and implemented in this country. Is the division of power between state and nation a matter of constitutional principle or political power? Is federalism necessary, or has America outgrown it? How is the shifting balance of power in national-state relations linked to the tension between equality and freedom that characterizes the American political value system? Does federalism promote pluralist or majoritarian politics?

Unsafe at Any Speed
Mothers Against Drunk Driving (MADD) campaigned hard to get drunken drivers off the road. Their strategies included national advertising — and national legislation. They also took aim at state legislatures, urging tougher sanctions for driving "under the influence."

FEDERALISM AND AMERICAN IDEOLOGY: MYTHS AND METAPHORS

The delegates who met in Philadelphia in 1787 were charged with repairing weaknesses in the Articles of Confederation. Instead, they solved the problem of making one nation out of thirteen independent states by writing a new Constitution and inventing a new political form: *federal* government. Under **"federalism,"** then, two or more governments would exercise power and authority over the same people and the same territory. Thus, people living in Pennsylvania would be citizens of both Pennsylvania and the United States. Although the governments of the United States and of Pennsylvania would share certain powers (the power to tax, for instance), other powers would belong exclusively to one or the other. As Madison saw it, "The federal Constitution forms a happy combination . . . the great and aggregate interests being referred to the national, and the local and particular to state governments."[2] Thus, the power to coin money belongs to the national government, whereas the power to grant divorces remains a state prerogative. Yet, as the history of American federalism reveals, drawing the line between "great and aggregate" on the one hand and "local and particular" on the other has not always been easy. (The everyday expression that Americans use to refer to their central government serves to muddy the waters even more. People usually refer to the central government headquartered in Washington, D.C., as the "federal government." Technically speaking, however, we have a federal *system* of government that includes both *national* and *state governments*. To avoid confusion in this chapter, we shall use the term *national government* rather than *federal government* when we are referring to the central government.)

Federalism offered a solution to the problem of diversity in America. It also provided a new model. Though federal systems are fairly rare, as Compared With What? 4.1 shows, a number of other nations have adopted them, often to deal with their own special forms of diversity.

The Mythology of American Federalism

The founding of America is a comparatively recent and well-documented event; yet, like the foundings of Rome and of other ancient states, the beginning of the American republic has been a source of much political mythology. Stories about the founding serve the same function myths do—they present part of the people's beliefs and help to explain current political practices. The concept of federalism and the political maneuvering from which it was born have given rise to two competing and contradictory myths. Like many myths, each of these may have some kernel of truth. Determining just what that truth is, however, can be difficult, if not impossible.

The first of these two myths, called **dual federalism,** interprets the Constitution as a compact among sovereign states. This view stresses **states' rights,** a concept that reserves to the states all rights not specifically conferred on the national government. It also envisions a rigid wall of separation between nation and state. The second myth plays down the role of the states and sees the Constitution as an agreement made by the *people*. The second view, known as **cooperative federalism,** emphasizes individuals, who are citizens of both state and nation and who may act in either capacity. In this view, any barrier between federal and state power is highly permeable and flexible. In general, dual federalism has been associated with conservatives, and cooperative federalism with liberals. However, this distinction may no longer be as sharp as it once was.

Dual federalism and cooperative federalism differ substantially in the way they interpret key sections of the Constitution, namely, Section 8 of Article I and the Tenth Amendment, which set out the terms of the relationship between the national and state governments. Article I, Section 8, enumerates the powers of the Congress and concludes with the **elastic clause,** which gives Congress the power to "make all Laws which shall be necessary and proper for carrying into Execution the foregoing Powers." The Tenth Amendment says that "powers not delegated to the United States by the Constitution, nor prohibited by it to the States, are reserved to the States respectively, or to the people."

Local Cops, National Cops

Governments share some powers. Local, state, and national governments have their own law-enforcing agencies. A local police officer (on the left) enforces local criminal laws — against murder, for example. The U.S. Marshals' Service is the oldest national law-enforcement agency. The presidentially appointed marshals and their support staffs (one of whom is pictured on the right) apprehend federal fugitives, transport federal prisoners, and, occasionally, prevent civil disturbances.

Compared With What? 4.1

Federalism Around the World

Question: What do the following nations have in common: Argentina, Australia, Austria, Brazil, Cameroon, Canada, the Federal Republic of Germany, India, Libya, Malaysia, Mexico, Nigeria, Switzerland, the Union of Soviet Socialist Republics, the United States of America, and Yugoslavia?

Answer: In the late 1960s, these were the only nations with a federal form of government. Since then, the citizens of Cameroon have voted for a unitary state, Nigeria has had a military coup, and Libya has become a "mass state" under Colonel Muammar Khadafy. That leaves only thirteen federal states, which makes them fairly rare.

Nation	Population (in millions)	Area (million sq. mi.)	Major Racial or Ethnic Groups	Major Languages	Major Religions
Argentina	29.6	1.1	97% European ancestry	Spanish	92% Roman Catholic
Australia	15.3	7.7	97% European ancestry	English	36% Anglican 33% Roman Catholic
Austria	7.6	0.764	98% Germanic	German	85% Roman Catholic
Brazil	122	3.29	60% Caucasian 30% Mixed 8% Black 2% Indian	Portuguese	93% Roman Catholic
Canada	25.2	9.92	45% British 29% French 23% Other European 1.5% Indian, Eskimo	English French	45% Roman Catholic 18% United Church 12% Anglican
Federal Republic of Germany	59	0.249	German	German	45% Roman Catholic 44% Protestant
India	746	3.28	72% Indo/Aryan 25% Dravidian 2% Mongoloid	Hindu English +14 others	83% Hindu 11% Moslem 2.6% Sikh Buddhist
Malaysia	14.1	0.329	50% Malay 36% Chinese 10% Indian	Malay Chinese English Tamil	Muslim Hindu Buddhist Confucianism Christian

Dual, or "Layer Cake," Federalism

In his first inaugural address, President Ronald Reagan noted that "the federal government did not create the states; the states created the federal government." In making this statement, Reagan affirmed his belief in the version of federalism that has as its central features states' rights, state sovereignty, dual federalism, and a particular interpretation of both Article I, Section 8, and the Tenth Amendment. It portrays the states as powerful components of the federal system—in some ways, the equals of the national government. After all, if the states did indeed create the nation, one might

Why do nations adopt a federal form of government? In theory, a federal system provides a means of recognizing local diversity while permitting some centralized authority. It also offers a defense against the national government's becoming too powerful. In practice, federalism is often used as a means of governing a large territory or a heterogeneous population (that is, a mixed population—one with many ethnic, religious, or linguistic groups, for example).

The table below contains some geographic and social characteristics of the federal nations and thus some clues as to why they use the federal form. For any nations that do not conform to the usual pattern, you might want to speculate about why they adopted federalism.

Nation	Population (in millions)	Area (million sq. mi.)	Major Racial or Ethnic Groups	Major Languages	Major Religions
Mexico	76	0.764	55% Indian-Spanish 29% American Indian 10% Caucasian	Spanish	97% Christian
Switzerland	6.5	0.015	Mixed European	65% German 18% French 12% Italian 1% Romansch	49% Roman Catholic 48% Protestant
Union of Soviet Socialist Republics	273.8	8.65	52% Russian 6% Ukrainian 5% Uzbek 4% Belorussian	Russian +18 others spoken by 1,000,000+	Russian Orthodox Muslim
United States	226	3.54	83% Caucasian 12% Black 5% Other	English	Protestant Roman Catholic Jewish
Yugoslavia		0.999	35% Serbian 19% Croatian 8.9% Muslim 7.8% Slovene 7.7% Albanian 5.9% Macedonians 5.4% Yugoslavs 2.5% Montenegrins	Serbo-Croatian Slovene Macedonian Albanian Hungarian Italian	41% Eastern Orthodox 32% Roman Catholic 12% Muslim

argue, the states are truly sovereign and, by implication, can set limits on the activities of the national government. Proponents of states' rights believe that the powers of the national government ought to be interpreted very narrowly. They insist that, in spite of the elastic clause, the activities of the national government should be confined strictly to those clearly mentioned in Article I, Section 8, of the Constitution. States' rights proponents support their view by quoting the Tenth Amendment provision that "the powers not delegated to the United States by the Constitution, nor prohibited by it to the States, are reserved to the States." They often downplay the last four words—"or to the people."

Through history, the viewpoint that has emphasized this Tenth Amendment provision has been tied to an idea called dual federalism and to a metaphor called "layer cake" federalism. Under dual federalism, the powers and functions of national and state governments are distinct and separable —as distinct and separable as the layers of a cake (see Figure 4.1 below). Each government is supreme in its own "layer" or sphere of action; the crumbs from one layer rarely, if ever, mix with those of the other layer. Furthermore, the appropriate dimensions of each layer are clearly fixed by the Constitution.

This understanding of federalism has found its way into some Supreme Court opinions, particularly in the late nineteenth and early twentieth centuries. For example, in *Hammer* v. *Dagenhart* (1918), which declared child labor laws unconstitutional, Justice William Day wrote that "the powers not expressly delegated to the national government are reserved" to the states and to the people. In writing this opinion, Day slightly revised the Constitution, for the Tenth Amendment does not say "expressly." He also went beyond the intent of the framers, who purposely left the word *expressly* out of the Tenth Amendment because they believed they could not possibly anticipate and specify every power that might be needed in the future to run a government. Those powers not specifically mentioned, but nonetheless necessary to make the enumerated powers effective, are usually said to be **implied** in Section 8 of Article I of the Constitution.[3]

The myths underlying the layer cake metaphor and dual federalism have been challenged on historical and other grounds. For example, if the national government is really a creation of the states, it is a creation of only thirteen states—those that ratified the Constitution. The other thirty-seven states were admitted *after* the national government existed and were created by that

Figure 4.1 ▬▬▬

**The Myths and
Their Metaphors**
*The two views of federalism may
be represented graphically.*

*The Myth of Dual Federalism:
The Layer Cake Metaphor*

Citizens cutting into the
political system will find
clear differences between
state and national powers,
functions, and responsibilities

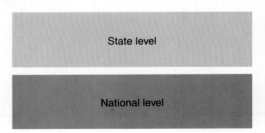

*The Myth of Cooperative Federalism:
The Marble Cake Metaphor*

Citizens cutting into the
political system at any point
will find national and state
powers, functions, and
responsibilities mixed and
mingled

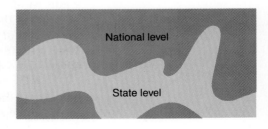

government out of land it had acquired. (To this day, the national government still owns a huge portion of the land in many states, particularly in the West. See Feature 4.1.) Another challenge to the myths embodied in dual federalism is that ratification in the original thirteen states took place in special conventions, not in state legislatures. Wasn't ratification, then, an act of the *people* rather than of the *states*? Indeed, the question of just where "the people" fit into the Constitution is not handled very well by those who prefer layer cake federalism. The full text of the Tenth Amendment says that powers not given to the national government shall be reserved to the states *or to the people*. By emphasizing the last four words, critics find grounds for rejecting the states' rights view. Instead, they ask: why can't the people assign more or less power to the national government? Why shouldn't the people exercise power or seek protection of their rights through the national government rather than through the state governments?

Cooperative, or "Marble Cake," Federalism

The second myth of federalism emphasizes the idea of the people as citizens of both state and nation. Advocates of this approach note that Article I, Section 8, clearly spells out a long list of congressional powers and then grants the national government the power to make laws that are *necessary and proper*. This view, which stresses the role of the national government, offers a "marble cake" metaphor as an alternative to the "layer cake" image. The marble cake metaphor presents the spheres of action of various levels of government not as separate layers but as intermingled parts of a cooperative federalism. Some scholars who support the marble cake image argue that the separateness of a layer cake has never really accurately described American federalism.[4] National and state governments have many common objectives and have often cooperated to achieve their shared goals. In the nineteenth century, for example, cooperation — not separation — made it possible to develop transportation systems and to establish land grant colleges. The layer cake might be a good model of what dual federalists *think* the relationship between national and state governments ought to be, but it does not square with the facts of American history.

However, marble cake federalism has also been challenged, and opponents note that the founders did want to distinguish between national and state powers. Marble cake federalism destroys such constitutional distinctions, according to these critics.

Both marble cake and layer cake federalism have enjoyed periods when they were considered appropriate models for the relations between levels of government. Conservatives, who favor freedom from the intrusions of national government, have frequently emphasized the layer cake approach. Liberals, often hoping to use the national government to bring about equality, have preferred the marble cake metaphor. The American political mythology has supported these two opposing views of what federalism ought to be, and supporters of each view see evidence for their arguments in the Constitution. But the Constitution is really only the starting point in the debate. The real meaning of American federalism might best be found in its implementation.

Feature 4.1

The Sagebrush Rebellion

One remnant of the fact that the U.S. government created most of the states out of land it had acquired is continued national ownership of huge tracts of land — nearly a third of the country, mostly in the western United States. For example, in 1979 the national government owned 96 percent of Alaska and 86 percent of Nevada.* National ownership of such vast areas of states has necessarily brought with it all sorts of difficulties for intergovernmental relations. Many western residents resent the presence and policies of the national landlord. To them, the national government seems to be slowing opportunities for development. On the other hand, environmentalists from all over the country believe that the national government has a duty to conserve the wilderness. In 1979, dissatisfied westerners banded together and began the "Sagebrush Rebellion," a movement — partly libertarian in inspiration — to divest the national government of its holdings and turn them over to states, localities, or individuals for development.

Sagebrush rebels were particularly upset by environmental and resource regulations and by the fact that national ownership of their land severely limited the growth and development of the West. For example, the expansion of such cities as Las Vegas and Santa Fe was held back by the fact that they are surrounded by public land that cannot be developed.

The rebels were particularly heartened in 1980 when Ronald Reagan proclaimed himself one of them. His appointment of James Watt as secretary of the interior was as much heralded by rebels as it was decried by environmentalists. But within four years, the rebellion died down, and Secretary Watt proclaimed himself a "rebel without a cause." And very little land was actually transferred from federal hands. Why had the rebels turned quiescent? For one thing, turning land over to state or local governments threatened to saddle those governments

*Frank J. Popper, "The Timely End of the Sagebrush Rebellion," *The Public Interest* (Summer 1984):61.

THE DYNAMICS OF FEDERALISM: LEGAL STICKS AND FINANCIAL CARROTS

Although the Constitution defines American federalism, the actual balance between national and state power has always been more a matter of politics than of formal authority. As a result, a discussion of federalism must do more than simply list the powers given to nation and state in the Constitution. The balance of power has shifted substantially since President James Madison agonized over the proper role the national government should play in funding roads. Today Washington has assumed functions never dreamed of in the nineteenth century.

Why have such power shifts occurred? In general, historical circumstances, not debates about the constitutional theory at the heart of the two federalism myths, have produced these shifts. For example, the greatest test of the states' rights position came when several southern states attempted to secede from the Union. This threat of secession challenged the supremacy of the national government, which was then established militarily on the bat-

with administrative and managerial challenges they did not welcome. Also, they would lose "replacement funds" provided by the national government to make up for lost tax revenue on national lands. Furthermore, westerners were suspicious of corporations that might get control of the land and keep the public off it entirely. In addition, during the recession of the early 1980s, there was little demand for the land, and not much of it could be sold off.

If the rebels didn't get rid of the national landlord, what did they get? Essentially, the rebellion was defused by offers of less regulation of the areas, more input from state and local governments, and more leasing of mineral rights. In addition, the acquisition of land for wildlife and park areas was slowed. Thus, by election time of 1984, Ronald Reagan had managed to still the Sagebrush Rebellion.

tlefields of the Civil War. But the Civil War by no means settled all questions about relations between governments in the United States. Many more subtle issues remained to be resolved, and new difficulties kept cropping up.

Some shifts in the federal balance of power resulted from specific constitutional changes. Several amendments have had an enormous impact, either direct or indirect, on the shape of the federal system. Examples include the due process and equal protection clauses of the Fourteenth Amendment,* the income tax permitted under the Sixteenth Amendment, and the Seventeenth Amendment provision for the direct election of senators. But the national government's use of "sticks" in the form of legislation and judicial interpretation and "carrots" in the form of grants and revenue sharing probably accounts for the most change in the national-state relationship. We shall discuss these political tools of change in this section and then in the following sections discuss their use in the development of American federalism.

---

*An amendment that was itself passed as one result of the Civil War.

Legislation and the Elastic Clause

The elastic clause of the Constitution gives Congress the power to make all laws that are "necessary and proper" to fulfill its responsibilities. By using this power in combination with its other listed powers, Congress has been able to increase the scope of the national government tremendously over the last two centuries—mainly in times of crisis and national emergency, such as the Civil War, the Great Depression of the 1930s, and both world wars. In general, the national government's role has grown as Congress has responded to needs and demands that state and local governments were unwilling or unable to meet.

Congress has used its legislative power to achieve goals at the state level in two ways: it has offered positive inducements to get states to comply with its wishes "voluntarily"; it has also forced compliance by threatening penalties. The Voting Rights Act of 1965 is a good example of legislation used as a stick to force compliance. Section 2 of Article I of the Constitution specifies that states should set voter qualifications. But the Fifteenth Amendment (1870) provides that no person should be denied the right to vote "on account of race, color, or previous condition of servitude." Before the Voting Rights Act, state election laws could not specifically deny blacks the right to vote, but they could require prospective voters to pass literacy tests or to pay poll taxes as part of the qualifications for voting. These requirements virtually disenfranchised blacks in many states. The Voting Rights Act was designed to correct this political inequality. The constitutional authority for this act was found in the elastic clause and in the second part of the Fifteenth Amendment, which gives Congress the power to enforce the amendment through appropriate legislation. Briefly, the Voting Rights Act gives officials of the

Signing Up to Vote
An elderly black woman registers to vote. Compared with actual voting, registering to vote is a time-consuming activity. After this woman's state failed to do the job, the national government stepped in to protect her rights under the Voting Rights Act of 1965.

national government the power to decide whether individuals are qualified to vote and requires that qualified individuals be permitted to vote in all elections—including primaries and national, state, and local elections.

Judicial Interpretation

The Voting Rights Act of 1965 was not a unanimous hit. Its opponents adopted the language of states' rights and dual federalism and insisted that the Constitution gives states the power to determine voter qualifications. Supporters of the act claimed that the Fifteenth Amendment guarantee of voting rights takes precedence over that power and gives the national government new responsibilities.

The conflict was ultimately resolved by the Supreme Court, which throughout our history has served as arbiter of the federal system, settling disputes concerning the powers of the national and state governments (see Chapter 13). These disputes are usually resolved when the Court decides whether new activities of the national government are constitutional. The Supreme Court has, on occasion, decided in favor of the states. Since 1937, however, it has almost always supported the national government in contests that involve the balance between national and state power.

Under Chief Justice Earl Warren in particular, the Court shifted the balance between the state and national governments by using the Fourteenth Amendment to extend various provisions of the Bill of Rights to the states. The Court's decisions seriously reduced the states' freedom to decide on such questions as what constitutes due process of law within their jurisdictions. For example, as a result of Court decisions concerning due process, citizens who are apprehended by the police must be read their constitutional rights, and those rights must be preserved by the arresting officer. Through the Supreme Court, the national government set minimum standards for due process, standards that the states would have to meet. These standards protect the freedom of individuals who are suspected of crimes, but critics argue that they hamper state officials in their job of maintaining order.

A series of reapportionment decisions resulted in further erosion of states' power in the early 1960s. Until that time, the states had specified the boundaries of voting districts, but some had failed to change the boundaries to reflect changes in the population. As a result, in some areas a very small number of rural voters were able to elect as many representatives as a very large number of urban voters. In deciding cases involving reapportionment, the Court set down the standard of "one man, one vote" and thus forced states to redraw their districts and to apportion their legislatures according to population.[5]

In the due process and reapportionment cases, the Supreme Court championed equality, by protecting individuals' rights that had been denied by states. Yet the Supreme Court is part of the national government. When it defends the rights of an individual against a state, it also substitutes a national standard for a state standard governing the relationship between state and individual. In the recent past, the substitution of national standards for state standards has generally favored equality over freedom while signaling a triumph for the nationalist view of federalism.

Grants-in-Aid and Revenue Sharing

In the last three decades, Washington's use of financial "carrots" has rivaled its use of legislation and judicial interpretation as means of shaping relations between national and state governments. Since the 1960s, state and local governments have looked to Washington for money more and more often. In 1960, the national government provided 15 percent of the funds spent by state and local governments; by 1980 the proportion had grown to 23 percent. The national government made this money available to states primarily through grants-in-aid and general revenue sharing.

A **grant-in-aid** is money paid by one level of government to another level, to be spent for a specific purpose. Grants-in-aid are frequently offered in accordance with standards or requirements prescribed by Congress. Often grants are awarded on a matching basis; that is, recipients make some contribution of their own, which is then matched by the national government. Grants take two general forms: categorical grants and block grants.

Categorical grants are targeted for very specific purposes, and restrictions on their use leave little discretion to the recipient government. Literally hundreds of categorical grant programs have been created, including those for

- Appalachian child welfare
- Disaster assistance, including removal of damaged timber
- Wildlife restoration
- Hazardous waste management
- Development of local facilities for runaway youths

Categorical grants may be further divided into formula grants and project grants. **Formula grants,** as their name implies, are distributed according to a particular formula, which specifies who is eligible for the grant and how much each eligible applicant will receive. The formulas used to distribute grant money vary from grant to grant and may include factors such as state per capita income, number of school-age children, urban population, and number of families below the poverty line. In 1981, 173 of the 534 categorical grants offered by the national government were formula grants. The remaining 361 grants were **project grants** — that is, grants awarded on the basis of competitive applications submitted by prospective recipients.

Block grants are awarded for more general purposes and allow recipients greater discretion in deciding how to allot grant money among specific programs. Block grants have been awarded for

- Law enforcement assistance
- Community development
- Comprehensive health services

General revenue sharing, first introduced by President Richard Nixon, places fewer restrictions on recipients than either categorical or block grants. A categorical grant, for example, might be given with a specification that it be used to promote ethnic heritage studies. A block grant might be offered only with the specification that it be used in elementary and secondary education; the recipient could decide to use part of the money to fund ethnic heritage studies and part to fund consumer education. The recipient might even choose another alternative — to put all of the money into consumer education and spend nothing on ethnic heritage studies. In this example, however, the block grant money must nevertheless be used for education. In contrast, revenue sharing money would be given to states or localities with virtually no restrictions on the purposes for which it could be spent. A recipient of revenue sharing funds might decide to spend the money on an educational program, such as ethnic heritage studies or consumer education, or the recipient might use the money to buy a new fire truck.

Grants-in-aid and revenue sharing are two ways to accomplish income redistribution. Money is collected by the national government from citizens of all fifty states and then reallocated to other citizens, supposedly for worthwhile social purposes. Grants have been used extensively to remove gross inequalities among states and their citizens. Yet the formulas used to redistribute this income are not impartial; they are themselves highly political and subject to long debates in Congress.

Regardless of the form it takes, money provided by the national government does not come without some strings attached. Many of the strings are intended to ensure that the money is used to achieve the purposes for which it was given; other regulations are designed to evaluate how well the grant has achieved its end. The national government may also stipulate that certain procedures be followed. For example, a recipient may be forced to adopt particular accounting procedures or to set up special agencies to ensure that the funds are administered properly, in accordance with the requirements of the national government.

The national government may also attach other restrictions to the money it grants. These restrictions are often designed to achieve some broad national goal, not necessarily related to the specific purpose for which the award has been made. For example, the Revenue Sharing Act was used to promote equality. The act does not tell governments *what* they must spend their revenue sharing money on; however, it does specifically prohibit discrimination based on race, color, sex, age, national origin, handicapped status, and religion in all state or local government activities that have been funded in any part by revenue sharing aid. The burden of proof is on the recipients, who must be able to show that they have not discriminated. The states have been more than willing to accept these limitations. The carrot of financial aid has become a powerful incentive for states to give up the freedom to set their own standards and to adopt those set by the national government.

THE DEVELOPING CONCEPT OF FEDERALISM: FROM LAYER CAKE TO MARBLE CAKE

A student of federalism once remarked that "each generation faced with new problems has had to work out its own version of federalism." Succeeding generations have used "sticks" and "carrots" to varying degrees and have shifted the balance between state and national power in both directions.

McCulloch v. Maryland

Early in the nineteenth century, a nationalist view of federalism apparently triumphed over a states' rights interpretation. In 1819, under Chief Justice John Marshall, the Supreme Court threw its weight behind the nationalist interpretation in its decision in *McCulloch* v. *Maryland*. In that case, the Court was asked to rule whether or not Congress had the power to establish a national bank and, if so, whether states had the power to tax that bank. In writing the majority opinion, Marshall supported a very broad interpretation of the "necessary and proper" clause of the Constitution. In a famous phrase, he proclaimed:

> Let the end be legitimate, let it be within the scope of the Constitution, and all means which are appropriate and which are plainly adapted to that end, which are not prohibited, but consistent with the letter and spirit of the Constitution, are constitutional.[6]

The Court's decision allowed a very broad interpretation of the elastic clause and clearly agreed that Congress had the power to charter a bank. But did states—in this case, Maryland—have the power to tax the bank? Arguing that "the power to tax is the power to destroy," Marshall insisted that states could not tax the national government because the powers of the national government came not from the states, but from the people. Thus Marshall embraced the second myth of federalism, which sees a direct relationship between the people and the national government, with no need for states as intermediaries. To assume that states had the power to tax the national government would be to give states supremacy over the national government. In that case, Marshall wrote, "the declaration that the Constitution, and the laws made in pursuance thereof, shall be the supreme law of the land is empty and unmeaning." Clearly, he reasoned, the framers of the Constitution did not intend to create a meaningless document. Therefore, they must have meant to give the national government all the powers necessary to accomplish its assigned functions, even if those powers could not be spelled out fully but could only be *implied*. Thus, the Marshall Court supported both the doctrine of implied powers and the doctrine of national supremacy.

States' Rights and Dual Federalism

Roger B. Taney became chief justice in 1836, and the Supreme Court began to shift the power balance back toward the states. The Taney Court recognized firm limits on the powers of the national government. As Taney saw it, the Constitution spoke "not only in the same words but with the same meaning and intent with which it spoke when it came from the framers." In the infamous Dred Scott decision (1857), for example, the Court decided that Congress had no power to prohibit slavery in the territories.[7]

Many people assume that the Civil War was fought over slavery, but it was not. The real issue was the character of the federal union—or federalism. At the time of the Civil War, regional variations between northern and southern states were considerable. The southern economy was based on labor-intensive agriculture, very different from the mechanized manufacturing that was developing in the North. As a result, southerners wanted cheap manufactured goods and cheap plantation labor. This led them to support both slavery and low tariffs on imported goods. The northern economy required almost exactly the opposite, and when northerners sought national legislation that threatened southern interests, southerners demanded states' rights. They even introduced the theory of **nullification** — the idea that a state could declare a particular action of the national government null and void and not applicable to it. The Civil War rendered the idea of nullification null and void, but it did not fully settle the balance between national and state power.

In the decades after the Civil War, the Supreme Court continued to place limits on national power, particularly when the national government attempted to regulate industry. In the late nineteenth and early twentieth centuries, the justices, who were influenced by contemporary economic theory, usually favored a laissez faire, or "hands off," approach to business. They frequently ruled that congressional legislation that limited the action of corporations was unconstitutional because it invaded the domain of the states. In 1918, for example, when Congress tried to use its power to regulate interstate commerce as the basis for legislation regulating child labor, the Court declared the legislation unconstitutional. The national government argued that national child labor legislation was needed because an individual state would not enact such legislation; to do so would increase the cost of labor in that state and make it less attractive to industry. The Court recognized this argument but was not persuaded, ruling that national legislation regulating

Made in the USA (1920)
A young factory worker in the early part of this century. The Supreme Court decided in 1918 that Congress had no power to limit child labor. That power belonged to the states, which resisted imposing limits for fear that such legislation would drive business to other (less restrictive) states.

child labor ran counter to both the commerce clause (of Article I, Section 8) and the Tenth Amendment. As Justice William Day wrote in *Hammer* v. *Dagenhart*:

> The commerce clause was not intended to give Congress a general authority to equalize conditions [of competition between the states]. If Congress can thus regulate matters intrusted to local authority . . . all freedom of commerce will be at an end, and the power of the states over local matters may be eliminated, and thus our system of government practically destroyed.[8]

The New Deal and Its Consequences

It took the Great Depression of the 1930s to test the limits of this theory of federalism. The problems of the Depression proved too extensive for either state governments or private businesses to handle. As a result, the national government assumed a heavy share of responsibility for providing relief and directing efforts toward economic recovery. Under the "New Deal," President Franklin D. Roosevelt's response to the Depression, Congress enacted various emergency relief programs to aid the unemployed. These measures often involved cooperation between national and state levels of government. For example, the national government offered the carrot of matching funds to stimulate state relief efforts. To receive these federal funds, however, states were usually required to provide administrative supervision or to contribute some money of their own. Relief efforts were centralized and removed from the hands of local bodies. Through the regulations it attached to funds, the federal government extended its power and control over states.[9]

The Supreme Court's view of the Depression differed from that of other branches of government, however. To the Court, the Depression was an accumulation of local problems, not a national problem demanding national action. In the Court's opinion, the whole structure of federalism was threatened when collections of local troubles were treated as one national problem. Justice Owen Roberts wrote in the decision in *U.S.* v. *Butler* (1936) that

> It does not help that local conditions throughout the nation have created a situation of national concern; for this is but to say that whenever there is a widespread similarity of local conditions, Congress may ignore constitutional limitations on its own powers and usurp those reserved to the states.[10]

In that decision and others, the Court struck down several pieces of regulatory legislation, including the National Industrial Recovery Act, which had been enacted to regulate wages, working hours, and business competition, among other things.

In 1937, though, with no change in personnel, the Court began to alter its course. It upheld such New Deal measures as the Social Security Act and the National Labor Relations Act as valid uses of congressional power. Perhaps the Court had studied the 1936 election returns and was responding to a new nationalist mood in the country. In any event, the Court gave up its effort to provide a rigid boundary between national and state power. Only a few years earlier, the Supreme Court had based its thinking about federalism on the Tenth Amendment, but in 1941, Justice Harlan Stone referred to it as "a truism that all is retained that has not been surrendered." In short, the

Court agreed that the layer cake had gone stale. From then on, the division of power in the federal system became less relevant, and relations *between* governments increased in importance.

Some see the New Deal era as "revolutionary," and there is no doubt that the period was critical in reshaping federalism in the United States. The national and state governments had cooperated before, but the increased extent of national-state interaction during Franklin D. Roosevelt's administration clearly made the marble cake the more accurate metaphor for American federalism. In addition, the size of the national government and its budget increased tremendously. But perhaps the most significant change was in the way Americans viewed both their problems and the role of the national government in providing solutions to those problems. Difficulties that had been seen as personal or local problems now became national problems requiring a national solution. The "general welfare," broadly defined, became a legitimate concern of the national government.

In other respects, however, the New Deal was not very revolutionary. Congress, for example, did not claim that any new powers were needed to deal with the nation's economic problems; it simply used the constitutional powers it had to suit the circumstances. And, from the late 1930s on, the Supreme Court upheld Congress's work.

Desegregation and the War on Poverty

During the 1950s and 1960s, the national government began to assume the task of promoting social equality by combating racism and poverty. Both of these problems had seemed impossible to solve on the state level. Matters of race relations had generally been left to the states and these issues were more or less ignored despite the constitutional amendments passed after the Civil War. Moreover, when the Supreme Court adopted the "separate but equal" doctrine in 1896, states were free to do as much — or as little — as they pleased about racial inequality.

In 1954, however, the Supreme Court decided in *Brown* v. *Board of Education* that separate was inherently unequal. This put the national government in the position of ordering the integration of public schools.[11] As the civil rights movement focused increasing national attention on the problems of discrimination, Congress passed two important pieces of legislation — the Civil Rights Act of 1964 and the Voting Rights Act of 1965. Through these acts, the national government used its legislative stick to outlaw racial discrimination in employment, in public accommodations, and in voting rights. The acts themselves sharply limited states' rights where the effect of those rights had been to deny equality; the acts promoted equality for all citizens, regardless of local customs.

In the 1960s, President Lyndon Johnson's War on Poverty added an enormous amount of social legislation and led to a massive increase in the scope of the national government. In an attempt to provide equality of opportunity and improve the quality of life throughout the United States, the national government used financial carrots — money — to introduce a number of new programs, including aid to elementary and secondary schools, school breakfasts and lunches, food stamps, vastly increased aid to higher education, and a huge array of economic development, public service, and employment training schemes. To administer these programs, government bureaucracies were enlarged—not just on the national level, but on the state level as well. In fact, state bureaucracies grew even faster than the national bureaucracy during the 1960s and 1970s.

Johnson's recipe for marble cake federalism included some new ingredients. Before 1960, nearly all intergovernmental assistance (that is, aid from one level of government to another) had gone from the national government to state governments. But the War on Poverty often included aid that was given directly to local governments or community groups as well.

As the national government grew to play a larger and more generally accepted role in providing funds to state and local governments, the key questions for federalism changed. National and state governments were no longer separate and distinct layers; they interacted. But how? The search for answers to that question led to a focus on **intergovernmental relations.** The various levels of American government have become highly interdependent and share functions. The study of intergovernmental relations looks at that web of interdependence, among other things, and the connections among government's personnel and policies. It also examines the influences that may be brought to bear on one level of government by another.

The political dynamics of intergovernmental relations since the 1960s have led to a new, if less appetizing, metaphor for federalism: **"picket fence" federalism** (see Figure 4.2). In this metaphor, the fence "rails" are the levels of government—national, state, and local—and the fence "slats" represent interests with their attendant lobbies and specialists, both inside and outside of government. The communities of interest represented by each slat make contact at each of the three levels of government. They are able to share information, develop common standards, and exert pressure on each level of government. Government officials themselves may move along the interest slats to influence officials on other rails. On a typical trip to Washington, for

Figure 4.2

"Picket Fence" Federalism
The picket fence model shows how functions cross government lines and also connect the officials who work at different levels of government.

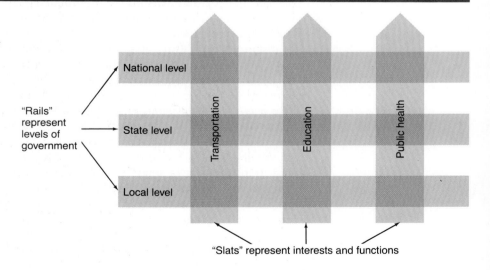

***Reach Out and
Touch Someone***
*The levels of government in the
federal system are now
intertwined. Here, in an
intergovernmental conference
call, New York Senators Daniel
Moynihan and Alphonse
D'Amato discuss funding
projects with New York
Governor Mario Cuomo and
New York City Mayor Ed Koch.*

instance, the head of a state department of education might have a morning meeting with members of the state's congressional delegation, making them aware of the state's educational needs and priorities. Next, he or she might have lunch with lobbyists from the National Education Association (NEA) before testifying before a congressional committee on education and meeting with officials from the U.S. Department of Education. Our tired official might return to the office the next day to find his or her opposite number from a neighboring state on the phone, hoping to find out how the visit went.

Since the 1960s, the national government has been willing to provide money for an increasing number of local programs. (See Figure 4.3 on the growth and decline of grants.) Money has been made available for such programs as rat control, jellyfish control, crime control, bikepath construction, urban gardening, rural fire protection, solid waste disposal, home insulation, and library services. Far from being unresponsive, Congress has become hyperresponsive. And Congress's willingness to spend national funds has led to the creation of new interest groups while increasing the importance of those that already exist. The result is not just pluralist democracy, but hyperpluralism, in which every conceivable interest has a group. Many smaller (and weaker) state groups have also united nationally to lobby for national solutions (via national money) to their local problems. A number of state and local governments have seen a need to lobby for their own interests — perhaps in self-defense.

The growth of government programs, the hyperresponsiveness of Congress, and the pressure of interest groups have led to a federal system that

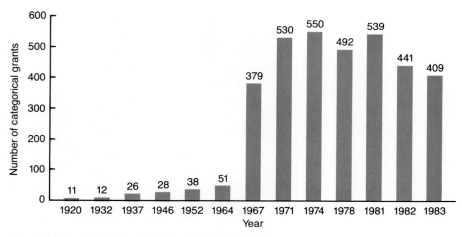

The Growth and Decline of Categorical Grants
National government programs grew during the New Deal and the War on Poverty. Cuts in programs during the Carter and Reagan years have stemmed the tide but hardly reversed it. (Source: Advisory Commission on Intergovernmental Relations [ACIR], The Federal Role in the Federal System: The Dynamics of Growth. *Washington, D.C.: ACIR, 1980, pp. 120, 121; ACIR,* Significant Features of Fiscal Federalism. *Washington, D.C.: ACIR, 1983, p. 120.)*

Figure 4.3 ━━━

critics describe as "overloaded and out of control." In keeping with the bakery-shop metaphors that are used to describe federalism, one commentator has suggested that layer cake federalism and marble cake federalism have now given way to "fruitcake" federalism—a federalism that is formless and indestructible and offers lots of plums for everyone.[12]

When the Advisory Commission on Intergovernmental Relations (ACIR), a group created by Congress to monitor the federal system, reviewed the operation of the federal system in 1980, it concluded that this fruitcake federalism was dysfunctional federalism—a federal system that just did not work. Over the last two decades, ACIR said, the system of intergovernmental relations had become "more pervasive, more intrusive, more unmanageable, more ineffective, more costly and more unaccountable."[13]

THE PENDULUM SWINGS BACK . . . MAYBE

Every president since Richard Nixon has expressed disenchantment with the hyperpluralist system of intergovernmental relations. Every president since Nixon has pledged to cut the size of the bureaucracy and return power to the states. Yet reform has been difficult to accomplish.

Nixon's New Federalism: Revenue Sharing

When Nixon came to office in 1969, he pledged to change a national government he characterized as "overly centralized, overbureaucratized . . .

unresponsive as well as inefficient." He dubbed his solution to the problem the "New Federalism" and claimed that it would channel "power, funds and authority . . . to those governments closest to the people."[14] He expected the New Federalism to help restore control of the nation's destiny "by returning a greater share of control to state and local authorities."

The centerpiece of Nixon's New Federalism was revenue sharing, in which the national government would turn tax revenues over to the states and localities to spend as they pleased. The revenue sharing plan had two parts: general revenue sharing and special revenue sharing. As discussed earlier, the former provided new money to be used in almost any way by state and local governments. Initially, Congress was quite willing to fund the general revenue sharing program. It was, after all, a new program, which meant that no one was required to give up anything for it. And 1972, the year in which it was enacted, was a year of fiscal crisis for cities and states. The program was quite popular with the governments it helped, but over several years it grew less popular with Congress. Members of Congress did not have the same control over revenue sharing funds that they had over the more traditional categorical grant programs. And they did not always have confidence in the state officials who would be receiving and administering the funds. Finally, many members of Congress grew irritated that, through revenue sharing, the national government was being asked to make up for poor taxation efforts by states and localities. As a result, Congress did not allow the funding for general revenue sharing to grow as much as the funding for categorical grant programs; by 1981 the states had lost most of the general revenue sharing benefits.

The second part of Nixon's New Federalism, **special revenue sharing,** consisted of a plan to consolidate existing categorical grant programs. Under the plan, money that was available for various existing categorical programs in a particular area (for example, health services) would be combined into one large block grant. Each state would then use its grant to meet its needs in that area, as it saw fit. However, Congress was unwilling to lose the political credit and control it had under the existing categorical grant system. In addition, the dynamics of intergovernmental relations worked against the consolidation of categorical grant programs; interest groups lobbied hard to keep their pet projects from being consolidated. As a result, special revenue sharing started only very slowly during the Nixon years.

For these reasons, Nixon's New Federalism was not very successful in slowing the flow of power from the states to the national government. The dollar amounts of aid continued to grow, and the numbers and kinds of programs that were funded continued to increase. The national government gave more aid to the states, and that aid carried with it more strings.

The perception that the federal system was bloated and out of control did take hold, however. In 1976 Jimmy Carter won the Democratic nomination and ran for president as an outsider who promised to reduce the size and cost of the national government. The amount of federal aid to states and localities (corrected for inflation) actually began to decline after 1978 (see Figure 4.4), but Carter's years in office did not mark a revolution in American federalism.

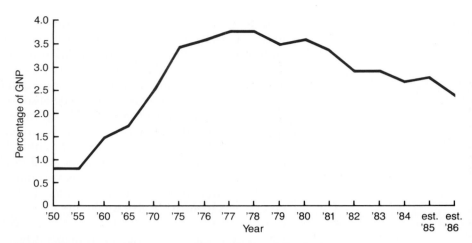

Federal Grants as a Percentage of Gross National Product
From 1955 to 1978, federal grants also consumed an ever-growing share of the gross national product (GNP). (Source: Special Analyses of the Budget of the United States Government, FY 1987, p. H-20.)

Figure 4.4 ■

Reagan's New Federalism: Budget Reductions

President Ronald Reagan took office promising a "new New Federalism," one that would "restore a proper constitutional relationship between the federal, state and local governments." He criticized the contemporary version of federalism, charging that "the federal system had been bent out of shape." The national government had become the senior partner in the intergovernmental relationship, treating "elected state and local officials as if they were nothing more than administrative agents for federal authority."

Under Reagan, New Federalism and spending cuts went hand in hand. Thus, he could not offer the carrot of new funding to make his program acceptable. In the first year of Reagan's administration, under his own version of special revenue sharing, Congress agreed to combine seventy-seven categorical grants into nine block grants. To build support for this plan, Reagan emphasized that state officials would have greater freedom in using their grant money. He pointed out that bureaucratic burdens would be reduced and, as a result, that it would be possible to run state and local programs at a lower cost. State officials were enthusiastic about the prospect of having greater control over the funds they received; they were much less enthusiastic when they realized that the amounts would be cut by approximately 25 percent. (See Figure 4.5.)

Reagan avoided some of the difficulties that other recent chief executives had experienced in their efforts to cut spending and consolidate programs. Part of his success stemmed from his appeal to majoritarian democracy, as

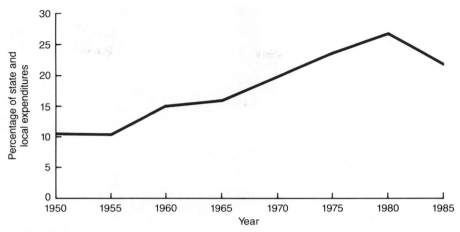

National Government Grants as a Percentage of State and Local Expenditures
States and localities had looked to Washington to provide larger and larger shares of their expenditures. But Reagan's New Federalism and his budget cuts forced states to come up with more of their own money. (Source: Special Analyses, Budget of the United States Government, FY 1987, p. H-20.)

Figure 4.5

opposed to the special interests characteristic of pluralist democracy. Interpreting his victory at the polls as a mandate, he had moved quickly, before interest groups were able to organize to oppose him. And, except for defense, his spending cuts were made across the board for the most part. Every group was hurt a little; no group could really complain that it was hurt more than others by the cuts.

This first round of new New Federalism took some of the plums out of fruitcake federalism but led to few other real changes in the federal system. In his 1982 State of the Union message, Reagan outlined a second round: he asked that more than forty programs that had previously required intergovernmental cooperation be put under state control. Initially, the national government would provide funds for these programs, but eventually the states themselves would be expected either to pick up the costs or to eliminate the programs.

Reagan's proposed exchange of programs like all suggestions for program swapping, was an intensely political matter, arousing intense political and ideological opposition. As one commentator put it, "Governors were suspicious; mayors were skeptical; and Congress was downright hostile."[15] As a result, the plan was abandoned by the Reagan administration. The effort to reshape the federal system continues, but in more piecemeal fashion — mainly through cuts in funding for programs that Reagan once offered to turn over to the states. But the task is not an easy one; as you saw at the beginning of this chapter, even a strong dual federalist like Reagan is not immune to appeals from certain interest groups.

Cities YES! Missiles NO!
*Under the Reagan adminis-
tration's domestic policy, New
Federalism has meant cuts in
national government funds for
the cities. Reagan's priorities
placed defense spending ahead
of domestic spending.*

OTHER GOVERNMENTS IN THE FEDERAL SYSTEM

We have concentrated in this chapter on the role the national government plays in shaping the federal system. Although the Constitution explicitly recognizes only state and national governments, the American federal system has spawned a multitude of other governments as well. In a recent count, the number exceeded 82,000!

The Kinds of Local Governments

The average American is a citizen of both nation and state, but also comes under the jurisdiction of various local government units. These units include **municipal governments,** which are the governments of cities. The municipalities (cities and towns) are, in turn, located in (or may contain or share boundaries with) counties, which are administered by **county governments.** In addition, the typical American also lives in a **school district,** which is responsible for administering local elementary and secondary educational programs. He or she may also be served by one or more **special districts,** which are government units created to perform particular functions, often when those functions are best performed across jurisdictional boundaries. Examples of special districts include the Port of New York Authority, the Chicago Sanitary District, and the Southeast Pennsylvania Transit Authority, whose main functions and jurisdictions are obvious from their names.

These local governments are created by state governments either in state constitutions or through other legislation. As a result, their organization, powers, responsibilities, and effectiveness may vary considerably from state to state. About forty states provide their cities with various forms of **home rule** — the right to enact and enforce legislation in certain administrative areas. By allowing a measure of self-government, home rule gives cities greater freedom of action than they would otherwise have. In contrast, county governments, which are the main units of local government in rural areas, tend to have relatively little legislative power, or none at all. Instead, county governments generally serve as administrative units of state government, performing the specific duties assigned to them under state law.

The functions of national, state, city, and county governments and of school and special districts often overlap. In practice, it is now virtually impossible to distinguish among these governments by using Madison's criterion of "great and aggregate" versus "local and particular" interests. Consider, for example, the case of the rural health officer, or "sanitarian":

> The sanitarian is appointed by the state under merit standards established by the federal government. His base salary comes jointly from state and federal funds, the county provides him with an office and office amenities and pays a portion of his expenses, and the largest city in the county also contributes to his salary by virtue of his appointment as a city plumbing inspector. It is impossible from moment to moment to tell under which governmental hat the sanitarian operates. His work of inspecting the purity of food is carried out under federal standards; but he is enforcing state laws when inspecting commodities that have not been in interstate commerce; and somewhat perversely he also acts under state authority when inspecting milk coming into the county from producing areas across the state border. He is a federal official when impounding impure drugs shipped from a neighboring state; a federal-state officer when distributing typhoid immunization serum; a state officer when enforcing standards of industrial hygiene; a state-local officer when inspecting the city's water supply; and [to complete the circle] a local officer when insisting that the city butchers adopt more hygienic methods of handling their garbage. But he cannot and does not think of himself as acting in these separate capacities. All business in the county that concerns health and sanitation he considers his business.[16]

If a health officer cannot manage to separate the city, state, county, and national functions he performs, can the ordinary citizen be expected to make sense of this maze of governments? Does the ordinary citizen really benefit from all this interwoven government?

So Many Governments: Advantages and Disadvantages

In theory at least, one benefit of breaking down and localizing government is that it brings government closer to the people. This localization, in turn, provides an opportunity for the people to participate in the political process and to have a direct impact on policies. Localized government conjures up visions of informed citizens deciding their own political fate in small local communities, which they know intimately — the New England town meeting repeated across the nation. Viewed from this perspective, the overlapping governmental structure appears quite compatible with a majoritarian view of democracy.

The reality is somewhat different, however. Studies have shown that people are much more likely to vote in national elections than in local elections; voter participation in purely local contests tends to be very low, even though the impact of the individual vote is much greater there. Furthermore, the fragmentation of powers, functions, and responsibilities among national, state, and local governments makes government as a whole seem very complicated and hence less comprehensible and accessible to ordinary people. In addition, citizens who are busy with the daily matter of making a living have only limited time to devote to public affairs, and involvement in politics can be very time consuming. All these factors tend to keep the citizen out of politics and to make government more responsive to organized groups, which have the resources — time, money, and know-how — to influence policies. Thus, instead of bringing government closer to the people and reinforcing majoritarian democracy, the system's enormous complexity tends to encourage pluralism.

Another possible benefit of having many governments is that they enable the country to experiment with new policies on a small scale. New programs or solutions to problems can be tested in one city or state or in a few such units. Successful programs can then be adopted by other states or by the nation as a whole. For this reason, states are sometimes referred to as "laboratories of democracy." For example, when Reagan asked for a constitutional amendment requiring a balanced national budget — that is, one in which expenditures may not be greater than income — he had a precedent. Many states have such a constitutional provision.

Finally, the large number of governments makes it possible for government to respond to the diversity of conditions that prevail in different parts of the country. States and cities differ enormously in population, size, economic resources, climate, and other characteristics — all the diverse elements that the political philosopher Montesquieu argued needed to be taken into account in formulating laws for a society. Smaller political units are better able to respond to particular local conditions and can generally do so more quickly. On the other hand, smaller units may be unable to muster the economic resources to respond to challenges. Nevertheless, the United States remains one nation regardless of its many local governments. The question of how much diversity that nation should tolerate in the way different states treat their citizens is important. Also important is the question of whether or not the national government (and, indirectly, the citizens of other states) should be called on to foot the bill for the problems that diversity produces.

ALL VISITORS REPORT

TO THE N Y S D E C

LOVE CANAL TASK FORCE

OFFICE - 9826 COLVIN BLVD

PRIOR TO ENTERING SITE

Playground Closed Today . . . and Forever
The ecological disaster at Love Canal in upper New York State, like many contemporary problems, seemed too big to handle on state or local levels. Additional discoveries of health risks in the environment (asbestos and radon exposure are two recent examples) will increase the call for assistance from the national government.

Throughout American history, differences between states have provided an impetus for the national government's playing a significant role in regional development. The national government's funds have been used to equalize disparities in wealth and development among states. Recently, differences between Sunbelt and Frostbelt have led to questions about this role. The development of the Sunbelt has been, and continues to be, helped considerably by national policies and projects. Tennessee Valley Authority (TVA) electrification and western irrigation projects were the results of national government spending; the South in particular was aided immensely by federal funding formulas designed to aid poorer areas of the country; and California has benefited from national largesse in the form of huge defense contracts. Overall, Sunbelt states have received more money from the government than they have paid in taxes. The Sunbelt communities in the West and South represent the new growth areas of the country, whereas the northern Frostbelt (at least those parts also nicknamed the "Rustbelt") is characterized by aging heavy industry in northeastern smokestack cities with declining tax bases.

Although Reagan has made a few exceptions to his ideological commitment to dual federalism (for example, his support of the uniform drinking age mentioned earlier), aid to the Rustbelt areas has not been one of them. Aid to the Rustbelt does not coincide with his budget-cutting requirements. At a time when the national government is trying to reduce domestic expenditures, it appears that the Rustbelt looks to the national government in vain. The problems of the smokestack cities are being treated as "local and particular matters" ineligible for national government solutions.

WHY FEDERALISM TODAY?

At the beginning of this chapter, we asked if federalism was still necessary. Today we can argue that many twentieth-century concerns, such as pollution control, protection of civil rights, and maintenance of a "safety net" of welfare benefits, really are "great and aggregate" national issues, which states cannot handle and which therefore require action at the national level. Perhaps the United States, like Cameroon, ought to give up federalism as an anachronism. Dual federalists and cooperative federalists would probably disagree on this issue. Their arguments also help to illustrate how the balance of power between nation and state affects the tension between equality and freedom that permeates the American political system.

Federalism: Some Issues of Freedom Versus Equality

Proponents of New Federalism and the layer cake image maintain that there are still many reasons for reducing the role of the national government and returning power to the states. Many of the arguments in favor of New Federalism emphasize the greater freedom individuals will have under it. Proponents of this position recognize that different states have different problems and resources, but assert that, by returning control to state governments, it will be possible to give more play to diversity. States would be free to experiment with different ways of meeting their problems. Innovation would be encouraged. States could compete with each other. People would then be free to choose the state government arrangement they preferred by simply "voting with their feet"—moving to another state.

In addition, the New Federalism proponents argue that the national government is too remote, that it is a prisoner of special interests, that it is not responsive to the public at large. The national government overregulates and tries to promote too much uniformity, according to this view. Moreover, these critics add, the size and complexity of the federal system leads to waste and inefficiency. States, on the other hand, are closer to the people and better prepared to respond specifically to local needs. If state governments were revitalized, individuals might believe that they could have a greater impact on decisionmaking. The quality of political participation would be improved.

To those on the other side of the debate, this portrait of the national ogre and the virtuous states seems distorted. Looking at the record, those who oppose New Federalism can show that, through history, states have not been responsive to various constituencies. The federal system allowed great inequalities and it supported racism. Blacks and city dwellers were often left virtually unrepresented by white state legislators who disproportionately served rural interests. Although state governments are supposed to be closer to the people, citizens have been less likely to participate in state-level politics than in national politics. In addition, states are not really equipped to handle the new burdens being thrust on them. These critics would assert that many state legislatures are still quite amateurish. In many states, legislatures are in session only a small part of the time, and the office of state legislator is a part-time job.

Finally, according to the opponents of New Federalism, the value of competition between the states must be debunked. Poor states left to their own devices would not be able to provide the same level of benefits that richer states could provide. But the citizens of all states, rich and poor, are also citizens of the United States. The national government plays an important role in protecting its citizens and in equalizing the burdens they bear. Part of that role is ensuring that some minimum standards are provided for their treatment. It is absurd to think that physical migration from state to state will bring social mobility, and the problems of the poor might very well be overlooked by the states. Competition between the states could degenerate into "competition in laxity," as states avoid strong actions to solve problems like pollution because the states are afraid of losing industry (see Feature 4.2). Far from being immune to the pressure of organized interests, states have fewer resources with which to resist powerful interests.

Federalism and Pluralism

As noted in Chapter 2, the foundation of American government was poured to support a structure conducive to pluralist democracy. Federalism is an important part of that foundation. How has the federal principle contributed to American pluralism? Do each of the competing views of federalism support pluralism?

The federal design was an attempt to allay citizens' fears that they might be ruled by majorities of citizens who were residents of far-removed regions and with whom they did not necessarily agree or share interests. The institutional design, by recognizing the legitimacy of states as political divisions, also recognized the importance of diversity. The existence and cultivation of a diversity of interests is a hallmark of pluralism.

Each of the two competing views of federalism supports pluralism, though in somewhat different ways. The states' rights–layer cake–New Federalist view emphasizes the value of decentralization through devolution of power to the states. It recognizes the importance of local rather than national standards. One could try to make an impact on the local system, but there would always

Feature 4.2

States at War: Tax Breaks and "Competition in Laxity"

The Philadelphia National Bank is incorporated in the state of Delaware. The Chase Manhattan Bank manages much of its credit card business from that state. Why? Delaware has long provided a congenial location for the incorporation of many firms. In 1981 its legislature decided to take advantage of loosening federal regulations on the banking industry to offer itself as the "Luxembourg of the U.S. for banking and financing." It would attempt to lure out-of-state banks by promising them freedom from taxation and regulation.

South Dakota had already eliminated ceilings on interest rates and had begun to permit banks to charge fees for credit cards. These concessions helped convince Citicorp to move its credit card operation from New York to South Dakota.*

In 1974 both industry representatives and Longshoremen's Union lobbyists warned California's legislature that it risked losing shipping business to Seattle unless it voted special tax breaks for cargo containers. The legislators responded quickly with a temporary tax exemption. With this limited success in California, the lobbyists moved on to Olympia, to see what Washington State legislators would be willing to do for them. Not to be outdone by the folks in Sacramento, the Washingtonians offered a permanent exemption; otherwise, they feared, Seattle risked losing out to Long Beach or Oakland. Finally, after this victory, the lobbyists returned to California and convinced the legislators there to match Washington's offer of a permanent exemption as well.

In the struggle to keep and attract industry, states engage in "bidding wars."† Each competes to offer businesses a variety of incentives to locate within its borders. The incentives take many forms: industrial development bonds, which are free of federal tax and thus carry lower-than-usual interest rates; tax exemptions; and freedom from regulation. As the examples show, the war between the states didn't end in 1865.

---

* Deil Wright, *Understanding Intergovernmental Relations,* 2nd ed. (Monterey, Calif.: Brooks/Cole, 1982), p. 348.

† Tina Rosenberg, "Wars Between the States," *The New Republic* (October 3, 1983).

---

be a variety of local systems from which to choose. By "voting with one's feet," a person could always choose to live where the set of arrangements was most pleasing. These factors tend to support pluralist democracy. However, when the New Federalists try to make a clear demarcation between national and state functions, they may be threatening a pluralist democracy that thrives on the presence of multiple overlapping power centers. Furthermore, the devolution of power might make the system too closed, too easily dominated by very few, very large interests.

In contrast, the nationalist–marble cake–cooperative federalist would be perfectly willing to override local standards for a national standard in the interests of promoting equality. Yet this view of federalism, particularly in its "picket fence" variant, has also been particularly conducive to pluralist democracy. It is highly responsive to all manner of group pressures, including pressure at one level from groups unsuccessful at other levels. By blurring the lines of national and state responsibility, as in the marble cake image, this version of federalism encourages petitioners to try their luck at whichever level of government offers the best chance of success.

SUMMARY

The federal design in the Constitution was the result of political bargaining. States feared giving up too much power to a central government. The division of powers sketched out in the Constitution was supposed to result in "great and aggregate" matters being turned over to the national government while "local and particular" concerns were left to the states. Exactly what counted as "great and aggregate" and what as "local and particular" could not be fully spelled out in advance. As a result, two competing federalist myths emerged. Dual, or layer cake, federalism preferred states over the national government and emphasized the separateness of the levels of government. Cooperative, or marble cake, federalism gave primacy to the national government and saw national and state governments working together to solve national problems. In its own way, each view supported the pluralist vision of democracy.

Over the years, the national government used the elastic clause together with other specific constitutional powers, such as the power over interstate commerce, to become involved in virtually every area of human activity. On the whole, the increased involvement of the national government has served to promote equality. The national government used both carrots and sticks to achieve its purposes. Through direct legislation, it outlawed racial discrimination in public accommodations. By offering categorical grant money, it stimulated states to provide money for highway safety programs. By threatening to withdraw highway funds, it compelled states to adopt a uniform drinking age. Through Supreme Court decisions, it made effective the national standards of the Bill of Rights, giving individuals protection against state governments. The power of the national government grew, while the power of state governments declined.

Yet the growth of the national government, particularly in the last twenty years, has also led to a system of intergovernmental relations which has become clogged. New Federalists have suggested decreasing the size of the national government, reducing federal spending, and turning programs over to states as a solution to the problem of an unwieldy intergovernmental system. Yet their opponents worry that, in their haste to cut, New Federalists will fail to see legitimate national interests at stake in too many programs and will turn over important national responsibilities to states unwilling and unable to assume them. Government, rather than being too responsive, will become unresponsive.

The federalism debate is likely to be important in the 1980s and will be couched in terms of the two competing mythologies of federalism, but, as in the past, the contest between these views will be settled by political means.

Key Terms

federalism
dual federalism
states' rights
cooperative federalism
elastic clause
implied powers
grant-in-aid
categorical grant
formula grant
project grant
block grant

general revenue sharing
nullification
intergovernmental relations
"picket fence" federalism
special revenue sharing
municipal government
county government
school district
special district
home rule

Selected Readings

Gittell, Marilyn, ed. *State Politics and the New Federalism*. New York: Longmans, 1986. A collection of works on intergovernmental relations that emphasizes the role of the states.

O'Toole, Laurence J., ed. *American Intergovernmental Relations*. Washington, D.C.: Congressional Quarterly, Inc., 1985. This general collection of readings includes classics on the subject as well as timely analyses of intergovernmental relations in the Reagan administration.

Reagan, Michael, and John Sanzone. *The New Federalism*. New York: Oxford University Press, 1981. A classic analysis of fiscal federalism with heavy emphasis on grants.

Walker, David B., *Toward a Functioning Federalism*. Cambridge, Mass.: Winthrop, 1981. This work critiques the overloaded system of intergovernmental relations and offers alternatives to them.

PART III

LINKING PEOPLE WITH GOVERNMENT

5

Public Opinion and Political Socialization

Fridays are different in Saudi Arabia. After prayers, criminals are paraded in the streets for public punishment. Murderers are beheaded, adulterers are flogged, and thieves have their hands chopped off. The Saudi government wants citizens to get the message: crime will not be tolerated. Saudi Arabia, which claims the lowest crime rate in the world, is indeed a country that values *order* greatly.

In contrast, the United States has one of the world's highest crime rates. Its homicide rate, for example, is three to ten times that of most other Western countries. Although no one is proud of this record, our government would never consider beheading, flogging, or dismembering as a means of lowering the crime rate. First, the Eighth Amendment to the Constitution forbids "cruel and unusual punishment." Second, the public would not tolerate such grisly punishment.

However, the public definitely is not squeamish about the death penalty (capital punishment) for certain crimes. The Gallup organization has polled the nation on this issue for fifty years. Except in 1957 and 1966, a clear majority of respondents have consistently favored the death penalty for murder.[1] In fact, public support for capital punishment has increased dramatically since the late 1960s. By 1985, 75 percent of all respondents favored the death penalty for murder, whereas only 17 percent opposed it. Substantial segments of the public also favored the death penalty for rape (45 percent), for airplane hijacking (45 percent), and for espionage (48 percent).

Government has been defined as the legitimate use of force to control human behavior. And legal execution of human beings who threaten the social order represents the extreme use of government force. In colonial times, the government could impose capital punishment for such antisocial behavior as denying the true God, cursing one's parents, adultery, witchcraft, or being a rebellious son.[2] In the late 1700s, however, some writers, editors, and clergy argued for abolishing the death sentence. The campaign intensified in the 1840s, and a few states responded by eliminating capital punishment. Pressures of the Civil War and its aftermath caused interest in this cause to wane until 1890, when New York State adopted the new technique of electrocution as the instrument of death. By 1917, twelve states had responded by passing laws against capital punishment. But the outbreak of World War I fed the public's suspicion of foreigners and fear of radicals, leading to renewed support for the death penalty. Reacting to this shift in public opinion, four states restored capital punishment.

The security needs of World War II and postwar fears of Soviet communism fueled continued public support for capital punishment. After the Red Scare subsided in the late 1950s, public opposition to the death penalty grew to a bare majority in 1957, but public opinion was neither strong enough nor stable enough to force state legislatures to outlaw the punishment. In keeping with the pluralist model of democracy, abolition efforts shifted from pressuring elected legislators to persuading the courts.

One of the major legal arguments was that capital punishment itself was cruel and unusual—and therefore unconstitutional. The public had not regarded capital punishment as either cruel or unusual in the 1780s, but two hundred years later, opponents contended that the execution of a human being by the state had *become* cruel and unusual. Their arguments had some

Many for and Few Against Capital Punishment
Public opinion polls show that an overwhelming majority of Americans favor capital punishment for murder, and substantial percentages also favor the death penalty for other crimes, such as rape, airplane hijacking, and espionage. The minority who oppose capital punishment tend to be civil libertarians who are opposed to government denial of freedom in general. However, some opponents also oppose the death penalty on religious grounds.

effect on public opinion; in 1966 a bare majority of respondents again opposed the death penalty for only the second time since the Gallup surveys began.

This shift in public opinion was reflected in a continuing reduction in the number of executions until, in 1968, executions were halted completely in anticipation of a Supreme Court decision. By then, however, public opinion had again reversed itself to favor capital punishment. Nevertheless, in 1972 the Court ruled, in a 5 to 4 vote, that the death penalty as imposed by existing state laws, was unconstitutional. Its decision was not well received in many states, and thirty-five state legislatures passed new laws to get around the Court ruling. Public approval of the death penalty jumped almost ten points and began climbing higher as the nation's homicide rate increased.

In 1976 the Supreme Court changed its position. It ruled that three of the new state laws—those that provided for consideration of the defendant and the offense before imposing the death sentence—*were* constitutional.

And the Court rejected the argument that punishment by death itself violates the Constitution. In its ruling, the Court also noted that public opinion favored the death penalty. Now endorsed by the courts, as well as by public opinion, death was again available to punish criminals. Nevertheless, few states used the penalty, and only three criminals were executed during the rest of the 1970s.

Does the death penalty help deter murder? Two-thirds of the public thinks that it does help.[3] What do people regard as the most humane method of execution? Most favor lethal injection (62 percent) over electrocution (18 percent). The gas chamber has more support (9 percent) than the old-fashioned firing squad (3 percent). But hanging (1 percent) is generally unpopular, and no one regards beheading as humane.

This history of public opinion on the death penalty reveals several characteristics of public opinion:

1. *The public's attitudes toward a given government policy vary over time, often dramatically.*   Specifically, opinions on capital punishment tend to fluctuate with threats to the social order. The public is more likely to favor capital punishment in times of war, fear of foreign subversion, and high crime rates.

2. *Public opinion places boundaries on allowable types of public policy.*   Thus, chopping off a hand is unacceptable as the criminal punishment for theft in the United States, but electrocuting a murderer in private (not in public) is all right.

3. *Citizens are willing to register opinions on matters outside their expertise.*   People clearly believe execution by lethal injection is more humane than asphyxiation in the gas chamber, and they prefer electrocution to hanging. How can the public know enough about execution to make such judgments?

4. *Governments tend to react to public opinion.*   State laws for and against capital punishment have reflected swings in the public mood. Moreover, the Supreme Court's 1972 decision against capital punishment came when public opinion on the death penalty was sharply divided; the Court's 1976 approval of capital punishment coincided with the rise in public approval of the death penalty.

5. *The government sometimes does not do what the people want.*   Although public opinion overwhelmingly favors the death penalty for murder, few states actually punish murderers with execution. The United States has averaged over 20,000 homicides annually in the 1980s, but fewer than 5 executions per year—although the execution rate is rising.

The last two conclusions bear on our discussion of the majoritarian and pluralist models of democracy in Chapter 2. This chapter will probe more deeply into the nature, shape, depth, and formation of public opinion in a democratic government. How do people acquire their opinions? What are the major lines of division in public opinion? How do individuals' ideology and knowledge affect their opinions? What is the relationship between public opinion and ideological type? First, we shall consider the place of public opinion in democratic government.

PUBLIC OPINION AND MODELS OF DEMOCRACY

The majoritarian and pluralist models of democracy differ greatly in their assumptions about the role of public opinion in democratic government. According to the classic majoritarian model, the government should do what a majority of the public wants. In contrast, pluralists argue that the public as a whole seldom demonstrates a clear and settled opinion on the day-to-day issues of government. At the same time, pluralists recognize that subgroups *within* the public do express opinions on specific matters—often and vigorously. The pluralist model requires government institutions that allow the free expression of opinions by these minority "publics." Pluralists see democracy at work when the opinions of many different publics clash openly and fairly over government policy.

Stop the Presses! Oops, Too Late . . .

As the 1948 election drew near, few people gave President Harry Truman a chance to defeat his Republican opponent, Thomas E. Dewey. Polling was still new, but virtually all the early polls showed Dewey far ahead. Most organizations simply stopped polling weeks before the election. The Chicago Daily Tribune *believed the polls and proclaimed Dewey's victory before the votes were counted. Here, the victorious Truman triumphantly displays the most embarrassing newspaper headline in American politics. Later it was revealed that the few polls taken closer to election day showed Truman catching up to Dewey, which demonstrates that polls estimate the vote only* at the time *they are taken.*

Thanks to opinion polling, we can better understand the choice between these two institutional models of democracy. Polling involves interviewing a sample of citizens to estimate public opinion as a whole (see Feature 5.1). **Public opinion** is simply the collected attitudes of citizens on a given issue or question. Opinion polling is such a common feature of contemporary life that we often forget that it is a modern invention, dating only from the 1930s (see Table 5.1). In fact, survey methodology did not mature into a powerful research tool until the advent of computers in the 1950s. Truly extensive knowledge of public opinion has been available only for the last thirty years.

Before polling became an accepted part of the American scene, politicians, journalists, and everyone else could argue about what "the people" wanted. Historians writing about America before the 1930s had to guess at public opinion by analyzing newspaper stories, politicians' speeches, voting returns, and travelers' diaries. When no one really *knows* what the people want, it is impossible for government to be responsive to public opinion. As discussed in Chapter 3, the founding fathers sought to build public opinion into our constitutional structure by electing representatives to one house of Congress according to population. Attitudes and actions in the House of Representatives would, the framers thought, reflect public opinion, especially on the crucial issues of government taxes and expenditures.

In practice, bills passed by a majority of elected representatives do not necessarily reflect the opinions of a majority of citizens. This would not have

Table 5.1

Gallup Poll Accuracy Record

One of the nation's oldest polls was started by George Gallup in the 1930s. The accuracy of the Gallup Poll in predicting national elections over nearly fifty years is summarized below. Although not always on the mark, its predictions have been fairly close to the election results. The poll was most notably wrong in 1948, when it predicted that Thomas Dewey would defeat President Harry Truman, underestimating Truman's vote by 5.4 percentage points. The average difference between the predicted and actual results for all twenty-five national elections is plus or minus 2.1 percentage points, which is within the margin of error expected for the samples of 1,500 that Gallup usually draws. Moreover, the accuracy of Gallup polls has increased over time, with better knowledge of survey research techniques.

Year	Final Survey	Winner	Election Results	Deviation	Year	Final Survey	Winner	Election Results	Deviation
1984	59.0%	Reagan	59.1%	−0.1	1958	57.0%	Democratic	56.5%	+0.5
1982	55.0	Democratic	56.1	−1.1	1956	59.5	Eisenhower	57.8	+1.7
1980	47.0	Reagan	50.8	−3.8	1954	51.5	Democratic	52.7	−1.2
1978	55.0	Democratic	54.6	+0.4	1952	51.0	Eisenhower	55.4	−4.4
1976	48.0	Carter	50.0	−2.0	1950	51.0	Democratic	50.3	+0.7
1974	60.0	Democratic	58.9	+1.1	1948	44.5	Truman	49.9	−5.4
1972	62.0	Nixon	61.8	+0.2	1946	58.0	Republican	54.3	+3.7
1970	53.0	Democratic	54.3	−1.3	1944	51.5	Roosevelt	53.3	−1.8
1968	43.0	Nixon	43.5	−0.5	1942	52.0	Democratic	48.0	+4.0
1966	52.5	Democratic	51.9	+0.6	1940	52.0	Roosevelt	55.0	−3.0
1964	64.0	Johnson	61.3	+2.7	1938	54.0	Democratic	50.8	+3.2
1962	55.5	Democratic	52.7	+2.8	1936	55.7	Roosevelt	62.5	−6.8
1960	51.0	Kennedy	50.1	+0.9					

Source: *Gallup Report* (December 1984):31. Reprinted by permission.

bothered the framers, for they never intended to create a full democracy, a government responsive to majority opinion. Although they wanted to provide for some input of public opinion, they had little faith in the masses' ability to decide all governmental issues. Nevertheless, the framers creatively relied on elected representatives to incorporate public opinion into the first large-scale attempt at democratic government.

Feature 5.1

Sampling a Few, Predicting to Everyone

How can a pollster tell what the nation thinks by talking to only a few hundred people? The answer lies in the statistical theory of *sampling*. Briefly, the theory holds that a sample of individuals selected by chance from any population will be "representative" of that population. This means that the traits of individuals in the sample — their attitudes, beliefs, sociological characteristics, and physical features — will reflect the traits in the whole population. Sampling theory does not say that the sample will exactly match the population, only that it will reflect the population within some predictable degree of accuracy.

Three factors determine the accuracy of a sample. The most important is *the way the sample is selected*. For maximum accuracy, the individuals in the sample must be chosen randomly. *Randomly* does not mean "at whim"; rather, it means that every individual in the population has the same chance of being selected.

For a population as large and widespread as that of the United States, direct random sampling of individuals by name is practically impossible. Instead, pollsters first divide the country into geographical areas. They then randomly choose areas and eventually sample individuals who live within those areas. This departure from strict random sampling does decrease the accuracy of the polling results, but only by a relatively small amount.

The second factor that affects the accuracy of sampling is *the amount of variation in the population*. If there were no variation in the population, every sample chosen would reflect the population's characteristics with perfect accuracy. But the greater the variation within the population, the greater the chance that one random sample will be different from another.

Finally, *the size of the sample* also affects its accuracy. The larger the sample, the more accurately it will represent the population. For example, a sample of four hundred individuals will predict accurately to a population within 6 percentage points (plus or minus), 95 percent of the time. A sample of six hundred will be accurate within 4 percentage points. (Surprisingly, when the population is very large compared with the sample — which is usually the case in opinion polling — the size of the population has essentially no effect on the sampling accuracy. Thus, a sample of, say, six hundred individuals selected within a city, a state, or even the nation will reflect the traits of its population with equal accuracy, within 4 percentage points. *Why* this is so is better discussed in a course on statistics.)

Most national samples, such as the Gallup Poll, involve about 1,500 individuals and are accurate within 3 percentage points, 95 percent of the time. As shown in Table 5.1, the voting predictions of the Gallup Poll for twenty-five national elections since 1936 have deviated from the voting results only an average of 2.1 percentage points. Even this small sampling error can lead to incorrect predictions in close elections. For purposes of estimating public opinion on political issues, however, a sampling error of 3 percentage points is acceptable.

Polls are subject to other methodological errors that have nothing to do with sampling theory. In particular, the questions they ask must be clear and carefully worded to avoid bias. For example, in surveys conducted during the Korean War, questions that mentioned the "communist invasion" tended to increase support for the war by 15 to 20 percentage points over essentially the same question without a mention of communism.* Survey methods are also likely to get superficial responses from busy respondents who will say anything, quickly, to get rid of a pesky interviewer. Recently, some newspaper columnists have even urged readers to *lie* to pollsters conducting polls outside voting booths, so as to confound election-night television predictions. But, despite its potential for abuse or distortion, modern polling has told us a great deal about public opinion in America.

---

*John E. Mueller, *War, Presidents and Public Opinion* (New York: John Wiley, 1973), p. 44.

Sampling methods and opinion polling have altered the debate about majoritarian and pluralist models of government. Now that we know how often government policy runs against majority opinion, it becomes harder to defend the U.S. government as democratic under the majoritarian view of democracy. As we have seen, Americans overwhelmingly favor the death penalty for murderers. Nevertheless, the Supreme Court once decided that existing state laws applying capital punishment were unconstitutional. Even after the Court approved new state laws as constitutional, very few murderers were actually executed. Consider, too, the case of prayer in the schools. The Supreme Court has ruled that no state or local government can require the reading of the Lord's Prayer or Bible verses in public school. Surveys continually show that a clear majority of Americans (over 60 percent) disapprove of that ruling.* Because government policy sometimes runs against settled majority opinion, the majoritarian model is easily attacked.

Which model is correct in its assumptions about public opinion? *Does* a majority of the public often hold clear and settled opinions on government policy? If public opinion is often divided, what are the bases of these divisions? What principles, if any, do people use to organize their beliefs and attitudes about politics? Exactly how do individuals form their political opinions? We shall pursue answers to these questions in this chapter. In subsequent chapters, we shall assess the effect of public opinion on government policies. The results should help you make up your own mind about the viability of the majoritarian and pluralist models for a functioning democracy.

THE DISTRIBUTION OF PUBLIC OPINION

A government that tries to respond to public opinion soon learns that citizens seldom think alike. Because people do not hold identical attitudes and beliefs, governments must pay attention to the way public opinion *distributes* among the choices on an issue. In particular, government must analyze the *shape* and the *stability* of the distribution.

Shape of the Distribution

The results of public opinion polls are often displayed on charts like those in Figure 5.1. The response categories are along the baseline. The heights of the columns indicate the percentages of those polled who gave each response. The *shape* of the opinion distribution refers to the pattern, or physical form, of all the responses when counted and plotted. Figure 5.1 depicts three idealized patterns of distribution—normal, skewed, and bimodal—superimposed on several actual survey items.[4]

Figure 5.1(a) shows how respondents to a 1984 national survey placed themselves along a liberal-conservative scale. The most frequent response, called the *mode*, was "moderate." Progressively fewer people classified themselves in each category toward the liberal and conservative extremes. The

---

*Five national surveys from 1974 through 1983 found an average of 61 percent disapproving this ruling. See James Allan Davis and Tom W. Smith, *General Social Surveys, 1972–1984: Cumulative Codebook* (Chicago: National Opinion Research Center, 1984), p. 132.

resulting shape of the graph resembles what statistical theory calls a **normal distribution**—a symmetrical bell-shaped distribution around a single mode. Opinions that are "normally distributed" tend to support politicians who favor moderation in government policies. At the same time, they allow for government policies that range to either side of the centrist position. Due to the spread of public opinion around the ideological center in the United States, government policies are allowed to shift rather significantly from liberal to conservative (and back again), but they never stray too far from the moderate center.

Figure 5.1(b) plots the percentages of those who agreed or disagreed with the statement "The private business system in the United States works better than any other system yet devised for industrial countries."[5] The shape of this graph is quite different from the symmetrical distribution of ideological attitudes. In this graph, the mode (containing the vast majority who agree with the statement) lies off to the left, leaving a "tail" (containing the few

Figure 5.1

Three Distributions of Opinion
Three smooth shapes of hypothetical distributions — normal, skewed, and bimodal — are superimposed on three actual distributions of responses to survey questions. Although the actual responses do not match the shapes exactly, they match closely enough to warrant describing the distribution of (a) ideological attitudes as approximately normal, (b) belief in capitalism as skewed, and (c) opinions on firing a communist teacher as bimodal.
(Sources: (a) James Allen Davis and Tom W. Smith, General Social Surveys, 1972–1984: Cumulative Codebook. *Chicago: National Opinion Research Center, 1984, p. 75. Sample size was 1,473. Only 2 percent of the sample said "don't know" or didn't answer the question. (b) 1981 Survey by Civic Service, Inc., reported in* Public Opinion 5. *October–November 1982:21. (c) James Allen Davis and Tom W. Smith,* General Social Surveys, 1972–1984: Cumulative Codebook. *Chicago: National Opinion Research Center, 1984, p. 98.)*

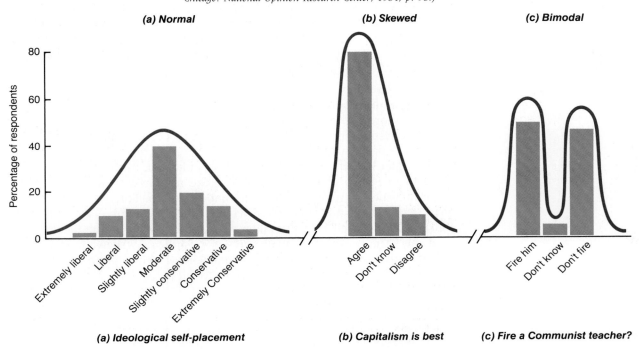

(a) Normal   **(b) Skewed**   **(c) Bimodal**

(a) Ideological self-placement   **(b) Capitalism is best**   **(c) Fire a Communist teacher?**

who disagree) on the right. Such an asymmetrical distribution is called a **skewed distribution.** The amount of "skew" in such a distribution (the proportion of respondents in the tail) is a matter of degree.

In a skewed distribution the opinions of the majority cluster around a point on one side of the issue. A skewed distribution indicates that less diversity of opinion exists than in a normal distribution. The skewed distribution of opinion in Figure 5.1(b) shows that most Americans are quite happy with capitalism as an economic system, which leaves a socialist little hope of winning an election by denouncing free enterprise. In fact, when consensus on an issue is so strong, those with minority opinions risk social ostracism and even persecution if they persist in voicing their opinions. If the public does not feel intensely about the issue, however, then politicians can sometimes discount a skewed distribution of public opinion. This has happened with the death penalty. Although most people favor capital punishment, it is not a burning issue for most of them, and politicians can usually ignore opinion on it without serious consequences.

Figure 5.1(c) plots percentages of respondents who favored or opposed firing a college teacher who was an admitted communist. Unlike either of the previous distributions, the responses plotted here fall into a **bimodal distribution.** Two categories are equally (or almost equally) chosen as the most frequent responses. Americans divide almost evenly over allowing an admitted communist (an opponent of capitalism) to teach in a college. Virtually half the population would fire him; nearly half would allow him to continue teaching. Because they split the community in nearly equal parts, bimodal distributions of opinion carry the greatest potential for political conflict, especially if those on both sides feel strongly about the issue.

Stability of the Distribution

A **stable distribution** of opinion is one that shows little change over time. Public opinion regarding important issues can change, but it is sometimes difficult to distinguish a true change in opinion from a difference in the way a question was worded. When the same question (or virtually the same question) produces significantly different responses over time, the surveys are more likely to be signaling true shifts in public opinion. When *different* questions produce similar distributions of opinion, the underlying attitudes are very stable.

Consider Americans' attitudes toward capitalism. In the 1981 survey illustrated in Figure 5.1(b), 79 percent of the respondents favored the U.S. private business system over any alternative system. Forty years earlier, in 1941, respondents had been asked whether they "would be better off if the concern you worked for were taken over and operated by the federal government." The responses at that time were also heavily skewed: 81 percent said that they preferred "business management." The nation's support of capitalism had barely changed over four decades.*

---

*These questions are not ideally matched, but other survey items about private enterprise yield comparable results. See Donald J. Devine, *The Political Culture of the United States* (Boston: Little, Brown, 1972), pp. 210–214.

***According to Our Poll, You're
Favored by Yuppies, 2 to 1***
*Pollsters should know, for
many of them fit the ''Yuppie''
definition as young, upwardly-
mobile professionals. Polling has
become a very important factor
in political campaigning, and
students who combine courses in
statistics, computers, and
political science sometimes find
employment in election
campaigns — or even start their
own firms.*

The public's self-placement on the standard liberal-conservative scale is another area that has remained surprisingly stable from the 1960s to the 1980s, as shown in Figure 5.2(a). Even in 1964, when liberal Lyndon B. Johnson won a landslide victory over conservative Barry Goldwater in the presidential election, more voters described themselves as conservative than as liberal. Indeed, this has been the public's ideological self-classification in every presidential election year since 1964.[6] Despite all the talk about the nation's becoming conservative in recent years, the fact is that most people did not describe themselves as liberal *at any time* during the past two decades. The public did become somewhat *more* conservative during that time (shifting about 5 percentage points toward the right), but they had considered themselves conservative to begin with.

Public opinion in America *is* capable of massive change over time, however. Moreover, these changes can occur on issues that were once highly controversial. A good example of a dramatic change in American public opinion is race relations, specifically integrated schools. A national survey in 1942 asked whether "white and Negro students should go to the same schools or separate schools." Only 30 percent of white respondents said that the students should attend the same schools. When the same research firm asked virtually the same question in 1984 (substituting "black" for "Negro"), 90 percent of the white respondents endorsed integrated schools. The change in opinion on this issue, as recorded over forty years, is graphed in Figure 5.2(b).

Some scholars writing on this trend in racial attitudes have commented on "(1) its massive magnitude, moving from a solid pro-segregation majority to an overwhelming pro-integration consensus; (2) its long duration,

Figure 5.2 ▬▬▬

Stability and Change in Public Opinion

Public opinion can remain stable over time on some issues, but it can also change dramatically on others. Figure 5.2(a) demonstrates great stability in respondents' ideological self-classifications in separate surveys in 1964 and 1984. Opinions at both times were approximately normally distributed around "moderate" as the modal category. (The 1964 distribution is slightly more compact, because the earlier survey had only five response categories.) Figure 5.2(b) shows how much public opinion on school integration has changed over four decades, moving from a majority opposed to school integration to nearly all in favor. (Sources: (a) Data for 1964 are from Lloyd A. Free and Hadley Cantril, The Political Beliefs of Americans. *New York: Simon & Schuster, 1968, p. 41. Data for 1984 come from the National Opinion Research Center (NORC) survey in Figure 5.1. (b) Surveys conducted by the NORC, reported in and recalculated from Tom W. Smith and Paul B. Sheatsley, "American Attitudes Toward Race Relations,"* Public Opinion *7. October–November 1984:15.)*

(a) Stability: Ideological Self-Placement

Percent classifying themselves by political ideology

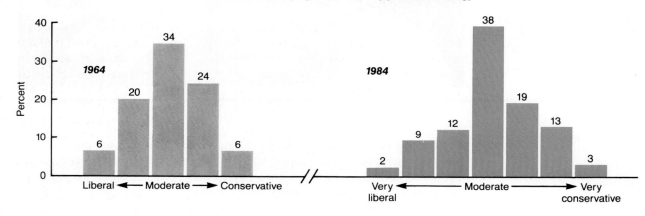

(b) Change: Opinions on School Integration

Percent saying that white and black students should go to same schools

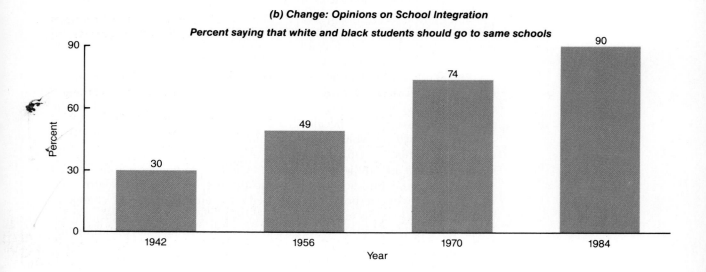

continuing over four decades; and (3) its steady relentless pace.''[7] The same scholars, however, note that white Americans have not become "colorblind." Despite their endorsement of integrated schools, only 23 percent favored busing to achieve racial balance. And whites were more willing to bus their children to a school with a few blacks than to one that was mostly black.[8] Thus, white opinion changed dramatically with regard to the *principle* of desegregated schools, but whites seemed divided on how that principle should be practiced. Seeking to explain this contradiction and the formation of political opinion in general, scholars cite the process of political socialization, the influence of various cultural factors, and the interplay of ideology and knowledge. In the next several sections, we will consider how these elements combine to affect public opinion.

POLITICAL SOCIALIZATION

Public opinion is grounded in political values. People acquire their values through a process of **political socialization,** or the complex process through which individuals become aware of political life, learn political facts, and form political values. Reflect for a moment on how *you* have been socialized about politics. What is your earliest recollection of a president? When did you first learn about political parties? If you identify with a party, how did you decide to do so? If you don't, why don't you? Who was the first liberal you ever met? The first conservative? How did you first learn about the hydrogen bomb? About the Soviet Union?

Obviously, the paths to political awareness, knowledge, and values differ among individuals, but most people are exposed to the same influences or *agents of socialization,* especially in childhood through young adulthood. These influences are the family, the school, and the community (including peers).

The Agents of Early Socialization

Like psychologists, scholars of political socialization place great emphasis on early learning. Both groups note two operating principles that characterize early learning:

- The **primacy principle.** What is learned first is learned best.
- The **structuring principle.** What is learned first structures later learning.[9]

Because most people learn first from their family, the family tends to be a very important agent of early socialization. The extent of family influence — and of the influence of other socializing agents — depends on the extent of our *exposure* to them, the amount of our *communication* with them, and our *receptivity* to them.[10]

Family. In most cases, exposure, communication, and receptivity are highest in family-child relations. From their families, children learn a wide range of values—social, moral, religious, economic, and political—that help shape their opinions. It is not surprising, then, that most people link their

One Nation . . .
Throughout America — as in every other country — young children are socialized into politics through the school system. The simple ceremony of raising the flag teaches students that they are part of a larger political system — the United States of America — no matter where they live. As Feature 5.2 points out, however, they may not always get the message straight in the beginning.

earliest recollections of politics with their families. One of the most politically important things that many children learn from their parents is party identification.

Children often learn party identification from their parents in much the same way that they learn their religion. Children are taught to imitate. When parents share the same religion, children almost always are raised in that faith. When parents differ on religion, children are likely to follow one or the other — not to adopt a different religion entirely. Similarly, parental influence on party identification is greater when both parents identify with the same party.[11] Overall, however, only about half of American voters identify with the same political party as their parents.*

Two crucial differences between party and religion may explain why youngsters are socialized into a religion much more surely and strongly than into a political party. The first is that most parents care a great deal more about their religion than about their politics. Therefore they are more deliberate in socializing their children with regard to religion. The second is that religious institutions themselves recognize the value of socialization and thus offer Sunday schools and other activities that are high on exposure, communication, and receptivity — reinforcing parental guidance. American political parties, on the other hand, sponsor few activities to win the hearts of little Democrats and young Republicans,† which leaves children open to counterinfluences in the school and community.

---

*Studying both parents and children in 1965 and 1973, Jennings and Niemi found that 57 percent of children shared their parents' party in 1965, but only 47 percent did in 1973. See M. Kent Jennings and Richard G. Niemi, *Generations and Politics* (Princeton, N.J.: Princeton University Press, 1981), pp. 90–91.
†The Communist party of the Soviet Union, in contrast, promotes the party image through the Young Pioneers, a group like a combined Boy Scout and Girl Scout organization.

School. According to some researchers, schools have an influence on political learning that is equal to or greater than that of parents.[12] We must, however, distinguish between primary and secondary schools on the one hand and institutions of higher education on the other. Primary schools introduce children to authority figures outside the family, such as the teacher, the principal, and the police officer. In so doing, these schools lay the foundation for accepting the social order. They also teach the nation's slogans and symbols—the Pledge of Allegiance, national anthem, national heroes, and holidays, for example. Elementary school teachers also stress the norms of group behavior and democratic decisionmaking, such as respecting others' opinions and choosing class officers by voting. In so doing, these teachers also emphasize the value of political equality.

Children do not always understand the meanings of the patriotic rituals and behaviors they learn in primary school (see Feature 5.2). In fact, much early learning about politics—in the United States and elsewhere—is more indoctrination than education. By the end of the eighth grade, however, children have begun to develop a differentiated view of government. At this point, children are more aware of collective institutions, such as Congress

---

Feature 5.2

The Goodyear Blimp over Washington

Elementary schools provide the first contact with American government for many young children. Sometimes the youngsters fail to get the message right at first. How many of you pledged allegiance to an "invisible" rather than an "indivisible" nation? Playwright Arthur Miller relates his own misunderstanding of the Pledge of Allegiance that he learned in primary school.

> ROXBURY, Conn. — I no longer remember how many years it took for me to realize I was making a mistake in the Pledge of Allegiance. With high passion, I stood beside my seat in my Harlem grammar school and repeated the Pledge to the Flag, which always drooped next to the teacher's desk. My feelings were doubtless warmed by my having two uncles who had been in the Great War, one in the Navy, the other as a mule driver in the Army who brought ammunition up to the front in France.
>
> Dirigibles were much in the news in the early 20's, and the Navy, as far as I was able to make out, owned them. Thus, the patriotic connection, which was helped along by the fact that nobody I had ever heard speaking English had ever used the word Indivisible. Or Divisible either, for that matter.
>
> None of which inhibited me from rapping out the Pledge each and every morning: ". . . One Nation in a Dirigible, with Liberty and Justice for All." I could actually see in my mind's eye hordes of faces looking down at Earth through the windows of the Navy's airships. The whole United States was up there, all for one and one for all—and the whole gang in that Dirigible. One day, maybe I could get to ride in it, too, for I was deeply patriotic, and the height of Americanism, as I then understood it, was to ride in a Dirigible. . . .

Source: Arthur Miller, "School Prayer: A Political Dirigible," *New York Times*, March 12, 1984.

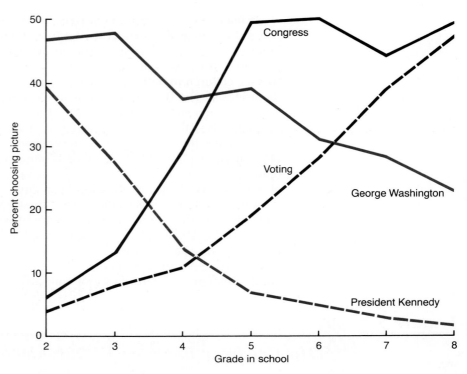

Children's Images of Government
In the earliest school years, political learning focuses on famous government leaders. Later, students are taught about government institutions. This figure shows how primary school students develop their political understanding from people to institutions. Students in different grades in the 1960s were given a series of pictures and were asked to pick the two that show best what our government is. By the eighth grade, voting and the Congress were chosen much more frequently than George Washington or even than President John F. Kennedy. (Source: David Easton and Jack Dennis, Children in the Political System. *New York: McGraw-Hill, 1969, p. 116. Copyright © 1969. Reprinted by permission of David Easton and Jack Dennis.)*

Figure 5.3

and elections, than they were earlier, when they tended to focus on single figures of government authority, such as the president (see Figure 5.3). In sum, most children emerge from elementary school with a sense of nationalism and an idealized notion of American government.[13]

Secondary schools continue the building of "good citizens." Field trips to the state legislature or the city council impress students with the majesty and power of government institutions. Secondary schools also offer more explicitly political content in their curricula, including courses in recent U.S. history, civics, and American government. As a result, high school seniors' ability to recognize political leaders improves dramatically compared with that of entering freshmen (see Figure 5.4). Better high school social studies teachers challenge students to think critically about American government and politics, but many others concentrate on teaching civic responsibilities.

Despite teachers' efforts to build children's trust in the political process, outside events can erode that trust when children grow up. Surveys of adults showed substantial drops in trust of the Washington government during the Watergate affair in 1974 and when American embassy personnel were held hostage in Iran in 1980. Nevertheless, recent survey data show that Americans' trust in their government is equal to or greater than that of citizens of

Figure 5.4

Knowledge of Political Leaders by Age Groups

Do people actually learn anything about politics during high school? They seem to, according to a study that asked children at ages thirteen and seventeen and young adults to write down the last names of people who held the public offices listed below. (Respondents were not penalized for spelling errors.) The percentage of correct responses increased for each age group, but the greatest increases occurred during the high school years, between ages thirteen and seventeen. (Source: Fred I. Greenstein, ''What the President Means to Americans,'' in James D. Barber, ed., Choosing the President. *Englewood Cliffs, N.J.: Prentice-Hall, 1974, p. 174.)*

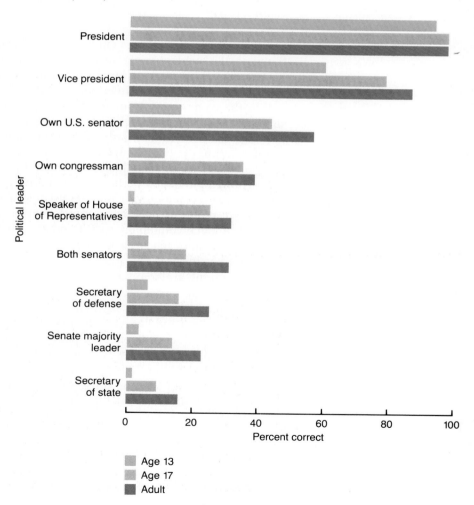

some other Western countries. Moreover, the same study revealed that Americans' pride in their country was considerably greater than that of the other respondents.[14]

Political learning at the college level can be very similar to political learning in high school or *very* different. The degree of difference is apt to increase if professors (or the texts they use) encourage their students to question authority. Questioning dominant political values does not necessarily mean rejecting them. For example, this text encourages you to recognize that freedom and equality — two idealized values in American culture — are often in conflict. It also invites you to view democracy in terms of competing institutional models, one of which challenges the idealized notion of democracy. These alternative perspectives are meant to instruct students in American political values, not subvert those values. College courses that are intended to stimulate critical thinking thus have the potential to introduce or develop in some students political ideas that are radically different from those they bring to the class — a characteristic that high school courses cannot always claim.

Community and peers.   One's community and one's peers are different but generally overlapping groups. *Community* refers to people of all ages who have contact with a person because they live or work near that person. *Peers* are friends, classmates, or coworkers, usually of similar age, who usually live within the community. Homogeneous communities — those with members similar in ethnicity, race, religion, or occupational status — can exert strong pressures on both children and adults to conform to the dominant attitude in the community. For example, neighbors can talk up the candidates of one party and criticize the candidates of the other, making it unpopular to voice a dissenting opinion. In particular, communities often display negative attitudes toward people outside the dominant social grouping. Communities of one ethnic group or religion are apt to be suspicious of members of other groups. Although community socialization is usually reinforced in the schools, schools sometimes teach ideas (such as sex education) that run counter to community values.

Peer groups are sometimes used by children and adults as a defense against community pressures. Adolescent peer groups are particularly useful against parental pressures. In their early years, children rely on peers to defend their dress and lifestyle rather than their politics. At the college level, however, peer group influence on politics can grow substantially, often fed by new learning that clashes with parental beliefs. A classic study of female students at Bennington College found that many became substantially more liberal than their affluent and conservative parents. A followup study twenty-five years later showed that their liberal attitudes had generally persisted, partly because their spouses and friends (peers) had supported their views.[15]

Continuing Socialization

Despite the importance of early learning, political socialization continues throughout life. As parental and school influences wane, peer groups (neighbors, fellow workers, and club members) assume a greater importance in promoting political awareness and in developing political opinions. Because adult knowledge of political events usually comes from the mass media — newspapers, magazines, television, and radio — the media themselves emerge as socialization agents. The role of television is especially important, since a majority of adults (64 percent in 1982) report that they rely on television for most of their information about politics.[16] (Ironically, studies indicate that television's effect on viewers' political knowledge is essentially *negative*. Reliance on television for news seems to *suppress* the ability to perceive differences between presidential candidates[17] and to *inhibit* knowledge about politics.[18])

Regardless of how people learn about politics as they grow older, they do gain a perspective on government that younger people lack. They are apt to measure up new candidates (and new ideas) in light of the old ones they remember. Their values also change to reflect their own self-interest. As voters age, for example, they begin to see more merit in government spending for social security than they did when they were younger. Finally, political learning comes simply through practice. An example is the simple act of voting, which voters do with increasing regularity as they mature.

SOCIAL GROUPS AND POLITICAL VALUES

No two people are influenced by precisely the same socialization agents in exactly the same way. As a result, each individual experiences a unique process of political socialization and forms a unique set of political values. Nevertheless, people with similar backgrounds do share various learning experiences; they thus tend to develop similar political opinions. In this section, we shall examine some links between people's social backgrounds and their political values. We shall refer to two questions that appeared on a 1984 survey and that are quoted at the top of Figure 5.5. (Other questions might not produce identical results but would probably show the same general tendencies.) They ask, in essence:

1. Would you allow an admitted communist to teach in a college?
2. Do you think that the government should reduce income differences between rich and poor people?[19]

The first question was introduced in Figure 5.1. Those who answer "no" are willing to deny freedom of speech to a teacher who favors changing the existing economic and political order. They apparently value order over individual freedom. Those who answer "yes" to the second question think that government should promote equality of income, even if that means taxing the rich more heavily (and thus reducing their freedom to use their money as they wish). These respondents apparently value equality over freedom.

Overall, the responses to each of these questions were divided approximately equally, with 50 percent of the respondents giving one answer and 50 percent giving the other. However, different percentages appear in the responses of those who differ on such socioeconomic factors as education, income, region, ethnicity, and religion. Their responses are shown in Figure 5.5 as positive and negative deviations (differences) in percentage points from

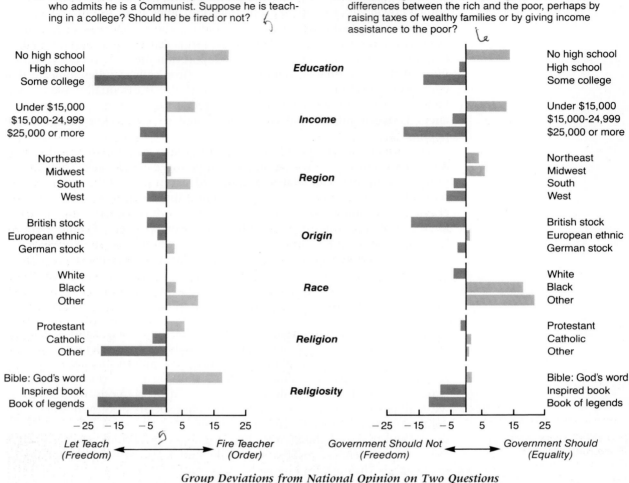

a. I should like to ask you some questions about a man who admits he is a Communist. Suppose he is teaching in a college? Should he be fired or not?

b. Should the government in Washington reduce income differences between the rich and the poor, perhaps by raising taxes of wealthy families or by giving income assistance to the poor?

Let Teach (Freedom) ← → Fire Teacher (Order)

Government Should Not (Freedom) ← → Government Should (Equality)

Group Deviations from National Opinion on Two Questions

Two questions — one on the dilemma of freedom versus order and the other on the dilemma of freedom versus equality — were asked of a national sample in 1984. Public opinion for the nation as a whole was equally divided on each question. The two graphs above show how respondents in several social groups deviated from overall public opinion. The longer the bars next to each group, the more its respondents deviated from the 50-50 split of public opinion. Bars that extend to the left show opinions that deviate toward freedom. Bars that extend toward the right show deviations away from freedom and toward order — Figure 5.5(a) — or equality — Figure 5.5(b). Note that different levels of education produce the largest and most consistent differences in opinion on these two questions. (Source: National Opinion Research Center, 1984 General Survey.)

Figure 5.5

the national averages of 50-50 on the two questions. For example, in Figure 5.5(a), groups whose bars extend to the right of the center line are above the national average in thinking that a communist should *not* teach in college; those whose bars extend to the left are below the average. In Figure 5.5(b), groups whose bars extend to the right of the center line are above the national average in thinking that the government *should* reduce income differences; again, those with bars extending to the left are below the average. Bars that extend to the right thus identify groups that are more likely than most Americans to sacrifice freedom for a given benefit of government: either equality or order.

Education

Education increases citizens' awareness and understanding of political issues. Education also underscores the value of free speech in a democratic society, thereby increasing our tolerance for those who dissent. This result is clearly shown in Figure 5.5(a), where higher levels of education correspond to a greater willingness to let an admitted communist teach. (That is, respondents with no high school education would tend to fire the teacher, whereas those with some college education would tend to let him teach.) When confronted with issues that involve a choice between personal freedom and social order, more highly educated respondents tend to choose freedom.

With regard to the role of government in reducing income inequality, Figure 5.5(b) shows that more education again gives rise to opinions in favor of freedom, this time over equality. The higher their level of education, the *less* respondents supported the redistribution of income. Some readers may think that educated people ought to favor a humanitarian role for government in aiding the poor. However, educated people tend to be wealthier people, who would be more heavily taxed to help the poor. Thus, in this case at least, the effect of education on public opinion is intertwined with the effect of income.

Is It the Government's Responsibility to Help?
Everyone feels uneasy at the sight of poverty in the presence of wealth. The question is, what should be done about poverty? Should the government step in to reduce income differences between the rich and the poor, perhaps by taxing the wealthy at higher rates and supplementing the income of the poor? Or should the government take no more from the wealthy than it does from the middle class, or even from the lower class?

Income

In many countries, differences in social class — based on one's social background and occupational status — divide people in their politics. In the United States, we have avoided the uglier aspects of class conflict, but here wealth sometimes substitutes for class. As shown in Figure 5.5, wealth is strongly related to opinions on government's role in promoting order and equality. Those with higher incomes are strongly opposed to government redistribution of income but only somewhat more likely to allow an admitted communist to teach. Thus we find that wealth and education have similar effects on these two issues. However, education has the stronger effect on opinions about order, whereas income has the stronger effect on opinions about equality.

Region

Early in our country's history, regional differences were politically important — important enough to spark a civil war between the North and the South. For nearly a hundred years after the Civil War, regional differences continued to affect politics. The South became virtually a one-party region, almost completely Democratic. The Midwest was long regarded as the stronghold of "isolationism" in foreign affairs. The moneyed Northeast was thought to control the purse strings of capitalism. And the rustic West pioneered its own mixture of progressive politics.

In the past, cultural differences among regions have been fed by regional differences in wealth. In recent decades, however, the movement of people and wealth away from the Frostbelt states in the Midwest and Northeast to the Sunbelt states in the South and Southwest has caused the regions to converge in per capita income over time, as graphed in Figure 5.6. One result of this equalization of wealth across regions is that the "Solid South" is no longer "solid" for the Democratic party. In fact, the South led the nation in voting for Richard Nixon, the Republican candidate for president in 1972, and was again strong for Republican Ronald Reagan in 1984.

We might expect, then, that there would be some difference in public opinion among the four major regions of the United States, but perhaps not much. Figure 5.6 shows that that is indeed the case. People in the South and West are only somewhat more likely to oppose government efforts to equalize income than people in the Midwest and Northeast. Regional differences are greater on the question of social order. Differences in opinion are strongest between the Northeast, where respondents are more likely to support freedom of speech, and the South, where they are more likely to prevent a communist from teaching. Despite these differences, regional effects on public opinion have faded compared with the effects of other social groupings.

The "Old" Ethnicity: European Origin

Beginning at the turn of the century, the major ethnic groups in American politics were immigrants from various European countries — for example, Ireland, Italy, Germany, and Poland — who came to the United States in waves during the late 1800s and early 1900s. These immigrants entered a country that had been founded by British settlers a hundred years or more earlier. The new immigrants found themselves in a strange land, usually without money and unable to speak the language. Moreover, their religious backgrounds—mainly Catholic and Jewish—differed from the predominant Protestantism of the earlier settlers. Local politicians saw these newcomers, who were concentrated in urban areas in the Northeast and Midwest, as a

Figure 5.6

Convergence in Income Across Regions, Across Time
At the beginning of the century, vast differences in wealth could be found among the nation's regions. The wealthiest people were located in the Northeast and on the West coast; the poorest were in the Southeast. Over time, these regional differences in income have narrowed dramatically. The figure below graphs per capita income as a percentage of the national average for eight different regions from 1900 to 1981. As the regions have converged toward equality in per capita income, they have lost a basis for political differences. (Source: Public Opinion 6. *February–March 1983:22. Reprinted with permission of American Enterprise Institute.)*

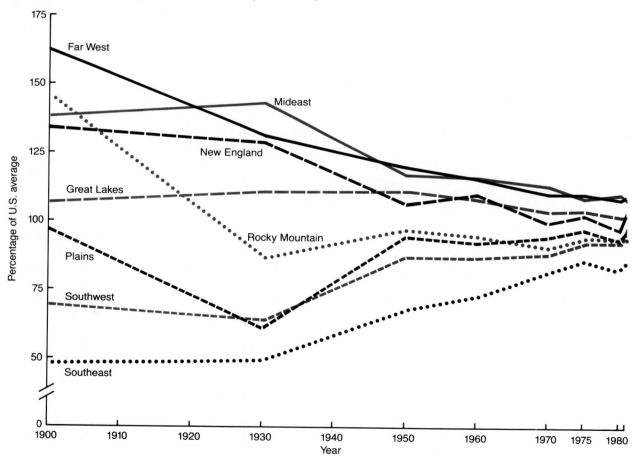

So You're Irish!
*Most young people today do
not realize that recent Irish
immigrants once stood at the
bottom of the social ladder in
American cities. Usually manual
laborers, they often worked at
the dirtiest and most dangerous
jobs, and they were herded into
ghettolike living areas. Like so
many other European ethnic
groups, the Irish used their
voting strength to win political
power and, eventually, access to
political office.*

new source of votes and soon mobilized them into politics. Holding jobs of
lower status, these urban ethnics became part of the great coalition of Democratic voters that President Franklin D. Roosevelt forged in the 1930s. For
years thereafter, studies of public opinion and voting behavior found consistent differences between their political preferences and those of the native
Anglo-Saxons.[20]

More recent studies of public opinion have shown a weakening of these
differences. Figure 5.5 on page 162 analyzes public opinion for three groups
of white ethnics, who account for almost 70 percent of the U.S. population.
Those of "British stock" (English, Scottish, Welsh) and "German stock" (German, Austrian, Swiss) each comprise about 20 percent of the sample. The
"European ethnics" (primarily Catholics and Jews from Eastern Europe,
Italy, and Ireland) comprise about 28 percent. The differences in opinions
among these groups are not large. However, Americans of British stock —
mostly "WASPs" (White Anglo-Saxon Protestants) — are markedly more opposed to government action to equalize incomes than are other European
whites. WASPs are also more likely to allow a communist to teach in college.
Despite these differences, national origin has lost some of its power in American politics. Simply put, European ethnics have been assimilated into America's "melting pot"; they are no longer very different from other white
Americans in language, education, or occupation.[21] But if this **"old" ethnicity** — European origin — is disappearing, a **"new" ethnicity** — race and
skin color — has arisen to take its place in American politics.

***We're Not Irish, but
We Can Win Too!***
*Reverend Jesse Jackson strikes a
victory pose with two Asian-
Americans in his 1984
campaign for the Democratic
nomination for president.
Jackson sought to assemble a
"Rainbow Coalition" consisting
of whites, blacks, Asians, and
Hispanics. Although he did not
win the nomination, he ran an
impressive campaign in a field
of nine announced candidates
and emerged with the third
largest group of convention
delegates, behind Walter
Mondale and Gary Hart.*

The "New" Ethnicity: Race

For many years after the Civil War, the racial issue in American politics was defined as "how the South should treat the Negro." The debate between North and South over this issue became a conflict of civil rights and states' rights—one in which "Negroes" were primarily objects and not participants. But with the rise of "black consciousness" and the grassroots civil rights demonstrations led by Dr. Martin Luther King and others in the 1960s, blacks themselves emerged as a political force. Through a series of civil rights laws backed by President Lyndon Johnson and northern Democrats in Congress, blacks secured effective voting rights in the South and exercised those rights more vigorously in the North. Although constituting only about 12 percent of the total population, blacks comprised sizable voting blocs in southern states and in urban areas in northern states. Like the European ethnics before them, American blacks were now courted for their votes; suddenly their opinions became politically important.

Blacks presently constitute the largest racial minority in American politics but not the only significant one. Another 5 percent of the population are Asians, American Indians (native Americans), and other nonwhites. Persons of Spanish origin—Hispanics—are also commonly regarded as a racial ethnic group, although many of them are white. According to the 1980 census, Hispanics constitute about 6 percent of the nation's population; moreover, they comprise up to 19 percent of the population in California and 21 percent in Texas.[22] Although they are politically strong in some communities, Hispanics have lagged behind blacks in nationwide political mobilization. However, they too are becoming a force to be reckoned with in electoral politics.

Two factors have caused blacks and members of other racial minorities to display similar political attitudes.[23] First, racial minorities tend to be low in **socioeconomic status** (a combination of education, occupational status, and income). Second, they have been targets of racial prejudice and discrimination. Figure 5.5 clearly shows the effects of racial groupings on political opinions. Blacks and other minorities (mostly Hispanics) distinctly favor government action to equalize incomes—favoring equality over freedom. Minorities also favor firing a communist teacher—a vote for order over freedom. Thus, minorities are more in favor of government action to promote both equality and order.

Religion

Since the last major wave of European immigration in the 1930s and 1940s, the religious makeup of the United States has remained fairly stable. Nearly 65 percent of those surveyed in 1984 were Protestant, about 25 percent identified themselves as Catholic, only 2 percent were Jewish, 2 percent claimed other religions, and 7 percent chose "none."[24] For many years, analysts had found strong and consistent differences in the opinions of Protestants, Catholics, and Jews. Protestants, compared with Catholics, revealed conservative attitudes, and Jews tended to be noticeably more liberal than even Catholics on most issues.

Over time, however, cultural assimilation has decreased attitudinal differences among religious groups, especially between Protestants and Catholics. Differences remained in 1984, but the edges had been softened, as shown in Figure 5.5 on page 162. There is virtually no difference of opinion among Protestants, Catholics, and others on the government's role in equalizing income. Differences do appear, however, in the question of freedom of speech. Protestants, who constitute the religious majority in America, tend toward order. Catholics tend toward freedom, and the other religious groups strongly favor freedom.

Perhaps for our purposes, Americans should be categorized not by "kind" of faith but by "degree" of faith. In other words, perhaps we should consider *religiosity,* not religion, as a factor. The 1984 survey measured religiosity by asking respondents about their attitudes toward the Bible. Did they think it should be taken literally as the actual word of God? Was it an inspired book, but not one that should be taken literally? Or was it only an ancient book of fables, legends, history, and moral precepts recorded by man?[25]

As Figure 5.5 indicates, the question that measured religiosity produced much greater differences of opinion than the question on religion. On the question of order, in fact, religiosity produced greater differences than for any other factor except education. Those who believed that the Bible is the word of God favored equality (mildly) and order (strongly) over freedom. Those in the other two groups—particularly those who viewed the Bible as a book of legends—chose freedom over both other values. Religion inevitably mixes with politics in the United States. As reported in Compared With What?

Compared With What? 5.1

The Importance of Religion

A comprehensive study of religious attitudes in the major Western countries found that religion played a larger role in the lives of citizens in the United States than in any other country. The graph below plots the percentage of respondents who said "very important" when asked "How important to you are your religious beliefs?"

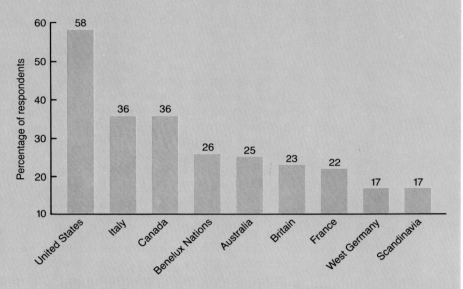

Source: *Public Opinion* 2 (March/May, 1979):38. Other response options were "fairly important," "not too important," and "not at all important." The surveys in the foreign countries were conducted in 1974 and 1975. The U.S. survey was taken in 1978. Reprinted with permission of the American Enterprise Institute.

5.1, the United States is a very religious country compared with other Western nations. The religious underpinnings of many Americans' political values must be considered when public opinion in the United States is assessed.

FROM VALUES TO IDEOLOGY

So far, we have studied differences in groups' opinions on two survey questions. Although responses to these questions reflect value choices between freedom and order and between freedom and equality, we have not yet interpreted group opinions in the context of political ideology. Political scientists generally agree that ideology enters into public opinion on specific issues, but they disagree on the extent to which people think in ideological terms.[26] However, they agree that ideological thinking within the public cannot be summarized simply in conventional liberal-conservative terms.

The Degree of Ideological Thinking in Public Opinion

In an early but important study, respondents were asked about the parties and candidates in the 1956 election.[27] Only about 12 percent of the sample volunteered responses that contained explicitly ideological terms (such as *liberal, conservative,* and *capitalism*). Most of the respondents (42 percent) evaluated the parties and candidates in terms of "benefits to groups"—farmers, workers, or businesspeople, for example. Others (24 percent) spoke more generally about "the nature of the times" (for example, inflation, unemployment, and the threat of war). Finally, a good portion of the sample (22 percent) displayed no classifiable issue content in their responses.

Subsequent research has shown somewhat greater ideological awareness within the electorate.[28] The proportion of **ideologues**—those credited with using ideological terms in their responses—jumped to 27 percent during the 1964 presidential contest between the Democratic candidate, ardent liberal Lyndon Johnson, and the Republican candidate, archconservative Barry Goldwater. Later studies found that the proportion of ideologues in samples of voters remained above 20 percent in subsequent presidential elections.[29] The tendency to respond to questions by using ideological terms is strongly related to level of education, which helps one to understand political issues and to relate them to one another. Personal experiences in the socialization process can also lead people to think ideologically. For example, children raised in strong union households may be taught to distrust private enterprise and to value collective action through the government.

True ideologues hold a consistent set of values and beliefs about the purpose and scope of government. Often people respond to questions in ways that *seem* ideological, even though they really fail to understand the underlying principles. For example, most respondents dutifully comply when they are asked to place themselves somewhere on a liberal-conservative continuum. The result, as shown in Figure 5.1, is an approximately normal distribution centering on "moderate" as the modal category. However, many people settle on "moderate" as the safe choice when they do not clearly understand the alternatives. In fact, "moderate" was chosen by 43 percent of those lacking a college education but by only 26 percent of those with a college education. Another study in 1984 gave respondents an alternative choice: the statement "I haven't thought much about it"—which allowed them to avoid placing themselves on the liberal-conservative continuum. In this study, 26 percent admitted that they had not thought much about liberalism or conservatism.[30] Thus, the extent of ideological thinking in America is considerably less than it might seem from responses to questions that ask people to describe themselves as liberals or conservatives.

The Quality of Ideological Thinking in Public Opinion

It is also not clear what people's ideological self-placement means in the 1980s. Originally, the liberal-conservative continuum represented a single dimension—attitudes toward scope of government activity. Liberals were in favor of more government action to provide public goods, and conservatives

Will They Be Liberals, Conservatives, or What?
A new group of immigrants is being sworn in as citizens of the United States during the centennial celebration of the Statue of Liberty, on July 4, 1986. The group gathered on this special occasion is quite different from the hordes of European immigrants who poured into the nation around the turn of the century and for decades afterward. Perhaps the young woman in the front row is wondering, as she steals a glance at Mikhail Baryshnikov, Russian émigŕe ballet dancer, is he a liberal, a conservative, or what?

were in favor of less. This simple classification is not as useful today. Many people who call themselves liberals no longer favor government activism in general, and many self-styled conservatives no longer oppose it in principle.

Chapter 1 proposed an alternative ideological classification based on relationships among the values of freedom, equality, and order. Liberals were described as people who believe that government should promote equality among its citizens, even if some freedom is lost in the process, but who oppose surrendering freedom to government-imposed order. Conservatives were described as not *opposing* equality in itself but putting a higher value on freedom than equality when the two conflict. However, conservatives are not above restricting freedom when threatened with loss of *order*. Thus, both groups value freedom, but one is more willing to trade freedom for equality, and the other is more inclined to trade freedom for order.

If you have trouble thinking about these tradeoffs on a single dimension, you are perfectly normal. The liberal-conservative "continuum" presented to respondents is really a two-dimensional space squashed into a straight line.* As a result, many people have difficulty deciding whether they are liberal or conservative, and others confidently choose the same point on the continuum for entirely different reasons. People describe themselves as liberal or conservative because of the symbolic value of the terms as much as for what they know about ideology.[31]

Studies of the public's ideological orientations find that two value-laden themes run through people's minds when they are asked to describe liberals and conservatives. One theme associates liberals with symbols of change and conservatives with preservation of traditional values. This theme corresponds to a separation of liberals and conservatives on the exercise of freedom and the maintenance of order.[32]

The other theme that differentiates liberals and conservatives is equality. The clash between freedom and equality underlay President Franklin D. Roosevelt's New Deal economic policies (social security, minimum wage legislation, farm price supports) in the 1930s. These policies carved out a more "interventionist" role for the government in Washington. Government intervention in the economy served to distinguish liberals from conservatives for decades afterward.[33] Attitudes toward government interventionism still underlie contemporary opinions of domestic policies.[34] Conservatives favor less government intervention and more individual freedom in economic activities. Liberals support intervention to promote their ideas of economic justice.

Ideological Types in the United States

Our ideological typology from Chapter 1, reproduced in Figure 5.7, incorporates these two themes. It classifies people as *liberals* if they favor equality over freedom but freedom over order. *Conservatives* favor the reverse set of values. *Libertarians* favor freedom over both equality and order — the opposite of *populists*. We can place respondents into these categories by cross-tabulating their answers to the two questions about equality and order. As shown in Figure 5.7, people's responses to these two questions show virtually no correlation, which clearly indicates that people do not decide about government activity according to a one-dimensional ideological standard.† Figure 5.7 can also be used to classify the sample according to the two dimensions in our ideological typology. There is substantial room for error in using only two issues to classify people in an ideological framework. Nevertheless, if the typology is worthwhile, the results should be meaningful, and they are.

---

*Milton Rokeach, *The Nature of Human Values* (New York: Free Press, 1973), also proposes a two-value model of political ideology grounded in the terminal values of freedom and equality (see especially Chapter 6). Rokeach's research found that positive and negative references to these two values permeated the writings of socialists, communists, fascists, and conservatives and clearly differentiated the four bodies of writing from one another (pp. 173–174). However, Rokeach built his two-dimensional model around only these two values and did not deal with freedom versus order.

†For the statistically minded, the product-moment correlation for the fourfold table is −.09.

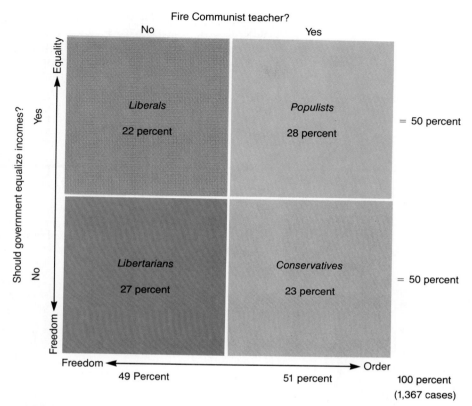

Respondents Classified by Ideological Type
Choices between freedom and order and between freedom and equality were represented by two survey questions that asked 1,367 respondents whether a communist should teach in college and whether the government should equalize income differences. People's responses to the questions showed no correlation, demonstrating that these value choices cannot be explained by a simple liberal-conservative continuum. Instead, their responses conform to four different ideological types.

Figure 5.7

The same 1,367 respondents in the 1984 sample in Figure 5.5 divided almost evenly among the four ideologies, with populists and libertarians only slightly more prevalent than conservatives and liberals. Although liberals are the smallest group, they still account for almost one-quarter of the public. These results are similar to findings for earlier years by other researchers who conducted more exhaustive analyses involving more survey questions. Using the same basic typology, these scholars classified substantial portions of their respondents in each ideological category in 1980.[35] It remains to be seen how these four categories relate to the conventional liberal-conservative continuum—if at all.

Figure 5.8 reports the respondents' self-placement as liberals or conservatives for each of our four ideological types. (The liberal-conservative continuum was reduced to three categories to simplify the analysis, and only college-educated respondents are reported to sharpen the findings.) Clearly, our liberals and conservatives—as determined by responses to two questions —were much more likely to describe themselves as liberals and conservatives than were those we classified as libertarians and populists. The populists (even respondents with college education) were unable to agree where they fit on the liberal-conservative continuum, and the libertarians showed nearly as much disagreement.

Figure 5.8

Ideological Self-Placement by Ideological Type
Respondents' attitudes toward government action to promote order and equality do not conform to the conventional liberal-conservative continuum. When college-educated respondents are divided into four ideological types, their patterns of self-placement confirm the typology. Those classified as liberals and conservatives in our typology are more likely to describe themselves as such. Populists and libertarians have more difficulty classifying themselves as either liberal or conservative.

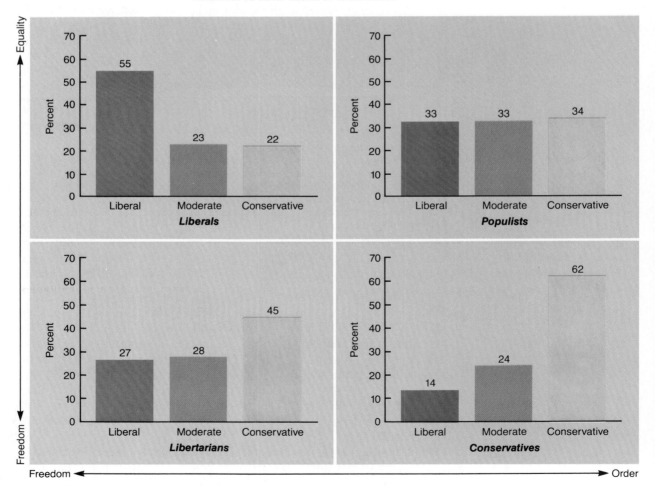

Obviously, most Americans' opinions do *not* fit a one-dimensional lib-eral-conservative continuum. If that continuum is expanded along another dimension, respondents can be analyzed more meaningfully.* Most Ameri-cans do not express opinions that are consistently liberal or conservative. In fact, most Americans hold combinations of opinions about the scope of gov-ernment action that are either populist or libertarian. However, there are important differences in ideological tendencies among the social groups in Figure 5.5.

Populists are prominent among minorities and others with low education and low income. These groups tend to look favorably on the benefits of government in general. *Libertarians* are concentrated among respondents with high education, with high income, from British stock, who live in the West, and who are not religious. These groups tend to be suspicious of government interference in their lives. *Conservatives* are found mainly in the South, and *liberals* are concentrated in the Northeast.

This more refined analysis of political ideology shows that there are fewer conservatives and liberals in the population than ideological self-placement would seem to indicate. Some of those who describe themselves as liberals or conservatives are more accurately described as populists or libertarians, but they are forced to make a choice along only one dimension. Moreover, many people who opt for the middle category, "moderate," are really pop-ulists or libertarians. But our analysis also indicates that many respondents who classify themselves as liberals and conservatives do conform to our ty-pology. Therefore, there is value in the liberal-conservative classification, as long as one understands its limitations.

THE PROCESS OF FORMING POLITICAL OPINIONS

Thus far, we have learned that people acquire their values through the so-cialization process and that different social groups develop different sets of political values. We have also learned that some people, but only a minority, think about politics ideologically, holding a consistent set of political attitudes and beliefs. However, we have not really discussed how people form opinions on any particular issue. In particular, how do those who are *not* ideologues —in other words, most citizens—form political opinions? We shall consider four factors: self-interest, political information, political leadership, and opin-ion schemas.

Self-Interest

Everyone is aware of the **self-interest principle,** which states that peo-ple prefer choices that benefit them personally. This principle plays an ob-vious role in opinion formation on government economic policies. Taxpayers

---

*The same conclusion was reached in a major study of British voting behavior. See Hilde T. Himmelweit et al., *How Voters Decide* (New York: Academic Press, 1981), pp. 138–141.

should prefer low taxes to high taxes; farmers should think more highly of candidates who promise them more support than of those who promise them less; and so on. The self-interest principle also operates, but less clearly, for some government policies outside of economics. Members of minority groups tend to see more personal advantage in government policies that promote social equality than do members of majority groups; teen-age males are more likely to oppose compulsory military service than are older people of either sex; and so on.

For many government policies, however, the self-interest principle plays little or no role, because the policies directly affect relatively few citizens. Outlawing of prostitution is one example; another is government policy on abortion. When such moral issues are involved in government policy, people form opinions based on their underlying values. When moral issues are not raised and when personal benefits are not involved, many people have trouble in relating to the question and thus in forming an opinion. This tends to be true of the whole subject of foreign policy, which few people interpret in terms of personal benefits. On such issues, many people have no opinion, or their opinions are not firmly held and are apt to change quite easily, given almost any new information.

Political Information

The United States today features compulsory education as far as high school and a relatively high literacy rate. It boasts an unparalleled network of colleges and universities entered by one-third of all high school graduates. Its citizens can obtain information from a variety of daily and weekly news publications. They can keep abreast of national and international affairs through nightly television news, which brings live coverage of world events via satellite from virtually anywhere in the world. Yet the average American citizen displays an astonishing lack of political knowledge.

In a 1978 survey, for example, only about half the electorate knew that their state was represented by two senators; only 30 percent knew that the term for a U.S. representative was two years; and less than one-quarter knew which two nations (the United States and the Soviet Union) were involved in the Strategic Arms Limitation Treaty (SALT) at the time it was being negotiated.[36] Citizens' knowledge of politics just before an election is no more impressive. Only 32 percent knew the names of their candidates for Congress in 1982, and barely 50 percent knew the names of their candidates for the Senate.[37]

But Americans do not let political ignorance stop them from expressing their opinions. They readily offer opinions on issues ranging from capital punishment to nuclear power to government handling of the economy. One consequence of having little information is shallow opinions that can easily change when new information becomes available. The result is a high degree of instability in public opinion poll results, depending on the way questions are worded and the occurrence of events that bear on the issue. One important type of event is a speech by a political figure who endorses (or opposes) the issue.

Political Leadership

Public opinion on specific issues is often shaped — and sometimes even *created* — by political leaders. A good example is public opinion on the Strategic Defense Initiative (SDI), the space-based weapons system that is often called "Star Wars." On March 23, 1983, President Ronald Reagan surprised the nation by announcing plans for a multibillion-dollar program to build a network of space satellites that could shoot down incoming enemy missiles using a new nuclear X-ray laser. SDI proved to be a highly controversial weapons system. The scientific community was deeply divided over whether it would be effective — or could even be built. The diplomatic community was divided over whether it would increase or reduce the chances of a world war. The economic community was divided over whether the nation could afford the vast expenditures SDI would require.

Nevertheless, 67 percent of the American people interviewed in the first month after President Reagan announced his program thought that the United States should try to develop the weapons system. Only 25 percent opposed the plan from the beginning, and a scant 8 percent had no opinion.[38] By August 1984, public support had slipped to 54 percent, and those with no opinion had increased to 12 percent. By July 1985, public support had dropped to 43 percent, and the number with no opinion had grown to 22 percent.[39]

Clearly, the initial showing of public opinion for the SDI proposal represented a flush of popular support for the president's foreign policy initiative without much understanding of its costs and consequences. As more information became available about the program over the next two years, it not only encountered more opposition, but, ironically, more people lacked an opinion about it. Of those who had an opinion, Republican voters favored the space-based system more than Democratic voters. Many supporters of SDI undoubtedly based their opinions on their favorable views of President Reagan — and many opposed it on contrary grounds. Others formed their opinions according to their faith in technology, their views of the Soviet threat, or other beliefs they held at the time.

Opinion Schemas

We have learned that only a minority of the population, about one person in five, can be classified as ideologues (those who regularly think about politics in ideological terms). Still, people do not come to new political issues with blank minds. Whether or not people approach politics with full-blown ideologies, they all interpret political issues in terms of some pre-existing mental structure.

Psychologists refer to the packet of pre-existing beliefs that people apply to specific issues as an **opinion schema** — a network of organized knowledge and beliefs that guides the processing of political information and that is focused on a particular subject.[40] An example of an opinion schema about Ronald Reagan is given in Figure 5.9, which represents part of a view that might be held by a conservative. Even this partial schema suggests the wide range of potential attitudes and beliefs concerning the president's views and policies on religion, communism, the budget, and so on. Moreover, a person's schema about Reagan will change as new information is acquired. A conservative acting on this opinion schema would be expected to support Reagan's SDI weapon system, which would in turn be incorporated into a revised opinion schema.

The schema concept provides a sharper tool for analyzing public opinion than the blunter concept of ideology. Opinion schemas relevant to politics may pertain to any political figure and to any subject — race, economics, foreign affairs, or farming, for example. Nevertheless, the more encompassing concept of ideology is hard to escape. Researchers have found that people tend to organize their personal schemas within a hierarchy of opinion that parallels broader ideological categories. A liberal's opinion schema about Reagan

Figure 5.9 ━━━

Hypothetical Opinion Schema About Ronald Reagan
People express opinions on issues, persons, or events according to pre-existing attitudes and beliefs that they associate with the question being asked. Psychologists sometimes refer to the network of attitudes, beliefs, and their relationships as an opinion schema. *Below is a hypothetical opinion schema that might be associated with Ronald Reagan in the memory of a conservative who voted for Reagan in the 1980 and 1984 presidential elections. (Source: From ''A Primer of Information-Processing Theory for the Political Scientist,'' by Reid Hastie, 1986, in Richard R. Lau and David O. Sears (eds.),* Political Cognition, *p. 32. Copyright 1986 by Lawrence Erlbaum Associates. Reprinted by permission.)*

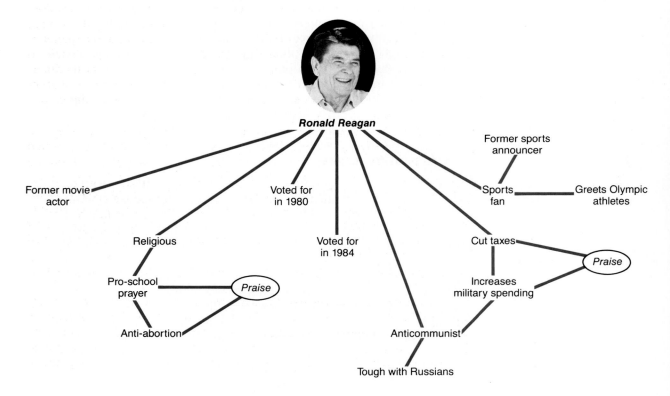

may not differ from a conservative's in the facts it contains, but it will differ considerably in its evaluation of those facts. In a liberal's schema, for example, anger might replace a conservative's praise for Reagan's stance against abortion. The main value of schemas for understanding how opinions are formed is that they remind us that opinion questions trigger many different images, linkages, and evaluations in the mind of each respondent. Given the complexity of factors in individual opinion schemas, it is surprising that researchers find as many strong correlations as they do among individuals' social backgrounds, general values, and specific opinions.

SUMMARY

Public opinion does not rule in America. On most issues, it merely sets general boundaries for government policy. Public opinion in America would not tolerate flogging criminals as a punishment for crime, but most Americans insist on death as the ultimate penalty for murderers. The shape of the distribution of opinion (normal, skewed, or bimodal) indicates how sharply the public is divided, with bimodal distributions harboring the greatest potential for political conflict. The stability of a distribution over time indicates how settled people are in their opinions. Because most Americans' ideological opinions are normally distributed around the "moderate" category and have been so for decades, government policies can vary from left to right over time without provoking severe political conflict.

People form their values through the process of political socialization. The most important socialization agents in early learning are family, school, community, and peers. Members of the same social group tend to experience similar socialization processes and thus to adopt similar values. People in different social groups, who hold different values, often express vastly different opinions. Differences in education, race, and religiosity produce sharper divisions of opinion today on questions of order and equality than differences in income, region, national ethnicity, and type of religion.

Although most people do not conceptualize politics in ideological terms, they readily classify themselves along a liberal-conservative continuum when asked to do so by pollsters. Many respondents—especially those without a college education—choose the middle category, "moderate," which seems to be a safe choice. Others classify themselves as liberals or conservatives for vague or contradictory reasons. Our two-dimensional framework for analyzing ideology according to the values of order and equality produces four ideological types: liberals, conservatives, libertarians, and populists. Classified according to our typology, libertarians and populists have trouble placing themselves on a liberal-conservative continuum; our liberals and conservatives do not.

According to the survey questions that we used to establish our typology, the four ideological types are roughly equal in size. A slight plurality of respondents are populists, wanting more government action to promote both order and equality. An almost equal number are libertarians, opposing government action for either purpose. Conservatives, who want the government to impose order but not equality, are in third place by a small amount. Liberals, who favor equality but not order, are the smallest group but still sizable at 22 percent.

In addition to ideological orientation, many other factors enter the process of forming political opinions. When individuals stand to benefit or to suffer from proposed government policies, they usually base their opinions on self-interest. When citizens lack information on which to base their opinions, they usually respond anyway, which leads to substantial fluctuations in poll results, depending on question wording and intervening events. In the absence of information, respondents are particularly susceptible to cues of support or opposition from political leaders. The various factors that impinge on the process of forming political opinions can be mapped out within an opinion schema, which is a network of beliefs and attitudes about a particular topic. The schema imagery helps us visualize how complex the process of forming opinions is. Nevertheless, the process is not completely idiosyncratic. People tend to organize their schemas according to broader ideological categories.

Which model of democracy, the majoritarian or the pluralist, is correct in its assumptions about public opinion? Sometimes the public shows clear and settled opinions on government policy, conforming to the majoritarian model. However, public opinion often is not firmly grounded in knowledge, and ideological biases often underlie public opinion. Moreover, politically powerful groups often divide on what they want government to do. This lack of consensus leaves politicians with a great deal of latitude in enacting specific policies, a finding that conforms to the pluralist model. Exactly how much latitude politicians have depends on how much the public actually participates in politics beyond registering opinions with pollsters. We turn to that question in Chapter 6.

Key Terms

public opinion	structuring principle
normal distribution	"old" ethnicity
skewed distribution	"new" ethnicity
bimodal distribution	socioeconomic status
stable distribution	ideologue
political socialization	self-interest principle
primacy principle	opinion schema

Selected Readings

Abramson, Paul R. *Political Attitudes in America: Formation and Change*. San Francisco: W. H. Freeman, 1983. Especially strong on how attitudes are studied and on continuity and changes of attitudes over time.

Maddox, William S., and Stuart A. Lilie. *Beyond Liberal and Conservative: Reassessing the Political Spectrum*. Washington, D.C.: Cato Institute, 1984. Uses an ideological typology similar to that in this chapter to analyze surveys in presidential elections from 1952 through 1980.

Manheim, Jarol B. *The Politics Within: A Primer in Political Attitudes and Behavior*. 2nd ed. New York: Longman, 1982. Focuses on the sociological and psychological process of opinion formation, presenting sophisticated arguments very clearly.

Miller, Warren E.; Arthur H. Miller; and Edward J. Schneider. *American National Election Studies Data Sourcebook, 1952–1978*. Cambridge, Mass.: Harvard University Press, 1980. A rich source of tables and graphs containing data from studies of voters in national elections from 1952 through 1978.

Public Opinion. A bimonthly magazine published by the American Enterprise Institute in Washington, D.C. The *best* monthly publication on contemporary public opinion in America.

Yeric, Jerry L., and John R. Todd. *Public Opinion: The Visible Politics*. Itasca, Ill.: F. E. Peacock, 1983. A standard text that pays special attention to the relationship between public opinion and government policy.

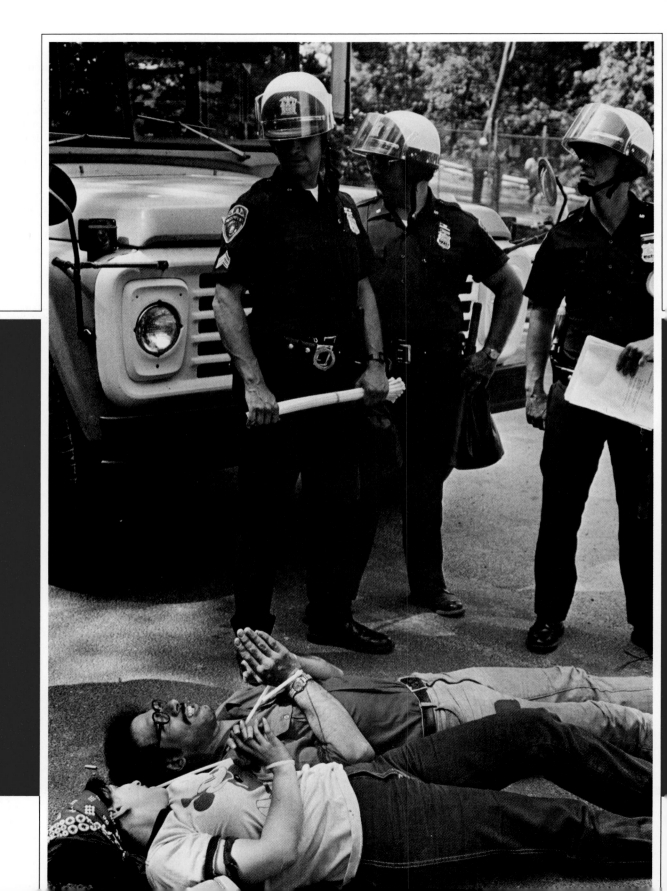

6

Participation and Elections

M ayor Richard J. Daley vowed, "Law and order will be maintained." Chicago was preparing to host the 1968 Democratic National Convention, and Daley had reason to be concerned. A variety of youthful antiwar protesters—ranging from hardcore revolutionaries to neatly dressed supporters of peace candidate Eugene McCarthy—planned to demonstrate against the Vietnam War at the convention. To enforce his vow, Daley put Chicago's 11,900-member police force on twelve-hour shifts. He also called up more than 5,000 Illinois National Guard troops and arranged for 6,500 federal troops to be flown in as reserves. In all, he had more than 23,000 law enforcement officers available to deal with the 8,000 to 10,000 demonstrators who actually showed up for the convention in late August.[1]

Skirmishes between the protesters and the police, the first line of Mayor Daley's defense, began before the convention formally opened. Daley had refused to allow the protesters to sleep on the grass in 1,200-acre Lincoln Park, far from the convention site. The dissident youths, most of them in their teens and twenties, tried to stay in the park after the 11:00 P.M. curfew but were easily driven out the first night. The clashes between the demonstrators and the police intensified on subsequent nights, and the National Guard troops were soon called in. As the convention began, the battleground shifted to Grant Park, just in front of the Conrad Hilton Hotel, where many delegates were staying. On the final night of the convention, a crowd estimated at three thousand taunted the police with cries of "Pig!" and fouler names and threw bricks and bottles. The police responded with tear gas and drawn nightsticks.

The orgy of beatings that followed was closely covered by the mass media. One eyewitness reporter wrote, "The sound of nightsticks smashing into skulls resounded through the park, mixed with shrieks and screams. 'Oh, no!' 'Oh, my God!' 'No, no, no!' " The reporter quoted a policeman: "If they'd gotten beaten like this when they were kids, they wouldn't be out here starting riots."[2] The police flailed at everyone in sight, injuring at least seventeen newsmen in that one night. During the week, more than 700 civilians and 83 police were injured. Of the 653 people arrested, only 91 were thirty years of age or older.[3]

Watching the conflict from their living rooms, a nationwide television audience heard horrified commentators criticizing the police for using excessive force on the young protesters. The public thought otherwise. People flooded the networks with mail, berating the television reporters and praising the police. A national poll taken two months later found that 75 percent of respondents with opinions on the riot thought that the police had used the right amount of force or should have used even more.[4]

As we learned in Chapter 5, about half the population chose order over freedom on the issue of allowing a communist to teach in college. On the subject of the Vietnam War, most of the public rejected freedom of organized protest and approved massive force to prevent demonstrators from disturbing the orderly conduct of the Democratic convention. Perhaps the public was simply fed up with the wave of protests against the war, the draft, capitalism, and social inequalities that characterized student activism in the 1960s.

Today's young people do not seem to engage in political protest as readily or as intently. The relatively few students who demonstrated in 1986 against college investments in South Africa met with only limited success. At Dartmouth College, a few conservative students even tore down the shantytown that other students had built to protest Dartmouth's South African investments. What has happened during the last two decades to alter the political behavior patterns of American youth? Why are Americans of all ages now so politically apathetic? Indeed, *are* Americans today really apathetic compared with those of other times and with citizens of other countries?

This chapter seeks to answer these and other important questions concerning popular participation in government. Whereas most people think of political participation primarily in terms of voting, other types of participation are sometimes more effective. The chapter begins by explaining different views of the role of participation in democratic government, distinguishing between conventional and unconventional participation. Then it evaluates the nature and extent of both types of participation in American politics. Next, the expansion of voting rights and voting in elections are studied as the major mechanism for mass participation in politics. Finally, the various forms of political participation are evaluated for the extent to which they serve the values of freedom, order, and equality or fit the majoritarian and pluralist models of democracy.

DEMOCRACY AND POLITICAL PARTICIPATION

"Government ought to be run by the people." That is the democratic ideal in a nutshell. But how much citizen participation, and what kind, is necessary for democratic government? Neither political theorists nor politicians, neither idealists nor realists, can agree on the answer. Champions of direct democracy believe that, if citizens do not participate *directly* in government affairs, making government decisions among themselves, then they should give up all pretense of democracy. More practical observers contend that people can govern indirectly through representatives whom they elect to act on their behalf. Moreover, they maintain that choosing leaders through **elections**—formal procedures for voting to make group decisions—is the only workable approach to democracy in a large, complex nation.[5]

The distinction between direct and indirect democracy appeared in Chapter 2, on theories and models of democracy. Indirect democracy inevitably relies on elections as the major mechanism allowing citizens to participate in government, and voting is central to the majoritarian model of government. But voting in elections is not the only means of political participation. In fact, the pluralist model of democracy relies less on voting and more on alternative modes of participation.

Citizen participation in elections is a necessary but not a sufficient condition for democratic government. Experience with authoritarian governments shows that the mere existence of elections does not guarantee the existence of democracy. The Soviet Union regularly holds elections in which more than 90 percent of the electorate turns out to vote, but the Soviet Union is not among the world's few democracies listed in Chapter 2 (see Compared With What? 2.1).

Where voting is the only form of political participation, there is no democracy. Both the majoritarian and the pluralist models of democracy assume that citizens engage in other forms of political behavior. For example, they expect citizens to meet to discuss politics, to form interest groups, to contact public officials, to campaign for political parties, to run for office, and even to protest government decisions.

Political participation can best be defined as ''those actions of private citizens by which they seek to influence or to support government and politics.''[6] This definition embraces both conventional and unconventional forms of political participation. In plain language, ''conventional'' behavior is behavior that is acceptable to the dominant culture in a given situation. Wearing a swimsuit at the beach is conventional; wearing one at a formal dance is not.

As is the case with all social analysis, some difficulties may arise in deciding whether particular political acts are conventional or unconventional. Nevertheless, the following distinction is useful in analyzing political participation:

Unconventional Political Participation

In August 1968, thousands of youthful antiwar protesters gathered in Chicago, where the Democrats were holding their national convention. Protests against the war had already forced President Lyndon Johnson not to seek re-election. Mayor Richard Daley vowed that the protesters would not disturb the convention's impending nomination of Hubert Humphrey, Johnson's vice president. Daley's police kept the youths from demonstrating at the convention, but the resulting violence did not help Humphrey, who lost to Richard Nixon in an extremely close election.

- ■ **Conventional participation** — Relatively routine behavior that uses the institutional channels of representative government, especially elections.
- ■ **Unconventional participation** — Relatively uncommon behavior that challenges or defies government channels and thus is personally stressful to participants and their opponents.

Voting and writing letters to public officials are examples of conventional political participation; staging sit-down strikes in public buildings and chanting slogans outside officials' windows are examples of unconventional participation. Unconventional participation makes the adrenalin flow or makes one fear for personal safety because he or she is doing something that is not approved by the dominant culture and thus is acting against the established order. Despite the importance of electoral and other forms of conventional participation to democratic government, the unconventional modes of participation — which sometimes lead to violent confrontations — are also important and need to be considered in discussing political participation in the United States. Our plan is to begin with unconventional modes of participation and to work toward the most visible form of conventional participation: voting in elections.

Conventional Political Participation

In the 1980s Republican Congressman Jack Kemp from New York addresses an orderly, attentive, neatly dressed group of Young Republicans in Washington, D.C. Today's youth are less inclined to engage in organized political protests and more inclined to participate in politics in conventional ways. It is hard to imagine such a well-groomed group of college students respectfully listening to a congressman in the turbulent 1960s.

UNCONVENTIONAL PARTICIPATION

On Sunday, March 7, 1965, a group of some six hundred people attempted to march fifty miles from Selma, Alabama, to the state capital at Montgomery. The marchers were demonstrating in favor of voting rights for blacks. (At the time, Selma had fewer than five hundred black voters registered, out of fifteen thousand who were eligible.[7]) Alabama Governor George Wallace declared the march illegal and sent state troopers to block its way. The two groups met at the Pettus Bridge over the Alabama River at the edge of the city of Selma. The marchers were beaten and trampled by troopers and deputy sheriffs — some on horseback — using clubs, bullwhips, and tear gas. The day became known as "Bloody Sunday."

The march from Selma represented unconventional participation in politics. Marching fifty miles in a political protest is certainly uncommon; moreover, the march challenged the existing institutions, which prevented blacks from voting. From the beginning, the marchers knew that they would be in a stressful situation and that they would certainly be taunted by whites along the way. However, the blacks had been prevented from engaging in conventional behavior — voting in elections — for many decades, and they chose this unconventional method of dramatizing their cause.

Their march ended in violence because Wallace would not allow even this peaceful, albeit unusual, mode of expression. Unlike the antiwar protesters at the 1968 Democratic convention, the civil rights marchers themselves posed no threat of violence. Athough the brutal police response in Selma may have satisfied Wallace and other whites for the moment, the brutality also helped the rest of the nation realize the depth of the civil rights problem in the South. Unconventional participation is stressful and occasionally violent, but it is sometimes worth the risk.

Support for Unconventional Participation

Unconventional political participation has a long history in the United States. The Boston Tea Party in 1773, in which American colonists dumped a cargo of British tea into Boston Harbor, was only the first in a long line of violent protests against British rule, which led to rebellion and revolution. Nevertheless, we know less about unconventional political participation than about conventional participation. This is due to two main reasons. First, data on conventional means are easier to collect and thus more frequently studied. Second, political scientists are biased toward "institutionalized," or conventional, politics. In fact, some basic works on political participation explicitly exclude behavior that is "outside the system."[8] However, the waves of political protest that swept across Western Europe in the 1960s prompted researchers to conduct studies of political action in five nations, including the United States.[9]

The researchers asked people whether they had engaged in or approved of ten types of political participation outside of the electoral process. Responses for the United States are presented in Figure 6.1. Of the ten activities, only signing petitions was clearly regarded as conventional, in the sense that the behavior is nearly universally approved and widely practiced. Two of

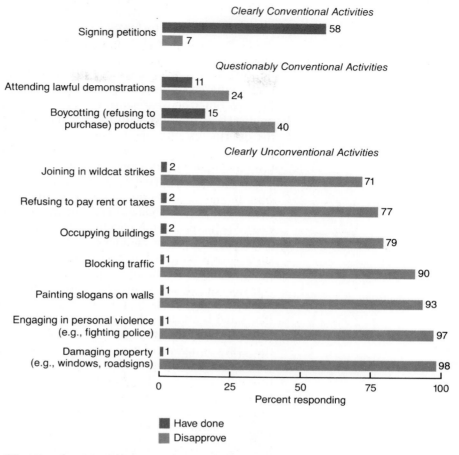

What People Regard as Unconventional Political Behavior
A survey of Americans asked whether they approved or disapproved of ten different forms of participation outside of the electoral process. The respondents disapproved of most of the ten forms, often overwhelmingly. Signing petitions is one form that was rarely disapproved and also widely done. But even attending lawful demonstrations (a right guaranteed in the Constitution) was disapproved by nearly 25 percent of the respondents and rarely practiced. Boycotting products was even more objectionable but more widely practiced. Attending demonstrations and boycotting products are only marginally conventional. The other seven forms are clearly unconventional. (Source: Samuel H. Barnes and Max Kaase, eds., Political Action. *Beverly Hills, Calif.: SAGE Publications, 1979, p. 545.)*

Figure 6.1 ▬▬▬

the other forms of behavior were doubtful, and the others were clearly unconventional.

Nearly one-quarter of the respondents disapproved of even "lawful demonstrations," and only one out of ten had ever participated in a lawful demonstration. What is and is not lawful is hard to determine, however. The antiwar demonstrators in Chicago had a constitutional right to assemble peaceably and to protest the war, but they did violate the law by trying to sleep in the park. The civil rights marchers also technically violated Governor

Wallace's decree. Because even lawful demonstrations are disapproved of by many and practiced by few, it might be argued that all demonstrations border on the unconventional. The same reasoning might apply to boycotting products — for example, refusing to buy lettuce or grapes picked by nonunion farm workers. Lawful demonstrations and boycotts are problem cases in deciding what is and is not conventional political participation.

The other acts in Figure 6.1 are clearly unconventional. In fact, when political acts interfere with daily living (such as blocking traffic) or involve the destruction of property (painting slogans) and physical violence, disapproval is nearly universal. No wonder the American public condemned the protesters and not the police at the 1968 Democratic convention.

Why this overwhelming disapproval of most unconventional political action? The reason is not simply that Americans see such tactics as failing in their purpose. Respondents in the survey were also asked whether they thought each type of action was effective or ineffective. Most did feel that unconventional political actions are ineffective, but there were more people who thought such actions were effective than who personally approved of them.[10] What, then, accounts for the rejection of unconventional behavior?

The researchers on the project suggested the following explanation. Non-institutionalized political protest has been used mainly by **outgroups** — groups that have been denied access to channels of political influence, which are controlled by the **ingroup.** For example, Mayor Daley denied permission for the Chicago antiwar demonstrators to sleep in the park, although granting permission could have averted the initial clashes. When government authorities confront and resist outgroups, unconventional political action tends to erupt in violence as the authorities use force to impose order. The ingroup thus sees the direct action of opposed groups as violent and its own actions as nonviolent.[11] Mayor Daley, for instance, justified his police force's behavior by describing the antiwar protesters as "terrorists."

Effectiveness of Unconventional Participation

Does unconventional participation ever work, especially when it provokes violence? Yes. Antiwar protesters discouraged President Lyndon Johnson from seeking re-election, and they heightened public concern over the United States' participation in the Vietnam War. American college students who disrupted campuses in the late 1960s and early 1970s helped end the military draft in 1973, and — as we shall study more closely later — they were surprised by speedy passage of the Twenty-Sixth Amendment, which lowered the voting age to 18. Notable successes also resulted from the unconventional politics of the civil rights movement. Dr. Martin Luther King, Jr., relied on "direct action" in leading the 1957 Montgomery bus boycott (sparked by Rosa Parks's refusal to surrender her seat to a white man; see Chapter 1, page 6). **Direct action** involved assembling crowds to confront businesses and local governments and to demand equal treatment in public accommodations and government. The civil rights movement involved over a thousand such newsworthy demonstrations nationwide — 387 in 1965 alone.[12] As with

Charming 1 bedrm; good loc.; low rent; blacks only
Students at numerous college campuses in 1986 protested college investments in South Africa because of its policy of apartheid (radical separation of races). One form of peaceful protest involved building and sometimes living in shacks that represented the appalling shantytowns in which many South African blacks are forced to live. This one stood on the green at Dartmouth College but was torn down one night by conservative students who objected to its presence.

the march in Selma, many of these protests provoked violent confrontations between whites and blacks.

Denied opportunities for conventional political participation, the civil rights movement used unconventional politics to pressure Congress to pass a series of civil rights laws in 1957, 1960, 1964, 1968 — each one in some way extending federal protection against discrimination by reason of race, color, religion, or national origin. (The 1964 act also prohibited discrimination in employment on the basis of sex.)

In addition, the Voting Rights Act of 1965 put state electoral procedures under federal supervision, leading to increased registration of black voters and substantially higher rates of black voter turnout — especially in the South, where much of the violence occurred. Black protest activity (both violent and nonviolent) has also been credited with increased welfare support for blacks in the South.[13] Finally, we know that social change can occur, even when it is violently opposed at first. Twenty years after law enforcement officers beat civil rights marchers in Selma, state troopers and sheriff's deputies gave a protective escort to those who marched to commemorate Bloody Sunday (see Feature 6.1).

Although direct political action and the politics of confrontation sometimes work, it takes a special kind of commitment and willingness to sacrifice life and property to behave so unconventionally. Some studies show that direct political action appeals most to those who both (1) *distrust* the political

Feature 6.1

Selma, Alabama, Twenty Years Later

On March 7, 1965, civil rights marchers were beaten by Alabama state troopers and local law enforcement officers. The day became known as "Bloody Sunday." Twenty years later, on March 3, 1985, state troopers gave a protective escort to those who marched to commemorate Bloody Sunday. Some things do change.

SELMA, ALA., March 3 — More than 2,500 people paraded through the streets of this river city today, retracing the route of a group whose protest march 20 years ago marked a turning point in the movement for black voting rights in the South.

The demonstration today, led by Coretta Scott King and the Rev. Jesse Jackson, commemorated what is remembered as Bloody Sunday, when 600 civil rights protesters were beaten and routed by state troopers and mounted sheriff's deputies blocking their route toward Montgomery over the Edmund Pettus Bridge.

"When I think about Selma I think about blacks not being able to drink water when we were thirsty," said Mr. Jackson, speaking outside the Brown Chapel African Methodist Episcopal Church, where the marchers gathered 20 years ago. "Whenever our spirits are down and our hearts are heavy, we can always return to this landmark and remember how far we've come."

The violent confrontation on the bridge 20 years ago was captured by television news cameras and aired across the nation, provoking widespread protest and outrage and leading, later in 1965, to passage by Congress of the Voting Rights Act.

As one measure of the kinds of change that have occurred in central Alabama over the last 20 years, Joe T. Smitherman, the white man who is Mayor of Selma today as he was in 1965, was applauded as he presented keys to the city to the Rev. Mr. Jackson and another black leader, the Rev. Joseph E. Lowery, president of the Southern Christian Leadership Conference. . . .

Source: William E. Schmidt, "Selma Marchers Mark 1965 Clash," *New York Times*, March 4, 1985.

system and (2) have a strong sense of political *efficacy* — the feeling that they can do something to affect political decisions.[14] Whether or not this combination of attitudes will produce unconventional, system-challenging behavior depends on the extent of organized group activity.[15] The civil rights movement featured many such groups: the Southern Christian Leadership Conference (SCLC) of Martin Luther King, Jr.; the Congress of Racial Equality (CORE), founded by James Farmer; and the Student Non-Violent Coordinating Committee (SNCC), led by Stokely Carmichael — to mention a few.

The occurrence of unconventional behavior also depends on the extent to which individuals develop a *group consciousness* — identification with the group and awareness of its position in society, its objectives, and its intended course of action.[16] These factors were present among blacks and youth in the mid-1960s and are present today among blacks and women. Indeed, some authors contend that black consciousness has heightened the sense of system distrust and individual efficacy, producing more participation of different types by poor blacks than by poor whites.[17] Women's groups, such as the National Organization of Women (NOW), have also served to heighten women's consciousness, contributing to increased women's participation in politics — in both conventional and unconventional ways.

Unconventional Participation in America

Compared with citizens in the Netherlands, Britain, Germany, and Austria, Americans claim to "have done" as much or *more* in the way of unconventional behavior. Researchers have found that Americans were more likely to have participated in lawful demonstrations and were far more likely to have boycotted products of businesses for political reasons. Moreover, Americans were equally likely to have engaged in rent strikes, blocked traffic, painted political slogans, occupied buildings, damaged property, and fought with political opponents.[18] Contrary to the popular view that Americans are apathetic about politics, studies suggest that they are more likely to engage in political protests of various sorts than citizens in other democratic countries.

One might criticize these findings because the data were collected in 1974, following the civil rights activities of the 1960s and the student protests against the Vietnam War. However, protest activity was also prevalent at that time across western Europe. The national patterns of unconventional participation do not seem to be peculiar to those times.

Is there something wrong with our political system if so many Americans engage in unconventional methods of political participation? To answer this question, we must first learn how much Americans use conventional methods of participation.

CONVENTIONAL PARTICIPATION

A practical test of the democratic nature of any government is whether citizens can affect its policies by acting through its institutions — such as meeting with public officials, supporting candidates, and voting in elections. If people *must* operate outside governmental institutions in order to affect policies — as the civil rights movement had to do in the South — then the system is not democratic. Citizens should not have to risk life and property to participate in politics, and they should not have to take direct action to force their views to be heard within government. The objective of democratic institutions is to make political participation *conventional* — to ensure that ordinary citizens can engage in relatively routine, nonthreatening behavior to cause government to heed their opinions, interests, and needs.

Sometimes citizens in a democracy dramatize their positions by appearing in groups at a state legislature or a city council meeting, as when citizens protest a tax increase. Ordinarily, such demonstrations constitute conventional participation, for the participants do not risk their personal safety in demonstrating. If they have to worry about being beaten by police, the gov-

No Nukes Is Good Nukes
The 1979 accident leading to a near-meltdown at Pennsylvania's Three-Mile Island (TMI) nuclear electric power plant resulted in many demonstrations in opposition to nuclear power. This peaceful demonstration took place outside the Pennsylvania statehouse. Citizen concern over a nuclear tragedy led to a virtual standstill of nuclear power plant construction in the United States, even before the explosion and far more serious release of radioactivity at the Chernobyl nuclear plant in the Soviet Union in 1986.

ernment is certainly not democratic. Even in a democracy, however, violence can erupt between opposing groups demonstrating in a political setting—as between groups that stand for and against the legalization of abortion. The circumstances often determine whether organized protest is or is not conventional. In general, the less the threat to the participants, the more conventional organized protest is as an act of participation.

Several types of participation are conventional except in extreme circumstances. (For example, it would not have been conventional for a black to vote in Selma in the early 1960s). The most visible type of conventional participation is voting to choose candidates. However, we must not rush to study voting too quickly, for it will lead us away from considering less prominent but equally important types of political participation. In fact, these other forms of participation are in many ways even more important than voting, especially in the United States, where voting turnout is extremely low in comparison with that in most other democratic nations. We can divide conventional participation into two categories: actions that show *support* for government policies and those that try to change or *influence* policies.

Supportive Behavior

Supportive behavior includes purely ceremonial acts or other expressions of allegiance to government and country. As stated in Chapter 5, all governments try to cultivate support for the country and its form of government. Most governments use the country's educational system as the primary means of developing such generalized political support.[19] When American children recite the Pledge of Allegiance, they are being socialized into our political system. Although the children do not realize it, they are engaged in a form of supportive participation. When people graduate from school, get a job, acquire a home of their own, or decide to fly the American flag on holidays, they continue this form of political participation, showing support for the country and, by implication, for its political system. Many such ceremonial acts usually require little effort, knowledge, or personal courage — that is, they require little initiative on the part of the citizen. The simple act of turning out to vote is in itself a show of support for the political system.

Some people exercise greater initiative in demonstrating political allegiance by engaging in more "difficult" acts of participation, such as volunteering to serve as election judges in nonpartisan elections or organizing holiday parades. At times, more spirited citizens may allow their patriotism to cross the line into unconventional behavior. For example, they may disrupt the rallies of groups that they perceive as radical or somehow "un-American." Radical groups may threaten the political system with wrenching change, but superpatriots pose their own threat through misguided excesses of allegiance, which deny nonviolent means of dissent to others.

Influencing Behavior

Influencing behavior seeks to modify or even to reverse government policy to serve political interests. Attempts to influence government policy can be subdivided into those that seek *particular benefits* from government and those that have *broad policy objectives*.

Some citizens try to influence government to obtain benefits for themselves, for their immediate families, or for close friends. Two examples, which do not require much initiative, are voting to elect a relative to local office and voting against an increase in school taxes when one's own children have already left school. Serving one's own self-interest through the voting process is certainly acceptable to democratic theory. Each individual has only one vote, and no single voter can wangle particularized benefits from government through voting unless a majority of voters agree.

Political acts that require considerable knowledge and initiative are another story, however. Individuals or small groups who influence government officials to advance their self-interests may benefit without others' knowing about it. Those who quietly obtain particularized benefits from government present a serious challenge to a democracy. Pluralist theory holds that groups ought to be able to make government respond to their special problems and needs. On the other hand, majoritarian theory holds that government should not do what a majority would not want it to do. A majority of citizens might very well *not* want the government to do what any particular person or group seeks—if it imposes costs on them.

What might individual citizens or groups ask of their government, and how might they go about asking? They could ask courts to decide cases in their favor, or they could ask for services to be performed by their local government. We shall consider use of the courts first.

Few people realize that using the court system is a form of political participation. In fact, it is a form of particularized behavior that requires high personal initiative, for citizens are seeking to use the power of the state to serve their particular interests.[20] Although law is a mechanism for social control, it is also a way for citizens to press their rights in a democratic fashion. And because asserting legal rights depends on citizens' willingness and ability to initiate the legal process (knowing the law and being able to afford a lawyer), equality of resources also becomes an important issue.

Citizens may also ask for special services from their local government. Such requests may range from contacting the city forestry department to remove a dead tree in front of one's house to calling the county animal control center to deal with a vicious dog in the area. Studies of such "contacting" behavior as a form of political participation find that it tends not to be related to other forms of political activity but is related to the individual's socioeconomic status. Those of higher status are more likely to contact public officials.[21]

Citizens demand more of local than of national government. Whereas many people value self-reliance and individualism in national politics, most people expect local government to solve a wide range of social problems. A study of residents of Kansas City, Missouri, found that more than 90 percent thought it should be the city's responsibility to provide services in thirteen areas, including providing parks, setting standards for new home construction, demolishing vacant and unsafe buildings, ensuring that property owners clean up trash and weeds, and providing bus service. The researcher noted that "it is difficult to imagine a set of federal government activities about which there would necessarily be any more consensus—defense, environmental controls, and other areas. . . ."[22]

Several points emerge from this review of "particularized" forms of political participation. First, approaching government to serve one's particular interests is consistent with democratic theory, because it encourages input from an active citizenry. Second, particularized contact may be a form of participation unto itself, not necessarily related to other forms of participation, such as voting. Third, such participation tends to be used more by citizens who are advantaged in terms of knowledge and resources. Fourth, particularized participation may serve private interests to the detriment of the majority.

Influencing Broad Policies

We come now to what many scholars usually have in mind when they discuss political participation: activities that influence the selection of government personnel and government policies. This category can also be divided into acts that require little initiative (such as voting) and high initiative (attending political meetings or persuading others how to vote).

Even when it is used to influence policies, voting remains a "low-initiative" activity. "Policy" voting differs from voting to show support or to gain special benefits by its broader impact on the community or the society, rather than on the individual. Obviously, this distinction is not sharp; citizens vote for a number of reasons that mix allegiance, particularized benefits, and policy concerns. In addition to policy voting, many other low-initiative forms of conventional participation—wearing a campaign button, watching party conventions on television, posting a bumper sticker—are also connected with elections. In the next section, we shall focus on elections as a mechanism for participation. For now, we simply note that voting to influence policy can usually be regarded as a low-initiative activity. It actually requires more individual initiative to *register* to vote in the United States than to cast a vote on election day. We shall return to this observation later.

Other types of participation to affect broad policies require high citizen initiative. Running for office requires the most initiative; it is done by such a tiny portion of the public that we shall discuss it in the next chapter, along with campaigning. Many other political activities, such as attending party meetings and working in campaigns, are associated with the electoral process. Others, such as attending legislative hearings and writing letters to Congress, are not. These nonelectoral activities are a form of citizen-initiated contact with government officials, but the contacts are made to obtain governmental benefits for some group of people—for example, farmers, the unemployed, children, or oil producers. In fact, studies of citizen contacts in the United States conclude that about two-thirds deal with broader social issues and only one-third are for private gain.[23]

Citizens try to influence policies at all levels of government—local, state, and national. Congressional hearings are public events, sometimes broadcast over the mass media and occasionally held in various parts of the country. Especially since the end of World War II, the federal government has sought to increase citizen involvement in regulation and legislation by making information on government activities available to interested parties. For example, agencies are required to publish notices of impending regulations in the *Federal Register* and to make documents available to citizens on request without specifying need or purpose.

Conventional Participation in America

You may know someone who has participated in a congressional or administrative hearing. The odds are better, though, that you do not; such participation is a form of high-initiative behavior. It attracts relatively few people—those with high stakes in the outcome of the decision. How often *do* Americans contact government officials and engage in other forms of conventional political participation, compared with citizens in other countries?

The most common political behavior reported in a study of five countries was voting to choose candidates (see Compared With What? 6.1). However, Americans were *less* likely to vote than citizens in the other four countries.

Compared With What? 6.1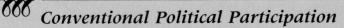

Conventional Political Participation

A cross-national study of political participation found that Americans were more likely than citizens in most other nations to engage in various forms of conventional political behavior—except voting. These findings clearly contradict the notion that Americans are politically apathetic.

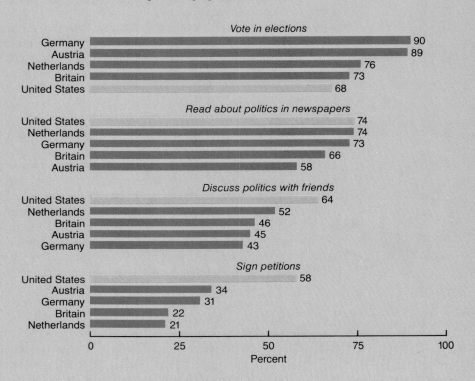

On the other hand, Americans were as likely (or substantially more likely) to engage in all of the other seven forms of conventional political participation —just as they did for the various measures of unconventional participation. Americans are thus more apt to engage in nearly all forms of unconventional *and* conventional political participation—*except* voting.

The researchers noted this oddity and wrote: "If, for example, we concentrate our attention on national elections we will find that the United States is the *least* participatory of our five nations." But looking at the other indicators, they found that "political apathy, by a wide margin, is lowest in the United States. Interestingly, the high levels of overall involvement reflect a rather balanced contribution of both . . . conventional and unconventional politics."[24] Clearly, low voting turnout in the United States constitutes some-

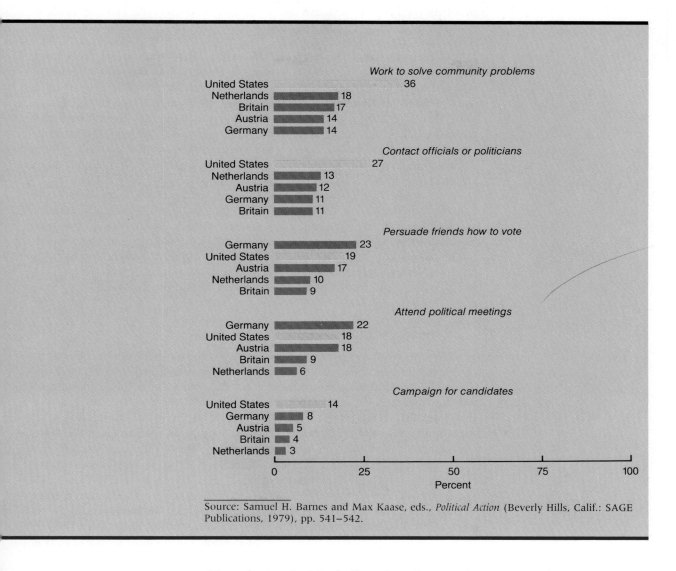

Source: Samuel H. Barnes and Max Kaase, eds., *Political Action* (Beverly Hills, Calif.: SAGE Publications, 1979), pp. 541–542.

thing of a puzzle. We shall work at that puzzle as we next focus on elections and electoral systems.

PARTICIPATING THROUGH ELECTIONS AND VOTING

The heart of democratic government lies in the electoral process. Whether or not a country holds elections and, if so, what kind constitute the critical differences between democratic and nondemocratic regimes.[25] Elections are important to democracy for their potential to institutionalize mass participation in government according to the three normative principles for procedural democracy discussed in Chapter 2. Electoral rules specify (1) *who* is allowed to vote, (2) *how much* each person's vote will count, and (3) *how many* votes are needed to win.

As defined earlier, elections are the institutions — the formal procedures — for making group decisions. **Voting** is the act that individuals perform when they choose among alternatives in an election. Two other terms need to be defined: **suffrage** and the **franchise.** Both mean simply "the right to vote." By formalizing political participation through rules for suffrage and counting ballots, electoral systems allow large masses of people, who individually have little political power, to wield great power. Electoral systems decide collectively who will govern and, in some instances, what government should do.

The simple fact of holding elections is less important than the specific rules and circumstances that govern voting. According to democratic theory's rule of universal participation, everyone should be able to vote. In practice, however, no nation grants universal suffrage. Every country has age requirements for voting, and all countries disqualify some inhabitants on various grounds: lack of citizenship, a criminal record, mental incompetency, and so forth. What is the record of enfranchisement in the United States?

Expansion of Suffrage

The United States was the first country to provide for general elections of representatives through "mass" suffrage, yet the franchise was far from universal. When our Constitution was framed, the idea of full adult suffrage was too radical to be seriously considered, much less adopted. Instead, the Constitution left the issue of enfranchisement to the states, stipulating only that individuals who could vote for "the most numerous Branch of the State Legislature" could also vote for their representatives to the U.S. Congress.

Initially, most states established taxpaying or propertyholding requirements for voting and thus limited political equality. Virginia, for example, required ownership of twenty-five acres of settled land or five hundred acres of unsettled land. The original thirteen states began to lift such requirements after 1800. Expansion of the franchise accelerated after 1815, with the admission of new "western" states (Indiana, Illinois, Alabama) where land was more plentiful and widely owned. By the 1850s, virtually all property and taxpaying requirements had been eliminated in all states, allowing the working class to vote — provided it was male and white. Extending the vote to blacks and women took more time.

Enfranchisement of blacks. The Fifteenth Amendment to the Constitution, adopted in 1870, forbade states to deny the right to vote "on account of race, color, or previous condition of servitude." However, the southern states of the old Confederacy soon evaded that provision by re-establishing restrictive requirements, such as poll taxes and literacy tests, that worked against blacks. Some southern states also cut blacks out of politics through a cunning circumvention of the Fifteenth Amendment. The amendment said nothing about voting rights in private organizations, so blacks were denied the right to vote in the "private" Democratic *primary* elections held to choose the party's candidates at the later general election. Since the Democratic party came to dominate politics in the South, the "white primary" effectively disenfranchised blacks despite the Fifteenth Amendment. Finally, in many areas of the South, blacks were discouraged from voting simply through threats of bodily harm if they tried it.

The extension of full voting rights to blacks came in two phases, separated by twenty years. In 1944 the Supreme Court decided in *Smith* v. *Allwright* that laws preventing blacks from voting in primary elections were unconstitutional, holding that party primaries were part of the continuous process of electing public officials. The Voting Rights Act of 1965, which followed Selma's Bloody Sunday by less than five months, suspended discriminatory voting tests against blacks. The voting rights act also authorized federal registrars to register voters in seven southern states where fewer than half of the voting age population had registered to vote in the 1964 election. For good measure, the Supreme Court in 1966 ruled in *Harper* v. *Virginia State Board of Elections* that poll taxes were unconstitutional. Though long in coming, these actions by the national government to enforce political equality within the states had dramatic results in increasing the registration of southern blacks, as shown in Figure 6.2.

Figure 6.2

Voter Registration in the South, 1960 and 1980
As a result of the Voting Rights Act of 1965 and other federal actions, black voter registration nearly doubled over the fifteen years before 1980. The interest in registering black voters also increased white voter registration. (Source: U.S. Bureau of the Census, Statistical Abstract of the United States, 1982–83. Washington, D.C.: U.S. Government Printing Office, 1983, p. 488.)

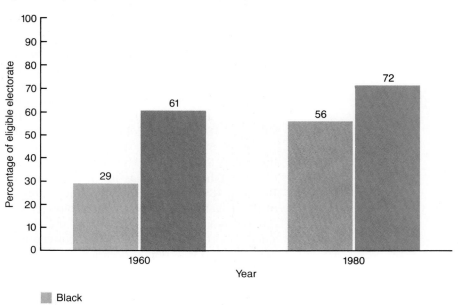

The Fight for Women's Suffrage . . .
Young people and minority groups are not the only groups who have resorted to unconventional means of political participation. In the late 1800s and early 1900s, women marched and demonstrated for equal voting rights.

Enfranchisement of women.   Enfranchisement of women in the United States is a less sordid story, but nothing to be proud of, for women had to fight long and hard to win voting rights. Until 1869, no women had the right to vote anywhere—in the United States or in the world.[26] However, women had begun to organize to obtain suffrage in the mid-1800s. Known as *suffragettes,* these early feminists at first had a limited impact on politics. The first victory for women's suffrage did not come until 1869, when Wyoming, while still a territory, granted women the right to vote. No state followed suit until 1893, when Colorado enfranchised women.

In the meantime, the suffragettes became more active. In 1884 they formed the Equal Rights party and nominated Belva A. Lockwood, a lawyer who could not herself vote, as the first woman candidate for the presidency.[27] Between 1896 and 1918, twelve other states adopted women's suffrage. Most of these were in the West, where pioneer women often departed from traditional women's roles. Nationally, the women's suffrage movement intensified, often employing the unconventional actions of marches and demonstrations—which occasionally invited violent attacks from men and even other women. In June of 1919, the U.S. Congress finally passed the Nineteenth Amendment to the Constitution, which forbids states to deny the right to vote "on account of sex." The amendment was ratified by the last state in August 1920, in time for the November election.

. . . And Against It
The early feminists in the United States encountered strong opposition to their fight to gain the vote. Their gatherings were occasionally disrupted by men—and sometimes other women—who were opposed to extending the right to vote to women.

Evaluating expansion of suffrage in America. The last major expansion of suffrage in the United States occurred in 1971 with the Twenty-Sixth Amendment to the Constitution, which forbids states to deny the right to vote to citizens eighteen years or older "on account of age." Thus, for most of its history, the United States has been far from the democratic ideal of universal suffrage. Voting rights were initially restricted to white male propertyowners or taxpayers, and various wealth requirements lasted until the 1850s. Through demonstrations and a constitutional amendment, women won the franchise less than seventy years ago. Through civil war, constitutional amendments, court actions, massive demonstrations, and congressional action, blacks finally became full voting citizens slightly more than twenty years ago. Our record has more than a few blemishes.

But compared with other countries, the United States looks pretty democratic.[28] Women did not gain the vote on equal terms with men until 1921 in Norway; until 1922 in the Netherlands; 1944 in France; 1946 in Italy, Japan, and Venezuela; 1948 in Belgium; and not until 1971 in Switzerland. It is difficult to compare experiences regarding the enfranchisement of minority racial groups, for most other democratic nations do not have such racial divisions. We should, however, note that the indigenous Maori population in New Zealand gained suffrage in 1867, but the aborigines in Australia were not fully enfranchised until 1967. And, of course, in notoriously undemocratic South Africa, blacks have no voting rights at all—despite their outnumbering the ruling whites by more than 4 to 1.

With regard to voting age, nineteen of twenty-seven countries that feature free elections also have a minimum voting age of eighteen (none has a lower age), and eight have higher age requirements. So, when judged against the rest of the world, the United States—which launched mass participation in government through elections—has as good a record of providing for political equality in voting rights as other democracies, and a better record than many.

Voting on Policies

Disenfranchised groups have struggled to gain voting rights because of the political power that is involved in mass voting. Belief in the ability of ordinary citizens to make political decisions and to control government through the power of the ballot box was strongest in the United States during the Progressive Era, which began around 1900 and lasted until about 1925. **Progressivism** was a philosophy of political reform that trusted the goodness and wisdom of the individual citizen and distrusted "special interests" (such as railroads and big corporations) and political institutions (such as political parties and legislatures).

Progressivism was headed by prominent political leaders, such as ex-president Theodore Roosevelt and Senator Robert La Follette of Wisconsin, and was supported by eminent scholars, such as historian Frederick Jackson Turner and philosopher John Dewey. Not content to vote for candidates chosen by party leaders, the Progressives championed the **direct primary** — a preliminary election, run by the state government, in which ordinary voters choose the candidates that the party will run in the subsequent general election.

Progressives also relied on the voting power of the masses to propose and to pass laws, thus approximating "direct democracy"—citizen participation in policymaking. They developed two voting mechanisms for policymaking (mentioned briefly in Chapter 2) that are still in use:

■ **Referendum**—A direct vote, by the people, either on an amendment to the state constitution or on a proposed law. The issues subject to vote are known as **propositions** when they are printed on the ballot. Twenty-five states permit popular referendums on laws, and all but Delaware require a referendum on constitutional amendments.

■ **Initiative**—A procedure by which ordinary voters can propose an issue to be decided by the legislature or by the people in a referendum. The procedure involves gathering the required number of signatures from registered voters (usually 5 to 10 percent of the total in a state, depending on the state) and submitting the petition to a designated state agency. About twenty states currently provide for some form of voter initiative.

There is no provision for either the initiative or the referendum at the national level, but both are widely used in many states. State legislatures in North Dakota and Oregon each voted on over 125 statutes initiated by citizens between 1898 and 1979. Nationwide, 754 citizen-initiated statutes were put to a vote during this period, and 38 percent were adopted.[29] Many more propositions are put to statewide popular vote. One scholar estimates that there have been more than 17,000 referendums since 1898 and more than 2,300 between 1968 and 1978 alone.[30] In fact, use of the initiative and the referendum for legislation is increasing. The institutional mechanisms built by the Progressives are still being used by today's reformers to approximate direct citizen participation in politics.

Sometimes citizens use the referendum to propose ideas that are unpopular with politicians. A prominent example is Proposition 13, a proposal submitted to California voters in 1978, which was designed to cut property taxes and drastically reduce government expenditures. Proposition 13 was opposed by most of the state's political, business, educational, communications, and labor leaders and was heavily attacked in the media. Nevertheless, the voters passed it by a landslide margin of 65 percent to 35 percent.

Politicians sometimes welcome a referendum in order to avoid deciding a hot issue themselves. Pornography is a hot issue of social order, and the citizens of Maine had their say on controlling pornography in a referendum on June 10, 1986. The referendum read: "Do you want to make it a crime to make, sell, give for value or otherwise promote obscene material in Maine?" It was proposed by the Maine Christian Civic League and backed by the Concerned Citizens for Decency, who sponsored television advertisements in which an expert on child abuse blamed pornography. The proposition was opposed by the American Civil Liberties Union (ACLU), feminists, and librarians. Its opponents sponsored television spots showing a leather-jacketed policeman supervising the burning of books, including *The Grapes of Wrath*, *The Color Purple*, and *The American Heritage Dictionary*. By a vote that ran about 2 to 1, the proposition was defeated.[31]

For Her, 13 Is a Lucky Number

In 1978, citizens in California were asked to vote on a very complex issue called Proposition 13. The issue called for an amendment to the state constitution to radically change the property tax system. Although opponents argued that it would force cutbacks in social programs, the proposition passed overwhelmingly and led to ''tax revolt'' referenda in other states.

What conclusion can be drawn about the Progressives' legacy of mechanisms for direct participation in government? One scholar who studied citizen use of the initiative and the referendum paints an unimpressive picture. He notes that in the 1980s an expensive "industry" developed which makes money circulating the petitions and then managing the large (and growing) sums of money needed to run a campaign to approve (or defeat) a referendum.[32] The money required to mount a statewide campaign has involved special interest groups in referendum politics rather than eliminating them. Not only is turnout usually lower in referendums than in other elections, but most voters confess they lack adequate knowledge for voting on ballot propositions. The author concludes:

> The expectations of the proponents of direct legislation that voters would read and study ballot propositions and then cast informed ballots have been substantially disproven. Voters are not better informed about propositions than they are about candidates. In fact, on most propositions, voters have not heard much prior to entering the voting booth. When voting for candidates, voters can at least utilize the party label if they possess no other information. Typically, however, voters do know something about state candidates and many know something about their issue positions.[33]

It is clear that citizens can exercise great power over government policy through the initiative and referendum mechanisms. What is not so clear is whether such direct democracy improves on the policies made by representatives elected for that purpose.

Voting for Candidates

We haved saved for last the most visible form of political participation: voting to choose candidates for public office. Voting for candidates serves democratic government in two ways. First, it allows citizens to choose the candidates they think would best serve their interests. If citizens chose candidates "like themselves" in personal traits or party affiliation, the elected officials would also tend to be like-minded on political issues. If public officials really thought like most of the voters, they would *automatically* reflect the majority's views when making public policy. The majority would not have to worry about monitoring the behavior of their public officials and directing their policymaking.

Second, voting allows the people to re-elect the officials they guessed correctly about and to kick out those they guessed wrong about. This is a very different function from the first. It makes public officials *accountable* for their behavior through the reward-punishment mechanism of elections. It assumes that officeholders are motivated to respond to public opinion by the threat of electoral defeat. It also assumes that the voters (1) know the candidates and their actions while in office and (2) participate actively in the electoral process. We shall take up the factors explaining voting choice in the next chapter. For now, we need to examine more closely Americans' reliance on elections to choose public officials.

In national politics, voters are content to elect only two executive offices —a president and a vice president—and to trust the president to appoint a

Compared With What? 6.2

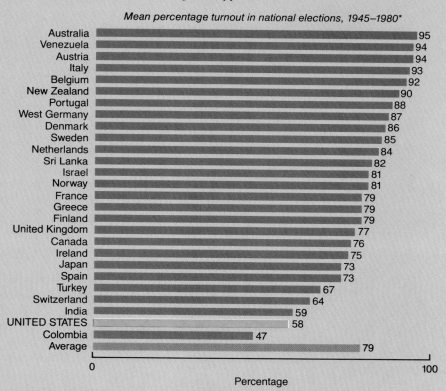

Voter Turnout in Democratic Nations

Americans participate in politics as much as or more than citizens in other nations in all forms of political behavior *except* voting. In fact, voting turnout in American presidential elections ranks near the bottom of voting rates for twenty-seven countries with competitive elections. As discussed in the text, the facts are correct, but the comparison is not as damning as it appears.

Mean percentage turnout in national elections, 1945–1980*

Country	Percentage
Australia	95
Venezuela	94
Austria	94
Italy	93
Belgium	92
New Zealand	90
Portugal	88
West Germany	87
Denmark	86
Sweden	85
Netherlands	84
Sri Lanka	82
Israel	81
Norway	81
France	79
Greece	79
Finland	79
United Kingdom	77
Canada	76
Ireland	75
Japan	73
Spain	73
Turkey	67
Switzerland	64
India	59
UNITED STATES	58
Colombia	47
Average	79

Percentage

*Number of elections varies from 2 to 14 with an average of 9.

Source: Ivor Crewe, "Electoral Participation," in David Butler et al., eds., *Democracy at the Polls* (Washington, D.C.: American Enterprise Institute, 1981), pp. 234–237. The turnout rates for each country are averaged over elections since 1945.

cabinet to round out his administration. But at the state and local levels, voters insist on selecting many administrative officials of secondary importance.

Not only does every state elect a governor (plus a lieutenant governor in forty-two of the fifty states), but forty-three elect an attorney general, thirty-eight a treasurer, thirty-six a secretary of state, twenty-five an auditor, and so on down through offices such as superintendent of education, secretary of agriculture, controller, board of education, and public utilities commissioners.[34] Elected county officials commonly include a sheriff, a treasurer, a clerk, a superintendent of schools, and a judge (often several). Even at the local level, all but about 600 of 15,300 school boards across the nation are elected.[35] Instead of trusting state and local chief executives to appoint lesser administrators (as we do for more important offices at the national level), we expect voters to choose intelligently among scores of candidates they meet for the first time on a complex ballot in the polling booth.

Americans seem to believe that there is no limit to voters' ability to make informed choices among candidates and thus to control government. The reasoning seems to be: "Elections are good; therefore, more elections are better, and the most elections are best." By this reasoning, the United States clearly has the best and most democratic government in the world, for it is the undisputed world champion at election holding. One scholar noted that America's supremacy in the field can be seen by comparing elections in the United States with elections in twenty-seven other democracies:

> No country can approach the United States in the frequency and variety of elections, and thus in the amount of electoral participation to which its citizens have a right. No other country elects its lower house as often as every two years, or its president as frequently as every four years. No other country popularly elects its state governors *and* town mayors; no other has as wide a variety of nonrepresentative offices (judges, sheriffs, attorneys general, city treasurers, and so on) subject to election. . . . The average American is entitled to do far more electing — probably by a factor of three or four — than the citizen of any other democracy.[36]

However, we learn from the same scholar's data (see Compared With What? 6.2) that the United States ranks at the bottom of these same twenty-seven countries in voting turnout! How can we square such a low voter participation rate with Americans' devotion to elections as an instrument of democratic government? To complicate matters further, how can we square the low voting turnout with other findings, discussed earlier, that establish the United States as the highest among five Western democratic nations in both conventional *and* unconventional political participation? Americans seem to participate at high levels in everything except elections.

EXPLAINING POLITICAL PARTICIPATION

As you have seen, political participation may be conventional or unconventional, may require much or little initiative, and may serve to support the government or to influence its decisions. Researchers have found that people who engage in one type of participation often do not engage in other types. For example, the same citizens who contact public officials (a conventional act requiring high initiative) to obtain special benefits (attempting to influence government decisions) may *not* vote regularly, participate in campaigns, or even contact officials about broader social issues. In fact, the "particularized contacting" of public officials stands by itself as a type of participation. Because this sort of participation serves individual interests rather than public purposes, it is not even viewed as *political* behavior by some people.

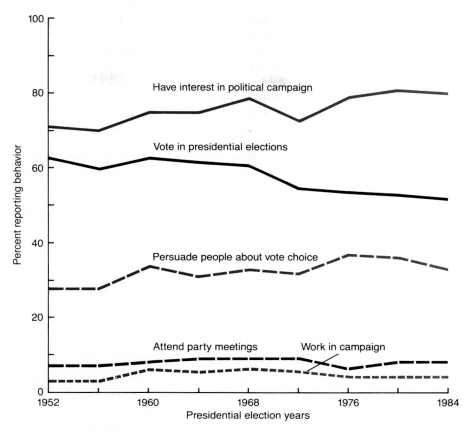

Electoral Participation in the United States over Time
Participation patterns over three decades show that Americans participate about as much or more in election campaigns in the 1980s as in the 1950s on every indicator except *voting turnout. The turnout rate dropped more than ten percentage points from 1952 to 1984. The drop in turnout compared with the other indicators also runs counter to the rise in educational level, constituting a puzzle that is discussed in the text. (Source: Warren E. Miller, Arthur H. Miller, and Edward J. Schneider,* American National Election Studies Data Sourcebook, 1952–1978. *Cambridge, Mass.: Harvard University Press, 1980. Data after 1978 came from the National Election Studies distributed by the Inter-University Consortium for Political and Social Research.)*

Figure 6.3

In this section, we shall examine some factors that affect the more obvious forms of political participation, with particular emphasis on voting. Our first task is to determine how much variation there is in patterns of participation within the United States over time.

Patterns of Participation over Time

Have Americans become more politically apathetic in the 1980s than they were in the 1960s? The answer lies in Figure 6.3, which graphs several measures of participation from 1952 through 1984. The graph shows a mixed pattern of participation over those thirty-two years. There is *stability* across time in the percentage of citizens who worked for candidates (3 to 6 percent) or who attended party meetings (6 to 9 percent) during presidential election years. Participation *increased* across time by 8 to 10 percentage points on two other indicators: interest in campaigns and persuading people how to vote. Participation *decreased* over time when measured as voting turnout in presidential elections (dropping from 63 to 52 percent). The plot has thickened. Not only is voting turnout low in the United States compared with that in other countries, but turnout has declined over time. Moreover, voting has decreased, while these other indicators of participation have increased. What is going on? Who votes? Who doesn't? Why? And does it really matter?

The Standard Socioeconomic Explanation

Researchers have found that social status is a good indicator of most types of *conventional* political participation. People with more education, higher

Figure 6.4 ━━━

Effect of Education on Political Participation in 1984
Education has a powerful effect on political participation in the United States. These data for a 1984 sample show that level of education is directly related to five different forms of conventional political participation. (Source: This analysis was based on the 1984 National Election Study distributed by the Inter-University Consortium for Political and Social Research.)

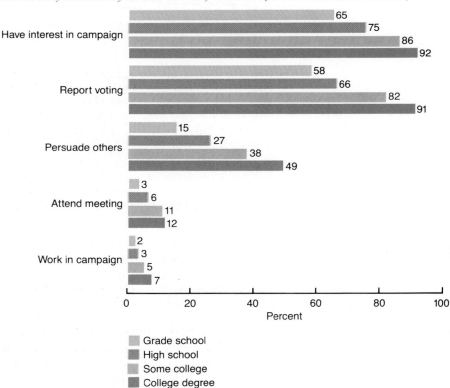

incomes, and white-collar or professional occupations tend to be more aware of the impact of politics on their lives, to know what can be done to influence government actions, and to have the necessary resources (time, money) to take action. They are thus more likely to participate in politics than people of lower status. This relationship between socioeconomic status and conventional political involvement has been dubbed the **standard socioeconomic model** of participation.[37]

Unconventional political behavior is less clearly related to socioeconomic status. Studies of unconventional participation in other countries have found that protest behavior was related to *low* status and especially to youth.[38] However, scattered studies of unconventional participation in the United States found that protesters (especially blacks) are often higher in socioeconomic status than those who do not join in protests.[39]

Obviously, socioeconomic status cannot account for all the differences in the ways people choose to participate in politics, even for conventional participation. Another important variable is age. As we noted above, young people are more likely to engage in political protests, but they are *less likely* to participate in conventional politics. Consistent with the learning model discussed in Chapter 5, voting rates tend to increase with age until about the age of sixty-five, when voting begins to decline due to physical infirmity.[40]

Two other variables—race and sex—have been related to participation in the past, but as times have changed, those relationships have altered as well. Blacks, who had very low participation rates in the 1950s, now participate at even *higher* rates than whites, when differences in socioeconomic status are taken into account.[41] Women have also exhibited low participation rates in the past, but sex differences in political participation have now virtually disappeared.[42] (The one exception is in attempting to persuade others how to vote, which women are less likely to do than men.[43])

Of all social and economic variables, education is the strongest single factor explaining most types of conventional political participation. The striking relationship between level of formal education and various types of conventional behavior in election campaigns is graphed in Figure 6.4.

Such a strong linkage between education and electoral participation raises questions about low voter turnout in the United States *both* over time and relative to other democracies. The fact is that the proportion of individuals with college degrees is greater in the United States than in other countries. Moreover, that proportion has been increasing steadily. Why, then, is voting turnout in elections so low—and why is it *declining?*

Our Low Voting Turnout

Voting is a low-initiative means of participating in politics that can satisfy all three motives for participation—to show allegiance to the nation, to seek particularized benefits, and to influence broad policy. Because voting turnout in the United States is relatively low, while other forms of participation are high and on the increase, we must seek explanations of low turnout that relate solely to the act of voting. We also need two kinds of explanations: one for the decline in voting within the United States over time and another for the low turnout in the United States as compared with that in other countries.

The decline in voting over time.   The graph of voting turnout over time in Figure 6.3 shows that the sharpest drop (6 percentage points) occurred between the 1968 and 1972 elections. It was during that period (in 1971, actually) that Congress proposed and the states ratified the Twenty-Sixth Amendment to the Constitution, which expanded the electorate by lowering the voting age from twenty-one to eighteen. Because people under twenty-one are much less likely to vote, they actually reduced the overall national turnout rate (the percentage of those eligible to vote who actually voted) when the voting age was lowered. Some observers estimate that the enfranchisement of eighteen-year-olds accounts for about 1 or 2 percentage points in the total decline in turnout since 1952.[44]

Researchers attribute most of the decline in turnout to changes in voters' convictions and attitudes regarding politics. One major factor is a decreasing belief that government is responsive to citizens and that voting does any good. Another important factor is a change in attitude toward political parties, along with a decline in the sense of party identification.[45] According to these psychological explanations, voting turnout in the United States is not likely to increase until the government does something to restore people's faith in the effectiveness of voting — with or without political parties. According to the age explanation, turnout in the United States is destined to remain a percentage point or two below its highs in the 1960s because of the lower voting rate of citizens under twenty-one.

U.S. turnout compared with others.   Given the high level of education in the United States and our greater than usual participation in other forms of political activity, voting turnout is much lower than might be expected compared with that in other countries. Scholars cite two factors to explain our low percentage of voters. The first is differences in voting laws and administrative machinery. In a few countries, voting is compulsory, and obviously, turnout there is extremely high. But there are other ways to encourage voting — declaring election days to be public holidays, providing for a two-day voting period, making it easy to cast absentee ballots. The United States does none of these things. Moreover, nearly every other democratic country places the burden of registration on the government rather than on the individual voter.

This is very important, for voting in the United States is a two-stage process, and the first stage — going to the proper officials to register — requires more initiative than the second stage — going to the polling booth to cast a ballot. In most American states, the registration process is separated from the voting process by both time (usually weeks in advance of the election) and geography (often done in the county courthouse, not the polling place). Moreover, registration procedures are often obscure and require calling around to find out what to do. Furthermore, people who move their residences (and roughly one-third of the population moves between national elections) must reregister. In short and using the terminology employed earlier, although voting requires little initiative, registration usually requires *high* initiative. If voting turnout is computed in relation to those who are *registered* to vote, then about 87 percent of Americans vote — a figure that moves the United States to the middle (but not the top) of all democratic nations.[46]

The second factor usually cited to explain low turnout in American elections is the lack of political parties that mobilize the vote of particular social groups, particularly lower-class and less-educated people. American parties do make an effort to get out the vote, but neither party is as closely linked to specific groups as parties are in many other countries, where certain parties work hand in hand with ethnic, occupational, or religious groups. Research shows that strong party-group linkages can significantly increase turnout.[47]

To these explanations for lower U.S. voting turnout — the burden of registration and the lack of strong party-group linkages — we can add another. Although the act of voting requires low initiative, the process of informing oneself about the scores of candidates on the ballot in American elections requires a great deal of initiative. Some people undoubtedly fail to vote simply because they feel inadequate to the task of deciding among candidates for the many offices on the ballot in U.S. elections.

Teachers, newspaper columnists, and public affairs groups tend to worry a great deal about low voting turnout in the United States, suggesting that it signifies some sort of political sickness — or at least that it gives us a bad mark for democracy. Some others who study elections closely seem less concerned. Voting turnout is only one indicator of political participation, and Americans tend to do better according to most other indicators. Moreover, one scholar argues:

> Turnout rates do not indicate the amount of electing — the frequency of occasion, the range of offices and decisions, the "value" of the vote — to which a country's citizens are entitled. . . . Thus, although the turnout rate in the United States is below that of most other democracies, American citizens do not necessarily do less voting than other citizens; most probably, they do more.[48]

Despite these words of assurance, the nagging thought remains that turnout ought to be higher, and various organizations mount "get-out-the-vote" campaigns at each election. Civic leaders often back these campaigns because they value voting for its contribution to political order.

PARTICIPATION AND FREEDOM, ORDER, AND EQUALITY

As you have seen, Americans do participate in government in a variety of ways and to a reasonable extent, compared with citizens of other countries. What is the relationship of political participation to the values of freedom, order, and equality?

Participation and Freedom

From the standpoint of normative theory, the relationship between participation and freedom is clear. Individuals should be free to participate in government and politics as they wish and as much as they wish. Indeed, they should be free to *avoid* participating if they so desire. Ideally, all barriers to participation (such as restrictive voting registration and limitations on campaign expenditures) should be abolished — as should any schemes for compulsory voting. In particular, we should not worry about low voting turnout, for citizens should have the freedom not to vote as well as to vote.

Freedom to participate also means that individuals may use their wealth, connections, information, organizational power (including sheer numbers in organized protests), or any other resource to influence government decisions, provided they do so legitimately. Of all these resources, the individual vote may be the weakest — and thus the least important — means of exerting political influence. Obviously, then, freedom as a value in political participation favors those with the resources to advance their own political self-interest.

Participation and Equality

The relationship between participation and equality is also clear. Each citizen's ability to influence government should be equal to that of every other citizen, so that differences in personal resources do not work against poor or otherwise disadvantaged citizens. Thus, *elections serve the ideal of equality better than any other means of political participation.* Formal rules for counting ballots — in particular, one person, one vote — negate differences in resources among individuals.

At the same time, groups of people who have few individual resources can combine their votes to wield political power. This power was exercised by various European ethnic groups (discussed in Chapter 5) whose votes won them entry into the sociopolitical system and allowed them to share in its benefits. More recently, blacks, Hispanics, and homosexuals have used their voting power to gain political recognition. However, minorities often had to use unconventional modes of participation to win the right to vote. As two major scholars of political participation put it, "Protest is the great equalizer, the political action that weights intensity as well as sheer numbers."[49]

Participation and Order

The relationship between participation and order is complicated. Some types of participation promote order and thus are encouraged by those who value order; other types promote disorder and are discouraged. Even giving women the right to vote was resisted by many citizens (men and women alike) for fear of upsetting the social order, of altering the traditional roles of men and women.

Either conventional or unconventional participation may result in the ouster of government officials, but the *regime* — the political system itself — is threatened more by unconventional participation. To maintain order, the government has a stake in converting unconventional participation to conventional participation whenever possible. One can easily imagine this tactic being used by authoritarian governments, but it is used by democratic governments as well.

Risking Lives for an Honest Election
You can see in the actions of these young Filipinos how precious a free and honest election can be. They linked arms to escort ballot boxes to the city hall for an honest count after the February 1986 presidential election. Agents of President Ferdinand Marcos, threatened with defeat by Corazon Aquino, began to tamper with the vote count. Although the National Assembly, which Marcos controlled, declared him the winner, the Filipino people rebelled at the fraudulent election and forced Marcos to flee the country, putting Aquino in the presidency that was stolen from her.

Recall the student unrest on college campuses during the Vietnam War. In private and public colleges alike, thousands of students stopped traffic, occupied buildings, destroyed property, struck classes, disrupted lectures, staged guerrilla theater, and behaved in other unconventional ways while protesting the war, racism, capitalism, their college presidents, the president of the United States, the military establishment, and all other establishments. (Today's students may think this list of actions is overdrawn. In fact, students did all these things at Northwestern University in Evanston, Illinois, after four students were killed by National Guardsmen in a demonstration at Kent State University in Ohio on May 4, 1970.)

Confronted by civil strife and disorder in the nation's institutions of higher learning, Congress took action. On March 23, 1971, it passed and sent to the states the proposed Twenty-Sixth Amendment, lowering the voting age

America's Largest Civil Rights Demonstration
On August 28, 1963, more than 200,000 blacks and whites participated in a Freedom March on Washington, D.C. Martin Luther King, Jr., one of the march's leaders, delivered his electrifying "I Have a Dream" speech from the steps of the Lincoln Memorial. The demonstrators pressed for legislation ensuring full civil rights for blacks, and their leaders were welcomed at the White House by President John F. Kennedy.

to eighteen. Three-quarters of the state legislatures had to ratify the amendment before it became part of the Constitution. Astonishingly, thirty-eight states (the required number) complied by June 30, establishing a new record for speedy ratification, cutting the old record nearly in half.[50] (Ironically, voting rights were about the only thing that students were not demanding.)

Testimony by four senators and one member of Congress before the Judiciary Committee stated that the eighteen-year-old vote was needed to "harness the energy of young people and direct it into useful and constructive channels," to keep students from becoming "more militant" and engaging "in destructive activities of a dangerous nature."[51] As one observer argued, the right for eighteen-year-olds to vote was not extended because youths demanded it, but because "public officials believed suffrage expansion to be a means of institutionalizing youths' participation in politics, which would, in turn, curb disorder."[52]

PARTICIPATION AND MODELS OF DEMOCRACY

Ostensibly, elections are institutional mechanisms that implement democracy by allowing citizens to choose among candidates or issues. However, elections serve other important purposes:

- *Elections socialize political activity.*   They transform what might otherwise consist of sporadic, citizen-initiated acts into a routine public function. This helps preserve government stability by containing and channeling away potentially more disruptive or dangerous forms of mass political activity.

- *Elections institutionalize mass influence in politics.*   They substitute an institutional mechanism for the informal sources of influence (such as strikes and riots) that might otherwise be used by the public.

- *Elections institutionalize access to political power.*   They permit ordinary citizens to play an important role in selecting political leaders.

- *Elections bolster the state's power and authority.*   The opportunity to participate in elections helps convince citizens that the government is responsive to their needs and wishes, which increases its legitimacy.[53]

Participation and Majoritarianism

Although the majoritarian model assumes that government responsiveness to popular demands comes through mass participation in politics, majoritarianism does not view participation very broadly. It favors conventional, institutionalized behavior of a narrow form — primarily, voting in elections. Because it relies on counting preferences to determine popular wishes, majoritarianism is strongly biased toward equality of citizens in political participation. Favoring collective decisions formalized through elections, majoritarianism offers little opportunity for motivated and resourceful individuals to exercise private influence over government actions.

Majoritarianism also reduces individual freedom in another way. By focusing on voting as the major means of mass participation, it narrows the scope of "conventional" political behavior. In this way, the mechanisms for participation in the majoritarian model restrict freedom by defining what political action is "orderly" and acceptable. By favoring "equality" and "order" in political participation, majoritarianism goes hand in hand with the ideological orientations of populists (see Chapter 1).

Participation and Pluralism

Resourceful citizens who seek the government's help with problems find a haven in the pluralist model of democracy. A decentralized and organizationally complex form of government allows many points of access and is well suited to various forms of conventional participation aside from voting. For example, wealthy people and well-funded groups can afford to hire lobbyists to press their interests in Congress. In one view of pluralist democracy, citizens are free to ply and wheedle public officials for selfish visions of the public good. From another viewpoint, pluralism offers citizens the opportunity to be treated as individuals when dealing with the government, to obtain or adjust policies in accordance with special circumstances, and to fulfill (insofar as is possible in representative government) their social potential through participation in community affairs.

SUMMARY

To have "government by the people," the people must participate in politics. Conventional forms of participation—contacting officials and voting in elections—come most quickly to mind. However, citizens can also participate in politics in unconventional ways—staging sit-down strikes in public buildings, blocking traffic, and so on. Most citizens disapprove of many forms of unconventional political behavior. Nevertheless, unconventional tactics have won various groups some important political rights, including women's right to vote and southern blacks' exercise of voting rights.

People are motivated to participate in politics for various reasons. They may be showing support for their country, seeking to obtain particularized benefits for themselves or their friends, or attempting to influence broad public policy. Their political actions may require very little political knowledge or personal initiative, or they may demand a great deal of both.

The press often paints an unflattering picture of political participation in America. Clearly, the proportion of the electorate that votes in general elections in the United States is far less than that in most comparable nations. When compared with other nations on a broader range of conventional and unconventional political behavior, however, the United States tends to show *more,* rather than less, citizen participation in politics. However, voting turnout in the United States suffers by comparison with that in other nations, because of differences in voter registration here and elsewhere. We also lack institutions (especially strong political parties) that increase voter registration and help bring those of lower socioeconomic status to the polls.

The tendency to participate in politics is strongly related to socioeconomic status. Education, one component of socioeconomic status, is the single strongest factor predicting conventional political participation in the United States. Because of the strong effect of socioeconomic status on political participation, the political system is potentially biased toward the interests of higher-status people. A pluralist democracy, which does provide many avenues for resourceful citizens to influence government decisions, tends to increase this potential bias.

A majoritarian democracy, which relies heavily on elections and the equality of the vote, offers citizens without great personal resources the opportunity to control government decisions through elections. However, elections also serve to legitimize government simply by involving the masses in government through voting. Whether or not the vote means anything depends on the nature of the voters' choices in the elections. The range of choice is a function of the nation's political parties, the topic of the next chapter.

Key Terms

election	voting
political participation	suffrage
conventional participation	franchise
unconventional participation	progressivism
outgroup	direct primary
ingroup	referendum
direct action	proposition
supportive behavior	initiative
influencing behavior	standard socioeconomic model

Selected Readings

Barnes, Samuel H., and Max Kaase, eds. *Political Action: Mass Participation in Five Western Democracies.* Beverly Hills, Calif.: SAGE Publications, 1979. The most important comparative study of both conventional and unconventional political participation.

Conway, M. Margaret. *Political Participation in the United States.* Washington, D.C.: CQ Press, 1985. Conway provides the best up-to-date review of survey data on conventional political participation.

Ginsberg, Benjamin. *The Consequences of Consent: Elections, Citizen Control and Popular Acquiescence.* Reading, Mass.: Addison-Wesley, 1982. A careful study of the functions of election, with considerable discussion of elections as mechanisms for government control of citizens.

Milbrath, Lester W., and M. L. Goel. *Political Participation.* Chicago: Rand McNally, 1977. One of the standard sources on political participation. It stresses sociological and psychological factors related to participation.

Verba, Sidney, and Norman H. Nie. *Participation in America: Political Democracy and Social Equality.* New York: Harper & Row, 1972. Analyzing data from surveys of citizens and political leaders, Verba and Nie have written one of the classic studies of political participation.

Wolfinger, Raymond E., and Steven J. Rosenstone. *Who Votes?* New Haven, Conn.: Yale University Press, 1980. This slim volume concentrates on determining and explaining nonvoting in the United States.

7

Political Parties, Campaigns, and Voting

Phil Gramm, formerly an economics professor at Texas A&M University, was first elected to Congress in 1978 as a Democrat from Texas's Sixth District. His constituents, who lived in fourteen counties between suburban Dallas and suburban Houston, were basically conservative. That suited Gramm, himself a staunch conservative, who found most of his Democratic colleagues in Congress too liberal. Nevertheless, he ran for reelection and won in 1980, the same year that Ronald Reagan was first elected president. Although Reagan was a Republican, he was Gramm's kind of president: anxious to cut back on social spending, eager to increase military spending. Gramm could work with Reagan.

In 1981 Phil Gramm won a seat on the House Budget Committee, an important committee that reviews the president's budget and prepares a version acceptable to the House. Gramm found his Democratic colleagues on the committee too willing to spend government money for social programs. He much preferred Reagan's cost-cutting, tax-cutting approach. Gramm began to meet with Reagan's director of the Office of Management and Budget (OMB), David A. Stockman, to reveal the Democrats' plans and to devise an alternative budget for 1982. Word soon leaked out, and several Democratic members of the Budget Committee objected to Gramm's participation in their meetings. The chairman of the House Democratic Caucus described Gramm as "the fox in the hen house."[1] By spring 1981, he stopped meeting with the Democrats.

However, Gramm began to meet with Republicans on the Budget Committee and even cosponsored (with its leading Republican) the key amendment to the budget resolution that substituted Reagan's economic blueprint for the one backed by the Democrats. Reagan's 1981 income tax cut, his cuts in domestic spending, and his increases in military spending owed much to Phil Gramm, Democrat from Texas — much to the dismay of the House Democratic leadership.

The Democratic voters in Texas were not dismayed, however, and reelected Gramm to the House in 1982. The Democratic leaders got their chance to even the score with Gramm in early 1983, when the committees were reorganized for the new Congress. Rarely does the party leadership try to discipline members for cooperating with the opposition; too many members would have to be punished, and the party has few available ways to discipline them. But Gramm had gone too far and was denied reappointment to the Budget Committee on January 3. Two days later, Gramm quit the Democratic party, resigned his newly won seat, and announced that he would run for re-election in the same district as a Republican.

A special election was called on February 12 in the normally Democratic Sixth District of Texas. Running as the sole Republican, Gramm faced nine Democratic challengers and a stray Libertarian. He defeated all ten opponents, winning the election with 55 percent of the vote. Whatever he had done in Congress, the voters approved and sent him back to do more of it. Not only did a triumphant Gramm return to Congress as a Republican, but the Republican party promptly rewarded him by appointing him to one of its seats on the Budget Committee! Two years later, Gramm's fame had outgrown his congressional district, and he ran for the United States Senate. He won easily and took his seat in 1985 as Republican senator from the state of Texas.

Phil Gramm's story is not a common one, but it illustrates some basic facts about the peculiar nature of American political parties. Each party has an ideological center of gravity, but each has supporters of varying political persuasions. Party attachment is important in elections, but its influence can be overcome. In short, parties are important in American politics, but they are not all-powerful. Why do we have political parties anyway? What functions do they perform? Are parties really necessary for democratic government, or do they just interfere in the relationship between citizens and government? This chapter will respond to these questions as it inquires into political parties, perhaps the most misunderstood institutions in American politics.

POLITICAL PARTIES AND THEIR FUNCTIONS

According to democratic theory, the primary means by which citizens control their government is voting in free elections. Most Americans agree that voting is important: 86 percent of those surveyed after the 1984 presidential campaign felt that elections made the government "pay attention to what the people think."[2] However, Americans are not nearly as supportive of the role played by political parties in elections. An overwhelming majority surveyed in 1980 (73 percent) believed that "the best way to vote is to pick a candidate regardless of party label." A clear majority (56 percent) thought that "parties do more to confuse the issues than to provide a clear choice on issues." In fact, almost half (49 percent) took the extreme position "It would be better if, in *all* elections, we put no *party labels on the ballot*."[3]

On the other hand, Americans are quick to condemn as "undemocratic" countries without parties (such as Saudi Arabia), as well as those with only one party (such as the Soviet Union). In truth, Americans have a love-hate relationship with political parties. Although parties are seen as necessary for democratic government, they are also viewed as somehow "obstructionist" and not to be trusted. This distrust is particularly strong among younger voters. A better appreciation of the role of political parties in democratic government may follow from an understanding of exactly what parties are and what they do.

Definitions

A **political party** is an organization that sponsors candidates for political office *under the organization's name*. The italicized part of this definition is important. True political parties **nominate** candidates for election to public office; in other words, they designate individuals as official candidates of the party. This function distinguishes the Democratic and Republican parties from interest groups such as the AFL-CIO and the National Association of Manufacturers. Interest groups often support candidates in various ways but do not nominate them to run *as their avowed representatives*. If they do, the interest groups then become political parties too. In short, it is the acceptance of political *labeling* by both candidate and organization that defines an organization as a party.

Most democratic theorists agree that a modern nation-state could not practice democracy without at least two political parties that regularly *contest*, or meet in, elections. (See Compared With What? 2.1. All nineteen countries rated as consensus democracies in Chapter 2 feature at least two competing parties.) In fact, the linkage between political parties and democracy is so close that many people define democratic government in terms of competitive party politics.

Parties contribute to democratic government through the functions they perform for the **political system** — the set of interrelated institutions that links people with government. We will consider four of parties' most important functions: (1) nominating candidates for election to public office; (2) structuring the voting choice in elections; (3) proposing alternative government programs; and (4) coordinating the actions of government officials.

Nominating Candidates

Political parties contribute to democratic government simply by fulfilling their definition and nominating candidates for election to public office. In the absence of parties, voters would be confronted with a bewildering array of self-nominated candidates, each seeking a narrow victory over others on the basis of personal friendships, celebrity status, or an appealing name. Parties provide a form of "quality control" for their nominees through the process of **peer review.** Party insiders, the nominees' peers, usually get to know potential candidates much better than the average voter does, and candidates are judged by their peers for acceptability as the party's representatives.

In nominating candidates, parties often do more than merely pass judgment on potential office seekers; sometimes they go so far as to recruit talented individuals to become party candidates. In this way, parties help not only to ensure a minimum level of quality for candidates who run for office, but also to raise the quality of the candidates offered to the voters.

Structuring the Voting Choice

Political parties also aid democratic government by structuring the voting choice — reducing the number of candidates on the ballot to those who have a realistic chance of winning. Established parties — those that have contested elections in the past — acquire a following of loyal voters, who guarantee the party's candidates a predictable base of votes. Parties that have won sizable portions of the vote in past elections are likely to win comparable portions of the vote in future ones. Thus, nonparty candidates are discouraged from running for office, and new parties are discouraged from forming. Consequently, the realistic choice is between candidates offered by the major parties. This focuses the election on the contest between parties and on candidates with established records, which reduces the amount of new information that voters need in order to make a rational decision.

Proposing Alternative Government Programs

Parties also help voters choose candidates by proposing alternative programs of government action — general policies that party candidates would pursue if they won control of government. Even if voters know nothing about

Eleanor Gives Her Blessing to the 1960 Democratic Ticket
The band was playing the Democrats' theme song, ''Happy Days Are Here Again!'' as John Kennedy (presidential candidate), Eleanor Roosevelt, and Lyndon Johnson (vice presidential candidate) appeared at a rally in the New York Coliseum just before the 1960 presidential election. Eleanor Roosevelt, a party leader in her own right, was the wife of President Franklin Roosevelt, who forged the Democratic coalition of Northern urban workers, Southerners, Catholics, Jews, and white ethnic minorities that replaced the Republican party as the majority party in America.

the qualities of the parties' candidates, they can vote rationally for candidates of the party that stands closest to the policies they favor. The specific policies advocated in an election campaign vary from candidate to candidate and from election to election. However, the types of policies advocated by candidates of the same party tend to differ from those proposed by candidates of other parties. Although there are exceptions, candidates of the same party tend to favor policies that fit their party's underlying political philosophy, or ideology. In many countries, parties often adopt labels that advertise their political stance (see Compared With What? 7.1).

Although the two major American parties have issue-neutral names, many minor parties in U.S. history have advertised their policies in their names: the Prohibition party, Farmer-Labor party, Socialist party, and so on. The ideological blandness of the names ''Democratic'' and ''Republican'' suggests that our parties are also undifferentiated in their policies. It may surprise you to learn that this is not true. The two major parties have regularly adopted very different policies in their platforms, which we will analyze at length later.

Coordinating the Actions of Government Officials

Finally, parties help coordinate the actions of public officials. Governments based on the separation of powers, like that of the United States, divide responsibilities for making public policy. The president, the leaders of the House, and the leaders of the Senate are not required to cooperate with one

Compared With What? 7.1

What's in a Name?

Many parties try to advertise their political philosophies in their names, and all parties certainly pay careful attention to the image they project through their choice of a party label.

The labels of the major U.S. parties — "Democratic" and "Republican" — do not themselves offer much of a clue to the two parties' policy orientations. But in other countries, the party label often symbolizes the party's policies. A study of party names across the world found that their symbols fell into four categories. Nearly half the parties made *ideological appeals* — describing themselves as "So-

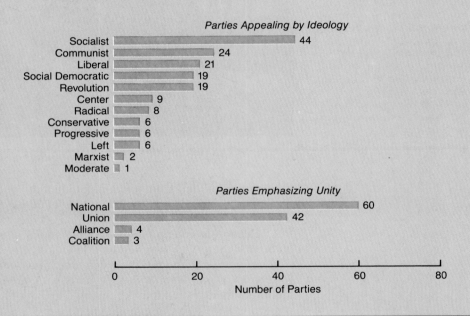

another. Political parties are the major means for bridging the separation of powers, to produce coordinated policies that are effective in governing the country. Individuals of the same party in the House, the Senate, and the presidency are likely to share political principles and thus to cooperate in making policy.

A HISTORY OF U.S. PARTY POLITICS

The two major U.S. parties are among the oldest in the world. In fact, the Democratic party, founded in 1828 but with roots reaching back into the late 1700s, has a strong claim to being the oldest party in existence. Its oldest rival is the British Conservative party, formed in 1832, two decades before cialist" or "Communist." About the same number used terms suggesting *self-government*, such as *democratic* or *people*. About one-quarter of the parties stressed *national unity*, using terms like *national* or *union* in their names. Only about 15 percent made explicit *group appeals*, identifying themselves as "Christian" or "labor." (The percentages add to more than 100 because some parties, such as the Christian Democrats, used more than one symbol.)

The appeal of democracy is so strong worldwide that nearly one-quarter of the parties employ the term in some form (democratic, democracy, democrats). *Republican* is not nearly as popular a term and was used by only eight parties outside the United States.

Source: This analysis was based on party names and translations from foreign languages in Alan J. Day and Henry W. Degenhardt, eds., *Political Parties of the World* (Detroit, Mich.: Gale Research Company, 1980).

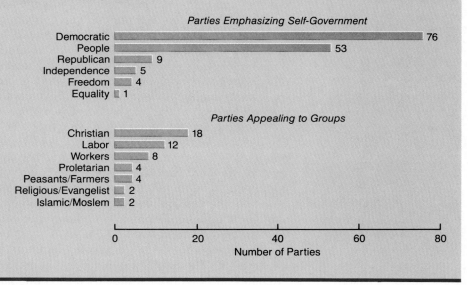

the Republican party formed in 1854. Both the Democratic and Republican parties have been supported by several generations of citizens and are part of American history. It is the parties' longevity, the fact that they have become *institutionalized* in our political process, that is most significant.

The Preparty Period

Today we regard party activities as normal, even essential, to American politics. It was not always so. The Constitution makes no mention of political parties, and none existed when the Constitution was written in 1787. Instead, it was common to refer to groups pursuing some common political interest as "factions." Although factions were seen as inevitable in politics, they were also considered dangerous. One argument for adopting the Constitution (as proposed in *The Federalist,* No. 51, see Chapter 3) was that its separation of powers and checks and balances would prevent factional influences from controlling the government.

Factions existed even under British rule. In colonial assemblies, supporters of the governor (and thus of the Crown) were known as "Tories" or "Loyalists," and their opponents were called "Whigs" or "Patriots." After independence, the arguments over whether or not to adopt the Constitution produced a different factional alignment. Those who backed the Constitution were loosely known as "federalists," and their opponents (naturally enough) were "antifederalists." At this stage, the groups could not be called "parties" because they did not sponsor candidates for election.

Elections then were vastly different from elections today. The Constitution provided for the president and vice president to be chosen by an **electoral college**—a body of electors who meet in the capitals of their respective states to cast ballots for president and vice president. Initially, these electors (one for each senator and representative in Congress) were chosen by state legislatures, not by the voters. Thus, presidential "elections" in the early years of the nation were decided by a few political leaders. They often met in small, frequently secret, groups called **caucuses,** to discuss candidates for public office. Often these caucuses were held among like-minded members of state legislatures and the national Congress. This was the setting for George Washington's election as the first president in 1789.

Washington can be classified as a federalist because he supported the Constitution, but he was not a factional leader and actually opposed factional politics. Possessing immense prestige and not aligned with factional groupings, Washington was unopposed for the office of president and was elected unanimously by the electoral college. During Washington's administration, however, the political cleavages sharpened between those who favored a stronger national government and those who wanted a less powerful, more decentralized government.

The first group, led by Alexander Hamilton, proclaimed themselves true "Federalists." The second group, led by Thomas Jefferson, labeled themselves "Republicans." (Although they used the same name, these were *not* Republicans as we know them today.) The Jeffersonians chose the name "Republicans" to distinguish themselves from the "aristocratic" tendencies of Hamilton's Federalists. The Federalists countered by calling the Republicans the "*Democratic* Republicans," attempting to link Jefferson's party to the disorder (and beheadings) spawned by the "radical democrats" in France following the French Revolution of 1789.

The First Party System: Federalists and Democratic Republicans

Washington was re-elected president unanimously in 1792, but his vice president, John Adams, won only after encountering opposition by a candidate backed by the Democratic Republicans. This brief skirmish foreshadowed the nation's first major party struggle over the presidency. Disheartened by the political split in his administration, Washington spoke out against "the baneful effects" of parties in his Farewell Address in 1796. Nevertheless, both parties continued after Washington retired from politics. (See "Two-Party Systems in U.S. History," Color Essay C, plate 7.)

In the election of 1796, the Federalists supported Vice President John Adams to succeed Washington as president. The Democratic Republicans backed Thomas Jefferson for president but could not agree on a vice presidential candidate. In the electoral college, Adams won 71 votes to Jefferson's 68, and both ran ahead of other candidates. Originally, the Constitution provided that the presidency went to the candidate who won the most votes in the electoral college, while the vice presidency went to the runner-up. So Adams, a Federalist, had to accept Jefferson, a Democratic Republican, as his vice president. Obviously, the Constitution's method of selecting the vice president did not anticipate a presidential contest between candidates from opposing political parties!

The party function of nominating candidates emerged more clearly in the election of 1800. Both parties caucused in Congress to nominate their candidates for president and vice president.[4] The result was the first true party contest for the presidency. The Federalists nominated John Adams and Charles Pinckney against the Democratic Republican ticket of Thomas Jefferson and Aaron Burr. This time, the Democratic Republican candidates won. However, the new party organization worked *too* well. The Democratic Republican electors cast all their votes for both Jefferson and Burr, with a resulting tie vote in the electoral college. Unfortunately, the presidency was to go to the candidate with the *most* votes.

Despite the fact that Jefferson was the party's presidential candidate and Burr, its vice presidential candidate, the House of Representatives was empowered by the Constitution to choose one of them as president. After seven days and thirty-six ballots (encouraged by the ambitious Burr), the House decided in favor of Jefferson.

The Twelfth Amendment, ratified in 1804, prevented a repeat of the troublesome election outcomes of 1796 and 1800. It required the electoral college to vote separately for president and vice president, implicitly recognizing that presidential elections would be contested by party candidates nominated for the separate offices but running on the same ballot.

In retrospect, we can see that the election of 1800 marked the beginning of the end for the Federalists, who lost the next four elections. By 1820 the Federalists had ceased to exist. The Democratic Republican candidate, James Monroe, was re-elected in the first presidential contest without party competition since Washington's time. (Monroe received all but one electoral college vote, which was reportedly cast against him so that Washington would remain the only president ever elected unanimously.) Ironically, the Era of Good Feelings under Monroe also marked the beginning of the end for his dominant Democratic Republican party.

Without opposition from another party, the Democratic Republicans lost their function of nominating candidates. The party continued to hold a congressional caucus to nominate candidates for president, but attendance dropped off, and the caucus of 1824 was poorly attended. Its nominee was challenged by three other Democratic Republicans, including John Quincy Adams and Andrew Jackson, who proved to be the most popular candidates among the voters in the ensuing election.

Until 1824, the parties' role in structuring the popular vote had been relatively unimportant, for relatively few people were entitled to vote. As explained in Chapter 6, states began to drop restrictive requirements for voting after 1800, and voting rights for white males expanded ever faster after 1815. With the expansion of suffrage, more states began allowing voters to choose presidential electors. The 1824 election was the first to feature selection of presidential electors through popular vote in most states. Still, the role of political parties in structuring the popular vote was not yet developed.

Although Jackson won a plurality of both the popular vote and the electoral vote in 1824, he did not win the necessary majority vote in the electoral college. The House of Representatives was again required to decide the winner. It chose the second-place John Quincy Adams (from the established state of Massachusetts) over the voters' choice, Jackson (from the frontier state of Tennessee). The factionalism among the Democratic Republican party leaders became so intense that the party split in two.

The Second Party System: Democrats and Whigs

The Jacksonian faction of the Democratic Republican party represented the common people in the expanding South and West and its members took pride in calling themselves simply "Democrats." Jackson ran again for the presidency as a Democrat in 1828, a milestone that marks the beginning of today's Democratic party. That election was also significant for being the first "mass" election in our history. Although many presidential electors had been chosen by popular vote in 1824, the total votes cast in that election numbered fewer than 370,000. By 1828, relaxed requirements for voting (and the use of popular elections to select presidential electors in more states) had increased the vote by more than 300 percent, to over 1.1 million.

As the electorate expanded, the parties changed. No longer could a few party members in Congress rely on close connections among relatively few political leaders in the state legislatures to control the vote cast in the electoral college. Parties now needed to campaign for votes cast by hundreds of thousands of citizens. Recognizing this new dimension of politics, parties responded with a new method for nominating presidential candidates.

Instead of the old method of selecting candidates in a closed caucus of party representatives in Congress, parties devised the **national convention.** These gatherings would let delegates from state parties across the nation choose candidates for president and vice president and adopt a statement of policies called a **party platform.** The first national convention was called in 1831 by the Anti-Masonic party, which was the first "third" party in American history to challenge the two major parties for the presidency. The Democrats adopted the convention idea in 1832 to nominate Jackson for a second term; so did their new opponents that year, the National Republicans.

The label "National Republicans" was applied to John Quincy Adams's faction of the former Democratic Republican party. We have already learned that the Jacksonian faction became today's Democratic party. However, the National Republicans did *not* become today's Republican party. Instead, Adams's followers called themselves *National* Republicans to signify their old

Federalist preference for a strong national government. But the symbolism did not appeal to the voters, and the National Republicans lost to Jackson in 1832.

Elected to another term, Jackson began to assert the power of the nation over the states (acting more like a National Republican than like a Democrat). His policies drew new opponents, who started calling him "King Andrew." A coalition of opponents composed of former National Republicans, Anti-Masons, and Jackson-haters then formed the Whig party in 1834.[5] The name harked back to the English Whigs, who opposed the powers of the British throne; thus the Whigs implied, even by their name, that President Jackson ruled like a king. For the next thirty years, Democrats and Whigs alternated in the presidency. However, the issues of slavery and sectionalism eventually destroyed the Whigs. Although the party had won the White House in 1848 and had taken 44 percent of the vote in 1852, the Whigs were unable to field a presidential candidate in the 1856 election.

The Present Party System: Democrats and Republicans

Meanwhile, in the early 1850s, antislavery forces (including Whigs, Free Soilers, and antislavery Democrats) began to organize. At meetings in Jackson, Michigan, and Ripon, Wisconsin, they recommended the formation of a new party, the Republican party, which would oppose the extension of slavery into the Kansas and Nebraska territories. It is *this* party, founded in 1854, that continues as today's Republican party.

The Republican party contested its first presidential election in 1856. Although it was an entirely new party, it took 33 percent of the vote. Moreover, its candidate (John Fremont) carried eleven states—all in the North. Then, in 1860, the Republicans nominated Abraham Lincoln. The Democrats were deeply divided over the slavery issue and actually split into two parties. The northern wing kept the name "Democratic party" and nominated Stephen Douglas. The southern Democrats ran John Breckinridge. A fourth party, the Constitutional Union party, nominated John Bell. Sectional voting was obvious in the election of 1860. Lincoln took 40 percent of the popular vote and carried every northern state. Breckinridge won every southern state. But all three of Lincoln's opponents together still did not win enough electoral votes to deny him the presidency.

The election of 1860 is regarded as the first of three "critical elections" in our nation's history.[6] A **critical election** produces a sharp change in the existing patterns of party loyalties among groups of voters. Moreover, this change in voting patterns, which is called an **electoral realignment,** does not end with that election. Rather, the altered party loyalties that are ushered in endure for several subsequent elections.[7] (For more information on the three critical elections, see Color Essay B, plates 2 and 3.) The critical election of 1860 divided the country between the northern states, which mainly voted Republican, and the southern states, which were overwhelmingly Democratic. The victory of the North over the South in the Civil War cemented Democratic loyalties in the South, particularly following the withdrawal of federal troops after the 1876 election.

Ike Gives His Blessing to the 1960 Republican Ticket
President Dwight Eisenhower was elected in 1952 as the first Republican president since Herbert Hoover lost his bid for reelection in 1932. Here Ike appears at a campaign rally in the New York City Coliseum just before the 1960 election. The Republican ticket consisted of Richard Nixon, who was vice president under Eisenhower, and Henry Cabot Lodge. Unfortunately for Nixon and Lodge, Eisenhower's endorsement was not enough to swing the election, and they lost to the Democratic ticket of John Kennedy and Lyndon Johnson.

For forty years, from 1880 to 1920, no Republican presidential candidate won even one of the eleven states of the Confederacy. The South's solid Democratic record earned it the nickname "Solid South." The Republicans did not puncture the Solid South until 1920, when Warren G. Harding carried Tennessee. Republicans also won five southern states in 1928 when the Democrats ran a Catholic candidate, Al Smith. Republican presidential candidates won no more southern states until 1952, when Dwight Eisenhower broke through the Democratic dominance of the South — ninety years after the partisan patterns had been set by the Civil War.

Eras of Party Dominance Since the Civil War

The critical election of 1860 established the Democratic and Republican parties as the major parties in the present two-party system. In a **two-party system,** most voters are so loyal to one or the other of the major parties that candidates from a "third" party — which means any minor party — have little chance of winning office. When third-party candidates do win (and occasionally they do), they are most likely to win offices in local or state elections. Since the present two-party system was established, relatively few minor party candidates have won election to the U.S. House, *very* few have won election to the Senate, and *not one* has won the presidency.

Although voters in most states have been divided in their loyalties between the Republicans and the Democrats, they have not always been *equally* divided. In some states, counties, or social groups, voters favor the Republicans, while voters in other areas or groups prefer the Democrats. When one party in a two-party system *regularly* enjoys support from most of the voters, it can be called the **majority party** and the other, the **minority party.** Over the lifetime of the present two-party system, there have been three different periods of balance between the two major parties.

A rough balance: 1860–1894. From 1860 through 1894, the Grand Old Party (or GOP, as the Republican party is sometimes called) won eight of ten presidential elections, which would seem to qualify it as the majority party. However, some of its success in presidential elections came from running Civil War heroes and from the North's domination of southern politics. Seats won in the House of Representatives are a better guide to breadth of national support, and an analysis of those shows that the Republicans and Democrats divided equally in winning congressional elections, each controlling the chamber for nine sessions through 1894.

A Republican majority: 1896–1930. The nation's second critical election, in 1896, transformed the Republican party into a true majority party. A Democrat (Grover Cleveland) was in the White House, and the country was in a severe economic depression. The Republicans nominated William McKinley, governor of Ohio and a conservative, who stood for a high tariff against foreign goods and sound money tied to the value of gold. Rather than tour the country seeking votes, McKinley ran a dignified campaign from his Ohio home.

The Democrats, already in trouble because of the depression, nominated the fiery William Jennings Bryan. In stark contrast to McKinley, Bryan advocated the free and unlimited coinage of silver—which meant cheap money

William Jennings Bryan: When Candidates Were Orators

Today a candidate would look silly waving his hands and shouting on television. But once candidates had to resort to such tactics to be effective with large crowds. One of the most commanding orators around the turn of the century was William Jennings Bryan, whose stirring speeches extolling the advantages of free and unlimited coinage of silver were music to the ears of thousands of Westerners and Southern farmers who heard him speak in person.

and easy payment of debts through inflation. Bryan was also nominated by the young Populist party, an agrarian protest party, which had previously proposed the "free silver" issue that Bryan adopted. (The Populist party was the basis of the book *The Wizard of Oz*, which you probably know as a movie but may not know as a political fable;[8] see Feature 7.1.) Businesspeople and conservative citizens were aghast at the Democrats' radical turn, and voters in the heavily populated Midwest and East surged toward the Republican party—many of them permanently.[9] The Republican McKinley carried every northern state east of the Mississippi. The Republicans also won the House and continued to control it for the next six elections.

The election of 1896 helped solidify the Republican majority in industrial America and forged a link between the Republican party and business. In the subsequent voter realignment, the Republicans emerged as a true majority party. The Republicans dominated national politics — except when Teddy Roosevelt's Progressive party split from the Republicans in 1912, allowing the Democrat Woodrow Wilson to win the presidency and giving the Democrats control of Congress. The GOP controlled the presidency, the Senate, and the House almost continuously from 1896 until the Wall Street crash of 1929, which burst big business's bubble and launched the Great Depression.

A Democratic majority: 1932 to the present.   The Republicans' majority status ended in the critical election of 1932 between incumbent president Herbert Hoover and the Democratic challenger, Franklin D. Roosevelt. Roosevelt promised new solutions to unemployment and the economic crisis of the Depression. His campaign appealed to labor unionists, middle-class liberals, and new European ethnic voters. These groups, added to Democratic voters in the Solid South, form the famous "Roosevelt coalition" of southerners, northern urban workers, Catholics, Jews, and white ethnic minorities. (The relatively few blacks who voted at that time tended to remain loyal to the Republicans—the "party of Lincoln.")

Roosevelt was swept into office in a landslide, carrying huge majorities into the House and Senate to carry out his liberal, activist programs. The electoral realignment prompted by the election of 1932 made the Democrats the majority party. Not only was Roosevelt re-elected in 1936, 1940, and 1944, but Democrats held control of both houses of Congress from 1933 through 1980—interrupted by only two years of Republican control in 1953 and 1954, during the Eisenhower administration.

In presidential elections, however, the Democrats have not fared so well since Roosevelt. In fact, they have won only four elections (Truman, Kennedy, Johnson, and Carter), compared with the Republicans, who have won six times (Eisenhower twice, Nixon twice, and Reagan twice). In Reagan's stunning 1980 election, Republicans wrested control of the Senate from the Democrats for the first time since 1954. In Reagan's even greater personal victory in 1984, Republicans held the Senate but could not gain control of the House. Moreover, the Democrats regained The Senate in 1986.

There are strong signs that the coalition of Democratic voters forged by Roosevelt in the 1930s has already cracked. Certainly the South is no longer "solid" for the Democrats. Since 1952, in fact, it has voted more consistently for Republican presidential candidates than for Democrats. The two-party

Feature 7.1

The Wizard of Oz: A Political Fable

Most Americans are familiar with *The Wizard of Oz* through L. Frank Baum's children's books or the 1939 motion picture, but few realize that the story was written as a political fable to promote the Populist movement around the turn of the century. Next time you see it, try interpreting the Tin Woodsman as the industrial worker, the Scarecrow as the struggling farmer, and the Wizard as the president, who is powerful only as long as he succeeds in deceiving the people. (Sorry, but in the book Dorothy's ruby slippers were only silver shoes.)

The Wonderful Wizard of Oz was written by Lyman Frank Baum in 1900, during the collapse of the Populist movement. Through the Populist party, Midwestern farmers, in alliance with some urban workers, had challenged the banks, railroads, and other economic interests that squeezed farmers through low prices, high freight rates, and continued indebtedness.

The Populists advocated government ownership of railroads, telephone, and telegraph industries. They also wanted silver coinage. Their power grew during the 1893 depression, the worst in U.S. history until then, as farm prices sank to new lows and unemployment was widespread. . . .

In the 1894 congressional elections, the Populist party got almost 40 percent of the vote. It looked forward to winning the presidency, and the silver standard, in 1896. But in that election, which revolved around the issue of gold versus silver, Populist Democrat William Jennings Bryan lost to Republican William McKinley by 95 electoral votes. Bryan, a congressman from Nebraska and a gifted orator, ran again in 1900, but the Populist strength was gone.

Baum viewed these events in both rural South Dakota—where he edited a local weekly—and urban Chicago—where he wrote *Oz*. He mourned the destruction of the fragile alliance between the Midwestern farmers (the Scarecrow) and the urban industrial workers (the Tin Woodsman). Along with Bryan (the Cowardly Lion with a roar but little else), they had been taken down the yellow brick road (the gold standard) that led nowhere. Each journeyed to Emerald City seeking favors from the Wizard of Oz (the President). Dorothy, the symbol of Everyman, went along with them, innocent enough to see the truth before the others.

Along the way they meet the Wicked Witch of the East who, Baum tells us, had kept the little Munchkin

people "in bondage for many years, making them slave for her night and day." She also had put a spell on the Tin Woodsman, once an independent and hardworking man, so that each time he swung his axe, it chopped off a different part of his body. Lacking another trade, he "worked harder than ever," becoming like a machine, incapable of love, yearning for a heart. Another witch, the Wicked Witch of the West, clearly symbolizes the large industrial corporations.

. . . The small group heads toward Emerald City where the Wizard rules from behind a papier-mâché façade. Oz, by the way, is the abbreviation for ounce, the standard measure for gold.

Like all good politicians, the Wizard can be all things to all people. Dorothy sees him as an enormous head. The Scarecrow sees a gossamer fairy. The Woodsman sees an awful beast, the Cowardly Lion "a ball of fire so fierce and glowing he could scarcely bear to gaze upon it."

Later, however, when they confront the Wizard directly, they see he is nothing more than "a little man, with a bald head and a wrinkled face."

"I have been making believe," the Wizard confesses. "I'm just a common man." But the Scarecrow adds, "You're more than that . . . you're a humbug."

"It was a great mistake my ever letting you into the Throne Room," admits the Wizard, a former ventriloquist and circus balloonist from Omaha.

This was Baum's ultimate Populist message. The powers-that-be survive by deception. Only people's ignorance allows the powerful to manipulate and control them. Dorothy returns to Kansas with the magical help of her Silver Shoes (the silver issue), but when she gets to Kansas she realizes her shoes "had fallen off in her flight through the air, and were lost forever in the desert." Still, she is safe at home with Aunt Em and Uncle Henry, simple farmers.

Source: Peter Dreier, *Today Journal*, February 14, 1986.
Copyright © Pacific News Service. Reprinted by permission.

Southerners Liked Ike
"I Like Ike!" was the popular Republican slogan in 1952 in Dwight Eisenhower's presidential campaign against Adlai E. Stevenson, II. Most people agreed—even in the South—and Eisenhower became the first Republican candidate since 1876 to win most of the Southern states as he swept to an easy victory. Eisenhower punctured the previously solid Democratic South and, since that time, Republican presidential candidates have run well in the region.

system in the United States may be undergoing yet another realignment, which could restore the Republican party to the majority status it enjoyed before the Great Depression.

THE AMERICAN TWO-PARTY SYSTEM

Our review of party history has focused on the major parties competing for presidential office. But even when concentrating on the major parties, we could not ignore the special contributions of certain minor parties, such as the Anti-Masonic party, the Populists, and the Progressives of 1912. In this section, we shall study the fortunes of minor, or "third," parties in American politics. We shall also account for the existence of only two major parties, explain how federalism helps the parties survive, and describe the voters' loyalties toward the two parties today.

Types and Examples of Minor Parties in America

Minor parties have continuously flecked the history of party politics in America. In the 1984 election, for example, fourteen minor parties sponsored presidential candidates. As shown in Table 7.1, all the minor party candidates in 1984 taken together won less than 1 percent of the vote—which is about

average. Minor parties seldom win enough votes to threaten the two dominant parties, but occasionally they do—depending on their *type*.[10]

■ **Bolter parties** are formed of factions that have split off from one of the
major parties. Six times in thirty presidential elections since the Civil
War, disgruntled leaders have "bolted the ticket" and challenged their
former parties. Bolter parties have occasionally won significant proportions of the vote. However, with the definite exception of Teddy Roosevelt's Progressive party in 1912 and the possible exception of George
Wallace's American Independent party in 1968, bolter parties have not
affected the outcome of the presidential election.

Table 7.1 ▬▬▬▬▬▬

Major and Minor Party Votes in the 1984 Election
If you think that the Democratic and Republican parties took all the votes in the 1984
election, guess again. They won only 99.33 percent of the vote; the remainder was divided
among 15 other candidates representing fourteen parties. The best showing was by David
Bergland, the candidate of the Libertarian party (see Feature 1.1, page 17).

Candidate	Party*	Official Popular Vote Total	Percent of Total Vote
Ronald Reagan	Republican	54,455,075	58.77
Walter F. Mondale	Democratic	37,577,185	40.56
John B. Anderson	National Unity Party of KY	1,479	0.00
Gerald Baker	Big Deal	892	0.00
David Bergland	Libertarian	227,204	0.25
Delmar Dennis	American	13,149	0.01
Earl F. Dodge	Prohibition	4,235	0.00
Gus Hall	Communist	36,225	0.04
Gavrielle Holmes	Workers World	2,656	0.00
Larry Holmes	Workers World	15,327	0.02
Sonia Johnson	Citizens	71,976	0.08
Lyndon LaRouche, Jr.	Independent	78,773	0.09
Arthur J. Lowery	United Sovereign Citizens	822	0.00
Mel Mason	Socialist Workers	24,681	0.03
Bob Richards	Populist	66,241	0.07
Dennis L. Serrette	Independent Alliance	46,809	0.05
Ed Winn	Workers League	10,789	0.01
Write-Ins		19,315	0.02
Total Votes		**92,652,842**	

Voting Age Population†	: 173,936,000	
Voter Turnout‡	: 53.27%	
Electoral Vote	: Reagan—525	Mondale—13

*Party designations may vary from one state to another.

†Projections of the *Population of Voting Age for States: November 1984*, Bureau of Census, Series
P-25, No. 948, April 1984.

‡Percentage of voting age population casting a vote.

Source: *FEC Journal of Election Administration* 12 (Summer 1985):12. Reprinted by permission.

- **Farmer-labor parties** represent farmers and urban workers who believe that they, the working class, do not get their share of society's wealth. The People's party, founded in 1892 and nicknamed "the Populist party," was the prime example of this type. The Populists won 8.5 percent of the vote that year and became the first third party since 1860 to win any electoral votes. Flush with success, it endorsed William Jennings Bryan, the Democratic candidate, in 1896 but met with defeat and quickly faded. Many Populist ideas were revived by labor and farm groups in the Progressive party in 1924, which nominated Robert La Follette. Although the party won 16.6 percent of the vote, it carried only La Follette's home state of Wisconsin. The party died in 1925. A Populist candidate ran in 1984 but received fewer than seventy thousand votes. However, populist ideas have been revived in Congress, where a Populist caucus, or group of representatives with similar ideas, claimed twenty-eight members in the House and Senate in 1986.*

- **Parties of ideological protest** go further than farmer-labor parties in criticizing the established system. These parties reject the prevailing doctrines and propose radically different principles — usually of a "leftist" nature, favoring more government activism. The Socialist party has been the most successful party of ideological protest. However, its high point was only 6 percent of the vote in 1912, and Socialist candidates for president never won a single state. In recent years, the sound of ideological protest has been heard more from rightist parties arguing for a radical disengagement of government from society. The Libertarian candidate in 1984, David Bergland, received more than 2.5 times the combined vote of five leftist candidates. However, Bergland himself won only one-quarter of one percent of the vote.

- **Single-issue parties,** as the category implies, are formed to promote one principle, rather than a general philosophy of government. The Anti-Masonic parties of the 1820s and 1830s, for example, opposed Masonic lodges and other secret societies. The Free Soil party of the 1840s and 1850s sought to abolish slavery. The Prohibition party, the most durable example of a party based on a single issue, opposed consumption of alcoholic beverages. Prohibition candidates consistently won from 1 to 2 percent of the vote in nine presidential elections from 1884 to 1916, and the party has run candidates in every presidential election since. The Prohibition candidate in 1984 polled 4,235 votes.

Third parties have thus been formed primarily to express discontent with the choices offered by the major parties and to work for their own objectives within the electoral system.[11] How have they fared? As *vote getters*, minor parties have not performed well, with two exceptions. First, bolter parties twice won more than 10 percent of the vote; no other type has ever won as much. Second, the Republican party originated in 1854 as a single-issue third

---

*Some members of the Populist caucus helped to found the New Populist Forum in 1985. The forum is intended to function as an interest group that would apply the populist philosophy in the tradition of populists 100 years ago to today's issues, and build political momentum among folks who still believe that government serves the interests of ordinary people in our country (*New Populist Forum* press release, 1986).

party opposed to slavery in new territories; in its first election, in 1856, the party came in second, displacing the Whigs. (Undoubtedly, the Republican exception to the rule has inspired the formation of other hopeful third parties.)

As *policy advocates*, minor parties have a better, but still clouded, record. If minor parties win few votes, it might be because their ideas are unpopular. A clear case of a major party adopting a minor party principle occurred in 1896. The Democrats accepted the Populist platform's "plank" (principle) of free silver coinage but went down to a defeat that stained the Democratic party for decades. Nevertheless, some important political ideas, such as women's suffrage, the graduated income tax, and the direct election of senators, have originated in third parties.[12]

Minor parties may perform their most useful function as *safety valves*. By forming a minor party, discontented groups have the opportunity to argue for their policies within the political system. Like the Free Soil party of the 1840s and 1850s and the Libertarians of today, they can contribute to the political dialogue of their times. If the presence of minor parties in elections indicates discontent, what should we make of the existence of fourteen minor parties in the 1984 election? Not much. Despite the proliferation of minor parties, the two major parties collected 99.33 percent of the vote. The number of third parties that appear in elections is less important than the total number of votes they receive.

Why a Two-Party System?

The history of party politics in the United States is essentially the story of two parties alternating in power. With relatively few exceptions, elections for national office and for most state and local offices are conducted within a two-party system. This pattern is unusual for democratic countries, where multiparty systems are more common. Why has U.S. politics narrowed to only two parties? The two most convincing reasons for the persistence of the two-party system in the United States are (1) the electoral system and (2) the process of political socialization.

Elections in the United States, unlike elections in many other countries, involve the twin principles of (1) *single winners* chosen by (2) a *simple plurality* of votes. That is, in the typical U.S. election, *one* office is contested by two or more candidates and is won by the single candidate who collects the *most* votes. Consider a state that is entitled to ten representatives in Congress. At present, the state is divided into ten congressional districts, and one representative is elected in each district. There are, however, other ways to elect the ten representatives. The state might have a single statewide election for all ten seats, with each party presenting a list of ten candidates. Voters could vote for the entire party list they preferred, and candidates would be elected from the top of each list according to the proportion of votes won by the party.

Lest you think that this alternative scheme of election is bizarre, you should know that some form of it is used in many democratic countries' multiparty systems. Such an electoral system, which awards legislative seats in proportion to votes won in elections, is known as **proportional representation.** It tends to produce (or to perpetuate) several parties, each of which has enough voting strength nationwide to elect some minimum number of candidates on its party list. In contrast, our system of single winners by simple plurality vote forces groups in society to work within one of the only two parties with any realistic chance of winning an election. Therefore, the system tends to produce only two parties.

The rules of our electoral system may explain why only two parties tend to form in specific election districts. But why do the *same* two parties (Democratic and Republican) operate within each state? The contest for the presidency is the key to this question. The presidential election can be won only by the single candidate who wins a *majority* of electoral votes across the entire nation. Presidential candidates must win votes under the same label in each state so that they can pool their states' electoral votes to win in the electoral college. The presidency is a big enough prize to produce uncomfortable coalitions of voters (such as southern white Protestants joining northern Jews and blacks in the Democratic party) just to win the electoral vote and the presidential election.

The American electoral system may force party politics into a two-party mold, but why must the same parties *reappear* from election to election? In fact, they have not. We have seen that the earliest two-party system pitted the Federalists against the Democratic Republicans. A later two-party system involved the Democrats and the Whigs. Over 130 years ago, the Republicans replaced the Whigs in what is our present two-party system. But, with modern issues so different from the issues then, why do the Democrats and Republicans persist? This is where *political socialization* comes into play. These two parties persist simply because they *have* persisted. After more than 100 years of political socialization, the two parties today have such a head start in structuring the vote that they discourage challenges from new parties. As you have seen, third parties still try to crack the two-party system from time to time, but most have little success.

The Federal Basis of the Party System

Studying the history of American parties by focusing on contests for the presidency is convenient and informative. It also oversimplifies party politics to the point of distortion. By concentrating only on presidential elections, we tend to ignore electoral patterns in the states, where elections often buck national trends. In a party's darkest defeats for the presidency, it can still claim many victories for state offices. These victories outside the arena of presidential politics give each party a base of support that keeps it running and keeps its machinery oiled for the next contest.

The Republican victories in the 1980 and 1984 presidential elections help illustrate how the states serve as a refuge for parties defeated for the presidency. Ronald Reagan carried 44 states in his landslide victory in 1980. Reagan swept 49 states in 1984—winning in *every* state but Minnesota, the home of his opponent, Walter Mondale. In 1980 the Republicans also won a majority in the Senate for the first time in twenty-eight years, and they kept that control in 1984. All this makes the 1980s sound like dark times for the Democrats, but in fact, they did very well indeed at the state level. Even

A Republican Majority?
Clearly, the movement in party identification in the United States in recent years has been toward the Republican party. National surveys still show, however, that the Democratic party has a slight edge within the eligible electorate. The Republicans have benefited greatly from the presidency of Ronald Reagan, who has been enormously popular with voters. A truer test of the party's appeal will come in 1988 when Reagan is not the Republican presidential candidate.

in the wake of Reagan's stunning 1984 victory, the Democrats kept control of the House of Representatives. They wound up controlling 34 state governorships to the Republicans' 16 (unchanged from before the election). They won control of 65 percent of the state legislatures, and they controlled the governorship, the upper house, and the lower house in 18 states compared to only 4 states for the Republicans.[13]

Reagan's strong victory in 1980 and his landslide in 1984 would make it seem that the Democrats are doomed for extinction. Perhaps in an earlier party era, when the existing parties were not so well institutionalized, that would have been so. However, the Democratic party not only remains alive but thrives within many states in our federal system. This separation of state politics from national trends affords each party a chance to lick its wounds after a presidential election debacle and to return to campaign optimistically four years later.

Party Identification in America

Many people take pride in saying that they vote for the person, not the party. Maybe they do, but most Americans readily identify with one of the two parties. The concept of **party identification** is one of the most important in political science. It refers to the voter's sense of psychological attachment to a party, which is not the same thing as *voting* for the party in any given election. Voting is a behavior; identification is a state of mind. For example, millions of southerners voted for Eisenhower for president in 1952 and 1956 while considering themselves Democrats. Across the nation, more people identify with one of the two major parties than reject a party attachment, considering themselves "independent" of either party.

The proportions of self-identified Republicans, Democrats, and Independents in the electorate are shown in Figure 7.1. Three significant points stand out.

Figure 7.1

Distribution of Party Identification over Time

In every presidential election since 1952, voters across the nation have been asked, "Generally speaking, do you usually think of yourself as a Republican, a Democrat, an Independent, or what?" Most voters readily admit to thinking of themselves as either Republicans or Democrats, but the proportion of those who regard themselves as Independents has increased over time. The Democrats' status as the majority party has also lessened over time. Nevertheless, most Americans today still identify with one of the two major parties, and there are still more Democrats than Republicans. (Source: Warren E. Miller, Arthur H. Miller, and Edward J. Schneider, American National Election Studies Data Sourcebook, 1952–1978. *Cambridge, Mass.: Harvard University Press, 1980, 1981, supplemented by data from the 1980 and 1984 National Election Studies conducted at the Center for Political Studies, University of Michigan, and distributed by the Inter-University Consortium for Political and Social Research.)*

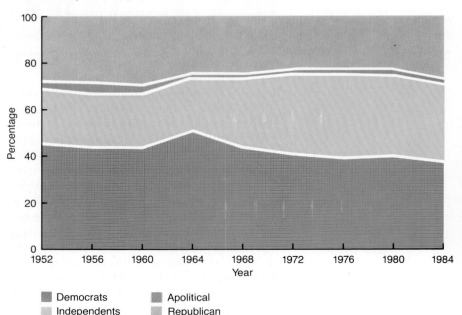

1. The proportion of Republicans and Democrats combined far exceeds the proportion of Independents in every year.

2. The proportion of Democrats consistently exceeds that of Republicans.

3. The proportion of Democrats has shrunk somewhat over time, to the benefit of both Republicans and Independents.

While a sense of party identification predisposes a citizen to vote for his or her favorite party, other factors may cause the voter to choose the opposition candidate. If such other factors cause individuals to vote against their party frequently, they may, over time, rethink their party preference and eventually switch. Apparently, this rethinking has gone on in the minds of many southern Democrats over time. In 1952 about 70 percent of white southerners thought of themselves as Democrats, and fewer than 20 percent thought of themselves as Republicans. By 1984 white Democrats were only 37 percent Democratic and 34 percent Republican.[14] Much of the nationwide growth in Republicans and Independents (and the parallel decline in Democrats) has been due to party switches among white southerners.

Who are the self-identified Democrats and Republicans in the electorate? Figure 7.2 analyzes party identification by social groups in 1984. Although there are still regional variations, region is not the critical differentiator that it once was. Democrats are still dominant in the South; Republicans are more prominent (but not dominant) in the north-central states. More important than region as reasons for party choice are socioeconomic factors. People of low education, low income, and less prestigious occupations tend to think of themselves as Democrats more than as Republicans. But the sharpest differences are based on such cultural factors as race and religion. Members of minority groups (especially blacks) overwhelmingly identify with the Democratic party. Those outside the dominant Protestant majority (especially Jews) are also significantly more likely to be Democrats. And people in unionist households are somewhat more likely to be Democrats.

Thus, despite the erosion of Democratic support among union workers and within the South, aspects of Roosevelt's old Democratic coalition can still be seen. Perhaps the major change in that coalition has been the loss of white European ethnic support and its replacement by support from blacks, attracted by the Democrats' backing of civil rights legislation in the 1960s.

Studies show that about half the citizens in the United States have adopted the parties of their parents. But it often takes time for a party identification to develop. About 59 percent of the youngest voters (those under twenty-one) claimed to be Independents in 1984, compared with only 38 percent of those between thirty-five and thirty-nine and 25 percent of those over sixty-five. This tendency for young voters to be Independents fits with their greater distrust of political parties as institutions. What concerns Democrats (and encourages Republicans) is the recent trend for younger voters (eighteen through twenty-nine) to identify with the Republican party. If this trend continues, the United States could experience a creeping electoral realignment, as older voters die and are replaced by new voters.

Once citizens find their political niches, they tend to stay there. The widespread and enduring sense of party loyalty among the American electorate tends to structure the vote before the election is even held, and even

Figure 7.2

Party Identification by Social Groups

Respondents to a 1984 survey were divided into eight different types of social groups — by income, education, sex, race, religion, occupation, union membership, and region — and analyzed for their self-descriptions as Republicans, Democrats, or Independents. Sex was found to have the least effect on party identification, and race, the greatest effect. (Source: 1984 National Election Study, distributed by the Inter-University Consortium for Political and Social Research.)

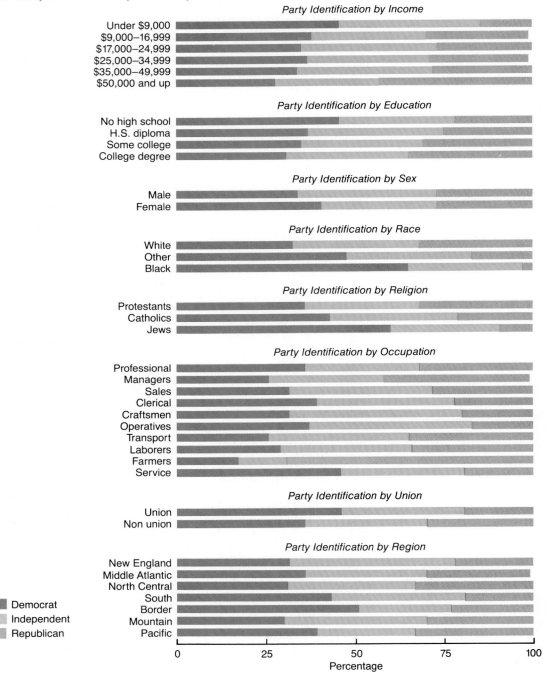

before the candidates are chosen. Later we shall examine the extent to which party identification determines voting choice. First we shall deal more with today's parties.

PARTY IDEOLOGY AND ORGANIZATION

George Wallace, a disgruntled Democrat who ran for president on the American Independent party ticket, complained that "there isn't a dime's worth of difference" between the Democrats and Republicans. Humorist Will Rogers said, "I am not a member of any organized political party—I am a Democrat." Wallace's comment was made in disgust; Rogers's in jest. Wallace was wrong; Rogers was close to being right. In this section, we shall attempt to dispel the myth that the parties do not differ significantly on issues and to explain how they are—or are not—organized.

Differences in Party Ideology

George Wallace notwithstanding, there *is* more than a dime's worth of difference between the two parties. In fact, the difference amounts to many billions of dollars, the cost of different government programs favored by each party. Democrats are more disposed to government spending to advance the social welfare (and hence to promote equality) than are Republicans. And social welfare programs cost money, a lot of money. (You will see exactly how much money in Chapters 15 and 16.) Republicans, on the other hand, are not averse to spending similar billions of dollars for the projects they consider important, such as national defense. President Reagan has portrayed the Democrats as big spenders, but the defense buildup during his administration cost the country one trillion, seven billion, nine hundred million dollars over four years.[15] (In numbers, that's $1,007,900,000,000.) And Reagan's Strategic Defense Initiative (the "Star Wars" space defense scheme) promises to cost many billions more, even by conservative estimates. These differences in spending patterns reflect some real philosophical differences between the parties.

One way to examine the differences between the two major parties is to look at the differences between the voters who identify with them. As shown in the middle portion of Figure 7.3, about one-quarter of Democrats described themselves as liberals, one-quarter as conservatives, and half as moderates in 1984. Republicans, however, were far more likely to be conservatives than liberals (by more than three to one). As discussed in Chapter 5, many ordinary voters do not "conceptualize" politics well or clearly in ideological terms. The ideological gap between the parties looms much larger when we focus on the party activists on the right- and left-hand sides of Figure 7.3. Half the delegates to the 1984 Democratic convention considered themselves liberals, and a clear majority of Republican delegates described themselves as conservatives.

Platforms: Freedom, equality, order. Surveys of voters' ideological orientations may reflect differences in self-image rather than actual differences in party ideology. For another test of party philosophies, we can look to the

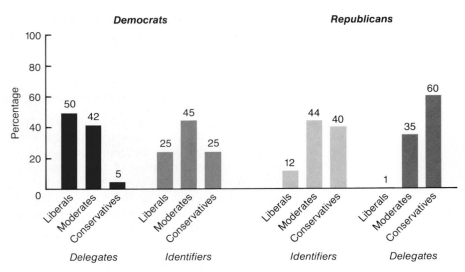

Ideologies of Party Voters and Activists in 1984
Contrary to what many people think, the Democratic and Republican parties differ substantially in their ideological centers of gravity. When citizens were asked to classify themselves on a scale of ideology, many more Republican than Democratic party identifiers described themselves as conservative. When delegates to the parties' national conventions were asked about their ideological orientations, the liberal-conservative split between the parties widened. (Source: New York Times, *August 24, 1984.)*

Figure 7.3

platforms adopted in party conventions. Although citizens feel that party platforms don't matter very much, they do matter a great deal to delegates at conventions. The wording of a platform plank often means the difference between victory and defeat for particular factions within the party. Delegates fight not only over the ideas, but also over the words and even the punctuation (see Feature 7.2) in a plank. Thus, platforms do provide a good statement of policy preferences among party activists.

The basic themes of the Democratic and Republican parties come through quite clearly in the following selections from their 1984 platforms. The Republican party's emphasis on *freedom* is visible in the platform's basic premise:

> From freedom comes opportunity; from opportunity comes growth; from growth comes progress. . . .
>
> If everything depends on freedom — and it does — then securing freedom, at home and around the world, is one of the most important endeavors a free people can undertake.
>
> Thus, the title of our Platform, "America's Future: Free and Secure," is more than a summary of our Platform's message. It is the essence.

The essence of the Democratic party's 1984 platform was fundamentally different. Whereas the Republicans emphasized freedom, the Democrats stressed *justice,* which was a code word for the social *equality* that Democrats envisioned:

> Fulfilling America's highest promise, equal justice for all: that is the Democratic agenda for a just future. . . .

The goal for the coming decades is not only full justice under the law, but *economic* justice as well. . . .

As Democrats and as Americans, we will make support for democracy, human rights, and economic and social justice the cornerstone of our policy.

Whereas both parties backed equal pay for equal work, the Democrats alone endorsed the more controversial idea of "equal pay for work of comparable worth" (see Feature 1.2 in Chapter 1).

Whereas the Republicans declared themselves "the party of limited government," the Democrats pledged to restore "an activist Government." However, the Republicans were more willing to use the power of the state to promote their view of social *order*. Their platform expressed "deep concern about gratuitous sex and violence in the entertainment media," and it promised to "vigorously enforce constitutional laws to control obscene materials." This issue did not concern the Democrats, who were more worried about violent acts directed at "gay men and lesbians"—an issue that did not concern the Republicans. Instead, the Republicans attacked the liberal experiments of the Democrats:

Worst of all, they tried to build their brave new world by assaulting our basic values. They mocked the work ethic. They scorned frugality. They attacked the integrity of the family and parental rights. They ignored traditional morality. And they still do.

These key statements of values cleanly separate the two parties on the values of freedom, equality, and order that underlie the dilemmas of government discussed in Chapter 1. According to the typology presented there, the

Feature 7.2

The Tax Plank: A Lesson in Grammar

The Democratic party held its 1984 convention in July, a month before the Republican convention. In his acceptance speech upon winning the Democratic nomination, Walter Mondale warned that taxes would have to be increased in order to decrease the huge federal budget deficit, no matter who won the election. He said, "Mr. Reagan will raise taxes, and so will I. He won't tell you. I just did." Mondale's candor stunned his audience and gave the Republicans a superb campaign issue. Reagan had already promised not to raise taxes; extreme conservatives within the Republican party sought to keep him at his word by leading a successful fight to eliminate a *comma* in the specific plank dealing with taxes in the Republican party platform:

The Proposed Republican Tax Plank

We therefore oppose any attempt to increase taxes which would harm the recovery and reverse the trend toward restoring control of the economy to individual Americans.

The Amended Republican Tax Plank

We therefore oppose any attempt to increase taxes, which would harm the recovery and reverse the trend toward restoring control of the economy to individual Americans.

According to rules of grammar, adding the comma makes the rest of the sentence a *nonrestrictive* rather than a *restrictive* clause. The net effect was to put the party on record as opposing not only tax increases that would harm the economy, but *any* tax increase — for *all* tax increases were regarded as harming the economy. Political activists are willing to spend time arguing such fine points in order to win points.

Republicans' 1984 platform clearly places their party in the conservative category and the Democrats' platform puts their party squarely into the liberal category.

Different, but similar.   The Democrats and the Republicans are thus quite different in ideological orientation. Nevertheless, many observers claim that the parties are really quite similar in ideology, especially when compared with other countries' parties. They *are* similar in that both are "capitalist" parties that reject government ownership of the means of production (see Chapter 1). A study of the Democratic and Republican party positions on four economic issues — ownership of the means of production, role in economic planning, redistribution of wealth, and providing for social welfare — found the Republican position consistently more opposed to government activity. Comparing these findings with data on party positions in thirteen other democracies, the researchers found about as much difference between the American parties as is usual within two-party systems. However, *both* American parties tend to be more conservative on economic matters than parties in other two-party systems. In most multiparty systems, the presence of strong socialist and antisocialist parties ensures that the range of ideological choice there is much greater than in our system — despite genuine differences between the Democrats and Republicans.[16]

National Party Organization

Most political observers would agree with Will Rogers's description of the Democrats as an unorganized political party. This used to be true of the Republicans, too, but that has changed over the last decade—at least at the national level. The distinction between levels of party structure must be kept in mind. American parties parallel our federal system: they have separate national and state organizations (and virtually separate local organizations, in many cases).

At the national level, each major party has three main organizational components:

- ■ *National convention.*   Every four years, each party convenes thousands of delegates from the states and the territories for the purpose of nominating a candidate for president. This national nominating convention is also the supreme governing body of the party. It determines party policy by enacting the platform, formulates rules to govern party operations, and designates a national committee, which is empowered to govern the party until the next convention.

- ■ *National committee.*   The **national committee** of each party is composed of party officials representing every state and including the chairpersons of every state party organization. Each party also adds other types of members, such as representatives of youth and ethnic groups. The membership of the Republican National Committee (RNC) is over 150, and there are more than 350 people on the Democratic National Committee (DNC). The chairperson of each national committee is chosen by the party's presidential nominee and then duly elected by the committee. If the nominee loses the election, the national committee usually replaces his chosen chairperson.

■ *Congressional campaign organizations.* Democrats and Republicans in the House and Senate maintain their own **congressional campaign organizations,** each of which raises its own funds to support its candidates in congressional elections. The fact that these are separate organizations tells us that the national party structure is quite loose; the national committee seldom gets involved with the election of any individual member of Congress. Moreover, even the congressional campaign organizations merely *supplement* the funds that senators and representatives raise on their own to win re-election.

It is tempting to think of the national party chairperson sitting at the top of a hierarchical party organization that runs through the state committees to the local levels. Few ideas could be more wrong. There is very little national direction of and even less national *control* over state and local election campaigns. In fact, the RNC and DNC do not direct or control even presidential campaigns. Individual candidates create their own campaign staffs to contest the party primary campaigns to win delegates who will support them for nomination at the party conventions. The successful party nominees then keep their winning staffs to contest the general election. The main role of a national committee is to cooperate with its candidate's personal campaign staff, in the hope of winning the election.

In this light, the national committees appear as relatively useless organizations. For many years, their role was essentially limited to planning for the next party convention. The committee would select the site, issue the "call" to state parties to attend, plan the program, and so on. In the 1970s, however, the roles of the DNC and RNC began to expand—but in different ways.

In response to street rioting during the 1968 Democratic convention (see Chapter 6), the Democrats created a special commission to introduce party reforms. The McGovern-Fraser Commission attempted to open the party to greater participation by women, minorities, and youth and to weaken local party leaders' control over the process of selecting future delegates. The commission formulated guidelines for state parties' selection of delegates to the 1972 Democratic convention. Included in these guidelines was the requirement that state parties take "affirmative action" — that is, do something — to ensure that women, blacks, and youth were included among their delegates "in reasonable relationship to the group's presence in the population of the state."[17] Many state parties rebelled at the imposition of such delegate quotas by sex, race, and age. Nevertheless, the DNC threatened to deny seating to any state delegation at the 1972 convention that did not comply with its guidelines.

Never before had a national party committee imposed such rules on a state party organization, but it worked. Even the powerful Chicago delegation, led by Mayor Richard Daley, was denied seating at the convention for violating the guidelines. And overall, blacks, women, and youth gained dramatically in representation at the 1972 Democratic convention. Although the party has since reduced its emphasis on quotas, these gains in minority representation have held up fairly well.

While the Democrats were engaged in this *procedural* reform, the Republicans were conducting *organizational* reform.[18] The RNC did little to open up its delegate selection process, for Republicans were not inclined to impose quotas on state parties through their national committee. Instead, the RNC strengthened its fund-raising, research, and service roles. Republicans acquired their own building and their own computer, and in 1976 they hired the first full-time chairperson of either national party. (Until then, the chairperson was only part-time or employed in some other career.) As RNC chairman, William Brock expanded the party's staff, launched new publications, started seminars, conducted election analyses, advised candidates, and did most of the things that national party committees had done routinely in other countries for years.

The vast difference between the Democratic and Republican approaches to "reforming" the national committees shows in the funds raised by the DNC and RNC during election campaigns. Since Brock's tenure as chairman of the RNC, the Republicans have raised three to four times the funds raised by the Democrats. This does not mean that the Republicans raised their money the easy way, from a few "fat cats." In fact, the Republicans received a larger proportion of their funds from smaller contributions (of less than $100), mainly through direct-mail solicitation. In short, the RNC has recently been raising far more money than the DNC from many more citizens, in a long-term commitment to improving its organizational services. Evidence of its efforts has appeared at the level of state party organizations.

State and Local Party Organizations

Earlier in our political history, both major parties were firmly anchored in strong state and local party organizations. Big-city party organizations, such as the Democrats' Tammany Hall in New York City and the Cook County Central Committee in Chicago, were prototypes of the **party machine.** The "machine" was a centralized party organization that dominated local politics by controlling elections — sometimes by illegal means, often by providing jobs and social services to urban workers in return for their votes. The social service functions of party machines were undercut as government expanded its role in providing unemployment compensation, aid to families with dependent children, and other social welfare programs. As a result, most local party organizations lost their ability to deliver votes and thus to determine the outcome of elections. However, machines are still strong in certain areas. In Nassau County, New York, for example, suburban Republicans have shown that they can run a machine as well as urban Democrats.[19]

The state organizations of both parties vary widely in strength, but Republican state organizations tend to be stronger than Democratic organizations.[20] The Republicans are likely to have larger budgets and staffs and tend to recruit candidates for more offices.

There seems to be little contact between state and national party organizations. In a survey of party chairpersons in twenty-seven states, most reported having "little involvement" in national committee affairs — even after the reforms by both national committees. However, the national contacts reported by state chairpersons do coincide with the way the RNC and DNC have developed their roles. Republicans at the state level received more staff assistance, poll data and research, financial help, and campaign instruction from the national organization. The only service that the DNC supplied more often than the RNC was "rule enforcement"[21] — reflecting the national party's enforcement of guidelines for selecting convention delegates. Otherwise, the dominant pattern in both parties was for the national organization *not* to intervene in state activities unless asked, and then only to supply services.

If strong party organization means that control is vested in the national headquarters, then *both* the Democrats and Republicans are, in Will Rogers's phrase, unorganized political parties. You will see this same decentralization in the way party candidates campaign for election and run the government after winning elections. In both activities, the party label is very important, but the party organization is not.

CAMPAIGNING FOR ELECTION

Winning public office at the federal or state level in the United States is a two-stage process. The first stage is to win the nomination of one of the two major parties, which is usually decided by an election within the party.* Once nominated, the candidate moves to the second stage: winning election to the office itself. Unless a candidate is lucky enough to run unopposed, each election must be won through an **electoral campaign,** an organized effort to persuade voters to choose one candidate over others competing for the same office.

A full-blown campaign waged by a creditable candidate against a formidable opponent proceeds through three broad stages:[22]

■ *Building the base.* Campaign workers must be recruited and organized to help publicize the candidate. Information about the electorate's past voting behavior must be acquired and analyzed. Funds to do all these things must be acquired, or sources of funds must be identified.

■ *Planning the strategy.* Arguments in favor of voting for the candidate and against the opposition must be incorporated into a campaign theme. The basic choices among strategies are running a *party-centered* campaign, which relies heavily on the voters' party identification and the party organization for resources; an *issue-oriented* campaign, which stresses policies that appeal to important groups; or a *personality-oriented* campaign, which emphasizes the candidate's personal qualities or image.

■ *Clinching the vote.* The candidate must meet with voting groups. The campaign theme must be publicized. Opposition arguments must be countered. Favorable voters must be mobilized to go to the polls on election day. The victory party must be planned.

---

*Of course, a candidate can be nominated by a third party or can run as an independent, but these routes are not usually successful.

Many factors help shape decisions at these three stages. The most important factor is whether the candidate is campaigning to win the nomination or to win the office itself.

Campaigning for the Nomination

The most important feature of the nomination process in American party politics is that it involves an *election*. National party leaders do not choose the party's nominee for president or even the party's candidates for House and Senate elections. Virtually no other parties in the world nominate candidates to the national legislature through primary elections. In more than half the world's parties, legislative candidates are chosen by local party leaders — and in most of those cases, even these choices must be approved by the national organization. In fact, in more than one-third of the world's parties, the national organization itself selects the party candidates.[23]

Primary elections.   In the United States, most aspiring party candidates are nominated through a **primary election,** a preliminary election conducted within the party to select candidates who will run for public office in a subsequent election. The parties' reliance on elections to nominate their candidates makes the nominating process highly decentralized, for it results from decisions of thousands, even millions, of the party rank and file.

There are different types of primary elections, depending on the state in which they are held. The most common type (used by about forty states) is the **closed primary,** in which voters must declare their support for the party before they are given the primary ballot containing the party's potential nominees. A handful of states uses the **open primary,** in which voters need not declare their party loyalty but must choose which party's primary ballot they take into the polling booth. In a **blanket primary,** currently used in only two or three states, voters receive a ballot containing each party's potential nominees and can help nominate candidates for all offices for each party.

A closed primary is thought to contribute to strong party organization, whereas a blanket primary is thought to weaken party organization. Nevertheless, the differences among types of primaries are minor compared with the fact that the parties hold elections to choose their candidates. This fact — that the nomination of most party candidates is in the hands of the party voters rather than the party leaders — contributes mightily to the decentralization of power in American parties. The decentralized nature of American parties is clearly illustrated in campaigns for the party nomination for president.

Nominating a presidential candidate.   Gone are the days when a presidential candidate could be chosen by top party leaders meeting in a "smoke-filled room" during the nominating convention — as the Republicans reportedly chose Warren G. Harding in 1920. For the last half-century, candidates have had to compete vigorously for the nomination by contesting in presidential primary elections across the country.

A **presidential primary** is a special primary used to select delegates to attend the party's national convention, which in turn nominates the presidential candidate. Although each state has its own legislation governing pres-

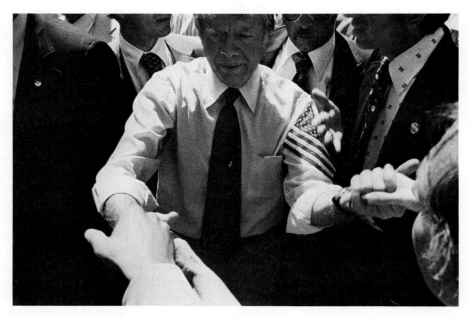

Campaigning Can Be Trying
Candidates for public office at all levels in the United States are expected to ''press the flesh'' with citizens who come to their campaign rallies. Here, even the folksy Jimmy Carter in his shirtsleeves indicates by his expression that he has pressed enough flesh for the day. The Secret Service agents who surround every presidential candidate become understandably nervous when their charge mingles with the crowd.

idential primaries, primaries tend to fall into three main types. In *delegate selection* presidential primaries (the most common type), voters are limited to choosing delegates who may or may not have declared for a presidential candidate. In the handful of *advisory preference* primaries, voters may pick delegates, but they also vote for a presidential candidate. The resulting presidential choice is not binding on the delegates. In the remaining *binding preference* primaries, voters also choose among the presidential candidates, but their choices bind delegates at the convention for lengths of time that vary depending on state law.

Primary elections were first used to select delegates to nominating conventions in 1912. In every election since, primaries have been held in at least twelve states and have always accounted for at least 33 percent of the delegates to the conventions.[24] The best-known presidential primary is held in tiny New Hampshire, with fewer than one million inhabitants, and its legislature is determined to be in the national spotlight once every four years by holding the *earliest* presidential primary. Because it is the first test of the candidates' popularity, they dutifully enter the New Hampshire primary, courting its relatively few voters to make a good early showing. Indeed, Gary Hart got an early boost in his bid for the 1984 Democratic nomination by beating the presumed frontrunner, Walter Mondale, in New Hampshire on February 28. Only 101,000 voters turned out for the Democratic presidential primary, but Hart took 37 percent to Mondale's 27 percent of the vote, surprising observers with his strength.

About thirty states held presidential primaries in 1984, selecting two-thirds of the delegates to both conventions. Most of the remaining one-third of convention delegates were chosen through a system of local party caucuses and state conventions. In the context of presidential nominations today, a

party caucus is a local meeting of party supporters to choose delegates to attend a subsequent meeting, usually at the county level. The delegates selected in the local caucus usually support one of the presidential candidates openly. The county meetings, in turn, select delegates to a higher level. The process culminates in a state convention, where delegates to the national convention are chosen.

In 1984, for example, the Democratic party in Iowa held its local party caucuses on February 20 in 2,495 meetings throughout the state. Approximately 85,000 voters participated in these local caucuses, with an average of 35 voters at each meeting.[25] After the caucus process ran its course and the state convention was held, months later, Mondale emerged with 35 of Iowa's delegates to Hart's 21, with 2 undecided.

Voter participation in the presidential nominating process tends to be much lower in caucus states than in primary states. And in no state did the caucus turnout represent more than 4 percent of the voting population. Nevertheless, nearly a million voters in twenty-seven caucus states participated in nominating the 1984 Democratic presidential candidate. Another fourteen million voters participated in twenty-nine Democratic presidential primaries.[26] Forcing prospective presidential candidates to campaign before hundreds of thousands of party activists in caucus states and millions of party voters in primaries has several consequences:

1. The uncertainty of the nomination process attracts many prospective candidates, especially when the party does not have a president seeking re-election. For example, the quest for the 1984 Democratic nomination began with nine aspirants. However, only three (Walter Mondale, Gary Hart, and Jesse Jackson) won enough primary victories to encourage them to stay in the race until the convention. Because the Constitution

Democratic Survivors Debate in 1984
The quest for the 1984 presidential nomination in the Democratic party began with nine official contenders. Through a complex series of state primaries, caucuses, and conventions, the group was winnowed to three—Walter Mondale (left), Jesse Jackson (center), and Gary Hart (right). In this picture, the three survivors fight for position in a televised debate that helped to determine their fates.

prevents President Reagan from seeking re-election, both parties will have an adequate supply of willing nominees in 1988.

2. Candidates usually cannot win the nomination unless they are favored by most party identifiers. There have been only two exceptions to this rule since 1936, when poll data first became available.[27] They were Adlai E. Stevenson II in 1952 and George McGovern in 1972. Both were Democrats; both lost impressively in the general election.

3. Candidates who win the nomination do it mainly on their own and owe little or nothing to the national party organization, which usually does not push a candidate. In fact, Jimmy Carter won the nomination in 1976 against a field of nationally prominent Democrats, even though he was a party outsider with few strong connections in the national party leadership.

Because primary elections are held among candidates of the same party, it makes no sense to follow a party-centered campaign strategy. Primaries are thus limited to some mix of the issue-oriented and the personality-oriented campaign strategies. Campaigns between different parties' candidates for election to office, however, can use the full range of strategies.

Campaigning for Office

By federal law, all seats in the House of Representatives and one-third of the seats in the Senate are filled in a **general election** held on the first Tuesday after the first Monday in November in even-numbered years. Every state uses the occasion of the federal general election to fill many state and local offices, which adds to the election's "generality." When the president is chosen every fourth year, the general election is also known as a *presidential* election. In the intervening years, it is known variously as a *congressional, midterm,* or *off-year* election.

In contrast to general election campaigns in most other countries (and in earlier periods of our history), relatively few campaigns today follow a party-centered strategy, emphasizing the candidate's party attachment. Often, the party name does not even appear in the candidate's campaign literature. When party-centered campaigns do occur, they are often conducted by candidates of the major party in areas that are traditionally strong for one party. Party-centered campaigns are also likely when a popular president is running for re-election, and challengers see an opportunity to ride in on his coattails. Otherwise, election campaigns for federal office tend to be highly personalistic, with candidates running as individuals rather than as a party team. Several factors contribute to this tendency:

1. Candidates who rely on personal campaign organizations to win party nominations in the primaries tend to keep the same staff through the general elections.

2. The decline of party identification in the electorate makes candidates less likely to rely on party-related appeals.

3. The increased use of electronic media, especially television, in campaigns requires that candidates personalize their messages.

How candidates personalize their messages depends on their choice of a personality-oriented or an issue-oriented strategy. Often the choice is dictated by events and by the raw material: the candidates. Ronald Reagan, an experienced actor, used television to great advantage in cultivating his image as a likable guy when he first ran for president in 1980. (See Chapter 9 for more discussion of the media in political campaigns.) Reagan's strategy was helped greatly by Jimmy Carter's negative, even "mean," image.[28] In 1984 Reagan was still viewed favorably as president by the electorate, and he was handed a valuable issue by Mondale's promise to raise taxes if elected. Campaign managers can sometimes be credited with devising an innovative theme cloaked in a brilliant electoral strategy, but usually election campaigns simply stress the candidate's obvious strengths and popular positions on issues. After that, the outcome depends on the efforts of the campaign organization and on the voters.

Campaign Financing

Speaking about election campaigns, House Speaker Thomas ("Tip") O'Neill once said, "As it is now, there are four parts to any campaign. The candidate, the issues of the candidate, the campaign organization, and the money to run the campaign with. Without money you can forget the other three."[29] Money is needed to pay for office space, staff salaries, telephone bills, postage, travel expenses, campaign literature, and, of course, advertising in the mass media.

Two major principles govern the funds needed to wage a victorious campaign. The first is that challengers need to raise more funds than **incumbents** — officeholders running for re-election. Challengers need more money for their campaign activities to overcome incumbents' advantages in name recognition. Ironically, it is usually easier for incumbents to raise money than it is for challengers, because incumbents can do favors for people while they are in office. People also expect that incumbents will be re-elected anyway.

If there is no incumbent in the election, the second principle applies: candidates of the minority party need to raise more funds than candidates of the majority party. Ironically, it is usually easier for candidates of the majority party to raise money. Candidates of the majority party have a better chance of winning, and people would rather contribute to winners than to losers. Thus, the political facts of life are that electoral challengers and minority party candidates need to raise a good deal of money to run victorious campaigns.

It is difficult to generalize about raising funds for political campaigns. Campaign financing now tends to be heavily regulated by federal and state governments, and regulations vary according to the level of the office — federal, state, or local. Even at the federal level, there are major differences in financing laws for presidential and congressional elections.

Regulating campaign financing. Strict campaign financing laws are relatively new to American politics. Early laws to limit campaign contributions and to control campaign spending were flawed in one way or another, and none clearly provided for administering and enforcing the legislation. During the party reform period of the early 1970s, Congress passed the 1971 *Federal*

Election Campaign Act (FECA), which imposed stringent new rules for full reporting of campaign contributions and expenditures. The weakness of the old legislation soon became apparent. In 1968, prior to the FECA, House and Senate candidates reported spending $8.5 million for their campaigns. With the FECA in force, the same number of candidates confessed to spending $88.9 million in 1972.[30]

The FECA has been amended several times since 1971, but the amendments have for the most part strengthened the law. A Federal Election Commission (FEC) now enforces limits on financial contributions to federal campaigns and requires full disclosure of campaign financial activity. The FEC also administers the public financing of presidential campaigns, which began with the 1976 election.

Financing presidential campaigns. Presidential campaigns have always been expensive, and raising the funds to support them was subject to abuse. Before the FEC took over funding presidential campaigns and regulating campaign finance, costs and fund raising had gotten out of hand. In the presidential election of 1972, the last election before public funding, President Nixon's campaign committee spent over $65 million, some of it obtained illegally, for which campaign officials went to jail. The new campaign finance law offered public funds for the primary and general election presidential campaigns under special conditions.

Candidates seeking *nomination* for president can qualify for federal funding by raising $5,000 (in private contributions no greater than $250 each) in each of twenty states. The FEC then matches these contributions up to one-half of the spending limit. The FEC spending limit for a candidate in the presidential primary election was fixed in the 1974 law at $10 million. However, because the law allowed for increases due to the cost of living and inflation, the primary election limit was $20.2 million in 1984.

The presidential nominees of the Democratic and Republican parties get a different deal when they campaign for *election*. They receive *twice* the primary election limit in public funds for the general election campaign ($40.4 million in 1984) *provided* that they spend only the public funds. Because every major candidate since 1976 has accepted public funding of his campaign, the costs for presidential campaigns have been held far below Nixon's 1972 record expenditure.

Note that the $40.4 million in public funds in 1984 were given directly to each candidate's campaign committee, not to the national committee of either party. However, the national committees are also limited by the FEC in what they can spend on behalf of their nominees. In 1984 the limit for national committees was a low $6.9 million. The FEC also limits individuals ($1,000) and organizations ($5,000) in the amount they may contribute to candidates per election. They are not limited, however, in the amount of *expenses* they may incur to promote candidates of their choice.*

The most obvious effect of public financing of presidential campaigns has been a limit on campaign costs. A second effect has been an equalization in

*A 1974 amendment to the FECA had established limits on both campaign contributions and expenditures. In *Buckley* v. *Valeo* (1976), the Supreme Court struck down the expenditure limits as an infringement on the freedom of speech, protected under the First Amendment.

the amounts spent by the major candidates in the general election. Both Reagan and Mondale spent their $40.4 million limit in the 1984 election. However, the Reagan campaign actually spent more than Mondale's, because the Republican national committee was able to raise funds to reach its own limit of $6.9 million. The Democratic national committee did not spend as much because it did not raise as much.

A third effect of public financing of presidential campaigns has been a continued "personalization" of the campaigns. Federal funds are given to the presidential *candidate* of each party, not to the party organization that the candidate represents. One might think that presidential candidates would coordinate their campaigns closely with those of others in their party running for Congress, that they would financially assist key senators or representatives caught in a tough fight for re-election. Presidential candidates may join congressional candidates in public appearances for mutual benefit, but presidential campaigns are usually isolated — financially and otherwise — from congressional campaigns.

EXPLAINING VOTING CHOICE

Individual voting choices can be analyzed as products of *long-term* and *short-term* forces. Long-term forces operate over a series of elections, predisposing voters to choose certain types of candidates. Short-term forces are associated with particular elections; they arise from a combination of the candidates and the issues of the time. *Party identification* is by far the most important long-term force affecting U.S. elections. The most important short-term forces are *candidate attributes* and their *policy positions*.

Party Identification

Most research on voting in presidential elections stems from a series of National Election Studies that originated at the University of Michigan. Comparable surveys have been conducted for every presidential election and most congressional elections since 1952. When respondents to the 1984 survey were asked at what point they had decided how to vote for president, nearly half (44 percent) said that they "knew all along" or had decided before the conventions.[31] This figure is only slightly higher than the average. In every presidential survey since 1952, about 40 percent of the voters have reported making up their minds before the candidates squared off in the general election campaign. And voters who make an early voting decision generally vote according to their party identification.

Figure 7.4 shows the effects of party identification on the presidential vote in 1984. Republicans voted 95 percent for Reagan, while Democrats voted 78 percent for Mondale. Independents split 68 percent for Reagan. This is a common pattern in presidential elections. The winner holds nearly all of the voters who identify with his party. The loser also holds most of his identifiers, but some percentage defects to the winner, due to the short-term forces surrounding the election. The winner usually gets most of the Independents, who split disproportionately for him, also on the basis of short-term forces.

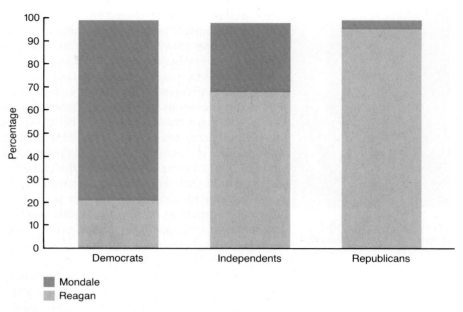

Effect of Party Identification on the Vote in 1984
Despite the long-term decline of party identification in America, party identification is still an important factor in voting choice. In 1984 about 95 percent of self-identified Republicans voted for Reagan, while Mondale received less than 80 percent of the vote of self-styled Democrats. Those who did not identify with a party, the Independents, voted almost 70 percent for Reagan. (Source: 1984 National Election Study conducted at the Center for Political Studies, University of Michigan, and distributed by the Inter-University Consortium for Political and Social Research.)

Figure 7.4 ▬▬▬

Because there are more Democrats than Republicans, the Democrats should benefit. Why, then, have Republican candidates won six out of nine presidential elections since 1952? For one thing, Democrats do not turn out to vote as consistently as Republicans. For another, Democrats defect more easily from their party identification. Defections are sparked by the short-term forces of candidate attributes and issues, which have favored Republican presidential candidates since 1952.

Candidate Attributes

Candidate attributes are especially important to voters who lack good information about a candidate's past behavior and policy stands — which means most of us. Lacking such information, voters search for clues about the candidate's likely behavior in office. Some fall back on their first-hand knowledge of marital status, religion, sex, and race in making political judgments. For example, most voters would rather have a "good guy" in the presidency than a "mean man." As we learned earlier, Ronald Reagan exuded a "good guy" image when he ran in 1980 against President Carter, who had acquired a reputation for being cross and ineffective. One analysis

Geraldine Ferraro, 1984
Democratic Vice Presidential
Candidate

of the 1980 presidential election calculated that such short-term differences in the candidates' perceived attributes cost Carter 4 percent of the vote.[32]

For some reason, the Democrats since 1952 have tended to nominate candidates who were personally flawed in many voters' eyes. In 1952 and in 1956, the Democrats nominated Adlai E. Stevenson II, whose "flaw" was that he was divorced. That may not seem like a flaw today, but it concerned voters in the 1950s. In 1960 the Democrats chose John F. Kennedy, whose flaw — to many Protestants — was being Catholic. Although he was a young, handsome, charismatic candidate of the majority party, who might have been expected to win easily, Kennedy did poorly among Protestant Democrats and barely edged Nixon out in one of the closest elections in history.

In 1984 the Democrats nominated Geraldine Ferraro for vice president; her flaw, for certain voters, was her sex. After an initial burst of enthusiasm for her nomination, many Democratic voters (especially in the South) came to resent a woman's being on the ticket. Divorced candidates and Catholics are commonplace in both parties now; some day women presidential candidates will be, too. The Democratic party may be ahead of the electorate's readiness to accept social change and thus may occasionally hurt itself at the polls because of its candidates' personal attributes. Remember that Democratic primary voters in 1984 also gave 18 percent of their vote to a black candidate, Jesse Jackson. Whichever party nominates the first black candidate may also pay a price at the polls.

Issues and Policies

Choosing between candidates according to personal attributes might be defended, but it is not rational voting according to democratic theory. Instead, citizens should vote according to the candidates' past performance and proposed policies. The candidates clearly differed on their policies in the presidential election of 1984. The Democratic challenger, Mondale, warned the public that, whoever was elected, the next president would have to raise taxes to reduce the huge budget deficit. President Reagan responded by vowing that *he* would not raise taxes after the election. The polls showed that voters preferred Reagan's promise to Mondale's.

Voters who choose between candidates on the basis of their policies are described as voting "on the issues." Unfortunately for democratic theory, most studies of presidential elections have shown that issues are less important than either party identification or candidate image as factors in voting. Only in 1972, when voters perceived George McGovern as too liberal for their tastes, did issue voting exceed party identification in importance.[33] Even that year, issues were less important than the candidate's image. According to the polls taken then, voters saw McGovern as weak and uncertain compared with their view of Nixon as strong and (ironically) highly principled.[34]

Nevertheless, there has been an increase in issue voting since the 1950s. Moreover, there is a closer alignment now between voters' positions on the issues and their party identification. For example, Democratic party identifiers — who are more likely than Republican identifiers to describe themselves as liberal — are now even more likely than Republican identifiers to favor government spending for social welfare and to allow abortions. The more closely

An Historic First in Politics
The Democratic nomination of Geraldine Ferraro for vice president of the United States marked the first time that a woman had been named to the presidential ticket of either major party. Although the Democrats lost, candidate Ferraro performed well as a campaigner, and she undoubtedly added to the credibility of women seeking the presidential nomination in both parties in the future.

party identification is aligned with ideological orientation, the more sense it makes to vote by party. In the absence of detailed information about candidates' positions, party identification becomes a handy and rational indicator of the candidates' policy positions.

Voting for Congress

The candidates for the presidency are listed at the top of the ballot in a presidential election, followed by candidates for other federal, state, and local offices. A voter is said to vote a **straight ticket** when he or she chooses only one party's candidates for all the offices. A voter who switches parties when choosing candidates for different offices is said to vote a **split ticket.** Such a voter might choose Reagan for president but cross over to the Democratic side of the ballot and vote for a Democratic member of Congress running for re-election.

Along with the decline of party identification, the amount of split-ticket voting has increased from about 30 percent of the voters in 1952 to more than half the voters in 1984. Split-ticket voting accounts for the Republicans' failure to win control of the House of Representatives in 1984, despite the fact that Reagan carried nearly every state in the presidential election. Many who voted for Reagan crossed over to vote for incumbent Democratic representatives. A total of 254 of the 435 congressional contests in 1984 pitted Democratic incumbents against Republican challengers, and 241 of the Democratic incumbents won.

A full explanation of the high rate of re-election for congressional incumbents is reserved for Chapter 10. In a nutshell, members of Congress have learned to use their powers of office to develop favorable impressions of themselves and their service to their districts. As a result, voting for congressional candidates has become increasingly detached from voting for presidents. As shown by the election of 1984, even Reagan's coattails were not strong enough to drag his party into control of the House of Representatives. In the words of a major scholar of congressional elections:

> Voters who choose presidents and members of Congress more or less independently of one another do not encourage collective responsibility; individual congressmen can escape the consequences of the collective failures of an administration and need not share their president's fate (and, therefore, interests).[35]

If citizens do not encourage the "collective responsibility" of the president and Congress through their voting behavior, perhaps the party organizations in Congress can hold the party members accountable to the party platform and the president's program. After all, one of the major functions of political parties is to coordinate the actions of government officials. Unfortunately, that is not what happens.

Taking Off the Gloves
Republican vice president George Bush pulled no punches against his Democratic opponent Geraldine Ferraro in the 1984 presidential campaign. The Republicans tried hard to focus voters' attention on Reagan's popularity rather than on Ferraro's gender or personality. In the end, a larger percentage of American women voted for Reagan in 1984 than in 1980.

POLITICAL PARTIES AND MODELS OF DEMOCRACY

The importance of political parties in democratic government depends on which model of democracy one chooses. Political parties as agents of government are much more important to the majoritarian model of democracy than to the pluralist model.

Parties and the Majoritarian Model

According to the majoritarian model of democracy, parties are essential to making the government responsive to public opinion. In fact, the ideal role of parties in majoritarian democracy has been formalized in the four principles of **responsible party government:**

1. Parties should present clear and coherent programs to voters.
2. Voters should choose candidates according to the party programs.
3. The winning party should carry out its program once in office.
4. Voters should hold the governing party responsible at the next election for executing its program.[36]

Let's evaluate how well these principles are fulfilled in American politics. You have learned that the Democratic and Republican platforms *do* differ clearly and that they are much more ideologically consistent than many people believe. The first principle is thus met fairly well. The second principle is only partially fulfilled. Most voters do have longstanding party identifications, which explain a great deal of their candidate choice. Although this is not the same thing as "choosing candidates according to their party programs," the alignment of party identifiers according to liberal-conservative ideology is fairly strong and increasing. However, the relationship between party identification and voting choice is often stronger in presidential than in congressional elections.

The third principle—that the winning party should carry out its program —is least applicable to American party politics. Regardless of which party wins the presidency, the president cannot count on his party members in Congress to vote solidly for his program. As will be explained in Chapter 10, members of Congress cater to their constituents in order to ensure their reelection. Accordingly, they often vote against their party's position when they think the vote would harm their district or state. In truth, political parties in America are too decentralized to enforce party discipline in congressional voting. Congressional candidates win their nominations on their own by contesting primary elections. Congressional candidates win elections mainly by raising their own funds and by running their own campaigns. The conditions for party discipline simply are not adequate to force members of Congress either to support their president's program or to oppose their opponent's program, as we saw in the case of Phil Gramm at the beginning of this chapter.

The fourth principle—that voters hold the governing party accountable at the next election for executing the party program—also does not apply in American politics. In fact, the "party program" tends to fade from sight soon after the convention that wrote the platform. While the party platform represents the views of delegates to the party convention, it may not reflect the views of the party's nominee for president. After the election, the winning candidate presents *his* legislative program, which may emphasize certain platform planks more than others and may neglect some entirely. Neither national party organization in America would pretend to force its platform on its winning presidential candidate. Instead, it is the *president's* legislative program, not the party platform, that party members in Congress are asked to support. The next presidential election becomes a referendum not so much on party government as on presidential government.

Parties and the Pluralist Model

Parties in the United States operate more in keeping with the pluralist model of democracy than with the majoritarian model. Instead of being the basic mechanisms through which citizens control their government, American parties function as two major interest groups. Our current parties press their own interests (electing and re-electing their candidates) in competition with others in the swirl of pluralist politics. Parties repeatedly bargain away platform principles for short-term electoral advantages.

Some scholars believe that stronger parties would contribute more to democratic government than our present weak ones, even if American parties could not then meet all the requirements of the responsible party model.[37] Even at present, our parties perform valuable functions in structuring the vote and proposing alternative government policies. Stronger ones might play a more valuable role in coordinating government policy.

SUMMARY

Political parties perform four important functions for a political system: they nominate candidates, structure the voting choice, propose alternative government programs, and coordinate the activities of government officials. Political parties have been performing these functions longer in the United States than in any other country. The Democratic party, founded in 1828, is the world's oldest political party. When the Republican party emerged as a major party after the 1856 election, it joined the Democrats to produce our present two-party system—the oldest party system in the world.

Our two-party system has experienced three critical elections, each of which realigned the electorate for years to come and affected the party balance in government. The election of 1860 established the Republicans as the major party in the North and the Democrats as the dominant party in the South. Nationally, the two parties were roughly balanced in Congress until the critical election of 1896. This election strengthened the link between the Republican party and business interests in the heavily populated Northeast and Midwest and produced a surge in voter support that made the Republicans the majority party nationally for more than three decades. The Great Depression produced conditions for the critical election of 1932, which transformed the Democrats into the majority party, giving them almost uninterrupted control of Congress until the present.

Minor parties have not enjoyed much electoral success in America, although they have contributed ideas to the Democratic and Republican platforms. The two-party system is perpetuated in the United States because of the nature of the electoral system and the socialization process, which results in most Americans' identifying with either the Democratic or the Republican party. The federal system of government has also helped the Democrats and Republicans survive major national defeats by sustaining them with electoral victories at the state level. However, the pattern of party identification has been changing in recent years, with more people becoming Independents and Republicans, to the decline of Democratic identifiers.

Party identifiers, party activists, and party platforms show consistent differences in ideological orientation between the two parties. Democratic identifiers and activists are more likely to describe themselves as liberal, while Republican identifiers and activists tend to be conservative. The 1984 Democratic party platform also showed a more liberal orientation by stressing equality over freedom, while the Republican platform was more conservative, concentrating on freedom but also emphasizing the importance of restoring social order. Organizationally, the Republicans have recently become the stronger party at both national and state levels, but both parties are very decentralized compared with parties in other countries.

The successful candidate for public office usually must campaign to win the party nomination as well as to win the general election. A major factor in the decentralization of American parties is their reliance on primary elections to nominate candidates. Candidates who have to campaign for the party nomination owe little to the party organization and retain their campaign organizations to help them win the general election. Even the dynamics of campaign financing requires candidates to rely mainly on their own resources or — in the case of presidential elections — on public funds. In either event, party organizations contribute relatively little toward candidates' campaign expenses.

The voting choice can be analyzed in terms of voters' party identifications, candidates' attributes, and candidates' policy positions. Party identification is still the most important long-term factor in shaping the voting decision, but few candidates rely on party preferences in their campaigns. Most candidates today run personalized campaigns stressing their attributes or their policies. In particular, votes for congressional candidates are highly tied to the personal relationships that incumbents have forged with their constituents. The high success rate of re-election for incumbent members of Congress helps insulate them from party pressures in policymaking.

American parties do not fulfill the ideals of responsible party government that fit with the majoritarian model of democracy. In particular, the parties are weak in carrying out their programs once in office, which makes it difficult for voters to hold a party accountable at the next election for government actions. American parties are better suited to the pluralist model of democracy, in which they can be viewed as major interest groups competing with lesser groups to further their own interests of re-election.

Returning to the four major functions performed by political parties, we can rate the American parties as follows: (1) high on nominating candidates; (2) very high on structuring the vote; (3) moderate on formulating alternative government programs; and (4) very low on coordinating the actions of officials in government. Still, political parties at least aspire to the noble goal of representing the wishes of most of the people. As you will see in the following chapter, interest groups do not even pretend as much.

Key Terms

political party
nominate
political system
peer review
electoral college
caucus
national convention
party platform
critical election
electoral realignment
two-party system
majority party
minority party
bolter party
farmer-labor party
party of ideological protest
single-issue party
proportional representation

party identification
national committee
congressional campaign
    organization
party machine
electoral campaign
primary election
closed primary
open primary
blanket primary
presidential primary
party caucus
general election
incumbent
straight ticket
split ticket
responsible party government

Selected Readings

Clubb, Jerome M.; William H. Flanigan; and Nancy H. Zingale. *Partisan Realignment: Voters, Parties, and Government in American History.* Beverly Hills, Calif.: SAGE Publications, 1980. This is a major statistical study of election returns for president and Congress from 1840 to 1978. The analysis focuses on identifying the realignment of voters, and it extends to the control of government and the role of political leadership in securing the realignment of voting blocs after a critical election.

Cotter, Cornelius P., et al. *Party Organizations in American Politics.* New York: Praeger, 1984. Cotter and associates studied the Democratic and Republican party organizations in twenty-seven states around 1980. They also surveyed county chairpersons in each state and interviewed members of the parties' national committees, producing the first major study of relationships among local, state, and national levels of party organization.

Crotty, William. *The Party Game.* New York: W. H. Freeman, 1985. In this slim volume, Crotty concisely surveys the history, structure, and role of political parties in American government. He concludes by speculating on the party system's future growth and capabilities.

Crotty, William, and John S. Jackson, III. *Presidential Primaries and Nominations.* Washington, D.C.: CQ Press, 1985. Crotty and Jackson cover the process of presidential selection, beginning at the declaration of candidacy and ending with the nomination at the national convention. They focus on how the nominating system has changed during the last three decades and on the political consequences of these changes.

Gitelson, Alan R.; M. Margaret Conway; and Frank B. Feigert. *American Political Parties: Stability and Change*. Boston: Houghton Mifflin, 1984. This is one of the major texts on party politics in the United States.

Hill, David B., and Norman R. Luttbeg. *Trends in American Electoral Behavior*. Itasca, Ill.: F. E. Peacock, 1983. Hill and Luttbeg provide a brief, readable, and informative review of the impact of party identification, issues, and images on voting behavior.

Nelson, Michael, ed. *The Elections of 1984*. Washington, D.C.: CQ Press, 1985. A series of eleven essays analyzes the 1984 presidential election for issues, campaign strategies, media effects, and political consequences.

Rosenstone, Steven J.; Roy L. Behr; and Edward H. Lazarus. *Third Parties in America: Citizen Response to Major Party Failure*. Princeton, N.J.: Princeton University Press, 1984. The authors not only provide an excellent review of the history of third-party movements in American politics, but they also analyze the factors that lead third-party voters and candidates to abandon the two major parties. They conclude that third-party efforts improve the performance of the party system.

Salmore, Stephen A., and Barbara G. Salmore. *Candidates, Parties, and Campaigns: Electoral Politics in America*. Washington, D.C.: CQ Press, 1985. The Salmores do an admirable job of summarizing the major characteristics of successful and unsuccessful electoral campaigns. They discuss campaigning before and after the introduction of television and pay special attention to the changing role of political parties in election campaigns.

8

Interest Groups

F

ew consumers realize that they pay a hidden tax of about $1,000 when they purchase a new American car. One might call this an "interest group tax," since it is the result of lobbying by American automobile companies and the United Auto Workers (UAW). Business and labor pushed Washington to enact restrictions on the import of cheap Japanese cars because their popularity was damaging the American automobile industry and putting many auto workers out of a job. The government responded in 1981 by pressuring Japanese auto manufacturers to accept "voluntary" yearly export quotas on cars shipped to the United States.

The result of the export quotas was that everybody profited except the American consumer. U.S. auto producers saw their financial picture brighten as a collective loss of $4 billion in 1980 gave way to profits of close to $9 billion each year in 1984 and 1985. Part of this change was due to a strengthening economy. But it also resulted from consumers' having to switch to American models because of the low supply of Toyotas, Hondas, and other imports. The United Auto Workers also saw the export restrictions as a success. The U.S. International Trade Commission estimated that the quotas saved about 44,000 American jobs. Ironically, the Japanese auto manufacturers did well too. Since the quotas altered the natural law of supply and demand, the Japanese were able to increase their car prices beyond the levels that would have been justified if they had shipped enough cars to meet the demand. By 1985, a comparably equipped Toyota Corolla sold for roughly $3,000 more in the United States than it did in Japan. Before the export restrictions went into effect, the difference was less than $500.

Because the quotas artificially raised the price of Japanese cars, the price of American cars could be kept higher — about $1,000 higher. Thus, even the consumer who never intended to buy a Japanese import ended up paying a huge hidden tax to keep American car companies and auto workers happy. The skyrocketing profits of U.S. auto makers led the Reagan administration to abandon the voluntary restraints formally in 1985. Yet the Japanese, fearing a political backlash in this country if they seized too much of the car market, kept to a self-imposed quota, although at a higher level of annual exports.[1]

This example of foreign car quotas illustrates some of the basic dynamics of interest group politics. All interest groups, or lobbies, claim that the policies they favor are "in the public interest" and can make a persuasive case for why society will benefit from the policy changes they recommend. Yet lobbies define the public interest in terms of policies that best serve their constituents. The United Auto Workers claimed that it would be to the nation's advantage to protect the jobs of U.S. workers rather than to export those jobs. This was a credible argument to other Americans, since no one wanted auto workers to lose their jobs. However, if consumers had known how much more they would have to pay for Japanese- *and* American-built cars because of those jobs, they might have thought differently about the issue. Would Americans really have supported the quotas if they had known that it would cost consumers $300,000 a year to protect *each* car manufacturing job in the United States?[2] Stated another way, might Americans have preferred a governmental process that did more to favor majoritarian interests — in this case, those of consumers — at the expense of the demands of such interest groups as car companies and the United Auto Workers?

In the end, the government must decide between competing interest groups' philosophies and stands on the issues. In analyzing interest group politics, we shall focus on a number of different questions. How do interest groups form? What kinds of people are most likely to be represented by interest groups? What tactics do different groups use to convince policymakers that their views are best for the nation? Why has the number of interest groups grown so rapidly in recent years?

INTEREST GROUPS AND THE AMERICAN POLITICAL TRADITION

An **interest group** is generally defined as "an organized body of individuals who share some goals and who try to influence public policy."[3] Some of the most prominent interest groups include the AFL-CIO (representing labor union members), the American Farm Bureau Federation (representing farmers), the Chamber of Commerce (representing businesspeople), and Common Cause (representing citizens concerned with reforming government). Interest groups are also called **lobbies,** and their representatives are referred to as **lobbyists.**

Interest Groups: Good or Evil?

A recurring debate in American politics concerns the relation of interest groups to a democratic society. Are interest groups a threat to the well-being of the political system, or do they contribute to its proper functioning? A favorable early evaluation of interest groups can be found in the writings of Alexis de Tocqueville, a French visitor to the United States in the early nineteenth century. During his travels, Tocqueville marveled at the array of organizations he found, and he later wrote that "Americans of all ages, all conditions, and all dispositions, constantly form associations" (see Compared With What? 8.1).[4] Tocqueville was suggesting that the ease with which we form organizations reflects a strong democratic culture. His comments have always been a source of pride for Americans.

James Madison offered a different perspective. Writing in *The Federalist,* Madison warned of the dangers of "factions," or the major divisions in American society. In *The Federalist,* No. 10, written in 1787, Madison said that it was inevitable that substantial differences would develop between factions. It was only natural that farmers would come to oppose merchants; tenants, landlords; and so on. Madison further reasoned that each faction would do what it could to prevail over the other factions. Each basic interest in society would try to persuade government to adopt policies that favored it at the expense of others. He noted that the fundamental causes of faction were "sown in the nature of man."[5]

But Madison argued against trying to suppress factions. He concluded that factions can be eliminated only by removing our freedoms: "Liberty is to faction what air is to fire."[6] Instead, Madison suggested that "relief" from

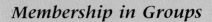 *Membership in Groups*

Alexis de Tocqueville's observation that "Americans form associations for the smallest undertakings"* may be an exaggeration, but Americans do seem to join groups in greater proportions than the people of other countries.

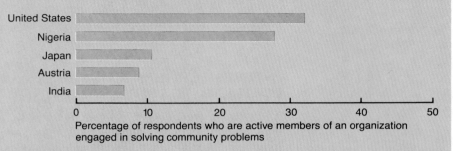

Percentage of respondents who are active members of an organization engaged in solving community problems

*Alexis de Tocqueville, *Democracy in America*, ed. Richard D. Heffner (New York: Mentor Books, 1956), p. 36.

Source: Sidney Verba, Norman H. Nie, and Jae-On Kim, *The Modes of Democratic Participation: A Cross-National Comparison* (Beverly Hills, Calif.: SAGE, 1971), p. 36. © 1971 Sage Publications Inc. Reprinted by permission of SAGE Publications Inc.

the self-interested advocacy of factions should come only through controlling the *effects* of such activity.[7] This relief would be provided by a democratic republic in which government would mediate between opposing factions. The structure of government would also ensure that even a majority faction could never come to suppress the rights of others.[8]

One's judgment of interest groups as "good" or "evil" depends on how strongly one is committed to freedom or equality (as discussed in Chapter 1). Giving people the freedom to organize lobbies does not guarantee that they will all end up with equally powerful interest groups acting on their behalf. Judgment is also influenced by whether one believes democracy works best if it abides by majoritarian or by pluralist principles (as discussed in Chapter 2). We shall return to these broader questions of democratic theory after explaining the operation of interest groups more fully.

The Roles of Interest Groups

The "evil" side of interest group politics is all too apparent. Each group pushes its own selfish interests, which, despite the group's claims to the contrary, are not always in the best interest of other Americans. The "good" side of interest group advocacy may not be as clear. What aspects of interest group activity benefit our political system?[9]

Representation.   Interest groups act to *represent* people before their government. Just as a member of Congress represents a particular constituency, so does a lobbyist. A lobbyist for the National Association of Broadcasters, for example, speaks for the interests of radio and television broadcasters when Congress or a government agency is considering a relevant policy decision.

Whether one has a political interest in the cement industry, excise taxes, endangered species, or any other significant, policy-related concern, it is desirable to have an active lobby operating in Washington. Members of Congress represent a multitude of interests — some of them conflicting — from their own districts and states. Administrators, too, are pulled in different directions and have their own policy preferences. Interest groups articulate their followers' preferences in a more direct and intense manner than government officials usually do.

If the Shoe Fits . . .
People often participate in politics by working through their lobbying organizations. Typically, the staff of the organization will ask members to write letters to their representatives and senators. Shoe manufacturers thought, however, that their request for protection from imports would attract more attention if their demands were written on pieces of leather cut in the shape of a shoe. Here, a staffer for Republican Senator John Warner of Virginia goes through her "mail."

Participation.   Interest groups are also vehicles for political *participation.* They provide a means by which like-minded citizens can pool their resources and channel their energy into collective political action. And individuals will band together because they know it is much easier to get government to listen to a group than to an individual. One farmer fighting for more generous price supports probably will not get very far, but thousands of farmers united in an organization stand a much better chance of getting policymakers to consider their plight.

Education.   As part of their efforts at lobbying and increasing their membership, interest groups help to *educate* their members, the public at large, and government officials. On one side of the liability insurance question are gathered the insurance companies, business groups, and the American Medical Association—organizations that have tried to demonstrate to the American people that excessive court awards have caused skyrocketing insurance premiums. Trial lawyers and consumer groups offer evidence on the opposite side; they attempt to convince the public that legislation curbing the size of awards is unwarranted because, first, insurance companies are still making money, and second, restrictions on awards will make it more difficult for injured people to collect damages. Through their testimony, policy statements, advertisements, fact sheets, and the media coverage of their activities, these competing groups have given Americans additional information about liability insurance to help them make up their minds.

Agenda building.   In a related role, interest groups bring new issues into the political limelight, through a process called **agenda building.** There are many problem areas in American society, but not all of them are being addressed by public officials. Interest groups make the government aware of these problem areas through their lobbying (advocacy) efforts, in order to ensure that something is done to solve them. After videocassette recorders (VCRs) became popular in the United States, competing lobbies raised a number of issues concerning copyright law and royalty payments to movie studios. The Motion Picture Association of America and the Electronic Industries Association (the trade group for VCR manufacturers) brought these issues to the fore by pressing Congress for action.[10]

Program monitoring.   Finally, interest groups engage in **program monitoring.** In other words, they follow government programs important to their constituents, keeping abreast of developments in Washington and in the local communities where policies are implemented. When problems emerge, interest groups push administrators to change policies in accordance with the group's program goals. They draw attention to agency officials' transgressions and even file suit to stop actions they consider unlawful. When the Department of Agriculture reduced food stamp benefits on the order of President Gerald Ford, the Food Research and Action Center acted on behalf of program recipients and took the department to court. The court sided with the lobbying group, and the original benefits were reinstated.

Interest groups do, then, play some positive roles in their pursuit of self-interest. But it is too soon to assume that the positive side of interest groups neatly balances the negative. Unanswered questions remain about the overall impact of interest groups on public policymaking. Most important, are the effects of interest group advocacy effectively controlled, as Madison believed they would be?

HOW INTEREST GROUPS FORM

Do some people form interest groups more easily than others? Are some factions represented while others are not? Pluralists assume that when a political issue arises, interest groups with relevant policy concerns begin to lobby. Policy conflicts are ultimately resolved through bargaining and negotiation between the involved organizations and government. Unlike Madison, who dwelt on the potential for harm by groups (factions), pluralists see groups in a beneficial light and argue that groups further democracy by broadening representation within the system.

A significant pluralist notion is that new interest groups naturally form when the need arises. David Truman outlined this idea in his classic work *The Governmental Process* (1951).[11] Truman said that an interest group originates when certain unorganized people are adversely affected by change. For example, if government threatens to regulate a particular industry, the firms comprising that industry will start a trade association to convince government not to take actions that will harm their financial well-being. Truman saw a direct cause-and-effect relationship in all of this: existing groups stand in equilibrium until some type of disturbance (such as falling wages or declining farm prices) forces new groups to form.

Truman's thinking on interest group formation seems similar to the "invisible hand" notion of classical economics: self-correcting market forces will remedy imbalances in the marketplace. But in politics there is no invisible hand—no force that automatically causes interest groups to develop. Truman's disturbance theory and other pluralist writings present only an idealized portrait of interest group politics in America. In real life, people do not automatically organize when they are adversely affected by some disturbance. A good example of this nonorganization can be found in Herbert Gans's book *The Urban Villagers*.[12] Gans, a sociologist, moved into a low-income Boston neighborhood during the late 1950s. This neighborhood, the "West End," had been targeted for urban redevelopment. The city regarded it as a slum and was going to tear down the existing buildings and replace them with modern ones. This meant that the people living there—primarily poor Italian Americans who very much liked their neighborhood—would have to be dispersed to other parts of the Boston area.

Few things in life are less pleasant than being evicted from one's home, so the situation in the West End would certainly qualify as a bona fide "disturbance" in Truman's scheme of interest group formation. Yet the West Enders put up hardly a fight to save their neighborhood. An organization started for that purpose attracted little support from residents. The West End remained unorganized; soon people were moved and buildings demolished.

The disturbance theory of interest group formation clearly fails to explain the case of Boston's West Enders. An adverse condition or change does not automatically ensure that an interest group will form. What, then, is the missing ingredient? Political scientist Robert Salisbury says that the quality of interest group leadership may be the crucial factor.

Interest Group Entrepreneurs

Salisbury likens the role of an interest group leader to that of an entrepreneur in the business world.[13] A business entrepreneur is one who starts new enterprises, usually at considerable personal financial risk. Salisbury says that an interest group entrepreneur or organizer will succeed or fail for many of the same reasons a business entrepreneur will succeed or fail. The **interest group entrepreneur** must have something attractive to "market" if he or she is going to convince members to join.[14] Potential members must be persuaded that the benefits they will receive outweigh their costs of joining. Someone starting a new union, for example, must convince workers that the union can win them wages high enough to offset the dues they will have to pay as members. The organizer of an ideological group must convince potential members that the group can effectively lobby the government to achieve their particular goals.

The development of the United Farm Workers Union illustrates the importance of leadership in an interest group's formation. This union is composed of men and women who pick crops, such as grapes and lettuce, in California and other parts of the Southwest. The work is backbreaking, performed in hot, desert climates. The pickers are predominantly poor, uneducated Americans of Hispanic background. For the most part, they have been unable to find opportunities other than unskilled farm labor.[15] Their chronically low wages and deplorable living conditions made these farm workers prime candidates for organization into a labor union.

Throughout the twentieth century there had been efforts to organize the pickers. Yet for many reasons, including distrust of union organizers, intimidation by employers, and lack of money to pay union dues, all such efforts had been failures. Then, in 1962, Cesar Chavez, a poor Mexican American, began to crisscross the Central Valley of California, talking to workers and planting the idea of a union. Chavez was a former farm worker himself (he first worked as a picker at the age of ten), and he was well aware of the difficulties that lay ahead for his newly organized United Farm Workers Union.

After a strike against grape growers failed in 1965, Chavez changed his tactics of trying to build a stronger union merely through recruiting a larger membership. Copying the black civil rights movement, Chavez and his followers marched 250 miles to the state capitol in Sacramento to demand help from the governor. This march and other nonviolent tactics began to draw sympathy from people who had no direct involvement in farming. Catholic clergy were attracted to the farm workers' movement since it seemed to help these poor members of the church. This support in turn gave Chavez greater credibility, and his followers cast him in the role of spiritual as well as political leader. At one point, he fasted for twenty-five days to show his commitment to nonviolence. Democratic Senator Robert Kennedy of New York, one of the most popular politicians of the day, joined Chavez when he broke his fast at a mass conducted on the back of a flat-bed truck in Delano, California.[16]

Cesar Chavez
Although many efforts had been made to organize migrant farm workers, none succeeded until Chavez's inspired leadership brought the United Farm Workers Union into existence. Growers bitterly resisted the unionization efforts, but economic pressures finally led many to the bargaining table.

Chavez became a respected and charismatic leader, and a small but significant number of Americans heeded his call to stop buying grapes. The growers, who had been intensely antagonistic toward the union, were finally hurt in their wallets. Under other economic pressures, they eventually agreed to recognize and bargain with the United Farm Workers Union. The union, in turn, helped its members through the wage and benefit agreements it negotiated.

Who Is Being Organized?

The case of Cesar Chavez is a persuasive example of leadership's importance in the formation of new interest groups. Despite many years of adverse conditions, efforts to organize the farm workers had failed miserably. The dynamic leadership of Cesar Chavez seems to have made the difference.

In addition to leadership, however, other very important factors were at work. The residents of Boston's West End and the California farm workers were poor, uneducated or undereducated, and politically inexperienced — factors that made it extremely difficult to organize them into interest groups. But if there had been a decision to redevelop a wealthy Boston neighborhood, an interest group would probably have formed immediately. The well educated and well off have more knowledge of how the system operates and more confidence that their actions can make a difference. Together, these attributes give people more incentive to devote their time and ample resources to organizing and supporting interest groups.

Every existing interest group has its own history, different from that of every other lobby. Yet the three variables that we have discussed help to explain why groups may or may not become fully organized. First, an adverse change or disturbance can contribute to people's awareness that they need political representation. However, change alone will not ensure that an organization forms, and organizations have been formed in the absence of such disturbances. Second, the quality of leadership is critical in the organization of interest groups. Some interest group entrepreneurs are more skilled at convincing people to join their organizations. Finally, the higher the social class of potential members, the more likely they are to know the value of interest groups and to participate in politics by joining them.

Since wealthy and better-educated Americans are more likely to form and join lobbies, they seem to have an important advantage in the political process. Nevertheless, as the United Farm Workers case shows, the poor and less educated are also capable of forming interest groups. The question that remains, then, is not *whether* the various opposing interests are represented, but *how well* they are represented. Or, in terms of Madison's premise in *The Federalist*, No. 10, are the "effects" of faction—in this case, the advantages of the wealthy and well educated—sufficiently "controlled"? Before we can answer this question, we need to turn our attention to the resources available to interest groups.

INTEREST GROUP RESOURCES

The strengths, capabilities, and effects of an interest group depend in large part on its *resources*. A group's most significant resources are its members, lobbyists, and money, including funds that can be contributed to political candidates. Not only is the sheer quantity of a group's resources important, but also the wisdom with which those resources are used.

Interest Group Members

One of the most valuable resources an interest group can have is a large and politically active membership. If a lobbyist is trying to convince a legislator to support a particular bill, it is tremendously helpful to have many group members living in the legislator's home district or state. A legislator who has not already taken a firm position on the bill might be swayed by the knowledge that the voters back home will be informed by that interest group of his or her votes on the issue. The National Rifle Association (NRA) is an effective interest group on Capitol Hill because its membership of three million cares so deeply about gun control. Members of Congress know that the NRA will inform its membership of how each senator and representative votes on proposed gun control bills and that NRA members might be influenced by that information when they go to the polls.

Members provide an organization not only with political muscle in its efforts to influence policy, but also with financial resources. The more money an organization can collect through dues and contributions, the more people it can hire to lobby government officials and monitor the policymaking process. These increased resources will also let the organization communicate with its members more and inform them better. The group's ability to work at maintaining its membership and attracting new members will also be directly affected.

Maintaining membership.   To keep the members it already has, an organization must persuade them that it is doing a good job in its advocacy efforts. A major tool for shoring up support among members is a newsletter or magazine. Through a publication, members can be informed and reminded of an organization's activities. Executives whose corporations belong to the National Association of Manufacturers (NAM) receive *Enterprise,* a business magazine; *Briefing,* a weekly newsletter that focuses on legislative and regulatory action in Washington; and the two-page *Issue Briefs,* which summarizes current public policy disputes. Members also have access, through a toll-free Washington number, to recordings describing matters of immediate concern to the NAM. Most lobbies provide more modest offerings for their members, but they usually have at least a newsletter.

Business, professional, and labor associations generally have an easier time holding onto members than do citizen groups. (**Citizen groups** are generally those whose basis of organization is a concern for issues unrelated to the members' vocations.) In many corporations, membership in a trade group constitutes only a very minor business expense. And, in some states, workers can be required to belong to the union that is the bargaining agent with their employer. Citizen groups, on the other hand, base their appeal on members' ideological sentiments. These groups face a difficult challenge: issue winds can blow hot and cold, and a particularly hot issue one year may not hold the same interest to citizens a few years later.

Attracting new members.   All interest groups constantly seek new members to expand their resources and clout. Groups relying on ideological appeals have a special problem, because the competition in most policy areas is intense. People concerned about the environment, for example, may receive invitations to join a seemingly limitless number of local, state, and national groups. Only a few of the national organizations are the National Wildlife Federation, Environmental Action, the Environmental Defense Fund, the Natural Resources Defense Council (NRDC), Friends of the Earth, the Wilderness Society, the Sierra Club, and the Environmental Policy Center.

One method of attracting new members which is being used more and more is **direct mail** — letters sent to selected audiences to promote the organization and to appeal for contributions. The advantage of direct mail is that separate letters can be sent to people in carefully targeted audiences. An organization can purchase a list of people who are likely to be sympathetic to its cause or trade lists with a similar organization. A group trying to fight legalized abortion, for instance, might use a list from a conservative magazine like the *National Review,* while a prochoice lobby might use that of the liberal *New Republic.* The main drawbacks to direct mail are its expense and low rate of return. A response rate of 2 percent of all those who receive membership or donation appeals is considered good. If the response rate falls below that level, a group's costs usually exceed the money returned. To maximize the chances of a good return, great care and thought are given to the design and content of letters. Letters often try to play on the reader's emotions and to create the feeling that the reader should be personally involved in the struggle.[17]

The free rider problem. The need for aggressive marketing by interest groups suggests that it is not easy to get people who sympathize with a group's goals to actually join and support it through voluntary contributions. Economists have called this difficulty the **free rider problem,** but we might call it, more colloquially, the "let George do it" problem.[18] The funding for public television stations illustrates this dilemma. Almost all agree that public television stations, which survive in large part through voluntary viewer contributions, are of great value. Yet not all of those who watch public television contribute on a regular basis. Why? Because they can watch the programs whether or not they are contributors. The "free rider" has the same access to a public television channel as the contributor.

The same logic holds true for interest group efforts. If a lobbying group wins some benefits, those benefits are not restricted to members of the organization. For instance, if the American Business Conference wins a tax concession from Congress for capital expenditures, all businesses falling within the provisions of the law can take advantage of the tax break. Thus many business executives might not support their firms' joining the American Business Conference, even though they might benefit from its efforts; they prefer instead to let others shoulder the financial burden.

The free rider problem increases the difficulty of attracting paying members, but it certainly does not make the task impossible. In fact, as we shall discuss below, the number of interest groups has grown significantly in recent years. Clearly, many Americans realize that if everyone decides to "let George do it," then the job simply won't get done. Millions of Americans contribute to interest groups because they feel a responsibility to help organizations that work on their behalf. However, a group's politics is not always the primary attraction for new members. Many organizations offer membership benefits having nothing to do with lobbying. Business trade associations, for example, offer publications about industry trends and effective management practices and organize conventions where members can learn, socialize, and occasionally find new customers or suppliers.

Lobbyists

Part of the money raised by interest groups is used to pay lobbyists, who represent the organizations before government. The lobbyists make sure that their organizations know what government is doing and that people in government know what their members want. Many organizations, especially those with members affected by government regulations, believe that it is imperative to have capable lobbyists stationed in Washington. Then, when an administrative agency issues new regulations, the group's representative can quickly interpret the regulations' content and implications for rank-and-file members. As William Utz of the National Shrimp Congress puts it, "The reaction time to new rules and regulations is faster if the headquarters is based in Washington. If you have an ear here, you can translate things as they happen."[19]

Lobbyists can be either full-time employees of the organization or employees of public relations or law firms who are hired on retainer. When hiring a lobbyist, an interest group looks for someone who knows his or her way around Washington. Lobbyists are valued for their experience and knowledge of how government operates. They are often people who have served in the legislative or executive branches, where they have had firsthand government experience. William Timmons, who heads his own lobbying firm, has attracted an impressive array of clients, such as the American Broadcasting Company, Anheuser-Busch, Chrysler, and Boeing. These companies know that Timmons's experience as a White House assistant for legislative liaison gives him a great deal of insight into the policymaking process, as well as valuable government contacts.[20]

Lobbying is so lucrative for those with the right kind of experience that nearly three hundred former members of Congress are part of the profession. As one old Washington saying has it, "They come to govern, they stay to lobby."[21]

By the nature of their location, many Washington law firms are drawn into lobbying. Corporations without their own Washington offices rely heavily on law firms to lobby for them before the federal government. Over time, lawyer-lobbyists tend to develop expertise in particular policy areas and are valued for their knowledge of the complexities of the policymaking process.

The most common image of a lobbyist is that of an "arm twister" — someone who spends most of the time trying to convince a legislator or administrator to back a certain policy. Usually lobbying is more subtle than that. The most typical interaction between lobbyists and policymakers is the transmission of information from lobbyist to government official (see Feature 8.1). Lobbyists constantly provide government officials and their staffs with data that support their organizations' policy goals. In recent years, for example, the American Iron and Steel Institute has tried to persuade the government to do more to protect the American steel industry from foreign competitors. As a result, the Institute's lobbyists try to supply members of Congress and officials in the Commerce Department with as much information as possible about declining employment, plant closings, and projected downward trends for American steel production.

But presenting data is not enough. A lobbyist must also build a compelling case, showing that the "facts" dictate that a change be made. What the lobbyist is really trying to do, of course, is to convince policymakers that his or her data deserve more attention and are more accurate than those presented by opposing lobbyists.

Political Action Committees

One of the organizational resources that can make a lobbyist's job easier is a **political action committee (PAC).** PACs pool campaign contributions from group members and donate those funds to candidates for political office. Under federal law, a PAC can give up to $5,000 for each separate election to a candidate for Congress. As Figure 8.1 shows, more and more interest groups are organizing PACs; the greatest growth has come from corporations, most of which were legally prohibited from operating such political com-

Feature 8.1

Liz Robbins, Lobbyist

Late Tuesday night, outside the Senate Chamber, a weary Sen. Pete Domenici spotted Elizabeth Robbins prowling the halls. He threw up his hands in mock frustration and sighed: "You've done us in with your lobbying on this one, Lizzie."

The Senate Budget Committee chairman was talking about a dispute over Medicaid funding between House and Senate budget conferees. The object of his compliment was the woman who is probably Washington's most successful lobbyist for federal aid for social services. Her clients include the California cities of San Francisco and Berkeley, the Michigan state legislature and, in special cases, New York City and Oneida County, N.Y. In the Medicaid dispute, she helped the state of Michigan escape a loss of about $40 million in aid in the coming fiscal year.

Even in a time of social-service cutbacks, Miss Robbins is a force in the legislative process. Much of her activity is defensive, aimed at preventing cutbacks or at reshaping budget proposals to meet her client's interest.

In a year when liberal lobbyists aren't doing well, Miss Robbins is doing better than most.

Rarely does a day pass when she isn't outside the House or Senate chamber, looking a bit disheveled, frequently a bit frantic and always carrying volumes of material on arcane subjects, such as "The Matching Formula for Title 20."

Sometimes, she'll flag a lawmaker with a polite "Senator" or "Mister Chairman." Usually, however, it's more like, "Hey Chris, we're going to move that amendment in conference tomorrow," or "Tom, we

got some problems on the cap." Whatever the greeting, most pay attention to Liz Robbins.

"Liz Robbins knows every button to push for almost every member," says Rep. Charles Wilson, the Texas Democrat who heads the newly formed Sunbelt Council that frequently competes with Miss Robbins' Northern industrial-state clients for federal money.

She is also a refutation of some myths about Washington lobbyists. While exaggerated stories abound about a few high-living women who call themselves lobbyists, Liz Robbins is considered as strait-laced as she is straightforward. She has a staff of only five, and lacks the fancy limousines and unlimited expense accounts of the high-powered corporate lobbyists.

Instead, she capitalizes on a willingness to put in many 16-hour days, on her personal contacts with hundreds of well-placed staffers and lawmakers and on an extraordinary knowledge of some complex subjects.

"She has a remarkable ability to really help members understand the practical effects of decisions they are making," says Sen. Thad Cochran, a conservative Mississippi Republican. "And she never misleads you."

It isn't easy, especially this year, for the 35-year-old lobbyist and her clients. She lost an effort to increase funds for day care and disabled children. And her habit of talking governmentese—there are lots of "glitches" and "minimum matches" in her conversation—confounds some lawmakers. . . .

Miss Robbins, unlike some liberal lobbyists, devotes a lot of time to cultivating conservatives. Even when she doesn't get their votes, she figures she softens their opposition. "I don't know of anybody up here

mittees until the law changed in 1974. There has also been rapid growth in the number of nonconnected PACs, ideological groups that have no parent lobbying organization and are formed only for the purpose of raising and channeling campaign funds. (Thus a PAC can be the campaign wing affiliate of an existing interest group, or it can be a wholly independent, unaffiliated group.) As Table 8.1 indicates, the amounts contributed by PACs to congressional candidates can be sizable. From Exxon PAC to SixPAC (which, as you might guess, represents the beer industry), everyone seems to be getting into the PAC game.

Why do interest groups form PACs? As Justin Dart, whose Dart Industries formed a PAC, put it, "Talking to politicians is fine, but with a little money they hear you better."[22] Dart's view seems cynical, but it contains more than

Liz Robbins — On the Run with Senator Dole

who doesn't like and respect her," says Sen. Orrin Hatch, the conservative Republican from Utah.

Such contacts paid off recently when the Senate voted to charge states interest on loans from the Unemployment Compensation Fund. That hurts states, such as Michigan, with heavy joblessness.

A champion of the provision in the House Ways and Means Committee was Louisiana Republican Hen-

son Moore, and after the vote Liz Robbins immediately sought him out. "I explained that Michigan already was taxing its business more than most other states," she recalls, "and with our high unemployment this would create a terrible hardship now."

She and the conservative Mr. Moore devised a compromise that would delay charging states such as Michigan any interest on such borrowing until future years. In the fiscal year starting October 1, [1981] Michigan will save an estimated $45 million it would have had to pay under the Senate bill. . . .

With such successes, Miss Robbins gets rave reviews from her clients. Shortly after she went to work for San Francisco several years ago, she started pushing for legislation to get the city a $200,000 grant for a breakwater for Fisherman's Wharf. "Ms. Robbins has been on our payroll for less than a month," crowed Mayor [Diane] Feinstein, "but with this federal allocation, she has already justified her annual salary." San Francisco pays her $56,000 of the $200,000 she grosses each year. About 75% of that total goes to pay staff and overhead. . . .

She clearly loves her work and delights in some of the lighter moments. A few years ago, she was urging a skeptical Sen. Bob Packwood to support a child-care bill. In the middle of her pitch, the Oregon Republican asked her if she played gin rummy, which she does. She then proceeded to win $12 from Sen. Packwood. She also got his vote on the child-care bill.

Source: Albert Hunt, "Lobbyist Liz Robbins Is Moving Force in Fight for U.S. Aid to Social Services," *Wall Street Journal,* July 31, 1981, p. 24. Reprinted from the *Wall Street Journal,* © Dow Jones & Company, Inc., 1981.

a kernel of truth. Lobbyists believe that campaign contributions help significantly when they are trying to gain access to a member of Congress. Members of Congress and their staffers are generally eager to meet with representatives of their constituencies, but their time is limited. However, a member of Congress or an administrative assistant would find it difficult to turn down a request for a meeting with a lobbyist from, for example, the National Association of Realtors, if that group's PAC had made a campaign contribution during the last election.

PACs, like most other interest groups, are highly pragmatic organizations; pushing a particular political philosophy takes second place to achieving immediate policy goals. Even though many corporate executives hold a strong free-market philosophy, for example, their company PAC would probably hold congressional candidates to a much more practical standard. Except for nonconnected ideological PACs, access to congressional offices is usually considered much more important than finding and supporting true believers. Former Democratic Representative Joseph Addabbo of New York, a relentless critic of the MX missile, the B-1 bomber, and many other major weapon systems, received more campaign contributions from defense contractors than did any other House member in the 1984 election. Although they disliked Addabbo's politics, defense contractors wanted as much access as possible to the chairman of the critically important House Appropriations Subcommittee on Defense.[23] As a group, corporations gave 78 percent of their contributions to incumbent members of Congress — many of them liberal and moderate Democrats — during the last two-year election cycle.[24]

The growing role of PACs in financing congressional campaigns has become the most controversial aspect of interest group politics. Critics believe that greater access to congressional offices brings greater influence over legislators. And access is increased by campaign contributions. It should come

Figure 8.1 ▬▬

The Growth of PACs
In 1974, a change in the law removed the prohibition that prevented most corporations from forming political action committees; in addition, other types of PACs have grown more numerous since that time. By the end of 1985, almost 4,000 PACs were registered with the Federal Election Commission.
(Source: Federal Election Commission Record, March 1986, p. 6.)

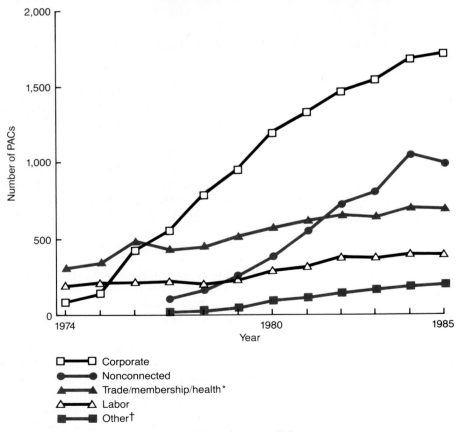

□—□ Corporate
●—● Nonconnected
▲—▲ Trade/membership/health*
△—△ Labor
■—■ Other†

* Until 1977, this category consisted of all but labor and corporate PACs.
† Includes PACs formed by corporations without capital stock and cooperatives.

Table 8.1

PACs: The Top Ten

The following groups contributed the largest amounts of money to candidates for federal office during the 1983–1984 election cycle.

1 Realtors Political Action Committee	$2,429,852
2 American Medical Association Political Action Committee	1,839,464
3 Build Political Action Committee of the National Association of Home Builders	1,625,539
4 National Education Association Political Action Committee	1,574,003
5 UAW-V-Cap (UAW Voluntary Community Action Program)	1,405,107
6 Seafarers Political Activity Donation (SPAD)	1,322,410
7 Machinists Non-Partisan Political League	1,306,497
8 Active Ballot Club, a Department of United Food and Commercial Workers International Union	1,261,974
9 Committee on Letter Carriers Political Education (Letter Carriers Political Action Fund)	1,234,603
10 National Association of Retired Federal Employees Political Action Committee (NARFE-PAC)	1,099,243

Source: Federal Election Commission, "FEC Final Report for '84 Elections Confirms Majority of PAC Money Went to Incumbents," December 1, 1985. Reprinted by permission of the Federal Election Commission.

as no surprise that corporate PACs contribute more to congressional candidates than does any other type of PAC. But, in a democracy, influence should not be a function of money; some citizens have little to give, but their rights nevertheless need to be protected. From this perspective, the issue is political equality. In the words of Republican Senator Robert Dole of Kansas, "there aren't any Poor PACs or Food Stamp PACs or Nutrition PACs or Medicare PACs."[25]

Still, strong arguments can be made for continuing PACs. They offer a means for people to participate in the political system. They permit many small givers to pool their resources and to fight the feeling that one person cannot make a difference. Moreover, with continually escalating campaign costs, many campaigns would be underfunded without PAC money. If this source of contributions were eliminated, it would be more difficult for candidates without personal wealth to make a credible try for Congress. Finally, proponents believe that restrictions on PACs would amount to restrictions on the personal freedom of political expression.

LOBBYING TACTICS

When an interest group decides to try to influence government on an issue, its staff and officers must develop a strategy, which may include a number of tactics aimed at various officials or offices. Together the tactics should use the group's resources as effectively as possible.

Keep in mind that lobbying extends beyond the legislative branch. Groups can seek help from the courts and administrative agencies as well as from Congress. Moreover, interest groups may have to shift their focus from one branch of government to another. After a bill becomes a law, for example, a group that lobbied for the legislation will probably try to influence the administrative agency responsible for implementing the new law. Some policy decisions will be left unresolved by legislation and will be settled through regulations. The lobby will want to make sure those decisions will be as close as possible to the group's preferences.

Three types of lobbying tactics will be discussed here: those aimed at policymakers and implemented through interest group representatives (direct lobbying); those that involve group members (grassroots lobbying); and those directed toward the public (information campaigns). We will also examine cooperative efforts of interest groups to influence government through coalitions.

Direct Lobbying

Direct lobbying refers to tactics that rely on a group representative's contact with a policymaker. The heart and soul of direct lobbying is *personal presentation* of a group's position. A recent survey of Washington lobbyists showed that 98 percent use direct contact with government officials to express their groups' views.[26] This interaction takes place when a lobbyist meets with a member of Congress, an agency official, or a staff member. As we noted earlier, the lobbyist in such meetings usually conveys his or her ar-

A Word with Representative Wright
Given the busy schedules of members of Congress, Washington fundraisers and Capitol Hill receptions offer the chance for many resourceful lobbyists to chat informally with a senator or representative. Texas Democrat Jim Wright (on the left) speaks with a lobbyist at one such affair. (In December 1986, Wright succeeded Tip O'Neill as Speaker of the House.)

guments in the form of data about a specific situation. If a lobbyist from, for example, the Chamber of Commerce meets with a member of Congress about a bill the organization backs, the lobbyist does not say (or even suggest), "Vote for this bill, or our people in the district will vote against you next time." Rather, he or she probably notes that "If this bill is passed, we're going to see hundreds of new jobs created back home." The member of Congress has no trouble at all figuring out that a vote for the bill can help in the next election.

Personal lobbying is a day-in, day-out process; it is not enough simply to meet with policymakers just before a vote or a regulatory decision. The basis of direct lobbying is to maintain contact with congressional and agency staffers, constantly providing them with pertinent data. Lobbyists at the American Gas Association, for instance, keep a list of 1,200 agency personnel who are "called frequently to share informally in association intelligence." The director of the group's lobbying efforts has a shorter list of 104 key administrators with whom he or she has met personally and "who could be counted on to provide information on agency decisionmaking."[27]

A related direct lobbying tactic is *testifying* at committee hearings when a bill is before the Congress. This tactic allows the interest group to put its views formally on record and to make them widely known when the hearing testimony is published. Although testifying is one of the most visible parts of lobbying, it is generally considered "window dressing." Most lobbyists believe that testimony usually does little by itself to persuade members of Congress.

Another direct but somewhat different approach is *legal advocacy*. Through this tactic, lawyers try to achieve a group's policy goals through litigation. For many years, the National Association for the Advancement of Colored People (NAACP) brought suits to overturn laws that allowed for racial segregation. The courts were a better target than Congress, since many members of Congress were strong segregationists from the South. This strategy eventually led to many favorable Supreme Court decisions, most notably the 1954 *Brown* v. *Board of Education* decision, which overturned school segregation.

Grassroots Lobbying

Grassroots lobbying involves an interest group's rank-and-file members and may also include people who are outside of the organization but who sympathize with its goals. Grassroots tactics, such as letter campaigns and protests, are often used in conjunction with direct lobbying by Washington representatives. Communications from a group's members to their representatives in Congress or to agency administrators add to the lobby's credibility in talks with these officials. A policymaker will be more concerned about what a lobbyist says when he or she knows that constituents are really watching his or her decisions.

Group members themselves occasionally go to Washington to lobby. More notable members, such as corporation presidents or local civic leaders, are more likely to do so. However, the most common grassroots lobbying tactic is *letter writing*. "Write your congressman" is not just a slogan out of a civics text. Legislators are highly sensitive to the content of their mail. Interest groups frequently attempt to stimulate letter writing through their regular publications or special alerts. They may even provide sample letters and print the name and address of specific policymakers. One organization that relies heavily on lobbying through the mail is the National Right to Work Committee. Opposed to compulsory unionism, this group can be counted on to generate angry letters every time a prolabor bill is being considered by Congress.

An organization will sometimes place ads in newspapers, asking the general public to write letters on a particular issue. This tactic is very expensive, however, and is used sparingly, generally by wealthy groups or by newly organized groups lacking a formal membership.

If people in government seem unresponsive to conventional lobbying tactics, a group might resort to some form of *political protest*. A protest or demonstration, such as picketing or marching, is designed to attract media attention to an issue (see Table 8.2). Protesters hope that television and newspaper coverage will help change public opinion and make policymakers more receptive to the group's demands. When three thousand farmers from the American Agriculture Movement drove tractors from their homes into Washington to show their disappointment with Carter administration farm policies, the spectacle attracted considerable publicity. Their unconventional approach increased the public's awareness of falling farm prices and stimulated the government to take some limited action.[28]

The main drawback to protest activity is that policymaking is a long-term, incremental process, whereas a demonstration is short-lived. It is difficult to sustain the anger and activism of group supporters and to keep large numbers of people involved in protest after protest, simply to keep the group's demands in the public eye. Notable exceptions were the civil rights demonstrations of the 1960s, which were sustained over a long period. National attention focused not only on the widespread demonstrations, but also on the sometimes violent confrontations between blacks and white law enforce-

Table 8.2

Protest as Theater
To bring their grievances to the attention of the American people through media coverage, interest groups will sometimes resort to unusual types of protests.

Protesters	Gripe	Demonstration
Cattle raisers	High cost of producing beef	"Beef-in": 47 steers and calves brought to Washington and put in pens on the Washington Mall
Motorcyclists	Law requiring cyclists to wear helmets	Bike-in at the Mall
Massachusetts People's Bicentennial Commission	"Tyranny" of big business	Dumping 100-pound sugar bags (actually filled with leaves) into Boston Harbor
Alaska Anti-Abortionists	Legalized abortion	Demonstrators chained themselves to a procedure table
American Agriculture Movement	Shrinking profits	Tractorcade into Washington
Greenpeace	Proposal to open one billion acres offshore for oil and gas exploration	Dumping marbles in Interior Department's lobby because Secretary Watt "lost his marbles" in making the proposal

From Jeffrey M. Berry, *The Interest Group Society*, p. 150. Copyright © 1984 by Jeffrey M. Berry. Reprinted by permission of Little, Brown and Company.

Grassroots Lobbyists
It is often said that the best lobbyists are the lobbyists back home. These Equal Rights Amendment proponents traveled to Washington to press their case because they know that members of Congress are greatly concerned about what their constituents think. A member's constituents are not necessarily united in their beliefs, however, as was the case with the divisive fight over the ERA.

ment officials. For example, the use of police dogs and high-power fire hoses against blacks marching in Alabama in the early 1960s angered millions of Americans who saw films of the confrontations on television news programs. The protests were a major factor in changing public opinion, which in turn hastened the passage of the Civil Rights Act of 1964 and the Voting Rights Act of 1965.[29]

Information Campaigns

As the strategy of the civil rights movement shows, interest groups generally feel that public backing adds strength to their lobbying efforts. And since all interest groups believe they are absolutely right in their policy orientations, they believe that they will get that backing if they make the public aware of their positions and the evidence that supports them. To this end, interest groups launch **information campaigns,** which are organized efforts to gain public backing by bringing the group's views to the public's attention. The underlying assumption is that public ignorance and apathy are as much a problem as the opposing views of competing interest groups. Various means are used to combat that apathy. Some are directed at the larger public, others at smaller audiences with longstanding interest in an issue.

Public relations is one information tactic. A public relations campaign might involve sending speakers to meetings in various parts of the country or producing literature such as pamphlets and handouts. A highly visible form of political public relations is newspaper and magazine advertising. Mobil Oil Corporation is well known for the way it uses print advertising to argue its point of view. Jewish and Arab partisans in the ongoing debate over the Middle East often lobby through print advertisements. Each side occasionally buys space in newspapers, especially the *New York Times* and the *Washington Post,* to lay out its position in detail. Newspaper and magazine advertising has one major drawback, however: it is extremely expensive. Consequently, few groups rely on it as their primary weapon.

Sponsoring *research* is another way interest groups press their cases. When a group believes that evidence has not been fully developed in a certain area, it may commission research on the subject. Disability rights groups have protected programs from would-be budget cutters by providing "lawmakers with abundant research findings demonstrating that it costs much more to keep people in institutions . . . than it does to utilize home and community living programs."[30]

Some groups believe that publicizing *voting records* of members of Congress is an effective means of influencing public opinion. These interest groups simply publish in their newsletters the record of how all members of Congress voted on issues of particular concern to the organization. Other groups prepare statistical indexes that compare the voting records of all members of Congress on selected key issues. Each member is graded (from 0 to 100 percent) according to how often he or she voted in agreement with the group's views. Thus the owners of small businesses who belong to the National Federation of Independent Business can assume that those members who receive a high score on the group's vote scorecard have usually voted in sympathy with their interests.

Coalitions

The final aspect of lobbying strategy that should be mentioned is **coalition building,** in which several organizations band together for the purpose of lobbying. This joint effort conserves or makes more effective use of the resources of groups with similar views. Coalitions often form among groups that have experience working together in the same policy area. On feminist issues, for example, organizations such as the National Organization for Women, the National Women's Political Caucus, the League of Women Voters, the American Association of University Women, and the Women's Equity Action League usually work cooperatively with one another.[31]

Most coalitions are informal, ad hoc arrangements. Groups have limited resources and prefer not to commit those resources to long-term coalitions. They might not always share an equal degree of enthusiasm on all issues. Sometimes even old friends end up on different sides of an issue. Government solutions to the acid rain problem, for instance, set coal companies from the West against coal producers from the East. In the West (where coal is low in sulfur), producers prefer a policy promoting the use of low-sulfur coal; eastern coal producers prefer scrubbers to reduce sulfur dioxide emissions.[32] Ad hoc coalitions that center around one immediate issue allow a group to keep its resource commitments flexible, while broadening those resources to increase the chances of influencing policymakers at key times.

THE GROWTH OF INTEREST GROUP POLITICS

The growing number of active interest groups is one of the most important trends in American politics. One survey of Washington-based lobbies showed that fully 30 percent of existing groups were formed between 1960 and 1980.[33] The greatest growth occurred in three types of interest groups: PACs (discussed earlier), citizen groups, and business lobbies.

The Public Interest Movement

Many recently formed citizen groups are commonly known as public interest groups. A **public interest group** is generally considered to have no economic self-interest in the policies it pursues.[34] For example, the members of an environmental group fighting for stricter clean air standards will receive no financial gain from the institution of such standards. The benefits to its members are largely ideological and aesthetic. In contrast, a corporation fighting against the same stringent standards is trying to protect its profits. A law that requires it to install expensive air-cleaning equipment can reduce stockholder dividends, depress salaries, and postpone expansion. Although both the corporation and the environmental group have valid reasons for their stands on the issue, their motivations are different. The environmental lobby is a public interest group; the corporation is not.

Ralph Nader Versus General Motors
When Nader (left) first attracted attention for exposing the defects in General Motors' Corvair, GM responded by hiring a private detective to investigate him. When the public learned of the investigation, it only added to Nader's credibility. GM soon realized that the consumer movement was not going to go away. Here, Nader debates GM's former president, Edward Cole, on the popular ''Phil Donahue Show.''

Many public interest groups that have appeared in the past two decades have become major actors in national politics. Common Cause, one of the best-known ''good government'' groups, pushes for campaign finance reform, ethics codes in government, and open congressional and administrative proceedings.[35]

The best-known public interest activist is Ralph Nader. He first came to the public's attention in 1966, when he exposed serious safety flaws in the General Motors Corvair. So damning was his indictment of the car that Corvair sales dropped significantly.[36] General Motors soon stopped producing the car. Nader now heads a small empire of public interest groups, such as the Aviation Consumer Action Project, the Public Citizen Litigation Group, and the Health Research Group.

Nader has a reputation as a relentless and driven lobbyist for consumer protection. He mercilessly criticizes politicians who disagree with him, treating them as ''enemies of the people,'' not as individuals who simply happen to hold different views (see Feature 8.2). Nader's self-righteousness is tempered by his dedication and zeal, and he lives an ascetic lifestyle with few visible comforts. Such characteristics have made him a highly effective advocate before Congress and administrative agencies.

Origins of the public interest movement. Traditionally, public interest lobbies have not been a major factor in Washington politics. Yet the upsurge of groups that began in the late 1960s did not prove to be as short-lived a

Feature 8.2

The Nader Method

Ralph Nader's unique personality and unusual lobbying style are the keys to his success. Although there is no official Nader ''manual,'' the following principles are a good guide to Nader's lobbying philosophy.

1. *Being Nice Gets You Nowhere.* Attack your friends as well as your enemies. Make policymakers fear your denunciations.
2. *Disdain Realistic Compromise — Promote Idealistic Solutions.* Appear to be unyielding. Compromises will be made whether you like it or not, so don't concede anything on your own.
3. *Never Get Caught on the Left.* Don't become identified with radicals or socialists — it will undermine your credibility. Talk about the need for true capitalistic competition.
4. *Mold the Media.* Be aggressive in dealing with reporters. Let reporters know that you are judging them on the way they serve the public interest.
5. *Information Is the Ultimate Weapon.* Kill them, not with kindness, but with information. Overwhelm them with research and studies so that the issue is discussed in terms of your ''facts,'' not theirs.
6. *Avoid Politics.* Place yourself above partisan politics. It's too difficult to have an impact on electoral politics, so why waste your resources?

Source: Adapted from Jeffrey M. Berry, ''Lessons from Chairman Ralph,'' *Citizen Participation* 1 (November–December 1979):3ff. Reprinted by permission of the Civic Education Foundation, Lincoln Filene Center, Tufts University.

An Image That Angered a Nation

Demonstrations by blacks during the early 1960s played a critical role in pushing Congress to pass civil rights legislation. This photo, in which vicious police dogs attacked demonstrators in Birmingham, Alabama, is typical of the scenes that were shown on the network news and placed in newspapers; they helped build public support for civil rights legislation.

phenomenon as many had expected. At first, most new groups were on the liberal side of the political spectrum. As discussed below, however, many new conservative groups have formed recently. Groups on both the left and the right have become more politically prominent. The public interest movement has been impressive in its collective scope and strength; many groups have been able to support themselves through the contributions of concerned citizens.

Why have so many public interest groups formed in the last two decades? The strongest roots of the movement grew from the civil rights and anti-Vietnam War activism of the 1960s.[37] In both cases, citizens with passionate beliefs about a cause felt they had no choice but to take aggressive, even abrasive, action. Dependence on political parties and the electoral process was not producing change in the "correct" direction. Collective citizen action had to be used instead.

The legacy of the civil rights and antiwar movements was the belief that citizens acting together were effective in influencing the direction of public policy. From the successes of these groups, Americans learned that ordinary citizens could have an impact on government if they organized into lobbies. (Most contemporary citizen groups no longer rely on the demonstrations that characterized these earlier movements. Instead, they channel the energy, resources, and outrage of their constituents into more conventional tactics, such as legislative lobbying and litigation.)

The late 1960s and early 1970s were also a time when Americans were becoming increasingly cynical about government. Loyalty to political parties was declining, too, as greater proportions of citizens told pollsters that they did not identify with either national party. If neither government nor political parties could be trusted to provide adequate representation in the nation's capital on such issues as preserving the environment or protecting consumers, the obvious alternative was membership in an ideological interest group.

Conservative reaction. Why conservatives were slower than liberals to mobilize is not altogether clear, but the new right-of-center groups appear in part to be a reaction to the perceived success of liberal groups. Like their liberal counterparts, these conservative groups cover a wide variety of policy areas; many concentrate on a narrow range of related issues. Most of them stand in direct opposition to causes espoused by liberal organizations. Phyllis Schlafly's Eagle Forum, for example, has fought long and hard against the Equal Rights Amendment and other positions favored by feminist groups.

Conservative groups are not merely mirror images of liberal citizen lobbies, however. A distinctive feature of the "New Right" is active participation by religious organizations. Most notable is the Moral Majority, a fundamentalist Christian group led by the Reverend Jerry Falwell. (Recently, Falwell announced that he was starting a new organization, the Liberty Federation; the Moral Majority will be a division of it.) The Moral Majority advocates policies that it considers to be in line with biblical teachings, such as permitting prayer in school and restricting abortions.[38] Falwell and a few others raise money for spiritual and political efforts through appeals in televised sermons. Some Americans who believe that the country is best served by a

Reverend Jerry Falwell and Friend
Falwell has played a central role in mobilizing fundamentalist Christians into a political force. The conservative political views of Falwell and his Moral Majority followers are highly compatible with the views of President Ronald Reagan, and the Republican party has made a concerted effort to court the fundamentalists.

complete separation of church and state are offended by the lobbying of the religious Right. But the religious Right believes that its moral duty is to see that Christian principles are embodied in government policy. The conflict between liberal critics and conservative, religious lobbies like the Moral Majority is more than a difference of opinion over specific policy decisions. Rather, it is a struggle to define the fundamental values that shape our society. And, as a spokesman for the American Coalition for Traditional Values notes, "somebody's values will prevail."[39]

During the Reagan presidency, conservative citizen groups have enjoyed substantial access to the White House, as lobbyists from these groups meet frequently with White House aides.[40] They cannot claim the same degree of success with Congress, though, where many of their most cherished goals— such as a constitutional amendment allowing school prayer—remain unattained. Nevertheless, the emergence of these groups and the resurgence of the Republican party have enhanced the conservative influence in America.

Business Lobbies

The number of business lobbies in Washington has also increased. Offices of individual corporations and of business trade associations are more in evidence than ever before. A **trade association,** such as the Mortgage Bankers Association or the National Electrical Manufacturers Association, is an organization that represents companies within the same industry. At one point during the 1970s, when the boom in business lobbying began, trade associations were moving their headquarters to Washington at an average of one every week.[41] A 1981 survey of corporations revealed that more than half of the organizations with a government relations office in Washington were started during the previous decade.[42] Corporations that already had offices in Washington typically upgraded those offices by adding staff.

The vast increase in business representation in Washington was in large part a response to the expanded scope of federal government activities during the 1960s and 1970s. As new regulatory agencies like the Environmental Protection Agency and the Consumer Product Safety Commission were created, many more companies found themselves affected by federal regulations. Corporations and trade groups located outside of Washington often found themselves *reacting* to policies already made, rather than participating in policy formulation. They saw a move to Washington—where the policymakers are —as necessary if they were to obtain information on pending government actions in enough time to act on it.

Ironically, the increase in government activity and in business lobbying followed directly from the "success" of liberal public interest groups, who are strong supporters of regulation to protect the environment and consumers. By the early 1970s, many businesspeople felt that the government was reacting to an agenda set primarily by citizen groups. This belief contributed to the founding of the Business Roundtable, a lobbying group with membership made up of about two hundred of the nation's largest companies. The Business Roundtable has become both a leading proponent of the business point of view and a symbol of business strength in Washington.

The increase in business advocacy in Washington was also fueled by the competitive nature of business lobbying. The reason for competition is that legislation and regulatory decisions never seem to apply uniformly to all of business; rather, they affect one type of business or one industry more than another. For example, with the advent of deregulation (and competition) in the phone industry, lobbyists from the differing segments of the industry have tried to influence public policy to suit their own companies' needs. AT&T, the regional phone companies (like Bell South and U.S. West), and the independent long-distance carriers don't see eye to eye because policies that help some companies to garner more business are likely to hurt other firms.[43]

This growth of business lobbies has reinforced and possibly expanded the overrepresentation of business in Washington politics. As Figure 8.2 shows, approximately half of all interest groups with a Washington office are either corporations or business trade associations. If organizations with a Washington lawyer or other kind of lobbyist on retainer are added to the total, the dominance of business in the lobbying population is even greater. Note, however, that the number of organizations or lobbyists is far from a perfect indicator of interest group strength. The AFL-CIO, which represents millions of union members, is more influential than a two-person corporate "listening post" office in Washington. Nevertheless, one cannot deny business's advantage in terms of Washington representation. And since business lobbies are able to draw on the institutional resources of corporations, they can fund their lobbying operations more easily than can groups who depend on voluntary individual contributions.

The Tax Lobbyist
Charls Walker is one of the most skilled business lobbyists in Washington. He holds a Ph.D. in economics and was a high-ranking official in the U.S. Treasury Department. Because of Walker's expertise and political skills, many large corporations hire him to lobby Congress on tax policy.

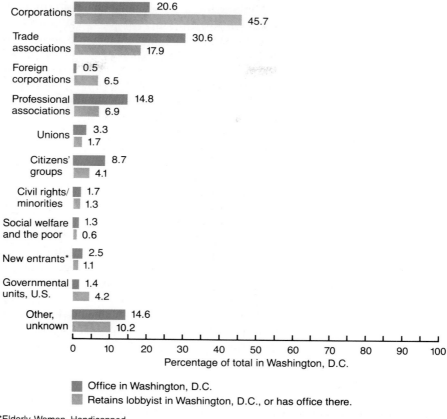

Percentage of total in Washington, D.C.

■ Office in Washington, D.C.

■ Retains lobbyist in Washington, D.C., or has office there.

*Elderly, Women, Handicapped

The Washington Interest Group Community
Although the interest group community is highly diverse, business organizations form the biggest part of that community. Corporations and trade associations are the most prevalent interest group actors in terms of having an office in Washington or, at the very least, employing a lobbyist there. (Source: Kay Lehman Schlozman and John T. Tierney, Organized Interests and American Democracy, *New York: Harper & Row, 1985, p. 67. Reprinted by permission of Harper and Row, Publishers, Inc. Adapted from the* Encyclopedia of Associations, *ed. Dennis S. Ashley. Gale Research.)*

Figure 8.2

EVALUATING INTEREST GROUPS

The pluralists who wrote during the 1950s and 1960s were right on one important point, but wrong on another. They argued that interest groups are at the center of the policymaking process. The growing number of groups in recent years seems to reflect a broad acceptance of this view by various sectors of American society. Although pluralist scholars never predicted perfect representation of affected interests, they did assume that representation would be more balanced than it is. What we have instead is a political system increasingly centered around interest group advocacy, but one in which some interests — most notably business — are much better represented than others. What are the consequences of this situation?

One consequence is that the large and growing number of interest groups works against a strengthening of our party system. Many activists find narrowly based interest groups more appealing than parties. The lobbies that these activists support work intensely on the few issues they care about most; parties often dilute issue stands to appeal to as broad a segment of the electorate as possible. Thus, many people who care deeply about public policy questions work to influence government through particular lobbies rather than through political parties. Interest in party reform has waned in the past few years. The satisfaction people feel with the work of their interest groups surely contributes to Americans' lack of concern for revitalizing the parties into more responsive policymaking bodies.

This lack of concern is unfortunate; interest groups can do no more than supplement the functions of parties. Most interest groups are small bodies concerned with only a few issues. Parties, however, can be instruments of majoritarian democracy. They can bring together broad coalitions of people and translate their concerns into large-scale social or economic change. Parties are particularly important because they can represent those who are not well represented by interest groups. As political scientist Walter Dean Burnham puts it, parties "can generate countervailing collective power on behalf of the many individually powerless against the relatively few who are individually — or organizationally — powerful."[44]

Most observers agree that stronger parties, which would provide a more majoritarian mechanism for influencing policy, are desirable. But few seem interested in reviving the parties if that means their own interest group will become less influential. Thus, if our party system undergoes a revival, it will be because of what the parties do to make themselves more appealing, not because people turn away from their interest groups.

Regulation of Interest Groups

Interest groups contribute to democratic government by representing their supporters' interests. However, concern that individual groups have too much influence or that interest group representation is biased in favor of certain segments of society prompts frequent calls for reform to weaken interest groups' influence. Yet, despite disenchantment with interest group politics, reform has remained elusive. As Madison noted, the problem is that it is difficult to limit interest group activity without limiting fundamental freedoms. The First Amendment guarantees Americans the right to petition their government, and lobbying is, at its most basic level, a form of organized petitioning.

One effort to reform lobbying was the Federal Regulation of Lobbying Act, passed in 1946. This law was intended to require all lobbyists to register and file expenditure reports with Congress. In practice, the law has been ineffective. A Supreme Court ruling has held that it applies only to persons or organizations whose "principal purpose" is influencing legislation.[45] This exempts many, if not most, of those who lobby. Periodic calls for stricter reform legislation continue, but it is difficult to see how such legislation would alter interest group behavior.

Linking People with Government

Presidential elections can decide more than which candidate becomes president; they can determine which coalition of voters dominates elections for national office. For example, the election of 1828—the nation's first with more than a million voters—not only chose Andrew Jackson from Tennessee over John Quincy Adams from Massachusetts but also established the voting power of western and southern farm states over the previously dominant northeastern manufacturing states. A presidential election that changes existing patterns of party loyalities among groups of voters across the nation for years afterward is called a critical election. *Scholars have identified only three elections—1860, 1896, and 1932—that showed significant changes in voting patterns and that "also began periods of unified party control of the presidency and both houses of Congress for as long as fourteen years" (J. Clubb, W. Flanigan, and N. Zingale,* Partisan Realignment, *1980). The election of 1860 (see next page), which chose Republican Abraham Lincoln over three others, set a pattern of regional voting, pitting northern Republicans against southern Democrats. In 1896, the populous and industrial east and midwest elected Republican William McKinley (who was probusiness) over Democrat William Jennings Bryan (spokesman for the rural west and south), and the Republicans emerged as the majority party. In 1932, Democrat Franklin Roosevelt won election with a coalition of southerners, northern urban workers, and religious and ethnic minorities that transformed the Democrats into the majority party. Ronald Reagan's election in 1984 was even more sweeping than Roosevelt's in 1932, but 1984 was not a critical election because Republicans did not win control of the House. Nevertheless, the proportion of Republican voters nationwide has been increasing recently, and the era of Democratic dominance, launched by Roosevelt, seems to be coming to a close.*

The Presidential Election of 1828

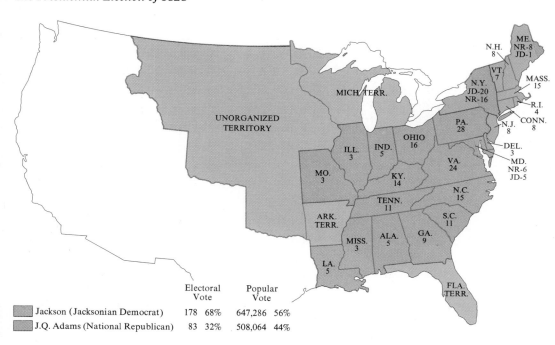

	Electoral Vote		Popular Vote	
Jackson (Jacksonian Democrat)	178	68%	647,286	56%
J.Q. Adams (National Republican)	83	32%	508,064	44%

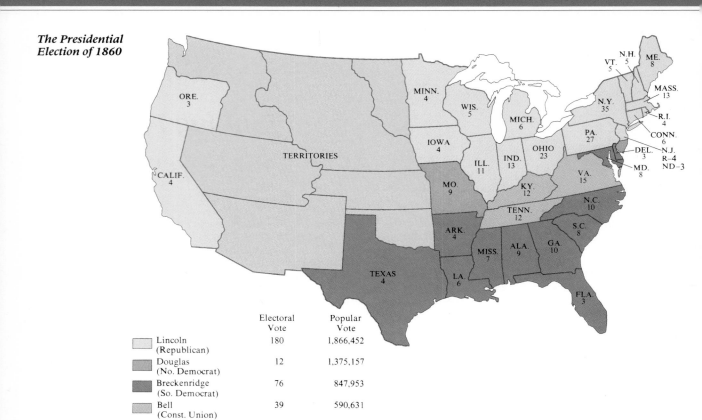

The Presidential Election of 1860

ORE. 3

CALIF. 4

TERRITORIES

MINN. 4

WIS. 5

MICH. 6

IOWA 4

ILL. 11

IND. 13

OHIO 23

MO. 9

KY. 12

TENN. 12

ARK. 4

MISS. 7

ALA. 9

GA. 10

TEXAS 4

LA. 6

FLA. 3

VA. 15

N.C. 10

S.C. 8

N.H. 5
VT. 5
ME. 8

N.Y. 35

MASS. 13

R.I. 4

CONN. 6

PA. 27

DEL. 3
MD. 8

N.J.
R–4
ND–3

	Electoral Vote	Popular Vote
Lincoln (Republican)	180	1,866,452
Douglas (No. Democrat)	12	1,375,157
Breckenridge (So. Democrat)	76	847,953
Bell (Const. Union)	39	590,631

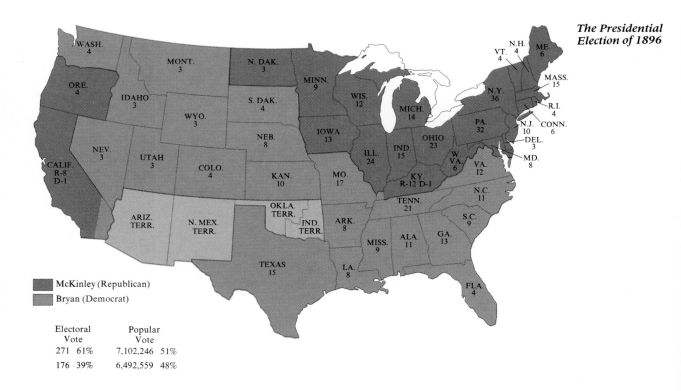

The Presidential Election of 1896

WASH. 4

ORE. 4

IDAHO 3

MONT. 3

N. DAK. 3

MINN. 9

WIS. 12

MICH. 14

NEV. 3

UTAH 3

WYO. 3

S. DAK. 4

NEB. 8

IOWA 13

ILL. 24

IND. 15

OHIO 23

W. VA. 6

CALIF. R–8 D–1

COLO. 4

KAN. 10

MO. 17

KY. R–12 D–1

VA. 12

ARIZ. TERR.

N. MEX. TERR.

OKLA. TERR.

IND. TERR.

ARK. 8

TENN. 21

N.C. 11

S.C. 9

TEXAS 15

MISS. 9

ALA. 11

GA. 13

LA. 8

FLA. 4

N.H. 4
VT. 4
ME. 6

N.Y. 36

MASS. 15

R.I. 4

CONN. 6

PA. 32

N.J. 10
DEL. 3
MD. 8

- McKinley (Republican)
- Bryan (Democrat)

Electoral Vote		Popular Vote	
271	61%	7,102,246	51%
176	39%	6,492,559	48%

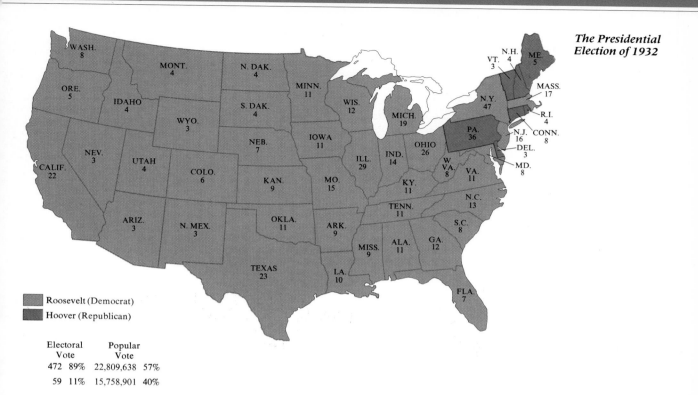

The Presidential Election of 1932

WASH. 8
ORE. 5
MONT. 4
N. DAK. 4
MINN. 11
IDAHO 4
S. DAK. 4
WIS. 12
WYO. 3
MICH. 19
NEV. 3
NEB. 7
IOWA 11
OHIO 26
CALIF. 22
UTAH 4
COLO. 6
ILL. 29
IND. 14
W. VA. 8
VA. 11
KAN. 9
MO. 15
KY. 11
ARIZ. 3
N. MEX. 3
OKLA. 11
ARK. 9
TENN. 11
N.C. 13
S.C. 8
MISS. 9
ALA. 11
GA. 12
TEXAS 23
LA. 10
FLA. 7
N.H. 4
VT. 3
ME. 5
MASS. 17
N.Y. 47
R.I. 4
N.J. 16
CONN. 8
PA. 36
DEL. 3
MD. 8

☐ Roosevelt (Democrat)
☐ Hoover (Republican)

Electoral Vote		Popular Vote	
472	89%	22,809,638	57%
59	11%	15,758,901	40%

The Presidential Election of 1984

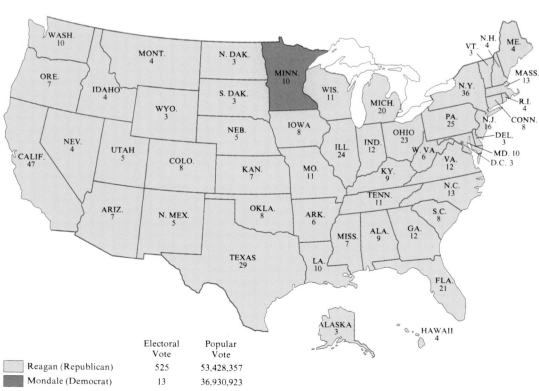

WASH. 10
ORE. 7
MONT. 4
N. DAK. 3
MINN. 10
IDAHO 4
S. DAK. 3
WIS. 11
WYO. 3
MICH. 20
NEV. 4
NEB. 5
IOWA 8
OHIO 23
CALIF. 47
UTAH 5
COLO. 8
ILL. 24
IND. 12
W. VA. 6
VA. 12
KAN. 7
MO. 11
KY. 9
ARIZ. 7
N. MEX. 5
OKLA. 8
ARK. 6
TENN. 11
N.C. 13
S.C. 8
MISS. 7
ALA. 9
GA. 12
TEXAS 29
LA. 10
FLA. 21
ALASKA 3
HAWAII 4
N.H. 4
VT. 3
ME. 4
MASS. 13
N.Y. 36
R.I. 4
N.J. 16
CONN. 8
PA. 25
DEL. 3
MD. 10
D.C. 3

		Electoral Vote	Popular Vote
☐	Reagan (Republican)	525	53,428,357
☐	Mondale (Democrat)	13	36,930,923

B–3

Population Composition of the United States

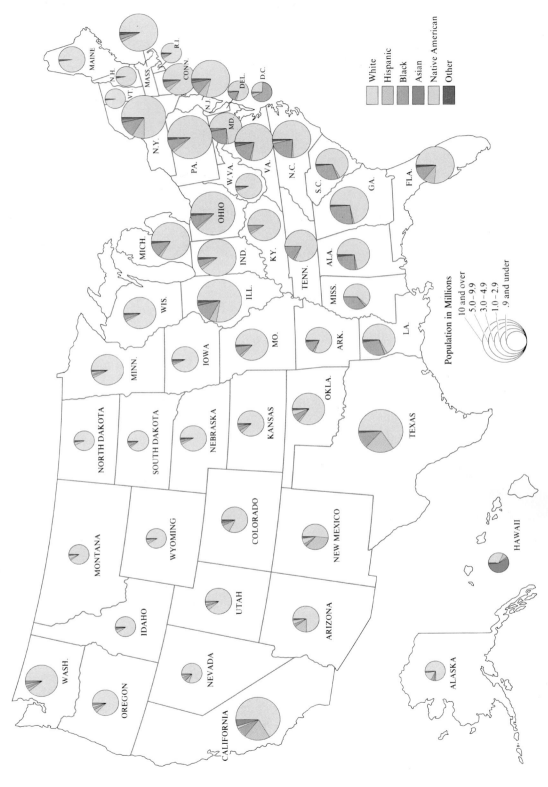

Legend:
- White
- Hispanic
- Black
- Asian
- Native American
- Other

Population in Millions
- 10 and over
- 5.0 – 9.9
- 3.0 – 4.9
- 1.0 – 2.9
- .9 and under

This map depicts the ethnic composition of the American states. Note that states in the extreme northeast (Maine, New Hampshire, and Vermont) have virtually no minorities, while other states (such as New Mexico, Texas, and California) have diverse mixes of nonwhite minority groups.

Immigration to the U.S. for each decade. Through 1976, figures are for years ending on June 30; beginning in 1977, years ended on Sept. 30.

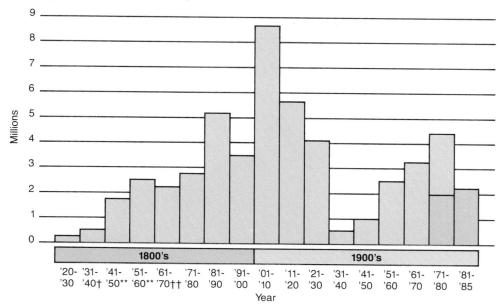

□ First five years of decade

*Oct. 1, 1819 to Sept. 30, 1830   †Oct. 1, 1830 to Dec. 31, 1840
**Calendar years   ††Jan. 1, 1861 to June 30, 1870

Since its founding, the United States has experienced two great waves of immigration. The first wave, which peaked during 1900–1910, carried immigrants from Europe. The second wave began after World War II and is still building. Most of these immigrants have come from Latin America and Asia, adding to the ethnic diversity of America.

Current Racial Mix of the United States

Hispanic people can be of any race. They make up 6.4 percent of the population.

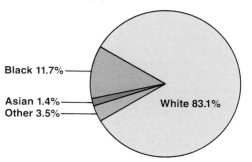

Black 11.7%
Asian 1.4%
Other 3.5%
White 83.1%

Feeding the Melting Pot

Percentage of immigrants by region of birth in each period. Numbers have been rounded.

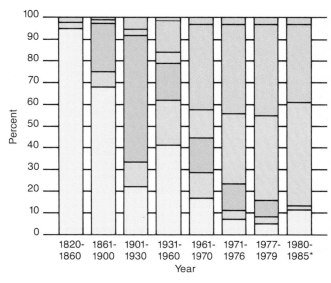

□ Northern and western Europe   ▨ Southern and eastern Europe
□ Latin America   □ North America
□ Asia   □ Other

*After 1979, figures for all of Europe are combined into one category.

Sources of Campaign Funding, 1983–84

HOUSE CANDIDATES

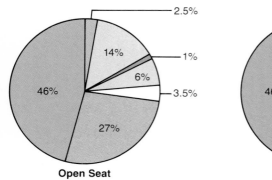

Open Seat

14% — 2.5%
1%
6%
46% — 3.5%
27%

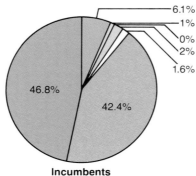

Incumbents

6.1%
1%
0%
2%
1.6%
46.8%
42.4%

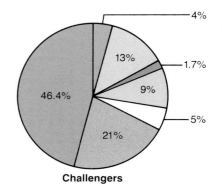

Challengers

13% — 4%
1.7%
9%
46.4%
5%
21%

SENATE CANDIDATES

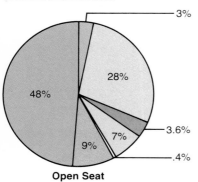

Open Seat

28% — 3%
48%
3.6%
9% 7%
.4%

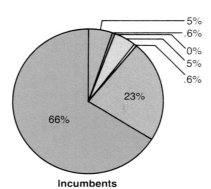

Incumbents

5%
.6%
0%
5%
.6%
66%
23%

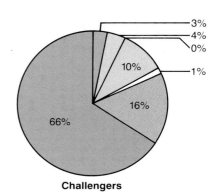

Challengers

3%
4%
0%
10%
1%
66%
16%

- ▨ Individual Contributions
- ▨ PAC Contributions
- ☐ Party Contributions
- ☐ Party Expenditures
- ▨ Candidate Contributions
- ☐ Candidate Loans
- ▨ Other Receipts

The sources of funds contributed to congressional campaigns vary greatly, depending on the candidate's political status. Candidates who contest for an open seat—one that does not have an incumbent running for reelection—receive funds in substantial amounts from many different sources. House and Senate incumbents rely far more heavily on contributions from PACs—political action committees. Candidates who challenge incumbents receive proportionately more support from their national party organizations, either in the form of contributions to their campaigns or direct expenditures on behalf of the candidate. But in all cases, the largest source of funding for congressional campaigns comes from individual contributions. The amount of money spent by candidates for the Senate and House has increased rather steadily from 1978 to 1984. For example, only about 20 Senate candidates ran "million dollar" campaigns in 1978 but more than 40 spent a million dollars campaigning in 1984. Whereas fewer than half of the House candidates spent more than $100,000 to be elected in 1978, far more than half spent that sum and more during campaigns in 1984. Candidates who challenged House incumbents usually spent less than their opponents simply because the challengers found it hard to raise funds to conduct their campaigns. In open contests without incumbents, both candidates were usually able to raise more campaign funds. While incumbents enjoy publicity from their office and need less campaign support to conduct a winning campaign, they tend to spend more in campaigning, simply because they find it easier to raise the funds to spend. PACs and private contributors are more willing to give funds to candidates who are likely to win, and incumbents are seldom defeated. Campaign contributions in 1984 also flowed more readily to Democratic incumbents in the House and to Republican incumbents in the Senate, because they headed the committees in the two chambers.

Campaign Spending*

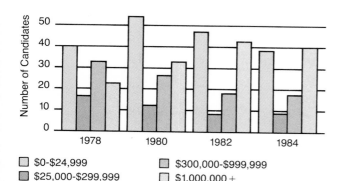

SENATE CANDIDATES

- □ $0-$24,999
- ■ $25,000-$299,999
- ■ $300,000-$999,999
- □ $1,000,000 +

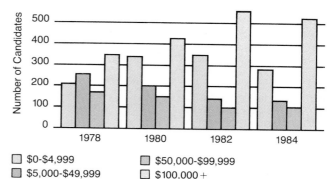

HOUSE CANDIDATES

- □ $0-$4,999
- ■ $5,000-$49,999
- ■ $50,000-$99,999
- □ $100,000 +

*Graph covers all campaign spending (primary, runoff and general) of candidates running in the general election.

Spending by House Candidates, 1984*

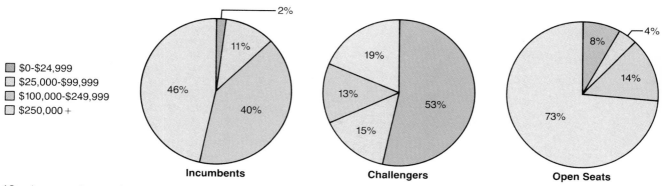

- ■ $0-$24,999
- □ $25,000-$99,999
- ■ $100,000-$249,999
- □ $250,000 +

Incumbents
2%
11%
46%
40%

Challengers
19%
13%
15%
53%

Open Seats
8%
4%
14%
73%

*Graph covers all campaign spending (primary, runoff and general) of major party candidates running in the general election.

Spending by House and Senate Candidates, 1983–84*

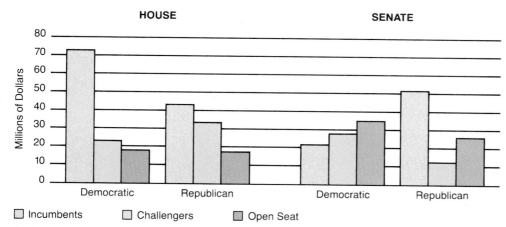

HOUSE   **SENATE**

Millions of Dollars

Democratic   Republican   Democratic   Republican

- □ Incumbents
- □ Challengers
- ■ Open Seat

*Includes spending by House and Senate candidates for 1984 or a future election or for retiring debts of former elections.

The Most Important Problem Facing the Country, 1935–1985

Since 1935, the Gallup organization has polled Americans several times each year asking what they think is the most important problem facing the United States. Gallup's list of the most frequent responses by year shows that the public's concern has alternated over time between issues of war and peace and issues pertaining to the economy. The only other issues that aroused the nation were labor unrest at the end of the 1940s, race relations in the late 1950s and early 1960s, and Watergate and energy issues in the 1970s. Over the last decade, the public has been mainly concerned with the high cost of living (inflation) and unemployment.

Year	Responses		
1985	Fear of war	unemployment	
1984	Unemployment	fear of war	
1983	Unemployment	high cost of living	
1982	Unemployment	high cost of living	
1981	High cost of living	unemployment	
1980	High cost of living	unemployment	
1979	High cost of living	energy problems	
1978	High cost of living	energy problems	
1977	High cost of living	unemployment	
1976	High cost of living	unemployment	
1975	High cost of living	unemployment	
1974	High cost of living	Watergate	energy crisis
1973	High cost of living	Watergate	
1972	Vietnam		
1971	Vietnam	high cost of living	
1970	Vietnam		
1969	Vietnam		
1968	Vietnam		
1967	Vietnam	high cost of living	
1966	Vietnam		
1965	Vietnam	race relations	
1964	Vietnam	race relations	
1963	Keeping peace	race relations	
1962	Keeping peace		
1961	Keeping peace		
1960	Keeping peace		

Year	Responses	
1959	Keeping peace	
1958	Unemployment	keeping peace
1957	Race relations	keeping peace
1956	Keeping peace	
1955	Keeping peace	
1954	Keeping peace	
1953	Keeping peace	
1952	Korean war	
1951	Korean war	
1950	Labor unrest	
1949	Labor unrest	
1948	Keeping peace	
1947	High cost of living	
1946	High cost of living	
1945	Winning war	
1944	Winning war	
1943	Winning war	
1942	Winning war	
1941	Keeping out of war	winning war
1940	Keeping out of war	
1939	Keeping out of war	
1938	Keeping out of war	
1937	Unemployment	
1936	Unemployment	
1935	Unemployment	

Campaign Financing

Much of the debate over interest groups and political reform centers around the role PACs play in financing congressional campaigns. As the costs of political campaigning escalate sharply, politicians have to raise larger and larger sums. During the 1970s, Congress took some important steps aimed at reforming campaign financing practices. Strong disclosure requirements now exist, so that the source of all significant contributions to candidates for federal office is part of the public record. Public financing of presidential campaigns is also provided for; taxpayer money is given in equal amounts to the major parties' presidential nominees.

Reformers have also called for public financing of congressional elections, to reduce the alleged influence of PACs in Congress. Public financing and other schemes designed to reduce the percentage of campaign funds supplied by PACs are meant to reduce interest groups' advantage in gaining access to and sympathy from members of Congress and their staffers. Yet incumbents usually find it easier to raise money from PACs than their electoral challengers do, and they have been reluctant to change this part of the law. It is often said that "money is the mother's milk of politics," and Congress doesn't want to turn off the flow.

The debate over PACs is another manifestation of the sharp underlying tension between the principles of freedom and equality. For many, restrictions on PACs represent restrictions on their personal freedoms. Shouldn't people have the right to join with those who think as they do and contribute

to the candidates of their choice? For others, though, PAC contributions seem less a matter of freedom of political expression than some people's freedom to use their wealth to further their own special interests. Critics charge that PACs favor those who can most afford to donate money by giving them increased access to those in government. They further argue that the consequence of PAC giving is to reinforce, if not expand, the inequities between rich and poor.

SUMMARY

Interest groups play many important roles in our political process. They are a means by which citizens can participate in politics, and they communicate their members' views to those in government. Interest groups differ greatly in the resources at their disposal and in the tactics they use to influence government. The numbers of interest groups has grown sharply in recent years, including an upsurge in political action committees.

Despite growth and change in the nature of interest groups, the fundamental dilemma identified by Madison over two hundred years ago endures. In a free and open society like the United States, groups form to pursue policies that favor themselves at the expense of the broader national interest. Madison hoped that the solution to this problem would come through the structure of our government and through the heterogeneity and dispersion of the population.

To a certain extent, Madison's expectation has been borne out. The natural differences between groups that oppose each other has kept us from the tyranny of any one faction. Yet the interest group system remains unbalanced, with some segments in society (particularly business and those high in education and income) considerably better organized than others. The growth of citizen groups has reduced this disparity somewhat, but there are still significant inequities in how well different interests are represented in Washington.

The inequities in interest group representation have led most contemporary interest group scholars to reject a key proposition of the early pluralists: that the freedom to form lobbies produces a healthy competition between opposing groups and that the compromises emerging from that competition lead to policies that fairly represent the divisions in society. Pluralism has instead meant that business and professional groups have the advantage because of their greater wealth and ease of organization. Pluralist democracy clearly compromises the principle of political equality as stated in the maxim "one person, one vote." Formal political equality is certainly more likely to occur outside of interest group politics, in elections between candidates from competing political parties — which better fits the majoritarian model of democracy.

Despite the inequities of the interest group system, little general effort has been made to restrict interest group activity. Madison's dictum that suppressing political freedoms is worse than suppressing interest group activity has generally guided public policy. Yet, as the problem of PACs demonstrates, government has had to set some restrictions on interest groups. PACs' giving unlimited contributions to political candidates would undermine confidence in the system; the wealthiest groups would appear to be buying influence on Capitol Hill. Some feel that is happening now, pointing to a dozen groups, each of which contributed over a million dollars to candidates for federal office during the last election. Where to draw the limit on PAC activity remains a thorny problem, since there is little consensus on how to balance the conflicting needs of our society.

Key Terms

interest group
lobby
lobbyist
agenda building
program monitoring
interest group entrepreneur
citizen group
direct mail

free rider problem
political action committee (PAC)
direct lobbying
grassroots lobbying
information campaign
coalition building
public interest group
trade association

Selected Readings

Berry, Jeffrey M. *The Interest Group Society*. Boston: Little, Brown, 1984. An analysis of the growth of interest group politics.

Berry, Jeffrey M. *Lobbying for the People*. Princeton, N.J.: Princeton University Press, 1977. A study of eighty-three public interest groups active in national politics.

Cigler, Allan J., and Burdett A. Loomis, eds. *Interest Group Politics*. Washington, D.C.: Congressional Quarterly, 1983. This reader includes fifteen separate essays on lobbying groups.

Lowi, Theodore J. *The End of Liberalism*. 2nd ed. New York: Norton, 1979. A critical analysis of the role accorded to interest groups in our society.

Olson, Mancur, Jr. *The Logic of Collective Action*. New York: Schocken, 1968. Olson, an economist, looks at the free rider problem and the rationality of joining lobbying organizations.

Sabato, Larry J. *PAC Power*. New York: Norton, 1984. An insightful and well-written account of how PACs operate.

Schlozman, Kay Lehman, and John T. Tierney. *Organized Interests and American Democracy*. New York: Harper & Row, 1985. A valuable and comprehensive study that draws on an original survey of Washington lobbyists.

9

The Mass Media

LIVE! — from *Beirut*! — it's TV DIPLOMACY! — that fascinating, irresponsible, and *dangerous* media game that confuses making news with reporting news! Starring Dan Rather, Tom Brokaw, and Peter Jennings — with special guests Nabih Berri and the Shi'ite gunmen. Also appearing — courtesy of TWA — this week's airplane hostages! Stay tuned, but first this message. . . .

Although this wasn't exactly how the television networks handled the hijacking of TWA flight 847 in 1985, it's close. On June 14, 1985, TWA flight 847, carrying 145 passengers (mostly Americans) out of Athens and bound for Rome, was hijacked by a group of Shi'ite Muslim gunmen and forced to fly to Beirut, Lebanon. Thus began one of the most extraordinary episodes in broadcast journalism. Via television, viewers not only became eyewitnesses to a terrorist event but also saw television reporters shaping the event through their participation in it.

Soon after landing in Beirut, the hijackers demanded refueling, took off for Algiers, returned to Beirut, flew back to Algiers, and returned to Beirut once more. By this time, the terrorists had released all but thirty male passengers and three TWA crew members. To prove they meant business, the terrorists also beat and then shot a male passenger and dumped his body on the runway.

The hijackers demanded media coverage to pressure Israel to release seven hundred Shi'ite prisoners. The news media rushed reporters to the Beirut airport, where television cameras zoomed in on the plane parked in a remote corner, captured the sights and sounds of sporadic gunfire, and

This Is Your Captain Speaking
The pilot of the TWA plane hijacked in 1985 speaks with television reporters on the runway of Beirut's airport. One of the hijackers is holding a pistol to his head. ABC television news broadcast this brief interview to its national audience, which helped to dramatize international terrorism. In the end, the hijackers got what they wanted: the release of hundreds of Shi'ite prisoners held by Israel.

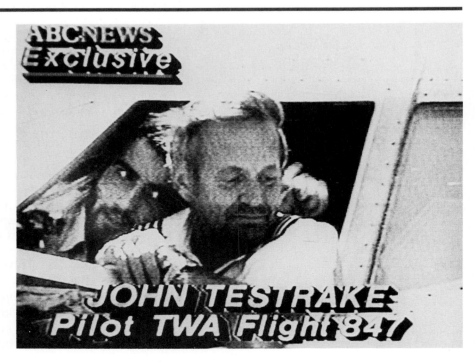

ABC NEWS Exclusive

JOHN TESTRAKE
Pilot TWA Flight 847

showed the body of the passenger shot by the hijackers. The gunmen communicated with the press through the plane's captain. Occasionally, they fired at television cameramen or reporters. The situation was, as they say, made for TV.

All three major networks filled the air with coverage of the hostage crisis, not only on scheduled news programs but also in specials and numerous special bulletins. CNN, the twenty-four-hour cable news service, covered little else. The networks competed to scoop each other, and they catered to the hijackers in the process. On June 19, ABC News correspondents Charles Glass and Julie Flint, standing on the runway, were granted an exclusive on-camera interview with three TWA crew members guarded by their gun-wielding captors. ABC scored another coup on the June 28 edition of "Good Morning America," when David Hartman spoke by telephone with Nabih Berri, a Lebanese government official with close connections to the gunmen's sect, who let Hartman interview three hostages who were with Berri in his headquarters. "Good Morning America" also showed the wife of one of the hostages speaking from Cyprus via satellite with her captive husband in Berri's office. She then spoke with Berri (ironically, Lebanon's minister of justice), who offered her words of comfort. Even the industry publication *Broadcasting* referred to this incident as "a classic example of the theater of the absurd."[1]

The other networks scored their own coups. NBC flew six hostage families to Frankfurt, putting them up in hotels in return for exclusive interviews when the captives were released. Dan Rather of CBS taped an interview with Berri in which the two all but started negotiations for the hostages' release. Berri, who clearly backed the Shi'ite cause, told Rather, who was ostensibly representing the United States "If they [the Israelis] took the seven hundred [Shi'ite prisoners] to a neutral country, I am ready to send all the Americans here with their plane to the same country, to make the exchange."[2]

Eventually the hostages (and the Shi'ite prisoners) were released with no additional deaths. What was wrong with the media coverage of this event? First, coverage was largely driven by ratings, not by news judgment. Because it was a sensational event, perfect for television viewing, the networks milked it for more than it was worth. Each network devoted more than 60 percent of its nightly news to the Beirut hostage situation, for sixteen days from capture to release,[3] exaggerating its importance in comparison with other political events. Second, the media played into the hands of the hijackers, who were allowed to portray themselves as humane terrorists who were nice to their prisoners. The terrorists were also able to stir up public opinion for the U.S. government to pressure the Israelis to release their Shi'ite prisoners. Finally, the media probably increased the appeal of hijacking as a political weapon, by helping to resolve the incident in a way favorable to the terrorists. Thus, freedom of the press has threatened the social order.

The mass media are clearly important to communication in a democratic government, but the media cause problems as well as solve them. What is the nature of the mass media in America? What events have influenced their development in the United States? Who owns the media, and to what extent are they regulated by the government? In this chapter, we shall assess their objectivity and examine the impact the media have on politics.

PEOPLE, GOVERNMENT, AND COMMUNICATIONS

"We never *talk* anymore" is a common lament among people who are living together but not getting along very well. In politics, too, citizens and their government need to communicate in order to get along well. **Communication** is the process of transmitting information from one individual or group to another. **Mass communication** is the process by which individuals or groups transmit information to large, heterogeneous, and widely dispersed audiences. The **mass media** refer to the technical devices employed in mass communication. The mass media are commonly divided into two types:

1. **Print media** communicate information through the publication of written words. Prime examples of print media are daily newspapers and popular magazines. Because books seldom have very large circulations relative to the population, they are not normally included as mass media.

2. **Broadcast media** communicate information electronically through spoken words. Prime examples of broadcast media are radio and television. Although the telephone also transmits spoken words, it is typically used for more targeted communications and is not normally included within the mass media.

In the United States, the mass media are in business to make money, which they make mainly by selling advertising through their major function of entertainment. We are more interested in the five specific functions the mass media serve for the political system: *reporting* the news, *interpreting* the news, *socializing* citizens about politics, *influencing* citizens' attitudes and behavior, and *setting the agenda* for government action.

Our special focus is on the role of the mass media in promoting communication about a government to its citizens *and* from citizens to their government. In totalitarian governments, information flows more in one direction (from government to people) than in the other. In democratic governments, information must flow freely in both directions; a democratic government can be responsive to public opinion only if its citizens can make their opinions known. Moreover, the electorate can hold government officials accountable for their actions only if voters know what their government has done, what it is doing, and what it plans to do. Because the mass media provide the major channels for this two-way flow of information, they have the dual capability of reflecting *and* shaping our political views.

Mass media are not the only means of communication between citizens and government. In the four previous chapters, we discussed other "linkage mechanisms" that also promote such communication — certain agents of socialization (especially schools), elections, political parties, and interest groups. Certain linkage mechanisms communicate better in one direction than in the other. Primary and secondary schools, for example, commonly instruct young citizens about government rules and symbols, whereas election results usually send messages from voters to government. Parties and interest groups more often foster communications in both directions. The mass media, however, are the only linkage mechanisms that *specialize* in communication.

No, but I Saw the Movie
Actors Robert Redford and Dustin Hoffman played Washington Post *reporters Carl Bernstein and Bob Woodward in the film,* All the President's Men. *The book by Bernstein and Woodward helped reveal Nixon's role in the Watergate scandal. Here the actors meet on the set with John Dean, former counsel to President Richard Nixon, and Maureen Dean, who was often shown in the audience when her husband was testifying at the Senate Watergate hearings, implicating Nixon in the coverup. Dean himself pleaded guilty of participating in the affair.*

Although we shall concentrate on political uses of the four most prominent mass media—newspapers, magazines, radio, and television—you should understand that political content can also be transmitted through other mass media, such as recordings and motion pictures. Rock groups like the Talking Heads and Gang of Four often express political ideas in their music, and motion pictures can convey particularly intense images of political life.

In the 1976 film *All the President's Men,* Dustin Hoffman and Robert Redford played the two *Washington Post* reporters (Carl Bernstein and Bob Woodward) who doggedly exposed the Watergate scandal that culminated in President Richard Nixon's 1974 resignation. This motion picture dramatized a seamy side of political life that contrasted sharply with the idealized view of the office. More recently, *Rambo: First Blood, Part Two* (1985) starred Silvester Stallone as a superhero who returns to Vietnam ("This time, to win!") to rescue American MIAs. Compared with earlier films about Vietnam (for example, *Coming Home, The Deerhunter, Apocalypse Now!*), which portrayed war as a terrifying hell, Stallone's *Rambo* implied that soldiering can be glorious. His film also conveyed the message that military force can be an effective way of solving difficult international problems.

DEVELOPMENT OF THE MASS MEDIA IN THE UNITED STATES

Although the film and record industries sometimes convey political messages, they are primarily entertainment industries. Our focus will be on the mass media in the news industry—on print and broadcast journalism. The development of the mass media in the United States reflects the growth of the country, technological inventions, and political attitudes toward the scope of government—as well as the need to entertain.

Newspapers

When the Revolutionary War broke out in 1775, thirty-seven news-papers (all weeklies) were being published in the colonies.[4] Most of them favored the colonists' side against the British, and they played an important part in promoting the Revolution. However, these weekly papers could not be regarded as instruments of mass communication. Their circulations were small (usually a thousand copies or so), and they were relatively expensive. Type had to be set by hand, the presses printed quite slowly, transportation was costly, and there were few advertisers to defray the costs of publication. However, politicians of the day quickly saw the value of the press and started papers that printed their own views. During George Washington's administration, for example, the Federalists published the *Gazette of the U.S.,* and the Republicans countered with the *National Gazette.*

The first newspapers were therefore mainly political organs, financed by parties and advocating their causes. Newspapers did not move toward independent ownership and large circulation until the 1830s, with the publication of two successful dailies (the *New York Sun* and the *New York Herald*) that sold for just a penny. Inventions spurred the growth of the news industry. The telegraph (invented in 1837) eventually replaced carrier pigeons for transmitting news and led to simultaneous publication of news stories in papers across the country. The rotary press (1847) soon enabled publishers to print much more quickly and cheaply.

According to the 1880 census, 971 daily newspapers and 8,633 weekly newspapers and periodicals were then published in the United States. Most larger cities had multiple newspapers—New York had 29 papers, Philadelphia 24, San Francisco 21, and Chicago 18. Competition for readers grew fierce among the big-city dailies. Toward the latter part of the nineteenth century, imaginative publishers competed for readers by entertaining them with photographs, comic strips, sports sections, advice to the lovelorn, and stories of sex and crime. The sensational reporting of that period came to be called **yellow journalism** — after the "Yellow Kid," a comic strip character featured in the *New York World,* published by Joseph Pulitzer (the same Pulitzer honored in the Pulitzer prizes for distinguished journalism).[5] Contests calculated to sell papers were also popular with publishers, and some promotional schemes had lasting political consequences. Pulitzer raised funds to put the Statue of Liberty on its pedestal after Congress turned down a request for $100,000 for that purpose. Each person who donated to the cause had his or her name printed in the *New York World*'s list of donors. And William Randolph Hearst, publisher of the rival *New York Journal,* helped get the nation into a war with Spain. When the U.S. battleship *Maine* blew up mysteriously in Havana harbor on February 15, 1898, Hearst proclaimed it the work of enemy agents, charging his readers to "Remember the Maine!"

By the 1950s, intense competition among big-city dailies had nearly disappeared. New York, which had 29 papers in 1880, had only 3 by 1969. This pattern was repeated in every large city; most were left with only 3, 2, or just 1 major paper. As a result of the rise of new cities that accompanied general population growth, however, the number of daily newspapers published (and the papers' combined circulation) remained about the same nationally. In 1950, a total of 1,772 daily papers had a circulation of 53.8 million; in 1983, a total of 1,701 papers had a circulation of 62.6 million.[6]

The daily paper with the largest circulation in 1985 (about 2 million copies) is the *Wall Street Journal,* which appeals to a national audience because of its extensive coverage of business news. The *New York Times,* which many journalists consider the best newspaper in the country, sells only about a million copies, placing it fifth in circulation nationally. Even in New York, the *Times* sells fewer copies than the sensationalist, tabloid-size *New York Post.* Neither the *Times* nor the journalistically respected *Wall Street Journal* carries any comic strips, which no doubt limits their mass appeal. They also print more political news and more news analyses than most readers want to confront (see Feature 9.1).

Magazines

Magazines differ from newspapers primarily in the nature of their coverage, their frequency of publication, and the quality of their production. In contrast to the broad coverage of daily papers, many magazines focus on narrow topics such as sports. Even news-oriented magazines cover the news in a more specialized manner than newspapers. Magazines and newspapers differ not only in content, but also in the way they are presented. Newspapers are printed on inexpensive paper and are expected to be discarded; magazines are printed more carefully on durable stock, which allows them to be read over several days or weeks. This increased durability has allowed magazines to be more important as forums for opinion than as news reports. As such, magazines of public affairs have had relatively small circulations and select readerships, making them questionable as mass media.

Feature 9.1

Front Pages of Four Major Daily Newspapers

Even if a rose is a rose, a newspaper is not necessarily a *newspaper*. Some papers, like the *Wall Street Journal* and the *New York Times,* pride themselves on providing thorough coverage of the news (the *Times'* motto is "All the News That's Fit to Print") and in-depth analyses of major national and international news events. Neither paper may feature (or even cover) the local fires or street crimes headlined in other papers, which cater to more popular tastes for violence and human interest stories.

Differences among papers can often be judged simply by examining their front pages. Papers that are oriented to popular entertainment have punchy graphics to catch the eye of readers who do not intend to spend a good part of the day studying the news. Compare the front pages of the *Wall Street Journal* and the *New York Times* with those of *USA Today* and the *New York News* —all published on the same day, July 17, 1986. Both the *Journal* and the *Times* are published for the serious news reader and use few gimmicks to draw readers.

The above description certainly applies to the earliest public affairs magazines published in the mid-1800s, such as *Nation, McClure's,* and *Harper's.* Nevertheless, these magazines were often politically influential—especially in framing arguments against slavery and later in publishing exposés, by such writers as Lincoln Steffens and Ida Tarbell, of political corruption and business exploitation. These writers, derisively called **muckrakers** (a term derived from a special rake used to collect manure), practiced an early form of investigative reporting. Because their writings were lengthy critiques of the existing economic and political order, they found a more hospitable outlet in magazines of opinion than in newspapers of mass circulation.

Three more specialized weekly news magazines—*Time* (founded in 1923), *Newsweek* (1933), and *U.S. News and World Report* (1933)—have enjoyed much larger circulations (from 1 million to 2 million copies in 1985). The audiences of these three magazines are not as large as the nearly 18 million buyers of *Reader's Digest,* or the 17 million readers of *TV Guide,* or even the

The *Journal* does not even publish photographs—any-where—except in advertisements. *USA Today* and the *New York News,* on the other hand, appeal to people who read the paper less to learn about political developments than to keep abreast of popular culture. The *News,* with its huge and provocative headlines and big oversized photographs, outsells the *Times* in New York, and the colorful *USA Today* is closing fast on the *Journal* in national sales. Founded only in 1982, *USA Today* uses punchy graphics in a ''busy'' layout to appeal to readers socialized by hours of television viewing.

4.6 million consumers of *National Enquirer.* Nevertheless, these prominent weekly news magazines not only qualify as mass media, but also substitute for the lack of widely read national newspapers.

Radio

Regularly scheduled and continuous radio broadcasting began in 1920 on stations KDKA in Pittsburgh and WWJ in Detroit. Both stations claim to be the first commercial station, and both did broadcast returns of the 1920 election of President Warren G. Harding. However, the news was available on only 5,000 radio receivers, and those were operated mainly by technical experts. Five years later, there were more than 2.5 million receivers, mostly in American homes. By 1940 more than 860 stations served nearly 30 million homes.[7] The number of radio stations mushroomed to more than 3,000 in 1950.[8]

The first radio network, the National Broadcasting Company (NBC), was formed in 1926. The Columbia Broadcasting System (CBS) was created in 1927, followed by the American Broadcasting System (ABC) and the Mutual Broadcasting System. By linking together thousands of local stations, the four major networks transformed radio into a national medium. Millions of Americans were able to hear the president of the United States, Franklin D. Roosevelt, deliver his first "fireside chat" in 1933, soon after his inauguration. However, the first coast-to-coast broadcast did not occur until 1937, when listeners were shocked by an eyewitness report of the mooring and subsequent explosion of the dirigible *Hindenburg* in New Jersey.

Because the public could sense reporters' personalities over radio in a way they could not in print, broadcast journalists quickly became national celebrities. Edward R. Murrow, one of the most famous radio news personalities, broadcast news of the merger of Germany and Austria by shortwave from Vienna in 1938 and later gave stirring reports of German air raids on London in World War II.

Television

Experiments with television began in France in the early 1900s. By 1937 seventeen experimental television stations were operating in the United States. In 1939 President Roosevelt appeared on television at the New York World's Fair. By 1940 twenty-three television stations were operating on a more

Listening to the President Before Television Took Over
Before television, friends often gathered around a radio to hear the president make an important address. In 1941, American soldiers, friends, and visiting relatives gathered in the Army YMCA on Governors Island in New York to hear President Franklin Roosevelt's warning of approaching war. Of course, the message had a special meaning for this group. Still, see how intently they are listening to what the president is saying. Maybe we should consider using radio instead of television for critically important speeches.

regular basis, and — repeating the feat of radio twenty years earlier — two stations broadcast the returns of the 1940 election and Roosevelt's re-election.[9]

The onset of World War II froze the development of television technology, but following the war growth in the medium exploded. When peace returned in 1945, only eight television stations were broadcasting. By 1950 ninety-eight stations were covering the major population centers of the country, but only 9 percent of American households had television receivers.

The first commercial color television broadcast came in 1951, as did the first coast-to-coast broadcast — President Harry Truman's address to delegates at the Japanese Peace Treaty Conference in San Francisco. The same year, Democratic Senator Estes Kefauver of Tennessee called for public television coverage of his committee's investigation of organized crime. For weeks, people with television sets invited their neighbors to watch underworld crime figures answering questions before the camera. And Senator Kefauver became one of the first politicians to benefit from television coverage. Previously unknown and representing a small state, he nevertheless entered the 1952 Democratic presidential primaries, and won many of them. His performance in the primaries in 1952 led to his nomination as the Democrats' vice presidential candidate in 1956.

The number of television stations increased to over five hundred in 1960, and 87 percent of households had television receivers. By 1980 the United States had more than eight hundred commercial and three hundred educational television stations, and virtually every household (98 percent) had

How Young and Handsome He Looks!

Television revolutionized presidential politics by allowing millions of voters to look closely at the candidates' faces and to judge their personalities in the process. This closeup of John Kennedy during a debate with Richard Nixon in the 1960 campaign showed Kennedy to good advantage. Closeups of Nixon, on the other hand, made him look as though he needed a shave. Because Kennedy won one of the closest elections in history, one wonders whether Kennedy's good looks on television made the difference.

receivers. Now, television claims by far the largest audiences of the mass media (see Figure 9.1.) From television's beginning, most stations were linked into networks founded by three of the four major radio networks. (Only the Mutual Broadcasting System did not make the transition into television.) At present, about 85 percent of commercial television stations are affiliated with either NBC, CBS, or ABC. Many of the early "anchormen" on network news programs (for example, Walter Cronkite) came to the medium with years of experience as radio broadcast journalists. Now that the news audience could actually see the broadcasters as well as hear them, news personalities became even greater celebrities. When he retired from anchoring the "CBS Evening News" in 1981, Walter Cronkite emerged as one of the most trusted and influential people in America.

Figure 9.1 ━━

Audiences of Selected Media Sources

Television, newspapers, and magazines differ sharply in their appeal to mass audiences as news sources. The difference shows clearly when we compare the figures for the average number of homes that are tuned nightly to each of the three major network news programs with the figures for the circulation of the three top news magazines, the eight top newspapers, and the two largest opinion magazines. Clearly, television news enters many more homes than does news from the other media. All three news magazines (which are published only weekly) have more readers than any daily newspaper, and opinion magazines reach only a small fraction of the usual television news audiences. (Sources: Average television news audiences for September 1983 through March 1984 are from the Nielsen Television Index; *newspaper circulations for September 20, 1985, are from* Editor & Publisher, International Yearbook, 1986; *magazine circulation figures are from* Standard Periodical Directory, 1985–86.)

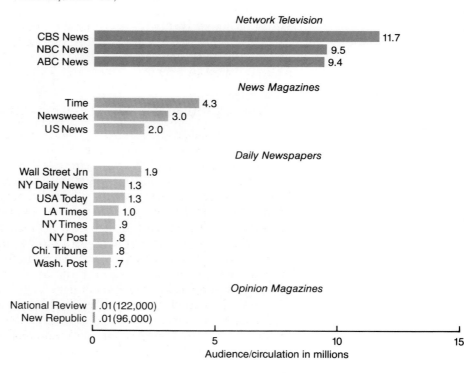

Just as the appearance of the newscaster became important for television viewers, so did the appearance of the news itself. Television's great advantage over radio—that it *showed* people and events—both contributed to the impact of television news coverage and to some extent determined the news that television chose to cover. Television was particularly partial to events that had *film value* (visual impact). Organized protests and fires are examples of events that "show well" on television, so television tends to show them. Violent conflict of any kind, especially unfolding dramas that involve weapons, rate especially high in visual impact, which accounts for television's all-consuming coverage of the 1985 hijacking in Beirut. However, television is not alone among the mass media in focusing on news that appeals to its audience's emotions. The 1890s newspapers that engaged in yellow journalism also played on emotions. In fact, private ownership of the media ensures that news will be selected for its audience appeal (see Figure 9.1).

PRIVATE OWNERSHIP OF THE MEDIA

In the United States, private ownership of the media is an accepted, largely unquestioned fact. Indeed, government ownership of the media strikes most Americans as an unwarranted violation of liberty. It can, in fact, interfere with the "marketplace of ideas" and result in one-way communication, from government to citizens. When the government controls the news flow, the people have little chance either to learn what the government is doing or to pressure it to behave differently. In the Soviet Union, for example, the major newspaper, *Pravda* (which means "Truth" in Russian), is operated by the Communist party. A second daily paper, *Isvestia* (which means "News" in Russian), is operated by the government itself. The distinction between the two newspapers is not important, for they do not compete with each other. Even the Russians joke about their papers: "In *Truth* there is no news, and in *News* there is no truth."

Consequences of Private Ownership

The print media (both newspapers and magazines) are privately owned in other Western democratic countries, but the broadcast media usually are not. In most countries, both radio and television tend to be run by the government, often as monopolies. Except for "public television" (and "public radio," which is less well known), the electronic media are privately owned in the United States. Private ownership of both print and broadcast media gives the American news industry more political freedom than any other in the world, but it also makes the media more dependent on advertising revenues to cover their costs and to make a profit. Because advertising revenues are tied to the size of the audience, the news operations of mass media in America must appeal to the audiences they serve.

One might think that the likelihood of a story's being covered in the media depends on its political significance, educational value, or broad social importance. The sad truth is that most potential news stories are not judged by such grand criteria. The primary criterion of a story's **newsworthiness** is usually its audience appeal, as judged by its *high impact* on readers or listeners; its *sensationalist* aspect (as exemplified by violence, conflict, disaster, or scandal); its treatment of *familiar* people or life situations; its *close-to-home* character; and its *timeliness*.[10]

Reliance on audience appeal has led the news industry to calculate its audience very carefully. The print media can easily determine their circulations through sales, but the broadcast media must estimate their audiences through various sampling techniques. Because both print and broadcast media have reason to inflate their estimated audiences (and thereby to tell advertisers that they reach more people than they actually do), a separate industry has arisen to rate audience size impartially. The rating reports have resulted in a "ratings game," in which the media try to increase ratings regardless of the consequences for news delivery. Some television stations favor "happy talk" on local news broadcasts—witty on-the-air exchanges among reporters, sportscasters, and meteorologists. Other stations use the "eyewitness" approach, showing a preponderance of film with human-interest, humorous, or violent content. Many stations combine the two, often pleasing viewers, but perhaps not informing them properly.

The news function of the mass media in the United States cannot be separated from the main function of the privately owned media: entertainment. Entertainment increases audiences, which increases advertising revenues. Of the four hours or so that the average American spends watching television every day, only about ninety minutes are devoted to news or documentaries; the remainder goes to entertainment, movies, or sports.[11] More than 60 million newspapers circulate daily among the population, but more than 60 percent of their content is devoted to advertising.[12] Only a portion of the remaining newspaper space is devoted to news of any sort, and only a fraction of the news space can be classified as "political" news (excluding fires, robberies, murder trials, and so on).

Concentration of Private Ownership

Media owners can make more money by increasing their audiences, either by enlarging existing audiences or by acquiring additional publications or stations. In fact, there is a decided trend toward concentrated ownership of the media, which raises the prospect that a few major owners could control the news flow to promote their own political interests—much as political parties influenced the content of early newspapers. Although the number of daily newspapers has remained approximately the same over the last thirty-five years, the number of *independent* newspapers has declined as more papers have been acquired by newspaper chains (two or more newspapers in different cities under the same ownership). Most of the more than 150 newspaper chains are small, owning fewer than ten papers.[13] Some, however, are very large. The Gannett newspaper chain, for example, owns eighty-seven newspapers throughout the United States—including *USA Today*, the newspaper with the third largest circulation in the nation. Only about four hundred dailies are still independent, and many of these papers are too small and unprofitable to invite acquisition.

At first glance, ownership concentration in the television industry does not seem to be a problem. Although there are only three major networks, the networks usually do not own their affiliates. Nearly half of all the communities in the United States are served by eight or more stations.[14] This figure suggests that the electronic media offer enough diversity of views to balance ownership concentration. Like newspapers, however, television stations in different cities are sometimes owned by the same group. In 1985, for example, the Capcities/ABC group owned eight television stations—one each in New York, Los Angeles, Chicago, Philadelphia, San Francisco, Houston, Fresno, and Raleigh-Durham—serving 24 percent of the television market. A group of five stations owned by CBS covers 21 percent of the market, and five NBC stations cover 20 percent.[15]

Ownership concentration can also occur across the media. Sometimes the same corporation will own a television station, a radio station, and a newspaper in the same area. For example, the Chicago Tribune Company owns the *Chicago Tribune* (Chicago's largest daily newspaper); the *New York Daily News* (the nation's second largest paper); six television stations in major cities (including WGN-TV in Chicago, WPIX-TV in New York, and KTLA-TV in Los Angeles), serving 19 percent of the market; and several radio stations across the country.

Some people fear such concentration of media under a single owner, and government has recognized these fears in regulating media ownership.

GOVERNMENT REGULATION OF THE MEDIA

Although most of the mass media in the United States are privately owned, they do not operate completely free of government regulation. The broadcast media, however, operate under more regulations than the print media, due initially to technical factors in broadcasting. In general, government regulations of the mass media fall into three categories: (1) technical, (2) structural, and (3) content.[16]

Technical Regulations

The broadcast media confront certain technical limitations not faced by the print media. The number of electronic airwaves available for broadcasting radio and television signals is limited. In the early days of radio, stations that operated on similar frequencies in the same area often jammed each other's signals, and neither could broadcast clearly. At the early broadcasters' insistence, Congress passed the Federal Radio Act of 1927, which declared that the public owned the airwaves and that private broadcasters could use them only by obtaining a license from the Federal Radio Commission. Thus, government regulation of broadcasting was not "forced" on the industry by socialist politicians; it was requested by capitalist owners who wanted the government to impose order on the use of the airwaves.

The Federal Communications Act of 1934 updated the Federal Radio Act of 1927 and forms the basis for current regulation of the broadcasting industry. The 1934 act replaced the five-person radio commission with the

Federal Communications Commission (FCC), consisting of seven members (no more than four of them from the same political party) chosen by the president for terms of seven years. Because the commissioners serve overlapping terms — beginning and ending in different years — and can be removed from office only through impeachment and conviction, the FCC is considered an independent regulatory agency — it is insulated from political control by either the president or Congress. (Independent regulatory agencies are discussed in Chapter 12.) The FCC today is charged with regulating interstate and foreign communication by radio, television, telephone, telegraph, cable, and satellite.

The government's regulatory powers in technical areas go beyond granting licenses, however. For example, the FCC determined the standard for color television in 1950 by choosing a CBS-developed transmission system over a competing one by RCA. Moreover, in the early 1960s, Congress required all television sets manufactured for sale in interstate commerce to receive both VHF (very high frequency) channels 2 through 13 and UHF (ultra high frequency) channels 14 through 83. Both regulations again helped the broadcast industry by assuring the public that the television sets being sold would receive the signals being transmitted.

Structural Regulations

The FCC also regulates the structure of the electronic media — the organization of broadcasting companies and their interrelationships. As radio began broadcasting to millions of citizens, the FCC became concerned about concentrating too much power in the hands of a single owner. Concerned that the National Broadcasting Company — which operated both a "red" and

Earwitness News Reporting
Journalists who attempted to cover the American invasion of the tiny Caribbean island of Grenada in 1983 were reduced to waiting off shore and listening to battle reports on the radio. The Grenada incident was unlike other recent confrontations — World War II, the Korean War, and Vietnam, for example — in that it represented the first time in recent American history that the government prevented journalists from accompanying U.S. troops during an invasion.

a "blue" network until 1943 — had grown too big, the FCC ordered NBC to sell its blue network, leading to the creation of the American Broadcasting Company. Also during the 1940s, the FCC adopted its **duopoly rule,** which prohibits any company from owning more than one AM, one FM, or one television station in a single community.[17]

In the early 1950s, the FCC adopted its **7-7-7 rule,** which limited to seven the number of AM, FM, and television stations a single company could own. This ceiling was set when there were fewer than two hundred television stations and fewer than three thousand radio stations. But by 1984 the number of commercial television stations had grown to nearly nine hundred, and the number of radio stations had nearly tripled, to over eight thousand. A majority of commissioners appointed by President Reagan thus opted to relax FCC regulations by expanding the ownership rule to a **12-12-12 rule,** which would benefit several large media groups — such as Gannett — that are at or near the current limit on ownership of television stations. Looking ahead to 1990, the FCC anticipates an end to all ownership restrictions.[18] If that occurs, the FCC will have abandoned a principle that it once enforced vigorously — limiting media control.

Regulation of Content

The First Amendment to the Constitution prohibits Congress from abridging the freedom of the press. Over time, "the press" has come to be interpreted as *all* the mass media. As one might expect, the press — particularly the print media — has interpreted "freedom of the press" in the broadest possible way, citing the Constitution for its right to print any news it wants to print. Over the past two hundred years, the courts have decided numerous cases to define exactly how far freedom of the press extends under law. The most important of these cases, which are often quite complex, are discussed in Chapter 17. Usually the courts have struck down government attempts to censor the press and to restrain it from publishing or broadcasting information, events, or opinions that it finds newsworthy. One notable exception is during wartime, when courts have supported censorship in the publishing or broadcasting of such information as the sailing schedules of troop ships or the movements of troops in battle. Otherwise, the courts have recognized a strong constitutional case against press censorship. This stand has given the United States some of the freest, most vigorous news media in the world (see Compared With What? 9.1).

Again, however, the broadcast media endure some regulation of the content of their news coverage that is not applied to the print media. The basis for the FCC's regulation of content lies in its charge to ensure that radio (and, later, television) stations would "serve the public interest, convenience, and necessity." Broadcasters operate under three constraints rooted in the Federal Communications Act of 1934. The FCC's **equal opportunities rule** provides that, if a broadcast station gives or sells time to a candidate for any public office, it must make available an equal amount of time under the same conditions to all other candidates for that office. The **fairness doctrine** obligates broadcasters to discuss public issues and to provide fair coverage to each side of those issues. Finally, the **reasonable access rule** requires that

Compared With What? 9.1

Freedom of the Press

The United States guarantees freedom of the press in the First Amendment to the Constitution. This alone does not distinguish the United States from other nations of the world, however; nearly all of them recognize freedom of the press in some form. But specifying freedom of the press in a nation's constitution is not enough to guarantee freedom of the press in practice. A recent survey of government control of the news media in 157 countries classified the print and broadcast media into three categories: free, partly free, and not free. For example, both types of media were judged to be free in the United States; neither was classified as free in the Soviet Union; and in France, the print media were free, but the broadcast media were only partly free. In all, the print media were free in only 34 percent of the countries, and the broadcast media were even less likely to be free (23 percent).

Moreover, two-thirds of the governments operated their own official news agencies, either in addition to or in lieu of private news services. In the Soviet Union, for example, the only news service is that of the government news agency, TASS, which alone decides what news to disseminate to the rest of the world and within the Soviet Union. In the United States, which has no government news agency, the three private television networks and other private news agencies — such as the Associated Press (AP) and United Press International (UPI) — contribute to freedom of the press.

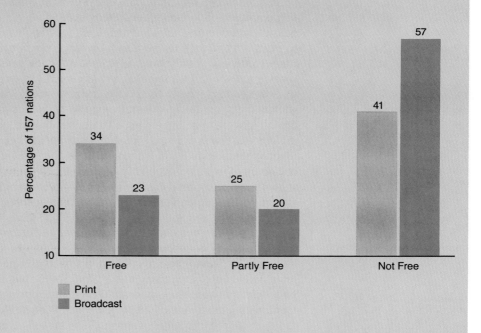

Source: Raymond D. Gastil, *Freedom in the World: Political Rights and Civil Liberties 1984–1985* (Westport, Conn.: Greenwood Press, 1985), pp. 64–67.

stations make their facilities available for the expression of conflicting views or issues from all responsible elements in the community.

These regulations seem unobjectionable to most people, but they are at the heart of a developing controversy about deregulation of the broadcast media. Note that *none* of these regulations is imposed on the print media, which has no responsibility to give equal treatment to political candidates that it opposes, to give fair coverage to all sides of an issue, or to express conflicting views from all responsible elements of the community. In fact, one aspect of a free press is its ability to champion causes that it favors (such as erecting the Statue of Liberty or starting a war with Spain) — without having to argue the case for the other side. The broadcast media have traditionally been treated differently, under the assumption that they were licensed by the FCC to operate as semimonopolies.[19] With the rise of one-newspaper cities and towns, however, there is now actually more competition among television stations than among newspapers in virtually every market area. Critics who advocate dropping the equal opportunities, fairness, and reasonable access regulations argue that the broadcast media should now be just as free as the print media to decide which candidates they endorse and which issues they support.

The FCC itself seems to have swung toward this view. In 1985 it asked Congress to abolish the fairness doctrine on the grounds that it "chills and coerces speech."[20] In its hundred-page report, the FCC provided examples of broadcasters who had sidestepped controversies rather than risk a court challenge under the fairness doctrine. If Congress does eliminate the fairness doctrine and related provisions of the Federal Communications Act, it may dramatically change the way television transmits news to the American people. One might expect the content and coverage of television news to become more like that in newspapers — taking more partisan stands and backing particular viewpoints. If so, the effect on public opinion may be substantial, given the importance of television as a source of news for most Americans.

REPORTING THE NEWS

"News," for most journalists, is an important event that happens in a current twenty-four-hour period. A presidential news conference or an explosion in the Capitol would qualify as news. And a national political convention certainly qualifies as news, although it may not justify the fourteen thousand media representatives who covered the 1984 Democratic National Convention. Who decides what is important? The media, of course. In this section, we discuss how the media cover political affairs, what they choose to report (which then becomes "news"), and whether the media are biased in their reporting.

Covering Politics

All the major news media seek to cover political events through first-hand reports from journalists on the scene. For example, the *New York Times* alone has about 35 reporters in Washington, D.C. Because so many significant political events occur in the nation's capital, Washington has by far the largest press corps—about 3,500—of any city in the United States.

About one-third of these correspondents are assigned to cover the White House. Since President Theodore Roosevelt first provided a special room for reporters in the White House in 1902, the press has had special access to the presidency. In fact, reporters even enjoyed informal personal relationships with the president as late as Truman's administration. Today the media's relationship with the president is itself mediated through the Office of the Press Secretary and the Office of Media Liaison.

White House correspondents cover the presidency largely by hanging around the press room, waiting for news to materialize. Material for their stories routinely comes in one of three forms, each carefully crafted by the White House to control the news output.[21]

The most frequent form is the *news release*—a prepared text distributed to reporters with the hope that it will be used verbatim. A *news briefing,* held daily by tradition, enables reporters to question the press secretary about news releases. A *news conference* involves questioning high-level officials in the executive branch—including the president on occasion. News conferences appear to be freewheeling, but precise answers to expected questions tend to be carefully rehearsed.

Occasionally, news conferences are given *on background,* meaning that the information can be quoted but the source must not be identified precisely. A vague reference—"a senior official says"—is all right. (When he was secretary of state, Henry Kissinger himself was often the "senior official" reporting on foreign policy developments.) Information disclosed *off the record* cannot even be printed. Journalists who violate these well-known rules risk losing their welcome at the White House.

Most reporters in the Washington press corps are accredited to sit in the House and Senate press galleries, but only about four hundred cover Congress exclusively.[22] Most of the news about Congress comes from innumerable press releases issued by its 535 members and from its unending supply of congressional reports. Thus, a journalist can report on Congress in many ways without hanging around its press galleries.

Not so long ago, individual congressional committees only allowed radio and television coverage of their proceedings on special occasions—as Senator Estes Kefauver did during his committee's investigation of organized crime, and as the Senate Select Committee did during the Watergate investigation. Congress banned microphones and cameras from its chambers proper until 1979, when the House permitted live coverage. Even then, the leadership controlled the views being televised. Nevertheless, televised broadcasts of the House were surprisingly successful—thanks to C-SPAN (the Cable Satellite Public Affairs Network), which is linked to more than 1,500 cable systems across the country and which developed a cultlike following among hundreds of thousands of regular viewers. To share in the television exposure, a majority of senators voted to begin television coverage of their chamber in 1986.

In addition to these recognized news channels, selected reporters occasionally benefit from *leaks* of information released by officials who are guar-

McCarthy Sees Red — Everywhere
Republican Senator Joseph McCarthy from Wisconsin expounds his views on the communist menace in America during the televised Senate Army-McCarthy hearings in 1954. McCarthy had been accused of improper influence in his investigation of alleged subversion in the Army. In this early television coverage of congressional activities, a national audience witnessed bitter clashes between McCarthy and Joseph Welch (with hand on head), special counsel to the Army. McCarthy was cleared of these charges, but he was later condemned by the Senate itself for abusing its committees.

anteed anonymity. Officials may leak news to interfere with others' political plans or to float ideas ("trial balloons") past the public and other political leaders so as to gauge their reactions. Sometimes one carefully placed leak will turn into a gusher of media coverage through the practice of *pack journalism* — the tendency of journalists to chase after a morsel of news. Often the story hounded by the pack simply does not offer enough substance to sustain pursuit, and the chase is abandoned as quickly as it was begun.

Presenting the News

Media executives, news editors, and prominent reporters function as **gatekeepers** in directing the news flow: they decide which events to report and how to handle the elements in the stories that they choose to report. Only a few individuals—no more than twenty-five on the average newspaper or news weekly and fifty on each of the major television networks—qualify as gatekeepers and thus define the news for public consumption.[23] They are usually very selective in choosing what goes through the gate.

It is impossible for the media to communicate *everything* about public affairs. There is neither space in newspapers or magazines nor time on television or radio to do so. Time limitations impose especially severe constraints on television news broadcasting. Each half-hour network news program, without commercials, leaves only about twenty minutes for the news. The average story lasts about one minute, and few stories run longer than two minutes. The typical script for an entire television news broadcast would fill less than two columns of one page of the *New York Times*.[24]

A parade of unconnected one-minute news stories, flashing across the television screen every night, would boggle the eyes and minds of viewers. To make the news understandable and to hold viewers' attention, television editors and producers group stories together within overarching themes. The stories themselves concentrate on individuals, because individuals are tangible and identifiable to audiences, whereas political institutions are not. The presidency is an exception, because that institution is conveniently embodied in the president. When television covers Congress, however, it tries to personify Congress by focusing on prominent, quotable leaders, such as the Speaker of the House or the majority leader of the Senate. Such personification tends to distort the character of the institution for the purpose of gaining audience acceptability. This approach also encourages **horse race journalism,** in which election coverage becomes a matter of "who's ahead?" Elections end up in the television news as contests between individuals rather than as confrontations between parties and platforms.

Campaigning for office is a type of political news that lends itself to media coverage, especially if the candidates create a **media event** — a situation that is too "newsworthy" to pass up. "Walkin' Lawton" Chiles won his U.S. Senate seat by walking 1,003 miles down the Florida peninsula in the 1970s, drawing considerable press attention along the way. Dan Walker strolled into the Illinois governor's mansion using the very same approach. Not to be outdone, Bob Graham drew press coverage by working on one hundred different blue-collar jobs in one hundred days, in his successful campaign for the Florida governorship in 1978.

One study of news content in city newspapers, local television, and network television found that the network news contained a higher percentage of items about government and politics (involving the presidency, Congress, domestic policy, foreign affairs, and so on) than the city's daily newspapers and substantially more than the local television news (see Figure 9.2).[25] In comparison with the other media, newspapers emphasized stories about crime and justice (including individual crimes, police items, and so on). Local television news programs dealt more with economic and social issues (including issues involving business and labor, environment and transportation, education, and so on). Remember, however, that this study calculated only the *relative* coverage of news in the media. Although the network news reports a higher percentage of news about government and politics, its coverage of each story tends to last less than two minutes, whereas daily papers usually discuss the same story in greater depth.

Is Reporting Biased?

News professes to reflect reality, yet critics of modern journalism contend that this reality is colored by the way it is interpreted through the ideological biases of the owners and editors (the gatekeepers) and by the reporters themselves.

The argument that news is politically biased has two sides. On the one hand, news reporters are criticized for sharing a liberal ideology that colors the "reality" they portray in words and in recorded images. On the other hand, wealthy and conservative media owners are suspected of reinforcing

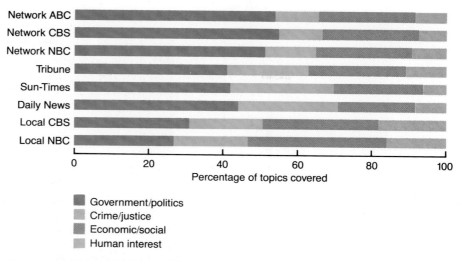

Government/politics
Crime/justice
Economic/social
Human interest

Frequency of News Topics in Different Sources
Where you get your news to some extent determines the news that you get. This conclusion emerges from a count of the news topics in eight sources — three network evening news programs, three major Chicago daily newspapers, and two local news broadcasts — for nine months in 1976. All three television networks reported proportionately more news about government and politics than did the newspapers, which in turn reported proportionately more than the local television news did. Stories about economic and social matters (business and labor affairs, environment and transportation issues, and education and religion) were most popular on local television, along with human interest features. The newspapers tended to report more about crime and justice. (Source: Doris A. Graber, Mass Media and American Politics, *2nd ed. (Washington, D.C.: CQ Press, 1984), pp. 83–84.)*

Figure 9.2

the existing order by serving a relentless round of entertainment that numbs the public's capacity for critical analysis.

Although the picture is far from clear, available evidence seems to confirm the charge of liberal bias among reporters in the major news media. A study of the voting behavior of 240 reporters and broadcasters employed by such media giants as the *New York Times,* the *Washington Post,* the *Wall Street Journal, Time, Newsweek, U.S. News and World Report,* CBS, NBC, and ABC supports that idea. In presidential elections from 1964 through 1976, these elite media journalists voted for the Democratic candidate more than 80 percent of the time.[26] Moreover, a 1985 *Los Angeles Times* survey of 2,703 news and editorial staffers on 621 papers found that 55 percent of the journalists described themselves as liberal, compared with a figure of only 23 percent for the general public.[27]

Another careful analysis of 625 news stories about the 1984 presidential campaign, as broadcast by all three television networks, measured ideological leaning and the "spin" put on the news by the tone of the reporting.[28] The authors illustrate "spin" by citing Dan Rather's characterization of candidate Reagan's campaign train trip through Ohio (which was hard news) as "a photo-opportunity train trip, chock full of symbolism and trading on Harry Truman's old turf." Counting positive spin as "good press" and negative spin

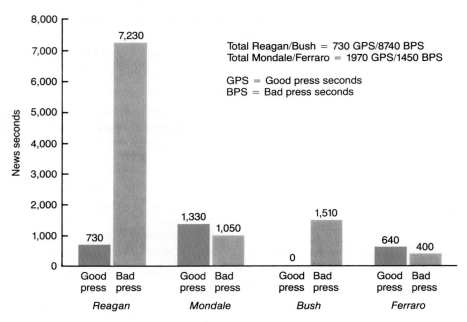

TV News Bias in the 1984 Presidential Campaign
A team of researchers studied tape recordings of the evening news broadcasts for all three networks from Labor Day through Election Day, 1984. They identified 625 news items discussing the presidential and vice presidential campaigns. Each story was scored on a number of dimensions, including the "spin" given to the story by the reporter's positive or negative tone or remarks in discussing the candidate. A piece with positive spin—tone or remarks favorable to the candidate—was defined as "good press" and a piece with a negative spin was defined as a "bad press." The graph above shows the number of news seconds that the researchers scored as good press (GPS) or bad press (BPS) for each of the candidates. Ronald Reagan's bad-press total was ten times his good-press total. His Republican running mate, George Bush, had no good press and 1,500 seconds of bad press. Walter Mondale and his running mate, Geraldine Ferraro, had a slightly favorable ratio of good press to bad press. Compared with the Republican presidential candidates, the Democratic ticket enjoyed substantially more favorable campaign coverage in the network news, but Reagan enjoyed four times the coverage given to Mondale. (Source: Maura Clancey and Michael J. Robinson, "General Election Coverage: Part I," Public Opinion 7, December– January 1985:50. Reprinted with permission of American Enterprise Institute.)

Figure 9.3 ━━

as "bad press," the authors found that Reagan's bad press total of news seconds on television was *ten times* that of his good press (see Figure 9.3). The comparison for Bush was even worse, since he got no good press at all. Conversely, Democratic candidates, Walter Mondale and Geraldine Ferraro, enjoyed a slightly favorable ratio of good press to bad press and therefore considerably more favorable campaign coverage.

Such analyses tend to reinforce charges of a liberal bias in the media. No doubt they helped spur conservative Republican Senator Jesse Helms from North Carolina to encourage his fellow conservatives to *buy* CBS, which he saw as an especially liberal network, and thus become "Dan Rather's boss."

("Rather Biased" was the slogan of this unsuccessful campaign to purchase the CBS network.)

Although most journalists in the 1985 *Los Angeles Times* survey classified themselves as liberal, they also described the newspapers for which they worked as more conservative (pro-Reagan and probusiness) than liberal (42 to 28 percent). To some extent, working journalists are at odds with their own editors, who tend to be more conservative. The editors, in their function as gatekeepers, tend to tone down the liberal biases of their own reporters.[29]

If media owners and their editors were indeed conservative supporters of the status quo, they could be expected to support officeholders over challengers in elections. However, the campaign news that emerges from both print and broadcast media tends in the other direction. One researcher who found evidence of liberal bias in the 1984 presidential campaign had also studied the 1980 campaign, when Reagan was the challenger and Jimmy Carter the incumbent president.[30] In that campaign, the media covered Carter more negatively than his conservative challenger. Taking both election years into consideration, the researcher concluded that there is virtually no *continuing* ideological or partisan bias on the evening television news. Instead, what was seen as partisan bias or ideology in both 1980 and 1984 was a bias against *incumbents* and *frontrunners*. "But," he concludes, "that is journalism, not partisanship."[31]

According to this reasoning, if journalists have any pronounced bias, it is against politicians. When an incumbent runs for re-election, journalists may feel a special responsibility to counteract his or her advantage by putting a different partisan spin on the news.[32] Thus, whether the media coverage of campaigns is seen as pro-Democratic (and therefore liberal) or pro-Republican (and therefore conservative) depends on which party is in office at the time. When the media cover other types of political news, editors undoubtedly check some of their reporters' liberal tendencies.

POLITICAL EFFECTS OF THE MEDIA

Virtually all citizens must rely on the mass media for their political news. Although television news programs claim far larger audiences than news magazines and newspapers, many people may watch television news programs for their entertainment value without learning much about politics. In this section, we shall examine where citizens acquire their political knowledge, look at what people learn from the media, and probe media effects on elections and on the political agenda.

Where the Public Gets Its News

Until the early 1960s, most people reported getting more of their news from newspapers than from any other source. As shown in Figure 9.4, in the mid-1960s, television nudged out newspapers as the public's major source

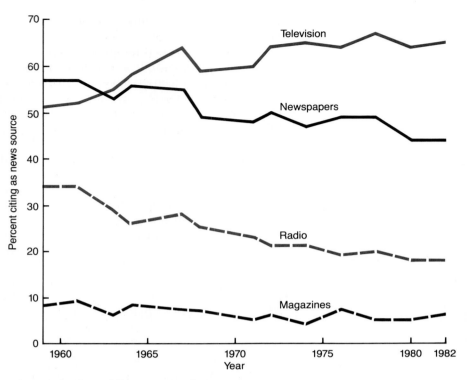

Changes in the Public's Sources of News
For about a quarter of a century, the Roper Organization has put this question to a national sample: "I'd like to ask you where you usually get most of your news about what's going on in the world today—from the newspapers or radio or television or magazines or talking to people or where?" Up until twenty-five years ago, newspapers were cited as the main source of news for people in the Roper sample. In the early 1960s, television replaced radio, and the gap between the two has grown rather steadily. Radio has declined dramatically as a source of news, but magazines have retained most of their audience over time. (Source: Roper Organization, Trends in Attitudes Toward Television and Other Media: A Twenty-Four Year Review. Television Information Office Publication, *1983, p. 5. The percentages do not total 100 because people were allowed to cite more than one news source.)*

Figure 9.4

of news. By the 1980s, about two-thirds of the public cited television as their news source, compared with less than one-half who named newspapers and less than one-fifth who relied on radio. Not only is television the public's most important source of news, but television news is also rated as more trustworthy than newspaper news—by a margin of more than two to one (see Figure 9.5).

Some people prefer television to newspapers as a source of news simply because they cannot read very well. According to a recent literacy test conducted by the U.S. Census Bureau, 13 percent of adults living in the United States are illiterate in English.[33] Although some people who failed the census test were immigrants, 9 percent of those who spoke English as their native language failed as well. Others who are literate in English may not be interested enough to plow through printed matter, when they can simply tune in a good-looking reporter on television and see colored pictures at the same time. It is not surprising, therefore, that people with different levels of education employ different media as news sources. For example, in 1984 people with only grade-school educations were more apt to report watching the network television news every day than were people with a college degree (52 to 46 percent). However, the college-educated were more likely to report reading a daily newspaper (52 to 34 percent) and a weekly news magazine (38 to 6 percent).[34]

Figure 9.5

Credibility of the News Media

In the same survey that asked people about their sources of news, the Roper Organization also asked, ''If you got conflicting or different reports of the same news story from radio, television, the magazines and the newspapers, which of the four versions would you be most inclined to believe?'' Here, the gap between television and newspapers is even greater — and it, too, has been growing. By the 1980s, more people saw television as the most credible news source than all the other media combined. (Source: Roper Organization, Trends in Attitudes Toward Television and Other Media: A Twenty-Four Year Review. *Television Information Office Publication, 1983, p. 6;* The American Polity: The People and Their Government, *by Everett Carll Ladd. W. W. Norton and Company, Inc. © 1985, p. 490. Reprinted by permission.*

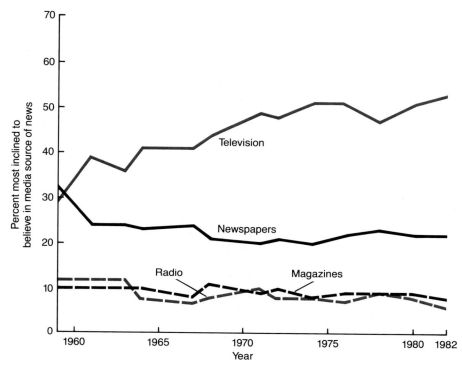

What People Remember and Know

About half the population reports watching the network news daily, and another 20 percent say that they watch the network news three or four times a week. Even those who are not faithful watchers of television news hear political news on the radio or read it in newspapers and news magazines. In short, an overwhelming majority of the American public is exposed to news through at least one of the mass media. Nevertheless, most people appear to have learned very little about the news that has bombarded them for hours every day. When a national survey asked, "Over the last twelve months [1983–1984], which news event would you say you remember the most?" over 40 percent of the sample answered "nothing" or recalled nonpolitical events as what they remembered most about the year's news.[35] For those who recalled *some* political news, Israel's long seige and bombing of Beirut in the summer of 1984 emerged as the most memorable event (cited by 14 percent). Many people did not even have a clear idea of what was political and what was not: "Murders and murderers totally outdistanced foreign wars or foreign anything. For example, homicidal maniacs, as a class, proved seven times as memorable as the brutal war between Iran and Iraq."[36]

The public did little better in recalling domestic political news, even when prompted. Although the survey was conducted at the height of the 1984 presidential primary campaign, over 60 percent of the respondents gave incorrect answers to a question that asked whether "during the Reagan years the inflation rate has gotten worse, leveled off, or gotten better?" (It had gotten better, and at least 33 percent should have chosen that alternative even by guessing among the choices.) Didn't the people remember *anything* specific from all those hours of television viewing? Yes, without prompting, 44 percent could identify the commercial slogan that Walter Mondale had used to criticize Gary Hart—"Where's the beef?"[37]

The authors drew several conclusions from their study: that the public knows *less* about politics than journalists or politicians think; that, for many people, news is not politics; and that slogans can penetrate public indifference about political affairs, when hard news cannot.[38]

How can it be that so many people are so ignorant of political affairs when they are exposed to so much news in the media? Perhaps the message is in the medium of television, which most people cite as their major news source. Several studies have found that increased exposure to television news has a numbing effect on a person's capacity to discriminate among news messages. A comparison between *viewers'* and *readers'* ability to explain reasons for their Senate voting choices in 1974 found that reading more newspapers produced more reasons but watching more television news did not.[39] In fact, the researchers found evidence that watching television actually tended to *inhibit* knowledge about politics. A later study of subjects' abilities to distinguish presidential candidates Gerald Ford and Jimmy Carter on campaign issues in 1976 found that regular television viewers saw no more difference between the candidates than those who neither watched nor read the news on a regular basis.[40] For people with similar levels of education, heavy television watching actually had a *suppressing* effect on the ability to see differences between candidates.

Why should this be? We know that television tends to squeeze public policy issues into one-minute or, at most, two-minute fragments, which makes it difficult to explain candidates' positions. Television also tends to cast abstract issues in personal terms to enhance the visual image that the medium is required to convey. Thus, viewers may become more adept at visually identifying the candidates and knowing their personal habits than at knowing their positions on issues. Finally, the television networks, which are licensed by the government, are concerned about being fair and equal in their coverage of the candidates, which may result in equalizing candidates' positions as well. Newspapers, which are not licensed by the government, enjoy more latitude in choosing which candidates they cover and how they cover them. Whatever the explanation, the wonders of television seem to have contributed little to citizens' knowledge of public affairs. Indeed, electronic journalism may work against the citizen knowledge that democratic government requires.

There is also evidence to suggest that those people who rely on television to follow politics are more confused and cynical than those who do not.[41] This problem may be even more acute where foreign affairs are concerned, since most of the public has relatively little interest in foreign affairs, but the networks tend to "overreport" them.[42] Watching events unfold in countries they know little about, the public usually witnesses conflict, criticism, and controversy. Not knowing what to think or whom to believe, the public responds "by becoming more cynical, more negative, and more critical of leadership and institutions."[43]

Election Outcomes

The mass media are well known for their success in advertising a product so that people will buy it. In politics, the parallel of advertising a product is advertising a candidate; the parallel of buying the product is voting for the candidate. Political advertising in the form of posters, buttons, and slogans has a long history in American election campaigns. What is different about campaign advertising through the mass media, especially television, is the use of **spot advertising** techniques similar to those that sell beer and beauty aids — very brief, but very frequent, positive mentions of the product (the candidate). Dwight Eisenhower's 1952 campaign for the presidency moved national politics into the television age when it hired the advertising firm of Batten, Barton, Durstine & Osborne to create spot campaign ads for the first time in politics.

Over the years, political advertisements have become more sophisticated — and more expensive. The 1984 Reagan and Mondale campaigns spent about $25 million each on television ads.[44] Reagan's advertising campaign was handled by an all-star group of advertising professionals called the "Tuesday Team," whose spot advertisements were considerably slicker than those Eisenhower used in the 1950s. Their famous "Russian bear" spot seductively implied that Reagan could be counted on to keep a strong defense against the Soviet Union (see Feature 9.2). Political advertising, of course, is used by both sides. Mondale hired D. H. Sawyer Associates to conduct his own multimillion-dollar campaign.

Feature 9.2

Never Trust the Russian Bear

This slick, subtle spot was prepared by a group of advertising all-stars called the Tuesday Team, who were assembled to handle the campaign to re-elect Ronald Reagan in 1984. The idea for this spot came from Hal Riney, who was the writer and the voice of many Gallo wine ads. The production cost for this one spot was $80,000, which included the rental of a bear trained to step backward when it walked into a hidden wire at the end of the commercial. The finished ad was shown to one hundred "focus groups" — small groups of people sharing similar sociological characteristics (white suburban housewives, black professionals, and so on) to test it before airing. The spot was also aired in selected markets, and viewers were phoned to see if they remembered it. The recall rate was 75 percent, in an area in which 50 percent recall is quite good.

Source: Edwin Diamond and Stephen Bates, "The Ads," *Public Opinion* 7 (December–January, 1985): 57.

(Camera up on a grizzly, lumbering across a hilltop, crossing a stream, forging through underbrush. A drum plays incessantly, like a heartbeat, over ominous chords.)

Announcer *(Hal Riney)*: There's a bear in the woods. For some people, the bear is easy to see. Others don't see it at all. Some people say the bear is tame. Others say it is vicious and dangerous. Since no one can really be sure who's right, isn't it smart to be as strong as the bear?

(The bear walks slowly along a ridge, silhouetted against the sky; it looks up, stops suddenly and takes a step backward. The camera pulls back to show a man standing a few yards away, facing the bear. A gun is slung over his shoulder. He too is silhouetted.)

Announcer: If there is a bear.

Closing graphic: "President Reagan: Prepared for Peace."

© Hal Riney & Sons. Reprinted by permission.

Of course, carrying campaign advertising is not the only way that the media can influence political behavior. As we have seen, the mass media news reports during the 1984 presidential campaign gave more favorable press to Mondale and Ferraro than to Reagan and Bush. If the news media are as powerful as many people claim, how can they bombard a candidate with "bad press" — as the media did with Reagan — without causing the voters to decide against the candidate? The author of the 1980 and 1984 studies of media bias offers this explanation:

> Reagan was able to work through or around his press — virtually any incumbent can, as long as *conditions* are favorable. The fact is, no president needs good press. He only needs good news . . . . The electorate will almost never pay serious attention to spin or campaign issues agenda if things are good. . . . The networks, outside of presenting hard news and fact, have far less influence on voters than most critics — and most campaign managers — assume.[45]

According to this view, the most important factor in shaping a voter's decision is *what* the news is, not *how* it is reported. This point seems elementary, but it is too frequently forgotten in assessments of the mass media's ability to influence attitudes and behavior.

Another way of looking at the matter is that the greatest source of bias in the media lies not in ideology but in simple coverage. Little or no coverage is even worse than unfavorable coverage because of *selective perception* — the tendency for individuals to filter out messages that do not conform to their existing beliefs. According to this view, the press certainly was biased in reporting the Reagan campaign — but biased *toward* Reagan, who received four times the coverage given to Mondale. Thus, media bias may be more important in *amount* of coverage than in its favorable or unfavorable nature.

Setting the Political Agenda

An *agenda* is a list of things to do or to consider, and a **political agenda** is a list of issues that need government attention. Those who *set* the political agenda are those who define the issues for discussion and debate among government decisionmakers. Like the tree that falls in the forest without anyone to hear it, an issue that does not get on the political agenda will not have anyone in government working on its behalf.

The mass media in the United States have traditionally played an important role in defining the political agenda. As we have seen, newspaper publisher William Randolph Hearst helped put war with Spain on the political agenda in 1898. The muckrakers' magazine articles helped put political and business reforms on the political agenda in the early 1900s. Radio helped put the Nazis' rise in power on the American political agenda in the late 1930s. Television, which reaches daily into virtually every home, has an even greater potential for setting the political agenda.

Today's newspapers also heighten the public's concern about particular social issues. Crime is a good example. Certain types of crime — particularly murder — are especially attractive to the media, which tends to distort the incidence of crime in its reporting. A study of newspaper coverage of crime in nine cities found more attention given to violent crimes (murder, rape, and assault) than was justified by official police statistics. In addition, the study found that newspapers in recent years have given increased attention to political crimes — such as assassinations or political kidnappings — and to violent crimes committed outside the metropolitan areas served by the papers.[46] The author concluded that, although newspapers helped put "combating crime" on the political agenda, they also distorted the extent and even the nature of the problem, confusing local policymakers about what should, or could, be done.

The Shot Seen 'Round the World
Millions of Americans watching the network news one night during the Vietnam war witnessed a South Vietnamese army officer (our ally) executing a captured Viet Cong prisoner. This striking photo of the same incident appears to capture the moment of impact. Television showed the public the truly ugly aspects of war and helped mobilize sentiment for withdrawal.

At the national level, the major news media help set the political agenda for politicians by what they choose to report. One study of Washington reporters identified eleven organizations that comprise the "inner ring" of influence in Washington: the three major television network news organizations (NBC, CBS, and ABC); the two leading news wire services (Associated Press and United Press International); three newspapers with national influence (the *Washington Post,* the *New York Times,* and the *Wall Street Journal*); and three major news weeklies (*Time, Newsweek,* and *U.S. News & World Report*).[47] Top government leaders closely follow the news reported daily in these sources. (The president receives a digest of the news in these sources plus confidential reports from government agencies.) Much of what these news media report works its way into the political agenda at one level or another.

Socialization

We discussed the major agents of political socialization in Chapter 5, but, for reasons of emphasis and space, we did not include the mass media among them. Young people, who rarely follow the news by choice, nevertheless acquire political values through the entertainment function of the broadcast media. Years ago, children learned from radio programs; now they learn from television. What they learned then, however, was very different from what they are learning now. In the "golden days of radio," youngsters listening to the popular radio drama "The Shadow" heard over and over again that "Crime does *not* pay . . . the *Shadow* knows!" Action programs — such as "The FBI in Peace and War" and "Gangbusters!" — taught children that the major federal and state law enforcement agencies would inevitably catch criminals and put them behind bars. In program after program — "Dragnet," "Junior G-Men," "Crime Fighters" — the message never varied: criminals are bad, the police are good, criminals get caught, and criminals are severely punished for their crimes.

Needless to say, television today does not portray the criminal justice system in the same way — even in police dramas. Consider the hit prime-time show "Miami Vice," starring Don Johnson and Philip Michael Thomas as Crockett and Tubbs. According to one researcher, who watched virtually every episode, the program communicates these themes about law enforcement:

- The federal government is evil — the Central Intelligence Agency (CIA) or the Drug Enforcement Agency (DEA) often intervenes for shadowy reasons to protect killers and drug pushers tracked down by Crockett and Tubbs.

- The criminal justice system is suspect — the criminals caught by Crockett and Tubbs are usually released by judges soon after they are arrested (so justice is better served if the crooks are blown away instead).[48]

In general, "Miami Vice" is cynical about humanity outside the station house. Only material goods — a black Ferrari Daytona, a sleek sailboat, a powerful speedboat, an elegant Armani suit — can be trusted.

These themes are not unique to "Miami Vice," and another theme — violence — is common to all contemporary television police dramas. "Dempsey and Makepeace" and "Cagney and Lacey" depict violence more vividly than any sound effects man on "Gangbusters!" could. One cannot establish the exact effect of these messages—distrust of federal law enforcement, disrespect of the criminal justice system, cynicism and materialism, and functional violence—on impressionable youngsters, but one would be hard pressed to argue that modern television helps prepare law-abiding citizens through its entertainment programs.

The media play further contradictory roles in the socialization process. In one role, the media promote popular support for government by joining in the celebration of national holidays, heroes' birthdays, political anniversaries, and civic accomplishments. The media coverage of the hundredth anniversary of the Statue of Liberty exemplifies the media's contribution to a sense of national pride. In their other role, the U.S media erode public confidence by publicizing citizen grievances, by airing investigative reports of agency malfeasance, and by giving front-page and prime-time coverage to assorted political critics, protesters, and even terrorists and assassins. Some critics contend that the media give too much coverage to government's opponents, especially to those who engage in unconventional opposition. However, strikes, sit-ins, violent confrontations, and hijackings draw large audiences and thus are very newsworthy to the mass media.

EVALUATING THE MEDIA IN GOVERNMENT

We have described the major political functions of the mass media. What contributions do the media make to democratic government? What effects do they have on freedom, order, and equality?

Contributions to Democracy

As noted earlier, the communication flow in a democracy must move in two directions: from government to citizens and from citizens to government. In fact, thanks to the privately owned media, political communication in the United States seldom goes directly from the government to citizens without passing *through* the media. This is important because, as we have seen, news reporters tend to be highly critical of politicians; they instinctively search for inaccuracies in fact and weaknesses in argument. Some have characterized the news media and government as adversaries—each mistrusting the other and locked in competition for popular favor. To the extent that this is true, the media serve both models of democracy well by improving the quality of information transmitted to people about their government.

The mass media also transmit information *from citizens to government* by reporting citizens' reactions to political events and government actions. Before sample surveys were used, a collection of newspaper stories from across the country passed for public opinion on political affairs. After commercial polls (such as the Gallup and Roper polls) were established in the 1930s, newspapers began to report more reliable readings of public opinion, and opinion surveys soon became important fare for journalists as well as for politicians. By the 1960s, the media (both national and local) began to conduct their own surveys. In the 1970s, survey research groups became formal divisions of some news organizations. Occasionally, print and electronic media joined forces to conduct major continuing national surveys.

The media now have the tools to do a better job of reporting mass opinion than ever before, and they are using those tools extensively. The well-respected *New York Times*/CBS poll conducts surveys that are aired first on the "CBS Evening News" and then analyzed at length in the *Times*. In fact, of forty-nine *Times* stories on the 1984 campaign the week before the election, poll results were cited in 57 percent and received major or important discussion in 30 percent.[49] While polls sometimes create opinions just by asking the question, the net effect has been to generate more accurate knowledge of public opinion and to report that knowledge back to the public. Although widespread knowledge of public opinion does not guarantee government responsiveness to popular demands, such knowledge is required if government is to function according to the majoritarian model of democracy.

The mass media are less important in the pluralist model of democracy, for specialized interest groups — such as the Farm Bureau, the National Education Association (NEA), and the National Rifle Association (NRA) — can inform their members of government action through specialized publications or mass mailings. Interest groups can use the same means of communication to urge their members to write Congress, and they are increasingly advertising in the media to generate public support for their special interests. But for political communication to and from the public as a whole, there is no substitute for the mass media.

Effects on Freedom, Order, and Equality

The media in the United States have played an important role in advancing equality, especially racial equality. Throughout the civil rights movement of the 1960s, the media gave national coverage to conflict in the South, as black children tried to attend white schools or as civil rights workers were beaten and even killed in the effort to register black voters. Partly because of media coverage, civil rights were elevated on the political agenda as new coalitions were formed in Congress to pass new laws promoting racial equality. Women's rights have also been advanced through the media, which focused national attention on the National Organization for Women (NOW) and others working for sexual equality. In general, the mass media offer spokespersons for any disadvantaged group an opportunity to state their case before a national audience and to work for a place on the political agenda.

Although the media are quite willing to mobilize government action to infringe on personal freedom for equality's sake, they resist attempts to infringe on freedom of the press to promote order. The media, far more than the public, regard freedom of the press as sacrosanct. For example, 98 percent of the 2,703 journalists surveyed by the *Los Angeles Times* opposed allowing a government official to prevent publication of a story seen as inaccurate, compared with only 50 percent of the public. Whereas the public felt that certain types of news should never be published — "exit polls saying who will win an election, secret documents dealing with national security issues, the names of CIA spies, photographs that invade people's privacy" — journalists are more reluctant to draw the line anywhere.[50]

On the topic of press freedom, the media operate as an interest group in a pluralist democracy. The media's interest in reporting whatever they wish whenever they wish certainly erodes government's efforts to maintain order. Three examples should illustrate the point.

- The media's sensationalist coverage of the Beirut hijacking fits a general pattern of media coverage given to all sorts of terrorist activities. By publicizing terrorism, the media give terrorists exactly what they want, making it more difficult to reduce terrorist threats to order.

- The portrayal of brutal killings and rapes on television, often in the guise of entertainment, has produced "copycat" crimes, those admittedly committed "as seen on TV."

- The national publicity given to deaths from adulterated drugs (for instance, Tylenol capsules laced with cyanide) has prompted similar tampering with other products.

Freedom of the press is a noble value and one that has been important to our democratic government. But we should not ignore the fact that sometimes we pay a price for pursuing it without qualification.

SUMMARY

The mass media transmit information to large, heterogeneous, and widely dispersed audiences through either print or broadcasts. The main function of the mass media is entertainment, but the media also perform the political functions of reporting news, interpreting news, influencing citizens' attitudes and behavior, setting the political agenda, and socializing citizens about politics.

The mass media in the United States are privately owned and are in business to make money, which they do mainly by selling their services to advertisers according to audience size. Both print and electronic media determine which events are newsworthy according to their audience appeal. In fact, it was the rise of mass-circulation newspapers in the 1830s that produced a politically independent press in the United States. In their aggressive competition for readers, newspapers often engaged in sensational reporting, a charge sometimes leveled at today's media.

The broadcast media operate under government technical, structural, and content regulations, which tend to equalize the coverage of political contests more on radio and television than in newspapers and news magazines.

The major media maintain staffs of professional journalists in major cities across the world to report news as it breaks. Washington, D.C., has the largest press corps in the United States, and nearly one-third of the Washington correspondents concentrate on the presidency. Because Congress is a more decentralized institution, it is covered in a more decentralized manner. All professional journalists recognize rules for citing sources that guides their reporting. What actually gets reported in the media depends on its gatekeepers, the publishers and editors.

Although more people today depend on television than on newspapers for news, those with more education rely more on newspapers. Newspapers usually do a more thorough job of informing the public about politics. Despite citizens' heavy exposure to news in the print and electronic media, their ability to retain much political information is shockingly low. Despite the media's vaunted reputation for influencing behavior, American voters are quite able to ignore the bad press the media might give to an incumbent and re-elect him or her anyway. Sheer amount of coverage given to a candidate may be the most important source of press bias.

In terms of interpreting the news, the media elite, including reporters from the major television networks, tends to be more liberal than the public, as judged by journalists' tendency to vote more Democratic than Republican and by their own self-descriptions. However, if the media elite systematically demonstrates pronounced bias in its actual news reporting, it tends to work against incumbents and frontrunners, regardless of their party, rather than for liberal Democrats.

From the standpoint of majoritarian democracy, one of the most important effects of the media is in communicating from the people to the government through the media's heavy reporting of public opinion polls. The media jealously defend the freedom of the press, even to the point of encouraging disorder by criticizing the government and by giving extensive publicity to violent protests, terrorist acts, and other threats to order.

Key Terms

communication
mass communication
mass media
print media
broadcast media
yellow journalism
muckraker
newsworthiness
Federal Communications
    Commission
independent regulatory agency

duopoly rule
7-7-7 rule
12-12-12 rule
equal opportunities rule
fairness doctrine
reasonable access rule
gatekeeper
horse race journalism
media event
spot advertising
political agenda

Selected Reading

Altschull, J. Herbert. *Agents of Power: The Role of the News Media in Human Affairs.* New York: Longman, 1984. A critical study of the media, giving special attention to the role of ideology in the press and including cross-national comparisons.

Graber, Doris A. *Mass Media and American Politics.* 2nd ed. Washington, D.C.: CQ Press, 1984. Covers the mass media specifically for their political coverage and impact.

Turow, Joseph. *Media Industries: The Production of News and Entertainment.* New York: Longman, 1984. This short book concentrates on the production of news in the mass media and is historical in scope.

Ulloth, Dana R.; Peter L. Klinge; and Sandra Eells. *Mass Media: Past, Present, Future.* St. Paul, Minn.: West, 1983. A readable text that provides convenient statistical information about the growth of the mass media.

INSTITUTIONS
OF GOVERNMENT

10

The Congress

J immy Carter learned the hard way. In writing about his term as president, he complained that "Whenever tax measures were considered, we found ourselves fortunate if we left Congress with the same hide we wore in." Why this difficulty with tax legislation? To Carter the answer was simple, if depressing. During Carter's years in office, Congress did not have the fortitude to stand up to the "powerful and ravenous wolves" — the special interests — who were "determined to secure for themselves additional benefits at the expense of other Americans."[1]

Several years after Carter left office, Congress again found itself facing interest groups that stood in the way of tax reform. In 1985 the Reagan administration proposed a sweeping tax bill that would lower tax rates for most individuals and corporations. The revenue lost by these lower rates would be made up by eliminating certain tax deductions and tax credits — both of which have had the effect of lowering the tax burden for particular firms, industries, and individuals.

But what one person may see as a tax loophole, another may label (in Washington jargon) an "incentive to benefit the public interest." For example, one provision of the existing law that is targeted for elimination is the investment tax credit, which offers a significant reduction in federal taxes to companies that buy new machinery and equipment. One of the original reasons for the investment tax credit was to help the decaying "smokestack" industries, such as steel companies, which had to invest heavily in new and efficient machinery if they were to compete effectively with foreign manufacturers. Isn't it good public policy to have a tax code that helps industries in trouble, particularly when many jobs are at stake? And why should the steel industry lose its tax benefits when substantial tax breaks for other industries, such as oil and timber, were left largely in place?

Those who backed the tax reform move had an answer to these questions: by eliminating tax benefits that helped only selected industries, Congress could lower the highest corporate tax rate for all businesses from 46 percent of earnings to 34 percent. Other industries — for example, retailing, computer software, and publishing — would benefit from such a move toward tax equality. Many representatives of those industries believe that they were subsidizing favored industries like steel by paying a higher share of the nation's taxes.

The Reagan tax plan led to a classic confrontation between the majoritarian and pluralist views of democratic government discussed in Chapter 2. A majority of the public wanted simpler tax laws that would eliminate the maze of specialized deductions and credits and would result in lower tax rates. In opposition to that majority stood smaller interest groups that represented narrow segments of the population who wanted to preserve the deductions that benefited their members. They worked furiously to block various parts of the bill. In the end, the bill that emerged from Congress eliminated many — though not all — deductions that favored particular interests, while it lowered tax rates for the majority.

As explained in Chapter 2, democratic government needs institutional mechanisms that can translate public opinion into government policy. The five chapters in this part of the book cover Congress, the president, the bureaucracy, the courts, and the Washington community. In studying how these institutions operate in American government, we shall focus on their contributions to the majoritarian and pluralist versions of democracy. We shall be less concerned in these chapters with the concepts of freedom, order, and equality, which deal with the substance of public policy — discussed in Part V.

In every democratic country, the main institution for representing citizens' interests in government is an elected legislature. Two central questions emerge in studying Congress. First, when members of Congress vote on policy issues, whom do they *actually* represent? The second question concerns our preferences: "Whom *should* they represent?" We shall try to answer the first question, leaving you to think about the second one.

THE ORIGIN AND POWERS OF CONGRESS

In Chapter 3, we observed that the framers of the Constitution wanted to keep power from being concentrated in the hands of a few, but they were also concerned with creating a Union strong enough to overcome the weaknesses of the national government that existed under the Articles of Confederation. They argued passionately about how to structure the new government. In the end, they produced a legislative body that was as much an experiment as was the democracy of the new nation.

The Great Compromise

Compared with the legislatures of other Western democracies, our Congress is unusual in that it has two separate and powerful chambers: the House of Representatives and the Senate. A bill cannot become law unless it is passed in identical form by both chambers. The two-house, or **bicameral,** nature of the Congress has its origins in the negotiations that shaped the Constitution. When the Constitution was being drafted during the summer of 1787, "the fiercest struggle for power" centered on representation in the legislature.[2] The small states wanted all states to have equal representation in the Senate, but the more populous states preferred representation based on population because they did not want their power diluted. The Great Compromise broke the deadlock. The small states received the equal representation in the Senate that they advocated, but the House, where the number of each state's representatives would be based on population, retained the sole right to originate all money bills.

According to the Constitution, each state is to be represented by two senators, each of whom will serve for six years. Their terms of office are staggered, so that one-third of the Senate is elected every two years. As ratified, the Constitution also directed that senators were to be chosen by the state legislatures. However, the Seventeenth Amendment, adopted in 1913, provided for the election of senators by popular vote. As Table 10.1 shows, there are few formal qualifications for congressional office.

From the beginning, members of the House of Representatives have been elected by the people. Representatives serve two-year terms, and all House seats are up for election every two years. Because each state's representation

The Dome Goes Up
Construction of the Capitol Dome, 1857.

is in proportion to its population, the Constitution provides for a national census every ten years to adjust the seat allocation.

Until the first census, the Constitution fixed the number of representatives at 65. As the nation's population grew and new states were added to the Union, new seats were added to the House. (There were already 213 representatives after the census of 1820.)[3] At some point, however, a legislative body becomes too unwieldy to be efficient, and in 1929 the House decided to limit its growth by fixing its membership at 435. Population shifts (such as the recent growth in the nation's South and West) are reflected in **reapportionment** (or redistribution) of representatives among the states after each census is completed. In the reshuffling after the 1980 census, for example, Florida gained 4 seats and New York lost 5. California, the nation's most populous state, has 45 representatives, whereas six states have the constitutional minimum of 1 House member.

Each representative is elected from a particular congressional district within his or her home state; the number of districts in a state is equal to the number of representatives the state sends to the House. Before a series of Supreme

Table 10.1
Qualifications for Congressional Office

	Senator	Representative
Minimum age	30	25
Minimum years of citizenship	9	7
Requirement	Must be an inhabitant of the state he or she is to represent.	
Prohibition	Cannot hold any other federal office.	

Court rulings in the 1960s, states were not required to draw the boundaries of their districts in such a way that districts had approximately equal populations. As a result, some states' thinly populated rural districts had more representation in Congress than their number of residents warranted. The Court ruled that House districts, and all districts of houses and senates in state legislatures, had to be drawn so as to be reasonably equal in population.[4]

Duties of the House and Senate

The Great Compromise provided considerably different schemes of representation for the House and Senate, but the Constitution gives them essentially similar legislative tasks. Even the House's sole right to originate revenue bills, which was apparently coveted at the Constitutional Convention, is of limited consequence today, since all such bills must also be approved by the Senate.

There are at least a few important differences, however, in the constitutional duties of the two chambers. First, the House has the power of **impeachment,** which is the power to formally charge the president, vice president, and other "civil Officers" of the federal government with "Treason, Bribery, or Other High Crimes and Misdemeanors." The Senate is empowered to act as a court to try impeachments; a two-thirds vote of the senators present is necessary for conviction. Only one president — Andrew Johnson — has ever been impeached, and in 1868 the Senate came within a single vote of finding him guilty. More recently, the House Judiciary Committee voted in favor of impeaching President Richard Nixon for his role in the Watergate scandal, but he resigned in August 1974 before the full House of Representatives could vote. In 1986, the House voted a bill of impeachment against Harry E. Claiborne, a federal judge convicted of income tax evasion. Claiborne refused to resign his life-term office, so an impeachment trial was initiated in the Senate. After reviewing the evidence, the Senate voted to convict Claiborne on three of the four articles of impeachment brought by the House and removed him from office.

Another important difference between the duties of the Senate and the House is that the Senate has the sole power to affirm treaties with foreign nations. The president is empowered to *make* treaties, but they then must be submitted to the Senate, where treaties must be approved by a two-thirds majority. Because of this requirement, the executive branch generally considers the Senate's sentiments when it negotiates a treaty. At times, however, a president must try to convince a doubting Senate of a particular treaty's worth. Shortly after World War I, President Woodrow Wilson submitted to the Senate the Versailles Treaty, which contained the charter for the proposed League of Nations. Wilson had attempted to convince the Senate that the treaty deserved its support, and when the Senate refused to approve the treaty, it was a severe setback for Wilson.

The Senate must also approve such major presidential appointments as federal judges, ambassadors, and cabinet secretaries. Collectively, the House and Senate share many important powers, among them the powers to declare war, raise an army and navy, borrow and coin money, regulate interstate commerce, create federal courts, and establish rules for the naturalization of immigrants. The Congress may also "make all Laws which shall be necessary and proper for carrying into Execution the foregoing Powers."

Despite a lengthy enumeration of its powers in the Constitution, however, the question of what powers are appropriate to the Congress has generated substantial controversy. For example, although the Constitution may give Congress the sole power to declare war, many presidents have initiated military action on their own. And in other instances the courts have found that congressional actions have usurped the rights of the states.

ELECTING THE CONGRESS

If Americans do not like the job Congress is doing, they can try to change it by changing the people in Congress. With a congressional election every two years, the voters have frequent opportunities to express themselves.

The Incumbency Effect

Congressional elections offer voters a chance either to show their approval of Congress's performance or to "throw the rascals out," but voters seem to do more approving than rascal-throwing. This tendency is especially strong in the case of sitting members (or **incumbents**) of the House of Representatives. As one political scientist notes, with regard to this incumbency effect, when House incumbents seek re-election, their "success rate is spectacular."[5] In the majority of elections since 1950, more than 90 percent of all House incumbents' campaigns have ended in victory (see Figure 10.1).

Figure 10.1

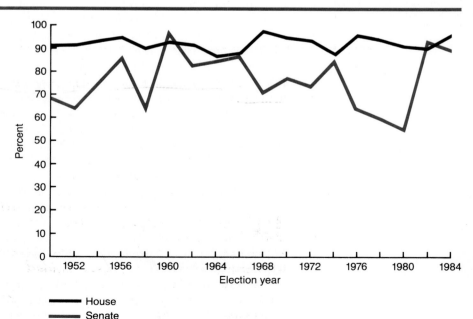

The Advantage of Incumbency
Figures represent the percentage of representatives and senators seeking reelection who won. The data include primary and general election defeats. (Source: Barbara Hinckley, Congressional Elections. *Washington, D.C.:* Congressional Quarterly, 1981, p. 39; Norman J. Ornstein et al., Vital Statistics on Congress, 1984–1985 Edition. Washington, D.C.: American Enterprise Institute, 1984, pp. 49–; and Congressional Quarterly Weekly Report, *November 10, 1984, pp. 2897–2907.*

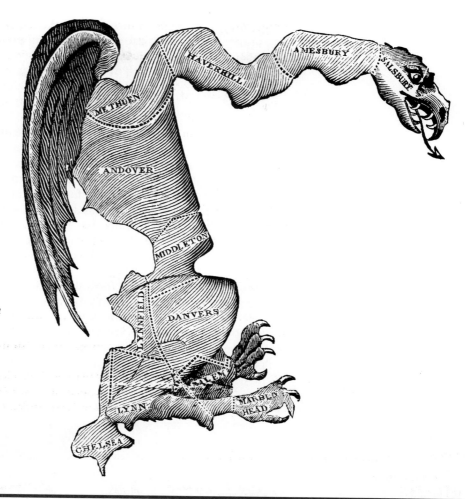

The Gerrymander
This 1812 cartoon lampoons a Massachusetts state senate district that was drawn in such a way as to ensure a Republican victory in the upcoming election. The term gerrymander *was coined then, combining the last name of Republican governor Elbridge Gerry with* salamander *(the cartoonist thought the peculiar shape of the district resembled this creature). Both the practice of drawing district boundaries for partisan gain and the term applied to it have survived into the 1980s.*

This high percentage may be surprising, since Congress as a whole is not held in particularly high esteem. When people are polled on the amount of confidence they have in major institutions, Congress scores much lower than the Supreme Court, the military, banks, and public schools.[6] People thus seem to distinguish between the *institution* of Congress and their own representatives and senators. But that still does not explain why incumbents do so well within their own districts and states.

Most research on the incumbency effect has focused on House elections. One explanation for the effect concerns **redistricting,** or the redrawing of congressional districts after census-based reapportionment. It is entirely possible for state legislatures to draw new districts to benefit the incumbents of one or both parties. This alteration of boundary lines for partisan advantage is commonly referred to as a **gerrymander.**

In truth, however, redistricting fails to explain the incumbency effect in the House as a whole. Statistics show that, after a reapportionment, redistricted and unredistricted seats end up approximately the same in terms of competitiveness.[7] Thus, although redistricting may be very helpful for an occasional incumbent, it doesn't explain why more than 90 percent of House incumbents are re-elected.

The Advantages of Incumbency in the House

If redistricting cannot explain the incumbency effect, then what can? Political scientists point to a number of other factors, including the American voter's increasing independence. Considerably less tied to political parties than their parents or grandparents were, contemporary voters are much more willing to split their tickets, voting for candidates of different parties. Given such a situation, the incumbent has a definite, strong advantage. Incumbents find it easier to get their names and records of accomplishments before the voters. Moreover, incumbents generally have an easier time attracting campaign resources than their challengers do.

Name and recognition.   Incumbents develop significant name recognition among the electorate simply because they *are* members of Congress. Their activities and speeches are fully reported by the local press. This process is aided by congressional staffs, who are adept at maximizing press coverage of their bosses' words and actions. Members of Congress are in high demand as speakers before local groups and, thanks to generous travel allowances

"Personalized" Letters
The mail that inundates each congressional office consumes a great deal of each representative's and senator's staff resources. The mail cannot be ignored—legislators want constituents to feel that they've taken a personal interest in their problem or concern. The autopen, like this one belonging to Democratic Senator Howard Metzenbaum of Ohio, offers a convenient way to personalize the letters that legislators are unable to sign by hand. Such machines can produce about 300 signatures an hour.

and easy air travel, they can make frequent trips between their districts and Washington, D.C.

Members of Congress make full use of the congressional **franking privilege** — the right to send mail free of charge — to ensure that constituents remain aware of their names, activities, and accomplishments. Their periodic newsletters, for example, almost always highlight successful efforts at winning funds and projects for the district, such as money to construct a highway or a new federal building. The newsletters also "advertise for business," by encouraging voters to phone or visit legislators' district offices if they need help with a problem. In turn, the large staffs that work for each member of Congress are able to do **casework** for people who approach the office — perhaps by tracking down errant social security checks or directing a small business owner to the appropriate federal agency. Constituents who are helped in this way usually remember who assisted them.

House incumbents enjoy a high level of voter support, even among constituents who do not know much about the incumbents. Polls show that at "any level of familiarity, voters are more inclined to mention something they like about the incumbent."[8] Voters tend to see their representatives as doing a good job and being helpful to constituents.[9]

Campaign financing.   In a race between an incumbent and a relatively unknown challenger, the incumbent's advantages of name recognition, office resources, and record of achievement translate directly into votes at election time. These advantages are often enough to cause a potentially strong challenger to shy away from an election battle and to wait for a more opportune time to run — perhaps when the incumbent retires or when his or her party seems headed for a fall.[10]

It should be clear that those who want to challenge an incumbent need especially solid financial backing. Challengers must spend large sums of money to run a strong campaign, with an emphasis on advertising — an expensive but effective way to bring their names and past accomplishments to the voters' attention. But, here again, the incumbent has the advantage. It is very difficult for challengers to raise campaign funds, because they have to overcome contributors' doubts that they can win. Political action committees (PACs) show a strong preference for incumbents, as we noted in Chapter 8 on interest groups. They tend not to want to risk offending an incumbent by giving money to a long-shot challenger. Thus, in the 1983–1984 election cycle, PACs contributed around $75 million to incumbents but little more than $17 million to challengers.[11] The attitude of the American Medical Association's PAC is fairly typical. "We have a friendly incumbent policy," says its director. "We always stick with the incumbent if we agree with both candidates."[12]

Nevertheless, although it is very difficult for a challenger to defeat a House incumbent, it is not impossible. The opposing party and unsympathetic PACs may target incumbents who seem vulnerable because of age, lack of seniority, or unfavorable redistricting. The result is a flow of campaign contributions to the challenger and an increased chance of victory. Other incumbents lose their seats in elections when the nation votes heavily for one party's candidates because of disappointment with the other party's control of the White House. In the 1980 election, for example, twenty-seven incumbent House Democrats were defeated in the general landslide that swept Ronald Reagan into office.[13]

Incumbency in the Senate

As Figure 10.1 shows, incumbency is less of an advantage in Senate elections than in House elections. There is no simple explanation for this difference, but one important factor is the greater visibility of challengers for Senate seats. These challengers usually are prominent individuals (including governors and incumbent representatives), and their names and reputations are known to many voters. In addition, Senate challengers often run better-funded campaigns than their House counterparts, and Senate races attract more public interest and press coverage. All these factors tend to reduce the "identification gap" between incumbent and challenger, resulting in more competitive races for the Senate.

Whom Do We Elect?

We elect and then re-elect to Congress people who do not comprise a cross-section of American society. For example, in terms of occupational backgrounds, most members of Congress are professionals — primarily lawyers and businesspeople (see Table 10.2). Although nearly one-third of the American labor force works in blue-collar jobs, there are virtually no former blue-collar workers in Congress.[14] And, although the typical American does not have a college degree, the typical member of Congress holds both undergraduate and graduate degrees.

The number of blacks in the House has grown modestly, but blacks are still underrepresented relative to their proportion in the population. Not a

Table 10.2 ▬▬▬▬▬▬▬▬
Members' Occupational Backgrounds
Business and law continue to be the most common backgrounds for members of the House and the Senate.

	House		Senate	
	Eighty-Third Congress (1953)	*Ninety-Eighth Congress (1983)*	*Eighty-Third Congress (1953)*	*Ninety-Eighth Congress (1983)*
Occupation*				
Agriculture	53	26	22	9
Business or banking	131	138	28	29
Engineering	5	5	5	0
Medicine	6	6	1	1
Education	46	43	17	12
Law	247	200	59	61
Journalism	36	22	10	7

*Some members are listed under more than one occupation. (Source: Norman J. Ornstein, et al., *Vital Statistics on Congress, 1984–1985 ed.* Washington, D.C.: American Enterprise Institute, 1984, pp. 21 and 24. Reprinted by permission.)

single black currently serves in the Senate. Women, who make up half the population of the United States, are represented by only 2 percent of the Senate. This is not to say that Congress discriminates against minorities — after all, the voters select the membership of Congress. But the underrepresentation of women and blacks in Congress surely reflects larger, historical patterns of opportunity — or lack of it — in American society. The predominance of white-collar professionals in Congress also reflects the advantages of wealth and education that make it easier for upper-middle-class people to enter politics.

If a "representative" legislative body is one that is a mirror image of the electorate, then Congress certainly doesn't qualify as one. Yet the correspondence between the social characteristics of the population and the membership of Congress is only one way to look at the question of representation. A more crucial measure may be how well the members of Congress represent their constituents' views as they make policy decisions while writing laws. In the next several sections, we shall examine the legislative process. Then, near the end of the chapter, we shall return to the subject of representation.

THE DANCE OF LEGISLATION: AN OVERVIEW

Most people think of the job of a member of Congress in terms of that individual's role in making laws. When members of Congress pass legislation, they decide on public policy. The process of writing bills and getting them passed is relatively simple in the sense that it consists of only a small number of specific steps. But the process is also complex because legislation can be treated in many different ways at each step. In this section, we shall examine the simple and straightforward process by which laws are made. Then, in the next few sections, we shall discuss some of the details and complexities of that process.

After a **bill,** or proposed new law, is introduced in either house, the next step is its assignment to an appropriate committee of that chamber for study (see Figure 10.2). A banking bill, for example, would be assigned to the Banking, Finance, and Urban Affairs Committee in the House or to the Banking, Housing, and Urban Affairs Committee in the Senate, depending on where it had been introduced. When a committee actively considers a piece of legislation assigned to it, the bill is usually referred to a specialized subcommittee. The subcommittee may hold hearings, and legislative staffers may do research on the bill. The original bill will probably be modified or revised and, if finally passed in some form, it will then be sent back to the full committee. A bill that is approved by the full committee is *reported* (that is, sent) to the entire membership of that chamber, where it may be debated, amended, and either passed or defeated.

House and Senate procedures differ from each other in a small way: bills coming out of House committees must go to the Rules Committee before going before the full House membership. The Rules Committee attaches a "rule" to the bill, governing the coming floor debate, typically specifying the

Figure 10.2

The Legislative Process
The process by which a bill becomes a law is subject to much variation. The diagram at right depicts the typical process that a bill might follow. It is important to remember that a bill can fail to survive any of these stages because of lack of support.

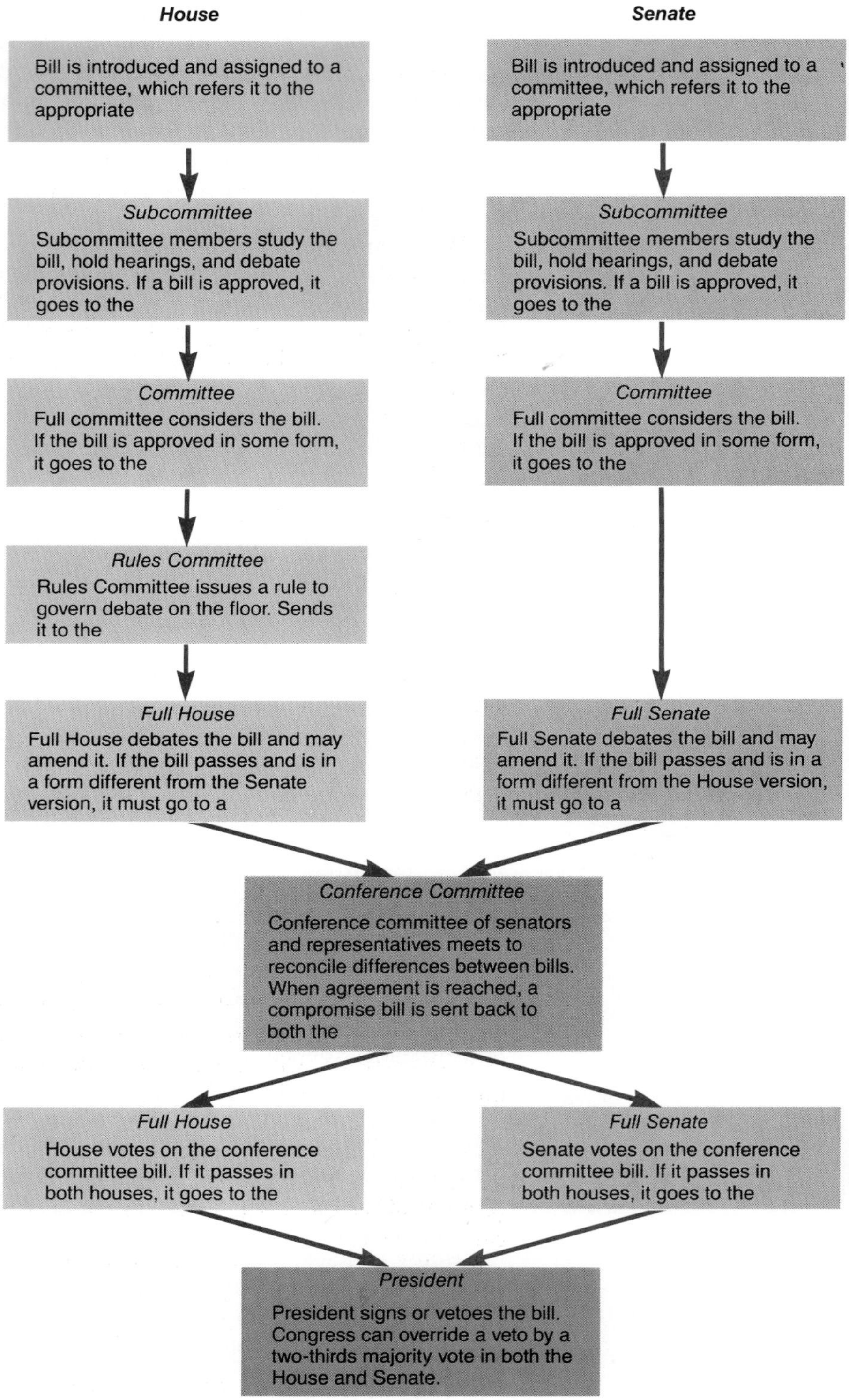

House

Bill is introduced and assigned to a committee, which refers it to the appropriate

Subcommittee
Subcommittee members study the bill, hold hearings, and debate provisions. If a bill is approved, it goes to the

Committee
Full committee considers the bill. If the bill is approved in some form, it goes to the

Rules Committee
Rules Committee issues a rule to govern debate on the floor. Sends it to the

Full House
Full House debates the bill and may amend it. If the bill passes and is in a form different from the Senate version, it must go to a

Senate

Bill is introduced and assigned to a committee, which refers it to the appropriate

Subcommittee
Subcommittee members study the bill, hold hearings, and debate provisions. If a bill is approved, it goes to the

Committee
Full committee considers the bill. If the bill is approved in some form, it goes to the

Full Senate
Full Senate debates the bill and may amend it. If the bill passes and is in a form different from the House version, it must go to a

Conference Committee
Conference committee of senators and representatives meets to reconcile differences between bills. When agreement is reached, a compromise bill is sent back to both the

Full House
House votes on the conference committee bill. If it passes in both houses, it goes to the

Full Senate
Senate votes on the conference committee bill. If it passes in both houses, it goes to the

President
President signs or vetoes the bill. Congress can override a veto by a two-thirds majority vote in both the House and Senate.

length of the debate and the types of amendments that can be offered. The Senate has no comparable committee, though restrictions on the length of floor debate can be reached through unanimous consent agreements.

Even if a bill on the same subject is passed by both houses of Congress, the Senate and House versions are typically different from each other. In that case, a conference committee, composed of legislators from both houses, will work out the differences and develop a compromise version. That version is then sent back to both houses for another floor vote. If this bill passes both houses, it is sent to the president for signature or veto.

When the president signs the bill, it becomes law. If the president **vetoes** (or disapproves) the bill, it will be sent back to the Congress with his reasons for rejecting it. The bill can then become law only if Congress overrides the president's veto by a two-thirds vote of each house. If the president neither signs nor vetoes the bill within ten days (Sundays excepted) of receiving it, the bill becomes law — with one exception: if Congress adjourns within the ten days, the president can let the bill die through a **pocket veto**, by not signing it.

A bill's content can be changed at any stage of the process, in either house. Lawmaking (and thus policymaking) in Congress has many access points for those who wish to influence legislation. This openness tends to fit with the pluralist model of democracy. As a bill moves through the dance of legislation, it is amended again and again, in a search for the consensus that will get it passed and signed into law. The process can be tortuously slow and often fruitless. Derailing legislation seems easier than enacting it. The process gives groups frequent opportunities to voice their preferences and, if necessary, to thwart their opponents. One foreign ambassador stationed in Washington aptly described the twists and turns of our legislative process when he noted that "in the Congress of the U.S., it's never over until it's over. And when it's over, it's still not over."[15]

HOW ISSUES GET ON THE CONGRESSIONAL AGENDA

The formal legislative process begins when a member of Congress introduces a bill. In the House, members drop new bills in the "hopper," a mahogany box near the front rostrum where the speaker presides. In the Senate, a senator gives his or her bill to one of the Senate clerks or introduces it from the floor.[16] But before a bill can be introduced to solve a problem, someone must perceive that a problem exists or that an issue needs to be resolved. In other words, the problem or issue must somehow find its way onto the congressional agenda. *Agenda* actually has *two* meanings in the vocabulary of political scientists. The first is that of a narrow, formal agenda, such as a calendar of bills to be voted on. The second meaning refers to the broad, imprecise, and unwritten agenda that consists of all the issues an institution is considering. We are using the term here in its second sense.

When one looks at what Congress is working on at any one time, it seems as if many of the issues on its agenda have been around forever. Foreign aid, the national debt, and social security have come up in just about every recent session of Congress. Yet all issues begin at some point in time. For example, acquired immune deficiency syndrome (AIDS), a deadly disease most commonly transmitted through sexual contact among homosexuals and blood exchanges especially among intravenous drug users, is a very recent issue. Now that AIDS has been recognized as a tragic and widespread health problem, Congress must deal with appropriations (allocations of funds) for research on the disease.

How did this and other issues become part of the broad congressional agenda? In the case of AIDS, the need for congressional action was relatively clear; when public health officials began to document an increasing number of deaths from the disease, the seriousness of the situation demanded government funding to help researchers find a cure. Likewise, a highly visible event can prompt action. An explosion on November 20, 1968, in the Consolidated Coal Company's Number 9 mine in West Virginia, which killed all seventy-eight miners trapped there, prompted government action on mine safety.[17]

Often, though, it is not a single situation or event that causes Congress to act. In many instances, a small group of members of Congress or even a single member has tried for years to get Congress to recognize a new problem or to enact a novel solution to an older problem. For years, these figures may be lone voices in the wilderness, but sometimes they are joined by many more members or by politically stronger figures. This certainly was the case for the *flat tax*, which was promoted energetically by two Republicans — Representative Jack Kemp of New York and Senator Robert Kasten of Wisconsin — and by two Democrats — Representative Richard Gephardt of Missouri and Senator Bill Bradley of New Jersey. The basic idea of the flat tax is to simplify the tax code, reduce people's tax rates, and eliminate tax loopholes. The flat tax seemed to be a good idea that was going nowhere, until President Reagan embraced a modified version and asked Congress to pass a bill that included the provisions described earlier in this chapter. The power of the presidency was, in this case, responsible for tax reform's being actively considered by Congress.

Within Congress, the party leaders and committee chairs have the best opportunity to influence the political agenda. National insurance for catastrophic illness is a case in point. According to a survey of leaders in national health policymaking, only a minority believed that catastrophic illness insurance was a prominent issue (14 percent in 1977 and 33 percent in 1978). But when Russell Long, chairman of the Senate Finance Committee, announced in 1979 that his committee would work up a bill on catastrophic illness insurance, the figure jumped to 92 percent. "In other words, a key congressional committee chairman single-handedly set a major portion of the policy agenda in health by his intention to move on health insurance."[18]

Although congressional leaders and committee chairs have the opportunity to move issues onto the agenda, they rarely act capriciously, seizing upon issues without rhyme or reason. They often bide their time, waiting for other members of Congress to learn about an issue, as they attempt to accurately gauge the level of support. Sometimes the advocacy efforts of an interest group will increase members' support of an issue, or at least their awareness of it. When chairs or party leaders — or, for that matter, rank-and-file members — sense that the time is ripe for action on a new issue, they are often spurred on by the added incentive of knowing that sponsorship of an important bill can enhance their own image. In the words of one observer, "Congress exists to do things. There isn't much mileage in doing nothing."[19]

COMMITTEES: THE WORKHORSES OF CONGRESS

Woodrow Wilson once observed that "Congress in session is Congress on public exhibition, whilst Congress in its committee-rooms is Congress at work."[20] His words are as true today as when he wrote them over one hundred years ago. A speech given on the Senate floor, for example, may convince the layperson, but it is less likely to influence other senators. Indeed, few of them may even hear it. The real nuts-and-bolts work of lawmaking takes place when and where the various congressional committees meet.

The Division of Labor Among Committees

The House and Senate are divided into committees for the same reason that other large organizations are broken into specialized groups or divisions — to develop and use expertise in specific areas. At IBM, for example, different groups of people design computers, write software, assemble hardware, and sell the company's products. Each of these tasks requires an expertise that may have little to do with the other major tasks that the company must perform. Likewise, in Congress, decisions on weapons systems require a specialized knowledge that is of little relevance to decisions on, for example, reimbursement formulas for health insurance. It makes sense for some members of Congress to spend more time examining defense issues, becoming increasingly expert as they do so, while others concentrate on health matters.

Eventually, though, all members of Congress have to vote on each bill that emerges from the committees. Those who are not on a particular committee depend on committee members to examine the issues thoroughly, to find compromises on controversial questions, and to bring forward a sound piece of legislation that has a good chance of being passed. Each member will, of course, decide individually on the bill's merits. But once it reaches the House or Senate floor, members may get to vote on only a handful of amendments (if any at all) before they must cast their yeas and nays for the entire bill.

Standing committees. Although various kinds of congressional committees exist, one form, the standing committee, is predominant. **Standing committees** are permanent committees that specialize in a particular area of legislation — for example, the House Judiciary Committee or the Senate Environment and Public Works Committee (see Table 10.3). Most of the day-to-day work of drafting legislation takes place in these twenty-two House committees and sixteen Senate committees. There are typically thirty to forty members on each standing committee in the House, and fifteen to twenty senators on each Senate committee. The proportions of Democrats and

Table 10.3
Standing Committees of Congress

Standing Committees of the Senate

Agriculture, Nutrition, and Forestry	Finance
Appropriations	Foreign Relations
Armed Services	Governmental Affairs
Banking, Housing, and Urban Affairs	Judiciary
Budget	Labor and Human Resources
Commerce, Science and Transportation	Rules and Administration
Energy and Natural Resources	Small Business
Environment and Public Works	Veterans' Affairs

Standing Committees of the House

Agriculture	Interior and Insular Affairs
Appropriations	Judiciary
Armed Services	Merchant Marine and Fisheries
Banking, Finance, and Urban Affairs	Post Office and Civil Service
Budget	Public Works and Transportation
District of Columbia	Rules
Education and Labor	Science and Technology
Energy and Commerce	Small Business
Foreign Affairs	Standards of Official Conduct
Government Operations	Veterans' Affairs
House Administration	Ways and Means

Source: *Committees and Subcommittees of the 99th Congress,* supplement to *Congressional Quarterly Weekly Report,* April 27, 1985. Copyrighted material reprinted with permission, Congressional Quarterly Inc.

Republicans on a standing committee generally reflect party proportions in the full House or Senate, and each member of Congress serves on only a small number of committees.

With a few exceptions, standing committees are further broken down into subcommittees. The House Agriculture Committee, for example, has ten separate subcommittees. Subcommittees exist for the same reason the "parent" committees exist: members acquire expertise by continually working within the same, fairly narrow policy areas.

Other congressional committees.   Members of Congress may also serve on joint, select, and conference committees. **Joint committees** are made up of members of both the House and the Senate. Like standing committees, the small number of joint committees are concerned with particular policy areas. The Joint Economic Committee, for instance, analyzes the country's economic policies. Joint committees operate similarly to standing committees, but they are almost always restricted from reporting bills to the House or Senate.

A **select committee** is temporary and created for a specific purpose; it is disbanded when its purpose has been served. Select committees are established to deal with special circumstances or with issues that either overlap

The Conference Committee
When a conference committee convenes, the chairs of the House and Senate committees that wrote the competing versions of the legislation play pivotal roles. At this conference, House Budget Committee Chairman William Gray, Democrat of Pennsylvania, and Senate Budget Committee Chairman Pete Domenici, Republican of New Mexico, talk informally before the session begins.

or are not included in the areas of expertise of standing committees. The Senate committee that investigated the Watergate scandal was a select committee, created for that purpose only.

A **conference committee** is also a temporary committee and is created only to work out differences between the House and Senate versions of a specific piece of legislation. Members are appointed from the standing committees or subcommittees that originally handled and reported the legislation to each house. Depending on the nature of the differences and the importance of the legislation, a conference committee may exist for only hours or for weeks on end. When the conference committee agrees on a compromise, the bill is reported to both houses of Congress. Each house may either approve or disapprove the compromise; they cannot amend or change it in any way.

Congressional Expertise and Seniority

Once appointed to a committee, a representative or senator has great incentive to remain on it and to gain increasing expertise over the years. That incentive can be translated as influence in Congress, and that influence will increase as the member's level of expertise grows. Influence also grows in a more formal way, with **seniority,** or years of consecutive service on a committee. In the quest for expertise and seniority, members tend to stay on the same committees. Sometimes, however, they will switch places when they are offered the opportunity to move to one of the high-prestige committees (like Ways and Means or Appropriations in the House) or to a committee that handles legislation of vital importance to their constituencies.

In a committee, the member of the majority party with the most seniority usually becomes the committee chair. (The majority party in each house controls committee leadership.) Other high-seniority members of the majority party become subcommittee chairs, while their counterparts from the minority party gain influence as *ranking minority members*. With about 140 subcommittees in the House and 90 in the Senate, there is a great deal of power and status available to members of Congress.

Unlike seniority, expertise does not follow merely from length of service. The ability and effort expended by the individual member can make a major difference in the role of a committee member. When he first came to the Senate in 1973, Democrat Sam Nunn of Georgia began to pursue his interest in military affairs. As a member of the Senate Armed Services Committee, he quickly established a reputation for doing his homework on defense issues, as well as for developing pragmatic and well-reasoned policy views. Other members ask Nunn for advice on defense issues. Recently, Republican senators Arlen Specter of Pennsylvania and Daniel Evans of Washington sought out Democrat Nunn for his views on the MX missile before they cast their votes on this controversial weapon. As one senator put it, "Sam is very much the key vote on defense matters."[21]

Committee Reform

The committee system and the seniority system that determine the leadership of committees came under sharp attack during the 1970s. The push for reform came primarily from liberal and junior members of the House who "chafed under the restrictions on their participation and policy influence that the old, committee-dominated regime imposed. The committee chair, often in collaboration with the ranking minority member, dominated the panel."[22]

Although this internal distribution of influence had long been in place, it especially rankled the new, change-oriented members who first came to Congress in the wake of a decade of protest and agitation over civil rights and the Vietnam War. In a time of declining strength in the major political parties, they also felt more independent and less tied to the traditional system. In the 1974 election, the Democrats won in a landslide, and seventy-five new "Watergate babies" entered the House on the Democratic side.[23]

During this decade, a number of select committees were established to study the organization of the House and Senate. While not all of their reforms were adopted, many significant changes were made. The power of the subcommittees in relation to their parent committees was enhanced; the number of subcommittees was increased; and House Democrats (the majority party) forbade their members to serve as chairs of more than one subcommittee. Also in the House, the seniority system was weakened by new rules that held that seniority did not have to be followed in the selection of committee chairs. In 1975 the House Democrats voted out three aging and unpopular committee chairmen, thereby serving notice on all committee chairs that autocratic rule would not be tolerated. An earlier change by House Democrats had eliminated the committee chairs' power to appoint subcommittee chairs.

There was considerably less reform in the Senate. The smaller number of members in that body guarantees virtually all senators in the majority

Committee Deliberations
It is in the committees and subcommittees of Congress that most of the work on legislation takes place. Committee members closely examine the provisions of a bill and consider various alternatives and policy compromises.

party at least one subcommittee chair. Moreover, the Senate's greater national visibility makes its members less dependent on their committee activities or seniority to gain recognition and influence. As one study concludes, "Committees are simply less crucial to the pursuit of personal goals in the Senate than in the House."[24] In the House, however, the changes brought about a greater decentralization of influence within the body. Although some changes also strengthened the position of the Speaker of the House, their general thrust was to make subcommittees more autonomous and powerful.

Drafting Legislation

How committees and subcommittees are organized within Congress is ultimately significant because much public policy decisionmaking takes place there. An important first step in drafting legislation is a decision to hold committee hearings on an issue. When members of a committee perceive that there is a problem needing their attention, hearings will be held to take testimony from witnesses who have some specialized knowledge on the subject. A decision to hold hearings places the issue on the committee's agenda, though there is no assurance that enough agreement will be mustered to get the bill out of committee. Research by committee staff typically supplements the hearings as a source of information for the committee members.

Committee hearings can involve theatrics to draw public attention — especially in the form of television coverage. When the House Judiciary Subcommittee on Administrative Law held hearings on alleged malpractice in military hospitals, it did not restrict its list of witnesses to the experts who had done relevant research. Rather, it called witnesses like Dawn Lambert, a former member of the Navy, who sobbed as she told the committee that she had been left sterile by a misdiagnosis and a botched operation that had left a sponge and a green marker inside her. It was an irresistible story for the evening network news, and the committee hearings succeeded in bringing the malpractice problem to light.[25]

Subcommittee or committee meetings held to actually debate and amend legislation are called **markup sessions.** The process by which committees reach decisions varies. In many committees, there is a strong tradition of decision by consensus. The chair, ranking minority member, and others in such committees work hard, in formal committee sessions and in informal meetings, to find a middle ground on issues that divide committee members. Other committees are more conflictual; their members exhibit strong ideological and partisan sentiments. One House member on Education and Labor said there was so much division that "You can't get a resolution praising God through this Committee without having a three-day battle over it."[26]

The skill of an individual committee or subcommittee chair can strongly influence the way a committee handles its drafting of legislation. Some chairs are quite gifted at understanding what makes the other members tick and have the patience and diligence to lead the bargaining between those holding different views until a consensus decision is reached. The legendary Wilbur Mills, an Arkansas Democrat and former chairman of the tax-writing House Ways and Means Committee, was brilliant at helping his committee reach agreement on the complex and controversial issues before it. To the committee members, he was "a shaper of decisions, not a dictator. . . . an extremely skillful leader who responds to them in such a way that his conclusions, drawn from their discussions, become their conclusions."[27] Mills, like all other committee chairs, wanted to develop a reasonable bill that would pass when the entire chamber voted on it.

Committees: The Majoritarian and Pluralist Views

It is both advantageous and desirable to bring as much expertise as possible to the policymaking process, and the committee system has done just that. But government by committee vests a tremendous amount of power in the committees and subcommittees of Congress — especially in committee leadership. This is particularly true of the House, which, as noted above, is more decentralized in its patterns of influence and is more restrictive in the degree to which legislation can be amended on the floor. A committee can bury a bill by not reporting it to the full House or Senate. The influence of committee members extends even further, to the floor debate on a bill and, later, to the conference committee that is charged with developing a compromise version of the bill.

This vesting of policy-area power in many committees and subcommittees tends to remove that power from the majority political party and thus to operate against majoritarianism. At the same time, the committee system enhances the force of pluralism in American politics. Representatives and senators are elected by the voters in particular districts and states, and they tend to seek membership on the committees whose decisions are most important to those constituencies. Members from farm areas, for example, seek membership on the House and Senate agriculture committees. Westerners like to serve on the committees dealing with public lands and water rights. Urban liberals like the committees that handle social programs. As a result, the various committees are predisposed to writing legislation favorable to those who are most affected by their actions.

This is not to say that committee members care only about being re-elected and simply pass legislation that will win them votes back home. Rather they are genuinely sympathetic to their constituents and can usually rationalize that good policy for their constituents is good policy for the nation as a whole.

A meeting of the whole House or Senate, to vote a bill up or down, may seem to be an example of majoritarianism at work. The views of the collective membership of each body may reasonably approximate the diverse mix of interests in the United States.[28] Committee decisionmaking also anticipates what is acceptable to the entire membership. Still, by the time the broader membership begins to debate the legislation on the floor, many crucial decisions have already been made in committees with a much narrower constituency in mind. Clearly, the internal structure of Congress gives small groups of members, with intense interests in particular policy areas, a disproportionate amount of influence over those areas.

LEADERS AND FOLLOWERS IN CONGRESS

Above the committee chairs is another layer of authority in the organization of the House and the Senate. The Democratic and Republican leaders in each house work to maximize the influence of their own party, at the same time trying to keep their house of Congress functioning smoothly and efficiently. The operation of the two houses is also influenced by the rules and norms that each chamber has developed over the years.

The Leadership Task

Each of the two parties in each of the two houses has an elected leader. In the House of Representatives, the leader selected by the majority party is the **Speaker of the House** who, gavel in hand, chairs the sessions from the ornate rostrum at the front of the House chamber. The counterpart in the opposing party is the **minority leader.** The majority party chooses the Speaker at its *caucus*, a closed-door meeting of the party. The majority and minority parties then "slate" their candidates for Speaker at the opening session of Congress. The official election follows strict party lines, affirming the majority party's caucus decision. The losing minority party candidate becomes the minority leader. The Speaker is a constitutional officer, though the Constitution merely says the House shall have one, without listing the Speaker's duties. The minority leader is not mentioned in the Constitution, but that post has evolved into an important party position in the House.

The vice president of the United States is directed by the Constitution to be the "President of the Senate." But a vice president does not usually come to the Senate chamber unless there is the possibility of a tie vote, in which case he may break the tie. The **president pro tem** (president "for the time"), elected by the majority party, is supposed to chair the Senate in the vice president's absence, but by custom this constitutional position is entirely honorific.

The real power in the Senate resides in the party position of **majority leader.** As in the House, the top position in the opposing party is that of *minority leader.* Technically, the majority leader does not preside (members rotate in the president pro tem's chair), but he does schedule legislation in consultation with the minority leader. More broadly, the majority leader, the minority leader, and the handful of other party leaders below them play a critical role in getting bills through the Congress. The most significant function that leaders play is steering the bargaining and negotiating over the content of legislation. When an issue divides their party, their house, the two houses, or their house and the White House, the leaders must take the initiative to work out a compromise solution.

Sometimes this action can be quite direct. When months of wrangling over social security and defense spending brought the budgetary process to a halt in 1985, Democrat Tip O'Neill of Massachusetts, then the Speaker of the House, met with Republican President Ronald Reagan. O'Neill and Reagan struck a deal: the House Democrats would agree to a higher level of defense spending and the president would accept the Democrats' insistence that social security benefits not be cut.[29]

Usually, though, the work of party leaders is much less dramatic. Day in, day out, they meet with other members of their house to try to strike deals that will yield a majority on the floor. It is often a matter of finding out if one faction will give up a policy preference in exchange for another concession. Beyond trying to engineer tradeoffs that will win votes, the party leaders

A Meeting in the Speaker's Office
Although some turn-of-the-century Speakers of the House ruled with an iron fist, modern-day Speakers and other party leaders must rely on their skills as negotiators. Speaker Tip O'Neill of Massachusetts (seated), was an adept mediator, juggling the many conflicting interests among House Democrats. O'Neill served as Speaker for a decade until his retirement from Congress at the end of 1986. He confers here with fellow Democrats (from the left) Dan Rostenkowski of Illinois, Richard Gephardt of Missouri, Ari Weiss (a member of his staff), and Jim Wright of Texas.

The Johnson Treatment

During his tenure as Senate Majority Leader during the 1950s, Lyndon Johnson was well known for his style of interaction with other members. In this unusual set of photographs, we see Johnson applying the treatment to Rhode Island Democrat, Theodore Francis Green. Washington journalists Rowland Evans and Robert Novak offered the following description of the "Johnson treatment": "Its tone could be supplication, accusation, cajolery, exuberance, scorn, tears, complaint, the hint of threat. It was all of these together. It ran the gamut of human emotions. Its velocity was breathtaking, and it was all in one direction. Interjections from the target were rare. Johnson anticipated them before they could be spoken. He moved in close, his face a scant millimeter from his target, his eyes widening and narrowing, his eyebrows rising and falling. From his pockets poured clippings, memos, statistics. Mimicry, humor, and the genius of analogy made The Treatment an almost hypnotic experience and rendered the target stunned and helpless." (Rowland Evans and Robert Novak, Lyndon B. Johnson: The Exercise of Power. *New York: New American Library, 1966, p. 104; as cited in Robert L. Peabody,* Leadership in Congress. *Boston: Little, Brown, 1976, pp. 341–342.)*

---

must persuade others (often powerful committee chairs) that theirs is the best deal possible. Senator Robert Dole of Kansas aptly described himself as the "majority pleader" in his role as Senate majority leader.[30]

Party leaders are coalition builders, but not kingmakers. Gone are the days when leaders ruled the House and the Senate with iron fists. Even as recently as the 1950s, strong leaders dominated the legislative process. Senate Majority Leader (and later President) Lyndon B. Johnson made full use of his intelligence, parliamentary skills, and forceful personality to direct the Senate. When he approached individual senators for one-on-one persuasion, "no one subjected to the 'Johnson treatment' ever forgot it."[31] In today's Congress, though, rank-and-file representatives and senators will not stand for such domination by the leadership. Yet there is no doubt that contemporary leaders have an impact on policy outcomes in Congress. As one expert concluded, "Although leadership contributions may be marginal, most important political choices are made at the margins."[32]

Rules of Procedure

The operation of the House and Senate is structured by both formal *rules* and informal *norms* of behavior. Rules in each chamber are mostly matters of parliamentary procedure. Rules, for example, govern the scheduling of legislation, outlining when and how certain types of legislation may be brought to the floor. Rules, such as those concerning the *germaneness*, or relevance, of floor amendments, also differ in the two chambers. In the House, amendments must be directly germane to the bill at hand. In the Senate, except in certain specified instances, senators may add amendments that are not germane to the bill at hand.

As noted earlier, an important difference between the two chambers is the House's use of its Rules Committee to govern floor debate. Without a similar committee to act as a "traffic cop" for legislation approaching the floor, the Senate relies on *unanimous consent agreements* to set the starting time and length of debate. If one senator objects to such a motion, it cannot take effect. Senators do not routinely object to unanimous consent agreements, however, because they need such arrangements when a bill of their own awaits scheduling by the leadership.

If a senator wants to stop a bill badly enough, he or she may start a **filibuster**—that is, he or she may try to talk a bill to death. By historical tradition, the Senate gives its members the right of unlimited debate. During a 1947 debate, Idaho Senator Glen Taylor "spoke for $8\frac{1}{2}$ hours on fishing, baptism, Wall Street, and his children." The record for holding the floor belongs to Republican Senator Strom Thurmond of South Carolina, for his 24-hour, 18-minute marathon.[33]

After a 1917 filibuster by a small group of senators killed President Wilson's bill to arm merchant ships—a bill favored by a majority of senators—the Senate finally adopted a means of shutting off debate. Rule XXII, since amended, sets a limit on the length of debate after **cloture** is voted. A cloture vote is scheduled after sixteen senators sign a petition requesting such action. It now takes sixty senators to invoke cloture to shut off debate.[34] Cloture was successfully invoked against the southerners' filibuster against the far-reaching Civil Rights Act of 1964, paving the way for passage of this historic legislation.

Norms of Behavior

Both houses have codes of behavior that help keep them running. These codes are largely unwritten norms, though some of them are eventually written into House or Senate rules. Members of Congress recognize that personal conflict must be eliminated (or minimized), lest Congress dissolve into bickering factions unable to work together. One of the most celebrated norms is that members show respect for one another in their public deliberations. During floor debate, members who may be bitterly opposed refer to each other in such terms as "My distinguished colleague" or "My good friend the senior Senator from . . . ."

Members of Congress are only human, of course, and tempers do occasionally flare (see Feature 10.1). For example, when Democrat Barney Frank

Feature 10.1

Congressional Fighting Just Isn't What It Used to Be

Congressional fighting has gone sadly downhill in recent years and is now a pretty tacky and occasional pastime. The lawmakers are far removed from the early-nineteenth-century days when duels off the floor were regarded as a natural extension of quarrels on it.

A half-century of such irregular combat was climaxed in 1839 when Representative William Graves of Kentucky killed Representative Jonathan Cilley of Maine in a duel, and Congress, to preserve its ranks from further depletion, passed an antidueling law. But, twenty-five years later, Representative John Potter of Wisconsin was able to avert a duel only by choosing as his weapons Bowie knives, not then readily obtainable in the District of Columbia.

In the old days, floor fights were sometimes literally that. When Representative Roger Griswold of Connecticut debated personal cowardice with Matthew Lyon of Vermont in 1798, Lyon climaxed the exchange by spitting in his face, and then, to make sure Griswold had not missed his point, he hit him with the tongs from the House fireplace. Two motions to censure the combatants failed. . . .

Senate brawling, on the whole, has been less frequent than the House variety and more rigorously condemned after the fact. In 1850, while Senator Henry Foote of Mississippi was speaking on the floor, Senator Thomas Hart Benton of Missouri made menacing gestures and advanced toward Foote's desk. Foote drew his pistol and ostentatiously cocked it, but cooler heads intervened. An investigating committee recommended censure of both men, but the Senate took no action.

A half-dozen years later, Senator Charles Sumner of Massachusetts was sitting at his desk in the chamber after a session during which he had attacked Senator A. P. Butler of South Carolina for advocating optional slavery in Kansas and Nebraska. Butler's nephew, Representative Preston Brooks of South Carolina, came into the chamber shouting angrily at the abolitionist and beat him over the head with a heavy cane. Sumner fell to the floor bleeding and unconscious and was unable to return to the Senate for the rest of that year. His Massachusetts constituents re-elected him in the fall, however, and he was finally well enough to reclaim his seat in 1859, more than three years later. . . .

In 1902, charges of lying led to a Senate chamber fistfight between the two South Carolina members, John McLaurin and "Pitchfork Ben" Tillman (so known because he had threatened to stick one into Grover Cleveland). The two men were unanimously voted in contempt of the Senate. Five days later, after an inquiry and separate apologies, each was censured for "breach of the privileges and dignity of this body." Tillman was a Populist and, like some other members of that noisy agrarian movement, tended to attract criticism that often bordered on physical attack. Another Populist Senator, Thomas Gore of Oklahoma, was as blunt as the best of them but was sheltered from reprisal by the fact that he was blind. One day, after a particularly bitter debate, an infuriated opponent whispered to Gore, "If you weren't blind, I'd thrash you within an inch of your life." The Oklahoman snapped to an ally, "Blindfold that ruffian and aim him in my direction."

Source: Warren Weaver, Jr., *Both Your Houses* (New York: Praeger, 1972), pp. 47–49. Copyright © The New York Times Company. Reprinted by permission.

of Massachusetts was angered by what he thought were unusually harsh charges against the Democratic party, made by Republican Robert Walker of Pennsylvania, Frank rose to ask the presiding officer if it was permissible to refer to Walker as a "crybaby." When he was informed that it was not, Frank sat down, having made his point without technically violating the House's code of behavior.[35]

Another norm of expected behavior is that individual members should be willing to bargain with each other. Members of Congress know that policymaking is a process of give and take and that they must search for a compromise with those with whom they disagree.

On some bills, it may be that one side has the votes needed for passage and has no need to bargain with those on the other side. Many issues, however, are complex and have many different provisions, and some bargaining on them is necessary if a bill is to be passed. When a conference committee met on a bill aimed at imposing economic sanctions on the white supremacist government of South Africa, there were many different, passionately held views. At one point, liberal Democratic Representative Parren Mitchell of Maryland pushed Republican Senator Richard Lugar of Indiana to accept the Democratic position on banning South African gold coins (Krugerrands), saying, "I'm pleading with you today, you and your Senate conferees, I'm pleading with you to take that one quantum step so that this nation can hold up its head high in the international community. Let's go ahead and vote for the ban on Krugerrands." Subsequently the Senate conferees agreed to accept the ban on Krugerrands in exchange for House acceptance of the Senate position against banning new investment in South Africa.[36]

It is important to point out that members of Congress are not expected to violate their consciences on policy issues, simply to strike a deal. They are expected, however, to listen to what others have to offer and to make every effort to reach a reasonable compromise. Members realize that if each of them sticks rigidly to his or her views, they will never agree to anything. Moreover, few policy matters are so clear-cut that compromise will destroy one's position.

Consequently, members of Congress are willing bargainers, who enter the lawmaking process with a rough idea of which provisions they are willing to yield on, which they would give up entirely, and which they feel they cannot yield on. Most of this horsetrading goes on in committee, with the chair usually playing a pivotal role in putting together a deal and coming up with a reportable bill. The norms for such committee bargaining on the House Ways and Means Committee are instructive:

> If a member asks a reasonable price, and Rostenkowski [Democratic chairman, from Illinois] makes the deal, the agreement is clear: the member must then vote for the final package. If a member asks a price that the chairman cannot or will not pay, then there are no obligations on either side; the member is free to oppose the bill, and the chairman is free to follow his own advice and kick the member's brains in, making no concession to his special concerns.[37]

One form of bargaining is **logrolling.** This amounts to legislative back scratching, in which members of Congress exchange votes on separate bills or amendments. Logrolling led to passage of the Food Stamp Act of 1964. The urban liberals in favor of this program were shy of a majority in the House. At around the same time, a bill providing cotton and wheat subsidies was also in trouble since it lacked votes for passage. Some of the southern Democrats and northern Republicans who were unenthusiastic about food stamps but desperately wanted the cotton-wheat bill to pass bargained willingly with the liberals. In turn, there were urban liberals who cared more about getting the food stamp bill through than about voting against an agriculture bill they opposed. In the end, logrolling provided enough votes for both the food stamp bill and the cotton-wheat bill to win approval on the House floor.[38]

Lawmaking requires that leaders be attentive to their followers. Members of Congress have many opportunities to present and argue their claims. Although members can apply the brakes to the congressional process, the rules and norms encourage cooperation among competing interests in order for Congress to function. Compromise enables the leadership to forge majorities from these competing interests. This description of legislative leadership fits the pluralist model of democracy.

THE LEGISLATIVE DECISIONMAKING ENVIRONMENT

As legislation emerges from committee and is scheduled for floor debate, how do legislators make up their minds on how they will vote? In this section, we will examine the broader legislative environment that affects decisionmaking in Congress. More specifically, we will look at the roles of political parties, interest groups, colleagues, staff, the president, and constituents as sources of information for and influence on legislators.[39]

Political Parties

U.S. legislative parties are quite independent of the national parties. One very important reason for this is that the national parties do not control the nominations of House and Senate candidates. Candidates receive the bulk of their funds from individual contributors and political action committees, not from the national parties. In short, members of Congress are highly independent of their parent parties. The party leadership in each house does, however, try to influence the rank and file. Individual members may, for example, need their party leaders' assistance on legislation they have worked on; members will therefore have an incentive to cooperate with those leaders. Members rarely vote as solid blocs when the yeas and nays are called on bills up for a floor vote. However, most members of one party often vote against most of the other in a *party unity vote* — in which a majority of Democrats opposes a majority of Republicans. In recent years, the proportion of party unity votes has increased; in 1985, for example, more than half of all the recorded votes in both chambers were between opposing party majorities.[40]

Within each party, there are major regional differences in members' tendencies to support their party. In 1985, 80 percent or more of the *Northern* Democrats in both chambers voted with their party, and 80 percent or more of the *Southern* Republicans voted with theirs. Occasionally, most Southern Democrats joined with a majority of Republicans to form a **conservative coalition** — a voting alliance of Republicans and Southern Democrats against the Northern Democrats. This alliance occurred on about 15 percent of the votes in 1985. The conservative coalition won nearly 90 percent of the time that it appeared. It is clear that, although strong party allegiance shows up on about half of the votes in Congress, definite regional differences exist within the parties. When Southern Democrats abandon their party to vote with Republicans, the resulting coalition seldom loses.

Interest Groups

The interaction of lobbyists and legislators is not limited to conversations about what the lobbyist does or does not want out of a bill. Legislators often know where a lobbying group stands on an issue because they know whom the organization represents. For instance, a legislator does not need to be told whether the AFL-CIO favors an increase in the minimum wage. The key is for lobbyists to provide useful and reliable information. AFL-CIO lobbyists try to provide congressional offices with reports and research analyses describing why an increase in the minimum wage would not be inflationary or reduce competitiveness in world markets, but would raise the working poor's standard of living and reduce welfare payments.

Lobbies are often disparagingly referred to as "pressure groups," though political scientists prefer to use a more neutral term. Nevertheless, interest groups *do* try to pressure Congress. One of the most effective forms of pressure is having constituents back home present members of Congress with their version of the facts. Members of Congress aren't re-elected by Washington lobbyists — it's the people back home who cast the ballots. One study calls this the "Utah plant manager theory" of lobbying. A Utah senator may not want to take time out of his hectic schedule to speak with a lobbyist from an industry trade group, but if the manager of a Utah plant in this same industry comes to Washington and wants to see the senator, the senator is more likely to agree to a meeting. He doesn't want the manager to go back home and tell all the workers (voters) in the plant that the senator was too busy to hear about that industry's problems.[41]

Colleagues

Lobbyists and interest group members from back home will present legislators with the facts and arguments that most strongly support their groups' policy preferences. But what if the legislator feels that he or she needs a more objective view of a bill? The legislator may very well turn to a fellow representative or senator. One reason is the expertise that comes with committee specialization. It is easy for a member to find an extremely knowledgeable colleague, who can offer a quick analysis of the legislative choices. A second reason is that other representatives and senators form a peer group, and strong bonds of trust, friendship, and professional respect develop over time within that peer group.

Consultation with colleagues comes not only through informal conversations, but also through various formal groupings of legislators. Half of the state delegations in the House meet regularly to discuss issues of mutual concern.[42] There are numerous other groupings, or *caucuses*, who work together on issues that particularly concern them or their constituents. In the House, for example, there are bipartisan caucuses for steel, coal, and Irish affairs. One of the better-known groups is the Congressional Black Caucus, which is composed of the twenty or so blacks who serve in the House. Finally, there are partisan groupings of legislators, such as House groups like the Democratic Study Group and the Republican's Conservative Opportunity Society.

Staff

The number of congressional staff members has risen dramatically in recent years. In the mid-1950s, House members had about 2,500 personal staffers. By 1981, the figure had grown to about 7,500. For the same time period, Senate personal staffs grew from around 1,000 to about 4,000 people.[43] The number of staff members assigned to congressional committees has grown significantly as well.

These larger staffs have helped members of Congress to handle an increasing workload. Staffers reliably represent their bosses' interests during the day-in, day-out negotiations over legislation.[44] Staffers are particularly helpful in involving their bosses in new issues that will increase their influence both with constituents and within Congress. More broadly, one scholar notes, "The increased use of personalized, entrepreneurial staffs has helped Congress retain its position as a key initiator of federal policy, despite the growing power of the executive branch."[45]

The President

Unlike members of Congress, who are elected by voters in individual congressional districts, the president is elected by voters across the entire nation. The president therefore has a better claim to representing the nation than does any single member of Congress. One can also argue, however, that the Congress *as a whole* has a better claim than the president to representing the majority of voters. In fact, when Congress and the president differ, opinion surveys sometimes show that Congress's position on a given bill more closely resembles the majority view; at other times, these surveys show that the president's position accords with the majority. Nevertheless, presidents

Schneider and Staffer
The staff in each legislator's office handles a variety of tasks, including handling casework and press relations, doing research, monitoring legislation, writing speeches, and meeting with constituents and interest group representatives. The hurried and full days that confront members of Congress mean that they must sometimes meet with staffers in a spare moment between other pressing obligations, as Claudine Schneider, Republican representative from Rhode Island (left), is doing here.

capitalize on their popular election and usually act as though they are speaking for the majority.

During the twentieth century, the public's expectations of what a president can accomplish in office have grown enormously. We now expect the president to be our "chief legislator." The American public looks to the president to introduce legislation on the major issues of the day and to use his influence to push bills through Congress. This is much different from our early history, when presidents felt constrained by the constitutional doctrine of separation of powers and had to have members work confidentially for them during legislative sessions.[46]

The White House is involved not only in the writing of bills, but also in their development as they wind their way through the legislative process. If a bill is not to the White House's liking, it will try to work out a compromise with key legislators and then have the legislation amended. On issues of the greatest importance, the president himself will meet with individual legislators to persuade them to vote a certain way. To monitor more mundane, day-to-day congressional activities and lobby for the broad range of administration policies, there are hundreds of legislative liaison personnel working for the executive branch.

Although members of Congress will grant presidents a leadership role in proposing legislation, they jealously guard their power to debate, shape, pass, or defeat any legislation the president proposes. Congress often clashes sharply with the president when his proposals are seen as ill advised.

Constituents

A crucial factor in any legislator's consideration of a bill is the way his or her **constituents** — citizens who live and vote in the legislator's district or state — feel about the issue. As much as members of Congress may want to please the party leadership or the president by going along with their preferences, they must think about what the voters back home want. Should they displease enough people with the way they vote, they might lose their seats in the next election.

In considering the influence of all these factors in the legislator's environment, it is important to keep in mind that legislators also have strong views of their own. They come to Congress deeply committed to working on some key issues and do not need to be pressured into activity on them or into voting a certain way. Indeed, their strong views on some policy questions can come into conflict with what their constituents want. We will discuss this problem in detail later in this chapter.

Of all these possible sources of influence, which are the most important? Unfortunately, there is no one way of measuring them. However, in one interesting and straightforward study, political scientist John Kingdon asked a sample of House members how they made up their minds on a variety of issues. He found that colleagues and the constituency were more likely to have an impact than the other factors listed here. Kingdon cautioned, however, that the decisionmaking process in Congress is complex and that no single factor "is important enough that one could conclude that congressmen vote as they do" because of its influence.[47]

OVERSIGHT: FOLLOWING THROUGH ON LEGISLATION

It is often said in Washington that "knowledge is power." If Congress is to retain its influence over the programs it creates, it must be aware of how they are being administered by the agencies responsible for them. To that end, legislators and their committees engage in **oversight,** the process of reviewing agency operations to determine whether an agency is carrying out policies as Congress intended.

As the executive branch has grown and policies and programs have become increasingly complex, oversight has become more difficult. The sheer magnitude of executive branch operations is staggering. On a typical weekday, for example, over a hundred pages of new agency regulations are issued. Even with the division of labor in the committee system, it is no easy task to determine how good a job an agency is doing in implementing a program.

Congress performs its oversight function in a number of different ways. The most visible oversight activity is the hearing. Hearings may be part of a routine review, or they may be prompted by information revealing a major problem with a program or with an agency's administrative practices. The failure of the Penn Square Bank of Oklahoma City in 1982 caused serious problems for the entire financial system, because a number of major banks had purchased loan portfolios from Penn Square. It turned out that bank examiners had known for a couple of years before the collapse that Penn Square was lending hundreds of millions of dollars without making sure that those borrowing the money had sufficient collateral. The House Banking, Finance, and Urban Affairs Committee asked the Comptroller of the Currency to testify so members could ask him why his agency had failed to act when it found out that Penn Square was violating standard banking practices. The committee needed to find out if new and tougher laws were necessary.[48]

Another way Congress keeps track of what departments and agencies are doing is to request reports on specific agency practices and operations. Two reporters for the *Washington Post* noted the volume of material that Congress requests from the Defense Department:

> Along with the Pentagon's wish list in the 1985 defense budget, Congress asked for a little paper work on the side.
>
> First, the Defense Department had to supply more than 20,000 pages of detailed justifications for the money requested.
>
> Piled atop that were 440 reports and 257 studies demanded by Congress. . . .
>
> Furthermore, before a dispirited Pentagon stopped counting in 1983, Defense Department witnesses in one year logged 1,453 hours of testimony before 91 congressional committees and subcommittees. During the same year, the military responded to 84,148 written queries from Capitol Hill and 592,150 telephone requests, numbers officials believe are on the rise.[49]

Despite this onslaught of information, much escapes congressional attention. To deal with the breadth of executive branch activity, Congress has, as noted earlier, greatly expanded its staffing. In addition to increasing personal and committee staff sizes, Congress created two new specialized offices in the 1970s — the Congressional Budget Office and the Office of Technology Assessment — to do sophisticated analyses of agency operations and proposals.

The longer-standing Government Accounting Office (GAO) and the Congressional Research Service of the Library of Congress also do in-depth studies for Congress.

For all its available resources, though, Congress is routinely criticized for not doing more in the way of oversight. Many argue that members of Congress have little reason to spend much time on oversight. It is seen as rather tedious, unglamorous work that will win few points from the voters back home. With so many pressing tasks competing for their time, members of Congress may push oversight aside for other, more compelling activities, such as talking to constituents in the home district.[50]

It is clear that members of Congress are pulled in many different directions by demands on their time (see Table 10.4). Still, members do not ignore their oversight responsibilities and may in fact do much more than is popularly perceived. Research has shown that the amount of time committees devote to oversight hearings has risen significantly.[51] The main reason why members spend time on oversight, even though it might not always get their name in the newspapers back home, is that they care about making good public policy. A study of the food stamp program found that, through most of the program's history, oversight has been conducted by a small band of legislators who "sought out the issue and worked on it with great energy, imagination, and fervor. Although their individual views differed, these members of Congress were moved to act because they believed current food stamp policy to be incompatible with their own prescription for a fair and just society."[52]

Table 10.4

The Representatives' Day — No Time for Quiet Reflection

A House survey of its members reveals that the "average" representative spends his or her day in the following manner. (Time is given in hours and minutes.)

On the Floor and in Committee	Time	In the Office	Time	In Other Locations in Washington, Including Capitol Hill	Time
In the House chamber	2:53	With constituents	17	With constituents in Capitol	9
In committee meetings	43	With organized groups	9	At events	33
Hearings	9	With others	20	With leadership	3
Business	4	With personal and committee staff	53	With other members	11
Markup	27			With informal groups	8
Other	3	With other members	5	In party meetings	5
In subcommittee meetings	39	Answering mail and signing letters	46	Personal time	28
Hearings	17			Other	25
Business	5	Preparing legislation and speeches	12	Subtotal	2:02
Markup	15	Reading	11	*Other*	*Time*
Other	2	On telephone	26	Other time spent	1:40
In conference meetings	10				
Subtotal	4:25	Subtotal	3:19	Total	11:26

Source: Commission on Administrative Review, U. S. House of Representatives, *Administrative Reorganization and Legislative Management* (95th Congress, 1st session, H. Doc. 95-232), pp. 17–19.

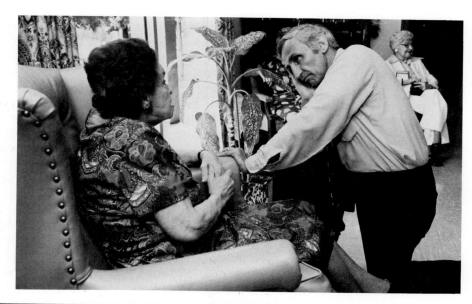

Mazzoli at Home
Members of Congress work extraordinarily hard at keeping in touch with their constituents. The work week in Washington is commonly followed by a trip back home to the district or state, to give speeches, meet with voters, and talk with local office holders. Here House Democrat Romano Mazzoli listens to one of his constituents from Louisville, Kentucky.

THE DILEMMA OF REPRESENTATION

When candidates for the House and Senate campaign for office, they routinely promise to work hard for their district's or state's interests. When they get to Washington, though, they all face the troubling dilemma with which we began this chapter: what their constituents want may not be what the people across the nation want.

Presidents and Shopping Bags

In doing the research for his book *Home Style*, political scientist Richard Fenno accompanied a small number of representatives on trips back to their home districts. On one such trip, he was in an airport with a congressional aide, waiting for the representative's plane from Washington to land. When the congressman arrived, he told Fenno and the aide that "I spent fifteen minutes on the telephone with the president this afternoon. He had a plaintive tone in his voice and he pleaded with me." The congressman's side of the issue had prevailed over the president's, and he was elated by his victory in Washington. When the three men reached the aide's car, the congressman saw the back seat piled high with campaign paraphernalia: shopping bags printed with the representative's name and picture. "Back to this again," he sighed.[53]

Every member of Congress lives in two worlds—the world of presidents and the world of personalized shopping bags. A typical work week in the life of a representative means that, when the work in Washington is done, he or she boards a plane and flies back to the district. There the representative spends time meeting with individual constituents and giving speeches and answering questions before civic groups, church gatherings, business associations, labor unions, and the like. A survey of House members during a nonelection year showed that each made an average of thirty-five trips back to the district, spending an average of 138 days there.[54]

A popular criticism of members of Congress is that they are out of touch with the people they are supposed to represent. This charge hardly seems justified. Members of Congress work extraordinarily hard at keeping in touch with voters. However, working hard to find out what is on constituents' minds is one thing, but acting on that knowledge is something else. If members of Congress know that their constituents prefer a certain policy, are they bound to follow that preference?

Trustees or Delegates?

The debate over whether legislators should vote according to their consciences or their constituencies has never been resolved. One position holds that legislators must be free to vote in line with what they think best. This view has long been associated with the eighteenth-century English political philosopher Edmund Burke (1729–1797). Burke, who served in Parliament, told his Bristol constituents in a speech that "You choose a member, indeed; but when you have chosen him, he is not a member of Bristol, but he is a member of *Parliament*."[55] Burke reasoned that the representative is sent by his constituents to vote as he thinks best. As a **trustee,** the representative is obligated to consider the views of constituents but is not obligated to vote according to those views if he or she thinks they are misguided.

The opposite position is that the legislator is duty bound to represent the majority view of constituents. According to this view, he or she is a **delegate** with instructions from the people at home on how to vote on critical issues. A member of Congress who considers his or her role as that of a delegate must be prepared to vote against his or her own policy preferences. This was the case with former representative Jerry Patterson, a California Democrat. Patterson had long felt that the MX missile was too unreliable a weapon to be worth its cost. Yet during a 1984 roll call vote on the House floor, he cast his vote *for* building the MX missile. Why? Because many workers in his district were employed by Northrop, Rockwell, and other defense contractors working on the missile. Patterson was lobbied hard by those representing labor and management, who desperately wanted to keep the MX in production. In the end, the district won out over Patterson's own sentiments. Patterson said of his actions, "The reality is that you're elected every two years, and the reality is that your job is to represent your constituents. You've got to do that, and you should do that."[56]

Thus, members of Congress are subject to two opposing forces. While the interests of the district push them toward the role of delegates, the larger national interest calls on them to be trustees. As one member of Congress put it, "There is a heavy responsibility to represent the people of the district and the country at large, . . . both [to] make your own decisions and to represent [others]."[57] As a result, there are few who act consistently as either delegates or trustees.

But even if Congress is not clearly a body of trustees or of delegates, it is more apt to take the delegate role on issues that are of great concern to constituents.[58] If jobs are at stake in the district, the member of Congress knows that there is considerable concern back home over how he or she votes. But although constituents in a suburban Los Angeles district may care a great deal about the MX missile, they are not likely to care much about federal farm loan policy, since there aren't many farms there. Consequently, the district's representative can act as a trustee on issues affecting farmers, with little worry that large numbers of constituents will react negatively to how he or she votes on farm matters. Moreover, districts and states might be quite heterogeneous, and bills before Congress may affect competing interests back home rather differently (as in a business versus labor issue). In these cases, there is no clear-cut delegate role to adopt.

PLURALISM, MAJORITARIANISM, AND DEMOCRACY

The dilemma that individual members of Congress face in adopting the role of either trustee or delegate has broad implications for the way our country is governed. If legislators tend to act as delegates, then congressional policy-making is more pluralistic. Policies then reflect the bargaining that goes on among members of Congress who speak for different constituencies. If, instead, legislators tend to act as trustees and vote their consciences, policy-making becomes less tied to the narrower interests of districts and states. There is still no guarantee, however, that congressional actions in that case would represent what the people of this country wanted.

We shall end this chapter with a short discussion of the pluralist nature of Congress. But, first, to establish a frame of reference, we need to take a quick look at the more majoritarian type of legislature — the parliament.

Politics Is the Art of Compromise
American government is characterized by negotiation not only between the legislative and executive branches, but also between the two political parties. At this 1985 meeting, Republican President Ronald Reagan confers with Senate Majority Leader Robert Dole of Kansas and Senate Minority Leader Robert Byrd of West Virginia. (As a result of the November 1986 elections, the Democrats regained control of the Senate, and thus Byrd and Dole exchanged leadership positions.)

Parliamentary Government

Our legislative system is one in which the executive and legislative functions are divided between a president and a Congress who are elected separately. Most other democracies — for example, Britain and Japan — have parliamentary governments. In a **parliamentary system,** the chief executive is the leader whose party holds the most seats in the legislature after an election or whose party forms a major part of the ruling coalition. For instance, Margaret Thatcher became prime minister of Great Britain (head of the British government) because she was the leader of the Conservative party when it won a majority of seats in elections held in 1979 and again in 1983. She did not win her office directly in a national election. Although British voters knew that Mrs. Thatcher would become prime minister if her party won the election, they actually cast their votes for candidates in over six hundred parliamentary elections across the country. The only citizens who voted for Mrs. Thatcher were in her own district of Finchley. But voters across the nation put her in office by choosing Conservative candidates under her party leadership, in preference to candidates under the leadership of the opposition parties.

In a parliamentary system, government power is highly concentrated in the legislative leadership because the leader of the majority party is also the head of government. Moreover, parliamentary legislatures are usually composed of only one house or have a second chamber that is much weaker than the other. (In the British Parliament, the House of Commons makes the decisions of government; the other chamber, the House of Lords, is little more than an honorary debating club for distinguished members of society.) Parliamentary governments often lack a court that can invalidate acts of parliament. Under such a system, the government is usually in the hands of the party that controls the parliament. Without separation of government powers, there are seldom any checks on government action. The net effect is that parliamentary governments fit the majoritarian model of democracy to a much greater extent than congressional governments. (For another perspective, see Compared With What? 10.1.)

Pluralism Versus Majoritarianism in the Congress

Nowadays, the U.S. Congress is often criticized for being too pluralist and not majoritarian enough. The controversy over the federal budget deficit illustrates the points made by critics. By the mid-1980s, the federal government was spending roughly $200 billion more than it was taking in through taxes. According to a national poll in November 1985, 51 percent thought the national deficit was very serious.[59] Both Democrats and Republicans in Congress called for steps to reduce the budget deficit.

When the 1986 budget resolution was introduced in Congress, it contained some significant spending cuts intended to address the deficit. But as soon as the Senate began to consider it, the bargaining started in earnest. Many members refused to vote in favor of the budget resolution until they had protected programs that were of importance to their states. Democratic

Compared With What? 10.1

Form Follows Function in Legislative Architecture

Louis Sullivan, the famous architect, held that the form of a building should follow its function. This principle clearly applies in the layout of three legislative chambers in the United States, Britain, and the Soviet Union.

In the U.S. House of Representatives, members sit in a semicircle facing the Speaker of the House—Democrats to one side and Republicans to the other. Members formally address their remarks to the Speaker, rather than to one another, which tends to control debate and to mute partisanship. (The U.S. Senate is laid out in a similar way, but Senators have individual desks.)

In contrast, in the British House of Commons, members of the two major parties sit facing each other on benches on opposite sides of the chamber. It is an ideal setting for raucous, highly partisan debate that frequently degenerates into name-calling—which the impartial Speaker, in the middle, does his best to control. Not surprisingly, the British House of Commons has a much higher incidence of party-line voting than does the U.S. House of Representatives.

In the Supreme Soviet—the huge theater-like legislature of the U.S.S.R.—approximately 1,500 deputies gather for only a few days annually to sit and listen to their leaders, who are appropriately separated from the deputies and seated on the stage. No name-calling or even controlled debate occurs, and the deputies participate in these proceedings mainly by applauding decisions made elsewhere and reported to them by their leaders.

Three Legislative Chambers
Photos at the right show the U.S. House of Representatives (top), the British House of Commons (center), and the Supreme Soviet of the U.S.S.R.

Feature 10.2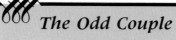

The Odd Couple

The capital's Odd Couple are not the fastidious Felix Unger and the slovenly Oscar Madison in the play by Neil Simon, but rather two members of Congress of opposite ideologies who have joined to win passage of several important health measures. One of them is Representative Henry A. Waxman, who is short, has an expanding waistline like others who have recently reached the age of 45, and is a Democrat from a heavily Jewish district in California who is accorded a 95 percent rating by the liberal Americans for Democratic Action. The other is Senator Orrin G. Hatch, tall and so athletically lean that he does not look his 50 years, a Utah Republican who is a Bishop in the Mormon Church and who votes with the conservative Americans for Constitutional Action 95 percent of the time. . . .

Both men say that their concerns for health rise above their deep political and philosophical differences. "Henry and I expect to establish a health policy that will satisfy both liberals and conservatives," Senator Hatch said the other day.

Their legislative power comes from their chairmanships, with Mr. Waxman heading the House Energy and Commerce Subcommittee on Health and the Environment and Mr. Hatch leading the Senate Labor and Human Resources Committee. These are some of the measures that they have pushed along together:

- A bill designed to increase the sales of lower-priced unbranded medicines has passed in Congress.

- A measure that mandates sterner health warnings on cigarette labels has been passed in the House and is being held up in the Senate only by a parliamentary maneuver that the bill's sponsors are confident of overcoming.

- A law intended to encourage the development and marketing of medicines that do not have great commercial potential has already produced such an "orphan" drug for the treatment of Tourette's syndrome, a rare disease.

The Washington pressure cooker creates such odd couples from time to time, and Representative Waxman and Senator Hatch have specific, pointed evidence to prove it. At a birthday luncheon for Mr. Waxman at the Mayflower Hotel this week, the association of generic drug companies thanked him and Mr. Hatch by presenting them with nightshirts with the slogan "Politics Makes Strange Bedfellows.". . .

According to a Senate aide, the cooperation between the two legislators began at a House-Senate conference in 1981 at which Mr. Waxman made a strong case

Senator Edward Zorinsky of Nebraska would not agree to vote for the budget until some funds were restored for farm programs vital to Nebraska. Republican Senator William Cohen of Maine signed on only after he secured more money for rural housing, which would aid Maine's large rural population. Other senators won increased funding for the Small Business Administration, the Amtrak railroad system, student loans, and the Jobs Corps. Republican Senator Mark Andrews of North Dakota initially spoke for many senators when he harshly criticized the budget. But when Andrews won agreement from the White House to back a plan for more grain exports, he reversed his position. "It's amazing how fast I can support a turkey," Andrews said, speaking of what he thought was a poor bill.[60] For those who favor a ma-

Representative Henry A. Waxman (left) and Senator Orrin G. Hatch.

for the orphan drug legislation. Senator Hatch had no strong position on the measure at that point, but he did want something else, a law to benefit Utah residents who maintained that they had suffered a higher incidence of leukemia as a result of nuclear bomb tests in Nevada in the 1950's and 1960's. Each got what he wanted in the compromise, and the partnership was under way.

The two legislators, despite their agreements, do not try to hide their differences.

"We disagree on abortion," said Mr. Waxman, who favors the view that a woman should have the right to choose to have an abortion. "Senator Hatch has identified with the Moral Majority, and I reject the idea that it is either moral or represents the majority. He is for the school prayer amendment and I am against it. We will disagree on those issues, but we have to see that we can agree on one day and fight on the next."

Source: I. Molotsky, "This Odd Couple Focuses on Health," *New York Times*, September 14, 1984. Copyright © 1984 by The New York Times Company. Reprinted by permission.

joritarian system, Andrews's description certainly fits the budget that the Senate eventually passed. The bargaining among members of Congress considerably reduced the proposed budget cuts. Moreover, this type of bargaining is not unusual; as you saw earlier in this chapter, congressional norms encourage it (see Feature 10.2). And bargaining always seems to "soften" a policy decision.

Many would conclude from such episodes that Congress should become less pluralist and more majoritarian. How else is it to attack such serious problems as the national deficit? Yet those who favor pluralism are quick to point out Congress's merits. For example, many different constituencies were well served by the budget deliberations described above. The restoration of spending cuts through bargaining did not always result in money wasted on frivolous projects; the money was usually put back into programs of value to particular constituencies. Students in need of college loans, farmers in need of financial aid, and the rural poor in need of housing benefited from the current congressional system.

Proponents of pluralism also argue that the makeup of Congress generally reflects that of the nation. Certainly some members of Congress represent farm areas, some represent oil and gas areas, some represent low-income inner cities, some represent places where there are many factories and union workers, and so on. They point out that, after all, America itself is pluralistic, with a rich diversity of economic, social, religious, and racial groups. Even if your own representatives and senators don't represent your particular viewpoint, it's likely that some others in Congress do.[61]

An alternative to today's highly pluralist Congress is one that would operate on strictly majoritarian principles. For this kind of system to work, we would need strong parties—as described by the principles of responsible party government in Chapter 7. That is, congressional candidates for each party would have to stand relatively united on the major issues. Then the majority party in Congress would act on a clear mandate from the voters—at least on the major issues discussed in the preceding election campaign. This would be quite different from the pluralist system we now have, which furthers the influence of interest groups and local constituencies in national policymaking. Which is better: a Congress that considers and responds to the majority's view on policy matters (the majoritarian model) or a Congress that considers and responds to the demands of individual constituencies (the pluralist model)?

SUMMARY

Congress plays a central role in our governmental process through its lawmaking functions. It writes the laws of the land and attempts to oversee their implementation. It helps to educate us about new issues as they appear on the political agenda. Most important, members of Congress represent their constituents, trying to ensure that interests from home and from around the country are heard during the policymaking process.

We count on Congress to do so much that criticism about how well it does its job is inevitable. Some strengths are still apparent, however. The committee system fosters expertise; the representatives and senators who know the most about particular issues have the most influence over them. Members of Congress work long hours and try to keep in close touch with their constituents. This "keeping in touch" through frequent trips home is also a form of campaigning, helping them in their efforts to be re-elected. The many advantages of incumbency make elections an uphill battle for challengers, particularly those running against House members. Incumbents have an overwhelming advantage in raising campaign funds because PACs want to keep on good terms with them.

One important feature of the congressional policymaking process is constant bargaining and compromise. Some find this disquieting, wishing that there were less dealmaking and more adherence to principle. This view is in line with the desire for a more majoritarian system, in which congressional parties would be strong and unified. Others defend the congressional system, noting that this is a large, complex, and pluralistic nation. With so many divergent interests in this country, they say, policy should be developed through bargaining among various interests.

There is no clear-cut answer on whether a majoritarian or a pluralist legislative system provides better representation for voters. As you have seen, our congressional system tends to favor a pluralist model of democracy more than a majoritarian one. Congress can be defended as serving minority interests, which might otherwise be neglected (or even harmed) by an unthinking or uncaring majority. But Congress can also be criticized for being overly responsive to special interests at the expense of the majority of Americans.

Key Terms

bicameral
reapportionment
impeachment
incumbent
redistricting
gerrymander
franking privilege
casework
bill
veto
pocket veto
standing committee
joint commitee
select committee
conference committee

seniority
markup session
Speaker of the House
minority leader
president pro tem
majority leader
filibuster
cloture
logrolling
conservative coalition
constituents
oversight
trustee
delegate
parliamentary system

Selected Readings

Dodd, Lawrence C., and Bruce I. Oppenheimer. *Congress Reconsidered,* 3rd ed. Washington, D.C.: Congressional Quarterly, 1985. This collection of essays pulls together much of the latest research on Congress.

Fenno, Richard F., Jr. *Congressmen in Committees.* Boston: Little, Brown, 1973. A classic study of how legislators' goals affect committee operations.

Fenno, Richard F., Jr. *Home Style.* Boston: Little, Brown, 1978. An analysis of how House members interact with constituents during visits to their home districts.

Jacobson, Gary C. *Money in Congressional Elections.* New Haven, Conn.: Yale University Press, 1980. Jacobson demonstrates how levels of spending affect congressional candidates' election chances.

Mayhew, David R. *Congress: The Electoral Connection.* New Haven, Conn.: Yale University Press, 1974. A provocative argument that members of Congress are single-minded seekers of re-election.

Peabody, Robert L. *Leadership in Congress.* Boston: Little, Brown, 1976. A comprehensive examination of leadership patterns in the House and Senate.

11

The Presidency

I n early April of 1952, while American troops were fighting in Korea, the steelworkers' union was poised to go out on strike. The union's labor contract with the steel companies had expired at the end of 1951, but the workers had stayed on the job for several months while negotiations continued. Now, with no new contract in sight, they were about to stop working, to back up their contract demands.

Harry Truman, who was president at the time, had a number of alternatives to choose from — all of them unpleasant. He could simply let the labor dispute run its natural course, allowing the strike to take place. But the steel industry was vital to the war effort; Truman's secretary of Defense had warned him that if a strike cut off steel production, American and South Korean troops could be endangered by a shortage of ammunition.

Truman could also invoke the Taft-Hartley Act, thereby forcing the steelworkers to remain on the job for an eighty-day cooling-off period. This would give labor and management more time to reach a settlement, but it would be extremely unpopular with union members, who had already worked almost one hundred days without a contract. And Truman, a Democrat, was sensitive to the concerns of organized labor, which was a mainstay of his party. Furthermore, Taft-Hartley had become law when Congress overrode Truman's veto of the bill in 1947, and it might seem hypocritical for him to utilize it. The president's last alternative was to ask Congress to pass a law allowing him to take control of the steel industry. However, Truman's popularity was so low at the time that he probably could not have persuaded Congress to pass such a controversial bill.

Truman chose none of these alternatives, deciding instead to issue an executive order through which he, as president, seized control of the steel industry. Both he and his attorney general, Tom Clark, believed that he had the *inherent* power to do so in a crisis, even though that power was not explicitly detailed in the Constitution. Further, in an unusual breach of judicial ethics, the chief justice of the Supreme Court, Fred Vinson, privately advised Truman to go ahead with the seizure, since he considered the president to be on solid legal ground.

Truman's executive order met with a storm of criticism, but he was convinced he had done the right thing. "Tell 'em to read the Constitution," Truman said. "The president has the right to keep the country from going to hell." The steel companies, however, contended that the president did not have the right to take control of private firms and immediately took their case to court. In a momentous decision, the Supreme Court agreed with the steel companies, citing the constitutional separation of powers and saying that Truman had, in effect, acted as lawmaker, whereas the Constitution provides that only Congress can make the laws of the land. Truman's executive order was nullified, and the ensuing strike lasted fifty-three days before a settlement was finally reached.[1]

Truman's attempt to seize control of the steel industry illustrates some of the conflicts surrounding the office of president of the United States. For example, to what degree should the president be constrained within our system of checks and balances? To what extent must the president rely on his formal powers, and in what situations should he use informal powers?

And finally, how does the presidency function: is the presidency primarily an instrument of *pluralist* democracy, serving small but vocal constituencies, or does it operate to promote *majoritarian* democracy, responding primarily to popular desires as expressed through public opinion?

THE CONSTITUTIONAL BASIS OF PRESIDENTIAL POWER

When the justices of the Supreme Court ruled on the steel industry case, they cited the founders' intention to limit the powers of the presidency. When the presidency was created, the colonies had just fought a war of independence; their reaction to British domination focused on the autocratic rule of King George III.

The delegates to the Constitutional Convention were extremely wary of unchecked power. They were determined not to create a presidential office whose occupant could become an all-powerful, dictatorial figure.

The delegates' fear of a powerful presidency was counterbalanced by an obvious need for strong leadership. The earlier Articles of Confederation — which did not provide for a single head of state — had failed to bind the states together into a unified nation. In addition, the governors of the individual states had generally proved to be inadequate leaders because they had few formal powers. The new nation was conspicuously weak; its Congress had no power to compel the states to obey its legislation. With the failed Confederation in mind, John Jay wrote to George Washington, asking him, "Shall we have a king?"[2]

The idea of establishing an American royalty was far from popular among the delegates to the Constitutional Convention, but they knew that some type of executive office had to be created (see Compared With What? 11.1). Their task was to provide national leadership without allowing the opportunity for tyranny.

Initial Conceptions of the Presidency

Some of the delegates to the convention wanted a president who was chosen by the Congress and largely subservient to that body. The idea of a presidential council or committee was also considered. Initial approval was given to a plan that called for a single executive, chosen by the Congress for a seven-year term and ineligible for re-election.[3] But some of the delegates continued to argue for a strong president who would be elected independently of Congress.

The final shape of the presidency reflected the "checks and balances" philosophy that became so influential in shaping the Constitution. In the minds of the delegates, important limits were imposed on the presidency through the powers that were specifically delegated to the Congress and the courts. Those counterbalancing powers would act as checks or controls on presidents who might try to expand the office beyond its proper bounds.

Compared With What? 11.1

Head of State or Head of Government?

In the United States, we elect a president to be both *head of government*, which means that he directs and executes government policy, and *head of state*, which means that he is the nation's ceremonial leader and its symbol of sovereignty. Only about one-quarter of the nations with representative legislatures also have popularly elected heads of state. The accompanying graph, which plots the method of selecting the head of state for 54 nations, shows that a plurality (18) still have a hereditary monarch as head of state. Those 18 nations include Belgium, Denmark, the Netherlands, Norway, Sweden, Britain, and some countries in the British Commonwealth. Parliaments choose the head of state in one-quarter of the nations — Israel is one example — and a council of political leaders chooses the head of state in a few other countries.

The United States is one of only eight countries in the group that combines the positions of head of state and head of government (shown in the red portions of the graph). France, in contrast, has a popularly elected president, but its government is headed by a prime minister who makes policy with the support of parliament. Because he possesses both offices, our president's latent powers are greater than those of any prime minister. Whereas a prime minister represents the political party that heads the government at the time, the president personifies the nation and its historical traditions — as the Queen does in Britain. Opponents can criticize a prime minister without criticizing the nation, but personal attacks on the president may seem to some to border on attacks on the nation. This implied criticism happens frequently in the area of international relations, where critics of the president's foreign policy may be told that they are being disloyal to the United States.

Powers of the President

The responsibilities of American presidents are set forth in Article II of the Constitution. But in view of the importance of the office, the constitutional description of the president's duties is surprisingly brief and vague. This vagueness has led to repeated conflict over the limits of presidential power.

There were undoubtedly many reasons for Article II's lack of precision. One reason was no doubt the difficult task of providing and at the same time limiting presidential power. Furthermore, the framers of the Constitution had no model — no existing presidency — on which to base the office and, in fact, disagreed sharply over the nature of that office. Their description of the presidency might have been more precise if they had had less confidence in George Washington, the obvious choice for the first president. According to one account of the Constitutional Convention, "when Dr. Franklin predicted on June 4 that 'the first man put at the helm will be a good one,' every delegate knew perfectly well who that first good man would be."[4] The delegates had great trust in Washington; they had no fear that he would try to misuse the office.

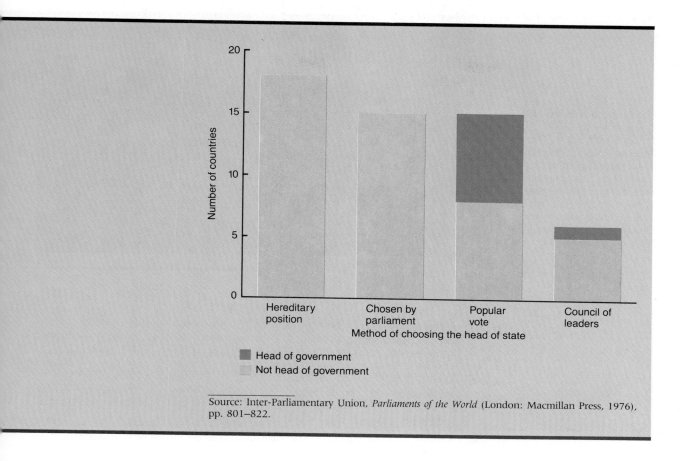

Source: Inter-Parliamentary Union, *Parliaments of the World* (London: Macmillan Press, 1976), pp. 801–822.

The major duties and powers that the delegates did list for Washington and his successors can be summarized as follows:

■ *Serve as administrative head of the nation.*   The Constitution gives little guidance on the president's administrative duties. It states merely that "the executive Power shall be vested in a President of the United States of America" and that "he shall take Care that the Laws be faithfully executed." These imprecise directives have been interpreted to mean that the president is to supervise and offer leadership to various departments, agencies, and programs created by Congress. In practice, a chief executive spends much more time making policy decisions for his cabinet departments and agencies than he does trying to enforce existing policies.

■ *Act as commander in chief of the military.*   In essence, the Constitution names the president as the highest ranking officer in the armed forces. But it gives Congress the power to *declare* war. The framers no doubt intended Congress to control the president's military power; yet presidents have initiated military action without the approval of Congress. The entire Vietnam War was fought without a congressional declaration of war.

The Commanders and the Commander in Chief
During World War II President Franklin Roosevelt visited the troops at an American base in Sicily. There, the commander in chief met with General Dwight Eisenhower (to FDR's left), who would win the presidency himself in 1952. At the far left is the legendary General George Patton.

- *Convene Congress.* The president can call Congress into special session on "extraordinary Occasions," though this has been done only rarely. He must also periodically inform Congress of "the State of the Union."

- *Veto legislation.* The president can **veto** (disapprove) any bill or resolution passed by Congress, with the exception of joint resolutions that propose constitutional amendments. Congress can override a presidential veto with a two-thirds vote in each house.

- *Appoint various officials.* The president has the authority to appoint federal court judges, ambassadors, cabinet members, other key policymakers, and many lesser officials. Many appointments are subject to Senate confirmation.

- *Make treaties.* With the "advice and consent" of at least two-thirds of those senators voting at the time, the president can make treaties with foreign powers. The president is also to "receive ambassadors," which presidents quickly interpreted as the right to recognize other nations.

- *Grant pardons.* The president can grant pardons to individuals who have committed "Offenses against the United States, except in Cases of Impeachment."

THE EXPANSION OF PRESIDENTIAL POWER

The framers' limited conception of the president's role has given way to a considerably more powerful executive office. In this section, we shall look beyond the presidential responsibilities explicitly listed in the Constitution and examine additional sources of presidential power, which presidents have used to expand the authority of the office. First, we shall look at the claims that presidents make about "inherent" powers implicit in the Constitution.

Second, we shall turn to congressional grants of power to the executive branch. Third, we shall discuss the influence that comes from a president's political skills. Fourth, we shall analyze how a president's popular support affects his personal power. And finally, we shall look at the tremendous expectations the public has come to have for such a powerful office.

The Inherent Powers

Several presidents have assumed power by taking actions that exceeded commonly held notions of the president's proper authority. These men justified what they had done by saying that the actions fell within the **inherent powers** of the office. From this broader perspective, presidential power derives not only from those duties clearly outlined in Article II, but also from inferences that may be drawn from the Constitution.

Like Truman in the steel industry case, presidents who act under what they consider to be their inherent powers force Congress and the courts either to acquiesce to such actions or to restrict them. Unlike Truman, some presidents have succeeded; those who did left a legacy to their successors in the form of a permanent expansion of presidential authority. One early use of the inherent power of the presidency occurred during George Washington's tenure in office. The British and French were at war and Washington was under some pressure from members of his own administration to show favoritism toward the French. He reacted instead by issuing a proclamation of strict neutrality, which angered many who harbored anti-British sentiments; the ensuing controversy provoked a constitutional debate. Critics noted that the Constitution does not include a presidential power to declare neutrality. Defenders of Washington's decision said that the president had inherent powers to conduct diplomacy. In the end, Washington's decision was not overturned by Congress or the courts and thus set a precedent in the area of foreign affairs.[5]

Such actions have often come at critical points in the nation's history. During the Civil War, for example, President Abraham Lincoln issued a number of orders that exceeded the accepted limits of presidential authority. One of these orders increased the size of the armed forces far beyond the congressionally mandated ceiling, even though the Constitution gives only Congress the power "to raise and support armies." And, because military expenditures would then have exceeded military appropriations, Lincoln clearly had also acted to usurp the taxing and spending powers conferred on Congress by the Constitution. In another order, Lincoln instituted a blockade of Southern ports; with this order, he essentially committed acts of war against the Confederacy without the approval of Congress.

Lincoln's defense of his conduct was that the urgent nature of the South's challenge to the Union gave him no choice but to act without waiting for congressional approval. His rationale was simple: "Was it possible to lose the nation and yet preserve the Constitution?"[6] In other words, Lincoln circumvented the Constitution in order to save the nation. Subsequently, Congress and the Supreme Court approved Lincoln's actions. That approval gave added legitimacy to a theory of inherent powers of the presidency—a theory that over time has transformed the presidency.

Preserving the Union
During the Civil War, Abraham Lincoln took many controversial actions that expanded the authority of the presidency. Lincoln (pictured with his generals at Antietam, Maryland) strongly influenced the nature of the office through his emergency measures.

Any president who lays claim to new authority runs the risk of being rebuffed by Congress or the courts and thus being hurt politically. After Andrew Jackson vetoed a bill reauthorizing a national bank, he ordered William Duane, his secretary of the treasury, to withdraw all federal deposits and to place them in state banks. Duane refused, claiming that he was under the supervision of both Congress and the executive branch; Jackson responded by firing him. The president's action angered many Congress members who believed that Jackson had overstepped his constitutional bounds, since the Constitution does not actually state that a president may remove his cabinet secretaries. Although that prerogative is now taken for granted, Jackson's presidency was weakened by the controversy. His censure by the Senate was a slap in the face, and he was denounced even by members of his own party. It took many years for the president's right to remove cabinet officers to become accepted practice.[7]

Congressional Delegation of Power

Presidential power has grown when presidents have successfully challenged Congress, but in many other instances Congress has willingly delegated power to the executive branch. As the American public has pressured Washington to solve various problems, Congress, through a process called **delegation of powers,** has given the executive branch more responsibility to administer programs to solve those problems. One example of delegation of legislative power occurred in the 1930s, during the Great Depression, when

Congress gave Franklin Roosevelt's administration wide latitude to do what it thought was necessary to solve the nation's economic ills.

When Congress concludes that the government needs flexibility in its approach to a problem, the president is often given great freedom in how or when to implement policies. President Richard Nixon, for example, was given discretionary authority to impose a freeze on wages and prices in an effort to combat escalating inflation. If Congress had been forced to debate the timing of this freeze, merchants and manufacturers would surely have raised their prices in anticipation of the event. Nixon was able to act suddenly, and the freeze was imposed without forewarning. (Congressional delegation of authority to the executive branch is discussed in more detail in Chapter 12 on the bureaucracy.)

At other times, however, Congress acts on the belief that too much power is accumulating in the executive branch, and it passes legislation reasserting congressional authority. During the 1970s, many representatives and senators agreed that Congress's role in the American political system was declining and that presidents were exercising power that rightfully belonged to the legislative branch. The most notable reaction was passage of the War Powers Resolution in 1973, which was directed toward ending the president's ability to pursue armed conflict without explicit congressional approval. Congress has also moved to prevent presidents from impounding (refusing to spend) money appropriated by Congress.[8]

The President's Power to Persuade

A president's influence in office comes not only from his assigned responsibilities, but also from his personal skills. How effectively a president uses the resources of his office will also determine how good his chances will be of achieving his goals. One of the best analyses of how a president uses those resources is offered by political scientist Richard Neustadt. In his classic book *Presidential Power,* Neustadt develops a model of how presidents gain, lose, or maintain their influence. Neustadt's initial premise is simple enough: "Presidential *power* is the power to persuade."[9] Presidents, for all their resources—a skilled staff, extensive media coverage of presidential actions, the great respect for the office—must still depend on others' cooperation to get things done. Harry Truman echoed Neustadt's premise when he said, "I sit here all day trying to persuade people to do the things they ought to have sense enough to do without my persuading them. . . . That's all the powers of the President amount to."[10]

The abilities displayed in bargaining, dealing with adversaries, and choosing priorities, according to Neustadt, separate mediocre from above-average presidents. A president makes choices about which policies to push and which to put aside until more support can be found. He decides when to accept compromises and when to stand on principles. He must know when to go public and when to work behind the scenes.

Often, a president faces a dilemma in which all the alternatives carry some risk. After Dwight Eisenhower took office in 1953, he had to decide what stance to take with regard to Joseph McCarthy, the Republican senator from Wisconsin. McCarthy had been largely responsible for creating a national hysteria over alleged communists in government. He made many wild and reckless charges, damaging a number of innocent people's careers by accusing them of communist sympathies. Many people looked to Eisenhower to control McCarthy — not only because he was president, but also because he was a fellow Republican. Yet Eisenhower chose not to confront McCarthy, worrying about his own popularity. He worked instead behind the scenes, with a "hidden-hand" strategy, to do what he could to weaken McCarthy. Politically, Eisenhower seems to have made the right choice; McCarthy soon discredited himself.[11] Eisenhower's performance can be criticized, however, as weak moral leadership. If he had strongly denounced the senator, he might have helped stop the McCarthy witch hunt sooner.

A president's political skills are especially important in affecting outcomes in Congress (see Feature 11.1). The chief executive cannot intervene in every legislative struggle. He must choose his battles carefully and then try to use the force of his personality and the prestige of his office to forge an agreement among differing factions. Lyndon Johnson was one of the best of our modern presidents in bargaining with others to get his legislation passed. Johnson once got religious leaders Billy Graham and Francis Cardinal Spellman to go for a swim in the White House pool and then took the opportunity to push them into resolving a church-state dispute that was holding up an education bill in Congress.[12]

Neustadt stresses in his study of presidential power that a president's influence is related to his professional reputation and prestige. When a president pushes hard for bills that Congress eventually defeats or emasculates, the president's reputation is hurt. He is perceived by the public as not doing a very good job, and Congress becomes even less likely to cooperate with him in the future. Thus, presidents do not want to lose support by backing bills that will end up in the headlines as "President's Bill Goes Down to Defeat in House." President Jimmy Carter hurt himself during his term by putting his prestige on the line for bills proposing welfare reform, hospital cost containment, and an Agency for Consumer Protection — none of which passed. Yet the other side of this coin is that presidents cannot easily avoid controversial bills, especially if campaign promises were made. If a president backs only sure things, he will be credited with little and perceived as too cautious.

The Public and the President

Neustadt's analysis suggests that a popular president is more persuasive than an unpopular one. A popular president has more power to persuade because public support is a resource that can be used in the bargaining process. Congress members who know that the president is highly popular back home have more incentive to cooperate with the administration. If the president and his aides know that a member of Congress does not want to be seen as hostile to the president, they can apply more leverage to achieve a favorable compromise in a legislative struggle.

The most common way of assessing presidential popularity is to look at national polls. Since 1938, the Gallup Poll has asked a sample of Americans

Feature 11.1   The Reagan Touch

It had been raining most of the morning . . . when President Reagan came out of his personal lodge at the Presidential hideaway in the Catoctin Mountains to greet 15 Democratic Congressmen. He had invited them up for lunch and a bit of lobbying. As luck would have it, the sun came out, gleaming over the wet foliage, a few minutes before the cars arrived. The President in cowboy boots, brown slacks and a beige, Western-style shirt, stood on his doorstep to shake hands with each Congressman personally. For half an hour they all swapped small talk over coffee, orange juice, and Bloody Marys on the flagstone patio overlooking a rustic country-club setting of terraced gardens, a swimming pool and nearby woods. Then the President walked them to Laurel Lodge where his chefs had set out a buffet of hot dogs, hamburgers, potato salad, chili beans and fresh corn.

After lunch, President Reagan stood up. "Now for the commercial," he smiled, launching into a brief pitch for his three-year tax-cut package which was due for a showdown vote in the House of Representatives three days hence. He asked for the support of the group, most of them still publicly uncommitted. "If you have any questions," the President offered, "I'd be happy to answer them."

Dave McCurdy, a freshman Democrat from Oklahoma, wanted to know how the President answered the charge that his was "a rich man's tax cut" that did less than the Democrats for middle-income America.

"With our third year, those people in the $15,000-to-$30,000 income bracket would actually do better under our bill than under the two-year Democratic bill," Mr. Reagan replied. There was room for debate on this point, but no one contested his answer. Bill Hefner, a fourth-term Democratic conservative from North Carolina, was worried about the third-year tax cut adding to the 1984 budget deficit. "If your economic assumptions are off on interest rates and unemployment and inflation by a couple of points and we're locked into the tax cut and you're faced with a $70 to $80 billion deficit," he challenged the President, "what are you going to do? Cut defense or Social Security?"

"I don't know why everybody's so concerned about the third year, when they'll give business tax cuts for seven years and when spending programs go on for years and years and years," the President answered. "Eighty percent of our business is small business and these people need to be able to plan ahead. The third year gives predictability. If you accept the Democratic plan, we'll never have a third year."

Ike Skelton of Missouri was concerned that indexing income-tax rates to inflation after 1984 would crimp the Pentagon budget. "Nobody's more concerned about defense than I am," the President countered, "and if there were some kind of international crisis, we would correct that with new legislation. We could go back in there and fix it." Richard Shelby of Alabama liked the indexing idea. "You can count on me," he told the President. "I'm going to do everything I can. I believe your package is superior."

Most of the others remained noncommittal and the President did not press them for a decision. It was the classic Reagan charm treatment: no hard sell, no demand for commitments, but a willingness to listen and talk, and a flattering sense of access and importance. Later on, aides would follow up, offering the Oklahomans a Presidential pledge to fight any windfall-profits tax on natural gas, telling the Georgians the President would oppose large peanut imports in the future. President Reagan's job was softening them up. As they drove away, he said to one aide: "Gee, I wonder if we did any good with those fellows today."

The answer is that after his rousing partisan television speech the next night, touching off what House Speaker Thomas P. O'Neill Jr., called "a telephone blitz like this nation has never seen" on behalf of the Reagan tax package, the President got 12 of the 15 Democratic votes he courted at Camp David that afternoon.

Source: Hedrick Smith, "Taking Charge of Congress," *New York Times Magazine;* August 5, 1981, pp. 12–13. Copyright © 1981 by The New York Times Company. Reprinted by permission.

whether they approved of the way the president was doing his job. Four decades of such approval ratings, plotted in Figures 11.1(a) through 11.1(f), give a good view of the heights and depths of presidential popularity over time. Two patterns are immediately evident. First, the basic trend for most presidents is to move from high popularity to low popularity. Second, every president experiences ups and downs. In general, a president receives the most support upon taking office. Over time, however, public approval changes in response to events and presidential actions. Notice what happened to Gerald Ford's rating after he issued a blanket pardon of Richard Nixon for any illegal activities he may have engaged in during the Watergate episode.

The general decline in presidential popularity through a term in office has been explained by the concept of a **coalition of minorities**:[13] the idea

Figure 11.1

Presidential Popularity: John F. Kennedy to Ronald Reagan
Since the late 1930s, the Gallup Poll has asked a sample of Americans, "Do you approve or disapprove of the way [the present officeholder] is handling his job as president?" Plotting the percentages of approval for the presidents' performance shows that most presidents have lost support over time. Lyndon Johnson's rating, for example, sank almost steadily from great popularity to the depths of disapproval (which discouraged him from running for re-election). Richard Nixon's percentages, however, plunged more steeply than

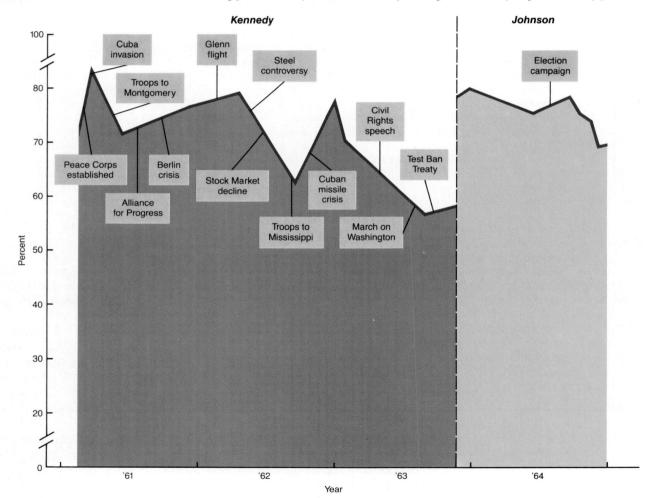

that different groups of voters become dissatisfied with the president's handling of particular issues of concern. While campaigning for office, the president encourages all sectors of society to believe he is for them. After he is in office, the president cannot possibly deliver on all his promises, and the groups that fail to get what they want become disaffected. The coalition of minorities begins to criticize the president. Moreover, the president's vulnerability is exploited by other leaders for their own political gains. The result

---

anyone else's — moving from a high of 68 percent in January 1973 to a low of 28 percent in less than nine months (he resigned a year later). Ronald Reagan's popularity, relatively high at the end of 1985, dropped significantly in the fall of 1986, when it was revealed that there were secret U.S. arms sales to Iran and that the profits from these sales were being funneled to the Contras in Nicaragua. (Gallup Opinion Index Report 182, October-November 1980.)

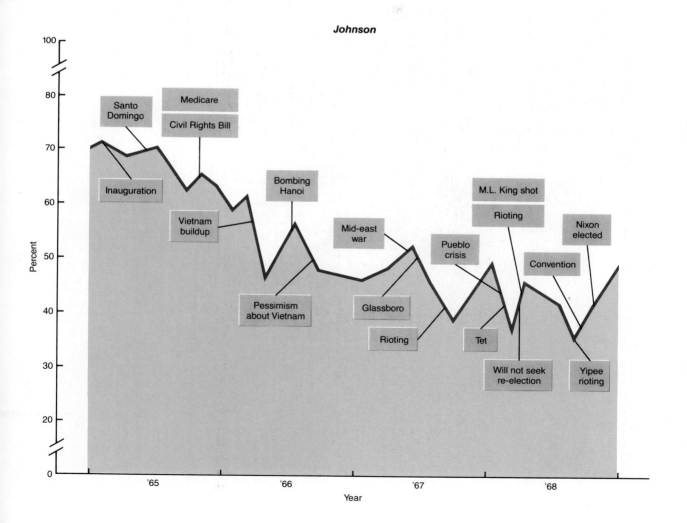

is a continuing assault on presidential popularity, and the president's level of approval drops from its initial heights.

The sharp peaks and valleys in presidential popularity (within the usual overall pattern of decline) can be explained by several factors. First, public approval of the job done by presidents is affected by *economic conditions,* such as inflation and unemployment.[14] A strong economy buoyed Eisenhower's popularity during his first term, but a recession during the middle of his second term brought his rating down. Second, presidents are affected by *unanticipated events* of all types that occur during their administrations. When American embassy personnel were taken hostage in Teheran by militantly anti-American Iranians, Carter's popularity soared. This "rally 'round the flag" support for the president eventually gave way to frustration with Carter's inability to gain the hostages' release and his popularity plummeted. The third main factor that affects presidential popularity is American involve-

Figure 11.1 continued

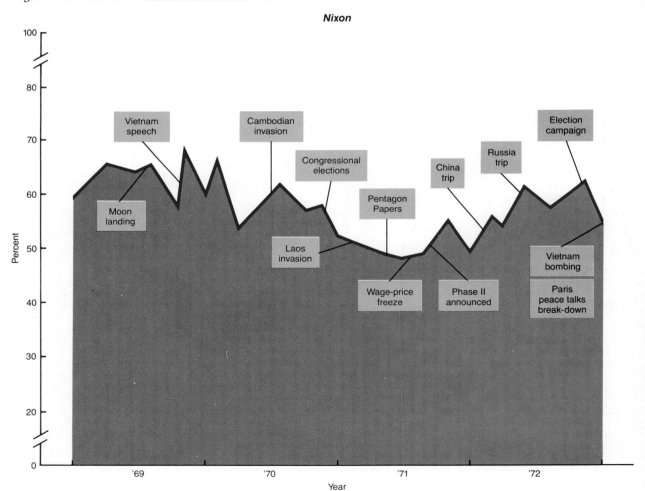

ment in a *war*, which can erode public approval. This was the case when Johnson led the country during the escalation of the American effort in Vietnam.[15]

Great Expectations

Contemporary Americans become dissatisfied with their presidents for still one more reason: we expect so much from them in the first place. The president has come to be viewed as much more than chief executive of our government; the president is expected to be a moral leader as well as a political one (see Table 11.1). The presidential family is regarded with reverence and subjected to intense media scrutiny. The president is part king, part savior, and part wise man. In times of crisis, he is seen as the best hope for saving us from our enemies or even from ourselves. One observer notes

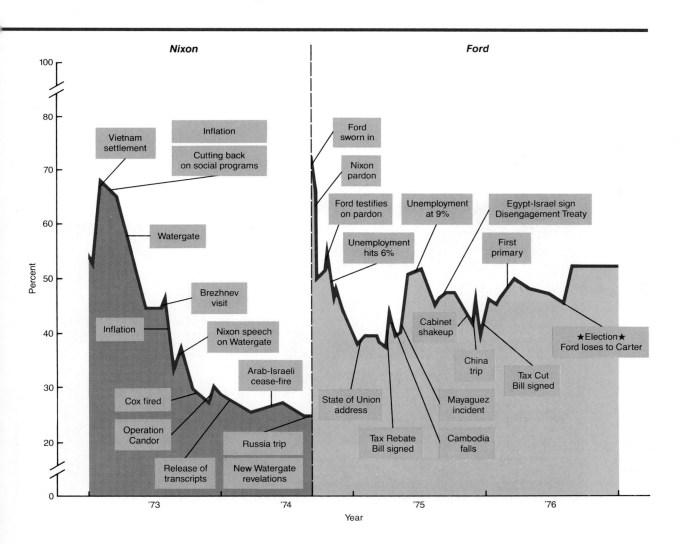

that "the election of a president is an almost religious task; it intimately affects the life of the spirit, our identity. Who the man is determines in real measure who we are."[16]

Why do Americans put so much faith in the presidency? One reason is the common tendency to believe that great people shape great events. This "great man" view of history is, in a sense, a shortcut in understanding the dynamics of policymaking. To the average citizen, the governmental process is complex and confusing. An individual who is dissatisfied with the performance of the economy might have to spend considerable time learning about the forces that shape it — such as the Federal Reserve Board's money supply policy, the balance of payments with foreign countries, and the government's taxing and spending policies — to adequately understand why the economy is acting the way it is. One might be tempted to believe instead that economic performance is determined by presidential judgment. It is much easier to assume that the president always makes the critical difference in the

Figure 11.1 continued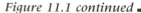

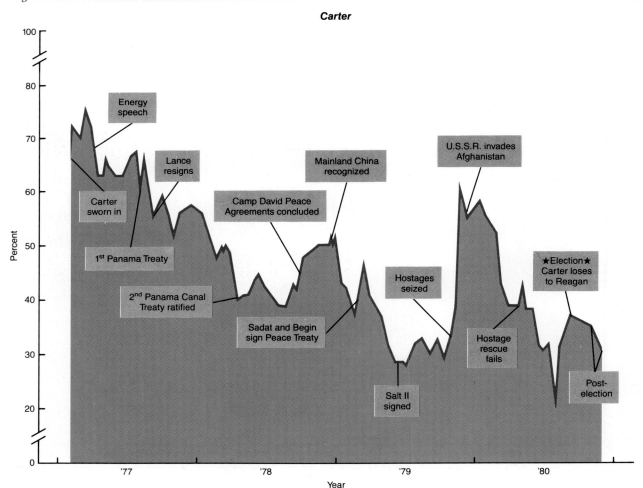

Table 11.1
What Would You Think if the President . . . ?

Behavior	% Would Strongly Object
If he smoked marijuana occasionally	70
If he told ethnic or racial jokes in private	43
If he were not a member of a church	38
If he used tranquilizers occasionally	36
If he used profane language in private	33
If he had seen a psychiatrist	30
If he wore blue jeans occasionally in the Oval Office	21
If he were divorced	17
If he had a cocktail before dinner each night	14

Source: Gallup Survey, Fall 1979, in George C. Edwards and Stephen J. Wayne, *Presidential Leadership* (New York: St. Martin's Press, 1985), p. 100. Reprinted by permission.

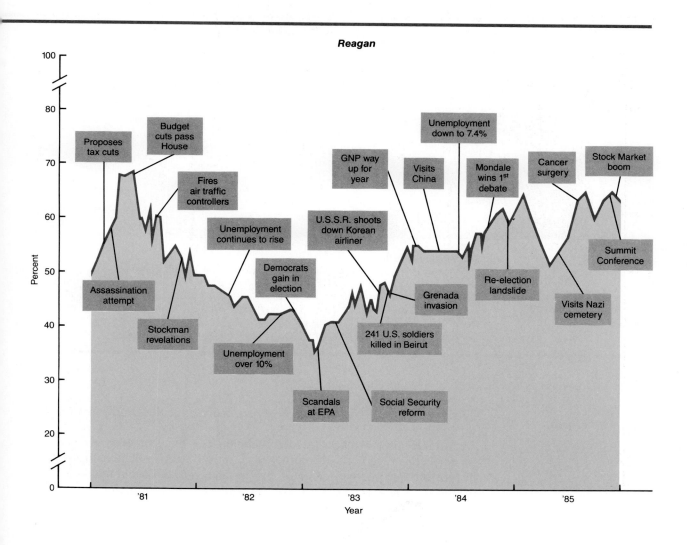

The Hostage Crisis
On November 4th, 1979, more than fifty Americans were taken hostage in Teheran, Iran. Despite efforts to win the hostages' release, the Iranian government refused to let them go. The public became frustrated and grew critical of the administration's failure to get the hostages back, and President Carter's chances for re-election were damaged. At the very end of his term, an agreement was finally reached. The Americans were released on January 20, 1981, the day Carter left office and Ronald Reagan was inaugurated.

direction of public policy than to try to analyze all the factors underlying such policy.

An intriguing explanation of why the public's expectations have become so exaggerated is Thomas Cronin's work on the **textbook presidency,** or the portrait that textbooks paint of the president's role. Cronin makes a compelling case that texts have played a significant role in giving Americans unrealistic expectations about the presidency. In his examination of college-level texts of the 1950s and 1960s, Cronin found that the authors consistently inflated the powers and responsibilities of the office. For example, he cites one text on the presidency as saying, ''There is virtually no limit to what the President can do if he does it for democratic ends and by democratic means.''[17]

Cronin found in these texts a general pattern in which the president is identified as the central figure in national and international politics. He is the ''strategic catalyst for progress,'' the ''engine of change to move this nation forward.'' Roosevelt pulled the nation out of the depths of the Depression. Eisenhower went to Korea and stopped the war there. Kennedy pledged that America would put a man on the moon within a decade.[18] The tone of these books suggests that we need great presidents to solve great problems (see Color Insert C, plate 8).

By the 1970s, textbook descriptions of the presidency began to change. With the Vietnam War and the Watergate scandal, the presidency went through a period of reappraisal. Some scholars considered Vietnam a ''presidential war'' because, as noted earlier, there was no congressional declaration of war. To many this seemed to be an abuse of the president's inherent powers. And nothing could have been more disillusioning about the presidency than Watergate. Nixon's willingness to conspire with his aides to cover up crimes by political associates stands in stark contrast to the trust Americans have traditionally placed in the office.

Bound for Glory
Ronald Reagan is very effective at drawing on the symbols and pageantry of the presidency. In this whistle-stop campaign swing through Ohio in 1984, he gave his speeches from the same Pullman car that Harry Truman used in his famous come-from-behind victory over Republican Thomas Dewey in 1948.

This reassessment of the presidency led to critical studies with titles like *The Imperial Presidency*[19] and *Choosing Our King.*[20] A more balanced view of the presidency emerged, and scholars now emphasize the constraints on the presidency, as well as its potential for good. But myths die hard, and it will take many years for the revised textbook presidency to take hold in people's minds. The public still seems to believe that the president is the "engine of change." As Americans yearn for a change in the quality of their lives or in the direction of public policy, they still see the president as the vehicle for accomplishing what they want, no matter how difficult or even impossible the task. Thus, when Reagan promised in the 1980 campaign that he would significantly cut taxes, dramatically increase defense spending, not cut necessary services to the poor and elderly, and balance the budget by 1984, the American public was ready to believe he could do it. Wanting an economic miracle, they elected not just a mere mortal, but someone they hoped would be a miracle worker.

Unfortunately, the more we expect from presidents, the greater the likelihood that we will be disappointed. The growth of presidential responsibilities and the growth of excessive expectations makes it easier for presidents to be measured as failures. Indeed, one presidential scholar goes so far as to argue that "the presidency has become an impossible job."[21]

PRESIDENTIAL ELECTIONS: THE ELECTORAL CONNECTION

Our faith in American democracy is based on the belief that a link exists between the sentiments of voters and the actions of elected officials. How is that link forged? How does a president put together his electoral coalition?

The Electoral College

The Constitution requires only that a candidate for the office of president be a natural-born citizen, at least thirty-five years old, who has actually lived in the United States for a minimum of fourteen years. The delegates to the Constitutional Convention decided not to let individual voters choose the president directly. Instead, the delegates devised a system in which electors are chosen in their states, and those electors in turn vote for the president. The assumption was that the electors would be educated leaders and would show better judgment in their choices for president than would rank-and-file citizens. The founders did not, however, anticipate that political parties would develop and that voters would soon be able to cast their ballots for electors openly supporting a party candidate. One legacy of the system of having electors cast ballots on behalf of voters in their states does remain, however. Occasionally an elector fails to follow the voters' preference. The electors have complete freedom; they are bound neither to a candidate nor to a party. In 1972, one elector from Virginia voted for John Hospers of the Libertarian party rather than for Richard Nixon. This left Nixon with 520 electoral votes.[22]

In the **electoral college,** each state is accorded one vote for each of its senators and representatives. California, the state with the largest population, has forty-seven electoral votes in the electoral college — a total of its forty-five representatives and two senators. Six small states qualify for only one representative and therefore have only three electoral votes each. (The Twenty-Third Amendment to the Constitution awards three electoral votes to the District of Columbia, even though it elects no voting members of Congress.) After each census, the number of electoral votes for each state is recalculated to reflect population changes that may reduce or increase the number of representatives the state sends to Washington.

In recent years, the greatest population growth has come in the so-called Sunbelt states (the South, the Southwest, and California); consequently, their proportionate share of electoral votes has grown as well. This increase has come at the expense of the Frostbelt states of the Northeast and Midwest (see Figure 11.2).

If no candidate receives a majority when the electoral college votes, the election is thrown into the House of Representatives. The House votes by state, with each state casting one vote for a single presidential candidate. (This means that Delaware, for example, has the same voting strength as New York.) The candidates for election by the House are the top three finishers in the general election. A presidential election has gone to the House only twice in American history, the first time in 1800 and the second in 1824. Both cases occurred before a stable two-party system had developed.

The most troubling aspect of the electoral college is the possibility that, despite winning a plurality or even a majority of popular votes, a candidate could lose the election in the electoral college. These losses can result when one candidate wins many of his states by a very large amount, while the other candidate wins many of his states by a slim margin. Whether a candidate wins a state by 5 votes or 500,000 votes, he wins *all* that state's electoral votes.* Indeed, this has happened in three elections, most recently in 1888, when Grover Cleveland received 48.6 percent of the popular vote to Benjamin Harrison's 47.9 percent. Cleveland nevertheless trailed Harrison in the electoral college, 168 to 233, and Harrison was elected president.

This peculiar feature of our system has led to calls for abolition of the electoral college. Reformers argue that it is simply wrong to have a system that allows a candidate who receives the most popular votes to lose the election. Would the next president be regarded as the legitimate "winner" by the American people if he or she received a minority of popular votes? Reform plans that call for direct election of the president would institute a purely majoritarian means of choosing the president. However, defenders of the electoral college point out that this system, warts and all, has been a stable one. It might be riskier to replace it with a new arrangement that could alter our party system or the way presidential campaigns are conducted. Tradition has in fact prevailed, and recent proposals for fundamental reform have come nowhere close to adoption.

---

*The one exception is in Maine, where 2 of the state's 4 electoral votes are awarded by congressional district. The presidential condidate who carries each district wins a single electoral vote.

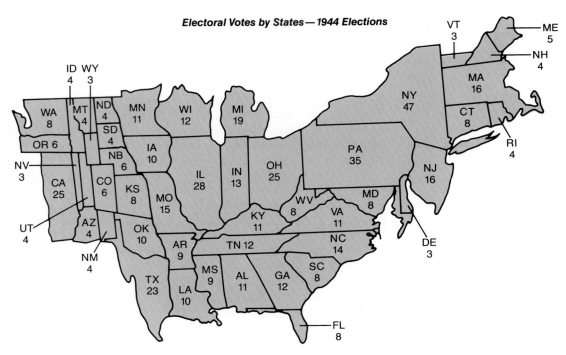

Electoral Votes by States — 1944 Elections

Population Shifts and the Electoral College
As the population has moved away from the Frostbelt and into the Sunbelt, the electoral college clout of the northern industrial states has diminished. At the same time, the Sunbelt states of Florida, Texas, and California have become more significant in national elections. The size of each state in these maps reflects its proportion of votes in the electoral college.

Figure 11.2

Winning the Presidency

In his farewell address to the nation, Jimmy Carter lashed out at the interest groups that had bedeviled his presidency. Interest groups, he said, "distort our purposes because the national interest is not always the sum of all our single or special interests." Carter went on to note the president's singular responsibility: "The president is the only elected official charged with representing all the people."[23] Carter, like all other presidents, was quick to recognize the dilemma of majoritarianism versus pluralism when he took office. The president must try to please countless separate constituencies while at the same time trying to do what is best for the whole country.

It is easy to stand on the sidelines and say that presidents should always try to follow a majoritarian path — pursuing policies that reflect the preferences of most citizens. Simply by running for office, candidates align themselves with particular segments of the population. As a result of their electoral strategy, their identification with activists in their party, and their own political views, candidates come into office with an interest in pleasing some constituencies more than others.

Electoral Votes by States—1984 Elections

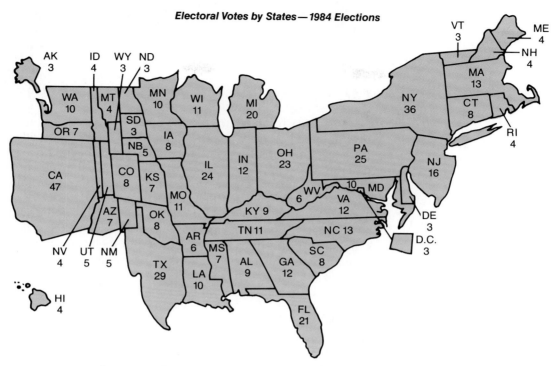

Source: *Presidential Elections Since 1784* (Washington, D.C.: Congressional Quarterly, 1975), p. 35, and *Elections '84* (Washington, D.C.: Congressional Quarterly, 1984), p. 78. James Q. Wilson, *American Government: Institutions and Policies,* 3rd edition. © 1986 D.C. Heath and Company, p. 321. Used with permission.

Each candidate attempts to put together a winning electoral college co-alition that will give at least the minimum 270 (out of 538) votes needed for election. The two major party candidates begin with a traditional base of party support, which they then try to expand. Republican candidates know that the western states have favored their party in recent presidential elections. A Democrat looks to the industrial states of the Northeast for the foundation of an electoral coalition. A candidate does not appeal to states, of course, but to the kinds of voters concentrated in them. For a Democrat like 1984 presidential nominee Walter Mondale, organized labor, which is stronger in the Northeast than in the West, is a major building block of any winning coalition.

As the campaign proceeds, the candidates try to win votes by appealing to different groups of voters through their stands on various issues. They promise that when they take office they will take certain actions that will appeal to people holding a particular view on an issue. For example, among the many stands Reagan took as a candidate during the 1980 campaign were positions against affirmative action, against court-ordered busing for school integration, for a constitutional amendment outlawing abortion, against "excessive" environmentalism that threatens economic growth, against gay rights ordinances, for a constitutional amendment permitting school prayer, against gun control, against a peacetime draft, for quick decontrol of oil and gas prices, for a 30 percent cut on individual income taxes, and for abolishing the Department of Education.[24] For Reagan and other candidates, such policy stands are typically related to long-held views about government and are not simply expedient ways to attract voters.

Just as each candidate attracts voters with his stands on particular issues, he will offend others who are committed to the opposite side of these issues. Reagan's emphasis on economic growth, which downplayed the need for environmental protection, surely helped him win the votes of businesspeople. On the other hand, it gave those concerned about environmental problems more reason to vote for the Democratic candidate, Carter. Because issue stands can cut both ways—attracting some voters and driving others away—candidates are often tempted to finesse an issue by being deliberately vague. Candidates might hope that voters will put their own interpretations on ambiguous stands. If the tactic works, the candidate will attract some voters without offending others. During the 1968 campaign, Nixon said he was committed to ending the war in Vietnam, but gave few details about how he would accomplish that end. He wanted to appeal not only to those who were in favor of military pressure against the North Vietnamese but also to those who wanted quick military disengagement.[25]

Candidates cannot, however, be deliberately vague about all issues. A candidate who is noncommittal on too many issues appears wishy-washy or indecisive. And future presidents do not build their political careers without working strongly for and becoming associated with important issues and constituencies. As a result, presidents enter office with both a majority of voters on their side and a close identification with particular issue constituencies.

... And Losing It

Winning the voters' support and keeping it are two different ball games. The electoral "mandate" that the voters have given the winning candidate is a rather vague directive for presidential action, and this mandate tends to become more and more fragile over time. As noted earlier, presidential popularity can be eroded by a coalition of minorities.

Even a landslide at the polls does not ensure solid, consistent support throughout a president's term. Lyndon Johnson crushed his Republican opponent, Barry Goldwater, in the 1964 election, winning 61 percent of the popular vote and all but six states. Nevertheless, that popularity went into a steep decline in response to the growing unpopularity of the war in Vietnam and a backlash against Johnson's liberal social welfare programs. Even his remarkable influence with Congress began to dissipate. The Democrats lost forty-seven seats in the House in the congressional elections of 1966; this in turn made it even harder for the president to lead. In the spring of 1968, with his administration under fire and a strong challenge brewing within his own party against his renomination, Johnson withdrew from the presidential race.

A major problem that the president faces in translating his mandate into action is the separation of powers that makes Congress independent of the executive branch. His own party may not even have majorities in the two houses. Not once during the eight years of the Nixon and Ford presidencies did the Republicans control the House or the Senate. But even presidents who have majorities in both houses of Congress may find their congressional "allies" unwilling to follow on some major issues. Committee and party leaders have their own, independent electoral bases, and their electoral fortunes are largely independent of the president's.

With constraints on their ability to move Congress, the inevitable unpopular choices that presidents must make, and the real difficulties involved in actually *solving* problems, presidents may find it extremely hard to meet all the goals they set for their administrations. With all this in mind, one might easily agree with the argument that the presidency is an "impossible job." Yet not all presidents are doomed to failure. Dwight Eisenhower left office after eight years with relatively high popularity with the American people. And, despite alienating many constituencies in his first term, Ronald Reagan was able to convince a large majority of Americans that his policies were necessary medicine for a sick economy. After a strong economic upturn preceding the 1984 election, he won a strong endorsement for his administration's general approach when he beat Walter Mondale in a landslide (see Table 11.2).

Table 11.2

One-Term Presidents, Two-Term Presidents
Since the Twenty-Second Amendment to the Constitution was passed in the wake of Franklin Roosevelt's unprecedented election to a fourth term, presidents have been forbidden to run for a third term. The amendment first applied to Eisenhower, but he was the last president to serve two full terms. Ronald Reagan is bucking recent history, though, and at this writing he is close to filling out a full two terms.

President	Reason for Leaving
Dwight Eisenhower (1953–1961)	Served limit of two full terms.
John Kennedy (1961–1963)	Assassinated in Dallas, Texas, on November 22, 1963.
Lyndon Johnson* (1963–1969)	Withdrew from race for Democratic nomination after challenger, Senator Eugene McCarthy, scored well in the New Hampshire primary.
Richard Nixon (1969–1974)	Forced to resign after evidence implicated him in criminal conspiracy associated with the Watergate break-in.
Gerald Ford (1974–1977)	Defeated by Jimmy Carter in the general election.
Jimmy Carter (1977–1981)	Defeated by Ronald Reagan in the general election.
Ronald Reagan (1981–)	Re-elected in 1984.

*If a vice president assumes the presidency with fewer than two years of the previous president's term left, he is permitted to run for two full terms of his own. In this case, however, Johnson chose not to run for a second full term.

THE EXECUTIVE BRANCH ESTABLISHMENT

As a president tries to maintain the support of his electoral coalition through the policies he pursues, he is able to draw on the great resources of the executive branch of government. Inside the White House, the president has his own staff to help him formulate policy. Of course, there is the vice president, whose duties within the administration vary according to his relationship with the president. The president's cabinet secretaries—the heads of the major departments of the federal government—play a number of roles, including a critical management function in administering the programs falling within their jurisdiction. Finally, within the departments and agencies and operating at a level below that of the president's appointees, are the career bureaucrats. These bureaucrats (who will be discussed in the next chapter), have great expertise in program operations to offer to the administration in power.

The White House Staff

A president depends heavily on his key aides. They advise him on his most crucial political choices, devise the general strategy the administration will follow in pursuing congressional and public support, and control access to the president to ensure that he has enough time for his most important tasks. Consequently, he needs to trust and respect these top staffers; many of an entering president's inner circle of assistants will be long-time associates.

Presidents typically have a chief of staff, who may be a first among equals or, in some administrations, dominant in the staff. H. R. Haldeman, Nixon's chief of staff, played this stronger role, with unquestioned authority to run the White House for the president. He ran a highly disciplined operation,

The Reagan Team
Each president organizes his staff in the way that suits his own needs and preferences. During Ronald Reagan's first term, he had three key aides at the top of his senior staff. In his second term, he has had a strong chief of staff, Donald Regan (second from the right of the president), atop the staff hierarchy.

frequently prodding staff members to work harder and faster. Haldeman also felt that part of his role was to "take the heat" for the president by assuming responsibility for many of the more unpopular decisions that were made. "Every president needs a son of a bitch, and I'm Nixon's."[26] Hamilton Jordan, chief of staff during the Carter administration, did not dominate the White House staff in the same way. His primary job "was to settle interagency conflict and make sure that the implementation of presidential policy was well supervised."[27]

Presidents also have a national security adviser to provide them with a daily briefing on foreign and military affairs and longer-range analyses on issues confronting the administration. A Council of Economic Advisers is also located in the White House. One or more senior domestic policy advisers help the president determine the administration's basic approach to such areas as health, education, and social services. Below these top aides are large staffs that serve them and the president. These staffs are organized around certain functional specialties. Some staff members work on "political" matters, such as liaison with interest groups, relations with ethnic and religious minorities, and party affairs. There is a staff that deals exclusively with the press and a legislative liaison staff to help push the administration's bills through Congress. The large Office of Management and Budget (OMB) analyzes budget requests, is involved in the policymaking process, and examines agency management practices. This extended White House executive establishment is known as the **Executive Office of the President**.

There is no agreed-upon "right way" for a president to organize his White House staff. Each president makes changes from the previous operation to create the structure that will work best for him. Eisenhower, the former general, wanted clear lines of authority and a hierarchical structure that mirrored a military command. One factor that influences how a president uses his senior staff is the degree to which he delegates authority to them. Jimmy Carter immersed himself in the policymaking process to ensure that he made all the significant decisions. Early in his administration, he told his staff, "Unless there's a holocaust, I'll take care of everything the same day it comes in."[28] (This explains in large part why Hamilton Jordan's role as chief of staff was less powerful than Haldeman's during the Nixon years.) President Ronald Reagan has delegated much more to his staff, preferring to concentrate on the broad issues facing his administration. Some say, however, that Reagan has delegated too much and does not spend enough time analyzing policy options.

Despite the formal organization of the White House staff, it suffers from the same "turf wars" that plague other large organizations. This struggle over authority stems not only from personal ambition and political differences, but also from overlapping jurisdictions. One common source of conflict is between the secretary of state (a member of the cabinet) and the president's national security adviser; each wants primacy in influencing the administration's foreign policy. Henry Kissinger, who served as Nixon's national security adviser, was extraordinarily shrewd in devising ways to gain advantage over Secretary of State William Rogers. One of his tactics, for example, was to create "backchannels" through which information from the field would come to him secretly, bypassing the Department of State. Kissinger did this "not

Consultation in the Oval Office

Henry Kissinger (pictured in the center) was an influential foreign policy adviser for two presidents. He served as national security adviser for Richard Nixon and then as Nixon's secretary of state. He remained as secretary of state in the Ford administration. During this period, Kissinger played a critical role in developing policies toward the Vietnam War, détente with the Soviet Union, and relations with China.

only to keep control of an ongoing negotiation but also to prevent his peers and subordinates from finding out what was going on."[29] Presidents, however, often find it more useful to hear competing policy views than to depend on one person.

The Vice President

The vice president's primary function is to serve as standby equipment, only a heartbeat away from the presidency itself (see Feature 11.2). Traditionally, vice presidents have not been used in any important advisory capacity. Instead, presidents tend to give them political chores—campaigning, fund raising, and "stroking" the party faithful. This is often the case because vice presidential candidates are chosen for reasons that have more to do with the political campaign than with governing the nation. One of the primary reasons Richard Nixon chose Spiro Agnew, a relatively inexperienced governor of Maryland, to be his running mate in 1968 was that Agnew would not outshine the colorless Nixon. John Kennedy chose Lyndon Johnson of Texas for the vice presidential slot in 1960 because he thought Johnson would help him carry the South. Johnson proved to be of help in the election, but once Kennedy was in office, he made little use of his vice president. After Johnson became president, he was sometimes openly contemptuous of his own vice president, Hubert Humphrey of Minnesota. One participant at a meeting recalled the following interaction:

> President Johnson allotted the loquacious Hubert H. Humphrey five minutes in which to speak (*"Five minutes,* Hubert!"); then Johnson stood by, eyes fixed on the sweep second hand of his watch, while Humphrey spoke, and when the Vice President went over the limit, pushed him, still talking, out of the room with his own hands.[30]

An exception to the usual pattern was Jimmy Carter's vice president, Walter Mondale. Carter was wise enough to realize that Mondale's experience in the Senate could be of great value to him, especially since Carter had never served in Congress. Ronald Reagan has also given George Bush substantive work to do, though Bush does not seem to play as major a role as Mondale did. How a president uses his vice president often depends less on objective criteria than on the chemistry between the two people.

Feature 11.2

Who's President When the President Can't Be?

What happens if a president dies in office? The vice president, of course, becomes the new president. But what happens if the vice president died earlier or left office for some reason? What happens if the president becomes senile or is disabled by illness? These are questions that the authors of the Constitution failed to resolve.

The nuclear age has made these questions more troubling. When President Woodrow Wilson suffered a stroke in 1919, it meant that the country was without effective leadership for a time, but the lack of an active president during that period did not endanger the lives of all Americans. Today, with the possibility of nuclear attack, national security dictates that the nation have a commander in chief at all times. The Twenty-Fifth Amendment, which was ratified in 1967, specifies a mechanism for replacing a living president in case he cannot carry out the duties of his office. A president can declare himself unable to carry on, or the vice president and the cabinet can decide collectively that the president is incapacitated. In either case, the vice president becomes acting president and assumes all powers of the office. In 1981, when President Reagan was seriously wounded in an assassination attempt and had to undergo emergency surgery, the Twenty-Fifth Amendment was not invoked by the vice president and the cabinet. Four years later, when Reagan underwent cancer surgery, he sent a letter to Vice President George Bush transferring the power of the office to him at the moment the president was anesthetized. Eight hours later, Reagan reclaimed his authority. Under the Twenty-Fifth Amendment, if the president and the cabinet disagree about whether he is able to resume his duties, Congress must ultimately decide.

The Twenty-Fifth Amendment also provides that the president select a new vice president in the event that office becomes vacant; the president's choice must be approved by a majority of both houses of Congress. Gerald Ford became vice president in this manner when Spiro Agnew resigned after pleading no contest to charges of income tax evasion and accepting bribes. Later, when Richard Nixon resigned, Ford chose Nelson Rockefeller as his vice president.

The Cabinet

The president's **cabinet** is composed of the heads of the departments in the executive branch (see Table 11.3) and a small number of other key officials, such as the head of the Office of Management and Budget and the ambassador to the United Nations. The cabinet has expanded greatly since Washington formed his initial cabinet of the attorney general and the secretaries of state, treasury, and war. Clearly, the growth of the cabinet reflects the growth of government responsibility and intervention in areas such as energy, housing, and transportation.

In theory, the members of the cabinet constitute an advisory body that meets with the president to debate major policy decisions. In practice, however, cabinet meetings have been described as "vapid non-events in which there has been a deliberate non-exchange of information as part of a process of mutual nonconsultation."[31] One Carter cabinet member called meetings "adult Show-and-Tell."[32] Why is this so? First, the cabinet has become rather large. Counting department heads, other officials of cabinet rank, and presidential aides, it becomes a body of at least twenty people—a size that many presidents find unwieldy for the give-and-take of political decisionmaking. Second, most cabinet members have limited areas of expertise and simply cannot contribute much to deliberations on areas they know little about. The secretary of defense, for example, would probably be a poor choice to help decide important issues of agricultural policy. Third, although cabinet members have impressive backgrounds, they are not necessarily personally close to the president or easy for him to work with. The president often chooses

Table 11.3
The Cabinet

Department	Created
State	1789
Treasury	1789
Defense†	1789
Justice‡	1789
Interior	1849
Agriculture	1862
Commerce	1913
Labor	1913
Health and Human Services*	1953
Housing and Urban Development	1965
Transportation	1966
Energy	1977
Education	1979

*The Department of Health, Education, and Welfare became the Department of Health and Human Services in 1979 when an independent Department of Education was established.

†The War Department was created in 1789. The Defense Department was created in 1949.

‡The attorney general was a member of the first cabinet. The Justice Department was established in 1870.

Source: *Statistical Abstract of the United States: 1985* (Washington, D.C.: U.S. Bureau of the Census, 1984), p. 311.

cabinet members on the basis of their reputations, and he often does not know them beforehand. His choices may also be guided by a need to give his cabinet some racial, ethnic, geographical, sexual, or religious balance.

Finally, modern presidents do not rely on the cabinet to make policy because they have such large White House staffs, which offer most of the advisory support they need. In contrast to cabinet secretaries, who may be pulled in different directions by the wishes of the president and the wishes of their department's clientele groups, White House staffers are likely to see themselves as responsible to the president alone. Thus, despite the periodic calls for the cabinet to play more of a role as a collective decisionmaking body, cabinet meetings seem doomed to be little more than academic exercises. In practice, presidents prefer the flexibility of drawing on ad hoc groups, specialized White House staffs, and the advisers and cabinet secretaries with whom they feel most comfortable.

More broadly, presidents use their personal staffs and the larger Executive Office of the President to centralize control over the entire executive branch. The vast size of the executive branch and the number and complexity of decisions that must be made each day pose a challenge to the White House. President Reagan, for example, has used a new staff unit in the Office of Management and Budget to review proposals by regulatory agencies. In sum, to make the most of the White House's political goals and policy preferences, modern presidents have encouraged their various staffs to play increasingly important roles in executive branch decisionmaking.[33]

THE PRESIDENT AS NATIONAL LEADER

With an election behind him and the resources of his office at hand, a president is ready to lead the nation. Each president enters office with a general vision of how the government should approach policy issues. During his term, a president spends much of his time trying to get Congress to enact legislation that incorporates his general philosophy and specific policy preferences.

From Political Values . . .

Presidents differ greatly in their views of the role of government. Lyndon Johnson had a strong liberal ideology on domestic affairs, believing that government has a responsibility to help disadvantaged Americans. After his landslide victory in 1964, Johnson articulated his vision of justice in his inaugural address:

> . . . justice was the promise that all who made the journey would share in the fruits of the land.
>
> In a land of wealth, families must not live in hopeless poverty. In a land rich in harvest, children just must not go hungry. In a land of healing miracles, neighbors must not suffer and die untended. In a great land of learning and scholars, young people must be taught to read and write.
>
> For more than thirty years that I have served this nation, I have believed that this injustice to our people, this waste of our resources, was our real enemy. For thirty years or more, with the resources I have had, I have vigilantly fought against it.[34]

The Transfer of Power
Vice President Lyndon Johnson was with President John Kennedy during his fateful visit to Dallas for some political fence-mending with Texas Democrats. After Kennedy was pronounced dead at Parkland Hospital, Johnson returned to the airport, where federal judge Sarah Hughes (lower left) boarded Air Force One to administer the presidential oath of office. Standing next to Johnson was Lady Bird, his wife (left), and Kennedy's widow, Jacqueline (right). Five days after he was sworn in, Johnson gave a nationally televised address before a joint session of Congress. In a memorable phrase symbolizing the stability of the presidency, Johnson declared, ''Let us continue.''

Johnson used *justice* and *injustice* as code words for *equality* and *inequality*. They were used six times in his entire speech, whereas *freedom* was used only twice. Johnson used the mandate from his landslide and the resources of his office to press for a ''just'' America, or what he termed ''The Great Society.''

To achieve his Great Society, Johnson sent Congress an unparalleled package of liberal legislation. He launched such projects as the Job Corps (which created centers and camps offering vocational training and work experience to youths aged sixteen to twenty-one); Medicare (which provided medical care for the elderly); and the National Teacher Corps (which funded teachers to work in impoverished neighborhoods). Supported by huge Democratic majorities in Congress during 1965 and 1966, he had tremendous success in getting his proposals through. Liberalism was in full swing.

Exactly twenty years after Johnson's inaugural speech, Ronald Reagan took his oath of office for the second time and then addressed the nation. Reagan reasserted his conservative philosophy. He emphasized *freedom*, using the term fourteen times, and failed to mention *justice* or *equality* once. In the following excerpts, the term *freedom* is highlighted for easy reference:

> By 1980, we knew it was time to renew our faith, to strive with all our strength toward the ultimate in individual *freedom* consistent with an orderly society. . . . We will not rest until every American enjoys the fullness of *freedom*, dignity, and opportunity as our birthright. . . . Americans . . . turned the tide of history away from totalitarian darkness and into the warm sunlight of human *freedom*. . . . Let

history say of us, these were golden years—when the American Revolution was reborn, when *freedom* gained new life, when America reached for her best. . . . *freedom* and incentives unleash the drive and entrepreneurial genius that are at the core of human progress. . . . From new *freedom* will spring new opportunities for growth. . . . Yet history has shown that peace does not come, nor will our *freedom* be preserved by good will alone. There are those in the world who scorn our vision of human dignity and *freedom*. . . . Human *freedom* is on the march, and nowhere more so than in our own hemisphere. *Freedom* is one of the deepest and noblest aspirations of the human spirit. . . . America must remain *freedom's* staunchest friend, for *freedom* is our best ally. . . . Every victory for human *freedom* will be a victory for world peace. . . . One people under God, dedicated to the dream of *freedom* that He has placed in the human heart.[35]

Reagan turned Johnson's philosophy on its head, declaring that "government is not the solution to our problem. Government is the problem." During his presidency, Reagan worked to undo many welfare and social service programs. For example, Reagan proposed in 1981 that funding for the Job Corps be reduced by 40 percent, though Congress refused to go along. He was more successful in getting Congress to cut back on food stamps (a program started during the Kennedy administration) through reduced benefits and eligibility restrictions. Food stamp legislation called for outlays to be reduced by 14 percent over the next three years.[36]

. . . To Policy Agenda

The roots of particular policy proposals can thus be traced to the more general political ideology of the president. He surely outlined that philosophy of government during his campaign for the White House. But when the hot rhetoric of the presidential campaign meets the cold reality of what is possible in Washington, the newly elected president must make some hard choices about what he will push for during the coming term. These choices are reflected in the bills the president submits to Congress, as well as in the degree to which he works for their passage. The president's bills, introduced by his allies in the House and Senate, always receive a good deal of initial attention. In the words of one Washington lobbyist, "when a president sends up a bill, it takes first place in the queue. All other bills take second place."[37]

The president's role in legislative leadership is largely a twentieth-century phenomenon. Not until after the Budget and Accounting Act of 1921 was passed did executive branch departments and agencies have to clear their proposed budget bills with the White House. Before this, the president did not even coordinate proposals for how much the executive branch would spend on all the programs it administered. Later, Franklin Roosevelt required that, in addition to budget bills, all other major legislative proposals by an agency or department be cleared by the White House. No longer could a department submit a bill without White House support.[38]

Roosevelt's impact on the relationship between the president and Congress went far beyond this new administrative arrangement for coordinating legislative proposals. With the nation in the midst of the Depression that began in 1929, Roosevelt moved boldly when he took office in 1933 with an ambitious array of legislative proposals. During the first hundred days Congress was in session, it enacted fifteen significant laws, including the

Agricultural Adjustment Act, the Civilian Conservation Corps, and the National Industrial Recovery Act. Never had a president demanded — and received — so much from Congress. Roosevelt's legacy was that the president would henceforth provide aggressive leadership for Congress by providing it with his own legislative program.

Although the president's central role in our political system guarantees that he can always command attention for his agenda, his first year in office is crucial to his program's overall success. As you have seen, the president enters office with the support of a majority of citizens; if his popularity drops, however, his honeymoon with Congress can end quickly. Whereas the coalition of minorities expands to chip away slowly at the president's majority support, his popularity can quickly plummet when major problems of general importance are not solved — even if they are beyond the president's control. An obvious example is the rise in oil prices that led to surging inflation during the Carter administration.

After his first election in 1980, Reagan was warned by David Stockman, who would become director of the Office of Management and Budget, that it was important for the administration to get up to speed quickly. "Things could go very badly during the first year, resulting in incalculable erosion of GOP momentum, unity, and public confidence."[39] The administration did act decisively, and quick passage of Reagan's budget and tax cuts produced key victories and a great deal of respect for the new president.

The President as Chief Lobbyist

When presidents like Roosevelt and Truman first became heavily involved in preparing legislative packages, political scientists were apt to describe the process as one in which "the president proposes and the Congress disposes." In other words, once the president sends his legislation to Capitol Hill, Congress decides on its own what to do with it. Over time, though, presidents have become increasingly active in all stages of the legislative process. The president is expected not only to propose legislation, but also to make sure that it passes. His role as "chief lobbyist" is illustrated by John Kennedy's first year in office, during which time he

> held thirty-two Tuesday morning breakfasts with congressional leadership, ninety private conversations with congressional leaders that lasted an hour or two, coffee hours with 500 legislators, bill signing ceremonies with a similar number, and in all approximately 2,500 separate contacts with congressmen exclusive of correspondence.[40]

The president's efforts to influence Congress are reinforced by a staff of specialists on his legislative liaison staff. In addition to liaison personnel in the White House, all departments and major agencies have legislative specialists as well. These department and agency people work with the White House staff, which coordinates the administration's lobbying on major issues.

The **legislative liaison staff** is the communications link between the White House and Congress. As a bill makes its way slowly through Congress, liaison staffers advise the president or a cabinet secretary on the problems that are emerging. They specify what parts of a bill are in trouble and may have to be modified or dropped. They tell their boss what amendments are likely to be offered, which members of Congress need lobbying, and what the chances are for passage of the bill with or without certain provisions. Decisions must then be reached about how the administration should respond to such developments. For example, when the Reagan White House realized it was still a few votes short of victory on a budget bill in the House, it reversed its opposition to a sugar price-support bill. This attracted the votes of representatives from Louisiana and Florida, two sugar-growing states, for the budget bill. The White House preferred not to call what happened a "deal" but noted that "adjustments and considerations" had been made[41] (see Figure 11.3).

Figure 11.3 ━━━

Support for the President in Congressional Voting
The extent to which individual representatives and senators support the president in their congressional voting patterns can be measured by the presidential support score, *computed by* Congressional Quarterly, *a Washington, D.C., publication that specializes in reporting on Congress.* Congressional Quarterly *reviews all the public messages and statements of the president to determine what legislation he favored and opposed. After analyzing all recorded roll call votes in a session of Congress,* Congressional Quarterly *assigns to each representative and senator a presidential support score, indicating the percentage of time that the member backed the president's position during the session. The graph shows that, regardless of party, the average member of the House and Senate supported the president somewhat more than half the time. When the list is broken down by party, a clear pattern emerges: Republican members are far more likely to support Republican presidents, and Democratic members, to support Democratic presidents.*

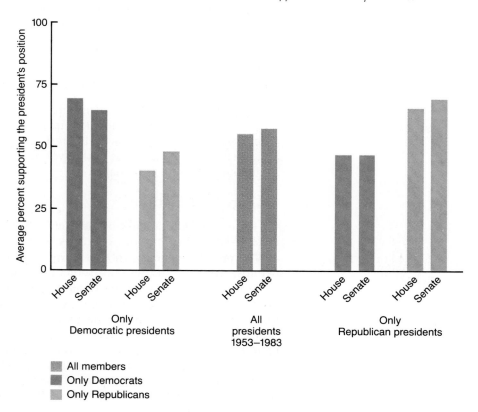

A certain amount of the president's job is stereotypical "arm twisting" — pushing reluctant legislators to vote a certain way. Yet most day-in, day-out interactions tend to be more subtle, as liaison staff tries to build consensus around a bill by working cooperatively with members of Congress. When a congressional committee is working on a bill, liaison people talk to committee members individually, to see what concerns they have and to help fashion a compromise if some of the members differ with the president's position. As one experienced White House lobbyist put it, "I think it is important to try to develop an individual relationship with the members, to get to know their problems and what their interests are and to gain their confidence."[42]

The White House also works directly with interest groups in its efforts to build support for legislation. Presidential aides try to persuade the Washington lobbyists of groups interested in particular bills to activate the most effective lobbyists of all: the voters back home. Interest groups can quickly reach the constituents who are most concerned about a bill. One White House aide said with admiration, "The Realtors can send out half a million Mailgrams within 24 hours. . . . If they have a hundred target congressmen, they can get out 100,000 Mailgrams targeted by district."[43]

Although much of the presidential staff's work with Congress is done in a cooperative spirit, agreement cannot always be reached. When Congress passes a bill the president opposes, he may veto it and send it back to Congress. As noted earlier, Congress can override a veto with a two-thirds majority of those voting in each house. Presidents use their veto power sparingly, but the threat that a president will veto an unacceptable bill increases his bargaining leverage with members of Congress as he pushes them to accept a policy compromise more to his liking.

THE PRESIDENT AS WORLD LEADER

The president's leadership responsibilities extend beyond the Congress and the nation, into the international arena. Each administration tries to further what it sees as the United States' interests in relations with allies, adversaries, and the developing countries of the world. In this role, the president can act as diplomat or as crisis manager.

Foreign Relations

Presidents like to think of themselves as leaders of the Western democracies — the noncommunist countries of Europe, Japan, Canada, Australia, and a few other nations. (As you learned in Chapter 2, there are only about twenty to thirty countries that fit the different criteria political scientists use to define a democracy.) The president does become the focal point for the Western bloc's relations with the Soviet Union and China, the two communist superpowers. There is no formal alliance of all the Western democracies, but the United States has entered into military alliances with many of them. The most important of these is the North Atlantic Treaty Organization (NATO), composed of the United States, Canada, and most of the countries of Western Europe. These countries depend on our nuclear shield and troop commitments as deterrents to potential aggression.

A New Era
Richard Nixon's dramatic trip to the People's Republic of China in 1972 signaled an end to the Cold War hostility between the United States and the communist regime. Nixon and Chinese premier Zhou Enlai toast the beginning of friendlier relations between the two countries.

Although the leadership of the United States is based on this nation's long-term economic and military might, the president has little formal diplomatic control over other democratic countries. America's allies have interests of their own and strong internal reasons for wanting to remain independent of this country. Inherent nationalism, economic necessity, differing political philosophies, and the vision of their own leaders give countries like France, Italy, and England reasons to stake out an independent role in world politics. France and West Germany, for example, have taken significant steps on their own to improve relations with the Soviet Union and with the countries of Eastern Europe aligned with Moscow.

As in his dealings with Congress, a president must lead the allies with his powers of persuasion. He must act deftly, pushing the various heads of state to follow America's lead in foreign policy, but not pressuring them so much that they become resentful and uncooperative. Jimmy Carter's effort to boycott the 1980 Olympic games in Moscow illustrates the difficulty recent presidents have had in leading the allies. After the Soviet Union sent its troops into neighboring Afghanistan because it feared that a hostile regime might come to power, President Carter felt that the Western democracies needed to respond to the Soviet aggression. Despite widespread anger and revulsion over the Soviet Union's actions, many allies (such as France and Great Britain) did not comply with Carter's request to boycott the games and went ahead and sent their athletes to Moscow.

Presidential diplomatic skills are tested in another way in their relations with the Soviet Union, the other great nuclear power. The president must regard the Soviet Union as an adversary but at the same time develop a

The Handshake of Peace
One of the crowning achievements of Jimmy Carter's presidency was the role he played in helping to forge a peace treaty between Egypt and Israel. Egyptian president Anwar Sadat (left) and Israeli prime minister Menachem Begin (right) came to the presidential retreat at Camp David in Maryland. For thirteen days Carter was a mediator in the negotiations between the two sides. After the historic accords were reached, the three flew by helicopter to the White House, where they signed the initial agreements.

sound working relationship with its leaders. The primary concern of the president—and of his counterpart, the leader of the Communist party in the Soviet Union—is achieving the right level of armament and arms control. Each country wants to remain militarily strong, but each also has a real interest in limiting the arms race because of spiraling costs, the worry that the other country might achieve a clear weapons superiority, and a general desire to reduce international tensions.

Presidents are constrained in directing our relations with the Soviet Union by public opinion, Congress, and this country's longstanding anticommunist ideology. As presidents and their advisers develop policy, they anticipate the reactions of critics. Yet recent presidents have also played an important role in leading the United States out of the Cold War—the years following World War II when there was enormous distrust of and hostility toward the Soviet Union. President Nixon pursued *détente*, an easing of tensions between the two countries, which resulted in an arms control agreement (SALT I). Ford and Carter pursued détente as well, leading to the SALT II accords during the Carter administration. (SALT II was never ratified by the Senate, but the two countries continue to pledge adherence to it. In 1986, however, the Reagan administration said it was prepared to abandon the accords, while at the same time it pushed for further arms control negotiations with the Soviets.)

It is also the general goal of all presidents to pull the developing countries into closer, friendlier relations with the United States. At the very least, presidents try to keep such countries from falling under communist domination. For example, the Reagan administration feels that the Marxist government of Nicaragua is a threat to the rest of Central America and has given support to guerrillas fighting the Nicaraguan regime. Presidents can also face problems with developing countries that are our allies. Over the years, the United States has supported a number of dictatorial leaders because such support suited our strategic needs. The American support of the Shah of Iran, for example, angered the people of Iran, who associated the Shah's repressive regime with the United States. Since the Iranian revolution, Iranians have considered the United States a great enemy.

Crisis Management

Periodically the president faces a grave situation in which conflict is imminent or a small conflict threatens to explode into a larger war. Handling such episodes is a critical part of the president's job. In this era, when we must put enormous trust in the one person with the power to pull our nuclear trigger, voters may make the candidates' personal judgment and intelligence primary considerations in how they cast their ballots. A major reason for Republican Barry Goldwater's crushing defeat in the 1964 election was his warlike image. Goldwater's bellicose rhetoric scared many Americans, who, fearing that he would be too quick to resort to nuclear weapons, voted for Lyndon Johnson instead.

A president must be able to exercise good judgment and remain cool in crisis situations. John Kennedy's behavior during the Cuban missile crisis has become a model of effective crisis management. When it was discovered that the Soviet Union had placed missiles in Cuba that were capable of delivering nuclear warheads against the United States, government leaders interpreted it as an unacceptable threat to this country's security. Kennedy drew on a group of senior aides, including top people from the Pentagon, to advise him on possible military and diplomatic actions. An armed invasion of Cuba and air strikes against the missiles were two of the options considered. In the end, Kennedy decided on a less dangerous response to the Soviet move: implementing a naval blockade of Cuba. The Soviet Union thought better of further challenging the United States and soon agreed to remove its missiles.[44] For a short time, though, the world held its breath over the very real possibility of a nuclear war.

Are there guidelines for what a president should do in times of crisis? Drawing on a range of advisers and opinions is certainly one.[45] Not acting in unnecessary haste is another. But there is little to go on beyond these rather general rules. Almost by definition, each crisis is a unique event. Sometimes all of the open alternatives carry substantial risks. And, almost always, time is of the essence. Such a situation arose when Cambodia captured the American merchant ship *Mayaguez* off its coast in 1975. Not wanting to wait until the Cambodian government moved the seamen inland, where there would be little chance of rescuing them, President Gerald Ford immediately sent in the Marines. Unfortunately, forty-one American soldiers were killed in the fighting, "all in vain because the American captives had shortly before the attack been released and sent across the border into Thailand."[46] Even so, Ford can be defended for making the decision he did; he did not know what the Cambodians would do. World events are unpredictable and, in the end, presidents must rely on their own judgment in crisis situations.

PRESIDENTIAL CHARACTER

How does the public assess which presidential candidate has the best judgment and a character suitable to the office? Americans must make a broad evaluation, considering the candidates' personalities and leadership styles. Once presidents are in office, the public continues to evaluate them on the basis of their personal qualities.

A president's actions in office reflect something more than ideology and politics. They also reflect the inner forces that give rise to his basic character. Much of any adult's character is formed in childhood, and many individual traits can be traced to early experiences. Lyndon Johnson, for example, had a troubled relationship with his father, who questioned his son's masculinity. Johnson recalled that, when he ran away from home after wrecking his father's car, his father phoned him and said that people in town were calling Lyndon "yellow" and a coward.[47] Johnson biographer Robert Caro notes another crucial episode in young Lyndon's life — a humiliating beating he took at the hands of a dance partner's jealous boyfriend. In front of family

A Difference in Character
Political scientist James Barber's analysis of presidential personality leads him to classify Calvin Coolidge as a passive-negative type. Coolidge's motto, "Let well enough alone," says much about his approach to the presidency. Barber labels John Kennedy an active-positive type, noting he had an "inner confidence" that "freed him to grow as president."

Table 11.4

Barber's Typology of Presidential Character

Energy	Enjoyment	
	Positive	*Negative*
Active	Active-Positives F. Roosevelt Truman Kennedy Ford Carter	Active-Negatives Wilson Hoover Johnson Nixon
Passive	Passive-Positives Taft Harding Reagan	Passive-Negatives Coolidge Eisenhower

Source: James Barber, *The Presidential Character,* 3rd ed. (Englewood Cliffs, N.J. Prentice-Hall, 1985). Reprinted by permission.

and friends, "blood was pouring out of Lyndon's nose and mouth, running down his face and onto the crepe-de-chine shirt."[48]

Was Lyndon Johnson overly concerned about his masculinity? Did this psychological problem make it difficult for him to extricate the United States from the Vietnam War? Another Johnson biographer, Doris Kearns, argues that Johnson wanted to make sure he "was not forced to see himself as a coward, running away from Vietnam."[49] Nonetheless, it is almost impossible to establish the roots of Johnson's behavior as president, and some might find connections between childhood humiliations and presidential policy decisions rather speculative. Others, however, feel that *psychobiography* — the application of psychological analysis to historical figures — has enormous potential as an approach to studying political leaders.

Whatever their roots, the personality characteristics of presidents clearly have an important effect on their success or failure in office. Richard Nixon had such an exaggerated fear of what his "enemies" might try to do to him that he created in the White House a climate that nurtured the Watergate break-in and coverup. Franklin Roosevelt, on the other hand, was certainly aided in office by his relaxed manner and self-confidence.

In an innovative study, *The Presidential Character,* James David Barber classifies all presidents according to two basic character dimensions. The first is the degree of energy presidents put into their job. In this regard, Barber sees presidents as tending to be either *active* or *passive*. The second dimension is the degree to which presidents find their work enjoyable. Here Barber classifies presidents as either *positive* or *negative* toward their work. Does a president "seem to experience his political life as happy or sad, enjoyable or discouraging"?[50] Table 11.4 shows how various presidents are classified within Barber's framework.

Barber suggests that active-positives are best suited in personality to fill the office of president. They lack the rigidity and defensiveness of presidents like Johnson and Nixon, for example. But, as Barber points out, active-positives are not free of character-based problems. Their need to get results may push them into ill-considered action.

It is easy to quibble with some of Barber's conclusions. "Passive" seems to be an exaggerated description of Ronald Reagan, for instance. He has not shied away from the vigorous use of presidential power, and Reagan's first year in office was notable for aggressiveness, not passivity. It may be that Barber's fourfold categorization is far too limited to do justice to the variety of personality styles that have characterized our presidents.

Interesting as it is, Barber's analysis of presidents hardly provides a fool-proof way to choose presidents. Candidates don't come neatly labeled as having a healthy or an unhealthy presidential character. Although voters make their own estimations of how presidents will behave in office, there is no guarantee that those evaluations will turn out to be accurate. And a candidate's character must still be weighed along with other factors, including ideology, party affiliation, and stances on specific issues.

SUMMARY

When the founding fathers met to design the government of this new nation, they had trouble shaping the office of president. They struggled to find a balance between producing an office that was powerful enough to provide unified leadership and ensuring that presidents could not use their powers to become tyrants or dictators. The initial conceptions of the presidency have been transformed slowly over time, as presidents have adapted the office to meet the nation's changing needs. The trend has been to expand presidential power. Some of this expansion has come from presidential actions under claims of inherent powers. Congress has also delegated a great deal of power to the executive branch, further expanding the role of the president.

Because the president is elected by the entire nation, he can claim to represent all citizens when proposing policy. This broad electoral base equips the presidency to be an institution of *majoritarian* democracy — compared with Congress's structural tendencies toward *pluralist* democracy. Whether the presidency actually operates in a majoritarian manner depends on several factors — the individual president's perception of public opinion on political issues, the relationship between public opinion and the president's political ideology, and the extent to which he is committed to pursuing his values through his office.

Presidents' success in getting programs through Congress is related to their political skills and their power to persuade. Presidents are in a stronger position when their popularity is high, but popularity usually declines over time. Americans become dissatisfied with incumbents because presidents cannot please all constituencies.

The American people tend to exaggerate the powers of the president and are easily disappointed when incumbents fail to bring about the changes they want. But if presidents are not the all-powerful miracle workers they are sometimes made out to be, neither are they helpless, pitiful giants.

The executive branch establishment has grown rapidly, and even the White House has become a sizable bureaucracy. Newer responsibilities of the twentieth-century presidency are particularly noticeable in the area of legislative leadership. Contemporary presidents are expected to be policy initiators for Congress, as well as chief lobbyists who must guide their bills through the legislative process.

Key Terms

veto
inherent powers
delegation of powers
coalition of minorities
textbook presidency

electoral college
Executive Office of the President
cabinet
legislative liaison staff
presidential character

Selected Readings

Cronin, Thomas E. *The State of the Presidency*. 2nd ed. Boston: Little, Brown, 1980. An insightful and original look at the modern presidency.

Greenstein, Fred I. *The Hidden-Hand Presidency*. New York: Basic Books, 1982. Greenstein analyzes the leadership style of Dwight Eisenhower, paying particular attention to his handling of the McCarthy problem.

Lowi, Theodore J. *The Personal President*. Ithaca, N.Y.: Cornell University Press, 1985. In Lowi's eyes, the decline of our party system has helped give rise to a direct relationship between contemporary presidents and the people.

Nelson, Michael, ed. *The Presidency and the Political System*. Washington, D.C.: Congressional Quarterly, 1984. This collection of original essays covers a wide range of topics.

Neustadt, Richard E. *Presidential Power*, rev. ed. New York: John Wiley, 1980. Neustadt's classic study examines the president's power to persuade.

Pious, Richard M. *The American Presidency*. New York: Basic Books, 1979. This work focuses on the Constitution and the growth of presidential power.

Rockman, Bert A. *The Leadership Question*. New York: Praeger, 1984. A comprehensive analysis of the factors affecting presidential leadership.

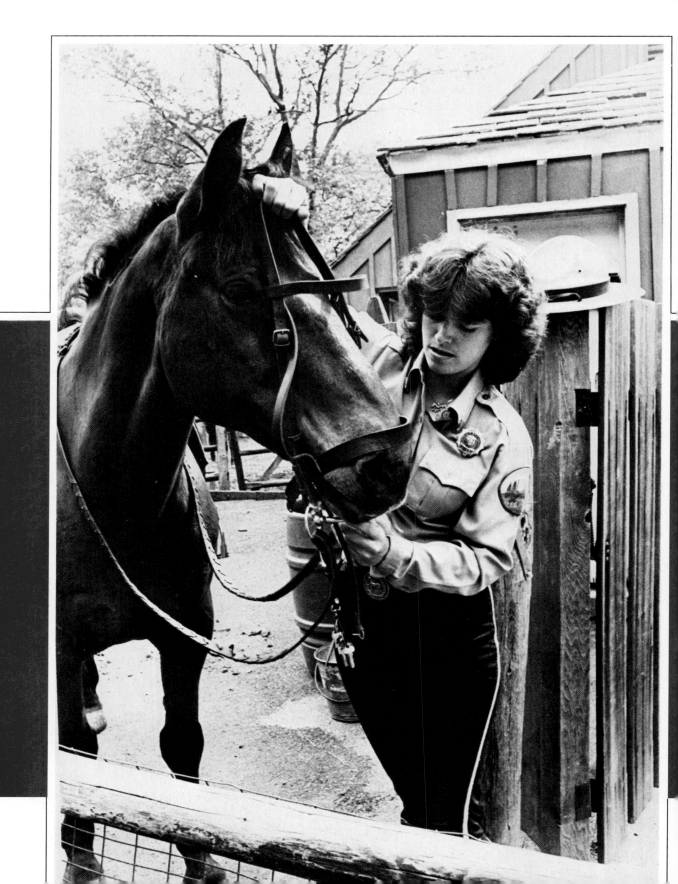

12

The Bureaucracy

T he public knows her as Baby Jane Doe. She was born in October 1983 with a number of severe birth defects, including spina bifida (a failure of the spinal cord to close), an abnormally small head, and water on the brain. Her parents were told that, with corrective surgery, she could live into her twenties but would be severely retarded, paralyzed from the waist down, and bedridden. Without the surgery, life expectancy was less than two years. After much anguish, the couple decided to forgo the surgery and let their baby face an early death.

The Reagan administration was not willing to let parents make such decisions on their own. It had recently set up a hot line in the Department of Health and Human Services, to receive reports of hospitals' failing to protect the rights of handicapped infants. Administrators notified about Baby Doe became concerned about her right to life; they went to court to obtain the child's medical records as a basis for deciding on further intervention.

The parents, Dan and Linda, bitterly disagreed with the administration's contention that it should be involved in deciding their child's future. In Dan's words, federal officials "can't feel what we're feeling now. They can talk about life, but they can't feel what we feel for our baby."[1] To the administration, however, the question was straightforward: who speaks for the baby alone? Its answer was: the federal bureaucracy.

The fight over Baby Doe reversed the usual conservative and liberal roles. President Ronald Reagan's conservative administration was theoretically committed to reducing the bureaucracy's reach into everyday life, but in this case it tried to establish a new and highly controversial role for a bureaucracy. The conservative *Wall Street Journal* castigated the administration's efforts as the work of "medico-legal busybodies" dedicated to harassing parents and physicians.[2] The *Journal* and many liberals argued that parents must have the freedom to make these difficult decisions themselves. The Reagan administration countered with the traditional liberal argument that only a federal bureaucracy could ensure that children were treated in an equitable and fair manner. In the end, the Supreme Court sided with Dan and Linda, concluding that federal law did not sanction such government intervention.

This conservative-liberal role reversal, although interesting, is not the most important aspect of the Baby Doe case. At the core of the case is a fundamental question about American politics: to what degree should the federal government use its power to promote order, in this case by protecting human life? Or, alternatively, to what degree must government respect individuals' freedom to lead their lives without its interference?

In analyzing the federal bureaucracy in this chapter, we shall focus on its potential for infringing on individual freedom in the pursuit of order and equality. We shall also assess the bureaucracy's contribution to democratic government according to the pluralist and majoritarian models. In addressing these broad issues, we shall ask — and answer — a number of related questions: To what extent does the bureaucracy merely follow the directions of Congress in implementing the laws of the land, and to what extent does it act on its own? How responsive is the bureaucracy to the president's wishes? How are agencies and departments influenced by ordinary citizens and by interest groups? Who, in short, controls the bureaucracy in our democracy?

THE DEVELOPMENT OF THE BUREAUCRATIC STATE

A nation's laws and policies are administered, or put into effect, by a variety of departments, agencies, bureaus, offices, and other government units, which together are known as its bureaucracy. The word **bureaucracy** actually means any large, complex organization in which employees have very specific job responsibilities and work within a hierarchy of authority. The employees of these government units, who are quite knowledgeable within their narrow areas, have become known somewhat derisively as **bureaucrats.**

The inevitability of bureaucracies in modern societies has not made their role any less controversial. Bureaucracies make decisions not merely about minor details of public policy, but sometimes also about the fundamental

Faces of the Bureaucracy
Some of the functions of the bureaucracy are longstanding, like coining and engraving money. Indeed, this governmental task is mentioned in the Constitution. Other governmental responsibilities are more recent and may reflect changes in science or technology. This government biologist works for the U.S. Center for Disease Control in Atlanta.

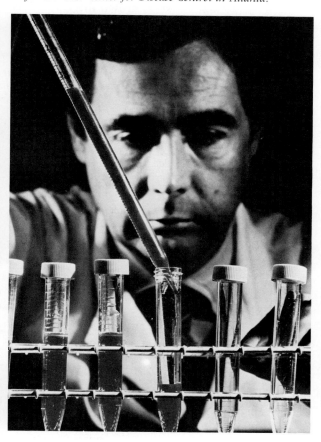

nature of policy. The basic conflict over just how far the bureaucracy should go in creating policies that promote equality of opportunity or individual freedom arises hundreds of times a day in Washington. And, although Americans may hold sharply divided opinions about government's role in specific policy areas, they seem more able to agree that government — specifically, the bureaucracy — tries to do too much.

The Growth of American Government

American government seems to have grown without limit during this century. As one observer noted wryly, "The assistant administrator for water and hazardous materials of the Environmental Protection Agency presided over a staff larger than Washington's entire first administration."[3] Yet, even during Washington's time, bureaucracies were necessary. No one argued then about the need for a postal service to deliver the mail or a Department of the Treasury to maintain a system of currency.

Government at all levels (federal, state, and local) has grown enormously. In recent years most growth has taken place in state and local government, while the federal work force has remained relatively stable (see Figure 12.1). There are a number of major reasons why our government has grown the way it has.

Figure 12.1

Government Employment
The figures below indicate the number of employees working at the federal, state, and local levels of government at different points in time. The federal government figure is for civilian employees only.

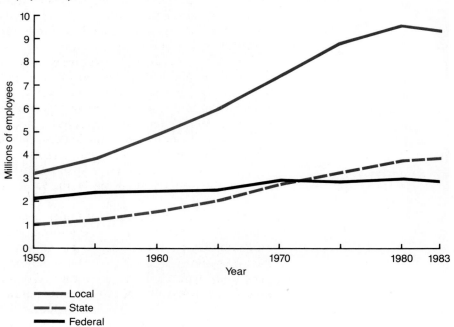

Science and technology.   One reason government has grown so much is the increasing complexity of society. George Washington did not have an assistant administrator for water and hazardous materials because there was no obvious need for one. A National Aeronautics and Space Administration (NASA) was not necessary until rockets were invented.

Even longstanding departments have had to expand to keep up with technological and societal changes. The Department of Agriculture has grown in part in response to advances in biology, chemistry, and nutrition. Greater understanding of soil, seeds, and pests has created more opportunities for government to provide services to farmers, to help them grow more disease-resistant crops and larger, more cost-efficient harvests.

Business regulation.   Another reason government has grown is that public philosophy toward business has changed. During the nineteenth century, the prevailing rule for government regulation of business was **laissez faire** — a French term that can be freely translated as "let them (business-people) do as they please." Business was held to be generally autonomous, and government intervention in the economy was considered inappropriate. This philosophy began to change toward the end of the nineteenth century, as more Americans became aware that laissez faire did not always bring about highly competitive markets that benefited consumers. Rather, business sometimes formed oligopolies like the infamous "sugar trust," a small group of companies that controlled virtually the entire sugar market.

Gradually, government intervention came to be viewed as necessary to protect the integrity of business markets. And, if government was to effectively police unfair business practices, it needed administrative agencies. Over the course of the twentieth century, new bureaucracies were organized to regulate specific industries. The Securities and Exchange Commission (SEC), for securities trading; the Interstate Commerce Commission (ICC), for surface transportation; and the Federal Communications Commission (FCC), for television, radio, and telephone, are just a few such agencies.

Through bureaucracies like these, government became a referee in the marketplace, developing standards of fair trade, setting rates, and licensing individual businesses for operation. As new problem areas emerged, government added new agencies, thereby expanding the scope of its activities. During the 1960s, for instance, the public became increasingly aware that some design flaws in automobiles made them unnecessarily unsafe. For example, sharp, protruding dashboard knobs caused a car's own interior to be dangerous on impact. Congress responded to public demands for change by creating the National Highway Traffic Safety Administration in 1966.*

Social welfare.   General attitudes about government's welfare responsibilities have changed too. An enduring part of American culture has been an emphasis on self-reliance. People are expected to overcome adversity on their own and to succeed on the basis of their own skills and efforts. In years past, those who could not take care of themselves had to hope that their families or primitive local programs would help them.

---

*Its original name was the National Highway Safety Agency.

People in this country were slow to accept government in the role of "thy brother's keeper." Only in the wake of the Great Depression did the government begin to take steps to provide income security. In 1935 the Social Security Act became law, creating the social security fund that workers pay into and then collect income from during old age. A small part of that act was a provision for impoverished families, which evolved into Aid to Families with Dependent Children (AFDC), the nation's basic welfare program.

The belief in progress.   A larger, stronger central government can also be traced to Americans' firm belief in the idea of progress. Another thread that runs through American culture is faith in our ability to solve problems. No problem is too big or too complicated. This attitude is typified by President John F. Kennedy's commitment in 1961 to put a man on the moon by 1970.

NASA in Good Times . . .
For many years NASA has been a highly respected government agency. It seemed to embody the "can do" spirit of America. With the moon landing in 1969, NASA fulfilled President John F. Kennedy's commitment to put a man on the moon before the decade was out.

. . . And in Bad Times
In January 1986, the space shuttle Challenger *exploded shortly after takeoff, and all seven crew members perished. The Rogers Commission, which investigated the tragedy, revealed serious flaws in NASA's management practices, which further stained the agency's image.*

Califano's Antismoking Campaign
Joseph Califano was an enterprising secretary of health, education, and welfare in President Jimmy Carter's administration. He may have been too enterprising, though—the White House viewed him as disloyal and he was removed in 1979.

As difficult as the task seemed when he made the pledge, a man walked on the moon on July 20, 1969. This same spirit leads politicians to declare "War on Poverty" or "War on Cancer" through massive programs of coordinated and well-funded activities. Many people believe that the private sector cannot undertake such large-scale programs and that government must be responsible for them. When government does make a major new effort, it often requires the creation of a new bureaucracy. Thus new agencies, such as the National Cancer Institute, come into being when we want government to do more in a particular area.

Ambitious administrators. Finally, government has grown because agency officials have expanded their organizations and staffs to take on added responsibilities. An imaginative and ambitious agency administrator looks for more ways to conscientiously serve his or her clients. New programs are developed, which lead to new authority. Larger budgets and staffs are, in turn, necessary to support that authority. For example, despite President Jimmy Carter's reluctance to involve himself in the controversy over smoking, health, and government tobacco subsidies, his secretary of health, education, and welfare, Joseph Califano, declared that smoking was "Public Enemy Number One" and launched a major antismoking campaign.[4] Likewise, members of Congress may push for new agencies and programs that favor interest groups they want to please.

Can Government Be Reduced in Size?

In recent years we have witnessed a movement toward reducing the size of the bureaucracy. Americans seem to want less of this country's total financial resources to go into funding the government. Ronald Reagan campaigned on a promise to cut bureaucracies, which he said were wasteful, and to get government "off the back" of the American people. Nondefense budget cuts enacted at his urging led to reductions in the size and range of some bureaucratic activities. The initial rounds of budget cutting were followed by further pressure to reduce the size of government as the public grew dissatisfied with the large budget deficits (in some years exceeding $200 billion) that emerged during the Reagan years.

Presidents and members of Congress face a tough job when they try to reduce the size of the bureaucracy; each government agency performs a service some sector of society wants. As a group, bankers surely favor the laissez-faire capitalist principles of a free market and of minimal government intervention. Few bankers voiced those principles, however, when mismanagement at Continental Illinois, one of the nation's largest banks, led it to the brink of insolvency in 1984. A run on the bank by the holders of large, uninsured deposits pushed the bank toward failure. Continental's failure would have had a destabilizing impact on the entire banking system. When that failure became imminent, the Federal Reserve Board and the Federal Deposit Insurance Corporation (FDIC), two of the agencies that regulate the nation's banking industry, stepped in, put billions of dollars into the bank, and guaranteed every dollar of deposits. In this case, bankers were happy to have "big government" regulate a member of their industry out of its difficulties.[5]

Bankers are not the only group that wants to be protected by the federal government. Farmers need the price supports of the Department of Agriculture. Builders profit from programs offered by the Department of Housing and Urban Development (HUD). And labor unions want a vigorous Occupational Safety and Health Adminstration (OSHA). Thus, efforts to cut an agency's scope are almost always resisted by interest groups having a stake in that agency.

Still, despite their political support, agencies are not immune to change. It is rare for a department or agency to be completely abolished. However, it is not uncommon for one to undergo a major reorganization, in which programs are consolidated and the size and scope of activities are reduced.[6] Other programs, such as government-sponsored job training, can lose support if they are perceived to be working poorly. As funds are cut, bureaucracy positions are eliminated.

In sum, attitudes about the size of government are somewhat paradoxical. Many believe that government is too big, that it tries to do too much, and that it intrudes too much into our daily lives. Still, substantial reductions in the scope of government activity are unusual, because individual agencies carry out programs that protect or benefit some constituency. Those constituencies, in turn, work hard to protect their agencies from would-be budget cutters.

This paradox is just one more manifestation of the tension between majoritarianism and pluralism. What the broader public wants — a smaller federal government — is undermined by the strong preferences of different segments of society for government to perform some valuable function for them. Lobbies that represent these segments work strenuously to convince Congress and the administration that their agency's particular part of the budget is vital and that any cuts ought to come out of some other agency's hide. Those other agencies, however, are also likely to have strong supporters. Even so, change is possible. Shifting national priorities can bring about reductions in an agency's scope. And, in recent years, public opinion and large budget deficits have generally kept the government from moving into new areas of domestic policy.

BUREAUS AND BUREAUCRATS

The bureaucracy is often discussed as if it were a giant octopus with countless arms. The Washington bureaucracy is, in reality, a disjointed collection of departments, agencies, bureaus, offices, and commissions. Each is a bureaucracy in its own right.

The Organization of Government

By examining the basic types of government organizations, we can better understand how the executive branch operates. We shall pay particular attention to their relative degree of independence and their relationship to the White House.

Departments.   **Departments** are the largest units of the executive branch, covering broad areas of government responsibility. As noted in the previous chapter, the heads of these departments, the secretaries, form the president's cabinet along with a few other key officials. The current cabinet departments are State, Defense, Justice, Treasury, Interior, Agriculture, Commerce, Labor, Health and Human Services, Housing and Urban Development, Transportation, Energy, and Education. Each of these massive bureaucracies is broken down into subsidiary bureaus, offices, services, and agencies. The National Park Service, for example, is just one of a number of offices and bureaus within the Department of the Interior; it is itself a very large bureaucracy with many subsidiary divisions (see Figure 12.2). The director of the National Park Service reports to the assistant secretary of the interior for fish and wildlife and parks, who in turn reports to the secretary of the interior, who in turn reports to the president of the United States.

Independent agencies.   Within the executive branch, there are approximately sixty **independent agencies**[7] that are not part of any cabinet department. Rather, they stand alone and are controlled in varying degrees by the president. Some, such as the Central Intelligence Agency (CIA), are directly under the president's control. Others, such as the Federal Communications Commission, are structured as **regulatory commissions.** Each is run by a small number of commissioners (usually an odd number, which helps to prevent tie votes), appointed to fixed terms by the president. Some commissions were formed to guard against unfair business practices. Others were formed to police the side effects, or **externalities,** of business operations, such as polluted air emitted by a factory. Still others were formed to protect the public from unsafe products. They are outside the direct control of the White House so that they will be freed from the pressures of the political process and the partisan considerations that shape it.

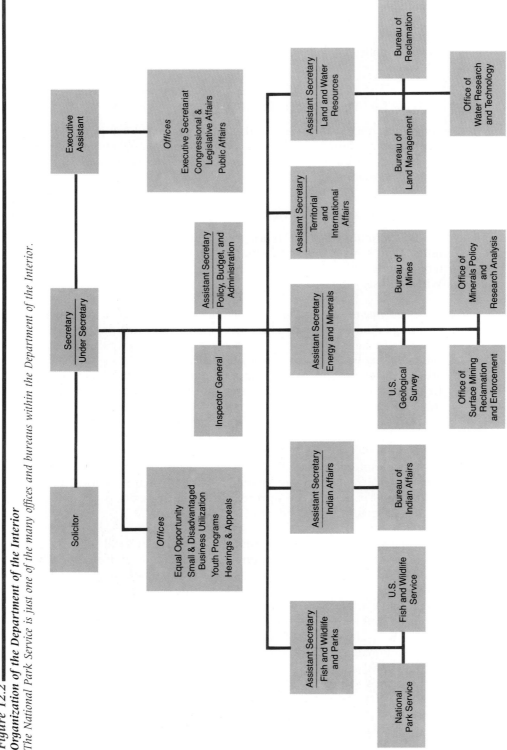

Figure 12.2
Organization of the Department of the Interior
The National Park Service is just one of the many offices and bureaus within the Department of the Interior.

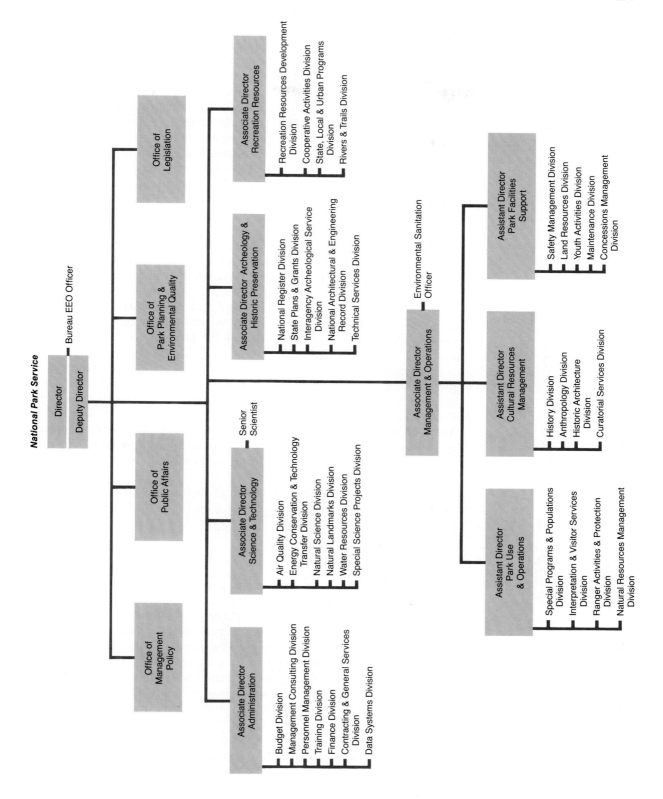

Nevertheless, these agencies are hardly immune to political pressures. They are lobbied fervently by client groups and must consider those groups' demands when making policy. If the Consumer Product Safety Commission is considering safety standards for chain saws, for example, the chain saw industry will do all it can to convince the agency to either drop the standards or issue them in a form the industry considers least objectionable.

The president exerts influence on these agencies through his power to appoint new commissioners when terms expire or when resignations create openings. During President Carter's administration, his appointed chairman of the Federal Trade Commission (FTC), Michael Pertschuk, led a vigorous proconsumer commission. The Reagan administration, however, took a different stand when it exerted its influence over the FTC. Reagan's appointed chairman, free-market economist James Miller, gave the Reagan forces a numerical advantage on the five-member board. Under Miller's leadership, the FTC reversed its policy of industrywide checks for false advertising in favor of investigations that responded only to specific complaints filed with the agency. From the viewpoint of consumer advocates, this reversal meant that the FTC would be less aggressive in protecting Americans from false advertising. From business's standpoint, it meant that the FTC would stop going on "fishing expeditions."[8] Whatever one's point of view, a significant policy shift occurred as a direct result of the presidential change.

Government corporations.   Finally, Congress has also created a small number of **government corporations.** The services these executive branch agencies perform theoretically could be provided by the private sector, but Congress has decided that the public would be better served if they had some link with the government. For example, the federal government maintains a postal service because it feels that Americans need low-cost door-to-door service for all kinds of mail, not just for mail on profitable routes or mail that requires special services.

In some cases, too, the financial incentive is insufficient for the private sector to engage in a particular activity. This is the case with the financially troubled Amtrak train line.

The Civil Service

The federal bureaucracy is staffed by around 2.7 million civilian employees, who account for less than 3 percent of the U.S. work force. Americans have a tendency to stereotype all these government workers as faceless paper pushers, but the federal work force is actually quite diverse. Government workers include forest rangers, FBI agents, typists, foreign service officers, computer programmers, policy analysts, public relations specialists, security guards, librarians, agency executives, engineers, and people from literally hundreds of other occupations — including 25,000 metalworkers, 18,000 plumbers, and 10,000 painters and paperhangers.[9]

An important feature of the federal bureaucracy is that most of its workers are hired under the requirements of the **civil service.** The creation of the civil service was spurred by the assassination of President James Garfield by an unbalanced and dejected job seeker. Congress responded by passing the Pendleton Act of 1883, which established the Civil Service Commission (now the Office of Personnel Management). The act's purpose was to reduce *patronage* — the practice of filling government positions with the president's political allies or cronies. The civil service attempts to ensure that government jobs will be filled on the basis of merit and that employees will not be fired for political reasons. Over the years, job qualifications and selection procedures have been developed for most government positions.

About 87 percent of federal workers are employed outside of Washington.[10] One reason for this distribution is to make government offices accessible to the people they serve. The Social Security Administration, for example, has to have offices within a reasonable distance of most Americans, so that its many clients have somewhere to take their questions, problems, and paperwork. Another reason why the national government spreads its offices is to distribute jobs and income across the country. The government's Center for Disease Control could easily have been located in Washington, but it is in Atlanta instead. Likewise, the NASA headquarters for space flights is located in Houston. Members of Congress, of course, like to place some of the "pork barrel" back home, so that their constituents will credit them with the jobs and money that federal installations create.

Given the enormous variety of federal jobs, it is no surprise that employees come from all walks of life. Studies of the social composition of the civil service *as a whole* indicate that it does mirror the American population on such important characteristics as father's occupation, education, income, and age.[11] There is also substantial representation of minorities (24 percent) and women (35 percent) within the federal government.[12] However, in higher-level policymaking positions, the work force is skewed much more sharply toward white males and those born into families of higher occupational status.

On the Front Line

Most civil servants work outside of Washington. These customs agents are employed in Brownsville, Texas.

Around eight thousand employees in the higher level of the civil service form the **Senior Executive Service** (SES). Created by the Civil Service Reform Act of 1978, the SES offers the president and his top aides some flexibility in the assignment of high-level administrators. SES managers considered ineffectual can be transferred to other government positions. Cash performance bonuses can also be awarded to keep talented SES officials in government. However, studies of the SES show that it has so far had a rather limited impact.[13]

The 1978 law also makes it somewhat easier to fire truly incompetent civil servants. Yet civil servants still enjoy substantial protections and the right to an extensive appeals process if they are fired.[14]

Presidential Control over the Bureaucracy

Reforms such as the civil service have effectively insulated the vast majority of government workers from party politics. An incoming president can appoint fewer than 1 percent of all executive branch employees. Still, presidential appointees fill the top policymaking positions in the government. Thus, each new president establishes an extensive personnel review process to find appointees who are both ideologically compatible and highly qualified in their field. Although the president selects some people from his campaign staff, most of his political appointees have not been campaign workers. Instead, his cabinet secretaries, assistant secretaries, agency heads, and the like tend to be drawn directly from business, universities, or government itself. Only two of the eleven members of President Richard Nixon's last cabinet had extensive political experience before their appointment. Only three of Carter's original cabinet members could be described as "ambassadors from interest group constituencies," and five had Ph.D.'s.[15]

Presidents often come to believe that they have insufficient control over the bureaucracy because so few of their own people are in each agency and department. Some have argued that civil service reforms have gone too far and that it is time to give the president more positions to fill with loyalists. As one critic put it, "The people we elect no longer have a chance to change government, because they can't change the people who make it up."[16] President Kennedy echoed this sentiment when he complained that the State Department was a "bowl of jelly" and that giving an instruction to State was like putting it in a dead letter box.[17]

Although presidents become frustrated with the federal bureaucracy, they are hardly helpless, pitiful giants. As the example of the FTC's change in leadership illustrates, presidential appointees can have a substantial impact on their agencies. Recent research shows that presidential appointees are very influential in bringing new issues onto the political agenda, whereas civil servants have comparatively little impact.[18] But the question remains: should there be more political appointments in the federal government, so that the president can make the bureaucracy more responsive to his wishes? Those who answer in the affirmative argue that presidents might be able to fulfill more of their campaign promises if they had greater control over the bureaucracy. But others point out the value of a stable, experienced work force that implements policy in a consistent fashion.

POLICYMAKING: FORMAL PROCESSES

The sprawling diversity of the executive branch leaves many Americans with the impression that federal bureaucracies are complex, impenetrable organizations. Bureaucratic actions and policies often appear irrational to ordinary citizens who know little of how government officials reach their decisions. Many Americans wonder why agencies sometimes actually *make* policy rather than merely carry it out. Administrative agencies are, in fact, authoritative policymaking bodies, and their decisions on substantive issues are legally binding on the citizens of this country.

Administrative Discretion

What are executive agencies set up to do? First of all, Cabinet departments and independent agencies are creatures of the Congress. Congress creates a new department or agency by passing a law that describes each organization's mandate, or *mission*. As part of that mandate, Congress grants to the agency a certain amount of authority to make policy decisions. Congress long ago recognized that it has neither the time nor the expertise in highly technical areas to make all policy decisions. Ideally, it sets general guidelines for policy, and an agency is expected to act within those guidelines. The latitude that Congress gives agencies to make policy in the spirit of their legislative mandate is called **administrative discretion.**

The Department of Transportation has used its discretionary policymaking authority to address the problem of alcohol and drug abuse by railway engineers. A departmental study showed that, during an eight-year period, alcohol- or drug-impaired judgment caused a minimum of forty-five train accidents resulting in thirty-four fatalities. In response, the Transportation Department set forth policies that not only ban drug and alcohol use on the job but also require preemployment drug screening, allow spot checks of employees for drugs, and permit voluntary worker treatment without fear of firing.[19]

Critics of bureaucracy frequently complain that agencies are granted too much discretion. In his book *The End of Liberalism*, Theodore Lowi argues that Congress commonly gives vague directives in its initial enabling legislation, instead of truly setting guidelines. Agencies are charged with protecting the "public interest" but are left to determine on their own what policies best serve the public.[20] These critics believe that members of Congress assign too much of their responsibility for difficult policy choices to unelected administrators.

Congress is often vague about its intent when setting up a new agency or program. Sometimes this vagueness occurs because the problem is clear cut but the solution is not. Congress nevertheless feels a pressure to act. It therefore creates an agency or program to show that it is concerned and responsive and assumes that administrators will eventually develop specific solutions. For example, the initial enabling legislation in 1934 for the Federal Communications Commission recognized a need for regulation in the burgeoning radio industry. The growing number of stations would soon have made it difficult to listen to the radio because of interference between overlapping frequencies. Congress avoided many sticky issues by leaving the FCC

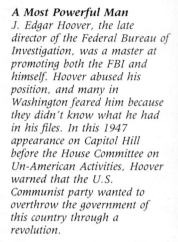

A Most Powerful Man
J. Edgar Hoover, the late director of the Federal Bureau of Investigation, was a master at promoting both the FBI and himself. Hoover abused his position, and many in Washington feared him because they didn't know what he had in his files. In this 1947 appearance on Capitol Hill before the House Committee on Un-American Activities, Hoover warned that the U.S. Communist party wanted to overthrow the government of this country through a revolution.

with the ambiguous directive that broadcasters should "serve the public interest, convenience, and necessity."[21] In other cases, a number of "obvious" solutions to a problem may be available, but members of Congress cannot agree on which one is best. One compromise is to set deliberately ambiguous policy guidelines for the agency that is created to solve the problem. Its administrators are then saddled with the responsibility for turning ambiguities into specific policy decisions.[22]

The wide latitude Congress gives bureaucratic agencies often leads to charges that government is "out of control" and a "power unto itself." These claims are frequently exaggerated.[23] Administrative discretion is not a fixed commodity; Congress does have the power to express its displeasure by reining agencies in with additional legislation. If Congress is displeased with an agency's actions, it can pass laws invalidating specific policies. This method of control may seem cumbersome, but Congress has periodic opportunities to amend the original legislation that created a program or agency. Over time, Congress makes increasingly detailed policy decisions, often affirming or modifying previous agency decisions.[24]

Informal contacts with members of Congress also influence administrators. Through such communication, legislators can clarify exactly which actions they prefer administrators to take. And administrators listen because they are wary of offending members of the committees and subcommittees that oversee their programs and, particularly, their budgets. Contacts with legislators also let administrators explain problems facing their agencies, justify their decisions, and even negotiate compromises on unresolved issues. Overall, the bureaucracy seems to be neither out of control nor off on its own in the area of policymaking.

Institutions of Government

U.S. House Districts and Changes after the 1980 Census

Legend:
- States gaining districts
- States losing districts
- States with no change

Projected Congressional Apportionment, 2000

States are apportioned seats in the 435-member House of Representatives according to population. Following the national census in 1980, the Census Bureau revised the number of seats to which each state was entitled due to changes in population since 1970. The redistribution of seats shown for 1980 reflects the shift of population from the northeast toward the southwest. If the rate of population change remains constant, the distribution of congressional districts in the year 2000 would look as shown at right. The western and sunbelt states would gain even more seats at the expense of the midwest and northeast.

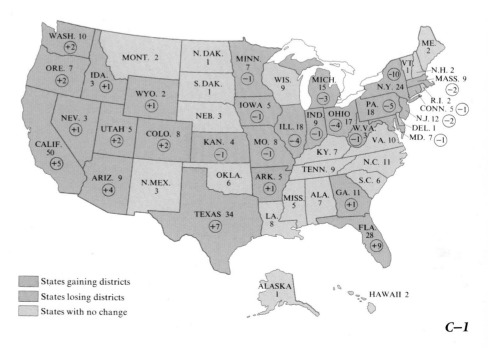

Legend:
- States gaining districts
- States losing districts
- States with no change

C–1

The Heart of Washington, D.C.

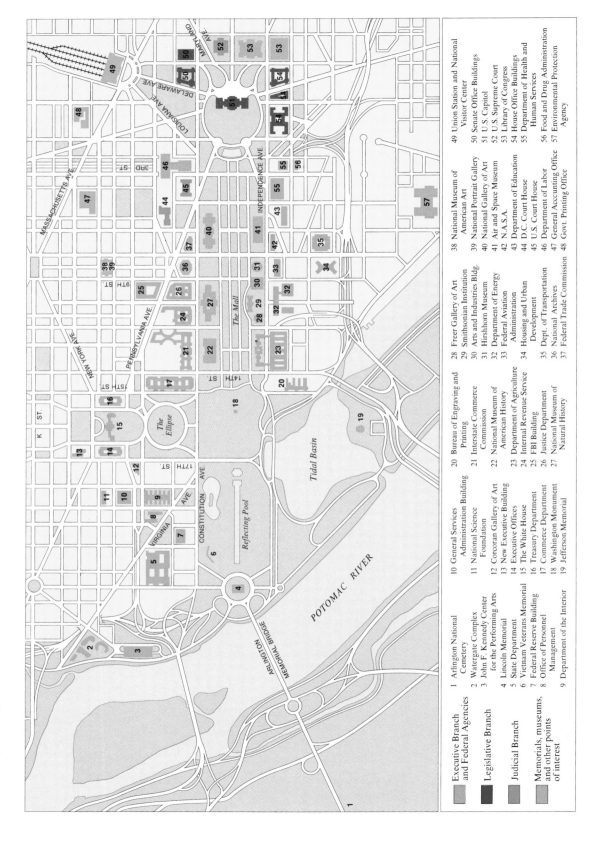

Executive Branch and Federal Agencies

Legislative Branch

Judicial Branch

Memorials, museums, and other points of interest

1 Arlington National Cemetery
2 Watergate Complex
3 John F. Kennedy Center for the Performing Arts
4 Lincoln Memorial
5 State Department
6 Vietnam Veterans Memorial
7 Federal Reserve Building
8 Office of Personnel Management
9 Department of the Interior

10 General Services Administration Building
11 National Science Foundation
12 Corcoran Gallery of Art
13 New Executive Building
14 Executive Offices
15 The White House
16 Treasury Department
17 Commerce Department
18 Washington Monument
19 Jefferson Memorial

20 Bureau of Engraving and Printing
21 Interstate Commerce Commission
22 National Museum of American History
23 Department of Agriculture
24 Internal Revenue Service
25 FBI Building
26 Justice Department
27 National Museum of Natural History

28 Freer Gallery of Art
29 Smithsonian Institution
30 Arts and Industries Bldg.
31 Hirshhorn Museum
32 Department of Energy
33 Federal Aviation Administration
34 Housing and Urban Development
35 Dept. of Transportation
36 National Archives
37 Federal Trade Commission

38 National Museum of American Art
39 National Portrait Gallery
40 National Gallery of Art
41 Air and Space Museum
42 N.A.S.A.
43 Department of Education
44 D.C. Court House
45 U.S. Court House
46 Department of Labor
47 General Accounting Office
48 Govt. Printing Office

49 Union Station and National Visitor Center
50 Senate Office Buildings
51 U.S. Capitol
52 U.S. Supreme Court
53 Library of Congress
54 House Office Buildings
55 Department of Health and Human Services
56 Food and Drug Administration
57 Environmental Protection Agency

The United States Capitol

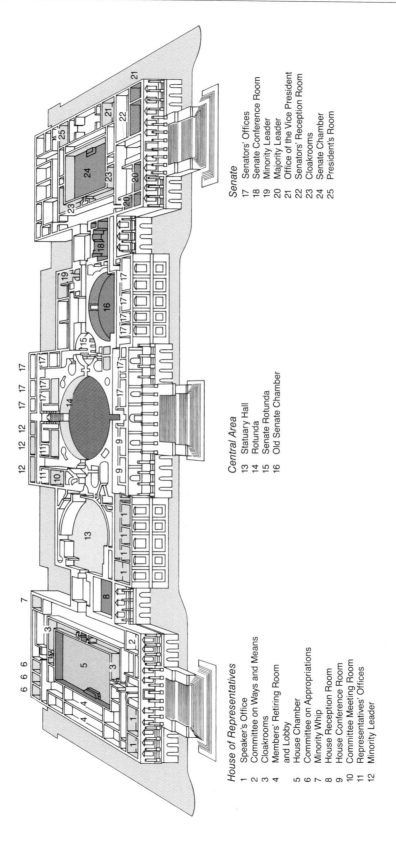

House of Representatives
1 Speaker's Office
2 Committee on Ways and Means
3 Cloakrooms
4 Members' Retiring Room and Lobby
5 House Chamber
6 Committee on Appropriations
7 Minority Whip
8 House Reception Room
9 House Conference Room
10 Committee Meeting Room
11 Representatives' Offices
12 Minority Leader

Central Area
13 Statuary Hall
14 Rotunda
15 Senate Rotunda
16 Old Senate Chamber

Senate
17 Senators' Offices
18 Senate Conference Room
19 Minority Leader
20 Majority Leader
21 Office of the Vice President
22 Senators' Reception Room
23 Cloakrooms
24 Senate Chamber
25 President's Room

The White House

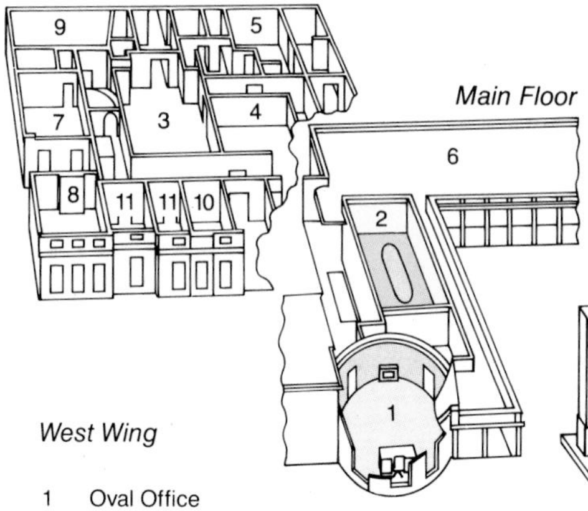

Main Floor
9
5
7
3
4
6
8
11
11
10
2
1

West Wing

1 Oval Office
2 Cabinet Room
3 West Lobby
4 Roosevelt Room (conference room)
5 Presidential Press Secretary
6 Press Room
7 Vice President's Office
8 Chief of Staff
9 National Security Advisor
10 Director of Communications
11 Assistants to the President

Third Floor
Second Floor
17
16
18
19
12
13
14
15
First Floor
Ground Floor

Mansion

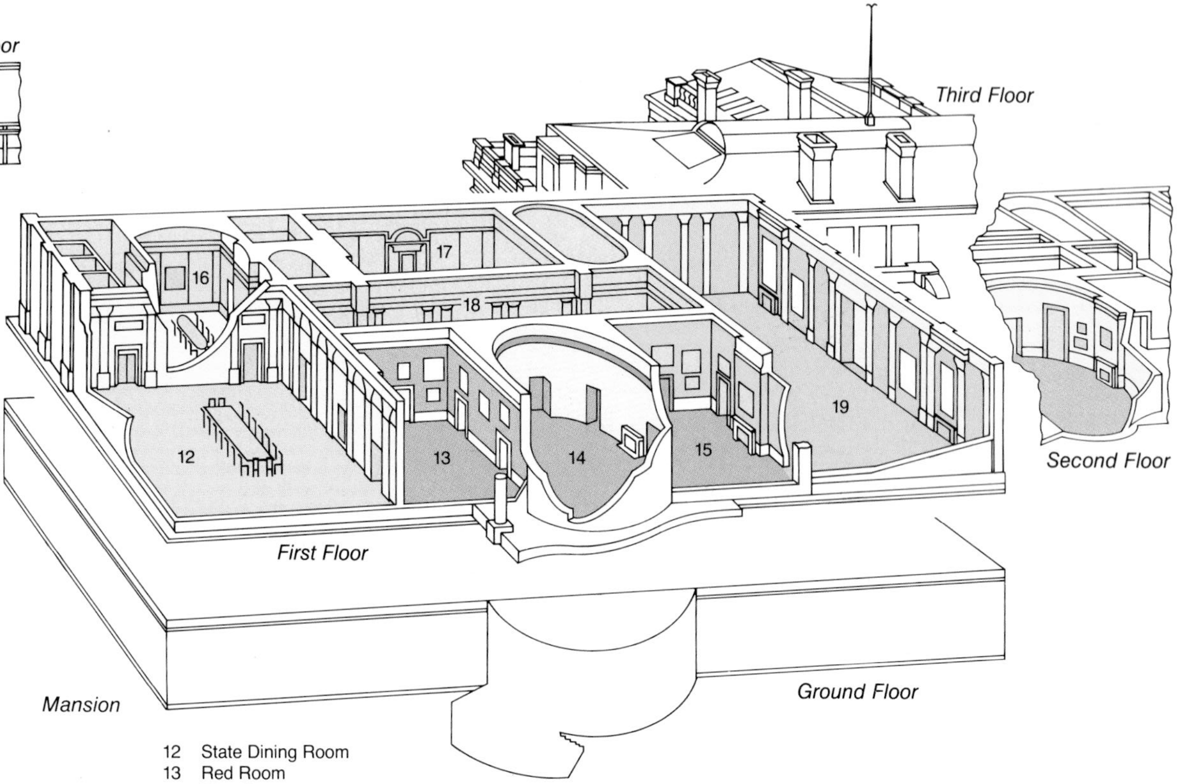

12 State Dining Room
13 Red Room
14 Blue Room
15 Green Room
16 Private Dining Room
17 Main Lobby
18 Cross Hall
19 East Room

The Supreme Court

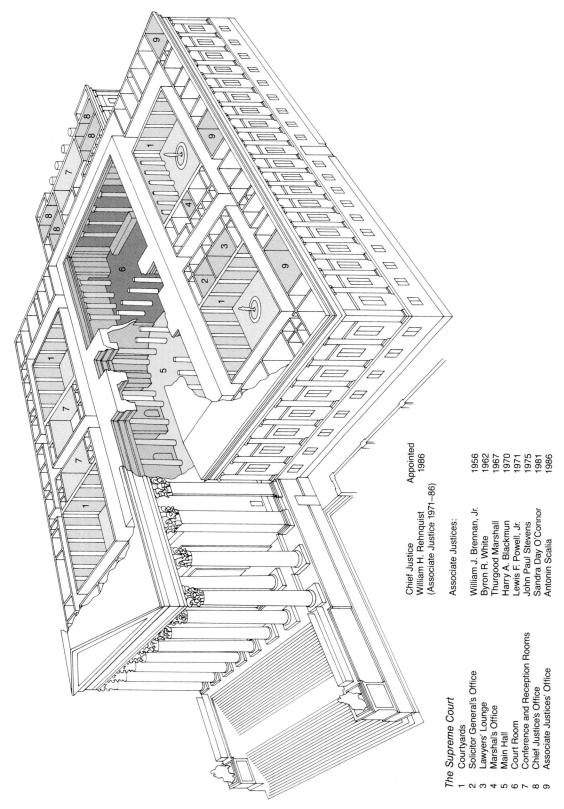

The Supreme Court

1 Courtyards
2 Solicitor General's Office
3 Lawyers' Lounge
4 Marshal's Office
5 Main Hall
6 Court Room
7 Conference and Reception Rooms
8 Chief Justice's Office
9 Associate Justices' Office

	Appointed
Chief Justice	
William H. Rehnquist	1986
(Associate Justice 1971–86)	
Associate Justices:	
William J. Brennan, Jr.	1956
Byron R. White	1962
Thurgood Marshall	1967
Harry A. Blackmun	1970
Lewis F. Powell, Jr.	1971
John Paul Stevens	1975
Sandra Day O'Connor	1981
Antonin Scalia	1986

U.S. Circuit Courts of Appeals and U.S. District Courts

Circuit boundaries
District boundaries
State boundaries

At the base of the federal court system are ninety-four district courts, each headed by a single federal judge. Each state has at least one district court; larger states have more. Judgments from district courts can be appealed to one of twelve circuit courts of appeals, where they are heard before three judges. However, only a fraction of the cases decided in district courts ever come before the appeals courts, and only a tiny fraction of these are reviewed by the Supreme Court.

Presidential success in congressional voting is determined by computing the percentage of instances that Congress supported the president when he had announced his position on votes before each chamber. Although useful as a measure of a president's influence with Congress, these percentages do not distinguish between votes crucial to a president and those less so. Nevertheless, Democratic presidents tended to be more successful in Congress than Republican presidents, who usually faced Democratic majorities.

Presidential Success Scores*

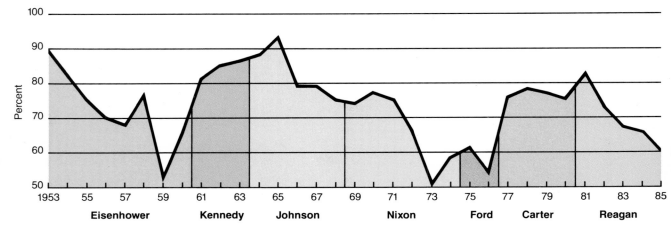

*Percentage based on votes on which presidents took a position.

Two-Party Systems in U.S. History

1789	Washington unanimously elected President				**PRE-PARTY PERIOD**
1792	Washington unanimously reelected				

Year	**Federalist**	**Democratic-Republican**			Period
1796	Adams				
1800	—	Jefferson			
1804	—	Jefferson			**FIRST PARTY SYSTEM**
1808	—	Madison			
1812	—	Madison			
1816	—	Monroe			

1820	Monroe		**"ERA OF GOOD FEELING"**
1824	J.Q. Adams		

Year	System	**Democratic**	**National-Republican** / **Whig**
1828		Jackson	
1832		Jackson	
1836	**SECOND PARTY SYSTEM**	Van Buren	
1840			Harrison
1844		Polk	
1848		—	Taylor
1852		Pierce	

Year	System	Constitutional Union / Southern Democrat	Democratic	Populist	**Republican**
1856			Buchanan		
1860		Constitutional Union / Southern Democrat	—		Lincoln
1864			—		Lincoln
1868	**THIRD PARTY SYSTEM**		—		Grant
1872			—		Grant
1876			—		Hayes
1880			—		Garfield
1884	**ROUGH BALANCE**		Cleveland		—
1888			—		Harrison
1892			Cleveland		—
1896			—	Populist	McKinley

Year	System	Democratic	Progressive	**Republican**
1900		—		McKinley
1904		—		T. Roosevelt
1908		—		Taft
1912	**REPUBLICAN DOMINANCE**	Wilson	Progressive	—
1916		Wilson		—
1920		—		Harding
1924		—		Coolidge
1928		—		Hoover

Year	System	Democratic	States' Rights	Republican
1932		F.D. Roosevelt		—
1936		F.D. Roosevelt		—
1940		F.D. Roosevelt		—
1944	**DEMOCRATIC DOMINANCE**	F.D. Roosevelt		—
1948		Truman	States' Rights	—
1952		—		Eisenhower
1956		—		Eisenhower
1960		Kennedy		—
1964		Johnson		—

Year	Democratic	American Independent / Independent	Republican
1968	—	American Independent	Nixon
1972	—		Nixon
1976	Carter		—
1980	—	Independent	Reagan
1984	—		Reagan

Party politics in the United States can be analyzed in terms of three different two-party systems. The third (and present) party system first appeared in the presidential election of 1856. In the more than one hundred years that have elapsed since that time, the Democrats and Republicans have alternated irregularly in power, each enjoying a long period of dominance. Although the Republicans have won the presidency more frequently than the Democrats over the last three decades, the Democrats have dominated in Congress and in state capitals.

Presidential Greatness

In 1982, the Chicago Tribune asked 49 leading historians and political scholars to rate all past presidents on a descending scale from 5 (best) to 0 (worst) in five categories: leadership qualities, accomplishments and crisis management, political skills, quality of appointments, and character and integrity. Lincoln ranked at the top, and Franklin Roosevelt edged out Washington for second place. Among more recent presidents, Eisenhower, Johnson, and Kennedy all rated far higher than Ford, Carter, and Nixon. Nixon's ranking suffered by his extraordinarily low score for character and integrity—the lowest that the scholars gave to any president in history.

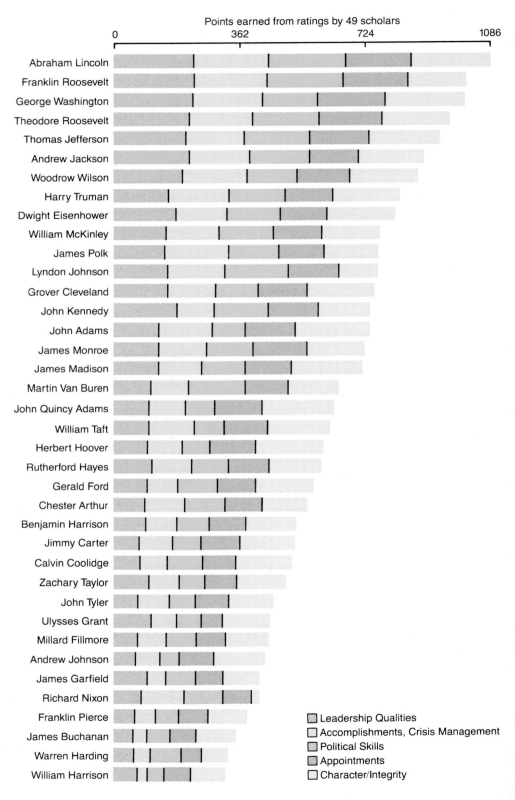

Points earned from ratings by 49 scholars

Leadership Qualities
Accomplishments, Crisis Management
Political Skills
Appointments
Character/Integrity

Rulemaking

The policymaking discretion that Congress gives to agencies is exercised through formal administrative procedures, usually either *rulemaking* or *adjudication*. **Rulemaking** is the administrative process that results in the issuance of regulations. And **regulations,** in turn, are rules that govern the operation of various government programs. In administering the Clean Air Act, for example, the Environmental Protection Agency (EPA) has had to formulate regulations specifying the permissible amounts of pollutants, such as nitrogen oxides and sulfur dioxide, that factories can emit. Although highly technical, such regulations are not trivial. Clean Air Act regulations have forced industries to spend millions of dollars to reduce their plants' pollution.

Since they are authorized by congressional statutes, regulations have the effect of law. In theory, the policy content of regulations follows from the intent of the legislation. As already noted, however, Congress does not always express clear intent. The discretion available to administrative agencies frequently produces political conflict during the rulemaking process on important regulations. One such case involved the Federal Trade Commission's use of its general rulemaking authority to regulate the funeral industry. The FTC began its investigation in 1972, acting on complaints from people who felt they had been taken advantage of during the emotion-laden process of arranging a relative's funeral. After extensive research and numerous public hearings, a final version of the regulations was published in 1979. The rules required funeral homes to give itemized price lists and to quote prices over the phone. The National Funeral Directors Association and others in the industry launched a strong counterattack that resulted in Congress's suspending the rules to allow further analysis of them. (One member of Congress criticized the rules as another occasion when government interference hurt the productivity of an industry.) When the revised regulations were issued, a congressional effort to overturn them failed. After a court challenge by the industry also failed, they went into effect in 1984.[25]

The steps in the rulemaking process are set by the Administrative Procedure Act, first passed in 1946 and amended many times since. The act was meant to ensure that regulations are developed in an open and systematic manner, with a mechanism to let all affected parties voice their opinions. Rulemaking takes place when administrators feel that a *general* rule is needed to govern some aspect of a program. Research is then done on the various solutions that can be imposed, such as determining the economic impact of each alternative. Hearings might be held to gather information from outside experts and from the people or businesses that will be affected. Drafts of major regulations that an agency wants to adopt are reviewed by the Office of Management and Budget, which makes sure that they conform to the administration's policy objectives. The next step is for the proposed regulations to appear in the *Federal Register*. This official government document is published daily and contains each newly proposed or final regulation of departments and agencies. After the proposed regulations appear, the public has the opportunity to comment by writing letters to the agency. Administrators will evaluate the public's comments (many of which come from interest groups) along with congressional opinion and will consult with higher administration officials if necessary. When they have reviewed the comments, administrators will decide whether any changes should be made. Only then are the final regulations worked out and published in the *Federal Register*.

Since regulations have the effect of law, they are written in "legalese" to anticipate any potential court challenges (see Feature 12.1). Lawyers are called on not only to write regulations, but also to interpret them for affected constituencies. But the central issue concerning administrative rulemaking is neither the obscure language of regulations nor the nature of the rulemaking process itself. Rather, it is that regulations require individuals and corporations to act in certain prescribed ways, often against their own self-interest. Steel companies, for example, would certainly prefer to make their own decisions about how much, if anything, they should spend to reduce pollution.

Government, however, must balance society's need for clean air with the steel companies' needs to sustain profitable operations and to compete effectively against foreign companies. When the EPA writes regulations that specify the details of that balance, the agency becomes the object of criticism from both those who would like government to do more and those who would like it to do less. The EPA is in many ways taking the "heat" for Congress,

Feature 12.1

Want to Know Why There Are So Many Lawyers in Washington? Read This

After a regulation is written, it reads somewhat like the one reprinted below. The complex and esoteric nature of regulations is a boon to lawyers, who are able to make handsome livings lobbying regulatory agencies and explaining the regulations of those agencies to clients.

The following regulation from the National Highway Transportation Administration amends existing safety standards for hydraulic brake systems.

S5.1 *Service brake systems.* Each passenger car and each multipurpose passenger vehicle, truck and bus with a GVWR of 10,000 lbs. or less, and each school bus with a GVWR of greater than 10,000 lbs, shall be capable of meeting the requirements of S5.1.1 through S5.1.6 under the conditions prescribed in S6, when tested according to the procedures and in the sequence set forth in S7. Each multipurpose passenger vehicle, truck, and bus (other than a school bus) with a GVWR greater than 10,000 lbs. shall meet the requirements of S5.1.2 and S5.1.3 under the conditions specified in S6 when tested according to the procedures and in the sequence set forth in S7. Except as noted in S5.1.1.2 and S5.1.4, if a vehicle is incapable of attaining a speed specified in S5.1.1, S5.1.2, S5.1.3, or S5.1.6, its service brakes shall be capable of stopping the vehicle from the multiple of 5 mph that is 4 to 8 mph less than the speed attainable in 2 miles, within distances that do not exceed the corresponding distances specified in Table II. If a vehicle is incapable of attaining a speed specified in S5.1.4 in the time or distance interval set forth, it shall be tested at the highest speed attainable in the time or distance interval specified.

Source: *Federal Register*, January 2, 1981, p. 55 (49 C.F.R., pt. 571).

because Congress has the ultimate responsibility for pollution policy—a responsibility it has delegated in part to the EPA.

Adjudication

Rulemaking is a *quasi-legislative* process because it develops generally applicable rules, just as Congress does when it passes a law. **Adjudication,** however, is a *quasi-judicial* process. It is used to resolve *individual conflicts,* much as trials are used in a court of law. Adjudicatory proceedings in an agency determine whether a person or business is failing to comply with the law or with agency rules.

Congress delegates adjudicatory authority to certain agencies because it anticipates conflicts over the interpretation of laws and regulations and because it does not have time to settle all the fine points of law when it writes statutes. The National Labor Relations Board (NLRB), which acts as a mediating institution for business-labor disputes, is an example of an agency that relies heavily on adjudication.

Adjudication decisions are made by administrative law judges, who are technically their agencies' employees. Yet they are strictly independent in their actions and cannot be removed except for gross misconduct. Adjudicatory proceedings allow each party to present its side of the case and allow the judge to search for any information that will be helpful in reaching a decision. Somewhat less formal than a court trial, the proceeding is still adversarial in nature. In NLRB cases, the party that loses may appeal to the five-member board, which has set up five three-member panels to review decisions.[26]

POLICYMAKING: INFORMAL POLITICS

The formal procedures used in rulemaking are only part of the policymaking process. When a new regulation is being considered and the evidence and arguments on all sides have been presented, how does an administrator reach a decision? Few important policy decisions can be calculated with the efficiency of a computer. Rather, policy decisions emerge from human beings' weighing and judging complex problems that frequently have no completely satisfactory solutions.

The Science of Muddling Through

Administrative decisions are subject to many influences and constraints. In a classic analysis of policymaking, "The Science of Muddling Through," Charles Lindblom compared the way policy should ideally be made with the way it is formulated in the real world.[27] Lindblom's analysis highlighted the difficulties of reaching a "rational" decision. The scenario for the idealized decisionmaking process begins when an administrator tackles a problem by ranking his or her values and objectives. After those objectives are clarified, all possible solutions to the problem are given thorough consideration. Alternative solutions are analyzed in a comprehensive manner that takes all relevant factors into account. The final choice will be the most effective means of achieving the desired goal and solving the problem.

Lindblom claimed that this "rational-comprehensive" model was as inaccurate as it was ideal. To begin with, policymakers have great difficulty defining precise values and goals. Administrators at the Department of Energy, for example, want to ensure that supplies of home heating oil are sufficient each winter. At the same time, they want to reduce dependence on foreign oil. The two goals are not fully compatible. How can administrators precisely rank these and other goals of the nation's energy policy?

Real-world decisionmaking parts company with the ideal in another way: the chosen policy cannot always be the most effective means to the desired end. Even if a tax at the pump is the most effective way of maintaining order by reducing oil consumption during a shortage, legislators and administrators might fear that motorists' anger at such a freedom-restricting tax would make the theoretically "right" decision politically unthinkable. Thus the "best" policy is often the one on which the most people can agree. But political compromise between differing viewpoints may mean that the government will go only part of the way toward solving a problem.

A final point critics of the rational-comprehensive model raise is that policymaking can never be based on truly comprehensive analysis. If a secretary of energy ordered a comprehensive study of all alternative energy sources and relevant policy considerations for the next two decades, he or she could not possibly find time to read it. A truly thorough investigation of the subject could produce thousands of pages of text. Instead, the secretary of energy usually relies on short staff memos outlining a limited range of feasible solutions for immediate problems. Time is of the essence, and problems are frequently too pressing to await complete and final study.

In short, policymaking tends to be *incremental,* with policies and programs changing bit by bit, step by step. Decisionmakers are constrained by incomplete information, competing policy objectives, opposing political forces, and time pressures. They choose from a limited number of feasible options that are almost always modifications of existing policies rather than wholesale departures.

Influences on Decisionmaking

Policymakers do not make decisions in isolation. Instead, administrators make decisions within two basic contexts. First, the internal structure of a bureaucracy affects decisionmaking. Formal lines of authority, approval procedures, the quality and extent of research, and coordinating committees between divisions are all part of this internal structure. The bureaucracy's external environment — including interest group pressures, public opinion, congressional preferences, and White House goals — also influences decisionmaking.

In large, complex organizations, many people are involved in making any important decision. Although one administrator will probably have ultimate responsibility for each decision, that administrator's staff is often highly influential in developing the chosen policy. A top administrator has many duties and, as noted earlier, does not have the time to personally research and analyze each issue.

The administrator of the Occupational Safety and Health Administration, for example, works with a large number of professional staffers, many of whom are experts in the technologies of various industries. When the OSHA administrator wants something done about workers' exposure to lead in a car battery plant, he or she needs the advice of agency experts. The administrator also needs advice from staff members on the political ramifications of any new battery plant standards. Will the new machinery required by regulations be so expensive that small plant owners will prefer to take their chances by not complying? Can battery company executives persuade members of Congress to pressure the agency to reverse itself? Will labor unions find the safety regulations too lenient and do what they can to block them?

Thus, when administrators evaluate policy options, they must consider the reactions of both those in the external environment, such as interest groups, and those with whom they work inside the bureaucracy. Yet these constraints do not completely tie administrators' hands. Agency or bureau chiefs can make their influence felt by focusing problem solving on solutions they favor. Much of an administrator's time, however, can be taken up trying to build a united coalition within the agency (or between the agency and other government bureaucracies) in favor of the policy compromise that comes closest to his or her point of view.

The Bureaucrat

How an organization makes decisions and performs its tasks is greatly affected by the people who work there — the bureaucrats. Americans often find that their interactions with bureaucrats are frustrating because bureaucrats "go by the book," are inflexible, or delay matters by saying they need permission from a superior before they can do anything. Top administrators can also become frustrated with the bureaucrats who work for them.

Why do people act "bureaucratically"? Individuals who work for large organizations cannot help but be affected by the "culture of bureaucracy," even in their everyday speech (see Feature 12.2). Modern bureaucracies develop explicit rules and standards in order to promote efficiency of operations and fairness in treating clients. But within each organization, *norms* (informal, unwritten rules of behavior) also develop and influence the way people act on the job. The Veterans Administration (VA), for example, for many years had an official rule that medical care was to be provided only to veterans in need of hospitalization; more routine treatment should be left to private physicians. Doctors working for the VA thought this rule was irrational, and among them a norm developed whereby they would provide routine care under the guise that it was needed prior to a hospital admission.[28]

Other forces are also at work. An employee of a bureaucracy is positioned somewhere in a large hierarchy. To advance in the hierarchy, the employee must impress his or her direct superior. This means not only doing a good individual job, but also being a cooperative member of the supervisor's staff. It is easy to stereotype bureaucrats as overly cautious, never-rock-the-boat

Feature 12.2

English as a Foreign Language

One of the most irritating characteristics of the bureaucrat is a tendency to use *jargon*, or a specialized vocabulary peculiar to an occupation. A less-than-kind definition is "gibberish." In the language of bureaucracy, a simple sentence, such as "Based on the evidence, we decided to close the Denver office," might become "A determination was made from the decision matrix that the relevant output variables indicated that a termination of the department's regional office at Denver was necessitated at this time."

Why does jargon rear its ugly head in the bureaucracy? One reason is that jargon is often mistaken as a sign of professionalism. Some people assume that the use of specialized terms reflects a command of their subject matter. Another reason is that many bureaucrats receive graduate training in the social sciences, where jargon breeds and multiplies. They then bring to government all the specialized vocabulary of political science, sociology, and economics.

The principal reason for the ascent of jargon over English in the bureaucracy may be the decline in writing skills. It's far easier to write several long, complex, jargon-laden sentences than it is to write one that is short and crystal clear.

If you're thinking about entering government, take the following "aptitude" test. How many of these words in "bureaucratese" can you define? (Answers appear below.)

1. Parameters	6. Formatting
2. Interdigitate	7. Proactive
3. Prioritize	8. Window of opportunity
4. GIGO	9. Highly scenario-dependent
5. Interface	10. Career deceleration

Answers:

(1) Boundaries   (2) To work together   (3) Rank   (4) Garbage in, garbage out. (Or, in other words, if the data you put into the computer are worthless, then so will be your results.)   (5) See interdigitate   (6) Designing   (7) Opposite of reactive   (8) The time is ripe   (9) It all depends   (10) You're fired.

types. But bureaucracies, like corporations or any other organization, have their share of ambitious, aggressive individuals who are willing to take risks to advance themselves and their ideas.

At first glance, the bureaucrat may seem to be a completely negative sort of creature. That creature does, however, have its positive side. The desire to please superiors makes people work hard. In some bureaucracies, a strong sense of mission develops, and the resulting *esprit de corps* motivates workers. The U.S. Forest Service is a familiar example of an agency with highly committed workers. This agency's effectiveness in its operations is clearly enhanced by the attractiveness of the forest ranger's job to many people. Forest rangers see their position as more than just another job, and their performance reflects that commitment.[29]

Bureaucrats' caution and close adherence to agency rules also have their brighter sides. It would be unsettling if government employees were highly independent and interpreted the rules as they pleased. Simply put, bureaucrats "go by the book" because the "book" is composed of the laws and regulations of this country, as well as the internal rules and norms of a particular agency. Americans expect to be treated equally before the law, and bureaucrats work with that expectation in mind.

PROBLEMS IN POLICY IMPLEMENTATION

The development of policy in Washington is the end of one part of the policymaking cycle but the beginning of another. After policies have been developed, they must be implemented. **Implementation** is the process of putting specific policies into operation. Ultimately, bureaucrats must convert policies on paper into policies in action. For example, the Social Security Administration could issue a new set of policies designed to get people receiving disability payments to return to work when they are physically capable. No set of regulations can possibly anticipate all injuries suffered on the job. And medical opinion on even a single case can differ. How much can be left to the discretion of social security bureaucrats in local offices? What if they err and take benefits away from people who really cannot work?

It is important to study implementation, because policies do not always do what they were designed to do. Some of the most persistent problems in implementation are due to vague directives, faulty coordination, decentralization of authority, and imprecise evaluation of success.

Vague Directives

It is difficult to implement a policy when that policy is not clearly stated. Policy directives to bureaucrats in the field sometimes lack clarity and leave lower-level officials with too much discretion. The source of such vague regulations is often vague legislation. Congress, for example, included in the Elementary and Secondary School Act of 1965 a program of grants to meet the "special needs of educationally deprived children." The Act did not, however, spell out who qualified as educationally deprived. The administering agency, the U.S. Office of Education, passed the money on to the states without providing highly specific eligibility criteria. As a result, the money was spent for a variety of purposes, not all of which were beneficial to deprived children.[30]

Vague directives crop up as problems particularly at the time a program is first put into operation. Knowing that this problem exists, however, and finding the best way to solve it are two different things.

Faulty Coordination

Programs frequently cut across the jurisdictions of a number of agencies. Effective policy implementation sometimes fails to materialize because the agencies involved have trouble coordinating their efforts. An economic development program in Oakland, California, lagged badly because many agencies had jurisdiction over various parts of the project. One study found that, during a seven-year period, there were thirty different stages for decisions that required seventy agreements among various bureaucracies.[31]

A turf war can break out when different agencies begin competing for leadership in a policy area. The fight against illegal drugs has been hampered by bickering over leadership and jurisdiction between the Drug Enforcement Agency and the Customs Service.[32]

Decentralization of Authority

A problem related to faulty coordination is the dispersal of authority in the federal system. Even when the federal government is unified in its objectives, it sometimes must share authority over a program with state and local officials. When President Lyndon B. Johnson declared his War on Poverty, Community Action Agencies were its front-line soldiers. Johnson intended that these local agencies would design a "comprehensive attack on poverty" in their communities, because local people supposedly knew more about poverty in their own cities than the bureaucrats in Washington did.

Many of these Community Action Agencies turned out to be disappointments. Some came under the control of local government officials who were not aggressive in dealing with the poverty problem. Others were ineffective for the opposite reason; local officials viewed them as rivals because they were independent of city hall.[33]

Decentralization does not always result in such failures, but it usually means a tradeoff is inevitable. Decentralization does tap local imagination and initiative, but at some risk: local administrators may not use funds as originally envisioned by the program's designers, and squabbling between local political factions may reduce the program's effectiveness.

Imprecise Evaluation of Success

Sometimes a program's implementation is hampered because there is no reliable way to measure its success. If a program's effectiveness cannot be measured accurately, policymakers must operate in the dark. They do not have the necessary information to judge whether a policy is working well, needs modification, or should be scrapped altogether.

An interesting example of how important accurate evaluation is and how difficult it is to obtain comes from the Head Start program. Head Start, which was begun in the 1960s, was designed to help low-income and minority students do better in school. These students were placed in preschool enrichment programs, with the hope that this "head start" would help them do as well as those from more privileged backgrounds. The initial results were disappointing. Children who had been in Head Start programs did not do appreciably better in school than similarly deprived children who had not been in the program. This outcome weakened political support for Head Start, since there seemed to be little justification for spending money on it. Yet longer-term studies now show that preschool enrichment programs *can* have positive effects on school performance.[34]

Although obstacles to effective implementation can create an impression that nothing will succeed, programs can and do work. Problems in the implementation process demonstrate why time, patience, and continual analysis are necessary ingredients in successful policymaking. To return to a term we used earlier, implementation is by its nature an *incremental* process, in which trial and error lead to policy adjustments.

REFORMING THE BUREAUCRACY

American citizens do not hesitate to criticize the bureaucracy. They complain that it is too big, too intrusive, too costly and inefficient, and too unresponsive. Presidents, members of Congress, and agency administrators constantly try to come up with reforms that address these complaints. In recent years, reform efforts have included reorganization, deregulation, citizen participation, and analytical budgeting.

Reorganization

One of the most common attempts at improving the bureaucracy's performance is **reorganization.** For instance, two or three bureaus in a department might be combined to reduce overlap. Or responsibility for running a program might be taken from one agency and given to another that runs programs in the same general area. When departments or agencies are reorganized, administrators sometimes find ways of improving the delivery of services, saving money, or both.

Reorganization lets the government adapt to new responsibilities and priorities. The creation of the Department of Energy during the Carter administration was a large-scale effort at reorganization. In the wake of an Arab oil embargo in 1973, support began to grow for a coherent, coordinated energy policy that would make the United States less dependent on foreign supplies. Administrative units in the various departments and agencies that dealt with energy problems were pulled together into one large, new department. By 1981, however, America was less concerned about its energy future, and Ronald Reagan proposed eliminating the Energy Department and dispersing some of its programs to other cabinet departments or agencies. Congress refused to go along with Reagan's reorganization plan; it did, however, cut the department's budget, which was one of the president's primary goals.

Interest groups and members of Congress who are trying to protect valued programs often oppose administrative reorganizations. In addition, bureaucrats themselves can be formidable obstacles. For example, the Pentagon makes periodic efforts to centralize such management functions as purchasing, in order to save money by eliminating overlapping jobs and by standardizing equipment. But interservice rivalries among the army, navy, and air force consistently plague such efforts. Civilian bureaucrats in the Pentagon even failed at one point to get all the branches of the service to adopt a common belt buckle for uniforms. Although the escalating cost of high-technology weapons systems has renewed pressure for Pentagon reorganization, major breakthroughs have yet to come about.[35]

Deregulation

Many people believe that government is too involved in **regulation,** or intervention in the natural workings of business markets to promote some socially desired goal. For example, government might regulate a market to ensure that products pose no danger to consumers. Through **deregulation** the government lessens its role and lets the natural market forces of supply and demand take over. Indeed, nothing is more central to capitalist philosophy than the belief that the free market will efficiently promote the balance of supply and demand. Some important moves toward deregulation have taken place recently, notably in the airline, trucking, financial services, and telecommunications industries.

In the case of the airlines, the Civil Aeronautics Board (CAB) had been determining fares and controlling access to routes. The justification for these regulatory efforts was that they would prevent overloads, both in the sky and at airport facilities, and would ensure some service to all parts of the nation. But regulation had a side effect: it reduced competition among airlines, and that worked to the disadvantage of consumers. Congress responded by passing a law in 1978 mandating deregulation of fares and routes, and the airlines became more competitive. New carriers entered lucrative markets, fares decreased, and price wars broke out. In smaller cities, which major carriers no longer had to serve, smaller "commuter" airlines offered essential services. In retrospect, it is clear that government was overregulating the airline industry.

The question of how much regulation (or deregulation) is enough leads to a larger question about the role of the federal government (and therefore the bureaucracy) in American society. Conservatives tend to believe that government regulation of business should be minimal, giving both consumers and producers as much personal freedom as possible. Liberals, however, believe the free market offers citizens inadequate protection from unfair or dangerous business practices.

What about the bureaucrats themselves? How do they view regulation? Compared With What? 12.1 reports the attitudes of politicians and bureaucrats in six countries regarding the "preferred degree of state involvement in the economy and society."

The regulation of prescription drugs by the Food and Drug Administration (FDA) is another illustration of how difficult it can be to decide where to draw the fine line between regulation and the free market. To promote safety, the FDA requires thorough testing of new prescription drugs before they can be sold to consumers. But while the years drag on before the FDA is satisfied with a new drug's safety, a useful drug that can reduce suffering may be kept out of the hands of sick people. Drug manufacturers argue that the FDA should speed up its testing and approval process, to get new drugs out to those who need them. Not insignificantly, earlier approval would also permit drug companies to begin recouping their investments in research and development earlier.

The other side of the coin is that faster licensing of drugs can be dangerous. The harmful side effects of drugs may not come to light for years; in the intervening period, unforeseen effects can cause serious harm to users and may increase their risks of cancer. Never too far from the minds of congressional and agency officials who would have to take responsibility for

Dole on the Job
Cabinet secretaries are key policymakers in the executive branch. In addition to their involvement in the development of policy, they must play a management role overseeing the performance of their department in carrying out program responsibilities. Here Secretary of Transportation Elizabeth Dole takes a first-hand look at the job of air traffic controllers.

deregulation is the thalidomide case. The William S. Merrill Company purchased the license to market this drug, already available in Europe, and filed an application with the FDA in 1960. The company then began a protracted fight with FDA bureaucrat Dr. Frances Kelsey, who was assigned to evaluate the thalidomide application. She demanded that the company abide by all FDA drug testing requirements, despite the fact that the drug was already in use in other countries. She and her superiors resisted pressure from the company to bend the rules a little and expedite approval. Before Merrill had conducted all the FDA tests, news came pouring in from Europe that some women who had taken thalidomide during pregnancy were giving birth to babies without arms, legs, or ears. Strict adherence to government regulation protected American mothers from the same tragedy.

Citizen Participation

A very different kind of reform effort is citizen participation. **Citizen participation programs** encourage interaction between bureaucrats and their clients. For example, before federal Community Development Block Grant (CDBG) funds can be used in a local area, a hearing must be held to let citizens comment on the proposals. Ideally, citizen input then becomes an important factor in the decisionmaking of bureaucrats administering the CDBG funds.

Citizen participation programs arose out of a belief that bureaucracies are too far removed from the people they serve. The hope is that policymakers will fashion policies that are more in line with what citizens really want and that citizens will feel more confident about the governmental process because they have participated in it. The citizen participation movement was set in motion by the Johnson administration's War on Poverty legislation. The Economic Opportunity Act of 1964 stated that poverty program administrators

Compared With What? 12.1

Bureaucrats' and Politicians' Attitudes Toward State Involvement

In all the countries surveyed, bureaucrats were more likely than politicians to occupy the middle position, favoring the "present balance." But U.S. bureaucrats were more likely than those in other countries to favor "much more" state involvement. Some readers might interpret the deviant American pattern as conclusive proof of a "liberal bias" within the federal bureaucracy. Others might explain the pattern by noting that *all* of the other countries already experience a great deal more "state involvement" than we do in the United States, causing bureaucrats in other countries to be more satisfied with the "present balance."

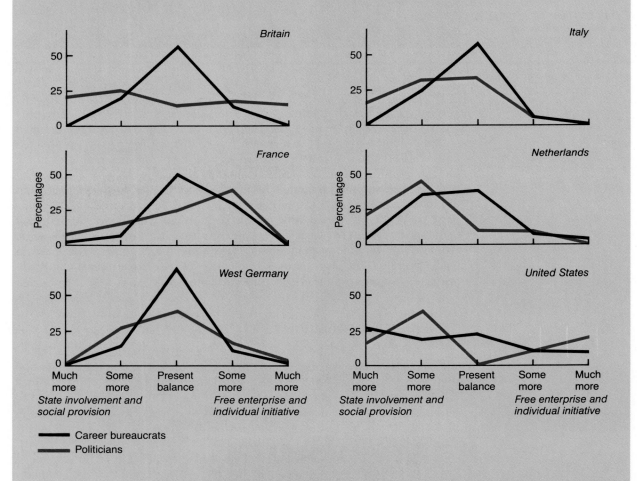

Source: Adapted from Figure 5–1 in Joel D. Aberbach, Robert D. Putnam, and Bert A. Rockman, *Bureaucrats and Politicians in Western Democracies* (Cambridge, Mass.: Harvard University Press, 1981), p. 122.

should include "maximum feasible participation" by the poor in their policy-making deliberations. In the following ten years, more than 150 new citizen participation programs were started.

The programs themselves have had mixed results, and many are best described as "rituals."[36] Often, citizens express their views at hearings held mainly for show, and these groups exert little substantive influence. Because bureaucrats have not been eager to share their power with citizens' groups, many comply with the letter—but not with the spirit—of the requirements.

Nevertheless, some citizen participation programs have been successful. Some bureaucracies have involved local citizens and citizens' groups extensively in their policymaking processes. The Army Corps of Engineers' "fish-bowl planning process" was a concerted effort to make project planning highly visible in affected communities and to involve citizens in project deliberations from the beginning. Citizens who participated gave the planning process high marks.[37]

Federal citizen participation programs diminished in importance when Reagan was elected. To his administration, these programs represent the views of liberal environmentalists and consumers. As a result, the Reagan administration has placed little value on the programs.[38] Whether citizen participation will emerge as an effective administrative reform in the future remains to be seen.

Analytical Budgeting

In recent years, a reform often imposed on the federal bureaucracy is **analytical budgeting.** In an effort to keep bureaucracies from spending any more than necessary to meet their program goals, various administrations have sought to bring sophisticated analysis to the budgeting process. Such budget tools as *cost-benefit analysis* and the Carter administration's *zero-based budgeting* are examples. Although different methods have been used, the basic idea is the same: force administrators to think rigorously about alternative means of achieving their policy objectives and to choose the most cost-effective means.

For example, if the Department of Defense wants to develop a new weapons system, how should it make its decision? Defense Department officials could simply conclude that the cruise missile is an effective battle weapon and therefore ought to be built. But, instead of looking at strategic considerations alone, their analysis could combine cost calculations with measures of combat effectiveness. One analysis compared three types of cruise missiles (air-, ground-, and sea-launched) with other weapons systems. On the basis of purchase price alone, ground- and sea-launched cruise missiles were the most expensive. But when a method of analysis called "life-cycle costing," which took into account long-term operating and support service expenditures, was used, ground- and sea-launched missiles emerged as the least expensive alternative (per warhead).[39]

Many programs are not susceptible to the type of quantitative analysis of costs and benefits that analytical budgeting requires. How does one calculate the value of grants for medical research that may at some later date save lives? Analytical budgeting is further compromised by political considerations. Administration officials are not eager to offend their constituents.

The federal government's water reclamation projects are cases in point. They are especially popular with western farmers who have received low-cost water to irrigate their fields. Strict cost-benefit analyses of many of these projects show that they offer too little benefit at too great a cost. Stated another way, taxpayers are unnecessarily subsidizing western farmers who could well afford to pay more for the irrigation water they receive. The subsidies endure, though, because the *political* costs for ending them are too great. Western politicians are not about to let analytical budgeting put an end to something their constituents want so badly.[40]

Looking back on the various efforts at analytical budgeting, one scholar writes, "Practices of both Republican and Democratic administrations indicate that nonpolitical budgets based on business practices of economy and efficiency are largely unknown outside the rhetoric of textbooks."[41]

SUMMARY

As the scope of government activity has grown during the twentieth century, an accompanying growth has taken place in the number and size of government bureaucracies. The executive branch has evolved into a complex set of departments, independent agencies, and government corporations. Such bureaucracies are important to study because they are policymaking bodies. Through the administrative discretion granted to them by Congress, bureaucracies make policy decisions that have the force of law. In making policy choices, agency decisionmakers are influenced by their external environment, especially Congress, interest groups, and the White House. Decisionmakers are also influenced by internal norms and the need to work cooperatively with others in the agency.

The controversy and conflict surrounding bureaucratic policymaking reflect broader differences in the American political system and the clash of values underlying U.S. politics. Whether policy involves funeral practices, action on the Clean Air Act, or standards for chain saws, one issue is fundamental: to what degree should the federal government intervene to protect Americans in the name of order or to promote their welfare in the name of equality? At what point does protection for some citizens rob others of the freedom to lead their lives as they want?

The division exists between those who want administrative agencies to more aggressively protect citizens from harmful or unfair business practices and those who want agencies to do less. This division also usually represents the line that divides the views of liberals and conservatives. However, conservatives can sometimes find reasons why the government should take action on social issues, and liberals can find reasons why the government should not interfere. Businesspeople, too, can find many reasons for the government to regulate aspects of their own industry, even though they generally believe in deregulation.

Although we can all find bureaucratic activities of which we approve or disapprove, Americans tend to be critical of bureaucracy in general. It is commonly faulted for being unresponsive, delivering services poorly, or wasting money. Reforms, like citizen participation or reorganization are commonly put forward as means of improving bureaucratic performance. But ultimately critics must face the relationship of bureaucracy to democracy.

The most serious charge is that bureaucracy is out of control of the people. In fact, there are substantial controls on the bureaucracy from the White House, the other branches of government, interest groups, and public opinion. Still, to many Americans, the bureaucracy seems too big, too costly, and too intrusive. It is difficult to reduce the size and scope of bureaucratic activity because pluralism characterizes our political system. The entire executive branch may appear too large, and each of us can point to agencies that we believe should be reduced or eliminated. Yet each bureaucracy has its supporters. To farmers, the Department of Agriculture performs vital services. Unions care greatly about the Department of Labor. Scholars want the National Science Foundation protected. And home builders would not want Housing and Urban Development programs cut back. Bureaucracies survive because they perform services that some people want very badly.

Key Terms

bureaucracy
bureaucrat
laissez faire
department
independent agency
regulatory commission
externality
government corporation
civil service
Senior Executive Service

administrative discretion
rulemaking
regulation (rule)
adjudication
implementation
reorganization
regulation
deregulation
citizen participation program
analytical budgeting

Selected Readings

Downs, Anthony. *Inside Bureaucracy.* Boston: Little, Brown, 1967. A rigorous analysis of bureaucratic behavior.

Heclo, Hugh. *A Government of Strangers.* Washington, D.C.: Brookings Institution, 1977. A look at the uneasy relationship between career bureaucrats and political appointees.

Meier, Kenneth J. *Regulation.* New York: St. Martin's, 1985. A helpful, detailed introduction to regulation in America.

Pressman, Jeffrey L., and Aaron B. Wildavsky, *Implementation.* 3rd ed. Berkeley: University of California Press, 1984. A classic case study of why programs don't always work out.

Rourke, Francis E. *Bureaucracy, Politics, and Public Policy.* 3rd ed. Boston: Little, Brown, 1984. An excellent introduction to bureaucracy, with a very useful analysis of the relationship between agencies and their clientele.

Seidman, Harold. *Politics, Position, and Power.* 3rd ed. New York: Oxford, 1980. An authoritative account of the politics of reorganization.

Wilson, James Q., ed. *The Politics of Regulation.* New York: Basic Books, 1980. A collection of essays that describes regulatory practices of different Washington agencies.

13

The Courts

Justice Felix Frankfurter commented, "This is the first indication that I have ever had that there is a God." What provoked this extraordinary comment? Chief Justice Fred M. Vinson had died unexpectedly on September 8, 1953. Frankfurter despised Vinson as a leader and disliked him as a person. Now Vinson's sudden death cast new light — and perhaps new hope — on the school segregation cases known collectively as *Brown* v. *Board of Education.*

The issue of public school segregation had been argued in the United States Supreme Court in late 1952. The justices were deeply divided, and Vinson supported upholding racial segregation in the United States. Since it was clear the justices were not ready to reach a decision, they set the school segregation cases for reargument the following year.

Frankfurter's caustic remark reflected the critical role Vinson's replacement as chief justice would play as the Court tackled the desegregation issue. On September 30, 1953, in his very first appointment, President Dwight D. Eisenhower chose California Governor Earl Warren as chief justice. The president would later regret his choice.

Following reargument in December 1953, the new chief justice led the Court from division to unanimity on the issue of school segregation. Unlike his predecessor, Warren began the secret conference to decide the segregation issue with a strong statement: that segregation was contrary to the Thirteenth, Fourteenth, and Fifteenth Amendments to the Constitution. "Personally," remarked the new chief justice, "I can't see how today we can justify segregation based solely on race." Moreover, if the Court were to uphold segregation, he argued, it could do so only on the theory that blacks were inherently inferior to whites. As the discussion proceeded, Warren's opponents were cast in the awkward position of appearing to support racism.

Five justices were clearly on Warren's side, making six votes; two were prepared to join the majority if Warren's opinion satisfied them. With only one clear holdout, Warren set about the task of satisfying his colleagues' concerns. In the months that followed, Warren met with them individually in their chambers. They maintained an extraordinary level of secrecy about their impending decision and the reasons that would accompany it. Finally, in April 1954, Warren approached Justice Stanley Reed, whose vote would make the opinion unanimous. "Stan," said the chief justice, "you're all by yourself in this now. You've got to decide whether it's really the best thing for the country." Ultimately Reed joined. On May 17, 1954, the Supreme Court unanimously decided against racial segregation in public education and signaled the end of legally created or governmentally enforced segregation of the races in the United States.[1]

Judges confront conflicting values in specific cases submitted to them for decision, and tough cases call for fine distinctions among competing values. In crafting these distinctions, judges make policy through their decisions because other judges tend to accept rulings made in similar cases. Therefore, although they are made for *particular* cases, court decisions influence policy when they are cited as the basis for decisions in *similar* cases. In this way, the judicial process moves from the specific to the general. One judge in one court can make public policy to the extent that he or she can influence other decisions. According to democratic theory, however, the power to

A Last Oyez
*Earl Warren (1891–1974)
retired from his post as the
fourteenth chief justice of the
United States on June 23, 1968,
after sixteen years of service on
the nation's highest court. A
true liberal, Warren led a Court
that actively preferred equality
to freedom and that preferred
freedom to order. These decisions
brought calls for Warren's
impeachment from the Congress,
located in the Capitol building
in the background. One of
Warren's last official acts was
to administer the oath of office
to his successor, Warren
Earl Burger.*

make law resides only in the people or in their representatives in an elected legislature.

American courts are deeply involved in the life of the country and its people. Some courts, like the Supreme Court of the United States, make fundamental policy decisions vital to the preservation of freedom, order, and equality. Yet most courts, including the Supreme Court, are largely beyond democratic control. Courts shape policies that form the very heart of American democracy. They can undo the work of representative institutions and therefore represent a difficult problem for democratic theory. Because court rulings — especially Supreme Court rulings — extend far beyond any particular case, they present a potential problem for democratic government. Judges are students of the law, but they remain human beings. They have their own opinions about the value of freedom, order, and equality in our society. Although all judges are constrained by statutes and precedents from expressing their personal values in their decisions, some judges are more prone than others to interpret laws in the light of their beliefs.

Judges are said to exercise **judicial restraint** when they hew closely to statutes and previous cases in reaching their decisions. Judges are said to exercise **judicial activism** when they are apt to interpret existing laws and rulings more loosely and to interject their own values in court decisions. In recent history, many activist judges have tended to trade freedom for equality in their decisions, which has linked the concept of judicial activism with liberalism. However, there is no necessary connection between judicial activism and liberalism. If judges interpret existing statutes and precedents more loosely to trade freedom for order, they are still activists—conservative activists. How do courts exercise political power within the pluralist model? Are judges simply politicians in black robes, making decisions independent of popular control? This chapter attempts to answer such questions as it explores the role of the judiciary in American political life.

CONFERRING FEDERAL JUDICIAL AUTHORITY

Article III of the Constitution created "one supreme Court." The founders were divided on the need for additional courts for the national government, so they deferred to Congress the decision to create a federal court system. Those who opposed the creation of the federal courts believed that such a system would usurp the authority of the state courts.[2] Congress considered the issue in its first session and, in the Judiciary Act of 1789, gave life to a system of federal courts that would coexist with the courts in each state, but be independent of them.

Fifteen months after the Constitution's ratification, President George Washington signed the Judiciary Act of 1789. The act set the number of Supreme Court justices at six (that number has now grown to nine). On the same day, Washington sent the Senate the first nominations to the Supreme Court.

The Judiciary Act also created thirteen district courts, three circuit courts, and one judgeship for each of the thirteen district courts. The **district courts** were to be the trial courts of the federal government; one would be located in each state and would serve as the primary access to federal judicial power. Their **jurisdiction,** or authority to exercise judicial power, was limited at first to deciding only admiralty and maritime questions—the shipping and commerce cases that arise on the high seas and in navigable U.S. waters.

The three circuit courts created by the act functioned for the most part as trial courts, resolving disputes between citizens of different states or between the U.S. government and foreign citizens, as long as more than $500 was at stake. The **circuit courts** also shared some power with state courts to hear and decide federal questions—disputes arising from the Constitution, federal laws, and treaties. But most such questions were expected to be raised and answered in the state courts.* Each circuit court was to be composed of two Supreme Court justices (who were required to travel the geographical area known as the "circuit") and one district judge.

In sum, the Constitution and the Judiciary Act of 1789 created three different types of federal courts (district courts, circuit courts, and one Supreme Court) staffed by two kinds of judges (district court judges and Su-

---

* The circuits were also empowered to hear some appeals from decisions of the district courts.

preme Court justices) and conferred on them the limited authority to decide some, though not all, cases or controversies. Indeed, then and now, the distinguishing characteristic of the federal courts is their limited jurisdiction: they can exercise only as much authority as Congress deems necessary—in any event, no more power than the Constitution itself allows.

Chief Justice John Marshall (1755–1835)
Marshall clearly ranks as the "Babe Ruth" of the Supreme Court. Both Marshall and the Bambino transformed their respective games and became symbols of their institutions. Scholars now recognize both men as originators—Marshall of judicial review, and Ruth of the modern age of baseball.

Federal Judicial Supremacy

In the early years of the republic, the federal judiciary was not considered a particularly powerful branch of government. It was difficult to recruit Supreme Court justices during this period. John Jay, the first chief justice, refused to resume his duties in 1801 because he concluded that the Court could not muster the "energy, weight, and dignity" to contribute to national affairs.[3] Several distinguished statesmen refused appointments and several others, including Oliver Ellsworth, the second chief justice, resigned.

Judicial Review of the Other Branches

When John Marshall, an ardent Federalist, was appointed chief justice in 1801, a period of profound change began for the Court that so many notables had shunned. Shortly after Marshall's appointment, the Court confronted a question of fundamental importance to the future of the new republic: if a federal law and the Constitution conflict, which should prevail? This question arose in the case of *Marbury* v. *Madison* (1803), which involved a controversial series of last-minute political appointments (see below).* The ensuing litigation hinged on the concept of the Supreme Court's **original jurisdiction,** or its authority to hear a case before any other court does.

The Constitution confers original jurisdiction on the Supreme Court to hear and decide "all Cases affecting Ambassadors, other public Ministers and Consuls, and those in which a State shall be a Party." Cases falling under the Supreme Court's original jurisdiction are tried and decided in the Court itself; such cases begin and end there. The largest part of the Supreme Court's jurisdiction, then and now, extends only to cases that have been tried, decided, and re-examined as far as the law permits in other federal or state courts. These referred cases fall under the Supreme Court's **appellate jurisdiction.** The Court exercises judicial power under its appellate jurisdiction only because Congress gives it the authority to do so. This congressional control is another example of the checks and balances principle embodied in the Constitution. Thus, the power of the federal courts depends on a grant of jurisdiction from the legislative branch.

---

* Courts publish their opinions in volumes called *reporters*. Today, the United States Report is the official reporter for the U.S. Supreme Court. For example, the Court's opinion in the case of *Brown* v. *Board of Education* will be cited as 347 U.S. 483 (1954). This means that the opinion in the Brown case begins on page 483 of Volume 347 in the U.S. Report. The citation also includes the year of the decision. In this example, the Court decided the Brown case in 1954.

   Before 1875 the official reports of the Supreme Court were published under the names of private decision compilers. For example, the case of *Marbury* v. *Madison* is cited as 1 Cranch 137 (1803). This means that the case of Marbury against Madison is found in Volume 1, compiled by reporter William Cranch, starting on page 137.

"What's Going On Here?"
Sometimes, court opinions do not yield easily to understanding by reporters (or by judges, as this cartoon suggests). Several readings may be required to grasp the issues and the arguments, which can be embedded in the complexities of the legal process.

The case of *Marbury* v. *Madison* began on March 2, 1801, when an obscure Federalist, William Marbury, was designated as a justice of the peace in the District of Columbia. Marbury and several others were appointed to government posts created in the last days of the Adams administration. In the rush to conclude that administration's work, Secretary of State John Marshall failed to deliver to Marbury (and the other appointees) the documents that would have made their appointments official before the end of Adams's term at midnight, March 3, 1801. The documents, known as *commissions,* were duly signed by President John Adams and affixed with the Great Seal of the United States by Marshall, Adams's secretary of state. But they remained undelivered, tucked away in the secretary of state's desk. The newly arrived Jefferson administration had little interest in completing these appointments by delivering the commissions; there were qualified Jeffersonians who would welcome the jobs.

Marbury and three others brought suit in the Supreme Court to have their commissions delivered by the new secretary of state, James Madison. Marbury claimed that the Judiciary Act of 1789 gave the Court the power to order Madison to do so. Marbury contended that Section 13 of the Judiciary Act gave the Supreme Court original jurisdiction by authorizing the Court to issue writs of mandamus to United States officials. (*Mandamus* means "we command," and a **writ of mandamus** is a court order directing an official to act.)

The Court faced two alternatives. It could issue the writ, but in all likelihood, Madison would ignore it. In this case, the nation's highest court would risk ridicule by a rebuff over a trifling issue. The Court's other option was to deny the writ that Marbury requested. However, given the explicit authority in Section 13, a failure to act would mean the retreat of a Court that feared its actions would not be obeyed. The Court found a novel solution that avoided either ridicule or retreat.

On February 24, 1803, the Court held, through the forceful argument of Chief Justice Marshall, that Marbury had a right to his commission and that it should be delivered to him. The Court concluded, however, that it lacked the power to order the commission delivered. Although Marbury based his suit on the Court's power to issue writs of mandamus, the Court viewed the act granting that power as expanding its original jurisdiction, which was restricted by the Constitution. Hence, a provision of an act of Congress was in conflict with a provision of the Constitution. Can "an act repugnant to the constitution . . . become the law of the land?" asked the chief justice.

Marshall's logic was elegant. He argued that the Constitution was "the fundamental and paramount law of the nation" and that "an act of the legislature repugnant to the constitution is void." In other words, the Constitution takes precedence over acts of the legislature, namely, Congress. The last part in Marshall's argument vested in the judges the power to weigh legislative acts in relation to the Constitution:

> It is emphatically the province and duty of the judicial department to say what the law is. Those who apply the rule to particular cases, must of necessity expound and interpret that rule. . . . If a law be in opposition to the constitution, if both the law and the constitution apply to a particular case, so that the court must either decide that case conformably to the law, disregarding the constitution; or conformably to the constitution, disregarding the law; the court must determine which of these conflicting rules governs the case. This is the very essence of judicial duty.[4]

Marbury v. *Madison* thus established the Supreme Court's power of **judicial review** — the power to declare congressional acts invalid because they violate the Constitution.* Subsequent cases extended this principle to presidential acts.

John Marshall surely took a measure of political delight from the Court's decision. Though the decision blocked the Adams appointments, it was also a stiff rebuke of the Jefferson administration. By a "masterwork of indirection," John Marshall had expanded the potential power of the Supreme Court to equal or exceed that of the other branches of government. Should a congressional act or, by implication, a presidential act conflict with the Constitution, the Supreme Court claimed the power to declare the act void. The judiciary would be a check on the legislative and executive branches, consistent with the checks and balances principle embedded in the Constitution. Though Congress and the president may wrestle with the constitutionality of their actions, the Supreme Court remains the final authority on the meaning of the Constitution because it possesses the power of judicial review.

The exercise of judicial review appears to run counter to democratic theory: an unelected branch checks an elected branch in the name of the Constitution. Losers in the courts can still press their claims in Congress, however, by calling for a constitutional amendment to reverse a Court

---

* The Supreme Court had earlier upheld an act of Congress in *Hylton* v. *United States*, 3 Dall. 171 (1796). By striking down a portion of the Judiciary Act of 1789, *Marbury* v. *Madison* stood for a component of judicial power that had never before been exercised.

decision. In addition, the Court can also reconsider its previous decisions. Although infrequent, reversals of Court decisions demonstrate the continuing struggle among competing interests, consistent with the pluralist model.

Judicial Review of State Government

The establishment of judicial review of federal laws made the Supreme Court the arbiter of the national government. When acts of the federal government conflict with the Constitution, the Supreme Court can declare those acts invalid. Do state laws in conflict with the federal Constitution suffer a similar fate?

In *Fletcher* v. *Peck* (1810), the Supreme Court reached the conclusion that state laws in conflict with the Constitution are indeed void. The case, which began in a lower federal court, claimed that a Georgia law violated Article I, Section 10, of the Constitution: "No State shall . . . pass any . . . Law impairing the Obligation of Contracts."

In this case, a thoroughly corrupt Georgia legislature had approved the sale of vast portions of the state to a group of land speculators. The legislators were in on the deal and stood to reap huge rewards because the selling price was far below the property's real value. However, when most of the legislators were voted out of office, the new lawmakers repealed the land deal. In an opinion by Chief Justice Marshall, the Supreme Court held that the land deal repeal was an impairment of the contract obligations guaranteed by the U.S. Constitution. And the U.S. Constitution is supreme law. The case of *Fletcher* v. *Peck* was an early example of invalidation of state law in conflict with a provision of the Constitution.

When state laws conflict with the U.S. Constitution, the federal courts, including the Supreme Court, can declare such laws invalid. Judicial review thus embraces the power to invalidate state laws. But the states continued to resist this yoke of national supremacy, until their resistance erupted into civil war. Though federal judges were empowered to give supremacy to the Constitution, could state judges be yoked to the federal judiciary's views? After all, the states and the federal government were equal sovereigns, according to advocates of states' rights. The views of state judges deserved consideration and respect equal to that given to the views of federal judges.

The advocates of strong states rights conceded that the supremacy clause of the Constitution (Article VI) obligates state judges to follow the Constitution when it conflicts with state law. They maintained, however, that the states were bound only by their own interpretation of the Constitution. Relying again on the Judiciary Act of 1789, the Supreme Court argued that it possessed the authority to review state courts' decisions that called for interpretation of federal law. National supremacy required the Supreme Court to impose uniformity on federal law; otherwise, the Constitution's meaning would vary from state to state. The people, not the states, had ordained the Constitution, and the people had subordinated state power to the Constitution in order to establish a viable national government with supreme authority.

These decisions by John Marshall's Supreme Court established another component of federal judicial authority — the Court's power to review state court decisions resting on an interpretation of federal laws or the Constitution. Together they establish the power of the federal courts to declare federal, state, and local acts invalid if they violate the Constitution; the supremacy of federal laws or treaties when they conflict with state and local laws; and the role of the Supreme Court as the final authority on the meaning of the Constitution. But this political might — the power to undo decisions of the representative branches of national and state governments — was in the hands of persons appointed essentially for life. Frequent use of this power would highlight the Court's undemocratic character; infrequent use would mask it. Put bluntly, the Court is potentially a very undemocratic institution.

The Exercise of Judicial Review

The Supreme Court opinions that argued for judicial review echoed the views of Alexander Hamilton's essay, *The Federalist*, No. 78. Written during the ratification debates surrounding the adoption of the Constitution, Hamilton's essay maintained that the judiciary would be the weakest of the three branches of government because it lacked "the strength of the sword or the purse." Beyond comparison the weakest of the three branches, the courts have "neither FORCE nor WILL, but only judgment."

Hamilton's essay was a defense of legislative supremacy, but he argued that judicial review was an essential barrier to legislative oppression. He recognized that the power to declare government acts void implied the superiority of the courts over the other branches. But this power, argued Hamilton, simply reflects the will of the people declared in the Constitution as compared with the will of the legislature declared in its statutes. Judicial independence, embodied in life tenure and protected salaries, minimizes the risk that judges will deviate from the commands of the Constitution by assuring the appointment of judges with the skill and intelligence to discern its meaning. Since the Constitution is a fundamental law, a conflict between a legislative act and a constitutional provision will be correctly resolved by judges, independent of executive or legislative control. If the judges make a mistake, the people or their representatives possess the means to correct the error. Judicial review, according to Hamilton, does not lead to judicial supremacy.[5] Impeachment and amendment are checks on judicial power, but both require extraordinary majorities.

The Supreme Court has exercised its power of judicial review more often against the states than against the federal government, and more frequently in this century than previously. The fact that there are more state laws than federal laws probably provides the Supreme Court with more targets for the exercise of its power. Judges are lifetime appointees free from direct congressional or presidential influence. When they exercise the power of judicial review, the judges may operate counter to majoritarian rule by undoing the actions of the people's elected representatives. Compared With What? 13.1 gives us some idea of how common judicial review is among other governments, democratic and nondemocratic.

Is the Court out of line with majority sentiment? Or, is the Court simply responding to pluralist demands — the competing demands of interest groups that turn to the courts to make public policies? We will return to these questions later in this chapter.

Compared With What? 13.1

Judicial Review

The U.S. Constitution does not explicitly give the Supreme Court the power of judicial review. In a controversial interpretation, the Court inferred this power from the text and structure of the Constitution. Other countries sought to avoid political controversy about the power of courts to review legislation by explicitly providing for the power in their constitutions. Japan's constitution, inspired by the American model, went beyond it in providing that "the Supreme Court is the court of last resort with power to determine the constitutionality of any law, order, regulation, or official act."

The essential objection to the American form of judicial review is the unwillingness to place judges, who are usually appointed for life, above representatives appointed by the people. The European concept of judging involves adjudicating, but not "creatively" interpreting the constitutions or laws. Some constitutions even make explicit the denial of judicial review. For example, Article 28 of the Belgian constitution (1831) firmly asserts that "the authoritative interpretation of laws is solely the prerogative of the Legislative authority."

The logical basis of judicial review — that government is responsible to higher authority — can take interesting forms in other countries. Judges may invoke a higher authority than the constitution — God, an ideology, or an ethical code. Some constitutions place ideology (for example, communism) or religion above their constitutions. Iran and Pakistan provide for an Islamic review of all legislation (Pakistan also has the American form of judicial review).

By 1980 about sixty countries had adopted some form of judicial review. Australia, Brazil, Burma, Canada, India, Japan, and Pakistan give their courts a full measure of judicial review power. All but Japan have *federal* governments. Governments with relatively consistent experience with judicial review share some common characteristics: stability, competitive political parties, distribution of power (akin to separation of powers), a tradition of judicial independence, and a high degree of political freedom. Is judicial review the cause or the consequence of such characteristics? More likely than not, judicial review contributes to stability, judicial independence, and political freedom. And separation of powers, political freedom, and judicial independence contribute to the effectiveness of judicial review.

Switzerland also has a federal form of government. However, its Supreme Federal Court is empowered by its constitution to rule on the constitutionality of cantonal laws, the laws of the Swiss equivalent to our state laws. The Supreme Federal Court lacks the power to nullify laws passed by the Swiss Federal Assembly. The Swiss people, through a constitutional initiative or a popular referendum, exercise the sovereign right to determine the constitutionality of federal law. In Switzerland, the people are truly supreme.

These views are found in Henry J. Abraham, *The Judicial Process*, 4th ed. (New York: Oxford University Press, 1980), pp. 295–322; and Ivo D. Duchacek, *Power Maps: Comparative Politics of Constitutions* (Santa Barbara, Calif.: ABC-CLIO, 1973), pp. 216–219.

THE ORGANIZATION OF THE FEDERAL COURTS TODAY

The Supreme Court sits at the apex of a system of lower federal courts established and granted authority by Congress. The federal courts coexist with state courts (see Figure 13.1). The main entry points for the federal court system are the federal district courts, where litigation begins. Each state has at least one federal district court,[6] and no district straddles more than one state.* The federal **courts of appeals** sit between the federal district courts on the bottom and the U.S. Supreme Court at the top of the judicial pyramid. The courts of appeals, like the Supreme Court, are appellate courts, reviewing cases that were decided in another forum. There are thirteen courts of

* There is one insignificant exception. The district court for the district of Wyoming includes the portions of Yellowstone National Park within Montana and Idaho.

appeals. The nation is divided into regions (or "circuits") where the courts convene.

Most federal courts hear and decide a wide array of cases; the judges are generalists. But, from time to time, Congress has created courts with specialized tasks. One of the oldest of these is the U.S. Claims Court, created in

Figure 13.1

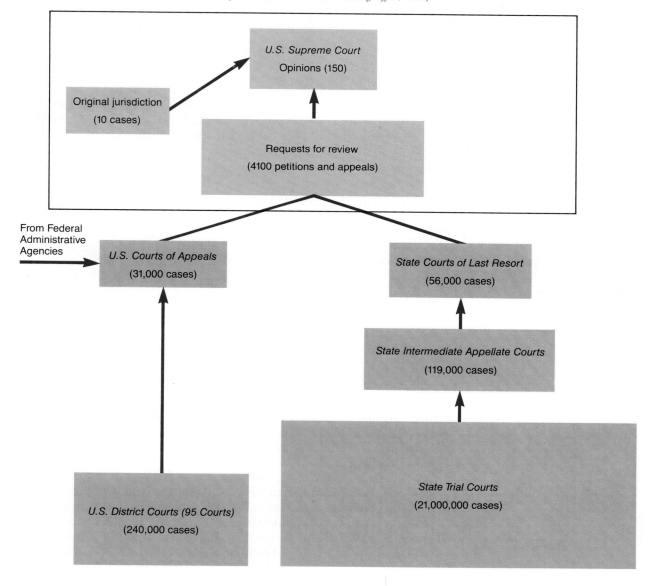

The Federal and State Court Systems

The Supreme Court of the United States was created by the Constitution (Article III). All other federal courts were created by Congress. State courts were created by state constitutions. Most litigation in the United States occurs in state courts. (Sources: State Court Caseload Statistics, Annual Report, 1984. *Williamsburg, Va.: National Center for State Courts, 1986;* Annual Report of the Director of the Administrative Office of the United States Courts *(Washington, D.C.: Government Printing Office, 1985)*

1855, which decides claims against the United States that are permitted by statute. The Court of Customs and Patent Appeals was created in 1910 to address appeals arising from the Claims Court and to provide a special forum for patent questions. It became part of the new Court of Appeals for the Federal Circuit in 1981. To add folly to confusion, some "courts," such as the Tax Court and the Court of Military Appeals, are part of the executive branch, though their decisions can be appealed to the federal courts.[7]

The Federal District Courts

Today, there are ninety-five federal district courts in the United States, where more than five hundred district court judges dispense federal justice. In most cases, these courts serve as the entry points to the federal court system. Note that each state has its own court system, as does the District of Columbia, and the vast majority of cases will be resolved in the state systems. When trials occur in the federal system, they will take place in the federal district courts.

Civil and criminal law. The criminal code is legislation that regulates individual conduct and spells out punishments for violations. Crime is a violation of this code. Courts decide criminal and civil cases. The government prosecutes **criminal cases,** in which crime is a violation of public order. Maintaining public order through the criminal law is largely a state and local function, however. Federal criminal cases represent only a fraction of all criminal cases prosecuted in the United States. **Civil cases** involve private disputes arising from such matters as accidents, contractual obligations, and divorce. The government can be a party to such disputes, called upon to defend as well as to allege wrongs.

Sources of litigation. Today the federal courts decide

1. Federal criminal cases authorized by federal law (for example, robbery of a federally insured bank or interstate transportation of stolen securities).
2. Civil cases brought by individuals, groups, or government for alleged violation of federal law (for example, failure of a municipality to implement pollution control regulations required by a federal agency).
3. Civil cases brought against the federal government when authorized by federal law (for example, enforcement of a contract between a manufacturer and a government agency).
4. Civil cases between citizens of different states when the matter in controversy exceeds $10,000 (for example, when a citizen of New York sues an Alabama driver in an Alabama federal court for damages stemming from an auto accident in Alabama).

Most cases never run the gamut of the court system. Often the parties will settle their own dispute. One side or the other will simply use a lawsuit as a threat to exact a concession from an opponent. Less frequently, cases will end with **adjudication,** a court judgment resolving the parties' claims and ultimately enforced by government power. When district judges adjudicate cases, they usually offer written reasons to support their decisions. If the issues or the circumstances are novel, the judges can publish their **opinions,** explanations justifying the judgment, making them available to others.

The United States Courts of Appeals

Some litigants persist beyond district court adjudication by appealing their cases to one of the U.S. courts of appeals. Cases in the district courts resolved by final judgments and decisions of federal administrative agencies can be appealed to the courts of appeals. These thirteen courts, with a corps of 159 full-time judges, handled nearly thirty thousand cases in 1986. As regional courts, they are identified by the term *circuit,* a carryover from the original circuit courts created in 1789. Eleven of the circuits encompass two or more states. The U.S. Court of Appeals for the District of Columbia is an exception; it is a circuit unto itself. The U.S. Court of Appeals for the Federal Circuit is an exception of a different sort. It combined the Court of Claims

Searching for the Law
Judge Learned Hand (1872–1961) served as a federal judge for 52 years, a record unequaled in the twentieth century. Although many jurists regarded Hand as a leading contender for a Supreme Court seat, he never managed to get the coveted appointment. His public reputation rested on his unusual name, his eloquent style, and his physiognomy (note the bushy eyebrows and square, strong features). Many of Hand's 3,000 opinions are still cited for their lucidity and powerful reasoning. Hand was perhaps the greatest judge of his generation; his achievements stemmed from ''the great way in which he dealt with a multitude of little cases.''

and the Court of Customs and Patent Appeals and specializes in cases involving the infringement of patents, among other cases exclusively within its reach.

Appellate court proceedings.   Appellate court proceedings are public, but they usually lack courtroom drama. Appellate courts have no jurors, witnesses, or cross-examinations; these are features of the trial courts. Issues on appeal turn on the rulings in the trial courts, however. For example, in the course of a criminal trial, a federal district judge permits the introduction of evidence that convicts a defendant. The defendant appeals on the ground that the evidence was obtained in the absence of a valid search warrant and thus was inadmissible. The admissibility of the evidence is the issue on appeal.

Litigants frequently attempt to settle their dispute while it is on appeal. For example, when a Texas state court issued an $11 billion judgment against the Texaco Oil Company in 1985, settlement discussions began immediately, at the same time that Texaco planned its appeal. Occasionally litigants abandon their appeals for want of resources or resolve. Most of the time, however, appellate courts adjudicate cases.

The courts of appeals are regional courts in which panels of three judges render judgments. The judges receive written arguments known as **briefs** (which are also sometimes employed in trial courts). Often, the judges hear oral argument and question to probe the lawyers' briefs.

Precedent and decisionmaking.   One of the three judges will attempt to summarize the panel's views, though each judge remains free to disagree with the reasons or with the judgment. When appellate judges write and publish opinions, their influence can reach well beyond the immediate case. For example, a lawsuit turning on a statute's meaning will produce a rule that can then serve as a **precedent** for subsequent cases, that is, the decision provides a reason for deciding similar cases in the same way. Although district court judges will sometimes write and publish their opinions, it is the exception rather than the rule at that level. At the appellate level, however, precedent requires opinions in writing.

Decisionmaking according to precedent is central to the operation of the legal system, providing continuity and predictability. This bias in favor of existing decisions is captured by the Latin expression *stare decisis,* meaning "let the decision stand." The legal system's use of precedent and the principle of stare decisis tends over time to reduce uncertainty in the meaning and application of legal obligations.

Judges on the courts of appeals direct their energy to correcting errors introduced in district court proceedings and making policy in the course of writing opinions. These opinions frequently modify or create rules of law. When judges create or modify law, they are engaging in policymaking. Thus, judges make policy by interpreting and thereby amending the law. Judges are politicians, in the sense that they exercise political power, but the black robes that distinguish judges from other politicians signal constraints on their exercise of power.

The policymaking function of judging occurs in two different ways. Occasionally judges employ rules from prior decisions in the absence of legislation. We refer to this body of rules as the **common** or **judge-made law**. The roots of the common law lie in English legal decisions. Contracts, property, and **torts** (an injury or wrong to the person or property of another) are common-law domains. The second area of lawmaking by judges involves litigants' disputing the application of a statute enacted by the legislature. The judges' interpretation of legislative acts is called **statutory construction.** The application of the statute may not always coincide with the words of the statute. Judges seek the legislature's intent from committee hearings and debates in Congress. The court determines the meaning of the law if these sources do not unlock the statute's meaning. With or without legislation to guide them, judges on the courts of appeals and district courts look to the relevant opinions of the Supreme Court for authority to decide the issues currently before them.

Though the Supreme Court remains the final word, its decisions often fail to address the precise issue confronting lower court judges. This means that federal judges below the Supreme Court exercise political power every bit as effective as that of the High Court's justices themselves. For example, federal judges in Alabama were called upon to decide whether, in light of the Supreme Court's decision in *Brown* v. *Board of Education,* Alabama's racially segregated public transportation facilities violated the Constitution's equal protection clause. Applicable Supreme Court precedents appeared to go in opposite directions, and three federal judges from the deep South had to decide which path to take (see Feature 13.1).

Uniformity of law.   Decisions by the courts of appeals assure a measure of uniformity in the application of national law. For example, similar issues are dealt with in the decisions of different district judges. These decisions may be inconsistent or in conflict. The courts of appeals harmonize such decisions to ensure that the law is uniform in its application.

The regional character of the courts of appeals undermines the uniformity that they attempt to maintain, however, because these courts are not bound by the decisions of other circuits. The law in one court of appeals may not be viewed as the law in another. Federal laws can be applied differently within the United States. The percolation of cases up through this system of courts virtually guarantees that at some point two or more courts of appeals will state different views of the law on the same set of relevant facts.

This tendency toward conflicting decisions between the intermediate courts can be corrected by review in the Supreme Court of the United States, where policymaking, not error correcting, is the paramount goal.

THE SUPREME COURT OF THE UNITED STATES

Above the west portico of the Supreme Court building are inscribed the words EQUAL JUSTICE UNDER LAW. At the opposite end of the building, above the east portico, are the words JUSTICE THE GUARDIAN OF LIBERTY (see Feature 13.2 on page 478). These mottos reflect the Court's difficult task: achieving a just balance among the values of freedom, order, and equality

Feature 13.1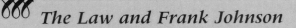

The Law and Frank Johnson

Judge Frank Johnson issued many path-breaking decisions from the federal court-house in Montgomery, Alabama. Appointed by President Dwight D. Eisenhower, Johnson ordered the integration of public parks, interstate bus terminals, restaurants and restrooms, and libraries and museums. In 1964 Johnson applied the one-person, one-vote principle for the first time in state legislative apportionment. In 1971 he held that patients in state mental hospitals have a constitutional right to treatment. And in 1976 he ordered the reform of the Alabama prison system on the ground that the conditions of confinement violated the constitutional rights of prisoners.

In this selection from an interview with journalist Bill Moyers, Johnson recalls his participation in *Browder* v. *Gayle* (1955). The case was a direct challenge to the Supreme Court's 1896 decision in *Plessy* v. *Ferguson,* which had held that separate but equal public transportation facilities were constitutionally acceptable. The Browder decision desegregating the Montgomery buses was the first time (in Johnson's memory, at least) when a district court had ever overruled a decision of the Supreme Court. It was also the first extension of the landmark 1954 Supreme Court decision in *Brown* v. *Board of Education.* The Browder case was decided by a special three-judge district court. Participating with Judge Johnson were Judges Richard Rives and Seybourne H. Lynne.

Moyers: Anybody call you and say, "My God, Johnson, you don't know what you've done," or "Do you know what you've done?"

Johnson: Well, they didn't put it in those words.

M: How did they put it?

J: I don't think I was subjected to vilification, I don't think I was subjected to the feeling of hate comparable to that which Judge Rives was subjected. Judge Richard Rives and I are the ones that decided that case. (Judge Lynne dissented.) Judge Rives had grown up here in Montgomery. He had practiced law here in Montgomery. He was one of the most able — recognized as one of the most able lawyers in the South. President Truman appointed him to the federal bench. He'd been on the bench about four years when I came on in '55. He helped swear me in in this courtroom. But Judge Rives' roots were here. He was one of them. He wasn't a

when they conflict. Consider how these values conflicted in two controversial cases that the Court faced concerning abortion and school desegregation.

Abortion pits the value of order — the government's responsibility for protecting life — against the value of freedom — a woman's right to decide whether or not she will give birth. In the abortion cases beginning with *Roe* v. *Wade,* the Supreme Court extended the right to privacy (an expression of freedom) to cover a woman's right to terminate a pregnancy. The Court determined that, at the beginning of pregnancy, a woman has the right to an abortion, free from government-imposed constraint. But the Court also recognized that, toward the end of pregnancy, government interest in protecting the fetus's right to life normally will outweigh a woman's right to an abortion.

foreigner that had been imported from the hills of north Alabama [where Johnson was born and raised]. And it was said by several people, and probably in the newspapers—I think I recall—here in Montgomery, "Well, we didn't expect any more out of that fellow from up at north Alabama, but Richard Rives is one of our own, and we did expect more out of him, and he's forfeited the right to be buried in Confederate soil." And that's how strong it was.

M: When you were discussing that case in your private chambers, after it had been argued—

J: The junior member of the court votes first. The senior member of the court votes last. That's followed throughout the system. That's to keep the senior member from influencing the junior member in his vote.

M: And you voted first?

J: So, Judge Rives says, "Frank, what do you think about this case?" "I don't think segregation in *any* public facilities is constitutional. Violates the equal protection clause of the Fourteenth amendment, Judge." That's all I had to say. It didn't take me long to express myself. The law was clear. And I might add this, Bill, the law to me was clear in practically every one of these cases that I've decided where race was involved. I had no problem with the case where we outlawed the poll tax, charging people to vote. I had no problem with the museums, the libraries, the public parks, or any public facilities. The law will not tolerate discrimination on the basis of race.

M: When you said this to Judge Rives, what did he say?

J: Well, when it came Judge Rives' time to vote, he says, "I feel the same way."

M: And that was it.

J: Absolutely. Sure. Sure. Well, I don't guess we deliberated over ten minutes at the outside.

M: History seems to require more dramatic moments than that.

J: There are rarely ever any dramatic moments in a judge's conference room. It's a cold, calculated, legal approach.

Source: Bill Moyers' Journal, "Judge: The Law & Frank Johnson—Part 1." Transcription, pp. 8–10. © 1980 by Educational Broadcasting Corporation. Reprinted by permission

School desegregation pits the value of equality—equal educational opportunities for minorities—against the value of freedom—the rights of white parents to send their children to neighborhood schools. In the school desegregation cases of the 1950s, the Supreme Court carried the banner of racial equality by striking down state-mandated racial segregation in public education. This decision helped launch a revolution in race relations in the United States. The justices recognized the disorder such a decision would create in a society accustomed to racial bias, but in this case equality clearly outweighed order. Twenty-four years later, the Court was still embroiled in controversy over equality when it upheld racial considerations in university admissions, in the Bakke case. In securing the equality of blacks, the government then had to confront the charge that it was denying equality to whites.

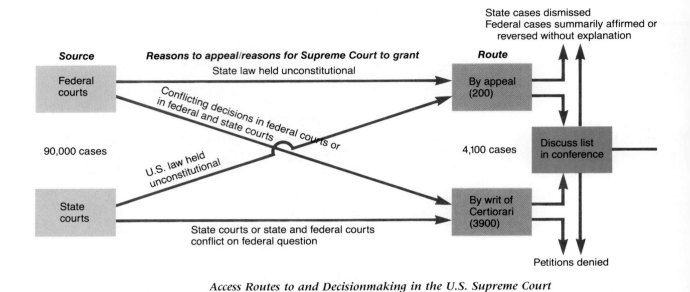

Access Routes to and Decisionmaking in the U.S. Supreme Court
Cases travel different routes to reach the Supreme Court's docket, and the reasons that

Figure 13.2

The Supreme Court is a national policymaker. Because its decisions have far-reaching impact on all of us, it is vital that we understand how it reaches such momentous decisions. With this understanding, we can evaluate how the Court fits within our model of democracy.

Access to the Court

Bringing a case to the Supreme Court requires attention to the formal rules of access and sensitivity to the interests of the justices. The idea that any person can bring a case to the Supreme Court remains true only in theory, not in fact. (We chart Supreme Court access and decisionmaking in Figure 13.2)

A case can enter the U.S. Supreme Court following a decision in one of the courts of appeals.* A case can also enter the Supreme Court from the highest court of a state. Two conditions must be met, however. First, the case must reach the end of the line in the state court system. Litigants cannot jump at will from state to federal arenas of justice. Second, the case must raise a **federal question,** an issue covered under the Constitution, federal laws, or treaties. But even for these cases, Supreme Court review is not easily

---

* On rare occasions, cases can be brought to the Supreme Court after judgment in the district court but before consideration by a court of appeals. This happened in *United States* v. *Nixon,* 418 U.S. 683 (1974). The urgency of an authoritative decision in the Watergate tapes case short-circuited a decision in the court of appeals. A small class of cases can be heard in the first instance before special three-judge district courts with appeals directly to the Supreme Court. See Feature 13.1.

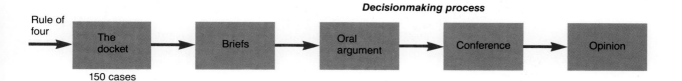

Decisionmaking process

Rule of four → The docket (150 cases) → Briefs → Oral argument → Conference → Opinion

support each route are different. The steps in the decision of a case depend on the route taken. The chart above shows the routes some typical cases would take.

obtained. Since 1925, the Court has exercised substantial (and, today, nearly complete) control over its **docket,** a technical term for the Court's agenda. This control lets the Court select a relative handful (150) of cases as most worthy of consideration from the more than 4,000 requests it receives each year. This selectivity enhances the Court's policymaking function. For the vast majority of the cases left unreviewed by the Court, the decision of the lower court stands.

The Supreme Court's caseload stems from two sources. A few cases (seventeen in 1983) derive from the Court's original jurisdiction, conferred by Article III, Section 2, of the Constitution (for example, legal disputes between states). The Court is the first and only forum in which such cases are resolved. The Court hears few such cases today, however, usually referring original jurisdiction cases to a *special master,* often a retired judge. He or she reviews the parties' contentions and recommends to the justices an appropriate resolution, which they are free to accept or reject.

The second and main source of cases is review of state and lower federal court decisions, in the Court's appellate jurisdiction. Such cases arrive at the Court mainly by two well-traveled routes,* the contours of which are found in congressional statutes. The most common route is by petition for writ of certiorari. The **writ of certiorari** is an order from the Supreme Court to a lower court to prepare the record in a case and send it up for review. (*Certiorari* is a Latin word meaning "to be certified.") The Court can either grant or deny such petitions as it wishes. No congressional acts or Court rules

---

* A third route (known as *certification*) is rarely invoked.

Feature 13.2

The Marble Palace

The Supreme Court of the United States sits east of the Capitol in a building designed both to embrace the majesty of the law and to elevate its occupants to the status of Platonic guardians. The Corinthian-style marble building was completed in 1935 at a cost of $10 million. Until it settled in its permanent home, the Court had occupied makeshift, hand-me-down quarters in nearly a dozen places (including two taverns) since its first session in Feburary 1790.

Each justice has a suite of offices, including space for several law clerks—top graduates from the nation's elite law schools who serve for a year or two.

The courtroom is eighty-two feet by ninety-one feet, with a forty-four-foot high ceiling and twenty-four columns of Italian marble. The room is dominated by marble panels, which were sculpted by Adolph A. Weinman. Directly above the mahogany bench, which is angled so that all the justices can see and hear each other, are two marble figures depicting ''majesty of law'' and ''power of government.'' A tableau of the Ten Commandments is located between the figures.

The Court begins its official work-year on the first Monday of October, known as the October Term. During its public sessions, when appeals are argued or the justices announce opinions, the court marshal (dressed in cutaways) pounds the gavel at exactly 10 A.M. and announces:

> The honorable, the chief justice and the associate justices of the Supreme Court of the United States: Oyez. Oyez. Oyez. All persons having business before the honorable, the Supreme Court of the United States, are admonished to draw near and give their attention, for the Court is now sitting. God save the United States and this honorable Court.

Then the justices enter in black robes from behind a velvet curtain, led by the chief justice and followed by the other justices in order of seniority.

Oral argument is usually limited to thirty minutes for each side. Few attorneys argue appeals regularly before the Court, so the awe and significance of the moment can overwhelm even seasoned advocates.

Sometimes the intensity of an argument before the court was too much for a lawyer to endure. Solicitor General Stanley Reed once fainted while arguing a case before his brethren-to-be. One day a private practitioner completely lost the thread of his argument and began to babble incoherently. [Chief Justice Charles Evans] Hughes tried to aid him by asking simple questions about the case. Seeing that this further bewildered the lawyer, Hughes took the brief and completed the argument that counsel was unable to make. . . .

There were other occasions when the utmost restraint was necessary to maintain the dignity of the court. . . . A New York attorney argued so vehemently that his false teeth popped out of his mouth. With amazing dexterity he scooped up the errant dentures almost before they hit the counsel's table in front of him and flipped them back into his mouth, with scarcely a word interrupted. Not a smile ruffled the dignity of the bench, but the Justices' pent-up mirth broke into gales of laughter when they reached safe havens of privacy.*

---

* Merlo J. Pusey, *Charles Evans Hughes*, Vol. 2. (New York: Macmillan, 1951), pp. 674–675.
Source: *Congressional Quarterly's Guide to the U.S. Supreme Court.* (Washington: Congressional Quarterly, 1979), pp. 761, 769–772. Reprinted by permission.

guarantee that petitions will be granted, and the standards spelled out by the Court offer it substantial latitude in such cases.[8] A typical petition might seek review of a criminal defendant's claim that his conviction was obtained without adequate legal assistance, a right he maintains is conferred by the Sixth Amendment of the U.S. Constitution. He has probably made this argument at his trial in a state court and employed it in his appeal to the highest court in his state, where typically his appeal on constitutional grounds has been denied. Now he petitions for certiorari in the Supreme Court, where his request is a "long shot" vying with thousands of others for the justices' limited attention.

The second route to the Court is by **appeal,** in which review rests on standards spelled out in the jurisdictional statutes enacted by Congress. In theory, the Court is obligated to hear and decide cases arising on appeal. In practice, however, the issue of jurisdiction remains within the justices' discretion in nearly all circumstances. For example, suppose a group of litigants in federal court has challenged the validity of a state law setting grooming standards for public school students. The ground for the challenge is that the standards deny the students due process of law, as guaranteed by the Constitution's Fourteenth Amendment. The district court invalidates the state law and the court of appeals affirms (upholds) the district court decision. The litigants then take their case to the Supreme Court by the appeal route, since the case falls under the appeals category defined by statute. But the justices have set the requirement that, for the Court to hear an appeal, the federal question must be a substantial one, and the determination of substantiality is left entirely up to the justices. The Court has affirmed without opinion the lower court decision in many grooming standards cases on the ground that the federal issues involved in such cases are insubstantial.

Occasionally, Supreme Court review is essential. For example, in 1985 Congress passed sweeping budget-cutting legislation. The budget-cutting law provoked considerable controversy, and its constitutionality was repeatedly brought into question. Congress provided for judicial review of the law before a special three-judge district court and then by appeal directly to the Supreme Court. On the day President Ronald Reagan signed the law, a member of Congress filed a federal lawsuit claiming that the law was unconstitutional. In July 1986, the Supreme Court ruled that the across-the-board spending cuts mandated by the law were unconstitutional because they encroached on presidential authority by giving executive power to the comptroller general. Since the comptroller general can be removed only by Congress, the budget-cutting law put a congressional officer in the unconstitutional role of dictating to the president.

For the vast majority of cases, however, the two main routes (see Figure 13.2) to the Supreme Court—by certiorari and by appeal—are largely within the justices' control. The most frequent result by either route is the same: no Supreme Court review. Without further review, the decision of the lower court stands.

Review is not granted unless, by an unwritten rule known as the **rule of four,** four or more justices agree that a case warrants full consideration (submission of briefs and oral argument). All nine justices, with advance preparation by their law clerks, make these judgments at their biweekly conferences. The justices convene alone and in secret to add cases to their docket and to vote on the previously argued cases. The chief justice will have prepared and circulated to all the justices a "discuss list" of worthy petitions and appeals (cases on the discuss list are then subject to the rule of four in conference). A petition not on the list will be struck from conference consideration unless a justice wishes to add it. Most cases, even those discussed in conference, are denied review. The dismissal of an appeal for want of a substantial federal question or the denial of a petition for writ of certiorari carries little or no value as a ruling by the Court, since no reasoned explanation accompanies the Court's order denying review.

The Solicitor General

Some scholars have searched for explanations of the Court's docket-control decisions. One theory suggests that the justices look to clues in the requests for review for signs of an important case.[9] The most powerful sign is a recommendation by the solicitor general to grant or deny review either in a case in which the federal government is a party or in other cases in which the solicitor general's recommendation is sought by the Court.

The solicitor general is appointed by the president and is the third-ranking official in the Justice Department. He represents the federal government before the Supreme Court. His duties include deciding whether the government should appeal from lower federal court decisions in which the government has lost; reviewing and modifying, when necessary, the briefs filed in government appeals; and deciding whether the federal government should file an *amicus curiae* (Latin for "friend of the court") **brief*** in any appellate court.[10] His purpose is to present a unified executive branch policy in the federal courts.

The solicitor general plays two different, and occasionally conflicting, roles. First, he is an advocate for the president's policy preferences; second, as an officer of the Court, he traditionally defends the institutional interests of the federal government. Sometimes the institutional interest prevails. For example, the Reagan administration was committed to the return of power to the states. But the solicitor general argued for the exercise of federal power in his defense of a federal law setting wage requirements for a city-owned mass transit system. In a sharp blow to the administration, the Court held that the Constitution placed no specific limit on congressional power to interfere in state and local affairs.[11]

The solicitor general's office is like a specialized law firm within the Justice Department. Members of that office collectively possess more experience arguing issues before the Supreme Court than any other organization in the nation. In 1985, it had twenty-two lawyers analyzing lower federal court decisions to determine whether to ask for Supreme Court review. If the Court grants review in a case in which the federal government is a party, either the solicitor general himself or one of his deputies will argue the government's position before the High Court.

---

* Amicus briefs can be filed by other parties with permission of the Court. This permits groups and individuals with an interest in the litigation (but not a party to it) to influence the Court's thinking and, perhaps, its decision.

Solicitors general have usually acted with considerable restraint in recommending the granting or denial of review before the Court. By recommending only cases of general importance, they increase their credibility. Since the justices must consider the potential impact of their grant or denial of review, the credibility of the particular solicitor general's recommendations can enhance or diminish his influence.

Rex E. Lee, who was solicitor general from 1981 to 1985, acknowledged in an unusually candid interview that he had refused to make arguments that members of the Reagan administration had urged on him. "I'm not the pamphleteer general; I'm the solicitor general. My audience is not 100 million people; my audience is nine people. . . . Credibility," Lee remarked, "is the most important asset that any solicitor general has."[12]

The solicitor general is a powerful figure in the legal system despite limited visibility. Though he lacks the limelight shining on the nine justices, the solicitor general's influence in arguing cases before the Court has earned him the informal title of "the Court's tenth justice."

Supreme Court Decisionmaking

Our knowledge of the dynamics of decisionmaking on the Supreme Court, or on multijudge courts in general, is all second-hand; only the justices attend the Court's Wednesday and Friday conferences. By tradition, however, the justices first shake hands in a gesture of harmony. The chief justice then begins the discussion by offering a brief summary of each case's merits; the other justices follow in descending order of seniority. Since the justices usually make their positions known in the course of discussion, there is little need for a formal vote. In the past, however, a formal vote followed discussion in every case. At that time, the most junior justice voted first, and the process continued in order of seniority until the chief justice voted last.

Kinds of court action. The voting outcome is the **judgment,** the decision on who wins and who loses. Justices often disagree, not only on winners and losers, but also on the reasons supporting their judgments. This should not be surprising, given nine independent minds and issues that can be approached in several ways.

The next task after the judgment calls for the justices in the majority to draft an opinion setting out the reasons in support of their judgment. The **argument** is the kernel of the opinion, its logical content separated from facts, rhetoric, and procedure. If all the justices agree with the judgment and the reasons supporting it, then the opinion is unanimous. A justice can agree with the judgment, upholding or striking down a claim, based on different reasons. Such agreement is called **concurrence.** A justice can **dissent** if he or she disagrees with the judgment. Such dissents often explain the reasons for a justice's disagreement.

In the Court's early period, each justice delivered his own opinion in every case, without attempting to join forces with his colleagues. This practice was abandoned after Marshall's appointment to the Court. During his first four years as chief justice, the Court handed down twenty-six opinions in twenty-six cases. Of these, Marshall drafted and delivered twenty-four. Marshall changed the opinion practice and he thereby gave coherence and power to the Court.[13]

Opinion assignment. Following the conference, the chief justice writes the majority opinion or assigns the responsibility to another justice in the majority. If the chief justice is not in the majority, the writing or assigning responsibility rests with the most senior associate justice in the majority. The assigning justice may consider many factors in allocating the crucial opinion-writing task: workload, expertise, public opinion—but above all, the author's ability to hold the majority together. If the drafting justice holds an extreme view on the issues in a case, he or she may give little weight to the views of more moderate colleagues, perhaps encouraging them to withdraw their votes. On the other hand, assigning a more moderate justice to draft an opinion might reduce the risk of shifting the vote but weaken the argument on which the opinion is to rest.

Strategies on the Court. Beyond these formalities, we know that the Court is more than the sum of its formal processes. The justices exercise real political power. If we start with the assumption that the justices will attempt to stamp their own policy views on the cases they review, then we should expect patterns of behavior typical of a political institution far different from the Court's as revealed in its public pronouncements. Perceptive scholars and journalists have pierced the veil that shrouds the Court from direct public view.[14] Cases that reach the Supreme Court's docket pose difficult choices, and the justices must sort out these dilemmas in virtually every case they decide. Because they grapple with such conflicts on a daily basis, the justices probably possess well-defined ideologies reflecting their value preferences.

The beliefs of most justices can be located on the liberal-conservative axis of political values. Such liberal justices as Thurgood Marshall and William J. Brennan, Jr., prefer freedom to order and equality to freedom. In contrast, conservative justices — William Rehnquist and Sandra Day O'Connor, for example — prefer order to freedom and freedom to equality. These choices translate into policy preferences as the justices struggle to win votes or retain coalitions.

We know that the justices also vary in intellectual ability, advocacy skills, social graces, stubbornness, and so on. For example, Chief Justice Charles Evans Hughes had a photographic memory and came to each conference armed with well-marked copies of Supreme Court opinions. Few justices were his match in such debates. It is reasonable to expect that a justice will attempt to win colleagues to his or her side by the forcefulness of drafts and memoranda, demonstrating that his or her colleagues' interests will be furthered by agreeing with or harmed by opposing his or her position. We should expect the justices to make occasional, if not regular, use of friendship, ridicule, and patriotism to mold their opponents' views.

A justice might adopt a long-term strategy of influencing the appointment of like-minded colleagues in order to marshal additional strength on the Court. Chief Justice (and former President) William Howard Taft bombarded

President Warren G. Harding with recommendations and suggestions whenever a Court vacancy was announced. Taft was especially determined to block the appointment of anyone who might side with the "dangerous twosome," Justices Oliver Wendell Holmes and Louis D. Brandeis.

Opinion writing. Opinion writing is the justices' most critical function. It is not surprising, then, that they spend much of their time drafting opinions. The justices usually call on their law clerks — elite law school top graduates who serve for a year or two — to assist in opinion preparation and other tasks.

On the occasion of his eightieth birthday and after more than thirty years of service on the Supreme Court, Justice Brennan offered a rare account of the process of preparing and exchanging memoranda and drafts leading to a final, acceptable Court opinion.

> It's startling to me every time I read these darned things to see how much I've had in the way of exchanges and how the exchanges have resulted in changes of view both of my own and of colleagues. And all of a sudden at the end of the road, we come up with an agreement on an opinion of the Court.[15]

The authoring justice distributes a draft opinion; the other justices circulate criticisms and suggestions. An opinion may have to be rewritten several times to accommodate perfectionists or wavering colleagues who remain unpersuaded by the majority draft. Justice Felix Frankfurter was a perfectionist; some of his opinions went through thirty or more drafts. Justices can change their votes, and perhaps alter the judgment, up until the official announcement of the decision. And the justices announce their decisions only when they are ready. Often the most controversial cases pile up in a backlog as the coalitions on the Court vie for support or sharpen their criticisms. On the day the Court announces decisions, the authoring justices read or summarize their opinions from the courtroom. Copies of these opinions, known as slip opinions, are then distributed to interested parties and to the press.

Justices in the majority frequently try to muffle or stifle dissent in order to encourage institutional cohesion. The justices must be keenly aware of the slender foundation of their authority, which rests largely on public respect. That respect is tested whenever the Court ventures into areas of controversy. Banking, slavery, and Reconstruction policies embroiled the Court in controversy in the nineteenth century. Freedom of speech and religion, racial equality, and privacy have led the Court into controversy in this century.

The chief justice. The chief justice is only one of nine justices, but he can play important roles based on his authority. If the chief justice does not play these roles, someone else will.[16] Apart from his role in docket control decisions and his direction of the conference, the chief justice can also be a social leader, generating solidarity within the group. Sometimes, a chief justice can embody intellectual leadership. Finally, the chief justice can provide policy leadership, directing the Court toward a general policy position. Perhaps only John Marshall could lay claim to social, intellectual, and policy leadership roles. (Docket control did not exist during Marshall's time, nearly 180 years ago.) Warren E. Burger, who resigned as chief justice in 1986, was a lackluster leader in all three roles.

The Supreme Court, 1986 Term: The Starting Nine
Chief Justice William H. Rehnquist (center) with the associate justices. From left, Sandra Day O'Connor, Lewis F. Powell Jr., Thurgood Marshall, William J. Brennan Jr., William H. Rehnquist, Byron R. White, Harry A. Blackmun, John Paul Stevens, and Antonin Scalia.

When he presides at the conference, the chief justice can exercise some control over the discussion of issues, although independent-minded justices are not likely to succumb to his views. For example, at the end of the conference on *Brown* v. *Board of Education,* Chief Justice Warren had six firm votes for his position that segregated public schools were unconstitutional. Two other justices indicated that they would join the majority if an opinion could be written to satisfy their concerns. In the months that followed, Warren talked frequently with his colleagues to minimize the possibility of dissenting or concurring opinions. By April 1954, only one holdout remained. Justice Warren's patriotic appeals had made both the decision and the opinion unanimous.[17]

The chief justice's power to cast the last vote can be used to moderate the majority's view, even if the chief justice's interest is in the minority. Suppose the vote in conference is 6 to 2 before the chief justice casts his vote. A vote with the majority gives the chief justice the power to assign the opinion writing to himself or to a justice who is closer to the minority viewpoint, where the chief justice's principles lie. In the 1972 abortion case of *Roe* v. *Wade,* for instance, Justice William O. Douglas charged that Chief Justice Burger abused his power by voting with the majority to overturn a state antiabortion statute, even though Burger's true sentiments lay with the minority two votes. Douglas threatened to issue a sharply worded concurrence rebuking the chief justice's use of the opinion-assignment power. His colleagues convinced Douglas that the Court's reputation would suffer by airing the dispute in public, so the opinion was never published.[18]

JUDICIAL RECRUITMENT

Neither the Constitution nor federal law imposes formal requirements for appointment to the federal courts, except for the condition that, once appointed, district court and appeals judges must reside in the district or circuit to which they are appointed. The president appoints judges to the federal courts, and all nominees must be confirmed by the Senate.

State courts operate somewhat similarly. Governors appoint judges in nearly half the states. Other states select their judges by partisan or nonpartisan election.[19] Nominees in some states must be confirmed by the state legislature. In the remaining states, judges must be confirmed in general elections that are held several years after appointment. Contested elections for judgeships are unusual. Criminal charges of widespread corruption in Chicago courts, where judges are elected, failed to unseat incumbents. Most voters paid no attention whatsoever.

The Appointment of Federal Judges

The Constitution states that federal judges hold their commissions "during good behavior," which means, in practice, for life.* A president's judicial appointments are thus likely to survive his administration and can be viewed as his political legacy. The appointment power assumes that the president exercises control over such appointments and that he is free to identify candidates and appoint judges who will favor his policies.

Judicial vacancies occur when sitting judges die, retire, or resign from the bench. Vacancies also arise when Congress creates additional judgeships to meet growth in litigation. The president then nominates a candidate who must be confirmed by the Senate. Because the president's role in the appointment process is represented by the Justice Department, the department will have screened candidates prior to formal nomination, even subjecting serious contenders to FBI investigation. The department and the Senate vie for control in the appointment of district court and appeals judges.

The "advice and consent" of the Senate.   For district court and appeals vacancies, the appointment process hinges on the nominees' acceptability to the senator for the president's party from the state in which the vacancy arises. The power of these senators was such that they could suggest a single name for a vacancy and hold out until he or she was nominated.[20]

The practice of **senatorial courtesy** forces presidents to share the nomination power with members of the Senate. Through this practice of asking for a senator's opinion of a nominee, the Senate will not confirm a nominee who is opposed by the senior senator in the president's party in the nominee's state. The practice is accomplished by failure to return a form, called a "blue slip." In the absence of the blue slip, the chairman of the Senate Judiciary Committee, which reviews all judicial nominees, will not schedule a confirmation hearing, effectively killing the nomination.

---

* Only five federal judges have been removed by impeachment in nearly two hundred years; nine resigned before formal impeachment charges could be lodged; and only four have ever been convicted of felonies (serious criminal conduct).

Though the Justice Department is still sensitive to senatorial prerogatives, senators can no longer submit a single name for a vacancy. The department was once a passive funnel for the evaluation of candidates, but no longer. It will search for acceptable candidates and poll the appropriate senator for his or her reaction to them.

The Senate Judiciary Committee conducts a hearing for each judicial nominee. The chair exercises a measure of control in the appointment process, beyond the power of senatorial courtesy. If a nominee is objectionable to the chair, he or she can delay a hearing or hold up other appointments until the president and the Justice Department consider some alternative. Obstreperous behavior does not win a politician much influence in the long run, however. Committee chairs are usually loathe to place obstacles in a president's path, especially when they may want presidential support for their own policies and constituencies.

The American Bar Association. The American Bar Association (ABA), the largest organization of lawyers in the United States, has been involved in screening candidates for the federal bench since 1946.[21] At the president's behest, the ABA's Standing Committee on the Federal Judiciary routinely rates the competence, integrity, and judicial temperament of prospective appointees. Using a four-value scale ranging from "exceptionally well qualified" to "not qualified," the committee interviews fellow lawyers capable of evaluating the candidates' professional and personal qualifications.

Presidents are not always inclined to agree with the committee's judgment, in part because its objections may mask disagreements with a candidate's political views. For instance, in 1985 the ABA revealed that the committee furnished lists of prospective nominees to groups seeking to challenge appointments on ideological grounds.[22] However, a poor ABA rating can weaken a candidate's chances, since the ratings become public knowledge. Occasionally, a candidate deemed "not qualified" is nominated and even appointed, but the overwhelming majority of appointees to the federal bench since 1946 have had the ABA's blessing.

Reagan and the Federal Judiciary

After little more than three months into his administration, President Ronald Reagan abolished, by executive order, the merit selection panels created by his predecessor, Jimmy Carter. Carter had aimed at appointing judges of higher quality than did his predecessors. The quality of his appointments is debatable. One finding is clear, however. Carter appointed substantially more blacks, women, and Hispanics to the federal bench than did any of his predecessors or his successor. Of course, time and scholarship — not political grandstanding — will render an independent judgment of judicial skills.

A small group of top-level Reagan administrators now meets every Thursday afternoon to approve or reject Justice Department recommendations for the federal bench. Reagan has generally heeded senatorial recommendations for the district courts and, like Carter, has held a firmer rein on appointments to the appeals courts. To date, only 7 percent of Reagan's 231 appointments have been black or Hispanic. In contrast, 20 percent of Carter's

Judge and Company
Judge Norma Johnson, seated here, was appointed by President Jimmy Carter in 1980 to the United States District Court for the District of Columbia. She was the first black woman appointed to that court. Judge Johnson is assisted by two law clerks, who serve for a year or two. Although the most coveted clerkships are in the Supreme Court, clerking for other federal and state judges can pay big dividends. In 1986, some major New York law firms were offering bonuses of several thousand dollars for new recruits with prior clerkship experience in the federal courts.

258 judges were from those groups,[23] but these differences may simply reflect heavier black and Hispanic representation among Democrats than among Republicans.

It nevertheless seems clear that Reagan has sought out nominees with particular policy preferences in order to leave his stamp on the judiciary well into the twenty-first century. In contrast to his predecessors, Reagan has used the nation's law schools for judicial talent the way major league baseball managers use farm teams. With the right statistics, a professor can move to the major leagues: in this case, one of the federal district or appellate courts. Carter's liberal values disposed him to seek judges committed to equality; Reagan's conservative values disposed him to favor judges who were more committed to order. Reagan may well surpass Carter in the extent to which he will reshape the federal courts in his own image.

In the first five years of his administration, Reagan appointed more than 220 federal judges without a hitch. Then, in 1986, the Republican-dominated Senate balked at two Reagan nominees. The Judiciary Committee killed Jefferson Beauregard Sessions' nomination to the district court. His racist-tinged remarks led to his demise. This was only the second time in this century when the committee blocked a nomination.

Shortly thereafter, the committee failed to approve but nevertheless reported the nomination of Daniel Manion to the U.S. Court of Appeals. The committee Democrats, joined by two Republicans, faulted Manion for his shoddy spelling and syntax and questioned his commitment to upholding federal law. In Manion's defense, one Republican senator declared, "Who cares if he can write. The real question is, is he fair?"

The question of Manion's judicial competence also served as a smoke-screen for his ideology. It seems that, while he was a state senator, Manion sponsored a bill allowing the posting of the Ten Commandments in public school classrooms, although the Supreme Court had ruled, just one year before, that such legislation violated the First Amendment's establishment clause. Vote trading and cloakroom maneuvering brought an end to the bitter Senate debate and gave the nomination to Manion.

Appointment to the Supreme Court

The announcement of a vacancy on the High Court usually causes quite a stir. Campaigns for Supreme Court seats are commonplace, but rarely visible to the public. Hopeful candidates contact their friends in the administration and urge their influential lawyer and judge friends to do the same on their behalf. Some candidates never give up hope. Judge John J. Parker, whose nomination to the Court was defeated in 1930, tried in vain to rekindle interest in his appointment several times until he was well past the age — usually the early sixties — when appointments are made.[24]

The president is not shackled by senatorial courtesy when it comes to nominating a Supreme Court justice, because an appointment to the High Court attracts more intense public scrutiny than lower-level appointments. This media scrutiny is what limits a president's choices and focuses attention on the Senate's "advice and consent" function.

Of the 140 men and 1 woman nominated to the Court, 26 — or more than 1 in 5 — have failed to receive Senate confirmation. Only 4 rejections have come in this century, the last 2 during the Nixon administration. The most important factor in the rejection of a nominee is partisan politics. Twelve candidates were rejected because the presidents who nominated them were "lame ducks" or because the party in control of the Senate anticipated victory for its candidate and sought to deny the incumbent president an important political appointment.[25] Only 2 nominees were rejected on the ground that they were unqualified. The most recent of these was federal judge G. Harrold Carswell, who was nominated by President Richard M. Nixon in 1970.

Since 1950, 14 of 18 Supreme Court nominees have had prior judicial experience in federal or state courts. This "promotion" from within the judiciary may be based on the view that a judge's opinions are good predictors of his or her positions on the High Court. After all, a president will want powerful lifetime appointees to be sympathetic to his views. Federal or state court judges holding lifetime appointments are likely to state their views frankly in their opinions. In contrast, the policy preferences of High Court candidates who have been in political office or in legal practice must be based on the conjectures of professional associates, on the text of a speech to the local Rotary Club, or on speeches on the floor of the legislature. Whether appointments arise from the judiciary or elsewhere, the predictability of subsequent Supreme Court behavior has limits.

The resignation of Chief Justice Warren Burger in July 1986 gave Ronald Reagan the chance to elevate Associate Justice William H. Rehnquist to the position of chief justice and to appoint Antonin Scalia, who was a judge in a federal court of appeals, as Rehnquist's replacement. Rehnquist faced stern

AN EXTRAORDINARY SESSION OF THE SUPREME COURT WILL BE HELD ON THE EVENING OF MARCH 9.

Not Quite All My Children
If you think these Supreme Court justices are listening to a 1937 soap opera, guess again. President Franklin D. Roosevelt was angered when a conservative majority on the Court blocked his New Deal legislation. In a ''Fireside Chat'' on the evening of March 9, 1937, Roosevelt sought public support for his proposal to enlarge (or pack) the Court under the guise of assisting the elderly justices in the performance of their duties.

questioning from liberal critics during his Senate confirmation hearings. His opponents failed to identify the ''smoking gun'' that would stop confirmation in the Republican-controlled Senate. Both Rehnquist and Scalia avoided detailed defenses of their judicial records and argued that judicial independence required that they not be called to account before the Senate. Both judges also ducked issues that might come to the Court for fear of compromising their impartiality.

Both Rehnquist and Scalia are strong and articulate conservatives. They will continue to prefer freedom to equality and order to freedom on the Court's docket. Rehnquist's leadership role should strengthen the Court's conservative wing in the years ahead.

In recent political history, inconsistency between expectations and actual performance has caught up with two presidents. Dwight D. Eisenhower thought little of his first appointee, Chief Justice Earl Warren. Eisenhower labeled the appointment ''one of the two biggest mistakes I made in my administration.''[26] Harry S Truman considered his appointment of Justice Tom C. Clark the biggest mistake of his presidency. "It isn't so much that he's a *bad* man," said Truman. "It's just that he's such a dumb son of a bitch. He's about the dumbest man I think I've ever run across."[27]

THE LEGAL PROFESSION

If the judiciary is one link in the chain that connects law and politics, then the legal profession is the raw material from which that link is forged. An understanding of judges and the power they wield can be aided by an understanding of the legal profession, for every judge has been baptized in the law and practices its craft.

Growth in the Legal Profession

Today, the number of lawyers in the United States exceeds 650,000.[28] This translates to 1 lawyer for every 354 people. Twenty-five years ago, there was 1 lawyer for every 700 people. The rate of growth in the legal profession will probably continue to outpace the rate of population growth through the end of the century.

The public's perception of the legal profession still leaves much to be desired. In national surveys conducted between 1973 and 1977, lawyers were ranked at or near the bottom in terms of confidence when compared with fifteen other groups or institutions.[29] What is the attraction of a profession that generates so little confidence? Market forces can account for some of the allure. We know that in 1983 the average salary of experienced lawyers was $85,000. If we could include in this average the salaries of all lawyers regardless of experience, the figure would probably drop to far less than the $100,000 average salary of physicians. But lawyers' salaries would still be substantially greater than for other professions.[30] Salaries for newly minted lawyers heading for elite New York law firms reached $65,000 in 1986; some firms offered additional superbonuses for clerkship experience in the federal courts and state supreme courts. The glamour of legal practice strengthens the attraction of its great financial rewards.

There are other reasons for the popularity of the legal profession and the unquenchable demand for legal services. Materialism and individualism in American culture encourage dispute. Federalism provides separate legal systems for each state plus the national government. Advertising can now create demand for legal services, too. Finally, the principles of separation of powers and of checks and balances make governing difficult and sometimes impossible. When political institutions act, they often do so in a crucible of compromise, deferring critical issues to the courts. When representative institutions prove incapable of action, the task often falls on the courts and lawyers. Pluralist democracy operates when groups are able to press their interests on, and even challenge, the government. The expression of group demands in a culture that encourages lawsuits thrusts upon the courts all manner of disputes and interests. Is it any wonder that America needs all the lawyers it can train?[31]

United States Attorneys

The Justice Department is responsible for the faithful execution of the laws under the president's authority. The main administrators of federal law enforcement are the ninety-five U.S. attorneys, appointed by the president with the advice and consent of the Senate. Unlike federal judges, these appointees serve at the pleasure of the president and are expected to relinquish their positions when the reins of government change hands.

There is a U.S. attorney in each federal judicial district. Their staffs of assistant attorneys vary roughly with the amount of federal litigation in the district. U.S. attorneys possess considerable discretion, which makes them powerful political figures in any community. Their decision to prosecute or not affects the wealth, freedom, rights, and reputation of the individuals and organizations in the district.

These attorneys for the government are usually free of political control, despite their lack of lifetime appointment.[32] Yet the position commands media attention and serves political ambitions. In 1969 President Richard Nixon appointed Jim Thompson U.S. attorney for the northern district of Illinois (covering the Chicago metropolitan area). Thompson vowed to root out political corruption, and his office successfully prosecuted several leading Democrats active in Chicago and Illinois politics. The notches on his briefcase earned Thompson the public exposure that helped launch his successful campaign to become governor of Illinois in 1976.

THE CONSEQUENCES OF JUDICIAL DECISIONS

Lawsuits represent the tip of an iceberg of disputes; most disputes never surface in the courts. Of all the lawsuits begun in the United States, the overwhelming proportion end without a court judgment. Many civil cases are settled, or the parties give up, or the courts dismiss the claims because they are beyond the legitimate bounds of judicial resolution.

Most criminal cases end by **plea bargaining,** in which defendants admit guilt, usually with some expectation that punishment will be less severe than if they had gone to trial. Only about 20 percent of criminal cases in the federal trial courts are tried; an equally small percentage of civil cases are adjudicated. The fact that a judge sentences a criminal defendant to ten years in prison or that a court holds a company liable for $11 billion in damages does not guarantee that the defendant or the company will give up either freedom or assets. In the case of the criminal defendant, the grounds for appeal following trial and conviction are well traveled and, if nothing else, serve to delay the day when no alternatives to prison remain. In civil cases, the immediate consequence of a judgment may also be an appeal, which delays the day of reckoning.

Punishment

One of the most important tasks exercised by federal judges is the imposition of punishment on convicted criminal offenders. Order and stability are government goals. Punishment is one means of securing these goals, but punishment necessitates the denial of liberty, perhaps even the denial of life, to some. The penalties for violation of federal law are set by congressional statute, but judges retain considerable flexibility for setting a sentence — by fine, imprisonment, probation (which is supervision without imprisonment), or a combination of these. The sentence should fit the defendant and the circumstances of the crime.

The deprivation of life, liberty, or wealth is an awesome responsibility, and judges usually approach it with the gravity it deserves. However, the exercise of this responsibility is inconsistent with one fundamental concept of justice: that the punishment imposed should not vary with the judge imposing it. If judicial decisions are too idiosyncratic, then judges will appear to lack the objectivity that breeds respect for law. And respect for law is the source of judicial power.

In a classic study conducted by the Federal Judicial Center — the research and training arm of the federal courts — different judges were asked to impose sentences on a group of identical defendants. Fifty judges were asked to sentence twenty "paper" defendants after reviewing detailed reports on each one. The study demonstrated that identical defendants would be given widely different sentences depending on the sentencing judge. For example, one judge meted out an eighteen-year prison sentence and a $5,000 fine to a defendant who pleaded guilty to a bank robbery charge. Another judge rendered a five-year prison sentence to the same defendant for the same offense. In a case involving interstate transportation of stolen securities, one judge sentenced the defendant to three years in prison, while another judge found that one year of probation was adequate. Moreover, few of the judges were themselves consistent in meting out stiff or lenient punishment. Neither political values, experience, nor age could account for the substantial disparity in judicial behavior.[33]

After years of debate, the Congress finally agreed to restrain federal judicial discretion in sentencing. In 1985 it created a sentencing commission (composed of judges, lawyers, and academics) to develop benchmark sentences. Departures from the benchmarks would require an explanation by the sentencing judge. And sentences can now be appealed by defendants and prosecutors. Whether these reforms will instill new respect for the judiciary remains to be seen, however.

Supreme Court Implementation and Impact

To *implement* decisions requires courts to rely on others to translate policy into action. Supreme Court justices, for example, must hold their majorities together and, if possible, strive for unanimity in their judgments. This need forces compromises in their opinions, which fosters uncertainty in the policies they articulate. Ambiguous or poorly crafted opinions enable opponents to avoid policies or limit their application. When the Supreme Court issued its order in 1955 to desegregate public school facilities "with all deliberate speed," judges opposed to the Court's policy dragged their feet to delay implementation. In the early 1960s, the Supreme Court struck down official public sponsorship of prayers and Bible reading in public schools. Yet state court judges and attorneys general reinterpreted the High Court's decision to mean

Communicating to Court and Congress
Although the justices work in isolation from the public, they are not immune to public opinion. These pro-choice demonstrators in front of the Supreme Court aim their remarks at a decision that reversed a lower court decision denying the use of federal funds to pay for poor women's abortions. Across the plaza separating the Court from the Capitol building, Students for Life demonstrators take a recess from their efforts to reverse by constitutional amendment the Supreme Court's 1973 abortion decision.

that only *compulsory* prayer or Bible reading was unconstitutional and that state-sponsored voluntary prayer or Bible reading was acceptable.[34]

Because the Supreme Court confronts issues freighted with deeply felt social values or fundamental political beliefs, its decisions have *impact* beyond the immediate parties in the dispute. The Court's 1973 decision legalizing abortion generated heated public reaction. The justices were barraged with thousands of denunciatory letters. Antiabortion groups vowed to overturn the decision. Proabortion groups moved to protect the right they had won. Within eight months of the decision, more than two dozen constitutional amendments were introduced in Congress, though none managed to carry the extraordinary majority required for passage. Opponents of the decision achieved a modest victory with the passage of a provision forbidding the use of federal funds for abortions except when the mother's life is in jeopardy. A local Boston prosecutor captured national attention when he pressed criminal charges against a physician who failed to save the life of a fetus while performing a sixth-month abortion. (The jury returned a guilty verdict, but the case was overturned on appeal.) Even presidential politics in 1976 was affected by the Court's decision. Though Jimmy Carter had defeated Gerald Ford for the presidency, a Washington state elector refused to cast his ballot in the electoral college for Gerald Ford, who carried the state. In an act of defiance, he cast his ballot for Ronald Reagan (who was not a candidate in 1976) on the grounds that Carter and Ford were equally unacceptable in their moderate stands on abortion.[35]

Public Opinion and the Courts

Implementation is rarely simple; impact is usually far-reaching and complex. Yet obedience to the law is an accepted feature of American public opinion. This provides the courts with widespread support. Except for a handful of leading constitutional questions, most Americans remain ignorant of legal decisions.

Democratic theorists have a difficult time reconciling a commitment to representative democracy with electorally unaccountable judges who possess the power to undo legislative or executive acts. This difficulty may simply be a problem for theorists, however, because the policies coming from the Supreme Court rarely seem out of line with the majority.[36] Public opinion polls in several controversial areas reveal that the Court rarely departs from majority sentiment or the trend toward such sentiment.

A study of Court decisions enlarging or narrowing minority rights between 1937 and 1980 shows that this was an exceptionally active period for the use of judicial review. Public opinion polls for the same period indicated that the Court was not out of step with public sentiment—instead, the Court decisions were "surprisingly consistent with majoritarian principles."[37] Decisions in the area of minority rights were supported by a growing minority of Americans and, in some cases, by a clear majority. The Court also refrained from ruling or ruled with equivocation in areas characterized by highly negative public opinion, such as marijuana use, busing to achieve school integration, and homosexual conduct.

In the abortion rights area, the public was and still is sharply divided. This continuing division may explain why the issue refuses to die despite the Supreme Court's repeated enforcement of its initial 1973 decision. The Court clearly defied the wishes of the majority on only one issue: school prayer. In this area, too, majority sentiment today remains incompatible with the Court's position. Controversy will continue as long as public sentiment remains divided.

THE CHANGING ROLE OF THE COURTS

The main issue in evaluating the role of the courts as policymakers in democratic government is this: how far should judges stray from the letter of existing statutes and precedents? Supporters of the majoritarian model would argue that the courts should adhere to the letter of the law and refrain from injecting their own values into their decisions. If the law places too much emphasis (or not enough) on equality or order, according to the majoritarians, it is up to the elected legislature—not the courts—to change the law. In contrast, those who support the pluralist model maintain that the courts are yet another policymaking branch of government and interested parties should try to find a like-minded judge who will favor their values when rendering a court decision.

Against this background of conflicting values, the exercise of judicial power in new domains, coupled with the litigious character of American society, continues to attract more controversial cases into the courts. Many are outrageous, and most are surely dismissed, but the presence of such suits on court dockets suggests a new perception of the judiciary today. For example, the Italian Historical Society of America sued to prohibit the U.S. Postal Service from issuing a stamp commemorating Alexander Graham Bell's invention of the telephone. The society contended in federal court that the telephone was actually invented by Antonio Meucci. In another case, a loyal group of Washington Redskin fans brought suit in federal court to overturn a critical referee decision denying the Redskins a victory in a game against the St. Louis Cardinals.[38] The span of issues confronting the courts is nearly as broad as the social, political, and economic diversity of American life.

New rights created by congressional acts fuel many of today's controversies. For example, Congress declares that there shall be no sex discrimination in university programs. Enacted with such vagueness that few members can object, such a statute provides considerable latitude for judicial interpretation. The judges face the nearly impossible task of determining whether a university practices sex discrimination when it spends more money on men's athletics than on women's athletics.

Courts create rights in the name of the Constitution. For example, several federal appellate courts, though not the Supreme Court, have recognized a right to adequate care in state-run mental hospitals, contending that the denial of a patient's liberty must be justified in terms of treatment. The absence of treatment is thus a denial of due process of law, a right guaranteed by the Fifth and Fourteenth Amendments. The creation of new rights and the reduction in traditional impediments to litigation place ever-increasing responsibilities on the courts. The courts then become arenas for political conflict with litigants, either individually or in groups, vying for benefits. This vision of the courts fits the pluralist model of government.

The traditional view of litigation is as a contest between two parties disputing issues arising from transpired events. Moreover, the issues are contained within the circumstances of the case, and the parties initiate the dispute and control its progress.[39] Relaxation of these elements thrusts the federal courts into an adminstrative or legislative role. For example, Federal District Judge W. Arthur Garrity, Jr., gained national attention when he assumed the administration of the Boston public school system in 1976 to ensure its desegregation, and held it until 1985. Judge Frank Johnson supervised the administration of the Alabama mental hospitals and prison system in order to ensure enforcement of constitutionally protected rights.[40] Johnson's decree went so far as to specify the maximum number of inmates for every foot of urinal troughs.

These are but two examples of a growing number of disputes that pit the authority of the federal courts against representative institutions through the enforcement of constitutional or statutory rights. Under normal conditions, the people of Boston select their school administrators, and the people of Alabama, through their elected representatives, make policies for their state institutions. If the courts fit the pluralist model and provide access to all groups seeking redress, then the charge that judges can trump elected government officials loses its sting. Some observers contend that courts are *countermajoritarian*—that they often act against the wishes of the majority, especially when courts defend freedom over order. It is clear that courts sometimes make decisions that run counter to the opinion of the majority. According to one sense of justice, that is precisely what courts are supposed to do: make difficult but fair decisions, however unpopular they may be. Nevertheless, making decisions that conflict with public opinion causes occasional problems for courts.

Today, judges usually shrink from the tug of contemporary political conflict while they exercise political power. Their power rests precisely on their legitimacy, the belief that their decisions are correct and proper. The correctness or propriety of their decisions could be called into question if judges behaved like other politicians.

Chief Justice William H. Rehnquist recently observed that judges in courts of last resort, such as the Supreme Court, work in an insulated atmosphere, hearing oral arguments, reading briefs, and writing opinions. They maintain contact with the rest of the world the way most of us do, through newspapers, conversation, books, and film. But "somewhere . . . beyond the walls of the courthouse," remarked Rehnquist, "run currents and tides of public opinion which lap at the courthouse door." Tides of sufficient strength and duration will affect the cases within that courthouse.

> Judges . . . can no more escape being influenced by public opinion in the long run than can people working at other jobs. And if a judge coming on the bench were to hermetically seal himself off from all manifestations of public opinion, he would accomplish very little; he would not be influenced by public opinion, but instead by the state of public opinion at the time he came on the bench.[41]

Both judges and elected representatives feel the current of public opinion. But unlike judges, representatives can institute policies at any time regardless of the past. In contrast, judges must await issues and resolve them by relying on previous decisions. Representatives must answer at regular intervals to the people by running for election; judges need answer only to their consciences.

The frustration that the framers built into government makes courts an attractive forum for the resolution of competing claims of individuals or groups. As long as courts remain accessible to all substantial claims, then courts fit the pluralist model of democracy.

SUMMARY

The power of judicial review, claimed by the Supreme Court in 1803, placed the judiciary on an equal footing with Congress and the president as a branch of the federal government. The principle of checks and balances can restrain judicial power through congressional control of jurisdiction and presidential control of the appointment power. Restrictions on judicial power have been infrequent, leaving the federal courts to exercise considerable influence through judicial review and statutory interpretation.

The federal court system has three tiers, beginning with the district courts, proceeding to the courts of appeals, and then to the apex, the Supreme Court. The majority of disputes end in the district courts. The ability of judges to make policy increases from trial courts to appellate courts.

Lawsuits are just a small part of all disputes; most are settled or abandoned. The exercise of judicial power affects the equality and freedom of groups and individuals. The Supreme Court, free to draft its own agenda through the discretionary control of its docket, serves to harmonize conflicting interpretations of national law and to articulate and supervise the enforcement of constitutional rights. It is assisted at this crucial stage by the solicitor general, who represents the executive branch of government before the High Court. His influence with the justices affects their docket-control decisions.

Rules of law emerge from the lawyer's representation of clients in the accepted tradition of negotiation and litigation. From the nation's lawyers arise the nation's judges, whose political allegiances and policy preferences are usually a necessary condition for a coveted appointment by the president to the federal bench. Presidents choose judges on the basis of their political beliefs. Preferences toward freedom, order, and equality go a long way to explain many such appointments. The president and senators from his party share power, uneasily sometimes, in the appointment of district and appellate judges. The president has more leeway in the nomination of Supreme Court justices. Reagan's appointments to the federal courts will leave his conservative stamp on the judiciary into the twenty-first century.

Justice Benjamin N. Cardozo observed, "[T]he great tides and currents which engulf the rest of men, do not turn aside in their course, and pass the judges by."[42] Litigation thrusts upon the courts the exigencies of modern life. The character of litigation is changing, bringing new issues to America's courtrooms and new threats to the power and legitimacy of the judiciary. By retaining the traditional trappings of judicial authority, the law appears unchanging. The issues confronting the nation's courts are a far cry from those litigated two hundred years ago. In addition to the responsibility of balancing freedom and order, the judges must now balance freedom and equality. Appointed judges undoing the work of representative institutions vexes democratic theorists. We have argued that the courts fit within the pluralist model and are often in step with the prevailing sentiment.

The Corinthian-style marble building that we know as the Supreme Court of the United States captures the dilemmas of government. Within the courtroom columns, the justices aim to balance values in conflict and to ensure an orderly, peaceful society. We shall examine some of these conflicts in Chapters 17 and 18.

Key Terms

judicial restraint
judicial activism
district court
jurisdiction
original jurisdiction
appellate jurisdiction
writ of mandamus
judicial review
courts of appeal
criminal case
civil case
adjudication
opinion
brief
precedent
stare decisis

common (judge-made) law
torts
statutory construction
federal question
docket
writ of certiorari
appeal
rule of four
amicus curiae brief
judgment
argument
concurrence
dissent
senatorial courtesy
plea bargaining

Selected Readings

Abraham, Henry J. *Justices and Presidents: A Political History of Appointments to the Supreme Court,* 2nd ed. New York: Oxford University Press, 1985. This highly readable book examines the critical relationship between justices and presidents from the appointment of John Jay in 1789 through the appointment of Sandra Day O'Connor in 1981.

Baum, Lawrence. *American Courts: Process and Policy.* Boston: Houghton Mifflin Company, 1986. A review of trial and appellate courts in the United States, addressing their activities, describing their procedures, and exploring the processes that affect them.

Coffin, Frank M. *The Ways of a Judge: Reflections from the Federal Appellate Bench.* Boston: Houghton Mifflin Company, 1980. This is a closeup look at the workings of a federal appellate court, the work ways of its chief judge, and his description of how he reaches decisions.

Ely, John Hart. *Democracy and Distrust.* Cambridge, Mass.: Harvard University Press, 1980. A carefully argued appraisal of judicial review, attempting to identify and justify the guidelines for the Supreme Court's application of a 200-year-old Constitution to conditions of modern life.

Jacob, Herbert. *Law and Politics in the United States.* Boston: Little, Brown and Company, 1986. An accessible introduction to the American legal system with an emphasis on linkages to the political arena.

Posner, Richard A. *The Federal Courts: Crisis and Reform.* Cambridge, Mass.: Harvard University Press, 1985. A provocative, comprehensive and lucid analysis of the institutional problems besetting the federal courts. Written by a distinguished law professor, now a federal appellate judge.

Wasby, Stephen L. *The Supreme Court in the Federal System,* 2nd ed. New York: Holt, Rinehart and Winston, 1984. A thorough study of the Supreme Court's internal procedures, its role at the apex of national and state court systems, and its role in the political system.

14

The Washington Community

General Alton Slay left the Air Force after many years of service, but he did not really retire. Instead he began a second, highly lucrative career as a consultant. His one-man firm, Slay Enterprises, Inc., works for companies that want to do business with the Department of Defense. His clients include Lockheed, United Technologies, and Raytheon, three of the nation's largest defense contractors. Such prized clients sought Slay out because of his military experience as head of both the Air Force Flight Test Center and Systems Command, where he oversaw the production of air force planes. Not coincidentally, those airplanes were built by companies like Lockheed and other subsequent clients of Slay Enterprises.

Defense contractors hire a consultant like Alton Slay because they need his expertise to win Pentagon contracts. Who knows the ins and outs of Pentagon contracts better than an ex-general? Apparently, Slay is well worth his fees; former Pentagon colleagues say that he has helped his "new clients find their way to success and continued good fortune in the politics of selling weapons to the military."[1]

Like Alton Slay, Anne Wexler knows her way around Washington. And, like Slay, she has worked in both the private and the public sectors. After beginning her political career as a liberal, anti-Vietnam War activist, Wexler later worked for the Commerce Department and for the Carter White House, doing liaison work with interest groups. After President Jimmy Carter was defeated in 1980, she and two colleagues started a lobbying firm. A conservative Republican, Nancy Reynolds, soon joined the firm to lend it a bipartisan flavor that might broaden its appeal.

Wexler's political savvy was soon recognized by vice presidential candidate Geraldine Ferraro, who brought her into the campaign as a senior adviser to help fashion strategy and respond to developing political events. After the campaign, Wexler went back to her firm — now called Wexler, Reynolds, Harrison & Schule — to work on behalf of its largely corporate clientele, which included Aetna Life & Casualty, General Motors, and the National Football League. Her experience and political skills have paid off handsomely, though some of her liberal colleagues consider her one of the many who come to Washington to do good and end up doing very well.[2]

Alton Slay and Anne Wexler are only two of the thousands of Washingtonians who work *on* the government rather than *for* it. Although they are in the private sector, they are part of the group of individuals and organizations that propels the governmental process forward. They are part of the **"Washington community"** — the people inside and outside of government who work on public policy issues.

In previous chapters, we have analyzed the major institutions of the federal government: Congress, the presidency, the bureaucracy, and the courts. Here we turn to private sector actors in Washington politics. We will focus on five important segments of Washington's service economy: law firms, consulting firms, think tanks, public relations firms, and trade associations. Each of these enterprises plays a vital role in the governmental process. Collectively, they provide an important link between the public and government policymakers, enabling citizens and private sector policy experts to communicate their opinions and knowledge to those in government.

Wexler and Reynolds
Anne Wexler (left), a well-known Democrat, and Nancy Reynolds, a Republican, are two of the principals in a lobbying firm. The bipartisan nature of their firm is not unusual—public relations and lobbying firms want clients to believe they have access to important policymakers in both parties.

After examining each of these segments of the Washington community, we will turn to the interrelationships between private sector actors and government decisionmakers. These ongoing relationships, or *issue networks*, form a significant part of the policymaking process. Instead of concentrating on how policy is made *within* an institution such as Congress or the courts, we will look at how policy is made *across* institutions. Policies move back and forth between institutions, and issue networks composed of government officials and private sector actors often engage in informal bargaining and negotiating that leads to policy decisions.

In terms of the majoritarian-pluralist conflict, issue networks allow small but active constituencies to achieve policy goals they consider vital to their well-being. They thereby contribute to the tension between the majoritarian pressures that push government to do what is best for the entire population and the reality that that population is not as well represented in Washington politics as are some subgroups within it. In other words, what benefits those subgroups may not be in the best interests of the rest of the country.

Before turning to the private sector of Washington and its connections with government, we shall take a brief look at life in the nation's capital. Washington is a unique city—some say it is a world in itself. What are the special qualities that give that world its character and make it so appealing to live and work in?

WASHINGTON: A CITY AT THE CENTER

"Washington," said President John F. Kennedy, "is a town of northern charm and southern efficiency." Indeed, Washington is a city of contrasting cultures: North and South, black and white, rich and poor, public sector and private sector. People outside of Washington, though, perceive it not so much as a city divided within itself but as a city divided from the rest of the country. In 1976 Democratic presidential candidate Jimmy Carter proudly told campaign audiences that he was a "Washington outsider." In 1980 Republican candidate Ronald Reagan spoke disparagingly of the "Washington buddy system." Both men were kinder than former presidential candidate George Wallace, who ridiculed "pointy-headed, briefcase-totin' bureaucrats" for running the government in defiance of common sense.[3] And many Americans simply regard Washingtonians as arrogant and out of touch with the feelings of average citizens.

Washington *is* different from other cities. Its major "industries" are government and firms trying to influence government. Data from the 1980 census show that Washingtonians have the highest annual median income per family of any major city in the country: $27,515, compared with $19,903 nationally. The percentage of Washingtonians who are college graduates (32 percent) is the highest in the nation and twice the national average.[4]

Beyond statistics, there is an attitude that sets Washingtonians apart, a pervasive feeling that their city is the true center of the nation. It is where the most important people live and the most important decisions are made. Washingtonians exude a smugness of being "in the know" and believing that, when people from Washington speak, others listen. Yet, for all its arrogance, the city has its share of insecurities. Washingtonians are upset by the thought that New Yorkers regard the nation's capital as a "hick" town. And Washington has never overcome its embarrassment over its baseball team's (the perennially cellar-dwelling Washington Senators) move to Texas.

Despite the town's relative affluence, money is not the main measure of social status in Washington. *Power* —the ability to influence important decisions—is. Many Washingtonians' career goals are based on coming closer to the centers of power. For bureaucrats, this means climbing the ladder to ever-higher levels of administration. For legislators, aspirations run to committee chairs and party leadership posts. For congressional aides, senior positions on personal or committee staffs beckon.

In a less structured way, those outside of government have a similar objective—to become increasingly influential in the decisionmaking process. Their route to power is more indirect and sometimes involves going back and forth between jobs in the public sector and jobs in the private sector.

Washington, Then and Now
Washington, D.C., has changed a great deal since the mid-1800s, as pictured in the early rendering at top right. The photograph below shows a view of K Street in downtown Washington, where the tenants include trade associations, law firms, consulting firms, and others involved in the government service industry.

But whatever their training or backgrounds, most people who are not currently in the government must strive to gain access to key government officials. Lawyers, lobbyists, and public relations specialists know that they cannot do their jobs properly unless people in government are willing to listen to them.

Washington has changed dramatically since it became the nation's capital in 1800 (see Feature 14.1). The private sector service industry of public

Feature 14.1

Washington's Washington

In its early years, the United States had a government without a home. After the Revolutionary War, the Congress shifted its meetings about among New York, Philadelphia, Trenton, Princeton, and Annapolis. Having no building of its own in these cities, Congress had to take what it could get, often sharing offices with the state or local government. To add insult to injury, the Congress was not always a welcome guest. Meeting in Philadelphia (the City of Brotherly Love) in June 1783, the members of Congress were set upon by an unruly mob of Revolutionary militiamen, who demanded payment of overdue wages. When the state of Pennsylvania refused to provide adequate protection from further attacks, the Congress secretly adjourned and fled to Princeton, New Jersey.

Feeling that a permanent home of their own would give them the respect they deserved, the congressmen decided to select a capital where they would have exclusive authority. Yet they were unable to choose one among themselves, and in 1790 they finally threw up their hands and delegated the decision to President George Washington. The Congress's only requirement was that the new capital be located in the center of the nation, along a 105-mile stretch of the Potomac River. Once the president selected the actual site, the government proceeded to pay $66.50 an acre for land that was reputedly worth about one-fifth that amount.

President Washington and other national leaders hoped that the new capital would become one of the great cities of the world. They wanted it to become like Paris or Rome, a center of culture, commerce, and national life. They were bitterly disappointed. When the government held its first auction of 10,000 parcels of Washington land in 1791, only 35 lots could be sold. Auctions over the next two years proved to be similar failures and were subsequently suspended because of the embarrassment. It was simply the case that almost nobody wanted to move to Washington.

When the government officially took residence in Washington in 1800, its members found it to be a depressing, miserable little town. It had only 109 stone or brick buildings; the rest of the dwellings were shanties or huts. The city attracted virtually no private enterprise in its early years. Excluding slaves, there were fewer than ten thousand residents as late as 1820, for those not employed by the government found little reason to move there. Those in government hardly found the city to their liking either. Supreme Court justices and congressmen spent much of the year in their home towns, traveling to Washington only when their government body was in session.

In retrospect, it seems that Washington failed to become an important city in its first decades because the people of the new nation had only a limited interest in what went on there.

This view is found in James Sterling Young, *The Washington Community* (New York: Columbia University Press, 1966), pp. 13–37.

relations and consulting firms did not exist then. James Sterling Young has written of Washington in its earliest years:

> No national association made the government's headquarters their headquarters, and few came on errands to Washington. [of] Resident lobbyists, in the modern definition of the term, there were none. . . . Outsiders eager to assist and manipulate the operations of government were conspicuous by their absence; the drama of national politics in early Washington was played without this supporting cast of characters whom big government and a complex industrial society have since attracted to the residence of power.[5]

This "supporting cast of characters" is now as much a part of the Washington scene as government itself. The 400,000 government employees in Washington are outnumbered by the 700,000 employees of the private sector. Not all of the latter work at jobs having to do with influencing government, but the number of those who do is growing faster than for those who work for government itself. Indeed, a real economic boom has taken place in Washington, in large part because of the tremendous growth of firms "designed to hook the bureaucracies into their client groups."[6] One cannot really understand Washington without some understanding of these nongovernmental organizations.

LAW FIRMS

Nothing better symbolizes the connection between Washington's private sector and the federal government than its law firms. The practice of law in Washington is largely a matter of representing clients who have some problem with the government. And this representation does not take place primarily in the courts. Rather, most Washington lawyers do their business before regulatory agencies and the Congress. Typically, a Washington lawyer will act on behalf of a corporation or a trade association that has an interest in policies being developed by the government. If the Federal Communications Commission (FCC) is formulating regulations governing cable television, cable broadcasters will want their views to be heard. The FCC's decisions may affect the way they run their businesses, as well as their profitability.

Why are Washington-based lawyers so useful to clients who want to influence decisions in Washington? Why can't a corporation, for example, simply rely on its own executives to lobby the government? First, the decisions of government (statutes, regulations, and court opinions) are couched in "legalese" (see Feature 12.1). Clients need someone with not only a sophisticated understanding of a particular policy area but also an ability to decipher and interpret technically complex documents. Second, even though many firms are represented by a Washington trade association, some situations require more extensive representation than a trade group can provide. Lawyers in private practice provide the most readily available pool of talent that can offer the needed services. Third, those wanting to influence government need someone who is well acquainted with the committee or agency making the policy, who knows the key people on the government side, and who has a reputation as an expert in that policy area. Law firms are full of exactly such experts.

Washington lawyers are probably better described as **lawyer-lobbyists,** since they most often use their backgrounds and expertise to influence government. Many Washington law firms have reputations as effective advocates before government. The big, well-known firms can bill corporate clients at a rate of $200 or more per hour for a senior partner's time. Partners — those who share in the annual profits of a firm — can expect salaries in the range of $100,000 to $300,000 a year.[7]

The success of Covington & Burling, Washington's largest law firm, can in part be attributed to its early start in government advocacy work. Founded in 1919, it was one of the first firms to recognize the government's tentative steps toward regulation as an opportunity. Some early clients included industrial giants like DuPont and General Motors. Today the firm has around two hundred partners and associates, and one member estimates that it has represented "twenty percent of the companies on *Fortune*'s list of the five hundred top corporations."[8]

Beyond the top firms, many individuals have reached the pinnacle of success in practicing Washington law. Lawyers like Tommy Boggs (see Feature 14.2) or Joseph Califano, a former aide to President Lyndon B. Johnson and a member of the Carter administration cabinet, attract important and wealthy clients because they have a reputation for being extremely skillful in influencing government. Attorneys who attract numerous clients to their firms are known as "rainmakers." They bring business to the firm because of their professional reputations, social connections, or familiarity with clients from previous government experience. When Republican Senate Majority Leader Howard Baker of Tennessee announced his retirement from Congress in 1984, the Washington office of Vinson & Elkins hired him for around $700,000 to $800,000 a year. Clearly, the partners thought that someone with such exceptional experience and connections would make a lot of rain for the firm.[9]

Washington Law as a Growth Industry

Washington law has been one of America's great growth industries. As Figure 14.1 shows, the number of lawyers in Washington has skyrocketed in recent years. There are roughly three times as many lawyers practicing in Washington as in Los Angeles, a city three times its size.[10]

What has stimulated this growth? A major factor is the regulatory spiral. As new regulatory agencies, such as 1970's Environmental Protection Agency (EPA) and Occupational Safety and Health Administration (OSHA), began to issue thousands of pages of regulations a year, more and more businesses found themselves directly affected by what went on in government. Any time

Figure 14.1 ▬▬▬

Washington Lawyers
The number of lawyers in Washington, D.C., has increased sharply in recent years. Many of these lawyers represent clients who want to influence government policymaking.

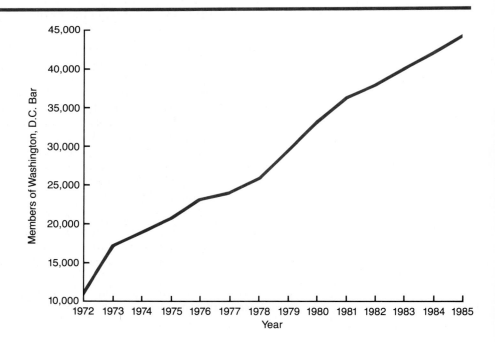

Feature 14.2

Tommy Boggs, Worth a Million

The best thing that ever happened to Tommy Boggs may have been losing his one and only race for Congress. Out of the ashes of that defeat has come an extraordinary career as a lawyer-lobbyist. Now in his mid-forties, Boggs is considered by many to be the most effective lobbyist in Washington.

Politics is in Boggs's blood. His late father, Hale Boggs, was a Democratic representative from Louisiana. His mother, Lindy, took Hale's place in the House of Representatives after he died in a plane crash. After graduating from Georgetown University's night law school, Tommy was hired by James Patton to join Patton's small, four-lawyer firm. Since then, the firm has grown to eighty lawyers, and its letterhead now reads "Patton, Boggs & Blow." Around town, it is known simply as "the Boggs firm."

The *Washington Post* calls Patton, Boggs & Blow "the young, swashbuckling state-of-the-art Washington lobbying house of its era," and Tommy Boggs gave it that reputation. There is no magic in Boggs's approach: he combines hard work and assiduous attention to detail with a superb understanding of the legislative process and of the complex areas of public policy — such as tax law — that his clients are involved in. Fellow lobbyist Robert McCandless describes him this way: "Being a good lobbyist is like running a good restaurant. You've got to spend a helluva lot of time in the kitchen. Tommy does." He also knows how important money is and puts a lot of effort into raising and channeling campaign funds from clients to members of Congress.

Boggs's clientele reads like a *Who's Who* of American business. One of his most notable achievements was helping to get the Chrysler bailout bill through Congress. The giant auto manufacturer was teetering near bankruptcy, and its management felt that only federal loan guarantees would allow it to raise the cash needed to stay in business. The bill overcame strong opposition, was passed, and has kept the company not only alive but also highly profitable.

For his efforts, Boggs earns around a million a year. But the satisfaction goes beyond the riches his work brings him. "I really enjoy playing the game," he says.

These views are found in Albert R. Hunt, "Thomas Boggs Offers Full-Service Lobbying for a Diverse Clientele," *Wall Street Journal*, March 23, 1982; Paul Taylor, "Gladiators for Hire — Part II," *Washington Post*, August 1, 1983; and "Briefing," *New York Times*, February 27, 1986.

an agency considers changing a regulation, those affected need to be advised of its implications. (One Washington attorney referred to the expanding federal regulation of energy that began in the 1970s as a "public service employment program for lawyers.")[11] Clients often want their attorneys to influence the outcome.

The importance of legal representation in Washington has produced another interesting trend. Major law firms with headquarters located in other cities have opened Washington branch offices in self-defense. In 1965 only 45 branch offices were located in Washington; by 1983 the number had reached 247.[12] These firms believe that they can best serve clients who are having problems with a regulatory agency by having their own lawyers in Washington. And this tactic keeps them from losing clients to Washington firms.

Specialty Law Firms

Despite the presence of so many large, prestigious firms, the structure of the Washington legal establishment is really quite diverse. Many small and medium-size firms do quite well. One way a small firm can distinguish itself is by specializing in a particular area of the law. By becoming known as highly expert in the workings of one agency or program, smaller firms can attract a clientele with a specialized interest.

The law firm of Epstein & Becker, which works almost exclusively in the health care field, is a case in point. Attorneys from Epstein & Becker will, for example, advise clients who wish to set up a health maintenance organization (HMO), a prepaid health plan for consumers. Epstein & Becker can guide applicants through the administrative maze of federal laws and regulations governing HMOs.[13]

Public interest law firms form another part of the Washington bar. There are a number of these organizations, which use the courts to try to protect what they consider to be the "people's interest." Public interest law firms are advocacy organizations, taking on only those issues that fit their ideological perspectives. Like their counterparts in larger corporate firms, these organizations handle administrative lobbying as well as court suits. The Public Citizen Litigation Group, for instance, has won many lawsuits, including one allowing pharmacies to advertise prescription drug prices.

When the public interest movement emerged as a strong force in the late 1960s and early 1970s, almost all of the new public interest law firms were on the liberal side of the political spectrum. These attorneys believed that it was their responsibility to counter the influence of large corporations, which are always well represented by lawyers. In the past few years, however, some conservative public interest law firms have set up shop in Washington. One of these organizations, the Capital Legal Foundation, sued CBS on behalf of General William Westmoreland, who alleged that he was libeled by a network documentary on the Vietnam War. (The program claimed that he deliberately misled policymakers about estimates of enemy troop strength.) The Capital Legal Foundation's interest in the case seemed to be to punish and influence the CBS news division, which the group regards as too powerful

Westmoreland Takes on CBS
The legal work of General William Westmoreland's libel suit against CBS news was assumed by the Capital Legal Foundation, a conservative public interest law firm. Many conservatives were angry at CBS's conclusions about Westmoreland and, more broadly, at what they saw as a liberal bias on the part of the network.

and too liberal. But, after the law firm had spent more than $3 million on the case, adverse trial testimony led the organization and Westmoreland to agree to an out-of-court settlement that clearly favored CBS.

CONSULTING FIRMS

Not all government work is done by government workers. Federal departments and agencies spend enormous sums of money hiring people outside of government to conduct research, collect data, and perform policy and organizational analyses. Such outsiders hired by the government are called **consultants.** Consulting firms are profit-seeking businesses, and they are big business in Washington, where hundreds of firms compete for government contracts.

The Nature of Government Consulting

Consulting is not aimed solely at government, however. Consulting firms can be found all over the country, and many do little or no government work. Some firms work exclusively on business consulting, offering specialized services such as market research or management studies.

What do *government* consultants do? It is best to begin with the concept of *contracting out*. An agency may decide that it needs to *contract out*, to seek outside help in performing some job, because it lacks staff or expertise or believes that its own people might not be fully objective in their assessments. If it hires a consultant, that individual signs a contract spelling out the services to be provided and the amount of money to be paid for them. For example, an agency may need a computer program to deal with a new and highly complex problem. If it does not have programming expertise, the agency could award a contract to a computer consulting firm to have the work done. When the work is complete, the contract has been fulfilled, and the agency has no further financial obligation to the consultant. This is a much more efficient way of spending agency funds than hiring a new bureaucrat who would have to be kept on the payroll indefinitely. Thus contracting out makes sense when there is no constant, year-round work to be done or when an agency simply does not have the expertise to solve the problem at hand.

Much contracting out is done for technical services, such as auditing, computer work, or data collection, and seems far removed from the political process. More directly related to government decisionmaking are studies that evaluate programs and analyze policy options. Government agencies spend hundreds of millions of dollars a year on such consulting contracts. For example, the National Institute of Education hired Abt Associates of Cambridge, Massachusetts, to evaluate how altering federal aid formulas would affect school districts. Under the three-year, $3.7 million contract, Abt followed thirteen school districts and found that awarding money on the basis of educational performance rather than family income made little difference in either the services that would be purchased with federal aid or the cost of those services.[14]

A common criticism of this kind of consulting is that many studies do not warrant spending the taxpayers' money. There is ample evidence that a significant portion of policy consulting work is simply not worth doing or paying for. One congressional study of Defense Department consultants revealed that 17 percent of the projects they undertook were "of questionable value."[15] And everyone in Washington has a favorite horror story about a consulting contract that was an outright "boondoggle." A classic example is a Department of Transportation contract for $225,000, under which Stanford Research Institute consultants were asked to forecast transportation costs in the year 2025 under conditions of widespread guerrilla warfare.[16]

Another problem with consulting is that studies dealing with important issues sometimes end up having negligible impact. An agency might contract with skilled analysts, who produce a first-rate piece of research, and then disregard the study. Why does this happen? One reason is that a major study can often take a year or more to complete, by which time policy or personnel changes may have reduced its urgency. In other cases, a study's recommendations, even though well thought out, might not be politically feasible. A third reason is that the people requesting the study might not have the power to make the necessary policy changes. Finally, as one scholar notes, "the process of evaluation suggests change."[17] Change in program operations could mean that some people in the agency would lose authority, in which case they would fight to stop proposed changes.

Getting the Contract

Criticism of the relationship between the government and consulting firms has also been directed at the way in which contracts are handed out. Even though many contracts are awarded competitively, to the lowest bidder, other contracts are offered, in the language of the Washington bureaucracy, on a "sole source" basis. The Defense Department study cited above found that 82 percent of the contracts it examined were awarded without competitive bidding.[18] An agency can select a consulting firm without accepting competing bids on the grounds that the chosen consultant is uniquely qualified to do the job.

Consultants' familiarity with certain programs and agency officials helps them to obtain both competitive and noncompetitive contracts. Individuals can be uniquely qualified to consult for an agency because they used to work in it. When they write a proposal, they have an advantage in knowing the problems or approaches the agency is most interested in. Charles R. Owens, who worked for the Cost of Living Council and the Federal Energy Office, drafted oil price regulations during his stay in government. When he left the bureaucracy, he founded Charles R. Owens Associates, which became a leading consulting firm in the area of oil price controls.[19] Some consultants use their familiarity with their former agencies to help others get government contracts. Ex-General Alton Slay, introduced at the beginning of this chapter, is one of many consultants who help corporations like Lockheed generate business with the government.

By its very nature, consulting work is unpredictable. Firms cannot always be assured of winning enough contracts to keep all their employees. This uncertainty puts tremendous pressure on a firm's top executives to find and win consulting jobs. As one Washington consultant put it, "The people who work as consultants to the federal government generally are aggressive and competitive. You've got to be to survive. You don't sit passively and wait for people to call—it just doesn't work that way."[20]

THINK TANKS

"Think tank" is a common expression for an institution in which scholars engage in public policy research. Think tanks are staffed largely by people who have graduate degrees in the social sciences and strong interests in some aspect of public policy. The purpose of Washington-based think tanks, such as the Brookings Institution and the American Enterprise Institute (discussed below), is to sponsor studies pertinent to the debate over selected issues facing the country. And they can take "their case directly to the Congress, the media, and the public—to the marketplace of ideas."[21]

Unlike consulting firms, think tanks are nonprofit organizations. Most think tanks do not rely on government (or private) contracts for their existence. Although they may do some government work, they receive the bulk of their funding from foundation grants, their own endowments, corporate gifts, and proceeds from sales of their publications. Since they do not have to chase after consulting jobs, think tanks have the freedom to choose their own areas of study. Most sponsor broad, scholarly studies that are directed

A Forum at the American Enterprise Institute
Think tanks often sponsor conferences and forums on current issues and political developments. This forum at the American Enterprise Institute brought together leading political commentators and political scientists to discuss "Ronald Reagan and the American Dream."

toward a large audience inside and outside of government and that may take years to complete. The results of some think tank studies, such as *Policy Making for Social Security*[22] or *The New Congress*,[23] are published as books.

Some think tanks focus their efforts on one broad policy area; for example, the Urban Institute, which focuses on urban policy issues, or the Joint Center for Political Studies, which does research on blacks. Others, such as the left-leaning Institute for Policy Studies or the right-leaning Heritage Foundation, have distinct ideological perspectives. Still others strive toward a more "mainstream" point of view. Of all the think tanks in Washington, probably the best known are the Brookings Institution and the American Enterprise Institute; both address a broad range of policy questions and produce highly respected studies.

The Brookings Institution

The Brookings Institution is located in a large, gray, austere building near Washington's Dupont Circle. The institution was founded in the early part of this century by Robert Somers Brookings, a St. Louis businessman. The money he left began an endowment that continues to fund a significant part of the institution's yearly budget. Brookings sponsors and performs studies in foreign, domestic, and economic policy. Its senior fellows are scholars with national reputations, and its publications are frequently used as texts in university political science and economics courses across the country. It is particularly well known for its analyses of federal budgetary policy.

Although it is strictly nonpartisan, Brookings has a reputation as a Democratic think tank. Its staff does have a liberal bent, and many Brookings staffers are called on when a Democrat enters the White House. When Jimmy Carter became president, for example, a number of Brookings scholars took prominent positions in his administration. Among them were Charles Schultze, who became chairman of the Council of Economic Advisers, and Henry Aaron, who filled a top position in the Department of Health and Human Services. Aaron was given responsibility for developing an administration initiative on welfare reform; not coincidentally, he had earlier published a Brookings monograph titled *Why Is Welfare So Hard to Reform?*[24] When the Democrats are not in power, Brookings is often referred to as the "government in exile."

The American Enterprise Institute

The American Enterprise Institute (AEI) was slower to develop its strong reputation than was Brookings. Started in 1943 and funded almost exclusively from corporate gifts, the institute tended to parrot whatever big business was saying at the time. Now, however, AEI has become fiercely independent and employs top scholars in the social sciences. However, AEI still retains an overall conservative perspective; it is sometimes referred to as "the Brookings of the Right."

Like Brookings, AEI is highly respected in Washington for the quality of its work. It produces a steady stream of nationally distributed books, monographs, and conference proceedings. One particular area of research emphasis is current regulatory practices. AEI economists tend to look for market solutions to policy problems; in line with its conservative outlook, many AEI studies reflect a general goal of reducing government regulation.

Brookings, AEI, and other think tanks have a common purpose: to influence government policy by providing useful research studies. As the Heritage Foundation's Burton Pines put it, "We are one of those few public organizations . . . who believe that ideas have consequences, ideas count, and it's worth fighting the war of ideas."[25] Beyond that common ground, though, think tanks differ greatly in their political views and their areas of policy expertise. They are like little universities without students — places where scholars can quietly go about their business of trying to find answers to this country's most pressing problems. Those located in Washington have a special perch to sing from.

PUBLIC RELATIONS FIRMS

Washington-based **public relations firms** are hired by clients that want their interests promoted aggressively. These firms' clients are usually corporations or trade associations that need help in influencing government or the public. At the same time, a client may want a public relations firm to change a negative public image. In short, Washington public relations firms combine lobbying with image building.

A good example of this combination occurred a few years ago when the Food and Drug Administration (FDA) banned the use of saccharin, an artificial low-calorie sweetener. Tests showed that saccharin caused cancer in rats; as a result, companies that used saccharin in diet drinks and other diet products were faced with a serious problem. They would have to fight the FDA ban and at the same time convince the public that they weren't selling bottled cancer. These manufacturers turned to a Washington public relations firm, which immediately rounded up a number of scientists who disputed the FDA's findings. An educational and promotional campaign quickly reassured the public and played a large part in eventually lifting the ban on saccharin.[26]

Public relations firms can also prepare free editorials for radio, TV, and newspapers. Small-town newspapers and radio stations in particular do not have the staff to prepare enough news. They depend, of course, on the networks and wire services for most of what they broadcast or print. But independent sources can also approach them with already-prepared material in the form of editorials or news stories. For example, Fraser Associates prepared material on pending labor law legislation for its client, the business-backed National Action Committee on Labor Law Reform. Newspapers like the Henderson, Kentucky, *Gleaner Journal,* the Delhi, New York, *Republican-Express,* and the Mentor, Ohio, *News-Herald* all carried almost-identical editorials attacking the legislation, from the material Fraser Associates sent them.[27]

Robert Gray, Public Relations Specialist
Robert Gray (right) is a Washington insider, known for his access to policymakers. Gray built the largest public relations firm in Washington, staffing it with men and women experienced in government or media work. Here he has a warm greeting for Republican Senator John Warner of Virginia.

Public relations is a lucrative business in the United States. The two largest firms are Hill and Knowlton, and Burson-Marsteller, each with over $75 million in yearly fee billings.[28] The largest public relations operation in Washington is Gray and Company, with close to 200 employees. (In 1986 Gray and Company was sold to Hill and Knowlton; Hill and Knowlton's existing branch office in Washington is to be merged into the Gray office.)[29] One way smaller firms successfully compete against a giant like Gray and Company is to find a particular market niche. Fenton Communications, for example, is known for its public relations work on behalf of "progressive" causes. In a typical job, the Fenton company arranged schedules and publicity for a group of eleven foreign notables who came to Washington to protest U.S. "intervention in Central America."[30]

Washington public relations offices are often heavily staffed with individuals who have experience working for the media or government. Those with backgrounds in government try to use their connections with people still in government to aid and attract clients. At Gray and Company, employees include Gary Hymel, a former aide to the Speaker of the House; Daniel Murphy, a former admiral in the Navy and aide to Vice President George Bush; Bruce Fein, a former counsel at the Federal Communications Commission; and Diana Aldridge, a former aide to Democratic Senator Edward Kennedy of Massachusetts. Robert Gray, the firm's founder, is a friend of Ronald Reagan and chaired the president's inaugural committees in 1981 and 1985.[31] Corporate clients assume that someone who has been an intimate of the president can get a foot in the door, have phone calls returned, and exert some influence with policymakers.

Public relations firms have an image problem, however. Many people react negatively to the whole idea of public relations. A public relations campaign assumes that people's minds can be changed by some type of promotion or advertising, but people don't like to think that they can be swayed by would-be persuaders. Consequently, corporate clients want something more than slick advertising campaigns that the public might not buy. Public relations firms have responded by becoming increasingly sophisticated in their Washington operations. They offer a diversified set of services aimed at helping clients influence issues as they develop. They know that advertising and publicity must be complemented by long-term lobbying efforts if their clients are to achieve their goals.

TRADE ASSOCIATIONS

As defined in Chapter 8, **trade associations** are organizations of firms in the same basic industry. The Grocery Manufacturers of America is, not surprisingly, composed of firms in the grocery business. The National Machine Tool Builders Association, the American Apparel Manufacturers Association, and the American Maritime Association are similarly organized. Many trade association activities have little to do with politics. They keep members abreast of marketing and manufacturing developments in their respective industries, publish association newsletters and magazines, and sponsor conventions and gatherings where members can meet and possibly do business together.

Yet trade associations are also political groups because they represent their members' interests before the government. They are, in short, the lobbying arms of individual industries, and their political role is becoming increasingly important. As noted in Chapter 8, the number of trade associations with headquarters in Washington increased significantly in response to the growth in regulatory agencies and federal regulation in the 1960s and 1970s. Between 1971 and 1981, the percentage of all trade associations with headquarters in Washington grew from 19 percent to 29 percent. The more than three thousand trade groups located in Washington are a principal source of employment in Washington's private sector, now employing around eighty thousand people.[32]

Trade associations do much more than lobby Congress when an occasional vote comes up. Day in and day out, they monitor the congressional committees and administrative agencies that oversee the programs or industries with which they are concerned. Experienced trade association representatives maintain regular contact with policymakers, supplying them with relevant information when they can. These lobbyists are particularly interested in finding out about proposed legislation or possible changes in regulations that may affect their members. As one association head noted, "Every time HUD [the Department of Housing and Urban Development] hiccups, 20 construction industry associations hold a meeting."[33]

SUBSYSTEM POLITICS

We have now discussed the key private sector organizations and individuals in the Washington community: lawyers, lobbyists, consultants, scholars, and public relations specialists. All of them attempt to influence government and the policymaking process. To best serve their own or their clients' interests, they must develop reputations for excellence in intensely competitive fields. And in Washington, "excellence" means, more than anything else, technical mastery of one's policy area. Members of the community must strive to know their narrow specialties better than anyone else in the field. But these people who sell their expertise must also develop political relationships that will let them put their knowledge to work. In short, they must work toward becoming part of what political scientists call a **subsystem**—a group of individuals, both inside and outside of the government, who together develop policy in a specific area.[34]

Government by Policy Area

It is easy to examine Washington politics and policymaking by looking at the institutions of American government—Congress, the White House, the bureaucracy, and the courts—as separate, self-contained political bodies. Each is characterized by its own set of policymaking procedures, different patterns of personnel recruitment, and particular responsibilities that have been assigned by the Constitution or have evolved over the years. But policymaking is actually a dynamic process involving all these institutions inter-

Washington Talk
It is often said in Washington that "information is power." Members of the Washington community are constantly trying to find out what's on the mind of policymakers. At this reception officials from the American Trucking Association, a trade group, talk with Betty Jo Christian, a member of the Interstate Commerce Commission.

acting with one another. And, as we have seen, policymaking also involves people from the private sector.

Suppose that Congress is considering amendments to the Clean Air Act; institutions other than Congress will become active participants in the process. The Environmental Protection Agency, for example, will try to shape the final outcome of the legislation, because it will eventually have to administer the law. Similarly, there will be concern at the White House, since the Clean Air Act affects such vital sectors of the economy as the steel and coal industries. As a result, officials from both the White House and the EPA will work with members of Congress and with the appropriate committee staffs to ensure that their interests are protected. At the same time, lobbyists representing corporations, trade associations, and environmental groups will do their best to influence Congress, agency officials, and White House aides. The trade associations, in turn, might hire public relations firms to sway public opinion toward industry's point of view. Outside experts from think tanks and universities might be asked to testify at hearings or to serve in an informal advisory capacity concerning the technical, economic, and social impact of the proposed amendments.

When Congress does enact the new amendments, the policymaking process does not end; it enters a new phase. First, administrative regulations need to be drawn up. This is the function of the bureaucracy—that is, of the EPA— but key congressional committee members and officials from the Office of Management and Budget (OMB), acting on behalf of the White House, will monitor the process closely. Interest group lawyers will also work to influence the regulations' content. Once the new law and its regulations are put into effect, the EPA might hire consultants to assess their impact. If an interest group's lawyers feel that the regulations harm its members and have not been drawn up to follow Congress's original intent, they might take the agency to court. And if Congress and agency officials become aware of emerging problems, then new amendments will be proposed, and the process will begin anew.

Thus policymaking on the Clean Air Act neither ends nor takes place within only one institution. Rather, such policymaking takes place among a group of actors from various institutions, all of whom have some interest in the act. What these actors have in common is membership in a *policy subsystem*. Such subsystems differ from policy area to policy area and vary considerably in their degree of influence over final policy outcomes.

Subsystems are important not only as an aspect of the overall policymaking process, but also as another example of the conflict between majoritarianism and pluralism. To what extent do the actors in subsystems reflect majority opinion? Are subsystems dominated by the most powerful interest groups? Alternatively, do subsystems play a mediating role between competing interest groups within each policy area?

From Iron Triangles . . .

The idea of examining Washington politics by looking at policy areas rather than at single institutions is not new. Research by an earlier generation of political scientists and journalists described subsystems as tight-knit groups composed of a small number of key individuals. For example, Douglass Cater described the sugar subsystem (or "subgovernment") of the late 1950s as follows:

> Political power within the sugar subgovernment is largely vested in the Chairman of the House Agricultural Committee who works out the schedule of quotas. It is shared by a veteran civil servant, the director of the Sugar Division of the U.S. Department of Agriculture, who provides the necessary "expert" advice for such a complex marketing arrangement. Further advice is provided by Washington representatives of the domestic beet and cane sugar growers, the sugar refineries, and the foreign producers.[35]

Three key components of a subsystem are evident in Cater's description. First are *congressional committees* or *subcommittees*. In an agricultural policy area such as sugar, members of the congressional agriculture committees (*not* the entire Congress) are involved. In the sugar subsystem, the chairman of the House Agriculture Committee was the critical player. Second is the particular *agency* or *bureau* that administers the program in question. In this "subgovernment," Cater identified a single bureaucrat who acted on behalf of the Department of Agriculture in sugar policymaking. The third component is a small number of *lobbyists* representing the agency's central clients — in this case, the growers, refineries, and foreign producers.

Subsystems like the one that existed for sugar policymaking were often called **iron triangles.** The term *iron* referred to one very important property of subsystems. They were largely autonomous and closed, and outsiders had a great deal of difficulty penetrating them. Even presidents were said to have difficulty influencing iron triangles, which endured over time and changed little when new administrations came into power. Even job changes did not break up these close working relationships, because an individual who left one component of an iron triangle often became associated with one of the other two components. A person who left the administrative agency, for example, might become a lobbyist for one of the client groups involved in the same subsystem. Likewise, a staff member of a congressional committee might take a job with a client group or go to work for the agency with which he or she had been dealing. Iron triangles worked well for those involved because participants shared similar policy views and tried to reach a consensus that would benefit all concerned. In such a mutual self-help arrangement, policymaking can be described as a process of "three-sided backscratching."[36]

. . . to Issue Networks

Today, subsystems are still central to the policymaking process, but political scientists no longer describe them as "iron triangles." About fifteen years after Cater, political scientist Hugh Heclo pointed out that "the iron triangle concept is not so much wrong as it is disastrously incomplete."[37] What happened during the last two decades to make the iron triangle description inadequate?

Of central importance was the proliferation of interest groups. A growing number of interest group representatives have come to Washington, intent on becoming part of the policy subsystems relevant to their organizations' interests. Unless they are hostile to a group's policy views, members of Congress do not usually want to exclude representatives of constituents back home. Thus, as newly represented groups pushed to get into a Washington subsystem, the triangles turned out to be more porous than the term *iron* suggests.

Change also came to Congress. For a variety of reasons, it began to decentralize its internal structure, and the number of subcommittees began to grow. As a result, it became more difficult for one or two members of Congress to control a particular policy area. The increasing overlap of policymaking authority among subcommittees worked to open up the policymaking process to interested parties.[38]

Policymaking in a particular area is still influenced by a community of activists from the public and private sectors. But now these subsystems tend to be more open and accessible to a broader range of players. Heclo calls these new subsystems **issue networks,** defined as "a shared-knowledge group having to do with some aspect . . . of public policy."[39]

Unfortunately, there is no graphic image as crisp as that of an iron triangle to represent an issue network. But if the boundaries of an issue network are fuzzy, the glue that holds its members together is readily apparent: it is technical mastery of their particular policy area. The members of Congress, committee staffers, agency officials, lawyers, lobbyists, consultants, scholars, and public relations specialists—those who interact with one another as part of a Washington issue network — have in common a detailed knowledge of a particular program or set of programs. And the complexity of today's policy problems makes that knowledge extremely difficult to acquire.

EXPERTISE WITHIN SUBSYSTEMS

The iron triangles may have rusted through, and contemporary issue networks may be much more open to new participants, but there is still a significant barrier to admission into a subsystem. One must have the required expertise to enter the community of activists and politicians who influence policy development in an issue area.

Take, for example, the case of oil policymaking. One observer concludes that "the days when the Washington representative of a major oil company could visit the Office of Oil and Gas to find relief for his company's problems are over."[40] At the same time, he finds that "strong energy subsystems [issue networks] continue to thrive."[41] In short, the oil subsystem is broader than it once was.

Yet entry into these energy subsystems still depends on mastering the technical complexities of the oil business. It is easy to understand why. When one looks at the issues addressed during a period of expanding regulation of the domestic oil industry, there is no end to seemingly obscure and complicated policy questions. How were "original costs" to be distinguished from "reproduction costs"? Was it fair for "secondary and tertiary production" to be exempted from "base period volumes"? Did drilling that yielded "new pays" or "extensions" qualify as "new" oil or "old" oil for pricing purposes?[42]

Those in an issue network speak the same language. They can participate in the negotiation and compromise of policymaking because they can offer concrete, detailed solutions to the problems at hand. They understand the substance of policy, the way Washington works, and one another's viewpoints.

The "In-and-Outers"

One reason participants in an issue network have such a good understanding of the needs and problems of others in the network is that job switches within subsystems continue to be common. When someone wants to leave his or her current position but remain in Washington, the most obvious place to look for a job is in the same policy field. For these **"in-and-outers,"** knowledge and experience remain relevant to a particular issue network no matter which side of the fence the people are on.

The most typical — and most frequently criticized — pattern of job switching is to work in government for a number of years, build up knowledge of a policy area, and then take a lobbying job. Trade associations; corporations; and law, consulting, and public relations firms generally pay much higher salaries than the government. And these private sector firms pay not just for experience and know-how, but for connections with government. When the Washington lobbying firm of Black, Manafort, and Stone hired James C. Healy, a former aide to the Democratic chairman of the House Ways and

Clark Clifford, Private Citizen and Public Servant
Clark Clifford (at left speaking with President Johnson) has had a celebrated career moving back and forth between the private sector and government service. As a young attorney he went to work for President Truman. Later, after many years as a Washington lawyer, he went back into government as the secretary of defense for Lyndon Johnson. He returned to private practice when Johnson left office in 1969.

Means Committee, it knew that this in-and-outer would give them better access to that critical tax-writing unit. Corporations that want to influence the committee can choose among many Washington firms. Black, Manafort, and Stone can make a convincing case to prospective clients that Healy's phone calls to the House Democratic leadership are returned.[43]

Sometimes congressional staffers or high-ranking agency officials will "cash in their chips" by starting their own firms rather than going to work for an existing firm. Despite the competition, those with valuable government experience and their peers' respect can quickly establish themselves as the people with the right expertise and the right contacts in a particular policy field. This was certainly the case with Susan J. Williams and Terrence L. Bracy. Both served as assistant secretaries of transportation in the Carter administration. When they started Bracy Williams & Company in 1981, they had little trouble attracting clients in the transportation field. Among other clients, Bracy Williams was retained by the Air Line Pilots Association, the

Michael Deaver, Before the Fall

This photo of top-Reagan-aide-turned-lobbyist Michael Deaver, which appeared on the cover of Time *magazine, has come to symbolize the brazenness with which high-powered Washington lobbyists flaunt their access to key policymakers. Posing for the* Time *photographer in the back of his chauffeur-driven Jaguar, Deaver seemed to want the world to know that no one had better access than he did. Ironically, shortly after this picture appeared, allegations surfaced that Deaver had violated the Ethics in Government Act.*

CSX railroad company, and the Quixote Corporation, which manufactures highway crash barriers.[44]

One constraint on in-and-outers is the Ethics in Government Act, which specifies that any senior executive branch official refrain from lobbying his or her former agency for a year after leaving the government. Former officials must also wait two years to lobby any agency on an issue on which they were personally and substantially involved. Former presidential aide Michael Deaver was accused of violating the act after he resigned from the Reagan White House in 1985. Allegations against Deaver included charges that, while still in the White House, he participated in meetings concerning Canadian complaints about acid rain. Less than a year later, Deaver had set up his own firm and was lobbying on behalf of the Canadian government. Investigators have not yet determined whether Deaver should be charged with violating the Ethics in Government Act.

Movement within a subsystem also flows the other way: individuals from the private sector are often tapped for a government position within the same subsystem. After President Reagan took office, he chose William Sullivan, Jr., as an associate administrator of the Environmental Protection Agency. Previously, Sullivan had headed the Steel Communities Coalition, an industry group fighting to have pollution control standards relaxed because they were having an adverse impact on financially ailing steel companies. At the EPA, Sullivan's job included enforcing air pollution standards.[45]

Examples of Issue Differences

All issue networks have in common the requirement of expertise and familiarity among participants. However, contemporary subsystems differ greatly in operations, depending on their issue areas. In other words, the nature of the issue itself affects the type of subsystem surrounding it. A comparison of the issue networks for food stamp policy and defense procurement policy illustrates this effect.

The food stamp network. Since its inception in 1961, the food stamp program has offered assistance to the nation's poor. Those who qualify receive scrip that may be used to buy food at the grocery store. For most of the food stamp program's history, administrators in the Department of Agriculture and lobbyists representing poor people's groups have had an adversarial relationship. Citizen groups have been highly critical of most administrations for not spending enough on food stamps. For budgetary or ideological reasons, most administrations have tried to restrict program participation. When food stamp officials have been hostile toward these citizen groups, the groups' lobbyists have worked with liberal members of Congress; those members of Congress have, in turn, tried to pressure the administration.

An exception to this pattern occurred during the liberal Carter administration. Citizen group lobbyists were appointed to the key policymaking positions dealing with food and nutrition in the Department of Agriculture. These lobbyists-turned-administrators were quick to bring their former citizen group colleagues into the policymaking process. Thus the Washington-based Food Research and Action Center and the Community Nutrition Institute had nearly unlimited access to administrators and played a major advisory role in this issue network. But their smoothly running, consensual subsystem, consisting of congressional liberals, lobbyists, and administrators, was upended when the Reagan administration took office. The new administration proposed drastic cutbacks in food stamp program spending. Newly appointed Reagan conservatives in the Department of Agriculture, antagonistic toward pro–food stamp groups, closed the door to them.[46]

Experience has thus shown that the food stamp issue network is neither autonomous, unified, nor stable. The White House has frequently exerted control over the program, and ideological and partisan factors have had a major influence on food stamp policy.

The defense procurement network.   It is more accurate to speak of *several* issue networks in defense procurement than to speak of a single subsystem. Different defense contractors deal with different offices within different services, depending on the specific weapon they are promoting. All the subsystems surrounding the procurement of weapons systems are, however, much further removed from partisan politics and ideological swings than is the food stamp network. The complexity of modern weapons systems, the worrisome nature of national security in a nuclear age, and the common interests of private and public sector actors help to make these issue networks highly autonomous. One recent study indicated that

> decisions on defense policy and weapons procurement rest almost entirely in the hands of insiders and policy experts, walled off from outsiders and alternative perspectives. The policy-makers, whose expertise is real and necessary, are also people and organizations with interests to protect and promote.[47]

Although controversies occasionally erupt over the need for a particular weapons system, most policymaking on weapons selection receives little outside scrutiny. There are few (if any) powerful interest groups fighting against the Pentagon's weapons procurement procedures. There is some conflict, however, between different defense contractors, who can find themselves competing when they try to sell the Pentagon slightly different versions of the same weapon.

Defense Department procurement officials are often hired away by the private sector firms they dealt with while in government. Each year, hundreds of officers in the armed services move to jobs with defense contractors like Lockheed, Boeing, and General Dynamics (see Feature 14.3). This promotes consensual, cooperative interaction between buyers and sellers of weapons systems.

SUBSYSTEMS AND DEMOCRACY

The involvement of subsystems in policymaking has given rise to a set of interrelated questions or fears regarding issue networks. Has our government become too fragmented into distinct policymaking networks? Are some issue networks beyond popular control? Has the increasing complexity of public policy given technical experts too much policymaking authority? Are we, in short, a government of subgovernments?

This issue was raised in Chapter 2. There we noted that, for many years, political scientists have described American democracy as one in which many constituencies energetically try to influence policies that are of primary concern to them. Policymaking is seen as a response to these groups rather than to the majority will. This is a considerably different conception of democracy than the more traditional view that policies reflect what most of the people want. It is, in fact, a pluralist, rather than a majoritarian, view of American government.

The case of the food stamp network reminds us that not every subsystem dominates policymaking in its issue area. Still, many analysts suggest that American government is becoming increasingly captive to issue networks (see

Feature 14.3

The Armed Forces: A Great Place to Start!

An ad campaign aimed at young people encourages them to consider the armed forces because they're a "great place to start." The message is that young adults learning a skill in the armed services will acquire an important credential for the job hunt when their military obligation ends. And, of course, that job training comes at Uncle Sam's expense. The same logic apparently holds for many senior officers. Although they may not have entered the military with much thought for acquiring skills for their retirement, those with the right military experience can land lucrative jobs working for defense contractors.

Defense contractors want experienced military officers to help them win contracts. They worry that it may not be enough just to have a good product. As one industry spokesperson put it, "We need everything we can get. This is a very competitive business." Critics charge that the ex–military officers are able to win favorable treatment for their new employers.

The "revolving door" pattern is pervasive. In one three-year period, 1,437 military officers with the rank of major or higher left the armed services to take a position with a defense contractor. Among those who left to join the private sector:

Colonel Harvey M. Paskin, who supervised the development of the radar for the F-16 fighter jet for the Air Force, left to work for Westinghouse on the radar for the F-16.

Lieutenant Colonel John W. O'Neal, who worked for the Joint Chiefs of Staff as the officer in charge of the Ground Mobile Command Center, left to join TRW as the senior planner for the Ground Mobile Command Center.

Major General Henry B. Stelling, Jr., was vice commander of the Electronics Systems Division at an air base but left to join the Defense Electronics Operations division of Rockwell International.

Colonel James C. Crosby was head of the Army Defense Board, which tested the Divad antiaircraft system, but left to work for Ford Aerospace, chief contractor for the Divad system.

Colonel William E. Crouch, Jr., served as the commander of Army Aviation Development Test Activity at Fort Rucker, Alabama, until he became Fort Rucker branch manager for Hughes Helicopter. Hughes's equipment is frequently tested at that Army facility.

Colonel Sherwin Arculis was responsible for testing remotely piloted vehicles, such as reconnaissance drones, for the Army, but moved to a job with Lockheed's Missiles and Space division. There he became manager for logistical support to the Army's remotely piloted vehicle program.

Source: Adapted from Fred Kaplan, "Military's 'Revolving Door' with Business," *Boston Globe,* January 15, 1984. Reprinted by permission.

Compared With What? 14.1). They point especially to the complexity of such contemporary policy issues as nuclear power, toxic wastes, and air pollution. The more technically complex the issue, the more elected officials must depend on a technocratic elite for policy guidance. And technical expertise, of course, is a chief characteristic of those in an issue network.

At first glance, it may seem very desirable to have policymaking highly influenced by technical experts. As political scientists Randall Ripley and

Compared With What? 14.1

Bureaucrats, Legislators, and Lobbyists

The patterns of interaction among bureaucrats, legislators, and lobbyists differ considerably among Western democracies. The figures at right indicate the percentage of bureaucrats in each country reporting that they have "regular" contact with legislators and representatives of client groups. Subsystem politics contributes to the high level of interaction that U.S. bureaucrats have with legislators and interest group representatives.

Country	Percentage of bureaucrats reporting "regular" contacts with —	
	Members of parliament	Representatives of clientele groups
Britain	5	67
Netherlands	16	64
Sweden	31	No data*
Italy	50	59
Germany	74	74
United States	64	93

* Swedish respondents were asked about five interest groups; those data are excluded from this analysis as noncomparable. (Source: Adapted from Joel D. Aberbach, Robert D. Putnam, and Bert A. Rockman, *Bureaucrats and Politicians in Western Democracies.* Cambridge, Mass.: Harvard University Press, 1981, p. 230.) Reprinted by permission.

Grace Franklin note, "Some would argue that the dominance of subgovernments in much policymaking is good and works in the public interest because genuine experts are placed in charge of issues."[48] This line of thinking is appealing because we often consider "politics" to be a barrier to effective problem solving.

Yet dependence on technocrats works to the advantage of interest groups, who employ policy experts to maximize their influence with government. Seen in this light, issue networks become less appealing. Interest groups — at least those with which we do not personally identify — are seen as selfish. They pursue policies that favor their constituents rather than the national interest. In contrast, policymaking that is influenced more by a broader set of participants or by the public at large may seem more democratic.

Although the expertise of interest group representatives and other members of the Washington community is valued by those in government, there is a more fundamental reason why they are allowed to enter issue networks. Although Americans believe that the majority should rule, they also believe that government should be open and accessible to the people. If some constituency has a problem, they reason, government ought to listen to it. The practical consequence of this view is that government must be open to interest groups. And it is interest group lobbyists — and those they hire from the Washington community, such as lawyers and public relations specialists — who go before government. It is, of course, possible for rank-and-file members of an interest group to become involved through letter writing and other tactics, but professional lobbyists handle most contacts with government.

The presence of subsystems is thus something of a dilemma. Americans want the government to hear their views. At the same time, the government's willingness to work with lobbying groups through issue networks works against majoritarianism. Too often, public policy decisions turn out to be better for the subsystem than for the larger public. Moreover, not every constituency is equally well represented in issue network politics. Defense contractors and food stamp recipients, for example, have had considerably different levels of influence within their respective issue networks. As presently constituted, subsystems do not promote equal representation of interests. Instead, they reflect the existing inequality of resources between different segments of American society.

SUMMARY

The policymaking process in Washington involves many people outside of the legislative, judicial, and executive branches of government. Washington's private sector — made up of law firms, consulting firms, think tanks, public relations firms, and trade associations — is an integral part of Washington politics. The growth of these government service industries reflects the changing nature of Washington politics. Government expanded greatly during the 1960s and 1970s, when new regulatory agencies were created to deal with a widening variety of business and social concerns. The number of interest groups rose dramatically, and many new business and citizen groups established offices in Washington. This expanding universe of lobbies drew on growing numbers of lawyers, consultants, public relations firms, and other experts to influence government policy.

Policymaking can be viewed as an ongoing process of interaction between those within government and those outside of it, through issue networks that deal with particular policy areas. Each network is a means of communication, through which information and policy ideas are exchanged. Consultants and scholars from think tanks join experts working on behalf of interest groups, agency officials, and members of Congress in various issue networks. Generally, these contemporary subsystems are more open to new participants than the old iron triangles were. Despite their similarities, however, individual issue networks differ greatly in influence and autonomy.

The ever-increasing complexity of public policy issues also puts a premium on expertise. Those with expertise in a given area are in the best position to influence policy in that area.

Political scientists view issue networks with some concern. Issue networks facilitate the representation of many interests in the policymaking process. But they sometimes also allow small, aggressive constituencies to prevail over the broader interests of the nation. In essence, issue networks embody a dilemma of choosing a majoritarian or a pluralist model of democracy. It is easy to say that the majority should rule. But in the real world, the majority tends to be far less interested in issues than are the constituencies most directly affected by them. It is also easy to say that those most affected by issues should have the most influence. Experience teaches us, however, that such influence leads to policies that favor the well represented, at the expense of those who should be at the bargaining table but are not.

Key Terms

"Washington community"   trade association
lawyer-lobbyist   subsystem
consultant   iron triangle
"think tank"   issue network
public relations firm   "in-and-outer"

Selected Readings

Adams, Gordon. *The Politics of Defense Contracting: The Iron Triangle.* New Brunswick, N.J.: Transaction Books, 1982. An examination of the close relationship between defense contractors and government officials.

Berry, Jeffrey M. *Feeding Hungry People: Rulemaking in the Food Stamp Program.* New Brunswick, N.J.: Rutgers University Press, 1984. A study of the food stamp issue network.

Cater, Douglass. *Power in Washington.* New York: Vintage Books, 1964. One reporter's view of how policy is formulated in Washington.

Chubb, John E. *Interest Groups and the Bureaucracy.* Stanford, Calif: Stanford University Press, 1983. Chubb analyzes the relationship between interest groups and agencies for different energy subsystems.

Dodd, Lawrence C., and Richard L. Schott. *Congress and the Administrative State.* New York: Wiley, 1979. The authors trace the evolution of subsystems and institutional reform in Congress.

Ripley, Randall B., and Grace A. Franklin. *Congress, the Bureaucracy, and Public Policy.* 3rd ed. Homewood, Ill.: Dorsey Press, 1984. Ripley and Franklin look at subsystem politics in different policy arenas.

PART V

MAKING PUBLIC POLICY

15

The Economics of
Public Policy

onald Reagan, the movie actor, had a bad experience with income taxes, and he described it in his 1965 autobiography, *Where's the Rest of Me?*[1] Success in films had given Reagan a high income and a high standard of living, but it had also put him in a high tax bracket:

> True, I'd been making handsome money ever since World War II, but that handsome money lost a lot of its beauty and substance going through the 91 per cent bracket of the income tax.[2]

He complained that his nightclub bills, which were running $750 a month, were considered to be "purely personal and thus not deductible for computing income tax." Because of his high tax rate, Reagan wrote, "I had to earn about eight dollars for very dollar I was spending."[3] Reagan was upset with a government that took away so much of his income.

According to tax tables for the early 1950s, Reagan's tax rate put his taxable income above $200,000. Despite his high income, Reagan got into tax trouble.

> The tragic fact in this evil day of progressive taxation is that, once behind, it is well-nigh impossible to earn your way out. Like most fellows in uniform, I had taken advantage of the right to defer income tax until after the war, so I returned to civilian life with a good income, a high tax rate, and a debt. . . . The day for repayment came and so did a polite fellow in a gray suit. When I opened the front door, almost his very first words were, "Where is it?"[4]

This encounter with the Internal Revenue Service had a lasting effect on Ronald Reagan. As a movie star, he had to pay the government 91 percent of his net earnings over $200,000. In comparison, taxpayers earning the median family income of $3,300 in 1950 were only in the 25 percent tax bracket. Reagan believed that his high rate amounted to government confiscation of his income, which discouraged him from making more money by making more pictures.

Ronald Reagan, the president, did not forget his encounter with the government tax collectors. Although the maximum tax rate had dropped to 70 percent before he took office, Reagan quickly pushed through a 1981 tax bill that cut the top rate to 50 percent. He also advocated sweeping tax reform — which included a much greater reduction in the top tax bracket — as the major domestic policy objective of his administration. And he got what he wanted. On October 22, 1986, President Reagan signed into law a comprehensive tax reform bill that eliminated numerous tax shelters while reducing both individual and corporate rates. Beginning in 1988, the top tax bracket will be 28 percent, compared with 50 percent in 1986.

Why did Reagan succeed in his tax reform when others had failed before him? Is Reagan's personal victory in restructuring the income tax rates also a victory for the average taxpayer, or will the lower rates benefit primarily the rich? And what is the relationship between taxing and spending? Can the government budget be balanced only by cutting spending, or will taxes also need to be raised eventually? We shall grapple with these and other questions about the economics of public policy in this chapter.

GOVERNMENT PURPOSES
AND PUBLIC POLICIES

In Chapter 1, we noted that virtually all citizens are willing to accept limitations on their personal freedom in return for various benefits of government. The major purposes of government were defined as maintaining order, providing public goods, and promoting equality. Governments vary in how much they value each of these broad purposes, as reflected in their public policies. A **public policy** is a general plan of action adopted by government to solve a social problem, counter a threat, or make use of an opportunity. For example, governments may formulate policies for lowering unemployment, reducing crime in cities, or negotiating with the Soviet Union.

Governments may also fail to adopt a policy for dealing with a troublesome situation; instead they may just "muddle through" somehow until the problem goes away — or until it becomes too great to ignore. Government policies may be carefully developed and then turn out to be effective, or they may be hastily drawn and ineffective or even counterproductive. But the reverse may also be true; deliberately constructed policies may end up as total disasters, and quick fixes may work just fine. Regardless of their ultimate effectiveness, however, all policies have this in common: they are the *means* by which government pursues certain *goals* within specific *situations*. People disagree over public policies because they disagree over one or more of these ingredients: the goals that government should have, the means that should be tried to fulfill them, and the perception of the situation.

Consider the social problem of poverty. Everyone deplores poverty, but people differ as to whether reducing poverty should be a goal of government action. Even those who think that the government ought to fight poverty are divided over the proper means. Some favor government job programs for the unemployed poor; others favor specific aid programs, such as the food stamp program; and still others favor a "minimum income" for all Americans. Finally, people may disagree over the extent of poverty in the United States. How many of the nation's 230 million people do *you* think live in poverty? Fewer than a million? Between 10 and 20 million? More than 30 million? How you perceive the problem makes a difference in how you evaluate the alternative policies aimed at reducing poverty.

A 1984 report of a subcommittee of the House Ways and Means Committee found that *35 million* Americans lived in poverty in 1983.[5] That number is 15.2 percent of the population! If you accept this finding as fact, you probably want government to do something about the problem. However, you might think that the finding exaggerates the extent of poverty. What is "poverty" anyway? The Census Bureau defines the "poverty threshold" differently according to the number of people in a family. In 1983, it was $5,277 for a single person or $10,612 for a family of four.[6] Even if you agree that people with such low incomes are "poor," you may dispute the count of people below the poverty threshold as pure fabrication by faceless bureaucrats. In that case, you may pooh-pooh the problem and deny the need for activist policies designed to aid 35 million people. Even if you accept the fact of poverty *and* the need for government action, what should be the policy?

The Law Says ''Butt Out!''
Government regulations against smoking in public areas are intended to protect the public health. As of now, smoking is not widely regarded as morally repugnant behavior that should be completely banned. But remember that the sale and distribution of alcoholic beverages once was prohibited by the Constitution.

As you will see in Chapter 16, it is difficult to formulate satisfactory policies to reduce poverty. The congressional report cited above concluded that more people were poor in 1983 than in 1965, when President Lyndon Johnson launched his ''War on Poverty'' and committed the nation to spending billions of dollars to win it.

What can governments do to achieve their goals? Stripped to their essentials, here are the options: a government can *demand* that citizens do this or not do that; it can try to *persuade* citizens to behave in certain ways; it can *take* from individuals or *give* to individuals; or it can *do what is required* itself. These categories exhaust the various overt actions that governments demonstrate in their policies. Unfortunately, knowing these categories is not the same as understanding government's objectives in demanding, persuading, taking, giving, or doing. We need concepts that will help us analyze the purposes behind a government's overt actions.

At the broadest level, public policies can be usefully analyzed according to whether they prohibit, protect, promote, or provide. Some policies are

Oil Rigs Floating on a Sea of Tax Benefits
The government can tailor its tax policies to promote certain business activities. The oil and coal industries have long enjoyed various tax deductions for expenses incurred in energy exploration. In 1984, the federal government lost about $3 billion in revenues as a result of tax benefits to these industries.

intended to *prohibit* behavior that the government regards as morally repugnant. Murder, robbery, and rape are obvious examples of outlawed behavior in every society. Governments that emphasize order tend to specialize in policies of prohibition, which instruct people what they must not do — such as drink liquor, have abortions, or engage in homosexual relations.

Government policies can also *protect* activities, things, or special groups of citizens. For example, taxes were once levied on colored oleomargarine (the butter substitute) to reduce its sales and thus protect the dairy industry from competition. Regulations concerning the testing of new drugs are intended to protect citizens against harmful side effects, and government rules about safety in the workplace are enacted to protect workers. As discussed in Chapter 12, governments defend such regulations as serving the public good, but some people regard most protective legislation as unwarranted government interference in the marketplace or in private lives.

Policies can also *promote* social activities that are important to the government. Governments occasionally rely on persuasion through advertising

The Post Office on Madison Avenue
Before the days of electronic media and sophisticated Madison Avenue advertising techniques, the federal government tried its hand at promoting government programs through persuasive poster art. This 1929 poster tried to convince Americans that everybody was sending letters by air mail. The government's objective was to help support the fledgling airline industry.

to promote certain activities — urging people to "Buy Bonds" or to join the army, for example. To really get things done, governments sometimes become very generous. To promote railroad construction in the 1860s, Congress granted railroad companies huge tracts of public lands along the right-of-way through western states. However, the most important way in which government can promote activities is through favorable treatment within the tax structure.

The technical term for this form of government promotion is **tax expenditure,** for it amounts to a loss of government revenue due to the favorable tax treatment. For example, the government encourages people to buy their own homes by allowing them to deduct, from their taxable income, the amount of money they pay in mortgage interest. In 1984, this tax expenditure cost the federal government nearly $23 billion. And, of course, churches and private educational institutions often pay no property taxes to state and local governments.

Finally, public policies can *provide* benefits directly to citizens. The benefits can be either public or private. *Public benefits* are facilities or services which all citizens share, such as mail service, roads, schools, street lighting, libraries, and parks. *Private benefits* are those that go to certain classes of citizens — poor people, farmers, veterans, and even college students. Public benefits are the more difficult to deliver to citizens, since they require either the construction of facilities (such as roads, dams, or sewer systems) or organizations to provide services (such as transportation, electric power, and garbage collection). Private benefits are simply payments to individuals, like food stamps, subsidies, pensions, and loans. These payments are made because the recipients are thought to be particularly needy or politically powerful, or both.

Not every policy neatly matches just one of these four purposes, for policies sometimes serve multiple purposes. For example, a policy of subsidizing farmers might be viewed as protecting the family farm or promoting farming as well as providing private benefits. Nevertheless, most policies have a dominant underlying objective. We classify farm subsidies as providing private benefits simply because they have neither encouraged individuals to enter farming nor protected the family farm as an institution. In fact, most farm subsidies go to the largest farms.

Governments rely on different legislative techniques to achieve their policy objectives. Some laws simply forbid or require certain behavior. For example, the Constitution forbids interfering with the free exercise of religion, and Congress has passed laws requiring employers to pay men and women equally for equal work. We shall examine such prohibitions and requirements more closely in Chapters 17 and 18, on civil liberties and civil rights. In this chapter, we shall focus on taxing and spending, which the government employs creatively in public policies designed to protect, promote, and provide.

THEORIES OF ECONOMIC POLICY

Taxing and spending are major policy tools of government. How policymakers use these tools depends on their beliefs about (1) how the economy functions and (2) the proper role of government in economic life. The American economy is so complex that no policymaker knows exactly how it works. Policymakers rely on economic theories to explain its functioning, and there are nearly as many theories as economists (see Feature 15.1). Unfortunately, different theories (and economists) often predict quite different outcomes. One source of difference is the simplifying assumptions that are part of every economic theory, and which differ from theory to theory. Another problem is the difference between an idealized theory and the real world. Yet in spite of disagreement among economists, a knowledge of basic economics is needed to understand government approaches to public policy.

We shall be concerned only with economic policy in a *market economy* — one in which the prices of goods and services are determined through the interaction of sellers and buyers (that is, through supply and demand). Such economies are typical of the consumer-dominated societies of western Europe and the United States. *Nonmarket economies* rely on government planners to determine both the prices of goods and the amounts that are produced. (This

Feature 15.1

Economics: The Dismal Science

Thomas Carlyle, a nineteenth-century British social critic, characterized economics as "the dismal science." Although Carlyle was speaking in a different context, his phrase has stuck. If being a science requires agreement on fundamental propositions among its practitioners, then the prospects for economics as a science are surely dismal. When twenty-seven standard propositions in economic theory were put to almost a thousand economists in five Western countries, they did not agree on a single proposition. Consider this example: "Reducing the role of regulatory authorities (e.g., in air traffic) would improve the efficiency of the economy." One-third of the economists "generally disagreed," 30 percent "generally agreed," and 34 percent "agreed with provisions." When learned economists do not agree on basic propositions in economic theory, practical politicians are free to choose theories that fit their views of the proper role of government in economic life.

The Economists

This view is found in Bruno S. Frey, et al., "Consensus and Dissension among Economists: An Empirical Inquiry," *American Economic Review*, 74 (December 1984): 986–994.

is characteristic of the Soviet Union and most eastern European communist societies.) In nonmarket economies, the government owns and operates the major means of production. However, market economies often exhibit a mix of government and private ownership. For example, Britain has considerably more government-owned enterprises (railroads, broadcasting, housing, and utilities) than the United States.

Market economies are loosely called "capitalist" economies, signifying that private individuals sell goods for a profit in a free, or open, market. The competing theories of market economies differ largely on how "free" the market should be, and what government should do to direct its economy through intervention.

Laissez Faire Economics

The French term *laissez faire* was introduced in Chapter 1 and discussed again in Chapter 12. It describes an absence of any government economic control. The economic doctrine of laissez faire likens the operation of a completely free market to the process of evolution. Economic competition will weed out the weak and preserve the strong. In the process, the economy will prosper and everyone will eventually benefit.

Advocates of laissez faire economics are fond of quoting Adam Smith's *The Wealth of Nations*. In this 1776 treatise, Smith argued that each individual, pursuing his own selfish interests in a free market, was "led by an invisible hand to promote an end which was no part of his intention." Smith's "invisible hand" is used to justify the belief that the narrow pursuit of business profit serves the broad interests of society. Laissez faire advocates maintain that government interference with business only tampers with the laws of nature, obstructing the workings of the free market.

Keynesian Theory

One problem with laissez faire economics is its insistence that government should not do anything about **economic depressions,** which are periods of high unemployment and business failures, or about raging **inflation,** which is characterized by price increases linked to a decrease in the value of the currency. Inflation is generally measured by the *Consumer Price Index* (see Feature 15.2). Since the industrial revolution of the mid-nineteenth century, capitalist economies have suffered through many cyclical fluctuations in which "boom" is followed by "bust." The United States experienced more than fifteen of these **business cycles** — expansions and contractions of business activity, the first stage accompanied by inflation and the second stage by unemployment (see Color Essay D, plates 1 and 2). No one had a theory that would explain these cycles acceptably until the Great Depression of the 1930s, which left one out of every four workers unemployed in 1932.

That was when John Maynard Keynes, a British economist, explained business cycles as resulting from imbalances between aggregate demand and productive capacity. **Aggregate demand** is the money available to be spent for goods and services by consumers, business, and government. **Productive capacity** is the total value of goods and services that can be produced when the economy works at full capacity. (The total value of the goods and services *actually* produced is called the **gross national product.**)

When demand exceeds productive capacity, people will pay more for the available goods, resulting in price inflation. When productive capacity exceeds demand, producers cut back their output of goods, resulting in unemployment. When many people are unemployed for an extended period, the economy is in a depression. Keynes theorized that government could stabilize the economy (and flatten or eliminate business cycles) by controlling the level of aggregate demand.

Keynesian theory holds that aggregate demand can be adjusted through a combination of fiscal and monetary policies. **Fiscal policies** involve changes

The Consumer Price Index

Inflation in the United States is measured most commonly with the *Consumer Price Index* (CPI). The CPI measures changes in the cost of a fixed "market basket" of more than 400 goods and services, as computed monthly by the Bureau of Labor Statistics from weekly diaries of expenses kept in 4,800 households. Another 4,800 households provide information on major purchases over three-month periods. Additional information on prices comes from a monthly sample of more than 18,000 retail outlets.

The CPI is hardly a perfect yardstick. A Ford sedan bought in 1976 is not the same as a Ford sedan bought in 1986. To some extent, a price difference will reflect a change in quality as well as a change in the value of the dollar. For example, an improvement in fuel economy improves the car's quality and justifies a somewhat higher price. The CPI is also slow to reflect changes in purchasing habits, which are contrary to the concept of a *fixed* market basket. Wash-and-wear apparel was tumbling in the dryer for several years before the government agreed to include it as an item in the market basket.

These are minor issues compared with the weighting given over time to the cost of housing. Until 1983, the cost of purchasing and financing a home accounted for 26 percent of the CPI. This large weighting neglected the facts that many people rent, rather than buy, homes and that few people buy a home every year. A better measure of shelter costs is the cost of renting houses similar to those that are owned. This method of calculating shelter costs dropped the weighting given to housing in the CPI, from 26 percent to 14 percent. Before the correction, the CPI overstated the rise in prices affecting the average citizen during the period of inflation beginning in the late 1960s.

Owing to the legislative technique for *price indexing* (or simply *indexing*), many government payments are adjusted periodically for changes in the cost of living as reflected in the CPI. This is true for federal civil service and military pension payments, social security benefits, and food stamp allowances. Moreover, many union wage contracts with private businesses are indexed to the CPI. Because the CPI virtually always increases each year, so do government and wage payments tied to the CPI. In a way then, indexing payments according to the CPI adds to both the growth of government spending and inflation itself.

Despite its faults, the CPI is at least a consistent measure of prices and will likely continue to be used as the basis for adjustments to wages, benefits, and payments affecting millions of people.

These views can be found in David S. Moore, *Statistics: Concepts and Controversies*, 2nd ed. (New York: Freeman, 1985), pp. 238–241.

in government spending and taxing. When demand is too low, government should either spend more itself or cut taxes, which would give the people more money to spend. When demand is too great, the government should either spend less or raise taxes, which would give people less money to spend. **Monetary policies** operate more indirectly on the economy through changes in the money supply. If the amount of money in circulation increases, demand will increase and price inflation will occur. Decreasing the money supply decreases aggregate demand and inflationary pressures.

Keynesian theory has been widely adopted by capitalist countries seeking to control their economies through a mix of fiscal and monetary policies. At one time or another, virtually all have used the Keynesian technique of **deficit financing**—spending beyond government income—to combat an economic slump. Deficit financing aims at injecting extra money into the economy to stimulate aggregate demand. Although governments can print extra money to finance deficits, that *really* would cause inflation. Most deficits are financed by funds borrowed through the issuing of government bonds, notes, or other securities. The theory holds that small deficits can be paid off with budget surpluses after the economy recovers.

Because Keynesian theory requires government to play an active role in controlling the economy, it runs counter to laissez faire economics. Before Keynes, no administration in Washington would undertake responsibility for maintaining a healthy economy. In the year in which Keynes died, Congress passed the *Employment Act of 1946*, fixing *under law* "the continuing responsibility of the federal government to . . . promote maximum employment, production and purchasing power." It also created a **Council of Economic Advisers** (CEA) within the Executive Office of the President to provide advice on maintaining a stable economy. The CEA normally consists of three economists (usually university professors) appointed by the president with Senate approval. Aided by a staff of about twenty-five people (mostly economists), the CEA helps the president prepare his annual Economic Report, also required by the 1946 act. The chair of the CEA is usually a major spokesperson for the administration's economic policy. However, the CEA has been significantly less important under President Reagan, primarily because Reagan's views on economics have not always coincided with the theories of the economists on the council. Nevertheless, many people regard the mandate of the 1946 Employment Act as a prime source of "big government" in America. Even such a conservative president as Richard Nixon admitted that "we are all Keynesians now."

Monetarism

While most economists accept Keynesian theory in its broad outlines, they differ over its political utility. Some especially doubt the value of fiscal policies in controlling inflation and unemployment. They feel that government spending programs take too long to enact in Congress and to implement through the bureaucracy. As a result, they say, jobs are created not when they are needed but rather years later, when the crisis may have passed and when it is time for government spending to be reduced. Furthermore, government spending is easier to start than to stop, because the groups favored by each spending program tend to defend that program even when it is no longer needed. A similar criticism applies to tax policies. Politically, it is much easier to cut taxes than to raise them. In other words, Keynesian theory requires that governments be able to quickly begin *and* end spending, and that they be able to quickly cut *and* raise taxes. But in the real world, these fiscal tools are easier to use in one way than in the other.

Monetarists despair of the fiscal tools of Keynesian economics and favor reliance on monetary policies—changing the nation's money supply. Major monetary policies in the United States are under the control of the Board of Governors of the **Federal Reserve System,** which acts as the central bank of the United States. Established in 1913, "the Fed" (as it is called) is not a single bank but a banking system with centralized and decentralized features. At its top, the Board of Governors is composed of seven members appointed by the president for staggered terms of fourteen years. The board is directed by a chairman who serves a four-year term that overlaps the president's term of office. This complex arrangement was intended to make the board independent of the president and even Congress, for the Fed funds its own operations. An independent board, the reasoning went, would be able to make financial decisions for the nation without regard to political implications.

The Fed controls the money supply through three main activities. It can change the *reserve requirement,* which is the amount of cash that member banks must keep on deposit in a regional Federal Reserve Bank. An increase in the reserve requirement decreases the amount of money a bank has available to lend. The Fed can also change its *discount rate,* the interest rate that member banks have to pay to borrow money from a Federal Reserve Bank. Finally, it can *buy and sell government securities* (such as U.S. Treasury notes and bonds) on the open market. When it buys securities, it pays out money and thus puts more money into circulation, and vice versa. These and other monetary activities are essential parts of an overall economic policy, but they lie outside the direct control of the president and in the hands of the Fed.

Because the Fed operates independently of the president, problems sometimes arise in coordinating economic policy. For example, the president might want the Fed to lower interest rates to stimulate the economy, but the Fed might resist for fear of inflation. Such policy clashes often pit the chairman of the Federal Reserve Board directly against the president of the United States. It takes a strong personality to resist the president, but few people rise to the powerful position of chairman of the Federal Reserve Board by being shy. The last two chairmen clashed, on occasion, with presidents of both parties. Although the Fed's economic policies are not perfectly insulated from political concerns, they are sufficiently independent so that the president is not able to control monetary policy without the Fed's cooperation. This means that the president cannot be held completely responsible for the the state of the economy — despite the Employment Act of 1946.

"Supply-Side" Economics

When Ronald Reagan came to office in 1981, he embraced a school of thought called **supply-side economics** to deal with the double-digit inflation that the nation was experiencing. As we have noted, Keynesian theory suggests that inflation is due to an excess of aggregate demand over supply, and the standard Keynesian solution is to reduce demand (for example, by increasing taxes). Supply-siders argued that inflation could be lowered more effectively by increasing supply. (That is, they stressed the *supply side* of the economic equation.) Specifically, they favored tax cuts to stimulate investment (which, in turn, would lead to the production of more goods) and proposed less government regulation of business (again to increase productivity). Economist Arthur Laffer popularized the supply-side argument with

***Volcker Smokes
and Reagan Fumes***
*The cigar-smoking Paul Volcker
was appointed chairman of the
Federal Reserve Board in 1979
by Jimmy Carter, who liked
Volcker's tight-fisted monetary
policies. Reagan reappointed
him in 1983 to chair the Fed for
a second four-year term.
However, Reagan's desire to
lower the discount rate
(reducing the dollar's value
overseas and thus improving
trade) eventually led to an
organizational clash. And, in a
rare show of disunity, the board
outvoted Volcker 4 to 3 in early
1986 — thanks to four members
who had been appointed by
Reagan.*

reference to the "Laffer curve" (supposedly drawn on the back of a napkin in a burst of inspiration). It suggested that higher taxes decrease the incentive to work and thus produce less, not more, government revenue.

To support their theory, supply-side economists pointed to a tax cut which was enacted during John Kennedy's administration (1961–1963). It stimulated investment and thus raised the total national income. As a result, the government took in as much tax revenue under the tax cut as it had before taxes were cut. Supply-siders also argue that the rich should receive *larger* tax cuts than the poor, because the rich have more money to invest. The benefits of the increased investment will then "trickle down" to working people in the form of additional jobs and income.

In a sense, supply-side economics represents a move toward laissez faire economics in the form of less government regulation and less taxation. Supply-siders believe that government interferes too much with the efforts of individuals to work, save, and invest. That was exactly the point that Ronald Reagan, the movie actor, grasped when he was in the 91 percent income tax bracket. Because the government took so much of his income, he simply quit working for the year after he moved into that bracket. Obviously, supply-side economic philosophy was well suited to a president who favored individual freedom.

Inspired by supply-side theory, Reagan proposed (and got) massive tax cuts in the *Economic Recovery Tax Act of 1981*. Individual tax rates were reduced by 23 percent over a three-year period, and the tax rate for the highest income group was cut from 70 to 50 percent. Reagan also launched a program to deregulate businesses. According to the theory, these actions would generate

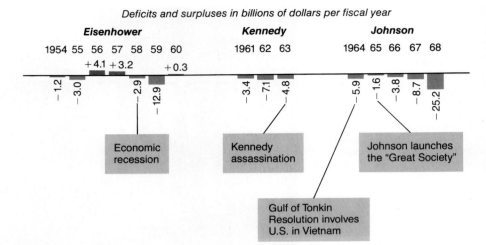

Budget Deficits over Time
There are several ways to calculate budget deficits. As shown here, the deficit is expressed in
terms of current dollars, *which are dollars evaluated as of the time of the deficit. Owing to*
inflation, however, dollars usually lose value over time. The effects of inflation can be
eliminated by plotting deficits in terms of constant dollars, *which are dollars whose value*
has been adjusted to a given year. Deficits can also be viewed as a percentage of the gross

Figure 15.1

extra government revenue and thus make spending cuts unnecessary. Nevertheless, Reagan also cut funding for some domestic programs, such as aid to
families with dependent children and food stamps. But he also proposed
major increases in military spending. This blend of tax cuts, deregulation,
cuts in spending for social programs, and increases in spending for the military became known, somewhat disparagingly, as *Reaganomics.*

How well did Reaganomics succeed? During Reagan's first term in office,
annual price inflation fell 8.6 percentage points—from 12.4 percent in 1980
to 3.8 percent in 1983. However, many economists credit the drop in the
inflation rate to the tight-money policies of the Federal Reserve Board, which
raised interest rates. The higher interest rates cut back business investments,
producing a recession and unemployment.[7] Unfortunately, and in spite of
supply-side theory, the tax cut was accompanied by a massive drop in tax
revenues. Reagan had promised that his economic policies would balance
the federal budget by 1984, but the lower tax revenues produced the largest
budget deficits ever (see Figure 15.1).

PUBLIC POLICY AND THE BUDGET

To most people—college students included—the federal budget is B-O-R-
i-n-g. To national politicians, it is the script for high drama. The numbers,
categories, and percentages that numb normal minds cause politicians' nos-
trils to flare and hearts to pound. Politicians pore over the president's budget
as soon as it is published, because it predicts the likely winners and losers in
public policy. The president's budget is only a forecast of incoming and out-

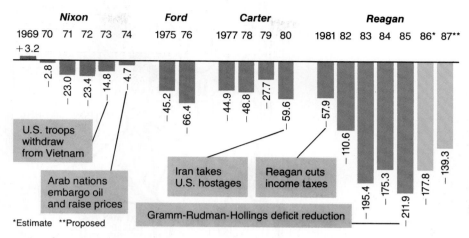

	Nixon						Ford			Carter					Reagan					

1969 70 71 72 73 74   1975 76   1977 78 79 80   1981 82 83 84 85 86* 87**
+3.2

-2.8
-23.0
-23.4
-14.8
-4.7

U.S. troops withdraw from Vietnam

Arab nations embargo oil and raise prices

*Estimate **Proposed

-45.2
-66.4
-44.9
-48.8
-27.7
-59.6
-57.9
-110.6
-195.4
-175.3
-211.9
-177.8
-139.3

Iran takes U.S. hostages

Reagan cuts income taxes

Gramm-Rudman-Hollings deficit reduction

national product, which also eliminates the effects of inflation. Reagan's budget deficits appear huge when expressed in current dollars. Although they are less intimidating when computed in the other, more appropriate ways, they still represent the largest postwar deficits compiled by any president. (Source: U.S. Advisory Commission on Intergovernmental Relations, *Significant Features of Fiscal Federalism, 1985–1986.*)

going dollars, so it leaves hope that potential losers can gain by changing the numbers. But the plot thickens as potential winners also scheme to ensure that the president's budget survives attempts to change it in Congress.

Prior to 1921, Congress itself prepared the budget under its constitutional authority to raise taxes and appropriate funds. The budget was formed piecemeal by enacting a series of laws that originated in the many committees involved in the highly decentralized process of authorizing expenditures, appropriating funds, and raising revenue. No one was responsible for the "big picture"—the budget as a whole. The president's role was limited mainly to approving the revenue and appropriations bills, just as he approved other pieces of legislation. In fact, even executive agencies submitted their budgetary requests directly to Congress, and not to the president.

This early process of congressional budgeting (such as it was) worked well enough for a nation of farmers, but not for an industrialized nation with a growing population. Soon after World War I, Congress realized that the budgeting process needed to be centralized. With the *Budgeting and Accounting Act of 1921*, it thrust the responsibility for preparing the budget onto the president. The act established a Bureau of the Budget to assist the president in submitting "his" budget to Congress each January. Of course, Congress retained its constitutional authority to raise and spend funds, but now Congress would begin its work from the president's budget. Furthermore, all executive agencies' budget requests had to be funneled through the new Bureau of the Budget (which became the Office of Management and Budget in 1970). These requests were centrally reviewed, and those consistent with the president's overall economic and legislative program were incorporated into the president's budget.

The Nature of the Budget

The federal budget is complex; there is no denying that. But its basic elements are not beyond understanding. We begin with some definitions. The *Budget of the United States Government* is a thick document containing the annual financial plan that the president is required to submit to Congress. It applies to the next **fiscal year** (FY), the strange period the government uses for accounting purposes. Currently, the fiscal year runs from October 1 to September 30. The budget is named for the year in which it *ends*. Thus, the FY 1987 budget applied to the twelve months from October 1, 1986, to September 30, 1987. Broadly speaking, the budget states how much government agencies will be authorized to spend for programs (their **budget authority**); how much they are expected to spend (called **budget outlays** or expenditures); and how much is expected in taxes and other revenues **(receipts)**. (The relationship of authority to outlays is diagrammed in Figure 15.2.) For example, President Reagan's proposed FY 1987 budget contained authority for expenditures of $1,102 billion, but it provided for spending (outlays) of "only" $994 billion. Reagan's budget anticipated receipts of $850 billion, leaving a deficit of $144 billion — the difference between receipts and outlays.

As a document, the budget contains more than numbers. It also explains individual spending programs in terms of national needs, agency missions, and basic programs, and it analyzes proposed taxes and other receipts. Not surprisingly, the budget document is huge, and it is intimidating to the ordinary citizen. Reagan's FY 1987 budget contained over 500 pages and weighed more than five pounds. Nevertheless, its publication was anxiously awaited by reporters, lobbyists, and political analysts seeking to learn the president's plan for government spending in the coming year.

Preparing the President's Budget

The budget that the president submits to Congress each January results from a process that begins the previous spring under the supervision of the **Office of Management and Budget** (OMB). OMB is located within the Executive Office of the President and is headed by a director who is appointed by the president with the approval of the Senate. OMB, with a staff of nearly

Figure 15.2

Relationship of Budget Authority to Budget Outlays
The federal budget is a complicated document. One source of confusion for people studying the budget for the first time is the relationship of budget authority to budget outlay. These two figures differ because of sums that are carried over from prior years and to future years. The diagram below helps explain the relationship; all amounts are in billions of dollars. The new *budget authority for FY 1987 is in red and the* unspent *authority from prior years is in gray. Only $758.7 billion of the FY 1987 budget authority is expected to be spent in FY 1987, while $343.3 billion will be carried over for spending in future years. Similarly, $235.3 billion in funds authorized in prior years will be spent in FY 1987. (Source:* Congressional Quarterly Weekly Report, *February 8, 1986, p. 248. Copyright material reprinted with permission Congressional Quarterly Incorporated.)*

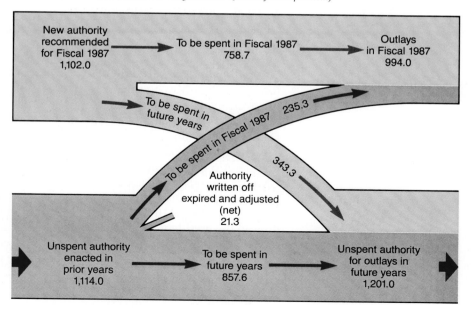

David Stockman: He Kissed and Told
David A. Stockman enjoyed a meteoric career in politics. He was elected to Congress in 1976 from Michigan. A self-described libertarian, Stockman argued vigorously for reduced government spending and tax rates. Soon after his election in 1980, Ronald Reagan asked Stockman to head the OMB. Only 34 years of age, Stockman became the most forceful exponent of Reagan's principles and one of the most powerful men in government. However, he revealed in an embarrassing interview in the December 1981 issue of Atlantic Monthly *that ''none of us really understands what's going on with all these numbers.'' Nevertheless, Reagan kept him on until 1985, when Stockman resigned to write a book.*

600, is the most powerful domestic agency in the bureaucracy, and its director, who sits in the president's cabinet, is one of the most powerful figures in government. President Reagan picked David Stockman, a young congressman who vigorously advocated cutting government spending, as his first OMB director and the architect of his budgetary policies.

The OMB initiates the budget process each spring by meeting with the president to discuss the economic situation and his budgetary priorities. The OMB then sends broad economic guidelines to every government agency and requests their initial projections of funds that will be needed for the next fiscal year. The OMB assembles this information and makes recommendations to the president, who settles on more precise guidelines. By the summer, the agencies are asked to prepare budgets based on the new guidelines. By the fall, they submit their formal budgets to the OMB, where budget analysts scrutinize agency requests for cost and consistency with the president's legislative program. A lot of politics occurs at this stage, as agency heads frequently try to go around the OMB to plead for their pet projects with presidential advisers and perhaps even the president himself. Political negotiations may extend into the early winter—often to the last possible moment before the president's budget goes to the printer.

The voluminous, carefully printed, and neatly bound document, which the president must submit to Congress within fifteen days after it convenes each January, looks like the product of a faultless process of social accounting. However, this large, impressive document is far from final. The members of Congress are interested in the content of the president's budget, rather than its appearance. In giving the president the responsibility for preparing the budget, they have provided themselves with a starting point for their own work on the federal budget.

Passing the Congressional Budget

There is something old, something new, and something drastic in the process that the Congress now uses in reacting to the president's budget.

Something old: the traditional committee structure. The old procedure, in which tasks are divided among a number of committees, has been retained from the early days of congressional budgeting. Those committees include

- **Tax committees,** which are responsible for raising the revenue to run the government. The Ways and Means Committee in the House and the Finance Committee in the Senate consider all proposals for taxes, tariffs, and other receipts contained in the president's budget.

- **Authorization committees** (such as the House Armed Services Committee and the Senate Committee on Banking, Housing, and Urban Affairs), which have jurisdiction over particular legislative subject matter. The House has nineteen committees that can authorize spending and the Senate has sixteen. Each one pores over the portions of the budget that pertain to its area of responsibility.

- **Appropriations committees** that decide which of the programs passed by the authorization committees will actually be funded (that is, given money to spend). As an example, the House Armed Services Committee might decide to build a new line of tanks for the army, and even get its decision enacted into law. Nevertheless, the tanks will never be built unless funds are appropriated for that purpose by the appropriations committees. Thirteen distinct appropriation bills are enacted each year to fund the country.

Two major problems are inherent in a budgeting process that involves three distinct kinds of congressional committees. First, the two-step spending process (first *authorization* and then *appropriation*) is very complex; it offers wonderful opportunities for interest groups to get into the budgeting act. Second, because one group of legislators in each house plans for revenues and many other groups plan for spending, no one is responsible for the budget as a whole. Congress has, however, added a new committee structure that addresses these problems. This structure should combat the pluralist politics inherent in the old procedures and should allow budget choices to be made in a more majoritarian manner, by votes in both chambers.

Something new: the Budget Committee structure. When Congress in 1921 gave the president the responsibility for initially preparing the budget, its members surrendered considerable authority to the president. Congress attempted to regain control of the budgeting process in 1947, 1948, 1949, and 1950, but these efforts failed to overcome jurisdictional squabbles between the revenue and appropriations committees and to soothe the vanities of their chairs, threatened with loss of power.

Overall control of the budget was important to Congress for several reasons. First, members of Congress are politicians, and politicians want to wield power, rather than watch someone else wield it. Second, the Constitution established Congress, not the president, as the "first branch" of government and the people's representatives; this act legitimated its institutional jealousy. Third, Congress as a body often disagreed with presidential spending priorities, but it was unable to present a coherent alternative budget. Congress as an *institution* could not mount a serious challenge to the president's budgetary views.

After bitter spending fights with President Nixon in the late 1960s and early 1970s, Congress finally passed the Budget and Impoundment Control Act of 1974. That act fashioned a typically political solution to the problem of wounded egos and trampled jurisdictions that had frustrated previous

---

Reagan's FY 1987 Budget Rises from the Dead
Even before President Reagan's budget document was officially transmitted to the Congress, critics announced it "DOA" (Dead on Arrival). At 7:30 A.M. on February 5, 1986, those reporters who were lined up outside the Government Printing Office to buy the budget as soon as it went on sale were startled by the siren and flashing lights of an approaching ambulance. The ambulance stopped right at the door, and attendants carried out a stretcher bearing the still form of Paul Olkhovski, an employee of the Office of Management and Budget. Suddenly, he rose Lazarus-like from the dead, wielding a copy of the president's budget, very much alive.

Table 15.1 ━━━━━━━━

Timetable for the Congressional Budget Process
Since the Budget and Impoundment Control Act of 1974, which set up the current congressional budgeting process, Congress has attempted to discipline itself with a budget timetable. Congress met its own deadlines relatively well from 1975 to 1980 in adopting its initial budgetary resolution, but it has done less well since that time. The schedule below, which was adopted in 1985, moved the budgetary resolution deadline up one month to April 15, giving Congress more time to complete reconciliation and action on the annual appropriations bills, but Congress fell behind schedule again in 1986.

Budget Process Timetable: Fiscal Years 1987–1991

February 15	CBO issues annual report to Budget Committees.
February 25	Committees submit views and estimates to Budget Committees.
April 1	Budget Committee reports budget resolution.
April 15	Congress completes budget resolution.
June 10	House Appropriations Committee reports last annual appropriation bill.
June 15	Congress completes reconciliation.
June 30	House completes action on annual appropriation bills.
August 15	OMB and CBO estimate deficit for upcoming fiscal year.
August 20	OMB and CBO submit report to Comptroller General.
August 25	Comptroller General submits report to President.
September 1	Initial presidential reduction order issued (if required).
September 5	Deadline for President to propose reduction in defense contracts.
October 1	Initial presidential reduction order effective; fiscal year begins.
October 5	OMB and CBO submit revised report to Comptroller General.
October 10	Comptroller General submits revised report to President.
October 15	Final presidential reduction order issued (if required) and becomes effective.
September–October	Congressional alternative to presidential order, if any, developed and adopted.
November 15	Comptroller General compliance report issued.

Source: Committee on the Budget, U.S. Senate, *Gramm-Rudman-Hollings and the Congressional Budget Process: An Explanation* (1986), p. 21.

attempts to change the budgeting procedure. All the tax and appropriations committees (and chairpersons) were retained, and *new* House and Senate **Budget Committees** were superimposed on the old committee structure. The Budget Committees supervised a new comprehensive budget review process, aided by a new **Congressional Budget Office**. The CBO, with a staff of over 200, acquired a budgetary expertise equal to that of the president's OMB, so it could prepare credible alternative budgets for Congress.

At the heart of the 1974 budgetary process was a timetable of budget resolutions to be adopted by Congress (see Table 15.1). Although the original timetable has since been modified, it is still used as a means of disciplining the procedure. In March, about two months after receiving the president's budget, the Budget Committees propose an initial budget resolution that sets overall budget totals and spending levels, broken down into twenty-one different "budget functions" such as national defense, agriculture, and health.

In addition, the budget resolution provides for the reconciliation of differences between amounts that the authorization committees have authorized for spending and the amounts allocated in the budget functions. In effect, the budget resolution directs each authorization committee to "reconcile," or match, the amount it has authorized for spending with the amount it is being given to spend. The reconciliation process sometimes requires that authorization committees actually change an existing law. A change in the law is needed when spending is covered by an **entitlement** program, such as social security, which says that those who qualify for benefits are legally entitled to them.

By April 15, both houses are supposed to have agreed on a single budget resolution to guide their further work on the budget during the summer. Appropriations must be completed in the House by June 30, and in the Senate by the start of the fiscal year, October 1. Throughout all congressional activity during this time, the levels of spending set by majority vote on the budget resolution are constraints on pluralist politics in Congress.

This process (or one very much like it) was implemented in 1975 and worked reasonably well for the first few years. Congress regained some capability to structure the budget as a whole, rather than merely alter pieces of it. However, Congress encountered increasing difficulty in enacting its budget resolutions according to its own timetable. The problem became more severe under the Reagan administration, as the president submitted annual budgets with huge deficits. Reagan kept to his economic game plan, resisting any tax increases to reduce the deficits and trying to cut social spending even more while increasing military spending. For its part, Congress reversed the spending priorities but refused to propose a tax increase without presidential cooperation.

Something drastic: Gramm-Rudman-Hollings.   Alarmed by the huge deficits in President Reagan's budgets, frustrated by Reagan's refusal to raise taxes, and stymied by their own inability to eliminate the deficits, members of Congress were ready to try almost anything. Republican Senators Phil Gramm of Texas and Warren Rudman of New Hampshire proposed drastic action to force a balanced budget. In September 1985 they introduced a bill officially titled the *Balanced Budget and Emergency Deficit Control Act*. It soon was co-sponsored by Democratic Senator Ernest Hollings of South Carolina and became known as **Gramm-Rudman-Hollings.**

Simply put, Gramm-Rudman-Hollings mandated that the budget deficit be lowered to a specified level each year until the budget is balanced in FY 1991 (see Figure 15.3). If Congress did not meet the mandated deficit level in any year, across-the-board budget cuts were to be made by the Comptroller General, who heads the General Accounting Office. Because the Comptroller General is an agent of Congress, many experts thought that the law encroached on the president's constitutional power to execute the law. Moreover, few members of Congress liked the arbitrary nature of across-the-board budget cuts; most were uneasy with the legislation, which many judged as unconstitutional, unwise, and unworkable. Nevertheless, three months after it was introduced, Gramm-Rudman-Hollings became law when President Reagan signed it on December 12, 1985.

Senator Rudman described his own bill and its success as "a bad idea whose time has come." Frustration at repeated congressional inability to cut the deficit was so great that Gramm-Rudman-Hollings sailed through on a

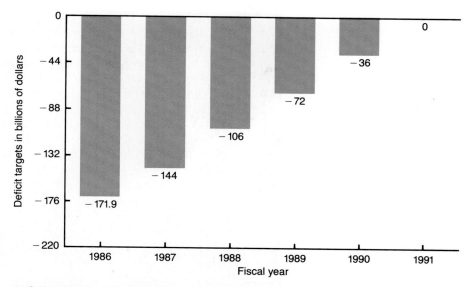

Deficit Reduction Timetable for Gramm-Rudman-Hollings
*The 1985 deficit reduction law, known as Gramm-Rudman-Hollings for its Senate
sponsors, aims at reducing the federal deficit by stages, resulting in a balanced budget by
FY 1991. It requires the president to prepare a budget that stays within specified deficit
levels each year. Because economic conditions can change between the time the president
submits the budget in January and the start of the fiscal year in October, Congress provides
for a midyear check on the deficit estimates. On August 15, the OMB and CBO produce
their own estimates of the budget deficit for the upcoming fiscal year. If the average of these
two estimates exceeds the year's target deficit, automatic across-the-board cuts are made —
half from defense programs and half from nondefense programs — to achieve the desired
deficit level. (Source: Committee on the Budget, U.S. Senate,* Gramm-Rudman-Hollings and the
Congressional Budget Process: An Explanation, *1985, p. 21.)*

Figure 15.3

wave of exasperation. The bill was not considered by congressional committees in the usual manner; nor was it subjected to formal economic, procedural, or legal analysis. No one really knew what the legislation would do
— except that it would allow Congress to escape hard choices as to which
programs to cut or whose taxes to raise so as to reduce the deficit. Republican
Senator Robert Packwood (Oregon) confessed to the Senate, "I pray that
what we are about to undertake will work."[8]

On March 1, 1986, the previously obscure Comptroller General, Charles
A. Bowsher, made the first series of automatic cuts under Gramm-Rudman-
Hollings. Although Congress had decided not to reach the full deficit target
the first year (FY 1986) and to cut only $11.7 billion from the projected
deficit, that small reduction gave Congress a taste of its own medicine. Under
the law, Bowsher had to apply the cuts equally to domestic and military
programs. He sliced 4.3 percent from every domestic and defense program,
project, and activity, except those programs that were specifically exempted;
the latter included social security, several programs for the poor, and Reagan's
Strategic Defense Initiative. Thus, $824 million was cut from price-support

Deficit Hitchhikers
Senators Warren Rudman, Phil Gramm, and Ernest Hollings give the ''thumbs up'' sign prior to the favorable conference committee vote on their historic legislation to reduce the federal deficit in stages by FY 1991.

payments to farmers, who simply found their checks decreased by 4.3 percent. Federal meat and poultry inspectors were laid off for nine days over the remainder of the year, closing some meat-packing plants, which cannot work without inspectors. The Public Health Service cut its annual immunization survey. On the military side, $200 million was cut from personnel, $900 million from procurement, and so on.

The across-the-board budget-cutting mandated by Gramm-Rudman-Hollings reduces funding for all programs without regard for their value to the nation. Its net effect is to weaken all programs through underfunding. In that respect, Gramm-Rudman-Hollings represents a failure of the legislative process, in which elected representatives are expected to decide how public funds should be spent. Of course, one might also argue that the process had failed well before Gramm-Rudman-Hollings was enacted, when Congress failed to raise revenues to pay for the government services it supported.

Soon after it became law, Gramm-Rudman-Hollings was challenged in federal court, and the Supreme Court confirmed what many expected—that it was unconstitutional to give the comptroller functions which belong to the president. But to preserve the budget reductions already made under the law, Congress itself quickly enacted all of Bowsher's cuts. And to try to keep Gramm-Rudman-Hollings in effect, Congress considered entrusting future across-the-board cuts to the OMB. (Congress had hoped to avoid giving this power to a presidential agency.) At present, no one really knows how long Congress can live with the automatic budget-cutting monster it created.

TAX POLICIES

So far we have been concerned mainly with the spending side of the budget, for which appropriations must be enacted each year. The revenue side of the budget is provided by overall tax policy, which is designed to provide a continuous flow of income without annual legislation. On occasion, however, tax policy is significantly changed to accomplish one or more of several objectives: (1) to adjust overall revenue to meet budget outlays, (2) to make the tax burden more equitable for taxpayers; and (3) to help control the economy by raising taxes (thus decreasing aggregate demand) or by lowering taxes (thus increasing demand).[9]

In his first year in office, President Reagan requested and got a significant change in tax policy. Personal income taxes were lowered by 25 percent over a three-year period, for a total revenue loss of $750 billion. According to the supply-side economic theory that Reagan embraced, that massive tax cut should have stimulated the economy and yielded even more revenue than was lost—if not in the first year then soon afterward. That did not happen. Revenues lagged badly behind spending, and the deficits grew.

Still, Reagan would not agree to raise taxes, and few politicians dared mention a tax hike. Democratic candidate Walter Mondale tried it in the 1984 presidential election and was beaten badly. The Democratic leadership in Congress and many leading Republicans believed that taxes must be raised to cut the deficit, but no one was willing to propose an increase. For his part, Reagan remained adamant. Once he invoked Clint Eastwood's line from the "Dirty Harry" character in *Sudden Impact* and dared Congress to "Make my day" by proposing an increase he could shoot down with his veto.

Reagan went further, by requesting fundamental changes in tax policy. He urged Congress to enact sweeping tax reform that would (1) lower still further the rate for the highest income tax bracket; (2) reduce the number of tax brackets; (3) eliminate virtually all the tax "loopholes" through which many wealthy people escaped paying taxes; and (4) be *revenue neutral*, in the sense that it would bring in no more and no less revenue than the earlier tax policy.

Tax Reform

A strange thing often happens to tax reform proposals: they become so heavily influenced by interest groups seeking special benefits that they end up working contrary to their original purpose. The same might have happened to Reagan's tax reform, but it did not. His basic goals were met with relatively few major changes.

Reagan's success in the House was due to several factors. First, two influential Democrats, Representative Richard Gephardt of Missouri and Senator Bill Bradley of New Jersey, had proposed a "Fair Tax" reform plan of their own in 1982 very much along the lines of President Reagan's. Second, the Democrats were worried that President Reagan would outflank them on the tax reform issue, as he had on tax increases in the 1984 presidential election, and they were determined that it would not happen again. Third, Reagan's proposals were backed by the powerful support of Democratic

Representative Dan Rostenkowski, chairman of the Ways and Means Committee in the House (where all revenue bills must begin).

In fact, immediately after the president announced his plan on national television, Rostenkowski appeared to publicly endorse the president's broad objectives. (Some people called it the "Ron 'n Rosty" show.) Commenting on the politics of tax reform, Rostenkowski said, "Anyone who wants to get in front of this train is going to get hit pretty hard."[10]

Actually, Reagan's tax proposals encountered less difficulty in the Democratic House than they did in the Republican Senate. For a time it seemed that Senator Robert Packwood of Oregon, chairman of the Senate Finance Committee, would not be able to keep special interests from restoring proposed tax deductions and inserting special favors in the Senate version of the reform bill. In fact, Senator Packwood himself proposed special benefits for the lumbering industry in his home state.

Special one-time benefits are *always* granted in tax bills, to obtain the votes needed to pass them. In legislative terminology, these provisions are called "transition rules." For example, Republican Senator Pete Wilson of California obtained a $7 million exception for the Walt Disney Company, to protect tax benefits for films in production; Republican Senator John Heinz of Pennsylvania got a $500 million refund of unused investment tax credits for troubled steel mills; Democratic Senator David L. Boren of Oklahoma negotiated two special exemptions for the Phillips Petroleum Company; and so on.[11] The House bill contained even more transition rules than the Senate bill, amounting to a loss of $26 billion. The problem in the Senate was that special interests were going beyond short-term exceptions and pressing for special deductions for the future.

Just as it appeared that fundamental tax reform would be scuttled in the Senate, the atmosphere changed — literally over a single historic weekend — and the Finance Committee removed many of the interest group ornaments that had been hung on the massive bill. The Senate approved a 1,489-page tax bill that, in spirit, was similar to the House bill, although specific tax rates, exemptions, and other details differed significantly; those had to be hammered out during weeks of grueling conference committee meetings.

The bill that eventually emerged from the House-Senate conference committee gave President Reagan pretty much what he wanted. It represented one of the most sweeping tax policy changes in history. By eliminating many deductions, the new policy reclaimed a great deal of revenue that had been lost through tax loopholes, to corporations and wealthy citizens with clever tax accountants. That revenue is to pay for a general reduction in tax rates for individual citizens. By eliminating many tax brackets, the new tax policy approached the idea of a "flat tax" — one that requires everyone to pay at the same rate. A flat tax has the appeal of simplicity, but it violates the principle of **progressive taxation,** by which the rich pay proportionately higher taxes than the poor. That principle is used by governments to redistribute wealth and thus promote equality.

In general, the larger the number of tax brackets, the more progressive the tax can be. The 1985 tax code included fourteen tax brackets, ranging from 11 percent to 50 percent. As an interim step for 1987, the number of

Here's to Tax Reform!
Senator Robert Packwood and Representative Dan Rostenkowski toast their joint accomplishment: getting agreement on a tax reform bill in the House-Senate conference committee in August 1986. Packwood, chairman of the Senate Finance Committee, and Rostenkowski, chairman of the House Ways and Means Committee, were the chief negotiators in the tax reform bill conference committee.

brackets was reduced to five, ranging from 11 to 38.5 percent. Thereafter, there will be only two rates: 15 and 28 percent. While people like the idea of reduced rates and tax simplification, polls showed that they were not generally in favor of doing away with progressive taxation. When asked whether taxpayers should "pay the same rate of tax" or whether they should "pay very different rates depending on their incomes," most respondents (72 percent) preferred multiple rates.[12] Although Reagan pledged "to break apart the shackles and liberate America from tax bondage,"[13] most people did not think they were in bondage.

Public Opinion on Federal Taxes

Ironically, the American public was not worked up over taxes as much as President Reagan was. When asked in 1984 which of five different economic problems "was worst these days," the public ranked federal income tax levels at the *bottom* of the list; it was chosen by only 5 percent of a national sample of registered voters. At the top was the size of the federal deficit (identified by 34 percent), followed by unemployment (33 percent), high interest rates (19 percent), and inflation (9 percent).[14] Of course, people do not like to pay taxes, and they would rather pay less in taxes than more. Nevertheless, high tax rates have not been a burning public issue. In a 1985 survey, more people (51 percent) thought they paid "about the right amount" of taxes than "too much" (45 percent).[15] This is what pollsters usually find; only a tiny portion of the American public sees high taxes as a major problem.

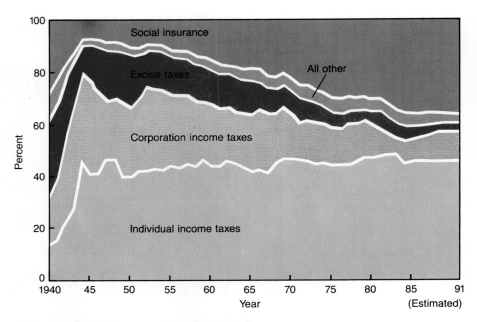

Percentage Composition of Federal Budget Receipts, 1940–1985
*The graph shows the relative composition of federal receipts (revenues) from 1940 to 1985.
It clearly indicates that the percentage obtained through income taxes has changed very
little since the mid-1940s, whereas the proportion obtained through social security taxes has
more than quadrupled during the same period. In fact, many lower-income people pay
more in social security taxes than they do in income taxes. (Source: Historical Tables, Budget
of the United States Government, 1987, Tables 1.1 and 1.2.)*

Figure 15.4

However, the overwhelming majority resists paying *more* taxes, even to reduce the deficit.[16]

Comparing Tax Burdens

One way to compare tax burdens is to examine taxes over time in the
same country; another is to compare taxes in different countries at the same
time. By comparing taxes over time in the United States, we find that the
tax burden of U.S. citizens has indeed been growing. For the average family,
the percentage of income that goes to all federal, state, and local taxes doubled to 23 percent from 1953 to 1980. During the same time, the taxes of
wealthy families increased by two-thirds to 33 percent of their income.[17]

However, the income tax has not been the major culprit in the increasing
tax bite at the federal level. As shown in Figure 15.4, which graphs the
composition of federal budget receipts over time, the proportion contributed
by income tax has remained fairly constant since the end of World War II.
The largest increases came in social security taxes, which have risen steadily
to pay for the government's largest single social welfare program, aid to the
elderly.

Another way of comparing tax burdens is to examine tax rates in various countries. As you can see in Compared With What? 15.1, Americans' taxes are quite low, compared with those in nineteen other democratic nations. Only Japan (which has a very small military budget) and Spain rank below the United States. Despite talk about "high taxes," the U.S. tax burden is not large compared with taxes in other major democratic nations.

Compared With What? 15.1

Tax Burdens in Twenty Countries

All nations impose taxes on their citizens, but some nations impose a heavier tax burden than others. This graph compares tax burdens as a percentage of gross domestic product — GNP minus the value of goods produced outside the country. The percentages include national, state, and local taxes and social security contributions. By this measure, the U.S. government extracts less in taxes from its citizens than the governments of most other democratic nations. At the top of the list stands Sweden, well known as a "social welfare" state, which consumes about 50 percent of its gross domestic product in taxes.

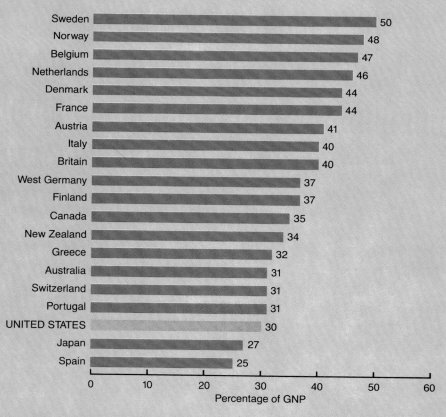

Source: *Statistical Abstract of the United States, 1985*, p. 850.

SPENDING POLICIES

The federal government spends hundreds of billions of dollars every year. Where does the money go? Figure 15.5 allocates $994 billion in outlays in President Reagan's FY 1987 budget, according to the nineteen major budgetary functions. The largest amount by far (nearly 30 percent of the total budget) was earmarked for national defense. The next largest outlay was for social security, and the third largest was interest on the accumulated national debt, which alone consumes around 15 percent of all government spending.

To understand current expenditures, it is a good idea to examine federal expenditures over time. (Refer to Plate 1 of Color Essay D for a graphic illustration of the budget outlays in four major categories since 1940 by percentage.) The effect of World War II is clear; spending for national defense rose sharply after 1940, peaked at about 90 percent of the budget in 1945, and fell to about 30 percent in peacetime. The percentage allocated to defense rose again in the early 1950s, reflecting rearmament in the Cold War with the Soviet Union. Thereafter, the share of the budget devoted to defense decreased rather steadily (except for the bump during the Vietnam War in the late 1960s) until that trend was reversed by the Reagan administration in the 1980s.

Government payments to individuals consistently consumed less of the budget than national defense until 1971. Since then, payments to individuals have accounted for most of the federal budget, and they have been increasing. Net interest payments also increased substantially in recent years, reflecting the rapidly growing federal debt. Note that "all other" government outlays have been squeezed by pressure from payments for national defense, to individuals, and for interest on the national debt.

Because of continuing price inflation, one would expect government expenditures to increase rather steadily in dollar amounts. However, federal spending has far outstripped inflation. To show this, Figure 15.6 graphs government receipts and outlays as a percentage of GNP, which eliminates the effect of inflation. It indicates that federal spending has increased from about 15 percent of GNP soon after World War II to nearly 25 percent, most recently at the expense of the federal deficit. There are two major explanations for this steady increase in government spending. One explanation is bureaucratic, the other is political.

Incremental Budgeting . . .

The bureaucratic explanation of spending increases involves the notion of **incremental budgeting:** bureaucrats, in compiling their budget funding requests for next year, ask for the amount they got this year plus some *increment* to fund new projects. Members of Congress pay little attention to the size of the agency's budget for the current year (the largest part of that budget) but focus instead on the extra money (the increment) requested for next year. As a result, few programs are ever cut back, and spending continually increases.

Incremental budgeting produces a sort of bureaucratic momentum that continually pushes up federal spending. Once an agency is established, it attracts a clientele that defends its existence and that supports the agency's

Figure 15.5

President Reagan's FY 1987 Budget by Function

Federal budget authorities and outlays are organized into twenty-one budget functions, two of which (allowances and offsetting receipts) are mainly for bookkeeping purposes. The graph below shows expected outlays for each of the nineteen substantive functions in President Reagan's FY 1987 budget. The final budget differed somewhat from this distribution because the Congress did not accept all of the president's spending proposals, but the proportions remained about the same. (Source: Congressional Quarterly Weekly Report, *February 8, 1986, pp. 256–257.)*

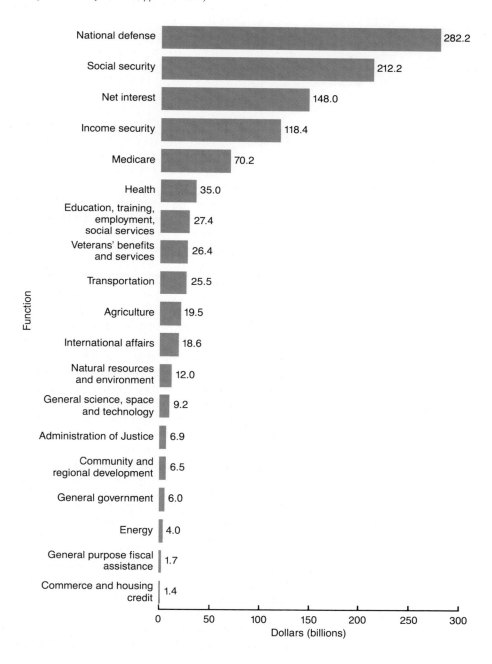

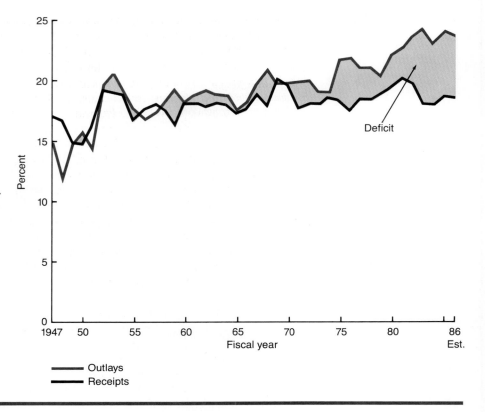

Government Outlays and Receipts as Percentage of GNP

We can see the growth of government spending — and the rising federal debt — by plotting budget outlays and receipts against each other over time. In this graph, outlays and receipts are expressed as a percentage of GNP, to control for inflation and to demonstrate that both government spending and taxes have been taking a progressively larger share of the nation's productive output. (Source: Office of Management and Budget, Fiscal Year 1987 Budget of the United States Government: Historical Tables, *pp. 2–6 and 2–7.)*

Figure 15.6

requests for extra funds to do more year after year. Domestic spending cuts under President Reagan have, however, substantially checked the practice of incremental budgeting. For example, his FY 1987 budget cut $9.5 billion (almost 18 percent) from the Agriculture Department budget by eliminating housing, water and sewer construction programs, rural electrification and telephone programs, and the agriculture extension service.[18] The $8 billion college student aid program was cut by $2 billion.

Such major cuts interfere with incremental budgeting and force closer scrutiny of budgetary proposals by agencies and members of Congress alike. As a result, agencies are now more likely to engage in a form of analytical budgeting, discussed in Chapter 12, in which existing programs are justified in terms of their effectiveness. Nevertheless, President Reagan found it impossible to reduce government spending enough to balance the budget, because politics had put most of the budget beyond his control.

. . . And Uncontrollable Spending

Certain spending programs are effectively immune to budget reductions because they have been (1) enacted into existing law and (2) enshrined in politics. For example, social security legislation guarantees certain benefits to participants in the program when they retire from employment. The same applies for such entitlement programs as Medicare, veterans' benefits, and various welfare programs. Because these payments have to be made under existing law, they represent **uncontrollable outlays.** In Reagan's FY 1987 budget, nearly 75 percent of federal budget outlays are uncontrollable or relatively uncontrollable — social security and railroad retirement, 20.8 percent; other payments to individuals, 20.3 percent; prior year contracts, 18 percent; net interest, 14.4 percent; and other open-ended programs, 1 percent. Most of the remaining 25.6 percent was earmarked for defense, which Reagan had pledged to increase. Less than 10 percent remained to absorb the cuts.[19]

To be sure, Congress could change the laws to end entitlement payments, and it does make minor modifications to them through the budget reconciliation process. But politics argues against major reductions. The only major social program that Reagan did not cut was the $212 billion social security program — the largest single domestic program and, according to many surveys, the most popular one. (Even Senator Gramm, coauthor of Gramm-Rudman-Hollings, admitted that trying to cut spending for the elderly is "not winnable." His mother, in her eighties, told her son to "keep your mouth shut" when it came to that part of the budget.) Reagan tried to cut Social Security during his first year in office, but he encountered such opposition that he became its staunch defender.

What spending cuts would be popular or even acceptable to the public? After the 1984 election, voters were asked which of ten expense items in the federal budget should be increased and which reduced. Most respondents favored spending either at the current level or at increased levels for *all of them* — the environment, defense, crimefighting, social security, medicare, education, science and technology, assistance to blacks, jobs for the unemployed, and even food stamps.[20] In a 1985 survey proposing ten specific ways of trimming government expenses, voters rejected all but two of the ten cuts. They approved only of ending loans to college students whose familes make more than $30,000 a year and of cutting federal support for opera, music, and dance.[21]

How much could the government save by cutting federal support for opera, music, and dance? The entire budget of the National Endowment for the Arts in FY 1987 was $144 million. While that is not a trivial amount, it would not help much in reaching the *$144 billion* deficit target in Gramm-Rudman-Hollings. In fact, the government could save more by eliminating the $154 million for military bands that is hidden in the $300 billion defense budget.[22]

The largest *controllable* expenditure, amounting to 17 percent of the total budget, is in the area of defense. Because Reagan wanted to increase defense spending, not cut it, he had to focus his cuts on controllable civilian or domestic programs. But those programs account for only 8.5 percent of the budget, and no president can substantially reduce federal spending by snipping away at such a relatively small federal outlay. Surveys did show support for cuts in defense spending in 1986,[23] but otherwise the public wants to have its cake and eat it too. Americans have grown accustomed to such domestic programs as social security, Medicare, student loans, and farm subsidies. But they do not like the idea of paying for these government benefits through increased taxes.

But He Doesn't Look Like Scrooge!
Thousands of citizens turn out for a rally in front of the Washington Monument to protest President Reagan's spending priorities. They are opposed to his support of defense spending and his cuts in spending for social welfare programs. Unfortunately for their cause, they are carrying a picture of Reagan at his likeable, movie-star best. It is hard to work up anger against that particular personage.

TAXING, SPENDING, AND ECONOMIC EQUALITY

As we noted in Chapter 1, the most controversial purpose of government is to promote equality, especially economic equality. Economic equality can be promoted only at the expense of economic freedom, for it requires government action to redistribute wealth from the rich to the poor. One means of accomplishing this redistribution of wealth is through government tax policy, and especially through a progressive income tax. The intent of the progressive income tax is rarely to produce equality of outcome; it aims only at reducing inequalities by assisting the poor. But as you will see, our current income tax policies do not serve even this limited objective very well.

The federal government has levied an income tax every year since 1913, when the Sixteenth Amendment gave it the power to do so. From 1964 to 1981, people who reported taxable incomes of $100,000 or more paid a top tax rate of 70 percent or more, while those with lower incomes paid taxes at progressively lower rates. How have government spending and tax policies during this period affected economic equality in America?

Government Effects on Economic Equality

In a major recent study, researchers examined the effects of transfer payments and tax policies on different income groups from 1966 to 1985.[24] **Transfer payments** are payments to individuals through programs such as social security, unemployment insurance, and food stamps. The researchers found that social spending (transfer payments) had a definite effect in reducing income inequality in 1980, just before the Reagan era. Families in the lowest-income tenth of the population paid 33 percent of their income in federal, state, and local taxes, but they also received payments from all levels of government that almost equaled their earned income. Thus the lowest income group enjoyed a net benefit from government due to transfer payments — but *not* because of tax relief. Ironically, families with the top 1 percent of income paid proportionately *less* of their income in taxes (about 28 percent). But the rich received only 1 percent of their income in transfer payments and thus suffered a net loss from government.[25]

How, you may ask, can people in the lowest income group pay a higher percentage of their income in taxes than those in the very highest group? That is the combined result of federal, state, and local tax policies. Only the federal *income tax* is progressive, with rates rising as income rises. The federal payroll tax that funds social security is highly *regressive;* its effective rate decreases as income increases beyond a certain point. Everyone pays at the same rate (7.05 percent in 1985), but the tax is levied only up to a maximum wage ($39,000 annually in 1985). There is no payroll tax at all on wages over that amount. Thus, in 1985, the effective rate of the payroll tax was about 9 percent for the lowest income group, and only 1 percent for the very top income group.

State and local sales taxes are equally regressive. Poor and rich pay the same flat tax rate on their purchases; but the poor spend almost everything they earn on purchases that are taxed, whereas the rich are able to save. So while the effective sales tax rate for the lowest income group was 7 percent, that for the top 1 percent was only 1 percent.[26]

In general, the nation's tax policies at all levels not only favored the wealthy, but they also favored those who drew their income from capital rather than labor.[27] The tax code contained many examples; here are three:

1. The tax on income from the sale of stock (called "capital gains") was typically less than the tax on income from salaries.

2. The tax on earned income (salaries and wages) was withheld from paychecks by employers under federal law; the tax on unearned income (interest and dividends) was not. Instead, the government depended on the good faith of investors to report all their unearned income.

3. There was *no federal tax at all* on investments in certain securities, such as municipal bonds.

Effects of Taxing and Spending Policies over Time

In 1966, at the beginning of President Lyndon Johnson's "Great Society" programs, the poorest fifth of American families had 4.3 percent of the nation's income after taxes and transfer payments, while the richest fifth had 45.7 percent. In 1980, after many billions of dollars in social spending and before President Reagan's cutbacks in social spending, the poorest fifth had 4.3 percent of the nation's income and the richest fifth had 48.0 percent (see Figure 15.7).[28] In short, there was virtually no change in the distribution of income. In fact, the rich had become relatively richer.

Everyone recognizes that some degree of inequality is inevitable (and perhaps even desirable). There may be some kind of limit to economic equality, and the United States may already have reached it. That would prevent government policies from equalizing the income distribution, no matter what was tried. To find out, we should look to other democracies to see how much equality they have been able to sustain. That has been done for six other countries; of those, only in France is as much as 46 percent of total income received by the top fifth of the population. In Canada, Italy, West Germany, Britain, and Sweden that percentage runs from 42 down to 37 percent.[29] The comparison suggests that our society has measurably more economic inequality than others. The question is, why?

Democracy and Equality

Although the United States is a democracy that prizes political equality for its citizens, its record in economic equality is not as good. In fact, its distribution of *wealth* — which includes not only income but ownership of savings, housing, automobiles, stocks, and so on — is strikingly unequal.

Figure 15.7

Distribution of Total Family Income in 1966 and 1980
The 20 percent of families with the highest income actually received more than 40 percent of the total income of all families in the United States (after taxes and transfer payments have been taken into account). At the bottom end of the scale, the poorest 20 percent of families received less than 5 percent of total family income. Note that, despite fourteen years of progressive taxation and social welfare programs, the distribution of income actually became more unequal. Of course, it would have been even more unequal *without transfer payments, most of which go to the poor. (Source: Joseph A. Pechman,* Who Paid the Taxes, 1966–85? *(Washington, D.C.: The Brookings Institution, 1985), p. 74.)*

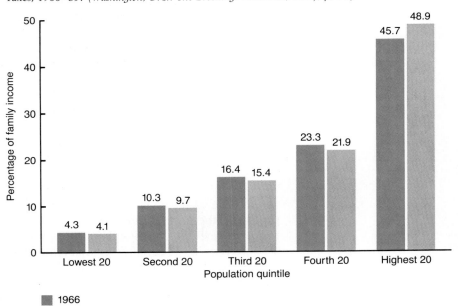

1966
1980

According to the Census Bureau, the top 12 percent of American families control almost 40 percent of household wealth. Moreover, the distribution of wealth by ethnic groups is alarming. The typical white family—which has an annual income more than 1.7 times that of blacks and 1.5 times that of Hispanics—has more than *11 times* the accumulated wealth of black families and nearly *8 times* the wealth of Hispanic families.[30] If democracy means government "by the people," why do the people not share more equally in the nation's wealth? If one of the purposes of government is to promote equality, why do government policies not work that way?

One scholar theorizes that interest group activity in a pluralist democracy distorts government attempts to promote equality. His analysis of pluralism sees "corporations and organized groups with an upper-income slant as exerting political power over and above the formal one-man–one-vote standard of democracy."[31] As you learned in Chapters 8 and 14, the pluralist model of democracy rewards those groups who are well organized and well funded.

Consider one concrete example of how well-organized and well-funded groups can secure tax advantages. As noted earlier, federal income tax is withheld by law from "earned" income (salaries and wages) but not from "unearned" income (interest and dividends). President Reagan surprised the financial world by proposing to withhold taxes from unearned income as part of his overall economic plan, and Congress made it the law in the summer of 1982. Financial institutions were given a year to devise procedures for withholding 10 percent of dividend and interest payments for income tax (the withholding was to begin July 1, 1983). Led by the American Bankers' Association, the banking interests urged their depositors to write legislators to protest the law; they even handed out sample letters that could be sent to members of Congress.

Some people, who apparently had never declared their bank interest as income, indignantly protested this "new" tax. Washington was flooded with mail stimulated by local banks and savings and loan associations. Congress had to hire temporary employees to answer letters from aroused high income taxpayers (who are also high turnout voters). President Reagan and many members of Congress were furious at the American Bankers' Association, which spent more than $300,000 in its effort to have the law repealed. Democratic Representative Thomas J. Downey of New York said that if withholding was repealed, "We send a signal that the Congress of the United States is a group of patsies to every well-organized group in America."[32] Nevertheless, Congress did back down, and withholding from unearned income was repealed only weeks before it was to go into effect.

What would happen if federal tax policy were determined according to principles of majoritarian rather than pluralist democracy? Perhaps not much —if public opinion is any guide. Public opinion in the United States shows little sentiment for redistributing wealth by increasing the only major progressive tax, the income tax. If federal taxes *must* be raised, Americans strongly favor a national sales tax over increased income taxes.[33] Because a sales tax is a flat tax, paid by rich and poor at the same rate, it would have a regressive effect on income distribution, promoting inequality rather than equality. The public also prefers a weekly $10 million national lottery to an increase in the income tax.[34] Because poor people chance more of their income on winning a fortune through lotteries than do rich people, lotteries (run by eighteen states in 1985) also contribute to income inequality through the tax system.

A majoritarian might argue that most Americans fail to understand the inequities of the federal tax system. However, a majoritarian *cannot* argue that the public demands "fairer" tax rates which take from richer citizens to help poorer ones. If it did, the lowest income families might receive a greater share of the national income than they do. Instead, economic policy is determined mainly through a complex process of pluralist politics that preserves nearly half the income in the hands of the top 20 percent of the families.

President Reagan's new tax plan is supposed to make wealthy people and corporations pay more taxes by eliminating tax shelters and other loopholes. We shall see how well that works. But even if it does work as intended, the move away from progressive taxation is also a move away from the idea of using tax policy to redistribute income.

SUMMARY

Public policies can be separated into those that prohibit, those that promote, those that protect, and those that provide. This is not an airtight typology, but it is useful in analyzing a complex subject. Governments typically employ their powers to tax and spend as a major tool of public policy. In fact, governments have begun to use their economic tools to control the business cycles in market economies. However, the extent to which government intervenes in the economy is a major issue in public policy.

Laissez faire economics holds that the government should keep its hands off the economy. Keynesian theory holds that government should take an active role in dealing with inflation and unemployment, using fiscal and monetary policies to produce the desired levels of aggregate demand. Monetarists believe fiscal policies are unreliable and prefer to rely on control of the money supply to control aggregate demand. Supply-side economists, who have been influential under the Reagan administration, focus on controlling the supply of goods and services rather than the demand for them.

Policy winners and losers are foretold in the federal budget for each fiscal year. Congress thrust the responsibility for the budget on the president in 1921, and then unsuccessfully tried to regain control of the budgeting process after World War II. Later, Congress managed to restructure the process under House and Senate Budget Committees. The new process worked well for a while, but it deteriorated under the huge deficits in the Reagan budgets.

Because so much of the budget involves military spending and uncontrollable payments to individuals, it is virtually impossible to balance the budget by reducing what remains—mainly spending for nonentitlement domestic programs. With President Reagan firmly against a tax increase, Congress accepted the drastic Gramm-Rudman-Hollings deficit reduction law of 1985. Under that law, deficits were to be reduced by stages, through automatic across-the-board cuts if necessary, until the budget was balanced by FY 1991.

Although President Reagan was against a tax hike, he pushed for sweeping tax reform. The result was a simplified tax plan with fewer loopholes for avoiding taxation, fewer tax brackets, and a significantly lower rate for the top bracket. But even with the heavily progressive tax rates of the past, the federal tax system did little to redistribute income. Government transfer payments to individuals did, however, help to reduce income inequalities. Nevertheless, the distribution of income in the United States in 1980 was nearly identical to the distribution in 1966. Moreover, there is less income equality in the United States than in most major Western nations.

Pluralist democracy as practiced in the United States has allowed well organized and well financed interests to manipulate tax and spending policies to their benefit. A poorer and larger but unorganized segment of society generally fails to obtain such benefits.

Key Terms

public policy
tax expenditure
economic depression
inflation
business cycle
aggregate demand
productive capacity
gross national product
Keynesian theory
fiscal policies
monetary policies
deficit financing
Council of Economic Advisers
monetarists
Federal Reserve System
supply-side economics
fiscal year

budget authority
budget outlays
receipts
Office of Management and Budget
tax committees
authorization committees
appropriations committees
Budget Committees
Congressional Budget Office
reconciliation
entitlement
Gramm-Rudman-Hollings
progressive taxation
incremental budgeting
uncontrollable outlays
transfer payments

Selected Readings

Committee on the Budget, U.S. Senate. *Gramm-Rudman-Hollings and the Congressional Budget Process: An Explanation*. Washington, D.C.: U.S. Government Printing Office, 1986. This short committee report succinctly explains the congressional budget process and the workings of the new budget reduction law.

Page, Benjamin A. *Who Gets What from Government?* Berkeley: University of California Press, 1983. Argues the case for equality of outcome. Contains good data on the distribution of income.

Palmer, John L., and Isabel V. Sawhill (eds.) *The Reagan Record: An Assess-* ment of America's Changing Domestic Priorities. Cambridge, Mass.: Ballinger, 1984. A series of studies of policies during Reagan's administration; chapters on the economy, the budget, social policy, business, and family incomes are especially relevant.

Pechman, Joseph A. *Who Paid the Taxes, 1966–1985?* Washington, D.C.: The Brookings Institution, 1985. Clear description of who paid what taxes by a noted authority.

Wildavsky, Aaron. *The Politics of the Budgetary Process*. 4th ed. Boston: Little, Brown, 1984. The standard study on budgetary politics, by one of the first analysts of incremental budgeting.

16

Domestic Policy

Government Policies and Individual Welfare

The Growth of the American Welfare State / Reduction of the Welfare State

Policies That Provide: Social Insurance

Social Security / Medicare

Policies That Provide: Public Assistance

Poverty and Public Assistance / Cash Assistance: AFDC / Necessary Nutrition: Food Stamps

Policies That Provide: Agriculture

Origins of the Farm Problem / The "Traditional" Solution / Some Consequences of Farm Policy / A New Direction?

The Jessen family's farm in the rolling hills near Chariton, Iowa, is small but idyllic. The Jessens — Mom, Dad, and three kids — tend a herd of dairy cows that produces enough milk for hundreds of families. Their hogs could provide enough meat to feed fifteen families for a year. But amid their bounty, the Jessens are in trouble; they are deeply in debt, and the cows and hogs are pledged to a lender. The Jessens would face ruin if they sold or butchered any of their animals. To supplement their budget, the Jessens receive food stamps each month.

Thousands of farmers like the Jessens, battered by the worst economic conditions for farming since the 1930s, are turning to government welfare programs for help. American farmers prize their self-sufficiency, but many are desperately trying to reduce expenses to save their debt-ridden farms. Many will fail, though not for want of trying.[1]

Three hundred and fifty miles away, Dorothy Sands, 37, and her family of six children, two grandchildren, and three house-guests live in a three-room, ramshackle apartment without heat or amenities. The apartment building — worn-out, vacant, garbage-strewn, and vermin-infested — is one of many similar structures on Chicago's blighted West Side. Nearly all the neighborhood's residents are black, and more than half receive public assistance (welfare). Dorothy Sands has been on the welfare rolls continuously for twenty-eight years and seems likely to remain there. Sands has given up; she has lost her initiative and her self-reliance. She and her family now live at the minimal standard: $868 a month in government support payments and food stamps. Somehow, in a land of promise and plenty, Sands is lost in an abyss of urban squalor and decay.[2]

American agriculture still towers over many of the nation's industries, and it remains the biggest earner of export revenue. Yet farmers like the Jessens face ruin while surrounded by plenty. Although America is one of the freest and richest countries in the world, Dorothy Sands and her family can take little comfort from the nation's liberties and wealth. Why is American farming in jeopardy; and why can't we solve the problems of self-perpetuating inner-city poverty?

In this chapter, we shall concentrate on government's effort to frame policies in three areas: social insurance, public assistance, and agriculture. These policies provide Americans with income, nutrition, and health care. For each area, we shall inquire into the origins and politics of specific policies, the manner in which policies address the issues, and the effects of policies once they are implemented.

There are several reasons for selecting these particular areas for scrutiny. First, the goal of policies that provide is to alleviate some of the consequences of economic inequality. Yet poverty and inequality remain as features of American life. Second, government expenditures in these three areas represent more than one-quarter of the total annual output of goods and services in the United States.[3] This is a sizable piece of the American pie; informed citizens ought to know how their resources are allocated, and why they are so allocated. Moreover, agricultural programs represent the fastest growing area of domestic spending. And third, these three areas pose some of the most vexing problems involving the conflict of democratic values.

GOVERNMENT POLICIES AND INDIVIDUAL WELFARE

The most controversial purpose of government is to promote social and economic equality among its citizens. To do so may conflict with the freedom of those citizens, for it requires government action to redistribute income from rich to poor. This choice between freedom and equality constitutes the modern dilemma of government; it has been at the center of many of the major conflicts in U.S. public policy since World War II. On the one hand, most Americans believe that government should help the needy. On the other hand, they do not want to sacrifice their own standard of living to provide government handouts to those whom they may perceive as shiftless and lazy.

The Growth of the American Welfare State

At one time governments confined their activities to the minimal protection of persons and property—to ensuring security and order. Now, however, almost every modern nation may be characterized as a **welfare state,** a concept that stresses government's function as the provider and protector of individual well-being through economic and social programs. **Social welfare** encompasses government programs that are developed to provide the necessary minimum living standards for all citizens. Income for the elderly, health care, subsidized housing, and nutrition are among the concerns addressed by government social welfare programs.

The recent history of U.S. government support for social welfare policies is sketched in Figure 16.1. In 1960, twenty-six cents of every dollar of federal spending went to payments for individuals. In 1970, thirty-three cents of every dollar went to payments for individuals. And, in 1980, slightly less than half of each federal dollar went to individuals. Today, federal spending for individuals has fallen off a few percent from the 1980 level, but the U.S. government clearly remains a provider of social welfare, despite changes in administrations.

The origins of social welfare as government policy go back to the Industrial Revolution, when the mechanization of production resulted in a shift from home manufacturing to large-scale factory production. As more and more people worked for wages, many more were subjected to the dreadful consequences of the loss of employment due to injury, sickness, old age, or economic conditions. The sick, the aged, and the disabled were tended, for the most part, by charities. The poor were confined to poorhouses or almshouses, which were little more than shacks to warehouse the impoverished. For, in the eighteenth and nineteenth centuries, poverty was viewed as a disgrace. Poor people were viewed as lazy and incompetent. (Indeed, many Americans still hold this view.) Relief was purposely made disagreeable to discourage dependence on outside assistance.

America today is far from being a welfare state in the same sense as Sweden or Great Britain; those nations provide many more medical, educational, and unemployment benefits to their citizens. However, the United States does have some social welfare functions. To understand social welfare

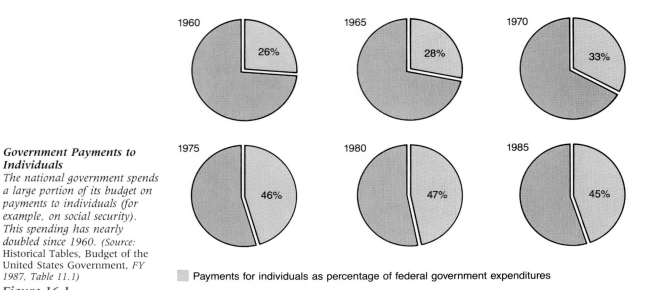

Government Payments to Individuals

The national government spends a large portion of its budget on payments to individuals (for example, on social security). This spending has nearly doubled since 1960. (Source: Historical Tables, Budget of the United States Government, *FY 1987, Table 11.1)*

Figure 16.1

Payments for individuals as percentage of federal government expenditures

policies in the United States, you must first understand the significance of a major event — the Great Depression — and two presidential plans for extending the scope of government — the "New Deal" and the "Great Society."

The Great Depression. Throughout its history, the U.S. economy has experienced alternating good times and hard times, generally referred to as *business cycles*. An **economic depression** is a severe, long-lasting downturn in a business cycle. The **Great Depression** was, by far, the longest and deepest setback that the American economy has ever experienced. It began with the stock market crash of 1929 (on October 29, 1929, now known as Black Tuesday) and did not end until the start of World War II. By 1932, one out of every four U.S. workers was unemployed, and millions more were underemployed. No other event has had a greater effect on the thinking and institutions of government in the twentieth century.

The forces that had previously stemmed such declines no longer were operative: there were no more frontiers, no growing exports, no new technologies to boost employment. Unchecked, unemployment spread like an epidemic. And the crisis fueled itself. Workers who lost their source of income could no longer buy the food, goods, and services that kept the economy going. Thus, private industry and commercial farmers tended to produce more than could be sold profitably. Closed factories, surplus crops, and idle workers were the consequences.

The Great Depression generated powerful ironies. Producers, seeking to restore profits, trimmed costs by replacing workers with machines, which only increased unemployment. Workers were jobless because machines produced so much that their services were no longer needed. People went hungry because so much food had been produced that it could not be sold profitably; dumping it was cheaper than taking it to market.

The industrialized nations of Europe were also hit hard. The value of U.S. exports fell while the value of its imports was increasing; this led to high tariffs, which strangled trade and fueled the Depression. From 1929 to 1932, more than 44 percent of the nation's banks failed. Farm prices fell by more than half in the same period. Marginal farmers lost their land, and tenant farmers succumbed to mechanization. The uprooted — tens of thousands of dispossessed farm families, with their possessions atop their cars and trucks — headed west in a hopeless quest for opportunity.

The New Deal. In his speech accepting the presidential nomination at the 1932 Democratic National Convention, Franklin Delano Roosevelt (then governor of New York) made a promise: "I pledge you, I pledge myself, to a new deal for the American people." Though this **New Deal** was never defined, it became the label for measures advocated by the Roosevelt administration to stem the Depression. Some scholars regard these measures as the most imaginative burst of domestic policy in the nation's history. Others see them as the source of massive government growth without matching benefits.

President Roosevelt's New Deal was composed of two phases. The first, which ended in 1935, was aimed at boosting prices and lowering unemployment. The second phase, which ended in 1938, was aimed at aiding the forgotten people: the poor, the aged, the unorganized working men and women, and the farmers. The Supreme Court stymied Roosevelt's first-phase reform efforts by declaring major New Deal legislation unconstitutional, beginning in 1935. A majority of the justices maintained that, in the legislation,

A Human Tragedy
The Great Depression idled millions of Americans. By 1933, when President Herbert Hoover left office, about one-fourth of the labor force was out of work. The few available jobs attracted long lines of able-bodied workers.

Congress had exceeded its constitutional authority to regulate interstate commerce.

The Democrats won overwhelming popular support for their efforts at relief and recovery. The voters returned Roosevelt to office in a landslide election in 1936. But the Supreme Court continued its opposition to New Deal legislation. That prompted Roosevelt to advocate an increase in the number of justices on the Court; his goal was to appoint justices sympathetic to the legislation enacted by the Democrats. However, Roosevelt's attack on the Court, coupled with increasing labor violence, alarmed conservatives and put the New Deal on the defensive. Yet within a few months of the 1936 election, the Supreme Court began to yield to a view of expanded federal power; in an abrupt about-face, the Court now upheld New Deal policies stemming from the second phase. (It was, said one wag, "the switch in time that saved nine.")

The New Deal programs were opportunistic; they were not guided by, or based on, a single political or economic theory. They were aimed at relief for the needy, recovery for the nation, and long-range reform for the economy. Administration of the programs called for government growth; funding for the programs required higher taxes. Government could no longer rely on either the decentralized political structure of federalism or the market forces of laissez faire capitalism to bring the country out of its decline. The

Facing the Great Depression
The human tragedy of the Depression can be seen in the faces of this migrant mother and her children. They were unsuccessful in their search for work in Weslaco, Texas, in 1939. Desperate farmers, forced from their land by foreclosure, trooped from town to town in search of jobs or food. The health, nutrition, and shelter of millions of Americans suffered as a consequence of the Depression.

New Deal embodied the belief that a complex economy required centralized government control.

Poverty and unemployment remained, however, despite the best efforts of the Democrats. By 1939, 17 percent of the work force (more than 9 million people) was still unemployed. Only World War II was able to provide the economic surge needed to yield lower unemployment and higher prices, the elusive goals of the New Deal. Though real uncertainty remains as to the economic value of the New Deal reforms, those policies did begin long-range trends toward government expansion. And another torrent of domestic policymaking burst forth three decades after the New Deal.

The Great Society.   John F. Kennedy's election in 1960 brought to Washington public servants sensitive to the persistence of poverty and concerned for the needs of minorities. But Kennedy's narrow victory margin was far from a mandate to improve their plight. At first, Kennedy proposed technical and financial aid for depressed areas and programs for upgrading the skills of workers in marginal jobs. Kennedy and influential members of his administration were moved to action by politics as much as poverty. By 1962, with the economy faltering again, the Kennedy administration proposed substantial tax breaks for middle- and upper-income groups. But many low-income Americans remained untouched by the administration's programs.

Kennedy's assassination in November 1963 provided the backdrop for new policies founded on equality and proposed by his successor, Lyndon Baines Johnson. In his 1965 State of the Union address, President Johnson offered his own version of a New Deal; his vision for the **"Great Society"** included a broad array of programs designed to redress political, social, and economic inequality. Some of these programs had already been enacted, whereas others were still in the planning stage. The Civil Rights Act of 1964 was aimed at erasing racial discrimination from most areas of American life. The Voting Rights Act of 1965 had as its goal the elimination of voting restrictions that discriminated against blacks and other minorities. Both statutes prohibited conduct that was inconsistent with political and social equality.

Another part of Johnson's Great Society plan was based on the traditional American belief that social and economic equality could be attained through increased equality of educational opportunity. The Elementary and Secondary Education Act of 1965 provided, for the first time, direct federal aid to local school districts, based on the number of low-income families in each district. Later, the federal government was able to use the threat of withholding federal school aid (under the Civil Rights Act of 1964) to dramatically increase the pace of school integration in the South.

Still another vital element of the Great Society was the **War on Poverty.** The major weapon in this war was the Economic Opportunity Act of 1964; its proponents promised that it would eradicate poverty in ten years. The act encouraged a variety of local community programs to educate and train people for employment; among these programs were college work-study, summer employment for high school and college students, loans to small businesses, a domestic version of the Peace Corps (called VISTA, for Volunteers in Service to America), educational enrichment for preschoolers, and legal services for the poor. It offered opportunity: a hand up, rather than a handout.

The act also established the Office for Economic Opportunity (OEO), which was the administrative center for waging the War on Poverty. Its basic strategy was to involve the poor themselves in administering the programs, in the hope that they would know which programs would best serve the needs of the poor. Federal money was channeled directly to Community Action Programs to fight local poverty through local groups. This approach avoided such vested interests as state and local government bureaucrats and political machines. But it also led to new local controversies by shifting the control of federal funds from local politicians to other groups. (In one notorious example, the Blackstone Rangers, a Chicago street gang, received support in the War on Poverty.)

In 1967, the Johnson administration responded to pressure from established local politicians by requiring that poverty funds be distributed through certified state and local agencies. In addition, all sectors of the community (including business, labor, and civic leaders) would now be represented, along with the poor, in administering Community Action Programs.

The War on Poverty eventually sputtered and disappeared as funding was diverted to the Vietnam War. Although it had achieved little in the way of income redistribution, it did do much to make the poor aware of their political power. Candidates representing the poor ran for political office, and officeholders paid increasing attention to the poor. The poor also found that they could use the legal system to their benefit. For example, with legal assistance from the OEO, low-income litigants were successful in striking down state laws requiring a minimum period of residency before poor people could receive public assistance.[4]

Some War on Poverty programs remain as established features of government. (Among these are the work-study program that enables many college students to finance their educations.) Yet poverty also remains; and the evidence suggests that it may once again be on the rise. Public attitudes toward poverty have changed, however, since the Great Depression. Though one in every four Americans still thinks poor people are lazy, the vast majority are sympathetic to the plight of the needy. Americans realize that poverty results from forces beyond the control of most individuals, such as shifts in the economy.

Social welfare policy is based on the premise that society has an obligation to provide for the minimum welfare of its members. In a recent national survey, the poor and nonpoor agreed that government should protect its citizens against the risks that they are powerless to combat. Americans expressed a clear conviction that money and wealth ought to be more evenly shared by a larger percentage of the population. The label "welfare state" reflects this protective role of government.

By meeting minimum needs, government welfare policies attempt to promote equality. New Deal policies were aimed at meeting the needs of the poor by redistributing income: people with greater incomes paid progressively higher taxes; the wealthy paid to alleviate poverty. Today's liberals tend to follow in the New Deal path. They are willing to curtail economic freedom somewhat in return for economic equality. As a result, their policies aim at providing direct income subsidies and government jobs. Today's conservatives avoid this government-as-provider approach, preferring economic

Have a Nice Day
This unemployment office was not designed to be inviting; it is one way for government to discourage dependence on assistance. The office processes claims for assistance filed by people who become unemployed through no fault of their own. A cooperative state-federal assistance plan was enacted in 1935; in 1985, an eligible person could receive maximum weekly benefits of about $150 for a period of 26 weeks or longer.

freedom to government intervention. Their policies aim at curbing inflation and reducing government spending, on the theory that a rising economic tide lifts all boats.[5]

Reduction of the Welfare State

A spirit of equality—equality of opportunity—had motivated the reforms of the 1960s, and many of these reforms carried over to the 1970s. But the overwhelming election of Ronald Reagan in 1980 and his landslide reelection in 1984 forced a reexamination of social welfare policy.

In a dramatic departure from his predecessors (Republicans as well as Democrats), Reagan shifted emphasis from economic equality to economic freedom. He questioned whether government alone should continue to be responsible for shouldering the economic and social well-being of less fortunate citizens. And, to the extent that government should bear this responsibility, he maintained that state and local governments could do so more efficiently than the federal government.

Reagan has lent his support to the "truly needy" and to the preservation of a "reliable safety net of social programs," by which he means the core programs begun in the New Deal. But his administration has abolished a number of federal social welfare programs and has redirected others. Reagan has proposed sharp cutbacks in housing assistance, welfare, the food stamp program, and education and training programs. He also has trimmed the most basic of American social welfare programs—social security—although cuts here were less severe than in other areas.[6]

So far, Congress has checked some of the president's proposed cutbacks; many Great Society programs remain in force, though at lower funding levels. Overall spending on social welfare programs (as a proportion of gross national product) has declined to about mid-1970s levels. But the dramatic growth in the promotion of social welfare that began with the New Deal has ended. Ronald Reagan's focus on the federal budget deficit will no doubt restrict efforts to expand the government's social welfare role.

POLICIES THAT PROVIDE: SOCIAL INSURANCE

Insurance is a device for guaranteeing an individual against loss. Since the late nineteenth century, there has been a growing tendency for governments to offer **social insurance,** which is a government-backed guarantee against loss by individuals, without regard to need. The most common forms of social insurance guard against losses due to worker injury, sickness, and disability; due to old age; and due to unemployment. The first example of social insurance in the United States was workers' compensation. Beginning early in this century, most states provided a system of insurance that compensated workers who lost income because they were injured in the workplace.

Social insurance benefits are distributed to recipients without regard for their economic status. Old-age benefits, for example, are paid to all people —rich or poor—who reach the required age. In most social insurance programs, employees and employers contribute to a separate fund from which later disbursements are made to recipients.*

Social insurance programs are examples of **entitlements**—benefits to which every eligible person has a legal right, and which government cannot deny. Federal entitlement programs consume about sixty cents of every dollar of government spending; one of the largest entitlement programs is social security.

Social Security

Social security is social insurance that provides economic assistance to persons faced with unemployment, disability, or old age; it is financed by taxes on employers and employees. Initially, social security benefits were distributed only to the aged, the unemployed, and poor people with dependent children. Today, social security provides medical care for the elderly and income support for the disabled.

---

*Examine your next paycheck stub. It should indicate your contribution to FICA (the Federal Insurance Contribution Act). This is your social security tax.

Origins of social security.   The idea of social security came late to the United States. As early as 1883, Germany enacted legislation to protect workers against the hazards of industrial life. Most European nations adopted old-age insurance after World War I; many provided income support for the disabled and income protection for families faced with the death of the principal wage earner. In the United States, however, the needs of the elderly and unemployed were left to private organizations and individuals. Hard work and savings were the American way to avoid dependency in old age. But the widespread unemployment and loss of savings resulting from the Great Depression vividly demonstrated that this was simply not enough. Although twenty-eight states had old-age assistance programs by 1934, neither private charities nor state and local governments—nor both together—could cope with the prolonged unemployment and distress that resulted from the Depression. A national policy was necessary to deal with a national crisis.

The first important step came on August 14, 1935, when President Franklin Roosevelt signed the **Social Security Act;** that act has become the cornerstone of the modern American welfare state. The act's framers developed three approaches to the problem of dependency. The first approach provided social insurance in the form of old-age and surviving-spouse benefits, and cooperative state-federal unemployment assistance. A program was created to provide income to retired workers, to ensure that the elderly did not have to retire into poverty. This was to serve as a floor of protection against income loss for the elderly. (Americans usually identify social security only with this program.) In addition, an unemployment insurance program, financed by employers, was created to provide payments for a limited time to workers who were laid off or dismissed for reasons beyond their control.

The second approach was aid to the destitute in the form of grants-in-aid to the states. The act established the first permanent federal commitment to provide financial assistance to the needy aged, needy families with dependent children, the blind, and (since the 1950s) the permanently and totally disabled.

The third approach provided health and welfare services through federal aid to the states. Included were health and family services for crippled children and orphans, and vocational rehabilitation for the disabled.

How social security works.   The social security old-age benefits program is administered directly by the federal government through the Social Security Administration. Old-age retirement revenue goes into a separate *trust fund* (there is a separate fund for each social security program), which means that this revenue can be spent only for the old-age benefits program. Benefits, in the form of monthly payments, begin when an employee reaches retirement age, which today stands at 65. (People can retire as early as age 62, but then they must accept reduced benefits.) The retirement age is slated to increase gradually over the next several years to 67.

Many Americans believe that each person's social security contributions (the FICA tax taken out of each paycheck) are set aside specifically for his or her retirement like a savings account.[7] But social security doesn't operate quite like that. Rather, the federal government imposes a tax on employees and employers: the social security revenue generated today pays benefits to

Listen to Your Elders
Democratic representative Claude Pepper of Florida was only 79 when he posed with two 100-year-old constituents who testified before the House Select Committee on Aging in 1979. Still active in 1986, Pepper continues to be the driving force behind government programs that provide assistance to the nation's elderly.

those who have already reached retirement age. Thus, social security (and social insurance generally) is not a form of savings; it is a pay-as-you-go tax system. Today's workers support today's elderly.

When the social security program began, it had few beneficiaries and many contributors. During its infancy, the program could provide relatively large benefits with low taxes. In 1937, for example, the tax rate was 1 percent, and there were nine workers shouldering the benefits of each retiree. As the program matured and more people retired, the ratio of workers to recipients decreased. In 1982, for example, the social security system paid benefits to 35 million people and collected revenues from 110 million; the FICA tax rate was 6.7 percent.

At one time, federal workers, members of Congress, judges, even the president were omitted from the social security system. Today, however, there are few exceptions. Universal participation is essential if the system is to operate well, since it is not a savings program but a tax program. If participation were not compulsory, there would be insufficient revenue to provide benefits to present retirees. So government, which is the only institution that can coerce, requires that all employees and their employers contribute. Of course, government coercion imposes restrictions on freedom, but few can recognize or resist those restrictions. Consider, for example, the plight of Valentine Y. Byler, an Amish farmer. He declined to participate in the social security system because his faith directs its members to care for one another. In 1961, the Internal Revenue Service seized Byler's three horses and sold them at auction to collect $308.96 in unpaid social security taxes.[8]

Those people who currently pay into the system will receive retirement benefits that are financed by future participants. As with a pyramid scheme or chain letter, success depends on the growth of the base. If the birth rate remains steady or grows, then future wage earners will be able to support today's contributors when they retire. If the economy expands, then there will be more jobs, more income, and a growing wage base to tax for increased benefits to retirees. But suppose the birth rate declines or unemployment rises and the economy falters. Then contributions can decline to the point at which benefits exceed revenues. Thus, despite general approval of social security as policy, its pyramidal character is its Achilles' heel. Social security is a coercive government program in which everyone appears to get more than he or she pays in. How is that possible? An answer can be found in the politics of widely distributed benefits.

Who pays? Who benefits? "Who pays?" and "Who benefits?" are two important questions of politics, and they apply directly to social security. In 1968, the Republican party platform called for automatic adjustments that would increase social security payments as the cost of living increased. The theory was simple: as the cost of living rises, so should retirement benefits; otherwise, the benefits would be paid in "shrinking dollars." With an expanding economy and a growing wage base, there would be ample revenues to cover the increased benefits. Cost-of-living adjustments (COLAs) became a political football in 1969 as the Democrats and Republicans tried to outdo each other by suggesting larger increases for retirees. The result was a significant expansion of the social security program, far in excess of the cost of living. The beneficiaries were the retired, who were beginning to flex their political muscle. The alienation of such a constituency could change an election.[9]

In 1972, the Congress adopted automatic adjustments in benefits and in the wage base on which contributions are assessed, so that revenue would expand when benefits grew. This approach set social security on automatic pilot. If inflation exceeds 3 percent, then the automatic adjustment goes into effect. (Politicians nonetheless fear retribution at the polls if there is not some annual adjustment. When it appeared that inflation would fall below 3 percent in 1986, the bidding game re-emerged as senators facing re-election challenged their colleagues to deny added benefits that social security recipients deserved.)

There was no assurance, however, that revenue growth would equal or exceed the growth in social security expenditures. And, in fact, when "stagflation" took hold in the 1970s, the entire social security system was jeopardized. (*Stagflation* is high unemployment coupled with high inflation.) Stagflation gripped the social security system in an economic vise: unemployment meant a reduction in revenue; high inflation meant growing benefits. This one-two punch drained social security trust fund reserves to critically low levels in the late 1970s and early 1980s. In addition, a reduced birth rate meant that, in future, fewer workers would support more retirees. Higher taxes — a distasteful political alternative — loomed as the only alternative except for paying for social security out of general revenues, that is, income taxes. Social security was on the verge of becoming a public assistance program like welfare. But in 1983, shortly before existing social security benefit funds were exhausted, Congress and President Reagan agreed to a rescue calling for two painful adjustments: increased taxes and reduced benefits.

The changes enacted in 1983 may indeed guarantee the future of the social security system. However, although policymakers have not generally fared well in predicting future economic conditions, it is those conditions that will determine the success or failure of the system. When today's workers retire, tomorrow's workers will have to support them. As longevity increases, the burden on future workers will also increase, for greater numbers of re- tirees will require greater retirement benefits. In addition, starting in the next century, a relatively smaller pool of workers will carry the revenue burden. Despite various revenue-generating plans, higher taxes or reduced benefits may be the only means for assuring the viability of social security.[10]

Today, no one argues against the need for social security. The real debate surrounds the extent of coverage and the level of benefits. "The [Social Se- curity] Act is the most successful program of the modern state," declared Nobel Prize laureate Paul Samuelson. Yet Milton Friedman, another Nobel laureate, labeled the act "a sacred cow that no politician can criticize." How can two world-class economists maintain such dramatically different views? Samuelson is a liberal in the Keynesian tradition; he favors equality over freedom. Social security lifted the elderly from destitution by redistributing income from workers (with growing incomes) to the elderly (with little or no income). Friedman is a libertarian and a monetarist; he favors freedom over equality. Since social security limits freedom in return for economic equality, Friedman would no doubt prefer that the program be scaled back or even eliminated. The political risks associated with social security cutbacks are too great, however, for most politicians to bear.

Medicare

The social security system provides economic assistance conditioned on unemployment, disability, or old age. In 1962, the Senate considered ex- tending social security benefits to provide hospitalization and medical care for the elderly. In opposing the extension, Democratic Senator Russell Long of Louisiana declared that "We are not staring at a sweet old lady in bed with her kimono and nightcap. We are looking into the eyes of the wolf that ate Red Riding Hood's grandma."[11] Long was concerned that there would be no way to limit this new direction in government assistance to the elderly. Other opponents echoed the opposition of the American Medical Association (AMA), which perceived government control of medicine in virtually any step that government would take toward providing medical care. Long and others won the battle that day. Three years later, however, the Social Security Act was amended to provide **Medicare,** or health care for all people over 65.

Origins of Medicare. Public opinion clearly supported some form of national health insurance as early as 1945. That idea became entangled in the cold war, however, at a time when there was a growing crusade against communism in America.[12] The AMA, representing the nation's physicians, mounted and financed an all-out campaign to link national health insurance (so-called socialized medicine) with socialism; the campaign was so success-ful that the prospect of a national health policy vanished while anticom-munist sentiment rose.

Both proponents and opponents tried to link their positions to deeply rooted American values: the advocates of national health insurance empha-sized equality and fairness; the opponents stressed individual freedom. In the absence of a clear public mandate as to the *kind* of insurance (publicly funded or private) that might be wanted, the AMA was able to marshal political influence to prevent any national insurance at all.[13]

By 1960, however, the terms of the debate had changed. The focus was no longer fixed on the clash of freedom and equality. Now the issue of health insurance was cast in terms of assistance to the aged, and a groundswell of support forced it onto the national agenda.[14]

The Democratic victory in 1964 and the advent of President Johnson's Great Society made some form of national health policy almost inevitable. On July 30, 1965, Johnson signed a bill that provided a number of health benefits targeted at the elderly and poor. Fearful of the AMA's power to punish its opponents, the Democrats confined their efforts to a compulsory hospitalization insurance plan for the elderly. (This is known today as Part A of Medicare.) In addition, they passed a form of the alternative Republican plan, which called for voluntary government-subsidized insurance to cover physician's bills. (This is known today as Part B of Medicare.)*

Medicare today. Part A of Medicare is compulsory insurance which covers certain hospital services for persons 65 and older. Workers pay a tax. Retirees pay premiums deducted from social security payments. Payments for covered services are made directly to participating hospitals and other qualifying facilities by the federal government; they are limited to the rea-sonable costs of medically necessary services. In 1985, 30.3 million people were enrolled in Part A. The government spent $41.5 billion under the pro-gram in 1984.

Part B of Medicare is a voluntary program of medical insurance for per-sons 65 and older, who pay the premiums. The insurance covers the services of physicians and other qualified providers; payments for those services are based on reasonable charges or on set fees. In 1985, 29.9 million people were enrolled; the government spent $22 billion for Part B benefits in 1984. In 1986, the monthly premium was $16.10 for this insurance.[15]

The fears that Senator Long voiced in 1962 seem to have become reality: Medicare costs soared out of control almost from the start. In 1987, Medicare costs are expected to exceed $75 billion, representing a fourfold increase in ten years. Moreover, the trust fund supporting hospitalization costs appears headed for bankruptcy by the mid-1990s unless spending can be reduced (by curtailing benefits) or income can be increased (by raising taxes).[16]

One attempt at cost containment makes use of economic incentives in the hospital treatment of Medicare patients. The plan seems to have had the

---

*A third program, added a year later, is called *Medicaid*; it provides medical aid to the poor through federally assisted state health programs. Medicaid is a need-based comprehensive med-ical and hospitalization program for the poor. Need is the only criterion; if you are poor, you qualify. Medicaid today covers 21.4 million people at a cost in 1984 of $34.3 billion.

desired economic benefits, but it raises a question regarding the endangerment of elderly patients' health. Medicare payments to hospitals have been based on the length of a patient's stay; the longer the stay, the more revenue the hospitals earned. This payment approach encouraged overconsumption of health care and longer hospital stays, since the government, as insurer, was paying the bill. In 1985, however, the government switched to a new payment system under which hospitals are paid a fixed, preset fee based on the patient's diagnosis. If the patient's stay costs more than the fee schedule allows, the hospital pays the difference. On the other hand, if the hospital treats a patient for less than the fixed fee, then the hospital reaps the profit. This new system provides an incentive for hospitals to discharge patients sooner and, perhaps, before they are completely well.

POLICIES THAT PROVIDE: PUBLIC ASSISTANCE

Public assistance is what most people mean when they use the term "welfare" or "welfare payments"; it is government aid to individuals who can demonstrate a need for that aid. Public assistance is directed toward those who lack the ability or resources to provide for themselves or their families.

Public assistance programs instituted under the Social Security Act are known today as *categorical assistance programs*. They include (1) old-age assistance for the needy elderly not covered by old-age pension benefits, (2) aid to the needy blind, (3) aid to needy families with dependent children, and (4) aid to the totally and permanently disabled. Though adopted initially as stop-gap measures during the Depression, these programs have now become entitlements. They are administered by the states, although the bulk of the funding comes from the federal government's general tax revenues. Because the states also contribute to the funding of their own public assistance programs, the benefits tend to vary from state to state.

Poverty and Public Assistance

The federal government requires that national standards be used in the administration of state welfare programs. It distributes resources to the states based on the proportion of each state's population that is living in poverty. That proportion is, in turn, determined on the basis of a federal **poverty level,** or poverty threshold, which is the minimum cash income that will provide for a family's basic needs. The poverty level is calculated as three times the cost of an economy food plan, a market basket of food that provides a minimally nutritious diet. (The threshold is computed in this way because research suggests that the poor spend one-third of their income on food.*)

---

*Though it has been the source of endless debate, today's definition of poverty retains remarkable similarity to its predecessors. As early as 1795, a group of English magistrates "decided that a minimum income should be the cost of a gallon loaf of bread, multiplied by three, plus an allowance for each dependent." See Alvin L. Schorr, "Redefining Poverty Levels," *New York Times*, May 9, 1984, p. 27

The poverty level, is, of course, only a rough measure for distinguishing the poor and the nonpoor, but it is fairly simple to apply. Using it is like using a wrench as a hammer: It works, but not very well.

The poverty level varies with family size; and it is adjusted each year to reflect changes in consumer prices. In 1984, the poverty threshold for a family of four was $10,609.[17] This is income *before* taxes. If the poverty threshold were viewed as disposable income (in other words, income *after* taxes), then the perceived proportion of the population living in poverty would be increased.

Some critics believe that more than cash income should be used in computing the poverty level and determining the number of Americans who fall below it. The current computation fails to take into account such noncash benefits as food stamps, health benefits (Medicaid), and subsidized housing. Presumably, the inclusion of these noncash benefits would decrease the proportion of individuals living below the poverty level.

Critics notwithstanding, the poverty threshold has been calculated for many years as a total cash income. At the very least, that yardstick allows us to chart our progress against poverty. Figure 16.2 shows that poverty in the United States has declined from its peak years around 1960. The elderly have made the most progress, with blacks and whites progressing about equally. Nevertheless, in 1984 poverty was still the economic condition of more than one in ten whites and more than one in three blacks. Despite soaring social welfare spending during the 1970s, poverty retains a tight hold on the American population. And, as is reported in Figure 16.3, it has begun to creep back up to mid-1960 levels.

Figure 16.2

Poverty Rates by Groups, 1959 and 1984
The condition of being poor affects blacks, whites, and the elderly unequally. A smaller percentage of all Americans live in poverty today than in 1959, when income information was first collected systematically.
(*Source: Bureau of the Census,* Money Income and Poverty Status of Families and Persons in the United States: 1984, *Current Populations Reports, Series P-60, No. 149, Table 15, p. 21.*)

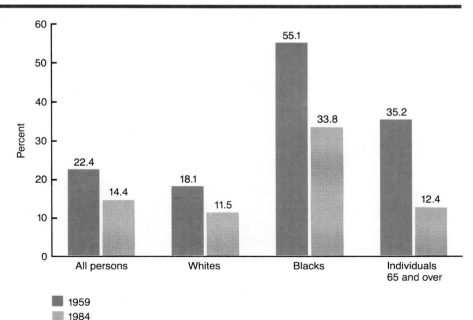

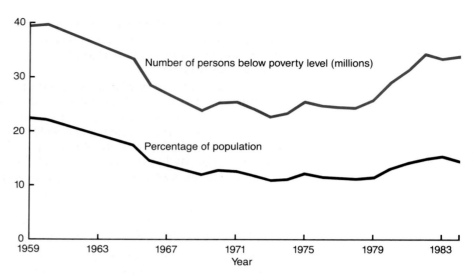

Poverty in the United States, 1959 to 1984
The graph shows the percentage of the population below the poverty level, in the given years. The number of Americans who are living below the poverty level has been increasing since 1978. (Source: Bureau of the Census, Money Income and Poverty Status of Families and Persons in the United States: 1984, *Current Population Reports, Series P-60, No. 149, Table 15, p. 21.)*

Figure 16.3

Cash Assistance: AFDC

The largest public assistance program is **Aid to Families with Dependent Children (AFDC),** which was created in the Social Security Act of 1935. In 1983, the federal government spent $14 billion in public assistance programs authorized by the Social Security Act; of this, the AFDC program cost $13.8 billion, and it provided assistance to roughly 11 million persons each month.[18] The program acknowledges federal government responsibility to help care for children who have been deprived of parental support through death, disability, or desertion. Previously, these children commonly had been cared for in orphanages.

AFDC benefits are distributed in cash through the states, and AFDC is the basic cash assistance program for poor families. The typical AFDC family lives in a large urban area and consists of a mother under thirty and two children under eight; more than half the AFDC recipients are white, and 40 percent are black. Eligibility for AFDC automatically qualifies recipients for Medicaid and other forms of public assistance. But recipients must first go through a complicated qualifying process, because government is very wary of giving money to persons who might in any way be regarded as undeserving. The process has four parts, as illustrated in Figure 16.4:

1. *Family composition test.* Generally speaking, an applicant for AFDC benefits must be a single parent living with at least one child under age eighteen. In half the states recipients can be married, but the principal wage earner must be unemployed.

2. *Assets test* (varies from state to state). Assets are savings, clothing, and furniture. The federal government sets a limit on the value of the assets an AFDC family can possess (in 1985, it was $1,000). However, states can impose stricter limits.

3. *Determination of need* (varies from state to state). A family is considered to be in need if its income is below a "need standard" set by each state. Only families with incomes below the need standard qualify for benefits.

4. *Benefit calculation.* Each state establishes a payment standard for determining benefits. (In half the states, the payment standard is below the need standard.) For qualifying families, the difference between the payment standard and family income is the AFDC benefit.

Necessary Nutrition: Food Stamps

The federal **food stamp program** has the goal of improving the diets of members of low-income households by supplementing their food purchasing power. The federally funded program is administered through local agencies, which distribute the stamps to needy individuals and families. The stamps are actually coupons that can be used to purchase any food meant for human consumption.

Food stamps originated in Roosevelt's New Deal years, as a dual-purpose program aimed at confronting the "unsettling contradiction between unprecedented destitution and deprivation on the one hand and excessive agricultural production on the other."[19] The program accomplished its twin goals of feeding the hungry and helping the farmers, and then became dormant when the economy rebounded in World War II. But the problem of hunger remained. Later administrations either denied that there was a substantial problem of hunger in America or instituted generally ineffective programs in which surplus commodities (lard, rice, flour, butter, and cheese) were distributed to the poor in amounts too small to assure adequate nutrition.

The revival of the food stamp program was the top legislative priority of Democratic Representative Leonor Sullivan of Missouri during the 1950s. Sullivan's dogged determination kept the idea alive through the Eisenhower and Kennedy administrations, until Congress provided a substantially ex-

Figure 16.4 ▬▬

AFDC Qualification Process
A family seeking AFDC benefits must complete a four-step process. Some steps vary from state to state. (Source: Tom Joe and Cheryl Rogers, By the Few, for the Few: The Reagan Welfare Legacy, *p. 25. Lexington, Mass.: Lexington Books, 1985. © 1985, Lexington Books. Reprinted by permission.)*

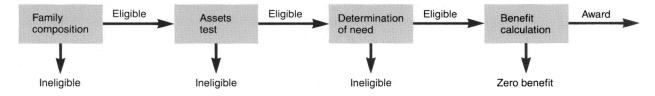

Food Stamps
Food stamps are misnamed. They are not lick'em stamps at all but coupons that can be used to purchase any food meant for human consumption. (This rules out kitty litter and deodorants, for example.) In 1983, nearly one in every ten Americans received an average of $43 per month in food "stamps."

panded program in the Food Stamp Act of 1964. At first, administrators were fearful that the distribution of free stamps would encourage a black market for the stamps. That is, if the stamps provided more food than was necessary, recipients would be tempted to sell their excess stamps. The solution was to require recipients to purchase stamps with a portion of their incomes. In return, they would receive stamps whose value was equal to the purchase price *plus* an additional amount. As family income rose, the additional amount declined. Unfortunately, this purchase plan did not work well, because people who needed food stamps often lacked the cash with which to buy them. Moreover, even the most generous food stamp allotment was not enough to ensure adequate nutrition.

Meanwhile, critics continued to point to the inadequacies of government nutrition policy. The Citizens' Crusade Against Poverty, a liberal advocacy group formed in 1965, collected evidence on the extent of hunger and malnutrition in the United States. Several other public interest groups joined the so-called "hunger lobby," and the poor also lobbied on their own behalf: more than 3000 people participated in "The Poor People's March on Washington" in 1968. They camped on the mall east of the Lincoln Memorial and presented their demands to the Secretary of Agriculture. A CBS television documentary called "Hunger in America" focused on the problem of government ineffectiveness in combatting hunger.

Some concessions were granted by the government, but they proved inadequate and new advocates for the poor joined the lobbying effort. Finally, the Nixon administration introduced significant changes in the food stamp program. Food stamp allotments were increased to ensure a nutritionally adequate diet, and the purchase price of the stamps was reduced. Later, in 1977, the need to purchase food stamps was eliminated entirely. By the end of the decade, the problem of hunger appeared on the verge of being solved.

The food stamp and AFDC programs are structured to work jointly. Recall that AFDC benefits vary from state to state. Food stamp benefits are, however, set nationally, so that in states which offer lower AFDC benefits, participants receive larger food stamp allotments. In 1983, the food stamp program cost the government $11.8 billion. The 21 million participants (nearly one in ten Americans) received an average of $43 per month in food stamps.

The Reagan administration has attempted to curtail the food stamp program and has had a measure of success. More than a million people lost their food stamp benefits entirely as a result of spending cuts in 1984, and benefits were reduced for many others.[20] The administration maintained that this was not as heartless as it appeared: most of those who lost their benefits had incomes in excess of 130 percent of the poverty level. At the same time, the Reagan administration increased its distribution of surplus food to the poor. But there is no established and workable distribution system, and the food that is given away (often five-pound blocks of American cheese) qualifies only as a nutritional supplement, and not as the basis of a nourishing diet.

A Not-So-Merry Christmas
Many Americans rely on public and private programs to eke out an existence. In spite of efforts of private charities to fill the needs of the homeless and hungry, like this Christmas Day soup line in Boston, most people must eventually turn to the government to supply the aid they need if they are to survive.

Ronald Reagan once observed that "In the war on poverty, poverty won." Americans tend to agree. About half of all Americans regard the liberal welfare policies of the 1960s as making things "somewhat better" for the poor; only 10 percent maintain that those policies made the poor much better off. But 90 percent of Americans seem convinced that poverty will remain a persistent problem, in part because 70 percent believe that government doesn't know enough about how to eliminate poverty.[21]

Government provides many Americans with benefits. According to the Bureau of the Census, 39.1 million of the nation's 83.6 million households received federal government benefits in 1984. Nearly 40 percent of all households received some form of social security or other benefits for which they did not have to demonstrate need. Nearly one-fifth of those households also participated in need-based programs, including food stamps, subsidized housing, school lunch programs, and Medicaid. Is the United States generous in the benefits it confers? Do the costs seem to be in line with the benefits? Some evidence that might help you form an opinion is presented in Compared With What? 16.1.

POLICIES THAT PROVIDE: AGRICULTURE

According to a *New York Times*/CBS News poll conducted in February 1985, the vast majority of Americans view farming as a good way of life, embodying the virtues of stability, hard work, and occasional sacrifice.[22] Two hundred years ago America was a nation of farmers, but today America's farmers make up less than 3 percent of the population. Yet despite their declining numbers, American farmers have managed to bring in bumper harvests. Agriculture remains a large industry (much larger than, for example, the automobile, banking, and publishing industries); and it accounts for the nation's highest export earnings.[23] Nonetheless, this bucolic picture of performance and plenty is, in reality, riddled with problems.

Origins of the Farm Problem

The federal government's agricultural policies were confined to research and education until the Depression, when farm prices and income plunged. The collapse of the nation's economy brought the farming industry near to ruin. To preserve American farming and the nation's farmers, the free market in farm products — in which supply and demand determine price — had to be constrained. The result was government policies aimed at raising and stabilizing prices and at controlling production.

As part of Roosevelt's New Deal, Congress passed an Agricultural Adjustment Act in 1933. The act, an effort to boost farm prices and farmers' purchasing power, placed a tax on the processors of seven basic commodities (wheat, cotton, field corn, hogs, rice, tobacco, and dairy products). The tax proceeds were used to pay benefits to farmers who agreed to reduce their production of those commodities. The decline in production would force prices up, increasing farm income and encouraging the production of other crops. With lower but stable production of specific crops, supply and demand would maintain prices at a level that would avert catastrophe.

Compared With What? 16.1

Social Insurance Costs and Benefits

This table compares old-age and health insurance taxes or premiums and benefits in four countries. Note that West Germany exacts the highest tax for old-age benefits, while Great Britain imposes the smallest tax. France offers the most generous retirement benefits: retirement at age 60 with a benefit guarantee of 75 percent of the worker's wages during the last work year. Americans retire later (at age 65) and with a somewhat lower retirement benefit.

Health insurance premiums are lowest in the United States and highest in France, where there is no ceiling on payments. France, West Germany, and Great Britain offer total health care for everyone. But in the United States, such care is limited to the aged and the poor. In a sense, Americans get what they pay for.

Individual Social Welfare Costs and Benefits
(all currencies converted to dollars)

COSTS (1983)	France	West Germany	Great Britain	United States
Old Age				
Maximum employee payments	$ 865	$ 2,400	$ 850	$ 1,930
Maximum employer payments	1,220	2,400	1,000	1,930
Income ceiling for calculating payments	14,900	25,800	9,500	35,700
Health Insurance				
Maximum employee payments	5.5%	1,100	*	465
Maximum employer payments	12.6%	1,100	*	465
Income ceiling for calculating payments	no ceiling	19,300	*	35,700
BENEFITS **Old Age (1980)**				
Age at retirement (M/F)	60/60	65/65	65/60	65/65
Replacement wage rate (percentage of last year of wages)	75	49	47	66
Health Insurance				
Duration	unlimited	unlimited	unlimited	limited
Hospitalization	complete	complete	complete	some limits
Medical Care	free	free	free	limited
Coverage	all	all	all	aged & poor

*In Great Britain, comprehensive payments covered under "Old Age"

Sources: *Comparative Tables of the Social Security Schemes in the Member States of the European Communities, Situation at 1 July 1984.* European Communities. Commission. 13th ed. (1985). *Statistical Abstract of the United States, 1985.* Table 642.

In 1936, the Supreme Court declared the 1933 act an unconstitutional exercise of the Congressional taxing power.[24] But majority sentiment would not be thwarted; the Court soon reversed its stand on New Deal policies in general and farm policy in particular. By 1938, Congress had enacted a similar agricultural act, which the Supreme Court upheld as a valid legislative exercise of its power over interstate commerce.[25]

Government intervention in the market for farm products has, since that time, moderated the effects of business cycles on farmers. But that intervention has also encouraged much overproduction, which, in turn, has increased the cost of government farm policy. Agriculture programs cost the government almost $26 billion in 1985. Even allowing for inflation, this is more than four times the cost just a decade earlier.[26] Yet farmers have come to depend on government help to absorb their bumper crops. In the absence of government assistance, many farmers would face certain ruin.

The "Traditional" Solution

Today's agricultural policy is based on the 1938 act. It involves three concepts — price supports, direct income subsidies, and production controls — which have been translated into programs aimed at protecting and promoting American agriculture.

Price supports are the means that government uses to maintain at least a minimum price for certain commodities. The federal government uses loans that are not really loans as the chief mechanism for agricultural price supports. To see how they work, suppose you are a wheat farmer. The government offers to lend you a certain amount of money, say $3.30, for each bushel of wheat that you are willing to place in a government-approved granary. The crop will serve as collateral for the loan. You could, of course, sell the wheat on the open market, but there may be good reasons for putting the grain in storage — at least for a while. For example, if all farmers were to put their wheat on the market at the same time, the glut would force the price down. You would do better to wait for the price to rise again.

Suppose you agree to place 10,000 bushels of wheat in storage; at $3.30 a bushel, you receive a loan of $33,000. Now, if the market price of the wheat rises above the $3.30 loan rate, you can remove your grain from storage, sell it, repay the loan, and pocket the difference. If the market price remains below the loan rate, then you simply keep the loan and the government keeps the wheat. In effect, the loan has become the price floor for wheat. If such *support prices* are adjusted regularly for inflation and other economic factors, they tend to act as insurance against market fluctuations. But when they are higher than the market price, they tend to stimulate the very overproduction that government seeks to moderate (see Figure 16.5).

Direct income subsidies (also called *deficiency payments*) are cash payments to farmers. Unlike price supports, they do not prop up the prices of farm products. Instead, they reimburse the farmer for the cost of producing a crop when that cost is greater than the market price or loan rate for the crop. This form of assistance assures farmers of an adequate income when market prices fall below the cost of production. In 1976, for example, bumper crops in grain-importing countries reduced the world demand for American

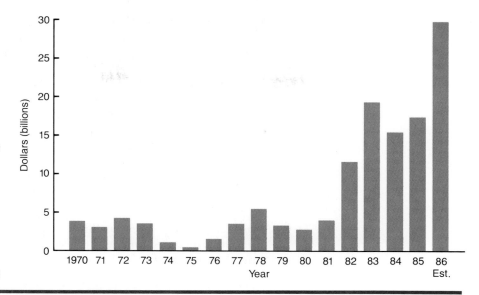

The Cost of Farm Price Supports
Government spending for the farm price-support program rose dramatically in the 1980s, and it is likely to continue to rise under the new farm law. These figures include spending for wheat, corn, other feed grains, rice, soybeans, peanuts, sugar, cotton, dairy products, honey, wool, and mohair. (Copyright © 1986 by The New York Times Company. Reprinted by permission.)

Figure 16.5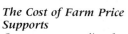

grains. Farmers held huge surpluses and could sell them only at depressed prices. Direct income subsidies protected the farmers from the effects of nature's bounty.

Let's continue with our wheat farming example. Recall that the loan rate for a bushel of wheat is $3.30. Now suppose that the government determines that the national average cost for producing a bushel of wheat is $4.38; it sets that as its *target price*. You have taken a "loan" of $33,000 from the government in exchange for 10,000 bushels of wheat. You would also receive a direct income subsidy payment from the government for the difference between the target price of $4.38 per bushel and the loan rate of $3.30 per bushel. This would add another $10,800 to your bank account, to cover your costs of production and to help feed, clothe, and care for your family. Of course, you would not receive the subsidy if the market price rose above the target price; but then you would not have taken the government loan either. In effect, direct income subsidies protect farmers against losses that result from increased production costs; they are a form of public assistance to farmers, paid from general tax revenues.

The same tax revenue that pays for Medicaid, food stamps, and AFDC benefits pays for direct income subsidies and price supports. A third farm program — production controls — shifts some costs from the taxpayer to the consumer.

Production controls are agreements that call for farmers to plant less of a particular crop. Smaller plantings mean smaller harvests, so that demand for the crop will force the price to rise; and the higher price is paid directly by the consumer who purchases the product. Production controls are voluntary agreements, but only farmers who are willing to limit production are eligible for direct income subsidies and price supports. Freedom in this case becomes a gamble, and most farmers opt for the protection of government farm programs.

Some Consequences of Farm Policy

According to the many variations of "Murphy's Law," if something can go wrong, it will. American agriculture in the 1980s was an apt demonstration of that truth: everything that could go wrong, did. A world recession reduced international demand for U.S. crops. At the same time, the value of the dollar soared, making American agricultural exports more expensive and less competitive. And foreign growers produced crop surpluses, which they marketed aggressively. As a result, America's share of the world agricultural market declined sharply.

Overproduction.   Congress reviews and modifies farm policy every four years. In retrospect, we can see that the price supports set in the 1981 farm policy were too high; they were much higher than the market prices for the basic farm commodities (see Feature 16.1). This led farmers to sell much of their output to the government at the higher support prices. Huge surpluses of farm commodities bulged from government storehouses. As an example, by 1983, the government was buying 10 percent of the milk produced in the United States at a cost of $3 billion; it was storing the equivalent of about 16 billion pounds of milk in the form of butter, cheese, and powdered milk. Even after donations to needy countries and to food assistance programs at home, the government still held in reserve a veritable mountain of butter.

Recall that the support price establishes a price floor for farmers. It also establishes a price ceiling for foreign competitors. The biggest market for American grains is outside the United States. But if the support price is high, American farmers would rather sell their grain to the government; at the

Getting out of hand

Feature 16.1

A Honey of a Deal

Established in 1949, the honey support program was designed to assure a sufficient supply of honeybees for pollinating the nation's fields and orchards. In the last decade, the program's costs have soared.

Under the program, commercial beekeepers receive loans from the Government at the rate of 65 cents a pound, using honey as collateral.

Since the Government price is higher than the wholesale price, now 40 cents a pound, beekeepers have found it profitable to forfeit on their loans and pay the Government back with honey.

This year beekeepers are expected to forfeit 115 million pounds of honey, costing the Government about $100 million in purchase and storage costs. The Agriculture Department recently estimated that only 1 percent of the nation's 211,000 beekeepers were receiving these support payments since most American beekeepers were hobbyists owning fewer than 25 hives.

As recently as 1980, when the market price for honey nearly equaled the Government price, the Government acquired just six million pounds at a cost of about $3 million.

Source: *New York Times*, November 23, 1985. Copyright © 1985 by The New York Times Company. Reprinted by permission.

same time, foreign competitors can more easily sell their grain at a price just below the support price, which makes their product more attractive to grain-importing nations. This is exactly what happened: the high support price encouraged the loss of foreign markets by American farmers.

High target prices in the 1980s also encouraged overproduction, since a bigger crop meant a fatter direct income subsidy check. Farmers overproduced, and their bumper crops increased the cost of the government farm program. Then, when the government stockpiles reached capacity and had to be sold, market prices fell. The government's loss from buying at high prices (from farmers) and selling low sent the actual cost of the farm policy to unexpected heights. Government economists had projected in 1981 that farm policy costs for 1983 to 1986 would be $11 billion. The actual costs exceeded $60 billion.

Government farm policy has encouraged overproduction to the point where farm production now far exceeds the market's ability to absorb it. It has been predicted that by 1989, American farmers will depend on the government for 70 percent of their net income, compared to about 25 percent in 1984.[27] As you will see, this outpouring of federal revenue forced a careful reexamination of farm policy in 1985.

Farm debt.   The government encouraged farmers to borrow in order to expand their operations, at the same time it was cushioning farmers from the effects of the market. From 1969 to 1981, farm land use expanded by 54 million acres. Farm techniques improved as well. And the federal government

Another Human Tragedy
The year 1986 will go down in American history as one of the most difficult and most painful that the American farmers have faced in recent times. Many farm families found themselves in the position of the family shown here, threatened with the loss of both home and livelihood as their farms were put up at auction.

subsidized farm borrowing, at rates below inflation through the 1970s. There seemed to be reason enough for expansion: a devaluation of the dollar made American farm products attractive and broadened foreign markets. Grain sales abroad were increasing. And economists predicted high prices and growing markets through the 1980s and beyond. Of course, farm expansion meant more debt, but larger farms held the promise of larger incomes. For many, the gamble appeared to be worth the risk.

But many of the farmers who expanded in the 1970s faced a severe credit crunch in the 1980s. Inflation dropped sharply. The government's encouragement of cultivation brought bumper harvests. From 1972 to 1982, the nation's corn crop burgeoned from 5.6 billion bushels to 8.4 billion bushels. American farmers, dependent on foreign markets for sales of one-half to two-thirds of their products, ended up with monster surpluses and mountainous debts.

Despite their bountiful harvests, many farmers could not generate enough income to cover their loans or mortgages. The value of farm land, which depends on the income it produces, slid downward. Because they were deeply in debt, farmers had trouble getting operating loans with which to buy seed and fertilizer for planting; their devalued land could barely serve as collateral. By the mid-1980s, the interest owed to banks by farmers had grown to $21 billion per year, whereas total farm income reached only $23 billion. Foreclosure and ruin seemed a certainty for many, especially younger farmers who had bought land when prices were high and could no longer borrow enough money to sustain their operations. Some farmers, like the Jessens, swallowed their pride and turned to public assistance, including food stamps, in an effort to hold on to their way of life.

A New Direction?

Given the many failures of the 1981 farm policy, it was clear that Congress would carefully rethink the status quo in 1985. The prospect of a new farm policy attracted lobbies of every stripe, including groups representing chicken producers, hog farmers, pesticide manufacturers, supermarkets, and banks. It seemed that every group had a farm policy to present. Even the Fertilizer Institute, which represents 292 fertilizer manufacturing and distributing companies and had never had a farm policy in its entire 102-year history, had one in 1985.

The Reagan administration's farm plan called for the immediate elimination of price and income supports. The only way to break the spiral in which government spending causes overproduction which causes more spending was to withdraw government support for agriculture and return to a free market. At the opposite end, some farmers—a vocal minority—called for a farmer referendum to establish mandatory production controls. Prices would rise if production limits could be imposed equally on all farmers. But the only consensus that emerged from congressional hearings, debates, and lobbying was that the 1981 policy was not working. Juggling the old programs in new ways proved to be the only politically viable approach.

The 1985 Farm Security Act, approved by Congress in December 1985, headed in a new direction. The new farm bill was eleven months in gestation; it weighed in at a hefty 13 pounds. Congress took a step—but only a step —toward the free market advocated by President Reagan. First, price supports were lowered below market levels. This would ensure that farmers sold to markets, not to government. Second, income subsidies were maintained at their previous levels. Since these payments are geared to production, more farmers will receive bigger government checks than ever. And third, farmers were required to set aside 20 to 30 percent of their land to qualify for the subsidies. (This is not likely to reduce production, because farmers usually set aside their least productive land.)

The Farmers' Cause Takes Center Stage
Art came to imitate life in the 1980s as Hollywood took up the farmers' cause. Several ''save the farm'' movies (for example, Places in the Heart, Country, *and* The River) *depicted the farmers' grim plight. At a congressional hearing in Washington, actresses Jessica Lange (left), Jane Fonda (center), and Sissy Spacek (right) argued for government legislation to protect real farmers from financial ruin.*

In theory, the new farm policy aims to remove all government support of farming at some point in the future. In practice, government has lowered the floor but added some pillows. Lower support prices mean that government need not bear the burden of the market and that American farm products will be more competitive in world markets. For farmers, reduced support prices will be counterbalanced by heavier direct income subsidies — at least for the time being. But lower price supports will also mean that some farmers who expanded in the 1970s will be forced out of farming.

Government farm policy has now inched toward a free market. As a consequence of this shift, some farmers will be forced from a lifestyle that is envied by many Americans. One alternative is a return to policies by which government substitutes for the market, imposing order and security through its control of prices. By all accounts, however, that policy was at the core of America's farm crisis.[28] The other alternative is to mandate equitable production limits on all farmers, in an effort to boost prices. That alternative trades away freedom in return for order and equality. To deal responsibly with these conflicts is the challenge of democracy.

SUMMARY

Many domestic policies that provide benefits to individuals and promote economic equality were instituted during the Great Depression. Today, government plays an active role in providing benefits to the poor, the elderly, and the disabled. Such domestic policies aim to alleviate conditions that individuals are powerless to prevent. This is the social welfare function of the modern state.

Government confers benefits to individuals through social insurance and public assistance. Public assistance (welfare) hinges on proof of need; social insurance does not require a demonstration of need. In one form of social insurance — old-age benefits — a tax on workers pays the elderly's benefits. Aid for the poor comes from government's general tax revenues.

Programs to aid the elderly and the poor have been transformed into entitlements, which are rights that accrue to eligible persons. Some entitlements hinge on need, which is often defined in terms of income: persons with incomes below a given level satisfy the need condition. These government programs have reduced poverty, especially among the elderly. However, poverty retains a grip on the population, and it is creeping up to levels that Americans have not seen since the 1960s.

Farm policy today traces its roots to the New Deal and still involves three basic programs: price supports, direct income subsidies, and production controls. These also provide benefits that cushion farmers from the hazards of economic cycles, overproduction, high production costs, and (to an extent) foreign competition. These government farm programs encouraged overproduction and expansion at the same time that foreign markets were being claimed by foreign competitors. As a result, government ended up footing the bill for the nation's plenty. The newest farm policy is an attempt to free up the market for agricultural products.

Key Terms

welfare state
social welfare
economic depression
Great Depression
New Deal
Great Society
War on Poverty
social insurance
entitlements
social security

Social Security Act
Medicare
public assistance
poverty level
Aid to Families with Dependent
  Children (AFDC)
food stamp program
price supports
direct income subsidies
production controls

Selected Readings

Berry, Jeffrey M. *Feeding Hungry People: Rulemaking in the Food Stamp Program.* New Brunswick, N.J.: Rutgers University Press, 1984. A thorough examination of the evolution of the food stamp program and the relationships among Congress, the Department of Agriculture, and interest groups.

Ferrara, Peter J. *Social Security: The Inherent Contradiction.* San Francisco: The Cato Institute, 1980. Argues that the pay-as-you-go feature of Social Security inevitably clashes with the desirability of a savings policy.

Galston, William A. *A Tough Row to Hoe: The 1985 Farm Bill & Beyond.* Lanham, N.Y.: University Press of America, 1985. Provides an excellent overview of the problems and prospects of agricultural policy today.

Joe, Tom, and Cheryl Rogers. *By the Few for the Few.* Lexington, Mass.: Lexington Books, 1985. An engaging study of the changes in AFDC wrought by the Reagan administration, and the negative effects of those changes on incentives for welfare recipients to work.

Murray, Charles. *Losing Ground.* New York: Basic Books, 1985. A controversial assessment of American social policy from 1950 to 1980; argues that by attempting to remove the barriers to the good life for the poor, policymakers have created a poverty trap.

Schwarz, John E. *America's Hidden Success.* New York: Norton, 1983. A measured defense of the success of social policy from 1960 to 1980; argues the achievements of the Great Society and should be read in conjunction with Murray.

Starr, Paul. *The Social Transformation of American Medicine.* New York: Basic Books, 1982. The definitive work on the evolution of the American health care system of doctors, hospitals, health plans, and government programs.

17

Order and
Civil Liberties

C ountless generations of American Sunday school students have heard the story: "In the beginning God created the heaven and the earth." So says the Book of Genesis, in a story familiar to hundreds of millions of people around the world. The Genesis story of the sudden creation of the universe, energy, and life from nothingness is at the foundation of Christian and Judaic belief; with such broad appeal, it seems an unlikely subject for a legal battle. Yet in 1981 it was at the core of a dispute that pitted Arkansas' power to control its public school curriculum against the U.S. constitutional mandate that the government "shall make no law respecting an establishment of religion."

Arkansas had long been a stronghold of Christian fundamentalism, which adheres to a literal interpretation of the Bible and a belief in the infallibility of the Scriptures. Scientific advances, most notably Charles Darwin's theory of evolution, had challenged the fundamentalists' central premises. But with political might on their side, the fundamentalists were successful in legislating evolution out of the Arkansas public school curriculum through the mid-1960s. In 1968, however, Arkansas' forty-year-old antievolution statute was declared unconstitutional, and Darwin's theory entered Arkansas classrooms for the first time.[1]

Thirteen years later, the state of Arkansas attempted to return Genesis to its classrooms. In March 1981, Governor Frank D. White signed into law the Balanced Treatment for Creation-Science and Evolution-Science Act, following its speedy enactment by the Arkansas legislature. The upshot of this action was to require the teaching of the Book of Genesis, as "creation-science," in the Arkansas public schools, in order to balance the teaching of the Darwinian view, which the legislators labeled "evolution-science."

Shortly after the governor signed the act, it was challenged by Reverend Bill McLean and others representing students, teachers, and nonfundamentalist religious denominations. The challenge took place in the Federal District Court in Little Rock, where opponents of the act sought an injunction against the Arkansas Board of Education to prevent the enforcement of the law. (An **injunction** is a court order either compelling or constraining an action by an individual or a government.) McLean claimed that the new law violated the establishment of religion clause of the U.S. Constitution.

Throughout this nation's history, such cases have arisen over conflicts between basic values. Here the clash involved government-imposed order versus individual freedom. The Arkansas government had an interest in preserving social order (the established patterns of authority in society) through the control of public institutions—in this case, the public schools. In particular, the state wanted to direct the public school curriculum in a manner consistent with the religious beliefs of many (perhaps a majority) of its citizens. McLean had an interest in religious freedom and maintained that government may not impose any religious belief on its citizens. Obviously, the exercise of one interest would infringe on the exercise of the other. And, just as obviously, both sides had merit, because each defended a value we recognize as vital to democratic rule. In the American political system, such controversies are often resolved by the courts.

How well do the courts respond to these value clashes, which pit order against freedom in some cases and freedom against equality in others? Is any one of the values we have discussed — freedom, equality, or order — ever unconditional? In this chapter we shall explore some value conflicts that have been resolved by the judiciary. You should be able to judge from these cases and their decisions whether American government has met the challenge of democracy by finding the appropriate balance between freedom and order and between freedom and equality.

The value conflicts described in this chapter revolve around claims or entitlements that rest on law. In the case of *McLean* v. *Arkansas Board of Education,* McLean claimed his right to religious freedom was based on the Constitution itself. Arkansas' claim that it could direct the operation of its public schools rested on the very purpose of government—to maintain order. Although we shall concentrate on conflicts over constitutional issues, you should realize that the Constitution is not the only source of people's rights. Government can—and does—create rights through laws and regulations (see Feature 17.1).

We shall begin this chapter with the Bill of Rights and the role of the First Amendment in the original struggle — the conflict between freedom and order. Next we shall turn to the Fourteenth Amendment and the limits it placed on the states. Finally, in Chapter 18, we shall examine the Fourteenth Amendment's promise of equal protection, which sets the stage for the modern dilemma of government: the struggle between freedom and equality.

THE BILL OF RIGHTS

You may recall from Chapter 3 that the Constitutional Convention of 1787 did not add a list of individual liberties — a bill of rights — to the national government's charter. James Madison proposed a bill of rights, because "it will kill the opposition [to ratification] everywhere," but he privately referred to the addition of such restraints on the national government as the "nauseous project of amendments." During the ratification debates, it became clear that the omission of a bill of rights was the most important obstacle to the Constitution's adoption by the states.

The ten ratified amendments imposed limits on the national government but not on state governments. One of the amendments that failed to gain congressional approval sought to limit the *states'* infringement on the rights of conscience, press, speech, and jury trial in criminal cases. Madison regarded this proposed amendment as the "most valuable of the whole list," but it failed to muster the required two-thirds vote in the Senate. The Supreme Court was repeatedly pressed to extend the amendments' restraints to the states, but similar restrictions were not placed on state powers until the adoption of the Fourteenth Amendment in 1868. Until then, protection from repressive state governments had to come from state bills of rights.

The U.S. Constitution guarantees Americans a large constellation of rights and liberties, and in this chapter we explore a portion of this constellation. Two terms, *civil rights* and *civil liberties,* are often used interchangeably in this context, although their meanings differ. **Civil rights** are powers or privileges that are guaranteed to individuals and protected from arbitrary removal at the hands of the government or individuals. Two examples of civil rights are

Feature 17.1   *Up (and Down) in Smoke*

Though the Constitution is a significant source of rights, it is not the only source of citizen entitlements conferred by law. Government can confer rights through laws like the Civil Rights Act of 1964 or through regulations issued by federal agencies, such as the Civil Aeronautics Board (CAB), which regulated air travel until 1985 when it was abolished and many of its functions were transferred to other agencies. Which values conflict in the following example?

It was a variation on the "Three Little Pigs" at 15,000 feet. When the non-smoker huffed and the smokers puffed, the pilot brought their plane down.

Capt. Larry Kinsey was piloting Eastern Flight 1410 . . . when "an in-surrection" between smokers and nonsmokers led him to land the 8 A.M. shuttle flight from Washington to New York at the Baltimore-Washington Airport. . . . The problem developed when a [nonsmoking attorney from a Washington firm] was seated in the smoking section of the filled 727. While the plane was still on the ground, he demanded that his area be made non-smoking, and it was, but passengers in nearby seats were apparently not informed so they lit up. At that point, just about everyone fumed.

[A] spokesman for the airline said that the nonsmoker had first been offered a seat on the next flight. When he turned down that offer, and a call for a volunteer to change seats went unanswered, the nonsmoking section was expanded. The Civil Aeronautics Board has ruled that airlines must pro-vide enough seats in a nonsmoking section to accommodate all nonsmokers.

When the other passengers began smoking . . . the pilot ordered them to stop, but they refused.

"It was silly and childish," said a passenger. "I haven't seen a display like this since kindergarten. We had to land the plane and sort out everybody's dollies and metal toys."

After the nonsmoker threatened legal action against the airline because those around him were assaulting him with smoke, Captain Kinsey, the pilot, appealed to everyone's sense of reason. . . . By now, the plane was in the air. The pilot said if the situation remained unstable, he would land the plane at the nearest airport. And that is what he did.

Source: *New York Times*, December 6, 1979, p. 1. Copyright © 1979 by The New York Times Company. Reprinted by permission. Reprinted with permission, the Associated Press.

the right to vote and the right to trial in criminal cases. Today, civil rights have also come to include the goals of laws that further certain ideals. The Civil Rights Act of 1964, for example, furthered the ideal of equality by establishing the right to nondiscrimination in places of public accommoda-tions and the right to equal employment opportunity. We shall discuss civil rights and their ramifications in Chapter 18.

Civil liberties are freedoms that are guaranteed to individuals. These guarantees take the form of negative restraints on government. For example, the First Amendment declares that "Congress shall make no law abridg-ing . . . the freedom of speech." Such restraints declare what the government *cannot* do; in contrast, civil rights declare what the government *must* do or provide. Civil liberties are the subject matter of this chapter.

Actually, the Bill of Rights combines civil rights and civil liberties. When we refer to the rights and liberties of the Constitution, we shall mean the protections enshrined in the Bill of Rights: freedom of religion, of speech and the press, of assembly and petition; the rights of the criminally accused; the requirement of due process; and the equal protection of the laws. These rights and liberties are found in the first ten amendments to the Constitution and in the Fourteenth Amendment.[2]

FREEDOM OF RELIGION

> Congress shall make no law respecting an establishment of religion, or prohibiting the free exercise thereof.

Religious freedom was very important to the colonies (and, following independence, to the states) and that importance is reflected in its position in the Bill of Rights: first, in the very first amendment. Freedom of religion is guaranteed by the Constitution in two clauses. The first (called the **establishment clause**) forbids any law respecting the establishment of religion; the second (called the **free exercise clause**) prevents the government from interfering with the exercise of religion. Together they ensure that government can neither promote nor inhibit religious beliefs or practices. Note that these clauses restrain Congress from using a power that it never possessed; they do, however, explicitly express the absence of that power.

Carting Religious Freedom
Americans are a religious people. Court cases interpreting the establishment and free exercise clauses of the First Amendment stir deep feelings. Religious and nonreligious minorities, such as the Amish and the atheists, have frequently served as standard bearers for these two interrelated but sometimes conflicting constitutional guarantees.

Freedom to follow one's faith was a central force in the colonization of America. Nevertheless, in 1789 several state constitutions expressed a bond between religion and government. Delaware, for example, required its citizens to affirm the doctrine of the Trinity; and four states (New Hampshire, Massachusetts, Connecticut, and South Carolina) insisted on a belief in Protestantism.[3] In 1787, many Americans, especially in New England, maintained that government could and should foster religion, certainly Protestantism. Many more Americans were in agreement, however, that this was a state government issue and that the federal government possessed no authority to meddle in religious affairs. The religion clauses were drafted in this spirit.[4] But, as in the case of many other constitutional provisions, the Supreme Court has avoided absolute interpretations of the religion clauses. Thus, freedom to believe is unlimited, but freedom to *practice* a belief may be limited. Direct governmental benefits to religion are forbidden, but indirect governmental benefits for religious activities with secular purposes are permitted. For example, government contributions to churches and synagogues confer direct benefits to religion. Books on nonreligious subjects purchased by government for use in all schools — public, private, and parochial — confer indirect benefits.

Americans are a religious people. You may recall from Chapter 5 that America ranks first among eleven major industrialized nations in the proportion of its citizens who believe in God (see Compared With What? 5.1, p. 169). Since the overwhelming majority of Americans are religious, majoritarian theorists could argue that government support for religion is permissible. These critics would agree that the establishment clause should be interpreted as barring government support of a *single* faith, but they might also maintain that government should support all religions. Such support, according to majoritarian theorists, would be consistent with the wishes of the majority and true to the language of the Constitution. The Court has rejected this kind of reasoning and, in the process, has been tarred with the claim that it undermines democracy. This criticism may be true with regard to majoritarian democracy, but the freedom protected by the Supreme Court can be justified in terms of the basic values of democratic government.

The Establishment Clause

The provision that "Congress shall make no law respecting an establishment of religion" bars government sponsorship or support of religious activity. The Supreme Court has consistently affirmed that the establishment clause requires government to maintain a position of neutrality toward religions and in cases that involve choices between religion and nonreligion. However, the clause has never been held to bar all assistance that incidentally aids religious institutions. In this section, we shall consider the application of the clause to public support for parochial education and for religion in general, to prayer in the public schools, and to curricula encouraging biblical instruction.

Government support of religion. In 1879 the Supreme Court contended, in Jefferson's words, that the establishment clause erected "a wall of separation between church and state." By 1947 the justices appeared to breach the wall, when they upheld a local government program providing free transportation to parochial school students.[5] The breach seemed to widen in 1968, when the Court sustained as constitutional a government program in which state-purchased textbooks were loaned to parochial school students.[6] The program's purpose, reasoned the majority, was to further educational opportunity. The loan was made to the students, not to the schools, and the benefits were realized by the parents, not by the church.

Government aid to church schools has limits, however. In **Lemon v. Kurtzman** (1971),[7] the Supreme Court struck down a state program authorizing parochial schools' purchase of secular services, such as salaries for teachers hired to give instruction in secular subjects. The justices proposed a three-pronged test for constitutionality under the establishment clause: the questioned statute must have a secular legislative purpose, such as lending books to parochial school students; its primary effect must not be the advancing or inhibiting of religion; and it must not involve the government in an excessive entanglement with religion. A law missing any prong would be unconstitutional. The program in the *Lemon* case failed on the last ground: the state would have to constantly monitor the teachers it financed, to ensure that they did not include religious instruction in their secular lessons. For example, the state would be required to monitor mathematics lessons to ensure that the instruction did not reinforce religious dogma. But such supervision would entangle the government in religious activity, violating the Constitution's prohibition.

Does the display of religious artifacts on public property violate the establishment clause? In *Lynch* v. *Donnelly* (1984),[8] the Court upheld, by a vote of 5 to 4, placing a publicly funded Christmas Nativity scene on public property, surrounded by commercial symbols of the Christmas season (for example, Santa and his sleigh). While conceding that the creche had religious significance, Chief Justice Warren E. Burger, writing for the majority, maintained that the display did fit within a legitimate secular purpose: the celebration of a national holiday. Second, the display did not have the primary effect of benefiting religion; the religious benefits were "indirect, remote and incidental." And, third, the display led to no excessive entanglement between religion and government. The justices hinted at relaxation of the establishment clause by asserting their "unwillingness to be confined to any single test or criterion in this sensitive area." The upshot of the Nativity scene case was an "acknowledgment" of the religious heritage of the majority of Americans, even though the Christmas holiday is a vivid reminder to religious minorities of their separateness from the dominant Christian culture. Government risks social disruption in supporting the dominant faith, thus reinforcing feelings of alienation among minority faiths and the nonreligious.

School prayer. The Supreme Court has consistently viewed prayer in public schools as government encouragement of religion. In 1962 it struck down the daily reading of the following twenty-two-word, nondenominational prayer in New York's public schools:

> Almighty God, we acknowledge our dependence upon Thee, and we beg Thy blessings upon us, our parents, our teachers, and our country.

Justice Hugo L. Black, speaking for a 6-to-1 majority, held that official state approval of prayer was an unconstitutional attempt on the part of government to establish a religion. This decision, in *Engle* v. *Vitale*,[9] drew a storm of protest.

The following year, the Court struck down a state law calling for daily Bible reading and recitation of the Lord's Prayer in the Pennsylvania public schools.[10] The readings and recitation were defended on the grounds that they taught literature, perpetuated traditional institutions, and inculcated moral virtues. Nevertheless, the Court held that the state's involvement violated the government's constitutionally imposed neutrality in matters of religion. Given the degree of religious sentiment in the United States, the burden on individual children on whose behalf such unpopular suits are brought can be overwhelming.

New challenges on the issue of school prayer continue to find their way to the Supreme Court; each is a reminder of the pluralist nature of American democracy. Access to the courts can vent widely held and strongly felt religious convictions. But government risks disorder when it continually frustrates strongly held majority views. The outcomes offer little immediate comfort to the majority of Americans who favor school prayer.

If the Constitution bars school prayer, does it also bar silent meditation in school? In *Jaffree* v. *Wallace*, decided in 1985, the Court struck down a series of Alabama statutes requiring elementary school teachers to observe a moment of silence for meditation or voluntary prayer at the beginning of each school day.[11] In a 6-to-3 decision, the Court renewed its use of the "*Lemon* test" and reaffirmed the principle of government neutrality between religion and nonreligion. The Court found that the purpose of the statutes was to endorse religion; however, a majority of the justices hinted that a straightforward moment-of-silence statute that steered clear of religious endorsements might pass constitutional muster.

Creation-science and evolution-science. In the introduction to this chapter, we discussed the case of *McLean* v. *Arkansas Board of Education* but did not give you the decision. In early 1982, following a ten-day trial in which scientists and philosophers testified on both sides, Federal District Judge William Ray Overton ruled that the Arkansas law violated the establishment clause.[12] Overton concluded that creation science was inspired solely by the Book of Genesis and had no scientific foundation.

The law failed the first part of the prevailing *Lemon* test: its primary purpose was to advance fundamentalist beliefs. Although a significant majority of Americans believe that creation science should be taught, or at least do not oppose such teaching in the public schools, Overton captured the purpose of the protections enshrined in the Bill of Rights. "The application and content of First Amendment principles are not determined by public opinion polls or by a majority vote. . . . No group, no matter how large or small, may use the organs of government, of which the public schools are the most conspicuous and influential, to foist its religious beliefs on others."[13]

Under the establishment clause, a neutral position between religion and nonreligion may prove to be the most difficult to maintain. Toleration of the

Papal Prayers on Public Property
In 1979, Pope John Paul conducted the largest religious ceremony ever held in the United States when he said Mass for 1.5 million people in Chicago's Grant Park. Advocates holding absolute positions on the First Amendment were at odds: the free exercise clause warranted the activity, but the establishment clause argued against it. The judiciary continues to struggle with the delicate and emotional issue of religion in American life.

dominant religion at the expense of other religions risks *minority* discontent, but support for no religion (neutrality between religion and nonreligion) risks *majority* discontent. Support for all religions at the expense of nonreligion poses the least risk for the maintenance of order.

The Free Exercise Clause

The free exercise clause of the First Amendment states that "Congress shall make no law . . . prohibiting the free exercise [of religion]." The Supreme Court has struggled to avoid absolute interpretations of this restriction so as not to violate its complement, the establishment clause. Suppose that Congress grants exemptions from military service to individuals who have religious scruples against participation in war. Such actions could be construed as violating the establishment clause by favoring some religious groups over others. But if Congress required military service for these conscientious objectors, government would run afoul of the free exercise clause by forcing the objectors to engage in activities violating their religious beliefs.

In free exercise cases, the justices have distinguished religious beliefs from actions based on such beliefs. Beliefs are inviolate and thus beyond the reach of government control; but antisocial actions are not protected by the First Amendment.

Saluting the flag. Government compulsion clashed with religious freedom in 1940, when the Court considered the first of two cases involving compulsory flag saluting in the public schools. In *Minersville School District* v. *Gobitis*,[14] a group of Jehovah's Witnesses challenged the compulsory flag salute on the ground that the action forced them to worship graven images, which their faith forbids. Government order won in an 8-to-1 decision. The "mere possession of religious convictions," wrote Justice Felix Frankfurter, "which contradict the relevant concerns of a political society does not relieve the citizen from the discharge of political responsibilities."

Three years later, however, the Court reversed this policy in ***West Virginia State Board of Education v. Barnette***.[15] This time, the Court saw a larger issue: whether anyone could be compelled to salute the flag against his or her will. The *Gobitis* case was decided on the narrower issue of religious belief versus the flag salute. In *Barnette*, the justices chose instead to focus on the broader issue of freedom of expression, overriding the salute. In stirring language, Justice Robert H. Jackson argued in the majority opinion that no one could be compelled by the government to declare any belief.

> If there is any fixed star in our constitutional constellation, it is that no official, high or petty, can prescribe what shall be orthodox in politics, nationalism, religion, or other matters of opinion or force citizens to confess by word or act their faith therein. If there are any circumstances which permit an exception, they do not now occur to us.[16]

Drugs as sacrament. The use of hallucinogenic drugs as part of the religious sacrament raises yet another type of free exercise problem. The Supreme Court has never provided a definitive statement on the issue, but some guidance can be found in state court decisions. For example, the California Supreme Court held in 1964 that the use of peyote (an illegal but nonaddictive hallucinogen) was central to the ritual of Navajo Indians who were members of the Native American Church of California.[17] In that case, the court weighed the free exercise of religion against the state's interest in maintaining order and protecting the Navajo community. It found that "the scale tips in favor of the constitutional guarantee."

The issue of drugs as sacrament involves other cults as well. The Rastafarians and members of the Ethiopian Zion Coptic Church smoke marijuana in the belief that it is the body and blood of Christ. Obviously, the freedom to practice religion, taken to an extreme, can be used as a license for illegal conduct. But even when such practices stem from deeply felt convictions, government resistance to such activities is understandable, and the result is inevitably a clash between religious freedom and social order.

The Supreme Court does not take an absolute view on the meanings of rights and liberties; to do so would create unsolvable problems between the government and its citizens. Consider, for example, the 1983 religious rally held for Pope John Paul in Chicago's Grant Park. In the absolutist view, Chicago would be required to permit the rally under the free exercise clause of the First Amendment; simultaneously, under the establishment clause, the city would have to prohibit the holding of that rally on public property. Since a rally cannot be both held and not held, courts have struggled with solutions that avoid immobility and divisiveness.

FREEDOM OF EXPRESSION

> Congress shall make no law . . . abridging the freedom of speech, or of the press.

The initial versions of the **speech clause** and the **press clause** of the First Amendment were introduced by James Madison in the House of Representatives on June 8, 1789. One of these early proposals provided that "the people shall not be deprived of their right to speak, to write, or to publish their sentiments, and the freedom of the press, as one of the great bulwarks of liberty, shall be inviolable." That version was rewritten several times and then merged with the religion clauses to yield the First Amendment that we recognize today.

The original House debates on the proposed speech and press clauses are uninformative. There is no record of debate in the Senate or in the states during the ratification stage. But careful analysis of the records of the period supports the view that the press clause prohibited only the imposition of **prior restraint,** or censorship before publication. Publishers could not claim protection from punishment if works that had already been published were later deemed improper, mischievous, or illegal.

The sparse language of the First Amendment seems perfectly clear: "Congress shall make no law . . . abridging the freedom of speech, or of the press." Yet a majority of the Supreme Court has never agreed that this "most majestic guarantee" is absolutely inviolable.[18] Historians have long debated the framers' intentions regarding the **free expression clauses.** The dominant view is that the clauses confer the right to unrestricted discussion of public affairs.[19] Other scholars, examining much the same evidence, concluded that few, if any, of the framers clearly understood the clause; moreover, prosecution for seditious statements (statements inciting to insurrection) was not ruled out by the First Amendment.[20]

The passage of the national government's Sedition Act of 1798 lends credibility to the latter claim. The act punished "false, scandalous and malicious writings against the government of the United States," seemingly in direct conflict with the new free expression clauses. President John Adams's administration used the Sedition Act in 1798 to punish its political opponents for expressing contempt of the government and its public officials. Thomas Jefferson and his allies in turn attacked Adams's use of the act and supported a broad view of the protection afforded by the First Amendment. The libertarian view represented by Jefferson and his supporters serves as the basis for the modern perspective on the First Amendment free expression clauses. Today, the clauses are deemed to bar most forms of prior restraint (which is consistent with the initial understanding). In addition, according to the current interpretation, they also bar after-the-fact prosecution for political and other discourse.

The Supreme Court has evolved two approaches to the resolution of claims based on the free expression clauses. First, government can regulate or punish the advocacy of ideas, but only if it can prove that such advocacy is both "directed to inciting or producing imminent lawless action" and "likely to produce such action." And, second, government can impose reasonable restrictions on the *flow* of ideas and, consequently, discourage or limit the communication of ideas.

Suppose, for example, that a political party advocates unilateral disarmament as part of its campaign. Government cannot regulate or punish that party for advocating unilateral disarmament because the standards of proof — that the act be directed to inciting or producing imminent lawless action and that the act be judged likely to produce such action — do not apply. But government can impose restrictions on the way those candidates communicate what they are advocating — for example, by blaring their campaign messages from loudspeakers in residential neighborhoods at 3 A.M. We concentrate on the development of the first approach in this chapter.

To return to the Adams case, the fines imposed on Adams's critics under the Sedition Act were later repaid by an act of Congress, and President Thomas Jefferson, Adams's successor, pardoned those who had been convicted and sentenced under the law. But far subtler restrictions on free expression were sewn into the fabric of American society. As Mark Twain once remarked, "The American people enjoy three great blessings — free speech, free press and the good sense not to use either."[21]

Freedom of Speech

The starting point for any modern analysis of free speech is the **clear and present danger test** formulated by Justice Oliver Wendell Holmes in the Supreme Court's unanimous decision in *Schenck* v. *United States* (1919).[22] Schenck and his fellow defendants were convicted under a federal criminal statute for attempting to disrupt World War I military recruitment by distributing leaflets claiming that conscription was unconstitutional. The government viewed such behavior as threatening to public order. At the core of the Court's opinion, Holmes wrote:

> The character of every act depends upon the circumstances in which it is done. . . . The most stringent protection of free speech would not protect a man in falsely shouting fire in a theatre and causing a panic. . . . The question in every case is whether the words used are used in such circumstances and are of such a nature as to create a *clear and present danger* that they will bring about the substantive evils that Congress has a right to prevent. It is a question of proximity and degree. When a nation is at war many things that might be said in time of peace are such a hindrance to its effort that their utterance will not be endured so long as men fight and that no Court could regard them as protected by any constitutional right [emphasis added].[23]

Because the anticonscription actions of the defendants in the Schenck trial were deemed to create a clear and present danger to the United States at that time, the defendants' convictions were upheld. Holmes himself later frequently disagreed with a majority of his colleagues in applying his "clear and present danger" test. The test helps to distinguish advocacy of ideas, which is protected, from incitement, which is not protected.

In an oft-quoted dissent in *Abrams* v. *United States* (1919), Holmes revealed his deeply rooted resistance to the suppression of ideas. The majority had upheld criminal convictions for leaflet distribution denouncing the war and U.S. opposition to the Russian Revolution. Holmes wrote:

> When men have realized that time has upset many fighting faiths, they may come to believe even more than they believe the very foundations of their own

conduct that the ultimate good desired is better reached by free trade in ideas—that the best test of truth is the power of the thought to get itself accepted in the competition of the market, and that truth is the only ground upon which their wishes safely can be carried out. That at any rate is the theory of our Constitution.[24]

In 1925 the Court issued a landmark decision in *Gitlow v. New York*.[25] Gitlow was arrested for distributing copies of a "Left Wing Manifesto" calling for the establishment of socialism by strikes and class action in any form. Gitlow was convicted under a *state* criminal anarchy law; Schenck and Abrams had been convicted under a *federal* law. A majority of the justices affirmed Gitlow's conviction, holding that the First Amendment speech and press provisions applied to the states through the due process clause of the Fourteenth Amendment. Justices Holmes and Louis D. Brandeis argued in dissent that Gitlow's ideas did not pose a clear and present danger. "Eloquence may set fire to reason," conceded the dissenters. "But whatever may be thought of the redundant discourse before us, it had no chance of starting a present conflagration."

The protection of advocacy faced yet another challenge in 1948 when eleven members of the Communist party were charged with violating the Smith Act—a federal law making the advocacy of force or violence against the United States a criminal offense. The leaders were convicted, although the government introduced no evidence that they actually urged people to commit specific violent acts. Although the Supreme Court mustered a majority for its decision to uphold the convictions under the act, it could not get a majority to agree on the reasons in support of that decision. The largest bloc of four justices announced the plurality opinion in 1951, arguing that the government's interest was substantial enough to warrant criminal penalties. The justices interpreted the threat to government to be the gravity of the advocated action, "discounted by its improbability." In other words, a single, soap-box orator advocating revolution stands a low chance of success. But a well-organized and highly disciplined political movement advocating revolution in the tinderbox of world conditions stands a greater chance of success. In broadening the meaning of a clear and present danger, the Court held that the government was justified in acting preventively rather than waiting until the revolution is about to occur.[26]

By 1969, however, the pendulum had swung back in the other direction, and the justices began to show a stronger preference for freedom. That year, in *Brandenburg v. Ohio*, a unanimous Supreme Court decision extended the freedom of speech to new limits. Clarence Brandenburg, the leader of the Ohio Ku Klux Klan, had been convicted under an Ohio statute for remarks he made at a Klan rally. His remarks, which had been filmed by a television crew invited to cover the meeting, included threats against government officials.

The Court reversed Brandenburg's conviction because the government failed to prove that the danger was real, not imaginary. The Court went even further and declared that threatening speech is protected by the First Amendment unless the government can prove that the goal is to produce lawless action and that a high probability exists that such action will occur.[27] The ruling offered wider latitude for the expression of political ideas than ever before in the nation's history.

Symbolic Expression

Symbolic expression, or nonverbal communication, generally receives less protection than pure speech. One form of symbolic expression that was protected by the Constitution is illustrated by ***Tinker v. Des Moines Independent County School District*** (1969), a case in which three public school students wore black armbands to school to protest the Vietnam War.[28] Principals in their school district had prohibited the wearing of armbands on the ground that such conduct would provoke a disturbance, and the students were suspended from school. The Supreme Court overturned the suspensions. Justice Abe Fortas declared for the majority that the principals had failed to show that the forbidden conduct would substantially interfere with appropriate school discipline.

> Undifferentiated fear or apprehension is not enough to overcome the right to freedom of expression. Any departure from absolute regimentation may cause trouble. Any variation from the majority's opinion may inspire fear. Any word spoken, in class, in the lunchroom, or on the campus, that deviates from the

---

Hair Today, Hawk Tomorrow
Schools and other public institutions sometimes seek to regulate matters of personal choice. According to some people, hair styles should not be subject to government control because they are forms of symbolic expression. Some courts — although not the Supreme Court — have held that hair styles may contain elements of nonverbal communication (expressions of nonconformity), thus raising questions about First Amendment protection.

views of another person may start an argument or cause a disturbance. But our Constitution says we must take this risk.[29]

Dress codes and hairstyles, especially in the 1960s and 1970s, have provoked several constitutional challenges, but the Supreme Court has avoided decision in these areas. Public school and state college authorities have maintained that such regulations are essential to the control of their institutions. Students have argued that personal appearance is a form of symbolic expression protected from government by the Constitution. The U.S. courts of appeals remain divided on personal appearance codes. Some courts of appeals have held that hair length rules are unconstitutional unless the school can prove that a particular hairstyle disrupts the educational process. Other courts of appeals have held that the length of a student's hair falls outside constitutional protections. But in case after case, the Supreme Court has declined to grant review on the personal appearance issue, casting nonconformity and school authority in perpetual uncertainty.

A free speech exception: Fighting words. "Fighting words" are a notable exception to the protection of free speech. In *Chaplinsky* v. *New Hampshire* (1942), a Jehovah's Witness was convicted under a state statute for calling a city marshal a "God-damned racketeer" and "a damned fascist" in a public place. The Supreme Court upheld Chaplinsky's conviction on the theory that **fighting words** — utterances that "inflict injury or tend to incite an immediate breach of the peace" — do not convey ideas and thus are not subject to First Amendment protection.

The definition of *fighting words* was made much more exclusive just seven years later. Father Arthur Terminiello, a vicious anti-Semite and suspended Catholic priest from Alabama, addressed the Christian Veterans of America, a right-wing extremist group, in a Chicago hall. The packed audience inside heard Father Terminiello call the jeering crowd of 1,500 angry protesters outside the hall "slimy scum," while he ranted on about the "Communistic Zionistic" Jews of America, evoking cries of "kill the Jews" and "dirty kikes" from his listeners. The crowd outside the hall heaved bottles, bricks, and rocks, while the police attempted to protect Terminiello and his listeners inside. Finally, the police arrested Terminiello for breaching the peace.

Terminiello's speech was far more serious than Chaplinsky's. Yet the Supreme Court struck down Terminiello's conviction on the ground that provocative speech, even speech that stirs people to anger, is protected by the First Amendment. "Freedom of speech," wrote Justice William O. Douglas in the majority opinion, "though not absolute . . . is nevertheless protected against censorship or punishment, unless shown likely to produce a clear and present danger of serious substantive evil that rises far above public inconvenience, annoyance, or unrest."[30]

This broad view of speech protection brought a stiff rebuke in Justice Robert O. Jackson's dissenting opinion:

> The choice is not between order and liberty. It is between liberty with order and anarchy without either. There is danger that, if the Court does not temper its doctrinaire logic with a little practical wisdom, it will convert the constitutional Bill of Rights into a suicide pact.[31]

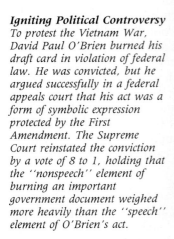

Igniting Political Controversy
To protest the Vietnam War, David Paul O'Brien burned his draft card in violation of federal law. He was convicted, but he argued successfully in a federal appeals court that his act was a form of symbolic expression protected by the First Amendment. The Supreme Court reinstated the conviction by a vote of 8 to 1, holding that the ''nonspeech'' element of burning an important government document weighed more heavily than the ''speech'' element of O'Brien's act.

The times seem to have caught up with the idealism that Jackson criticized in his colleagues. In *Cohen v. California* (1971), a nineteen-year-old department store employee sought to express his opposition to the Vietnam War. He wore a jacket emblazoned with ''FUCK THE DRAFT. STOP THE WAR.'' The young man, Paul Cohen, was charged in 1968 under a California statute which prohibits ''maliciously and willfully disturb[ing] the peace and quiet of any neighborhood or person [by] offensive conduct.'' He was found guilty and sentenced to thirty days in jail. On appeal to the U.S. Supreme Court, Cohen's conviction was reversed. The Court reasoned that the expletive he used, while provocative, was not directed toward anyone; besides, there was no evidence that people in ''substantial numbers'' would be provoked into physical contact by Cohen's actions. In recognizing that ''one man's vulgarity is another's lyric,'' the Court protected two elements of speech: the emotive (the expression of emotion) and the cognitive (the expression of ideas).[32]

Another exception: Obscenity.   Obscene material—otherwise known as ''dirty'' words, books, magazines, films, or such—is entirely excluded from constitutional protection.[33] This exclusion rests on the Supreme Court's review of historical evidence surrounding freedom of expression at the time of the Constitution's adoption. The Court observed that blasphemy, profanity, and obscenity were colonial crimes, but obscenity was not a developed area of the law at the time of the adoption of the Bill of Rights. Difficulties arise, however, in determining what is obscene and what is not. Justice William Brennan Jr. defined obscene material as that which ''deals with sex in a manner appealing to the prurient interest.''[34] But the identity of obscenity has proved elusive; no objective definition seems adequate. Justice Potter Stewart will long be remembered for his solution to the problem of identifying obscene materials. He declared that he could not define it. "But," he added, "I know it when I see it."[35]

In its last major attempt to clarify constitutional standards governing obscenity, the Court declared that a work—play, film, or book—is obscene and may be regulated by government if the work taken as a whole appeals to the prurient interest; the work portrays sexual conduct in a patently offensive way; and, taken as a whole, the work lacks serious literary, artistic, political, or scientific value (*Miller* v. *California*, 415 U.S. 15, 1973). Local community standards, not national standards, would govern the determination. Through this last stipulation, the Court tried to free itself from the nagging problem of reviewing state court obscenity findings; but the justices also recognized that judicial review is essential to prevent "unbridled discretion" in obscenity determinations.[36]

Freedom of the Press

The First Amendment guarantees that government "shall make no law . . . abridging the freedom . . . of the press." Although it was adopted as a restriction on the national government, the free press guarantee has been held since 1925 to apply to state and local government as well.

The ability to collect and report information without government interference was (and still is) regarded as being at the core of a free society. The print media continue to use and defend this freedom, which was conferred on them by the framers. The electronic media must, however, accept government regulation that stems from the scarcity of broadcast frequencies.

Defamation of character. **Libel** is the written defamation of character.* A person who believes his or her name and character have been harmed by false statements in a publication can institute a lawsuit against the publication and seek monetary compensation for the damage. Such lawsuits can impose limits on freedom of expression. At the same time, however, false statements may impinge on the rights of individuals. In a landmark decision, in **New York Times Co. v. Sullivan** (1964),[37] the Supreme Court declared that freedom of the press takes precedence—at least when the defamed individual is a public official. The Court unanimously agreed that the First Amendment prohibits punishment for publishing statements, even false ones, about the official conduct of public officials except when such statements are made with actual malice (with knowledge that they are false or in reckless disregard of their truth or falsity). Citing John Stuart Mill's 1859 essay "On Liberty," the Court declared that "Even a false statement may be deemed to make a valuable contribution to public debate, since it brings about 'the clearer perception and livelier impression of truth, produced by its collision with error'. "

Three years later, the Court extended this protection to include suits brought by any public figures, whether or not they are public officials. **Public figures** are people who assume roles of prominence in the affairs of society or who thrust themselves to the forefront of public controversy—including

---

Slander is the oral defamation of character. The durability of the written word usually means that libel is a more serious accusation than slander.

officials, actors, writers, television personalities, and others. These people must show that there was actual malice if they are to punish publishers who print false statements about them.

Two interesting lawsuits that applied these libel standards against public figures in 1985 demonstrate the special protection of the press under the First Amendment. Israeli general Ariel Sharon sued *Time* magazine for $50 million in damages in a libel suit. *Time* claimed that an Israeli commission had found that Sharon played a part in the 1982 massacre of Palestinian civilians in Lebanon. Sharon convinced the six-member jury that the magazine statement was defamatory and that the statement was false, but he failed to convince the jury that *Time* had lied or acted recklessly. Although the magazine statements were false, this was insufficient for Sharon to win a libel judgment.

American general William C. Westmoreland had to overcome tougher odds. In 1982, CBS broadcast a documentary charging Westmoreland with under-reporting enemy troop strength during the Vietnam War. (Westmoreland was commander of American forces in Vietnam from 1964 to 1968.) Westmoreland sued CBS for libel and sought $120 million in damages. He had to prove that the program was false and that CBS acted with reckless disregard of the truth or falsity of its claims. After two and a half years of litigation and an eighteen-week trial, Westmoreland abandoned his suit when he realized that he could not prove that the charges against him were false. Few plaintiffs prevail because the burden of proof they must carry is so great. Press freedom is the beneficiary.

Prior restraint and the press. In the United States, freedom of the press has meant primarily immunity from prior restraint, or censorship. The Supreme Court's first encounter with a law imposing prior restraint on a newspaper was in *Near* v. *Minnesota* (1931).[38] Jay Near—as abusive and obnoxious a hero as one could imagine—published a scandal sheet in Minneapolis, in which he attacked local officials, charging that they were implicated with gangsters.[39] Minnesota officials had obtained an injunction to prevent Near from publishing his newspaper under a state law permitting such actions against periodicals deemed "malicious, scandalous, and defamatory."

The Supreme Court struck down the law, declaring that prior restraints are a special burden on a free press. The need for a vigilant and unrestrained press was expressed forcefully by Chief Justice Charles Evans Hughes: "The fact that the liberty of the press may be abused by miscreant purveyors of scandal does not make any the less necessary the immunity of the press from previous restraint in dealing with official misconduct."[40] The Court recognized that prior restraint may be permissible in exceptional circumstances, but it did not specify those circumstances. Nor has it yet done so, although the Court was sorely pressed in two modern cases involving prior restraint.

The first of these cases occurred in a time of war, a period when the tension between government order and individual freedom often tends to peak. In 1971 Daniel Ellsberg, a special assistant in the Pentagon's Office of International Security Affairs, delivered portions of a classified Defense Department study to the *New York Times* and the *Washington Post*. By making the documents public, he hoped to discredit the Vietnam War and thereby end it. The highly secret study documented the history of U.S. involvement

Stamp Out Secrecy!
In 1971, Daniel Ellsberg transmitted classified documents on U.S. involvement in Vietnam to the New York Times *and the* Washington Post. *The Federal Employees for Peace awarded him this ''declassified'' stamp for really big jobs. The government awarded him an indictment for theft of government property and for violation of the Espionage Act. Two years later, however, a federal judge dismissed the indictment after the Watergate investigation disclosed that the government had wiretapped Ellsberg's phone and that the CIA had sponsored a burglary of Ellsberg's former psychiatrist to obtain his files.*

in the war. The Justice Department sought to restrain the *Times* and the *Post* from publishing the documents, contending that publication would prolong the war and become a diplomatic embarrassment. The case was quickly brought before the Supreme Court, which delayed its summer adjournment to hear oral argument.

Three days later, in its 6-to-3 decision in **New York Times v. United States** (1971),[41] the Supreme Court concluded that the government had not met the heavy burden of proving that immediate, inevitable, and irreparable harm would follow publication. The majority's view was expressed in a brief, unsigned *per curiam* (Latin for ''by the Court'') opinion, although individual and collective concurring and dissenting views added nine opinions to the decision. Two justices maintained that the First Amendment offered absolute protection against government trespass, no matter what the situation. But the other justices again left the door ajar for the imposition of prior restraint, if only in the most extreme and compelling circumstances. The result was hardly a ringing endorsement of press freedom; nor was it a full affirmation of the public's right to all the information that is vital to the debating of public issues.

In the second case, a Wisconsin federal district court issued an order preventing a monthly magazine, *The Progressive*, from publishing technical material concerning the production of a hydrogen bomb. The material was far from a do-it-yourself guide to thermonuclear weaponry, and the publisher maintained that the article merely combined information that was available in public documents. Nevertheless, the district judge found that the article contained concepts vital to the operation of the bomb, and that these concepts were not in the public domain. Thus, the nation's first imposition of prior restraint against a publication was accomplished. The judge reasoned that a mistake in ruling against the government would far outweigh a mistake in ruling against the magazine: a mistake "against the United States would pave the way for thermonuclear annihilation for us all. In that event, our right to life is extinguished and the right to publish becomes moot."[42] Unfortunately, the dispute never reached the Supreme Court. The legal proceedings against the magazine were abandoned because similar information on nuclear weapons was published by other periodicals.

Press freedom versus law enforcement.   The courts have consistently held that freedom of the press does not override the requirements of law enforcement. A Louisville, Kentucky, reporter who had researched and written an article about drug activities was called before a grand jury to identify people he had seen in possession of marijuana or in the act of processing hashish. The reporter refused to testify, maintaining that freedom of the press shielded him from inquiry. In a closely divided decision, the Supreme Court in 1972 rejected this position. The Court declared that no exception, even a limited one, exists to the rule that every citizen has a duty to give his or her government whatever testimony he or she is capable of giving.[43]

A divided Supreme Court maintained again in 1978 that journalists are not protected from the demands of law enforcement when the Court upheld a lower court's warrant to search a Stanford University campus newspaper office for photographs of a violent demonstration.[44] Thus, the investigation of criminal conduct seems to be treated as a special area in the maintenance of order by government—an area in which the Supreme Court is not willing to provide the press with extraordinary protection of its freedom.

The Right to Peaceable Assembly and Petition

The final clause of the First Amendment states that "Congress shall make no law . . . abridging . . . the right of the people peaceably to assemble, and to petition the Government for a redress of grievances." The roots of the right of petition can be traced to the Magna Carta, the charter of English political and civil liberties granted by King John at Runnymede in 1215. The right peaceably to assemble arose much later. Historically, this section of the First Amendment should read "the right of the people peaceably to assemble" *in order to* "petition the government."[45] Today, however, the right of peaceable assembly stems from the same root as free speech and free press and is held to be equally fundamental. Government cannot prohibit meetings for peaceable political action. And government cannot brand as criminals those who assist in conducting such meetings.[46]

The rights of assembly and petition have merged with the guarantees of free speech and a free press under the more general freedom of expression. Possession of the right to assemble and to petition the government implies the freedom to express one's thoughts and beliefs.

The clash of interests in cases involving these rights illustrates a continuing effort to define and apply fundamental principles. The concept of freedom has been tempered by the need for order and stability. And when there is a confrontation between these basic values, the justices of the Supreme Court, who are responsible only to their consciences, strike the balance. Such clashes are certain to occur again and again. Freedom and order conflict when public libraries become targets for community censors, when religious devotion interferes with military service, when individuals and groups express views or hold beliefs at odds with majority sentiment. These conflicts between freedom and order, and between minority and majority viewpoints, are part and parcel of politics and government at home and abroad. How do other nations rank on the degree of civil liberties they guarantee their citizens? And is freedom increasing or declining in the world? For some answers, see Compared With What? 17.1.

APPLYING THE BILL OF RIGHTS TO THE STATES

Recall that the major purpose of the Constitution was to structure the division of power between states and nation. Even before it was amended, the Constitution did set some limits on both the nation and the states with regard to citizens' rights. Both governments were barred from passing **bills of attainder,** which are legislative acts that make an individual guilty of a crime without a trial. They were also prohibited from enacting **ex post facto laws,** which declare an action a crime after it has been performed. And both states and nation were barred from impairing the **obligation of contracts,** which compels the parties in a contract to carry out its terms and, if necessary, requires the government to ensure that they do so.

Recall, too, that James Madison was unsuccessful in his effort to include in the Bill of Rights an amendment that would limit *state* infringements on the basic rights of citizens. As a result, the Bill of Rights seemed to limit only national authority. Nevertheless, various litigants pressed the claim that these guarantees reached beyond the federal government and into the states.

For example, in the case of *Barron* v. *Baltimore* (1833), two wharf owners sued the city of Baltimore because their property had been made useless when Baltimore diverted some streams. The wharf owners maintained that the Fifth Amendment provision that "private property shall not be taken for public use without just compensation" applied to the states with the same force as to the national government. Chief Justice John Marshall affirmed what seemed plain from the Constitution's language and from "the history of the day" (the events surrounding the Constitutional Convention): the provisions of the Bill of Rights served only as limits on national authority. "Had the framers of these amendments intended them to be limitations on the powers of the state governments," continued Marshall, "they would have . . . expressed that intention."[47]

Many similar—and similarly unsuccessful—claims were pressed on the Supreme Court, despite the clarity of Marshall's rejection. Individuals were offered the promise of constitutional protection from state infringement on their freedoms only when the Fourteenth Amendment was adopted in 1868. That amendment's due process clause has served as the linchpin that binds the states to the provisions of the Bill of Rights.

Compared With What? 17.1

Civil Liberties Around the World

Raymond D. Gastil has surveyed freedom around the world for several years. One of his objectives is to produce a comparative assessment of civil liberties. He uses a seven-point comparative scale ranking nations from 1 (the greatest degree of freedom) to 7 (the least degree of freedom). The goal is a system in which most observers would judge nations with lower ratings to be freer than nations with higher ratings. Of course, no nation is absolutely free or unfree.

In countries rated 1, the expression of political opinion has an outlet in the press, especially when the intent of that expression is to affect the legitimate political process. In addition, in those countries no major medium of expression serves as a simple conduit for government propaganda. The courts protect the individual; people cannot be punished for their opinions; there is respect for private rights and desires in education, occupation, religion, and residence; and law-abiding citizens do not fear for their lives because of their political activities.

Moving down the scale from 2 to 7, we see a steady loss of civil freedoms. Compared with a rating of 1, the police and the courts in nations with a rating of 2 have more authoritarian traditions. In some cases, they may simply have a less institutionalized or secure set of liberties, such as in Portugal or Greece. Nations rated 3 or below may have political prisoners and varying forms of censorship. Frequently, their security services practice torture. States rated 6 almost always have political prisoners; usually the legitimate media are completely under government supervision; there is no right to assembly; and, often, narrow restrictions apply to travel, residence, and occupation. However, at 6, there may still be relative freedom in private conversations, especially at home; illegal demonstrations can or do occur; and underground literature circulates. At 7 on the scale, there is pervasive fear; little independent expression, even in private; almost no public expressions of opposition to the regime; and imprisonment or execution is swift and sure.

The degree of freedom within a nation varies with shifts in the political regime. The states in **boldface type** have experienced a decline in civil liberties from 1984 to 1985. The states in *italic boldface type* have experienced an increase in civil liberties from 1984 to 1985.

Source: Raymond D. Gastil, *Freedom in the World: Political Rights and Civil Liberties, 1984–1985* (Westport, Conn.: Greenwood Press, 1985), pp. 10, 13, 20–21, 23; and *Freedom at Issue* (No. 88), p. 11 (January–February 1986).

The Fourteenth Amendment: Due Process of Law

Section 1. . . . No *State* shall make or enforce any law which shall abridge the privileges or immunities of citizens of the United States; nor shall any *State* deprive any person of life, liberty, or property, without due process of law [italics added for emphasis].

Rating of Nations by Civil Liberties, 1985

Most Free **1**	Australia Austria Belgium Belize Canada	Costa Rica Denmark Iceland Ireland Italy	Japan Luxembourg Netherlands New Zealand Norway	St. Kitts-Nevis Sweden Switzerland United Kingdom United States

2	Argentina
	Bahamas
	Barbados
	Brazil
	Cyprus (G)
	Dominica
	Fiji
		Finland
		France
		Germany (W)
		Greece
		Israel
		Kiribati
		Mauritius
			Nauru
			Papua New
			  Guinea
			Portugal
			St. Lucia
			St. Vincent
			Spain
				Trinidad and
				  Tobago
				Tuvalu
				Uruguay
				Venezuela

3	Antigua and Barbuda Bolivia Botswana Colombia	Cyprus (T) Dominican Rep. *Ecuador* Grenada Honduras	India Jamaica Panama Peru	**Philippines** Solomons Tonga Western Samoa
4	Egypt **El Salvador** Gambia **Guatemala**	Kuwait Lebanon Malta Mexico	Nepal Senegal Sri Lanka	Thailand **Uganda** Vanuatu
5	Bahrain Bangladesh Bhutan **Brunei** Chile China (Taiwan) Guinea Guyana Hungary	Ivory Coast Jordan Kenya Korea (S) Lesotho Liberia Malaysia Maldives Morocco	Nicaragua Nigeria Pakistan Paraguay Poland Qatar Sierra Leone Singapore Tunisia	Turkey United Arab Emirates Yemen (N) Yugoslavia Zambia

6	Algeria
	Burkina Faso
	Burundi
	Central African
	  Republic
	China
	  (Mainland)
	Comoros
	Congo
		Cuba
		Czechoslovakia
		Djibouti
		Gabon
		Germany (E)
		Ghana
		Guinea-Bissau
		Haiti
		Indonesia
			Iran
			Libya
			Madagascar
			Mali
			Mauritania
			Niger
			Oman
			Rwanda
			Seychelles
				South Africa
				Sudan
				Suriname
				Swaziland
				Tanzania
				Togo
				Transkei
				Zimbabwe

7 *Least Free*	Afghanistan Albania Angola Benin Bulgaria Burma Cambodia	Cameroon Cape Verde Is. Chad **Equa. Guinea** Ethiopia Iraq Korea (N)	Laos Malawi Mongolia Mozambique Romania Sao Tome and Principe	Saudi Arabia Somalia Syria USSR **Vietnam** Yemen (S) Zaire

Most protections enshrined in the Bill of Rights now apply as limitations on the states. And many of the standards that limit federal authority serve equally to limit the states' authority. These changes have been achieved through the Supreme Court's interpretation of the due process clause of the Four-teenth Amendment: "nor shall any State deprive any person of life, liberty, or property, without due process of law." Cases involving this clause show that constitutional guarantees are often championed by unlikely litigants and that freedom is not always the victor.

The Fourteenth Amendment was first interpreted in the *Slaughter-House Cases* (1873).[48] Some New Orleans butchers who had been excluded from a state-chartered slaughterhouse monopoly sought to break the monopoly with the Constitution's new weapon, the Fourteenth Amendment, which aimed at state action adverse to certain fundamental rights. Justice Samuel F. Miller, speaking for a sharply divided Supreme Court, denied the relief the butchers sought. The core of his argument was that the overwhelming purpose of the Civil War amendments (the Thirteenth, Fourteenth, and Fifteenth) was the freedom, security, and protection of the emancipated black man. The Court gutted the "privileges and immunities clause" when it declined to depart from the theory that fundamental rights stem from state, not national, citizenship. In brief, the Court stated, the Fourteenth Amendment imposed no additional restrictions on the states.

Miller's position was short-lived, however. The justices had two options in their effort to apply the provisions of the Bill of Rights to the states. They could overrule the *Slaughter-House* decision, but this was unlikely given their commitment to *stare decisis*. (This Latin phrase means "let the decision stand" and refers to a principle that guides judges and lawyers to agree with decisions that have been made previously unless compelling reasons call for new precedents.) Instead, the justices searched for another constitutional provision to carry the weight; they found it in the due process clause.

The Fundamental Freedoms

In 1897, without fanfare, the Supreme Court reversed the position it had taken in *Barron* v. *Baltimore*. The states, the Court said, would be limited by the Fifth Amendment's prohibition on taking of private property without just compensation.[49] The Court accomplished its goals by absorbing that prohibition into the due process clause of the Fourteenth Amendment, which applies to the states. Now one Bill of Rights protection—but only that one —limited both the states and the national government.

The inclusion of other Bill of Rights guarantees within the due process clause faced a critical test in ***Palko* v. *Connecticut*** (1937).[50] Frank Palko had been charged with first-degree murder. He was convicted instead of second-degree murder and sentenced to life imprisonment. The state of Connecticut appealed and won a new trial; this time Palko was found guilty of first-degree murder and sentenced to death. Palko appealed this second conviction on the ground that it violated his protection against double jeopardy, guaranteed to him by the Fifth Amendment. This protection applied to the states, he contended, because of the Fourteenth Amendment's due process clause.

The Supreme Court upheld Palko's second conviction. In his majority opinion, Justice Benjamin N. Cardozo formulated principles that were to direct the Court's actions for the next three decades. He noted that some Bill of Rights guarantees—such as freedom of thought and speech—are fundamental; these fundamental rights are absorbed by the Fourteenth Amendment's due process clause and are applicable to the states. These rights are essential, argued Cardozo, because "neither liberty nor justice would exist if they were sacrificed." Other rights, such as trial by jury, although valuable and important, are not essential to liberty and justice, and are therefore not absorbed by the due process clause. "Few would be so narrow or provincial," Cardozo claimed, "as to maintain that a fair and enlightened system of justice" would be impossible without these other rights.[51] In other words, only some Bill of Rights provisions — those tagged as "fundamental" — were absorbed into the due process clause and made applicable to the states. Because protection against double jeopardy was not one of them, Frank Palko died in Connecticut's gas chamber in April 1938.

The next thirty years constituted a period of slow but perceptible change in the standard for determining whether or not a Bill of Rights guarantee was fundamental. The reference point was transformed from the idealized "fair and enlightened system of justice" of the *Palko* case to the more realistic "American scheme of justice." During that period, in case after case, the continual testing of guarantees resulted in the finding that they were indeed fundamental. By 1969 the *Palko* decision appeared an empty shell; most of the Bill of Rights guarantees had been found applicable to the states (see Table 17.1).

The Supreme Court finally overturned the *Palko* decision on June 23, 1969, Chief Justice Earl Warren's last day of service as a member of the Court. He and a majority of his colleagues had come to recognize that "*Palko*'s roots had been cut away years ago."[52] Although nearly all the guarantees of the Bill of Rights apply today to government at all levels, the controversy over these safeguards continues.

Criminal Procedure: The Meanings of Constitutional Guarantees

"The history of liberty," remarked Justice Felix Frankfurter, "has largely been the history of observance of procedural safeguards."[53] The safeguards embodied in the Fourth through Eighth Amendments to the Constitution specify *how* government must behave in criminal proceedings. Their application as *limits on the states* has reshaped American criminal justice in the last thirty years.

The application of these safeguards to the states has followed a two-step process. The first step requires the judgment that a guarantee asserted in the Bill of Rights also applies to the states. The second step requires that the judiciary give specific meaning to that guarantee. If the judiciary simply calls on the states to define and enforce their own versions of the guarantee, then that definition will probably vary from state to state — and citizens' rights will vary similarly. If the rights are fundamental, their meaning cannot vary — it would seem to follow that the meaning must be uniform. But life is not quite so simple under the U.S. Constitution. The idea of federalism was sewn into the constitutional fabric, and the Supreme Court recognizes that there may be more than one way to prosecute the accused while heeding fundamental rights.

Consider, as an example, the right to a jury trial in criminal cases, which is guaranteed by the Sixth Amendment. This right was made obligatory for the states in *Duncan* v. *Louisiana* (1968).[54] The Supreme Court later held that

Table 17.1
Cases Applying the Bill of Rights to the States

Amendment	Case	Date
I.		
Congress shall make no law respecting an establishment of religion,	*Everson* v. *Board of Education*	1947
or prohibiting the free exercise thereof;	*Cantwell* v. *Connecticut*	1940
or abridging the freedom of speech,	*Gitlow* v. *New York*	1925
or of the press;	*Near* v. *Minnesota*	1931
or the right of the people peaceably to assemble,	*DeJonge* v. *Oregon*	1937
and to petition the Government for a redress of grievances.	*DeJonge* v. *Oregon*	1937
II.		
A well regulated Militia, being necessary to the security of a free State, the right of the people to keep and bear Arms, shall not be infringed.		
III.		
No soldier shall, in time of peace be quartered in any house, without the consent of the Owner, nor in time of war, but in a manner to be prescribed by law.		
IV.		
The right of the people to be secure in their persons, houses, papers, and effects, against unreasonable searches and seizures, shall not be violated,	*Wolf* v. *Colorado*	1949
and no Warrants shall issue, but upon probable cause, supported by Oath or affirmation, and particularly describing the place to be searched, and the persons or things to be seized.	*Aguilar* v. *Texas*	1964
V.		
No person shall be held to answer for a capital, or otherwise infamous crime, unless on a presentment or indictment of a Grand Jury,		
except in cases arising in the land or naval forces, or in the Militia, when in actual service in time of War or public danger;		
nor shall any person be subject for the same offence to be twice put in jeopardy of life or limb;	*Benton* v. *Maryland*	1969

the right applied to all nonpetty criminal cases—those in which the penalty upon conviction was more than six months' imprisonment.[55] But the Court did not require that state juries have twelve members, the number required for federal criminal proceedings. Jury size was permitted to vary from state to state, although the minimum number was set at six. Furthermore, the federal requirement of a unanimous jury verdict was not imposed on the states. As a result, even today many states do not require unanimous verdicts for criminal convictions. Some observers question whether criminal defendants in those states enjoy the same rights that defendants in unanimous-verdict states are granted.

In contrast to the right to jury trial, the right to an attorney, guaranteed by the Sixth Amendment, left no room for state variations after the Supreme Court declared it to be fundamental. Clarence Earl Gideon was a penniless vagrant accused of breaking into and robbing a Florida pool hall. (The "loot" was mainly change taken out of vending machines.) Because Gideon could not afford a lawyer, he asked the state to provide him with legal counsel for

Amendment	Case	Date
nor shall be compelled in any criminal case to be a witness against himself,	*Malloy* v. *Hogan*	1964
nor be deprived of life, liberty, or property, without due process of law;		
nor shall private property be taken for public use, without just compensation.	*Chicago, B. & Q. R. Co.* v. *Chicago*	1897

VI.

Amendment	Case	Date
In all criminal prosecutions, the accused shall enjoy the right to a speedy	*Klopfer* v. *North Carolina*	1967
and public trial	*In re Oliver*	1948
by an impartial	*Parker* v. *Gladden*	1966
jury	*Duncan* v. *Louisiana*	1968
of the State and district wherein the crime shall have been committed, which district shall have been previously ascertained by law,		
and to be informed of the nature and cause of the accusation;	*Lanzetta* v. *New Jersey*	1939
to be confronted with the witnesses against him;	*Pointer* v. *Texas*	1965
to have compulsory process for obtaining witnesses in his favor,	*Washington* v. *Texas*	1967
and to have the Assistance of Counsel for his defence.	*Gideon* v. *Wainwright*	1963

VII.

Amendment	Case	Date
In Suits at common law, where the value of the controversy shall exceed twenty dollars, the right of trial by jury shall be preserved,		
and no fact tried by a jury, shall be otherwise reexamined in any Court of the United States, than according to the rules of common law.		

VIII.

Amendment	Case	Date
Excessive bail shall not be required,		
nor excessive fines imposed,		
nor cruel and unusual punishments inflicted.	*Robinson* v. *California*	1962

IX.

Amendment	Case	Date
The enumeration in the Constitution, of certain rights, shall not be construed to deny or disparage others retained by the people.	*Griswold* v. *Connecticut*	1965

his trial. The state refused Gideon's request, and he was subsequently convicted and sentenced to five years in the Florida State Penitentiary. From his cell, Gideon appealed to the U.S. Supreme Court, claiming that his conviction should be struck down because his Sixth Amendment right to counsel had been denied. (Gideon was also without counsel in this appeal; he filed a hand-lettered "pauper's petition" with the Court, after studying law texts in the prison library. However, when the Court agreed to consider his case, he was assigned a prominent Washington attorney, Abe Fortas, who later became a Supreme Court justice.)

In its landmark decision in **Gideon v. Wainwright** (1963), the Court set aside Gideon's conviction and extended to the states the Sixth Amendment's right to counsel.[56] Gideon was retried, but this time, with the assistance of a lawyer, he was found not guilty.

In subsequent rulings that stretched over more than a decade, the Court specified at what points a defendant was entitled to a lawyer in the course of a criminal proceeding (from arrest to trial, appeal, and beyond). All states

A Pauper's Plea

Clarence Earl Gideon, penniless and without a lawyer, was convicted and sent to prison for breaking into and robbing a pool hall. At his trial, Gideon pleaded with the judge: "Your Honor, the U.S. Constitution says I am entitled to be represented by counsel." The judge was required by state law to deny Gideon's request. Undaunted, Gideon continued his quest for recognition of his Sixth Amendment right to counsel. He was turned down at every stage until the Supreme Court granted his penciled petition for assistance. The Court granted Gideon the right he advocated with such conviction.

were bound by these pronouncements. In state as well as federal proceedings, legal assistance had to be furnished to those who did not have the means to hire their own attorneys.

During this period the Court also came to grips with another issue involving procedural safeguards: when those accused of crimes remain ignorant of their constitutional rights, safeguards are useless. Ernesto Miranda was arrested in Arizona for kidnapping and raping an eighteen-year-old woman. After the police questioned him for two hours and the woman identified him, Miranda confessed to the crime. He was convicted in an Arizona court on the basis of that confession—although he was never told he had the right to counsel and the right to refrain from incriminating himself. Miranda appealed his conviction, which was overturned by the Supreme Court in 1966.

The Court based its decision in *Miranda* v. *Arizona*[57] on the Fifth Amendment privilege against compelled self-incrimination. According to the Court, informal compulsion had been exerted by the police during in-custody questioning. Warnings were required, the Court argued, to dispel the coercion inherent in custodial police interrogation. The warnings were not required if a person was only in custody or if a person was only subject to questioning without arrest. However, the combination of interrogation *and* custody was sufficiently intimidating to require neutralizing statements prior to questioning. These statements, known today as the **Miranda warnings,** declare in part that:

- You have the right to remain silent.
- Anything you say can be used against you in court.
- You have the right to talk to a lawyer of your own choice before questioning.
- If you cannot afford to a hire a lawyer, a lawyer will be provided without charge.

In each area of criminal procedure, the justices have had to grapple with the two steps in the application of constitutional guarantees to criminal defendants: the application of a right to the states and the definition of that right. The *Gideon* case illustrates the right to counsel applied uniformly from state to state. The *Duncan* case illustrates the application of the right to jury trial with variation from state to state. Finally, the *Miranda* case illustrates that government has a duty to inform its citizens so that they can claim the full measure of their constitutional rights.

The problems balancing freedom and order can be formidable. A primary function of government is to maintain order. What should be done when an individual's freedom is infringed for the sake of order? Consider the guarantee expressed in the Fourth Amendment: "The right of the people to be secure in their persons, houses, papers, and effects, against unreasonable searches and seizures, shall not be violated." This right was made applicable to the states in *Wolf* v. *Colorado* (1949).[58] Following the *Palko* approach, the Court found that the core of the amendment—security against arbitrary police intrusion—was a fundamental right. The Court thus declared that citizens were to be protected from illegal searches by state and local government. But how? The federal courts had long followed the **exclusionary rule,** which holds that evidence obtained from an illegal search and seizure cannot be used in a trial. And, of course, if that evidence is critical to the prosecution, the conviction is lost. But the Court declined to take the second step: applying the exclusionary rule to the states. Instead, it permitted the states to decide on their own how to handle the fruits of an illegal search. The upshot of *Wolf* v. *Colorado* was that the evidence used to convict a defendant was declared to be obtained illegally, but his conviction on the basis of that illegal evidence was affirmed.

The justices again considered the exclusionary rule twelve years later in **Mapp v. Ohio** (1961).[59] Dolree Mapp had been convicted of possessing "obscene materials" after an admittedly illegal search of her home for a fugitive. Her conviction was affirmed by the Ohio Supreme Court, and she appealed to the U.S. Supreme Court. Mapp's attorneys argued for a reversal based on freedom of expression, contending that the confiscated materials were protected by the First Amendment. However, the Court elected to use the *Mapp* case to give meaning to the constitutional guarantee against unreasonable search and seizure. In a 6-to-3 decision, the justices declared that "all evidence obtained by searches and seizures in violation of the Constitution is, by [the Fourth Amendment], inadmissible in a state court." Mapp had, therefore, been convicted illegally.

The decision was historic. It placed the exclusionary rule safely within the confines of the Fourth Amendment and required all levels of government to operate according to the provisions of that amendment. Failure to do so would result in the acquittal of otherwise guilty defendants.

The *Mapp* case launched a divided Supreme Court on a troublesome course. The Court has, since that time, attempted to determine the application of the exclusionary rule. For example, the Court continues to struggle with police use of sophisticated electronic eavesdropping devices and the search of movable vehicles. In each case, the justices must confront a rule that appears to handicap the police while it offers freedom to persons whose guilt has been established by the illegally seized evidence. The *Mapp* case forced the Court to confront a classic democratic dilemma: the justices had to choose freedom or order. If they tipped the scale toward freedom, guilty parties would go free and perhaps engage in criminal conduct again. If instead they chose order, a stamp of government approval would be given to police conduct in violation of the Constitution. Such is the challenge of democracy.

THE NINTH AMENDMENT AND PERSONAL AUTONOMY

The adoption of the Bill of Rights in 1791 made explicit those rights that the national government could not abridge. But did this adoption carry with it the assumption that other rights not specified in the amendments could nevertheless be abridged by government?[60] An answer to this question may be found in the ambiguous language of the Ninth Amendment, which states: "The enumeration in the Constitution, of certain rights, shall not be construed to deny or disparage others retained by the people."

The amendment and its history remain an enigma. The evidence supports two different views. The amendment may protect unenumerated rights, or the amendment may simply protect state governments against the assumption of power by the national government.[61] The significance of the amendment remained dormant until 1965 when the Supreme Court employed it in the protection of privacy, a right unenumerated in the Constitution.

The Abortion Controversy

In *Griswold* **v.** *Connecticut*,[62] the Court struck down, by a vote of 7 to 2, a seldom-used Connecticut statute that made the use of birth control devices a crime. Justice William O. Douglas's majority opinion asserted that the "specific guarantees in the Bill of Rights have penumbras," (areas of partial illumination) that give "life and substance" to specific Bill of Rights guarantees. Several specific guarantees in the First, Third, Fourth, and Fifth Amendments create a zone of privacy, Douglas argued, and this zone is protected by use of the Ninth Amendment and applicable to the states by virtue of the Fourteenth Amendment's due process clause (see Feature 17.2).

Three of the justices gave added emphasis to the relevance of the Ninth Amendment, which, they contended, protected fundamental rights derived from those specifically enumerated in the first eight amendments. This view was in sharp contrast to the position expressed by the two dissenters, Justices Hugo L. Black and Potter Stewart. They argued that, in the absence of some specific prohibition, the Bill of Rights and the Fourteenth Amendment do not license judicial annulment of state legislative policies, even if those policies are abhorrent to the judge.

Griswold v. *Connecticut* established the principle that the Bill of Rights as a whole creates a right to make certain intimate personal choices, including the right of married people to engage in sexual intercourse for reproduction or merely for pleasure. This zone of personal autonomy, protected by the Constitution, gave comfort in 1973 to litigants who sought to invalidate state

Making Public Policy

Major changes in federal spending over time can be seen by plotting the percentage of annual budget outlays since 1940 for four major expense categories. In the 1940s, spending for World War II consumed more than 80 percent of the federal budget. Defense again accounted for most federal expenditures during the Cold War in the 1950s. Since then, the military's share of expenditures has declined while payments to individuals (mostly social security benefits) have increased dramatically. Also, the proportion of the budget paid in interest on the federal debt has increased substantially since the 1970s.

Keynesian economic theory was designed to control the occurrence of business cycles—*rhythmic expansion and contraction of business activity accompanied by inflation and unemployment (see graph on following page)— through government use of fiscal and monetary economic policies. Although the federal government regularly uses such policies to control the economy, the government has not eliminated business cycles, as shown by the wavy graph of industrial production in the United States since 1964. Nevertheless, no one can say how wildly the cycles might have fluctuated in the absence of government intervention in the economy.*

Federal Government Outlays

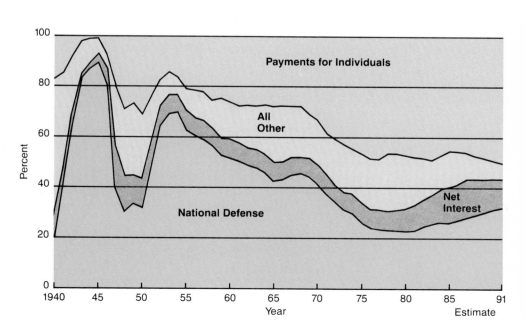

The American Economic Experience over Two Decades

U.S. industrial production index (1967 = 100)

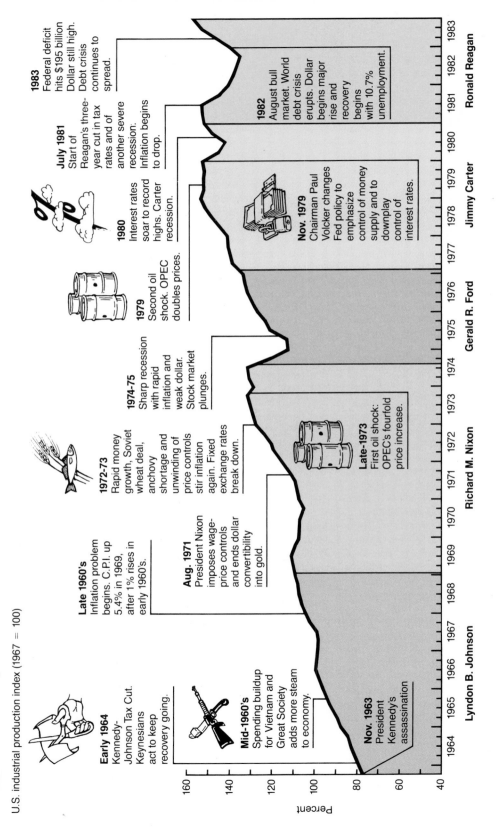

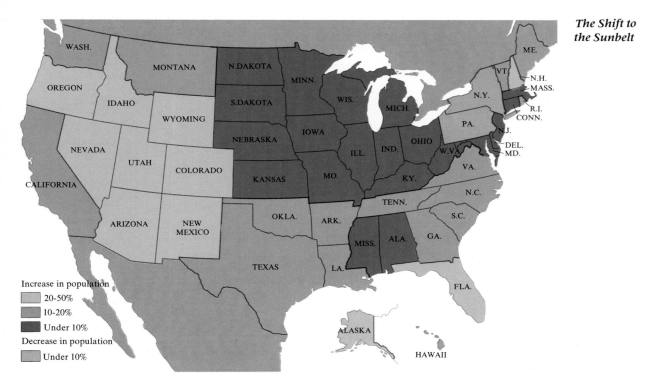

Increase in population
- 20-50%
- 10-20%
- Under 10%

Decrease in population
- Under 10%

The southwest experienced dramatic population growth from 1970 to 1980 as the prospect for jobs led many people to leave the "rustbelt" (or "frostbelt") of the northeast and midwest for states in the "sunbelt." The pattern of federal funding has done little to stop this migration. The map below shows the relationship between the amount of taxes paid to Washington by citizens in each state and the money returned to the states through federal spending. States with ratios below 1.00 paid more in taxes than they received back in spending, while those states with ratios over 1.00 paid less than they received.

The Flow of Federal Funds

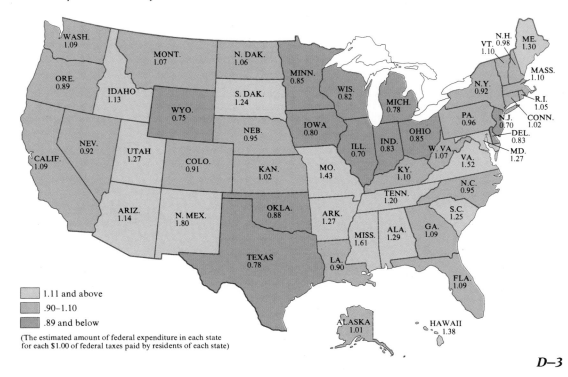

- 1.11 and above
- .90–1.10
- .89 and below

(The estimated amount of federal expenditure in each state for each $1.00 of federal taxes paid by residents of each state)

The west and east coasts are the regions that are most successful in obtaining defense contracts. California leads the nation in per capita share, followed by New England. This coastal/central split can also be seen in the economic profile of the United States. The central states have been hurt by the nation's decline as an exporter of agricultural goods, raw materials, and manufacturing. The coastal states, on the other hand, have benefited from the concentration of high technology firms in states such as California and Massachusetts and from the growth of the service sector.

The Flow of Defense Dollars

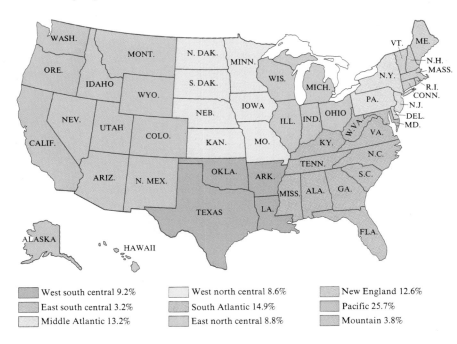

West south central 9.2%	West north central 8.6%	New England 12.6%
East south central 3.2%	South Atlantic 14.9%	Pacific 25.7%
Middle Atlantic 13.2%	East north central 8.8%	Mountain 3.8%

The Bicoastal Economy

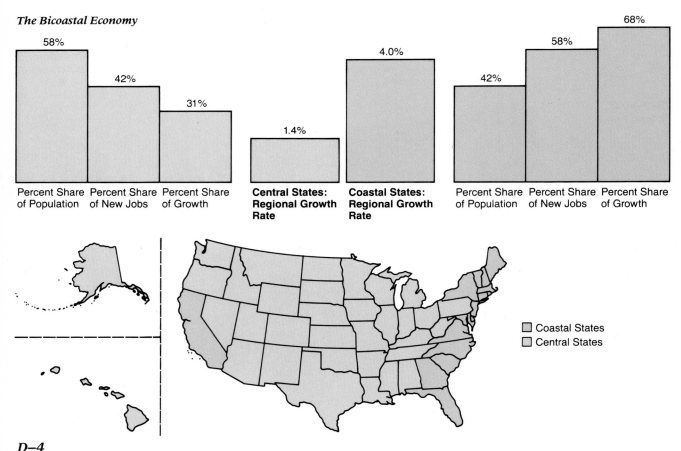

58% — Percent Share of Population
42% — Percent Share of New Jobs
31% — Percent Share of Growth

1.4% — Central States: Regional Growth Rate
4.0% — Coastal States: Regional Growth Rate

42% — Percent Share of Population
58% — Percent Share of New Jobs
68% — Percent Share of Growth

☐ Coastal States
☐ Central States

Metropolitan Areas of the United States and the Interstate Highway System

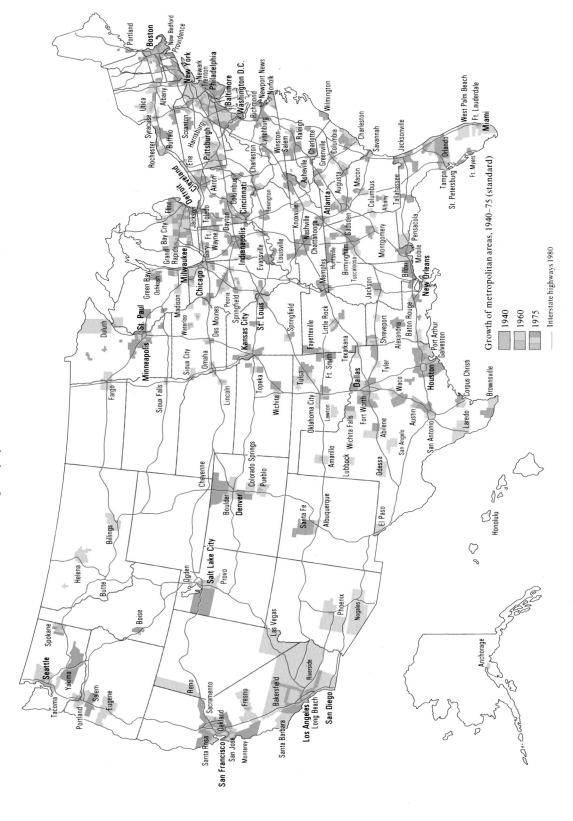

Growth of metropolitan areas, 1940–75 (standard)

1940
1960
1975
Interstate highways 1980

Military Bases and Forces on Foreign Territory

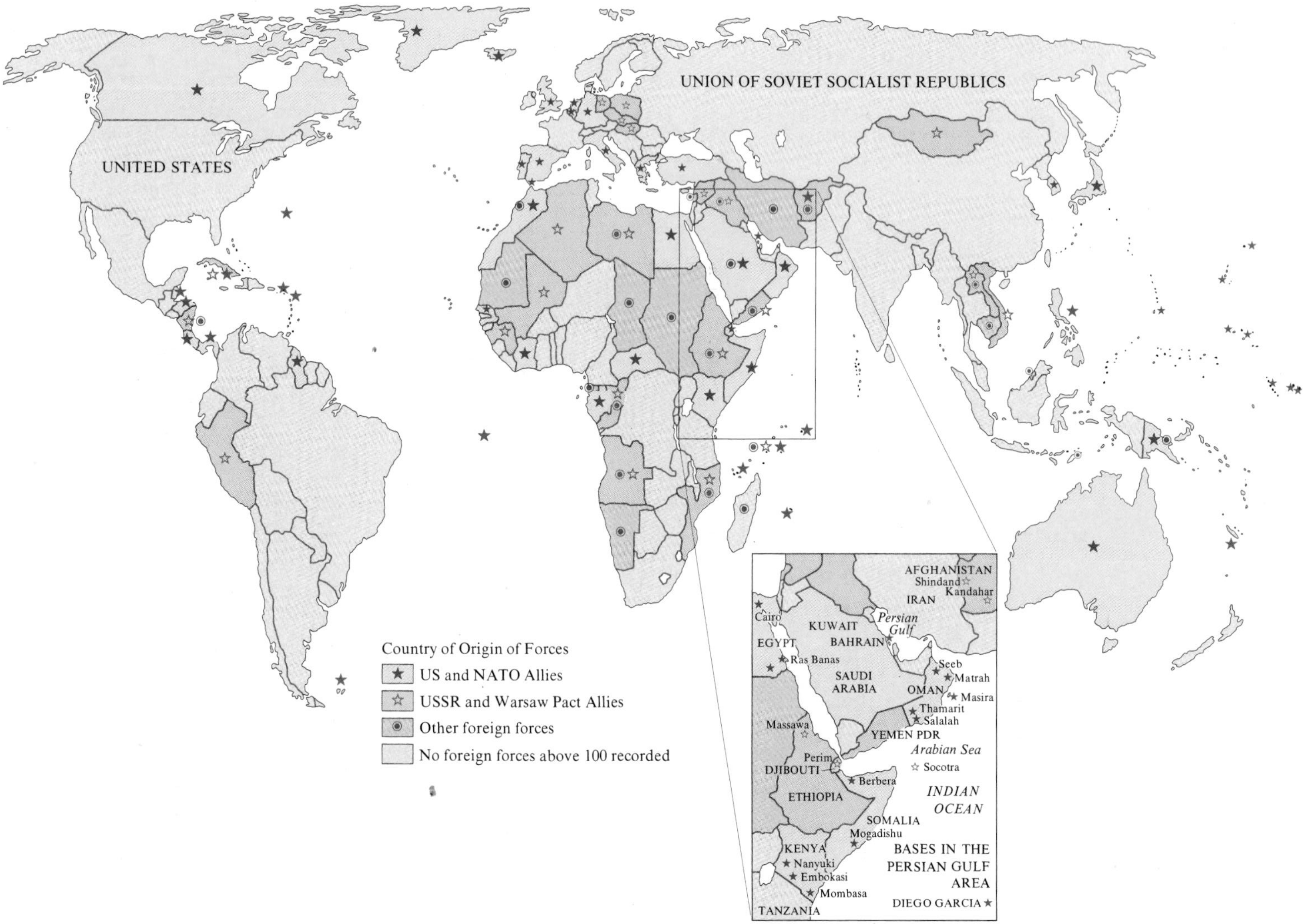

UNION OF SOVIET SOCIALIST REPUBLICS

UNITED STATES

Country of Origin of Forces

★ US and NATO Allies

☆ USSR and Warsaw Pact Allies

◉ Other foreign forces

No foreign forces above 100 recorded

Inset: BASES IN THE PERSIAN GULF AREA

AFGHANISTAN
Shindand ☆
☆ Kandahar

IRAN

Persian Gulf

KUWAIT
BAHRAIN ★
SAUDI ARABIA

EGYPT
Cairo ★
★ Ras Banas

★ Seeb
Matrah ★
OMAN ★ Masira
Thamarit ★
★ Salalah

YEMEN PDR

Arabian Sea

☆ Socotra

INDIAN OCEAN

Massawa ★
Perim ★
DJIBOUTI
★ Berbera

ETHIOPIA

SOMALIA
Mogadishu ★

KENYA
★ Nanyuki
Embokasi ★
★ Mombasa

TANZANIA

DIEGO GARCIA ★

American-Soviet Relations, 1948–1983

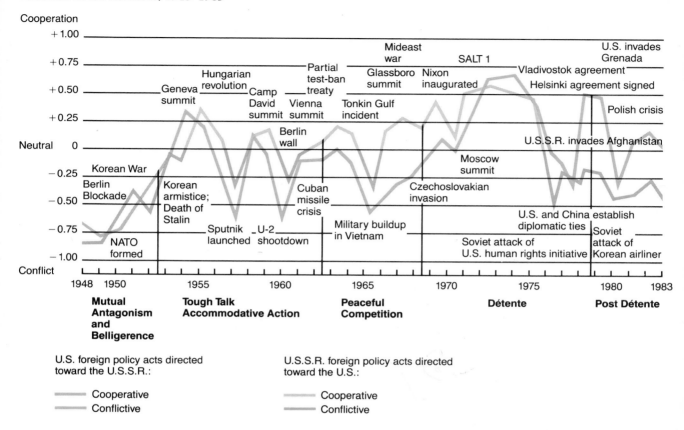

This graph plots the net result of the percentage of positive and negative foreign policy "acts"—letters, diplomatic exchanges, media criticism, troop movements, and so on—directed annually by the United States toward the Soviet Union and vice versa. Positive acts showed cooperation, and negative ones indicated antagonism and conflict. Until 1975, the pattern of American-Soviet relations was one of ups and downs along a gradual rise toward cooperation under the policy of detente, which originated during the Nixon administration. Since then, the two nations have vacillated in relations, mostly around the negative side.

The Soviet Union and the United States together have over a million troops stationed on foreign territory. The U.S. military presence is felt in 40 countries and territories, including 385,000 troops in Japan and in Europe (where they form part of the NATO force) and 95,000 in other countries. The Soviet Union has 640,000 troops stationed in the Warsaw Pact countries and Mongolia, and it maintains 115,000 troops fighting in Afghanistan. In addition, it has about 23,000 military personnel stationed abroad in 22 foreign countries. Other nations with significant military presences abroad include Britain and France, each with about 90,000 troops stationed in some former colonies, and Cuba, which has about 32,000 soldiers supporting some revolutionary regimes in Africa and the Middle East.

The organization Freedom House annually rates nations (see following page) according to their practice of political rights—whether they permit competitive elections—and civil liberties—whether they allow freedom of expression. In free countries, citizens participate in fully competitive elections and the press enjoys the right to criticize the government. Partly free states are governed with some degree of popular consensus, although they may hold political prisoners and practice some press censorship. Citizens in countries that are not free cannot voice their desires for a change in government policy. Such nations almost always hold political prisoners, control the press, and restrict travel, residence, and occupation.

The Map of Freedom

- Free countries
- Partly free countries
- Not free countries

Free countries

1 Antigua and Barbuda	22 France	44 St. Kitts-Nevis
2 Argentina	23 Germany (W)	45 St. Lucia
3 Australia	24 Greece	46 St. Vincent
4 Austria	25 Grenada	47 Solomons
5 Bahamas	26 Honduras	48 Spain
6 Barbados	27 Iceland	49 Sweden
7 Belgium	28 India	50 Switzerland
8 Belize	29 Ireland	51 Trinidad and Tobago
9 Bolivia	30 Israel	52 Tuvalu
10 Botswana	31 Italy	53 United Kingdom
11 Brazil	32 Jamaica	54 United States
12 Canada	33 Japan	55 Uruguay
13 Colombia	34 Kiribati	56 Venezuela
14 Costa Rica	35 Luxembourg	
15 Cyprus (G)	36 Mauritius	
16 Denmark	37 Nauru	
17 Dominica	38 Netherlands	
18 Dominican Republic	39 New Zealand	
19 Ecuador	40 Norway	
20 Fiji	41 Papua New Guinea	
21 Finland	42 Peru	
	43 Portugal	

Partly free countries

57 Bahrain	63 Cyprus (T)	85 Morocco
58 Bangladesh	64 Egypt	86 Nepal
59 Bhutan	65 El Salvador	87 Nicaragua
60 Brunei	66 Gambia	88 Pakistan
61 Chile	67 Guatemala	89 Panama
62 China (Taiwan)	68 Guyana	90 Paraguay
	69 Hungary	91 Philippines
	70 Indonesia	92 Poland
	71 Iran	93 Qatar
	72 Ivory Coast	94 Senegal
	73 Jordan	95 Sierra Leone
	74 Kenya	96 Singapore
	75 Korea (S)	97 So. Africa
	76 Kuwait	98 Sri Lanka
	77 Lebanon	99 Swaziland
	78 Liberia	100 Thailand
	79 Madagascar	101 Tonga
	80 Malaysia	102 Tunisia
	81 Maldives	103 Turkey
	82 Malta	104 Uganda
	83 Mexico	105 United Arab Emirates
	84 Morocco	106 Vanuatu

107 W. Samoa	
108 Yemen (N)	
109 Yugoslavia	
110 Zambia	
111 Zimbabwe	

Not free countries

112 Afghanistan	126 China (Mainland)	148 Mozambique
113 Albania	127 Comoros	149 Niger
114 Algeria	128 Congo	150 Nigeria
115 Angola	129 Cuba	151 Oman
116 Benin	130 Czechoslovakia	152 Romania
117 Bulgaria	131 Djibouti	153 Rwanda
118 Burkina Faso	132 Equatorial Guinea	154 São Tome & Princip
119 Burma	133 Ethiopia	155 Saudi Arabia
120 Burundi	134 Gabon	156 Seychelles
121 Cambodia	135 Germany (E)	157 Somalia
122 Cameroon	136 Ghana	158 Sudan
123 Cape Verde Is.	137 Guinea	159 Suriname
124 Central African Rep.	138 Guinea-Bissau	160 Syria
125 Chad	139 Haiti	161 Tanzania
	140 Iraq	162 Togo
	141 Korea (N)	163 USSR
	142 Laos	164 Vietnam
	143 Libya	165 Yemen (S)
	144 Malawi	166 Zaire
	145 Mali	
	146 Mauritania	
	147 Mongolia	

Feature 17.2

The Birth of a New Right

In 1965 the Supreme Court confronted a state criminal statute that prohibited the use of birth control devices and giving medical advice in their use. Two people were convicted under the law for giving birth control advice to married couples and for prescribing contraceptives. In the conference following argument, the justices were divided 7 to 2 in favor of declaring the law unconstitutional but were unable to articulate a clear theory on which to base their decision. Justice William O. Douglas stated the simplest rationale on which the statute could be invalidated. Douglas viewed the law as violating the First Amendment's guarantee of freedom of association. This right, which was officially recognized by the Court in 1958, protected the advancement of beliefs and ideas. The problem was that the right of association did not appear to protect *conjugal* association. Justice Hugo L. Black spoke sarcastically of the Douglas position in the conference. To Black, the right of association meant the right of assembly, and the right of husband and wife to assemble in bed seemed to him to be an entirely new interpretation of right of assembly.

Douglas nevertheless drafted his opinion along right of association lines, since he saw this right emanating from specific provisions in the Bill of Rights. But within a day of the opinion's distribution, Justice William J. Brennan, Jr., urged Douglas to abandon the right of association argument because it had little to do with the advocacy protected by that right. Instead, Brennan suggested that Douglas use the same approach but rest the decision on the right to privacy. Douglas followed Brennan's suggestion and circulated a new draft opinion, which recognized a constitutional right to privacy formed by the *penumbras*, or "partial shadows," cast by specific guarantees in the Bill of Rights. Thus the right to privacy was officially born.

The constitutional right to privacy created by the Court in 1965 would spawn one of the most controversial decisions of the modern Supreme Court. In *Roe v. Wade*, decided in 1973, the Court struck down state antiabortion laws on the ground that they violate the right of privacy, which was now held to include the right of women to terminate pregnancies.

The right to privacy has limits, however. In 1986, in a 5-to-4 decision, the Court refused to extend the right to privacy to cover the decision of two consenting adults to engage in homosexual acts. Choices fundamental to heterosexual life—whether to marry, to conceive a child, to carry a pregnancy to term—are still protected by the zone of privacy.

See Bernard Schwartz, *The Unpublished Opinions of the Warren Court* (New York: Oxford University Press, 1985), Ch. 7.

antiabortion laws. But rights are not absolute, and in weighing the interests of the individual against the interests of the government, the Supreme Court found itself caught in a flood of controversy that has yet to ebb.

In *Roe v. Wade* (1973),[63] the Supreme Court in a 7-to-2 decision declared unconstitutional a Texas law making it a crime to obtain an abortion except for the purpose of saving the mother's life. Justice Harry A. Blackmun, who authored the majority opinion, could not point to a specific constitutional guarantee to justify the Court's ruling. Rather, the decision rested on the right to privacy embraced within personal liberty protected by the Fourteenth Amendment's due process clause. The Court declared that, in the first three months of pregnancy, the abortion decision must be left to the woman and her physician. Furthermore, a woman's right to end her pregnancy can be defeated only by "compelling" state interests. In the interest of protecting the mother's health, states may restrict but not prohibit abortions in the second three months of pregnancy. Finally, in the last three months of pregnancy, states may regulate or even prohibit abortions to protect the life of the fetus except when medical judgment determines that an abortion is necessary to preserve the mother's life. In all, the laws of forty-six states were affected by the Court's ruling.

The case of *Roe* v. *Wade* illustrates the freedom-versus-order dilemma in another form. Antiabortion laws abridge freedom—the ability to make fundamental personal choices without interference. But antiabortion laws also fulfill the need for order—the protection of life (including unborn life) and the safety of citizens. In balancing freedom and order, the Supreme Court created a controversy that centered around the rightfulness of the Court's own political power.

The dissenters—Justices Byron R. White and William H. Rehnquist— were quick to point out what critics have frequently repeated since the decision: the Court's judgment was directed by its own dislikes, not by any constitutional compass. In the absence of guiding principles, the critics assert, the justices simply substituted their views for the views of the state legislatures whose abortion regulations were invalidated.[64]

Today, more than fourteen years after the landmark decision, political controversy still churns around *Roe* v. *Wade*. In 1976 Congress severely restricted the use of federal funds for reimbursement of abortion costs. The Supreme Court sustained this restriction of federal funds, known as the **Hyde Amendment,** in 1980. The Court issued a strong reaffirmation of *Roe* v. *Wade* when it struck down government-imposed restrictions on abortion procedures in 1983. This reaffirmation is not likely to deter abortion opponents, heal the divisions within the Court, or resolve the difficult issues that loom ahead as medical risks to various abortion procedures decrease.

President Ronald Reagan's 1981 nomination of Sandra Day O'Connor as the Court's 102nd justice focused attention on the strength of the abortion issue. It dominated public debate on O'Connor's fitness for judicial office. She was roundly condemned by antiabortion groups, though the opposition was hardly enough to stop her appointment as the first woman to the High Court. As if to prove his commitment to an antiabortion policy, in 1982 Reagan endorsed a constitutional amendment that would have reversed the Court's abortion decision in *Roe* v. *Wade*.

The abortion issue will not fade from view, and the Court continues to struggle with it. In 1986 the justices held unconstitutional a Pennsylvania law that required doctors to provide detailed information about risks and alternatives to women seeking abortions. The law also required that two doctors be present at late-term abortions and that the procedures most likely to produce live births be used as long as women were not put at significantly greater risk. These provisions were designed to deter women from having abortions and to require doctors to risk the health of pregnant women in order to save late-term fetuses. The Court concluded that the law had invaded the private sphere of individual liberty protected by the Constitution.[65]

Although antiabortion groups denounced it, advocates of abortion rights hailed the decision as a victory. The real significance of the decision, however, was the depth of division registered within the Court. The justices split 5 to 4, and the dissenters, Justices Rehnquist, White and O'Connor, authored three unusually harsh opinions. Chief Justice Burger voted for the first time in dissent, urging a re-examination of the *Roe* decision.

Burger resigned from the Court effective July 1986, and Reagan made a two-part replacement to fill the vacancy. Justice William Rehnquist was appointed from the Court to replace Burger as chief justice, and Judge Antonin Scalia was appointed to fill Rehnquist's seat on the Court. These changes do not shift the balance of opinions found in the Burger Court. But with Rehnquist's appointment as chief justice, a consistent dissenter on the abortion issue will now lead the Court. If Reagan is able to make another appointment, one of the majority justices could be the person replaced. Such an appointment could reverse the outcome, which, in all likelihood, will return the abortion issue to the state legislatures where it first arose.

Personal Autonomy, Sexual Orientation, and the Right to Die

The right to privacy cases may have opened a Pandora's box of divisive social issues. Does the right to privacy embrace private homosexual acts between consenting adults? Consider the recent case of Michael Hardwick, who was arrested in his Atlanta bedroom while having sex with another man. In a standard approach to prosecuting homosexuals, he was charged under a state criminal statute with the crime of sodomy, which means any oral or anal intercourse. The police said that they had gone to his home to arrest him for failing to pay a fine for drinking in public. Although the prosecutor dropped the charges, Hardwick sued to challenge the law's constitutionality and won in the lower courts.

Gay Power
Homosexual rights advocates had reason for dismay in the Supreme Court's 1986 decision upholding state laws against sodomy. Recognition of homosexual rights by the federal government now seems many years off. Homosexual activists will shift their efforts to gain legal protection from the national level to the state and city levels. Twenty-four states no longer make sodomy a crime. Other states will follow suit if gays can muster enough support in their state legislatures to repeal existing sodomy laws.

The conflict between freedom and order lies at the core of the case. "Our legal history and our social traditions have condemned this conduct uniformly for hundreds and hundreds of years," argued Georgia's attorney. Constitutional law, he continued, "must not become an instrument for a change in the social order." Hardwick's attorney, a noted constitutional scholar, said that government must have a more important reason than "majority morality to justify regulation of sexual intimacies in the privacy of the home." He maintained that the case involved two precious freedoms: the right to engage in private sexual relations and the right to be free from government intrusion in one's home.[66]

Twenty-six states have removed criminal penalties against private homosexual acts between consenting adults. The remaining twenty-four states still outlaw homosexual sodomy, and nineteen of them outlaw heterosexual sodomy as well. As a result, the Hardwick case was closely followed by homosexual rights groups and some civil liberties groups. Fundamentalist Christian groups and defenders of traditional morality expressed deep interest in the outcome, too.

In a bitterly divided ruling in 1986, the Court held that the Constitution does not protect homosexual relations between consenting adults, even in the privacy of their own homes. The logic of the privacy cases in the areas of contraception and abortion seemed to compel a right to personal autonomy — to make one's own choices unconstrained by government. But the 5-to-4 majority maintained that only heterosexual choices — whether and whom to marry, whether to conceive a child, whether to have an abortion — fall within the zone of privacy advanced by the Court in its earlier rulings.[67] "The judiciary necessarily takes to itself further authority to govern the country without express constitutional authority" when it expands the list of fundamental rights "not rooted in the language or design of the Constitution" wrote Justice Byron White, the author of the majority opinion. The march toward increased personal freedom seems to have come to a halt; the government's concern for social order — established patterns of authority — has prevailed.

Pluralism provides one solution to the problems that result from the Court's choice. If state legislatures can enact laws making certain acts punishable, then they can also repeal those laws. Opponents to the Georgia statute now must mobilize support and force a change that half the states have already adopted. However, such a solution offers little comfort to Americans who viewed the Constitution's zone of privacy as protection for their most intimate decisions and actions.

Does the right to make intimate personal decisions also include the right to die? Elizabeth Bouvia, a twenty-eight-year-old quadriplegic cerebral palsy victim, wants to remove a feeding tube that is keeping her alive. She is paralyzed, bedridden, and in severe pain. In supporting her request, a California appeals court recently declared that the "right to die is an integral part of our right to control our own destinies so long as the rights of others are not affected." The government commitment to protecting and preserving life clashes with the individual's interest in terminating that life. The balance between life and death leaves little room for compromise, which has been the hallmark of court decisions confronting the challenge of democracy.

CONSTITUTIONALIZING PUBLIC POLICIES

The issue embedded in *Griswold* and *Roe* is more fundamental and more disturbing for democracy than the surface issues of privacy and personal autonomy. By shrouding a policy in the Constitution, the Court removes that policy from the legislative arena, where the people's will can be expressed through the democratic process. Specific constitutional guarantees pose little threat of usurping democratic functions, because there are inherent limits in specific constitutional commandments. But the abortion controversy demonstrates to many critics that the judges now may place under the cloak of the Constitution a host of public policies that were once debated and resolved by the democratic process. By elevating a policy to constitutionally protected status (as the Court did with abortion), the judges assume responsibilities that have traditionally been left to the political branches to resolve. If we trust appointed judges to serve as uniquely qualified guardians of democracy, then our fears may be illusory. If we trust democratically crafted solutions for such policy questions, then the fears may be well grounded. The controversy will continue as the Supreme Court strikes a balance between freedom and order. But in holding the balance, the justices must wrestle among themselves and with their critics over whether the Constitution authorizes them to fill the due process clause with fundamental values that cannot easily be traced to constitutional text, history, or structure.

Though the courts may be "the chief guardians of the liberties of the people," they ought not have the last word, argued the great jurist Learned Hand, because

> [A] society so riven that the spirit of moderation is gone, no court *can* save; that a society where that spirit flourishes, no court *need* save; that in a society which evades its responsibilities by thrusting upon the courts the nurture of that spirit, that spirit in the end will perish.[68]

SUMMARY

In establishing a government of limited powers, the framers were compelled to assure the states and the people, through the Bill of Rights, that their freedom would not be infringed upon by the new government. In their interpretation of these ten amendments, the courts, especially the Supreme Court, have taken on the task of balancing freedom and order.

Religious freedom in the First Amendment calls for government neutrality toward religions and between religion and nonreligion. Religious beliefs are inviolate, but antisocial actions in the name of religion are not protected by the Constitution.

Freedom of expression encompasses freedom of speech and freedom of the press. These freedoms have never been held to be absolute, though they have been given a far greater measure of protection than other freedoms in the Bill of Rights. The courts have protected only some forms of symbolic expression in the name of the First Amendment. Press freedom has had broad constitutional protection, since a free society depends on the ability to collect and report information without government interference. The rights of peaceable assembly and petition stem from the same freedom protecting speech and press. Each of these freedoms is equally fundamental.

The adoption of the Fourteenth Amendment offered individuals protection from state infringements on their freedoms. The due process clause became the vehicle for applying specific provisions of the Bill of Rights, one at a time in case after case, as limitations against the states. The designation of a right as fundamental also called for a definition of that right. The Supreme Court has tolerated some variation from state to state in the meaning of some constitutional rights. The Court has also imposed a duty on government to inform citizens of their rights so that those rights may be exercised.

The Supreme Court became embroiled in controversy as it fashioned new fundamental rights from the Constitution. The right to privacy served as the basis for the right of women to terminate a pregnancy, which in turn suggested a right to personal autonomy. The abortion controversy is more divisive than ever before, and the justices have called a halt to the extension of personal privacy in the name of the Constitution.

New appointments to the Supreme Court will probably force the justices to consider whether they have cloaked their preferences in the Constitution. By offering constitutional protection to public policies, the courts risk removing decisions from the democratic branches, where the people can have their say through elected representatives. One thing is certain, however: the challenge of democracy requires the constant balancing of freedom and order.

Key Terms and Cases

injunction
civil rights
civil liberties
establishment clause
free exercise clause
Lemon v. *Kurtzman*
*West Virginia State Board of
Education* v. *Barnette*
speech clause
press clause
prior restraint
free expression clauses
clear and present danger test
Gitlow v. *New York*
Brandenburg v. *Ohio*
Tinker v. *Des Moines Independent
County School District*

symbolic expression
fighting words
Cohen v. *California*
libel
New York Times Co. v. *Sullivan*
public figures
New York Times v. *United States*
bills of attainder
ex post facto laws
obligation of contracts
Palko v. *Connecticut*
Gideon v. *Wainwright*
Miranda warnings
exclusionary rule
Mapp v. *Ohio*
Griswold v. *Connecticut*
Roe v. *Wade*
Hyde Amendment

Selected Readings

Baker, Liva. *Miranda: Crime, Law and Politics*. New York: Atheneum, 1983. Baker uses the *Miranda* case as a vehicle for explaining the American legal system. Baker traces the case from its origin to its landmark resolution.

Berns, Walter. *The First Amendment and the Future of Democracy*. New York: Basic Books, 1976. Berns contends that the Supreme Court is steadily eroding the conditions of civil liberty.

Brigham, John. *Civil Liberties and American Democracy*. Washington, D.C.: CQ Press, 1984. A survey of U.S. civil rights and liberties organized around basic concepts (privacy, entitlements).

Haiman, Franklyn C. *Speech and Law in a Free Society*. Chicago: University of Chicago Press, 1981. A thorough survey of the meaning of the First Amendment. Haiman argues that no special significance attaches to the separate speech and press clauses.

Levy, Leonard W. *The Emergence of a Free Press*. New York: Oxford University Press, 1985. This new work revises Levy's original scholarship, *The Legacy of Suppression*, which caused a stir when it was published. Levy maintained that the generation that adopted the Constitution and the Bill of Rights did not believe in a broad view of freedom of expression, especially in the area of politics. His new position, based both on new evidence and on continued criticism of his original thesis, is that Americans were more tolerant of government criticism but that the revolutionary generation did not intend to wipe out seditious libel with the adoption of the First Amendment.

Lewis, Anthony. *Gideon's Trumpet*. New York: Random House, 1964. The moving story of Clarence Earl Gideon's claim to assistance of counsel guaranteed by the Sixth Amendment.

18

Equality and
Civil Rights

A polite employment notice might have read, "Whites only. Others need not apply." Such pronouncements recall a long, painful, and shameful period of U.S. history during which black Americans were subjected to the indignities of racial prejudice — a period that stretched from colonization through the nation's bicentennial. Yet this particular pronouncement also summarized the sentiments of a New York labor union, Local 28 of the Sheet Metal Workers' International Association, as late as 1986.

Local 28 refused to admit blacks or Hispanics from 1913, when it was established, until 1969; and even then, only a few nonwhites were permitted to join. When New York City attempted to assign six minority trainees to sheet metal contractors working on city projects, Local 28 walked off the job. Its white members were steadfast in their opposition to nonwhites.

The list of ruses used by Local 28 to avoid the entry of nonwhites seemed endless. The local required special examinations and a high school diploma for entrance, simply to bar nonwhites; neither had any bearing on job performance. Union funds were used to provide special tutoring to members' friends and relatives who were taking the entrance exams. Local 28 declined to keep records on the racial composition of its membership, in an attempt to avoid charges of discrimination.

Discrimination is an act of irrational hatred or suspicion of a specific race, religion, or other group. Government policies that tolerated racial discrimination thus abetted **racism,** a belief that human races have distinct characteristics and that one's own race is superior and has a right to rule others. Today, American government rejects the racism of its past. Instead, government policies in employment, housing, and education attempt to erase discrimination root and branch, and thus to promote equality.

In 1975, a federal court concluded that Local 28 had violated Title VII of the Civil Rights Act of 1964, which bars employment discrimination on account of race, color, religion, sex, and national origin. The court established a 29 percent nonwhite membership goal, based on the percentage of nonwhites in the New York City labor pool; the court also gave the union six years to achieve that goal. This decision was justified, said the court, by Local 28's long and persistent pattern of discrimination. But the union failed to institute employment programs that would boost minority membership; and it continued to erect new barriers as quickly as the courts struck them down.

Finally, after more than twenty years of state and federal litigation, the federal court required Local 28 to accept equal numbers of white and non-white apprentices to achieve the 29 percent nonwhite membership. To ensure that minority apprentices would be employed, Local 28 was required to assign to contractors one apprentice for every four experienced workers. Such requirements have been fiercely opposed by many Americans. Policies that are aimed at achieving equality often generate hostility. Why? The answer is complex. To arrive at it, we shall trace the development of American civil rights.

The history of civil rights in the United States has been mainly a story of the search for social and economic equality in American democracy. That search has gone on for more than a century — since the Civil War — and has

A Sad Legacy
In World War II, Congress authorized the detention and relocation of Japanese residents in the western United States, including native-born American citizens of Japanese ancestry. More than 110,000 men, women and children — most of them loyal Americans — were incarcerated and dispossessed simply because they were of Japanese heritage. Laws prejudicial to racial and other minorities are ordinarily forbidden, yet the Supreme Court upheld the law in 1944. This episode was the only occasion on which the Court gave constitutional protection to an explicit legislative act of racial inequality.

not yet been completed. It has primarily involved the civil rights of black citizens, whose subjugation roused the passions of a nation. Their struggle has been a beacon illuminating similar struggles faced by Hispanic Americans, Native Americans, and women. Each group confronted discrimination, sometimes subtle and sometimes overt. Yet each group achieved a measure of success by pressing its interests on government, even challenging government. These challenges and the responses have shaped our evaluation of democracy.

Recall that **civil rights** are powers or privileges that are guaranteed to individuals and protected from arbitrary removal at the hands of government or individuals. (Rights need not be confined to humans. Some advocates claim that animals have rights, too.) In this chapter we concentrate on the rights guaranteed by the constitutional amendments adopted after the Civil War and by laws passed to enforce those guarantees. Prominent among them is the right to equal protection of the laws. This right remained a promise rather than a reality well into the twentieth century, when government began promoting social and political equality for groups that had been disadvantaged by prejudice.

THE CIVIL WAR AMENDMENTS

The Civil War Amendments were adopted to provide freedom and equality to black Americans. The Thirteenth Amendment, which was ratified in 1865, provided the freedom; it states simply that

> Neither slavery nor involuntary servitude . . . shall exist within the United States, or any place subject to their jurisdiction.

The Fourteenth Amendment was adopted three years later. It provides first that the freed slaves are citizens:

> All persons born or naturalized in the United States and subject to the jurisdiction thereof, are citizens of the United States and of the State wherein they reside.

Next, as discussed in Chapter 17, it prohibits the states from abridging the "privileges or immunities of citizens of the United States" or depriving any person of "life, liberty, or property without due process of law." The Fourteenth Amendment then provides for equality under the law by declaring that no state shall

> deny to any person within its jurisdiction the equal protection of the laws.

The Fifteenth Amendment, adopted in 1870, added a measure of political equality:

> The right of citizens of the United States to vote shall not be denied or abridged by the United States or by any State on account of race, color, or previous condition of servitude.

The amendment did not prohibit the use of other means for denying citizens the right to vote. Thus, being female was still sufficient cause to bar the enfranchising of half the black population, along with half of all whites. Nonetheless, American blacks were free and politically equal — at least according to the U.S. Constitution.

Early Supreme Court Interpretations

In 1866 the Congress passed a Civil Rights Act that gave the federal government some authority over the treatment of blacks by state courts. Later, in the Civil Rights Act of 1875, Congress attempted to guarantee equality to blacks in places of public accommodation (such as streetcars, inns, parks, and theaters).

Meanwhile, the Supreme Court seemed intent on weakening attempts to ensure the civil rights of black citizens. Recall from Chapter 17 that, in the *Slaughter House Cases* (1873), the Court ruled that the Civil War Amendments had not changed the relationship between the state and national governments.[1] In other words, state citizenship and national citizenship remained separate and distinct; the Fourteenth Amendment did not enlarge the rights guaranteed by U.S. citizenship. The amendment was thus (temporarily, at least) stripped of its power to secure the Bill of Rights guarantees for black citizens.

From this beginning, the Court continued to shrink constitutional protections for blacks. In 1876, in *United States* v. *Cruikshank,* the justices crippled congressional attempts to enforce the rights of blacks. A group of Louisiana whites had used violence and fraud to prevent blacks from exercising basic constitutional rights, including the right of peaceable assembly. The justices held that the rights allegedly infringed were not federally protected rights and that therefore Congress was powerless to punish the persons who violated them.[2] On the very same day, the Court ruled that the Fifteenth Amendment did not guarantee all citizens the right to vote; instead, it only listed grounds that *could not be used to deny* that right.[3] And in the *Civil Rights Cases* (1883) the Court struck down the public accommodations section of the Civil Rights Act of 1875. The justices declared that the federal government could prohibit only *state action* discriminating against blacks; private acts of discrimination or acts of omission by a state were beyond the reach of federal power. The Court refused to view racial discrimination as a badge of slavery that the federal government could prohibit.[4]

The results of such decisions seem obvious in retrospect. In the matter of voting rights, for example, states that wanted to bar black men from the polls simply used nonracial means to do so. One popular barrier to Negro voting was the **poll tax,** first instituted by Georgia in 1877. This was a tax of $1 or $2 on every citizen who wished to vote. The tax was no burden on white citizens. However, many blacks were tenant farmers, deeply in debt to white merchants and land owners; they were hardly ever able to put together more than a few pennies. Other bars to black suffrage included the requirement that the voter had attained a particular level of education or that he owned property — and even that the voter had a grandfather who was eligible to vote before 1867 (that is, three years before the Fifteenth Amendment declared that race could not be used to deny the right to vote).[5] Intimidation and violence were also used to keep blacks from the polls.

The Roots of Racial Segregation

Well before the Civil War, the South was characterized by widespread but informal **racial segregation,** in which blacks lived and worked separately from whites. After the war, southern states began to enact "Jim Crow" laws that *required* segregation. With the nullification of the Civil Rights Act of 1875, such laws proliferated. Blacks were required to live in separate — and generally inferior — areas of towns and cities; they were restricted to separate and inferior sections of hospitals, to separate cemeteries, separate drinking and toilet facilities, separate sections of streetcars, trains, schools, jails, parks, and every other public accommodation. Each day, in countless ways, they were reminded of the inferior status accorded them by white society.

In 1892, Homer Adolph Plessy — who was seven-eighths Caucasian — took a seat in a "whites only" car of a Louisiana railroad train. He refused to move to the car reserved for blacks and was arrested, and his case reached the Supreme Court. Plessy argued that Louisiana's law requiring racial segregation on its trains was an unconstitutional infringement of both the privileges or immunities and the equal protection clauses of the Fourteenth Amendment. The Supreme Court disagreed. The majority decision in ***Plessy v. Ferguson*** (1896) upheld state-imposed racial segregation based on the

Separate and Unequal
The Supreme Court gave constitutional protection to racial separation on the theory that states could provide "separate but equal" facilities for blacks. But racial separation meant unequal facilities, as these two water fountains dramatically illustrate. The Supreme Court struck a fatal blow against the "separate but equal" doctrine in its landmark 1954 ruling, Brown *v.* Board of Education.

concept of **separate-but-equal** facilities for blacks.[6] The lone dissenter was John Marshall Harlan (the first of two distinguished justices with the same name). Harlan, who envisioned a "color-blind Constitution," wrote:

> We boast of the freedom enjoyed by our people above all other peoples. But it is difficult to reconcile that boast with a state of the law which, practically, puts the brand of servitude and degradation upon a large class of our fellow citizens, —our equals before the law. The thin disguise of "equal" accommodations for passengers in railroad coaches will not mislead any one, nor atone for the wrong this day done.

Three years later, the Supreme Court extended the separate-but-equal doctrine to the schools.[7] The justices ignored the fact that black educational facilities (and most other "colored only" facilities) were far from equal to those reserved for whites. Thus, by the end of the nineteenth century, racial segregation was firmly and legally entrenched in the American South. Several decades would have to pass before there was any discernible change.

THE DISMANTLING OF SCHOOL SEGREGATION

Denied the right to vote, blacks sought access to political power in other parts of the political system. The National Association for the Advancement of Colored People (NAACP) began the campaign for black civil rights. It was founded in 1909 by W. E. B. Du Bois and others, both black and white, with the goal of ending racial discrimination and segregation. The plan was to attack the separate-but-equal doctrine in two parts — first by pressing for fully equal facilities for blacks, and then by proving the unconstitutionality of segregation. The process would be a slow one, but the strategies involved did not require a large organization or heavy financial backing (and, at the time, the NAACP had neither).*

Pressure for Equality . . .

In 1935 Lloyd Gaines graduated from Lincoln University (a black college) in Missouri and applied to the state law school. Gaines was rejected because he was black. Missouri refused to admit blacks to its all-white state law school; instead, the state policy was to pay the costs of blacks who were admitted to out-of-state law schools. With the support of the NAACP, Gaines appealed to the courts for admission to the University of Missouri Law School. In 1938 the Supreme Court mandated that he be admitted. Under the *Plessy* doctrine, Missouri could not shift its responsibility to provide an equal education onto other states.[8]

Two later cases helped reinforce the requirement that segregated facilities be equal in all major respects. One of these was brought by Heman Sweatt (again with the help of the NAACP). Sweatt had been denied entrance to the all-white University of Texas Law School because of his race. A federal court ordered the state to provide a black law school that Sweatt could attend; the state responded by renting a few rooms in an office building and hiring two black lawyers as teachers. Sweatt refused to attend this so-called "black law school" and took his case to the Supreme Court.[9]

Similarly, George McLaurin had been refused admission to a doctoral program in education at the all-white University of Oklahoma because he was black. There was no equivalent program for blacks in the state. McLaurin sought a federal court order to admit him, but under pressure from the *Gaines* decision the university amended its procedures and admitted McLaurin "on a segregated basis." The sixty-eight-year-old McLaurin was restricted to hastily designated "colored only" sections of a few rooms. He appealed this obvious lack of equal facilities to the Supreme Court under the direction of the NAACP.[10]

The Supreme Court ruled on the tandem *Sweatt* and *McLaurin* cases in 1950. The justices unanimously found that the facilities in each case were inadequate for black students: the separate "law school" provided for Sweatt did not approach the quality of the white University of Texas; and the restrictions placed on McLaurin, through his segregation from other students within the same institution, would result in an inferior education. Both Sweatt and McLaurin had to be admitted to full student status at their respective state universities. But the Court avoided reexamination of the separate-but-equal doctrine.

---

*In 1939, the NAACP established an offshoot called the NAACP Legal Defense and Education Fund, Inc., to work on legal challenges while the main organization concentrated on lobbying as its principal strategy.

... And Pressure for Desegregation

These decisions—especially the *McLaurin* case—seemed to indicate that the time was right for an attack on segregation itself. In addition, public attitudes regarding race relations were slowly changing from the predominant racism of the nineteenth and early twentieth centuries. Black troops had fought with honor—albeit in segregated military units—in World War II. Blacks and whites were working together in unions and in service organizations like the National Council of Churches.

President Harry S Truman risked his political future in his strong support of black civil rights. In 1947 he established the President's Committee on Civil Rights. That committee's report, issued the same year, became the agenda for the civil rights movement over the next two decades. It called for federal laws prohibiting racially motivated brutality, segregation, and poll taxes and

Anger Erupts in Little Rock
The school board in Little Rock, Arkansas, attempted to implement a court-approved desegregation program. The first step called for the admission of nine blacks to Central High School on September 3, 1957, but when they appeared for classes, the governor sent in the national guard to prevent their attendance. Police escorts could not control the mobs that gathered around the school on September 23, when the black students once again attempted to attend classes. Two days later, under the protection of federal troops ordered by President Eisenhower to enforce the court order, the students were admitted. Mob violence and hostility led the school board to seek a postponement of the desegregation plan, but the Supreme Court, meeting in special session in the summer of 1958, affirmed the Brown *decision and ordered the desegregation plan to proceed as scheduled.*

for guarantees of voting rights and equal employment opportunity. In 1948, as commander-in-chief, Truman ordered the **desegregation** (the ending of authorized racial segregation) of the armed forces. And in 1947, under Truman, the U.S. Department of Justice had begun to submit briefs to the courts in support of civil rights. Perhaps the department's most important intervention was in **Brown v. Board of Education of Topeka**. This was an NAACP-supported attempt to secure the desegregation of the nation's public schools.

Linda Brown was a black child whose father sought to enroll her in a white public school in Topeka, Kansas. The white school was close to Linda's home; the walk to the black school required that she cross a dangerous set of railroad tracks. Brown's request was refused because of Linda's race. A federal district court found that the black public school was, in all major respects, equal in quality to the white school; therefore, by the *Plessy* doctrine, Linda was required to go to the black public school. Brown appealed that decision.

Brown v. *Board of Education of Topeka* reached the Supreme Court in 1952, along with four similar cases, brought in Delaware, South Carolina, Virginia, and the District of Columbia. (All were supported by the NAACP and coordinated by Thurgood Marshall, who would later become the first black justice of the Supreme Court.) These five public school cases squarely challenged the separate-but-equal principle. By all "tangible" measures (such as standards for teacher licensing, teacher-pupil ratios, and library facilities) the two school systems in each case — one white, the other black — were equal. Legally imposed separation of the races was at issue.

The cases were argued in 1953; but they were set for reargument at the request of the justices. On May 17, 1954, Chief Justice Earl Warren, who had joined the Court less than a year before, delivered a single opinion covering four of the cases. (In Chapter 13 we examined how he approached the school segregation cases after they were argued.) Warren spoke for a unanimous Court when he declared that "in the field of public education the doctrine of 'separate but equal' has no place. Separate educational facilities are inherently unequal, depriving the plaintiffs of the equal protection of the laws."[11] Segregated facilities generate in black children "a feeling of inferiority . . . that may affect their hearts and minds in a way unlikely ever to be undone." In short, state-imposed public school segregation violates the Fourteenth Amendment's equal protection clause.

A companion case to *Brown* challenged the segregation of public schools in Washington, D.C.[12] This segregation was imposed by Congress, but the equal protection clause protected citizens only against *state* violations. There was no equal protection clause restraining the national government. It was unthinkable for the Constitution to impose a lesser duty on the federal government than on the states. In this case the Court decided that the racial segregation requirement was an arbitrary deprivation of liberty without due process of law, which is a violation of the Fifth Amendment.

The Court deferred the implementation of the school desegregation decisions until the following year. Then, in **Brown v. Board of Education of Topeka II,** it commanded that school systems desegregate "with all deliberate speed."[13] Desegregation was to proceed under the direction of the lower federal courts.

Some states quietly implemented the *Brown* decree. Others did little to desegregate their schools. And many communities in the South defied the Court, sometimes violently. Some states paid the tuition of white students who attended private schools; others ordered that desegregated schools be closed.

This resistance, along with the Supreme Court's "all deliberate speed" order, placed a heavy burden on federal judges to dismantle what were by now fundamental social institutions in their own communities.[14] Gradual desegregation under the *Brown* decree was, in some cases, no desegregation at all. For that reason, in 1969, a unanimous Supreme Court ordered that the operation of segregated school systems must stop "at once."[15]

Two years later, the Court approved several remedies to achieve integration, including busing, racial quotas, and the pairing or grouping of noncontiguous school zones. In **Swann v. Charlotte-Mecklenburg County Schools** the Supreme Court affirmed the right of lower courts to order the busing of children to assure school desegregation. But these remedies applied only to **de jure segregation** (government-imposed segregation), not to **de facto segregation** (segregation that is not the result of government influence).[16]

Like school desegregation itself, the busing of school children came under heavy attack in both the North and the South. Busing was viewed as a possible remedy in many northern cities, where schools had become segregated not by law, but because many white families had left the cities for the suburbs; as a result of this "white flight," inner-city schools had become predominantly black, whereas suburban schools were almost all white. Increasingly, busing became the target of legislative politics. Public opinion was opposed to the busing approach. Congress sought limits on busing as a remedy. In 1974, a closely divided Supreme Court ruled in **Milliken v. Bradley** that lower courts could not order busing across school district boundaries to achieve racial balance unless each district had practiced racial discrimination, or unless school district lines had been drawn to achieve racial segregation.[17] This case reversed the trend started by the *Brown* decision—the trend toward favoring all efforts at integrating the public schools. It meant an end to extensive school integration in metropolitan areas. And a growing call for "Freedom now!" signaled black frustration with the idea of equality that, for many, still remained only a promise.

THE CIVIL RIGHTS MOVEMENT

Although the NAACP had concentrated on school desegregation, it had also made headway in other civil rights areas. The Supreme Court responded to NAACP's efforts of the mid- to late 1940s by outlawing the white-only primary elections that were being held in the South and by declaring them to be in violation of the Fifteenth Amendment. The Court also declared segregation on interstate bus routes to be unconstitutional and desegregated restaurants and hotels in the District of Columbia. Despite these and other decisions which chipped away at existing barriers to equality, black citizens were still being denied political power, and segregation remained a fact of daily life (see Feature 18.1).

Feature 18.1

American Racism as International Handicap

In August 1955, the ambassador from India, G.L. Mehta, walked into a restaurant at the Houston International Airport, sat down, and waited to order. But Texas law required that whites and blacks be served in separate dining facilities. The dark-skinned diplomat, who had seated himself in a whites-only area, was told to move. The insult stung deeply and was not soon forgotten. From Washington, Secretary of State John Foster Dulles telegraphed his apologies for this blatant display of racism, fearing that the incident would injure relations with a nation whose allegiance the United States was seeking in the Cold War.

Such embarrassments were not uncommon in the 1950s. Burma's minister of education was denied a meal in a Columbus, Ohio, restaurant; and the finance minister of Ghana was turned away from a Howard Johnson's restaurant just outside the nation's capital. Secretary Dulles complained that segregationist practices were becoming a "major international hazard," a threat to U.S. efforts to gain the friendship of Third World countries. Americans stood publicly condemned as a people who did not honor the ideal of equality.

Thus when the attorney general appealed to the Supreme Court to strike down segregation in public schools, his introductory remarks took note of the international implications. "It is in the context of the present world struggle between freedom and tyranny that the problem of racial discrimination must be viewed," he warned. The humiliation of dark-skinned diplomats in Washington, D.C., "the window through which the world looks into our house," was damaging to American interests. Racism "furnished grist for the Communist propaganda mills."

Source: Mary Beth Norton *et al., A People and a Nation: A History of the United States,* 2nd ed. (Boston: Houghton Mifflin, 1986), Vol. II, p. 867.

Dwight D. Eisenhower, who became president in 1953, was not as concerned with civil rights as his predecessor. He chose to stand above the battle between the Supreme Court and those who resisted the Court's decisions. He even refused to reveal whether he agreed with the Court's *Brown* decision. "It makes no difference," Eisenhower declared, because "the Constitution is as the Supreme Court interprets it."[18]

Eisenhower enforced school desegregation with reluctance when the safety of school children was involved, but he appeared unwilling to do much more to advance racial equality. That goal seemed to require the political mobilization of the people — black and white — into what is now known as the **civil rights movement.**

Civil Disobedience

The call to action was first sounded by Rosa Parks, a black Montgomery, Alabama, maid. In December 1955, Parks boarded a city bus on her way home from work. The city's Jim Crow ordinances required blacks to sit in the back of the bus and, when asked, to give up their seats to whites. Tired

A Speech Electrifies a Nation
Martin Luther King, Jr. was a Baptist minister who believed in nonviolent peaceful protest in the spirit of India's Mahatma Gandhi. King helped to coordinate civil rights activities, starting with the Montgomery, Alabama, bus boycott in 1955.
  More than a quarter of a million people—whites as well as blacks—gathered in August 1963 at the Lincoln Memorial to demonstrate their support for civil rights. King gave a spellbinding oration. "I have a dream," he told the crowd, "that one day this nation will rise up and live out the true meaning of its creed: 'We hold these truths to be self-evident, that all men are created equal.' "
  King was assassinated in 1968 in Memphis, Tennessee.

after the day's work, Parks took an available seat in the front (white) section of the bus; she refused to give up her seat when asked to do so by the driver and was arrested and fined $10 for violating a city ordinance.

Montgomery's black community responded to Parks' arrest with a boycott of the city's bus system. (A **boycott** is a refusal to do business with a firm or individual, as an expression of disapproval or as a means of coercion.) Blacks walked or used car pools or simply did not make trips that were not absolutely necessary. As the bus company moved closer to bankruptcy and downtown merchants suffered from the loss of black business, city officials began to harass blacks, hoping to frighten them into ending the boycott. But Montgomery's black citizens now had a leader—a charismatic twenty-seven-year-old Baptist minister named Martin Luther King, Jr.

King urged the people to persevere in the boycott, and they did. A year after the boycott began, the Supreme Court ruled that segregated transportation systems violated the equal protection clause of the Constitution (see Feature 13.1 on page 474). The boycott proved to be an effective weapon against whites who were resolved to maintain their power and institutions.

In 1957, Martin Luther King, Jr., helped organize the Southern Christian Leadership Council (SCLC) to coordinate civil rights activities. King was totally committed to nonviolent direct action to bring racial issues into the light. He advocated **civil disobedience,** the willful—but nonviolent—violation of laws that were regarded as unjust.

Another tactic in the fight against Jim Crow was the *sit-in*. On February 1, 1960, four black students from North Carolina Agricultural and Technical College in Greensboro sought service at a white lunch counter. They were refused service and, when they would not leave, were abused verbally and physically. Still they would not move, until finally they were arrested. Soon there were similar sit-in demonstrations throughout the South, and then into the North. The Supreme Court upheld the actions of the demonstrators, but the unanimity that had characterized the Court's earlier decisions was gone (see Feature 18.2).

The Civil Rights Act of 1964

In 1961 a new administration came into power, headed by President John F. Kennedy. At first Kennedy did not seem to be committed to civil rights. However, the movement gained momentum, and more and more whites became aware of the abuse being heaped on sit-in demonstrators, on "Freedom Riders" who tested unlawful segregation on interstate bus routes, and on individuals attempting to help blacks register to vote in southern states. These volunteers were being jailed, beaten, and killed for advocating activities that whites took for granted.

Then, in the fall of 1962, President Kennedy ordered federal troops to ensure the safety of James Meredith, the first black to attend the University of Mississippi. In early 1963 Kennedy enforced the desegregation of the University of Alabama. And in April 1963 television viewers were shocked to see film of a march in Birmingham, Alabama, during which sheriff's deputies attacked peaceful demonstrators with dogs, fire hoses, and cattle prods. (The idea of the march was to provoke confrontations with white officials in an effort to compel the federal government to intervene on behalf of blacks.) Finally, in June 1963, Kennedy asked Congress for legislation that would outlaw segregation in public accommodations.

Two months later, Martin Luther King, Jr., organized and led a march on Washington, D.C., to show support for the civil rights movement. More than 250,000 people, black and white, gathered peaceably at the Lincoln Memorial to hear King speak. "I have a dream," he told them, "that my little children will one day live in a nation where they will not be judged by the color of their skin but by the content of their character."[19]

Kennedy's public accommodations bill had not yet been passed by Congress when, on November 22, 1963, Kennedy was assassinated. His successor, Lyndon B. Johnson, considered civil rights to be his top legislative priority, and within months Congress passed the Civil Rights Act of 1964. The quick passage of the act was, in part, a reaction to Kennedy's death. But it was almost surely also a reaction to such brutal acts as the bombing of the Sixteenth Street Baptist Church in Birmingham while Sunday school was in session; four young black girls were killed in the explosion.

Civil rights laws had been passed by Congress in 1957 and 1960, but they dealt primarily with voting rights. The 1964 act was the most comprehensive legislative effort to erase racial discrimination from American life. It was enacted after the longest debate in Senate history, and only after the first successful use of cloture to end a civil rights filibuster.

The bill had to avoid the grip of Southern conservatives in the House and the Senate. Because it was grounded in both Section 5 of the Fourteenth Amendment (which gives Congress the power to enforce that amendment) and the commerce clause of Article 1, the bill was sent to two committees in each chamber. The House Judiciary Committee and the Senate Commerce

Feature 18.2

A Right to Discriminate?

The Supreme Court led by Chief Justice Earl Warren did more to vindicate civil rights than any other government institution. But it came perilously close to depriving the civil rights movement of a powerful weapon: the sit-in. The justices were divided over vital issues of freedom and equality.

The Court confronted four sit-in cases in 1964. In each case, blacks sat down in restaurants or at lunch counters and refused to leave without being served. In the principal case, *Bell* v. *Maryland,* the sit-in occurred in Baltimore. The demonstrators were arrested and then convicted for violating state trespass laws.

At the conference to decide the merits, the Chief Justice urged his colleagues to "get to the 'raw' of the problem." His position was that the convictions violated the equal protection clause of the Fourteenth Amendment. Said Warren: "As long as the demonstrators behave themselves, the owner can't have police to help to throw them out. The state then unconstitutionally enforces discrimination."

The justices were deeply divided; Warren gathered only three votes in addition to his own. The majority sided with Justice Hugo L. Black, who delivered an emotional statement in which he recalled his "Pappy," who ran a general store in Alabama: surely he had the right to decide whom he would serve or would not serve. Black had been in the vanguard of Fourteenth Amendment protections in the relatively easy cases like *Brown* v. *Board of Education.* Here, however, the conflict pitted freedom (even freedom to discriminate) against equality; the majority preferred freedom.

The division brought several exchanges of opinions, some brimming with emotion. Justice William J. Brennan, Jr., expressed his fear that an affirmance of the sit-in convictions might cripple the Civil Rights Act. Title II, barring discrimination in places of public accommodation, was then the subject of a Senate filibuster. Brennan counseled delay until the legislative outcome was clear, urging the justices to avoid the constitutional question before them. Instead, he argued that the sit-in convictions should be overturned on the basis of a Baltimore public accommodations law enacted after the demonstrators were convicted. The convictions were still pending when the city law was adopted. This had the effect, argued Brennan, of nullifying the trespass violations.

Ultimately, Brennan's view prevailed, and his majority opinion was announced shortly before passage of the Civil Rights Act of 1964. Had Black's opinion prevailed, the history of American civil rights might have been different; that opinion could have weakened, if not defeated, the nation's most comprehensive effort to erase racial discrimination from American life.

See Bernard Schwartz, *The Unpublished Opinions of the Warren Court* (New York: Oxford University Press, 1985), pp. 143–190.

Committee were chaired by supporters of the bill, so it was certain to be brought to the floor of each chamber for a vote.

Among its many provisions, the act:

1. Entitled all persons to "the full and equal enjoyment" of goods, services, and privileges in places of public accommodation without discrimination on the ground of race, color, religion, or national origin.
2. Established the right to equality in employment opportunities.
3. Strengthened voting rights legislation.
4. Created the Equal Employment Opportunity Commission (EEOC), charging it to hear and investigate complaints of job discrimination.*
5. Provided that funds could be withheld from federally assisted programs that were administered in a discriminatory manner.

The last of these provisions had a powerful impact on school desegregation when Congress passed the Elementary and Secondary Education Act in 1965. That act provided for billions of federal dollars in aid for the nation's schools; the threat of losing those funds spurred local school boards to formulate and implement new desegregation plans.

The 1964 act faced an immediate constitutional challenge. Its opponents argued that the Constitution does not forbid acts of private discrimination. But a unanimous Supreme Court upheld the law in *Heart of Atlanta Motel* v. *United States* (1964), declaring that acts of discrimination impose substantial burdens on interstate commerce and thus are subject to congressional control.[20] In a companion case, *Katzenbach* v. *McClung* (1964), the owners of a small barbecue restaurant had refused to serve blacks and had sought to stop enforcement of the law. Ollie McClung maintained that he had the freedom to serve or not serve customers in his own restaurant. The justices, however, upheld the government's prohibition of McClung's racial discrimination on the ground that a substantial portion of the food served in his restaurant had moved in interstate commerce.[21] The Civil Rights Act of 1964 was vindicated by reason of the congressional power to regulate interstate commerce, rather than on the basis of the Fourteenth Amendment.

Other civil rights legislation soon followed under Johnson's Great Society:

■ The Economic Opportunity Act of 1964, which focused on education and training in the fight against poverty.

■ The Voting Rights Act of 1965, which empowered the Attorney General to send voter registration supervisors to areas in which fewer than half the eligible minority voters had been registered. That act has been credited with doubling black voter registration in the South in only five years.

■ The Fair Housing Act of 1968, which banned discrimination in the rental or sale of most housing.

In addition, the Twenty-Fourth Amendment, which banned poll taxes, was ratified in 1964.

---

*Since 1972, the EEOC has had the power to institute legal proceedings on behalf of employees who allege that they have been victims of illegal discrimination.

Racial Violence and Black Nationalism

The mid- and late 1960s were marked by increased violence, on the part of both those who demanded their civil rights and those who refused to relinquish them. Violence against civil rights workers was confined primarily to the South, where volunteers continued to work for desegregation and the registering of black voters. Among the atrocities that incensed even complacent whites were the bombings of dozens of black churches; the murder of three young civil rights workers in Philadelphia, Mississippi, in 1964 by a group of whites that included sheriff's deputies; police violence against a group of demonstrators who had started out on a peaceful march from Selma, Alabama, to Montgomery in 1965; and the assassination of Martin Luther King, Jr., in Memphis in 1968.

Black violence took the form of rioting in black ghettos of Northern cities. Civil rights gains had mainly been focused on the South. Northern blacks had the vote and were not subject to Jim Crow laws. Yet most lived in poverty, experienced extremely high unemployment, and, when they were

The March on Montgomery, 1965
Under the leadership of Martin Luther King, Jr., and his crusade of nonviolence, Southern blacks joined in a massive march on Montgomery, Alabama, in the cause of black voter registration. Later in the 1960s, such nonviolent protests all but disappeared, as a new militancy set the tone for the cause of civil rights.

employed, were paid lower wages for generally more menial jobs than whites. Their segregation in inner-city ghettos, although not sanctioned by law, was nevertheless real; their voting power was of little moment because they constituted a small minority of the Northern population. The solid gains made by Southern blacks added to their frustration, and starting in 1964 they took to the streets, burning and looting. Riots in 168 cities and towns followed King's assassination in 1968.

The lack of progress toward equality for Northern blacks was an important factor in the rise of a black nationalist movement in the 1960s. The Black Muslims, led by Malcolm X until his assassination in 1965, called for separation from whites rather than integration, and for violence in return for violence. The Black Panther Party denounced the values of white America. In 1966, Stokely Carmichael, then chairman of the Student Nonviolent Coordinating Committee (SNCC), called on blacks to assert "Black Power" in their struggle for civil rights. Organizations that previously had espoused integration and nonviolence now began to argue that blacks needed power more than they needed white friendship.

The black nationalist movement promoted and instilled pride in black history and culture, and toward the end of the decade colleges and universities began to institute black studies programs for their students. More black citizens were voting than ever before, and their voting power was evident: increasing numbers of blacks were being elected to public office. Thus, in 1967 Cleveland's voters elected Carl Stokes as the first black mayor of a major American city. And by 1969, black representatives were able to form the Congressional Black Caucus. These achievements became incentives for other groups who also faced impediments to equality.

CIVIL RIGHTS FOR OTHER MINORITIES

The civil rights won by black Americans apply, of course, to all Americans; recent civil rights laws and court decisions are aimed at protecting members of all minority groups. In the United States, however, equality has been granted most slowly to nonwhite minorities. In this section we briefly discuss the civil rights struggles of two such minorities—Native Americans and Hispanic Americans.

Native Americans

During the eighteenth and nineteenth centuries, U.S. government policy toward American Indians, or Native Americans, was characterized by the taking of Indian lands, the geographic isolation of Indians on reservations, and then political and social isolation. Government policy was often enforced with violence and riddled with broken promises. The agency system for administering Indian reservations kept Native Americans poor and dependent on the federal government.

It was not until 1924 that Indians were given U.S. citizenship. Until then they were considered solely as members of tribal nations whose relations

Wounded Knee,
South Dakota
Wounded Knee conjures up a
bitter image for Native
Americans. On that site, in
1890, government troops
massacred two hundred sick and
hungry men, women, and
children who were mistakenly
believed to be armed for revolt.
In 1973, militant members of
the American Indian Movement
seized hostages at Wounded
Knee to express their anger with
both federal government policies
and the actions of conservative
Indian leaders. Some Indians
who sided with the federal
marshals were dismissed by the
militants as ''Uncle Toma-
hawks.'' Here, Indians and
government officials walk
around a teepee as they seek a
negotiated settlement at a
powwow.

with government were subject to treaties made with the United States. The
Native American population suffered badly during the Depression, primarily
because the poorest people were affected most, but also through inept administration of Indian reservations. Poverty remained on the reservations well
after the Depression was over, and Indian lands continued to shrink through
the 1950s and into the 1960s—in spite of signed treaties and the religious
significance of portions of those lands. In the 1960s, for example, a part of
the Hopi Sacred Circle, which is considered the source of all life in tribal
religion, was strip-mined for coal.

Anger bred of poverty, unemployment, and frustration with an uncaring
government exploded into militant action in November 1969, when several
American Indians seized the abandoned Alcatraz Island in San Francisco Bay.
The group cited an 1868 Sioux treaty which entitled them to the possession
of unused federal lands; they remained on the island for a year and a half.
In 1973, armed members of the American Indian Movement seized eleven
hostages at Wounded Knee, South Dakota—the site of an 1890 massacre of
the Sioux by U.S. cavalry troops. They remained there, occasionally exchanging gunfire with federal marshals, for 71 days.

In 1946 Congress had passed legislation establishing an Indian Claims
Commission to compensate Native Americans for land that had been taken
from them. In the 1970s, the Native American Rights Fund and other groups
used that legislation to win important victories. Lands were returned to tribes
in the midwest and in the states of Oklahoma, New Mexico, and Washington.

In 1980, the Supreme Court ordered the federal government to pay the Sioux $117 million plus interest for the Black Hills of South Dakota, which had been stolen from them a century before. Other cases, involving land from coast to coast, are still pending.

Hispanic Americans

In the 1920s, large numbers of Mexican and Puerto Rican immigrants came to the United States in search of employment and a better life. They were welcomed by business people who saw in this wave of immigration a source of cheap labor. Many of the Mexicans became farm workers, but both groups settled mainly in crowded, low-rent inner-city districts: the Mexicans in the southwest, and the Puerto Ricans primarily in New York City. Both groups formed their own *barrios,* or communities, within cities, where they maintained the customs and values of their homelands.

Like blacks who had migrated to Northern cities, most of the new Hispanic immigrants found poverty and discrimination there. And, again like poor blacks and Native Americans, they were hit hard by the Depression. About one-third of the Mexican-American population (mainly those who had been migratory farm workers) returned to Mexico during the 1930s.

World War II gave rise to another influx of Mexicans, who this time were courted to work farms primarily in California. But by the late 1950s, most farm workers were living in poverty—blacks and whites as well as Mexican-Americans. Those Hispanic Americans who lived in cities had fared little better. Yet millions of Mexicans continued to cross the border into the United States, both legally and illegally. Their effect was to depress the value of farm labor in California and the Southwest.

In 1965, Cesar Chavez led a strike of the United Farm Workers' Union against growers in California. The strike lasted several years but resulted in somewhat better pay, working conditions, and housing for workers.

In the 1970s and 1980s, the Hispanic American population continued to grow. The 20 million Hispanics living in the United States in the 1970s were mainly Puerto Rican and Mexican-American, but they had been joined by immigrants from the Dominican Republic, Colombia, Cuba, and Ecuador. They were, to an extent, helped by recent civil rights legislation, but nonetheless were among the poorest and least educated groups in the United States. Their problems are similar to problems faced by other nonwhites; but, in addition, almost all Hispanics had to overcome the further difficulty of learning and using a new language.

The exercise of clout requires Hispanics to vote and gain representation. Voter registration and voter turnout among Hispanics is lower than among other groups. Language is an impediment for many Hispanics; with few or no Spanish-speaking voting officials, low registration levels may be inevitable. Voter turnout depends on effective political advertising, and Hispanics are not targeted as often as other groups with political messages that they can understand. Despite these impediments, however, Hispanics have started to exercise a measure of political power. They have gained some access to political power through their representation in coalitions that dominate policymaking on minority-related issues.[22]

Some Hispanic leaders believe that the problems of low voter registration and low voter turnout will not be solved until Hispanics exercise greater political clout — "brown power." Although many of America's Hispanics speak the same language, they came here from different countries and they differ in many ways. "We need a Spanish Bobby Kennedy or Martin Luther King," observed one leader. "Right now he's just not here."[23]

GENDER AND EQUAL RIGHTS: THE WOMEN'S MOVEMENT

Until the early 1970s, laws that affected the civil rights of women were based on traditional views of the relationship between men and women. **Protectionism** — the policy of sheltering women from life's cruelties — best characterized that relationship. Thomas Jefferson, author of the Declaration of Independence, believed that

> Were our state a pure democracy there would still be excluded from our deliberations women, who, to prevent deprivation of morals and ambiguity of issues, should not mix promiscuously in gatherings of men.[24]

And protected they were, through sexually discriminatory laws involving mainly employment but other areas as well. Women were also "protected" from voting until early in the twentieth century.

Protectionist Laws

The demand for women's rights arose out of the Abolitionist movement and was based primarily on the Fourteenth Amendment's prohibition of laws that "abridge the privileges or immunities of citizens of the United States." However, the courts consistently rebuffed challenges of state protectionist laws. In 1873, the Supreme Court upheld an Illinois statute that prohibited women from practicing law. The justices maintained that the Fourteenth Amendment did not affect a state's authority to regulate admission of members to the bar.[25] In a concurring opinion, Justice Joseph P. Bradley articulated the common protectionist belief that women were unfit for certain occupations: "Man is, or should be, woman's protector and defender. The natural and proper timidity and delicacy which belongs to the female sex evidently unfits it for many of the occupations of civil life."

The protectionist approach reached a peak in 1908 when the Court upheld an Oregon law limiting the number of hours that women were permitted to work. The decision was rife with sexist assumptions about the nature and role of women, and it gave wide latitude to laws that protected the "weaker sex."[26] It also led to protectionist legislation that barred women from working more than forty-eight hours a week and from employment calling for workers to lift more than thirty-five pounds. Thus, women were locked out of jobs that called for substantial overtime (and overtime pay); they were, instead, shunted to jobs suited to their abilities, as perceived by men.

Political Equality for Women

As we noted toward the beginning of this chapter, the Fifteenth Amendment (as interpreted by the Supreme Court) prohibited the use of race in denying a person the right to vote. But gender remained a legal ground for denying the vote to female citizens. In 1869, Francis and Virginia Minor sued a St. Louis, Missouri, registrar for not allowing Virginia Minor to vote. In its decision in *Minor* v. *Happersett* (1875), the Supreme Court held that the Fourteenth Amendment did not confer the right to vote on all citizens or require that the states permit women to vote.[27]

The *Minor* decision clearly blocked the road to women's suffrage, but it did not stop efforts to reach that goal. In 1878, Susan B. Anthony, a women's rights activist, convinced a U.S. senator from California to introduce a constitutional amendment requiring that "the right of citizens of the United States to vote shall not be denied or abridged by the United States or by any State on account of sex." The amendment was introduced and voted down a number of times over the next twenty years. However, a number of states — primarily in the Midwest and West — did grant limited suffrage to women.

The movement for women's suffrage now became a political battle to amend the Constitution. In 1917, 218 women from 26 states were arrested when they picketed the White House to demand the right to vote. Nearly 100 went to jail — some for days, others for months. Hunger strikes and forced feedings followed. The movement culminated in the adoption in 1920 of the **Nineteenth Amendment,** which protects women's right to vote in the wording first suggested by Susan B. Anthony.

Meanwhile, the Supreme Court continued to act as the benevolent protector of women. Women had entered the work force in significant numbers during World War I, and they did so again during World War II; but they received lower wages than the men they replaced. Often the justification was (again) the "proper" role of women as mothers and homemakers. Since men were expected to be the principal providers, it followed that women's earnings were less important to the family's support. But because women were expected to stay at home, women needed — and obtained — less education than men. And because they lacked education, women tended to qualify only for low-paying, low-skill jobs with little chance of advancement. The concept of a "proper" role for women continued to shape policies that discriminated against them. The goal of social and economic equality for women remained hidden until the 1960s.

Prohibiting Sex-Based Discrimination

The movement to provide equal rights to women advanced a step with the passage of the Equal Pay Act of 1963. That act requires equal pay for men and women doing similar work. However, state protectionist laws still had the effect of restricting women to jobs that were not usually taken by men. Where employment was stratified by sex, equal pay was an empty promise. Women needed equal opportunity for employment, free from the restrictions of protectionism. They got it in the Civil Rights Act of 1964 and later legislation.

The purpose of the 1964 Civil Rights Act was to eliminate racial discrimination in America. In its proposed form, Title VII of the act forbade employment discrimination based on race, color, religion, and national origin—but not gender. In an effort to scuttle this provision during House debate, Democrat Howard W. Smith of Virginia proposed an amendment barring job discrimination based on sex. Smith's purpose was to make the law unacceptable. His effort to ridicule the law brought gales of laughter to the debate, but Democrat Martha W. Griffiths of Michigan used Smith's strategy against him. With her support, Smith's amendment carried, as did the act.[28] The jurisdiction of the Equal Employment Opportunity Commission was also extended to cover cases of sex discrimination, or **sexism.**

Subsequent women's rights legislation was motivated by the pressure for civil rights, as well as a resurgence of the women's movement, which had subsided after the adoption of the Nineteenth Amendment. One particularly important law was Title IX of the Education Amendments Act of 1972, which prohibited sex discrimination in federally aided education programs. Another boost to women came from the Revenue Act of 1972, which provided tax credits for child-care expenses. In effect, the act subsidized parents with young children so that women could enter or remain in the work force. However, the high-water mark in the effort on behalf of women's rights was the Equal Rights Amendment, which we shall discuss shortly.

Stereotypes Under Scrutiny

After nearly a century of broad deference to government actions protecting the role of women, the Supreme Court began to take a closer look at gender-based protectionist distinctions. In 1971 it struck down a state law which gave men preference over women in administering the estate of a person who died without naming an administrator. The state maintained that the law reduced court workloads and avoided family battles; however, the Court dismissed those objectives because they were not important enough to sustain the use of gender distinctions.[29] Two years later, the justices declared that the paternalism of earlier ages operated to "put women not on a pedestal, but in a cage."[30] They then proceeded to strike down several gender-based laws that either prevented or discouraged departures from "proper" sex roles. In *Craig* v. *Borden* (1976) the Supreme Court at last developed a workable standard for reviewing such laws: gender-based distinctions could be justified only if they serve some important government purpose.[31]

The objective in claims of gender-based discrimination is to end sexual stereotypes while fashioning public policies that acknowledge *relevant* differences between men and women. Perhaps the most controversial issue in the 1980s is the idea of "comparable worth," which would require employers to pay comparable wages for different jobs that are of about the same worth to an employer, even if one job might be filled predominantly by women and another mainly by men. The goal is a job standard that takes into account both the legal equality of men and women and the relevant physiological differences.[32]

The Equal Rights Amendment

Women have not enjoyed the same rights as men. Policies protecting women have been woven into the legal fabric of American life based largely but not entirely on sexual stereotypes. That protectionism limited the freedom of women to compete with men on an equal footing in social and economic endeavors. The Supreme Court has been noticeably hesitant to extend the principles of the Fourteenth Amendment beyond issues of race. If constitutional interpretation imposes such a limit, then it can be overcome only by a constitutional amendment.

The **Equal Rights Amendment (ERA)** was first introduced in 1923 by the National Women's Party, one of the few women's action groups that

The End of an Era
The death knell for a national Equal Rights Amendment (ERA) pealed on July 1, 1982, three votes short of ratification. ERA proponents have urged adoption of similar laws in the states.

did not disband after the passage of the Nineteenth Amendment. The ERA declared that "Equality of rights under the law shall not be denied or abridged by the United States or any State on account of sex." It remained bottled up in committee in every Congress until 1970, when Representative Martha Griffiths filed a discharge petition to report it to the House floor for a vote. Griffiths' effort brought House passage of the ERA, but the Senate scuttled it by attaching a section calling for prayer in the public schools.

A national coalition of women's rights advocates generated enough support to get the ERA through the proposal stage in 1972. Its proponents now had seven years in which to obtain ratification of the amendment by thirty-eight state legislatures, as required by the Constitution. By 1977 they were three states short of that goal, and three states had rescinded previous ratification. For some reason, the national coalition that had worked so effectively to move through the proposal stage seemed to lack the political strength to jump the ratification hurdle. Then, in an unprecedented action, Congress extended the ratification deadline. The ERA died as a national cause on July 1, 1982, when the time for ratification ran out; it was still three states short of adoption.

The failure to ratify the ERA stands in stark contrast to the quick passage of many laws that now protect women's rights. But in fact there was little audible opposition to women's rights legislation: if years of racial discrimination called for government redress, then so did years of gender-based discrimination. Furthermore, laws protecting women's rights required only the amending of civil rights bills or the passage of similar bills.

The situation was quite different with regard to the ERA. The amendment quickly acquired an opposition, including many women who had supported women's rights legislation. By 1973, ERA opponents had begun a strong campaign to fight ratification. And, as the opposition grew stronger, especially from women who wished to maintain their traditional role, state legislators came to realize that there were risks involved in ERA support. It takes an extraordinary majority to amend the Constitution, which is equivalent to saying that it takes only a committed minority to thwart majority will. (See Compared With What? 18.1.)

The ERA is still alive at the state level, at least at the moment. Sixteen states have laws on their books requiring their governments to observe sexual equality; however, no state has added an ERA provision since 1977, despite five attempts. The latest battle for an ERA was decided in 1986 by referendum in Vermont, a state that traditionally favored women's rights. (Its state university was one of the first to admit women.) Though every major political figure endorsed the amendment and polls demonstrated popular support, the referendum was defeated. Opponents of the measure, including Phyllis Schlafly's Eagle Forum and the Catholic Church, waged a pitched battle to defeat it. Supporters of Vermont's ERA knew that they had a very hard sell. One supporter, a seventy-four-year-old woman from Montpelier, offered her argument to a group of state politicians:

> The opponents want to roll back the clock to what they think were the good old days. But I was there, and those days weren't all that good. Vermont is better than most states, but why not go the rest of the way, and give us our full rights as citizens? Do it for Grandma.[33]

Compared With What? 18.1

Barriers for Women Fall

Feminist activism has had an impact on American perceptions of gender distinctions in politics. In 1974, more than one-third of the public agreed with the statement "Women should take care of running their homes and leave running the country up to men." That attitude has been on the decline; by 1982, slightly more than one-fourth of the public agreed with the same statement.

How do these American attitudes compare with public attitudes in other countries? Such a comparison is not an easy one, because it is difficult to find an exact match to the question posed to the American public. But one survey question, posed in 1983 to people in four European countries, comes very close: "It is sometimes said that 'politics should be left to men.' How far would you agree or disagree?"* The percentage results of that survey question appear in the table at right.

*Euro-Barometer 19: Gender Roles in the European Community, April 1983.

To the extent that the questions posed are comparable, American attitudes about women in politics fall roughly midway between those in the United Kingdom (with the lowest approval) and those in West Germany (with the highest approval). In fact, Americans come closest to Italians in their attitude toward women — at least in politics.

Country	Percent agreeing that "politics should be left to men"
France	22
West Germany	40
Italy	25
United Kingdom	18

AFFIRMATIVE ACTION: EQUAL OPPORTUNITY OR EQUAL OUTCOME?

In his vision of the "Great Society," President Lyndon Johnson linked economic rights with civil rights, and equality of result with equality of opportunity. "Equal opportunity is essential, but not enough," he declared. "We seek not just legal equity but human ability, not just equality as a right and a theory but equality as a fact and equality as a result." This commitment led to programs that were meant to overcome the residual effects of past discrimination. Such programs, known as **affirmative action** programs, involve steps taken by businesses, schools, and other institutions to expand opportunities for women and members of minority groups.

Typical affirmative action programs run the gamut from recruitment of minority applicants to preferential treatment for members of minority groups or women in areas such as job training and professional education, employment, and the letting of government contracts. The goal of such programs is to move beyond equality of opportunity to assure equality of outcome — very much as the busing of school children was used to ensure that the schools were indeed integrated. Numerical goals, quotas and timetables for the selection of women and minorities are the most aggressive forms of affirmative action; for that reason they generate the most hostility within the majority. In this latter type of program, a specific number of places in a law school might be reserved for minority candidates; or a contract for military equipment might specify that 10 percent of the work be subcontracted to minority-owned firms.

Reverse Discrimination

The Supreme Court confronted an affirmative action quota program for the first time in ***Regents of the University of California v. Bakke*** (1978).[34] Allan Bakke, a thirty-five-year-old white man, had twice applied for admission to the University of California Medical School at Davis. He was rejected both times. The school had reserved sixteen places in each entering class of one hundred for "qualified" minorities, as part of the university's affirmative action program. Bakke's qualifications (college grade point average and test scores) exceeded those of any of the minority students admitted in the two years when Bakke's applications were rejected. Bakke contended, first in the California courts and then in the Supreme Court, that he was excluded from admission solely on the basis of race. He contended that this *reverse discrimination* was prohibited by the Fourteenth Amendment's equal protection clause and by the Civil Rights Act of 1964.

The Supreme Court decision in the *Bakke* case contained six opinions and spanned 154 pages. But even after careful analysis of the decision, it was

***Rights Affirmed;
Dreams Fulfilled***
Allan Bakke, a 38-year-old engineer, was rejected twice from the Medical School of the University of California at Davis despite the fact that he scored well above most candidates admitted under a special minority admissions program. Bakke filed a lawsuit, which eventually forced the Supreme Court to examine the constitutionality of affirmative action programs. Bakke finally won his admission in 1978. In a complicated opinion, however, the justices upheld the use of race as one of several permissible criteria in such programs. Bakke was awarded his degree in 1982.

difficult to discern what the Court had decided — for there was no majority opinion. Four of the justices contended that any racial quota system supported by government violated the Civil Rights Act of 1964. Justice Lewis F. Powell, Jr., agreed and thus cast the deciding vote ordering the medical school to admit Bakke. However, in his opinion, Powell argued that the rigid use of racial quotas as employed at UC Davis violated the equal protection clause of the Fourteenth Amendment. The remaining four justices held that the use of race as a criterion in admissions decisions in higher education was constitutionally permissible. Powell joined that opinion as well, contending that the use of race was permissible as *one of several* admission criteria. Thus, in this one case, the Court managed to minimize white opposition to the goal of equality (by finding for Bakke) while extending gains for racial minorities through affirmative action.

Other cases followed. Through collective bargaining, the United Steelworkers of America and the Kaiser Aluminum and Chemical Corporation introduced a voluntary plan for affirmative action in 1974. The plan gave blacks preference for admission to craft training programs. Brian Weber, a white applicant, was rejected from a training program, despite the fact that he had more seniority than any of the minority applicants. Weber charged that he was the victim of reverse discrimination, which was forbidden by the Civil Rights Act of 1964. In a 5-to-2 decision, the Supreme Court upheld this voluntary affirmative action plan.[35] A year later, in 1980, the Court upheld, by a vote of 6 to 3, a federal law that set aside 10 percent of public works funds for minority businesses.[36] Then, in 1984, the Court confronted a difficult choice between the desire to uphold traditional values in employment and the desire to eradicate the effects of discrimination.

The city of Memphis, Tennessee, had agreed to an affirmative action order to increase the proportion of minority employees in its fire department. Later, the city was forced to lay off workers; traditional work rules specify that the last employees hired are the first to be laid off. The question arose as to whether affirmative action exempted the minority firefighters (who were the last ones hired) from this traditional seniority rule. In a 6-to-2 decision, the Court held that firefighter layoffs must proceed by seniority, unless minority employees could demonstrate that they were actual victims of the city's discrimination.[37] This meant that the minority firefighters targeted for layoffs would have to prove that they would have been employed if not for the city's discriminatory actions. Since such proof is difficult, and perhaps impossible, to establish in most cases, the decision upheld layoffs based on seniority.

Victims of Discrimination

The Memphis decision raised a troublesome question: Do all affirmative action programs, and not just layoffs, apply solely to actual victims of past discrimination? The Supreme Court delivered a partial answer in May 1986 when it struck down a school board layoff plan giving preference to members of minority groups. The decision in **Wygant v. Jackson Board of Education** was a complicated one, with five separate opinions. The suit was brought by white teachers who had been laid off by the school board. The board layoff plan favored black teachers in an effort to redress general societal discrimination and to maintain sufficient role models for black students. But the Court ruled that these purposes were insufficient to force certain individuals to shoulder the severe impact of such layoffs. Hiring goals impose a diffuse burden on society, argued Justice Lewis F. Powell, Jr., for the Court. But layoffs of innocent whites, he continued, "impose the entire burden of achieving racial equality on particular individuals."[38]

Recall, from the beginning of this chapter, that New York sheet metal workers' Local 28 had engaged in persistent discrimination, and that a remedy was ordered by a lower federal court. The union sought review in the Supreme Court. Local 28 argued, this time with the support of the Reagan administration, that the membership goal ordered by the lower courts was unlawful because it extended race-conscious preferences to individuals who were not identified victims of Local 28's admittedly unlawful discrimination.

In *Local 28* **v.** *the EEOC*, the justices voted 6 to 3 in support of race-conscious affirmative action that would benefit individuals who were not the actual victims of discrimination.[39] The justices maintained that such remedies are particularly appropriate against employers or unions that have engaged in persistent or extreme discrimination. With regard to the use of a numerical goal to increase minority membership in the union, the justices split 5 to 4. The majority maintained that such a goal furthered the government's interest in remedying obvious past discrimination and provided the only way to measure the union's progress in eliminating discriminatory practices.

Equality: Lower and Upper Limits

Americans want equality, but they differ on the extent to which government should provide it.[40] This, as well as our attitudes toward affirmative action, can be explained in terms of conflicting values.

Most Americans support **equality of opportunity.** This form of equality provides all individuals with the same chance to get ahead; it glorifies personal achievement through free competition and permits everyone to climb the ladder of success. Special recruitment efforts aimed at qualified minority or female job applicants illustrate equal opportunity in action. But after continued application of the equal opportunity principle, some individuals get ahead and others lag behind. This divergence tends to perpetuate the advantages of those who are ahead of the pack and the disadvantages of those who lag behind. Equality of outcome corrects this consequence.

Americans express less commitment to **equality of outcome,** which means greater uniformity in social, economic, and political power for people. Equality of outcome can occur only if we restrict the free competition that is derived from equality of opportunity. The restriction comes by way of policies that establish lower and upper limits on personal achievement. The lower limit is a "floor" below which individuals will not be allowed to fall. The upper limit is a "ceiling" above which individuals cannot rise. The right to vote and special recruitment efforts are examples of policy floors. "One person, one vote" and job quotas are examples of policy ceilings. Each places a limit on individual control or initiative, though with different results.

Handicapped People Have Rights, Too
The Rehabilitation Act of 1973 prohibits discrimination against handicapped people in programs that receive federal funds. Today, a majority of disabled Americans believe that their quality of life has improved, and they credit the 1973 law for their gains. Nevertheless, the everyday life of many handicapped Americans contains many seemingly small but extraordinarily difficult situations that most other people take for granted — revolving doors, flights of stairs, and buses without lifts.

A floor takes political, economic, or social power from those at the top and gives it to those on the bottom. People may move closer but their relative positions on the "power ladder" don't change. Hiring preferences, for example, provide places for minorities and women. But a ceiling limits individual advancement; it bars a person on the ladder from climbing higher and permits someone else to move ahead. A ceiling thus alters positions on the ladder — and that can lead to opposition. Explosive outbursts occur when Americans realize that their positions on the ladder will be affected by equal-outcome policies. Job quotas that benefit minorities and women also bar innocent white men from advancement. Individual initiative clashes with quotas. In other words, freedom clashes with equality.

SUMMARY

The Fourteenth, Fifteenth, and Sixteenth Amendments were adopted to provide full civil rights to black Americans. Yet in the late nineteenth century the Supreme Court interpreted the amendments very narrowly, declaring that they did not restrain individuals from denying civil rights to blacks and that they did not apply to powers that were reserved to the states. Such interpretations had the effect of denying the vote to most blacks, institutionalizing racial segregation, and according an inferior status to blacks in almost every facet of daily life.

Through a series of court cases covering two decades, segregation in the schools was slowly dismantled. The school desegregation campaign culminated in the *Brown* cases of 1954 and 1955; in those cases a now supportive Supreme Court declared segregated schools to be inherently unequal and thus unconstitutional. The Court also ordered the desegregation of all schools and upheld the use of busing to do so.

Gains in other civil rights areas came more slowly, primarily as a result of the civil rights movement of the late 1950s and 1960s. The movement was led by Rev. Martin Luther King, Jr., until his death in 1968. King believed strongly in civil disobedience and nonviolence, tactics which helped secure equality in voting rights, public accommodations, higher education, housing, and employment opportunity.

Civil rights activism and the civil rights movement worked to the benefit of all minority groups and, in fact, of all Americans. Among the former are American Indians, who obtained some redress for past injustices, and Hispanic Americans, who feel that they have yet to enjoy economic equality. In addition, civil rights legislation has removed the paternal protectionism that was, in effect, legalized discrimination against women in education and employment.

Affirmative action programs were instituted to counteract the results of past discrimination. They provided preferential treatment for minorities in a number of areas that affect economic opportunity and well-being. In spite of their discriminatory nature, these programs have had Supreme Court support when society in general bears the burden, rather than particular innocent individuals.

Equality can take two forms: equality of opportunity and equality of outcome. Americans support equality of opportunity but are divided, sometimes deeply, on equality of outcome. Equality of outcome operates by imposing upper and lower limits on individual achievement. Americans object most to policies that impose ceilings, such as the use of numerical goals, because they restrict individual freedom and alter positions on the ladder of success that Americans profess to climb. The challenge of pluralist democracy is to balance these conflicting values.

Key Terms and Cases

discrimination
racism
civil rights
poll tax
racial segregation
Plessy v. *Ferguson*
separate-but-equal doctrine
desegregation
Brown v. *Board of Education of Topeka*
Brown v. *Board of Education of Topeka II*
Swann v. *Charlotte-Mecklenberg County Schools*
de jure segregation
de facto segregation
Milliken v. *Bradley*

civil rights movement
boycott
civil disobedience
protectionism
Nineteenth Amendment
sexism
Equal Rights Amendment (ERA)
affirmative action
Regents of the University of California v. *Bakke*
Wygant v. *Jackson Board of Education*
Local 28 v. *the EEOC*
equality of opportunity
equality of outcome

Selected Readings

Baer, Judith A. *Equality Under the Constitution: Reclaiming the Fourteenth Amendment.* Ithaca, N.Y.: Cornell University Press, 1983. Explores the early American concept of equality and reexamines the debates surrounding the adoption of the Fourteenth Amendment; points to new areas of struggle in the application of the equality principle to children, the aged, the disabled, and homosexuals.

Bass, Jack. *Unlikely Heroes.* New York: Simon and Schuster, 1981. Chronicles the efforts of four federal appellate judges in the deep South to enforce the desegregation mandate of the *Brown* decision.

Browning, Rufus P.; Dale Rogers Marshall; and David H. Tabb. *Protest is Not Enough.* Berkeley, Calif.: University of California Press, 1984. A recent study of black and Hispanic political activities and their translation into representative voices in the policymaking of ten California cities.

Deloria, Vine, Jr., and Clifford M. Lytle. *The Nations Within.* New York: Pantheon, 1984. A thorough discussion of Native American policies from the "New Deal" to the present; examines the drive for Indian self-determination and self-government.

Kessler-Harris, Alice. *Out to Work: A History of Wage-Earning Women in the United States.* New York: Oxford University Press, 1982. An informative history analyzing the forces motivating women to work and the effect of work on family roles.

Kluger, Richard. *Simple Justice.* New York: Knopf, 1976. A monumentally detailed history of the desegregation cases; examines the legal, political, and sociological events culminating in *Brown* v. *Board of Education.*

Verba, Sidney, and Gary R. Orren. *Equality in America: The View from the Top.* Cambridge, Mass.: Harvard University Press, 1985. Two political scientists isolate different meanings of equality and then analyze the opinions of American leaders on the application of equality of opportunity and equality of outcome across a range of policy areas.

Yates, Gayle Graham. *What Women Want: The Ideas of the Movement.* Cambridge, Mass.: Harvard University Press, 1975. Identifies different perspectives in the women's movement and traces their evolution from early feminist thinking to recent positions.

19

Foreign and Defense Policy

President Ronald Reagan argued his case: "You can't fight helicopters piloted by Cubans with Band-Aids and mosquito nets." The administration wanted $70 million in military aid as part of a $100-million package earmarked for the Nicaraguan rebels, or "Contras." A clear majority of House members favored support for the Contras — nonlethal, nonmilitary, humanitarian support. Military expenditures had been prohibited since 1984, when Congress discovered the CIA had financed the mining of Nicaraguan harbors. Now, in June 1986, the administration had returned, seeking authorization to transfer some Pentagon funds to provide military aid for the Contras. The same issue had been before the House just three months earlier, and the administration had lost narrowly, by a vote of 210 to 222. This time, too, observers expected a close vote.

In the debate on the measure, each side introduced what it considered appropriate historical analogies. The president's supporters reminded their listeners about the 1930s, when the democracies had appeared reluctant to defend themselves and thus encouraged fascist states to indulge in the expansionism that ultimately led to World War II. They also recalled President Harry Truman's postwar commitment to help defend Greece and Turkey against communist expansion. The lessons of American history plainly showed, the president's supporters argued, that America should stand up against totalitarianism and nip it in the bud.

Opponents of the aid package had their own analogies. They pointed to the more recent Vietnam experience as an example of the limits of military power and the danger that small commitments might escalate into large ones. They feared that requests for American money today might be followed by requests for American troops in the future. Several members equated the bill with the Tonkin Gulf Resolution, which gave President Lyndon Johnson congressional backing for his actions during the Vietnam War.

Both sides agreed on the fundamental goals of U.S. foreign policy in Latin America: the United States had to protect its national security interests by maintaining order. However, the two sides disagreed on the nature of the threat to order in Latin America and also on how to deal with it.

In the House debate, forces friendly to the administration pointed out that the Nicaraguan rulers were Marxists who could provide a base for Soviet expansion on the American continent. The regime threatened the stability of the Latin American democracies and ultimately of the United States, according to those who backed Reagan's request. These members of Congress emphasized repression by the Sandinistas (the ruling faction in Nicaragua). The Sandinistas had denied basic freedoms of speech, press, and religion; they were also unwilling to hold free and fair elections. The Reagan administration's official preferred strategy was to give American military aid to the Contras, who were seeking to overthrow the Sandinistas. This aid was, in turn, supposed to increase pressure on the Sandinista regime to bargain with the Contras and establish a more democratic government.

The administration's foes in Congress offered a different interpretation. They spent less time discussing the repressiveness of the Sandinista regime. After all, they said, for forty years the United States had supported the rule of the Somoza family in Nicaragua and the Somozas were notorious violators of human rights — and, for that matter, so were the Contras whom we were currently backing. Instead, the congressional opponents of military aid argued that the real sources of instability in Latin American society lay in inequality. As long as most Latin Americans suffered from poverty, illiteracy, and ill health, Latin America would offer a breeding ground for political turmoil, which the Soviets would always be happy to use to their advantage. Military aid was not the way to attack these problems; diplomacy and development assistance were better suited to the task of keeping order south of our border. In addition, those opposing military aid argued, the Contras were not up to the job assigned to them. The Contras had been unable to inspire great popular uprisings in their support; in fact, they had been unable to hold a single town. If the Sandinistas were to be brought to the conference table, the opponents of the aid package warned, it would cost much more than $100 million in aid to the Contras. The president's opposition feared that the final bill for the administration's policy would be much higher.

When the debate ended and the votes were tallied in June 1986, the president had won by a narrow margin of 221 to 209. Reagan had scored a significant victory, but it was not based on the kind of overwhelming bipartisan support that presidents dream of for their foreign policy. Moreover, opposition to aiding the Contras increased after Congress learned in November that the administration had secretly sold arms to Iran and had used the profits, deposited in a Swiss bank account, to funnel additional funds to the Contras.

Since the war in Vietnam, bipartisan support for foreign policy has been hard to come by. Why? In this chapter, we shall try to answer that question by looking at the breakdown of the post–World War II foreign policy consensus and the emergence of the two conflicting foreign policy paradigms, or world views, that characterized the House debate on Contra aid. These

Freedom Fighters?
President Reagan repeatedly referred to the Nicaraguan rebels (the Contras) fighting against the Marxist Sandinista government as ''Freedom Fighters,'' comparing them to colonists fighting in our American revolution. Here young Contra troops in the hills of northern Nicaragua show their enthusiasm for battle.

paradigms give very different weights to the values of order, freedom, and equality and rely on very different tools to promote those values.

Why did President Reagan win on the June 1986 vote, especially after having lost on the same question so recently? What did the public think about aiding the Contras? Where does the public fit into the foreign policy process? Is foreign policymaking a majoritarian, a pluralist, or an elitist enterprise? Spending for national defense is the second largest item in the federal budget. Do we spend too much on defense? Or not enough? We consider these and other questions in this chapter.

TWO POLICY PARADIGMS

The Contra aid debate is a good illustration of the rift that has characterized American foreign policymaking since the Vietnam War. Two opposing viewpoints have emerged, and they can be represented by the Munich paradigm and the Vietnam paradigm.

The Munich, or Pearl Harbor, Paradigm

In the first view, the Vietnam War itself was fought in a "noble cause": to overcome communist aggression. America and its South Vietnamese allies could have won in Vietnam — if only this country had had the will to prevail and had allowed the military to do the job they were trained to do. According to this first view, the United States must be willing to intervene, militarily if necessary, anywhere on the globe to put down the major threat to order and freedom in the world: Soviet-inspired communist aggression.

Some political scientists have called this viewpoint the **Munich,** or **Pearl Harbor, paradigm** because it reflects the influence of the events that led to World War II. The Soviets have replaced Hitler as the central threat to peace, and the split between East and West has become the most important division in world politics. Until proved otherwise, all communists are believed to be fundamentally the same, and the hand of the Soviet Union is generally behind communist actions, according to those who support this view. The primary goal of U.S. foreign policy must be to promote order by containing communist expansion. The United States must commit itself to preventing a Soviet takeover of the globe and must be prepared to move against each and every instance of Soviet aggression. Therefore, America must maintain a strong military. The Munich paradigm essentially represents the outlook of the Reagan administration.

The Vietnam Paradigm

The second view, the **Vietnam paradigm,** is quite different and takes as its point of departure the Vietnam experience rather than World War II. Its adherents believe that American involvement in Vietnam resulted from a tragic failure — the country's failure to realize that all left-wing revolutionary movements are not necessarily directed from Moscow but may instead be the product of internal nationalist forces. Although the Kremlin is always willing to exploit unrest, it cannot create it out of nothing. Revolutions in Third World countries are more likely to spring from factors such as poverty and nationalism than to be fabricated by the Soviet Union. From this perspective, the split between rich nations and poor nations is more important than the East-West division. And, although order is certainly important, America should not oppose the egalitarian desires of Third World nations. Furthermore, if a right-wing regime is suppressing individual freedom and promoting inequality, the United States should not back that regime just because its rulers are anti-Soviet.

Proponents of the Vietnam paradigm also argue that military solutions are not the most effective way to "win the hearts and minds" of people in other countries. Their approach rejects the U.S. role of "world policeman" and fears any overseas intervention, which could be a prelude to full-scale troop commitments. The United States should beware of intervention anywhere in the world, lest it find itself in "another Vietnam." The tools preferred by those holding this view include "the four D's": diplomacy rather than military force; détente (the relaxation of tensions between East and West); disarmament and arms control; and development aid to overcome the inequalities that breed disorder and that allow communist movements to thrive.

At the end of the Vietnam War, political scientists suggested that a "paradigm shift" might be taking place and that a new foreign policy consensus might form around the Vietnam paradigm.[1] They expected that this world view would eventually dominate, as those clinging to the older standpoint either converted or died. To some extent, the dominance of the Vietnam paradigm depended on the "Vietnam generation" moving into positions of power. Today, the idea that the Vietnam experience might serve as the core of such a consensus seems more dubious. For one thing, it is not at all clear that there is a single Vietnam view shared even by members of the Vietnam generation.[2] For another, as we have indicated, Reagan's approach to foreign affairs fits much more neatly into the Munich mold. His victory on Contra aid undermines any suggestion that he is just a survivor of the older breed whose world view is doomed to extinction in the near future.

The 1980s have brought crises in the Middle East, southern Africa, and Central and South America. What is at stake for the United States in these areas? What are the root causes of turmoil? What approach should the United States take in dealing with these problems? To answer such foreign policy questions, each citizen draws heavily on his or her political orientation and values. And since those values may be both complex and multidimensional, it is perhaps unwise to expect a simple, clear consensus on America's role in the world. Perhaps the pluralism of viewpoints that characterizes American domestic politics carries over into foreign politics as well. The essential agreement that existed during the period between World War II and Vietnam may have been an exception rather than the rule. Any discussion of these issues, though, requires a better understanding of the historical context of modern American foreign policy.

U.S. VALUES AND INTERESTS: THE HISTORICAL CONTEXT

The question "What is at stake for the United States in Central America, or southern Africa, or the Middle East, or anywhere else?" is just a way of asking how events there affect America's national interest. Above all else, the goal of American foreign policy is to preserve our national security. The difficult parts of foreign policymaking are interpreting just what "national security" means in practice and deciding exactly what is required to preserve it. To protect our security interests must we also prohibit the spread of communism at all costs, everywhere in the world?

From Isolationism to Globalism

Americans have not always viewed their national security interests in global terms. Throughout most of the nineteenth century the limits of American national security interests were those staked out by the Monroe Doctrine of 1823. Under its principles, the United States rejected any European efforts to colonize in the Western hemisphere; and, for its part, the United States agreed not to involve itself in European politics. The basic posture toward Europe was isolationist—Americans wanted little to do with the Old World.

As the nineteenth century wore on, however, the United States did become increasingly involved in the affairs of non-European nations. For example, the United States expanded its power in the Pacific, acquiring the Hawaiian islands and the Philippines. And U.S. foreign policy toward Latin America showed strong **interventionist** tendencies. However, the U.S. in-

Join the Navy, Save the World
Superpower status today gives global scope to American national security interests. The U.S. role of world policeman has roots in World War I, when Americans were encouraged to join the Navy and save the world.

terventions in Latin America were relatively small matters that cost fairly little and did not require much of a military commitment. America's defense and foreign policy establishments remained small.

World War I marked the United States' first serious foray into European politics. In 1917 the rhetoric of our entry — "to make the world safe for democracy" — underscored the moralistic and idealistic tone of America's approach to international politics at that time. At the Versailles Peace Conference in 1919, President Woodrow Wilson championed the League of Nations as a device for preventing future wars. When the Senate refused to ratify the Versailles treaty, and thus blocked America's entry into the League, the brief moment of American internationalism ended. For the next two decades, the United States maintained its familiar isolationist posture, except for intervention in Latin America — this time in Nicaragua.

In 1939, America's security interests were still narrowly defined, and the military establishment that was needed to defend those interests was quite small. At the outbreak of the Second World War (September 1939), the United States had no draft or compulsory military service; there were 334,473 men in the armed forces, and defense expenditures amounted to about $1.3 billion (roughly equal to 1.5 percent of the GNP at that time).[3] No American troops were garrisoned abroad, and the country was not party to any military alliance. The oceans represented America's first line of defense.

But World War II brought a dramatic change in America's orientation toward the world. (See Figure 19.1, which graphically depicts the growth of the military, for example.) In 1949 — four years after the war had ended — approximately 5.5 percent of the GNP was being spent on the army, navy, and air force, and 1,615,360 persons were on active duty with the U.S. military.[4] Also in 1949, the United States concluded the first of many peacetime alliances: the North Atlantic Treaty, which created the North Atlantic Treaty Organization (NATO). Under this treaty, America permanently committed itself to the defense of Western Europe. Western Europe, not the Atlantic Ocean, was now recognized as America's first line of defense to the east. To reinforce the U.S. commitment, American occupation troops stayed on in Europe, and the wartime draft was continued to provide the necessary manpower. In addition, the U.S. attitude toward international organizations changed after World War II. These institutions were now seen as providing the basis for world order. Thus America became the driving force in founding the United Nations and also supported the establishment of a World Court. American isolationism appeared to be gone for good, replaced by a new **globalism.** The United States had become a superpower, and American national security interests were now global in scope.

Containment and Korea

Superpower status carried a price. An important debate in 1949 involved the question of how to think about defense spending. Paul Nitze and other Defense and State Department officials suggested, in a document known as NSC-68, that the American view of defense spending might have to be altered radically. Not only would Americans have to spend more money on defense

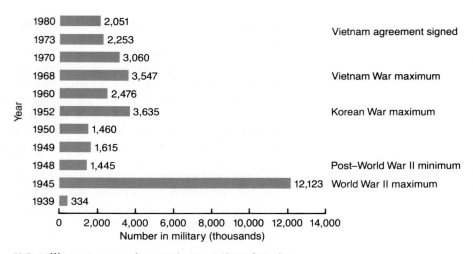

U.S. Military Personnel on Active Duty in Selected Years
As America assumed its role as a superpower, a corresponding buildup occurred in the U.S. armed forces.

Figure 19.1

during peacetime, but they would also have to give defense spending a higher priority than spending on domestic social programs. The foreign policy consensus being forged at the end of the 1940s was clearly internationalist — with a strong militarist flavor. The Soviet Union, America's wartime ally, now appeared to be the principal threat to order. The Soviets dominated Eastern Europe; their communist ideology was expansionistic; and America feared the growth of Soviet power. Powerful European conflicts had drawn America into war twice in twenty-five years; the Soviets, left unchecked, might well do it again.

In this view (heavily shaped, no doubt, by the recent experience of the rise of Hitler), the Soviets sought world domination and were bent on extending the communist system into "every nook and cranny" of the globe. Frustrating the Kremlin's design would mean, among other things, cutting budgets for purposes other than defense and foreign assistance, even if these cuts meant deferring certain desirable domestic programs.[5] For the first time ever in peacetime, Americans were called upon to give priority to defense spending over domestic spending—that is, to guns over butter. America was not in an actual shooting war, or "hot war," with the Soviets, but the adversarial nature of U.S.–Soviet relations was clear. A new term was invented to describe the situation: **Cold War.**

The Cold War would require commitment and sacrifice. The American course of action, as sketched out by State Department official George Kennan, had to be "longterm, patient but firm and vigilant containment."[6] **Containment** meant that Soviet power had to be kept from expanding further; it had to be held in check as though it were in a container. A return to isolationism was impossible, as Truman had proclaimed in a speech justifying economic and military aid to Greece and Turkey, because "totalitarian regimes imposed upon free peoples, by direct or indirect aggression, undermine the foundations of international peace and hence the security of the United States.''[7]

Besides relying on military preparedness, the Truman administration also developed economic tools to oppose Soviet expansion. Secretary of State George Marshall recognized that European nations that had been weakened economically by the war offered good targets for Soviet expansion. His European Recovery Plan (commonly known as the **Marshall Plan**) was developed to make Europe economically viable again. This program of foreign aid sent approximately $12 billion over a four-year period to help rebuild Europe.

While a clear American policy toward Europe was taking shape, new crises emerged in Asia. Mao Zedong (Mao Tse-tung) succeeded in driving out Chiang Kai-shek and installing a communist regime in China. It was generally believed in Washington that international politics was a *zero-sum game* — a situation in which one superpower's loss was the other's gain — and America's "loss" of China was therefore interpreted as a great victory for the Soviets. American policymakers who favored a more conciliatory position toward the Chinese suggested that all communism might not be Soviet communism. Their voices were soon drowned out when, on June 25, 1950, communist North Korea invaded noncommunist South Korea. The United States decided to intervene in the conflict to push the North Koreans out, but the decision was not simply to declare war or to send in troops.

Polishing the Coneheads
War often stimulates social change. During World War II, more than six million women entered the labor force, many doing jobs — such as making tailgunner cones for bombers — that had previously been done by men.

Instead, the United States asked that the United Nations send a force to quell the North Korean aggression. Because the Russians were boycotting the U.N. Security Council at the time and thus could not exercise their veto power, the American request was approved. The bulk of the U.N. force that was sent to Korea consisted of Americans.

The Korean War presented a stark contrast to the American image of what a war should be. World War II had been a "total war," and America had fully committed all its economic, human, and military resources to it. The goal of the Allies in the Second World War was total victory. After the fighting had begun, the time for political solutions was past. Only military solutions were acceptable.

In contrast, American economic and manpower commitments to the Korean conflict were much lower. General Douglas MacArthur, who commanded the U.N. force in Korea, was not permitted to use the atomic weapons that had ended World War II or (as he would have liked) to push an offensive into China after the Chinese communists entered the fighting. Policymakers on both sides pursued political solutions, trying to limit hostilities in order to avoid the outbreak of another world war. The conflict was finally ended when the countries involved agreed essentially to restore the original north-south boundary. The United States had successfully "contained" communism in Korea, but a Pandora's box had been opened and the problems that were released would beset the United States again in Vietnam. America's inability to translate enormous military and economic strength into consistent political success was proof that American power, though great, had limits.

Cold War Commitments Under Eisenhower and Kennedy

President Dwight Eisenhower generally continued Truman's Cold War peacetime policies, but with some important differences. He believed that the amount of money spent on defense should have limits. He also expressed concern about the ways in which the pursuit of global interests might affect America's democratic institutions. In his farewell address, Eisenhower warned against the power of the **military-industrial complex,** the "conjunction of an immense military establishment and a large arms industry," both lobbying for increased military spending. The growth of the military-industrial complex threatened pluralist democracy because it created an extremely powerful group united by two common interests—war and military spending. Eisenhower warned that its "total influence—economic, political, even spiritual—is felt in every city, every statehouse, every office of the federal government."[8] (For an example of the pervasiveness of the military-industrial complex in the 1980s, see Table 19.1, showing the distribution of defense contracts among the states; see also Color Essay D, plate 4.)

During the Eisenhower administration, U.S. defense policy was based primarily on the deterrent power of its nuclear weapons, not on the strength of its conventional (that is, non-nuclear) forces. The idea was that the Soviet leaders would hesitate to engage in aggressive actions because they understood that they risked massive retaliation from America's superior nuclear arsenal if the Cold War turned hot. Toward the late 1950s, however, the

Table 19.1
States and National Defense Contracts
President Dwight Eisenhower suggested that the military-industrial complex could become a pervasive force in American society. As this table shows, every state in the Union now receives substantial sums of money from defense-related contracts. Hundreds of thousands of jobs depend on these military-industrial related expenditures. As a result, Congress members who vote against defense spending may also be voting against jobs for people in their districts — a difficult thing to do. (Figures are in millions of dollars.)

State	1980	1981	1982	State	1980	1981	1982
Alabama	626	790	930	Montana	32	42	36
Alaska	251	323	327	Nebraska	100	106	140
Arizona	727	1,123	1,490	Nevada	50	78	109
Arkansas	112	154	452	New Hampshire	305	392	538
California	13,853	16,630	22,578	New Jersey	1,517	2,303	2,858
Colorado	510	935	1,072	New Mexico	286	383	455
Connecticut	3,867	4,492	5,897	New York	5,648	6,481	7,741
Delaware	240	236	239	North Carolina	651	825	828
D.C.	590	595	861	North Dakota	69	104	68
Florida	1,984	3,094	4,046	Ohio	1,617	2,436	3,300
Georgia	884	1,245	1,596	Oklahoma	420	621	563
Hawaii	315	591	511	Oregon	131	114	168
Idaho	19	28	77	Pennsylvania	2,166	2,374	3,052
Illinois	945	1,155	1,210	Rhode Island	261	235	285
Indiana	1,290	1,713	1,004	South Carolina	297	434	379
Iowa	283	312	339	South Dakota	17	54	51
Kansas	775	1,008	1,442	Tennessee	520	502	672
Kentucky	245	372	247	Texas	5,345	7,416	6,747
Louisiana	480	2,826	1,455	Utah	251	404	562
Maine	457	475	784	Vermont	124	167	202
Maryland	1,784	2,373	3,082	Virginia	3,344	3,591	4,050
Massachusetts	3,729	4,596	5,301	Washington	2,110	2,588	2,817
Michigan	1,696	1,735	1,572	West Virginia	86	89	101
Minnesota	1,048	1,159	1,434	Wisconsin	366	598	863
Mississippi	636	1,168	1,161	Wyoming	33	64	89
Missouri	3,191	4,349	5,294	Total	76,430	96,653	115,280

Source: U.S. Department of Defense, *Prime Contracts Awarded by State* (Washington, D.C.: U.S. Government Printing Office, annual).

Russians built up their own nuclear arsenal, and the two superpowers approached the possibility of **mutual assured destruction (MAD)** in a nuclear conflict. Against this new background, deterrence began to seem a less credible policy. American analysts such as Herman Kahn and Henry Kissinger argued that America should develop the strategies and weapons needed to fight a limited nuclear war.[9] In addition, there were demands that the United States beef up its conventional nonnuclear forces, so that the country would have a range of defense options from which to select.

This last idea, called **flexible response,** became a cornerstone of administration policy when John F. Kennedy became president. Kennedy shared the Cold War attitude of his two predecessors. In his inaugural address, he pledged to "pay any price, bear any burden, meet any hardship, support any friend, oppose any foe to assure the survival and success of liberty."[10]

To Kennedy, the struggle against Soviet communism was paramount. The two most dramatic foreign policy incidents of his administration were the failed Bay of Pigs invasion, in which U.S.-supported Cuban exiles invaded

Castro's communist Cuba, and the successfully managed Cuban missile crisis, in which an American naval blockade of the island forced the Soviets to remove missiles they had placed there. Both encounters were attempts to combat the perceived Soviet threat to U.S. security in the Western hemisphere.*

In the wake of the Cuban missile crisis, however, the United States and the Soviet Union moved to reduce the tension between the two countries. The two most notable steps were a nuclear test ban treaty (outlawing above-ground testing of nuclear weapons) and the installation of the Washington-Moscow teletype machine that has come to be known as the "hotline." In addition, the Kennedy administration pursued **nation-building policies,** which would shore up Third World countries economically, thereby making them less attractive targets for Soviet opportunism. Examples of these policies include the Alliance for Progress, a ten-year, $20-billion program of economic assistance to Latin America; the Peace Corps, through which Americans volunteered to help Third World countries with problems of development; and Food for Peace, a program that sold American agricultural commodities to less-developed countries on generous credit terms and also provided emergency food relief.

Kennedy's sensitivity to nation building in Third World countries did not outstrip his Cold War instincts, however. Once, while speaking about the Dominican Republic he made clear his hierarchy of preferred regime types: "There are three possibilities in descending order of preference: a decent democratic regime, a continuation of the [right-wing dictatorship under the] Trujillo [family], or a Castro regime. We ought to aim at the first but we really can't renounce the second until we are sure that we can avoid the third."[11] Inequality and right-wing threats to freedom were preferable to communist threats to freedom and the possibility of Soviet expansion.

One Kennedy commitment, involving both nation building and resistance to the Soviet threat, would later have a critical impact on American foreign policy. That commitment was in South Vietnam. Fearing a takeover by communist forces from North Vietnam, American governments had been sending aid and military advisers to South Vietnam for years. Under Kennedy, both were increased substantially. At the time of Kennedy's assassination in 1963, sixteen thousand American military advisers were stationed in South Vietnam to support the anticommunist government there. During the term of Lyndon Johnson, Kennedy's successor, the price of the Vietnam War would climb drastically in terms of both dollars and American lives.

Vietnam: The Challenge to America's Foreign Policy Consensus

In November 1963, just three weeks before President John Kennedy was assassinated, a United States-backed coup in South Vietnam resulted in the ouster and death of President Ngo Dinh Diem. Diem had not been a popular leader, and his regime was beset with instability. The weakness of the Diem regime undermined America's ability to "contain" the communist North

---

*It was during the Cuban missile crisis that Kennedy's willingness to "pay any price" seemed likely to be tested. Kennedy himself estimated the chances of war at that time as one in three.

War Is Hell
The Vietnam War entangled America in its longest military conflict. More than 57,000 Americans died in Southeast Asia. Despite first-aid from his marine buddy, this GI was to become another fatality as he lay mortally wounded in the Khe Sanh Valley of South Vietnam in 1967.

Vietnamese and their Viet Cong allies (the South Vietnamese communists). Although the Diem regime ended with the coup, political turmoil did not. One government succeeded another, but none proved capable of maintaining control for very long. Meanwhile, the military situation continued to deteriorate until, by early 1964, the Viet Cong controlled almost half of South Vietnam.

In August of that year, Congress passed the Gulf of Tonkin Resolution, which gave the president a virtual blank check in Vietnam. At first, Johnson ordered American bombing raids on the North; nevertheless, by early 1965, the military situation had become so bad that the president sent in U.S. ground forces. Eventually the United States had more than 500,000 combat troops in Vietnam. As the war escalated, casualties mounted, and no end to the conflict appeared in sight. Opposition to the undeclared war grew, on college campuses and elsewhere. The antiwar candidate, Democratic Senator Eugene McCarthy of Minnesota, challenged Johnson in the Democratic primaries. On March 31, 1968, Johnson halted the bombing in North Vietnam and announced that he would not seek another term as president. By August, a majority of Americans surveyed in a Gallup poll responded that they believed the United States had made a mistake in sending troops to Vietnam. That continued to be the majority view through the rest of the time America was involved in the conflict.

Richard Nixon, who succeeded Johnson, was well aware of the general dissatisfaction with the situation in Vietnam. He ran on a pledge to end the war through what came to be known as his "secret plan."* His method of achieving "peace with honor" depended on a strategy called **Vietnamization,** which meant turning more and more of the fighting over to the South Vietnamese. This tactic gradually led to a much-reduced American presence, fewer casualties, and smaller draft calls. A peace agreement was signed in 1973, and the remaining American troops left Vietnam. In April 1975, South Vietnam collapsed. The costs of the war were high; some of them are detailed in Feature 19.1. Others, however, cannot be counted so easily. The conflict deeply divided the American people and fragmented the Cold War consensus on American foreign policy.

Even while the war dragged on, President Nixon and his chief foreign policy adviser, Henry Kissinger, were making important changes in American foreign policy. The **Nixon doctrine** was an attempt to redefine America's overseas commitments and "steer a course between the past danger of over-involvement and the new temptation of underinvolvement."[12] In backing away from the rhetorical pledge of Kennedy's inaugural address, Nixon stated that America would no longer "conceive all the plans, design all the pro-grams, execute all the decisions and undertake all the defense of the free nations of the world." Instead, the United States would intervene only where "it makes a real difference and is considered in our interest."[13]

Nixon and Kissinger pursued **détente,** a policy aimed at reducing ten-sions between East and West. During the period of détente, Nixon visited Moscow for a summit meeting. The United States and the Soviet Union negotiated and signed the SALT agreement, which limited the growth of their nuclear arsenals and recognized the Soviet claim to "strategic parity" with the United States. Trade between the two countries increased, and a joint U.S.-Soviet space mission was planned.

Nixon also ended the decades of U.S. hostility toward the People's Re-public of China. Although that country was not accorded full diplomatic recognition until the Carter administration, both Kissinger and Nixon visited China and helped to open political and economic negotiations.

The theory of détente placed strong emphasis on the value of order — order based not only on military might but also on mutuality of interests among superpowers. Kissinger believed that if the Soviets and the Chinese were treated as legitimate participants in the international system, they would then have a vested interest in supporting world order. The two countries would also have less incentive to promote revolutionary challenges to inter-national stability. If the Soviets and the Chinese were bound to the United States through economic and political agreements, they would realize that their own interests would be served best through cooperation. Kissinger prac-ticed **linkage;** he attempted to use rewards and advantages in one area to promote Soviet compliance with his wishes in other areas.

Did the Soviets share Kissinger's vision? That is one of the major ques-tions in the evaluation of détente. Soviet involvement in Portugal, the Middle East, Angola, and, later, Afghanistan may be evidence that the Soviet view

---

*Cynics have noted that the plan was so secret that Nixon did not let it out until after he had been re-elected in 1972.

Feature 19.1

What Price Vietnam? Estimating the Costs of War

Everyone has heard it said that war brings incalculable human suffering, which the cold statistics of budget expenditures and casualty reports can never capture. True enough. But estimates of the cost of war usually include only the direct costs of the fighting; as a result, they vastly underestimate the true cost of war to the economy. Among the indirect costs are veterans' benefits, disability payments, and the like. While the original cost of the Korean conflict in terms of direct military expenditures has been put at about $20 billion, those who have attempted to come up with a more inclusive figure put the total closer to $165 billion.

When all the bills have come in for the war in Vietnam, what will its price be in dollars? In addition to war-specific spending, economists suggest that an estimate of the total cost of the war should include the following items:*

Economic Dislocation Caused by the War

Creation of budget deficits. At a time when war spending was at a level of approximately $72 billion a year, the U.S. budget deficit increased from $5 billion (1965) to $78.9 billion (1968).

Inflation. The rate of inflation had averaged 1.3 percent from 1960 to 1965 and shot up to the then–unheard of rate of 4.1 percent.

*Estimates courtesy of Robert S. Whitesell, Wabash College. Figures are given in August 1984 dollars.

Trade problems. In 1971 the United States had its first balance-of-trade deficit since 1893, with about $11.5 billion directly due to war expenditures.

Direct Costs and Opportunity Costs of the War

Direct military cost of the war	$ 469.5 billion
Foregone personal consumption	197.2 billion
Loss in income resulting from lost capital:	685.0 billion
Lost human capital: (Dead servicemen would have been expected to have earned this figure over their lifetimes. This figure does not include the losses of the disabled or the costs of drug addiction and psychological problems, so the estimate is low.)	54.5 billion
Cost of veterans' benefits to be paid over the next 100+ years (The final bills for Vietnam will come due far in the future. For example, from 1970 through 1974, the United States was still spending over 1 million dollars a year on veterans' benefits owed as a result of the Civil War.)	1,900 billion
Total:	$3,306.2 billion

Thus, the total bill for Vietnam will probably exceed $3.3 trillion dollars, an amount roughly seven times greater than the military cost of the war.

---

of détente was not the same as Kissinger's. On the other hand, after Watergate and related scandals weakened the Nixon presidency, Kissinger found himself unable to deliver on his promises to the Soviets. Specifically, his linkage politics came uncoupled when he was unable to secure legislative approval of provisions granting the Soviet Union a "most favored nation" trading status.

Critics have noted that neither Nixon's détente nor his attention to U.S.–Soviet relations brought about a successful end to the Vietnam War or a solution to the problem of the 1973 Arab oil embargo. In fact, Kissinger's concentration on East-West politics might have made him less able to deal with these concerns. Opponents of Nixon-Kissinger (and later of Ford-

Kissinger) foreign policy have also found fault with them for having been too cynical—for paying too much attention to power and interests and not enough to basic American ideals and human rights.

The Post-Vietnam Era

President Jimmy Carter's stance on foreign policy differed substantially from that of his predecessors. For example, he placed significant emphasis on human rights, leveling criticism—and sometimes even sanctions—at both friends and enemies with poor human rights records. In addition, Carter himself tended to downplay the Soviet threat throughout most of his administration. He usually viewed revolutions, whether in Nicaragua or in Iran, as largely the products of internal forces and not necessarily as Soviet-inspired. However, he did not hesitate to fault the Soviets for their lack of attention to human rights.

In contrast to the Nixon-Kissinger era, Carter leaned toward "open" (rather than secret) diplomacy, and his approach to foreign policy was sometimes criticized as overly idealistic. Nevertheless, his greatest foreign policy achievement, the Camp David Accords, stemmed from an isolated meeting he arranged between Egyptian President Anwar Sadat and Israeli Premier Menachem Begin at his presidential retreat in Maryland. Sealed off from the press for several days of very secret discussions, they produced an agreement that ended Israel's occupation of the Sinai peninsula.

Nevertheless, the Carter administration did not speak with one voice on foreign policy. U.N. Ambassador Andrew Young tended to emphasize Third World issues involving economic and political development, but National

Security Adviser Zbigniew Brzezinski continued to expend his energies on more traditional U.S.–Soviet issues.[14] Toward the end of Carter's term, following the Soviet invasion of Afghanistan, the president's own attitude toward the Russians hardened.

His successor, Ronald Reagan, brought into the Oval Office the firm belief that the Soviets were responsible for most of the evil in the world and that their hand could be found in any turmoil. Reagan attributed the instability in Central America (specifically, in El Salvador and Nicaragua) principally to the actions of the Soviets and their surrogates, the Cubans and the Sandinistas.

Reagan believed the best method of combating the Soviet threat was to renew American military strength, and the result was a huge increase in defense spending. In addition, the Reagan administration poured considerable money into aid for friendly Latin American governments.

As we noted at the beginning of this chapter, the view that the Soviets are responsible for all the world's turmoil is not necessarily shared by all American public officials; nor is it shared by all of America's neighbors and allies. The Contadora group (Mexico, Venezuela, Colombia, and Panama), for example, is working for peace in Central America on the basis of a very different analysis of its problems.

Critics have charged that, except for repeating the anti-Soviet theme, the Reagan administration has had a difficult time clarifying its foreign policy goals. For example, the administration sent the American marines to Lebanon with only vague and conflicting explanations of their mission. More than 240 marines lost their lives on that assignment. Nonetheless, the Reagan administration has pursued some consistent policies. It has begun a massive military buildup both as a deterrent and as a bargaining chip in talks with the Soviets. In a stated attempt to "restore American self-confidence" Reagan staged a military rescue of American students from the Cuban-backed regime of Grenada and sent our forces to bomb terrorist bases and other targets in Libya.

Conflicting Policy Paradigms and America's Foreign Policy Goals

This review of the history of U.S. foreign policy has highlighted a number of the goals this country has set. First among these has been the preservation of American freedom and independence. For much of American history, this meant staying away from the political tangles of Europe and the commitments involved in international alliances. The nation remained free to pursue the development of its own territory and to intervene, when necessary, in the affairs of other countries in the hemisphere. Today, most policymakers believe that American freedom can best be protected when international peace and stability are not threatened by communism. Thus, since the United States achieved superpower status, much of American foreign policy has been directed toward the goal of creating or preserving a "stable world order."

In its pursuit of order, the United States has used both conflict and cooperation. On one hand, the country's search for stability led to periods of détente with China and the Soviet Union. On the other hand, America has sometimes found itself "containing communism" by opposing, undermining, and intervening against revolutionary movements in Third World countries. The nation has also attempted to contain the greatest perceived threat to its freedom—the expansion of Soviet communism—by entering into a web of alliances around the globe. But alliances forged in the defense of freedom may also limit U.S. freedom, as this country discovered most painfully in Vietnam. Thus, under the Nixon doctrine, the United States has asserted that American *interests*, not American *commitments*, will be at the heart of future policy decisions.

The question of order is thus linked to the question of freedom. An important U.S. goal has been to spread American-style free institutions at both the national and the international levels. America backed the establishment of international organizations, such as the United Nations and the World Court, and also supports the development of capitalist economies and liberal political systems, with free elections and guarantees of basic human rights. Though some policymakers, including many members of the Carter administration, pressed American human rights standards even on friendly governments, policymakers have more often been willing to overlook violations of freedom by regimes that proclaim themselves to be anticommunist.

The question of order is linked not only to freedom, but also to equality. The East-West split still dominates many foreign policy decisions, but some observers attach increasing importance to the division of the world into rich versus poor nations (sometimes characterized as Third World nations versus industrialized nations, or North versus South). Supporters of this position argue that the real threat to international stability has its source in economic and political inequality, and that poverty creates opportunities for communism to take hold. These arguments support a foreign policy that relies heavily on economic development, interdependence, redistribution of wealth, and access to the political process, rather than on conflict and military might. Recent events, such as the Arab oil embargo, the Iranian hostage seizure, the war in Vietnam, and the troubles in Latin America, have tended to reinforce this viewpoint—at least for some policymakers.

The Munich paradigm and the Vietnam paradigm generally agree on the priority of the first goal—order—but they disagree sharply on how best to bring about order and how to weight the other two goals—freedom and equality. In a democracy, such a lack of consensus could seriously undermine the conduct of foreign policy. As early as 1837, Alexis de Tocqueville surveyed the American political scene and warned that democracy would face dangers in the area of foreign policy. He wrote, in *Democracy in America*:

> Foreign politics demand scarcely any of those qualities which are peculiar to a democracy; they require, on the contrary, the perfect use of almost all those in which it is deficient . . . a democracy can only with great difficulty regulate the details of an important undertaking, persevere in a fixed design, and work out its execution in spite of severe obstacles. It cannot combine its measures with secrecy or await their consequences with patience.[15]

How did the designers of the American Constitution expect to avoid the dilemmas associated with foreign policy? Some of the answers to that question can be found by examining the constitutional context of foreign policymaking.

FOREIGN POLICYMAKING: THE CONSTITUTIONAL CONTEXT

The Constitution clearly puts the president in charge of American foreign policy. However, the framers also built in a number of checks and balances to prevent the president from conducting American foreign policy without substantial cooperation from Congress. Various presidents have nevertheless found ways to sidestep these provisions when they felt it important to do so.

The Formal Division of Power

The Constitution gives the president four significant foreign policymaking powers:

- He is commander in chief of the armed forces.
- He has the power to make treaties (subject to the consent of the Senate).
- He appoints U.S. ambassadors and the heads of executive departments (also with the advice and consent of the Senate).
- He receives (and may refuse to receive) ambassadors from other countries.

The most important foreign policy power the Constitution gives to Congress is the power to declare war, which has been used only five times in U.S. history. However, Congress has become deeply involved in the foreign policy process in other ways. For example, Congress has used its *legislative* power to establish programs of international scope, and it has used its control over the nation's pursestrings to appropriate funds for such programs. Another way Congress has exercised power in the foreign policy area is by monitoring and controlling existing foreign policy programs through the congressional power to *spend* (or not to spend).

The Senate has not been shy about using its powers to approve treaties and to consent to presidential appointments. We have already noted that it refused to ratify the Versailles treaty. More recently, it refused to ratify the SALT II treaty with the Soviets, which was aimed at slowing the nuclear arms buildup. Using their power as commanders in chief, however, Presidents Carter and Reagan lived up to the terms of the unsigned treaty from its creation in 1979 until at least 1986.

Sidestepping the Constitution

Though the Constitution gives the president enormous power in the foreign policy area, it also places limits on that power. Presidents and their advisers have often found ingenious ways around these constitutional limitations. Among the innovative devices they have used are executive agreements, discretionary funds, transfer authority and reprogramming, undeclared wars, and special envoys. Since the Vietnam War, however, Congress has attempted to assert control over the use of these presidential tools. To some extent, the Nicaraguan aid debate was an example of congressional assertiveness, although the president seemed to win in the end.

An **executive agreement** is, as its name implies, a pact between the heads of two countries. Initially, such agreements were used to work out the tedious details of day-to-day international affairs. They were declared, in *U.S. v. Curtiss-Wright* (1936), to be within the inherent powers of the president and to have the legal status of treaties.[16] This status makes executive agreements an enormously powerful presidential tool. They are not subject to senatorial approval as treaties are; however, like treaties, they become part of the "law of the land." Until 1972 the texts of executive agreements did not even have to be reported to Congress. However, legislation passed that year now requires the president to send copies to the House and Senate foreign relations committees.

This requirement has not seriously affected the use of executive agreements, which has escalated dramatically since World War II. In the years from 1945 to 1983, executive agreements outnumbered treaties by a ratio of 17 to 1.[17] And presidents have used these agreements to make substantive foreign policy. In fact, senators have complained that the treaties now submitted for Senate approval deal with petty, unimportant matters, whereas serious issues are handled by executive agreement. Moreover, executive agreements are subject to very few limits. One observer noted that "the principal limitation on their use is political in nature — the degree to which it is wise to exclude the Senate from [its] constitutional foreign policy role."[18]

Presidents have used several devices to circumvent congressional control over the nation's finances, in order to pursue their own foreign policies. For one, the chief executive is provided with **discretionary funds** — large sums of cash that may be spent on unpredicted needs to further the national interest. Kennedy used discretionary funds to run the Peace Corps in its first year; Johnson used $1.5 billion of his funds in Southeast Asia in 1965 and 1966.[19]

Presidents can also employ various other accounting maneuvers to support their foreign policy endeavors. Money can be shifted from one use to another through the president's **transfer authority** or the **reprogramming** of funds. These powers allow executive departments the discretion to take money that Congress has approved for one purpose and to spend it on something else. Normally, reprogramming would have offered a promising means for the administration to send military aid to Nicaragua — except that Congress had specifically prohibited any redirection of funds for military use in Nicaragua. Finally, the president has control over the disposal of *excess stocks,* which include surplus or infrequently used equipment. The Central Intelligence Agency (CIA) has been an important beneficiary of excess stock disposal. Until specifically barred from doing so, the CIA could use excess stocks to supply the Contras.

A third important foreign policy tool not included in the Constitution is the **undeclared war.** Both Congress's power to declare war (or not to do so) and its power of the purse would seem to limit a president's ability to involve the United States in undeclared wars. But, under the Constitution, the president is commander in chief of the armed forces. In performing this constitutionally prescribed role, chief executives have claimed the right to commit American troops in emergency situations. America's "undeclared" wars, police actions, and other interventions have, in fact, outnumbered formal, congressionally declared wars by about 30 to 1. Since the last declared

Did You Hear the One About . . .
Although they were rival leaders of hostile blocs, Soviet Party Chairman Leonid Brezhnev and President Richard Nixon launched a period of détente between their nations. Meeting here in Moscow in 1972, they agreed on the Strategic Arms Limitation Treaty (SALT-I).

war ended in 1945, over 100,000 American servicemen and women have died in locations ranging from Korea and Vietnam to Lebanon, Grenada, the Dominican Republic, Cuba, El Salvador, and Libya — all without congressional declarations of war.

During the Vietnam conflict, congressional opponents of that war passed the **War Powers Resolution** to limit the president's ability to wage undeclared wars. Under this resolution, a president must "consult" with Congress in "every possible instance" before involving U.S. troops in hostilities. In addition, the president is required to notify Congress within forty-eight hours of committing troops to a foreign intervention, and he is prohibited from keeping troops there for more than sixty days without congressional approval (although he may take up to an additional thirty days to remove troops "safely"). President Nixon vetoed the War Powers Act as an unwarranted restriction on the president's constitutional authority, but it was passed over his veto. Other critics* of the legislation have charged that it does not limit presidential power, but instead allows the president to wage war at will for

---

*Including both conservative Republican Senator Barry Goldwater of Arizona and liberal Democratic Senator Thomas Eagleton of Missouri. The latter's feelings were succinctly summarized in the title of his book, *War and Presidential Power: A Chronicle of Congressional Surrender* (New York: Liveright, 1974).

up to sixty days. By the end of that period, a Congress might find it very difficult indeed to force the president to bring the troops home.

In the June 1986 debate on Nicaragua, House members who were wary of the United States' becoming involved in an undeclared war in Nicaragua added provisions limiting the use of American military personnel in the war zones.

Finally, a president may look for ways to get around the Senate's power to confirm presidential appointments. Actually, the Senate rarely rejects a presidential choice. However, senators have used confirmation hearings as opportunities for investigating the president's foreign policy activities. For example, while he served as national security adviser, Henry Kissinger claimed that executive privilege protected him from being summoned to testify before congressional committees. When President Nixon nominated him to be secretary of state, however, Senators were able to ask him, in the course of the confirmation process, about a variety of subjects, including his roles in the secret bombing of Cambodia and in wiretapping various news reporters and public officials. Another method presidents have used to avoid congressional power over appointments is to rely heavily on the White House staff, who are accountable to no one but the president, or to use **special envoys** or "personal representatives," who may perform a wide variety of foreign policy tasks. For example, Harry Hopkins served as President Franklin D. Roosevelt's personal representative on missions to London, Moscow, and elsewhere. More recently, Philip Habib served in this capacity in the Middle East, the Philippines, and, while Reagan was trying to win congressional support for his Nicaraguan aid package, in Central America.

FOREIGN POLICYMAKING: THE ADMINISTRATIVE MACHINERY

In general, then, American foreign policy is developed and administered by the executive branch, with the approval and funding of Congress. As America began to assume a larger role in world affairs following World War II, the existing foreign policy machinery began to appear inadequate. In 1947 Congress passed the National Security Act, which established three new organizations with important foreign policy roles: the Department of Defense, the National Security Council, and the CIA. In addition to these organizations, the other department within the executive branch that shares major foreign policymaking power and responsibility is the Department of State.

The Department of State

The department that has most to do with the overall conduct of foreign affairs is the Department of State. It helps to formulate and then executes and monitors the outlines and details of American policy throughout the world. Its head, the secretary of state, is the highest-ranking official in the cabinet; he is also, supposedly, the president's most important foreign policy adviser. However, different presidents have used the office of secretary of state in very different ways. Some, like John Kennedy, preferred to act as their own secretaries of state and appointed relatively weak figures to the post. Others, such as Dwight Eisenhower, appointed stronger individuals to the post (John Foster Dulles, during Eisenhower's administration). During his first term, Richard Nixon planned to control foreign policy from the White House. He appointed William Rogers as secretary of state but took much of his advice from Henry Kissinger, whose office was located in the White House.

Like other executive departments, the State Department is made up of political appointees and permanent employees selected under the civil service merit system. The former include deputy secretaries and undersecretaries of state and some—but not all—ambassadors; the latter include about 3,500 foreign service officers who alternate assignments between home and abroad. The department provides staff for U.S. embassies and consulates throughout the world. It has primary responsibility for representing America to the world and caring for American citizens and interests abroad. Although the foreign service is highly selective (fewer than 200 of the 15,000 who take the annual examination are appointed), the State Department is often criticized for a lack of morale and power. One often-cited reason is the damage that was done to the department in the 1950s by **McCarthyism**. With little or no evidence, Republican Senator Joseph McCarthy of Wisconsin and others charged that the department was riddled with communists who were engaged in selling out the country to the Soviets. Great numbers of Americans believed McCarthy's accusations; his "witch-hunts" not only ruined many individual careers but also left lasting scars on the department itself. As a result of such trauma, critics charge that bright young foreign service officers quickly realize that conformity is the best path to career advancement. As one observer put it: "There are old foreign service officers, and there are bold foreign service officers; but, there are no old, bold foreign service officers." Consequently, presidents may find the State Department's foreign policy machinery too slow and unwieldy. As President Kennedy remarked, "Bundy [Kennedy's national security adviser] and I get more done in one day in the White House than they do in six months in the State Department. . . . They never have any ideas over there, never come up with anything new."[20]

When Henry Kissinger became secretary of state in 1974, some hoped that his prestige within the Nixon administration would carry over to the department. By and large, however, Kissinger rarely used the department's facilities; he preferred instead to rely on subordinates who had been with him during his White House years.

Another difficulty faced by the State Department is the lack of a strong, built-in domestic constituency to exert pressure in support of its policies. This is in marked contrast with, say, the Department of Education, which might try to mobilize teachers to support their activities; or the Department of Agriculture, which might enlist farmers; or the Department of Defense, which might seek help from defense industries or veterans' groups. In a pluralist democracy, the lack of a natural constituency is a serious drawback for a department. The department is unable to count on powerful domestic allies to rally in support of its positions.

Foreign Policy High Five
Political scientist Henry Kissinger moved from the heights of the ivory tower to the heights of world power. He left his position in the government department at Harvard University to serve first as assistant to the president for national security affairs under Richard Nixon and later as secretary of state in the Nixon and Ford administrations.

The Department of Defense

The Department of Defense replaced two cabinet-level departments: the War Department and the Department of the Navy. It was created to provide the modern bureaucratic structure that was needed to manage America's much-increased peacetime military strength and to promote greater unity and coordination among the armed forces. At the same time, in keeping with the U.S. tradition of civilian control of the military, the new department was given a civilian head—the secretary of defense—a cabinet member who has authority over the military establishment. Successive reorganizations of the department (in 1949 and 1958) have given the secretary greater budgetary powers, control of defense research, and the authority to transfer, abolish, reassign, and consolidate functions among the military services. These powers enabled Robert McNamara, secretary of defense under Kennedy and Johnson, to make sweeping changes in military management procedures. Among other things, he attempted to involve the services in joint programs — in missile development, for example — in order to avoid duplication, inefficiency, and waste. In addition, during McNamara's tenure, the Pentagon's Office of International Security Affairs began to develop the department's own foreign policy positions based on both military and political factors.

As with secretaries of state, the power available to defense secretaries often depends on the secretary's own vision of the job and willingness to use the tools available. Strong secretaries of defense, including McNamara, Melvin Laird (under Nixon), and James Schlesinger (under Nixon and Ford), have wielded tremendous power. Currently, Caspar Weinberger, serving as

Reagan's secretary of defense, must be counted among the strongest figures in the administration.

Below the secretary, further reinforcing the principle of civilian control, are the civilian secretaries of the army, navy, and air force; below them are the military commanders of the three branches. These military leaders make up the Joint Chiefs of Staff (JCS). In addition to their roles as heads of their respective services, the JCS meet to coordinate military policy; they are also the primary military advisers to the president, the secretary of defense, and the National Security Council. As advisers, the JCS have broad responsibilities for developing positions on such matters as alliances, plans for nuclear and conventional war, nuclear targeting doctrine, and arms control and disarmament.

The National Security Council

The National Security Council (NSC) is a permanent group of advisers established to help the president integrate and coordinate the details of domestic, foreign, and military affairs as they relate to national security. By statute, the NSC consists of the president, the vice president, the secretaries of state and defense, and the chairman of the Joint Chiefs of Staff, as well as others who may be invited by the president. NSC discussions can cover a wide range of issues, including, for example, U.S. support for the Contras in Nicaragua, the political and military advantages of the Strategic Defense Initiative ("Star Wars" proposal), and revisions of U.S. policy in the Middle East. In theory, at least, NSC discussions offer the president an opportunity to solicit advice, while allowing key participants in the foreign policymaking process to keep abreast of the policies and capabilities of other departments.

The exact role played by the NSC has varied considerably under different presidents. Whereas Truman and Kennedy seldom met with the NSC, Eisenhower and Nixon brought it into much greater prominence. During the Nixon administration, the NSC was critically important in making foreign policy. Much of this importance derived from the role played by Henry Kissinger, Nixon's assistant for national security affairs (the title of the head of the NSC staff). Under Nixon and Kissinger, the NSC staff ballooned to over one hundred — in effect, a little State Department in the White House. Under President Reagan, there has been some effort to de-emphasize the policymaking role of the NSC and to confine its functions to coordination and communication.

The CIA and the Intelligence Community

Before World War II, the United States had no permanent agency specifically charged with gathering intelligence (that is, information) about the actions and intentions of foreign powers. Partly because of the desire to avoid intelligence failures of the sort that led to the Pearl Harbor disaster and partly in recognition of America's more internationalist role, Congress created the Central Intelligence Agency (CIA) in 1947.

The agency's charter lists two of its functions as (1) coordinating the information and data-gathering activities of various other government departments; and (2) collecting, analyzing, evaluating and circulating its own intelligence relating to national security matters. Most of these activities are relatively uncontroversial. By far the bulk of material obtained by the CIA comes from readily available sources: statistical abstracts, books, newspapers, and so on. The agency's *Intelligence Directorate* is responsible for these overt, or open, information-processing activities.

The charter also empowers the CIA "to perform such other functions and duties related to intelligence affecting the national security as the National Security Council shall direct." This vague clause has been used by the agency as its legal justification for the covert, or secret, activities undertaken by its *Operations Directorate*. These activities have included espionage, coups (in Iran in 1953 and Guatemala in 1954, for example), plots to assassinate foreign leaders (such as Fidel Castro), experiments exposing unsuspecting American citizens to mind-altering LSD, wiretaps, interception of the mail, and the infiltration of antiwar groups. As we noted at the beginning of the chapter, the CIA was providing military support and assistance to the Contras, including aid in mining Nicaraguan harbors, until Congress limited its activities. Allen Dulles, who was Eisenhower's CIA director, believed that covert activities are "an essential part of the free world's struggle against communism"; however, by the mid-1970s Senator Frank Church's description of the agency as a "rogue elephant rampaging out of control" seemed more apt. A presidential committee that investigated charges of CIA activity within the United States (then illegal under the CIA's charter) found that many of the agency's actions were "plainly unlawful."

CIA critics sometimes point out that the agency's existence has not ended major foreign policy "surprises" for the United States. Some gaffes have been the result of faulty intelligence (as in the case of the Bay of Pigs), but others were more the result of policymakers' failure to accept or interpret analyses properly. The CIA told President Johnson that bombing North Vietnam would not bring the North Vietnamese into submission. Johnson responded to CIA interpretations by remarking, "Policymaking is like milking a fat cow. You see the milk coming out, you press more and the milk bubbles and flows and just as the bucket is full the cow with its tail whips the bucket and all is spilled. That's what the CIA does to policymaking."[21] The usual response to intelligence failures is to investigate and then propose structural changes in institutions, but at least one analyst claims that "intelligence failure is political and psychological more often than it is institutional."[22] Even the best-designed intelligence network will not prevent the United States from being caught by surprise some of the time—at most, it might minimize the frequency or intensity of such surprises.

The basic dilemma posed by the CIA and the intelligence community, though, concerns the role of covert activities. Covert operations raise both moral and legal questions for a democracy. Are they, as Dulles suggested, "essential," or are they antithetical to a democracy that espouses open government, free elections, and the principle of self-determination? And if covert activities are deemed necessary and appropriate, how does one reconcile them with basic operating principles of American government? For example, should the principle of checks and balances be applied to secret operations? Though the CIA's covert activities were supposed to be approved by an NSC subcommittee, the president himself was not always briefed about them.

"Minor" operations were not even reported to NSC subcommittees. Political control of CIA activities was, in essence, sacrificed in the name of the secrecy necessary for successful operations. Congress has wrestled with these problems for more than a decade. In 1975 it passed the Hughes-Ryan amendment, which required all covert activities of the CIA to be reported to the appropriate congressional committees. In 1981, in the Intelligence Authorization Act, Congress required all intelligence agencies to inform appropriate committees not only of current covert operations but also of "significant *anticipated* operations." That act also reduced, from eight to two, the number of committees that must be informed of secret activities. But congressional dissatisfaction remains regarding the extent to which the intelligence community has complied with the law.

As we have seen, Tocqueville believed that part of democracies' weakness in foreign affairs stemmed from their inability to solve the dilemma of how to combine the secrecy necessary for foreign policy with the openness needed for democratic government. Practitioners of international relations have traditionally valued secrecy, but democratic theory requires that citizens know what their leaders are doing. As this discussion of the CIA shows, the dilemma continues to cause problems for American policymakers.

THE PUBLIC, THE MEDIA, AND FOREIGN POLICY

The other great difficulty Tocqueville anticipated for democracies in foreign affairs grew out of the changeable views of a mass electorate. He believed foreign relations required patience and persistence in the pursuit of long-term goals. But, as Tocqueville suggested, the public could be fickle and unwilling to set aside short-term gains for long-term security. Leaders who respond to domestic pressures and seek to appease the masses may then be forced to act in ways that are harmful to foreign policy interests. Their democratic responsiveness might well be detrimental to long-term foreign policy success.

How has the American democracy coped with this difficulty? To find the answer to that question, we will look at public opinion on foreign policy matters in terms of the majoritarian and pluralist models.

The Public and the Majoritarian Model

In Chapter 5, we showed that Americans as a group have little knowledge of politics but are nonetheless very willing to express their opinions about political issues. These findings hold for foreign affairs as well as (and perhaps even more than) domestic politics. Only about 15 percent of Americans are considered attentive to foreign affairs — that is, to the extent that they make an effort to find out what is happening internationally.

Americans are quick to tell policymakers what should be done, but they rarely can provide guidance on how to do it. Consider the public's response to a March 1969 poll on the Vietnam War. Of those polled, 52 percent — a clear majority — believed that our involvement in Vietnam was a mistake. But when respondents were asked, "What do you think the United States should do next in regard to the Vietnam situation?" their responses were as follows: wage all-out war, 32 percent; pull out of Vietnam, 26 percent; continue the present policy, 19 percent; end the war as soon as possible, 19 percent; other, 4 percent. Obviously, Americans were unhappy about the policies being pursued in Vietnam. However, they were unable to achieve a consensus on how to change those policies.

The public's opinions regarding foreign policy issues are also extremely volatile. The American people have historically been willing to "rally 'round the flag" and back presidential foreign policies, particularly in crisis situations. But they are willing to do so only for relatively short periods of time. Moreover, their foreign policy views can affect presidential elections. Thus, President Carter enjoyed increased public approval following the seizure of American hostages in Iran. And that added support helped him to victory over Senator Edward Kennedy of Massachusetts in the 1980 Democratic primaries. But his inability to resolve the hostage situation contributed to his defeat by Ronald Reagan a few months later.

Similarly, President Reagan's 1983 invasion of Grenada quickly garnered a great deal of popular support. But because that conflict was over within days, well before dissatisfaction could set in, approval never really wavered. More recently, the American bombing of Libya in reprisal for Libya's support of terrorism was enormously popular. In contrast, the president has been able to win little popular backing for aid to the Contras. Furthermore, his commitment of troops to Lebanon dragged on for over a year, with little popular support, until a terrorist bombing incident claimed 241 American lives and led briefly to a slight increase in support for our policies there. When support again waned and policy in Lebanon threatened to become an election issue, the president withdrew the marines. The moral to be drawn from these examples seems clear: a president had better be able to produce a short-run success or expect to lose his constituency — exactly what Tocqueville would have predicted.

If the American public is fickle in its foreign policy opinions, then how can we explain the consensus that prevailed after World War II? One observer suggests that it resulted from the "permissive mood" of the American people at that time. In general, Americans had been willing to follow the leader and to take their cues from policymakers, who were themselves in fundamental agreement.[23] Other analysts looked for a reasonably stable set of beliefs or assumptions held by the public.

To explain the current lack of consensus, political scientists have identified four different foreign policy orientations, which emerged in the mid-1970s. These, in turn, depend on the value that the individual attaches to two concepts: international cooperation and militant internationalism.[24] Those who support international cooperation tend to be aware of global interdependence, attuned to Third World issues, and concerned about economic inequality. Those who support militant internationalism are likely to see America as having global interests and a responsibility to check communist expansion, using military force if necessary. These two concepts seem to boil down to the two paradigms with which we began this chapter; however, it is more likely that they represent two different dimensions of a given person's orientation toward foreign policy. This means that an individual may accept

Mourning the Dead
President Reagan won popular support at home when he ordered the 1986 bombing of Tripoli, the capital city of Libya, in retaliation for terrorist activities encouraged and supported by Libyan leader Mu'ammar Qadhafi. There were few Reagan supporters in this crowd of several hundred Libyans who marched in a funeral procession in central Tripoli to mourn twenty victims of the American raid.

either cooperative internationalism or militant internationalism and reject the other, or accept both, or reject both. The four resulting foreign policy positions have been labeled internationalist, accommodationist, hardliner, and isolationist. They are outlined in Figure 19.2 and appear to be roughly comparable to the four ideological positions described in Chapter 1.

Taken together, these orientations suggest that Americans are mainly internationalist but differ on the form that internationalism should assume. Despite the splits in orientation, those who support the majoritarian model of democracy might claim, with some justification, that the people are capable of judging when a policy has become too painful or too costly to pursue. Yet, as we have noted, this does not mean that the public can make foreign policy. Or, to put it more strongly, any idea that American foreign policy is a reflection of mass opinion is crude and simplistic, since "policy formulation does not derive from the simple preferences of an uninformed, uninterested, unstable, acquiescent and manipulable 'public voice'."[25] In short, policymakers must look elsewhere for their cues. In foreign affairs, as in other areas of American politics, the majoritarian model does not really seem to describe American democracy.

Interest Groups and the Pluralist Model

Many people become interested in foreign policy issues when they perceive those issues as affecting them directly. Thus, auto workers and manufacturers may favor import restrictions on Japanese cars. People worried about the nuclear threat may support the freeze movement. Jewish citizens may pay particular attention to America's relations with Israel. These individuals may join unions and other organizations that present their policy positions to policymakers.

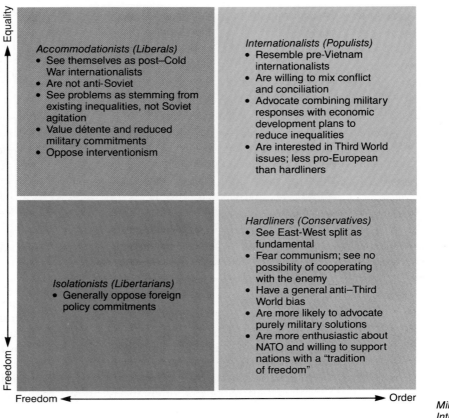

Cooperative
Internationalism

Equality

Accommodationists (Liberals)
- See themselves as post–Cold War internationalists
- Are not anti-Soviet
- See problems as stemming from existing inequalities, not Soviet agitation
- Value détente and reduced military commitments
- Oppose interventionism

Internationalists (Populists)
- Resemble pre-Vietnam internationalists
- Are willing to mix conflict and conciliation
- Advocate combining military responses with economic development plans to reduce inequalities
- Are interested in Third World issues; less pro-European than hardliners

Isolationists (Libertarians)
- Generally oppose foreign policy commitments

Hardliners (Conservatives)
- See East-West split as fundamental
- Fear communism; see no possibility of cooperating with the enemy
- Have a general anti–Third World bias
- Are more likely to advocate purely military solutions
- Are more enthusiastic about NATO and willing to support nations with a "tradition of freedom"

Freedom

Freedom ◀   ▶ Order

Militant
Internationalism

Four Orientations Toward Foreign Policy
In the absence of a clear foreign policy consensus, political scientists have identified four foreign policy orientations shared by Americans. It should be noted that, while one of these orientations is explicitly called "internationalist," all but one of them (isolationists) are essentially internationalist in outlook. Where they differ is on the nature of America's foreign policy problems and the appropriate methods for dealing with them. (Sources: Michael Maggiotto and Eugene Wittkopf, "American Public Attitudes Toward Foreign Policy," International Studies Quarterly (December 1981): 601–631; Ole Holsti, "The Three Headed Eagle: The United States and System Change," International Studies Quarterly (September 1979): 339–359; M. Mandelbaum and W. Schneider, "The New Internationalism," in K.A. Oye et al., eds., The Eagle Entangled: U.S. Foreign Policy in a Complex World (New York: Longman, 1979), pp. 34–88.)

Figure 19.2 ━━━

On foreign affairs issues, two of the most prominent kinds of lobbies have included businesses and unions, often seeking trade protection, and ethnic groups seeking support for their fellows in the "old country." More recently, and in keeping with the current lobbying boom in Washington, foreign governments have begun to hire high-powered Washington lobbying firms to represent their interests.

In general, the impact of these groups varies with the issue. But lobbying seems to be most effective when it takes place behind the scenes and deals with noncrisis issues that are not considered important by the public at large. Interest groups are more effective in maintaining support for the status quo than in bringing about policy changes.[26]

As with domestic issues, there is a tendency for foreign policy interest groups to counterbalance each other. The Turkish lobby may try to offset the Greek lobby; the Arms Control Association or the Federation of American Scientists may oppose the American Legion or the Veterans of Foreign Wars on issues of détente and military spending. The result may be that "foreign policy making resembles a taffy-pull: every group attempts to pull policy in its own direction while resisting the pulls of others, with the result that policy fails to move in any discernible direction. The process encourages solutions tending toward the middle of the road and maintenance of the status quo."[27] If this is so, one might argue that perhaps the pluralist model of democracy avoids some of the pitfalls Tocqueville envisioned in his writings about America. At least it would seem to offer the possibility of greater stability, if no greater long-term effectiveness.

The Media and Foreign Policy

A potentially powerful source of influence on both public attitudes and policymakers' actions is the media—television, newspapers, magazines, and radio. Do the media shape foreign policy? Television coverage of the Vietnam War is often thought to be one reason why people turned against that war (see Feature 19.2). Media attention to the Iranian hostage crisis kept the issue in the public eye for over a year.

Yet, the media's impact on the public is also limited. As noted above, most people simply do not follow foreign affairs or care much about foreign policy.

The media themselves try to cater to their audience and generally do not devote very much space or time to foreign policy issues. When they do, however, their impact on the general public tends to be more indirect than direct. One observer called it a "two-step" process.[28] The foreign policymakers and the "attentive public" obtain most of their information from the media. This information eventually filters down to the public through their communications with clergy, teachers, union officials, and other opinion leaders.

The media also function as foreign policy agenda setters (see Chapter 9). By giving play to a particular issue, policy, or crisis, the media are able to capture the public's consciousness and to focus attention on that issue. As in domestic affairs, the media "may not tell us what to think, but they tell us what to think about."[29]

The agenda-setter role of the media can impact foreign policymaking in another way. Recall that interest groups tend to be most effective in noncrisis situations that are not of general public concern. Thus, by calling attention to a particular issue, the media can dilute some of the effectiveness of organized special interest groups. And, in a crisis situation in which quick action is called for, media attention can even work to the detriment of an interest group. On the other hand, by keeping an issue before the public, the media can increase the likelihood that it will become the focus of some interest group's lobbying efforts.[30]

Feature 19.2

Press Coverage of Combat: Three Models

One area in which the requirements of democracy run headlong into the requirements of national security is the press coverage of military operations. Freedom of the press is one of the fundamental rights of citizens in a democracy, who must have access to accurate information to be able to judge their government's policies. In a democracy, the government responds to the people's will; it doesn't create that will. Yet in wartime, democratic governments and the press face a dilemma. The safety of soldiers and the success of military operations could be jeopardized if too much information were available to the public — and potentially to the enemy — too soon. But how much is too much, and who is to judge?

During World War II, war correspondents accompanied invading troops (after signing waivers releasing the U.S. government from any responsibility for their safety). The stories they filed were subject to military censorship and delay, ostensibly to protect the lives of American servicemen.

In Vietnam, by contrast, reporters were able to shoot film that appeared immediately on television news, with virtually no military censorship. Many people have credited the erosion of popular support for the war to the graphic portrayal of Vietnam horrors on the nightly television news. Some also argue that reduced domestic support for the war made it harder for American troops in the field; thus, indirectly, press coverage of the war in Vietnam may have undermined the safety of American fighting men.

In 1983, during the invasion of Grenada, news reporters were not permitted to land with the marines. Only after several days were they allowed access to the island and then only on a restricted basis. Despite a long tradition of allowing war correspondents in battle zones, the Department of Defense claimed that reporters were excluded because of concern for their safety. Journalists, however, charged that the Department of Defense was motivated far less by concern for reporters' safety than by the department's own interest in public relations — that is, in making sure that its own official version of the Grenada invasion was the one the American people received. The first films shown on network television following the invasion were produced by the Department of Defense and did not show fighting; rather, they dealt with the justification for the invasion by focusing on a cache of Cuban arms stored on Grenada. Obviously, the reporters argued, the department wanted to be sure that the invasion would be portrayed in a favorable light, so that the public would support it.

Which, if any, of the three press coverage models — World War II, Vietnam, or Grenada — puts democratic values and security demands in the proper balance?

THE FOREIGN POLICYMAKING PROCESS

Now that we have looked at the historical context of American foreign policy and the cast of characters involved, we should examine the policymaking process itself. How is foreign policy made? How was President Ronald Reagan able to turn his March 1986 defeat on aid to the Contras into a June 1986 victory?

Sources of Information
for the Executive Branch

By both constitutional position and practical control of resources, the president is the dominant actor in the foreign policymaking process. A president comes to the job with a paradigm or world view that helps him interpret and evaluate international events. And, as chief executive, he commands tremendous foreign policy resources, including information and personnel. The Pentagon, the State Department, and the CIA are among his main sources of information about the outside world and provide staffs to advise him on foreign policy and implement his decisions. Often his advisers will present conflicting information or offer different, even contradictory, advice. Their views on issues may be influenced by their positions in the bureaucracy — the secretary of state might lean more toward diplomacy, whereas the secretary of defense might push for a show of force. Advisers may compete for a president's ear or bargain among themselves to shape administration policy.

In addition to executive branch officials, a president's sources of foreign policy advice may include other, more removed, sources. For example, as the Reagan administration was formulating its Nicaraguan aid request, the president received a letter from congressional Democrats who had supported him in his request for nonlethal aid. They asked him to pursue diplomacy before asking for military aid. The foreign ministers of eight Latin American countries also called on the secretary of state to end U.S. support for the Contras.

One of the president's most important tasks in the foreign policymaking process can be deciding whom to believe — those who agree with his policy predispositions or those who challenge them. The wrong choice can be extremely costly. For example, some critics of the Johnson administration claim that Johnson preferred yes-men as advisers and was unwilling to listen to those within his administration who disagreed with him on Vietnam.

Congress and the President

When a president has decided on a policy, he may be able to carry it out without congressional approval if he has a clear constitutional mandate (for example, when recognizing another government or putting the marines on alert). When his legal authority is shakier and congressional approval appears unlikely, he may use the techniques we described in the section on "Sidestepping the Constitution" or go to Congress for the funds or authority to carry out his policy.

A president seeking congressional approval for a policy finds that his command of information and personnel gives him a considerable advantage over Congress. Although legislators have ample access to independent sources of information on domestic issues, their sources on foreign affairs are much more limited. Members of Congress may go on "fact-finding" tours — as did several representatives between the two votes on Nicaraguan aid. They may also get information from lobbyists, but in comparison with the president's sources of information, theirs are minuscule, and they are therefore heavily dependent on the executive branch for information.

Lonely at the Top
Being commander-in-chief of the armed forces is an awesome responsibility. Stunned by a resurgence of enemy activity during the Vietnam War in early 1968, President Lyndon Johnson decided not to seek re-election. Here in July 1968, the president listens to a tape-recorded message from his son-in-law, who was serving in the U.S. military in Vietnam.

The president may use his informational advantage to swing votes. Just two days after the March vote in the House on Contra aid (and shortly before the Senate voted 53 to 47 in favor of the request), the White House announced that fifteen hundred Nicaraguan troops had invaded Honduras in pursuit of the Contras. This release of information embarrassed House members who had voted against the president and may have helped him win support in the Senate.

In addition, the chief executive's personnel resources give him considerable ability to influence events. Many analysts argue, for example, that the incidents that sparked the Gulf of Tonkin Resolution during the Vietnam War were trumped-up — pretexts that President Johnson seized upon to expand American involvement. The House of Representatives, recognizing the ability of the executive branch to create and use incidents in faraway places, imposed limits on the use of American personnel in Nicaraguan combat areas.

Another potential disability of Congress in the foreign policy process is its fragmented authority over international issues. Different congressional committees have authority for the armed services, for foreign relations, for intelligence oversight, for foreign trade, and for development. There is no congressional equivalent of the National Security Council to bring even the appearance of coherence to the congressional approach to foreign policy. Granted, there are often disagreements within the executive branch. These may even spill over into the congressional arena. For example, a Pentagon official might quietly appeal to friendly members of the armed services committees to restore defense cuts made in the president's proposed budget. Disaffected officials might leak information. But, by and large, the executive is much better equipped to offer a unified approach to foreign policy.

Faced with these comparative disadvantages in terms of information, personnel, and organization, the general tendency is for Congress to accede to the president's foreign policy wishes. In the case of Contra aid, however, the influence of the Vietnam paradigm and the strong opposition mounted by the House leadership effectively tipped the scales against the Reagan administration in March.

Lobbies and the "Lobbyist in Chief"

While the legislation was pending before Congress, a considerable lobbying effort was made by both supporters and opponents of Contra aid. Supporters included the leaders of the United Nicaraguan Opposition (the Contra group that the United States backs) and various conservative organizations, including the National Endowment for the Preservation of Liberty, which launched its own $2 million pro-Contra campaign and hired a professional public relations and lobbying firm to represent the Contra cause. Arrayed on the other side were many members of the clergy, who publicized the human rights abuses of the Contras. The opponents of aid also had their own professional publicity firm.

The single most effective "lobbyist" on the issue, though, was not a lobbyist at all; it was the president. Back in March, White House staffers had used inflammatory rhetoric to brand those who opposed the administration as procommunist. This incensed many members of Congress. By June the administration had toned down its rhetoric, and Ronald Reagan began to use his power in a way that made him the best lobbyist for his cause. He made a conciliatory speech calling for a return to the kind of bipartisanship that had supported President Truman's request for aid to Greece and Turkey almost forty years earlier. He worked hard on the sixteen Republicans who had voted against him in March, assuring them that the aid was necessary.

He was able to convince five, including Chalmers Wylie of Ohio, who acknowledged that he had difficulty naming the countries of Central America and had decided to defer to the president's judgment, pointing out that "he's a very persuasive fellow."[31] The president was also able to convince three Democrats to change their votes, thus producing his new majority.

If Ronald Reagan was the best lobbyist for his own policy, Daniel Ortega, leader of the Sandinista government, was probably the worst lobbyist for his cause. Opponents of Contra aid found Ortega's Marxism increasingly difficult to defend. His trip to Moscow and the Nicaraguan incursion into Honduras made it difficult for wavering representatives to refute the Reagan analysis.

Policy Implementation

A president may decide on a course of action, and Congress may authorize it, but the policy still must be carried out. The question of who should carry out a particular policy is not always easily answered. Though each department or agency has its basic functions spelled out, there can be overlap. When there is, organizations may squabble over which one should perform a particular mission. At the outset of the Cuban missile crisis, for example, there were disputes between the CIA and the military concerning who should fly reconnaissance flights over Cuba.

On the Contra aid issue, some potentially divisive disputes over implementation surfaced after the bill had cleared the House. Specifically, these concerned the division of responsibility for the aid package. While technically the State Department administered the aid program, control over the newly authorized aid seemed to pass to the military and the CIA.

Congress, of course, is responsible for overseeing the implementation of programs. That means, among other things, monitoring the correct use and evaluating the effectiveness of programs. Here, too, the Contra aid question ran into some difficulties. Opponents of aid noted that the Contras were unable to account for much of the $27 million they had received previously. There were charges that much of the money had been diverted away from the revolutionary struggle in Nicaragua. In passing this new aid package, the House called for better financial accounting.

Public Opinion and Policymaking on the Contra Issue

What role did the general public play on the Contra aid issue? Essentially a passive one. Although the president had spoken out frequently on behalf of aid to the Contras, public opinion polls consistently showed that the public did not support the president on this issue. In a March 25, 1986, poll conducted by ABC News, 53 percent disagreed with the administration's proposal to send military aid to the Contras, and only 42 percent approved the plan. The president was unable to rally the people behind him. Since 1984, however, the public had become somewhat better informed on the issue (though not nearly as well informed as theorists of majoritarian democracy would prefer). Back in May of 1984, only 34 percent of people polled could correctly identify the side we were supporting in Nicaragua. By March 1986, that proportion had jumped to 50 percent.

Once again, the majoritarian model of democracy does not offer much help in understanding what happens in American politics. But, in the area of foreign policy in particular, a strong case can be made for another, anti-democratic theory, mentioned in Chapter 2, *elite theory*. The extent of presidential dominance in foreign policy makes it seem plausible that the foreign policymaking process is the preserve of an elite. Yet, as was pointed out in Chapter 2, if there is an elite, it is a very large one, and it is not able to win on every issue. Even the president's victory in June 1986 does not ensure that he will win the next time the issue is before Congress. Finally, if there *is* an elite controlling foreign policy, it is a much-divided elite, and divided elites offer fertile ground for pluralist politics.

DEFENSE POLICY

At the beginning of this chapter, we noted that adherents to the Munich and Vietnam paradigms differ in their attitudes about how and when to use the tools of American foreign policy. It would be far too simplistic to say that those influenced by the Munich paradigm see military force as the only choice, whereas those influenced by the Vietnam paradigm would never resort to force. But the two approaches do differ significantly in their attitudes on the role of the military, economic, and diplomatic resources of the United States. In this section and the next, we will explore issues concerning the military and economic tools available to policymakers and suggest some of the ways in which adherents to each of the two paradigms differ about their use.

How Much Should Be Spent?

Most people agree that, in order to protect national interests, the United States needs an adequate defense. But beyond that, agreement breaks down. What constitutes an adequate defense? To what extent should defense spending take priority over other kinds of spending?

President Reagan came to office committed to a strong national defense. He also pledged to cut the federal budget. During his administration, the federal government has trimmed back expenditures for domestic programs, while defense spending has increased enormously. In an argument reminiscent of the NSC-68 discussion during the Truman administration, the president maintains that the level of the defense budget is not really under his control — rather, it is established in Moscow. The adequacy of American defense can only be judged in comparison with that of our principal adversary, the Soviet Union (see Compared With What? 19.1). The United States has a political as well as a moral commitment to oppose communist expansion.

Critics of large defense budgets ask if the United States can defend itself adequately by investing huge amounts in sophisticated military hardware while cutting back on funds to develop "human capital" — that is, funds to prepare people to do the job. Reducing funds for programs such as children's nutrition or education may diminish the value of America's human capital. Arguably, both hardware and human beings are important to the national defense. In addition, other critics insist that high levels of defense spending may throw the entire federal budget out of line, creating budget deficits that may endanger the overall performance of the U.S. economy. A poorly performing economy could make the nation more vulnerable to outside pressures. A strong economy may be every bit as important to national security as a sound defense. But if increased defense outlays risk damaging the economy, the ironic result could be that more defense spending might make the United States less rather than more secure.

A final objection to enormous defense spending might be on the grounds of the moral and political effects of committing too much to the military. Eisenhower's warning about the military-industrial complex is a case in point. In a kind of vicious circle, military spending feeds powerful interests, which depend on that spending and in turn exert pressure to increase spending even more. As Table 19.1 shows, the sums involved are huge, and every state in the union receives them.

What Should Defense Money Buy?

Another important issue involved in defense policy is deciding what kind of defense is needed. In short, what should the defense budget be spent on? There are significant choices to be made concerning the personnel and equipment that will defend the country. One significant choice is whether to have a volunteer military force or to require service by some or all citizens. Other questions concern the kinds of weapons systems to build. What mix of nuclear and conventional forces should be used? How do different weapons fit into America's defense needs? Is a weapons system desirable because of the contribution it makes to defense requirements, or is it wanted for another purpose—as a bargaining chip to exact concessions from the Soviets in arms negotiations, for example?

The Reagan administration has been particularly supportive of high-technology weapons systems, both nuclear and conventional. It has championed the B-1 and Stealth bombers and worked hard to secure congressional authorization for the MX, a new generation of land-based intercontinental ballistic missiles (ICBMs). The Reagan administration also launched a large-scale American research and development effort called the Strategic Defense Initiative (SDI to its friends, "Star Wars" to its adversaries). This program is an attempt to build a system to defend against Soviet ICBMs. At present there is no defense against ICBMs other than deterrence—which depends on each superpower's refraining from the use of nuclear weapons out of fear of the consequences of retaliation.

Some opponents of weapons expenditures, including some of those who take their cues from the Vietnam paradigm, criticize these programs, not because they oppose all forms of military spending, but because they believe that certain systems do not meet the nation's defense needs. SDI, for example, has been criticized as both unworkable and far too expensive. Even a system that would defend perfectly against ICBMs would not halt the threat of nuclear

Compared With What? 19.1

U.S. Defense Spending

President Reagan has argued that the level of U.S. defense spending is set in Moscow. In other words, America's military spending must keep pace with that of the Soviet Union. This graph compares the total defense expenditures for the United States and the Soviet Union. It shows that the Soviet Union consistently outspends the United States. The picture changes, however, if we look at NATO versus Soviet bloc (Warsaw Pact) nations. (Figures are in billions of 1982 dollars.)

Legend:
- Other NATO
- Other Warsaw Pact
- U.S.
- Soviet Union

Source of data: U.S. Arms Control and Disarmament Agency, *World Military Expenditures and Arms Transfers* (Washington, D.C.: U.S. Government Printing Office, 1985).

extermination. Such technology would not be effective against sea-launched missiles fired from offshore submarines or cruise missiles flying close to the ground.

Defense critics also make a persuasive case against expenditures for large, costly, high-technology weapons. They argue that bigger and more expensive is not always better. Lower-technology weapons break down less frequently and require less maintenance. They are cheaper to repair and operate. As a result, troops are able to gain more training experience with them and can become more proficient at using them. Such experience could be critical in a combat situation.[32]

**Wheels of tracks, large or small,
U.S. or foreign-built . . .**

Guess what they've all got in common.

The most versatile combat vehicles in the world have one thing in common. They can all mount the combat-effective 25mm M242 BUSHMASTER automatic cannon.

In fact, over 3,500 BUSHMASTERs are now in service with the U.S. armed forces, and each month 80 more roll off the line at McDonnell Douglas Helicopter Company, currently the free world's largest producer of automatic cannons.

BUSHMASTER performance exceeds military requirements and goals on all counts . . . reliability, availability, maintainability, durability, accuracy and lethality. Join the growing ranks and put the lethal BUSHMASTER on your combat vehicle.

For further information, contact:
Ordnance Marketing
McDonnell Douglas Helicopter Company,
Culver City, CA 90230 USA,
telephone (213) 305-3260,
TELEX 182434 MD HC A CULV.

**MCDONNELL
DOUGLAS**

Made in the USA
Need to spruce up your tank? Buy the M242 BUSHMASTER automatic cannon from McDonnell Douglas. This advertisement shows that U.S. defense contractors are in business to sell to countries throughout the world. Actually, other countries — Sweden, Italy, and Israel, for example — market their weapons for international sales even more aggressively. Sale of military equipment is big business in any language.

Defense Policy and Foreign Policy

A final defense policy issue concerns the relationship between defense policy and foreign policy. Whereas Munich-paradigm adherents may think that a strong defense is the cornerstone of foreign policy, those influenced by the Vietnam paradigm reply that, although military power certainly confers some advantages, it is a very blunt instrument. Not every foreign policy objective can be achieved through the application of military force alone.

While the use of force may have helped the United States achieve its objectives in Grenada and Libya, other foreign policy tools must be used in more complicated situations, such as those in Lebanon or Central America.

ECONOMIC POLICY

Just as it would be incorrect to say that Vietnam-paradigm adherents oppose all use of force, it would also be incorrect to imply that Munich-paradigm supporters reject all methods short of force. The president's Contra aid package also contained substantial sums of money for economic aid to Central American democracies. Such aid is an example of one of many economic tools the United States has at its disposal in serving its foreign policy goals. Some economic tools, including development aid, preferential trade agreements ("most favored nation status"), and loans on favorable credit terms may be used as positive inducements or incentives for nations that support U.S. policies.

Other tools, such as boycotts and embargoes, may be used to punish nations of whose policies we do not approve. In recent years, under the Carter administration, the United States imposed a grain **embargo** against the Soviet Union—that is, the United States stopped wheat shipments to the Soviet Union—to convince the Russians to leave Afghanistan. Shortly after Castro took power in Cuba, the United States imposed a **boycott** on Cuban products—that is, it refused to allow its citizens to import Cuban sugar, cigars, and other goods.

Neither the grain embargo nor the boycott of Cuban goods has proved particularly effective in furthering foreign policy goals. After all, the Soviets were still in Afghanistan in 1986, and Castro's power in Cuba was still quite secure. The two policies did, however, have somewhat different effects at home. American pluralist democracy might help explain why one was dropped and the other remains in effect. American grain farmers were seriously hurt by the Soviet grain embargo. They were caught suddenly without a market for huge amounts of wheat that were originally destined for the Soviet Union. They were a vocal minority, the grain embargo became generally unpopular, and it was lifted by President Reagan. In contrast, a boycott of Cuban sugar is helpful to America's domestic sugar industry. A move to scrap the sugar boycott would be resisted not only by the large community of anti-Castro Cubans now living in this country, but also by the sugar industry, which would suddenly have to compete with cheaper Cuban sugar. Since there is no strong offsetting pressure to remove the boycott, it remains in place.

In addition to boycotts and embargoes, another essentially negative economic tool is the use of such import restrictions as tariffs, quotas, and non-tariff barriers (NTBs). (NTBs limit imports by setting product specifications for imported goods.) As we pointed out in Chapter 8, there may be strong domestic pressure for adopting import restrictions. Unions and manufacturers may want to prevent the goods of foreign competitors from flooding the American market and driving them out of business. Protectionist pressures on Congress have been growing recently; the president has usually opposed protectionism. Philosophically, he is committed to the value of free trade;

Japanese Compete for U.S. Markets
Japanese cars took a growing share of the American market in the 1970s and 1980s. Spurred by the U.S. auto industry, the government imposed import quotas on Japanese cars, which forced up prices. Ronald Reagan was opposed to such protectionism; he preferred the freedom of the marketplace and sought to avoid the closure of Japanese markets to U.S. goods.

practically, he argues, protectionism usually backfires. Countries whose products are kept out of the United States retaliate by refusing to import American goods. Finally, protectionism complicates the foreign policymaking process enormously. It is a distinctly unfriendly move to make toward nations that may be our friends and allies.

SUMMARY

In this chapter, we have argued that today's American foreign policy process is dominated by two competing paradigms or world views. One, the Munich paradigm, is shaped by World War II and the onset of the Cold War. The other, the Vietnam paradigm, analyzes events in terms of a framework shaped by the experience of Vietnam. While both paradigms share a commitment to order, they disagree on how order is best achieved and how the values of freedom and equality relate to it.

This split into two American foreign policy paradigms stands in marked contrast to the consensus that characterized American foreign policy between World War II and the Vietnam War. During that period, the United States assumed the role of a global superpower. As a nation relatively new to international affairs, the United States had to create larger foreign policy and defense establishments, leading to some concern that the nation might come to be dominated by a military-industrial complex.

In general, the "bipartisan-consensus foreign policy" during the period between World War II and Vietnam really meant presidential dominance of the process. During the period of foreign policy consensus, the public generally showed itself willing to follow its leaders in foreign policy matters, and Congress usually deferred to the president's judgment. Presidents for their part worked assiduously to avoid the possibility of congressional limitations on their power by relying on devices such as executive agreements. When the Vietnam War led members of Congress and the public to question their uncritical support of presidential leadership, many of the institutional innovations that enhanced the president's foreign policy powers came under attack. Various parts of the foreign policy apparatus came under new scrutiny intended to determine whether their activities fit into a democratic society in both theory and practice. The CIA in particular was an object of considerable attention.

The very existence of a secret intelligence agency poses a democratic dilemma: how can the secrecy needed for effective foreign policymaking be reconciled with open access to information? Or was Tocqueville right—is it simply impossible for a democracy to conduct foreign policy with skill? Although the public often seems to behave in foreign policy matters in ways Tocqueville would have predicted, by and large their impact on the foreign policymaking process is not very great. In foreign policy, the United States would appear to be no majoritarian democracy. Somewhat greater influence is wielded by interest groups, lending more support to a pluralist version. Yet, on the whole, foreign policy, much more than domestic policy, tends to be the preserve of the policymakers—but policymakers who are no longer of one mind.

Key Terms

Munich (Pearl Harbor) paradigm	Marshall Plan
Vietnam paradigm	military-industrial complex
isolationist	mutual assured destruction (MAD)
interventionist	flexible response
globalism	nation-building policy
Cold War	Vietnamization
containment	Nixon doctrine

détente   undeclared war
linkage   War Powers Resolution
executive agreement   special envoy
discretionary funds   McCarthyism
transfer authority   embargo
reprogramming   boycott

Selected Readings

Crabb, Cecil V. and Holt, Pat M. *An Invitation to Struggle*. Washington, D.C.: Congressional Quarterly Press, 1980. This work describes the interplay between Congress and the executive on foreign policy issues.

Fallows, James. *National Defense*. New York: Vintage Books, 1981. A critical look at American defense policy, which emphasizes the fit (or lack of fit) between weapons systems and the needs they are chosen to fill.

Nathan, James, and James Oliver. *United States Foreign Policy and World Order*. 3rd ed. Boston: Little, Brown, 1985. An excellent general history of American foreign policy since World War II.

Spanier, John, and Eric Uslaner. *American Foreign Policy Making and the Democratic Dilemmas*, 4th ed. New York: Holt, Rinehart and Winston, 1985. A brief examination of the policy process.

Appendices

THE DECLARATION OF INDEPENDENCE IN CONGRESS JULY 4, 1776

The unanimous declaration of the thirteen United States of America

When, in the course of human events, it becomes necessary for one people to dissolve the political bonds which have connected them with another, and to assume, among the powers of the earth, the separate and equal station to which the laws of nature and of nature's God entitle them, a decent respect to the opinions of mankind requires that they should declare the causes which impel them to the separation.

We hold these truths to be self-evident: That all men are created equal; that they are endowed by their Creator with certain unalienable rights; that among these are life, liberty, and the pursuit of happiness; that, to secure these rights, governments are instituted among men, deriving their just powers from the consent of the governed; that whenever any form of government becomes destructive of these ends, it is the right of the people to alter or to abolish it, and to institute new government, laying its foundation on such principles, and organizing its powers in such form, as to them shall seem most likely to effect their safety and happiness. Prudence, indeed, will dictate that governments long established should not be changed for light and transient causes; and accordingly all experience hath shown that mankind are more disposed to suffer, while evils are sufferable, than to right themselves by abolishing the forms to which they are accustomed. But when a long train of abuses and usurpations, pursuing invariably the same object, evinces a design to reduce them under absolute despotism, it is their right, it is their duty, to throw off such government, and to provide new guards for their future security. Such has been the patient sufferance of these colonies; and such is now the necessity which constrains them to alter their former systems of government. The history of the present King of Great Britain is a history of repeated injuries and usurpations, all having in direct object the establishment of an absolute tyranny over these states. To prove this, let facts be submitted to a candid world.

He has refused his assent to laws, the most wholesome and necessary for the public good.

He has forbidden his governors to pass laws of immediate and pressing importance, unless suspended in their operation till his assent should be obtained; and, when so suspended, he has utterly neglected to attend to them.

He has refused to pass other laws for the accommodation of large districts of people, unless those people would relinquish the right of representaton in the legislature, a right inestimable to them, and formidable to tyrants only.

He has called together legislative bodies at places unusual, uncomfortable, and distant from the depository of their public records, for the sole purpose of fatiguing them into compliance with his measures.

He has dissolved representative houses repeatedly, for opposing, with manly firmness, his invasions on the rights of the people.

He has refused for a long time, after such dissolutions, to cause others to be elected; whereby the legislative powers, incapable of annihilation, have returned to the people at large for their exercise; the state remaining, in the mean time, exposed to all the dangers of invasions from without and convulsions within.

He has endeavored to prevent the population of these states; for that purpose obstructing the laws for naturalization of foreigners; refusing to pass others to encourage their migration hither, and raising the conditions of new appropriations of lands.

He has obstructed the administration of justice, by refusing his assent to laws for establishing judiciary powers.

He has made judges dependent on his will alone, for the tenure of their offices, and the amount and payment of their salaries.

He has erected a multitude of new offices, and sent hither swarms of officers to harass our people and eat out their substance.

He has kept among us, in times of peace, standing armies, without the consent of our legislatures.

He has affected to render the military independent of, and superior to, the civil power.

He has combined with others to subject us to a jurisdiction foreign to our constitution, and unacknowledged by our laws, giving his assent to their acts of pretended legislation:

For quartering large bodies of armed troops among us;

For protecting them, by a mock trial, from punishment for any murders which they should commit on the inhabitants of these states;

For cutting off our trade with all parts of the world;

For imposing taxes on us without our consent;

For depriving us, in many cases, of the benefits of trial by jury;

For transporting us beyond seas, to be tried for pretended offenses;

For abolishing the free system of English laws in a neighboring province, establishing therein an arbitrary government, and enlarging its boundaries, so as to render it at once an example and fit instrument for introducing the same absolute rule into these colonies;

For taking away our charters, abolishing our most valuable laws, and altering fundamentally the forms of our governments;

For suspending our own legislatures, and declaring themselves invested with power to legislate for us in all cases whatsoever.

He has abdicated government here, by declaring us out of his protection and waging war against us.

He has plundered our seas, ravaged our coasts, burned our towns, and destroyed the lives of our people.

He is at this time transporting large armies of foreign mercenaries to complete the works of death, desolation, and tyranny already begun with circumstances of cruelty and perfidy scarcely paralleled in the most barbarous ages, and totally unworthy the head of a civilized nation.

He has constrained our fellow-citizens, taken captive on the high seas, to bear arms against their country, to become the executioners of their friends and brethren, or to fall themselves by their hands.

He has excited domestic insurrection among us, and has endeavored to bring on the inhabitants of our frontiers the merciless Indian savages, whose known rule of warfare is an undistinguished destruction of all ages, sexes, and conditions.

In every stage of these oppressions we have petitioned for redress in the most humble terms; our repeated petitions have been answered only by repeated injury. A prince, whose character is thus marked by every act which may define a tyrant, is unfit to be the ruler of a free people.

Nor have we been wanting in our attentions to our British brethren. We have warned them, from time to time, of attempts by their legislature to extend an unwarrantable jurisdiction over us. We have reminded them of the circumstances of our emigration and settlement here. We have appealed to their native justice and magnanimity; and we have conjured them, by the ties of our common kindred, to disavow these usurpations, which would inevitably interrupt our connections and correspondence. They, too, have been deaf to the voice of justice and of consanguinity. We must, therefore, acquiesce in the necessity which denounces our separation, and hold them, as we hold the rest of mankind, enemies in war, in peace friends.

We, therefore, the representatives of the United States of America, in General Congress assembled, appealing to the Supreme Judge of the world for the rectitude of our intentions, do, in the name and by the authority of the good people of these colonies, solemnly publish and declare, that these United Colonies are, and of right ought to be, FREE AND INDEPENDENT STATES; that they are absolved from all allegiance to the British crown, and that all political connection between them and the state of Great Britain is, and ought to be, totally dissolved; and that, as free and independent states, they have full power to levy war, conclude peace, contract alliances, establish commerce, and do all other acts and things which independent states may of right do. And for the support of this declaration, with a firm reliance on the protection of Divine Providence, we mutually pledge to each other our lives, our fortunes, and our sacred honor.

JOHN HANCOCK
and fifty-five others

THE CONSTITUTION OF THE UNITED STATES OF AMERICA*

Preamble

We the people of the United States, in order to form a more perfect union, establish justice, insure domestic tranquility, provide for the common defense, promote the general welfare, and secure the blessings of liberty to ourselves and our posterity, do ordain and establish this Constitution for the United States of America.

Article I

Section 1 All legislative powers herein granted shall be vested in a Congress of the United States, which shall consist of a Senate and a House of Representatives.

Section 2 The House of Representatives shall be composed of members chosen every second year by the people of the several States, and the electors in each State shall have the qualifications requisite for electors of the most numerous branch of the State Legislature.

No person shall be a Representative who shall not have attained to the age of twenty-five years, and been seven years a citizen of the United States, and who shall not, when elected, be an inhabitant of that State in which he shall be chosen.

Representatives and direct taxes shall be apportioned among the several States which may be included within this Union, according to their respective numbers, *which shall be determined by adding to the whole number of free persons, including those bound to service for a term of years and excluding Indians not taxed, three-fifths of all other persons.* The actual enumeration shall be made within three years after the first meeting of the Congress of the United States, and within every subsequent term of ten years, in such manner as they shall by law direct. The number of Representatives shall not exceed one for every thirty thousand, but each State shall have at least one

*Passages no longer in effect are printed in italic type.

Representative; *and until such enumeration shall be made, the State of New Hampshire shall be entitled to choose three, Massachusetts eight, Rhode Island and Providence Plantations one, Connecticut five, New York six, New Jersey four, Pennsylvania eight, Delaware one, Maryland six, Virginia ten, North Carolina five, South Carolina five, and Georgia three.*

When vacancies happen in the representation from any State, the Executive authority thereof shall issue writs of election to fill such vacancies.

The House of Representatives shall choose their Speaker and other officers; and shall have the sole power of impeachment.

Section 3 The Senate of the United States shall be composed of two Senators from each State, *chosen by the legislature thereof,* for six years; and each Senator shall have one vote.

Immediately after they shall be assembled in consequence of the first election, they shall be divided as equally as may be into three classes. The seats of the Senators of the first class shall be vacated at the expiration of the second year, of the second class at the expiration of the fourth year, and of the third class at the expiration of the sixth year, so that one-third may be chosen every second year; and if vacancies happen by resignation or otherwise, during the recess of the legislature of any State, the Executive thereof may make temporary appointments until the next meeting of the legislature, which shall then fill such vacancies.

No person shall be a Senator who shall not have attained to the age of thirty years, and been nine years a citizen of the United States, and who shall not, when elected, be an inhabitant of that State for which he shall be chosen.

The Vice-President of the United States shall be President of the Senate, but shall have no vote, unless they be equally divided.

The Senate shall choose their other officers, and also a President *pro tempore,* in the absence of the Vice-President, or when he shall exercise the office of President of the United States.

The Senate shall have the sole power to try all impeachments. When sitting for that purpose, they shall be on oath or affirmation. When the President of the United States is tried, the Chief Justice shall preside: and no person shall be convicted without the concurrence of two-thirds of the members present.

Judgment in cases of impeachment shall not extend further than to removal from the office, and disqualification to hold and enjoy any office of honor, trust or profit under the United States: but the party convicted shall nevertheless be liable and subject to indictment, trial, judgment and punishment, according to law.

Section 4 The times, places and manner of holding elections for Senators and Representatives shall be prescribed in each State by the legislature thereof; but the Congress may at any time by law make or alter such regulations, except as to the places of choosing Senators.

The Congress shall assemble at least once in every year, and such meeting *shall be on the first Monday in December, unless they shall by law appoint a different day.*

Section 5 Each house shall be the judge of the elections, returns and qualifications of its own members, and a majority of each shall constitute a quorum to do business; but a smaller number may adjourn from day to day, and may be authorized to compel the attendance of absent members, in such manner, and under such penalties, as each house may provide.

Each house may determine the rules of its proceedings, punish its members for disorderly behavior, and with the concurrence of two-thirds, expel a member.

Each house shall keep a journal of its proceedings, and from time to time publish the same, excepting such parts as may in their judgment require secrecy; and the yeas and nays of the members of either house on any question shall, at the desire of one-fifth of those present, be entered on the journal.

Neither house, during the session of Congress, shall, without the consent of the other, adjourn for more than three days, nor to any other place than that in which the two houses shall be sitting.

Section 6 The Senators and Representatives shall receive a compensation for their services, to be ascertained by law and paid out of the treasury of the United States. They shall in all cases except treason, felony and breach of the peace, be privileged from arrest during their attendance at the session of their respective houses, and in going to and returning from the same; and for any speech or debate in either house, they shall not be questioned in any other place.

No Senator or Representative shall, during the time for which he was elected, be appointed to any civil office under the authority of the United States, which shall have been created, or the emoluments whereof shall have been increased, during such time; and no person holding any office under the United States shall be a member of either house during his continuance in office.

Section 7 All bills for raising revenue shall originate in the House of Representatives; but the Senate may propose or concur with amendments as on other bills.

Every bill which shall have passed the House of Representatives and the Senate, shall, before it become a law, be presented to the President of the United States; if he approve he shall sign it, but if not he shall return it with objections to that house in which it originated, who shall enter the objections at large on their journal, and proceed to reconsider it. If after such reconsideration two-thirds of that house shall agree to pass the bill, it shall be sent, together with the objections, to the other house, by which it shall likewise be reconsidered, and, if approved by two-thirds of that house, it shall become a law. But in all such cases the votes of both houses shall be determined by yeas and nays, and the names of the persons voting for and against the bill shall be entered on the journal of each house respectively. If any bill shall not be returned by the President within ten days (Sundays excepted) after it shall have been presented to him, the same shall be a law, in like manner as if he had signed it, unless the Congress by their adjournment prevent its return, in which case it shall not be a law.

Every order, resolution, or vote to which the concurrence of the Senate and House of Representatives may be necessary (except on a question of adjournment) shall be presented to the President of the United States; and before the same shall take effect, shall be approved by him, or being disapproved by him, shall be repassed by two-thirds of the Senate and House of Representatives, according to the rules and limitations prescribed in the case of a bill.

Section 8 The Congress shall have power

To lay and collect taxes, duties, imposts, and excises, to pay the debts and provide for the common defense and general welfare of the United States; but all duties, imposts and excises shall be uniform throughout the United States;

To borrow money on the credit of the United States;

To regulate commerce with foreign nations, and among the several States, and with the Indian tribes;

To establish an uniform rule of naturalization, and uniform laws on the subject of bankruptcies throughout the United States;

To coin money, regulate the value thereof, and of foreign coin, and fix the standard of weights and measures;

To provide for the punishment of counterfeiting the securities and current coin of the United States;

To establish post offices and post roads;

To promote the progress of science and useful arts by securing for limited times to authors and inventors the exclusive right to their respective writings and discoveries;

To constitute tribunals inferior to the Supreme Court;

To define and punish piracies and felonies committed on the high seas and offenses against the law of nations;

To declare war, grant letters of marque and reprisal, and make rules concerning captures on land and water;

To raise and support armies, but no appropriation of money to that use shall be for a longer term than two years;

To provide and maintain a navy;

To make rules for the government and regulation of the land and naval forces;

To provide for calling forth the militia to execute the laws of the Union, suppress insurrections, and repel invasions;

To provide for organizing, arming, and disciplining the militia, and for governing such part of them as may be employed in the service of the United States, reserving to the States respectively the appointment of the officers, and the authority of training the militia according to the discipline prescribed by Congress;

To exercise exclusive legislation in all cases whatsoever, over such district (not exceeding ten miles square) as may, by cession of particular States, and the acceptance of Congress, become the seat of government of the United States, and to exercise like authority over all places purchased by the consent of the legislature of the State, in which the same shall be, for erection of forts, magazines, arsenals, dock-yards, and other needful buildings; —and

To make all laws which shall be necessary and proper for carrying into execution the foregoing powers, and all other powers vested by this Constitution in the government of the United States, or in any department or officer thereof.

Section 9 *The migration or importation of such persons as any of the States now existing shall think proper to admit shall not be prohibited by the Congress prior to the year 1808; but a tax or duty may be imposed on such importation, not exceeding $10 for each person.*

The privilege of the writ of habeas corpus shall not be suspended, unless when in cases of rebellion or invasion the public safety may require it.

No bill of attainer or ex post facto law shall be passed.

No capitation, or other direct, tax shall be laid, unless in proportion to the census or enumeration herein before directed to be taken.

No tax or duty shall be laid on articles exported from any State.

No preference shall be given by any regulation of commerce or revenue to the ports of one State over those of another; nor shall vessels bound to, or from, one State, be obliged to enter, clear, or pay duties in another.

No money shall be drawn from the treasury, but in consequence of appropriations made by law; and a regular statement and account of the receipts and expenditures of all public money shall be published from time to time.

No title of nobility shall be granted by the United States: and no person holding any office of profit or trust under them, shall, without the consent of the Congress, accept of any present, emolument, office, or title, of any kind whatever, from any king, prince, or foreign state.

Section 10 No State shall enter into any treaty, alliance, or confederation; grant letters of marque and reprisal; coin money; emit bills of credit; make anything but gold and silver coin a tender in payment of debts; pass any bill of attainder, ex post facto law, or law impairing the obligation of contracts, or grant any title of nobility.

No State shall, without the consent of Congress, lay any imposts or duties on imports or exports, except what may be absolutely necessary for executing its inspection laws: and the net produce of all duties and imposts, laid by any State on imports or exports, shall be for the use of the treasury of the United States; and all such laws shall be subject to the revision and control of the Congress.

No State shall, without the consent of Congress, lay any duty of tonnage, keep troops or ships of war in time of peace, enter into any agreement or compact with another State, or with a foreign power, or engage in war, unless actually invaded, or in such imminent danger as will not admit of delay.

Article II

Section 1 The executive power shall be vested in a President of the United States of America. He shall hold his office during the term of four years, and, together with the Vice-President, chosen for the same term, be elected as follows:

Each State shall appoint, in such manner as the legislature thereof may direct, a number of electors, equal to the whole number of Senators and Representatives to which the State may be entitled in the Congress; but no Senator or Representative, or person holding an office of trust or profit under the United States, shall be appointed an elector.

The electors shall meet in their respective States, and vote by ballot for two persons, of whom one at least shall not be an inhabitant of the same State with themselves. And they shall make a list of all the persons voted for, and of the number of votes for each; which list they shall sign and certify, and transmit sealed to the seat of government of the United States, directed to the President of the Senate. The President of the Senate shall, in the presence of the Senate and House of Representatives, open all the certificates, and the votes shall then be counted. The person having the greatest number of votes shall be the President, if such number be a majority of the whole number of electors appointed; and if there be more than one who have such majority, and have an equal number of votes, then the House of Representatives shall immediately choose by ballot one of them for President; and if no person have a majority, then from the five highest on the list said house shall in like manner choose the President. But in choosing the President the votes shall be taken by States, the representation from each State having one vote; a quorum for this purpose shall consist of a member or members from two-thirds of the States, and a majority of all the States shall be necessary to a choice. In every case, after the choice of the President, the person having the greatest number of votes of the electors shall be the Vice-President. But if there should remain two or more who have equal votes, the Senate shall choose from them by ballot the Vice-President.

The Congress may determine the time of choosing the electors and the day on which they shall give their votes; which day shall be the same throughout the United States.

No person except a natural-born citizen, *or a citizen of the United States at the time of the adoption of this Constitution,* shall be eligible to the office of President; neither shall any person be eligible to that office who shall not have attained to the age of thirty-five years, and been fourteen years a resident within the United States.

In cases of the removal of the President from office or of his death, resignation, or inability to discharge the powers and duties of the said office, the same shall devolve on the Vice-President, and the Congress may by law provide for the case of removal, death, resignation, or inability, both of the President and Vice-President, declaring what officer shall then act as President, and such officer shall act accordingly, until the disability be removed, or a President shall be elected.

The President shall, at stated times, receive for his services a compensation, which shall neither be increased nor diminished during the period for which he shall have been elected, and he shall not receive within that period any other emolument from the United States, or any of them.

Before he enter on the execution of his office, he shall take the following oath or affirmation: — "I do solemnly swear (or affirm) that I will faithfully execute the office of the President of the United States, and will to the best of my ability preserve, protect and defend the Constitution of the United States."

Section 2   The President shall be commander in chief of the army and navy of the United States, and of the militia of the several States, when called into the actual service of the United States; he may require the opinion, in writing, of the principal officer in each of the executive departments, upon any subject relating to the duties of their respective offices, and he shall have power to grant reprieves and pardons for offenses against the United States, except in cases of impeachment.

He shall have power, by and with the advice and consent of the Senate, to make treaties, provided two-thirds of the Senators present concur; and he shall nominate, and by and with the advice and consent of the Senate, shall appoint ambassadors, other public ministers and consuls, judges of the Supreme court, and all other officers of the United States, whose appointments are not herein otherwise provided for, and which shall be established by law: but Congress may by law vest the appointment of such inferior officers, as they think proper, in the President alone, in the courts of law, or in the heads of departments.

The President shall have power to fill up all vacancies that may happen during the recess of the Senate, by granting commissions which shall expire at the end of their next session.

Section 3   He shall from time to time give to the Congress information of the state of the Union, and recommend to their consideration such measures as he shall judge necessary and expedient; he may, on extraordinary occasions, convene both houses, or either of them, and in case of disagreement between them, with respect to the time of adjournment, he may adjourn them to such time as he shall think proper; he shall receive ambassadors and other public ministers; he shall take care that the laws be faithfully executed, and shall commission all the officers of the United States.

Section 4   The President, Vice-President and all civil officers of the United States shall be removed from office on impeachment for, and on conviction of, treason, bribery, or other high crimes and misdemeanors.

Article III

Section 1   The judicial power of the United States shall be vested in one Supreme Court, and in such inferior courts as the Congress may from time to time ordain and establish. The judges, both of the Supreme and inferior courts, shall hold their offices during good behavior, and shall, at stated times, receive for their services a compensation which shall not be diminished during their continuance in office.

Section 2   The judicial power shall extend to all cases, in law and equity, arising under this Constitution, the laws of the United States, and treaties made, or which shall be made, under their authority; — to all cases affecting ambassadors, other public ministers and consuls; — to all cases of admiralty and maritime jurisdiction; — to controversies to which the United States shall be a party; — to controversies between two or more States; — *between a State and citizens of another State;* — between citizens of different States; — between citizens of the same State claiming lands under grants of different States, and between a State, or the citizens thereof, and foreign states, citizens or subjects.

In all cases affecting ambassadors, other public ministers and consuls, and those in which a State shall be party, the Supreme Court shall have original jurisdiction. In all the other cases before mentioned, the Supreme Court shall have appellate jurisdiction, both as to law and fact, with such exceptions, and under such regulations, as the Congress shall make.

The trial of all crimes, except in cases of impeachment, shall be by jury; and such trial shall be held in the state where said crimes shall have been committed; but when not committed within any State, the trial shall be at such place or places as the Congress may by law have directed.

Section 3   Treason against the United States shall consist only in levying war against their, or in adhering to their enemies, giving them aid and comfort. No person shall be convicted of treason unless on the testimony of two witnesses to the same overt act, or on confession in open court.

The Congress shall have power to declare the punishment of treason, but no attainder of treason shall work corruption of blood, or forfeiture except during the life of the person attained.

Article IV

Section 1   Full faith and credit shall be given in each State to the public acts, records, and judicial proceedings of every other State. And the Congress may by general laws prescribe the manner in which such acts, records, and proceedings shall be proved, and the effect thereof.

Section 2   The citizens of each State shall be entitled to all privileges and immunities of citizens in the several States.

A person charged in any State with treason, felony, or other crime, who shall flee from justice, and be found in another State, shall on demand of the executive authority of the State from which he fled, be delivered up, to be removed to the State having jurisdiction of the crime.

No person held to service or labor in one State, under the laws thereof, escaping into another, shall, in consequence of any law or regulation therein, be discharged from such service or labor, but shall be delivered up on claim of the party to whom such service or labor may be due.

Section 3   New States may be admitted by the Congress into this Union; but no new State shall be formed or erected within the jurisdiction of any other State; nor any state be formed by the junction of two or more States, or parts of States, without the consent of the legislatures of the States concerned as well as of the Congress.

The Congress shall have power to dispose of and make all needful rules and regulations respecting the territory or other property belonging to the United States; and nothing in this Constitution shall be so construed as to prejudice any claims of the United States, or of any particular State.

Section 4   The United States shall guarantee to every State in this Union a republican form of government, and shall protect each of them against invasion; and on application of the legislature, or of the executive (when the legislature cannot be convened), against domestic violence.

Article V

The Congress, whenever two-thirds of both houses shall deem it necessary, shall propose amendments to this Constitution, or, on the application of the legislatures of two-thirds of the several States, shall call a convention for proposing amendments, which, in either case, shall be valid to all intents and purposes, as part of this Constitution, when ratified by the legislatures of three-fourths of the several States, or by conventions in three-fourths thereof, as the one or the other mode of ratification may be proposed by the Congress; provided *that no amendments which may be made prior to the year one thousand eight hundred and eight shall in any manner affect the first and fourth clauses in the ninth section of the first article;* and that no State, without its consent, shall be deprived of its equal suffrage in the Senate.

Article VI

All debts contracted and engagements entered into, before the adoption of this Constitution, shall be as valid against the United States under this Constitution, as under the Confederation.

This Constitution, and the laws of the United States which shall be made in pursuance thereof; and all treaties made, or which shall be made, under the authority of the United States, shall be the supreme law of the land; and the judges in every State shall be bound thereby, anything in the Constitution or laws of any State to the contrary notwithstanding.

The Senators and Representatives before mentioned, and the members of the several State legislatures, and all executive and judicial officers, both of the United States and of the several States, shall be bound by oath or affirmation to support this Constitution; but no religious test shall ever be required as a qualification to any office or public trust under the United States.

Article VII

The ratification of the conventions of nine States shall be sufficient for the establishment of this Constitution between the States so ratifying the same.

Done in Convention by the unanimous consent of the States present, the seventeenth day of September in the year of our Lord one thousand seven hundred and eighty-seven and of the Independence of the United States of America the twelfth. In witness whereof we have hereunto subscribed our names.

GEORGE WASHINGTON
and thirty-seven others

*Amendments to the Constitution**

Amendment I

Congress shall make no law respecting an establishment of religion, or prohibiting the free exercise thereof; or abridging the freedom of speech, or of the press; or the right of the people peaceably to assemble, and to petition the government for a redress of grievances.

Amendment II

A well-regulated militia being necessary to the security of a free State, the right of the people to keep and bear arms shall not be infringed.

Amendment III

No soldier shall, in time of peace, be quartered in any house without the consent of the owner, nor in time of war, but in a manner to be prescribed by law.

Amendment IV

The right of the people to be secure in their persons, houses, papers, and effects, against unreasonable searches and seizures, shall not be violated, and no warrants shall issue but upon probable cause, supported by oath or affirmation, and particularly describing the place to be searched, and the persons or things to be seized.

*The first ten amendments (the Bill of Rights) were adopted in 1791.

Amendment V

No person shall be held to answer for a capital, or otherwise infamous crime, unless on a presentment or indictment of a grand jury, except in cases arising in the land or naval forces, or in the militia, when in actual service in time of war or public danger; nor shall any person be subject for the same offense to be twice put in jeopardy of life or limb; nor shall be compelled in any criminal case to be a witness against himself, nor be deprived of life, liberty, or property, without due process of law; nor shall private property be taken for public use without just compensation.

Amendment VI

In all criminal prosecutions, the accused shall enjoy the right to a speedy and public trial, by an impartial jury of the State and district wherein the crime shall have been committed, which district shall have been previously ascertained by law, and to be informed of the nature and cause of the accusation; to be confronted with the witnesses against him; to have compulsory process for obtaining witnesses in his favor, and to have the assistance of counsel for his defense.

Amendment VII

In suits at common law, where the value in controversy shall exceed twenty dollars, the right of trial by jury shall be preserved, and no fact tried by a jury shall be otherwise reexamined in any court of the United States, than according to the rules of the common law.

Amendment VIII

Excessive bail shall not be required, nor excessive fines imposed, nor cruel and unusual punishments inflicted.

Amendment IX

The enumeration in the Constitution, of certain rights, shall not be construed to deny or disparage others retained by the people.

Amendment X

The powers not delegated to the United States by the Constitution, nor prohibited by it to the States, are reserved to the states respectively, or to the people.

Amendment XI

[Adopted 1798]

The judicial power of the United States shall not be construed to extend to any suit in law or equity, commenced or prosecuted aganst one of the United States by citizens of another state, or by citizens or subjects of any foreign state.

Amendment XII

[Adopted 1804]

The electors shall meet in their respective States, and vote by ballot for President and Vice-President, one of whom, at least, shall not be an inhabitant of the same State with themselves; they shall name in their ballots the person voted for as President, and in distinct ballots the person voted for as Vice-President, and they shall make distinct lists of all persons voted for as President, and of all persons voted for as Vice-President, and of the number of votes for each, which lists they shall sign and certify, and transmit sealed to the seat of government of the United States, directed to the President of the Senate; — the President of the Senate shall, in the presence of the Senate and House of representatives, open all the certificates and the votes shall then be counted; — the person having the greatest number of votes for President shall be the President, if such number be a majority of the whole number of electors appointed; and if no person have such majority, then from the persons having the highest numbers not exceeding three on the list of those voted for as President, the House of Representatives shall choose immediately, by ballot, the President. But in choosing the President, the votes shall be taken by States, the representation from each State having one vote; a quorum for this purpose shall consist of a member or members from two-thirds of the States, and a majority of all the States shall be necessary to a choice. And if the House of Representatives shall not choose a President whenever the right of choice shall devolve upon them, before *the fourth day of March* next following, then the Vice-President shall act as President, as in the case of the death or other constitutional disability of the President.

The person having the greatest number of votes as Vice-President shall be the Vice-President, if such number be a majority of the whole number of electors appointed; and if no person have a majority, then from the two highest numbers on the list the Senate shall choose the Vice-President; a quorum for the purpose shall consist of two-thirds of the whole number of Senators, and a majority of the whole number shall be necessary to a choice. But no person constitutionally ineligible to the office of President shall be eligible to that of Vice-President of the United States.

Amendment XIII

[Adopted 1865]

Section 1   Neither slavery nor involuntary servitude, except as a punishment for crime whereof the party shall have been duly convicted, shall exist within the United States, or any place subject to their jurisdiction.

Section 2   Congress shall have power to enforce this article by appropriate legislation.

Amendment XIV

[Adopted 1868]

Section 1   All persons born or naturalized in the United States, and subject to the jurisdiction thereof, are citizens of the United States and of the State wherein they reside. No State shall make or enforce any law which shall abridge the privileges or immunities of citizens of the United States; nor shall any State deprive any person of life, liberty, or property, without due process of law; nor deny to any person within its jurisdiction the equal protection of the laws.

Section 2   Representatives shall be apportioned among the several States according to their respective numbers, counting the whole number of persons in each State, excluding Indians not taxed. But when the right to vote at any election for the choice of Electors for President and Vice-President of the United States, Representatives in Congress, the executive and judicial officers of a State, or the members of the legislature thereof, is denied to any of the male inhabitants of such State, being twenty-one years of age and citizens of the United States, or in any way abridged, except for participation in rebellion, or other crime, the basis of representation therein shall be reduced in the proportion which the number of such male citizens shall bear to the whole number of male citizens twenty-one years of age in such State.

Section 3   No person shall be a Senator or Representative in Congress, or Elector of President and Vice-President, or hold any office, civil or military, under the United States, or under any State, who, having previously taken an oath, as a member of Congress, or as an officer of the United States, or as a member of any State legislature, or as an executive or judicial officer of any State, to support the Constitution of the United States, shall have engaged in insurrection or rebellion against the same, or given aid or comfort to the enemies thereof. Congress may, by a vote of two-thirds of each house, remove such disability.

Section 4 The validity of the public debt of the United States, authorized by law, including debts incurred for payment of pensions and bounties for services in suppressing insurrection or rebellion, shall not be questioned. But neither the United States nor any State shall assume or pay any debt or obligation incurred in aid of insurrection or rebellion against the United States, or any claim for the loss of emancipation of any slave; but all such debts, obligations, and claims shall be held illegal and void.

Section 5 The Congress shall have power to enforce, by appropriate legislation, the provisions of this article.

Amendment XV
[Adopted 1870]

Section 1 The right of citizens of the United States to vote shall not be denied or abridged by the United States or by any State on account of race, color, or previous condition of servitude.

Section 2 The Congress shall have power to enforce this article by appropriate legislation.

Amendment XVI
[Adopted 1913]

The Congress shall have power to lay and collect taxes on incomes, from whatever source derived, without apportionment among the several States, and without regard to any census or enumeration.

Amendment XVII
[Adopted 1913]

Section 1 The Senate of the United States shall be composed of two Senators from each State, elected by the people thereof, for six years; and each Senator shall have one vote. The electors in each State shall have the qualifications requisite for electors of [voters for] the most numerous branch of the State legislatures.

Section 2 When vacancies happen in the representation of any State in the Senate, the executive authority of such State shall issue writs of election to fill such vacancies: Provided, that the Legislature of any State may empower the executive thereof to make temporary appointments until the people fill the vacancies by election as the Legislature may direct.

Section 3 This amendment shall not be so construed as to affect the election or term of any Senator chosen before it becomes valid as part of the Constitution.

Amendment XVIII
[Adopted 1919, repealed 1933]

Section 1 After one year from the ratification of this article the manufacture, sale or transportation of intoxicating liquors within, the importation thereof into, or the exportation thereof from the United States and all territory subject to the jurisdiction thereof, for beverage purposes, is hereby prohibited.

Section 2 The Congress and the several States shall have concurrent power to enforce this article by appropriate legislation.

Section 3 This article shall be inoperative unless it shall have been ratified as an amendment to the Constitution by the legislatures of the several States, as provided by the Constitution, within seven years from the date of the submission thereof to the States by the Congress.

Amendment XIX
[Adopted 1920]

Section 1 The right of citizens of the United States to vote shall not be denied or abridged by the United States or by any State on account of sex.

Section 2 The Congress shall have power to enforce this article by appropriate legislation.

Amendment XX
[Adopted 1933]

Section 1 The terms of the President and Vice-President shall end at noon on the 20th day of January, and the terms of Senators and Representatives at noon on the 3d day of January, of the years in which such terms would have ended if this article had not been ratified; and the terms of their successors shall then begin.

Section 2 The Congress shall assemble at least once in every year, and such meetings shall begin at noon on the 3d day of January, unless they shall by law appoint a different day.

Section 3 If, at the time fixed for the beginning of the term of the President, the President-elect shall have died, the Vice-President-elect shall become President. If a President shall not have been chosen before the time fixed for the beginning of his term, or if the President-elect shall have failed to qualify, then the Vice-President-elect shall act as President until a President shall have qualified; and the Congress may by law provide for the case wherein neither a President-elect nor a Vice-President-elect shall have qualified, declaring who shall then act as President, or the manner in which one who is to act shall be selected, and such persons shall act accordingly until a President or Vice-President shall have qualified.

Section 4 The Congress may by law provide for the case of the death of any of the persons from whom the House of Representatives may choose a President whenever the right of choice shall have devolved upon them, and for the case of the death of any of the persons from whom the Senate may choose a Vice-President whenever the right of choice shall have devolved upon them.

Section 5 Sections 1 and 2 shall take effect on the 15th day of October following the ratification of this article.

Section 6 This article shall be inoperative unless it shall have been ratified as an amendment to the Constitution by the Legislatures of three-fourths of the several States within seven years from the date of its submission.

Amendment XXI
[Adopted 1933]

Section 1 The eighteenth article of amendment to the Constitution of the United States is hereby repealed.

Section 2 The transportation or importation into any State, Territory, or Possession of the United States for delivery or use therein of intoxicating liquors, in violation of the laws thereof, is hereby prohibited.

Section 3 This article shall be inoperative unless it shall have been ratified as an amendment to the Constitution by conventions in the several States, as provided in the Constitution, within seven years from the date of submission thereof to the States by the Congress.

Amendment XXII
[Adopted 1951]

Section 1 No person shall be elected to the office of President more than twice, and no person who has held the office of President, or acted as President, for more than two years of a term to which some other person was elected President shall be elected to the office of President more than once. But this article shall not apply to any person holding the office of President when this article was proposed by the Congress, and shall not prevent any person who may be holding the office of President, or acting as President, during the term within which this article becomes operative from holding the office of President or acting as President during the remainder of such term.

Section 2 This article shall be inoperative unless it shall have been ratified as an amendment to the Constitution by the legislatures of three-fourths of the several States within seven years from the date of its submission to the States by the Congress.

Amendment XXIII
[Adopted 1961]

Section 1 The District constituting the seat of Government of the United States shall appoint in such manner as the Congress may direct:

A number of electors of President and Vice-President equal to the whole number of Senators and Representatives in Congress to which the District would be entitled if it were a State, but in no event more than the least populous State; they shall be in addition to those appointed by the States, but they shall be considered for the purposes of the election of President and Vice-President, to be electors appointed by a State; and they shall meet in the District and perform such duties as provided by the twelfth article of amendment.

Section 2 The Congress shall have the power to enforce this article by appropriate legislation.

Amendment XXIV
[Adopted 1964]

Section 1 The right of citizens of the United States to vote in any primary or other election for President or Vice-President, for electors for President or Vice-President, or for Senator or Representative in Congress, shall not be denied or abridged by the United States or any State by reason of failure to pay any poll tax or other tax.

Section 2 The Congress shall have the power to enforce this article by appropriate legislation.

Amendment XXV
[Adopted 1967]

Section 1 In case of the removal of the President from office or of his death or resignation, the Vice-President shall become President.

Section 2 Whenever there is a vacancy in the office of the Vice-President, the President shall nominate a Vice-President who shall take office upon confirmation by a majority vote of both Houses of Congress.

Section 3 Whenever the President transmits to the President pro tempore of the Senate and the speaker of the House of Representatives his written declaration that he is unable to discharge the powers and duties of his office, and until he transmits to them a written declaration to the contrary, such powers and duties shall be discharged by the Vice-President as Acting President.

Section 4   Whenever the Vice-President and a majority of either the principal officers of the executive departments or of such other body as Congress may by law provide, transmit to the President pro tempore of the Senate and the Speaker of the House of Representatives their written declaration that the President is unable to discharge the powers and duties of his office, the Vice President shall immediately assume the powers and duties of the office as Acting President.

Thereafter, when the President transmits to the President pro tempore of the Senate and the Speaker of the House of Representatives his written declaration that no inability exists, he shall remume the powers and duties of his office unless the Vice-President and a majority of either the principal officers of the executive department(s) or of such other body as Congress may by law provide, transmit within four days to the President pro tempore of the Senate and the Speaker of the House of Representatives their written declaration that the President is unable to discharge the powers and duties of his office. Thereupon Congress shall decide the issue, assembling within forty-eight hours for that purpose if not in session. If the congress, within twenty-one days after receipt of the latter written declaration, or, if Congress is not in session, within twenty-one days after Congress is required to assemble, determines by two-thirds vote of both Houses that the President is unable to discharge the powers and duties of his office, the Vice-President shall continue to discharge the same as Acting President; otherwise, the President shall resume the powers and duties of his office.

Amendment XXVI
[Adopted 1971]

Section 1   The right of citizens of the United States, who are eighteen years of age or older, to vote shall not be denied or abridged by the United States or by any State on account of age.

Section 2   The Congress shall have power to enforce this article by appropriate legislation.

FEDERALIST NO. 10   1787

To the People of the State of New York: Among the numerous advantages promised by a well-constructed union, none deserves to be more accurately developed than its tendency to break and control the violence of faction. The friend of popular governments, never finds himself so much alarmed for their character and fate, as when he contemplates their propensity to this dangerous vice. He will not fail, therefore, to set a due value on any plan which, without violating the principles to which he is attached, provides a proper cure for it. The instability, injustice, and confusion introduced into the public councils, have, in truth, been the mortal diseases under which popular governments have everywhere perished; as they continue to be the favourite and fruitful topics from which the adversaries to liberty derive their most specious declamations. The valuable improvements made by the American constitutions on the popular models, both ancient and modern, cannot certainly be too much admired; but it would be an unwarrantable partiality, to contend that they have as effectually obviated the danger on this side, as was wished and expected. Complaints are everywhere heard from our most considerate and virtuous citizens, equally the friends of public and private faith, and of public and personal liberty, that our governments are too unstable; that the public good is disregarded in the conflicts of rival parties; and that measures are too often decided, not according to the rules of justice, and the rights of the minor party, but by the superior force of an interested and overbearing majority. However anxiously we may wish that these complaints had no foundation, the evidence of known facts will not permit us to deny that they are in some degree true. It will be found, indeed, on a candid review of our situation, that some of the distresses under which we labour have been erroneously charged on the operation of our governments; but it will be found, at the same time, that other causes will not alone account for many of our heaviest misfortunes; and, particularly, for that prevailing and increasing distrust of public engagements, and alarm for private rights, which are echoed from one end of the continent to the other. These must be chiefly, if not wholly, effects of the unsteadiness and injustice, with which a factious spirit has tainted our public administrations.

By a faction, I understand a number of citizens, whether amounting to a majority or minority of the whole, who are united and actuated by some common impulse of passion, or of interest, adverse to the rights of other citizens, or to the permanent and aggregate interests of the community.

There are two methods of curing the mischiefs of faction: The one, by removing its causes; the other, by controlling its effects.

There are again two methods of removing the causes of faction: The one, by destroying the liberty which is essential to its existence; the other, by giving to every citizen the same opinions, the same passions, and the same interests.

It could never be more truly said, than of the first remedy, that it was worse that the disease. Liberty is to faction what air is to fire, an aliment without which it instantly expires. But it could not be a less folly to abolish liberty, which is essential to political life, because it nourishes faction, than it would be to wish the annihilation of air, which is essential to animal life, because it imparts to fire its destructive agency.

The second expedient is as impracticable, as the first would be unwise. As long as the reason of man continues fallible, and he is at liberty to exercise it, different opinions will be formed. As long as the connection subsists between his reason and his self-love, his opinions and his passions will have a reciprocal influence on each other; and the former will be objects to which the latter will attach themselves. The diversity in the faculties of men, from which the rights of property originate, is not less an insuperable obstacle to an uniformity of interests. The protection of these faculties is the first object of government. From the protection of different and unequal faculties of acquiring property, the possession of different degrees and kinds of property immediately results; and from the influence of these on the sentiments and views of the respective proprietors, ensues a division of the society into different interests and parties.

The latent causes of action are thus sown in the nature of man; and we see them everywhere brought into different degrees of activity, according to the different circumstances of civil society. A zeal for different opinions concerning religion, concerning government, and many other points, as well as of speculation as of practice; an attachment to different leaders ambitiously contending for preeminence and power; or to persons of other descriptions whose fortunes have been interesting to the human passions, have, in turn, divided mankind into parties, inflamed them with mutual animosity, and rendered them much more disposed to vex and oppress each other, than to cooperate for their common good. So strong is this propensity of mankind, to fall into mutual animosities, that where no substantial occasion presents itself, the most frivolous and fanciful distinctions have been sufficient to kindle their unfriendly passions and excite their most violent conflicts. But the most common and durable source of factions, has been the various and unequal distribution of property. Those who

hold, and those who are without property, have ever formed distinct interests in society. Those who are creditors, and those who are debtors, fall under a like discrimination. A landed interest, a manufacturing interest, a mercantile interest, a moneyed interest, with many lesser interests, grow up of necessity in civilized nations, and divide them into different classes, actuated by different sentiments and views. The regulation of these various and interfering interests forms the principal task of modern legislation, and involves the spirit of the party and faction in the necessary and ordinary operations of the government.

No man is allowed to be a judge in his own cause; because his interest will certainly bias his judgment, and, not improbably, corrupt his integrity. With equal, nay, with greater reason, a body of men are unfit to be both judges and parties at the same time; yet what are many of the most important acts of legislation, but so many judicial determinations, not indeed concerning the right of single persons, but concerning the rights of large bodies of citizens? And what are the different classes of legislators, but advocates and parties to the causes which they determine? Is a law proposed concerning private debts? It is a question to which the creditors are parties on one side, and the debtors on the other. Justice ought to hold the balance between them. Yet the parties are, and must be, themselves the judges; and the most numerous party, or, in other words, the most powerful faction, must be expected to prevail. Shall domestic manufactures be encouraged, and in what degree, by restrictions on foreign manufactures? are questions which would be differently decided by the landed and the manufacturing classes; and probably by neither with a sole regard to justice and the public good. The apportionment of taxes, on the various descriptions of property, is an act which seems to require the most exact impartiality; yet there is, perhaps, no legislative act, in which greater opportunity and temptation are given to a predominant party to trample on the rules of justice. Every shilling, with which they overburden the inferior number, is a shilling saved to their own pockets.

It is in vain to say, that enlightened statesmen will be able to adjust these clashing interests, and render them all subservient to the public good. Enlightened statesmen will not always be at the helm: nor, in many cases, can such an adjustment be made at all, without taking into view indirect and remote considerations, which will rarely prevail over the immediate interest which one party may find in disregarding the rights of another, or the good of the whole.

The inference to which we are brought is, that the *causes* of faction cannot be removed; and that relief is only to be sought in the means of controlling its *effects*.

If a faction consists of less than a majority, relief is supplied by the republican principle, which enables the majority to defeat its sinister views, by regular vote. It may clog the administration, it may convulse the society; but it will be unable to execute and mask its violence under the forms of the constitution. When a majority is included in a faction, the form of popular government, on the other hand, enables it to sacrifice to its ruling passion or interest, both the public good and the rights of other citizens. To secure the public good, and private rights, against the danger of such a faction, and at the same time to preserve the spirit and the form of popular government, is then the great object to which our inquiries are directed. Let me add, that it is the great desideratum, by which alone this form of government can be rescued from the opprobrium under which it has so long laboured, and be recommended to the esteem and adoption of mankind.

By what means is this object attainable? Evidently by one of two only. Either the existence of the same passion or interest in a majority, at the same time, must be prevented; or the majority, having such coexistent passion or interest, must be rendered, by their number and local situation, unable to concert and carry into effect schemes of oppression. If the impulse and the opportunity be suffered to coincide, we well know that neither moral nor religious motives can be relied on as an adequate control. They are not found to be such on the injustice and violence of individuals, and lose their efficacy in proportion to the number combined together; that is, in proportion as their efficacy becomes needful.

From this view of the subject, it may be concluded, that a pure democracy, by which I mean a society consisting of a small number of citizens, who assemble and administer the government in person, can admit of no cure for the mischiefs of faction. A common passion or interest will, in almost every case, be felt by a majority of the whole; a communication and concert, results from the form of government itself; and there is nothing to check the inducements to sacrifice the weaker party, or an obnoxious individual. Hence, it is, that such democracies have ever been spectacles of turbulence and contention; have ever been found incompatible with personal security, or the rights of property; and have in general been as short in their lives, as they have been violent in their deaths. Theoretic politicians, who have patronized this species of government, have erroneously supposed, that by reducing mankind to a perfect equality in their political rights, they would, at the same time, be perfectly equalized and assimilated in their possessions, their opinions, and their passions.

A republic, by which I mean a government in which the scheme of representation takes place, opens a differ-

ent prospect, and promises the cure for which we are seeking. Let us examine the points in which it varies from pure democracy, and we shall comprehend both the nature of the cure and the efficacy which it must derive from the union.

The two great points of difference, between a democracy and a republic, are, first, the delegation of the government, in the latter, to a small number of citizens, elected by the rest; secondly, the greatest number of citizens, and greater sphere of country, over which the latter may be extended.

The effect of the first difference is, on the one hand, to refine and enlarge the public views, by passing them through the medium of a chosen body of citizens, whose wisdom may best discern the true interest of their country, and whose patriotism and love of justice, will be least likely to sacrifice it to temporary or partial considerations. Under such a regulation, it may well happen, that the public voice, pronounced by the representatives of the people, will be more consonant to the public good, than if pronounced by the people themselves, convened for the purpose. On the other hand the effect may be inverted. Men of factious tempers, of local prejudices, or of sinister designs, may by intrigue, by corruption, or by other means, first obtain the suffrages, and then betray the interest of the people. The question resulting is, whether small or extensive republics are most favourable to the election of proper guardians of the public weal; and it is clearly decided in favour of the latter by two obvious considerations.

In the first place, it is to be remarked that, however small the republic may be, the representatives must be raised to a certain number, in order to guard against the cabals of a few; and that however large it may be, they must be limited to a certain number, in order to guard against the confusion of a multitude. Hence, the number of representatives in the two cases not being in proportion to that of the constituents, and being proportionally greatest in the small republic, it follows, that if the proportion of fit characters be not less in the large than in the small republic, the former will present a greater option, and consequently a greater probability of a fit choice.

In the next place, as each representative will be chosen by a greater number of citizens in the large than in the small republic, it will be more difficult for unworthy candidates to practise with success the vicious arts, by which elections are too often carried; and the suffrages of the people being more free, will be more likely to centre in men who possess the most attractive merit, and the most diffusive and established characters.

It must be confessed, that in this, as in most other cases, there is a mean, on both sides of which inconveniences will be found to lie. By enlarging too much the number of electors, you render the representatives too little acquainted with all their local circumstances and lesser interests; as by reducing it too much, you render him unduly attached to these, and too little fit to comprehend and pursue great and national objects. The federal constitution forms a happy combination in this respect; the great and aggregate interests being referred to the national, the local and particular to the state legislatures.

The other point of difference is, the greater number of citizens, and extent of territory, which may be brought within the compass of republican, than of democratic government; and it is this circumstance principally which renders factious combinations less to be dreaded in the former, than in the latter. The smaller the society, the fewer probably will be the distinct parties and interests composing it; the fewer the distinct parties and interests, the more frequently will a majority be found of the same party; and the smaller the number of individuals composing a majority, and the smaller the compass within which they are placed, the more easily will they concert and execute their plans of oppression. Extend the sphere, and you take in a greater variety of parties and interests; you make it less probable that a majority of the whole will have a common motive to invade the rights of other citizens; or if such a common motive exists, it will be more difficult for all who feel it to discover their own strength, and to act in unison with each other. Besides other impediments, it may be remarked, that where there is a consciousness of unjust or dishonourable purposes, communication is always checked by distrust, in proportion to the number whose concurrence is necessary.

Hence, it clearly appears, that the same advantage, which a republic has over a democracy, in controlling the effects of faction, is enjoyed by a large over a small republic, — is enjoyed by the union over the states composing it. Does this advantage consist in the substitution of representatives, whose enlightened views and virtuous sentiments render them superior to local prejudices, and to schemes of injustice? It will not be denied that the representation of the union will be most likely to possess these requisite endowments. Does it consist in the greater security afforded by a greater variety of parties, against the event of any one party being able to outnumber and oppress the rest? In an equal degree does the increased variety of parties, comprised within the union, increase the security? Does it, in fine, consist in the greater obstacles opposed to the concert and accomplishment of the secret wishes of an unjust and interested majority? Here, again, the extent of the union gives it the most palpable advantage.

The influence of factious leaders may kindle a flame within their particular states, but will be unable to spread a general conflagration through the other states; a religious sect may degenerate into a political faction in a part of the confederacy; but the variety of sects dispersed over the entire face of it, must secure the national councils against any danger from that source: a rage for paper money, for an abolition of debts, for an equal division of property, or for any other improper or wicked project, will be less apt to pervade the whole body of the union than a particular member of it; in the same proportion as such a malady is more likely to taint a particular county or district, than an entire state.

In the extent and proper structure of the union, therefore, we behold a republican remedy for the diseases most incident to republican government. And according to the degree of pleasure and pride we feel in being republicans, ought to be our zeal in cherishing the spirit, and supporting the character of federalists.

JAMES MADISON

FEDERALIST NO. 51   1788

To the People of the State of New York: To what expedient then shall we finally resort for maintaining in practice the necessary partition of power among the several departments, as laid down in the constitution? The only answer that can be given is, that as all these exterior provisions are found to be inadequate, the defect must be supplied, by so contriving the interior structure of the government, as that its several constituent parts may, by their mutual relations, be the means of keeping each other in their proper places. Without presuming to undertake a full development of this important idea, I will hazard a few general observations, which may perhaps place it in a clearer light, and enable us to form a more correct judgment of the principles and structure of the government planned by the convention.

In order to lay a due foundation for that separate and distinct exercise of the different powers of government, which to a certain extent, is admitted on all hands to be essential to the preservaton of liberty, it is evident that each department should have a will of its own; and consequently should be so constituted, that the members of each should have as little agency as possible in the appointment of the members of the others. Were this principle rigorously adhered to, it would require that all the appointments for the supreme executive, legislative, and judiciary magistracies, should be drawn from the same fountain of authority, the people, through channels, having no communication whatever with one another. Perhaps such a plan of constructing the several departments would be less difficult in practice than it may in contemplation appear. Some difficulties however, and some additional expense, would attend the execution of it. Some deviations therefore from the principle must be admitted. In the constitution of the judiciary department in particular, it might be inexpedient to insist rigorously on the principle; first, because peculiar qualifications being essential in the members, the primary consideration ought to be to select that mode of choice, which best secures these qualifications; secondly, because the permanent tenure by which the appointments are held in that department, must soon destroy all sense of dependence on the authority conferring them.

It is equally evident that the members of each department should be as little dependent as possible on those of the others, for the emoluments annexed to their offices. Were the executive magistrate, or the judges, not independent of the legislature in this particular, their independence in every other would be merely nominal.

But the great security against a gradual concentration of the several powers in the same department, consists in giving to those who administer each department, the necessary constitutional means, and personal motives, to resist encroachments of the others. The provision for defense must in this, as in all other cases, be made commensurate to the danger of attack. Ambition must be made to counteract ambition. The interest of the man must be connected with the constitutional rights of the place. It may be a reflection on human nature, that such devices should be necessary to control the abuses of government. But what is government itself but the greatest of all reflections on human nature? If men were angels, no government would be necessary. If angels were to govern men, neither external nor internal controls on government would be necessary. In framing a government which is to be administered by men over men, the great difficulty lies in this: You must first enable the government to control the governed; and in the next place, oblige it to control itself. A dependence on the people is no doubt the primary control on the government; but experience has taught mankind the necessity of auxiliary precautions.

This policy of supplying by opposite and rival interests, the defect of better motives, might be traced through the whole system of human affairs, private as well as public. We see it particularly displayed in all the subordinate distributions of power; where the constant aim is to divide and arrange the several offices in such a manner as that each may be a check on the other; that the private interest of every individual, may be a sentinel over the public rights. These inventions of prudence cannot be

less requisite in the distribution of the supreme powers of the state.

But it is not possible to give to each department an equal power of self defense. In republican government the legislative authority, necessarily, predominates. The remedy for this inconveniency is, to divide the legislature into different branches; and to render them by different modes of election, and different principles of action, as little connected with each other, as the nature of their common functions, and their common dependence on the society, will admit. It may even be necessary to guard against dangerous encroachments by still further precautions. As the weight of the legislative authority requires that it should be thus divided, the weakness of the executive may require, on the other hand, that it should be fortified. An absolute negative, on the legislature, appears at first view to be the natural defense with which the executive magistrate should be armed. But perhaps it would be neither altogether safe, nor alone sufficient. On ordinary occasions, it might not be exerted with the requisite firmness; and on extraordinary occasions, it might be perfidiously abused. May not this defect of an absolute negative be supplied, by some qualified connection between this weaker department, and the weaker branch of the stronger department, by which the latter may be led to support the constitutional rights of the former, without being too much detached from the rights of its own department?

If the principles on which these observations are founded be just, as I persuade myself they are, and they be applied as a criterion, to the several state constitutions, and to the federal constitution, it will be found, that if the latter does not perfectly correspond with them, the former are infinitely less able to bear such a test.

There are moreover two considerations particularly applicable to the federal system of America, which place that system in a very interesting point of view.

First. In a single republic, all the power surrendered by the people, is submitted to the administration of a single government; and usurpations are guarded against by a division of the government into distinct and separate departments. In the compound republic of America, the power surrendered by the people, is first divided between two distinct governments, and then the portion allotted to each, subdivided among distinct and separate departments. Hence a double security arises to the rights of the people. The different governments will control each other; at the same time that each will be controlled by itself.

Second. It is of great importance in a republic, not only to guard the society against the oppression of its rulers; but to guard one part of the society against the injustice of the other part. Different interests necessarily exist in different classes of citizens. If a majority be united by a common interest, the rights of the minority will be insecure. There are but two methods of providing against this evil: The one by creating a will in the community independent of the majority, that is, of the society itself; the other by comprehending in the society so many separate descriptions of citizens, as will render an unjust combination of a majority of the whole, very improbable, if not impracticable. The first method prevails in all governments possessing an hereditary or self appointed authority. This at best is but a precarious security; because a power independent of the society may as well espouse the unjust views of the major, as the rightful interests, of the minor party, and may possibly be turned against both parties. The second method will be exemplified in the federal republic of the United States. While all authority in it will be derived from and dependent on the society, the society itself will be broken into so many parts, interests and classes of citizens, that the rights of individuals or of the minority, will be in little danger from interested combinations of the majority. In a free government, the security for civil rights must be the same as for religious rights. It consists in the one case in the multiplicity of interests, and in the other in the multiplicity of sects. The degree of security in both cases will depend on the number of interests and sects; and this may be presumed to depend on the extent of country and number of people comprehended under the same government. This view of the subject must particularly recommend a proper federal system to all the sincere and considerate friends of republican government: Since it shows that in exact proportion as the territory of the union may be formed into more circumscribed confederacies or states, oppressive combinations of a majority will be facilitated; the best security under the republican form, for the rights of every class of citizens, will be diminished; and consequently, the stability and independence of some member of the government, the only other security, must be proportionally increased. Justice is the end of government. It is the end of civil society. It ever has been, and ever will be pursued, until it be ob-

tained, or until liberty be lost in the pursuit. In a society under the forms of which the stronger faction can readily unite and oppress the weaker, anarchy may as truly be said to reign, as in a state of nature where the weaker individual is not secured against the violence of the stronger: And as in the latter state even the stronger individuals are prompted by the uncertainty of their condition, to submit to a government which may protect the weak as well as themselves: So in the former state, will the more powerful factions or parties be gradually induced by a like motive, to wish for a government which will protect all parties, the weaker as well as the more powerful. It can be little doubted, that if the state of Rhode Island was separated from the confederacy, and left to itself, the insecurity of rights under the popular form of government within such narrow limits, would be displayed by such reiterated oppressions of factious majorities, that some power altogether independent of the people would soon be called for by the voice of the very factions whose misrule had proved the necessity of it. In the extended republic of the United States, and among the great variety of interests, parties and sects which it embraces, a coalition of a majority of the whole society could seldom take place on any other principles than those of justice and the general good; and there being thus less danger to a minor from the will of the major party, there must be less pretext also, to provide for the security of the former, by introducing into the government a will not dependent on the latter; or in other words, a will independent of the society itself. It is no less certain than it is important, notwithstanding the contrary opinions which have been entertained, that the larger the society, provided it lie within a practicable sphere, the more duly capable it will be of self government. And happily for the *republican cause*, the practicable sphere may be carried to a very great extent, by a judicious modification and mixture of the *federal principle.*

JAMES MADISON

Presidents of the United States

	Party	Term
1. George Washington (1732–1799)	Federalist	1789–1797
2. John Adams (1735–1826)	Federalist	1797–1801
3. Thomas Jefferson (1743–1826)	Democratic-Republican	1801–1809
4. James Madison (1751–1836)	Democratic-Republican	1809–1817
5. James Monroe (1758–1831)	Democratic-Republican	1817–1825
6. John Quincy Adams (1767–1848)	Democratic-Republican	1825–1829
7. Andrew Jackson (1767–1845)	Democratic	1829–1837
8. Martin Van Buren (1782–1862)	Democratic	1837–1841
9. William Henry Harrison (1773–1841)	Whig	1841
10. John Tyler (1790–1862)	Whig	1841–1845
11. James K. Polk (1795–1849)	Democratic	1845–1849
12. Zachary Taylor (1784–1850)	Whig	1849–1850
13. Millard Fillmore (1800–1874)	Whig	1850–1853
14. Franklin Pierce (1804–1869)	Democratic	1853–1857
15. James Buchanan (1791–1868)	Democratic	1857–1861
16. Abraham Lincoln (1809–1865)	Republican	1861–1865
17. Andrew Johnson (1808–1875)	Union	1865–1869
18. Ulysses S. Grant (1822–1885)	Republican	1869–1877
19. Rutherford B. Hayes (1822–1893)	Republican	1877–1881
20. James A. Garfield (1831–1881)	Republican	1881
21. Chester A. Arthur (1830–1886)	Republican	1881–1885
22. Grover Cleveland (1837–1908)	Democratic	1885–1889
23. Benjamin Harrison (1833–1901)	Republican	1889–1893
24. Grover Cleveland (1837–1908)	Democratic	1893–1897
25. William McKinley (1843–1901)	Republican	1897–1901
26. Theodore Roosevelt (1858–1919)	Republican	1901–1909
27. William Howard Taft (1857–1930)	Republican	1909–1913
28. Woodrow Wilson (1856–1924)	Democratic	1913–1921
29. Warren G. Harding (1865–1923)	Republican	1921–1923
30. Calvin Coolidge (1871–1933)	Republican	1923–1929
31. Herbert Hoover (1874–1964)	Republican	1929–1933
32. Franklin Delano Roosevelt (1882–1945)	Democratic	1933–1945
33. Harry S Truman (1884–1972)	Democratic	1945–1953
34. Dwight D. Eisenhower (1890–1969)	Republican	1953–1961
35. John F. Kennedy (1917–1963)	Democratic	1961–1963
36. Lyndon B. Johnson (1908–1973)	Democratic	1963–1969
37. Richard M. Nixon (b. 1913)	Republican	1969–1974
38. Gerald R. Ford (b. 1913)	Republican	1974–1977
39. Jimmy Carter (b. 1924)	Democratic	1977–1981
40. Ronald Reagan (b. 1911)	Republican	1981–

Twentieth-Century Justices of the Supreme Court

Justice*	Term of Service	Years of Service	Life Span	Justice*	Term of Service	Years of Service	Life Span
Oliver W. Holmes	1902–1932	30	1841–1935	*Harlan F. Stone*	1941–1946	5	1872–1946
William R. Day	1903–1922	19	1849–1923	James F. Byrnes	1941–1942	1	1879–1972
William H. Moody	1906–1910	3	1853–1917	Robert H. Jackson	1941–1954	13	1892–1954
Horace H. Lurton	1910–1914	4	1844–1914	Wiley B. Rutledge	1943–1949	6	1894–1949
Charles E. Hughes	1910–1916	5	1862–1948	Harold H. Burton	1945–1958	13	1888–1964
Willis Van Devanter	1911–1937	26	1859–1941	*Fred M. Vinson*	1946–1953	7	1890–1953
Joseph R. Lamar	1911–1916	5	1857–1916	Tom C. Clark	1949–1967	18	1899–1977
Edward D. White	1910–1921	11	1845–1921	Sherman Minton	1949–1956	7	1890–1965
Mahlon Pitney	1912–1922	10	1858–1924	*Earl Warren*	1953–1969	16	1891–1974
James C. McReynolds	1914–1941	26	1862–1946	John Marshall Harlan	1955–1971	16	1899–1971
Louis D. Brandeis	1916–1939	22	1856–1941	William J. Brennan, Jr.	1956–	—	1906–
John H. Clarke	1916–1922	6	1857–1945	Charles E. Whittaker	1957–1962	5	1901–1973
William H. Taft	1921–1930	8	1857–1930	Potter Stewart	1958–1981	23	1915–
George Sutherland	1922–1938	15	1862–1942	Byron R. White	1962–	—	1917–
Pierce Butler	1922–1939	16	1866–1939	Arthur J. Goldberg	1962–1965	3	1908–
Edward T. Sanford	1923–1930	7	1865–1930	Abe Fortas	1965–1969	4	1910–1982
Harlan F. Stone	1925–1941	16	1872–1946	Thurgood Marshall	1967–	—	1908–
Charles E. Hughes	1930–1941	11	1862–1948	*Warren C. Burger*	1969–1986	17	1907–
Owen J. Roberts	1930–1945	15	1875–1955	Harry A. Blackmun	1970–	—	1908–
Benjamin N. Cardozo	1932–1938	6	1870–1938	Lewis F. Powell, Jr.	1972–	—	1907–
Hugo L. Black	1937–1971	34	1886–1971	William H. Rehnquist	1972–1986	14	1924–
Stanley F. Reed	1938–1957	19	1884–1980	John P. Stevens, III	1975–	—	1920–
Felix Frankfurter	1939–1962	23	1882–1965	Sandra Day O'Connor	1981–	—	1930–
William O. Douglas	1939–1975	36	1898–1980	*William H. Rehnquist*	1986–	—	1924–
Frank Murphy	1940–1949	9	1890–1949	Antonin Scalia	1986–	—	1936–

*The names of chief justices are printed in italic type.

Party Control of the Presidency, Senate, and House of Representatives 1901–1987

Congress	Years	President	Senate D	Senate R	Senate Other*	House D	House R	House Other*
57th	1901–1903	McKinley T. Roosevelt	31	55	4	151	197	9
58th	1903–1905	T. Roosevelt	33	57	—	178	208	—
59th	1905–1907	T. Roosevelt	33	57	—	136	250	—
60th	1907–1909	T. Roosevelt	31	61	—	164	222	—
61st	1909–1911	Taft	32	61	—	172	219	—
62d	1911–1913	Taft	41	51	—	228	161	1
63rd	1913–1915	Wilson	51	44	1	291	127	17
64th	1915–1917	Wilson	56	40	—	230	196	9
65th	1917–1919	Wilson	53	42	—	216	210	6
66th	1919–1921	Wilson	47	49	—	190	240	3
67th	1921–1923	Harding	37	59	—	131	301	1
68th	1923–1925	Coolidge	43	51	2	205	225	5
69th	1925–1927	Coolidge	39	56	1	183	247	4
70th	1927–1929	Coolidge	46	49	1	195	237	3
71st	1929–1931	Hoover	39	56	1	167	267	1
72d	1931–1933	Hoover	47	48	1	220	214	1
73d	1933–1935	F. Roosevelt	60	35	1	319	117	5
74th	1935–1937	F. Roosevelt	69	25	2	319	103	10
75th	1937–1939	F. Roosevelt	76	16	4	331	89	13
76th	1939–1941	F. Roosevelt	69	23	4	261	164	4
77th	1941–1943	F. Roosevelt	66	28	2	268	162	5
78th	1943–1945	F. Roosevelt	58	37	1	218	208	4
79th	1945–1947	Truman	56	38	1	242	190	2
80th	1947–1949	Truman	45	51	—	188	245	1
81st	1949–1951	Truman	54	42	—	263	171	1
82d	1951–1953	Truman	49	47	—	234	199	1
83d	1953–1955	Eisenhower	47	48	1	211	221	—
84th	1955–1957	Eisenhower	48	47	1	232	203	—
85th	1957–1959	Eisenhower	49	47	—	233	200	—
86th**	1959–1961	Eisenhower	65	35	—	284	153	—
87th**	1961–1963	Kennedy	65	35	—	263	174	—
88th	1963–1965	Kennedy Johnson	67	33	—	258	177	—

Sources: Department of Commerce, Bureau of the Census, *Statistical Abstract of the United States* (Washington, D.C.: U.S. Government Printing Office, 1980), p. 509, and *Members of Congress Since 1789*, 2d ed. (Washington, D.C.: Congressional Quarterly, 1981), pp. 176–177. Adapted from Barbara Hinckley, *Congressional Elections* (Washington, D.C.: Congressional Quarterly Press, 1981), pp. 144–145.

*Excludes vacancies at beginning of each session.

**The 437 members of the House in the 86th and 87th Congresses is attributable to the at-large representative given to both Alaska (January 3, 1959) and Hawaii (August 21, 1959) prior to redistricting in 1962.

Party Control of the Presidency, Senate, and House of Representatives 1901–1987 *(continued)*

Congress	Years	President	Senate			House		
			D	R	Other*	D	R	Other*
89th	1965–1967	Johnson	68	32	—	295	140	—
90th	1967–1969	Johnson	64	36	—	247	187	—
91st	1969–1971	Nixon	57	43	—	243	192	—
92d	1971–1973	Nixon	54	44	2	254	180	—
93d	1973–1975	Nixon Ford	56	42	2	239	192	1
94th	1975–1977	Ford	60	37	2	291	144	—
95th	1977–1979	Carter	61	38	1	292	143	—
96th	1979–1981	Carter	58	41	1	276	157	—
97th	1981–1983	Reagan	46	53	1	243	192	—
98th	1983–1985	Reagan	45	55	—	267	168	—
99th	1985–1987	Reagan	47	53	—	252	183	—
100th	1987–1989	Reagan	55	45	—	258	177	—

Glossary

adjudication   The settling of a case judicially. More specifically, formal hearings in which a business under agency scrutiny can present its position with legal counsel present. (12,13)

administrative discretion   The latitude that Congress gives agencies to make policy in the spirit of their legislative mandate. (12)

affirmative action   Programs that require businesses, schools, and other institutions to expand opportunities for women and members of minority groups. (18)

agenda building   The process by which new issues are brought into the political limelight. (8)

aggregate demand   The money available to be spent for goods and services by consumers, businesses, and government. (15)

Aid to Families with Dependent Children (AFDC) Created by the Social Security Act of 1935, this public assistance program places responsibility on the federal government to help care for children who have been deprived of parental support through death, disability, or desertion. (10)

analytical budgeting   A budgeting process that uses sophisticated analytical procedures such as cost-benefit analysis and zero-based budgeting to enable administrators to choose the most cost-effective means toward their program goals. (12)

anarchism   A political philosophy that opposes government in any form. (1)

appellate jurisdiction   The authority to hear cases that have been tried, decided, or re-examined in other courts. (13)

appropriations committee   A committee that decides which of the programs passed by the authorization committees of Congress will actually be funded. (15)

aristocracy   Literally, "rule by the best" citizens. Today, the "ruling elite," the individuals who head the nation's key financial, industrial, and communications institutions, are thought to govern a modern society as the aristocracy ruled traditional societies. (2)

authorization committee   The House has nineteen such committees and the Senate, sixteen. Each one studies the portions of the budget that pertain to its area of responsibility for the purpose of authorizing spending in that area. (15)

autocracy   A system of government in which the power to govern is concentrated in the hands of one individual. Also called *monarchy*. (2)

bicameral   Term describing a legislature with two houses, or chambers. (3,10)

bill   A legislative proposal introduced in either the House or Senate. (10)

Bill of Rights   The first ten amendments of the Constitution. They prevent the national government from tampering with fundamental rights and civil liberties, and emphasize the limited character of national power. (3)

bills of attainder   Legislative acts that pronounce an individual guilty of a crime without trial. (17)

bimodal distribution   In measuring public opinion, this distribution results when the two categories possible are equally (or almost equally) chosen as the most frequent response. (5)

blanket primary   A primary in which voters receive a ballot containing each party's potential nominees and can help nominate candidates for all offices for each party. (7)

block grant   Grants awarded for general purposes that allow the recipient great discretion in spending the grant money. (4)

bolter parties   Parties formed from factions that have split off from one of the major parties. (7)

boycott   A refusal to do business with a firm or

individual as an expression of disapproval or as a means of coercion. (18)

briefs Written arguments received by judges. (13)

broadcast media Forms of mass communication that relay the spoken word electronically. Examples are radio and television. (9)

budget committee A committee of Congress that supervises a comprehensive budget-review process. (15)

bureaucracy Any large, complex organization in which employees have very specific job responsibilities and work within a hierarchy. (12)

business cycle Expansions and constrictions of business activity, the first accompanied by inflation and the second by unemployment. (15)

cabinet A group of presidential advisers composed of the heads of the executive departments and a small number of key officials, such as the OMB director and the UN ambassador. (11)

capitalism The system of government that favors free enterprise (private businesses operating without government regulations). It is based on the theory that free enterprise is necessary for free politics. (1)

casework Specific deeds done for constituents by representatives' or senators' staffs, such as assisting with a problem a constituent may have with a bureaucratic agency. (10)

categorical grant Grants targeted for a specific purpose. (4)

caucus A closed meeting of the members of a political party to decide upon questions of policy and the selection of candidates for office. (7)

checks and balances A system of structuring the government that gives each branch some control over the other branches, thus distributing power equally. (3)

citizen group A group of people whose basis of organization is a concern for issues unrelated to the members' vocations. (8)

citizen participation programs Programs that encourage interaction between bureaucrats and their clients. (12)

civil cases Court cases that involve private disputes arising from such matters as accidents, contractual obligations, and divorce. (13)

civil disobedience The willful but nonviolent violation of laws that are regarded as unjust. (18)

civil liberties Freedoms guaranteed to individuals. They act as negative restraints on the government. (17)

civil rights Powers or privileges guaranteed to individuals and protected from arbitrary removal at the hands of government or individuals. (17,18)

civil rights movement Political mobilization of the people — black and white — to promote racial equality. (18)

civil service system The system of government appointments to the federal bureaucracy that insures that government jobs will be filled on the basis of merit and that employees will not be fired for political reasons. (12)

closed primary A primary in which voters must declare their support for the party before they are given the primary ballot containing the party's potential nominee. (7)

cloture The mechanism by which a filibuster is cut off. A vote of three-fifths of the Senate is necessary to invoke cloture. (10)

coalition building The final aspect of lobbying strategy, when several organizations band together for the purpose of lobbying. (8)

coalition of minorities The notion that different groups of voters become dissatisfied with the president's handling of particular issues of concern, thus accounting for a general decline in presidential popularity through a term in office. (11)

Cold War In the 1950s, a period of increased tension that stopped short of outright military conflict, during which the adversarial nature of U.S. – Soviet relations was clear. Americans were called upon to give priority to defense spending over domestic spending. (19)

commander in chief The president's title as the highest-ranking officer in the military. (11)

communication The process of transmitting information from one individual or group to another. (9)

communism A political system in which, in theory, ownership of all land and productive facilities is in the hands of the people, and all goods are equally shared. The production and distribution of goods is controlled by an authoritarian government. (1)

concept A generalized idea that subsumes various events, objects, or qualities under a common classification or label. (1)

concurrence Agreement by judges with a decision. (13)

confederation A loose association of independent states that agree to cooperate on specified matters. (3)

conference committee A temporary committee created only to work out differences between House and Senate versions of a specific piece of legislation. (10)

congressional campaign organization An organization maintained by a political party to raise funds to support its own kind in congressional elections. (7)

congressional delegation A process by which Congress delegates power or authority to the president to deal with various problems. (11)

consultants People from outside the government structure hired by government agencies to conduct research, collect data, and perform policy analysis. (13)

containment The idea that the Soviets have to be prevented from expanding further. (19)

Continental Congress The first political assembly to speak out and act collectively for the people of all the colonies. The first Continental Congress met in 1774 and adopted a statement of rights and principles that were later reflected in the Constitution. (3)

conventional participation Relatively routine behavior that is acceptable to the dominant culture in a given situation. (6)

cooperative federalism A system of government in which the emphasis is on the individual as a citizen of both state and nation, who may act in either capacity. The barrier between state and nation is flexible in cooperative federalism. (4)

cost-of-living adjustments (COLAs) Automatic adjustments that increase social security payments to beneficiaries as the cost of living increases. These represent a significant expansion of the social security program. (16)

Council of Economic Advisers (CEA) Created by the Employment Act of 1946, this group works within the executive branch to provide advice on maintaining a stable economy. (15)

criminal code Legislation that regulates individual conduct and spells out punishments for violations. (13)

critical election An election that produces a sharp change in the existing patterns of party loyalties among groups of voters. The election of 1860 is regarded as the first critical election. (7)

Declaration of Independence Drafted by Thomas Jefferson, this document proclaimed the rights of the colonists to revolt against the British government. (18)

de facto segregation Segregation that is not the result of government influence. (18)

deficit financing The Keynesian technique of spending beyond government income to combat an economic slump. Its purpose is to inject extra money into the economy to stimulate aggregate demand. (15)

de jure segregation Government-imposed segregation. (18)

democracy A system of government in which, in theory, the people rule, either directly or indirectly. (2)

democratic socialism A socialist form of government that also guarantees civil liberties such as freedom of speech and religion. In addition, it allows citizens to determine the extent of government activity through free elections and competitive political parties. (1)

departments The largest units of the executive branch, covering broad areas of government responsibility. The heads of these departments, or secretaries, form the president's cabinet. Examples: State, Defense, Justice, Agriculture, Health and Human Services. (12)

deregulation A bureaucratic reform by which the government lessens its role as a regulator of business and lets the natural market forces of supply and demand take their course. (12)

desegregation The ending of authorized segregation, or separation by race. (18)

détente A policy aimed at reducing tension between East and West. (19)

direct action An effective mode of unconventional participation that involves assembling crowds to confront businesses and local governments to demand equal treatment. (6)

direct democracy A system of rule in which all members of the group meet to make decisions while observing the principles of political equality and majority rule. (2)

direct income subsidies Cash payments to farmers that reimburse them for the cost of producing a crop when this cost is greater than the market prices or loan rate for the crop. (16)

direct lobbying Attempts to influence a legislator's vote that rely on a group representative's contact with the legislator. (8)

direct mail A method of attracting new members to an interest group by sending letters to people in carefully targeted audiences. (8)

discretionary funds Large amounts of cash that may be spent on unpredicted needs to further national interests. (19)

dissent A disagreement by a judge with a decision. (13)

district courts Trial courts of the federal government. (13)

docket A court's agenda. (10)

dual federalism An interpretation of the federalist argument that views the Constitution as a compact among sovereign states. This view assumes that the powers of the state and federal governments are fixed and stresses states' rights. (4)

duopoly rule The FCC-enforced rule that prohibits any company from owning more than one AM or FM radio station or one television station in a single community. (9)

economic depression Period of high unemployment and business failures; a severe long-lasting downturn in a business cycle. (15,16)

elastic clause See *necessary and proper clause.*

electoral campaign An organized effort to persuade voters to choose one candidate over others competing for the same office. (7)

electoral college A body of electors who meet in their state capitals to cast ballots for president and vice president. (7,11)

electoral realignment The change in voting pattern that occurs after a critical election. These altered party loyalties endure for several subsequent elections. (7)

empirical theories Factual generalizations that can be tested by observation. (1)

entitlements Benefits to which every eligible person has a legal right and that the government cannot deny. (16)

enumerated powers The powers explicitly granted to Congress by the Constitution. (3)

equality of opportunity The idea that each person is guaranteed the same chance to get ahead in life. (1,18)

equality of result The concept that society must see to it that people are equal. Under this conception, it is not enough for governments to provide people with equal opportunities for social advancement; governments should also design policies to redistribute wealth and status so that economic and social equality are actually achieved. (1,18)

equal opportunities rule Under the Federal Communications Act of 1934, if a broadcast station gives or sells time to a candidate for any public office, it must make available an equal amount of time under the same conditions to all other candidates for that office. (9)

Equal Rights Amendment (ERA) A constitutional amendment first introduced by the National Women's Party in 1923, it declares that "equality of rights under the law shall not be denied or abridged by the United States or any State on account of sex." (18)

establishment clause The clause in the First Amendment of the Bill of Rights that forbids the establishment of a state religion. (17)

exclusionary rule The rule that states that evidence obtained from an illegal search and seizure cannot be used in trial. (17)

executive agreement A pact between the heads of two countries. (19)

executive article Article II of the Constitution, which describes the qualifications for becoming president, the procedure for electing presidents through the electoral college, and the president's duties and powers. (3)

executive branch The law-enforcing branch of the government. (3)

ex post facto laws Laws that declare an action to be criminal *after* it has been performed. (17)

externalities Side effects of business operations. (12)

extraordinary majority Votes of approval greater than that of a simple majority. (6)

fairness doctrine An FCC regulation that obligates broadcasters to discuss public issues and to provide fair coverage to each side of those issues. (9)

farmer-labor parties Parties that represent farmers and urban workers who believe that the working class does not get its share of society's wealth. (7)

federalism The division of power among two or more governments. (3,4)

federal questions Issues covered under the Constitution, federal laws, or treaties. (13)

Federal Reserve System The central bank of the United States. Established in 1913, the "Fed" is not a single bank, but a banking system with centralized and decentralized features. (15)

filibuster A popular tactic in the Senate that involves speechmaking to delay action on a piece of legislation. (10)

fiscal policies Policies that involve government spending and taxing. (15)

fiscal year (FY) The twelve-month period from October 1 to September 30 used by the government for accounting purposes. The budget is named for the year in which it ends. (15)

flexible response The cornerstone defense policy of President John F. Kennedy, who shared the Cold War attitude of his two predecessors. It involved the strengthening of the country's nonconventional weapons so that the United States would have a range of defense options from which to select. (19)

food stamp program The federally funded program that distributes coupons that can be used to purchase food by needy families. (16)

formula grants Grants distributed according to a particular formula, which specifies who is eligible for the grants and how much each eligible applicant will receive. (4)

franchise   The right to vote. (6)

franking privilege   The right of members of Congress to send mail to constituents free of charge. (10)

free exercise clause   The clause in the First Amendment of the Bill of Rights that prevents the government from interfering with the exercise of religion. (17)

free expression clause   The still-controversial First Amendment clause that guarantees the right of freedom of speech. (17)

free rider problem   Because the benefits a lobbying group wins are not restricted to members of its organization, it is not easy to get people to join. They would rather enjoy a "free ride." (8)

gatekeepers   Media executives, news editors, and prominent reporters who direct the news flow. (9)

general election   An election that fills many state and local offices. When a president is chosen, this election is also known as the presidential election. In the intervening years, it is referred to as the congressional, midterm, or off-year election. (7)

general revenue sharing   A federal program introduced by President Richard Nixon that returned tax money to state and local governments to be spent largely as they wished. (4)

gerrymander   To redraw a congressional district intentionally to benefit one political party. (10)

globalism   The idea that the United States is a superpower whose national security and economic interests are now global, or worldwide, in scope. (19)

government   The legitimate use of force — including imprisonment and execution — to control human behavior. (1)

government corporations   Agencies that perform services that could be provided by the private sector. Either the financial incentive is insufficient for the private sector to perform the services, or Congress decides that the public would be better served if these services are linked with the government. (12)

Gramm-Rudman-Hollings Act   An act passed by Congress in September 1985 that seeks to reduce the deficit by a specified level until the federal budget is balanced in FY 1991. (15)

grant-in-aid   Money provided from one government to another to be spent for a specific purpose. These are often proffered with requirements that are prescribed by Congress. (4)

grassroots lobbying   Lobbying that involves rank-and-file interest-group members and would-be members. Grassroots tactics such as letter campaigns and protests are often used in conjunction with direct lobbying by Washington representatives. (8)

Great Compromise   Submitted by the Connecticut delegation to the Constitutional Convention of 1787 and thus also known as the Connecticut Compromise, this plan called for a bicameral legislature in which the House of Representatives would be apportioned according to population while the states would be represented equally in the Senate. (3)

Great Depression   The longest and deepest setback the American economy has ever experienced. It began with the stock market crash on October 12, 1929, and did not end until the start of World War II. (10)

Great Society   President Lyndon Johnson's broad array of programs designed to redress political, social, and economic inequality. (16)

gross national product (GNP)   The total value of the goods and services produced by the country during a year or part of a year. (15)

group consciousness   Identification with the group and awareness of its position in society, its objectives, and its intended course of action. (6)

Gulf of Tonkin Resolution   A congressional resolution that greatly increased President Lyndon Johnson's war-making power in the Vietnam conflict. (19)

Hobbes, Thomas   The seventeenth-century philosopher who wrote *Leviathan*, which claimed that government was necessary to preserve order. (1)

home rule   The right of certain administrative areas or countries to enact and enforce legislation. (4)

Hyde Amendment   A 1976 decision by Congress to restrict severely the use of federal funds for reimbursement of abortion costs; upheld by the Supreme Court in 1980. (17)

ideologues   Individuals who advocate a specific ideology, or set of ideas. (5)

impeachment   The power of the House to charge the president, vice president, and other civil officers of the federal government with "treason, bribery, or other high crimes and misdemeanors" and remove those people from office. (10)

implementation   The process of putting specific policies into operation. (12)

implied powers   Those powers that Congress requires in order to execute its enumerated powers. (3)

in-and-outers   Participants in an issue network who have a good understanding of the needs and problems of others in the network due to common job switches within subsystems. For these people, knowledge and experience remain relevant to a particular issue network no matter which side of the fence they work on. (14)

incremental budgeting A method of budget making that involves adding new funds (an increment) onto the amount previously budgeted for (last year's budget). (15)

incumbency effect The advantages of being in office that help a member of Congress win re-election, such as franking, staff, and name recognition. (10)

incumbents Officeholders running for re-election. (7)

independent agencies Agencies that are not part of any cabinet department; their heads are appointed by the president. Examples: National Aeronautics and Space Administration, Veterans Administration. (12)

indirect democracy A system of rule in which citizens participate by electing public officials to make government decisions for them. Also called *representative democracy.* (2)

inflation An economic condition characterized by price increases linked to a decrease in the value of the currency. Inflation is generally measured by the Consumer Price Index. (15)

influencing behavior Behavior that seeks to modify or even reverse government policy to serve political interests. (6)

information campaigns Organized efforts to gain public backing by bringing a group's views to public attention. (8)

in groups Groups of people who control channels of political influence. (6)

inherent power Authority claimed by the president that is not clearly specified in the Constitution. Typically, these powers stem from inferences that are drawn from the Constitution. (11)

initiative A procedure by which voters can propose an issue to be decided by the legislature or by the people in a referendum. It requires gathering a required number of signatures and submitting a petition to a designated agency. (2,6)

injunction A court order that compels or constrains an action by an individual or a government. (17)

institutional mechanisms Established procedures and organizations that translate public opinion into government policy. (2)

interest group An organized body of individuals who share some goals and who try to influence public policy. Also called a *lobby.* (2,8)

interest-group entrepreneur An interest-group organizer or leader. (8)

intergovernmental relations The interdependence and relationships among all levels of government and government personnel. (4)

interventionism A policy in which the United States involves itself in affairs of non-European nations. (19)

iron triangles Members of congressional committees, federal agencies or bureaus, and lobbies who work toward policy ends in a specific area. Iron triangles are difficult for other actors to penetrate. (14)

issue network A shared knowledge group having to do with some aspect of public policy. Issue networks are more open than iron triangles. (14)

Jim Crow laws Laws enacted by southern states that required racial segregation. (18)

joint committee A committee made up of members of both the House and the Senate. (10)

judicial activism A judicial philosophy whereby judges may interpret existing laws and rulings loosely and interject their own values in court decisions. (13)

judicial restraint A judicial philosophy whereby judges adhere closely to statutes and previous cases in reaching their decisions. (13)

judicial review The power to declare congressional (and presidential) acts invalid because they violate the Constitution. (13)

Keynesian theory A theory of the economy that states that demand can be adjusted through a combination of fiscal and monetary policies. (15)

laissez faire An economic policy that opposes any form of government intervention in business. (1)

lawyer-lobbyists Lawyers who are part of the Washington community and who use their training and expertise to influence government. (13)

legislative liaison staff A group of people forging the communications link between the White House and Congress. As a bill makes its way through Congress, liaison staffers advise the president or a cabinet secretary on the problems that emerge. (11)

libel The written defamation of character. (17)

libertarianism A system of belief that is opposed to all government action except that which is necessary to protect life and property. (1)

linkage In international relations, the idea of using rewards and advantages in one area of negotiation to promote another country's compliance with the first country's wishes in other areas of negotiation. Henry Kissinger attempted this policy with both the Soviets and the Chinese. (19)

lobby See *interest group.*

lobbyists Representatives of interest groups. (8)

Locke, John The seventeenth-century philosopher who wrote *Two Treatises of Government,* which contained the phrase "life, liberty, and property." His work strongly influenced the drafters of the Declaration of Independence. (1)

logrolling Legislative bargaining typified by members exchanging votes on bills. (10)

majoritarian model of democracy The classical textbook theory of democracy. It interprets government by the people as government by the majority of the people. (2)

majority leader The head of the majority party in the Senate. (10)

majority party The party that regularly enjoys support from the most voters. (7)

majority rule The rule — one of the basic principles of democratic theory — that states that a decision, when a choice is to be made among alternatives, must reflect the preference of the greater number choosing. (2)

markup sessions Meetings of congressional committee or subcommittee members to amend and prepare legislation for floor debate. (10)

Marshall Plan A post – World War II plan to restore European economic viability. The plan sent approximately $12 billion in aid to Europe over a four-year period. (19)

mass communication The process by which individuals or groups transmit information to large, heterogeneous, and widely dispersed audiences. (9)

mass media A term referring to the technical devices employed in mass communication. They are divided into two types, print media and broadcast media. (9)

Medicare A health-care program for all persons over the age of sixty-five. (16)

military-industrial complex The combined interests of the military establishment and the large arms industry. These two groups are united by two common interests: war and military spending. (19)

minority leader The head of the minority party in the Senate. (10)

Miranda warning The statement about rights police are required to make to a person before he or she is subjected to in-custody questioning. (17)

mode The most frequent response in a survey chart. (5)

monarchy See *autocracy.*

monetary policies Policies that operate more indirectly on the economy than do fiscal policies. If the amount of money in circulation increases, demand will increase and price inflation will occur. Decreasing the money supply decreases aggregate demand and inflationary pressures. (15)

muckrakers A term derived from a special rake used to collect manure. It is a common name for investigative reporters. (9)

Munich paradigm The view that the United States must be willing to intervene, militarily if necessary, anywhere on the globe to put down a major threat to order and freedom in the world. Also called the *Pearl Harbor paradigm.* (19)

mutual assured destruction (MAD) The capability each of the two great superpowers—the United States and the Soviet Union — has to destroy the other, ensuring that there would be no winner of a nuclear war. (19)

Nader, Ralph A well-known consumer activist and public interest watchdog; he heads a small empire of public interest groups, such as the Public Citizen Litigation group. (8)

national committee A committee of a political party composed of party chairpeople and party officials from every state. (7)

national convention A gathering of delegates of a single party from across the country to choose candidates for president and vice president and to adopt a party platform. (7)

nation-building policies Kennedy administration policies intended to shore up Third World countries economically, thereby making them less attractive targets for Soviet opportunism. (19)

necessary and proper clause The clause in the legislative article of the Constitution that gives Congress the means to execute the enumerated powers. This clause is the basis for Congress's implied powers. Also called the *elastic clause.* (3)

New Deal The label for measures advocated by the Roosevelt administration to alleviate the Depression. (16)

"new" ethnicity The newer outlook on the people comprising America's "melting pot," with the focus on race and color. (5)

New Jersey Plan In 1787, William Paterson, the head of the New Jersey delegation to the Constitutional Convention, introduced a set of nine new resolutions that would have, in effect, preserved the Articles of Confederation by amending rather than replacing them. The plan was defeated in the first major convention vote, seven states to three. (3)

Nineteenth Amendment This amendment to the Constitution, which was adopted in 1920, protects women's right to vote. (18)

Nixon Doctrine   An attempt to redefine America's overseas commitments. The doctrine sought to avoid both the over-involvement of the past and the temptation of future under-involvement. Instead, U.S. intervention would occur only where it made a "real difference" and was considered in our interest. (19)

nominate   To designate individuals as official candidates for the party. (7)

normal distribution   A bell-shaped curve of symmetrical distribution around a single mode. (5)

normative analysis   A process engaged in by close observers of government policies. They determine which values (norms) are harmed and which are helped by policy choices. (1)

normative theories   Statements that evaluate or prescribe conditions. (1)

nullification   The idea that a state could declare a particular action of the national government null and void and not applicable to the state. (4)

"old" ethnicity   A term covering the majority of people comprising America's "melting pot"—those who are of European origin. (5)

oligarchy   A system of government in which power is concentrated in the hands of a few. (2)

open primary   A primary in which voters need not declare their party loyalty but must choose which party's primary ballot they take into the polling booth. (7)

opinion schema   A network of organized knowledge and beliefs that guides the processing of political information and is focused on a particular subject. (5)

order   The establishment of law to preserve life and protect property. Maintaining order is the oldest purpose of government. (1)

original jurisdiction   The authority to hear a case before any other court does. (13)

out groups   Groups that have been denied access to channels of political influence controlled by in groups. (6)

parliamentary system   A system of government in which the chief executive is the leader whose party holds the most seats in the legislature after an election or whose party forms a major part of the ruling coalition. (10)

party caucus   A local meeting of party supporters to choose delegates to attend a subsequent meeting, usually at the county level. (7)

party identification   A concept that refers to the voters' sense of psychological attachment to a party, which is not the same thing as voting for the party in any given election. Voting is a behavior; identification is a state of mind. (7)

party machine   A centralized party organization that dominates local politics by controlling elections. (7)

party platform   The official policies of a national party. (7)

Pearl Harbor paradigm   See *Munich paradigm.*

peer review   Party insiders usually get to know potential candidates much better than the average voter does, and thus they judge the candidates for acceptability as the party's representatives. (7)

picket-fence federalism   A view of federalism that stresses the interdependence and interrelationships of the various levels of government when implementing programs. (4)

plea-bargain   A process by which defendants admit guilt, usually with some expectation that the punishment will be less severe than if they had gone to trial. (13)

pluralism   An alternative interpretation of democracy that evolved in the 1950s. This concept views modern society as a collection of groups of people who share religious, economic, and cultural interests. (2)

pocket veto   A veto that occurs when a bill is not signed by the president within ten days of congressional adjournment. (10)

police power   The authority of the government to maintain order and otherwise safeguard citizens' health, morals, safety, and welfare. (1)

political action committee (PAC)   An organization that pools campaign contributions from group members and donates those funds to candidates for political office. (8)

political agenda   A list of issues that need government attention. (9)

political equality   The state of being equal in the political world. For example, each citizen has the right to one and only one ballot in each election or decision. (1)

political ideology   A consistent set of values and beliefs about the proper purpose and scope of government. (1)

political participation   Actions of private citizens by which they seek to influence or support government and politics. (6)

political party   An organization that sponsors candidates for political office under the organization's name. (7)

political socialization   A complex process by which people acquire their political values. (5)

political system   A set of interrelated institutions that link people with government. (7)

poll tax   First instituted in Georgia in 1877, this was a tax of $1 or $2 on every citizen who wished to vote. It was no burden on white citizens, but it effectively disenfranchised the blacks. (18)

polyarchy A system of rule in which power is held by many people. (2)

populists A political group that views the government as an instrument to promote the advancement of the common people as opposed to the moneyed interests. (1)

poverty level An income below the poverty threshold, which is the minimum cash income that will provide for a family's basic needs. It is calculated as three times the cost of an economy food plan, a market basket of food that provides a minimally nutritious diet. (16)

precedent The judicial ruling on a case, which will then be consulted in subsequent cases. The decision provides a reason for handling similar cases in the same way. (13)

presidential character A typology developed by James David Barber that labels presidents on the basis of level of activity and the extent to which they find their work enjoyable. (11)

presidential primary A special primary used to select delegates to attend the party's national convention, which in turn nominates the presidential candidate. (7)

president pro tem The person elected by the majority party to chair the Senate in the vice president's absence. By custom, this constitutional position is entirely honorific. (10)

press clause The First Amendment guarantee of freedom of the press. (17)

primary election A preliminary election conducted within the party to select candidates who will run for public office in a subsequent election. (7)

print media A form of mass communication that transmits information through the publication of the written word. (9)

prior restraint Censorship before publication. (17)

procedural democratic theory A set of normative principles that state how a government ought to make decisions. (2)

production controls Agreements that call for farmers to plant less of a particular crop. (16)

productive capacity The total value of goods and services when the economy works at full capacity. (15)

program monitoring The following of government programs by interest groups. (8)

progressive taxation A system of taxation whereby the rich pay proportionately higher taxes than the poor. It is a principle used by governments to redistribute the wealth and thus promote equality. (3,15)

progressivism A philosophy of political reform based upon the goodness and wisdom of the individual citizen as opposed to special interests and political institutions. (6)

project grant A grant awarded on the basis of competitive applications submitted by prospective recipients. (4)

proportional representation An electoral system that awards legislative seats in proportion to votes won in elections. It tends to produce (or to perpetuate) several parties. (7)

propositions The issues to be voted on during a referendum. They are printed on the ballot. (6)

public assistance Government aid to individuals who can demonstrate a need for that aid. (16)

public good projects Projects that benefit all people but that are not likely to be produced by the voluntary acts of individuals. Financing for these projects is provided by taxes. (1)

public interest group A citizen group that generally is considered to have no economic self-interest in the policies it pursues. (8)

public opinion The collected attitudes of citizens on a given issue or question. (5)

public policy A general plan of action adopted by the government to solve a social problem, counter a threat, or make use of an opportunity. (14)

public relations firms Firms that combine lobbying with image building. These firms may help their clients influence the government, the public, or both. (14)

racial segregation Separation from society because of race. (18)

reapportionment Redistribution of legislative districts based on population movement. Congress is reapportioned after each census. (10)

reasonable access rule A rule that requires that broadcast stations make their facilities available for the expression of conflicting views or issues from all responsible elements in the community. (9)

reconciliation A matching of the amount a congressional committee has been authorized to spend with the money it has been given to spend. The reconciliation process sometimes requires the authorization committee to change an existing law. (15)

redistricting Redrawing of congressional districts after census-based reapportionment. (10)

referendum An election on a policy issue. (2)

regulation Government intervention in the natural workings of business markets to promote some socially desired goal. (12)

regulatory commissions   Commissions that control or direct some aspect of the economy. Commission heads are appointed by the president. Examples: Federal Communications Commission, National Labor Relations Board. (12)

representative democracy   See *indirect democracy*.

republicanism   A form of government in which power resides in the people and is exercised by their elected representatives. (3)

responsiveness   A decisionmaking principle, necessitated by representative government, the gist of which is that elected representatives should respond to public opinion, that they should do what the people want.

rights   The idea that every citizen is entitled to certain benefits of government. (1)

rulemaking   The quasi-legislative administrative process that results in the issuance of regulations. (12)

rule of four   An unwritten rule that requires that at least four justices agree that a case warrants consideration by the Supreme Court. (13)

ruling elite   The few individuals who head a nation's key financial, industrial, and communications institutions. (2)

select committee   A temporary committee created for a specific purpose and disbanded after that purpose is fulfilled. Select committees tend to be investigative in nature. (10)

self-interest principle   The principle that states that people prefer choices that benefit them personally. (5)

senatorial courtesy   A practice whereby the Senate will not confirm a nominee for a lower federal court judgeship who is opposed by the senior senator in the president's party in the nominee's state. (13)

Senior Executive Service (SES)   Created by the Civil Service Reform Act of 1978, the SES — approximately eight thousand employees in the higher level of the civil service — offers the president and his top aides some flexibility in the assignment of high-level administrators. (12)

seniority   Years of consecutive service on a particular congressional committee. A combinaton of seniority and majority party status is typically used to determine the committee chair. (10)

separate-but-equal doctrine   The concept of educating children of different races in schools that were supposedly of "equal" quality. This policy was enunciated by the Supreme Court in *Plessy* v. *Ferguson* (1896) but was declared unconstitutional by the court in *Brown* v. *Board of Education of Topeka* (1954). (18)

separation of powers   The assignment of law-making, law-enforcing, and law-interpreting functions to separate branches of government. (3)

seven-seven-seven rule   An FCC-enforced rule that limited to seven each the number of radio and television stations a single company could own. (9)

sexism   Sex discrimination. (18)

Shays's Rebellion   In early 1787, Daniel Shays, a Revolutionary War veteran, led a march to close a courthouse and thus prevent a foreclosure of farms by creditors. The following series of insurrections, which were named after Shays, dramatized the weakness of the newly created national government. (3)

Sierra Club   Founded by John Muir, the club is a conservation lobby whose goal is to protect American wildlands from economic use. (3)

single-issue parties   Parties formed to promote one principle rather than a general philosophy of government. (7)

skewed distribution   A public opinion graph in which the mode (containing the vast majority of respondents) lies off to one side, leaving a "tail" (containing the few who disagree) on the other. The amount of skew (the proportion of respondents in the tail) is a matter of degree. (5)

slip opinions   Copies of a judge's opinions, summarized from the courtroom, which are distributed to interested parties and the press. (13)

social equality   Equality in wealth, education, and status. (1)

social insurance   A government-backed guarantee against loss by individuals without regard to need. (16)

socialism   A form of rule in which the central government plays a strong role in regulating existing private industry and directing the economy, although it does allow some private ownership of productive capacity. (1)

social order   The established patterns of authority relationships in society. (1)

social security   Government-provided insurance that provides economic assistance to persons faced with unemployment, disability, or old age. It is financed by taxes on employers and employees. (16)

socioeconomic status   Position in society based on a combination of education, occupational status, and income. (5)

sovereignty   The power of self-rule. (3)

Speaker of the House   The presiding officer of the House of Representatives. (10)

special envoys   Personal representatives of the president who perform a wide variety of foreign policy tasks. (19)

split ticket A term used to describe what happens when a voter switches parties when choosing candidates for different offices on the ballot. (7)

spot advertising Brief but frequent campaign advertising on mass media. (9)

stable distribution An opinion poll that shows little change over time. (5)

standard socioeconomic model (of participation) The relationship between socioeconomic status and conventional political involvement. People of higher status and more education are more likely to participate than those of lower status. (6)

standing committee A permanent congressional committee that specializes in a particular substantive legislative area. (10)

stare decisis "Let the decision stand"; decisionmaking according to precedent. (13)

states' rights A concept whereby all rights not specifically conferred on the national government are reserved for the state. (4)

statutory construction A judge's interpretation of a legislative act. (13)

straight ticket The term used to describe what happens when a voter chooses only one party's candidates for all the offices. (7)

substantive democratic theory A theory that focuses on the substance of government policies rather than on the procedures followed in making those policies. (2)

subsystem A group of individuals, both inside and outside the government, who together develop a policy in a specific area. (14)

suffrage The right to vote. (6)

supply-side economics An economic policy intended to counter extreme inflation by increasing supply. (15)

supportive behavior Purely ceremonial acts or other expressions of allegiance to government and country. (6)

supremacy clause The clause in the Constitution that asserts that national laws take precedence over state and local laws when they are in conflict. (3)

tax committees Committees of Congress responsible for raising the revenue to run the government. (15)

tax expenditure The loss of government revenue due to favorable tax treatment. (15)

textbook presidency A term that refers to the inflated expectations the public has of the president. The concept stems from a study by Thomas Cronin of college-level texts in the 1950s and 1960s, which routinely exaggerated the powers and responsibilities of the presidency. (11)

think tank An institution in which scholars engage in public policy research. Brookings and the American Enterprise Institute are examples of think tanks that sponsor studies pertinent to the debate over selected issues facing the government, the public, or both. (14)

tort An injury or wrong to the person or property of another. (13)

totalitarianism A political philosophy that advocates unlimited power for the government to enable it to control all sectors of society. (1)

trade associations Organizations of firms in the same basic industry that keep members abreast of marketing and manufacturing developments. Trade associations also represent their members' interests before the government. (8,14)

transfer authority The power that allows executive departments the discretion to take money that Congress has approved and spend it on something else. Also called *reprogramming*. (19)

trustee A representative who is obligated to consider the views of the constituents but not obligated to vote according to those views if he or she thinks they are misguided. (10)

two-party system A political system in which two major political parties compete for control of the government. Candidates from a third party have little chance of winning office. (7)

uncontrollable outlays Required funding for programs that are protected by law. (15)

unconventional participation Relatively uncommon behavior that challenges or defies government channels and thus is personally stressful to participants and their opponents. (6)

undeclared war Military action, usually directed by the president, without benefit of a declaration of war from Congress. (19)

unitary government A form of government in which all power is centrally vested. (3)

universal participation The procedural conception of democracy that states that everyone should participate in government decisionmaking. (2)

veto The president's refusal to sign a bill into law. Congress can override a veto with a two-thirds vote in each house. (10,11)

Vietnamization Adopted by President Richard Nixon, this plan called for turning over more and more of the fighting in the Vietnam War to the South Vietnamese. This tactic finally led to the peace agreement in 1973. (19)

Vietnam paradigm The foreign policy view that accepts that not all left-wing revolutionary movements are necessarily directed from Moscow but instead can be a product of internal nationalist forces. The proponents of this paradigm also argue that military force is not the most effective way to ''win the hearts and the minds'' of people in other countries. (19)

voting   An act that individuals perform when they choose among alternatives in an election. (6)

War on Poverty   The major weapon of President Johnson's War on Poverty in America was the Economic Opportunity Act of 1964, which promised to eradicate poverty in ten years. (16)

War Powers Resolution   An act of Congress that limits the president's ability to wage undeclared war. (19)

Washington community   The public- and private-sector employees who work on public policy issues. (14)

welfare   A concept that stresses government's function as the provider and protector of individual well-being through economic and social programs. (10)

Wilderness Group   A conservation group based in Washington. (10)

writ of certiorari   An order from the Supreme Court to the lower court to prepare the record in a case and send it up for review. (13)

writ of mandamus   A court order directing an official to act. (13)

yellow journalism   The distorted, sensationalist reporting of stories that became popular toward the end of the nineteenth century. (9)

References

Chapter 1 / Freedom, Order, or Equality? / pp. 2–31

1. University of Michigan, Center for Political Studies of the Institute for Social Research, University of Michigan, *Election Study 1984.*
2. *1977 Constitution of the Union of Soviet Socialist Republics,* Article 11, in A. P. Blaustein and G. H. Flanz, eds., *Constitutions of Countries of the World* (Dobbs Ferry, N.Y.: Oceana Publications, 1971).
3. Karl Marx and Friedrich Engels, *Critique of the Gotha Programme* (New York: International Publishers, 1938), p. 10. Originally written in 1875 but published in 1891.
4. Milton Friedman, *Capitalism and Freedom* (Chicago: University of Chicago Press, 1962).
5. *Chicago Tribune,* May 3, 1986.
6. Jean Jacques Rousseau, *The Social Contract and Discourses,* trans. G. D. H. Cole (New York: Dutton, 1950), p. 5.
7. *Public Opinion* 5 (October–November 1982): 36.
8. Barbara G. Farah and Elda Vale, "Crime: A Tale of Two Cities," *Public Opinion* 8 (August–September 1985): 57.
9. See the argument in Amy Gutman, *Liberal Equality* (Cambridge, Eng.: Cambridge University Press, 1980), pp. 9–10.
10. See John H. Schaar, "Equality of Opportunity and Beyond," in J. Roland Pennock and John W. Chapman, eds., *Equality, NOMOS IX* (New York: Atherton Press, 1967), pp. 228–249.
11. Lawrence Herson, *The Politics of Ideas* (Homewood, Ill.: Dorsey Press, 1984), pp. 166–176.

Chapter 2 / Majoritarian or Pluralist Democracy? / pp. 32–60

1. *Public Opinion* (October–November 1982): 36.
2. "Pistols and Politics," *Chicago Tribune,* April 13, 1986.
3. Austin Ranney and Willmoore Kendall, *Democracy and the American Party System* (New York: Harcourt, Brace, 1956), p. 6.
4. Kenneth Janda, "What's in a Name? Party Labels Across the World," in F. W. Riggs, ed., *The CONTA Conference: Proceedings of the Conference on Conceptual and Terminological Analysis in the Social Sciences* (Frankfurt: Indeks Verlag, 1982), pp. 46–62.
5. This distinction is elaborated in Ranney and Kendall, pp. 12–13.
6. Candy Frank, "New England Town Meeting Reaching End of the Road," *Today Journal,* March 28, 1986.
7. Jean Jacques Rousseau, *The Social Contract and Discourses,* trans. G. D. H. Cole (New York: Dutton, 1950).
8. See Jane Mansbridge, *Beyond Adversary Democracy* (New York: Basic Books, 1982), for an analysis of democracy in action, both direct and indirect.
9. John Stuart Mill, *Considerations on Representative Government* (Indianapolis: Bobbs-Merrill, 1958).
10. See C. B. Macpherson, *The Real World of Democracy* (New York: Oxford University Press, 1975), pp. 58–59.
11. Austin Ranney, "Referendums and Initiatives 1984," *Public Opinion* 7 (December–January 1985): 16.
12. Use of modern information technology to improve citizen participation in politics is developed in Michael Margolis, *Viable Democracy* (New York: Penguin Books, 1979), especially Chapter 7. See also Benjamin R. Barber, *Strong Democracy: Participatory Politics for a New Age* (Berkeley: University of California Press, 1984), p. 307.
13. *New York Times,* April 15, 1986.
14. See Robert A. Dahl, *Dilemmas of Pluralist Democracy: Autonomy vs. Control* (New Haven, Conn.: Yale University Press, 1982), p. 5.
15. Robert A. Dahl, *Pluralist Democracy in the United States* (Chicago: Rand McNally, 1967), p. 24.
16. Seymour Melman, *Pentagon Capitalism: The Political Economy of War* (New York: McGraw-Hill, 1970).
17. Robert A. Dahl, "A Critique of the Ruling Elite Model," *American Political Science Review* 52 (June 1958): 463–469, at 466.
18. Thomas R. Dye, *Who's Running America? The Conservative Years* (Englewood Cliffs, N.J.: Prentice-Hall, 1986), p. 12. See also G. William Domhoff, *Who Rules America Now? A View for the Eighties* (Englewood Cliffs, N.J.: Prentice-Hall, 1983).
19. The most prominent study was Robert A. Dahl's research on decisionmaking in New Haven, Connecticut, in *Who Governs?* (New Haven, Conn.: Yale University Press, 1961). G. William Domhoff criticized Dahl's study in *Who Really Rules? New Haven and Community Power Reexamined* (New Brunswick, N.J.: Transaction Books, 1978). Nelson W. Polsby supported Dahl's basic findings in *Community Power and Political Theory: A Further Look at Problems of Evidence and Inference* (New Haven, Conn.: Yale University Press, 1980).
20. See Kenneth M. Dolbeare, *Democracy at Risk: The Politics of Economic Renewal*

(Chatham, N.J.: Chatham House, 1984), and Edward S. Greenberg, *The American Political System: A Radical Approach* (Boston: Little, Brown, 1986).

21. G. Bingham Powell, Jr., *Contemporary Democracies* (Cambridge, Mass.: Harvard University Press, 1982), p. 3.

22. U.S. Bureau of the Census, *Statistical Abstract of the United States, 1982–83* (Washington, D.C.: U. S. Government Printing Office, 1982), pp. 859–860.

Chapter 3 / The Constitution / pp. 62–105

1. Carl Bernstein and Bob Woodward, *All the President's Men* (New York: Warner Paperback, 1975).

2. *Ibid.*, p. 30.

3. Samuel Eliot Morison, *Oxford History of the American People* (New York: Oxford University Press, 1965), p. 182.

4. John Plamenatz, *Man and Society*, vol. 1 (New York: McGraw-Hill, 1963), pp. 162–164.

5. Extrapolated from U.S. Department of Defense, *Selected Manpower Statistics, FY1982* (Washington, D.C.), Table 2-30, p. 130, and *1985 Statistical Abstract of the United States* (Washington, D.C.: U.S. Government Printing Office, 1985), Tables 1 and 2, p. 6.

6. Joseph T. Keenan, *The Constitution of the United States* (Homewood, Ill.: Dow Jones–Irwin, 1975).

7. David P. Szatmary, *Shays' Rebellion: The Making of an Agrarian Insurrection* (Amherst, Mass.: University of Massachusetts Press, 1980), pp. 82–102.

8. Robert H. Jackson. *The Struggle for Judicial Supremacy* (New York: Knopf, 1941), p. 8.

9. Donald S. Lutz, "The Preamble to the Constitution of the United States," *This Constitution* 1 (September 1983): 23–30.

10. Richard E. Neustadt, *Presidential Power: The Politics of Leadership* (New York: John Wiley & Sons, Inc., 1960) p. 33.

11. Charles A. Beard, *An Economic Interpretation of the Constitution* (New York: Macmillan, 1913).

12. Leonard W. Levy, *Constitutional Opinions* (New York: Oxford University Press, 1986), p. 101.

13. Robert E. Brown, *Charles Beard and the Constitution* (Princeton, N.J.: Princeton University Press, 1956); Levy, pp. 103–104; and Forrest McDonald, *We the People: The Economic Origins of the Constitution* (Chicago: University of Chicago Press, 1958).

14. Max Farrand, *The Making of the United States Constitution* (New Haven, Conn.: Yale University Press, 1913), p. 207.

15. Walter Berns, *The First Amendment and the Future of American Democracy* (New York: Basic Books, 1976), p. 2.

16. Herbert J. Storing, ed., *The Complete Anti-Federalist*, 7 vols. (Chicago: University of Chicago Press, 1981).

17. Keenan, p. 21.

18. Jerold L. Waltman, *Political Origins of the U.S. Income Tax* (Jackson: University Press of Mississippi, 1985), p. 10.

19. Edward Meade Earle, ed., *The Federalist* (New York: Modern Library, 1937), p. xxi.

Chapter 4 / Federalism / pp. 106–140

1. Ronald Reagan, "National Minimum Drinking Age: Remarks on Signing HR4616 into Law (July 17, 1984)," *Weekly Compilation of Presidential Documents*, July 23, 1984, p. 1036.

2. James Madison, "The Federalist, No. 10, " in Alexander Hamilton, John Jay, and James Madison, *The Federalist Papers* (New York: Modern Library), p. 60.

3. Alpheus Mason and William Beaney, *The Supreme Court in a Free Society* (New York: W. W. Norton, 1968), pp. 70–71.

4. Daniel Elazar, *The American Partnership* (Chicago: University of Chicago Press, 1962); Morton Grodzins, *The American System* (Chicago: Rand McNally, 1966).

5. Baker v. Carr, 369 U.S. 186 (1962); Wesberry v. Sanders, 376 U.S. 1 (1964); Reynolds v. Sims, 377 U.S. 533 (1964).

6. McCulloch v. Maryland, 4 Wheat. 316 (1819).

7. Dred Scott v. Sanford, 19 How. 393 (1857).

8. Hammer v. Dagenhart, 247 U.S. 251 (1918).

9. James T. Patterson, *The New Deal and the States: Federalism in Transition* (Princeton, N.J.: Princeton University Press, 1969).

10. United States v. Butler, 297 U.S. 1 (1936).

11. Brown v. Board of Education of Topeka, 347 U.S. 483 (1954).

12. Aaron Wildavsky, "Bare Bones: Putting Flesh on the Skeleton of American Federalism," in ACIR, *The Future of Federalism in the 1980s*, (Washington, D.C.: U.S. Government Printing Office, 1981), p. 80.

13. Advisory Commission on Intergovernmental Relations, *The Federal Role in the Federal System* (Washington, D.C.: U.S. Government Printing Office, 1981), p. 101.

14. Richard Nixon, "Speech to National Governor's Conference, September 1,

1969," in *Congressional Quarterly Almanac* (1969), pp. 101A–103A.

15. Rochelle Stanfield, "States Come of Age in the Federal System," *National Journal*, January 12, 1985, p. 84.

16. Morton Grodzins, "The Federal System," in *Goals for Americans* (New York: Columbia University, The American Assembly, 1960), p. 265.

Chapter 5 / Public Opinion and Political Socialization / pp. 142–181

1. *Public Opinion* 8 (June–July 1985): 38–39.

2. *New York Times*, July 3, 1976.

3. *Public Opinion* 8 (June–July 1985): 39.

4. Most of the survey findings reported herein were computed from data collected by the National Opinion Research Center in 1984 as part of its series of General Social Surveys. The principal investigator was James A. Davis, and the Senior Study director was Tom W. Smith. The sample size in 1984 was 1,473 cases. These data were made available on computer tape by the Inter-University Consortium for Political and Social Research at the University of Michigan.

5. *Public Opinion* 5 (October–November 1982): 21.

6. Warren E. Miller, Arthur H. Miller, and Edward J. Schneider, *American National Election Studies Sourcebook, 1952–1978* (Cambridge, Mass.: Harvard University Press, 1980), pp. 94–95.

7. Tom W. Smith and Paul B. Sheatsley, "American Attitudes Toward Race Relations," *Public Opinion* 7 (October–November 1984): 15.

8. Smith and Sheatsley, 83.

9. Jerry L. Yeric and John R. Todd, *Public Opinion: The Visible Politics* (Itasca, Ill.: F. E. Peacock, 1983), p. 39.

10. Paul Allen Beck, "The Role of Agents in Political Socialization," in Stanley Allen Renshon, ed., *Handbook of Political Socialization: Theory and Research* (New York: Free Press, 1977), pp. 117–118.

11. M. Kent Jennings and Richard G. Niemi, *The Political Character of Adolescence: The Influence of Families and Schools* (Princeton, N.J.: Princeton University Press, 1974), p. 39.

12. Robert D. Hess and Judith V. Torney, *The Development of Political Attitudes in Children* (Chicago: Aldine, 1967).

13. Jarol B. Manheim, *The Politics Within* (New York: Longman, 1982), p. 83.

14. "Government Trust: Less in West Europe Than U.S." *New York Times*, February 16, 1986.

15. Theodore M. Newcomb, *Persistence and*

Social Change: Bennington College and Its Students After Twenty-Five Years (New York: John Wiley, 1967).

16. William Schneider, "Bang-Bang Television: The New Superpower," *Public Opinion* 5 (April–May 1982): 13.

17. Joseph Wagner, "Media Do Make a Difference: The Differential Impact of Mass Media in the 1976 Presidential Race," *American Journal of Political Science* 27 (August 1983): 423.

18. Peter Clarke and Eric Fredin, *Public Opinion Quarterly* 42 (Summer 1978): 150.

19. James Allan Davis and Tom W. Smith, *General Social Surveys, 1972–1984: Cumulative Codebook* (Chicago: National Opinion Research Center, 1984), p. 93. This question had seven response categories ranging from "government should do something to reduce income differences between rich and poor" (category 1) to "government should not concern itself with income differences" (category 7). Categories 1 through 3 were combined to represent the "government should" response, and categories 4 through 7 were combined to represent the "government should not" response.

20. For a recent review of these studies, see Stuart Rothenberg, Eric Licht, and Frank Newport, *Ethnic Voters and National Issues* (Washington, D.C.: Free Congress Research and Educational Foundation, 1982).

21. Nathan Glazer, "The Structure of Ethnicity," *Public Opinion* 7 (October–November 1984): 4.

22. *Statistical Abstract of the United States, 1982–83*, p. 32

23. Glazer, p. 5.

24. Davis and Smith, p. 111.

25. *Ibid.*, p. 132.

26. John Robinson, "The Ups and Downs and Ins and Outs of Ideology," *Public Opinion* 7 (February–March, 1984): 12.

27. Angus Campbell, Philip E. Converse, Warren E. Miller, and Donald E. Stokes, *The American Voter* (New York: John Wiley, 1960), ch. 10.

28. This research is not without criticism. See Eric R. A. N. Smith, "The Levels of Conceptualization; False Measures of Ideological Sophistication," *American Political Science Review* 74 (September 1980): 685–696.

29. Paul R. Hagner and John C. Pierce, "Correlative Characteristics of Levels of Conceptualization in the American Public: 1956–1976," *Journal of Politics* 44 (August 1982): 788.

30. National Election Study for 1984, pre-election survey, conducted by the Center for Political Studies, University of Michigan.

31. Pamela Johnston Conover, "The Origins and Meaning of Liberal-Conservative Self-Identifications," *American Journal of Political Science* 25 (November 1981): 621–622, and 643.

32. The relationship of liberalism to political tolerance is found by John L. Sullivan et al., "The Sources of Political Tolerance: A Multivariate Analysis," *American Political Science Review* 75 (March 1981): 102. See also Robinson, 13–15.

33. Herbert Asher, *Presidential Elections and American Politics* (Homewood, Ill.: Dorsey Press, 1980), pp. 14–20. Asher also constructs a two-dimensional ideological framework, distinguishing between the "traditional New Deal issues" and "new lifestyle" issues.

34. John E. Jackson, "The Systematic Beliefs of the Mass Public: Estimating Policy Preferences with Survey Data," *Journal of Politics* 45 (November 1983): 840–865, at 857.

35. William S. Maddox and Stuart A. Lilie, *Beyond Liberal and Conservative* (Washington, D.C.: Cato Institute, 1984), p. 68.

36. John C. Pierce, Kathleen M. Beatty, and Paul R. Hagner, *The Dynamics of American Public Opinion* (Glenview, Ill.: Scott, Foresman, 1982), p. 134.

37. Center for Political Studies, *1982 National Election Survey* (Ann Arbor, Mich.: Inter-University Consortium for Political and Social Research).

38. CBS News/New York Times, *National Surveys, 1983* (Ann Arbor, Mich.: Inter-University Consortium for Political and Social Research, 1985), p. 86.

39. *Public Opinion* 8 (August–September 1985): 33.

40. Pamela Johnston Conover and Stanley Feldman, "How People Organize the Political World: A Schematic Model," *American Journal of Political Science* 28 (February 1984): 96. For an excellent review of schema structures in contemporary psychology — especially as it relates to political science — see Reid Hastie, "A Primer of Information-Processing Theory for the Political Scientist," in Richard R. Lau and David O. Sears, eds., *Political Cognition* (Hillsdale, N.J.: Erlbaum, 1986), pp. 11–39.

Chapter 6 / Participation and Elections / pp. 182–219

1. *Time,* September 6, 1968, p. 21.
2. *Newsweek,* September 9, 1968, p. 39.
3. *Time,* September 6, 1968, p. 24.
4. John P. Robinson, "Public Reaction to Political Protest: Chicago 1968," *Public Opinion Quarterly* 34 (Spring 1970): 2.

5. G. Bingham Powell, "Party Systems and Political System Performance: Participation, Stability and Violence in Contemporary Democracies," *American Political Science Review* 75 (December 1981): 868. See Kirkpatrick, pp. 335–344, for the distinction between the best *conceivable* form of democracy and the best *possible* form.

6. Lester W. Milbrath and M. L. Goel, *Political Participation* (Chicago: Rand McNally, 1977), p. 2.

7. *New York Times,* March 4, 1985.

8. See Sidney Verba and Norman H. Nie, *Participation in America: Political Democracy and Social Equality* (New York: Harper & Row, 1972), p. 3.

9. Samual H. Barnes and Max Kaase, eds., *Political Action: Mass Participation in Five Western Democracies* (Beverly Hills, Calif.: SAGE Publications, 1979).

10. Barnes and Kaase, p. 552.

11. Max Kaase and Alan Marsh, "Political Action: A Theoretical Perspective," in Barnes and Kaase, p. 44.

12. Jonathan D. Casper, *The Politics of Civil Liberties* (New York: Harper & Row, 1972), p. 90.

13. David C. Colby, "A Test of the Relative Efficacy of Political Tactics," *American Journal of Political Science* 26 (November 1982): 741–753. See also Frances Fox Piven and Richard Cloward, *Poor People's Movements* (New York: Vintage Books, 1979).

14. Stephen C. Craig and Michael A. Maggiotto, "Political Discontent and Political Action," *Journal of Politics* 43 (May 1981): 514–522. But see Mitchell A. Seligson, "Trust, Efficacy and Modes of Political Participation: A Study of Costa Rican Peasants," *British Journal of Political Science* 10 (January 1980): 75–98, for a review of studies to the contrary.

15. Philip H. Pollock, III, "Organizations as Agents of Mobilization: How Does Group Activity Affect Political Participation?" *American Journal of Political Science* 26 (August 1982): 485–503.

16. Arthur H. Miller et al., "Group Consciousness and Political Participation," *American Journal of Political Science* 25 (August 1981): 495.

17. Richard D. Shingles, "Black Consciousness and Political Participation: The Missing Link," *American Political Science Review* 75 (March 1981): 76–91.

18. Barnes and Kaase, pp. 548–549.

19. David Easton and Jack Dennis, *Children in the Political System: Origins of Political Legitimacy* (New York: McGraw-Hill, 1969).

20. See Joel B. Grossman et al., "Dimen-

sions of Institutional Participation: Who Uses the Courts and How?" *Journal of Politics* 44 (February 1982): 86–114, and Frances Kahn Zemans, "Legal Mobilization: The Neglected Role of the Law in the Political System," *American Political Science Review* 77 (September 1983): 690–703, at 692.

21. See Sidney Verba and Norman H. Nie, *Participation in America: Political Democracy and Social Equality* (New York: Harper & Row, 1972), p. 69. Also see John Clayton Thomas, "Citizen-Initiated Contacts with Government Agencies: A Test of Three Theories," *American Journal of Political Science* 26 (August 1982): 504–522, and Elaine B. Sharp, "Citizen-Initiated Contacting of Government Officials and Socioeconomic Status: Determining the Relationship and Accounting for It," *American Political Science Review* 76 (March 1982): 109–115, at 114.

22. Elaine B. Sharp, "Citizen Demand Making in the Urban Context," *American Journal of Political Science* 28 (November 1984): 654–670, at 654 and 665.

23. Verba and Nie, p. 67; Sharp, 660.

24. Kaase and Marsh, p. 168.

25. David Butler, Howard R. Penniman, and Austin Ranney, *Democracy at the Polls: A Comparative Study of Competitive National Elections* (Washington, D.C.: 1981), p. 1.

26. Everett Carll Ladd, *The American Polity* (New York: W. W. Norton, 1985), p. 392.

27. Gorton Carruth and Associates, eds., *The Encyclopedia of American Facts and Dates* (New York: Thomas Y. Crowell, 1979), p. 330.

28. Ivor Crewe, "Electoral Participation," in Butler, Penniman, and Ranney, pp. 216–263, at pp. 219–223.

29. David B. Magleby, *Direct Legislation: Voting on Ballot Propositions in the United States* (Baltimore, Md.: The Johns Hopkins Press, 1984), pp. 36–39, 71.

30. Magleby, p. 70.

31. Matthew L. Wald, "In Maine, Obscenity Vote Brings Warnings of Purges and Plans for Prayer," *New York Times*, June 6, 1986, p. 8; *Chicago Tribune*, June 11, 1986, p. 17.

32. Magleby, p. 59.

33. Magleby, p. 198.

34. *The Book of the States 1984–85, Volume 25* (Lexington, Ky.: Council of State Governments, 1984), p. 45.

35. *Chicago Tribune*, March 10, 1985.

36. Crewe, p. 232.

37. Verba and Nie, p. 13.

38. Max Kaase and Alan Marsh, "Distribu-

tion of Political Action," in Barnes and Kaase, p. 186.

39. Milbrath and Goel, pp. 95–96.

40. Verba and Nie, p. 148.

41. Richard Murray and Arnold Vedlitz, "Race, Socioeconomic Status, and Voting Participation in Large Southern Cities," *Journal of Politics* 39 (November 1977): 1064–1072; Verba and Nie, p. 157.

42. Carol A. Cassel, "Change in Electoral Participation in the South," *Journal of Politics* 41 (August 1979): 907–917, at 917.

43. Ronald B. Rapoport, "The Sex Gap in Political Persuading: Where the 'Structuring Principle' Works," *American Journal of Political Science* 25 (February 1981): 32–48, at 42.

44. Stephen D. Shaffer, "A Multivariate Explanation of Decreasing Turnout in Presidential Elections, 1960–1976," *American Journal of Political Science* 25 (February 1981): 68–95, at 71; Paul R. Abramson and John H. Aldrich, "The Decline of Electoral Participation in America," *American Political Science Review* 76 (September 1982): 603–620.

45. Abramson and Aldrich, 519; Shaffer, 78 and 90.

46. David Glass, Peverill Squire, and Raymond Wolfinger, "Voter Turnout: An International Comparison," *Public Opinion* 6 (December–January 1984): 52.

47. G. Bingham Powell, "American Voter Turnout in Comparative Perspective," *American Political Science Review* 80 (March 1986): 25.

48. Crewe, p. 262.

49. Barnes and Kaase, p. 532.

50. *1971 CQ Almanac* (Washington, D.C.: Congressional Quarterly, 1972) p. 475.

51. Benjamin Ginsberg, *The Consequences of Consent: Elections, Citizen Control and Popular Acquiescence* (Reading, Mass.: Addison Wesley, 1982), p. 13.

52. Ginsberg, pp. 13–14.

53. This list is adapted from Ginsberg, pp. 6–7.

Chapter 7 / Political Parties, Campaigns, and Voting / pp. 220–267

1. *Congressional Quarterly Weekly Report*, January 8, 1983, p. 5.

2. Postelection interview of the 1984 National Election Study.

3. Alan R. Gitelson, M. Margaret Conway, and Frank B. Feigert, *American Political Parties: Stability and Change* (Boston: Houghton Mifflin, 1984), p. 317, emphasis added.

4. Noble E. Cunningham, Jr., ed., *The Making of the American Party System,*

1789 to 1809 (Englewood Cliffs, N.J.: Prentice-Hall, 1965), p. 123.

5. Richard B. Morris, ed., *Encyclopedia of American History* (New York: Harper & Row, 1976), p. 209.

6. See Jerome M. Clubb, William H. Flanigan, and Nancy H. Zingale, *Partisan Realignment: Voters, Parties, and Government in American History,* vol. 108, p. 163 (Beverly Hills, Calif.: SAGE Publications, 1980).

7. See Gerald Pomper, "Classification of Presidential Elections," *Journal of Politics* 29 (August 1967): 535–566.

8. For a more extensive treatment, see Henry M. Littlefield, "The Wizard of Oz: Parable on Populism," *American Quarterly* 16 (Spring 1964): 47–58.

9. Clubb, Flanigan, and Zingale, p. 99.

10. The following discussion draws heavily on Austin Ranney and Willmoore Kendall, *Democracy and the American Party System* (New York: Harcourt, Brace, 1956), chaps. 18 and 19.

11. See Steven J. Rosenstone, Roy L. Behr, and Edward H. Lazarus, *Third Parties in America: Citizen Response to Major Party Failure* (Princeton, N.J.: Princeton University Press, 1984), pp. 5–6.

12. *Ibid.*, p. 8.

13. *Public Opinion* 7 (December–January 1985): 26.

14. *Ibid.*, p. 34.

15. Bill Keller, "As Arms Buildup Eases, U.S. Tries to Take Stock," *New York Times*, May 14, 1985.

16. Robert Harmel and Kenneth Janda, *Parties and Their Environments: Limits to Reform?* (New York: Longman, 1982), pp. 27–29.

17. William Crotty and John S. Jackson, III, *Presidential Primaries and Nominations* (Washington, D.C.: CQ Press, 1985), p. 33.

18. John F. Bibby, "Party Renewal in the National Republican Party," in Gerald M. Pomper, ed., *Party Renewal in America: Theory and Practice* (New York: Praeger, 1980), pp. 102–115.

19. Tom Watson, "Machines: Something Old, Something New," *Congressional Quarterly Weekly Report*, August 17, 1985, p. 1619.

20. Cornelius P. Cotter et al., *Party Organizations in American Politics* (New York: Praeger, 1984), pp. 26–27.

21. Cotter et al., p. 63.

22. See Stephen A. Salmore and Barbara G. Salmore, *Candidates, Parties, and Campaigns* (Washington, D.C.: Congressional Quarterly Press, 1985), p. 13.

23. Kenneth Janda, *Political Parties: A Cross-National Survey* (New York: The Free Press, 1980), p. 112.

24. Crotty and Jackson, p. 16.
25. *Congressional Quarterly Weekly Report*, June 2, 1984, p. 1317.
26. *Ibid.*, p. 1316.
27. See James R. Beniger, "Winning the Presidential Nomination: National Polls and State Primary Elections, 1936–1972," *Public Opinion Quarterly* 40 (Spring 1976): 22–38.
28. Arthur H. Miller and Martin P. Wattenberg, "Throwing the Rascals Out: Policy and Performance Evaluations of Presidential Candidates, 1952–1980," *American Political Science Review* 79 (June 1985): 359–372, at p. 370.
29. Quoted in E. J. Dionne, Jr., "On the Trail of Corporation Donations," *New York Times*, October 6, 1980.
30. Federal Election Commission, *The First Ten Years: 1975–1985*, April 14, 1985, p. 1.
31. The findings reported here for 1984 were computed from the preliminary release of data made available through the Inter-University Consortium for Political and Social Research.
32. Miller and Wattenberg, p. 370.
33. David B. Hill and Norman R. Luttbeg, *Trends in American Electoral Behavior* (Itasca, Ill.: Peacock, 1983), p. 50.
34. Herbert Asher, *Presidential Elections and American Politics* (Homewood, Ill.: Dorsey Press, 1980), p. 196.
35. Gary C. Jacobson, *The Politics of Congressional Elections* (Boston: Little, Brown, 1983), p. 156.
36. The model is articulated most clearly in a report by the American Political Science Association, *Toward a More Responsible Two-Party System*, a special issue of *The American Political Science Review* 44 (September 1950). See also Gerald M. Pomper, "Toward a More Responsible Party System? What, Again?" *Journal of Politics* 33 (November 1971): 916–940.
37. See, for example, Gerald M. Pomper, ed., *Party Renewal in America*.

Chapter 8 / Interest Groups / pp. 268–301

1. Robert W. Crandall, "Detroit Rode Quotas to Prosperity," *Wall Street Journal*, January 29, 1986, and "The $1,000 Job Tax on Cars," *New York Times*, February 17, 1986, p. A16.
2. "The $1,000 Job Tax on Cars."
3. Jeffrey M. Berry, *The Interest Group Society* (Boston: Little, Brown, 1984), p. 5.
4. Alexis de Tocqueville, *Democracy in America*, ed. Richard D. Heffner (New York: Mentor Books, 1956), p. 198.
5. *The Federalist Papers*, Mentor ed. (New York: New American Library, 1961), p. 79.
6. *Ibid.*, p. 78.
7. *Ibid.*, p. 80.
8. See Robert A. Dahl, *A Preface to Democratic Theory* (Chicago: University of Chicago Press, 1956), pp. 4–33.
9. This discussion follows from Berry, pp. 6–8.
10. Steven Pressman, "Lobbying 'Star War' Flares as Movie Industry Fights Invasion of Video Recorders," *Congressional Quarterly Weekly Report*, June 4, 1983, pp. 1099–1103.
11. David B. Truman, *The Governmental Process* (New York: Knopf, 1951).
12. Herbert Gans, *The Urban Villagers* (New York: Free Press, 1962).
13. Robert H. Salisbury, "An Exchange Theory of Interest Groups," *Midwest Journal of Political Science* 13 (February 1969): 1–32.
14. See Mancur Olson, Jr., *The Logic of Collective Action* (New York: Schocken, 1968), and Terry M. Moe, *The Organization of Interests* (Chicago: University of Chicago Press, 1980).
15. Robert Coles, *Migrants, Sharecroppers, Mountaineers* (Boston: Little, Brown, 1971).
16. Peter Matthiessen, *Sal Si Puedes* (New York: Random House, 1969), and John G. Dunne, *Delano*, rev. ed. (New York: Farrar, Straus & Giroux, 1971).
17. Larry J. Sabato, *The Rise of Political Consultants* (New York: Basic Books, 1981), pp. 220–263.
18. See Olson.
19. Carol Greenwald, *Group Power* (New York: Praeger, 1977), p. 65.
20. David Rogers, "A Lobbyist's Fortuitous Position," *Wall Street Journal*, August 23, 1984, p. 42.
21. Paul Taylor, "Gladiators for Hire — Part I," *Washington Post*, July 31, 1983, p. A1.
22. Mark Green, "Political PAC-Man," *New Republic*, December 13, 1982, p. 24. On the influence of PACs, see Larry J. Sabato, *PAC Power* (New York: Norton, 1984), pp. 122–140.
23. Lynda Mapes, "For PACs It's the Gift, Not the Thought, That Counts," *Wall Street Journal*, November 1, 1984 p. 30.
24. Federal Election Commission, "FEC Releases Final Report on 1984 Congressional Races," December 8, 1985, p. 4.
25. Elizabeth Drew, "Politics and Money — I," *New Yorker*, December 6, 1982, p. 147.
26. Kay Lehman Schlozman and John T. Tierney, *Organized Interests and American Democracy* (New York: Harper & Row, 1986), p. 150.
27. John E. Chubb, *Interest Groups and the Bureaucracy* (Stanford, Calif.: Stanford University Press, 1983), p. 144.
28. Allan J. Cigler and John Mark Hansen, "Group Formation Through Protest: The American Agriculture Movement," in Allan J. Cigler and Burdett A. Loomis, *Interest Group Politics* (Washington, D.C.: Congressional Quarterly, 1983), pp. 84–109.
29. David J. Garrow, *Protest at Selma* (New Haven, Conn.: Yale University Press, 1978).
30. Roger P. Kingsley, "Advocacy for the Handicapped" (Paper delivered at the annual meeting of the American Political Science Association, Washington, D.C., September 1984), p. 10.
31. Anne Costain, "The Struggle for a National Women's Lobby," *Western Political Quarterly* 33 (December 1980): 476–491.
32. Schlozman and Tierney, p. 281.
33. Jack L. Walker, "The Origins and Maintenance of Interest Groups in America" (Paper delivered at the annual meeting of the American Political Science Association, New York, September 1981), p. 14.
34. Jeffrey M. Berry, *Lobbying for the People* (Princeton, N.J.: Princeton University Press, 1977), pp. 6–10.
35. Andrew S. McFarland, *Common Cause* (Chatham, N.J.: Chatham House, 1984).
36. Charles McCarry, *Citizen Nader* (New York: Saturday Review Press, 1972).
37. See David Vogel, *Lobbying the Corporation* (New York: Basic Books, 1978), pp. 21–68.
38. Frances Fitzgerald, "A Disciplined, Charging Army," *New Yorker*, May 18, 1981, pp. 53–141.
39. Rich Jaroslovsky, "Religious Right Counts on Reagan," *Wall Street Journal*, September 18, 1984, p. 64.
40. Martha Joynt Kumar and Michael Baruch Grossman, "The Presidency and Interest Groups," in Michael Nelson, ed., *The Presidency and the Political System* (Washington, D.C.: Congressional Quarterly, 1984), pp. 293–294.
41. David Vogel, "How Business Responds to Opposition" (Paper delivered at the annual meeting of the American Political Science Association, Washington, D.C., December 1979).
42. *Public Affairs Offices and Their Functions* (Boston: Boston University School of Management, 1981), p. 8.
43. Reginald Stuart, "The Telephone Lobby: No Longer a One-Company Shop," *New York Times*, August 4, 1985, p. F7.
44. Walter Dean Burnham, *Critical Elections*

and the Mainsprings of American Politics
(New York: Norton, 1970), p. 133.

45. United States v. Harriss, 347 U.S. 612
(1954).

**Chapter 9 / The Mass Media /
pp. 302–338**

1. *Broadcasting*, July 8, 1985, p. 33.
2. Steve Daley, "Hostages and Ratings,"
Chicago Tribune, June 30, 1985, sec. 5,
pp. 1, 4.
3. William C. Adams, "The Beirut Hostages: ABC and CBS Seize an Opportunity," *Public Opinion* 8 (August–
September 1985): 45.
4. S. N. D. North, *The Newspaper and Periodical Press* (Washington, D.C.: U.S.
Government Printing Office, 1884),
p. 27. This source provides much of
the information reported about newspapers and magazines prior to 1880.
5. Sidney Kobre, *The Yellow Press and
Gilded Age Journalism* (Tallahassee:
Florida State University Press, 1964),
p. 52.
6. *Statistical Abstract of the United States,
1985* (Washington, D.C.: U.S. Government Printing Office, 1986), p. 547.
7. *The Encyclopedia of American Facts and
Dates* (New York: Thomas Y. Crowell,
1979), pp. 467, 525.
8. *World Almanac and Book of Facts*, 1941
and 1951 issues.
9. Dana R. Ulloth, Peter L. Klinge, and
Sandra Eells, *Mass Media: Past, Present,
Future* (St. Paul, Minn.: West Publishing, 1983), p. 278.
10. Doris A. Graber, *Mass Media and American Politics* (Washington, D.C.: CQ
Press, 1984), pp. 78–79.
11. Roper Organization, *Trends in Attitudes
Toward Television and Other Media* (New
York: Television Information Office,
1983), p. 8.
12. *Statistical Abstract of the United States,
1982–83* (Washington, D.C.: U.S. Government Printing Office, 1984), p. 562.
13. *Editor & Publisher International Yearbook, 1984*, pp. 435–442.
14. Christopher H. Sterling and Timothy R.
Haight, p. 53
15. *Broadcasting*, May 27, 1985, p. 36.
16. Joseph Turow, *Media Industries: The
Production of News and Entertainment*
(New York: Longman, 1984), p. 18.
Our discussion of government regulation draws heavily on this source.
17. Joseph R. Dominick, *The Dynamics of
Mass Communication* (Reading, Mass.:
Addison-Wesley, 1983), p. 331.
18. *New York Times*, July 27, 1984, p. 1;
Wall Street Journal, July 27, 1984, p. 3.
19. Graber, p. 110.
20. "Fairness Rule Gags TV: FCC," *Chicago
Tribune*, August 8, 1965, Sec. 1, p. 3.

21. Graber, pp. 235–236
22. *Ibid.*, 241.
23. Graber, p. 72.
24. Austin Ranney, *Channels of Power: The
Impact of Television on American Politics*
(New York: Basic Books, 1983), p. 46.
25. Graber, pp. 82–83.
26. S. Robert Lichter and Stanley Roth-
man, "Media and Business Elites,"
Public Opinion 5 (October–November
1981): 42–46.
27. William Schneider and I. A. Lewis,
"Views on the News," *Public Opinion* 8
(August–September 1985): 7.
28. Maura Clancey and Michael J. Robinson, "General Election Coverage: Part
I," *Public Opinion* 7 (December–
January 1985): 49–54, 59.
29. *Ibid.*, 7–8.
30. Michael Robinson and Margaret Shee-
han, *Over the Wire and On TV: CBS and
UPI in Campaign '80* (New York: Russell Sage Foundation, 1983).
31. Michael J. Robinson, "The Media in
Campaign '84: Part II, Wingless,
Toothless, and Hopeless," *Public Opinion* 8 (February–March 1985): 43–48,
at 48.
32. Clancey and Robinson, 54.
33. Leslie Maitland Werner, "13% of U.S.
Adults Are Illiterate in English, a Federal Study Finds," *New York Times*,
April 21, 1986, pp. 1, 14.
34. Computed from data in the 1984 National Election Study, distributed by
the Inter-University Consortium for
Political and Social Research.
35. Michael J. Robinson and Maura Clancey, "Teflon Politics," *Public Opinion* 7
(April–May 1984): 14–18, at page 14.
36. *Ibid.*
37. *Ibid.*
38. *Ibid.*, p. 18.
39. Peter Clarke and Eric Fredin, "Newspapers, Television, and Political Reasoning," *Public Opinion Quarterly* 42
(Summer 1978): 143–160.
40. Joseph Wagner, "Media Do Make a
Difference: The Differential Impact of
Mass Media in the 1976 Presidential
Race," *American Journal of Political Science* 27 (August 1983): 407–430, at
415–417.
41. Michael J. Robinson, "American Political Legitimacy in an Era of Electronic
Journalism: Reflections on the Evening
News," in Douglas Caterr (ed.), *Television as a Social Force* (New York:
Praeger, 1975) pp. 97–139.
42. Graber, pp. 66–67, and Andrew Good-
man, "Television Images of the Foreign
Policy Process," (Ph.D diss., Northwestern University, 1985), chap. 11.
43. William Schneider, "Bang-Bang Television: The New Superpower," *Public

Opinion* 5 (April–May 1982): 13–15 at
13.
44. Edwin Diamond and Stephen Bates,
"The Ads," *Public Opinion* 7 (December–January 1985): 55.
45. Robinson, "The Media Campaign in
'84,'" pp. 47–48.
46. Herbert Jacob, *The Frustration of Policy:
Responses to Crime by American Cities*
(Boston: Little, Brown, 1984),
pp. 47–50.
47. Stephen Hess, *The Washington Reporters*
(Washington, D.C.: Brookings, 1981).
48. Ben Stein, " 'Miami Vice': It's So Hip
You'll Want to Kill Yourself," *Public
Opinion* 8 (October–November 1985):
41–43.
49. Thomas E. Patterson and Richard
Davis, "The Media Campaign: Struggle
for the Agenda," in Michael Nelson,
ed., *The Elections of 1984* (Washington,
D.C.: CQ Press, 1985), pp. 111–127, at
p. 124.
50. Schneider and Lewis, p. 11.

**Chapter 10 / The Congress /
pp. 340–381**

1. Jimmy Carter, *Keeping Faith* (New
York: Bantam Books, 1982), p. 84.
2. Clinton Rossiter, *1787: The Grand Convention* (New York: Mentor, 1968),
p. 158.
3. *Origins and Development of Congress*
(Washington, D.C.: Congressional
Quarterly, 1976), pp. 81–89.
4. Wesberry v. Sanders, 376 U.S. 1
(1964) (Congressional districts within
a state must be substantially equal in
population); Reynolds v. Sims, 377
U.S. 364 (1964) (State legislatures
must be apportioned on a population
basis).
5. Barbara Hinckley, *Congressional Elections*
(Washington, D.C.: Congressional
Quarterly, 1981), p. 37.
6. *The Gallup Report*, (July 1985): 3.
7. John A. Ferejohn, "On the Decline of
Competition in Congressional Elections," *American Political Science Review*
71 (March 1977): 166–176.
8. Gary C. Jacobson, *The Politics of
Congressional Elections* (Boston: Little,
Brown, 1983), pp. 91–92.
9. Hinckley, pp. 42–43.
10. Gary C. Jacobson and Samuel Kernell,
*Strategy and Choice in Congressional Elec-
tions* (New Haven, Conn.: Yale University Press, 1983).
11. "PAC Support of Incumbents Increases
in '84 Elections," Federal Election
Commission, May 19, 1985, p. 3.
12. Larry J. Sabato, *PAC Power* (New York:
Norton, 1984), p. 72.
13. Norman J. Ornstein et al., *Vital Statistics

on Congress, 1984–1985 ed. (Washington, D.C.: American Enterprise Institute, 1984), p. 45.

14. Charles O. Jones, *The United States Congress* (Homewood, Ill.: Dorsey Press, 1982), p. 65.

15. David Shribman, "Canada's Top Envoy to Washington Cuts Unusually Wide Swath," *Wall Street Journal*, July 29, 1985.

16. Walter J. Oleszek, *Congressional Procedures and the Policy Process*, 2nd ed. (Washington, D.C.: Congressional Quarterly, 1984), p. 73.

17. Roger Cobb and Charles Elder, *Participation in American Politics*, 2nd ed. (Baltimore, Md.: Johns Hopkins University Press, 1983), pp. 64–65.

18. John W. Kingdon, *Agendas, Alternatives, and Public Policies* (Boston: Little, Brown, 1984), p. 37.

19. *Ibid.*, p. 41.

20. Woodrow Wilson, *Congressional Government* (Boston: Houghton Mifflin, 1985), p. 79.

21. Steven V. Roberts, "Expertise on Budget of Military," *New York Times*, April 15, 1985.

22. Leroy Rieselbach, *Congressional Reform* (Washington, D.C.: Congressional Quarterly, 1986), p. 47.

23. Steven S. Smith and Christopher J. Deering, *Committees in Congress* (Washington, D.C.: Congressional Quarterly, 1984), pp. 35–57.

24. *Ibid.*, p. 271.

25. Philip M. Boffey, "Lawmakers Vow a Legal Recourse for Military Malpractice Victims," *New York Times*, July 9, 1985.

26. Richard F. Fenno, Jr. *Congressmen in Committees* (Boston: Little, Brown, 1973), p. 86.

27. John F. Manley, *The Politics of Finance* (Boston: Little, Brown, 1970), p. 109.

28. Robert Weissberg, "Collective vs. Dyadic Representation in Congress," *American Political Science Review* 72 (June 1978): 535–547.

29. Jacqueline Calmes, "President Fails to Unsnarl Budget Deadlock," *Congressional Quarterly Weekly Report*, July 13, 1985, p. 1355.

30. Andy Plattner, "Dole on the Job," *Congressional Quarterly Weekly Report*, June 29, 1985, p. 1270.

31. Roger H. Davidson, "Senate Leaders: Janitors for an Untidy Chamber?" in Lawrence C. Dodd and Bruce I. Oppenheimer, eds., *Congress Reconsidered*, 3rd ed. (Washington, D.C.: Congressional Quarterly, 1985), p. 228.

32. Robert L. Peabody, *Leadership in Congress* (Boston: Little, Brown, 1976), p. 9.

33. Jones, p. 322.

34. Oleszek, pp. 186–192.

35. Deborah Baldwin, "Pulling Punches," *Common Cause* (May–June 1985): 22.

36. John Felton, "Restive Congress Comes Close to Passing Anti-Apartheid Bill," *Congressional Quarterly Weekly Report*, August 3, 1985, p. 1527.

37. Steven V. Roberts, "A Most Important Man on Capitol Hill," *New York Times Magazine*, September 22, 1985, p. 55.

38. Randall B. Ripley, "Legislative Bargaining and the Food Stamp Act, 1964," in Frederic N. Cleveland and Associates, *Congress and Urban Problems* (Washington, D.C.: Brookings Institution, 1969), pp. 296–300.

39. This framework is adapted from John W. Kingdon, *Congressmen's Voting Decisions*, 2nd ed. (New York: Harper & Row, 1981).

40. Steve Blakely, "Partisanship in Congress Up Sharply in 1985," *Congressional Quarterly Weekly Report*, January 11, 1986, pp. 86–88.

41. Kay Lehman Schlozman and John T. Tierney, *Organized Interests and American Democracy* (New York: Harper & Row, 1985), p. 293.

42. Malcolm E. Jewell and Samuel C. Patterson, *The Legislative Process in the United States*, 4th ed. (New York: Random House, 1986), pp. 135–136.

43. Ornstein et al., p. 21.

44. Michael Malbin, *Unelected Representatives* (New York: Basic Books, 1980).

45. *Ibid.*, p. 240.

46. James Sterling Young, *The Washington Community* (New York: Harcourt, Brace, 1966).

47. Kingdon, *Congressmen's Voting Decisions*, p. 242.

48. Jeff Gerth, "Regulators Say Bank Failure Was 'Aberration,' " *New York Times*, July 16, 1982.

49. Fred Hiatt and Rick Atkinson, "Joint Chiefs of Congress," *Washington Post National Weekly Edition*, August 12, 1985, p. 6.

50. David R. Mayhew, *Congress: The Electoral Connection* (New Haven, Conn.: Yale University Press, 1974).

51. Joel D. Aberbach, "Changes in Congressional Oversight," *American Behavioral Scientist* 22 (May–June 1979): 493–515.

52. Jeffrey M. Berry, *Feeding Hungry People: Rulemaking in the Food Stamp Program* (New Brunswick, N.J.: Rutgers University Press, 1984), p. 122.

53. Richard F. Fenno, Jr., *Home Style* (Boston: Little, Brown, 1978), p. xii.

54. *Ibid.*, p. 32.

55. Louis I. Bredvold and Ralph G. Ross, eds., *The Philosophy of Edmund Burke* (Ann Arbor: University of Michigan Press, 1960), p. 148.

56. Steven V. Roberts, "On Arms, Jobs Are the Big Guns," *New York Times*, May 23, 1985.

57. Roger H. Davidson, *The Role of the Congressman* (New York: Pegasus, 1969), p. 120.

58. Warren E. Miller and Donald E. Stokes, "Constituency Influence in Congress," *American Political Science Review* (March 1963): 45–57.

59. *The Gallup Report*, (January–February, 1986): 37.

60. Jonathan Fuerbringer, "Two Budget Plans Lose Senate Votes," *New York Times*, May 9, 1985, and David Rogers, "House Democrats Face Tough Task in Meeting Budget Resolution Goals of Senate Republicans," *Wall Street Journal*, May 13, 1985.

61. Weissberg.

Chapter 11 / The Presidency / pp. 382–425

1. Robert J. Donovan, *Tumultuous Years* (New York: W. W. Norton, 1982), pp. 382–391; and Youngstown Sheet and Tube Co. v. Sawyer, 343 U.S. 579 (1952).

2. Louis W. Koenig, *The Chief Executive*, 4th ed. (New York: Harcourt, Brace, Jovanovich, 1981), p. 20.

3. Clinton Rossiter, *1787: The Grand Convention* (New York: Mentor, 1968), p. 148.

4. Rossiter, pp. 190–191.

5. Richard M. Pious, *The American Presidency* (New York: Basic Books, 1979), pp. 51–52.

6. Wilfred E. Binkley, *President and Congress*, 3rd ed. (New York: Vintage, 1962), p. 155.

7. Pious, pp. 60–63.

8. James L. Sundquist, *The Decline and Resurgence of Congress* (Washington, D.C.: Brookings Institution, 1981).

9. Richard E. Neustadt, *Presidential Power* (New York: John Wiley, 1980), p. 10.

10. Neustadt, p. 9.

11. Fred I. Greenstein, *The Hidden-Hand Presidency* (New York: Basic Books, 1982), pp. 155–227.

12. David Rosenbaum, "Aides Evoke Goals of Johnson Period," *New York Times*, April 20, 1985.

13. John E. Mueller, *War, Presidents, and Public Opinion* (New York: John Wiley, 1973).

14. Kristen Renwick Monroe, *Presidential Popularity and the Economy* (New York: Praeger, 1984).

15. Charles W. Ostrom, Jr., and Dennis M. Simon, "Promise and Performance: A

Dynamic Model of Presidential Popularity," *American Political Science Review* 79 (June 1985): 334–358.

16. Michael Novak, *Choosing Our King* (New York: Macmillan, 1974), p. 4.

17. Thomas E. Cronin, *The State of the Presidency*, 2nd ed. (Boston: Little, Brown, 1980), p. 81. The quotation is from Clinton Rossiter, *The American Presidency*, rev. ed. (New York: New American Library, 1960), p. 84.

18. Cronin, pp. 77–84.

19. Arthur Schlesinger, Jr., *The Imperial Presidency* (Boston: Houghton Mifflin, 1973).

20. Novak.

21. Theodore J. Lowi, "Ronald Reagan—Revolutionary?", in Lester M. Salamon and Michael S. Lund, eds., *The Reagan Presidency and the Governing of America* (Washington, D.C.: Urban Institute Press, 1984), p. 47.

22. *Elections '84* (Washington, D.C.: Congressional Quarterly, 1984), p. 87.

23. "Prepared Text of Carter's Farewell Address," *New York Times*, January 15, 1981.

24. Jeff Fishel, *Presidents and Promises* (Washington, D.C.: Congressional Quarterly, 1985), pp. 125–128.

25. Benjamin I. Page, *Choices and Echoes in Presidential Elections* (Chicago: University of Chicago Press, 1978).

26. Jeb Stuart Magruder, *An American Life* (New York: Atheneum, 1974), p. 58; as quoted in Benjamin Page and Mark Petracca, *The American Presidency* (New York: McGraw-Hill, 1983), p. 169.

27. Page and Petracca, p. 171.

28. Paul J. Quirk, "Presidential Competence," in Michael Nelson, ed., *The Presidency and the Political System* (Washington, D.C.: Congressional Quarterly, 1984), p. 135.

29. Seymour M. Hersh, *The Price of Power* (New York: Summit Books, 1983), p. 42.

30. Alexander Haig, *Caveat* (New York: Macmillan, 1984), p. 143.

31. Edward Weisband and Thomas M. Franck, *Resignation in Protest* (New York: Penguin, 1975), p. 139; as quoted in Cronin, p. 253.

32. Griffin B. Bell with Ronald J. Ostrow, *Taking Care of the Law* (New York: William Morrow, 1982), p. 45.

33. Terry M. Moe, "The Politicized Presidency," in John E. Chubb and Paul E. Peterson, eds., *The New Direction in American Politics* (Washington, D.C.: Brookings Institution, 1985), pp. 235–271.

34. *Public Papers of the President, Lyndon B. Johnson, 1965*, vol. I (Washington, D.C.: U.S. Government Printing Office, 1966), p. 72.

35. "Transcript of Second Inaugural Address by Reagan," *New York Times*, January 22, 1985.

36. John L. Palmer and Isabel V. Sawhill, eds., *The Reagan Record* (Cambridge, Mass.: Ballinger, 1984), pp. 366–368.

37. John W. Kingdon, *Agendas, Alternatives, and Public Policies* (Boston: Little, Brown, 1984), p. 25.

38. Richard E. Neustadt, "Presidency and Legislation: The Growth of Central Clearance," *American Political Science Review* 48 (September 1954): 641–671.

39. Paul C. Light, *The President's Agenda* (Baltimore, Md.: Johns Hopkins University Press, 1983), p. 45.

40. Page and Petracca, p. 248.

41. Seth King, "Reagan, in Bid for Budget Votes, Reported to Yield on Sugar Prices," *New York Times*, June 27, 1981.

42. Dom Bonafede, "The Tough Job of Normalizing Relations with Capitol Hill," *National Journal*, January 13, 1979, pp. 54–57.

43. Martha Joynt Kumar and Michael Baruch Grossman, "The Presidency and Interest Groups," in Nelson, p. 309.

44. See Robert Kennedy, *Thirteen Days* (New York: W. W. Norton, 1969), and Graham T. Allison, *Essence of Decision* (Boston: Little, Brown, 1971).

45. Alexander George, "The Case for Multiple Advocacy in Making Foreign Policy," *American Political Science Review* 66 (September 1972): 751–782.

46. Theodore J. Lowi, *The Personal President* (Ithaca, N.Y.: Cornell University Press, 1985), p. 185.

47. Robert A. Caro, *The Path to Power* (New York: Knopf, 1982), p. 131.

48. Caro, p. 135.

49. Doris Kearns, *Lyndon Johnson and the American Dream* (New York: Signet, 1977), p. 363.

50. James David Barber, *The Presidential Character*, 3rd ed. (Englewood Cliffs, N.J.: Prentice-Hall, 1985), p. 8.

Chapter 12 / The Bureaucracy / pp. 426–457

1. Pat Milton, "US Intervenes on behalf of Deformed Baby," *Boston Globe*, November 5, 1983.

2. "Big Brother Doe," *Wall Street Journal*, November 1, 1983.

3. Bruce D. Porter, "Parkinson's Law Revisited: War and the Growth of American Government," *Public Interest* 60 (Summer 1980): p. 50.

4. A. Lee Fritschler, *Smoking and Politics*, 3rd ed. (Englewood Cliffs, N.J.: Prentice-Hall, 1983), pp. 34, 160.

5. "Possible Nationalizing of Continental Illinois Raises Many Questions," *Wall Street Journal*, July 19, 1984.

6. Herbert Kaufman, *Are Government Organizations Immortal?* (Washington, D.C.: Brookings Institution, 1976).

7. Kenneth J. Meier, *Politics and the Bureaucracy* (North Scituate, Mass.: Duxbury Press, 1979).

8. "Advertisers Pleased by F.T.C. Plan," *New York Times*, March 24, 1984. See also Michael Pertschuk, *Revolt Against Regulation* (Berkeley: University of California Press, 1982).

9. Bureau of the Census, *Statistical Abstract of the United States, 1984–85* (Washington, D.C.: U.S. Government Printing Office, 1984), p. 326.

10. *Ibid.*, p. 322.

11. Kenneth J. Meier, "Representative Democracy: An Empirical Assessment," *American Political Science Review* 69 (June 1975): 532.

12. *Statistical Abstract*, pp. 322 and 326.

13. *Selected Findings from a Common Cause Study of the Senior Executive Service* (Washington, D.C.: Common Cause, 1984), and Adam Clymer, "Political Scientists See Little Impact of 1978 Civil Service Law," *New York Times*, May 3, 1982.

14. *Congressional Quarterly Almanac, 1978* (Washington, D.C.: Congressional Quarterly, 1979), pp. 818–822.

15. Nelson W. Polsby, "Presidential Cabinet Making," *Political Science Quarterly* 93 (Spring 1978): 16, 21; and Hugh Heclo, "Issue Networks and the Executive Establishment," in Anthony King, ed., *The New American Political System* (Washington, D.C.: American Enterprise Institute, 1978), pp. 105–115.

16. Charles Peters, "In the Capital, the Boss Can't Run the Store," *New York Times*, November 5, 1980.

17. Arthur Schlesinger, Jr., *A Thousand Days* (Greenwich, Conn.: Fawcett, 1967), p. 377.

18. John W. Kingdon, *Agendas, Alternatives, and Public Policies* (Boston: Little, Brown, 1984), pp. 23–37.

19. Christopher Conte, "U.S. Proposes Rules Aimed at Curbing Alcohol, Drug Abuse by Rail Operators," *Wall Street Journal*, June 7, 1984.

20. Theodore J. Lowi, *The End of Liberalism*, 2nd ed. (New York: Norton, 1979).

21. Doris A. Graber, *Mass Media and American Politics* (Washington, D.C.: Congressional Quarterly, 1980), p. 41.

22. Jerome T. Murphy, "The Education Bureaucracies Implement Novel Policy," in Allan Sindler, ed., *Policy and Politics in America* (Boston: Little, Brown, 1973), pp. 160–198.

23. Herbert Kaufman, "Fear of Bureauc-

racy: A Raging Pandemic," *Public Administration Review* (January–February 1981): 1–9.

24. Jeffrey M. Berry, *Feeding Hungry People: Rulemaking in the Food Stamp Program* (New Brunswick, N.J.: Rutgers University Press, 1984).

25. Pertschuk, p. 64, and Irvin Molotsky, "All Funeral Costs Must Be Itemized," *New York Times*, April 30, 1984.

26. Terry M. Moe, "Control and Feedback in Economic Regulation: The Case of the NLRB," *American Political Science Review* 79 (December 1985): 109–116.

27. Charles E. Lindblom, "The Science of Muddling Through," *Public Administration Review* 19 (Spring 1959): 79–88.

28. Michael Lipsky, *Street-Level Bureaucracy* (New York: Russell Sage Foundation, 1980), p. 21.

29. Herbert Kaufman, *The Forest Ranger* (Baltimore: Johns Hopkins University Press, 1960).

30. George C. Edwards, III, *Implementing Public Policy* (Washington, D.C.: Congressional Quarterly, 1980), p. 27. See also Daniel A. Mazmanian and Paul Sabatier, *Implementation and Public Policy* (Glenview, Ill.: Scott, Foresman, 1983), pp. 175–217.

31. Jeffrey L. Pressman and Aaron B. Wildavsky, *Implementation*, 3rd ed. (Berkeley: University of California Press, 1984), pp. 102–110.

32. Patricia Rachel, *Federal Narcotics Enforcement* (Boston: Auburn House, 1982).

33. Robert Nakamura and Frank Smallwood, *The Politics of Policy Implementation* (New York: St. Martin's, 1980), pp. 129–130. See also Daniel Moynihan, *Maximum Feasible Misunderstanding* (New York: Free Press, 1970).

34. "Absorbing the Head Start Lesson," *New York Times*, December 12, 1980, and Fred M. Hechinger, "Blacks Found to Benefit From Preschooling," *New York Times*, September 11, 1984.

35. Gerald F. Seib, "Pentagon Has Trouble Winning Cooperation Between the Services," *Wall Street Journal*, August 1, 1984.

36. Walter A. Rosenbaum, "Public Involvement as Reform and Ritual," in Stuart Langton, ed., *Citizen Participation in America* (Lexington, Mass.: Lexington Books, 1978).

37. Daniel Mazmanian and Jeanne Nienaber, *Can Organizations Change?* (Washington, D.C.: Brookings Institution, 1979).

38. Jeffrey M. Berry, "Maximum Feasible Dismantlement," *Citizen Participation* 3 (November–December 1981): 3–5.

39. John C. Baker, "Program Costs and Comparisons," in Richard K. Betts, ed., *Cruise Missiles* (Washington, D.C.: Brookings Institution, 1981), pp. 101–133, 573–595. Cited in Kent E. Portney, *Approaching Public Policy Analysis* (Englewood Cliffs, N.J.: Prentice-Hall, 1986), p. 104.

40. Howard E. Shumann, *Politics and the Budget* (Englewood Cliffs, N.J.: Prentice-Hall, 1984), pp. 37–43.

41. *Ibid.*, p. 43.

Chapter 13 / The Courts / pp. 458–499

1. Bernard Schwartz, *The Unpublished Opinions of the Warren Court* (New York: Oxford University Press, 1985), pp. 445–448.

2. Felix Frankfurter and James M. Landis, *The Business of the Supreme Court* (New York: Macmillan, 1928), pp. 5–14; and Julius Goebel, Jr., *History of the Supreme Court of the United States.* (New York: Macmillan, 1971), Vol. 1. *Antecedents and Beginnings to 1801.*

3. Robert G. McCloskey, *The United States Supreme Court* (Chicago: University of Chicago Press, 1960), p. 31.

4. 1 Cranch 137 177–178 (1803).

5. Garry Wills, *Explaining America: The Federalist* (Garden City, N.Y.: Doubleday, 1981), pp. 127–136.

6. Charles Alan Wright, *Handbook on the Law of Federal Courts,* 3rd ed. (St. Paul, Minn.: West, 1976), p. 7, n. 3.

7. *Ibid.*, pp. 11–12.

8. Rule 17 of the Supreme Court Rules sets out the guidelines. But see also Doris M. Provine, *Case Selection in the United States Supreme Court* (Chicago: University of Chicago Press, 1980).

9. Joseph Tanenhaus et al., "The Supreme Court's Certiorari Jurisdiction: Cue Theory," in Glendon Schubert, ed., *Judicial Decision-Making* (New York: The Free Press, 1963), pp. 111–132.

10. Provine, pp. 74–102.

11. Garcia v. San Antonio Metropolitan Transit Authority, 105 S.C. 1005 (1985).

12. Elder Witt, *A Different Justice: Reagan and the Supreme Court* (Washington, D.C.: CQ Press, 1986), p. 133.

13. *Congressional Quarterly's Guide to the U.S. Supreme Court* (Washington, D.C.: U.S. Congressional Quarterly Press, 1980), p. 741.

14. See, for example, Walter F. Murphy, *Elements of Judicial Strategy* (Chicago: University of Chicago Press, 1964), and Bob Woodward and Scott Armstrong, *The Brethren* (New York: Simon and Schuster, 1979).

15. *New York Times*, April 16, 1986, p. 18.

16. Stephen L. Wasby, *The Supreme Court in the Federal Judicial System*, 2nd ed.

(New York: Holt, Rinehart and Winston, 1984), p. 188.

17. Schwartz, pp. 446–447.

18. *Congressional Quarterly's Guide*, p. 740.

19. Herbert Jacob, *Justice in America*, 4th ed. (Boston: Little, Brown, 1984), pp. 113–127.

20. Harold W. Chase, *Federal Judges: The Appointing Process* (St. Paul: University of Minnesota Press, 1972).

21. Wasby, pp. 74–82.

22. *Wall Street Journal*, December 30, 1985, p. 8.

23. *U.S. News & World Report*, October 14, 1985, p. 61.

24. Peter G. Fish, "John J. Parker," *Dictionary of American Biography*, Supplement Six, 1956–1980, (New York: Charles Scribner's Sons, 1980), p. 494.

25. *Congressional Quarterly's Guide*, pp. 655–656.

26. Elmo Richardson, *The Presidency of Dwight D. Eisenhower* (Lawrence, Kan.: The Regents Press of Kansas, 1979), p. 108.

27. Merle Miller, *Plain Speaking: An Oral Biography of Harry S Truman* (New York: Berkley Publishing Co., 1973), pp. 225–226.

28. Barbara A. Curran, *The Lawyer Statistical Report* (Chicago: American Bar Foundation, 1985), p. 4.

29. *Public Opinion* 1 (July–August 1978): p. 37.

30. Bureau of Labor Statistics, *Occupational Outlook Handbook, 1984–1985* (Washington, D.C.: U.S. Government Printing Office, 1984).

31. Nicholas O. Berry, "Of Lawyers' Work, There Is No End," *New York Times*, December. 28, 1985, p. 19.

32. James Eisenstein, *Attorneys for the Government* (Baltimore, Md.: The Johns Hopkins University Press, 1980), p. 187.

33. Anthony Partridge and William B. Eldridge, *The Second Circuit Sentencing Study* (Washington, D.C.: The Federal Judicial Center, 1975).

34. Charles A. Johnson and Bradley C. Canon, *Judicial Policies: Implementation and Impact* (Washington, D.C.: CQ Press, 1984).

35. *Ibid.*, pp. 4–10.

36. Alexander M. Bickel, *The Least Dangerous Branch* (Indianapolis, Ind.: Bobbs-Merrill, 1962); Robert A. Dahl, "Decision-Making in a Democracy: The Supreme Court as a National Policy-Maker," *Journal of Public Law* 6 (1962): 279–295.

37. David G. Barnum, "The Supreme Court and Public Opinion: Judicial Decision Making in the Post–New Deal Period," *Journal of Politics* 47 (1985): 652–662.

38. Jethro K. Lieberman, *The Litigious Society* (New York: Basic Books, 1981).

39. Abram Chayes, "The Role of the Judge in Public Law Litigation," *Harvard Law Review* 89 (May 1976): 1281–1316.

40. "The *Wyatt* Case: Implementation of a Judicial Decree Ordering Institutional Change," *Yale Law Journal* 84 (1975): 1338–1347.

41. *New York Times*, April 17, 1986, p. 12.

42. Benjamin N. Cardozo, *The Nature of the Judicial Process* (New Haven, Conn.: Yale University Press, 1921), p. 168.

Chapter 14 / The Washington Community / pp. 500–530

1. This profile is adapted from Fred Kaplan, "Military's 'Revolving Door' with Business," *Boston Globe*, January 15, 1984.

2. The profile of Wexler is adapted from Robert W. Merry, "Lobbyist Wexler Advises Ferraro," *Wall Street Journal*, September 17, 1984.

3. John Herbers, "Capital Census: Far from Average," *New York Times*, May 7, 1982.

4. Herbers.

5. James Sterling Young, *The Washington Community* (New York: Columbia University Press, 1966), p. 25.

6. Nelson W. Polsby, "The Washington Community, 1960–1980," in Thomas E. Mann and Norman J. Ornstein, eds. *The New Congress* (Washington, D.C.: American Enterprise Institute, 1981), p. 11. See also Richard D. Lyons, "The 'Other Washington' Enjoys Boom; Private Sector Now Dominates Region," *New York Times*, January 20, 1981.

7. "Rise of the Power Brokers," *U.S. News and World Report*, March 10, 1980, p. 54.

8. Joseph C. Goulden, *The Superlawyers* (New York: Dell, 1973), p. 27, and "Rise of the Power Brokers," p. 53. See also Mark J. Green, *The Other Government* (New York: Grossman, 1975), pp. 16–44.

9. Stuart Taylor, Jr., "Senator Baker and the Art of Making Rain," *New York Times*, December 11, 1984.

10. Bryce Nelson, "A Gold Rush for Lawyers in Legal Hills of Washington," *Boston Globe*, December 8, 1980.

11. Steven V. Roberts, "Federal Magnetism Draws Law Firms," *New York Times*, January 11, 1978.

12. Edward O. Laumann and John P. Heinz, "Washington Lawyers and Others: The Structure of Washington Representation," *Stanford Law Review* 37 (January 1985): 467.

13. James W. Singer, "Practicing Law in Washington — An American Growth Industry," *National Journal*, February 2, 1978, p. 176.

14. James W. Singer, "Consultants — Helping Themselves by Helping Government," *National Journal*, June 24, 1978, p. 1002.

15. A. O. Sulzberger, Jr., "G.A.O. Seeks to Cut Defense Consultants," *New York Times*, April 7, 1981.

16. Gregg Easterbrook, "The Art of Further Study," *Washington Monthly* (May 1980): 19.

17. Aaron Wildavsky, "The Self-Evaluating Organization," *Public Administration Review* 32 (September–October 1972): 510.

18. Sulzberger.

19. Christopher Madison, "Energy Consultants — What Do They Do and Why Should They Be Doing It?" *National Journal*, August 30, 1980, p. 1444.

20. Singer, "Consultants," p. 1001.

21. Gregg Easterbrook, "Ideas Move Nations," *Atlantic Monthly* (January 1986): 66.

22. Martha Derthick, *Policy Making for Social Security* (Washington, D.C.: Brookings Institution, 1979).

23. Mann and Ornstein.

24. Henry J. Aaron, *Why Is Welfare So Hard to Reform?* (Washington, D.C.: Brookings Institution, 1973).

25. Bernard Weinraub, "Heritage Foundation 10 Years Later," *New York Times*, September 30, 1983.

26. Alvin P. Sanoff, "Image Makers Worry About Their Own Image," *U.S. News and World Report*, August 13, 1979, p. 59.

27. Michael R. Gordon, "The Image Makers in Washington — PR Firms Have Found a Natural Home," *National Journal*, May 31, 1980, pp. 888–889.

28. Philip H. Dougherty, "Hill & Knowlton to Buy Gray's Lobbying Firm," *New York Times*, June 4, 1986.

29. Dougherty.

30. Charles Mohr, "Market-Hunting in 'Progressive' P.R.," *New York Times*, April 21, 1984.

31. Ann Cooper, "Image Builders," *National Journal*, September 14, 1985, p. 2058–2059.

32. Robert H. Salisbury et al. "Soaking and Poking Among the Movers and Shakers" (Paper delivered at the annual meeting of the American Political Science Association, Washington, D.C., September 1984), and Paul Taylor, "Gladiators for Hire — I," *Washington Post*, July 31, 1983.

33. Steven V. Roberts, "Trade Associations Flocking to Capital as U.S. Role Rises," *New York Times*, March 4, 1978, p. 23.

34. See Randall B. Ripley and Grace A. Franklin, *Congress, the Bureaucracy, and Public Policy*, 3rd ed. (Homewood, Ill.: Dorsey Press, 1984), p. 8.

35. Douglass Cater, *Power in Washington* (New York: Vintage Books, 1964), p. 18.

36. Lawrence C. Dodd and Richard L. Schott, *Congress and the Administrative State* (New York: Wiley, 1979), p. 103.

37. Hugh Heclo, "Issue Networks and the Executive Establishment," in Anthony King, ed., *The New American Political System* (Washington, D.C.: American Enterprise Institute, 1978), p. 88.

38. Dodd and Schott, pp. 106–154.

39. Heclo, p. 103.

40. John E. Chubb, *Interest Groups and the Bureaucracy* (Stanford, Calif.: Stanford University Press, 1983), p. 68.

41. Chubb, p. 251.

42. John M. Blair, *The Control of Oil* (New York: Pantheon, 1976), pp. 354–370.

43. Thomas B. Edsall, "Republican Lobbyists Expanding; Advantages Seen After Landslide," *Washington Post*, December 16, 1984.

44. Richard Cohen, "Small Lobbying Firms Tout Their Policy Expertise and Client Contact," *National Journal*, January 14, 1984, p. 68.

45. Douglas R. Sease and Thomas Petzinger, Jr., "Steelmakers Cheer Two Reagan Nominees, But Others Question Their Impartiality," *Wall Street Journal*, July 5, 1981.

46. Jeffrey M. Berry, *Feeding Hungry People: Rulemaking in the Food Stamp Program* (New Brunswick, N.J.: Rutgers University Press, 1984).

47. Gordon Adams, *The Politics of Defense Contracting: The Iron Triangle* (New Brunswick, N.J.: Transaction Books, 1982).

48. As cited in Ripley and Franklin, pp. 207–208.

Chapter 15 / The Economics of Public Policy / pp. 532–571

1. Ronald Reagan with Richard G. Hubler, *Where's the Rest of Me?* (New York: Duell, Sloan and Pearce, 1965).

2. *Ibid.*, p. 245.

3. *Ibid.*, p. 233.

4. *Ibid.*

5. Subcommittee on Oversight, Committee on Ways and Means, U.S. House of Representatives, *Families in Poverty: Changes in the "Safety Net"* (Committee Print, 1984), p. 1.

6. *Social Security Bulletin* 48 (July 1985): 48.

7. Isabel V. Sawhill and Charles F. Stone, "The Economy: The Key to Success,"

in John L. Palmer and Isabel V. Saw-hill (eds.), *The Reagan Record* (Cambridge, Mass.: Ballinger, 1984), pp. 80–83.

8. *Congressional Quarterly Weekly Report,* December 14, 1985, p. 2605.

9. Richard A. Musgrave and Peggy B. Musgrave, *Public Finance in Theory and Practice,* 2nd ed. (New York: McGraw-Hill, 1976), p. 42.

10. *Chicago Tribune,* June 1, 1985.

11. Gary Klott, "Senators Won Many Exceptions in Bill to Aid Specific Taxpayers," *New York Times,* June 6, 1986.

12. *Public Opinion* 8 (February–March, 1985): 29.

13. George E. Curry, "The Ron 'n' Rosty Show Opens in Pa.," *Chicago Tribune,* June 1, 1985.

14. ABC/*Washington Post* Survey cited in *Public Opinion* 8 (February–March 1985): 21.

15. *New York Times,* January 24, 1985.

16. *Public Opinion* 8 (February–March 1985): 20.

17. Advisory Commission on Intergovernmental Relations, *Significant Features of Fiscal Federalism, 1981–1982,* p. 54.

18. *Congressional Quarterly Weekly Report,* February 8, 1986, p. 225.

19. *Congressional Quarterly Weekly Report,* February 8, 1986, p. 248.

20. National Election Study for 1984, conducted by the Center for Political Studies, University of Michigan.

21. *Public Opinion* 8 (February–March 1985): 19.

22. David Cole, "A Cymbal-Minded Defense Strategy," *New York Times,* July 14, 1986, p. 17.

23. *Gallup Report,* January–February, 1986, p. 30.

24. Joseph A. Pechman, *Who Paid the Taxes, 1966-85?* (Washington, D.C.: The Brookings Institution, 1985).

25. *Ibid.,* p. 53.

26. *Ibid.,* p. 80.

27. *Ibid.,* p. 73.

28. *Ibid.,* p. 74.

29. Charles F. Andrain, *Social Policies in Western Industrial Societies* (Berkeley: University of California Press, 1985), p. 194.

30. "Nation top-heavy with wealth," *Chicago Tribune,* July 19, 1986, p. 1; and *Statistical Abstract of the United States, 1985,* p. 446.

31. Benjamin I. Page, *Who Gets What from Government?* (Berkeley: University of California Press, 1983), p. 213.

32. *New York Times,* May 13, 1983,

33. Advisory Commission on Intergovernmental Relations, *Significant Features of Fiscal Federalism,* 1984 Ed. (Washington, D.C.: 1985), p. 139.

34. *Public Opinion* 8 (February–March 1985): 27.

Chapter 16 / Domestic Policy / pp. 572–603

1. *Chicago Tribune,* April 13, 1986, p. 1.

2. *Chicago Tribune,* October 6, 1985, p. 1.

3. *Social Security Bulletin, Annual Statistical Supplement, 1984–85,* Table 1, p. 64.

4. Shapiro v. Thompson, 396 US 618 (1969).

5. I. A. Lewis and William Schneider, "Hard Times: The Public on Poverty," *Public Opinion* Vol. 8 (June–July 1985), p. 2.

6. D. Lee Bawden and John L. Palmer, "Social Policy: Challenging the Welfare State," in John L. Palmer and Isabell V. Sawhill, eds., *The Reagan Record: An Assessment of America's Changing Domestic Priorities* (Cambridge, Mass.: Ballinger, 1984), pp. 177–215.

7. Paul Light, *Artful Work: The Politics of Social Security Reform* (New York: Random House, 1985), p. 63.

8. *Congressional Record,* June 26, 1961, 11307-08, as cited in Martha Derthick, *Policymaking for Social Security* (Washington, DC: Brookings Institution, 1979), p. 5.

9. Derthick, pp. 346–347.

10. Julie Kosterlitz, "Who Will Pay?" *National Journal,* March 8, 1985, pp. 570–574.

11. Derthick, p. 335.

12. Paul Starr, *The Social Transformation of American Medicine* (New York: Basic Books, 1982), pp. 279–280.

13. Starr, p. 287.

14. Theodore Marmor, *The Politics of Medicare* (Chicago: Aldine, 1973).

15. *Social Security Bulletin, Annual Statistical Supplement, 1984–85,* Tables 153 and 154, pp. 220–221.

16. *New York Times,* April 1, 1986, p. 12.

17. *Social Security Bulletin, Annual Statistical Supplement, 1984–85,* Table 7, p. 70.

18. *Social Security Bulletin, Annual Statistical Supplement, 1984–85,* Table 195, p. 254.

19. Jeffrey M. Berry, *Feeding Hungry People: Rulemaking in the Food Stamp Program* (New Brunswick, N.J.: Rutgers University Press, 1984), p. 21.

20. *New York Times,* October 25, 1984, p. 15.

21. Lewis and Schneider, pp. 3–7.

22. *New York Times,* March 7, 1985, p. 22.

23. *New York Times,* February 13, 1985, p. B7.

24. United States v. Butler, 297 US 1 (1936).

25. Mulford v. Smith, 307 US 38 (1939).

26. *Historical Tables, Budget of the United States Government, FY 1987,* Table 3.1.

27. *National Journal,* March 29, 1986, pp. 759–762.

28. *New York Times,* February 26, 1985, p. 20.

Chapter 17 / Order and Civil Liberties / pp. 604–641

1. Epperson v. Arkansas, 393 U.S. 96 (1968).

2. Learned Hand, *The Bill of Rights* (Boston: Atheneum, 1958), p. 1.

3. Leo Pfeffer, *Church, State, and Freedom* (Boston: Beacon Press, 1953), p. 106.

4. Leonard W. Levy, "The Original Meaning of the Establishment Clause of the First Amendment," in James E. Wood, Jr., ed., *Religion and the State* (Waco, Tex.: Baylor University Press, 1985), pp. 43–83.

5. Everson v. Board of Education, 330 U.S. 1, 16 (1947).

6. Board of Education v. Allen, 392 U.S. 236 (1968).

7. 403 U.S. 602 (1971).

8. 465 U.S. 668 (1984).

9. 260 U.S. 421 (1962).

10. Abington School District v. Schempp, 364 U.S. 203 (1963).

11. 105 S.Ct. 2479 (1985).

12. McLean v. Arkansas Board of Education, 529 F. Supp. 1255 (E.D. Ark. 1982).

13. *Ibid.,* 1274.

14. 310 U.S. 586 (1940).

15. 319 U.S. 624 (1943).

16. *Ibid.,* 642.

17. People v. Woody, 394, P.2d 813 (1964).

18. Laurence Tribe, *Treatise on American Constitutional Law* (St. Paul, Minn.: West, 1968), p. 566.

19. Zechariah Chafee, *Free Speech in the United States* (Cambridge, Mass.: Harvard University Press, 1941).

20. Leonard Levy, *Legacy of Suppression* (Cambridge, Mass.: Belknap Press, 1960).

21. As cited in William Cohen and John Kaplan, *Constitutional Law: Civil Liberty and Individual Rights,* 2nd ed. (Mineola, N.Y.: Foundation Press, 1982), p. 38.

22. 249 U.S. 46 (1919).

23. *Ibid.,* 52.

24. 205 U.S. 616 (1919).

25. 268 U.S. 652 (1925).

26. Dennis v. United States, 341 U.S. 494 (1951).

27. 395 U.S. 444 (1969).

28. 393 U.S. 503 (1969).

29. *Ibid.,* 508–509.

30. 337 U.S. 1 (1949).

31. *Ibid.,* 37.

32. 403 U.S. 15 (1971).

33. Roth v. United States, 354 U.S. 477 (1957).
34. *Ibid.*, 487.
35. Jacobellis v. Ohio, 378 U.S. 184, at 197 (concurring opinion).
36. Jenkins v. Georgia, 418 U.S. 153 (1974).
37. 376 U.S. 254 (1964).
38. 283 U.S. 697 (1931).
39. A detailed account of the case and its "hero" can be found in Fred W. Friendly, *Minnesota Rag* (New York: Random House, 1981).
40. 283 U.S. 697, 720.
41. New York Times v. United States, 403 U.S. 713 (1971).
42. United States v. Progressive, Inc., 467 F. Supp. 990 (W.D.Wis. 1979).
43. Branzenburg v. Hayes, 408 U.S. 665 (1972).
44. Zurcher v. Stanford Daily, 436 U.S. 547 (1978).
45. United States v. Cruikshank, 92 U.S. 542 (1876); *Constitution of the United States of America: Annotated and Interpreted* (Washington, D.C.: U.S. Government Printing Office, 1973), p. 1031.
46. DeJonge v. Oregon, 299 U.S. 353, 364 (1937).
47. 7 Pet. 243, 250 (1833).
48. 16 Wall. 36 (1873).
49. Chicago, B. & Q.R. Co. v. Chicago, 166 U.S. 226 (1897).
50. 302 U.S. 319 (1937).
51. *Ibid.*, 325
52. Benton v. Maryland, 395 U.S. 784 (1969).
53. McNabb v. United States, 318 U.S. 332, 347 (1943).
54. 391 U.S. 145 (1968).
55. Baldwin v. New York, 399 U.S. 66 (1970).
56. 372 U.S. 335 (1963).
57. 384 U.S. 486 (1966).
58. 338 U.S. 25 (1949).
59. 307 U.S. 643 (1961).
60. *The Federalist*, No. 84.
61. Paul Brest, *Processes of Constitutional Decision-making* (Boston: Little, Brown, 1975), p. 708.
62. 381 U.S. 479 (1965).
63. 410 U.S. 113 (1973).
64. See John Hart Ely, "The Wages of Crying Wolf: A Comment on *Roe v. Wade,* 82 *Yale Law Journal* 920 (1973).
65. Thornburgh v. American College of Obstetricians and Gynecologists, 54 *U.S. Law Week* 4618 (1986).
66. *New York Times*, April 1, 1986, p. 11.
67. Bowers v. Hardwick, 54 *U.S. Law Week* 4919 (1986).
68. Irving Dilliard, ed., *The Spirit of Liberty: Papers and Addresses of Learned Hand* (New York: Vintage Books, 1959), p. 125.

Chapter 18 / Equality and Civil Rights / pp. 642–673

1. Slaughter House Cases, 16 Wall. 36 (1873).
2. United States v. Cruikshank, 92 U.S. 542 (1876).
3. United States v. Reese, 12 U.S. 214 (1876).
4. Civil Rights Cases, 109 U.S. 3 (1883).
5. Mary Beth Norton et al., *A People and a Nation: A History of the United States,* 2nd ed. (Boston: Houghton Mifflin, 1986), Vol. II, p. 442.
6. Plessy v. Ferguson, 163 U.S. 537 (1896).
7. Cummings v. County Board of Education, 175 U.S. 528 (1899).
8. Missouri ex rel. Gaines v. Canada, 305 U.S. 337 (1938).
9. Sweatt v. Painter, 339 U.S. 629 (1950).
10. McLaurin v. Oklahoma State Regents, 339 U.S. 637 (1950).
11. Brown v. Board of Education of Topeka, 347 U.S. 487 (1954).
12. Bolling v. Sharpe, 347 U.S. 497 (1954).
13. Brown v. Board of Education of Topeka (II), 349 U.S. 294 (1955).
14. Jack W. Peltason, *Fifty-Eight Lonely Men,* rev. ed. (Urbana, Ill.: University of Illinois Press, 1971).
15. Alexander v. Holmes County Board of Education, 369 U.S. 19 (1969).
16. Swann v. Charlotte-Mecklenburg County Schools, 402 U.S. 1 (1971).
17. Milliken v. Bradley, 418 U.S. 717 (1974).
18. Richard Kluger, *Simple Justice* (New York: Knopf, 1975), p. 753.
19. Norton et al., p. 943.
20. Heart of Atlanta Motel v. United States, 379 U.S. 241 (1964).
21. Katzenbach v. McClung, 379 U.S. 294 (1964).
22. Rufus P. Browning, Dale Rogers Marshall, and David H. Tabb, *Protest Is Not Enough* (Berkeley, Calif.: University of California Press, 1984).
23. Norton et al., p. 987.
24. As cited in Martin Gruberg, *Women in American Politics* (Oshkosh, Wis.: Academia Press, 1968), p. 4.
25. Bradwell v. State, 16 Wall. 130 (1873).
26. Muller v. Oregon, 208 U.S. 412 (1908).
27. Minor v. Happersett, 21 Wall. 162 (1875).
28. John H. Aldrich, Gary J. Miller, Charles W. Ostrom, Jr., and David W. Rohde, *American Government: People, Institutions, and Policies* (Boston: Houghton Mifflin, 1986), p. 618.

29. Reed v. Reed, 404 U.S. 71 (1971).
30. Frontiero v. Richardson, 411 U.S. 677, 684 (1973).
31. Craig v. Borden, 429 U.S. 190 (1976).
32. Paul Weiler, "The Wages of Sex: The Uses and Limits of Comparable Worth," *Harvard Law Review,* Vol. 99 (June 1986), pp. 1728–1807.
33. *Wall Street Journal,* July 17, 1986, p. 44.
34. Regents of the University of California v. Bakke, 438 US 265 (1978).
35. United Steelworkers of America, AFL-CIO v. Weber, 443 U.S. 193 (1979).
36. Fullilove v. Klutznick, 448 U.S. 448 (1980).
37. Firefighters v. Stotts, 467 U.S. 561 (1984).
38. Wygant v. Jackson Board of Education, 476 U.S. (1986).
39. Local 28 of the Sheet Metal Workers' International Association v. EEOC, 54 U.S. Law Week 4984 (June 24, 1986).
40. Sidney Verba and Gary R. Orren, *Equality in America: The View from the Top* (Cambridge, Mass.: Harvard University Press, 1985), especially pp. 1–51.

Chapter 19 / Foreign and Defense Policy / pp. 674–718

1. Michael Roskin, "From Pearl Harbor to Vietnam: Shifting Generational Paradigms and Foreign Policy," *Political Science Quarterly* (Fall 1974): 563–588.
2. Ole Holsti and James Rosenau, "Does Where You Stand Depend on When You Were Born? The Impact of Generation on Post-Vietnam Foreign Policy Beliefs," *Public Opinion Quarterly* (Spring 1980): 1–22.
3. U.S. Bureau of the Census, *Historical Statistics of the United States: Colonial Times to 1970* (Washington, D.C.: U.S. Government Printing Office, 1975), pp. 1140–41.
4. *Ibid.*
5. See James A. Nathan and James K. Oliver, *United States Foreign Policy and World Order,* 2nd ed. (Boston: Little, Brown, 1981), p. 108.
6. "X" [George F. Kennan], "The Sources of Soviet Conduct," *Foreign Affairs* (July 1947): 575.
7. Harry S Truman, "Special Message to the Congress on Greece and Turkey (March 12, 1947)," in *Public Papers of the Presidents of the United States* (Washington, D.C.: U.S. Government Printing Office, 1963), p. 178.
8. Dwight D. Eisenhower, "Farewell Address," in *Public Papers of the Presidents of the United States* (Washington, D.C.: U.S. Government Printing Office, 1961), p. 616.

9. Herman Kahn, *On Thermonuclear War* (Princeton, N.J.: Princeton University Press, 1961); Henry Kissinger, *Nuclear Weapons and Foreign Policy* (New York: Harper & Row, 1957).

10. John F. Kennedy, "Inaugural Address (January 20, 1961)," in *Public Papers of the Presidents of the United States* (Washington, D.C.: U.S. Government Printing Office, 1961).

11. Quoted in Arthur M. Schlesinger, Jr., *A Thousand Days* (Boston: Houghton Mifflin, 1965), pp. 704–705.

12. Richard M. Nixon, "A Redefinition of the United States' Role in the World (February 25, 1971)," in *United States Foreign Policy — 1971* (Washington, D.C.: Department of State, 1972), p. 422.

13. Richard M. Nixon, *U.S. Foreign Policy for the 1970s: A New Strategy for Peace* (Washington, D.C.: U.S. Government Printing Office, 1970), p. 2.

14. James A. Nathan and James K. Oliver, *Foreign Policy Making and the American Political System* (Boston: Little, Brown, 1983), pp. 68–72.

15. Alexis de Tocqueville, *Democracy in America* (Oxford, Eng.: Oxford University Press, 1946), p. 161.

16. U.S. v. Curtiss-Wright Export Corporation, 299 U.S. 304 (1936).

17. Henry T. Nash, *American Foreign Policy: A Search for Security*, 3rd ed. (Homewood, Ill.: Dorsey Press, 1985), p. 160.

18. C. Herman Pritchett, "The President's Constitutional Position," in Tugwell and Cronin, *The Presidency Reappraised,* (New York: Praeger, 1977), p. 23.

19. Nathan and Oliver, *Foreign Policy Making,* p. 125.

20. Quoted in Schlesinger, p. 406.

21. Richard K. Betts, "Analysis, War and Decision Making: Why Intelligence Failures Are Inevitable, *World Politics* (October 1978): 64–65.

22. *Ibid.,* p. 61.

23. Gabriel A. Almond, *The American People and Foreign Policy* (New York: Praeger, 1960).

24. Michael Maggiotto and Eugene Wittkopf, "American Public Attitudes Toward Foreign Policy," *International Studies Quarterly* (December 1981): 601–631.

25. Charles W. Kegley and Eugene Wittkopf, *American Foreign Policy: Pattern and Process,* 2nd ed. (New York: St. Martin's Press 1982), p. 287.

26. Kegley and Wittkopf, pp. 262–263; Lester Milbrath, "Interest Groups and Foreign Policy," in James Rosenau, ed., *Domestic Sources of Foreign Policy* (New York: Free Press, 1967), 231–252.

27. Kegley and Wittkopf, p. 267.

28. Elihu Katz, "The Two-Step Flow of Communications, " *Public Opinion Quarterly* (Spring 1957): 61–78.

29. Kegley and Wittkopf, p.301.

30. Bernard C. Cohen, "The Influence of Special Interest Groups and Mass Media on Security Policy in the United States," in Charles W. Kegley and Eugene Wittkopf, eds., *Perspectives on American Foreign Policy* (New York: St. Martin's Press, 1983), pp. 222–241.

31. Quoted in "For Reagan, a Key House Win on 'Contra' Aid," *Congressional Quarterly,* June 28, 1986, p. 1447.

32. James Fallows, *National Defense,* (New York: Vintage Books, 1981).

Index to References

A-49

Index

Index

A-73

Supportive behavior, as conventional participation, 195
Support prices, agricultural, 596
Supreme Court, 473–485
  abortion decisions of, 634–637
  access to, 476–481
  on affirmative action, 668–669
  on Agricultural Adjustment Act of 1933, 596
  appellate jurisdiction of, 463
  appointment to, 486–487, 489–491
  arguing before, 479
  on black enfranchisement, 201
  building of, 478
  on capital punishment, 145–146
  chief justice of, 83, 484–485
  conduction of, 478–479
  on criminal procedure, 629–634
  decisionmaking in, 482–485
  early interpretations in civil rights cases, 646–647
  establishment of, 462
  federalism and, 114, 119, 122–125
  on freedom of speech, 620
  on freedom of the press, 621–623, 624
  on free expression clauses, 615–616
  on fundamental rights, 628–629
  on government support of religion, 611
  on Gramm-Rudman-Hollings bill, 556
  on homosexuality, 638
  implementation and impact and, 493–495
  interpretation of due process clause by, 627–628
  judicial review by, 98, 463–468
  judicial supremacy and, 463
  list of twentieth-century justices of, A19
  New Deal legislation and, 577–578
  nullification of Truman's executive order by, 384
  payment of Sioux for land and, 661
  power to review state government, 466–467
  protectionism of, 662, 663, 664
  Reagan and, 487–489
  on religious freedom, 610
  on rights of handicapped infants, 428
  on saluting the flag, 614
  on school desegregation, 460–461, 475, 493, 649–652
  on school prayer, 150, 493–494, 612
  on separate-but-equal facilities, 647–648
  on sit-ins, 656
  solicitor general of, 481–482
  on victims of discrimination, 669–670
  under Virginia Plan, 80
  on Watergate tapes, 66
Supreme Soviet, architecture of, 377
Surplus food, distribution of, 593
Swann v. Charlotte-Mecklenburg County Schools, 652
Sweatt, Heman, 649
Switzerland
  enfranchisement of women in, 203
  judicial review in, 468
Symbolic expression, 618–621

"fighting words" and, 619–620
  obscenity and, 620–621

Taft, William Howard, 483–484
Taft-Hartley Act, 384
Tammany Hall, 250
Taney, Roger B., federalism and, 122
Tarbell, Ida, 310
Target price, agricultural, 597
TASS, 320
Tax(es). See also Income tax; Public policy
  under Articles of Confederation, 75
  on commodity producers, 594, 596
  corporate, 342
  federalism and, 122
  poll, 201, 647
  progressive, 102–103, 558–559
  regressive, 567, 569
  Revolution and, 68–70
  for social security, 583–585, 586
Tax brackets, 558–559
Tax burdens, comparing, 560–561
Tax committees, congressional, 551
Tax Court, 470
Tax credit, elimination of, 342
Tax expenditure, public policy and, 538
Tax policies, 557–561
  comparing tax burdens and, 560–561
  effects over time, 567–568
  public opinion on, 559
  revenue neutral, 557
  tax reform and, 557–559
Tax reform, 557–559
  under Kennedy, 545
  under Reagan, 342, 393, 545–546
Taylor, Glen, 364
Tea, British duty on, 70
Tea Act of 1773, 70
Technical regulation, of media, 317–318
Technology, growth of government and, 431
Telegraph, newspapers and, 308
Telephone industry, see AT&T breakup
Television
  development of, 312–315
  funding for public stations and, 280
  political socialization and, 161, 333
  as source of news, 327–329
  suppressing effect on news recall and, 330–331
Television stations, ownership of, 317
Tennessee Valley Authority (TVA), 135
Terminiello, Arthur, 619
Terrorism. See also Iranian hostage crisis
  media coverage of, 304–305, 337, 705
Testifying
  journalists and, 624
  lobbying and, 287
Texaco Oil Company, 472
Textbook presidency, 400–401
Thalidomide, 453
Thatcher, Margaret, 376
Theory(ies)
  defined, 7
  empirical, 7
  normative, 8

Think tanks, 513–515
Third World, nation-building policies and, 686
Thurmond, Strom, 364
Timber industry, conflict over national forests and, 53
Time magazine, 310
  Sharon's suit against, 622
Timmons, William, 281
Tinker v. Des Moines Independent County School District, 618
Tocqueville, Alexis de, 692
  on interest groups, 271
Tories, 228
Torts, 473
Totalitarianism, 14
Town meetings, direct democracy in, 38
Townshend Act of 1767, 70
Trade associations, 517–518
  lobbying and, 295–296
Transfer authority, of president, 694
Transfer payments, 566–567
"Transition rules," 558
Transportation Department, see Department of Transportation
Treason, British penalty for, 73
Treaties
  president's power to make, 388, 693
  Senate power to make, 345
Trial, jury, 629–630
Truman, David, 275
Truman, Harry S., 313
  attempt to seize control of steel industry, 384
  Cold War and, 683
  disapproval of Clark, 490–491
  1948 polls and, 147 (fig.), 148 (fig.)
  support of civil rights, 650–651
Trust, in government, 159–160
Trustee, legislator's role as, 374–375
"Tuesday Team," 331, 332
Turner, Frederick Jackson, Progressivism and, 204
TVA, see Tennessee Valley Authority
Twain, Mark, 616
12-12-12-rule, 319
Two-party system, 236–245
  defined, 232
  eras of dominance since Civil War and, 232–236
  federal basis of, 240–241
  minor parties and, 236–239
  party identification and, 242–245
  reasons for, 239–240

UAW, see United Auto Workers
Unanimous consent agreements, Senate debate and, 364
Unanticipated events, presidential popularity and, 396
Uncontrollable outlays, spending increases and, 564–565
Unconventional political participation, 188–193
  defined, 187
  effectiveness of, 190–193

Illustration Credits (*continued from copyright page*)

Chapter 6: **Page 182 (Opener):** Alan Tannenbaum/ Sygma; **186:** UPI/Bettman Newsphotos; **187** and **191:** Paul Conklin; **194:** Lionel Delevingne/Stock, Boston; **202** and **203:** Library of Congress; **215** and **216:** AP/Wide World Photos.

Chapter 7: **Page 220 (Opener):** Richard Gordon/Archive; **225:** Library of Congress; **232:** AP/Wide World Photos; **233:** Library of Congress; **236:** AP/Wide World Photos; **241:** Martin A. Levick/Black Star; **253:** Gilles Peress/Magnum; **254:** UPI/Bettman Newsphotos; **260:** Eli Reed/Magnum; **261:** Taylor/Sygma; **262:** David Valdez/The White House.

Chapter 8: **Page 268 (Opener)** and **273:** Paul Conklin; **277:** Sam Sweezy/Stock, Boston; **283:** George Tames/NYT Pictures; **286:** Dennis Brack/Black Star; **289:** Michael D. Sullivan/TexaStock; **291:** AP/Wide World Photos; **293:** Charles Moore/Black Star; **294:** AP/Wide World Photos; **296:** John Ficara/ Woodfin Camp & Associates; **299:** ©1986, Wasserman for *The Boston Globe*. Reprinted with permission of the Los Angeles Times Syndicate.

Chapter 9: **Page 302 (Opener), 304,** and **307:** AP/Wide World Photos; **308:** Don Wright. *The Miami News;* **312:** Culver Pictures; **313:** United Press International/The National Archives; **318:** Urraca/Sygma; **323** and **333:** AP/Wide World Photos.

Chapter 10: **Page 304 (Opener):** James K.W. Atherton/ *The Washington Post;* **344:** The National Archives; **347:** Rare Books and Manuscripts Division, The New York Public Library, Aster, Lenox, and Tilden Foundation; **348:** ©Art Stein/Photo Researchers, Inc.; **357:** UPI/Bettman Newsphotos; **359:** Paul Conklin; **362** and **363:** George Tames/NYT Pictures; **369** and **373:** Paul Conklin; **375:** The White House/Black Star; **377**(top and middle): AP/Wide World Photos; **377**(bottom): TASS from Sovfoto; **379:** Paul Hosefros/NYT Pictures.

Chapter 11: **Page 382 (Opener):** Elliott Erwitt/Magnum; **388:** Franklin D. Roosevelt Library; **390:** The Bettman Archive; **400**(left): AP/Wide World Photos; **400**(right): Arthur Grace/Sygma; **401:** Jean-Louis Atlan/Sygma; **408:** Peter Souza/The White House; **410:** Gerald R. Ford Library; **414:** Lyndon Baines Johnson Library; **419** and **420:** AP/Wide World Photos; **422**(left): Culver Pictures; **422**(right): UPI/ Bettman Newsphotos.

Chapter 12: **Page 426 (Opener):** ©L. Druskis/Jeroboam, Inc.; **429**(left): J.P. Laffont/Sygma; **429**(right): B. Pierce/Sygma; **432**(top): NASA; **432**(bottom): Arthur Grace/Sygma; *433:* AP/Wide World Photos; **439:** Paul Conklin; **442:** UPI/Bettman Newsphotos; **453:** AP/Wide World Photos.

Chapter 13: **Page 458 (Opener):** Ken Regan/Camera 5; **461:** UPI/Bettman Newsphotos; **464:** Reprinted by permission: Tribune Media Services; **463:** National Portrait Gallery, Smithsonian Institution, Washington, D.C.; **471:** Dan Weiner; **478** and **479:** Supreme Court Historical Society; **485:** AP/Wide World Photos; **488:** Paul Conklin; **490:** U.S. Supreme Court; **494**(left): Paul Conklin; **494**(right): Jean-Louis Atlan/Sygma.

Chapter 14: **Page 500 (Opener):** Mark Godfrey/Archive; **503:** AP/Wide World Photos; **505**(top): Library of Congress; **505**(bottom): Paul Conklin; **509:** John Bowden/ Copyright *The Washington Post*. Reprinted by permission of the D.C. Public Library; **511:** Christopher Morris/Black Star; **514:** © Eric H. Poggenpohl; **519:** Michael D. Sullivan/ TexaStock; **523:** Lyndon Baines Johnson Library; **524:** Michael Evans/Sygma.

Chapter 15: **Page 532 (Opener):** ©Joel Gordon; **536:** Bohdan Hrynewych/Stock, Boston; **537:** Owen Franken/ Stock, Boston; **538:** National Archives; **540:** Reprinted by permission: Tribune Media Services; **545:** Owen Franken/ Sygma; **548:** Reprinted with permission of *Daily Texan;* **550:** Michael Evans/The White House; **552:** UPI/Bettman Newsphotos; **556:** James K.W. Atherton/THE WASHINGTON POST; **559:** Copyright 1986. Chicago Tribune Company. All rights reserved. Used with permission. **556:** Jean-Louis Atlan/Sygma.

Chapter 16: **Page 572 (Opener):** Betty Barry/The Picture Cube; **577:** Brown Brothers; **578:** Library of Congress; **581:** Owen Franken/Stock, Boston; **584:** UPI/Bettman Newsphotos; **592:** Bryce Flynn/Stock, Boston; **593:** George Rizer/*The Boston Globe*; **598:** Reprinted by permission: Tribune Media Services; **600:** Matthew Naythons/Gamma-Liaison; **601:** Terry Ashe/Sygma.

Chapter 17: **Page 604 (Opener):** AP/Wide World Photos; **609:** Jean-Louis Atlan/Sygma; **613:** AP/Wide World Photos; **618**(left): George Mars Cassidy/Click, Chicago; **618**(right): Paul Conklin; **620:** Hiroji Kubota/Magnum); **623:** UPI/Bettman Newsphotos; **632:** Flip Schulke/Black Star; **637:** Paul Conklin; **639:** ©1986, *Buffalo News*. Reprinted with permission of United Press Syndicate. All rights reserved.

Chapter 18: **Page 642 (Opener):** Bruce Davidson/Magnum; **645:** National Archives; **648:** Elliott Erwitt/Magnum; **650:** AP/Wide World Photos; **654:** UPI/Bettman Newsphotos; **658:** Frank Dandridge, *Life Magazine* ©1965 Time Inc.; **660:** UPI/Bettman Newsphotos; **665:** Paul Conklin; **668:** AP/ Wide World Photos; **671:** Felix Candelaria. Courtesy of the New York City Transit Authority.

Chapter 19: **Page 674 (Opener):** Jean-Louis Atlan/ Sygma **677:** Sygma; **680** and **683:** National Archives; **687:** AP/Wide World Photos; **690:** AUTH, Copyright ©1986 *Philadelphia Inquirer*. Reprinted with permission of Universal Press Syndicate; **695:** J.P. Laffont/Sygma; **698:** AP/Wide World Photos; **703:** UPI/Bettman Newsphotos; **708:** Lyndon Baines Johnson Library; **714:** McDonnell Douglas Helicopter Company; **716:** J.P. Laffont/Sygma.

Color Essay A: **Page 5:** Ben Shahn, *Bartolomeo Vanzetti and Nicola Sacco*. From Sacco-Vanzetti series of twenty-three paintings (1931-32). Tempera on paper over composition board, 10½ × 14½". Collection, The Museum of Modern Art, New York. Gift of Abby Aldrich Rockefeller.

Color Essay B: **Page 5**(top and bottom): Copyright ©1986 by the New York Times Company. Reprinted by permission. **8:** Gallup Report #243. December, 1985.

Color Essay C: **Page 6**(bottom): Copyrighted material reprinted with permission, Congressional Quarterly Inc. **8:** Copyright 1986. Chicago Tribune Company. All rights reserved. Used with permission.

Color Essay D: **Page 2:** Copyright ©1984 by the New York Times Company. **5:** From *The Times Concise Atlas of World History*. Distribution U.S.A. by Hammond Inc.; **6:** *World Military and Social Expenditures 1985* by Ruth Leger Silvard. Copyright ©1985 by World Priorities, Box 25140, Washington, D.C., U.S.A. **7:** Adapted from Professor Edward W. Azar's Conflict and Peace Data Bank. From *American Foreign Policy: Pattern and Process*. 2d ed., by Charles W. Kegley, Jr., and Eugene R. Wittkopf. Copyright ©1985 by St. Martin's Press Inc. Used with permission; **8:** Used with permission of Freedom House, 48 East 21 Street, N.Y., N.Y. 10010. Reproduced from ''Freedom at Issue,'' Jan.-Feb., 1986.